Fodor's 2016

FLORIDA

D0483598

WELCOME TO FLORIDA

With its accessible and varied pleasures, Florida is a favorite of many. Drawn to the colonial charm of St. Augustine, Miami's pulsing nightlife, the glitz of Palm Beach, or the quiet expanse of the Everglades, almost all visitors find something to love here. From the powdery white beaches of the Panhandle to the vibrant coral reefs of the Florida Keys, the ocean is always calling—for sailing, fishing, diving, swimming, and other water sports. Stray off the path a few miles, and you might glimpse a bit of the Florida of old, including cigar-makers and mermaids.

TOP REASONS TO GO

★ **Miami:** A vibrant, multicultural metropolis that buzzes both day and night.

★ **Beaches:** Surf-pounded on the Atlantic coast, powdery and pure white on the Gulf.

★ **Key West:** Quirky, fun, and tacky, it's both family-friendly and decidedly not.

★ **Golf:** Oceanfront and inland, some of the country's finest links are found here.

★ **Theme Parks:** The state has some of the biggest and best, not all of them Disney.

★ **Family Fun:** From shelling in Sanibel to meeting astronauts at Kennedy Space Center.

Fodor's FLORIDA 2016

Publisher: Amanda D'Acierno, *Senior Vice President*

Editorial: Arabella Bowen, *Editor in Chief*; Linda Cabasin, *Editorial Director*

Design: Tina Malaney, *Associate Art Director*; Chie Ushio, *Senior Designer*

Photography: Jennifer Arnow, *Senior Photo Editor*; Mary Robnett, *Photo Researcher*

Production: Linda Schmidt, *Managing Editor*; Evangelos Vasilakis, *Associate Managing Editor*; Angela L. McLean, *Senior Production Manager*

Maps: Rebecca Baer, *Senior Map Editor*; David Lindroth, Mark Stroud (Moon Street Cartography), *Cartographers*

Sales: Jacqueline Lebow, *Sales Director*

Marketing & Publicity: Heather Dalton, *Marketing Director*; Katherine Punia, *Publicity Director*

Business & Operations: Susan Livingston, *Vice President, Strategic Business Planning*; Sue Daulton, *Vice President, Operations*

Fodors.com: Megan Bell, *Executive Director, Revenue & Business Development*; Yasmin Marinaro, *Senior Director, Marketing & Partnerships*

Writers: Kate Bradshaw, Jennifer Greenhill-Taylor, Rona Gindin, Joseph Hayes, Lynne Helm, Jennie Hess, Jill Martin, Steve Master, Gary McKechnie, Jan Norris, Paul Rubio, Ashley Wright

Editors: Doug Stallings (Lead Editor), Bethany Beckerlegge

Production Editor: Elyse Rozelle

ISBN 978–1–101–87845–3

ISSN 0193–9556

All details in this book are based on information supplied to us at press time. Always confirm information when it matters, especially if you're making a detour to visit a specific place. Fodor's expressly disclaims any liability, loss, or risk, personal or otherwise, that is incurred as a consequence of the use of any of the contents of this book.

SPECIAL SALES

This book is available at special discounts for bulk purchases for sales promotions or premiums. For more information, e-mail specialmarkets@penguinrandomhouse.com.

PRINTED IN THE UNITED STATES OF AMERICA

10 9 8 7 6 5 4 3 2 1

CONTENTS

Fodor's Features

ABOUT THIS GUIDE

Fodor's Recommendations

Everything in this guide is worth doing—we don't cover what isn't—but exceptional sights, hotels, and restaurants are recognized with additional accolades. **Fodor's**Choice★ indicates our top recommendations. Care to nominate a new place? Visit Fodors.com/contact-us.

Trip Costs

We list prices wherever possible to help you budget well. Hotel and restaurant price categories from **$** to **$$$$** are noted alongside each recommendation. For hotels, we include the lowest cost of a standard double room in high season. For restaurants, we cite the average price of a main course at dinner or, if dinner isn't served, at lunch. For attractions, we always list adult admission fees; discounts are usually available for children, students, and senior citizens.

Hotels

Our local writers vet every hotel to recommend the best overnights in each price category, from budget to expensive. Unless otherwise specified, you can expect private bath, phone, and TV in your room. *Hotel reviews have been shortened. For full information, visit Fodors.com.*

Top Picks

★ **Fodor's**Choice

Listings

✉ Address
📨 Branch address
☎ Telephone
📠 Fax
🌐 Website
📧 E-mail
🎫 Admission fee
🕒 Open/closed times
[M] Subway
✥ Directions or Map coordinates

Hotels & Restaurants

🏨 Hotel
🛏 Number of rooms
🍽 Meal plans
✕ Restaurant
✍ Reservations
👔 Dress code
▭ No credit cards
[$] Price

Other

⇨ See also
☞ Take note
⛳ Golf facilities

Restaurants

Unless we state otherwise, restaurants are open for lunch and dinner daily. We mention dress code only when there's a specific requirement and reservations only when they're essential or not accepted. *To make restaurant reservations, visit Fodors.com.*

Credit Cards

The hotels and restaurants in this guide typically accept credit cards. If not, we'll say so.

EUGENE FODOR

Hungarian-born Eugene Fodor (1905–91) began his travel career as an interpreter on a French cruise ship. The experience inspired him to write *On the Continent* (1936), the first guidebook to receive annual updates and discuss a country's way of life as well as its sights. Fodor later joined the U.S. Army and worked for the OSS in World War II. After the war, he kept up his intelligence work while expanding his guidebook series. During the Cold War, many guides were written by fellow agents who understood the value of insider information. Today's guides continue Fodor's legacy by providing travelers with timely coverage, insider tips, and cultural context.

EXPERIENCE FLORIDA

WHAT'S WHERE

The following numbers refer to chapters.

2 Miami and Miami Beach. Greater Miami is hot—and we're not just talking about the weather. Art deco buildings and balmy beaches set the scene. Vacations here are as much about lifestyle as locale, so prepare for power shopping, club-hopping, and decadent dining.

3 The Everglades. Covering more than 1.5 million acres, the fabled "River of Grass" is the state's greatest natural treasure. Biscayne National Park (95% of which is under-water) runs a close second. It's the largest marine park in the United States.

4 The Florida Keys. This slender necklace of landfalls, strung together by a 113-mile highway, marks the southern edge of the continental United States. It's nirvana for anglers, divers, literature lovers, and Jimmy Buffett wannabes.

5 Fort Lauderdale with Broward County. The town *Where the Boys Are* has grown up. The beaches that first attracted college kids are now complemented by luxe lodgings and upscale enter-tainment options.

6 Palm Beach with the Treasure Coast. This area scores points for diversity.

Palm Beach and environs are famous for their golden sand and glitzy residents, whereas the Treasure Coast has unspoiled natural delights.

7 The Tampa Bay Area. Tampa's Busch Gardens and Ybor City are only part of the area's appeal. Culture vultures flock to St. Petersburg and Sarasota for concerts and museums, and eco-adventur-ers veer north to the Nature Coast.

8 The Lower Gulf Coast. Blessed with beaches, this was the last bit of coast to be settled. But as Naples's manicured golf greens and Fort Myers's mansions-cum-museums prove, it is far from uncivilized.

9 Orlando and Environs. Theme parks are what draw most visitors to the area, yet downtown Orlando, Kissim-mee, and Winter Park have enough sights, shops, and restaurants to make them destinations in their own right.

10 Walt Disney World. The granddaddy of attractions, Disney is four theme parks in one—Magic Kingdom, Animal Kingdom, Epcot, and Hollywood Studios. Plus, it has a pair of water parks and Downtown Disney (an entertainment zone featuring Cirque du Soleil).

11 Universal Orlando. The movies are brought to life at Universal Studios, while Islands of Adventure deliv-ers gravity-defying rides and special-effects surprises—and the Wizarding World of Harry Potter. Nearby Wet 'n Wild is full of watery adventures.

12 SeaWorld Orlando. Marine mammals perform in SeaWorld's meticulously choreographed shows, and thrill seekers find their adren-aline rush on coasters. Sister park Discovery Cove offers a daylong, swim-with-the-dolphins escape. At Aquatica water park, one slide even dips into a dolphin habitat.

13 Northeast Florida. Though time rewinds in historic St. Augustine, it's on fast-forward in Daytona Beach and the Space Coast, where horse-drawn carriages are replaced by race cars and rocket ships.

14 The Panhandle. South-ern gentility and redneck rambunctiousness make the Panhandle a colorful place—but it's the green gulf waters and sugar-white sand that keep devotees coming back.

FLORIDA TOP ATTRACTIONS

Walt Disney World

(A) Like one of Snow White's dwarfs, Orlando was sleepy until Uncle Walt turned this swampland into the world's most famous tourist attraction. Nowadays Walt Disney World is a 39-square-mile complex and growing, with four separate parks, scores of hotels, and satellite attractions. Thanks to innovative rides and dazzling animatronics, these parks feature prominently in every child's holiday fantasy. Walt Disney World also has grown-up amenities, including championship golf courses, sublime hotels and spas, and fine restaurants. If you have time for only one megapark, choose the original: Walt Disney World's Magic Kingdom. ⇨ *Chapter 10.*

South Beach

(B) You can't miss the distinctive forms, vibrant colors, and extravagant flourishes of SoBe's architectural gems. The world's largest concentration of art deco edifices is right here. The neighborhood also has enough beautiful people to qualify for the Register of Hippest Places. The glitterati, along with assorted vacationing hedonists, are drawn by übertrendy shops and a surfeit of celeb-studded clubs. Divine eateries are the icing—umm, better make that the ganache—on South Beach's proverbial cake. ⇨ *Chapter 2.*

Key West

(C) These 800-plus islands in the Florida Keys are at once a unique landmass and a mass of contradictions. At the far end of this island chain, Key West is the main attraction. Its laid-back vibe is intoxicating. Eating, drinking, water sports, sunset cruises, kayaking, and more drinking are high on the agenda. Visitors never grow tired of the walking tours through the gingerbread-house-filled streets and channeling the spirit of Ernest Hemingway, who lived and worked here. Today, touring his former digs and toasting his memory at

Sloppy Joe's Bar on Duval Street is almost mandatory. ⇨ *Chapter 4*.

Shopping in Fort Lauderdale and Miami

(D) The Sunshine State is a shopaholic's dream. Visitors travel from overseas with the sole purpose of shopping weekends at Fort Lauderdale's 2-mile, alligator-shape Sawgrass Mills outlet mall. The alfresco addition to the mall, The Colonnade Outlets, features more upscale stores like David Yurman, Valentino, and Prada. For true high-end shoppers, Bal Harbour Shops in the swanky Miami suburb is a collection of 100 haute couture shops, boutiques, and department stores. Restaurants and cafés, in tropical garden settings, overflow with style-conscious diners. A formidable rival to Bal Harbour's haute couture empire is Miami's growing Design District. ⇨ *Chapters 2 and 5*.

Universal Orlando

(E) With rides and attractions more geared toward adults and teens, Universal's two theme parks—Universal Studios and Islands of Adventure—deliver gravity-defying rides and special-effects extravaganzas based on popular television shows and films. At the Wizarding World of Harry Potter at Islands of Adventure, you'll get to see Hogwarts Castle and drink butter beer! ⇨ *Chapter 11*.

Kennedy Space Center

(F) Though there are enough wide-open expanses to justify the area's moniker, it was NASA that put the "space" in Space Coast—and this is its star attraction. Space memorabilia and aeronautic antiques, ranging from Redstone rockets to the *Apollo XIV* command module, turn an outing here into a trip back in time for anyone who lived through the space race. More down-to-earth types can also visit the Merritt Island National Wildlife

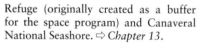

Refuge (originally created as a buffer for the space program) and Canaveral National Seashore. ⇨ *Chapter 13.*

Tampa Bay

(G) As a vibrant city with exceptional beaches, Tampa Bay is perfect for indecisive folks who want to enjoy surf and sand without sacrificing urban experiences. Families will love Busch Gardens, a major zoo and theme park. Football and hockey fans will relish the chance to see the Buccaneers and Lightning play. Baseball is big, too: the Rays are based here, and the Yankees descend annually for spring training. ⇨ *Chapter 7.*

The Dalí Museum

(H) St. Petersburg is home to a museum dedicated to the work of Salvador Dalí, showcasing the most comprehensive collection of the surrealist's artwork. This is the kind of first-class museum you'd expect to find in Paris or Madrid, but instead it's here on the Gulf Coast. The state-of-the-art glass building housing the museum is quite a spectacle in and of itself. ⇨ *Chapter 7.*

Sportfishing

(I) Islamorada in the Florida Keys holds steadfast to its claim as Sportfishing Capital of the World. Up in the Panhandle, Destin proves it is the World's Luckiest Fishing Village each October by inviting anglers young and old to compete in the monthlong Destin Fishing Rodeo. However, if you'd prefer to throw fish rather than catch them, head to Pensacola in late April for the Interstate Mullet Toss. (Participants line up to throw dead fish across the Florida–Alabama state line.) ⇨ *Chapter 14.*

Stand-Up Paddleboarding

(J) Also called "YOLO Boarding," paddleboarding involves jumping on what looks like a wide surf board and exploring calm waters with paddle in hand to push you forward. Requiring only a bit

of balance, almost anyone can do this (unlike surfing, which can be difficult to learn). Destin is paddleboard central, but you can enjoy the sport all over the Panhandle. ⇨ *Chapter 14.*

Palm Beach

(K) If money could talk, you'd hardly be able to hear above the din in Palm Beach. The upper crust started calling it home—during winter at least—in the early 1900s. And today it remains a ritzy, glitzy enclave for both old money and the nouveau riche (a coterie led by the Donald himself, who owns the landmark Mar-a-Lago Club). Simply put, Palm Beach is the sort of place where shopping is a full-time pursuit and residents don't just wear Polo—they play it. Ooh and aah to your heart's content; then, for more conspicuous consumption, continue south on the aptly named Gold Coast. ⇨ *Chapter 6.*

Broward's Inland Waterways

(L) Mariners should set their compass for Fort Lauderdale (aka the Venice of America), where vessels from around the world moor along some two dozen finger isles between the beach and the mainland. Tourists can cruise Broward County's 300 miles of inland waterways by water taxi and tour boat, or bob around the Atlantic in a chartered yacht. If you're in a buying mood, come in late October for the annual Fort Lauderdale International Boat Show. Billed as the world's largest, it has $3 billion worth of boats in every conceivable size, shape, and price range. ⇨ *Chapter 5.*

Little Havana

(M) On the streets of Miami's Little Havana, just west of downtown, salsa tunes blare and the smell of spicy chorizo fills the air. (You can get a good whiff of tobacco, too, thanks to the cigar makers who still hand-roll their products here.)

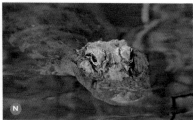

For nearly 50 years, the neighborhood's undisputed heart has been Calle Ocho, the commercial thoroughfare that hosts Carnaval Miami. The roaring 10-day block party each March culminates with the world's longest conga line. Ambience- and amenity-wise, it is as close as you'll get to Cuba without visiting the island itself. ⇨ *Chapter 2.*

The Everglades

(N) No trip to southern Florida is complete without seeing the Everglades. At its heart is a river—50 miles wide but merely 6 inches deep—flowing from Lake Okeechobee into Florida Bay. For an up-close look, speed demons can board an airboat that careens through the marshy waters. Purists, alternately, may placidly canoe or kayak within the boundaries of Everglades National Park. Just remember to keep your hands in the boat. The sharp saw grass and critters that call this unique ecosystem home (alligators, Florida

panthers, cottonmouth snakes, and horse-flies for starters) can add real cut, bite, or sting to your visit! ⇨ *Chapter 3.*

Sanibel Island

(O) Ready to do something slightly more vigorous than applying SPF 45 and rolling over? Trade beach-bumming for beach-combing in Sanibel, the Shell Capital of the World. Conchs, cockles, clams, coquinas—they're all here (the bounty is due to this barrier island's unusual east–west orientation). Of course, if you'd rather construct sand castles than do the Sanibel Stoop, you need only cross the 3-mile causeway to Fort Myers Beach. It has the finest building material and, every November, professional and amateur aficionados prove it during the American SandSculpting Championship. ⇨ *Chapter 8.*

Ringling Center for the Arts

(P) Sarasota, once winter headquarters for Ringling Bros. and Barnum & Bailey, is proud of its circus heritage. Ringling's former 32-room, 15-bathroom mansion is now the site of the Florida State University's Ringling Center for the Cultural Arts. Within this center, visitors who can't get enough of sawdust and sequins can see an impressive collection of vintage costumes, props, and parade wagons at the stunning Ringling Circus Museum. In addition, the center's John and Mable Ringling Museum of Art showcases 500 years of art, including an impressive collection of tapestries and paintings by Rubens. The adjacent Tibbals Learning Center houses a mind-boggling ¾-inch-scale miniature circus with almost a million pieces. ⇨ *Chapter 7.*

St. Augustine

(Q) History comes to life in St. Augustine . . . and the same can perhaps be said of the undead. Ghosts are plentiful, thanks to all the pirates, plunderers, and other lost souls who formerly lived in this deceptively quiet city. To hear lurid lore about local haunts, sign on for one of the nightly outings organized by Ghost Tours of St. Augustine. These 90-minute lantern-lighted walks recount spirited stories full of goose-bump-inducing details. You can also opt for a trolley ride and enter the old jail if you dare, or take a cruise through the harbor shadows in the summer. Top off your tour with an overnight stay at St. Francis Inn (St. Augustine's oldest hostelry) or the Casablanca Inn: both are reputedly haunted. ⇨ *Chapter 13.*

IF YOU LIKE

Animal Encounters

While Florida is known for one particular animated mouse, there is a lot of genuine wildlife here, too. In terms of biodiversity, the state ranks third in the country, with approximately 1,200 different kinds of critters.

■ **Alligators.** Florida has more than 1.3 million resident alligators. You can witness them doing inane tricks at places like **Gatorland** (⇨ *Chapter 9*), but gator spotting in the wild is far more rewarding. Everglades National Park teems with gators. The best place to get up close and personal with them is **Shark Valley** (⇨ *Chapter 3*), 45 miles west of Miami.

■ **Birds.** Poised on two major migratory routes, Florida draws about 500 species of birds—and the 2,000-mile **Great Florida Birding Trail** (⇨ *Chapter 8*) helps you track them down. Through detailed guides and highway signs, it identifies sites where you may spy anything from bald eagles to burrowing owls.

■ **Manatees.** They're nicknamed "sea cows" and resemble walruses. But Florida's official marine mammals are most closely related to elephants, which may account for their slow pace and hefty frames. For a chance at swimming with manatees in the wild, take an organized pontoon ride through **Crystal River** (⇨ *Chapter 7*), near the Upper Gulf Coast.

■ **Sea Turtles.** Ready for a late-night rendezvous with the massive leatherbacks and loggerheads that lumber onto Floridian beaches to lay their eggs between March and October? **Archie Carr National Wildlife Refuge** (⇨ *Chapter 6*), the Western Hemisphere's largest loggerhead nesting site, organizes turtle watches in June and July.

Life in the Fast Lane

The Sunshine State has been satisfying visitors' need for speed ever since Henry Ford and his snowbird buddies started using Ormond Beach as a test track. Today roller coasters, stock cars, supersonic jets, and spaceships add momentum to your vacation.

■ **Daytona Beach.** Daytona 500, NASCAR's most prestigious event, pulls in legions of devotees each February. But any time of year you can slip into a driving suit and then into the driver's seat of a Winston Cup–style stock car, courtesy of the Richard Petty Driving Experience at **Daytona International Speedway.** *See* ⇨ *Chapter 13*.

■ **Kennedy Space Center.** Whether you admire Buzz Aldrin or Buzz Lightyear, this spot has the right stuff. See a rocket launch or take your own giant leap with the **Astronaut Training Experience.** The half-day program consists of realistic training exercises culminating in a simulated mission. *See* ⇨ *Chapter 13*.

■ **Pensacola.** The **National Museum of Naval Aviation** displays 150-plus military aircraft and has motion-based simulators that let you "fly" an F/A-18. Better yet, the U.S. Navy Precision Flight Team (familiar to most of us as the Blue Angels) is based here, so you may get to observe them in action at 700 mph. *See* ⇨ *Chapter 14*.

■ **Tampa.** If you think the pursuit of happiness is a high-speed activity, head for **Busch Gardens,** Florida's premier roller-coaster location. SheiKra is one of the world's tallest dive coasters, Kumba features one of the world's largest vertical loops, and Montu (a gut-churning inverted coaster) delivers a g-force of 3.85. *See* ⇨ *Chapter 7*.

Something Old, Something New

You don't have to look far for "New Florida." It's evident in skyscrapers and sprawling suburbs, in malls, multiplexes, and the ubiquitous condo complexes that obscure parts of the coast. Yet it is easy enough to find reminders of the state's rich past.

■ **Apalachicola.** A booming cotton-and-lumber industry turned this Panhandle town into a bustling port in the 19th century. Now it's part of the Forgotten Coast. Hundreds of preserved buildings, ranging from antebellum warehouses to gracious Victorian-style homes, give it a time-warped appeal. *See ⇨ Chapter 14.*

■ **Coral Gables.** You can soak up 1920s architecture in Miami Beach. But in nearby Coral Gables you can soak *in* it at the **Venetian Pool**, a vintage municipal lagoon fashioned from a quarry. Back in the day it attracted Johnny Weissmuller, Esther Williams, and other legendary swimmers. *See ⇨ Chapter 2.*

■ **Cross Creek.** You can tour the Cracker-style house where Marjorie Kinnan Rawlings wrote *The Yearling* at **Marjorie Kinnan Rawlings Historic State Park** from October through July and visit the surrounding farm and grove year-round. *See ⇨ Chapter 13.*

■ **St. Augustine.** Fortify yourself at **Castillo de San Marcos.** Built by the Spanish to defend *La Florida,* this formidable 17th-century structure is America's oldest masonry fort. Even kids whose interest in architecture stops at Cinderella Castle will be impressed by its turrets, moat, and double drawbridge. *See ⇨ Chapter 13.*

Hitting the Greens

With more courses than any other state and weather that allows for year-round play, Florida is a dream destination for golfers. Ready to go for it? The tourism board's new, dedicated golf website (⊕ *www.golf.visitflorida.com*) will point you in the right direction.

■ **The Breakers.** Floridians' fascination with golf began in 1897 when the state's first course opened at this Palm Beach resort. (Rockefellers, Vanderbilts, and Astors are all listed in the guest book.) Today, the original 70-par **Ocean Course** offers spectacular Atlantic views and challenging shots on 140 acres. *See ⇨ Chapter 6.*

■ **PGA Village.** Owned and operated by the PGA, this Port St. Lucie venue boasts three championship courses designed by Tom Fazio and Pete Dye, plus a 35-acre **Golf Learning and Performance Center** that can turn weekend duffers into scratch players. A free museum of golf memorabilia is also on site. *See ⇨ Chapter 6.*

■ **Trump National Doral Miami.** The **Blue Monster** understandably grabs the spotlight here: the par-72 course has been a stop on the PGA tour for a half century. But the Miami resort has four other championship courses (including the new Golden Palm Course) as well as a Jim McLean golf school. *See ⇨ Chapter 2.*

FLORIDA'S BEST BEACHES

Bahia Honda State Park
Though the Florida Keys aren't renowned for beautiful sandy beaches, this is an exception. The 524-acre park has three superb beaches over 2.5 miles of sandy coastline at the crossroads of the Atlantic and the gulf, idyllic for swimming, snorkeling, kayaking, and fishing. Atlantic-facing Sandspur beach flaunts long stretches of powdery sands. *See* ⇨ *Chapter 4.*

Bowman's Beach, Sanibel Island
On Sanibel's secluded northwest end, this beach doubles as a shell hunter's paradise and a beach wanderer's great escape. For the former, the likelihood of leaving with a bag full of gorgeous shells is high. For the latter, the chance of serene, inspiring vistas is guaranteed. *See* ⇨ *Chapter 8.*

Caladesi Island State Park
Accessible only by ferry from Honeymoon Island State Recreation Area, this park offers pure white beaches, beautiful sunsets, and excellent bird-watching. *See* ⇨ *Chapter 7.*

Clearwater Beach
At what is arguably the state's best beach for families, kids and parents alike love the white stands and shallow, clear, warm waters by day, followed by sunset celebrations nightly, complete with musicians and artists. *See* ⇨ *Chapter 7.*

Fort de Soto Beach
Another winner of "America's Best Beach," the 1,136-acre park lies at the mouth of Tampa Bay, spread over five islands and housing 7 miles of beach, two fishing piers, and a 4-mile hiking/skating trail. The beaches are super packed on weekends but splendidly quiet on weekdays. *See* ⇨ *Chapter 7.*

Fort Lauderdale Beach
The former spring-break capital now plays host to a reinvented, more upscale beachfront; however, the downy sands and crystalline waters from the days of

Where the Boys Are haven't changed. The beach "scene" is found between Las Olas and Sunrise boulevards. *See ⇨ Chapter 5.*

John Pennekamp Coral Reef State Park

Florida's best bet for diving and snorkeling, this state park adjacent to the Florida Keys National Marine Sanctuary encompasses 78 square miles of ecological treasures, the majority of which are found underwater. Although the beaches here do attract families, the real draw is experiencing the underwater world of the 600 varieties of fish that call this park home. *See ⇨ Chapter 4.*

Panama City Beach

It may be Spring Break Capital of the World come March and April, but the rest of the year this 17-mile expanse of snowy-white sand and sparking emerald-green water attracts families from all across the Southeast to enjoy some awesome fun in the sun. Pier Park offers great shopping and watering holes on the streets opposite the beachfront hotels. *See ⇨ Chapter 14.*

Siesta Key Beach

Crowned "America's Best Beach" in 2012, this one boasts the finest quartz sands in the world. The sand is so fine and powdery it appears like piles of flour and squeaks under your feet when you walk on it. The 40-acre beach park of this island is exceptionally wide and long, providing ample space for families, romantics, and Sunday's Drum Circle celebration. *See ⇨ Chapter 7.*

South Beach

The legend of beautiful people is very much a reality on the sands parallel to deco-drenched Ocean Drive from 5th to 15th Street, and upscale Collins Avenue from 15th to 23rd Street. Expect diesel bodies, plastic surgery, hunky gay guys, pretentious partygoers, and random families coming to see what the fuss is all about. *See ⇨ Chapter 2.*

GREAT ITINERARIES

NORTHERN FLORIDA IN ONE WEEK

As much as South Florida centers on the present and future, northern Florida is more about the past. From America's oldest city—the circa 1565 St. Augustine—to the lost-in-time seaside communities along the 250-mile coastline of the Florida Panhandle, northern Florida embraces the architecture, simplicity, and pace of yesteryear. Beyond dedicated party towns, don't expect much in terms of nightlife or glitz. Do expect stunning, wide expanses of white-sand beach, day-caught seafood served up in no-frills settings, regions rich in marine life, excellent fishing, a family-friendly atmosphere and plenty of fun-in-the-sun.

St. Augustine

1 or 2 days. Start your journey through northern Florida in the nation's oldest city, which was founded by the Spanish in 1565. To explore the state's Spanish past, visit Castillo de San Marcos (its colonial-era fortress), the Colonial Quarter (a 2-acre living history museum of Florida life in the 16th, 17th, and 18th centuries), or stroll the streets of the Old City that grew up around the colonial quarter, giving you a chance to experience life in the past lane. A whole city block of historic houses built between 1790 and 1910 has been turned into the Dow Museum. But St. Augustine's future isn't all in the past. Peruse the many boutiques and indulge at the prolific restaurants that line the town center, stay in one of the many charming B&Bs, and discover why St. Augustine rivals Savannah and Charleston as one of America's most charming cities. To the east is Anastasia Island, a state park with a stunning beach. ⇨ *Chapter 13.*

Amelia Island and Vicinity

2 days. Head northeast beyond Jacksonville to reach prestigious Amelia Island, home to world-class beach resorts and wide swathes of family-friendly beaches. By day simply enjoy some fun-in-the-sun or beachcomb nearby undeveloped beaches for sand dollars and seashells. At night, search for nesting sea turtles. You can stay in one of Amelia Island's posh resorts, or for a similar experience that doesn't require such deep pockets, enjoy the beach action slightly south along one of the four quieter communities of Jacksonville Beaches, specifically Atlantic Beach or Ponte Vedra Beach. Jacksonville itself is a underrated vacation destination full of charm with a lively arts scene that often turns up on lists of the best places to live in the U.S. Take a short detour into Jacksonville one day to visit the Museum of Contemporary Art Jacksonville or the Jacksonville Zoo and Gardens, two of the area's world-class attractions. ⇨ *Chapter 13.*

Tallahassee

1 day. Drive west toward the Panhandle to get a true taste of the Old South in Spanish moss-draped Tallahassee, visiting one or two of the region's 71 plantations, such as Goodwood Museum and Gardens. Then get a dose of Old Florida at Edward Ball Wakulla Springs State Park, protected since the 1930s and famous as the jungle setting of the original Tarzan films, which today houses the largest and deepest freshwater spring in the world and plenty of manatees, alligators, and turtles, plus more than 180 species of birds. ⇨ *Chapter 14.*

Panama City Beach

1 or 2 days. Continue past the state capital to the 250-mile-plus belt known as Panhandle's Emerald Coast, heralded for its powdery white-sand beaches and sparkling water. If you take the coastal route, U.S. 98, along the way you may want to plan a stop in Apalachicola, a friendly and charming fishing town that's become a major regional tourist draw. Off the beach, this area feels more southern than South Florida. Sun-worship and indulge in gulf-to-table seafood in Panama City Beach, enjoying enhanced nightlife options that go beyond the typical spring break options. Take a boat tour out to St. Andrews State Park to tour protected Shell Island, one of the few places in the world where you can swim with dolphins in the wild. ⇨ *Chapter 14.*

Pensacola Beach

1 or 2 days. From Panama City Beach to Pensacola, take a relaxing drive along scenic Route 30A, passing nostalgia-inducing communities like WaterColor and Seaside, with an optional stop in glorious Grayton Beach, where kayaking ranks high on the agenda—or have lunch in the Panhandle's poshest subcity, Sandestin. At Pensacola Beach—one of the longest barrier islands in the world—enjoy such pursuits

as fishing, boating, water sports, or simply relaxing and soaking in the laid-back beach vibe. Time and interest permitting, take a half-day trip up to Florida Caverns State Park, one of the state's lesser-known treasures, where rangers lead insightful cave tours. ⇨ *Chapter 14.*

CENTRAL FLORIDA IN ONE WEEK

Theme parks, nature, and beaches—oh my! Central Florida lures in the masses with the prospect of thrilling rides, handshakes with Mickey Mouse, overall Disney magic, and simply basking in the frivolity of childhood, though its appeal spans far beyond man-made attractions. In fact, Central Florida also stakes claim to the state's most exceptional natural riches, including some of the country's superlative beaches (with accolades to prove it) and unparalleled nature encounters, such as swimming with manatees in the wild and bird-watching at Merritt Island National Wildlife Refuge.

Orlando

2 or 3 days. You could easily spend a week at Walt Disney World alone. But unless you're a die-hard theme park devotee, a few days is sufficient. Spend a few days park-hopping at Walt Disney World between The Magic Kingdom, Epcot, Disney's Hollywood Studios, and Disney's Animal Kingdom. Smaller kids may enjoy a quieter time at nearby Legoland, some 50 miles from Orlando. For more intense thrills, allow a day or two for movie magic at Universal Studios or heart-pumping rides at Islands of Adventure, where Harry Potter now reigns and draws crowds by the millions. If you are theme parked–out after two days (or never really liked them to begin with), survey the collection of modern paintings at the Orlando Museum of Art, stroll through the 50-acre Harry P. Leu Gardens, or visit Orlando's serene sister city, Winter Park. Boaters can take advantage of the area's numerous lakes, and golfers can link up on courses designed by the sport's biggest stars. ⇨ *Chapter 9, 10, and 11.*

Cape Canaveral

1 day. Head east from Orlando to discover one of Florida's best central coast treasures. Spend the day bird-watching at Merritt Island National Wildlife Refuge, have an out-of-this-world- experience at the Kennedy Space Center (and enjoy the interactive Space Shuttle *Challenger* exhibit), catch a wave like local surfing legend Kelly Slater in Cocoa Beach, or blissfully hit the beach at Canaveral National Seashore—a 24-mile undeveloped preserve where you lounge in the shelter of dunes, not the shadow of high-rises. Adrenaline junkies may want to reset their GPS for Daytona Beach. Its International Speedway, which has hosted NASCAR's Daytona 500 every February since 1959, is a must-see for stock-car enthusiasts (and the plane 'ole race-car curious). ⇨ *Chapter 13.*

Tampa

1 day. If you crave more theme park fun, scream through the hair-raising rides at Busch Gardens and admire the 2,000-animal zoo, intricately woven throughout the park. The more sports-minded, may want to catch one of Tampa Bay's myriad sporting events (the city has professional baseball, football, and hockey teams). Beach-lovers who didn't get enough sand and surf in Cape Canaveral may want to head over to Clearwater Beach to find some of central Florida's best sandy shores. At night, dine and imbibe in the Spanish-inflected Ybor City entertainment district. ⇨ *Chapter 7.*

St. Petersburg

2 days. Indulge in the culture and beaches of this sophisticated city, home to the riveting, world-class Salvador Dalí Museum, multiple art galleries, and a quaint, historic downtown. Hit the beach at Caladesi

Island State Park to the west of the city or Fort De Soto Park at the mouth of Tampa Bay, both winners of the national "America's Best Beach" competition. Or explore the colorful waterfront community of Gulfport and its Art Village, which is full of locally owned boutiques, galleries, and eclectic eateries. Beer-lovers will want to set aside time to explore the city's burgeoning craft beer scene. ⇨ *Chapter 7.*

Sarasota

1 day. Drive south to Sarasota to appreciate Florida's thriving arts scene and stay overnight on one of the western barrier islands, namely Longboat Key or Siesta Key, the latter home to the finest quartz sand in the world and one of America's best beaches. In Sarasota, visit the John and Mable Ringling Museum of Art to learn all about the history of the Ringling circus and enjoy John Ringling's mind-blowingly expansive art collection. The museum encompasses the entire Ringling estate and offers something for guests of all ages and interests. ⇨ *Chapter 7.*

Crystal River

1/2 day. As a half-day trip, nature lovers should proceed north to Crystal River, less than two hours north of St. Petersburg, where you can snorkel with the manatees that congregate in the warm waters

TIPS

■ Fly into and out of Orlando or Tampa, but you'll definitely need to rent a car.

■ In Orlando, a park-hopper pass will save you money and permit entry into multiple theme parks in a single day.

■ While within Disney World, leave your rental car in the hotel parking lot. Complimentary Disney buses transport you around this magical land.

■ The beaches around Tampa Bay and St. Petersburg are best on weekdays, when you are likely to have miles of sand all to yourself.

from November through March. It's one of the few places on the planet where you can legally interact with them in natural waters. In off-season months, get your nature fix with a dolphin-watching cruise through the Florida Aquarium, back in Tampa. ⇨ *Chapter 7.*

SOUTH FLORIDA IN ONE WEEK

Beautiful beaches and even more beautiful people, pulsing nightlife, striking architecture, fancy yachts, old money, new money, exotic wildlife, and stunning marine life—South Florida's got it all. One week is hardly enough to explore the region in detail, but it's enough for a sampler platter of this wildly popular vacation destination.

Fort Lauderdale

1 day. Whether you fly into Miami or right into Fort Lauderdale, make the Yachting Capital of the World and the Venice of America your first stop; it's only an hour from the Miami airport. Known for its expansive beaches, show-stopping resort hotels, exploding food scene, and burgeoning cultural scene, Fort Lauderdale has a lot to like, it may be hard to get your fill in a single day. Take to the waterways to appreciate this coastal beauty. Stroll picture-perfect Las Olas Boulevard, browsing the boutiques and enjoying the eclectic eateries lining Fort Lauderdale's principal thoroughfare. ⇨ *Chapter 5.*

Palm Beaches

1 day. Less than two hours north of Fort Lauderdale, the opulent mansions of Palm Beach's Ocean Boulevard give you a glimpse of how the richer half lives. For exclusive boutique shopping, art gallery browsing, and glittery sightseeing, sybarites should wander down "The Avenue" (that's Worth Avenue to non–Palm Beachers). The sporty set will find dozens of places to tee up in the Palm Beaches (hardly surprising given that the PGA is based here), along with tennis courts, polo clubs, even a croquet center. While there's also a less expensive side to Palm Beach, the area's famous hotels are significantly cheaper after Easter weekend, when the high season ends and the city feels like a different place entirely. ⇨ *Chapter 6.*

Treasure Coast

1 day. To balance the highbrow with the low-key, head northward for a tour of the Treasure Coast, from Stuart to Sebastian. The region is notable for its outdoor activities and Old Florida ambience. This region was named for the booty spilled by a fleet of Spanish galleons shipwrecked here in 1715 though these days you're more likely to discover manatees and golden surfing opportunities than actual gold. You can also look for the sea turtles that lay their own little treasures in the sands March through October. As you drive north, you may want to stop in Jupiter, especially if you're a dog lover, to see one of the state's most dog-friendly beaches. ⇨ *Chapter 6.*

Miami

2 or 3 days. Greater Miami lays claim to the country's most celebrated strand—South Beach—and lingering there tops most tourist itineraries. Once you've checked out the candy-color art deco architecture, take time off to ogle the parade of stylish people along Lincoln Road Mall, Ocean Drive, or at the bars, restaurants, and sleek swimming pools within the ever-growing number of trendy hotels in both South Beach and Mid-Beach. Do some credit card damage up in the posh beachfront city of Bal Harbour or inland in the see-and-be-seen Design District. Later, *merengue* over to Calle Ocho, the center of Miami's Cuban community, and pay a visit to bohemian Coconut Grove or the Wynwood Arts District for some more culture. ⇨ *Chapter 2.*

The Everglades

1/2 day. Miami is the only U.S. city with two national parks and a national preserve in its backyard, deeming it a

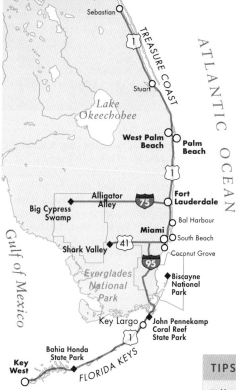

convenient base for eco-excursions. Especially if you stay three days, keep your car long enough to take a day trip to the Everglades. The easiest access point is Shark Valley, where you can bike along a trail teeming with alligators and herons. Alternatively, get a spectacular view of Florida's coral reefs from a glass-bottom boat in Biscayne National Park; and then spot some rare wood storks in Big Cypress Swamp, which is best explored via Alligator Alley (Interstate 75). ⇨ *Chapter 3.*

The Keys

2 or 3 days. Head south from the Florida mainland to the über-relaxing island chain, planning a pit stop at John Pennekamp Coral Reef State Park in Key Largo (which offers unparalleled snorkeling and scuba diving) or at Bahia Honda State Park farther south (it has ranger-led activities plus the Keys' best beach). Then plant yourself at the most famous key of all, Key West, where a come-as-you-are,

TIPS

■ You can fly into either Miami International Airport or Fort Lauderdale–Hollywood International Airport; pick whichever is cheaper.

■ You'll definitely need a rental car to get between most destinations in South Florida, but expensive parking, pedestrian-friendly streets, and taxis make a car unnecessary in both South Beach and Key West.

■ If you have time, drive from Miami to Key West, but flights back can be quick and cheap; check the drop-off charge for a one-way rental.

do-as-you-please vibe rules. The Old Town has a funky, laid-back feel, with prolific nods to Ernest Hemingway. If you haven't imbibed too much at one of the renowned watering holes, rent a moped to tour the rest of the island. Clear waters and abundant marine life make underwater activities another must. ⇨ *Chapter 4.*

WHEN TO GO

Although Florida is a year-round vacation venue, it divides the calendar into regional tourism seasons. Holidays and school breaks are major factors. However, the clincher is weather, with the best months being designated as peak periods.

High season in southern Florida starts with the run-up to Christmas and continues through Easter. Snowbirds migrate down then to escape frosty weather back home, and festivalgoers flock in because major events are held this time of year to avoid summer's searing heat and high humidity. Winter is also *the* time to visit the Everglades, as temperatures, mosquito activity, and water levels are all lower (making wildlife easier to spot).

Northern Florida, conversely, receives the greatest influx of visitors from Memorial Day to Labor Day. Costs are highest then, but so are temperatures. (In winter, when the mercury dips into the 40s, you'd get a chilly reception on Panhandle beaches.) Specific areas, like Panama City Beach or Daytona Beach, attract throngs—and thongs—during spring break, too. In the latter location, expect revved-up revelers during Speedweeks (late January and February) and Bike Week (early March).

Thanks to its theme parks, Central Florida is a magnet for children, meaning the largest crowds gather, logically enough, whenever class lets out. Lineups at attractions do shrink after they return to school, though this area's hopping all year, with large numbers of international families and kid-free adults coming in the off-season. Spring and fall shoulder seasons are the optimal time to visit, both weather-wise and price-wise.

Climate

Florida is rightly called the Sunshine State—areas like Tampa Bay report 361 days of sunshine a year! But it could also be dubbed the Humid State. From June through September, 90% humidity levels aren't uncommon, nor are accompanying thunderstorms. In fact, more than half of the state's rain falls during these months. Florida's two-sided coastline also makes it a target for tropical storms.

Hurricanes

The hurricane season begins on June 1 and lasts through November 1 (roughly half the year). However, big storms are much more likely in August and September. Chances are, you'll be just fine if you travel to Florida in June or July, though it's always a good idea to buy travel insurance in case something does happen. In the summer, frequent afternoon thunderstorms are common, especially inland in places like Orlando. On the coast, the weather is almost universally hot and muggy, and rain is common, especially later in the summer.

MIAMI AND
MIAMI BEACH

WELCOME TO MIAMI AND MIAMI BEACH

TOP REASONS TO GO

★ **The beach:** Miami Beach has been rated as one of the 10 best beaches in the world. White sand, warm water, and bronzed bodies everywhere provide just the right mix of relaxation and people-watching.

★ **Dining delights:** Miami's eclectic residents have transformed the city into a museum of epicurean wonders, ranging from Cuban and Argentine fare to fusion haute cuisine.

★ **Wee-hour parties:** A 24-hour liquor license means clubs stay open until 5 am, and after-parties go until noon the following day.

★ **Picture-perfect people:** Miami is a watering hole for the vain and beautiful of South America, Europe, and the Northeast. Watch them—or join them—as they strut their stuff and flaunt their tans on the white beds of renowned art deco hotels.

★ **Art Deco District:** Iconic pastels and neon lights accessorize the architecture that first put South Beach on the map in the 1930s.

1 Downtown. Weave through the glass-and-steel labyrinth of new condo construction to catch a game or a new exhibition.

2 Coconut Grove. Catch dinner and a movie, listen to live music, or cruise the bohemian shops.

3 Coral Gables. Dine and shop on family-friendly Miracle Mile, and take a driving tour of the surrounding neighborhoods.

4 Key Biscayne. Explore the pristine parks and stretches of award-winning beaches by boat, kayak, or foot.

5 Wynwood. Eat, shop, and gawk your way through this trendy, creative neighborhood north of downtown.

6 Midtown. Experience yuppie life in this residential enclave chock full of fabulous restaurants and lounges.

7 Design District. Browse the design showrooms and haute boutiques before dining at Miami's trendiest restaurants.

8 Little Haiti. Practice your Creole and sample Haitian food in this interesting ethnic neighborhood.

2

GETTING ORIENTED

Long considered the gateway to Latin America, Miami is as close to Cuba and the Caribbean as you can get within the United States. The 36-square-mile city is at the southern tip of the Florida peninsula, bordered on the east by Biscayne Bay. Over the bay lies a series of barrier islands, the largest being a thin 18-square-mile strip called Miami Beach. To the east of Miami Beach is the Atlantic Ocean. To the south are the Florida Keys.

9 Little Havana. Sip Cuban coffee, roll cigars, and play dominoes in the heart and soul of Cuba's exile community.

10 South Beach. People-watch from sidewalk cafés, admire art deco, and party 'til dawn at the nation's hottest clubs.

11 Mid-Beach. Experience the booming restaurant scene and trendy hotels just beyond South Beach.

12 Fisher and Belle Isle. Be near the pulse of Miami Beach but a man-made island away.

13 North Beach. Shop and relax in the quieter northern end of Miami Beach, which also encompasses Aventura, Bal Harbour, and Sunny Isles.

CUBAN FOOD

If the tropical vibe has you hankering for Cuban food, you've come to the right place. Miami is the top spot in the country to enjoy authentic Cuban cooking.

The flavors and preparations of Cuban cuisine are influenced by the island nation's natural bounty (yuca, sugarcane, guava), as well as its rich immigrant history, from near (Caribbean countries) and far (Spanish and African traditions). Chefs in Miami tend to stick with the classic versions of beloved dishes, though you'll find some variation from restaurant to restaurant, as recipes have often been passed down through generations of home cooks. For a true Cuban experience, try either the popular **Versailles** (⊠ *3555 S.W. 8th St.* ☎ *305/444-0240* ⊕ *www. versaillesrestaurant.com*) or classic **La Carreta** (⊠ *3632 S.W. 8th St.* ☎ *305/444-7501*) in Little Havana, appealing to families seeking a home-cooked, Cuban-style meal. For a modern interpretation of Cuban eats, head to Coral Gable's **Havana Harry's** (⊠ *4612 S. Le Jeune Rd.* ☎ *305/661-2622*). South Beach eatery **Puerto Sagua Restaurant** (⊠ *700 Collins Ave.* ☎ *305/673-1115*) is the beach's favorite Cuban hole-in-the-wall, open daily from 7 am to 2 am.

THE CUBAN SANDWICH

A great *cubano* (Cuban sandwich) requires pillowy Cuban bread layered with ham, garlic-citrus-marinated slow-roasted pork, Swiss cheese, and pickles (plus salami in Tampa, lettuce and tomatoes in Key West), with butter and/or mustard. The sandwich is grilled in a sandwich press until the cheese melts and all the elements are fused together. Try one at **Enriqueta's Sandwich Shop** (⊠ *2830 N.E. 2nd Ave.* ☎ *305/573-4681* ⊘ *Weekdays 6 am-4 pm, Sat. 6 am-2 pm*) in Wynwood, or **Exquisito Restaurant** (⊠ *1510 S.W. 8th St.* ☎ *305/643-0227* ⊘ *Daily 7 am-midnight*) in Little Havana.

KEY CUBAN DISHES

ARROZ CON POLLO

This chicken-and-rice dish is Cuban comfort food. Found throughout Latin America, the Cuban version is typically seasoned with garlic, paprika, and onions, then colored golden or reddish with saffron or *achiote* (a seed paste), and enlivened with a sizable splash of beer near the end of cooking. Green peas and sliced, roasted red peppers are standard toppings.

BISTEC DE PALOMILLA

This thinly sliced sirloin steak is marinated in lime juice and garlic and fried with onions. The steak is often served with *chimichurri* sauce, an olive oil, garlic, and cilantro sauce that sometimes comes with bread (slather bread with butter and dab on the chimichurri). Also try *ropa vieja*, a slow-cooked, shredded flank steak in a garlic-tomato sauce.

DESSERTS

Treat yourself to a slice of *tres leches* cake. The "three milks" come from the sweetened condensed milk, evaporated milk, and heavy cream that are poured over the cake until it's an utterly irresistible gooey mess. Also, don't miss the *pastelitos,* Cuban fruit-filled turnovers. Traditional flavors include plain guava, guava with cream cheese, and cream cheese with coconut. Yum!

DRINKS

Sip *guarapo* (gwa-RA-poh), a fresh sugarcane juice that isn't really as sweet as you might think, or grab a straw and enjoy a frothy *batido* (bah-TEE-doe), a Cuban-style milk shake made with tropical fruits like mango, *piña* (pineapple), or *mamey* (mah-MAY, a tropical fruit with a melon-cherry taste). For a real twist, try the *batido de trigo*—a wheat shake that will remind you of sugar-glazed breakfast cereal.

FRITAS

If you're in the mood for an inexpensive, casual Cuban meal, have a *frita*—a hamburger with distinctive Cuban flair. It's made with ground beef that's mixed with ground or finely chopped chorizo, spiced with pepper, paprika, and salt, topped with sautéed onions and shoestring potato fries, and then served on a bun slathered with a special tomato-based ketchup-like sauce.

LECHON ASADO

Fresh ham or an entire suckling pig marinated in *mojo criollo* (parsley, garlic, sour orange, and olive oil) is roasted until fork tender and served with white rice, black beans, and *tostones* (fried plantains) or *yuca* (pronounced YU-kah), a starchy tuber with a mild nut taste that's often sliced into fat sticks and deep-fried like fries.

By Paul Rubio   Three quarters of a century after the art deco movement, Miami remains one of the world's trendiest and flashiest hot spots. Luckily for visitors, South Beach is no longer the only place to stand and pose in Miami. North of downtown, the growing Wynwood and Design districts—along with nearby Midtown—are home to Miami's hipster and fashionista movements, and the South Beach "scene" continues to extend both north and west, with the addition of new venues north of 20th Street, south of 5th Street, and along the bay on West Avenue. The reopening of the mammoth Fontainebleau and its enclave of nightclubs and restaurants along Mid-Beach paved the way for a mid-beach renaissance, luring other globally renowned resorts, lounges, and restaurants into the neighborhood, such as the Soho Beach House and the Faena District Miami Beach, a multiblock project in mid-Beach by Argentinian icon and developer Alan Faena, scheduled for a 2017 completion.

Visit Miami today and it's hard to believe that 100 years ago it was a mosquito-infested swampland, with an Indian trading post on the Miami River. Then hotel builder Henry Flagler brought his railroad to the outpost known as Fort Dallas. Other visionaries—Carl Fisher, Julia Tuttle, William Brickell, and John Sewell, among others—set out to tame the unruly wilderness. Hotels were erected, bridges were built, the port was dredged, and electricity arrived. The narrow strip of mangrove coast was transformed into Miami Beach—and the tourists started to come. They haven't stopped since!

Greater Miami is many destinations in one. At its best it offers an unparalleled multicultural experience: melodic Latin and Caribbean tongues, international cuisines and cultural events, and an unmistakable joie de vivre—all against a beautiful beach backdrop. In Little Havana the air is tantalizing with the perfume of strong Cuban coffee. In Coconut Grove, Caribbean steel drums ring out during the Miami/Bahamas Goombay Festival. Anytime in colorful Miami Beach, restless crowds wait for entry to the hottest new clubs.

Many visitors don't know that Miami and Miami Beach are really separate cities. Miami, on the mainland, is South Florida's commercial hub. Miami Beach, on 17 islands in Biscayne Bay, is sometimes considered America's Riviera, luring refugees from winter with its warm sunshine; sandy beaches; graceful, shady palms; and tireless nightlife. The natives know well that there's more to Greater Miami than the bustle of South Beach and its Art Deco District. In addition to well-known places such as Ocean Drive and Lincoln Road, the less reported spots—like the burgeoning Design District in Miami, the historic buildings of Coral Gables, and the secluded beaches of Key Biscayne—are great insider destinations.

PLANNING

WHEN TO GO

Miami and Miami Beach are year-round destinations. Most people come from November through April, when the weather is close to perfect; hotels, restaurants, and attractions are busiest; and each weekend holds a festival or event. High season kicks off in December with Art Basel Miami Beach, and hotel rates don't come down until after the college kids have left after spring break in late March.

It's hot and steamy May through September, but nighttime temperatures are usually pleasant. Also, summer is a good time for the budget traveler. Many hotels lower their rates considerably, and many restaurants offer discounts—especially during Miami Spice in August and September, when a slew of top restaurants offer special tasting menus at a steep discount.

GETTING HERE AND AROUND

You'll need a car to visit many attractions and points of interest. If possible, avoid driving during the rush hours of 7–9 am and 5–7 pm—the hour just after and right before the peak times also can be slow going. During rainy weather, be especially cautious of flooding in South Beach and Key Biscayne.

AIR TRAVEL

Miami is serviced by Miami International Airport (MIA), 8 miles northwest of downtown, and Fort Lauderdale–Hollywood International Airport (FLL), 26 miles northeast. Many discount carriers, like Spirit Airlines, Southwest Airlines, and JetBlue, fly into FLL, making it a smart bargain if you're renting a car. Otherwise, look for flights to MIA, which recently underwent an extensive face-lift, improving facilities, common spaces, and the overall aesthetic of the airport.

CAR TRAVEL

Interstate 95 is the major expressway connecting South Florida with points north; State Road 836 is the major east–west expressway and connects to Florida's Turnpike, State Road 826, and Interstate 95. Seven causeways link Miami and Miami Beach, with I–195 and I–395 offering the most convenient routes; the Rickenbacker Causeway extends to Key Biscayne from I–95 and U.S. 1. The high-speed lanes on the left-hand side of I–95 require a prepaid toll pass called a "Sunpass," available in most drug and grocery stores or can be ordered by mail before your trip. It is sometimes included with your rental car (but you are billed for the tolls and associated fees later).

PUBLIC TRANSPORTATION

Some sights are accessible via the public transportation system, run by the **Metro-Dade Transit Agency,** which maintains 740 Metrobuses on 90 routes; the 23-mile Metrorail elevated rapid-transit system; and the Metromover, an elevated light-rail system. Those planning to use public transportation should get an EASY Card or EASY Ticket available at any Metrorail station and most supermarkets. Fares are discounted, and transfer fees are nominal. The bus stops for the **Metrobus** are marked with blue-and-green signs with a bus logo and route information. The fare is $2.25 (exact change only). Cash-paying customers must pay for another ride if transferring. Some express routes carry a surcharge of 40¢. Elevated **Metrorail** trains run from downtown Miami north to Hialeah and south along U.S. 1 to Dadeland. The system operates daily 5 am–midnight. The fare is $2.25; $0.60 transfers to Metrobus are available only for EASY Card and EASY Ticket holders. The free **Metromover** resembles an airport shuttle and runs on two loops around downtown Miami, linking major hotels, office buildings, and shopping areas. The system spans 4.4 miles, including the 1-mile Omni Loop and the 1-mile Brickell Loop. **Tri-Rail,** South Florida's commuter-train system, stops at 18 stations north of MIA along a 71-mile route. There's a Metrorail transfer station two stops north of MIA. Prices range from $2.50 to $6.90 for a one-way ticket.

Contacts Metro-Dade Transit Agency ☎ 305/891–3131 ⊕ www.miamidade. gov/transit/. **Tri-Rail** ☎ 800/874–7245 ⊕ www.tri-rail.com.

TAXI TRAVEL

Except in South Beach, it's difficult to hail a cab on the street; in most cases you'll need to call a cab company or have a hotel doorman hail one for you. Taxi drivers in Miami are notorious for bad customer service and not having credit card machines in their vehicles. These days, many people use Uber to avoid this taxi drama; however, in order to use Uber you must sign up with the company and have the Uber app installed on your smartphone. If using a regular taxi, note that fares run $2.50 for the first 1/6 of a mile and $2.40 every mile thereafter. Flat-rate fares are also available from the airport to a variety of zones (including Miami Beach) for $32. Expect a $2 surcharge on rides leaving from Miami International Airport or the Port of Miami. For those heading from MIA to downtown, the 15-minute, 7-mile trip costs around $22. Some cabs accept credit cards but not all, so ask when you get in.

Taxi Companies Central Cab ☎ *305/532-5555* ⊕ *www.centralcab.com* ☞ *Serving Miami Beach mainly.* **KB Village Taxi** ☎ *305/361-3111* ⊕ *www. kb-villagetaxi.com* ☞ *Serving Key Biscayne.* **Super Yellow Taxi** ✉ *3111 Northwest 27th Ave., Miami* ☎ *305/888-7777.* **Uber** ⊕ *www.uber.com.* **Yellow Cab** ☎ *305/444-4444.*

TRAIN TRAVEL

Amtrak provides service from 500 destinations to the Greater Miami area. The trains make several stops along the way; north–south service stops in the major Florida cities of Jacksonville, Orlando, Tampa, West Palm Beach, and Fort Lauderdale, but stations are not always conveniently located. The Auto Train (where you bring your car along) travels from Lorton, Virginia, just outside Washington, D.C., to Sanford, Florida, just outside Orlando. From there it's less than a four-hour drive to Miami. Fares vary, but expect to pay between around $275 and $350 for a basic sleeper seat and car passage each way. ■TIP➜ **You must be traveling with an automobile to purchase a ticket on the Auto Train.**

VISITOR INFORMATION

For additional information about Miami and Miami Beach, contact the city's visitor bureaus. You can also pick up a free Miami Beach INcard at the Miami Beach Visitors Center 10–4, seven days a week, entitling you to discounts and offers at restaurants, shops, galleries, and more.

Contacts City of Coral Gables ✉ *Coral Gables City Hall, 405 Biltmore Way, Coral Gables* ☎ *305/446-6800* ⊕ *www.coralgables.com.* **Coconut Grove Business Improvement District** ✉ *3390 Mary St., Suite 130, Coconut Grove, Miami* ☎ *305/461-5506* ⊕ *www.coconutgrove.com.* **Greater Miami Convention & Visitors Bureau** ✉ *701 Brickell Ave., Suite 2700, Miami* ☎ *305/539-3000, 800/933-8448 in U.S.* ⊕ *www.miamiandbeaches.com.* **Key Biscayne Chamber of Commerce and Visitors Center** ✉ *88 W. McIntyre St., Suite 100, Key Biscayne* ☎ *305/361-5207* ⊕ *www.keybiscaynechamber.org.* **Visit Miami Beach** ✉ *Visitor's Center, 1901 Convention Center Dr., Hall C, Miami Beach* ☎ *786/276-2763, 305/672-1270 Miami Beach Tourist Hotline* ⊕ *www.miamibeachguest.com.*

EXPLORING

If you'd arrived here 50 years ago with a guidebook in hand, chances are you'd be thumbing through listings looking for alligator wrestlers and you-pick strawberry fields or citrus groves. Things have changed. While Disney sidetracked families in Orlando, Miami was developing a unique culture and attitude that's equal parts beach town/big business, Latino/Caribbean meets European/American—all of which fuels a great art and food scene, as well as exuberant nightlife and myriad festivals.

To find your way around Greater Miami, learn how the numbering system works (or better yet, use a GPS). Miami is laid out on a grid with four quadrants—northeast, northwest, southeast, and southwest—that meet at Miami Avenue and Flagler Street. Miami Avenue separates east from west, and Flagler Street separates north from south. Avenues and courts run north–south; streets, terraces, and ways run east–west. Roads run diagonally, northwest–southeast. But other districts—Miami Beach, Coral Gables, and Hialeah—may or may not follow this system, and along the curve of Biscayne Bay the symmetrical grid shifts diagonally. It's best to buy a detailed map, stick to the major roads, and ask directions early and often. However, make sure you're in a safe neighborhood or public place when you seek guidance; cabdrivers and cops are good resources.

DOWNTOWN

Downtown Miami dazzles from a distance. America's third-largest skyline is fluid, thanks to the sheer number of sparkling glass high-rises between Biscayne Boulevard and the Miami River. Business is the key to downtown Miami's daytime bustle. However, the influx of massive, modern, and affordable condos has lured a young and trendy demographic to the areas in and around downtown, giving Miami much more of a "city" feel come nightfall. In fact, downtown has become a nighttime hot spot in recent years, inciting a cultural revolution that has fostered burgeoning areas north in Wynwood, Midtown, and the Design District, and south along Brickell Avenue. The pedestrian streets here tend to be very restaurant-centric, complemented by lounges and nightclubs.

The free, 4.4-mile, elevated commuter system known as the Metromover runs inner and outer loops through downtown and to nearby neighborhoods south and north. Many attractions are conveniently located within a few blocks of a station.

TOP ATTRACTIONS

Adrienne Arsht Center. Culture vultures and other artsy types are drawn to this stunning performing arts center, which includes the 2,400-seat Ziff Ballet Opera House, the 2,200-seat Knight Concet Hall, the Carnival Studio black-box Theater, and an outdoor Plaza for the Arts. Throughout the year, you'll find top-notch performances by local and national touring groups, including Broadway hits like *Wicked* and *Jersey Boys*, intimate music concerts, and showstopping ballet. Think of it as a sliver of savoir faire to temper Miami's often-over-the-top vibe. The massive development was designed by architect César Pelli, and stands as the largest American performing arts center constructed since the 1980s. Complimentary one-hour tours of the Arsht Center, highlighting the architecture and its public art, are offered every Saturday and Monday at noon. ⊠ *1300 Biscayne Blvd., at N.E. 13th St.* ☎ *305/949–6722 box office* ⊕ *www.arshtcenter.org.*

Freedom Tower. In the 1960s this ornate Spanish-baroque structure was the Cuban Refugee Center, processing more than 500,000 Cubans who entered the United States after fleeing Fidel Castro's regime. Built in 1925 for the *Miami Daily News,* it was inspired by the Giralda, an 800-year-old bell tower in Seville, Spain. Preservationists were pleased to see the tower's exterior restored in 1988. Today, it is owned by Miami Dade College (MDC), functioning as a cultural and educational center; it's also home to the MDC Museum of Art + Design, which showcases a broad collection of contemporary Latin art as well works in the genres of minimalism and pop art. ■ TIP→ Admission is free to both the tower

Downtown Miami

KEY

M Metromover Station

- - - Metromover

and museum. ✉ *600 Biscayne Blvd., at N.E. 6th St.* ☎ *305/237–7700* ⊕ *www.mdcmoad.org* ☾ *Wed.–Sun. noon–5 pm (3rd Sat. noon–8).*

HistoryMiami. Discover a treasure trove of colorful stories about the region's history at HistoryMiami, formerly known as the Historical Museum of Southern Florida. Exhibits celebrate the city's multicultural heritage, including an old Miami streetcar and unique items chronicling the migration of Cubans to Miami. Though HistoryMiami is not wildly popular with tourists, the museum's tours certainly are. You can take a wide range of walking, boat, coach, bike, gallery, and eco-history tours with varying prices, including culture walks through Little Haiti, informative and exciting Little Havana Arts & Culture Walks, and an evening of storytelling during the "Moon Over Miami" tour led by HistoryMiami historian, Dr. Paul George, where you'll float through downtown, learning all about Miami's early history hear circa the Tequesta Indians days. ✉ *101 W. Flagler St., between N.W. 1st and 2nd Aves.* ☎ *305/375–1492* ⊕ *www.historymiami.org* ✎ *$8; tour costs vary* ☾ *Mon.–Sat. 10–5, Sun. noon–5.*

Fodor'sChoice ★ **Pérez Art Museum Miami** (*PAMM*). Opened in December 2013, the Pérez Art Museum Miami, known locally as PAMM, shines as the city's first true world-class museum. This über-high-design architectural masterpiece on Biscayne Bay is a sight to behold. Double-story, cylindrical hanging gardens sway from high atop the museum, anchored to stylish wood trusses that help create this gotta-see-it-to-believe-it indoor/outdoor museum. Large sculptures, Asian-inspired gardens, sexy white benches, and steel frames envelop the property. Inside, the 120,000-square-foot space houses multicultural art from the 20th and 21st centuries, some of which were previously on display at the Miami Art Museum (note: downtown's Miami Art Museum no longer exists and the collection has now been incorporated into PAMM). Most of the interior space is devoted to temporary exhibitions, which have included the likes of *Ai Weiwei: According to What?* and *Edouard Duval-Carrié: Imagined Landscapes.* Even if you aren't a "museum type" per se, come check out this magnum opus over lunch at the Verde, the museum's sensational waterfront restaurant and bar. ■TIP➔ **Admission is free every first Thursday of the month and every second Saturday of the month.** ✉ *1103 Biscayne Blvd.* ☎ *305/375–3000* ⊕ *www.pamm.org* ✎ *$16* ☾ *Tues., Wed., and Fri.–Sun. 10–6, Thurs. 10–9.*

WORTH NOTING

FAMILY **Bayside Marketplace.** The Bayside Marketplace, a waterfront complex of entertainment, dining, and retail stores, was en vogue circa 1992 and remains popular due to its location near PortMiami. You'll find the area awash in cruise-ship passenger chaos on most days (it's definitely *not* a draw for locals), so expect plenty of souvenir shops, a Hard Rock Cafe, and stores like Wet Seal and Sunglass Hut. Many boat tours leave from the marinas lining the festival marketplace. ✉ *401 Biscayne Blvd.* ☎ *305/381–8972* ⊕ *www.baysidemarketplace.com.*

FAMILY **Jungle Island.** Originally located deep in south Miami and known as Parrot Jungle, South Florida's original tourist attraction opened in 1936 and moved closer to Miami Beach in 2003. Now on Watson Island, a small stretch of land between Downtown Miami and South Beach, Jungle Island is far more than a place where cockatoos ride tricycles; this interactive zoological park is home to just about every unusual and endangered species you would want to see (if you are into seeing them in zoolike settings that is), including a rare albino alligator, a liger (lion and tiger mix), and myriad exotic birds. With an emphasis on the experiential versus mere observation, the park now offers several new attractions and activities, including private beaches, treetop zip lining, aquatic activities, adventure trails, cultural activities, and enhanced VIP packages where you mingle with an array of furry and feathered friends. Jungle Island offers complimentary shuttle service to most Downtown Miami and South Beach hotels. ⊠ *Watson Island, 1111 Parrot Jungle Trail, off MacArthur Causeway (I–395)* ☎ *305/400–7000* ⊕ *www.jungleisland.com* ✍ *$34.95, plus $8 parking* ⊙ *Weekdays 10–5, weekends 10–6.*

FAMILY **Miami Children's Museum.** This Arquitectonica-designed museum, both imaginative and geometric in appearance, is directly across the MacArthur Causeway from Jungle Island. Twelve galleries house hundreds of interactive, bilingual exhibits. Children can scan plastic groceries in the supermarket, scramble through a giant sand castle, climb a rock wall, learn about the Everglades, and combine rhythms in the world-music studio. ⊠ *Watson Island, 980 MacArthur Causeway, off I–395* ☎ *305/373–5437* ⊕ *www.miamichildrensmuseum.org* ✍ *$18, parking $1/hr* ⊙ *Daily 10–6.*

COCONUT GROVE

A former haven for writers and artists, Coconut Grove has never quite outgrown its image as a small village. You can still feel the Bohemian roots of this artsy neighborhood, but it has grown increasingly mainstream and residential over the past 20 years. Posh estates mingle with rustic cottages, modest frame homes, and stark modern dwellings, often on the same block. If you're into horticulture, you'll be impressed by the Garden of Eden–like foliage that seems to grow everywhere without care. In truth, residents are determined to keep up the Grove's village-in-a-jungle look, so they lavish attention on exotic plantings even as they battle to protect any remaining native vegetation.

The center of the Grove still attracts its fair share of locals and tourists who enjoy perusing the small boutiques, sidewalk cafés, and cute galleries that remind us of the old Grove. Activities here are family-friendly with easy access to bayside parks, museums, and gardens.

TOP ATTRACTIONS

FAMILY **Patricia and Phillip Frost Museum of Science.** In summer 2016 the Patricia and Phillip Frost Museum of Science will relocate to its much larger (250,000-square-foot), hyper-modern, $300-million new home in downtown's Museum Park. Until then, the old incarnation of the museum remains in Coconut Grove, chock-full of hands-on sound, gravity, and electricity displays for children and adults alike. For animal lovers, its wildlife center houses native Florida snakes, turtles, tortoises, and birds of prey. Check the museum's schedule for traveling exhibits

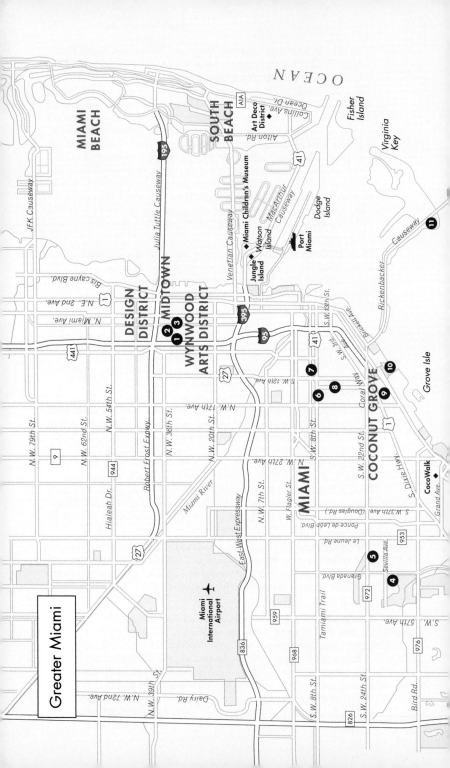

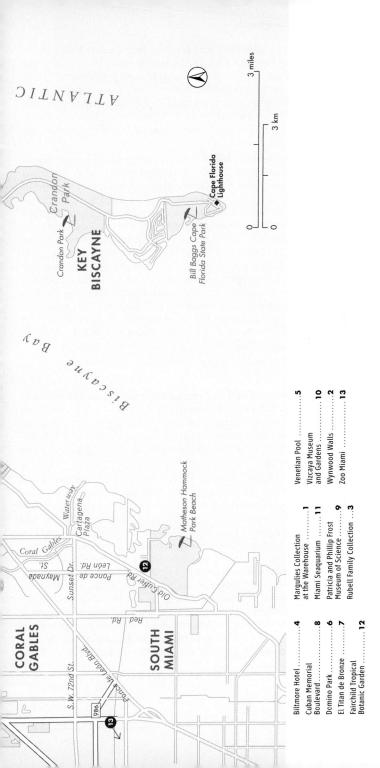

ATLANTIC

Crandon
Park

Crandon Park

**KEY
BISCAYNE**

Bill Baggs Cape
Florida State Park

◆ **Cape Florida
Lighthouse**

0   3 km

0   3 miles

Biscayne Bay

Waterway

Coral Gables

Cartagena
Plaza

Coral Gables

Maynada
St.

Sunset Dr.

Ponce de
León Rd.

Old Cutler Rd.

Matheson Hammock
Park Beach

**CORAL
GABLES**

Red Rd.

**SOUTH
MIAMI**

S.W. 72nd St.

Ponce de León Blvd.

986

that appear throughout the year. If you're here the first Friday of the month—called Fabulous First Fridays—stick around for the free star show at 7 pm and then gaze at the planets through two powerful Meade telescopes at the Weintraub Observatory. Also enjoy a laser-light rock-and-roll show nightly at 8, 9, 10, or 11 to the tunes of the Doors, Bob Marley, the Beatles, or Pink Floyd, to name a few. ⊠ *3280 S. Miami Ave.* ☎ *305/646–4200* ⊕ *www.miamisci.org* 🖅 *$14.95* ⊙ *Museum daily 10–6; planetarium varies.*

Fodor's Choice
★
Vizcaya Museum and Gardens. Of the 10,000 people living in Miami between 1912 and 1916, about 1,000 of them were gainfully employed by Chicago industrialist James Deering to build this European-inspired residence. Once comprising 180 acres, this National Historic Landmark now occupies a 30-acre tract that includes a rockland hammock (native forest) and more than 10 acres of formal gardens with fountains overlooking Biscayne Bay. The house, open to the public, contains 70 rooms, 34 of which are filled with paintings, sculpture, antique furniture, and other fine and decorative arts. The collection spans 2,000 years and represents the Renaissance, baroque, rococo, and neoclassical periods. The 90-minute self-guided Discover Vizcaya Audio Tour is available in multiple languages for an additional $5. Moonlight tours, offered on evenings that are nearest the full moon, provide a magical look at the gardens; call for reservations. ⊠ *3251 S. Miami Ave.* ☎ *305/250–9133* ⊕ *www.vizcaya.org* 🖅 *$18* ⊙ *Daily 9:30–4:30* ⊙ *Closed Tues.*

CORAL GABLES

You can easily spot Coral Gables from the window of a Miami-bound jetliner—just look for the massive orange tower of the Biltmore Hotel rising from a lush green carpet of trees concealing the city's gracious homes. The canopy is as much a part of this planned city as its distinctive architecture, all attributed to the vision of George E. Merrick more than a century ago.

The story of this city began in 1911, when Merrick inherited 1,600 acres of citrus and avocado groves from his father. Through judicious investment he nearly doubled the tract to 3,000 acres by 1921. Merrick dreamed of building an American Venice here, complete with canals and homes. Working from this vision, he began designing a city based on centuries-old prototypes from Mediterranean countries. Unfortunately for Merrick, the devastating no-name hurricane of 1926, followed by the Great Depression, prevented him from fulfilling many of his plans. He died at 54, an employee of the post office. Today Coral Gables has a population of about 47,000. In its bustling downtown more than 150 multinational companies maintain headquarters or regional offices, and the University of Miami campus in the southern part of the Gables brings a youthful vibrancy to the area. A southern branch of the city extends down the shore of Biscayne Bay through neighborhoods threaded with canals.

2

TOP ATTRACTIONS

Biltmore Hotel. Bouncing back stunningly from its dark days as an army hospital, this hotel has become the jewel of Coral Gables—a dazzling architectural gem with a colorful past. First opened in 1926, it was a hot spot for the rich and glamorous of the Jazz Age until it was converted to an army–air force regional hospital in 1942. Until 1968, the Veterans Administration continued to operate the hospital after World War II. The Biltmore then lay vacant for nearly 20 years before it underwent extensive renovations and reopened as a luxury hotel in 1987. Its 16-story tower, like the Freedom Tower in downtown Miami, is a replica of Seville's Giralda Tower. The magnificent pool is reportedly the largest hotel pool in the continental United States. ■TIP→ **Because it functions as a full-service hotel, your ticket in—if you aren't staying here—is to patronize one of the hotel's several restaurants or bars. Try to get a courtyard table for the Sunday champagne brunch, a local legend.** ⊠ *1200 Anastasia Ave., near De Soto Blvd.* ☎ *855/311–6903* ⊕ *www.biltmorehotel.com.*

FAMILY **Fairchild Tropical Botanic Garden.** With 83 acres of lakes, sunken gardens, a 560-foot vine pergola, orchids, bellflowers, coral trees, bougainvillea, rare palms, and flowering trees, Fairchild is the largest tropical botanical garden in the continental United States. The tram tour highlights the best of South Florida and exotic flora; then you can set off exploring on your own. The 2-acre Simons Rainforest showcases tropical plants from around the world complete with a waterfall and stream. The conservatory is home to rare tropical plants, including the Burmese endemic *Amherstia nobilis,* flowering annually with orchid-like pink flowers. The Keys Coastal Habitat, created in a marsh and mangrove area in 1995 with assistance from the Tropical Audubon Society, provides food and shelter to resident and migratory birds. The excellent bookstore–gift shop carries books on gardening and horticulture, and the Garden Café serves sandwiches and, seasonally, smoothies made from the garden's own crop of tropical fruits. ⊠ *10901 Old Cutler Rd.* ☎ *305/667–1651* ⊕ *www.fairchildgarden.org* 🎟 *$25* ☉ *Daily 7:30–4:30.*

FAMILY **Venetian Pool.** Sculpted from a rock quarry in 1923 and fed by artesian wells, this 820,000-gallon municipal pool had a major face-lift in 2010 and again in 2015. It remains quite popular because of its themed architecture—a fantasy version of a waterfront Italian village—created by Denman Fink. The pool has earned a place on the National Register of Historic Places and showcases a nice collection of vintage photos depicting 1920s beauty pageants and swank soirees held long ago. Paul Whiteman played here, Johnny Weissmuller and Esther Williams swam here, and you should, too (but no kids under age three). A snack bar, lockers, and showers make this must-see user-friendly as well. ⊠ *2701 De Soto Blvd., at Toledo St.* ☎ *305/460–5306* ⊕ *www.coralgables.com* 🎟 *$11; free parking across De Soto Blvd.* ☉ *Usually open Tues.–Sun. 11–4:30, but best to call ahead.*

OFF THE
BEATEN
PATH

Zoo Miami. Don't miss a visit to this top-notch zoo, 14 miles southwest of Coral Gables in the Miami suburbs. The only subtropical zoo in the continental United States, it has 320-plus acres that are home to more than 2,000 animals, including 40 endangered species, which roam on islands surrounded by moats. Amazon & Beyond encompasses 27 acres of simulated tropical rain forests showcasing 600 animals indigenous to the region, such as giant river otters, harpy eagles, anacondas, and jaguars. The Wings of Asia aviary has about 300 exotic birds representing 70 species flying free within the junglelike enclosure. The Samburu Giraffe Feeding Station facilitates personal interaction with these gentle giants as you hand-feed them veggies. There's also a children's zoo with a meerkat exhibit and an educational and entertaining wildlife show is given three times daily. ⊠ *12400 S.W. 152nd St. (1 Zoo Blvd.), Richmond Heights* ☎ *305/251–0400* ⊕ *www.zoomiami.org* ⊠ *$17.95; 45-min tram tour $4.95* ⊗ *Weekdays 10–5, weekends 9:30–5:30 (last admission 4).*

> ### SAIL AWAY
>
> If you can sail in Miami, do. Blue skies, calm seas, and a view of the city skyline make for a pleasurable outing—especially at twilight, when the fabled "moon over Miami" casts a soft glow on the water. Key Biscayne's calm waves and strong breezes are perfect for sailing and windsurfing, and although Dinner Key and the Coconut Grove waterfront remain the center of sailing in Greater Miami, sailboat moorings and rentals sit along other parts of the bay and up the Miami River, too.

KEY BISCAYNE

Once upon a time, the two barrier islands that make up the village of Key Biscayne (Key Biscayne itself and Virginia Key) were outposts for fishermen and sailors, pirates and salvagers, soldiers and settlers. The 95-foot Cape Florida Lighthouse stood tall during Seminole Indian battles and hurricanes. Coconut plantations covered two-thirds of Key Biscayne, and there were plans as far back as the 1800s to develop the picturesque island as a resort for the wealthy. Fortunately, the state and county governments set much of the land aside for parks, and both keys are now home to top-ranked beaches and golf, tennis, softball, and picnicking facilities. The long and winding bike paths that run through the islands are favorites for in-line skaters and cyclists. Incorporated in 1991, the village of Key Biscayne is a hospitable community of about 12,500, even though Virginia Key remains undeveloped at the moment. These two playground islands are especially family-friendly.

TOP ATTRACTIONS

FAMILY **Miami Seaquarium.** This classic family attraction stages shows with sea lions, dolphins, and other marine animals. The Crocodile Flats exhibit has 26 Nile crocodiles. Discovery Bay, an endangered mangrove habitat, is home to sea turtles, alligators, herons, egrets, and ibis. You can also visit a shark pool, a tropical reef aquarium, and West Indian and Florida manatees. A popular interactive attraction is the Stingray Touch Tank, where you can touch and feed cow-nose rays and southern stingrays. Another big draw is the Dolphin Interaction program, including the quite intensive Dolphin Odyssey ($210) experience and the lighter shallow-water Dolphin Encounter ($110). Make reservations for either experience. ⊠ *4400 Rickenbacker Causeway, Virginia Key*

☎ *305/361–5705* ⊕ *www.miamiseaquarium.com* ✉ *$40.99, parking $10 (cash only)* ⊙ *Daily 9:30–6, last admission 4:30.*

WYNWOOD

Fodor's Choice
★

North of downtown, the former downtrodden Wynwood neighborhood is developing, with an impressive mix of one-of-a-kind shops and art galleries, public art displays, see-and-be-seen bars, slick restaurants, and plenty of eye-popping graffiti. Wynwood's trendiness has proven infectious, also taking root in proximate neighborhoods. One thing is still missing from the emerging landscape: a decent hotel. On a positive note, it's kept the Wynwood vibe more local and less touristy. The downside: you'll need a vehicle to get here, and though in close proximity to one another, you'll also need a vehicle to get to nearby Midtown and The Design District.

Between Interstate 95 and Northeast 1st Avenue from 29th to 22nd streets lies the centerpiece of the edgy Wynwood neighborhood—the funky and edgy **Wynwood Art District** (⊕ *www.wynwoodmiami.com*), which is peppered with galleries, art studios, and private collections accessible to the public. Though the neighborhood hasn't completely shed its dodgy past, artist-painted graffiti walls and reinvented urban warehouses have transformed the area from plain old grimy to super trendy. The Wynwood Walls on Northwest 2nd Avenue between Northeast 25th and 26th streets are a cutting-edge enclave of modern urban murals. However, these avant-garde graffiti displays by renowned artists are just the beginning; in fact, almost every street is colored with funky spray-paint art, making the neighborhood a photographer's dream. Wynwood's retail space is a hodgepodge of cheap garment stores, upscale boutiques, and contemporary galleries (some by appointment only). First-timers may want to visit during Wynwood's monthly gallery walk on the second Saturday evening of each month, when studios and galleries are all open at the same time.

TOP ATTRACTIONS

Margulies Collection at the Warehouse. Make sure a visit to Wynwood includes a stop at the Margulies Collection at the Warehouse. Martin Margulies's collection of vintage and contemporary photography, videos, and installation art in a 45,000-square-foot space makes for eye-popping viewing. Admission proceeds go to the Lotus House, a local homeless shelter for women and children. ✉ *591 N.W. 27th St., between N.W. 5th and 6th Aves.* ☎ *305/576–1051* ⊕ *www.margu--lieswarehouse.com* ✉ *$10* ⊙ *Oct.–Apr., Wed.–Sat. 11–4.*

Fodor's Choice
★

Rubell Family Collection. Fans of edgy art will appreciate the Rubell Family Collection. Mera and Don Rubell have accumulated work by artists from the 1970s to the present, including Jeff Koons, Cindy Sherman, Damien Hirst, and Keith Haring. Admission always includes a complimentary audio tour; however, true art lovers should opt for a complimentary guided tour of the collection, offered Wednesday through Saturday at 3 pm. ✉ *95 N.W. 29th St., between N. Miami and N.W. 1st Aves.* ☎ *305/573–6090* ⊕ *rfc.museum* ✉ *$10* ⊙ *Dec.–May, Wed.–Sat. 10–5:30.*

Fodor's Choice **Wynwood Walls.** Between Northeast 25th and 26th streets on Northwest
★ 2nd Avenue, the Wynwood Walls are a cutting-edge enclave of modern
urban murals, reflecting diversity in graffiti and street art. More than 50
well-known and lesser-known artists have transformed 80,000 square
feet of warehouse walls into an outdoor museum of sorts (and a photographer's dream). The popularity of the walls spawned the neighboring
Wynwood Doors, an industrial space rife with metal roll-down gates
also used as blank canvases. Even more recently, the Outside the Walls
project is spreading the Walls love across the neighborhood, as artists
are commissioned to transform Wynwood's surrounding warehouses
and building spaces into singular pieces of painted art. ⊠ *2520 N.W.
2nd Ave.* ⊕ *www.thewynwoodwalls.com.*

MIDTOWN

Northeast of Wynwood, Midtown (⊕ *www.midtownmiami.com*) lies
between Northeast 29th and 36th streets, from North Miami Avenue
to Northeast 2nd Avenue. This subcity is anchored by a multitower
residential complex with prolific retail space, often housing the latest
and greatest in dining and shopping trends.

DESIGN DISTRICT

North of Midtown, from about Northeast 38th to Northeast 42nd
streets and across the other side of Interstate 195, the Design District
(⊕ *www.miamidesigndistrict.net*) is yet another 18 blocks of clothiers,
antiques shops, design stores, and bars and eateries. The real draws here
are the interior design and furniture galleries as well as über-high-end
shopping that's oh-so Rodeo Drive (and rivals Bal Harbour in North
Beach).

Right outside Little Haiti's boundaries, running from 50th to 77th
streets along Biscayne Boulevard, is the MiMo Biscayne Boulevard Historic District, known in short as the MiMo District. This strip is noted
for its Miami Modernist Architecture and houses a number of boutiques
and design galleries. It's sometimes seen as the latest extension of the
growing Design District (with much cheaper rents). Within this district
and in the neighborhoods to the east—collectively known as Miami's
"Upper East Side"—several new restaurants are beginning to open.

LITTLE HAITI

Once a small farming community, Little Haiti is the heart and soul of
Haitian society in the United States. In fact, Miami's Little Haiti is the
largest Haitian community outside of Haiti itself. While people of different ethnic backgrounds have begun to move into the neighborhood,
people here are still surprised to see tourists. However, owners of shops
and restaurants tend to be welcoming. Creole is commonly spoken,
although some people—especially younger folks—also speak English.
Its northern and southern boundaries are 85th Street and 42nd Street,
respectively, with Interstate 95 to the west and Biscayne Boulevard to
the east in its southern reaches, then Northeast 4th Court to the east

(two blocks west of Biscayne Boulevard). The best section to visit is along North Miami Avenue from 54th to 59th streets.

LITTLE HAVANA

Fodor's Choice
★
First settled en masse by Cubans in the early 1960s, after Cuba's Communist revolution, Little Havana is a predominantly working-class area and the core of Miami's Hispanic community. Spanish is the principal language, but don't be surprised if the cadence is less Cuban and more Salvadoran or Nicaraguan: the neighborhood is now home to people from all Latin American countries.

If you come to Little Havana expecting the Latino version of New Orleans's French Quarter, you're apt to be disappointed—it's not about the architecture here. Rather, it's a place to soak in the atmosphere. Little Havana is more about great, inexpensive food (not just Cuban; there's Vietnamese, Mexican, and Argentinean here as well), distinctive affordable Cuban-American art, cigars, and great coffee. It's not a prefab tourist destination—this is real life in Spanish-speaking Miami.

Little Havana's semiofficial boundaries are 27th Avenue to 4th Avenue on the west, Miami River to the north, and Southwest 13th Street to the south. Much of the neighborhood is residential; however, you'll quickly discover the area's flavor, both literally and figuratively, along Calle Ocho (Southwest 8th Street), between Southwest 11th and 17th avenues, which is lined with cigar factories, cafés selling guava pastries and rose petal flan, *botanicas* brimming with candles, and Cuban clothes and crafts stores. Your "Welcome to Little Havana" photo op shines on 27th Avenue and 8th Street. Giant hand-painted roosters are found scattered throughout the entire neighborhood, an artistic nod to their real-life counterparts that roam the streets here. You'll need to drive into Little Havana, since public transportation here is limited; but once on Calle Ocho, it's best to experience the neighborhood on foot.

TOP ATTRACTIONS

Cuban Memorial Boulevard. Four blocks in the heart of Little Havana are filled with monuments to Cuba's freedom fighters. South of *Calle Ocho* (8th Street), Southwest 13th Avenue becomes a ceiba tree–lined parkway known as Cuban Memorial Boulevard, divided at the center by a narrow grassy mall with a walking path through the various memorials. Among them is the *Eternal Torch of the Brigade 2506*, blazing with an endless flame and commemorating those who were killed in the failed Bay of Pigs invasion of 1961. Another is a bas-relief map of Cuba depicting each of its *municipios*. There's also a bronze statue in honor of Nestory (Tony) Izquierdo, who participated in the Bay of Pigs invasion and served in Nicaragua's Somozan forces. ⊠ *S.W. 13th Ave., between S.W. 8th and S.W. 12th Sts.*

Domino Park. If you're not yet ready to take advantage of the relaxed restrictions on travel to Cuba, watch a slice of old Havana come to life in Miami's Little Havana. At Domino Park, officially known as Maximo Gomez Park, guayabera-clad seniors bask in the sun and play dominoes, while onlookers share neighborhood gossip and political opinions. ■ TIP → There is a little office at the park with a window where you can get information on Little Havana; the office also stores the dominoes for the older gents who play regularly, but it's BYOD (bring your own dominoes) for everyone else. ✉ *801 S.W. 15th Ave.* ☎ *305/859–2717 park office.*

NEED A BREAK?

Las Pinareños Fruteria y Floreria. In the mood for something refreshing or a high-octane jolt? Try Las Pinareños, a *fruteria* (fruit stand) that serves *coco frio* (fresh, cold coconut juice served in a whole coconut), mango juice, and other *jugos* (juices), as well as Cuban coffees and Cuban finger foods. You can order your sweet, hot *cortadito* (coffee with milk) or a *cafecito* (no milk) from the walk-up window and enjoy it at one of the stools in front of the shop or sit at one of the tables inside the fruit and flower market. ✉ *1334 S.W. 8th St.* ☎ *305/285–1135.*

El Titan de Bronze. A peek at the intently focused cigar rollers through the windows doesn't prepare you for the rich, pungent scent that jolts your senses as you step inside the store. Millions of stogies are deftly hand-rolled at this family-owned cigar factory and retail store each year. Visitors are welcome to watch the rolling action (and of course buy some cigars). ✉ *1071 S.W. 8th St.* ☎ *305/860–1412* ⊕ *www.eltitancigars.com.*

SOUTH BEACH

Fodor's Choice
★
The hub of Miami Beach is South Beach (better known as SoBe), with its energetic Ocean Drive, Collins Avenue, and Washington Avenue. Here life unfolds 24 hours a day. Beautiful people pose in hotel lounges and sidewalk cafés, bronzed cyclists zoom past palm trees, and visitors flock to see the action. On Lincoln Road, café crowds spill onto the sidewalks, weekend markets draw all kinds of visitors and their dogs, and thanks to a few late-night lounges, the scene is just as alive at night. Farther north (in Mid-Beach and North Beach), the vibe is decidedly quieter.

TOP ATTRACTIONS

Española Way. There's a bohemian feel to this street lined with Mediterranean-revival buildings constructed in 1925. Al Capone's gambling syndicate ran its operations upstairs at what is now the Clay Hotel, a youth hostel. At a nightclub here in the 1930s, future bandleader Desi Arnaz strapped on a conga drum and started beating out a rumba rhythm. Visit this quaint avenue on a weekend afternoon, when merchants and craftspeople set up shop to sell everything from handcrafted bongo drums to fresh flowers. Between Washington and Drexel avenues the road has been narrowed to a single lane and Miami Beach's trademark pink sidewalks have been widened to accommodate sidewalk cafés and shops selling imaginative clothing, jewelry, and art. ✉ *Española Way, between 14th and 15th Sts. from Washington to Jefferson Aves.* ⊕ *www.myespanolaway.com.*

Holocaust Memorial. A bronze sculpture depicts refugees clinging to a giant bronze arm that reaches out of the ground and 42 feet into the air. Enter the surrounding courtyard to see a memorial wall and hear the music that seems to give voice to the 6 million Jews who died at the

2

hands of the Nazis. It's easy to understand why Kenneth Treister's dramatic memorial is in Miami Beach: the city's community of Holocaust survivors was once the second largest in the country. ✉ *1933–1945 Meridian Ave., at Dade Blvd.* ☎ *305/538–1663* ⊕ *holocaustmemorialmiamibeach.org/* ✉ *Free* ⊙ *Daily 9–sunset.*

FAMILY

Fodor's Choice
★

Lincoln Road Mall. This open-air pedestrian mall flaunts some of Miami's best people-watching. The eclectic interiors of myriad fabulous restaurants, colorful boutiques, art galleries, lounges, and cafés are often upstaged by the bustling outdoor scene. It's here among the prolific alfresco dining enclaves that you can pass the hours easily beholding the beautiful people. Indeed, outdoor restaurant and café seating take center stage along this wide pedestrian road adorned with towering date palms, linear pools, and colorful broken-tile mosaics. Some of the shops on Lincoln Road are owner-operated boutiques carrying a smart variety of clothing, furnishings, jewelry, and decorative elements. You'll also find typical upscale chain stores—H & M, American Eagle Outfitters, Forever 21, and so on. Lincoln Road is fun, lively, and friendly for people–old, young, gay, and straight—and their dogs.

Two landmarks worth checking out at the eastern end of Lincoln Road are the massive 1940s keystone building at 420 Lincoln Road, which has a 1945 Leo Birchanky mural in the lobby, and the 1921 Mission-style Miami Beach Community Church, at Drexel Avenue. The Lincoln Theatre (No. 541–545), at Pennsylvania Avenue, is a classical four-story art deco gem with friezes, which now houses H & M. At Euclid Avenue there's a monument to Morris Lapidus, the brains behind Lincoln Road Mall, who in his 90s watched the renaissance of his whimsical South Beach creation. At Lenox Avenue, a black-and-white art deco movie house with a Mediterranean barrel-tile roof is now the Colony Theater (1040 Lincoln Rd.), where live theater and experimental films are presented. ✉ *Lincoln Rd., between Washington Ave. and Alton Rd.* ⊕ *www.lincolnroadmall.com.*

QUICK
BITES

Lincoln Road is a great place to cool down with an icy treat while touring South Beach. If you visit on a Sunday, stop at one of the many juice vendors, who'll whip up made-to-order smoothies from mangoes, oranges, and other fresh local fruits.

Frieze Ice Cream Factory. A true South Beach original, this mom-and-pop ice cream shop serves what could very well be the best ice cream in Florida (except Azucar in Little Havana). Delight in mouthwatering homemade ice cream and sorbets including Indian mango, key lime pie, cashew toffee crunch, and chocolate decadence. ✉ *1626 Michigan Ave., just south of Lincoln Rd.* ☎ *305/538–0207* ⊕ *www.thefrieze.com.*

WORTH NOTING

Art Deco Welcome Center and Museum. Run by the Miami Design Preservation League, the center provides information about the buildings in the district. An official Art Deco Museum opened within the center in October 2014, and an improved gift shop sells 1930s–'50s art deco memorabilia, posters, and books on Miami's history. Several tours—covering

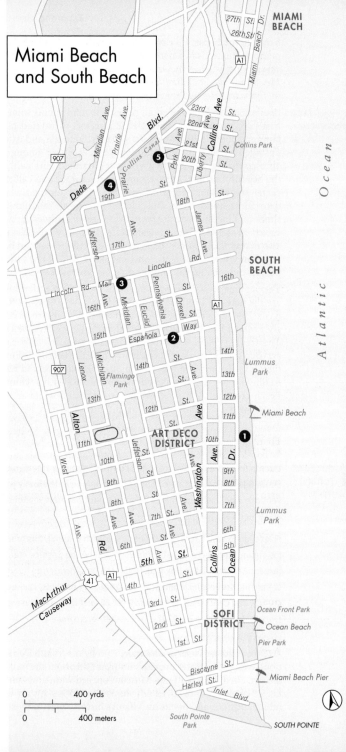

Miami Beach and South Beach

Lincoln Road, Española Way, North Beach, and the entire Art Deco District, among others—start here. You can choose from a self-guided iPod audio tour or join one of the regular morning walking tours at 10:30 every day. On Thursday a second tour takes place at 6:30 pm. Arrive at the center 15 minutes beforehand and prepurchase tickets online; all tours leave from the gift shop. All of the options provide detailed histories of the art deco hotels as well as an introduction to the art deco, Mediterranean revival, and Miami Modern (MiMo) styles found within the Miami Beach Architectural Historic District. Don't miss the special boat tours during Art Deco Weekend, in early January. *(⇨ For a map of the Art Deco District and info on some of the sites there, see the "A Stroll Down Deco Lane" in-focus feature.)* ⊠ *1001 Ocean Dr.* ☎ *305/672–2014, 305/531–3484 for tours* ⊕ *www.mdpl.org* ✉ *Tours $25* ⊗ *Gift shop and center daily 9:30–7; museum Tues.–Sun. 10–5.*

Bass Museum of Art. Special exhibitions join a diverse collection of European art at this museum whose original building is constructed of keystone and has unique Maya-inspired carvings. An expansion designed by Japanese architect Arata Isozaki houses another wing and an outdoor sculpture garden. Works on permanent display include *The Holy Family,* a painting by Peter Paul Rubens; *The Tournament,* one of several 16th-century Flemish tapestries; and works by Albrecht Dürer and Henri de Toulouse-Lautrec. Docent tours are by appointment but free with entry. Renovations to the museum will begin in June 2015. ⊠ *2100 Collins Ave.* ☎ *305/673–7530* ⊕ *www.bassmuseum.org* ✉ *$8* ⊗ *Wed.– Sun. noon–5, Fri. noon–9.*

MID-BEACH

Where does South Beach end and Mid-Beach begin? With the massive amount of money being spent on former 1950s pleasure palaces like the Fontainebleau and Eden Roc, it could be that Mid-Beach will soon just be considered part of South Beach. North of 23rd Street, Collins Avenue curves its way to 44th Street, where it takes a sharp left turn after running into the Soho House Miami and then the Fontainebleau resort. The area between these two points—and up until 63rd Street—is officially Mid-Beach. The area has been experiencing a renaissance since the $1 billion re-debut of the Fontainebleau resort in 2008. Investors have followed suit with major projects to revive the myriad former 1950s pleasure palaces of mid-Beach. Most recently, Argentinean developer Alan Faena has embarked on the neighborhood's latest $1 billion-plus mission: to restore the historic buildings along Collins Avenue from 32nd to 36th streets, creating new hotels, condos, and cultural institutions which will collectively become the Miami Beach Faena District.

FISHER AND BELLE ISLANDS

A private island community near the southern tip of South Beach, Fisher Island is accessible only by the island's ferry service. The island is predominantly residential with a few hotel rooms on offer at the Resort at Fisher Island Club. Belle Island is a small island connected to both the

mainland and Miami Beach by road. It is a mile north of South Beach and just west over the Venetian Causeway.

NORTH BEACH

Though often referred to collectively as "North Beach," there are several neighborhoods above Mid-Beach before reaching the Dade-Broward border. In Miami Beach proper, nearing the 63rd Street mark on Collins Avenue, Mid-Beach gives way to North Beach (until 87th Street), followed by Surfside (up until 96th Street).

BAL HARBOUR

At 96th Street, the town of Bal Harbour takes over Collins Avenue from Miami Beach. Bal Harbour is famous for its outdoor high-end shops; and if you take your shopping seriously, you may want to spend some considerable time in this area. The town runs a mere 10 blocks to the north before the bridge to another barrier island. After crossing the bridge, you'll first come to Halouver Beach Park, which is still technically in the village of Bal Harbour.

SUNNY ISLES BEACH

Beyond Haulover Beach (and on the same barrier island) is the town of Sunny Isles Beach. Once over the bridge, Collins Avenue bypasses several dozen street numbers, picking up again in the 150s; that's when you know you've arrived in the town of Sunny Isles Beach—an appealing, calm, and predominantly upscale choice for families looking for a beautiful beach, and where Russian may be heard as often as English. There's no nightlife to speak of in Sunny Isles, and yet the half dozen mega-luxurious skyscraper hotels that have sprung up here in the past decade have created a niche-resort town from the demolished ashes of much older, affordable hotels.

NORTH MIAMI

This suburban city, north of Miami proper, is comprised predominantly of older homes in its western reaches—many derelict—but also some snazzy rebuilds in the sections around Biscayne Bay and U.S.1. Several strip malls and restaurants line U.S. 1.

NORTH MIAMI BEACH

Don't let the name fool you. North Miami Beach actually isn't on the beach, but its southeastern end does but up against Biscayne Bay. Beyond the popular Oleta River State Park on the bay, the city offers little in terms of touristic appeal.

AVENTURA

West of Sunny Isles Beach and on the mainland are the high-rises of Aventura. This city is the heart and soul of South Florida's Jewish community as well as Miami's growing Russian community (along with Sunny Isles Beach). It is known for its high-end shopping opportunities, from the mega Aventura Mall to smaller boutiques in eclectic strip malls.

BEACHES

CORAL GABLES

FAMILY   **Matheson Hammock Park and Beach.** Kids love the gentle waves and warm (albeit often murky) waters of this beach in Coral Gables' suburbia, near Fairchild Tropical Botanic Garden. But the beach is only part of the draw—the park includes a boardwalk trail, a playground, and a golf course. Plus the park is a prime spot for kite-boarding. The man-made lagoon, or "atoll pool," is perfect for inexperienced swimmers, and it's one of the best places in mainland Miami for a picnic. Most tourists don't make the trek here; this park caters more to locals who don't want to travel all the way to Miami Beach. The park also offers a full-service marina. ■ TIP→ With an emphasis on family fun, it's not the best place for singles. Amenities: parking (fee); toilets. **Best for:** swimming. ⊠ *9610 Old Cutler Rd.* ☎ *305/665–5475* ⊕ *www.miamidade. gov/parks/matheson-hammock.asp* 🖅 *$5 per vehicle weekdays, $7 weekends* ⊙ *Daily sunrise–sunset.*

KEY BISCAYNE

Fodor's Choice   **Bill Baggs Cape Florida State Park.** Thanks to inviting beaches, sunsets, and a tranquil lighthouse, this park at Key Biscayne's southern tip is worth the drive. In fact, the 1-mile stretch of pure beachfront has been named several times in Dr. Beach's revered America's Top 10 Beaches list. It has 18 picnic pavilions available as daily rentals, two cafés that serve light lunches that include several Cuban specialties (Lighthouse Café, overlooking the Atlantic Ocean, and the Boater's Grill, on Biscayne Bay), and plenty of space to enjoy the umbrella and chair rentals. A stroll or ride along walking and bicycle paths provides wonderful views of Miami's dramatic skyline. From the southern end of the park you can see a handful of houses rising over the bay on wooden stilts, the remnants of Stiltsville, built in the 1940s and now protected by the Stiltsville Trust. The nonprofit group was established in 2003 to preserve the structures, because they showcase the park's rich history. Bill Baggs has bicycle rentals, a playground, fishing piers, and guided tours of the **Cape Florida Lighthouse,** South Florida's oldest structure. The lighthouse was erected in 1845 to replace an earlier one damaged in an 1836 Seminole attack, in which the keeper's helper was killed. Free tours are offered at the restored cottage and lighthouse at 10 am and 1 pm Thursday to Monday. Be there a half hour beforehand. **Amenities:** food and drink; lifeguards; parking; showers; toilets. **Best for:** solitude; sunsets; walking. ⊠ *1200 S. Crandon Blvd.* ☎ *305/361–5811* ⊕ *www. floridastateparks.org/capeflorida* 🖅 *$8 per vehicle; $2 per pedestrian* ⊙ *Daily 8–sunset.*

FAMILY   **Crandon Park Beach.** This relaxing oasis in northern Key Biscayne offers renowned tennis facilities, a great golf course, a family amusement center, and 2 miles of beach dotted with palm trees. The park is divided by Key Biscayne's main road, with tennis and golf on the bayside, the beaches on the oceanside. Families really enjoy the beaches here—the sand is soft, there are no rip tides, there's a great view of the Atlantic, and parking is both inexpensive and plentiful. However, on weekends, be prepared for a long hike from your car to the beach. There are bathrooms, outdoor showers, plenty of picnic tables, and concession stands. The family-friendly park offers abundant options for those who find it challenging simply to sit and build sand castles. Kite-board rentals and lessons are offered from the north water-sports concessions, as are kayak rentals. Eco-tours and nature trails showcase the myriad ecosystems of Key Biscayne including mangroves, coastal hammock, and seagrass beds. Bird-watching is great at the southern end of the park. The **Crandon's Family Amusement Center** at Crandon Park was once the site of a zoo. There are swans, waterfowl, peacocks, and dozens of huge iguanas running loose. Nearby you'll find a restored carousel (it's open weekends and major holidays 10:30–5, and you get three rides for $2), an old-fashioned outdoor roller rink, a dolphin-shape spray fountain, and a playground. **Amenities:** food and drink; lifeguards; parking (fee); showers; toilets; water sports. **Best for:** swimming; walking. ⌂ *6747 Crandon Blvd.* ☎ *305/361–5421* ⊕ *www.miamidade.gov/Parks/Parks/ crandon_beach.asp* ⊴ *$5 per vehicle weekdays, $7 weekends* ⊙ *Daily sunrise–sunset.*

SOUTH BEACH

Fodor's Choice
★

South Beach. A 10-block stretch of white sandy beach hugging the turquoise waters along Ocean Drive—from 5th to 15th streets—is one of the most popular in America, known for drawing unabashedly modelesque sunbathers and posers. With the influx of new luxe hotels and hotspots from 1st to 5th and 16th to 25th streets, the South Beach stand-and-pose scene is now bigger than ever and stretches yet another dozen plus blocks. The beaches crowd quickly on the weekends with a blend of European tourists, young hipsters, and sun-drenched locals offering Latin flavor. Separating the sand from the traffic of Ocean Drive is palm-fringed **Lummus Park**, with its volleyball nets and chickee huts (huts made of palmetto thatch over a cypress frame) for shade. The beach at **12th Street** is popular with gays, in a section often marked with rainbow flags. Locals hang out on 3rd Street beach, in an area called **SoFi** (South of Fifth) where they watch fit Brazilians play foot volley, a variation of volleyball that uses everything but the hands. Because much of South Beach leans toward skimpy sunning—women are often in G-strings and casually topless—many families prefer the tamer sections of Mid- and North Beach (save Halouver nude beach). Metered parking spots next to the ocean are a rare find. Instead, opt for a public garage a few blocks away and enjoy the people-watching as you walk to find your perfect spot on the sand. **Amenities:** food and drink; lifeguards; parking (fee); showers; toilets. **Best for:** partiers; sunrise; swimming; walking. ⌂ *Ocean Dr., from 5th to 15th Sts., then Collins Ave. to 25th St.*

NORTH BEACH

MIAMI BEACH

Haulover Beach Park. This popular clothing-optional beach is embraced by naturists of all ages, shapes, and sizes; there are even sections primarily frequented by families, singles, and gays. However, Haulover has more claims to fame than its casual attitude toward swimwear—it's also the best beach in the area for bodyboarding and surfing, as it gets what passes for impressive swells in these parts. Plus the sand here is fine-grain white, unusual for the Atlantic coast. Once you park in the North Lot, you'll walk through a short tunnel covered with trees and natural habitat until you emerge on the unpretentious beach, where nudity is rarely met by gawkers. There are volleyball nets, and plenty of beach chair and umbrella rentals to protect your birthday suit from too much exposure—to the sun, that is. The sections of beach requiring swimwear are popular, too, given the park's ample parking and relaxed atmosphere. Lifeguards stand watch. More active types might want to check out the kite rentals, or charter-fishing excursions. **Amenities:** food and drink; lifeguards; parking (fee); showers; toilets. **Best for:** nudists; surfing; swimming; walking. ⊠ *10800 Collins Ave., north of Bal Harbour, North Beach* ☎ *305/947–3525* ⊕ *www.miamidade.gov/ parks/haulover.asp* 🚗 *Parking $5 per vehicle weekdays, $7 weekends* ⊙ *Daily 8–sunset.*

NORTH MIAMI BEACH

FAMILY **Oleta River State Park.** Tucked away in North Miami Beach, this urban park is a ready-made family getaway. Nature lovers will find it easy to embrace the 1,128 acres of subtropical beauty along Biscayne Bay. Swim in the calm bay waters and bicycle, canoe, kayak, and bask among egrets, manatees, bald eagles, and fiddler crabs. Dozens of picnic tables, along with 10 covered pavilions, dot the stunning natural habitat, which was restored with red mangroves to revitalize the ecosystem and draw endangered birds, like the roseate spoonbill. There's a playground for tots, a mangrove island accessible only by boat, 15 miles of mountain-bike trails, a half-mile exercise track, concessions, and outdoor showers. **Amenities:** food and drink; parking (fee); showers; toilets; water sports. **Best for:** solitude; sunrise; sunset; walking. ⊠ *3400 N.E. 163rd St.* ☎ *305/919–1844* ⊕ *www.floridastateparks.org/park/Oleta-River* 🚗 *$6 per vehicle; $2 per pedestrian* ⊙ *Daily 8–sunset.*

WHERE TO EAT

Miami's restaurant scene has exploded in the past few years, with new restaurants springing up left and right every month. The melting pot of residents and visitors has brought an array of sophisticated, tasty cuisine. Little Havana is still king for Cuban fare, and Miami Beach is swept up in a trend of fusion cuisine, which combines Asian, French, American, and Latin cooking with sumptuous—and pricey—results. Locals spend the most time in Downtown Miami, Wynwood, Midtown, and the Design District, where the city's ongoing foodie and cocktail revolution is most pronounced. Since Miami dining is a part of the trendy nightlife scene, most dinners don't start until 8 or 9 pm, and may go well into the night. To avoid a long wait among the late-night partiers at hot spots, come before 7 pm or make reservations. Attire is usually casual-chic, but patrons like to dress to impress. Don't be surprised to see large tables of women in skimpy dresses—this is common in Miami. Prices tend to stay high in hot spots like Lincoln Road, but if you venture off the beaten path you can find delicious food for reasonable prices. When you get your bill, check whether a gratuity is already included; most restaurants add between 15% and 20% (ostensibly for the convenience of, and protection from, the many Latin American and European tourists who are used to this practice in their homelands), but supplement it depending on your opinion of the service.

Use the coordinate (✣ C2) at the end of each review to locate a property on the Where to Eat and Stay in the Miami Area map.

WHAT IT COSTS

	$	$$	$$$	$$$$
RESTAURANTS	under $16	$16–$20	$21–$30	over $30

Restaurant prices are the average cost of a main course at dinner or, if dinner is not served, at lunch.

DOWNTOWN

$$$$ ECLECTIC 🍴 **Azul.** A restaurant known for producing celebrity chefs and delivering dining fantasies of Food Network proportions, Azul is a Miami foodie institution. With its Forbes five-star, award-winning team, Azul offers a haute-cuisine experience on par with a two- or three-Michelin-star restaurant. Chefs fuse disparate ingredients, merging as decadent, gastronomic art. Headliners include dishes that pay homage to the Mandarin's Asian roots like the salmon tom ka gai with bok choy and a chicken-coconut panade and other global favorites like tuna poke with white soy, scallion, and macadamia nuts. Dine here, and you'll undoubtedly experience bold new taste sensations while enjoying one of the finest wine lists in the city and an incomparable skyline view. [$] *Average main: $48* ✉ *Mandarin Oriental, Miami, 500 Brickell Key Dr.* ☎ *305/913–8358* 🌐 *www.mandarinoriental.com/miami* ✍ *Reservations essential* ⏲ *Closed Sun. and Mon. No lunch* ✣ *D5.*

$$$$ FRENCH 🍴 **db Bistro Moderne Miami.** One of America's most celebrated French chefs, Daniel Boulud brings his renowned cooking to the Miami scene. The menu of Boulud's Miami outpost pays homage to Mediterranean cuisines and the specialties of his homeland. Begin with a cold plate from the fabulous raw bar or the signature house-smoked sturgeon; then feast on *escargots persillade* (wild burgundy snails simmered in parsley, garlic, salted butter with yellow tomatoes and wild mushrooms). For the main course, try the authentic *coq au vin,* which is sure to stir up memories of France through its robust taste and smell. There's a great $26 prix-fixe lunch during the workweek for Miami's business-lunch crowd. [$] *Average main: $31* ✉ *JW Marriott Marquis*

Miami, 255 Biscayne Blvd. Way ☎ *305/421–8800* 🌐 *www.dbbistro.com/miami* ✥ *D4.*

$$$ STEAKHOUSE Fodor's Choice ★ 🍴 **Edge, Steak & Bar.** It's farm-to-table surf-and-turf at this elegantly understated restaurant in the Four Seasons Hotel Miami, where hefty portions of the finest cuts and freshest seafood headline the menu, prepared by renowned chef Aaron Brooks. The innovative tartares are a surefire way to start the night right—try the corvina with baby cucumber, green apple, and a young celery-leaf, yellow-pepper sauce, or the ahi tuna with pickled shallots, watermelon, and mint. For the main event, Edge offers a variety of small, medium, and large cuts from the infrared grill, the most popular being the Black Angus filet mignon. For a more casual experience, enjoy your meal and the restaurant's artisan cocktails under the skies in the alfresco terrace, where you can also enjoy complimentary s'mores around the fire pits. Sunday brunch is also excellent with a well-stocked raw bar (including stone crabs in season), make-your-own taco station, and unlimited à la carte offerings that vary each week. [$] *Average main: $30* ✉ *Four Seasons Miami, 1435 Brickell Ave* ☎ *305/381–3190* 🌐 *www.edgerestaurantmiami.com* ✥ *D5.*

$$$ ECLECTIC Fodor's Choice ★ 🍴 **15th & Vine.** The signature restaurant of the überposh Viceroy Miami wows with a trifecta of sleek decor, delicious food, and a breathtaking backdrop from the property's famed terrace and deck hovering 15 stories above Brickell Avenue and Biscayne Bay. Seasonal menus tout contemporary American cuisine under global influences, all presented tapas-style. Dishes that stay on the menu year-round include bacon-wrapped dates; grilled flatbreads; Spanish pulpo (octopus) salad, and whole roasted snapper with Caribbean stir-fry. Socialization is easy from the high-top communal tables and alfresco seating around fire pits, while intimate tables fronting floor-to-ceiling windows or tucked outside among lush foliage promote further engagement. **■TIP→ In the evening, stroll across the massive pool terrace to the infinity stair observation deck for continued conversation over the views and under the stars.** [$] *Average main: $27* ✉ *Viceroy Miami, 485 Brickell Ave.* ☎ *305/307–5413* 🌐 *www.15thandvine.com* ✥ *D4.*

$$$$ PERUVIAN Fodor's Choice ★ 🍴 **La Mar by Gaston Acurio.** Don't have time to make a foodie pilgrimage to Lima, Peru? Not to worry; the next best thing beckons in downtown Miami. Peruvian celebrity chef Gaston Acurio has marked his U.S. debut at the dazzling Mandarin Oriental, Miami, offering a sublime menu and atmospheric, bay-side setting to match. Tour the far corners of Peru through La Mar's signature *cebiches* and *tiraditos,* freshly grilled street-style *anticuchos, causa* dishes (mashed potato topped with meat and vegetable toppings) and national libations, like the pisco sour. Eat inside the funky, contemporary, design-driven restaurant, replete with a living garden wall and an open anticucho kitchen and live cebiche bar, or bask in the Miami sun alfresco on the expansive terrace. [$] *Average main: $34* ✉ *Mandarin Oriental, Miami, 500 Brickell Key Dr.* 🌐 *www.mandarinoriental.com/miami* ✥ *D5.*

$$ SOUTHERN ITALIAN 🍴 **Moyé.** Gaining credibility as an excellent Italian restaurant *within Italy* is not easy, but Moyé, which translates to "this is the time" in the Bari dialect, has done exactly that. After six successful incarnations in the cradle of carb civilization, the first U.S. outpost of this

back-to-basics Italian restaurant concept instantly transports diners from the bustle of downtown Miami to *nonna's* kitchen in the Italian countryside. The restaurant hails from Italy's Puglia region (the "heel" of Italy's boot), and the menu focuses on authenticity and execution of classics perfected like the house-made burrata with white anchovies and oranges; *zuppa di pesce* (seafood stew in Puglia style); lasagna with homemade with meat ragu; and zucchini flan with scamorza cheese. Indeed, Moyé's time as a restaurant superstar is now! $ *Average main: $20* ⊠ *829 S.W. 1st Ave.* ☎ *305/372–5168* ⊕ *www.moyemiami.com* ⊹ *D5.*

$$$$
JAPANESE

✕ **NAOE.** By virtue of its petite size (eight patrons max) and strict seating times (at 6 and 9:30 nightly), the Japanese gem will forever remain intimate and original. And by virtue of its considerable price, it will inevitably require deep pockets; but this place is well worth the credit card debt. The all-inclusive menu changes daily, based on the day's best and freshest seafood, but always includes a bento box, soup, nigiri sushi, and dessert. Every visit ushers in a new exploration of the senses. Chef Kevin Cory prepares the gastronomic adventure a few feet from his patrons, using only the best ingredients and showcasing family treasures, like the renowned products of his centuries-old family *shoyu* (soy sauce) and sake brewery. From start to finish, you'll be transported to Japan through the stellar service, the tastes of bizarre sea creatures, and the smoothness of spectacular sakes. $ *Average main: $236* ⊠ *661 Brickell Key Dr.* ☎ *305/947–6263* ⊕ *www.naoemiami.com* ⌕ *Reservations essential* ☾ *Closed Sun. No lunch* ⊹ *D5.*

$
ECLECTIC
Fodor's Choice
★

✕ **Verde.** As if the high-design Pérez Art Museum Miami (PAMM) weren't cool enough, its waterfront restaurant is also making major waves across Biscayne Bay. The slick, contemporary Stephen Starr restaurant offers seating both indoors and out, with design-savvy decor and accessories true to its "green" name that blend seamlessly with the living walls and hanging gardens strewn across the museum's exterior. The exceptionally affordable, one-page menu features eclectic epicurean lunch plates that include a squash blossoms pizza, bigeye tuna tartare, a house chopped salad (with green goddess dressing), and gourmet cheeseburgers with applewood-smoked bacon and fries. ■TIP➜ **Museum admission is not required to eat here, but the restaurant is open only during museum hours, meaning lunch only, except on Thursday, when the museum remains open until 9.** $ *Average main: $14* ⊠ *Pérez Art Museum Miami, 1103 Biscayne Blvd.* ☎ *305/375–3000* ⊕ *www. pamm.org/dining* ☾ *Closed Mon. No dinner Fri.–Wed.* ⊹ *D4.*

COCONUT GROVE

$$
ECLECTIC

✕ **Lulu In the Grove.** At this eclectic sister to Green Street Cafe, red sofas and industrial communal tables commingle with ample bistro seating, while wraparound windows seamlessly merge the indoor and outdoor spaces. The menu is equally diverse, featuring classic American dishes with a twist (the fried green tomatoes with jalapeño ranch are a must-try) flecked with a few unexpected, yet soon-to-be-your-favorites, like the horizontally stacked fish tacos. The real highlight, however, is the red sangria, best enjoyed on a weekend afternoon while watching exotic and muscle cars purr along the picturesque street. The tapas-style presentations and ambience are best suited for social group outings versus solo or couple's dining. [$] *Average main: $20* ✉ *3105 Commodore Plaza* ☎ *305/447–5858* 🌐 *www.luluinthegrove.com* ✥ *C5.*

$$$ SEAFOOD FAMILY 🍴 **Monty's.** Connected to the Bayshore Landing Marina, Monty's has a Caribbean flair, thanks especially to live calypso and island music on the outdoor terrace. Though it has lost the luster it had back in the 1990s, it's still a fun, chill, kid-friendly place where Mom and Dad can kick back in the early evening and enjoy a beer and the raw bar while the kids dance to live music. The extensive menu offers a bit of everything, but the oysters on the half shell and the conch chowder are the best items. [$] *Average main: $25* ✉ *Bayshore Landing Marina, 2550 S. Bayshore Dr., at Aviation Ave.* ☎ *305/856–3992* ✥ *C5.*

$$ AMERICAN FAMILY 🍴 **Peacock Garden Café.** Reinstating the artsy and exciting vibe of Coconut Grove circa once-upon-a-time, this lovely spot offers an indoor-outdoor, tea-time setting for light bites. By day, it's one of Miami's most serene lunch spots. The lushly landscaped courtyard is lined with alfresco seating, drawing some of Miami's most fabulous ladies who lunch. Come evening, the café buzzes with a multigenerational crowd, enjoying the South Florida zephyrs and the delicious flatbreads, salads, homemade soups, and entrées. ■ **TIP→ Breakfast is also excellent.** [$] *Average main: $19* ✉ *2889 McFarlane Rd.* ☎ *305/774–3332* 🌐 *www.jaguarhg.com/peacockspot* ✥ *C5.*

CORAL GABLES

$$$ ECLECTIC Fodor's Choice ★ 🍴 **eating house.** Check your calorie counter at the door when you enter the hippest eatery in Coral Gables. This micro-restaurant sports long wait times, but you'll be talking about your meal here for months to come. The ever-changing small-plates menu teems with extreme culinary innovation and unexpected flavor combinations. Think: first fried cauliflower with lime cream, cotija cheese, and topped with layers of frito dust, followed by chicken "foie-ffles"—fried chicken, foie gras, and waffles smothered with candied bacon, maple syrup, and ranch dressing. Desserts are equally amazing. The famous "dirt cup" indeed resembles a soil-filled flowerpot. However, these roots are made of pretzels, hazelnuts, and *tierra nueva* chocolate ice cream; the "soil" is a mountain of crushed Oreos, and yes, that is a gummy worm in the "soil," adding a wonderfully campy touch to the dish's creativity. [$] *Average main: $23* ✉ *804 Ponce De Leon Blvd.* ☎ *305/448–6524* 🌐 *www.eatinghousemiami.com* ⊗ *No lunch weekends* ✥ *B5.*

$ CUBAN FAMILY 🍴 **El Palacio de los Jugos.** To the northwest of Coral Gables proper, this joint is one of the easiest and truest ways to see Miami's local Latin life in action. It's also one of the best fruit-shake shacks you'll ever come across (ask for a tropical juice of mamey or guanabana). Besides the rows of fresh tropical fruits and vegetables, and the shakes you can make with any of them, this boisterous indoor-outdoor market has numerous food counters where you can get just about any Cuban food—tamales, rice and beans, a *pan con lechón* (roast pork on Cuban bread), fried pork rinds, or a coconut split before you and served with a straw. Order your food at a counter, and eat it along with local families at rows of outdoor picnic-style tables next to the parking lot. It's disorganized, chaotic, and not for those cutting calories, but it's delicious and undeniably the real thing. [$] *Average main: $6* ✉ *5721 W. Flagler St., Flagami* ☎ *305/264–8662* 🌐 *www.elpalaciodelosjugos.com/en* 💳 *No credit cards* ✥ *B4.*

$$$$ CARIBBEAN 🍴 **Ortanique on the Mile.** Cascading *ortaniques*, a Jamaican hybrid orange, are hand-painted on columns in this warm, welcoming yellow dining room. Food is vibrant in taste and color, as delicious as it is beautiful. Though there is no denying that the strong, full flavors are imbued with island breezes, chef-partner Cindy Hutson's personal "cuisine of the sun" goes beyond Caribbean refinements. The menu centers on fish, since Hutson has a special way with it, and the West Indian Style Bouillabaisse is not to be missed. Ceviches and soups change nightly. The mojitos here—and the cocktails in general—are amazing. [$] *Average main: $33* ✉ *278 Miracle Mile* ☎ *305/446–7710* 🌐 *www.ortaniquerestaurants.com* ⏲ *No lunch weekends* ✥ *B5.*

$$$$ FRENCH 🍴 **Pascal's on Ponce.** This French gem amid the Coral Gables restaurant district is always full, thanks to chef-proprietor Pascal Oudin's assured and consistent cuisine. Oudin forgoes the glitz and fussiness often associated with French cuisine, and instead opts for a simple, small, refined dining room that won't overwhelm patrons. The equally sensible menu includes a creamy lobster bisque starter. The main course is a tough choice between oven-roasted duck with poached pears and diver sea scallops with beef short rib. Ask your expert waiter to pair dishes with a selection from Pascal's impressive wine list, and, for dessert, order the bittersweet-chocolate soufflé with chocolate ganache. [$] *Average main: $34* ✉ *2611 Ponce de León Blvd.* ☎ *305/444–2024* 🌐 *www.pascalmiami.com* ✍ *Reservations essential* ⏲ *Closed Sun. No lunch Sat.* ✥ *B5.*

$$$$ JAPANESE FUSION 🍴 **SushiSamba Coral Gables.** A flavor explosion of East-meets-South, SushiSamba beautifully mingles Japanese, Peruvian, and Brazilian cuisines to create an off-the-grid small-plates experience in the heart of Miracle Mile. The sleek 6,500-square-foot restaurant is at once modernist and welcoming. The colorful menu is divided into small hot plates, Samba Rolls, raw dishes, large plates, and skewers from the robata. Don't miss the divine *chicharrón de calamar,* a deliciously creative incarnation of fried calamari topped with tamarind sauce. Indulge in the crispy *taquitos*, stuffed with Maine lobster and hearts of palm. Feast on the specialty sushi roll unique to this location, the spicy Samba Coral Gables, which is loaded with steamed lobster, avocado, jalapeno, rice cracker, sweet chili, and key lime mayo. **■ TIP→ Save room for dessert. The Samba Split—a tower of dulce de leche ice cream, caramelized bananas, coconut flan, coconut mochi, and caramel popcorn—is even better than it sounds!** [$] *Average main: $36* ✉ *The Westin Colonnade Hotel, 180 Aragon Ave.* ☎ *305/448–4990* 🌐 *www.sushisamba.com* ✥ *B5.*

KEY BISCAYNE

$$$ MEXICAN 🍴 **Cantina Beach.** Leave it to Ritz-Carlton to bring a small, sumptuous piece of coastal Mexico to Florida's fabulous beaches. The pool- and ocean-side Cantina Beach showcases authentic and divine Mexican cuisine, including fresh guacamole made table-side. The restaurant also employs the region's only *tequilier*, mixing and matching 110 high-end tequilas. It's no surprise then that Cantina Beach has phenomenal margaritas. And the best part is that you can enjoy them with your feet in the sand, gazing at the ocean. [$] *Average main: $21* ✉ *The Ritz-Carlton Key Biscayne, Miami, 455 Grand Bay Dr.* ☎ *305/365–4500* 🌐 *www.ritzcarlton.com/keybiscayne* ✣ *D6.*

$$$$ ITALIAN 🍴 **Cioppino.** Few visitors think to venture out to the far end of Key Biscayne for dinner, but making the journey to the soothing grounds of this quiet Ritz-Carlton property on the beach is well worth it. Choose your view: the ornate dining room near the exhibition kitchen or the alfresco area with views of landscaped gardens or breeze-brushed beaches. Choosing your dishes may be more difficult, given the many rich, luscious Italian options, including imported cheeses, olive oils, risottos, and fresh fish flown in daily. Items range from the creamy *burrata* mozzarella and authentic pasta dishes to tantalizing risottos, all expertly matched with fine, vintage, rare, and boutique wines. An after-dinner drink and live music at the old-Havana-style Rumbar inside the hotel is another treat. [$] *Average main: $36* ✉ *The Ritz-Carlton Key Biscayne, Miami, 455 Grand Bay Dr.* ☎ *305/365–4500* 🌐 *www.ritzcarlton.com/keybiscayne* ✣ *D6.*

$$$ MODERN AMERICAN Fodor's Choice ★ 🍴 **Rusty Pelican.** Whether you're visiting Miami for the first or 15th time, a meal at the Rusty Pelican is a memorable experience. The legendary Key Biscayne restaurant underwent a major reinvention in 2012 and swapped rustic, nautical coziness for modern seaside elegance. Vistas of the bay and Miami skyline are sensational—whether you admire them through the floor-to-ceiling windows or from the expansive outdoor seating area, lined with alluring fire pits. The menu is split between tropically inspired small plates, ideal for sharing, and heartier entrées from land and sea. Standouts include corvina ceviche; baked crab cakes; and the crispy fried, whole local red snapper. [$] *Average main: $26* ✉ *3201 Rickenbacker Causeway* ☎ *305/361–3818* 🌐 *www.therustypelican.com* ✣ *D5.*

WYNWOOD

$$ ITALIAN 🍴 **Joey's.** Veneto-native chef Ivo Mazzon pays homage to fresh ingredients prepared simply in his small, modern Italian café, which offers a full line of flatbread pizzas, including the legendary *dolce e piccante* with figs, Gorgonzola, honey, and hot pepper—it's sweet-and-spicy goodness through and through. Joey's also serves the full gamut of Italian favorites. One of the first nongallery tenants and the first restaurant in the Wynwood Art District, it remains a favorite in the neighborhood despite an onslaught of fancy newcomers. The wine list is small but carefully chosen. [$] *Average main: $19* ✉ *2506 N.W. 2nd Ave.* ☎ *305/438–0488* 🌐 *www.joeyswynwood.com* ⏲ *No dinner Mon.* ✣ *D4.*

$ 🍴 **Panther Coffee.** Star-what? The eclectic coffee shop has made a triumphant return to Miami, and it goes by the name of Panther Coffee. The original location of the Miami-based specialty coffee roaster is smack in the center of the Wynwood Arts District (it has now expanded into Miami Beach and other South Florida neighborhoods), attracting a who's who of hipsters, artists, and even suburbanites to indulge in small-batch cups of joe and supermoist muffins and fresh-baked pastries. Baristas gingerly prepare every order, so prepare to wait a little for your macchiato. There are a few tables inside, but most prefer to multitask in the communal area outdoors (sipping, texting, talking, and people-watching all at once). It's open daily until 9. [$] *Average main: $5* ✉ *2390 N.W. 2nd Ave.* ☎ *305/677–3952* 🌐 *www.panthercoffee.com* ✥ *D4.*

CAFÉ
Fodor's Choice ★

$$$ 🍴 **Wynwood Kitchen & Bar.** At the center of Miami's artsy gallery-driven neighborhood, Wynwood Kitchen & Bar offers an experience that includes both cultural excitement and gastronomic fantasia. While you enjoy Latin-inspired small plates, you can marvel at the powerful, hand-painted murals characterizing the interiors and exteriors, which also spill out onto the captivating Wynwood Walls. Designed for sharing, tapas-style dishes include wood-grilled baby octopus skewers, lemon-pepper calamari, roasted beets, bacon-wrapped dates, and ropa vieja empanadas. It's best to allot a good chunk of time to thoroughly enjoy the creative food, the artist-inspired cocktails, and the cool crowd, and to venerate the sensational works of art all around you. [$] *Average main: $22* ✉ *2550 N.W. 2nd Ave.* ☎ *305/722–8959* 🌐 *www.wynwoodkitchenandbar.com* ✥ *C4.*

ECLECTIC
Fodor's Choice ★

MIDTOWN

$$$ 🍴 **Bocce.** A splendid slice of the Italian countryside thrives in Miami's trendy Midtown area, and the impressive 3,200-square-foot enclave houses a beautifully appointed rustic Italian restaurant, Miami's first official bocce court, and a throwback-style Italian market. Mosaic-tiled floors, antique mirrors, and exposed wood beams set the scene indoors while towering cypress trees, a traditional bocce court, and alfresco seating aplenty define the front patio. Spectacular design notwithstanding, it's the food that headlines the overall Bocce Bar experience. The small-plates sharing menu is a gastronomic tour through Italy with a modern twist. Dishes are beautifully presented, often accented by edible flowers, and never fall below a caliber of blow-your-mind deliciousness. [$] *Average main: $26* ✉ *3252 N.E. 1st Ave., No. 107* ☎ *786/245–6211* 🌐 *www.bocce-bar.com* ✥ *D4.*

MODERN ITALIAN

$$$$ 🍴 **Sugarcane Raw Bar Grill.** Midtown's most popular restaurant rages seven nights (and days) a week; and it's not hard to see why. The vibrant, supersexy, high-design restaurant perfectly captures Miami's Latin vibe while serving eclectic Latin American tapas and modern Japanese delights from three separate kitchens (robata, raw bar, and hot kitchen). Miami's easy-on-the-eyes crowd often begins the Sugarcane experience in the alfresco lounge, engaging in a fabulous mix of standing, posing, flirting, and sipping on delicious cocktails. Indoors, the trio of kitchens engineers some 60 small bites that include everything

JAPANESE FUSION
Fodor's Choice ★

from ceviche to sushi to bacon-wrapped dates and grilled maple-glazed sweet potatoes. Sugarcane has its fair share of out-of-the-ordinary dishes (think: barbecue spice pig's ear and oxtail paella) but it's the specialty sushi rolls—like the Night Crab Roll, filled with snow crab, shrimp tempura, and caper mustard—and the crudos—like the spicy local catch—that are most popular. [$] *Average main: $38* ✉ *3252 N.E. 1st Ave.* ☎ *786/369–0353* 🌐 *sugarcanerawbargrill.com* ✍ *Reservations essential* ✣ *D4.*

DESIGN DISTRICT

$$ PIZZA FAMILY Fodor's Choice ★

🍴 **Harry's Pizzeria.** Harry's is a neighborhood spot with some seriously good pizza, as one would expect as the second restaurant under Miami culinary darling Michael Schwartz and his team. The casual, friendly-yet-funky, ambience is inviting for all diner matchups: old chums, new dates, family members young and old. Seasonally inspired pizzas highlight locally sourced ingredients in unexpected, yet delicious, combinations as toppings for wood-fired, thin crusts. Fresh salads, snacks, and rotating daily dinner specials round out the menu. Also down the hatch are beverage options including craft beers, including Michael's Genuine Home Brew, great wines, Teamaker teas, and coffees in collaboration with fellow neighbor Panther Coffee. Simply sweet desserts like a chocolate chunk cookie or traditional zeppole with honey-whipped organic ricotta are crowd pleasers. [$] *Average main: $16* ✉ *3918 N. Miami Ave.* ☎ *786/275–4963* 🌐 *www.harryspizzeria.tumblr.com* ✣ *D3.*

$$$ MODERN GREEK Fodor's Choice ★

🍴 **Mandolin Aegean Bistro.** A step inside this 1940s house-turned-bistro transports you to *ya-ya*'s home along the Aegean Sea. The food is fresh and the service warm, matching its charming dining garden enveloped by a canopy of trees, a rustic wooden canopy, and traditional village furnishings. The menu of Greek and Turkish dishes sound simple enough, yet the raw flavors of excellent ingredients are memorable well beyond your meal. The food dazzles from beginning to end, commencing with flights of hummus, tzatziki, eggplant purees, and other authentic dipping sauces. Other noteworthy items include the signature Greek salad, grilled beef and lamb meatballs, a grilled Halloumi cheese sandwich, chicken kabobs, and fresh daily fish specials. Many of the herbs and produce used are picked right from the restaurant's organic garden next door. [$] *Average main: $24* ✉ *4312 N.E. 2nd Ave.* ☎ *305/576–6066* 🌐 *www.mandolinmiami.com* ✣ *D3.*

$$$ AMERICAN Fodor's Choice ★

🍴 **Michael's Genuine Food & Drink.** Michael's is often cited as Miami's top restaurant, and it's not hard to see why. This indoor-outdoor bistro in Miami's Design District is an evergreen oasis Miami dining sophisticates. Owner and chef Michael Schwartz aims for sophisticated American cuisine with an emphasis on local and organic ingredients. He gets it right. Portions are divided into small, medium, and large plates, and the smaller plates are more inventive, so you can order several and explore. Beautifully arranged combinations like crispy, sweet-and-spicy pork belly with kimchi explode with unlikely but satisfying flavor. Reserve two weeks in advance for weekend tables; also, consider brunch, but still make those reservations far in advance. [$] *Average main: $24* ✉ *130*

N.E. 40th St. ☎ *305/573–5550* ⊕ *www.michaelsgenuine.com* ⌣ *Reservations essential* ✚ *D3.*

LITTLE HAITI

$ ✕ **Chez Le Bebe.** Chez Le Bebe offers a short menu of Haitian home
CARIBBEAN   cooking—it's been going strong for 30 years and has been featured on shows like the Travel Channel's *Bizarre Foods with Andrew Zimmern* and *The Layover with Anthony Bourdain.* If you want to try stewed goat, this is the place to do it! Other dishes include tender and flavorful chicken, fish, oxtail, and fried pork; each plate comes with rice, beans, plantains, and salad, for around $15. $ *Average main: $15* ⊠ *114 N.E. 54th St.* ☎ *305/751–7639* ▭ *No credit cards* ✚ *D3.*

LITTLE HAVANA

$ ✕ **Azucar Ice Cream Company.** Balmy weather and sweet-tooth cravings
CAFÉ   are tempered at this ice cream shop specializing in homemade Cuban-
FAMILY   style scoops. More crafty than churning, flavors are inspired and derived from ingredients at nearby fruit stands, international grocery shops, and farmers' markets. A daily rotating menu fuses classics with innovative options (honey, pinot noir, lemon basil, Champagne grapefruit, rose, etc.), as well as creations that nod to its culturally rich location (café con leche, flan, and the signature Abuela Maria—made with Maria cookies, cream cheese, and guava). $ *Average main: $6* ⊠ *1503 S.W. 8th St.* ☎ *305/381–0369* ⊕ *www.azucaricecream.com* ✚ *C5.*

$ ✕ **El Exquisito Restaurant.** For a true locals' spot and some substantial
LATIN AMERICAN   Cuban eats in the heart of Little Havana, pop into Exquisito Restaurant, a local institution since the 1970s. The unassuming Cuban café serves up delectable, authentic Cuban favorites, including a great *cubano* (a grilled Cuban sandwich layered with ham, garlic-citrus-marinated slow-roasted pork, Swiss cheese, and pickles) and succulent yuca with garlic sauce. There's a quick-serve café on one side; next door is a full-service restaurant. A Cuban coffee is a whopping 75¢. $ *Average main: $14* ⊠ *1510 S.W. 8th St.* ☎ *305/643–0227* ⊕ *www.elexquisitomiami.com* ▭ *No credit cards* ✚ *C5.*

$$ ✕ **Hy-Vong Vietnamese Cuisine.** Florida's best Vietnamese food in the heart
VIETNAMESE   of Little Havana? It may sound bizarre, but Hy-Vong will have you
Fodor'sChoice   rethinking your drive to *Calle Ocho* for Cuban cuisine. In fact, people
★   are willing to wait on the sidewalk for hours to sample the delights at this tiny restaurant, like *cha gio* (Vietnamese spring rolls), fish panfried with mango or with *nuoc man* (a garlic-lime fish sauce), not to mention the pork *thit kho* (caramelized braised pork) stewed in coconut milk. Beer-savvy proprietors Kathy Manning and Tung Nguyen serve a half dozen top brews (Double Grimbergen, Peroni, and Spaten, among them) to further inoculate the experience from the ordinary—well, as ordinary as a Vietnamese restaurant on *Calle Ocho* can be. Arrive early to avoid long waits. $ *Average main: $17* ⊠ *3458 S.W. 8th St.* ☎ *305/446–3674* ⊕ *www.hyvong.com* ⊙ *Closed Mon. and Tues. No lunch* ✚ *B5.*

$ ✕**Las Pinareños Fruteria y Floreria.** In the mood for something refreshing
CUBAN or a high-octane jolt? Try Las Pinareños, a *fruteria* (fruit stand) that
serves *coco frio* (fresh, cold coconut juice served in a whole coconut),
mango juice, and other *jugos* (juices), as well as Cuban coffees and
Cuban finger foods. You can order your sweet, hot *cortadito* (coffee
with milk) or a *cafecito* (no milk) from the walk-up window and enjoy
it at one of the stools in front of the shop or sit at one of the tables
inside the fruit-and-flower market. $ *Average main: $7* ⊠ *1334 S.W.
8th St.* ☎ *305/285–1135* ✛ *C5.*

$ ✕**Versailles.** ¡*Bienvenido a Miami!* To the area's Cuban population,
CUBAN Miami without Versailles is like rice without black beans. First-timer
FAMILY Miami visitors looking for that "Cuban food on Calle Ocho" experi-
Fodor'sChoice ence, look no further. The storied eatery, where old émigrés opine daily
★ about all things Cuban, is a stop on every political candidate's campaign
trail, and it should be a stop for you as well. Order a heaping platter of
lechon asado (roasted pork loin), *ropa vieja* (shredded beef), or *picadillo*
(spicy ground beef), all served with rice, beans, and fried plantains. It's
not quite as good as true homemade Cuban food, but it's a requisite
stop in Little Havana. After overeating, battle the oncoming food coma
with a cup of the city's strongest *cafecito,* which comes in the tiniest of
cups but packs a lot of punch. Versailles operates a bakery next door
as well—take some *pastelitos* home. $ *Average main: $15* ⊠ *3555 S.W.
8th St.* ☎ *305/444–0240* ⊕ *www.versaillesrestaurant.com* ✛ *C5.*

SOUTH BEACH

$$$$ ✕**Bianca.** In a hotel where style reigns supreme, this high-profile res-
ITALIAN taurant provides both glamour and solid cuisine. The main attraction
of dining here is to see and be seen, but you may leave talking about
the food just as much as the outfits, hairdos, and celebrity appearances.
This Italian restaurant doles out some pretty amazing fare, including a
shaved baby-artichoke salad and truffle tagliatelle—perfection in every
bite. The dessert menu may seem a bit back-to-basics, with tiramisu
and cheesecake among the favorites, but these sweet classics are done
right. For something a bit more casual at the Delano, try sushi from
the Philippe Starck countertop sushi bar, Umi, at the front of the hotel.
$ *Average main: $50* ⊠ *Delano Hotel, 1685 Collins Ave.* ☎ *305/674–
5752* ⊕ *www.delano-hotel.com* ⌂ *Reservations essential* ✛ *H2.*

$$$$ ✕**BLT Steak.** This Ocean Drive favorite, renowned for seriously divine
STEAKHOUSE Gruyère cheese popovers and succulent steak and fish dishes, illuminates
the vibrant, open lobby of the snazzy Betsy Hotel. It has the distinc-
tion among all of Miami's steak houses of serving breakfast daily and
consistently impressing even the most finicky eaters. You can count
on the highest-quality cuts of USDA prime, certified Black Angus, and
American Wagyu beef, in addition to blackboard specials, and sushi
and raw-bar selections. Though the name may say steak, the fresh fish
is arguably the highlight of the entire menu—the sautéed Dover sole
with soy-caper brown butter is legendary. $ *Average main: $42* ⊠ *The
Betsy Hotel, 1440 Ocean Dr.* ☎ *305/673–0044* ⊕ *www.e2hospitality.
com/restaurants/* ✛ *G2.*

$$$ MODERN ITALIAN Fodor's Choice ★ **Dolce Italian.** Best known as a top contender on the Bravo TV show *Best New Restaurant,* Dolce Italian buzzes in the center of the South Beach action, doling out an irresistible menage à trois: great food, great ambience, and an easy-on-the-eyes crowd. Tucked into the first floors of the renovated Gale South Beach hotel, Miami's "it" crowd clamors for a table to see and be seen feasting on Dolce's spaghetti al pomodoro, *tartufata* pizza (with speck, spicy salami, and truffle oil), house-made mozzarella, roasted branzino, and meats from the Tuscan grill. Indeed, Italian-born chef Paolo Dorigato's menu is packed with modern incarnations of Italian classics that would make nonna proud. [$] *Average main: $24* ✉ *Gale South Beach, 1690 Collins Ave.* ☎ *786/975–2550* 🌐 *www.dolceitalianrestaurant.com* ✥ *G2.*

$$$$ SEAFOOD Fodor's Choice ★ **Joe's Stone Crab Restaurant.** In South Beach's decidedly new-money scene, the stately Joe's Stone Crab is an old-school testament to good food and good service. South Beach's most storied restaurant started as a turn-of-the-20th-century eating house when Joseph Weiss discovered succulent stone crabs off the Florida coast. A century later, the restaurant stretches a city block and serves 2,000 dinners a day to local politicians and moneyed patriarchs. Stone crabs, served with legendary mustard sauce, crispy hash browned potatoes, and creamed spinach, remain the staple. Though stone-crab season runs from October 15 to May 15, Joe's remains open year-round (albeit with a limited schedule) serving other phenomenal seafood dishes. Finish your meal with tart key lime pie, baked fresh daily. **■ TIP→ Joe's famously refuses reservations, and weekend waits can be three hours long—yes, you read that correctly—so come early or order from Joe's Take Away next door.** [$] *Average main: $45* ✉ *11 Washington Ave.* ☎ *305/673–0365, 305/673–4611 for takeout* 🌐 *www.joesstonecrab.com* ✍ *Reservations not accepted* ⏲ *No lunch Sun. and Mon. and mid-May–mid-Oct.* ✥ *G5.*

$$$$ JAPANESE FUSION Fodor's Choice ★ **Juvia.** High atop South Beach's design-driven 1111 Lincoln Road parking garage, Juvia commingles urban sophistication with South Beach seduction. Towering over the beach's art deco district, the restaurant rises as a bold amalgamation of steel, glass, hanging gardens, and purple accents—a true work of art high in the sky. Three renowned chefs unite to deliver an amazing eating experience that screams Japanese, Peruvian, and French all in the same breath, focusing largely on raw fish and seafood dishes. The see-and-be-seen crowd can't get enough; neither can we! [$] *Average main: $42* ✉ *1111 Lincoln Rd.* ☎ *305/763–8272* 🌐 *www.juviamiami.com* ✍ *Reservations essential* ✥ *F2.*

$$$ MEDITERRANEAN Fodor's Choice ★ **La Savina.** In an ultratrendy hotel like the Mondrian, it's refreshing to find a restaurant as timeless as La Savina. The Spanish Mediterranean–inspired fare includes grilled seafood and meats, "crudo" appetizers, charcuterie and cheese boards, and plenty of delectable salads and vegetables. Start with the shrimp crudo, poached in a vinaigrette of olives and tomatoes, followed by the sublime carrot salad, an exquisitely presented blend of raw and cooked carrots, pistachios, and feta cheese. Grilled fish and meat, such as the day-caught mahimahi and rib eye are cooked to perfection, basted in a salsa verde. While beach-appropriate lighter fare prevails on the menu, the vegetable sides are anything but.

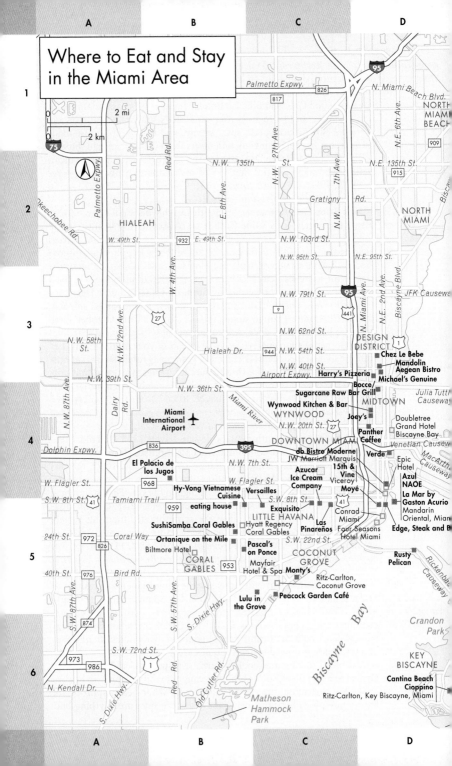

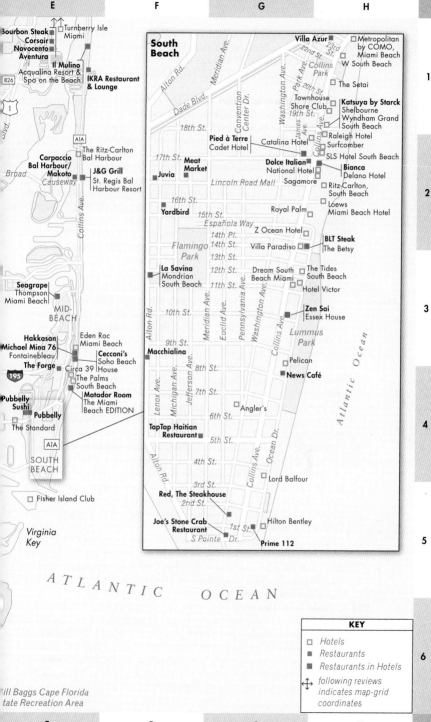

Gorge on the squash—grilled and candied then topped with marscapone cheese—or feast on the decadent, flash-fried cauliflower, dressed in yogurt and lemon. $ *Average main: $29* ⊠ *Mondrian South Beach Hotel, 1100 West Ave.* ☎ *305/514–1940* ⊕ *www.morganshotelgroup. com* ✧ *F3.*

$$$
ITALIAN
✕ **Macchialina Taverna Rustica.** Framed by exposed brick walls, decorated with daily specials chalkboards, and packed with gregarious patrons, this local foodie hangout feels like a cozy, neighborhoody, New England tavern. And with a gorgeous menu showcasing the prowess of chef Michael Pirolo, Macchialina Taverna Rustica nails the concept of modern Italian cuisine. Combining such great ambience and amazing eats, expect one helluva night. Start with some Italian-imported salumi, local *burrata,* or creamy polenta with sausage *ragu* and *cipollini* onions. Then, move on to the house-made pastas, perhaps the beet-filled *mezzaluna,* the *tagliolini al funghi,* or the spaghetti *con vongole,* before feasting on a lavish chicken or fish entrée. Save room for the house panna cotta, smothered in candied pistachios and balsamic-reduced strawberries. $ *Average main: $26* ⊠ *820 Alton Rd.* ☎ *305/534–2124* ⊕ *www.macchialina.com* ☾ *No lunch Mon.–Sat.* ✧ *F3.*

$$$$
STEAKHOUSE
✕ **Meat Market.** On Lincoln Road, where most of the restaurants emphasize people-watching over good food, this is one spot where you can find the best of both. Indeed, this is a meat market in every sense of the phrase, with great cuts of meat and plenty of sexy people passing by in skimpy clothes and enjoying fruity libations at the bar. Hard-core carnivores go wild over the 14-ounce center-cut prime New York steak as well as the "mixed-grill special," a creative trio of meats and seafood that changes nightly. There are plenty of excellent seafood options, as well. Try the cedar-paper salmon, topped with a spicy orange glaze, or the wood-grilled blackened local snapper, served atop celery root puree. $ *Average main: $40* ⊠ *915 Lincoln Rd.* ☎ *305/532–0088* ⊕ *www. meatmarket.net* ✧ *F2.*

$$
AMERICAN
✕ **News Café.** No trip to Miami is complete without a stop at this Ocean Drive landmark, though the food is nothing special. The 24-hour café attracts a crowd with snacks, light meals, drinks, periodicals, and the people parade on the sidewalk out front. Most prefer sitting outside, where they can feel the salt breeze and gawk at the human scenery. Seagrape trees shade a patio where you can watch from a quiet distance. Offering a little of this and a little of that—bagels, pâtés, chocolate fondue, sandwiches, and a terrific wine list—this joint has something for everyone. Although service can be indifferent to the point of laissez-faire and the food is mediocre at best, News Café is just one of those places visitors love. $ *Average main: $19* ⊠ *800 Ocean Dr.* ☎ *305/538–6397* ⊕ *www.newscafe.com* ⌦ *Reservations not accepted* ✧ *G4.*

$$$$
MODERN FRENCH
✕ **Pied à Terre.** This cozy, 36-seat French Contemporary restaurant with Mediterranean influence resides in the heart of South Beach, but it's everything the beach is not. Quiet, classic, and elegant, this hidden gastro-sanctuary within the historic Cadet Hotel forgoes glitz and gimmicks for taste and sophistication. The restaurant recalls the ambience of a bona fide, intimate Parisian eatery—the kind you'd randomly discover on a side street in the City of Light's 5th or 6th arrondissement—and

CHEAP EATS ON SOUTH BEACH

Miami Beach is notorious for overpriced eateries, but locals know that you don't always have to spend $30 for lunch or $45 for a dinner entree to have a good meal, even in overpriced South Beach. **Pizza Rustica** (✉ *8th St. and Washington Ave. and 667 Lincoln Rd.*) serves up humongous slices overflowing with mozzarella, steak, olives, and barbecue chicken until 4 am. **La Sandwicherie** (✉ *14th St. between Collins and Washington Aves.*) is a South Beach classic that's been here since 1988, serving gourmet French sandwiches, a delicious prosciutto salad, and healthful smoothies from a walk-up bar. **Lime Fresh Mexican Grill** (✉ *1439 Alton Rd., at 14th St.*) serves fresh and tangy fish tacos and homemade guacamole.

doles out succulent French contemporary cuisine enhanced by an excellent and reasonably priced wine list. [$] *Average main: $42* ✉ *Cadet Hotel, 1701 James Ave.* ☎ *305/531–4533* 🌐 *www.cadethotel.com* ✍ *Reservations essential* ⏲ *Closed Mon. No lunch* ✥ *G2.*

$$$$ STEAKHOUSE 🍴 **Prime 112.** This wildly busy steak house is particularly renowned for its highly marbleized prime beef, creamed corn, truffle macaroni and cheese, and buzzing scene: while you stand at the bar awaiting your table (everyone has to wait—at least a little bit), you'll clamor for a drink with all facets of Miami's high society, from the city's top real estate developers and philanthropists to striking models and celebrities (Lenny Kravitz, Jay-Z, and Matt Damon are among a big list of celebrity regulars). [$] *Average main: $46* ✉ *112 Ocean Dr.* ☎ *305/532–8112* 🌐 *www.mylesrestaurantgroup.com* ✍ *Reservations not accepted* ⏲ *No lunch weekends* ✥ *G5.*

$$$ ECLECTIC Fodor's Choice ★ 🍴 **Pubbelly.** This petite eatery, on a residential street in SoBe's western reaches, still attracts the who's-who of beach socialites, hipsters, and the occasional tourist coming to chow down on inventive Asian-Latin small plates, dumplings, charcuterie, and seasonal large plates by executive chef/owner Jose Mendin. From bay scallops bourguignon to short-rib tartare to *huitlacoche* (corn truffle) dumplings in squid ink black butter, Pubbelly constantly pushes the envelope on inventive cuisine, and locals simply can't get enough. Expect deservedly long wait times, especially on weekends. But not to worry, after a few rounds of craft beers, sake cocktails, and eclectic wines from the awesome drink menu, your table will be ready in no time! [$] *Average main: $28* ✉ *1418 20th St.* ☎ *305/532–7555* 🌐 *www.pubbelly.com* ✥ *E4.*

$$$$ JAPANESE 🍴 **Pubbelly Sushi.** The team behind South Beach's wildly popular Pubbelly gastropub has teamed up with sushi chef Yuki Ieto to create the Pubbelly Sushi, a 40-seat canteen doling out contemporary, Japanese-inspired sharing plates. Of course, you go light with the grade-A sashimi or meats from the *robata* (Japanese charcoal) grill, but the real fun lies in the flavor-rich "Snacks," "Pubbelly Rolls," and "New England Style Rolls." Start with Rock Shrimp Tempura "buffalo style" and graduate to the Bigeye Tuna Roll (spicy tuna over squares of crispy rice) and Navarro (salmon, crab, melted mozzarella, and fried onions).

Wash it all down with the house "vodkasake" cocktails. They're all deliciously addicting, but the Basil Berry (basil, strawberries, yuzu, sake) and Spicy Pina (jalapeño, pineapple, sake) go best with a steamy Miami evening. $ *Average main: $38* ⊠ *1424 20th St.* ☎ *305/531–9282* ⊕ *www.pubbellysushi.com* ⊹ *E4.*

$$$$
STEAKHOUSE

✕ **Red, the Steakhouse.** The carnivore glamour den seduces with its red-and-black dominatrix color scheme and overloads the senses with the divine smells and tastes of the extensive menu. Red boasts an equal number of seafood and traditional more meat offerings, each delicately prepared, meticulously presented, and gleefully consumed. Start with the tuna tartare, the mussels *diavolo*, or crisp chili calamari, and then continue with fresh lobster or the many variations of Angus beef prime. And don't forget about the dozen or so sides, often the most exciting part of any steak house experience. $ *Average main: $50* ⊠ *119 Washington Ave.* ☎ *305/534–3688* ⊕ *www.redthesteakhouse.com* ⊳ *Reservations essential* ⊹ *G5.*

$
CARIBBEAN

✕ **Tap Tap Haitian Restaurant.** Tap Tap is anything but SoBe glitz and glam, but this Haitian restaurant will instantly immerse you in Haiti's cuisine and culture. An extensive collection of Haitian folk art is displayed throughout this house-turned-restaurant, so much so that every wall, table, and chair doubles as a piece of colorful art. Menu highlights include *soup joumou* (pumpkin soup), *spagheti kreyol* (pasta, shrimp or herring, and a creole tomato sauce), *kabrit nan sos* (Bolinas goat stew in a mildly spicy tomato-based sauce), and grilled conch (when available). They also have an extensive vegetarian menu, including several vegan dishes. $ *Average main: $14* ⊠ *819 5th St.* ☎ *305/672–2898* ⊹ *F4.*

$$$$
MEDITERRANEAN

✕ **Villa Azur.** St. Tropez invades South Beach at this sceney resto-lounge where dinner doesn't usually begin until late (which is normal for the Miami crowd) and the Champagne-sipping continues until the wee hours of the morning (to sounds of awesome DJs).The restaurant fuses indoors and outdoors, merging prolific alfresco seating in a spacious, tree-lined courtyard with open-aired contemporary interior dining and relaxation areas (swaying chandeliers, white tufted couches, and whimsically accessorized library shelves). While Vueve Cliquot is a staple among patrons, the tropical-inspired cocktails and the selection from the in-house wine cellar, La Cave d'Azur, also impress. The exquisitely executed, French-Mediterranean cuisine is seafood-centric, beginning with colossal towers from the raw bar, then moving onto to light greens like the shaved artichoke and parmiagiano salad, and finishing with dishes such as dover sole *a la meunière.* $ *Average main: $45* ⊠ *309 23rd St.* ☎ *305/763–8688* ⊕ *www.villaazurmiami.com* ⊳ *Reservations essential* ⊗ *No lunch* ⊹ *H1.*

$$$
SOUTHERN

✕ **Yardbird Southern Table & Bar.** There's a helluva lot of Southern lovin' from the Lowcountry at this lively and funky South Beach spot. Miami's A-list puts calorie-counting aside for decadent nights filled with comfort foods and innovative drinks. The family-style menu is divided between "quick bites," "the bird," "plates," and "fixins," but have no doubt the "the bird" takes center stage (or plate) here. You'll rave about Mama's chicken biscuits, the chicken 'n' watermelon 'n' waffles, and Llewellyn's fine fried chicken, which requires a 27-hour marination and slow-cooking process. Oh, and then there are the sides, like house-cut fries with a buttermilk dipping sauce and bacon salt or the supercreamy macaroni and cheese. Don't plan on hitting the beach in a bikini the next day. [$] *Average main: $28* ✉ *1600 Lenox Ave.* ☎ *305/538–5220* 🌐 *www.runchickenrun.com* ✍ *Reservations essential* ✣ *F2.*

$$$ ASIAN FUSION Fodor's Choice ★

🍴 **Zen Sai.** In Miami's vortex of the fake and fabulous, it's rare to find a venue that's effortlessly cool, but Zen Sai is exactly that. The petite Asian eatery encompasses a small bar area and a small art deco–steeped dining veranda, enjoying a low profile among its larger-than-life neighbors. Dishes reflect a gastronomic tour of north Asia, largely focused on Japanese items for the American palate like robata-grilled meats, sushi rolls, and the heavenly 12-hour sweet yuzu and miso-marinated black cod. There's an extensive sake list to match, but don't forgo an opportunity to sample some of the beach's best cocktails. Zen Sai's artisanal libations remain true to the craft of cocktail making, using fresh and exotic ingredients for stellar results (lychee martinis with Kumosabe Nigori sake, Finlandia vodka, house-infused lychee syrup, and fresh lemon juice). [$] *Average main: $23* ✉ *Essex House Hotel, 1001 Collins Ave.* ☎ *786/276–5339* 🌐 *www.zensaisobe.com* 🕒 *No lunch* ✣ *G3.*

MID-BEACH

$$$ ITALIAN

🍴 **Cecconi's Miami Beach.** The wait for a table at this outpost of the iconic Italian restaurant is just as long as its counterparts in West Hollywood and London, and the dining experience just as fabulous. The food is great, but atmosphere here is everything. It's a real scene of who's who and who's eating what, cast in a seductive, vintage-chic setting across the courtyard of the Soho Beach House Miami. Without a doubt, the black-truffle-and-goat-cheese pizza, with huge hunks of black truffle, is the restaurant's most talked about dish. The fish carpaccios are light and succulent, while the classically hearty pastas and risottos provide authentic Italian fare. [$] *Average main: $27* ✉ *Soho Beach House Miami, 4385 Collins Ave.* ☎ *786/507–7902* 🌐 *www.cecconismiamibeach.com* ✍ *Reservations essential* ✣ *E3.*

$$$$ STEAKHOUSE

🍴 **The Forge.** Legendary for its opulence, this restaurant has been wowing patrons since 1968. After a face-lift in 2010, antiques, gilt-framed paintings, a chandelier from the Paris Opera House, and Tiffany stained-glass windows from New York's Trinity Church are the fitting background for some of Miami's best cuts. The tried-and-true menu also includes prime rib, bone-in fillet, lobster *gratinée*, chocolate soufflé, and sinful side dishes like creamed spinach and black truffle mac-and-cheese potpie. For its walk-in humidor alone, the over-the-top Forge is worth visiting. Automated wine machines span the perimeter of the restaurant and allow you to pick your own pour and sample several wines throughout your meal. [$] *Average main: $43* ✉ *432 Arthur Godfrey Rd.* ☎ *305/538–8533* 🌐 *www.theforge.com* 🕒 *No lunch* ✣ *E4.*

$$$$ CANTONESE

🍴 **Hakkasan Miami.** This stateside sibling of the Michelin-star London restaurant brings the haute-Chinese-food movement to South Florida, adding Pan-Asian flair to even quite simple and authentic Cantonese recipes, and producing an entire menu that can be classified as blow-your-mind delicious. Seafood and vegetarian dishes outnumber meat options, with the scallop-and-shrimp dim sum, Szechuan-style braised eggplant, and charcoal-grilled silver cod with Champagne and Chinese honey reaching new heights of excellence. **■ TIP→ It's dinner only here, except on weekends when the restaurant hosts a dim sum lunch.** Superb eats notwithstanding, another reason to experience Hakkasan is that it's arguably the sexiest, best-looking restaurant on Miami Beach. Intricately carved, lacquered-black-wood Chinois panels divide seating sections, creating a deceptively cozy dining experience for such a large restaurant. Dress to impress. [$] *Average main: $52* ✉ *Fontainebleau Miami Beach, 4441 Collins Ave., 4th fl.* ☎ *786/276–1388 after 4 pm, 877/326–7412 before 4 pm* 🌐 *www.hakkasan.com/locations/hakkasan-miami/* ✍ *Reservations essential* ⏲ *No lunch weekdays* ✥ *E3.*

$$
SPANISH
Fodor's Choice ★

🍴 **Matador Room.** In one Miami's most captivating and seductive settings, the latest headling restaurant by celebrity Chef Jean-Georges Vongerichten fuses Spanish, Caribbean, and Latin American gastronomy, presenting the result in a diverse (and surprisingly affordable) collection of small and large plates. Though the venue plays into a sexy matador theme, the name stems from the space's former incarnation—the eponymous, superglam supper club of yesteryear. Paying homage to its history by keeping the name, the space has now been thoroughly reinvented as well as augmented by the hanging gardens and braided lights of the alfresco Matador Terrace. Indulge on tropically inspired plates like peekytoe crab and corn fritters; wild gulf shrimp with sizzling garlic and chili oil; and charred Florida octopus with crispy potatoes and paprika emulsion. Pair the bites with equally superb libations like the epic pineapple elixir cocktail served in a massive copper pineapple. [$] *Average main: $20* ✉ *The Miami Beach Edition, 2901 Collins Ave.* ☎ *786/257–4600* 🌐 *www.matadorroom.com* ✥ *E4.*

$$$$
ECLECTIC
Fodor's Choice ★

🍴 **Michael Mina 74.** Celebrity Chef Michael Mina's sleek, tavern-style subterranean restaurant at the Fontainebleau is a daily celebration of gastronomic creativity, bold flavors, and Florida seafood. Dishes are served as shared plates, small and large, and include the likes of "Michael's Tuna Tartare," dressed and tossed tableside with Asian pear, pine nut, scotch bonnets, and sesame oil; and the Florida Snapper served atop succulent shrimp fried rice cakes and accented by thin slices of caramelized pineapple. Eye-catching food carts make rounds through the restaurant, offering rotating selections of daily appetizers and fresh shellfish. As hard as it may be to resist ordering a half dozen of Mina's savory selections, be sure to save room for dessert. The "Milk and Cookies" (tempura-fried cookie dough alongside a cup of malted milk foam) are not to be missed! [$] *Average main: $38* ✉ *Fontainebleau Miami Beach, 4441 Collins Ave.* ☎ *305/674–4636* 🌐 *www.michaelmina.net* ✍ *Reservations essential* ⏲ *No lunch* ✥ *E3.*

$$$$
ECLECTIC

🍴 **Seagrape.** Miami's homegrown celebrity chef and television personality Michelle Bernstein has returned to her Florida roots—literally and figuratively—for her latest buzzworthy eatery. In a vintage- chic, old Florida setting accessed through the breezeway of the snazzy Thompson Miami Beach hotel in the growing Mid-Beach district, Bernstein presents the best of the sunshine states's seafood, produce, and proteins, prepared simply yet skillfully such that each dish makes a statement.

Popular dishes include the local fish ceviche, the coriander roasted beet salad, and the Thai-style whole crispy Florida snapper. $ *Average main: $36* ⊠ *Thompson Miami Beach, 4041 Collins Ave.* ☎ *786/605–1043* ⊕ *www.seagrapemiamibeach.com* ✛ *E3.*

NORTH BEACH

BAL HARBOUR

$$$
MODERN ITALIAN

✕ **Carpaccio Bal Harbour.** As expected for its ritzy location, this upscale restaurant matches its high-fashion neighbors, albeit in a refreshing manner. There's no funky furniture nor slick decor, just simple white-clothed tables and charming Italian touches. Waiters don bow ties and coattails, even for lunch hours, yet are approachable in their knowledge and attentiveness. Made with the freshest ingredients, practically everything on the menu jumps out, though the handmade mozzarella antipasti, clam linguine, and namesake beef carpaccio are signature dishes. An extensive list of wines from Italy, California, and other worldly regions will perfectly complement your meal and offer a fitting end to a successful shopping excursion. ■ TIP➜ **You won't be alone appreciating the good service and food—Carpaccio is known for long lines wrapping around the restaurant, so it's best to try and snag a table early.** $ *Average main: $25* ⊠ *Bal Harbour Shops, 9700 Collins Ave.* ☎ *305/867–7777* ⊕ *www.carpaccioatbalharbour.com* ⌲ *Reservations not accepted* ✛ *E2.*

$$$$
MODERN FRENCH

✕ **J & G Grill.** In the ultraglamorous St. Regis Bal Harbour, celebrity Chef Jean-Gorges Vongerichten brings haute French fusion cuisine to the stunning Miami waterfront. The restaurant interiors flaunt a design sophistication that blends seamlessly with its host hotel. From beginning to end, a meal here is a true gastronomic tour de force, where dishes like the lobster bisque with butternut squash espuma and the porcini risotto with truffle brioche nary fall below the level of mind-blowing. While menu items change seasonally, there are always a number of can't-miss JG signatures such as the Crispy Poached Egg Caviar with vodka crème fraîche. Save room for the decadent desserts from pastry chef Antonio Bachour; his French-inspired delights are pure foodie fantasia. $ *Average main: $46* ⊠ *St. Regis Bal Harbour, 9703 Collins Ave.* ☎ *305/993–3300* ⊕ *www.jggrillmiami.com* ✛ *E2.*

$$$$
JAPANESE
Fodor's Choice
★

✕ **Makoto.** Stephen Starr's Japanese headliner, executed by celebrity Chef Makoto Okuwa, is one of the most popular restaurants in all of South Florida (and in this swanky shopping center, too). The ambience, service, and food all impress; and given its location in haute-couture central, the patrons definitely dress to impress. There are two menus, one devoted solely to sushi, sashimi, and maki; the other to Japanese cold and hot dishes like tempuras, meats, and vegetables grilled over Japanese charcoal (robata), rice and noodle dishes, and steaks and fish inspired by the Land of the Rising Sun. $ *Average main: $34* ⊠ *Bal Harbour Shops, 9700 Collins Ave.* ☎ *305/864–8600* ⊕ *www.makoto-restaurant.com* ✛ *E2.*

SUNNY ISLES BEACH

$$$$ RUSSIAN FAMILY

🍴 **IKRA Restaurant & Lounge.** Catering predominantly to a flashy Russian clientele, Ikra (Russian for "caviar") is a surprisingly good restaurant with abundant live entertainment in Sunny Isles, sure to please all nationalities. Don't let the stripmall location fool you. Once you step inside, each of the three rooms is decorated in true South Beach style, with long, flowing white curtains, whitewashed wood floors, and tiered mirrors that make a statement. The kitchen serves up taste sensations by three specialized chefs, who can handily produce both Ukranian and Mediterranean cuisine. As expected, the caviar list is rather incredible, but the standard menu items like the artichoke carpaccio with shaved truffle and the tuna tartare also impress. There are always a number of nightly specials, often one that involves fresh lobster, so be sure to inquire. And like most Russian entertainment venues, IKRA is very kid friendly. Live entertainment is on tap in the main room, where exceptionally talented singers belt out jazz, blues, and Top 40; and DJs spin sets between the live sessions. [$] *Average main: $31* ✉ *16850 Collins Ave., No. 106* ☎ *305/974–0081* 🌐 *www.ikramiami.com* ✍ *Reservations essential* ⏲ *No lunch* ✣ *E1.*

$$$$ ITALIAN

🍴 **Il Mulino New York - Sunny Isles Beach.** For more than two decades, Il Mulino New York has ranked among the top Italian restaurants in Gotham, so it's no surprise that the Miami outposts (one in Sunny Isles, one in South Beach) are similarly good. Even before the antipasti arrive, you may find yourself in a phenomenal carb coma from the complimentary fresh breads, the bruschetta, and fried zucchini. Everything that touches your palate is prepared to perfection, from simply prepared fried calamari and gnocchi pomodoro to the more complex scampi oregenata and ever-changing risottos. The Sunny Isle outpost is seductive, quiet, and intimate, and a favorite hangout of A-list celebs seeking a refined spot where crowds won't gawk over their presence. [$] *Average main: $52* ✉ *Acqualina Resort, 17875 Collins Ave.* ☎ *305/466–9191* 🌐 *www.ilmulino.com/miami* ✍ *Reservations essential* ✣ *E1.*

AVENTURA

$$$$ STEAKHOUSE

🍴 **Bourbon Steak.** Michael Mina's long-standing South Florida steak house has never gone out of style. The restaurant design is seductive, the clientele sophisticated, the wine list outstanding, the service phenomenal, and the food exceptional. Dinner begins with a skillet of fresh potato focaccia and chive butter. Mina then presents a bonus starter—his trio of famous fries (fried in duck fat) with three robust sauces. Appetizers are mainly seafood. The raw bar impresses and classic appetizers like the ahi tuna tartare are delightful and superfresh. Entrées like the Maine lobster potpie (with truffle cream) and any of the dozen varieties of butter-poached, wood-grilled steaks (from prime cuts to American Wagyu) are cooked to perfection. [$] *Average main: $57* ✉ *Turnberry Isle Miami, 19999 W. Country Club Dr.* ☎ *786/279–6600* 🌐 *www.michaelmina.net* ✍ *Reservations essential* ✣ *E1.*

$$$ MEDITERRANEAN Fodor's Choice ★

🍴 **Corsair.** At Corsair, *Chopped* judge Scott Conant doles out experiential, seasonally inspired farm-to-table fare prepared in Mediterranean style. From start to finish, each course serves as testimony to his deserved win on *Chopped All-Stars,* where he competed against other celebrity chefs to prove himself best-of-the-best. Even simple dishes like gnocchi pomodoro with basil and the roasted eggplant with burrata and tomato burst with complex flavors, ignited by use of fresh ingredients and skillful preparation. Larger plates, such as the decadent short rib beef of "lasagna" immersed in taleggio fonduta and the roasted diver scallops served over sunchoke puree and charred scallion salsa verde, also exemplify this caliber of blow-your-mind delectability. [$] *Average main: $28* ✉ *Turnberry Isle Miami, 19999 W. Country Club Dr.* ☎ *786/279–6800* 🌐 *www.turnberryislemiami.com* ⊕ *E1.*

WHERE TO STAY

Room rates in Miami tend to swing wildly. In high season, which is January through May, expect to pay at least $250 per night, even at value-oriented hotels. With a rebounding local economy and increased tourism, prices have skyrocketed since 2013, increasing up to 70% in some cases. Numerous hotels, previously affordable, have moved to our highest price category. In fact, it's common nowadays for rates to begin around $500 at Miami's top hotels. In summer, however, prices can be as much as 50% lower than the dizzying winter rates. You can also find great deals between Easter and Memorial Day, which is actually a delightful time in Miami. Business travelers tend to stay in downtown Miami, and most vacationers stay on Miami Beach, as close as possible to the water. South Beach is no longer the only "in" place to stay. Mid-Beach and downtown have taken the hotel scene by storm in the past few years and become home to some of the region's most avant-garde and luxurious properties to date. If money is no object, stay in one of the glamorous hotels lining Collins Avenue between 15th and 23rd streets. Otherwise, stay on the quiet beaches farther north, or in one of the small boutique hotels on Ocean Drive, Collins, or Washington avenues between 10th and 15th streets. Two important considerations that affect price are balcony and view. If you're willing to have a room without an ocean view, you can sometimes get a much lower price than the standard rate.

Hotel reviews have been shortened. For full information, visit Fodors.com. Use the coordinate (⊕ C2) at the end of each review to locate a property on the Where to Eat and Stay in the Miami Area map.

	WHAT IT COSTS			
	$	$$	$$$	$$$$
HOTELS	under $201	$201–$300	$301–$400	over $400

Hotel prices are the lowest cost of a standard double room in high season.

DOWNTOWN

Miami's skyline continues to grow by leaps and bounds. With downtown experiencing a renaissance of sorts, the hotel scene here isn't just for business anymore. In fact hotels that once relied solely on their Monday–Thursday traffic are now bustling on weekends, with a larger focus on cocktails around the rooftop pool and less a focus on the business center. These hotels offer proximate access to downtown's burgeoning food and cocktail scene, and historic sights, and are a short cab ride away from Miami's beaches.

$$$$
HOTEL

Conrad Miami. Occupying floors 16 to 26 of a 36-story skyscraper in Miami's burgeoning city center, this hotel mixes business with pleasure, offering easy access to the best of downtown. **Pros:** central downtown location; excellent service. **Cons:** poor views from some rooms; expensive parking. $ *Rooms from: $489* ⊠ *Espirito Santo Plaza, 1395 Brickell Ave.* ☎ *305/503–6500* ⊕ *www.conradhotels.com* ⤳ *185 rooms, 16 suites* ○ *No meals* ✛ *D5.*

$$
HOTEL

DoubleTree by Hilton Grand Hotel Biscayne Bay. Just 1 mile from Port-Miami at the north end of downtown, this waterfront hotel offers relatively basic, spacious rooms and convenient access to and from the cruise ships, making it a good crash pad for budget-conscious cruise passengers. **Pros:** marina; proximity to port. **Cons:** still need a cab to get around; dark lobby and neighboring arcade of shops; worn rooms. $ *Rooms from: $279* ⊠ *1717 N. Bayshore Dr.* ☎ *305/372–0313* ⊕ *www.doubletree.com* ⤳ *152 rooms, 50 suites* ○ *No meals* ✛ *D4.*

$$$
HOTEL

Epic Hotel. In the heart of downtown, Kimpton's pet-friendly, freebie-heavy Epic Hotel has 411 guest rooms, each with a spacious balcony (many of them overlook Biscayne Bay) and fabulous modern amenities—Frette linens, iPod docks, spa-inspired luxury bath products—that match the modern grandeur of the trendy common areas, which include a supersexy rooftop pool. **Pros:** sprawling rooftop pool deck; balcony in every room; complimentary wine hour, coffee, and Wi-Fi. **Cons:** some rooms have inferior views; congested valet area. $ *Rooms from: $399* ⊠ *270 Biscayne Blvd. Way* ☎ *305/424–5226* ⊕ *www.epichotel. com* ⤳ *411 rooms* ○ *No meals* ✛ *D4.*

$$$$
HOTEL
Fodor'sChoice
★

Four Seasons Hotel Miami. A favorite of business travelers visiting downtown's busy, business-centric Brickell Avenue, this plush sanctuary offers a respite from the nine-to-five mayhem—a soothing water wall greets you, the understated rooms impress you, and the seventh-floor, 2-acre-pool terrace relaxes you. **Pros:** condo rooms renovated in 2014; sensational service; window-side day beds; amazing gym and pool deck. **Cons:** no balconies; not near the beach. $ *Rooms from: $519* ⊠ *1435 Brickell Ave.* ☎ *305/358–3535* ⊕ *www.fourseasons.com/miami* ⤳ *182 rooms, 39 suites* ○ *No meals* ✛ *D5.*

$$$$
HOTEL

JW Marriott Marquis Miami. The marriage of Marriott's JW and Marquis brands created a truly tech-savvy, contemporary, and stylish business-minded hotel—you may never have seen another Marriott quite like this one. **Pros:** entertainment center; amazing technology; pristine rooms. **Cons:** swimming pool receives limited sunshine; lots of conventioneers on weekdays; congestion at street entrance. $ *Rooms from: $499* ⊠ *255 Biscayne Blvd. Way* ☎ *305/421–8600*

🌐 *www.jwmarriottmarquismiami.com* ⇨ *257 rooms, 56 suites* 🍴 *No meals* ✣ *D4.*

$$$$ HOTEL Fodor's Choice ★ **Mandarin Oriental, Miami.** At the tip of prestigious Brickell Key in Biscayne Bay, the Mandarin Oriental feels as exclusive as it does glamorous, with luxurious rooms, exalted restaurants, and the city's top spa, all of which marry the brand's signature Asian style with Miami's bold tropical elegance. **Pros:** impressive lobby; intimate vibe; ultraluxurious. **Cons:** man-made beach; small infinity pool; few beach cabanas. [$] *Rooms from: $599* ✉ *500 Brickell Key Dr.* ☎ *305/913–8288, 866/888–6780* 🌐 *www.mandarinoriental.com* ⇨ *326 rooms, 31 suites* 🍴 *No meals* ✣ *D5.*

$$$$ HOTEL **Viceroy Miami.** This hotel cultivates a brash, supersophisticated Miami attitude, likely stemming from its guest rooms decked out with dramatic Kelly Wearstler, Asian-inspired interiors and larger-than-life common areas designed by Philippe Starck. **Pros:** amazing design elements; exceptional pool deck and spa; sleek rooms. **Cons:** poor views from rooms; tiny lobby; some amenities shared with ICON Miami residents. [$] *Rooms from: $429* ✉ *485 Brickell Ave.* ☎ *305/503–4400, 866/781–9923* 🌐 *www.viceroymiami.com* ⇨ *150 rooms, 18 suites* 🍴 *No meals* ✣ *D4.*

COCONUT GROVE

Although this area certainly can't replace the draw of Miami Beach or the business convenience of downtown, about 20 minutes away, it's an exciting bohemian-chic neighborhood with a gorgeous waterfront.

$$ HOTEL **Mayfair Hotel & Spa.** Some 30 years strong, the five-story Mayfair Hotel & Spa still reflects Coconut Grove's bohemian roots, best exemplified by its eclectic exteriors: handcrafted wooden doors, one-of-a-kind decorative moldings, mosaic tiles inspired by Spain's Alhambra, and Gaudi-like ornaments adorning the rooftop pool deck. **Pros:** in the heart of walkable Coconut Grove; details in exterior design; in-house spa. **Cons:** limited lighting within rooms; interiors not as exciting as exteriors; car need to get to the beach. [$] *Rooms from: $239* ✉ *3000 Florida Ave.* ☎ *800/433–4555 reservations, 305/441–0000* 🌐 *www.mayfairhotelandspa.com* ⇨ *179 rooms* 🍴 *No meals* ✣ *C5.*

$$$ HOTEL **The Ritz-Carlton Coconut Grove, Miami.** This business-centric Ritz-Carlton hotel in the heart of Coconut Grove has a lively lobby and lounge that complements its sophisticated guest rooms—all with marble baths and private balconies. **Pros:** elevated pool deck; near Coconut Grove and Coral Gables shopping; excellent service. **Cons:** near residential area; more business- than leisure-oriented. [$] *Rooms from: $329* ✉ *3300 S.W. 27th Ave.* ☎ *305/644–4680, 800/241–3333* 🌐 *www.ritzcarlton.com* ⇨ *88 rooms, 27 suites* 🍴 *No meals* ✣ *C5.*

CORAL GABLES

Beautiful Coral Gables is set around its beacon, the national landmark Biltmore Hotel. It also has a couple of big business hotels and one smaller boutique property. The University of Miami is nearby.

$$$ HOTEL **Biltmore Hotel.** Built in 1926, this landmark hotel has had several incarnations over the years—including a stint as a hospital during World War II—but through it all, this grande dame has remained an opulent reminder of yesteryear, with its palatial lobby and grounds, enormous pool (largest in the lower 48), and distinctive 315-foot tower, which rises above the canopy of trees shading Coral Gables. **Pros:** historic property; gorgeous pool; great tennis and golf. **Cons:** in the suburbs; a car is necessary to get around. [$] *Rooms from: $343* ✉ *1200 Anastasia Ave.* ☎ *305/460–5364* 🌐 *www.biltmorehotel.com* *273 rooms, 39 suites* 🍴 *No meals* ✣ *B5.*

$$$ HOTEL **Hyatt Regency Coral Gables.** Within walking distance to the shops and businesses of Miami's most prestigious suburb and just 4 miles from Miami International Airport, the 250-room, Moorish-inspired Hyatt Regency Coral Gables mingles European charm with functionality. **Pros:** easy access to MIA; meets rigorous "green" standards; renovated in 2010. **Cons:** small bathrooms; far from beach; no spa. [$] *Rooms from: $319* ✉ *50 Alhambra Plaza* ☎ *305/441–1234* 🌐 *www.coralgables.hyatt.com* *250 rooms and suites* 🍴 *No meals* ✣ *B5.*

KEY BISCAYNE

There's probably no other place in Miami where slowness is lifted to a fine art. On Key Biscayne there are no pressures, there's no nightlife outside of the Ritz-Carlton's great live Latin music weekends, and the dining choices are essentially limited to the hotel (which has four dining options, including the languorous, Havana-style Rumbar).

$$$$ RESORT FAMILY Fodor's Choice ★ **The Ritz-Carlton Key Biscayne, Miami.** In this ultra-laid-back setting, it's natural to appreciate the Ritz brand of pampering with luxurious rooms, attentive service, five on-property dining options, and ample recreational activities for the whole family. **Pros:** on the beach; quiet; luxurious family retreat. **Cons:** far from South Beach; beach sometimes seaweed strewn; rental car almost a necessity. [$] *Rooms from: $499* ✉ *455 Grand Bay Dr.* ☎ *305/365–4500, 800/241–3333* 🌐 *www.ritzcarlton.com/keybiscayne* *365 rooms, 37 suites* 🍴 *No meals* ✣ *D6.*

SOUTH BEACH

If you are looking to experience the postcard image of Miami, look no further than South Beach. Most of the hotels along Ocean Drive, Collins Avenue, and Washington Avenue are housed in history-steeped art deco buildings, each one cooler than the next. From boutique hotels to high-rise structures, all South Beach hotels are in close proximity to the beach and never far from the action. Most hotels here cost a pretty penny, and for good reason. They are more of an experience than a place to crash (think designer lobbies, some of the world's best pool scenes, and unparalleled people-watching).

$$$ HOTEL **The Angler's.** This boutique hotel, one of several in Miami under the Kimpton brand, has an air of serenity and privacy that pervades this discreet little oasis of personality-driven villas (built in 1930 by

architect Henry Maloney) and modern tower units, together capturing the feel of a sophisticated private Mediterranean villa community. **Pros:** gardened private retreat; excellent service; daily complimentary wine hour. **Cons:** on busy Washington Avenue; not directly on beach. [$] *Rooms from: $379* ✉ *660 Washington Ave.* ☎ *305/534–9600* 🌐 *www.anglershotelmiami.com* 🛏 *24 rooms, 20 suites* 🍴 *No meals* ✥ *G4.*

$$ HOTEL Fodor's Choice ★ 🏨 **The Betsy Hotel.** An art deco treasure elegantly refurbished and totally retro-chic, The Betsy sits directly on world-famous Ocean Drive and delivers the full-throttle South Beach experience with style, pizzazz and cultural twist—the Betsy offers cultural programs year-round such as poetry readings, live jazz, and art shows. **Pros:** unbeatable location; superfashionable; great beach club. **Cons:** some small rooms; service can be hit or miss; no pool scene (but there's a rooftop scene). [$] *Rooms from: $265* ✉ *1440 Ocean Dr.* ☎ *305/531–6100* 🌐 *www.thebetsyhotel.com* 🛏 *41 rooms, 20 suites* 🍴 *No meals* ✥ *G2.*

$$ HOTEL Fodor's Choice ★ 🏨 **Cadet Hotel.** A former home to World War II air force cadets, this gem has been reimagined as an oasis in South Beach, offering the antithesis of the sometimes maddening jet-set scene with 34 distinctive rooms exuding understated luxury. **Pros:** excellent service; lovely garden and spa pool; originality. **Cons:** tiny swimming pool; limited appeal for the party crowd. [$] *Rooms from: $239* ✉ *1701 James Ave.* ☎ *305/672–6688, 800/432–2338* 🌐 *www.cadethotel.com* 🛏 *32 rooms, 3 suites* 🍴 *Breakfast* ✥ *G2.*

$ HOTEL 🏨 **Catalina Hotel & Beach Club.** The Catalina is the budget party spot in the heart of South Beach's hottest block and attracts plenty of twenty-somethings with its free nightly drink hour, airport shuttles, bike rentals, two fun pools, and beach chairs. **Pros:** free drinks; free bikes; free airport shuttle; good people-watching. **Cons:** service not a high priority; loud; rooms not well maintained. [$] *Rooms from: $183* ✉ *1720–1756 Collins Ave.* ☎ *305/674–1160* 🌐 *www.catalinahotel.com* 🛏 *190 rooms* 🍴 *No meals* ✥ *G2.*

$$$$ HOTEL Fodor's Choice ★ 🏨 **Delano Hotel.** The hotel that single-handedly made South Beach cool again in the 1990s is still making major waves across the beach as this Philippe Starck powerhouse continues to define the paradigm of South Beach decor and glamour. **Pros:** electrifying design; lounging among the beautiful and famous. **Cons:** crowded; scene-y; entry-level rooms are on small side. [$] *Rooms from: $429* ✉ *1685 Collins Ave.* ☎ *305/672–2000, 800/555–5001* 🌐 *www.morganshotelgroup.com/delano/delano-south-beach* 🛏 *184 rooms, 24 suites* 🍴 *No meals* ✥ *H2.*

$$$ HOTEL 🏨 **Dream South Beach Miami.** This trendy boutique hotel, which is right in the center of the South Beach action, merges two refurbished, archetypal 1939 art deco buildings as a single project of eclectic modernism, with whimsically decorated interiors in a result that is at once trippy and cool. **Pros:** awesome interior design; easy-on-the-eyes crowd; amazing location; pet-friendly. **Cons:** limited natural light in some rooms; lack of bathroom privacy; small pool. [$] *Rooms from: $309* ✉ *1111 Collins Ave.* ☎ *305/673–4747* 🌐 *www.dreamsouthbeach.com* 🛏 *108 rooms* 🍴 *No meals* ✥ *G3.*

$$ HOTEL 🏨 **Essex House.** This restored art deco gem is a favorite with Europeans desiring good location and a relatively no-frills, practical base—expect average-size rooms with midcentury-style red furniture and marble tubs. **Pros:** a social, heated pool; complimentary beer and wine hour weekdays; in-house sushi restaurant Zen Sai. **Cons:** small pool; not on the beach. [$] *Rooms from: $279* ✉ *1001 Collins Ave.* ☎ *305/534–2700* 🌐 *www.essexhotel.com* 🛏 *61 rooms, 15 suites* 🍴 *No meals* ✥ *G3.*

$$$$ HOTEL FAMILY 🏨 **Hilton Bentley Miami/South Beach.** Not to be confused with the budget-oriented Bentley Hotel down the street, the Hilton Bentley Miami is a contemporary, design-driven, and artsy boutique hotel in the emerging and trendy SoFi (South of Fifth) district, offering families just the right mix of South Beach flavor and wholesome fun while still providing couples a romantic base without any party madness. **Pros:** quiet location; style and grace; family-friendly. **Cons:** small pool; small lobby. [$] *Rooms from: $429* ✉ *101 Ocean Dr.* ☎ *305/938–4600* 🌐 *www.hilton.com* 🛏 *104 rooms, 5 suites* 🍴 *No meals* ✥ *G5.*

$$$$ HOTEL 🏨 **Hotel Victor.** After a Yabu Pushelberg face-lift in late 2013, the sleek Hotel Victor, originally influenced by Parisian designer Jacques Garcia, has replaced the dated jellyfish motif with a newer incarnation of bold modernism. **Pros:** views from pool deck; high hip factor; good service. **Cons:** small rooms; street noise from some rooms. [$] *Rooms from: $499* ✉ *1144 Ocean Dr.* ☎ *305/908–1462, 844/319–3854* 🌐 *www.hotelvictorsouthbeach.com* 🛏 *91 rooms* 🍴 *No meals* ✥ *G3.*

$$$$ HOTEL FAMILY 🏨 **Loews Miami Beach Hotel.** Loews Miami Beach, a two-tower 800-room megahotel with top-tier amenities, a massive spa, a great pool, and direct beachfront access, is a good choice for families, businesspeople, groups, and pet-lovers. **Pros:** top-notch amenities; immense spa; pets welcome. **Cons:** insanely large size; constantly crowded; pets desperate to go will need to wait several minutes to make it to the grass. [$] *Rooms from: $529* ✉ *1601 Collins Ave.* ☎ *305/604–1601, 800/235–6397* 🌐 *www.loewshotels.com/miamibeach* 🛏 *733 rooms, 57 suites* 🍴 *No meals* ✥ *H2.*

$$$ HOTEL 🏨 **The Lord Balfour.** Quickly making a name for itself in South Beach's emerging SoFi (South of Fifth) neighborhood, the luxurious, boutique, and retro-chic Lord Balfour hotel—now part of the Spain's RoomMate brand—exudes style, sophistication, and the full-throttle, present-day Miami Beach experience. **Pros:** great European crowd; whimsical interior design; excellent service. **Cons:** rooms on smaller side; occasional street noise from some rooms. [$] *Rooms from: $349* ✉ *350 Ocean Dr.* ☎ *855/471–2739, 305/673–0401* 🌐 *www.lordbalfour.room-matehotels.com* 🛏 *64 rooms* 🍴 *No meals* ✥ *G4.*

$$$$ RESORT 🏨 **Metropolitan by COMO, Miami Beach.** The luxury COMO brand brings its zen-glam swagger to South Beach, reinventing the art deco Traymore hotel into a 74-room, Paola Navone–designed boutique hotel that commingles brand signatures (excellent, health-driven cuisine, and myriad spa elements) with Miami panache. **Pros:** easy access to both South Beach and Mid-Beach; Como Shambhala toiletries; stylish "P" and "C" door magnets signal "Clean" or "Privacy." **Cons:** two people per room max; limited number of rooms with good views. [$] *Rooms from:*

$799 ⊠ 2445 Collins Ave. ☎ 305/695–3600 ⊕ www.comohotels.com/
metropolitanmiamibeach ➷ 74 rooms ⭘ No meals ✛ H1.

$$ ⛱ **Mondrian South Beach.** The Mondrian South Beach infuses life into
HOTEL   the beach's lesser-known western perimeter and rises as a poster child
of SoBe design glam—head to toe, the hotel is a living and function-
ing work of art, an ingenious vision of provocateur Marcel Wanders.
Pros: trendy; perfect sunsets; party vibe. **Cons:** busy lobby; doses of
South Beach attitude; no direct beach access. Ⓢ *Rooms from: $289*
⊠ 1100 West Ave. ☎ 305/514–1500 ⊕ www.morganshotelgroup.com/
mondrian/mondrian-south-beach ➷ 233 rooms, 102 suites ⭘ No
meals ✛ F3.

$$$$ ⛱ **National Hotel.** Fully renovated in 2014, the National Hotel maintains
HOTEL   its distinct art deco heritage (the chocolate- and ebony-hued pieces in
the lobby date back to the 1930s, and the baby grand piano headlines
the throwback Blues Bar) while also keeping up with SoBe's glossy new-
comers. **Pros:** stunning pool; perfect location; Blues Bar. **Cons:** street
noise on the weekends; smaller rooms in art deco tower. Ⓢ *Rooms
from: $549* ⊠ 1677 Collins Ave. ☎ 305/532–2311, 800/327–8370 res-
ervations ⊕ www.nationalhotel.com ➷ 116 rooms, 36 suites ⭘ No
meals ✛ H2.

$ ⛱ **Pelican Miami Beach.** Each awesome room of this Ocean Drive bou-
HOTEL   tique hotel is completely different, fashioned from a mix of antique
and garage-sale furnishings selected by the designer of Diesel's cloth-
ing-display windows. **Pros:** unique, over-the-top design; central Ocean
Drive location. **Cons:** rooms are so tiny that the quirky charm can
wear off quickly; not smoke-free. Ⓢ *Rooms from: $199* ⊠ 826 Ocean
Dr. ☎ 305/673–3373 ⊕ www.pelicanhotel.com ➷ 28 rooms, 4 suites
⭘ No meals ✛ G4.

$$$$ ⛱ **The Ritz-Carlton, South Beach.** Completely revamped and renovated in
HOTEL   2013, the smoking hot, art deco Ritz-Carlton, South Beach is a sur-
FAMILY   prisingly trendy, beachfront bombshell, with a dynamite staff, a snazzy
Club Lounge, and a long pool deck that leads right out to the beach.
Pros: luxurious renovated rooms; great service; pool with VIP cabanas;
great location. **Cons:** larger property; in-house restaurant Bistro ONE
LR often quiet; $28/night resort fee. Ⓢ *Rooms from: $749* ⊠ 1 Lin-
coln Rd. ☎ 786/276–4000, 800/542–8680 ⊕ www.ritzcarlton.com/
southbeach ➷ 375 rooms ⭘ No meals ✛ H2.

$$$ ⛱ **Royal Palm South Beach Miami.** The Royal Palm (formerly The James
RESORT   Royal Palm) is a daily celebration of art deco, Art Basel, modernity,
Fodor's Choice   and design detail. **Pros:** design blending contemporary style with South
★   Beach identity; impressive spa; multiple pools; unbeatable location.
Cons: small driveway for entering; older elevators. Ⓢ *Rooms from:
$383* ⊠ 1545 Collins Ave. ☎ 305/604–5700, 888/526–3778 reserva-
tions ⊕ www.royalpalmsouthbeach.com ➷ 234 studios, 159 suites
⭘ No meals ✛ G2.

$$$$ ⛱ **Sagamore, the Art Hotel.** This supersleek, all-white, all-suite hotel in
HOTEL   the middle of the action looks and feels like an edgy art gallery, filled
with brilliant contemporary works, the perfect complement to the posh,
gargantuan, 500-square-foot crash pads. **Pros:** sensational pool; great
location; good rate specials. **Cons:** can be quiet on weekdays; patchy

Wi-Fi. [$] *Rooms from: $489* ✉ *1671 Collins Ave.* ☎ *305/535–8088* ⊕ *www.sagamorehotel.com* ⌂ *93 suites* ⃝ *No meals* ✚ *H2.*

$$$$
RESORT
Fodor's Choice
★

🛏 **The Setai.** This opulent, all-suite hotel feels like an Asian museum: serene and beautiful, with heavy granite furniture lifted by orange accents, warm candlelight, and the soft bubble of seemingly endless ponds complemented by three oceanfront infinity pools (heated to different temperatures) that further spill onto the beach's velvety sands. **Pros:** quiet and classy; beautiful grounds; great celeb spotting. **Cons:** TVs are far from the beds; extremely high price point; many rooms lack ocean views. [$] *Rooms from: $871* ✉ *2001 Collins Ave.* ☎ *305/520– 6111, 888/625–7500 reservations* ⊕ *www.thesetaihotel.com* ⌂ *130 rooms and suites* ⃝ *No meals* ✚ *H1.*

$$$$
RESORT

🛏 **Shelborne Wyndham Grand South Beach.** After a major cash infusion from Wyndham hotels, the iconic Morris Lapidus–designed Shelborne hotel has reemerged as the retro-chic 200-room Shelborne Wyndham Grand South Beach, ushering in a new era of glory for both the brand and the hotel. **Pros:** location; prolific common spaces; Frette linens. **Cons:** entry-level rooms small; lack of balconies; long waits for food at in-house Morimoto restaurant. [$] *Rooms from: $489* ✉ *1801 Collins Ave.* ☎ *305/531–1271* ⊕ *www.shelbornewyndhamgrand.com* ⌂ *200 rooms and suites* ⃝ *No meals* ✚ *H1.*

$$$$
HOTEL

🛏 **Shore Club.** In terms of lounging, people-watching, partying, and poolside glitz, the Shore Club still ranks among the ultimate South Beach adult playgrounds; guests generally hang out in the minimalist lobby or by one of the two stylish pools, where a peek behind the cascading white curtains or palm trees can yield a celebrity, a scandal, or a make-out session. **Pros:** hip crowd; good restaurants and bars; nightlife in your backyard. **Cons:** spartan rooms; late-night music; major renovation to commence by September 2015. [$] *Rooms from: $439* ✉ *1901 Collins Ave.* ☎ *305/695–3100, 877/640–9500* ⊕ *www. morganshotelgroup.com/originals/originals-shore-club-south-beach* ⌂ *309 rooms, 79 suites* ⃝ *No meals* ✚ *H1.*

$$$$
RESORT
Fodor's Choice
★

🛏 **SLS Hotel South Beach.** Smack in the center of South Beach, the SLS Hotel marks designer Philippe Starck's triumphant large-scale return to South Beach; but this time he's teamed up with friends Sam Nazarian, Chefs José Andrés and Katsuya Uech, and Lenny Kravitz for the whimsical trip down the rabbit hole, creating the latest and greatest in the evolution of Miami's happening hotel/food/pool/beach scene. **Pros:** great in-house restaurants; masterful design; fun pool scene. **Cons:** sometimes small rooms; no lobby per se; $30/night resort fee. [$] *Rooms from: $415* ✉ *1701 Collins Ave.* ☎ *305/674–1701* ⊕ *www.slshotels. com/southbeach* ⌂ *127 rooms, 13 suites* ⃝ *No meals* ✚ *H2.*

$$$
HOTEL

🛏 **Surfcomber Miami, South Beach.** In 2012 the legendary Surfcomber joined the hip Kimpton Hotel group, spawning a fantastic nip-and-tuck that's rejuvenated the rooms and common spaces to reflect vintage luxe and oceanside freshness, and offering a price point that packs the place with a young, sophisticated, yet unpretentious crowd. **Pros:** stylish but not pretentious; pet-friendly; on the beach. **Cons:** small bathrooms; front desk often busy. [$] *Rooms from: $379* ✉ *1717 Collins*

Ave. ☎ *305/532–7715* 🌐 *www.surfcomber.com* 🛏 *182 rooms, 4 suites* 🍴 *No meals* ✥ *H2.*

$ HOTEL 🏨 **Townhouse Hotel.** Though sandwiched between the Setai and the Shore Club—two of the coolest hotels on the planet—the Townhouse doesn't try to act all dolled up: it's comfortable being the shabby-chic, lighthearted, relaxed fun hotel on South Beach (and rates include a Continental breakfast). **Pros:** a great budget buy for the style-hungry; direct beach access; hot rooftop lounge. **Cons:** no pool; small rooms not designed for long stays; some rooms accommodate only two. [$] *Rooms from: $155* ✉ *150 20th St., east of Collins Ave.* ☎ *305/534–3800* 🌐 *www.townhousehotel.com* 🛏 *69 rooms, 2 suites* 🍴 *Breakfast* ✥ *H1.*

$$$$ HOTEL Fodor's Choice ★ 🏨 **W South Beach.** Fun, fresh, and funky, the W South Beach represents the brand's evolution towards young sophistication, which means less club music in the lobby, more lighting, and more attention to the multimillion-dollar art collection lining the lobby's expansive walls. **Pros:** pool scene; masterful design; ocean-view balconies in each room. **Cons:** not a classic art deco building; hit-or-miss service; around 1K per night. [$] *Rooms from: $799* ✉ *2201 Collins Ave.* ☎ *305/938–3000* 🌐 *www.whotels.com/southbeach* 🛏 *213 studios, 135 suites* 🍴 *No meals* ✥ *H1.*

$$$ HOTEL 🏨 **Z Ocean Hotel South Beach.** The lauded firm of Arquitectonica designed the rooms and suites at this glossy and bold hideaway, including 27 rooftop suites endowed with terraces, each complete with Jacuzzi, plush chaise lounges, and a view of the South Beach skyline. **Pros:** incredible balconies; huge rooms; space-maximizing closets. **Cons:** gym is tiny and basic; not much privacy on rooftop suite decks. [$] *Rooms from: $369* ✉ *1437 Collins Ave.* ☎ *305/672–4554* 🌐 *www.zoceanhotelsouthbeach.com* 🛏 *79 suites* 🍴 *No meals* ✥ *G2.*

MID-BEACH

The stretch of Miami Beach called "Mid-Beach" is undergoing a renaissance, as formerly run-down hotels are renovated and new hotels and condos are built.

$ HOTEL 🏨 **Circa 39 Hotel.** Located in the heart of Mid-Beach, this stylish yet affordable boutique hotel pays attention to every detail and gets them all right, with amenities that include a swimming pool and sundeck complete with cabanas and umbrella-shaded chaises that invite all-day lounging. **Pros:** affordable; chic; intimate; beach chairs provided; art deco fireplace. **Cons:** not on the beach side of Collins Avenue. [$] *Rooms from: $180* ✉ *3900 Collins Ave.* ☎ *305/538–4900, 877/824–7223* 🌐 *www.circa39.com* 🛏 *96 rooms* 🍴 *No meals* ✥ *E4.*

$$$$ RESORT 🏨 **Eden Roc Miami Beach.** This grand 1950s hotel designed by Morris Lapidus retains its old glamour even after $230 million in renovations and expansions added sparkle to the rooms and grounds, renewing the allure and swagger of a stay at the Eden Roc. **Pros:** modern rooms; great pools; revival of Golden Age glamour. **Cons:** expensive parking; taxi needed to reach South Beach. [$] *Rooms from: $409* ✉ *4525 Collins Ave.* ☎ *305/531–0000, 855/433–3676 reservations* 🌐 *www.edenrocmiami.com* 🛏 *535 rooms, 92 suites* 🍴 *No meals* ✥ *E3.*

$$$$
RESORT
FAMILY
Fodor's Choice
★

⛭ Fontainebleau Miami Beach. Vegas meets art deco at this colossal classic, deemed Miami's biggest hotel after its $1 billion reinvention, which spawned more than 1,500 rooms (split among 658 suites in two new all-suite towers and 846 rooms in the two original buildings), 12 renowned restaurants and lounges, LIV nightclub, several sumptuous pools with cabana islands, a state-of-the-art fitness center, and a 40,000-square-foot spa. **Pros:** excellent restaurants; historic design mixed with all-new facilities; fabulous pools. **Cons:** away from the South Beach pedestrian scene; massive size; bizarre mix of guests. $ *Rooms from: $459 ✉ 4441 Collins Ave.* ☎ *305/535–3283, 800/548–8886* ⊕ *www.fontainebleau. com* ↝ *846 rooms, 658 suites* ⦿ *No meals* ✚ *E3.*

$$$$
RESORT
Fodor's Choice
★

⛭ The Miami Beach EDITION. At this reinvention of the 1955 landmark Seville Hotel by unlikely hospitality duo Ian Schrager and Marriott, historic glamour parallels modern relaxation from the palm-fringed marble lobby to the beachy guest rooms. **Pros:** hotel's got incredible swagger; hanging gardens in the alfresco area; great beachfront service. **Cons:** a bit pretentious; open bathroom setup in select rooms offers little privacy; near a particularly rocky part of Miami Beach. $ *Rooms from: $849 ✉ 2901 Collins Ave.* ☎ *786/257–4500* ⊕ *www.editionhotels.com/ miami-beach* ↝ *270 rooms, 24 suites* ⦿ *No meals* ✚ *E4.*

$$$$
HOTEL

⛭ Soho Beach House. The Soho Beach House is a throwback to swanky vibes of bygone decades, bedazzled in faded color palates, maritime ambience, and circa-1930s avant-garde furnishings, luring both somebodies and wannabes to indulge in the amenity-clad, retro-chic rooms as long as they follow stringent "house rules" (no photos, no mobile phones, no suits, and one guest only). **Pros:** trendy; two pools; fabulous restaurant; full spa. **Cons:** members have priority for rooms; lots of pretentious patrons; house rules are a bit much. $ *Rooms from: $495 ✉ 4385 Collins Ave.* ☎ *786/507–7900* ⊕ *www.sohobeachhouse.com* ↝ *55 rooms* ⦿ *No meals* ✚ *E3.*

$$$
RESORT

⛭ Thompson Miami Beach. Thompson's first foray outside of the urban realm and into the resort world has made a big splash in Miami's burgeoning Mid-Beach district with a beachfront classic art deco building reinvented by Martin Brudnizki to channel a colorful, modern incarnation of 1950s Florida glamour. **Pros:** valet only $5 for visitors dining on-property; excellent food and beverage; USB ports built into wall. **Cons:** small driveway; entry-level rooms are on the small side. $ *Rooms from: $399 ✉ 4041 Collins Ave.* ☎ *786/605–4041* ⊕ *www.thompsonhotels. com* ↝ *380 rooms* ⦿ *No meals* ✚ *E3.*

FISHER AND BELLE ISLANDS

$$$$
RESORT

⛭ Fisher Island Club Hotel & Resort. An exclusive private island, just south of Miami Beach but accessible only by ferry, Fisher Island houses an upscale residential community that includes a small inventory of overnight accommodations, including opulent cottages, villas, and junior suites, which surround the island's original 1920s-era Vanderbilt mansion. **Pros:** great private beaches; never crowded; varied on-island dining choices. **Cons:** not the warmest fellow guests; ferry ride to get on and off island; limited cell service. $ *Rooms from: $1037 ✉ 1 Fisher Island Dr.,*

Fisher Island ☎ *305/535–6000, 800/537–3708* 🌐 *www.fisherislandclub.com* 🛏 *50 condo units, 7 villas, 3 cottages* 🍴 *No meals* ✥ *E5.*

$$ RESORT 🏨 **The Standard Spa Miami Beach.** An extension of André Balazs's trendy and hip—yet budget-conscious—brand, this shabby-chic boutique spa hotel is a mile from South Beach on an island just over the Venetian Causeway and boasts one of South Florida's most renowned spas, trendiest bars, and hottest pool scenes. **Pros:** free bike and kayak rentals; swank pool scene; great spa; inexpensive. **Cons:** slight trek to South Beach; small rooms with no views. [$] *Rooms from: $269* ✉ *40 Island Ave., Belle Isle* ☎ *305/673–1717* 🌐 *www.standardhotels.com/spa-miami-beach* 🛏 *104 rooms, 1 suite* 🍴 *No meals* ✥ *E4.*

NORTH BEACH

BAL HARBOUR

$$$$ RESORT 🏨 **The Ritz-Carlton Bal Harbour, Miami.** In one of South Florida's poshest neighborhoods, the former ONE Bal Harbour exudes contemporary beachfront luxury design with decadent mahogany-floor guest rooms featuring large terraces with panoramic views of the water and city, over-the-top bathrooms with 10-foot floor-to-ceiling windows, and LCD TVs built into the bathroom mirrors. **Pros:** proximity to Bal Harbour Shops; beachfront; great contemporary-art collection. **Cons:** narrow beach is a bit disappointing; far from nightlife; $25 daily resort fee. [$] *Rooms from: $899* ✉ *10295 Collins Ave.* ☎ *305/455–5400* 🌐 *www.ritzcarlton.com/en/Properties/BalHarbourMiami* 🛏 *124 rooms, 63 suites* 🍴 *No meals* ✥ *E2.*

$$$$ RESORT Fodor's Choice ★ 🏨 **St. Regis Bal Harbour Resort.** When this $1 billion–plus resort opened in 2012, Miami's North Beach entered a new era of glamour and haute living, with A-list big spenders rushing to stay in this 27-story, 243-room, triple-glass-tower masterpiece. **Pros:** beachfront; beyond glamorous; large rooms. **Cons:** limited lounge space around main pool; limited privacy on balconies. [$] *Rooms from: $679* ✉ *9703 Collins Ave.* ☎ *305/993–3300* 🌐 *www.stregisbalharbour.com* 🛏 *227 rooms, 53 suites* 🍴 *No meals* ✥ *E2.*

SUNNY ISLES BEACH

$$$$ RESORT FAMILY Fodor's Choice ★ 🏨 **Acqualina Resort & Spa on the Beach.** On the heels of a complete room redesign in late 2014, Acqualina continues to raise the bar for Miami beachfront luxury, delivering a fantasy of modern Mediterranean opulence, with sumptuously appointed, striking gray- and silver-accented interiors, and expansive facilities. **Pros:** excellent beach; in-room check-in; luxury amenities; huge spa. **Cons:** no nightlife near hotel; hotel's towering height shades the beach by early afternoon. [$] *Rooms from: $825* ✉ *17875 Collins Ave.* ☎ *305/918–8000* 🌐 *www.acqualinaresort.com* 🛏 *54 rooms, 43 suites* 🍴 *No meals* ✥ *E1.*

AVENTURA

$$$$ RESORT FAMILY 🏨 **Turnberry Isle Miami.** Golfers and families favor this 300-acre tropical resort with jumbo-size rooms and world-class amenities, including a majestic lagoon pool (winding waterslide and lazy river included), an acclaimed three-story spa and fitness center, and two celeb chef

Cars whizz by the Avalon hotel and other art deco architecture on Ocean Drive, Miami South Beach.

restaurants- Michael Mina's Bourbon Steak and Scott Conant's Corsair restaurant. **Pros:** great golf, pools, and restaurants; free shuttle to Aventura Mall; situated between Miami and Fort Lauderdale. **Cons:** not on the beach; no nightlife. *Rooms from: $459* *19999 W. Country Club Dr.* *305/932–6200, 866/612–7739* *www.turnberryislemiami.com* *408 rooms, 29 suites* *No meals* *E1.*

NIGHTLIFE

One of Greater Miami's most popular pursuits is bar hopping. Bars range from intimate enclaves to showy see-and-be-seen lounges to loud, raucous frat parties. There's a New York–style flair to some of the newer lounges, which are increasingly catering to the Manhattan party crowd who escape to Miami and Miami Beach for long weekends. No doubt, Miami's pulse pounds with nonstop nightlife that reflects the area's potent cultural mix. On sultry, humid nights with the huge full moon rising out of the ocean and fragrant night-blooming jasmine intoxicating the senses, who can resist Cuban salsa with some disco and hip-hop thrown in for good measure? When this place throws a party, hips shake, fingers snap, bodies touch. It's no wonder many clubs are still rocking at 5 am. If you're looking for a relatively nonfrenetic evening, your best bet is one of the chic hotel bars on Collins Avenue, or a lounge away from Miami Beach in Wynwood, the Design District, or downtown.

The *Miami Herald* (*www.miamiherald.com*) is a good source for information on what to do in town. The Weekend section of the

THE VELVET ROPES

How to get past the velvet ropes at the hottest South Beach nightspots? First, if you're staying at a hotel, use the concierge. Decide which clubs you want to check out (consult *Ocean Drive* magazine celebrity pages if you want to be among the glitterati), and the concierge will email, fax, or call in your names to the clubs so you'll be on the guest list when you arrive. This means much easier access and usually no cover charge (which can be upward of $20) if you arrive before midnight. Guest list or no guest list, follow these pointers: Make sure there are more women than men in your group. Dress up: casual chic is the dress code. For men this means no sneakers, no shorts, no sleeveless vests, and no shirts unbuttoned past the top button. For women, provocative and seductive is fine; overly revealing is not. Black is always right. At the door: don't name-drop—no one takes it seriously. Don't be pushy while trying to get the doorman's attention. Wait until you make eye contact, then be cool and easygoing. If you decide to tip him (which most bouncers don't expect), be discreet and pleasant, not big-bucks obnoxious—a $10 or $20 bill quietly passed will be appreciated, however. With the right dress and the right attitude, you'll be on the dance floor rubbing shoulders with South Beach's finest clubbers in no time.

newspaper, included in the Friday edition, has an annotated guide to everything from plays and galleries to concerts and nightclubs. The "Ticket" column details the week's entertainment highlights. Or you can pick up the *Miami New Times* (⊕ *www.miaminewtimes.com*), the city's largest free alternative newspaper, published each Thursday. It lists nightclubs, concerts, and special events; reviews plays and movies; and provides in-depth coverage of the local music scene. *MIAMI* (⊕ *www.modernluxury.com/miami*) and *Ocean Drive* (⊕ *www.oceandrive.com*), Miami's model-strewn, upscale fashion and lifestyle magazines, squeeze club, bar, restaurant, and events listings in with fashion spreads, reviews, and personality profiles. Paparazzi photos of local party people and celebrities give you a taste of Greater Miami nightlife before you even dress up to paint the town.

The Spanish-language *El Nuevo Herald* (⊕ *www.elnuevoherald.com*), published by the *Miami Herald,* has extensive information on Spanish-language arts and entertainment, including dining reviews, concert previews, and nightclub highlights.

DOWNTOWN

BARS AND LOUNGES

Bin No.18. Pop into this bistro and wine bar before or after a show at the nearby Adrienne Arsht Center, or simply while the evening away here. The setting masters the fusing of style with charm, as seen with wine barrels that double as table bases, a blend of intimate and communal seating, a bar with open kitchen, and chandeliers adding just a hint of fanciness. The menu provides a good mix of seafood and meat, enjoyable to share or as personal dishes, but the real highlight is the wine list. Owner and Chef Alfredo Patino handpicks only from small importers of boutique wineries spanning the most famed regions to remote gem finds around the globe. ■TIP→ **The best time to explore new varietals is Tuesday, when the bottles are half-off.** ⊠ *275 N.E. 18 St., Suite 107, Downtown* ☎ *786/235–7575* ⊕ *www.bin18miami.com.*

Fodor's Choice ★ **Blackbird Ordinary.** This local watering hole has been around since 2011, but it's now trendier than ever. With a vibe that's a bit speakeasy, a bit dive bar, a bit hipster hangout, and a bit Miami sophisticate, it's hand's down one of the coolest places in the city and clearly appeals to a wide range of demographics. Mixology is a huge part of the Blackbird experience—so be prepared for some awesome artisanal cocktails. There's something going on every night of the week, and the stylish outdoor space is great for cocktails under the stars, movie screenings, and live music. ⊠ *729 S.W. 1st Ave.* ☎ *305/671–3307* ⊕ *www. blackbirdordinary.com.*

DANCE CLUBS

Club Space. Want 24-hour partying? Here's the place, which revolutionized the Miami party scene over a decade ago and still gets accolades as one of the country's best dance clubs. But depending on the month, Space wavers between trendy and empty, so make sure you get the up-to-date scoop from your hotel concierge. Created from four downtown warehouses, it has two levels (one blasts house music; the other reverberates with hip-hop), an outdoor patio, a New York–style industrial look, and a 24-hour liquor license. It's open on weekends only, and you'll need to look good to be allowed past the velvet ropes. Note that the crowd can sometimes be sketchy, and take caution walking around the surrounding neighborhood. ⊠ *34 N.E. 11th St.* ☎ *305/375–0001* ⊕ *www.clubspace.com.*

Fodor's Choice ★ **E11EVEN MIAMI.** A $40 million investment has transformed the former Gold Rush building into a nightclub with 600 square feet of LED video walls, intelligent lighting, and "Funktion-One" Resolution 6 sound system that pulses sports by day and beats by night, providing party-goers the 24/7 action they crave. Hospitality and VIP experiences are ample throughout the private lounges and $3-million champagne room on the second level; however, the real action is in "The Pit" featuring burlesque performances and intermittent Cirque du Soleil-style shows from a hydraulic-elevating stage. The fusion of theatrics and technology attracts an A-list clientele, and it's not unusual to catch a celebrity or two sporadically jumping on the decks. You may want to partake in a little pre-party on the third floor, where the intimate 50-seat Touché restaurant awaits with Italian cuisine and sushi bites by acclaimed Chef Carla Pellegrino. Live music on the adjacent rooftop lounge warms you up for the long evening—or morning—ahead. ⊠ *29 N.E. 11th St.* ☎ *305/829–2911* ⊕ *www.11miami.com.*

COCONUT GROVE

BARS AND LOUNGES

Vinos in the Grove. There's no swirling, sniffing, or pondering (unless you want to, of course); most are here to simply lean back and recoup from the day. Indeed this is a place to enjoy good wine without any airs. Socialization is easy via the staff, who are genuinely conversational with their wine knowledge; you can meet the locals in the casual outdoor seating area, which is front and center for the Grove activity. Inside, punched-out brick walls, chandeliers fastened from wineglasses, and chalkboard menus highlighting cheese plates add a quirky charm. ⊠ *3409 Main Hwy.* ☎ *305/442–8840* ⊕ *www.vinosinthegrove.com.*

CORAL GABLES

BARS AND LOUNGES

The Bar. One of the oldest bars in South Florida (est. 1946), the old Hofbrau has been reincarnated a few times and now goes by the name "The Bar." The no-frills joint has become an institution in the South Florida bar scene, though it remains totally nontouristy. A massive American flag hangs on the wall of this locals' hangout, arguably the only "cool" nightlife in suburban Coral Gables. Owned by the same folks as Blackbird Ordinary in downtown, The Bar delivers DJ-led tunes Wednesday through Saturday night and karaoke on Tuesday night. Oh, and they have pretty awesome, farm-fresh bar food, too, for both lunch and dinner. ⊠ *172 Giralda Ave., at Ponce de León Blvd., Coral Gables* ☎ *305/442–2730* ⊕ *www.thebargables.com.*

Fodor's Choice ★ **El Carajo.** The back of a BP gas station is perhaps the most unexpected location for a wine bar, yet for nearly 25 years a passion for good food and drink has kept this family-run business among Miami's best-kept secrets. Tables are in the old world–style wine cellar, stocked with bottles representing all parts of the globe (and at excellent prices). A waiter takes your order from the menu of exquisite cheeses and charcuterie, hot and cold tapas, paellas, and, of course, wine! Note that though this is an elusive spot, oenophiles are hardly deterred. Reservations are a must, as the place fills up quickly, especially since it closes by 10 pm weekdays, 11 pm weekends. ⊠ *2465 S.W. 17th Ave.* ☎ *305/856–2424* ⊕ *www.el-carajo.com.*

WYNWOOD

BARS AND LOUNGES

Cafeina Wynwood Lounge. This awesome Wynwood watering hole takes center stage during the highly social Gallery Night and Artwalk through the Wynwood Art District (⊕ *www.wynwoodartwalk.com*), the second Saturday of every month, which showcases the cool and hip art galleries between Northwest 20th and Northwest 36 streets west of North Miami Avenue. For those in the know, on any given Miami weekend, the evening either begins or ends this seductive, design-driven lounge with a gorgeous patio and plenty of art on display. It's simply a great place to hang out and get a true feel for Miami's cultural revolution.

It's open only Thursday–Saturday (5 pm to 3 am Thursday and Friday, 9 pm to 3 am Saturday). ⊠ *297 N.W. 23rd St., Wynwood* ☎ *305/438–0792* ⊕ *www.cafeinamiami.com.*

Wood Tavern. This is a neighborhood hangout where anything—and anyone—goes: suits mix with hoodies, fashionistas mingle with hipsters, but everyone in the crowd gives off a warm, welcoming vibe. The outdoor terrace is a block party scene with Latin bites served from grafitti-covered car countertops and bleacher-style stairs from which to people-watch or bob to the beats as the DJ jumps from Cypress Hill to Led Zepplin. The scene is a bit of a departure from the sultry nightlife typically associated with the Magic City (wine and cocktails are served in red plastic cups), but all in all it's an experience definitely worth checking out. ⊠ *2531 N.W. 2nd Ave.* ☎ *786/525–5955* ⊕ *www.woodtavernmiami.com.*

Wynwood Brewing Company. This family-owned craft brewery is hidden among the towering graffiti arts walls of Wynwood. Communal tables and ever-changing pop-up galleries by neighborhood artists make the taproom cozy; however, a peek through the window behind the bar reveals there is much more to the establishment: 15 pristine silver vats are constantly brewing variations of blond ale, IPA, barrel-aged strong ales, seasonal offerings, and national Gold Medalist the Robust Porter. All staff members are designated "Beer Servers" under the Cicerone Certification Program, ensuring knowledgeable descriptions and recommendations to your liking. ⊠ *565 N.W. 24 St.* ☎ *305/982–8732* ⊕ *www.wynwoodbrewing.com.*

MIDTOWN

BARS AND LOUNGES

Lagniappe. You may stumble upon this unassuming yet intriguing den across from the Midtown railroad tracks. Shelves house a selection of boutique-label wines with no corkage fee. Artisan cheeses and meats are also available for the plucking and can be arranged into tapas board displays. Once your selection is complete, take it back into the "living room" of worn sofas, antique lamps, and old-fashioned wall photos. Live musicians croon from the corner, with different bands each evening. Additional socialization can be found out in the "backyard" of mismatched seating and strung lighting, where as the evening wears on, you're apt to mingle and table-op among the international crowd. ⊠ *3425 N.E. 2nd Ave., Midtown* ☎ *305/576–0108* ⊕ *www.lagniappehouse.com.*

World of Beer - Miami Midtown. In Miami's trendy and unique Midtown blocks (sandwiched between the Design District to the north and Wynwood to the South), it may be surprising to find a chain establishment that feels pulled straight from the suburbs. However, the Florida-based chain World of Beer is a favorite local hangout in this artsy neighborhood. More than 500 different bottles and 50 rotating drafts of craft beer are on tap, and there are plenty of patrons that have tried them all. It's a laid-back scene, where you can just chat over a pint, and for many it provides an idyllic respite from Miami's scenesters, yuppies, and hipsters. ✉ *3252 N.E. 1st Ave., No. 112, Midtown, Miami, Florida, United States* ☎ *786/431–0347* ⊕ *www.worldofbeer.com/locations/midtown-miami.*

LITTLE HAVANA

LIVE MUSIC

Ball & Chain. Established in 1935 and steeped in legends of gambling, prohibition protests, the rise of budding entertainers Billie Holiday, Count Basie, and Chet Baker, and the development of Cuban-centric Calle Ocho, this storied nightlife spot has now been renovated and reestablished under its original name. The high-vaulted ceilings, floral wallpaper, black-and-white photos, and palm-fringed outdoor lounge nod to its torrid history and the glamour of Old Havana. Live music flows freely, as do the Latin-inspired libations and tapas of traditional Cuban favorites for an experience equally cultural as it is enjoyable. Reserved seating is available for a reasonable minimum. ✉ *1513 S.W. 8th St.* ☎ *305/643–7820* ⊕ *www.ballandchainmiami.com.*

SOUTH BEACH

BARS AND LOUNGES

Fodor's Choice ★ **Blues Bar.** Dedicate at least one night of your Miami vacation to an art deco pub crawl, patronizing the hotel bars and lounges of South Beach's most iconic buildings, including the National Hotel. Though it's a low-key affair, the nifty wooden Blues Bar here is well worth a stop. The bar is one of many elements original to the 1939 building that give it such a sense of its era that you'd expect to see Ginger Rogers and Fred Astaire hoofing it along the polished terrazzo floor. The adjoining Martini Room has a great collection of cigars, old airline stickers, and vintage Bacardi ads on the walls, but it's only available for private events. ✉ *National Hotel, 1677 Collins Ave.* ☎ *305/532–2311* ⊕ *www.nationalhotel.com.*

FDR at the Delano. The world's hottest DJs are on tap at this überexclusive subterranean lounge that caters to a stylish see-and-be-seen crowd. Seductive lighting illuminates the two-room, 200 person watering hole, decked out in dark and sexy decor. Bottle service is available for those with deep pockets. ✉ *1685 Collins Ave.* ☎ *305/924–4071* ⊕ *www.morganshotelgroup.com/delano/delano-south-beach.*

HaVen Lounge. This gastrolounge may be cozy by South Beach standards, but it's just as flashy under the glow of backlit architecture, main bar, and lounge tables in ever-changing hues. Wall-to-wall TVs that double as light installations provide additional hypnotic entertainment. Clever mixology matches the innovative ambience with smoky craft cocktails fusing fresh-fruit flavors with herbs. Your palate will be further appeased with an organic menu of sushi and Asian-inspired bites, interspersed with fresh interpretations of American classics (including duck burgers, Maytag blue tater tots, and jerk chicken brushed with scotch bonnet honey). ✉ *1237 Lincoln Rd., South Beach* ☎ *305/987–8885* ⊕ *www.havenlounge.com.*

Lost Weekend. Slumming celebs and locals often patronize this pool hall–resto–dive bar on quaint Española Way. The hard-core locals are serious about their pastime, so it can be challenging to get a table on weekends. However, everyone can enjoy the pinball machines, the bar grub, and the full bar, which has 150 kinds of beer (a dozen of which are on tap). Each night, Lost Weekend draws an eclectic crowd, from yuppies to drag queens to celebs on the down-low (and everyone gets equally bad service). So South Beach! ⊠ *218 Española Way* ☎ *305/672–1707.*

Mac's Club Deuce Bar. Although it's a complete dive bar—and not something you'd expect from glitzy South Beach, this circa-1964 pool hall attracts a colorful crowd of clubbers, locals, celebs, and just about anyone else. Locals consider it a top spot for an inexpensive drink and cheap thrills. ⊠ *222 14th St., at Collins Ave., South Beach, Miami Beach, Florida, United States* ☎ *305/531–6200* ⊕ *www.macsclubdeuce.com.*

Mynt Lounge. This is the quintessential celeb-studded, super-VIP, South Beach party where you may or may not be let in, depending on what you wear or who you know. It's the kind of place where back in the day LiLo would act out, Brit-Brit would chill out, and Paris Hilton would zone out, namely because of the club's "no paparazzi" policy. Admittedly, owner Romain Zago says that "Mynt is for the famous and fabulous." Every summer the lounge undergoes renovations to stay at the top of its game, revealing a slightly different look. ⊠ *1921 Collins Ave.* ☎ *305/532–0727* ⊕ *www.myntlounge.com.*

Palace Bar. South Beach's gay heyday continues at this fierce oceanfront bar where folks both gay and straight come to revel in good times, cheap cocktails, and great drag performances. Everyone's welcome, and there's no formal dress code. So for many, Speedos, tank tops, and two-pieces will do. The bar gets busiest in the afternoon and early evening; it's not really a late-night place. For out-of-towners, the Sunday Drag Brunch is a must. It's a true show-stopper—or car-shopper shall we say. Using Ocean Drive as a stage, drag queens direct oncoming traffic with street-side splits and acrobatic tricks in heels. ⊠ *1200 Ocean Dr.* ☎ *305/531–7234* ⊕ *www.palacesouthbeach.com.*

Fodor'sChoice ★ **Radio Bar.** What began as a pop-up bar on South Beach's emerging SoFi district in 2013 has evolved into a permanent local favorite, offering a basement-style party where the cool kids love to party, drink, and play. Radio Bar draws a diverse crowd of dressed-down locals, stylish yuppies, and consignment shop junkies. You'll quickly recognize the bar by the 600-foot radio tower that marks the back-door entrance. Inside, the bar serves awesome craft cocktails, local brews, and small bites. ⊠ *814 1st St.* ☎ *305/397–8382* ⊕ *www.radiosouthbeach.com.*

Fodor'sChoice ★ **The Regent Cocktail Club.** This classic cocktail bar recalls an intimate gentleman's club (and not the stripper kind) with strong masculine cocktails, dark furnishings, bartenders dressed to the nines, and the sounds of jazz legends in the background. The intimate space exudes elegance and timelessness. It's a welcome respite from South Beach's predictable nightlife scene. Cocktails—each with bespoke ice cubes—change daily and are posted on the house blackboard. ⊠ *Gale South Beach, 1690 Collins Ave.* ☎ *786/975–2555* ⊕ *www.galehotel.com/nightlife.*

Rose Bar. Tucked away inside the chic Delano hotel, the Rose Bar is a South Beach mainstay and an essential stop on any South Beach bar crawl. Now managed by Las Vegas's The Light Group, the Rose Bar mixes classic art deco architecture with the best in mixology (and a bit of Vegas bling). ⊠ *Delano Hotel, 1685 Collins Ave., South Beach, Miami Beach, Florida, United States* ☎ *305/674–5752* ⊕ *www. morganshotelgroup.com/delano/delano-south-beach.*

Skybar at the Shore Club. An entire enclave dedicated to alcohol-induced fun for grown-ups, the Skybar is actually a collection of adjoining lounges at the Shore Club, including the chic outdoor Red Room Garden, the seductively lit indoor Red Room, and the Rum Bar, all which teem with party-hungry visitors. ⊠ *Shore Club Hotel, 1901 Collins Ave.* ☎ *305/695–3100* ⊕ *www.morganshotelgroup.com/originals/ originals-shore-club-south-beach.*

DANCE CLUBS

Cameo. One of Miami's longest-running dance clubs, Cameo is constantly reinventing itself, but the result always seems to be the same—long lines filled with everyone claiming to be on the guest list, hoochie mamas wearing far too little clothing, a thuggish crowd, and some unsuspecting tourists trying to see what all the fuss is about. The combination makes for some insane partying, especially if the night is headlined by an all-star DJ. You'll find both plentiful dance space and plush VIP lounges. If you can brave the velvet rope, the rough crowd, and the nonsense described above, Saturday-night parties are the best. It's open Tuesday, Friday, and Saturday only. ⊠ *1445 Washington Ave., South Beach, Miami Beach, Florida, United States* ☎ *305/587–2272* ⊕ *www. cameomiami.com.*

Nikki Beach Club. Smack-dab on the beach, the full-service Nikki Beach Club was once upon a time a favorite of SoBe's pretty people and celebrities. Nowadays, it's filled with more suburbanites than the "in" crowd. Nikki's late-night parties are reserved for Sunday only. On Friday and Saturday, the Beach Club is opened from noon to 11 pm, and closing at 6 pm on weekdays. Visitors can eat at the Nikki Beach Restaurant, and get their food and drink on in the tepees, hammocks, and beach beds (expect rental fees). Sunday brunch at the club's restaurant is pretty spectacular. ⊠ *1 Ocean Dr., South Beach, Miami Beach, Florida, United States* ☎ *305/538–1111* ⊕ *www.nikkibeach.com/miami.*

Rec Room. Entering Rec Room is like stumbling upon an awesome basement party that just happens to be packed with the hottest people ever. Amy Sacco's subterranean space at the Gale pays homage to everything 1977 (memorabilia included) and features a collection of more than 3,000 vinyl records at the disposal of resident DJs. The vibe is totally speakeasy meets modern day—the easy-on-the-eyes crowd lets loose, free of inhibitions, jamming out to old-school hip-hop and eighties and nineties throwbacks. ⊠ *Gale South Beach, 1690 Collins Ave.* ☎ *786/975–2555* ⊕ *www.recroomies.com.*

Score. Since the 1990s, Score has been the see-and-be-seen HQ of Miami's gay community, with plenty of global hotties coming from near and far to show off their designer threads and six-pack abs. After moving in 2013 to Washington Avenue from it's longtime Lincoln Road location, this South Beach powerhouse shows no signs of slowing down. DJs spin five nights a week, but Planeta Macho Latin Tuesday is exceptionally popular, as are the weekend dance-offs—Filthy Gorgeous Friday and circuit party style Saturday. Dress to impress (and then be ready to go shirtless and show off your abs). ⊠ *1437 Washington Ave.* ☎ *305/535–1111* ⊕ *www.scorebar.net* ⊘ *Closed Mon. and Wed.*

Twist. Twist is a gay institution in South Beach, having been the late-night go-to place for decades, filling to capacity around 2 am after the beach's fly-by-night bars and more established lounges begin to die down (though it's in fact open daily from 1 pm to 5 am). There's never a cover here—not even on holidays or during gay-pride events. ⊠ *1057 Washington Ave.* ☎ *305/538–9478* ⊕ *www.twistsobe.com.*

LIVE MUSIC

Jazid. If you're looking for an unpretentious alternative to the velvet-rope nightclubs, this unassuming, live-music hot spot is a standout on the SoBe strip. The double-story venue stakes claim as the longest-running nightclub on Miami Beach. Expect live music Friday to Monday with eight-piece bands playing danceable Latin rhythms, as well as reggae, hip-hop, and fusion sounds. Other nights are dictated by DJ-led tunes, each night caters to a different genre. Call ahead to reserve a table. ⊠ *1342 Washington Ave., South Beach* ☎ *305/673–9372* ⊕ *www. jazid.net.*

MID-BEACH

BARS AND LOUNGES

The Broken Shaker. Popular with the Miami's cool crowd, this indoor/outdoor craft cocktail joint lures in droves to the adult-chic Freehand hostel to revel in the art of mixology and people-watching. The vibe is Brooklyn meets Miami: everyone's Instagraming everything in faded filters, and there's lots of man buns, facial hair, and girls that look like Lana del Rey (though they may claim they don't like her music). The drinks are pretty daring and definitely awesome with ingredients like green bean juice and kale juice complementing the top-shelf liquors. ⊠ *2727 Indian Creek Dr., Mid-Beach* ☎ *305/531–2727* ⊕ *thefreehand. com/miami/.*

DANCE CLUBS

Fodor'sChoice ★ **LIV Nightclub.** Since its 2009 opening, the Fontainebleau's LIV Nightclub has garnered plenty of global attention, and it shows no signs of stopping. It's not hard to see why LIV often makes lists of the world's best clubs—if you can get in, that is (LIV is notorious for lengthy lines, so don't arrive fashionably late). Past the velvet ropes, the dance palladium impresses with its lavish decor, well-dressed international crowd, sensational light-and-sound system, and seductive bi-level club experience. Sometimes the lobby bar, filled with LIV's overflow (and rejects), is just as fun as the club itself. ■TIP→ **Men beware: groups of guys entering**

LIV are often coerced into insanely priced bottle service. ⊠ *Fontaine-bleau Miami Beach, 4441 Collins Ave., Mid-Beach* ☎ *305/674–4680 for table reservations* ⊕ *www.livnightclub.com.*

FISHER AND BELLE ISLANDS

BARS AND LOUNGES

Lido Restaurant & Bayside Grill. With all due respect to wonderful food by Executive Chef Mark Zeitouni, many locals come to The Lido Restaurant & Bayside Grill with drinking as their top priority. By day, the colorful and chic, waterfront alfresco restaurant is idyllic for watching the bay-side boats and poolside hotties go by. In the evening, lights braided into the surrounding trees illuminate the terrace, sparking a seductive ambience. On weekdays from 4 to 7, the bar offers Sunset Service, their version of Happy Hour. ■TIP➜ The indoor, lobby-side Lido Bar and Lounge is great for a craft cocktail and a round of Ping-Pong, but the real scene is outdoors, on the opposite side of the hotel, at the Lido Restaurant & Bayside Grill. ⊠ *The Standard Spa Miami Beach, 40 Island Ave., Belle Isle* ⊕ *www.standardhotels.com/spa-miami-beach.*

SHOPPING

Beyond its fun-in-the-sun offerings, Miami has evolved into a world-class shopping destination. People fly to Miami from all over the world just to shop. The city teems with sophisticated malls—from multistory, indoor climate-controlled temples of consumerism to sun-kissed, open-air retail enclaves—and bustling avenues and streets, lined at once with affordable chain stores, haute couture boutiques, and one-off, "only in Miami"–type shops.

Following the incredible success of the Bal Harbour Shops in the highest of the high-end market (Chanel, Alexander McQueen, ETRO, and Hermès), the Design District has followed suit. Beyond fabulous designer furniture showrooms, the district's tenants now include Dior Homme, Rolex, and Prada. In addition, an entire LVMH mall is under construction at this writing to create more upscale retail space.

If you're from a region ripe with the climate-controlled slickness of shopping malls and food-court "meals," you'll love the choices in Miami. Head out into the sunshine and shop the city streets, where you'll find big-name retailers and local boutiques alike. Take a break at a sidewalk café to power up on some Cuban coffee or fresh-squeezed OJ and enjoy the tropical breezes.

Beyond clothiers and big-name retailers, Greater Miami has all manner of merchandise to tempt even the casual browser. For consumers on a mission to find certain items—art deco antiques or cigars, for instance—the city streets burst with a rewarding collection of specialty shops.

Stroll through Spanish-speaking neighborhoods where shops sell clothing, cigars, and other goods from all over Latin America or even head to Little Haiti for rare vinyl records.

COCONUT GROVE

ANTIQUES

Las Tias. A preferred spot for vintage fanatics and professional interior designers alike for its ever-changing collection of consignment furnishings at good pricing, Las Tias recently moved over from the Design District onto the eclectic 28th Lane in Coconut Grove, a burgeoning design strip of its own. The new space allows perusers to shop without feeling cramped, atypical of many antique and consignment stores, and easily uncover renowned brands of furniture, lighting, china, crystal, and more. A smaller section of vintage clothing and accessories by major designer houses can be found in the back. ⌂ *2638 S.W. 28th La.* ☎ *305/573–4198* ⊕ *www.lastias.com.*

CLOTHING

Maui Nix. Anchoring the corner of CocoWalk plaza, this Florida-based store sells anything and everything you might need for a trip to the beach. More beach storehouse than shack, the bleached-blond wood walls and racks display 100 surf and skate brands of apparel, shoes, accessories, and gear. Pair a Billabong sundress with a pooka bead necklace, Hurley hoodie with skateboard, Vans slip-ons with Oakely sunglasses or Beats headphones—the possibilities are endless for looking like a true "Grovite." ⌂ *CocoWalk, 3015 Grand Ave., No. 145* ☎ *305/444–6919* ⊕ *www.mauinix.com.*

MALLS

CocoWalk. Though this three-story, indoor-outdoor mall anchors the Grove's shopping scene, but it's long passed its 1990s heydey. Some chain stores like Victoria's Secret and Gap remain alongside a few specialty shops like Maui Nix. Touristy kiosks with cigars, beads, incense, herbs, and other small items are scattered around the ground level, and commercial restaurants and nightlife (Cheesecake Factory, Fat Tuesday, and Cinépolis Coconut Grove—a multiscreen, state-of-the-art movie theater with a wine bar and lounge and in-seat food service) line the upstairs perimeter. Overall, the space mixes the bustle of a mall with the breathability of an open-air market. Note that hanging out and people-watching is something of a pastime here for Miami suburbanites. ⌂ *3015 Grand Ave.* ☎ *305/444–0777* ⊕ *www.cocowalk.net.*

CORAL GABLES

BOOKS

FAMILY

Fodor's Choice

★

Books & Books, Inc. Long live the classic book store! Greater Miami's only independent, English-language bookshop, Books & Books, specializes in contemporary and classical literature as well as in books on the arts, architecture, Florida, and Cuba. The Coral Gables store is the largest of its four South Florida locations. Here, you can sip 'n' read in the courtyard lounge or dine at the old-fashioned in-store café while browsing the photography gallery. Multiple rooms are filled with myriad genres, making for a fabulous afternoon of book shopping; plus there's an entire area dedicated to kids. There are book signings, literary events, poetry, and other readings, too. Two smaller locations on Lincoln Road

Continued on page 105

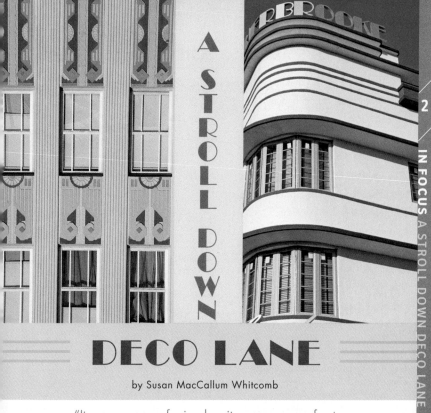

A STROLL DOWN

DECO LANE

by Susan MacCallum Whitcomb

"It was an age of miracles, it was an age of art,

it was an age of excess, and it was an age of satire."

—F. Scott Fitzgerald, *Echoes of the Jazz Age*

The 1920s and '30s brought us flappers and gangsters, plunging stock prices and soaring skyscrapers, and plenty of headline-worthy news from the arts scene, from talking pictures and the jazz craze to fashions where pearls piled on and sequins dazzled. These decades between the two world wars also gave us an art style reflective of the changing times: art deco.

Distinguished by geometrical shapes and the use of industrial motifs that fused the decorative arts with modern technology, art deco became the architectural style of choice for train stations and big buildings across the country (think New york's Radio City Music Hall and Empire State Building).

Using a steel-and-concrete box as the foundation, architects dipped into art deco's grab bag of accessories, initially decorating facades with spheres, cylinders, and cubes. They later borrowed increasingly from industrial design, stripping elements used in ocean liners and automobiles to their streamlined essentials.

The style was also used in jewelry, furniture, textiles, and advertising. The fact that it employed inexpensive materials, such as stucco or terrazzo, helped art deco thrive during the Great Depression.

MIAMI BEACH'S ART DECO DISTRICT

With its warm beaches and tropical surroundings, Miami Beach in the early 20th century was establishing itself as America's winter playground. During the roaring '20s luxurious hostelries resembling Venetian palaces, Spanish villages, and French châteaux sprouted up. In the 1930s, middle-class tourists started coming, and more hotels had to be built. Designers like Henry Hohauser chose art deco for its affordable yet distinctive design.

An antidote to the gloom of the Great Depression, the look was cheerful and tidy. And with the whimsical additions of portholes, colorful racing bands, and images of rolling ocean waves painted or etched on the walls, these South Beach properties created an oceanfront fantasy world for travelers.

Many of the candy-colored hotels have survived and been meticulously restored. They are among the more than 800 buildings of historical significance in South Beach's art deco district. Composing much of South Beach, the 1-square-mi district is bounded by Dade Boulevard on the north, the Atlantic Ocean on the east, 6th Street on the south, and Alton Road on the west.

Because the district as a whole was developed so rapidly and designed by like-minded architects—**Henry Hohauser, L. Murray Dixon, Albert Anis,** and their colleagues—it has amazing stylistic

unity. Nevertheless, on this single street you can trace the evolution of period form from angular, vertically emphatic early deco to aerodynamically rounded Streamline Moderne. The relatively severe Cavalier and more curvaceous Cardozo are fine examples of the former and latter, respectively.

To explore the district, begin by loading up on literature in the **Art Deco Welcome Center** (⊠ *1001 Ocean Dr.* ☎ *305/763–8026* ⊕ *www.mdpl.org*). If you want to view these historic properties on your own, just start walking. A four-block stroll north on Ocean Drive gets you up close to camera-ready classics: the **Clevelander** (1020), the **Tides** (1220), the **Leslie** (1244), the **Carlyle** (1250), the **Cardozo** (1300), the **Cavalier** (1320), and the **Winterhaven** (1400).

ARCHITECTURAL HIGHLIGHTS

Cavalier Hotel

FRIEZE DETAIL, CAVALIER HOTEL

The decorative stucco friezes outside the Cavalier Hotel at 1320 Ocean Drive are significant for more than aesthetic reasons. Roy France used them to add symmetry (adhering to the "Rule of Three") and accentuate the hotel's verticality by drawing the eye upward. The pattern he chose also reflected a fascination with ancient civilizations engendered by the recent rediscovery of King Tut's tomb and the Chichén Itzá temples.

Park Central Hotel

LOBBY FLOOR, PARK CENTRAL HOTEL

Terrazzo—a compound of cement and stone chips that could be poured, then polished—is a hallmark of deco design. Terrazzo floors typically had a geometric pattern, like this one in the Park Central Hotel, a 1937 building by Henry Hohauser at 640 Ocean Drive.

Essex House Hotel

CORNER FACADE, ESSEX HOUSE HOTEL

Essex House Hotel, a 1938 gem that appears permanently anchored at 1001 Collins Avenue, is a stunning example of Maritime deco (also known as Nautical Moderne). Designed by Henry Hohauser to evoke an ocean liner, the hotel is rife with marine elements, from the rows of porthole-style windows and natty racing stripes to the towering smokestack-like sign. With a prow angled proudly into the street corner, it seems ready to steam out to sea.

The Hotel

NEON SPIRE, THE HOTEL

The name spelled vertically in eye-popping neon on the venue's iconic aluminum spire—Tiffany—bears evidence of the hotel's earlier incarnation. When the L. Murray Dixon–designed Tiffany Hotel was erected at 801 Collins Avenue in 1939, neon was still a novelty. Its use, coupled with the spire's rocket-like shape, combined to create a futuristic look influenced by the sci-fi themes then pervasive in popular culture.

Jerry's Famous Deli

ENTRANCE, JERRY'S FAMOUS DELI

Inspired by everything from car fenders to airplane noses, proponents of art deco's Streamline Moderne look began to soften buildings' hitherto boxy edges. But when Henry Hohauser designed Hoffman's Cafeteria in 1940 he took moderne to the max. The landmark at 1450 Collins Avenue (now Jerry's Famous Deli) has a sleek, splendidly curved facade. The restored interior echoes it through semicircular booths and rounded chair backs.

ARCHITECTURAL TERMS

The Rule of Three: Early deco designers often used architectural elements in multiples of three, creating tripartite facades with triple sets of windows, eyebrows, or banding.

Eyebrows: Small shelf-like ledges that protruded over exterior windows were used to simultaneously provide much-needed shade and serve as a counterpoint to a building's strong vertical lines.

Tropical Motifs: In keeping with the setting, premises were plastered, painted, or etched with seaside images. Palm trees, sunbursts, waves, flamingoes, and the like were particularly common.

Banding: Enhancing the illusion that these immobile structures were rapidly speeding objects, colorful horizontal bands (also called "racing stripes") were painted on exteriors or applied with tile.

Stripped Classic: The most austere version of art deco (sometimes dubbed Depression Moderne) was used for buildings commissioned by the Public Works Administration.

(top) Hotel Marlin; (left) Sherbrooke Hotel; (right) U.S. Post Office in Miami Beach.

in South Beach and at the Bal Harbour Shops also carry great reads as does a petite outpost at the Miami International Airport. ⊠ *265 Aragon Ave., Coral Gables* ☏ *305/442–4408* ⊕ *www.booksandbooks.com* ⊗ *Sun.–Thurs. 9 am–11 pm, Fri. and Sat. 9 am–midnight.*

CLOTHING

ISA boutique. If you're one for lounging, sipping (on complimentary libations), and socializing while shopping, this is the ideal place. The highly curated selection here may appear stingy at first, yet nearly every piece is sure to catch your eye: glittery cocktail dresses by Betsy Moss, feminine gowns by Gracia, fresh jackets by Style Mafia, striking jewelry from the owner's design discoveries out of L.A., and statement belts and clutches. On-site alterations secure that your take-away pile is a perfect fit. The shop closes on Sunday. ⊠ *34 Giralda Ave., Coral Gables* ☏ *786/558–8027.*

FAMILY

Fodor's Choice

★

Nic Del Mar. Attending one of Miami's famed pool parties practically requires a trip to this upscale swimwear boutique. From the teeny weeny, to innovative one-pieces, to sporty cuts, the varied suit selection includes Mara Hoffman, Tori Praver, Acacia, and Zimmerman, many of which include matching children's styles for mini beach babes. Flowy coverups by the same labels and more can easily double as dinner dresses, while hats, totes, lotions, and even metallic temporary tattoos add a sun-kissed touch. Men's styles are also available. ⊠ *475 Biltmore Way, Suite 105* ☏ *305/442–8080* ⊕ *www.nicdelmar.com.*

Silvia Tcherassi. The famed, Miami-based Colombian designer's signature boutique in the Village of Merrick Park features ready-to-wear, feminine, and frilly dresses and separates accented with chiffon, tuille, and sequins. You'll see plenty of Tcherassi's designs on Miami's Latin power players at events and A-list parties. A neighboring atelier at 4101 Ponce de Leon Boulevard showcases the designer's bridal collection. ⊠ *Village of Merrick Park, 350 San Lorenzo Ave., No. 2140* ☏ *305/461–0009* ⊕ *www.silviatcherassi.com.*

MALLS

Village of Merrick Park. At this open-air Mediterranean-style, tri-level, shopping-and-dining venue, Neiman Marcus and Nordstrom anchor 115 specialty shops. Outposts by Michael Kors, Jimmy Choo, Tiffany & Co., Burberry, CH Carolina Herrera, and Gucci fulfill most high-fashion needs, and haute-decor shopping options include Brazilian contemporary-furniture designer Artefacto. International food favorite C'est Bon and pampering specialist Elemis Day-Spa offer further indulgences. ⊠ *358 San Lorenzo Ave.* ☏ *305/529–0200* ⊕ *www.villageofmerrickpark.com.*

ONLY IN MIAMI

Ramon Puig: La Casa de las Guayaberas. This clothing shop sells custom-made Ramon Puig guayaberas, the natty four-pocket dress shirts favored by older Cuban men and hipsters alike. Ramon Puig is known as "the King of Guayaberas," and his shirts are top of the line as far as guayaberas go. Hundreds are available off the rack. There are styles for women, too. A second outpost is in downtown Miami at 28 West Flager Street. ⊠ *5840 S.W. 8th St.* ☏ *305/266–9683* ⊕ *www.ramonpuig.com.*

SHOPPING DISTRICTS

Miracle Mile. The centerpiece of the downtown Coral Gables shopping district, lined with trees and busy with strolling shoppers, is home to a host of exclusive couturiers and bridal shops as well as some men's and women's boutiques, jewelry, and home-furnishings stores. The half-mile, "mile" runs from Douglas Road to LeJeune Road and Aragon Avenue to Andalusia Avenue, but many of the Gables' best nonbridal shops are found on side streets, off the actual mile. In addition, the street itself teems with first-rate restaurants—more than two-dozen—facilitating a fabulous afternoon of shopping and eating. ■TIP➔ If debating Miracle Mile versus Bal Harbour or the Design District, check out the others first. ⊠ *Miracle Mile (Coral Way), Douglas Rd. to LeJeune Rd., and Aragon Ave. to Andalusia Ave* ⊕ *www.shopcoralgables.com.*

WYNWOOD

ONLY IN MIAMI

FAMILY **Genius Jones.** This is a modern design store for kids and parents. It's the best—and one of the few—places to buy unique children's gifts in Miami. Pick up furniture, strollers, clothing, home accessories, and playthings, including classic wooden toys, vintage-rock T-shirts by Claude and Trunk, and toys designed by Takashi Murakami and Keith Haring. ⊠ *2800 N.E. 2nd Ave.* ☎ *305/571–2000* ⊕ *www.geniusjones. com.*

DESIGN DISTRICT

Fodor's Choice ★ Miami is synonymous with good design, and this ever-expanding visitor-friendly shopping district—officially from Northeast 38th to Northeast 42nd streets, between N. Miami Avenue and Northeast 2nd Avenue (though unofficially beyond)—is an unprecedented melding of public space and the exclusive world of design. High-design buildings don the creativity of architects like Aranda & Lasch, Sou Fujimoto, and the Leong Leong firm. Throughout the district, there are more than 100 showrooms and galleries, including Baltus, Animadomus, Kartell, Ann Sacks, Poliform USA, and Luminaire Lab. Upscale retail outlets also grace the district. Cartier, Dolce & Gabbana, Fendi, Marc Jacobs, Valentino, Giorgio Armani, Louis Vuitton, Prada, Rolex, and Scotch & Soda sit next to design showrooms. Meanwhile, restaurants like Michael's Genuine Food & Drink and Oak Tavern also make this trendy neighborhood a hip place to dine. Unlike most showrooms, which are typically the beat of decorators alone, the Miami Design District's showrooms are open to the public and occupy windowed, street-level spaces. The area also has its own website ⊕ *www.miamidesigndistrict.net.*

CLOTHING

Apt 606. One of the Design District's few men's stores to offer multiple designer brands takes a cue from its artsy neighborhood, offering a space that is more fashion gallery than boutique, with a modern black-and-white palette, immaculate layout, and accessories displayed on pedestals. From the pristinely organized racks hang fashion-forward jackets, knits, and pants by the likes of Alexander Wang, Raf Simmons, Surface to Air, BLK DNM, and celebrity underground favorite Public School. ⊠ *89 N.E. 40th St.* ☎ *305/573–3330* ⊕ *www.apt606.com.*

En Avance. This boutique offers a feminine compilation of on-the-cusp designers like Alexis, MSGM, Protagonist, Anjuna, and other young brands. Style and beauty enthusiasts will also enjoy the roving table displays of bespoke baubles, handbags, Assouline lifestyle books, and delicate lotions and potions. The owner's close connection with decorative artist Fornasetti brings to the store an extensive and exclusive selection of fashion-inspired furniture and accessories for the home. ⊠ *53 N.E. 40th St.* ☎ *305/576–0056* ⊕ *www.enavance.com.*

ONLY IN MIAMI

The Bazaar Project. Those looking for the rare and special need look no further than this boutique, curated by owner and Turkey-native Yeliz Titiz via her travels around the globe. Fashions, beauty, decor, and the wonderfully unusual exude the culture and craft akin to its respective region. Highlights include whimsical housewares and candles by Seletti, linens and Turkish rugs by Haremlique, French wallpapers by Koziel, and intriguing jewelry by Titiz's own line, Sura. ⊠ *4308 N.E. 2nd Ave.* ☎ *786/703–6153* ⊕ *www.thebazaarprojectshop.com.*

V°73. Though high rents in Miami's Design District have translated to more big-name tenants like Fendi and Giorgio Armani, a number of more singular offerings still thrive. One case in point is the exquisite boutique by Italian handbag designer Elisabetta Armellin. It's the artist's only U.S. store and offers a wealth of colorful and understated leather totes and accessories at a number of different price points, catering to a broader demographic than the Design District's typical black-card holders. ⊠ *4218 N.E. 2nd Ave.* ⊕ *www.v73.it/us_en.*

LITTLE HAITI

VINTAGE CLOTHING

Fly Boutique. After 13 years on South Beach, Fly Boutique found its new home in Miami's up-and-coming MIMO district, north of the Design District and bordering Little Haiti. This resale boutique is where Miami hipsters flock for the latest arrival of used clothing. 1980s glam designer pieces fly out at a premium price, but vintage camisoles and Levi's corduroys are still a resale deal. You'll find supercool art, furniture, luggage, and collectibles throughout the boutique. And be sure to look up—the eclectic lanterns are also for sale. ⊠ *7235 Biscayne Blvd.* ☎ *305/604–8508* ⊕ *www.flyboutiquevintage.com.*

Rebel. Rebel might be a little off the beaten path, though the trip here is well worth it. Half new, half vintage consignment, the goods offered here make you feel as if you are raiding your stylish friend's closet. Racks are packed with all different types of styles and designers—Flying Monkey, Ark & Co., Indah, Karina Grimaldi—requiring a little patience when sifting though. The store has a particularly strong collection of jeans, funky tees, and maxi dresses. ■ TIP➜ **Be throrough, as**

cute finds are within every nook and corner. ⌧ *6621 Biscayne Blvd., Upper East Side* ☏ *305/793–4104.*

LITTLE HAVANA

CIGARS

Sosa Family Cigars. At this retail outpost on Calle Ocho, the Sosa family sells their line of eponymous cigars, handmade at their nearby factory and distributed by the family-owned Antillian Cigar Corporation. The store offers some newly designed family stogies like Sosa Underground, 60 by Sosa, and Sosa Family Selection, as well as wide selection of tried-and-true premium and house cigars from around the world. It's one of the few cigar shops in Little Havana where you can sit and play dominoes while smoking. There's a selection of wines for purchase, too. Humidors and other accessories are also for sale here. ⌧ *3475 S.W. 8th St.* ☏ *305/446–2606* ⊕ *www.antilliancigars.com.*

ONLY IN MIAMI

FAMILY **La Casa de los Trucos.** This popular costume store first opened in Cuba in the 1920s; the exiled owners reopened it here in the 1970s. You'll find cartoon costumes, rock star costumes, pet costumes, couples costumes, you name it. If you come any time near Halloween, expect to stand in line just to enter the tiny store. Wooden, life-size costume cutouts in the parking lot make for great photo ops. ⌧ *1343 S.W. 8th St.* ☏ *305/858–5029* ⊕ *www.crazyforcostumes.com* ☾ *Closed Sun.*

SOUTH BEACH

ART GALLERIES

Britto Central. Though exhibited throughout galleries and museums in more than 100 countries, the vibrant, pop art creations by Brazilian artist Romero Britto have become most synonymous with Miami's playful spirt. His flagship gallery and store carries the full breach of his portfolio, including original paintings and sculptures, collectibles, and his signature interpretations in collaboration with some of America's most iconic characters and brands, including Disney and Coco-Cola. Home-decor accessories and tech gadgets with Britto's artistic touch are also available. ⌧ *818 Lincoln Rd.* ☏ *305/531–8821* ⊕ *www.britto.com.*

CLOTHING

Fodor'sChoice **Alchemist.** Synonymous with the pinnacle of design and fashion in the
★ Magic City, this boutique has so much personality that it requires not one but two cutting-edge spaces in the retail section of Lincoln Road's trendy Herzog and de Meuron–designed parking garage. There's an anchor store on street level, set in an extraordinary space of glass and steel, as well as a glass-encased studio for men's clothing and jewelry on the fifth floor. The price tags skew high, yet represent brands known for innovation and edge. Selections span statement pieces and accessories by Alaia, Givenchy, Moschino; jewelry on an artistry level including Cristina Ortiz, Lydia Courteille, and Stephen Webster; and fashions for the home by Tom Dixon. ⌧ *1111 Lincoln Rd., Carpark Level 5* ☏ *305/531–4815* ⊕ *www.shopalchemist.com.*

Atrium. You may consider not even packing a bag for your trip, as Atrium is truly a one-stop-shop covering every Miami fashion scenario. From lazy afternoons at the beach to biking on the boardwalk, from sophisticated dinners to nightlife fun, the corresponding men's and women's wear encompasses the latest trends and designers. The style risk-taker with a fashion-forward mind-set would perhaps best appreciate this boutique, though even the conservative might consider indulging in a statement piece or two. Miami is the place to let loose, after all. ⌧ *1931 Collins Ave.* ☎ *305/695–0757* ⊕ *www.atriumnyc.com.*

Base Superstore. This is the quintessential South Beach fun-and-funky boutique experience. Stop here for men's eclectic clothing, shoes, jewelry, and accessories that mix Japanese design with Caribbean-inspired materials. Constantly evolving, this shop features an intriguing magazine section, a record section, groovy home accessories, and the latest in men's swimwear and sunglasses. The often-present house-label designer may help select your wardrobe's newest addition. ⌧ *927 Lincoln Rd.* ☎ *305/531–4982* ⊕ *www.baseworld.com.*

Intermix. This modern New York–based boutique has the variety of a department store. You'll find fancy dresses, stylish shoes, slinky accessories, and trendy looks by sassy and somewhat pricey designers like Chloé, Stella McCartney, Marc Jacobs, Moschino, and Diane von Furstenberg. Its popularity on Collins Avenue has translated into a second, even bigger, outpost down the beach at Lincoln Road Mall, which opened in late 2014. There is yet another branch at the Bal Harbour Shops at 9700 Collins Avenue. ⌧ *634 Collins Ave., South Beach* ☎ *305/531–5950* ⊕ *www.intermixonline.com.*

ONLY IN MIAMI

Dog Bar. Just north of Lincoln Road's main drag, this over-the-top pet boutique caters to enthusiastic animal owners with a variety of unique items for the superpampered pet. From luxurious, vegan "leather" designer dog purse/carriers to bling-bling-studded collars to chic poopy bag holders, Miami's "original pet boutique" carries pretty much every pet accessory imaginable. You'll also find plenty of gourmet food and treats as well as a wide variety of fancy toys for dogs, large and small. ⌧ *1684 Jefferson Ave., South Beach* ☎ *305/532–5654* ⊕ *www.dogbar. com.*

Fodor'sChoice
★
The Webster Miami. Occupying an entire circa-1939 art deco building, the Webster is a tri-level, 20,000-square-foot, one-stop shop for fashionistas. This retail sanctuary carries ready-to-wear fashions by more than 100 top designers, plus in-store exclusive shirts, candles, books, and random trendy items you might need for your South Beach experience, a kind of haute Urban Outfitters for grown-ups. Too many choices? Sit down for a café au lait and pastry inside the store to mull over your future purchases. ⌧ *1220 Collins Ave., South Beach* ☎ *305/674–7899* ⊕ *www.thewebstermiami.com.*

SHOPPING DISTRICTS

Collins Avenue. Give your plastic a workout in South Beach shopping at the many high-profile tenants on this densely packed stretch of Collins between 5th and 10th streets, with stores like Steve Madden, Club

Monaco, MAC Cosmetics, Ralph Lauren, Kenneth Cole, and Intermix. Sprinkled among the upscale vendors are hair salons, spas, cafés, and such familiar stores as the Gap and Urban Outfitters. Be sure to head over one street east to Ocean Drive or west to Washington Avenue for a drink or a light bite, or go for more retail therapy on Lincoln Road. ✉ *Collins Ave. between 5th and 10th Sts.* ⊕ *www.lincolnroadmall.com/ shopping/collins-avenue.*

Fodor's Choice ★   **Lincoln Road Mall.** The eight-block-long pedestrian mall between Alton Road and Washington Avenue is the trendiest place on Miami Beach. Home to more than 200 shops, art galleries, restaurants and cafés, and the renovated Colony Theatre, Lincoln Road is like the larger, more sophisticated cousin of Ocean Drive. The see-and-be-seen theme is furthered by outdoor seating at every restaurant, where tourists and locals lounge and discuss the people (and pet) parade passing by. An 18-screen movie theater anchors the west end of the street, which is where most of the worthwhile shops are; the far east end is mostly discount and electronics shops. Due to higher rents, you are more likely to see big corporate stores like American Eagles Outfitters, H&M, and Victoria's Secret than original boutiques. However, a few emporiums and stores with unique personalities, like Atrium, Base, and Books & Books, remain. ✉ *Lincoln Rd. between Alton Rd. and Washington Ave.* ⊕ *www.lincolnroadmall.com.*

NORTH BEACH

BAL HARBOUR
CLOTHING

Le Beau Maroc. Shoppers can snag a piece of Moroccan exoticism and regality via pieces introduced to the United States for the very first time and available only within the boutique. Lavishly embellished couture kaftans by Souad Chraïbi and Siham Tazi, two of Morocco's most famed designers commissioned by a royal and celebrity clientele, can work for beach, day, and evening wear. Special orders created from the finest fabrics sourced from fashion houses Dior, Valentino, Hermes, Pucci, La Croix, Yves St. Laurent, Jakob Schlaepfer, and Ungaro are also available. Additional exclusive treasures are found at the "beauty bar," where you can adorn yourself with 18-carat gold Moroccan jewelry and the "liquid gold" of Marokissime, an elixir of 100% pure Moroccan argan and prickly pear oils coveted by Moroccan women for centuries for their beauty regimes. ✉ *9507 Harding Ave.* ☎ *305/763–8847* ⊕ *www.lebeaumaroc.com.*

100% Capri. This shop is one of only two stores by this brand in the United States. The collection is all pure linen (including the shopping bags). Designer Antonio Aiello sources and produces all pieces in Capri for an exciting interpretation that takes its wearers to exotic beach locales style-wise—and quite literally, given its clientele. You'll find clothing for women, men, and children, and even home goods with curated glass accessories brought over from Italy. Displays of gray, wood-slatted wall panels and pools of water build up the ambience, prompting you to linger longer. Now if only there was rosé.

Bal Harbour Shops, 9700 Collins Ave., No. 236 ☎ *305/866–4117* ⊕ *www.100capri.com/en.*

The Webster Bal Harbour. Though smaller than its sister store in South Beach, The Webster Bal Harbour is still sizable with 2,600 square feet to house high-level fashions for both men and women. Nearly every great contemporary luxury designer is represented (Chanel, Céline, Alaia, Valentino, Givenchy, Proenza Schouler, Stella McCartney, etc.), as well as emerging runway darlings. Fashionably impatient? The store can snag ready-to-wear pieces from the latest shows. It also carries exclusive pieces, a real feat considering its influential mall neighbors, including a continuous flow of capsule collections in collaboration with the likes of Calvin Klein, Marc Jacobs, and Anthony Vaccarello, to name a few. ⊠ *Bal Habour Shops, 9700 Collins Ave., No. 204* ☎ *305/868–6544* ⊕ *www.thewebstermiami.com.*

SHOPPING CENTERS AND MALLS

Fodor's Choice
★
Bal Harbour Shops. Beverly Hills meets the South Florida sun at this swank collection of 100 high-end shops, boutiques, and department stores, which currently holds the title as the country's greatest revenue-earner per square foot. Many European designers open their first North American signature store at this outdoor, pedestrian-friendly mall, and many American designers open their first boutique outside of New York here. The open-aired enclave includes Florida's largest Saks Fifth Avenue; an 8,100-square-foot, two-story flagship Salvatore Ferragamo store; and stores by Alexander McQueen, Gucci, Valentino, and local juggernaut the Webster. Restaurants and cafés, in tropical garden settings, overflow with style-conscious diners; in fact, people-watching on the terrace of the Japenese restaurant Makoto and Italian restaurant Carpaccio might be the best in Miami (even trumping South Beach). ⊠ *9700 Collins Ave.* ☎ *305/866–0311* ⊕ *www.balharbourshops.com.*

AVENTURA

JEWELRY

MIA Jewels. This jewelry and accessories boutique is known for its colorful gem- and bead-laden, gold and silver earrings, necklaces, bracelets, and brooches by lines such as Cousin Claudine, Amrita, and Alexis Bittar. This is a shoo-in store for everyone: you'll find things for trend lovers (gold-studded chunky Lucite bangles), classicists (long, colorful, wraparound beaded necklaces), and ice lovers (long Swarovski crystal cabin necklaces) alike. ⊠ *Aventura Mall, 19575 Biscayne Blvd., No. 1061* ☎ *305/931–2000.*

SHOPPING CENTERS AND MALLS

Fodor's Choice
★
Aventura Mall. This three-story megamall offers the ultimate in South Florida retail therapy. Aventura houses many global top performers including the most lucrative outposts of several U.S. chain stores, a supersize Nordstrom and Bloomingdale's, and 300 other shops like Façonnable, Dior, and MIA Jewels, which together create the fifth-largest mall in the United States. This is the one-stop, shop-'til-you-drop retail Mecca for locals, out-of-towners, and—frequently—celebrities. ⊠ *19501 Biscayne Blvd.* ☎ *305/935–1110* ⊕ *www.aventuramall.com.*

SPORTS AND THE OUTDOORS

Sun, sand, and crystal-clear water mixed with an almost nonexistent winter and a cosmopolitan clientele make Miami and Miami Beach ideal for year-round sunbathing and outdoor activities. Whether the priority is showing off a toned body, jumping on a Jet Ski, or relaxing in a tranquil natural environment, there's a beach tailor-made to please. But tanning and water sports are only part of this sun-drenched picture. Greater Miami has championship golf courses and tennis courts, miles of bike trails along placid canals and through subtropical forests, and skater-friendly concrete paths amidst the urban jungle. For those who like their sports of the spectator variety, the city offers up a bonanza of pro teams for every season. There's even a crazy ball-flinging game called jai alai that's billed as the fastest sport on Earth.

BASEBALL

FAMILY **Miami Marlins.** Miami's baseball team, formerly known as the Florida Marlins, moved into a new home in 2012, Marlins Park—a 37,442-seat retractable-roof, air-conditioned baseball stadium on the grounds of Miami's famous Orange Bowl. Go see the team that came out of nowhere to beat the New York Yankees and win the 2003 World Series. Home games are April through early October. ⊠ *Marlins Park, 501 N.W. 16 Ave., Little Havana* ☎ *305/480–1300, 305/480–2523 for tickets* ⊕ *marlins.com/tickets* ⬛ *$10–$395; parking from $20 and should be prepurchased online.*

BIKING

Perfect weather and flat terrain make Miami–Dade County a popular place for cyclists; however, biking here can also be quite dangerous. Be very vigilant when biking on Miami Beach, or better yet, steer clear and bike the beautiful paths of Key Biscayne instead.

Key Cycling. On an island where biking is a way of life, this Key Biscayne bike shop carries a wide range of amazing bikes and accessories in its showroom. Out-of-towners can rent mountain or hybrid bikes for $20 for two hours, $24 for the day, and $100 for the week. ⊠ *Galleria Shopping Center, 328 Crandon Blvd., Suite 121, Key Biscayne* ☎ *305/361–0061* ⊕ *www.keycycling.com.*

Miami Beach Bicycle Center. The easiest and most economical place for a bike rental on Miami Beach is this shop near Ocean Drive. Rent a bike for $5 per hour, $18 per day, or $80 for the week. All bike rentals include locks, helmets, and baskets. ⊠ *601 5th St., South Beach* ☎ *305/674–0150* ⊕ *www.bikemiamibeach.com.*

BOATING AND SAILING

Boating, whether on sailboats, powerboats, luxury yachts, WaveRunners, or windsurfers, is a passion in Greater Miami. The Intracoastal Waterway, wide and sheltered Biscayne Bay, and the Atlantic Ocean provide ample opportunities for fun aboard all types of watercraft.

Miami Beach residential buildings tower over the sand.

The best windsurfing spots are on the north side of the Rickenbacker Causeway at Virginia Key Beach or to the south at, go figure, Windsurfer Beach.

OUTFITTERS AND EXPEDITIONS

American Water Sports. It's easy to find your sea legs here with an expansive fleet of boats, including center consoles, bow riders, and the newest South Wind Vessels. More regal excursions are offered via yacht charters from a selection of 30-foot vessels to 100-foot megayachts with captain and crew who can take you around Star Island or down to Bimini via local cruising and extended excursion packages. Additional high-performance Jet Ski rentals allow for up-close exploration of the area solo or on guided tours. Those who simply want to play will appreciate an extra-large Ride Zone. ✉ *Monty's Marina, 2560 S. Bayshore Dr., Coconut Grove* ☎ *305/856–6559* ⊕ *www.americanwatersports.us.*

Miami Water Sports. Looking for the complete playground of water sports? Look no further than the picturesque Dinner Key Marina, formerly the Pan America Airways base of operations. Rentals include kayaks, paddleboards, and small boats. The extra intrepid can venture in parasailing, which offers particularly great views of downtown and South Beach from its Grove location, or rocket above the waters with flyboarding (where jet packs are placed on your feet for an Iron Man–like experience). Lessons are included in most activities. Bonus: free parking and lockers are included. ✉ *3400 Pan American Dr., Coconut Grove* ☎ *305/345–4104* ⊕ *www.miamiwatersports.com.*

Fodor's Choice ★ **Sailboards Miami.** Rent paddle boards and kayaks or learn how to windsurf from this permanent, roadside adventure outfitter, directly off Rickenbacker Causeway. These friendly folks say they teach more Windsurfers each year than anyone in the United States and promise to teach you to wind-surf within two hours—for $79. It's open Friday through Tuesday, from 10 to 5:30 ⊠ *Mile 6.5 on Rickenbacker Causeway, go right before bridge, Key Biscayne* ☎ *305/892–8992* ⊕ *www. sailboardsmiami.com.*

GOLF

Greater Miami has more than 30 private and public courses. Costs at most courses are higher on weekends and in season, but you can save by playing on weekdays and after 1 or 3 pm, depending on the course. Call ahead to find out when afternoon-twilight rates go into effect. For information on most courses in Miami and throughout Florida, you can visit ⊕ *www.floridagolferguide.com.*

Biltmore Golf Course. On the grounds of the historic circa 1926 Biltmore hotel, the Biltmore Golf Course provides a golf experience primarily for in-house guests, local residents, and those visiting the Coral Gables area. The 6,800-yard, 18-hole, par-71, championship golf course was designed in 1925 by Scotsman Donald Ross, the "it" golf designer of the Roaring Twenties. Today, the lush, well-maintained course is easily accessible thanks to its advanced online booking system, where you can easily reserve your tee time and decide between pricing, depending on the time of day and year (weekdays are cheaper; and the later, the cheaper it gets). There's a pro shop on-site, and golf instruction is available through the Biltmore Golf Academy or the more extensive, on-site Total Performance Golf programs. ⊠ *The Biltmore Hotel, 1210 Anastasia Ave., Coral Gables* ☎ *855/311–6903* ⊕ *www.biltmorehotel.com/golf* 🖭 *$120 for 9 holes, $230 for 18 holes* ⏳ *18 holes, 6800 yards, par 71.*

Fodor's Choice **Crandon Golf at Key Biscayne.** On the serene island of Key Biscayne,
★ overlooking Biscayne Bay, this top-rated, championship municipal golf course is considered one of the state's most challenging par 72 courses. The course also happens to be the only one in North America with a subtropical lagoon. The Devlin/Von Hagge–designed course has a USGA rating of 75.4 and a slope rating of 129 and has received national awards from both *Golfweek* and *Golf Digest*. The course is located on the south side of Crandon Park. Nonresidents should expect to pay $180 for a round during peak hours in peak season (mid-December– mid-April) and roughly half that off-season. Deeply discounted twilight rates of $56 apply after 2 pm. Tee times can be booked online. ⊠ *Crandon Park, 6700 Crandon Blvd., Key Biscayne* ☎ *305/361–9129, 855/465–3305 for tee times* ⊕ *www.golfcrandon.com* 🖭 *$180* ⏳ *18 holes, 7400 yards, par 72.*

The Senator Course at Shula's Golf Club. Deep in the suburbs of west Miami, the Senator Course at Shula's Golf Club boasts the longest championship course in the area (7,055 yards, par 72), a lighted par-3 course, and a golf school. The championship, classic-style Senator Course was originally designed in 1962 by Bill Watts, updated by Kipp Schulties in 1998, and completely refreshed in late 2013, with improvements that included sparkling new Champion Bermuda greens and new

Celebration Bermuda tees. Because of its remote location, green fees tend to be on the lower side, varying by season and time. You'll pay in the lower range on weekdays, more on weekends, and a third of prime-time rates after 2 pm. Golf carts are included. ✉ *7601 Miami Lakes Dr., 154th St. Exit off Rte. 826, Miami Lakes* ☎ *305/820–8088* ⊕ *www.shulasgolfclub.com* 🖻 *$130* ⚑ *18 holes, 7055 yards, par 70.*

Fodor'sChoice **Trump National Doral Miami.** Just west of Miami proper, Trump National ★ Doral Miami is best known for the par-72 Blue Monster course and the World Golf Championships–Cadillac Championship. The week of festivities planned around this March tournament, which offers $8.5 million in prize money, brings hordes of pro-golf aficionados to South Florida. But there's far more to the Trump golf grounds. There are four other renowned golf courses—the Greg Norman–designed Great White Course, the Raymon Floyd–redesigned Gold Course, the Jim McClean Signature Course, and the Red course (under renovation at press time)—and numerous other tournaments throughout the year; hence, golf enthusiasts flock here year-round. ✉ *4400 N.W. 87th Ave., 36th St. Exit off Rte. 826, Doral* ☎ *800/713–6725* ⊕ *www. trumphotelcollection.com/miami* 🖻 *Blue Monster Course, $450; Great White Course, $250; Gold Course, $190* ⚑ *Blue Monster Course: 18 holes, 7300 yards, par 72; Great White Course: 18 holes, 7200 yards, par 72; Gold Course: 18 holes, 6600 yards, par 70.*

GUIDED TOURS

BOAT TOURS

Island Queen Cruises. Working with nine boats, experiences on the very touristy Island Queen Cruises run the gamut—sunset cruises, dance cruises, fishing cruises, speedboat rides, and their signature, tours of Millionaire's Row, Miami's waterfront homes of the rich and famous. *The Island Queen, Island Lady,* and *Miami Lady* are three double-decker, 140-passenger tour boats docked at Bayside Marketplace that set sail daily for 90-minute narrated tours of the Port of Miami and Millionaires' Row. For the same tour with a lot more speed, take the tour on the high-speed *Bayside Blaster.* ✉ *401 Biscayne Blvd., Downtown* ☎ *305/379–5119* ⊕ *www.islandqueencruises.com* 🖻 *From $15.*

WALKING TOURS

Art Deco District Walking Tour. Operated by the Miami Design Preservation League, this is a 90-minute guided walking tour that departs from the league's welcome center at Ocean Drive and 10th Street. It starts at 10:30 am daily, with an extra tour at 6:30 pm Thursday. Alternatively, you can go at your own pace with the league's self-guided iPod audio tour, which also takes roughly an hour and a half. ✉ *1001 Ocean Dr., South Beach* ☎ *305/763–8026* ⊕ *www.mdpl.org* 🖻 *$25 guided tour, $20 self-guided audio tour.*

Little Havana Arts & Culture Walk. Cultural institution HistoryMiami (formerly the Historical Museum of Southern Florida) runs some fabulous art and cultural tours of Little Havana (spiked with plenty of Cuban coffees and cigars, of course). Enjoy the unique architecture of this ethnic enclave and community history by visiting art galleries, botanicas, cigar factories, and the Cuba Ocho Art and Research Center, featuring rare Cuban art from early 19th and 20th century. The two-hour tour is offered monthly and leaves from the juice stand and market Los Pinareños Fruteria at 10 am. Check the website ahead of time to book. ⊠ *1334 S.W. 8 St., Little Havana* ☎ *305/375–1621* ⊕ *www.historymiami.org/ tours/walking-tours* ⊴ *$30.*

SCUBA DIVING AND SNORKELING

Diving and snorkeling on the offshore coral wrecks and reefs on a calm day can be very rewarding. Chances are excellent that you'll come face-to-face with a flood of tropical fish. One option is to find Fowey, Triumph, Long, and Emerald reefs in 10- to 15-foot dives that are perfect for snorkelers and beginning divers. On the edge of the continental shelf a little more than 3 miles out, these reefs are just 1/4 mile away from depths greater than 100 feet. Another option is to paddle around the tangled prop roots of the mangrove trees that line the coast, peering at the fish, crabs, and other creatures hiding there.

Perhaps the area's most unusual diving options are its artificial reefs. Since 1981, Miami-Dade County's Department of Environmental Resources Management has sunk tons of limestone boulders and a water tower, army tanks, and almost 200 boats of all descriptions to create a "wreckreational" habitat where divers can swim with yellow tang, barracudas, nurse sharks, snapper, eels, and grouper. The website offers an interactive map of wreck locations. ⇨ *For the best snorkeling in Miami–Dade, head to Biscayne National Park. See the Everglades, Chapter 3, for more information.*

Divers Paradise of Key Biscayne. This complete dive shop and diving-charter service next to the Crandon Park Marina, includes equipment rental and scuba instruction with PADI and NAUI affiliation. Four-hour dive trips are offered Tuesday through Friday at 10:30, weekends 8:30 and 1:30. Night dives are offered Thursday at 5:30. ⊠ *Crandon Park Marina, 4000 Crandon Blvd., Key Biscayne* ☎ *305/361–3483* ⊕ *www. keydivers.com* ⊴ *$60* ⊘ *Closed Mon.*

Fodor'sChoice
★
South Beach Dive and Surf. Dedicated to all things ocean, this PADI 5-Star Dive Shop offers multiple diving and snorkeling trips weekly as well as surfboard, paddleboard, and skateboard sales, rentals and lessons. The Discover Scuba course (for non-certified divers) trains newcomers every Monday, Tuesday, Thursday, and Saturday at 8 am, which includes two dives in Key Largo's John Pennekamp Marine Sanctuary that same day. Night dives take place each Wednesday at 5, and wreck and reef dives on Saturday and Sunday at 7:30 am and noon. The center also runs dives in Key Largo's Spiegel Grove, the second-largest wreck ever to be sunk for the intention of recreational diving, and in the Neptune Memorial Reef, inspired by the city of Atlantis and created in part using the ashes of cremated bodies. The dive shop itself is located in the heart of South Beach, but boats depart from marinas in Miami Beach and Key Largo, in the Florida Keys. ⊠ *850 Washington Ave., South Beach* ☎ *305/531–6110* ⊕ *www.southbeachdivers.com.*

THE EVERGLADES

WELCOME TO THE EVERGLADES

TOP REASONS TO GO

★ **Fun fishing:** Cast for some of the world's fightingest game fish—600 species in all—in the Everglades' backwaters.

★ **Abundant birdlife:** Check hundreds of birds off your life list, including—if you're lucky—the rare Everglades snail kite.

★ **Cool kayaking:** Do a half-day trip in Big Cypress National Preserve or reach for the ultimate—the 99-mile Wilderness Trail.

★ **Swamp cuisine:** Want to chow down on alligator tail or frogs' legs? Or how about swamp cabbage, made from hearts of palm? Better yet, try stone-crab claws fresh from the traps.

★ **Gator-spotting:** This is ground zero for alligator viewing in the United States, and there's a good bet you'll leave having spotted your quota.

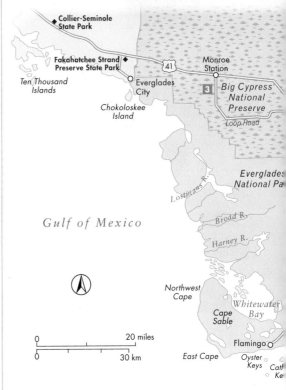

1 Everglades National Park. Alligators, Florida panthers, black bears, manatees, dolphins, bald eagles, and roseate spoonbills call this vast habitat home.

2 Biscayne National Park. Mostly under water, here's where the string of coral reefs and islands that form the Florida Keys begins.

Hialeah

95

Miami

836

Coral Gables

826

Kendall

997

Florida's Turnpike Extension

Tamiami Trail

41

Miccosukee Indian Village

Everglades Gator Park

Shark Valley

Everglades Safari Park

Observation Tower **1**

Homestead

Florida City

9336

Convoy Point

2

Biscayne National Park

Biscayne Bay

Boca Chita Key

Elliott Key

Adams Key

1

Barnes Sound

ATLANTIC OCEAN

Florida Bay

Florida Keys

...ake ...ght

...e Kemp ...ey

GETTING ORIENTED

3

The southern third of the Florida peninsula is largely taken up by protected government land that includes Everglades National Park, Big Cypress National Preserve, and Biscayne National Park. Miami lies to the northeast, with Naples and Marco Island to the northwest. Land access to Everglades National Park is primarily by two roads. The park's main road traverses the southern Everglades from the gateway towns of Homestead and Florida City to the outpost of Flamingo, on Florida Bay. To the north, Tamiami Trail (U.S. 41) cuts through the Everglades from Greater Miami on the east coast or from Naples on the west coast to the western park entrance at Everglades City at Route 29.

3 Big Cypress National Preserve. Neighbor to Everglades National Park, it's an outdoor-lover's paradise.

THE FLORIDA
EVERGLADES

by Lynne Helm

Alternately described as elixir of life or swampland muck, the Florida Everglades is one of a kind—a 50-mi-wide "river of grass" that spreads across hundreds of thousands of acres. It moves at varying speeds depending on rainfall and other variables, sloping south from the Kissimmee River and Lake Okeechobee to estuaries of Biscayne Bay, Florida Bay, and the Ten Thousand Islands.

Today, apart from sheltering some 70 species on America's endangered list, the Everglades also embraces more than 7 million residents, 50 million annual tourists, 400,000 acres of sugarcane, and the world's largest concentration of golf courses.

Demands on the land threaten the Everglades' finely balanced ecosystem. Irrigation canals for agriculture and roadways disrupt natural water flow. Drainage for development leaves wildlife scurrying for new territory. Water runoff, laced with fertilizers, promotes unnatural growth of swamp vegetation. What remains is a miracle of sorts, given decades of these destructive forces.

Creation of the Everglades required unique conditions. South Florida's geology, linked with its warm, wet subtropical climate, is the perfect mix for a marshland ecosystem. Layers of porous, permeable limestone create water-bearing rock,

soil, and aquifers, which in turn affects climate, weather, and hydrology.

This rock beneath the Everglades reflects Florida's geologic history—its crust was once part of the African region. Some scientists theorize that continental shifting merged North America with Africa, and then continental rifting later pulled North America away from the African continent but took part of northwest Africa with it—the part that is today's Florida. The Earth's tectonic plates continued to migrate, eventually placing Florida at its current location as a land mass jutting out into the ocean, with the Everglades at its tip.

EXPERIENCING THE ECOSYSTEMS

Eight distinct habitats exist within Everglades National Park, Big Cypress National Preserve, and Biscayne National Park.

ECOSYSTEMS	EASY WAY	MORE ACTIVE WAY
COASTAL PRAIRIE: An arid region of salt-tolerant vegetation lies between the tidal mud flats of Florida Bay and dry land. **Best place to see it: The Coastal Prairie Trail**	Take a guided boat tour of Florida Bay, leaving from Flamingo Marina.	Hike the Coastal Prairie Trail from Eco Pond to Clubhouse Beach.
CYPRESS: Capable of surviving in standing water, cypress trees often form dense clusters called "cypress domes" in natural water-filled depressions. **Best place to see it: Big Cypress National Preserve**	Drive U.S. 41 (also known as Tamiami Trail—pronounced Tammy-Amee), which cuts across Southern Florida, from Naples to Miami.	Hike (or drive) the scenic Loop Road, which begins off Tamiami Trail, running from the Loop Road Education Center to Monroe Station.
FRESH WATER MARL PRAIRIE: Bordering deeper sloughs are large prairies with marl (clay and calcium carbonate) sediments on limestone. Gators like to use their toothy snouts to dig holes in prairie mud. **Best place to see it: Pahayokee Overlook**	Drive there from the Ernest F. Coe Visitor Center.	Take a guided tour, either through the park service or from permitted, licensed guides. You also can set up camp at Long Pine Key.
FRESH WATER SLOUGH AND HARDWOOD HAMMOCK: Shark River Slough and Taylor Slough are the Everglades' two sloughs, or marshy rivers. Due to slight elevation amid sloughs, dense stands of hardwood trees appear as teardrop-shaped islands. **Best place to see it: The Observation Tower**	Take a two-hour guided tram tour from the Shark Valley Visitor Center to the tower and back.	Walk or bike (rentals available) the route to the tower via the tram road and (walkers only) Bobcat Boardwalk trail and Otter Cave Hammock Trail.
MANGROVE: Spread over South Florida's coastal channels and waterways, mangrove thrives where Everglades fresh water mixes with salt water. **Best place to see it: The Wilderness Waterway**	Picnic at the area near Long Pine Key, which is surrounded by mangrove, or take a water tour at Biscayne National Park.	Boat your way along the 99-mi Wilderness Waterway. It's six hours by motorized boat, seven days by canoe.
MARINE AND ESTUARINE: Corals, sponges, mollusks, seagrass, and algae thrive in the Florida Bay, where the fresh waters of the Everglades meet the salty seas. **Best place to see it: Florida Bay**	Take a boat tour from the Flamingo Visitor Center marina.	Canoe or kayak on White Water Bay along the Wilderness Waterway Canoe Trail.
PINELAND: A dominant plant in dry, rugged terrain, the Everglades' diverse pinelands consist of slash pine forest, saw palmettos, and more than 200 tropical plant varieties. **Best place to see it: Long Pine Key trails**	Drive to Long Pine Key, about 6 mi off the main road from Ernest F. Coe Visitor Center.	Hike or bike the 28 mi of Long Pine Key trails.

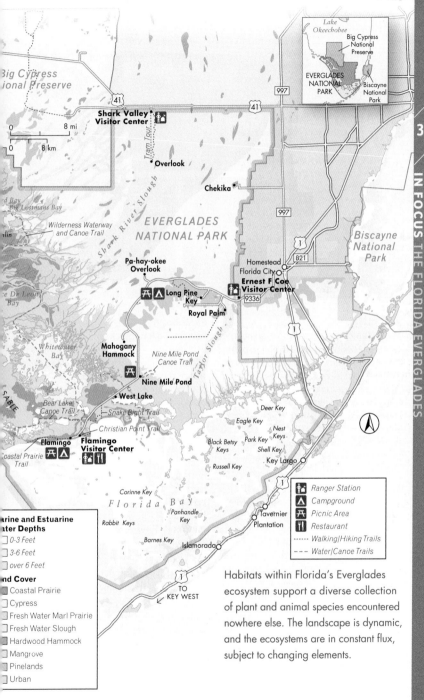

Big Cypress National Preserve

Shark Valley Visitor Center

Overlook

Chekika

Big Losmans Bay

Wilderness Waterway and Canoe Trail

EVERGLADES NATIONAL PARK

Pa-hay-okee Overlook

Long Pine Key

Royal Palm

Homestead
Florida City
Ernest F Coe Visitor Center
9336

Mahogany Hammock

Nine Mile Pond Canoe Trail

Nine Mile Pond

West Lake

Whitewater Bay

Bear Lake Canoe Trail

Snake Bight Trail

Christian Point Trail

Flamingo
Flamingo Visitor Center

Coastal Prairie Trail

Deer Key

Eagle Key

Nest Keys

Black Betsy Keys

Park Key

Shell Key

Russell Key

Key Largo

Corinne Key

F l o r i d a   B a y

Panhandle Key

Rabbit Keys

Barnes Key

Tavernier
Plantation

Islamorada

Biscayne National Park

Lake Okeechobee

Big Cypress National Preserve

EVERGLADES NATIONAL PARK

Biscayne National Park

TO KEY WEST

arine and Estuarine ater Depths
0-3 Feet
3-6 Feet
over 6 Feet

nd Cover
Coastal Prairie
Cypress
Fresh Water Marl Prairie
Fresh Water Slough
Hardwood Hammock
Mangrove
Pinelands
Urban

Ranger Station
Campground
Picnic Area
Restaurant
.... Walking/Hiking Trails
--- Water/Canoe Trails

Habitats within Florida's Everglades ecosystem support a diverse collection of plant and animal species encountered nowhere else. The landscape is dynamic, and the ecosystems are in constant flux, subject to changing elements.

FLORA

❶ Cabbage Palm

It's virtually impossible to visit the Everglades and not see a cabbage palm, Florida's official state tree. The cabbage palm (or sabal palm), graces assorted ecosystems and grows well in swamps. **Best place to see them:** At Loxahatchee National Wildlife Refuge (embracing the northern part of the Everglades, along Alligator Alley), throughout Everglades National Park, and at Big Cypress National Preserve.

❷ Sawgrass

With spiny, serrated leaf blades resembling saws, sawgrass inspired the term "river of grass" for the Everglades. **Best place to see them:** Both Shark Valley and Pahayokee Overlook provide terrific vantage points for gazing over sawgrass prairie; you also can get an eyeful of sawgrass when crossing Alligator Alley, even when doing so at top speeds.

❸ Mahogany

Hardwood hammocks of the Everglades live in areas that rarely flood because of the slight elevation of the sloughs, where they're typically found. **Best place to see them:** Everglades National Park's Mahogany Hammock Trail (which has a boardwalk leading to the nation's largest living mahogany tree).

❹ Mangrove

Mangrove forest ecosystems provide both food and protected nursery areas for fish, shellfish, and crustaceans. **Best place to see them:** Along Biscayne National Park shoreline, at Big Cypress National Preserve, and within Everglades National Park, especially around the Caple Sable area.

❺ Gumbo Limbo

Sometimes called "tourist trees" because of peeling reddish bark (not unlike sunburns). **Best place to see them:** Everglades National Park's Gumbo Limbo Trail and assorted spots throughout the expansive Everglades.

FAUNA

❶ American Alligator

In all likelihood, on your visit to the Everglades you'll see at least a gator or two. These carnivorous creatures can be found throughout the Everglades swampy wetlands.

Best place to see them: Loxahatchee National Wildlife Refuge (also sheltering the endangered Everglades snail kite) and within Everglades National Park at Shark Valley or Anhinga Trail. Sometimes (logically enough) gators hang out along Alligator Alley, basking in early morning or late-afternoon sun along four-lane I–75.

❷ American Crocodile

Crocs gravitate to fresh or brackish water, subsisting on birds, fish, snails, frogs, and small mammals.

Best place to see them: Within Everglades National Park, Big Cypress National Preserve, and protected grounds in or around Billie Swamp Safari.

❸ Eastern Coral Snake

This venomous snake burrows in underbrush, preying on lizards, frogs, and smaller snakes.

Best place to see them: Snakes typically shy away from people, but try Snake Bight or Eco Pond near Flamingo, where birds are also prevalent.

❹ Florida Panther

Struggling for survival amid loss of habitat, these shy, tan-colored cats now number around 100, up from lows of near 30.

Best place to see them: Protected grounds of Billie Swamp Safari sometimes provide sightings during tours. Signage on roadway linking Tamiami Trail and Alligator Alley warns of panther crossings, but sightings are rare.

❺ Green Tree Frog

Typically bright green with white or yellow stripes, these nocturnal creatures thrive in swamps and brackish water.

Best place to see them: Within Everglades National Park, especially in or near water.

● =Extremely Common ● =Very Common ● =Somewhat Common ● =Rare

BIRDS

❶ Anhinga

The lack of oil glands for waterproofing feathers helps this bird to dive as well as chase and spear fish with its pointed beak. The Anhinga is also often called a "water turkey" because of its long tail, or a "snake bird" because of its long neck.

Best place to see them: The Anhinga Trail, which also is known for attracting other wildlife to drink during especially dry winters.

❷ Blue-Winged Teal

Although it's predominantly brown and gray, this bird's powder-blue wing patch becomes visible in flight. Next to the mallard, the blue-winged teal is North America's second most abundant duck, and thrives particularly well in the Everglades.

Best place to see them: Near ponds and marshy areas of Everglades National Park or Big Cypress National Preserve.

❸ Great Blue Heron

This bird has a varied palate and enjoys feasting on everything from frogs, snakes, and mice to shrimp, aquatic insects, and sometimes even other birds! The all-white version, which at one time was considered a separate species, is quite common to the Everglades.

Best place to see them: Loxahatchee National Wildlife Refuge or Shark Valley in Everglades National Park.

❹ Great Egret

Once decimated by plume hunters, these monogamous, long-legged white birds with S-shaped necks feed in wetlands, nest in trees, and hang out in colonies that often include heron or other egret species.

Best place to see them: Throughout Everglades National Park, along Alligator Alley, and sometimes even on the fringes of Greater Fort Lauderdale.

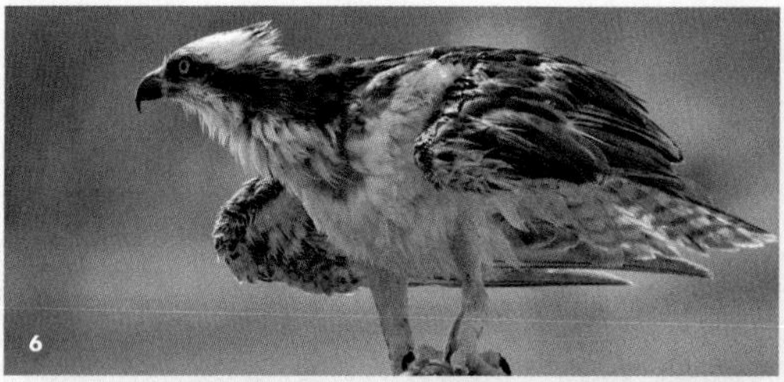

6

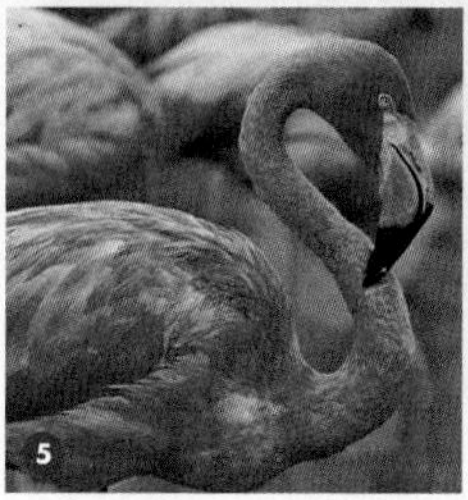

5

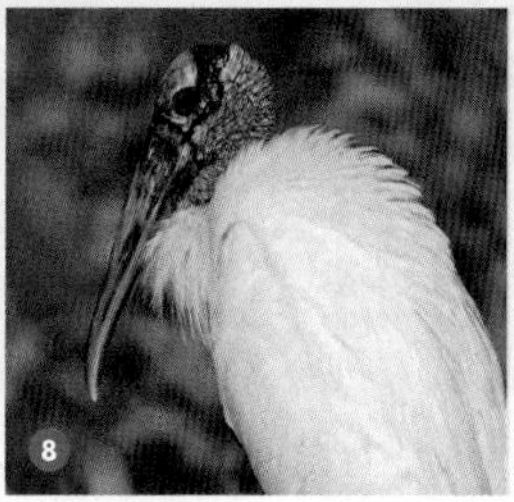

8

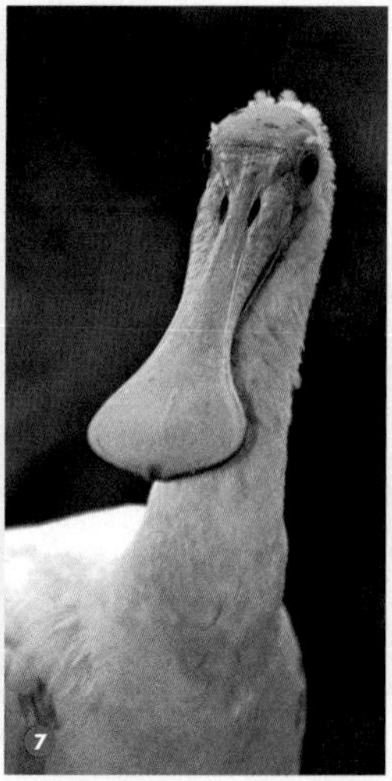

7

5 Greater Flamingo

Flocking together and using long legs and webbed feet to stir shallow waters and mud flats, color comes a couple of years after hatching from ingesting shrimplike crustaceans along with fish, fly larvae, and plankton.

Best place to see them: Try Snake Bight or Eco Pond, near Flamingo Marina.

6 Osprey

Making a big comeback from chemical pollutant endangerment, ospreys (sometimes confused with bald eagles) are distinguished by black eyestripes down their faces. Gripping pads on feet with curved claws help them pluck fish from water.

Best place to see them: Look near water, where they're fishing for lunch in the shallow areas. Try the coasts, bays, and ponds of Everglades National Park. They also gravitate to trees You can usually spot them from the Gulf Coast Visitor Center, or you can observe them via boating in the Ten Thousand Islands.

7 Roseate Spoonbill

These gregarious pink-and-white birds gravitate toward mangroves, feeding on fish, insects, amphibians, and some plants. They have long, spoon-like bills, and their feathers can have a touch of red and yellow. These birds appear in the Everglades year-round.

Best place to see them: Sandy Key, southwest of Flamingo, is a spoonbill nocturnal roosting spot, but at sunrise these colorful birds head out over Eco Pond to favored day hangouts throughout Everglades National Park.

8 Wood Stork

Recognizable by featherless heads and prominent bills, these birds submerge in water to scoop up hapless fish. They are most common in the early spring and often easiest to spot in the morning.

Best place to see them: Amid the Ten Thousand Island areas, Nine Mile Pond, Mrazek Pond, and in the mangroves at Paurotis Pond.

● =Extremely Common ● =Very Common ● =Somewhat Common ● =Rare

THE BEST EVERGLADES ACTIVITIES

HIKING

Top experiences: At Big Cypress National Preserve, you can hike along designated trails or push through unmarked acreage. (Conditions vary seasonally, which means you could be tramping through waist-deep waters.) Trailheads for the Florida National Scenic Trail are at Loop Road off U.S. 41 and Alligator Alley at mile marker 63.

What will I see? Dwarf cypress, hardwood hammocks, prairies, birds, and other wildlife.

For a short visit: A 6.5-mi section from Loop Road to U.S. 41 crosses Robert's Lake Strand, providing a satisfying sense of being out in the middle nowhere.

With more time: A 28-mile stretch from U.S. 41 to I–75 (Alligator Alley) reveals assorted habitats, including hardwood hammocks, pinelands, prairie, and cypress.

Want a tour? Big Cypress ranger-led exploration starts from the Oasis Visitor Center, late November through mid-April.

WALKING

Top experiences: Everglades National Park magnets: wheelchair accessible walkways at Anhinga Trail, Gumbo Limbo Trail, Pahayokee Overlook, Mahogany Hammock, and West Lake Trail.

What will I see? Birds and alligators at Anhinga; tropical hardwood hammock at Gumbo Limbo; an overlook of the River of Grass from Pahayokee's tower; a subtropical tree island with massive mahogany growth along Mahogany Hammock; and a forest of mangrove trees on West Lake Trail.

For a short visit: Flamingo's Eco Pond provides for waterside wildlife viewing.

With more time: Shark Valley lets you combine the quarter-mile Bobcat Boardwalk (looping through sawgrass prairie and a bayhead) with the 1-mi-long round-trip Otter Cave, allowing you to steep in subtropical hardwood hammock.

Want a tour? Pahayokee and Flamingo feature informative ranger-led walks.

The Anhinga Trail near the Royal Palm Visitor Center at Everglades National Park

BOATING

Top experiences: Launch a boat from the Gulf Coast Visitors Center or Flamingo Marina. Bring your own watercraft or rent canoes or skiffs at either location.

What will I see? Birds from bald eagles to roseate spoonbills, plus plenty of mangrove and wildlife—and maybe even some baby alligators with yellow stripes.

For a short visit: Canoe adventurers often head for Hells Bay, a 3-mile stretch about 9 mi north of Flamingo. Or put in at the Turner River alongside the Tamiami Trail in the Big Cypress National Preserve and paddle all the way (about eight hours) to Chocoloskee Bay at Everglades City.

With more time: Head out amid the Ten Thousand Islands and lose yourself in territory once exclusively the domain of only the hardiest pioneers and American Indians. If you've got a week or more for paddling, the 99-mile Wilderness Waterway stretches from Flamingo to Everglades City.

Want a tour? Sign on for narrated boat tours at the Gulf Coast or Flamingo visitor center.

BIRD WATCHING

Top experiences: Anhinga Trail, passing over Taylor Slough.

What will I see? Anhinga and heron sightings are a nearly sure thing, especially in early morning or late afternoon. Also, alligators can be seen from the boardwalk.

For a short visit: Even if you're traveling coast to coast at higher speeds via Alligator Alley, chances are you'll spot winged wonders like egrets, osprey, and heron.

With more time: Since bird-watching at Flamingo can be a special treat early in the morning or late in the afternoon, try camping overnight even if you're not one for roughing it. Reservations are recommended. (Flamingo Lodge remains closed after 2005 hurricane damage.)

Want a tour? Ranger-led walks at Pahayokee and from Everglades National Park visitor centers provide solid birding background for novices.

(top left) Tourists cruise the Everglades by airboat; (bottom left) Green Heron; (right) Eastern Meadowlark

THE BEST EVERGLADES ACTIVITIES

BIKING

Top experiences: Shark Valley (where bicycling is allowed on the tram road) is great for taking in the quiet beauty of the Everglades. Near Ernest F. Coe Visitor Center, Long Pine Key's 14-mile nature trail also can be a way to bike happily away from folks on foot.

What will I see? At Shark Valley, wading birds, turtles, and, probably alligators. At Long Pine Key, shady pinewood with subtropical plants and exposed limestone bedrock.

For a short visit: Bike on Shark Valley tram road but turn around to fit time schedule.

With more time: Go the entire 15-mi tram road route, which has no shortcuts. Or try the 22-mile route of Old Ingraham Highway near the Royal Palm Visitor Center, featuring mangrove, sawgrass, and birds (including hawks).

Want a tour? In Big Cypress National Preserve, Bear Island Bike Rides (8 mile round-trip over four to five hours) happen on certain Saturdays.

SNORKELING

Top experiences: Biscayne National Park, where clear waters incorporate the northernmost islands of the Florida Keys.

What will I see? Dense mangrove swamp covering the park shoreline, and, in shallow waters, a living coral reef and tropical fish in assorted colors.

For a short visit: Pick a sunny day to optimize your snorkeling fun, and be sure to use sunscreen.

With more time: Advanced snorkel tours head out from the park on weekends to the bay, finger channels, and around shorelines of the barrier islands. Biscayne National Park also has canoe and kayak rentals, picnic facilities, walking trails, fishing, and camping.

Want a tour? You can swim and snorkel or stay dry and picnic aboard tour boats that depart from Biscayne National Park's visitor center.

(top left) Biking near the Shark Valley Visitor Area. (top right) Snorkeling on the surface in the Atlantic Ocean.

DID YOU KNOW?

You can tell you're looking at a crocodile if you can see its lower teeth protruding when its jaws are shut, whereas an alligator shows no teeth when his mouth is closed. Gators are much darker in color—a gray-ish black—compared with the lighter tan color of crocodiles. Alligators' snouts are also much broader than their long, thin crocodilian counterparts.

THE STORY OF THE EVERGLADES

Dreams of draining southern Florida took hold in the early 1800s, expanding in the early 1900s to convert large tracts from wetlands to agricultural acreage. By the 1920s, towns like Fort Lauderdale and Miami boomed, and the sugar indus-try—which came to be known as "Big Sugar"—established its first sugar mills. In 1947 Ever-glades National Park opened as a refuge for wildlife.

Meanwhile, the sugar industry grew. In its infancy, about 175,000 tons of raw sugar per year was produced from fields totaling about 50,000 acres. But once the U.S. embargo stopped sugar imports from Cuba in 1960 and laws restricting acreage were lifted, Big Sugar took off. Less than five years later, the industry produced 572,000 tons of sugar and occupied nearly a quarter of a million acres.

Fast-forward to 2008, to what was hailed as the biggest conservation deal in U.S. history since the creation of the national parks. A trailblazing restora-tion strategy hinged on creating a water flow-way between Lake Okeechobee and the Everglades by buying up and flooding 187,000 acres of land. The country's largest producers of cane sugar agreed to sell the necessary 187,000 acres to the state of Florida for $1.75 billion. Environmentalists cheered.

But within months, news broke of a scaled-back land acquisition plan: $1.34 billion to buy 180,000 acres. By spring 2009, the restoration plan had shrunk to $536,000 to buy 73,000 acres. With the purchase still in limbo, critics claim the state might overpay for acreage appraised at pre-recession values and proponents fear dwindling revenues may derail the plan altogether.

The Big Sugar land deal is part of a larger effort to preserve the Everglades. In 2010, two separate lawsuits charged the state, along with the United States Environmental Protection Agency, with stalling Everglades cleanup that was supposed to begin in 2006. "Glacial delay" is how one judge put it. The state must reduce phosphorus levels in water that flows to the Everglades or face fines and sanctions for violating the federal Clean Water Act. The fate of the Ever-glades remains in the balance.

3

Updated by
Lynne Helm

More than 1.5 million acres of South Florida's 4.3 million acres of subtropical, watery wilderness were given national-park status and protection in 1947 with the creation of Everglades National Park. It's one of the country's largest national parks and is recognized by the world community as a Wetland of International Importance, an International Biosphere Reserve, and a World Heritage Site. Come here if you want to spend the day biking, hiking, or boating in deep, raw wilderness with lots of wildlife.

To the east of Everglades National Park, Biscayne National Park brings forth a pristine, magical, subtropical Florida. It's the nation's largest marine park and the largest national park within the continental United States boasting living coral reefs. A small portion of the park's 172,000 acres consists of mainland coast and outlying islands, but 95% remains submerged. Of particular interest are the mangroves and their tangled masses of stiltlike roots that thicken shorelines. These "walking trees," as some locals call them, have curved prop roots arching down from trunks, and aerial roots that drop from branches. The roots of these trees can filter salt from water and create a coastal nursery that sustains myriad types of marine life. You can see Miami's high-rise buildings from many of Biscayne's 44 islands, but the park is virtually undeveloped and large enough for escaping everything that Miami and the Upper Keys have become. To truly escape, grab scuba-diving or snorkeling gear and lose yourself in the wonders of the coral reefs.

On the northern edge of Everglades National Park lies Big Cypress National Preserve, one of South Florida's least developed watersheds. Established by Congress in 1974 to protect the Everglades, it comprises extensive tracts of prairie, marsh, pinelands, forested swamps, and sloughs. Hunting is allowed, as is off-road-vehicle use. Come here if you like alligators. Stop at the Oasis Visitor Center's boardwalk with alligators lounging underneath, and then drive Loop Road for a backwoods experience. If time and desire for watery adventure permits, kayak or canoe the Turner River.

Surrounding the parks and preserve are communities where you'll find useful outfitters: Everglades City, Florida City, and Homestead.

PLANNING

WHEN TO GO

Winter is the best, and busiest, time to visit the Everglades. Temperatures and mosquito activity are more tolerable, low water levels concentrate the resident wildlife, and migratory birds swell the avian population. In late spring the weather turns hot and rainy, and tours and facilities are less crowded. Migratory birds depart, and you must look harder to see wildlife. Summer brings intense sun and afternoon rainstorms. Water levels rise and mosquitoes descend, making outdoor activity virtually unbearable, unless you protect yourself with netting. Mosquito repellent is a necessity any time of year.

GETTING HERE AND AROUND

Miami International Airport (MIA) is 34 miles from Homestead and 47 miles from the eastern access to Everglades National Park. ⇨ *For MIA airline information, refer to the Miami chapter.* Shuttles run between MIA and Homestead. Southwest Florida International Airport (RSW), in Fort Myers, a little over an hour's drive from Everglades City, is the closest major airport to the Everglades' western entrance. On-demand taxi transportation from the airport to Everglades City is available from MBA Airport Transportation and costs $150 for up to three passengers ($10 each for additional passengers).

Contacts MBA Airport Transportation. MBA is the taxi concessionaire for Southwest Florida International Airport, providing transportation to Everglades City. Call for rates. ☎ 239/225–0428 ⊕ www.mbaairport.com.

HOTELS

Accommodations near the parks range from inexpensive to moderate and offer off-season rates in summer, when rampant mosquito populations discourage spending time outdoors, especially at dusk. If you're devoting several days to exploring the east-coast Everglades, stay in park campgrounds; 11 miles away in Homestead–Florida City, where there are reasonably priced chain motels and RV parks; in the Florida Keys; or in the Greater Miami–Fort Lauderdale area. Lodgings and campgrounds are also plentiful on the Gulf Coast (in Everglades City, Marco Island, and Naples, the latter with the most upscale area accommodations). *Hotel reviews have been shortened. For full information, visit Fodors.com.*

RESTAURANTS

Dining in the Everglades area centers on mom-and-pop places serving hearty home-style food, and small eateries specializing in fresh local fare: alligator, fish, stone crab, frogs' legs, and Florida lobster from the Keys. American Indian restaurants serve local favorites as well as catfish, Indian fry bread (a flour-and-water flatbread), and pumpkin bread. A growing Hispanic population around Homestead means plenty of authentic, inexpensive Latin cuisine, with an emphasis on Cuban and Mexican dishes. Restaurants in Everglades City, especially those along the river, specialize in fresh seafood including particularly succulent, sustainable stone crab. These mostly rustic places are ultracasual and often close in late summer or fall. For finer dining, head for Marco Island or Naples.

WHAT IT COSTS				
	$	**$$**	**$$$**	**$$$$**
RESTAURANTS	under $16	$16–$20	$21–$30	over $30
HOTELS	under $201	$201–$300	$301–$400	over $400

Restaurant prices are the average cost of a main course at dinner or, if dinner is not served, at lunch. Hotel prices are the lowest cost of a standard double room in high season.

ABOUT ACTIVITIES

⇨ *While outfitters are listed with the parks and preserve, see our What's Nearby section later in this chapter for information about each town.*

EVERGLADES NATIONAL PARK

45 miles southwest of Miami International Airport.

If you're heading across South Florida on U.S. 41 from Miami to Naples, you'll breeze right through the Everglades. Also known as Tamiami Trail, this mostly two-lane road skirts the edge of Everglades National Park and cuts across the Big Cypress National Preserve. You'll also be near the park if you're en route from Miami to the Florida Keys on U.S. 1, which cuts through Homestead and Florida City—communities east of the main park entrance. Basically, if you're in South Florida, you can't escape at least fringes of the Everglades. With tourist strongholds like Miami, Naples, and the Florida Keys so close, travelers from all over the world typically make day trips to the park.

Everglades National Park has three main entry points: the park headquarters at Ernest F. Coe Visitor Center, southwest of Homestead and Florida City; the Shark Valley area, accessed by Tamiami Trail (U.S. 41); and the Gulf Coast Visitor Center, south of Everglades City to the west and closest to Naples.

Explore on your own or participate in ranger-led hikes, bicycle or bird-watching tours, and canoe trips. The variety of these excursions is greatest from mid-December through Easter, and some adventures (canoe trips, for instance) typically aren't offered in sweltering summer. Among the more popular are the Anhinga Amble, a 50-minute walk around the Taylor Slough (departs from the Royal Palm Visitor Center), and the Early Bird Special, a 90-minute walk centered on birdlife (departs from Flamingo Visitor Center). Check with visitor centers for details.

War on Pythons

In 2013, Florida launched its first Python Challenge™ to put the kibosh on Burmese pythons, those deadly snakes literally squeezing the life out of Everglades wonders, from colorful birds to full-grown deer to gators.

The state-sponsored winter competition was a trailblazer, attracting amateurs and professionals alike from 38 states and Canada to help decimate this growing environmental threat. Sadly, only 68 pythons were captured of thousands estimated lurk in the Everglades.

Since then, the Challenge has been scrapped, although the state continues its war with a python removal program, issuing hunting permits to qualified applicants.

Even experienced Gladesmen with special permits to stalk these predators have trouble finding them—partly because tan, splotchy skin provides natural camouflage for slithering about and causing mayhem within the ecosystem. Unseasonably warm winter weather also leaves pythons, growing up to 26 feet long, without incentive to boldly expose themselves for sunning.

In 2012, the U.S. Department of the Interior—hailing a milestone in Everglades protection—announced a nationwide ban on the importation of Burmese pythons and other non-native, large constrictor snakes, including African pythons and the yellow anaconda.

No matter what the format for the state's effort to eradicate pythons, its war against invasive species and the efforts to protect Everglades wildlife continue unabated.   —Lynne Helm

PARK ESSENTIALS

Admission Fees The fee is $10 per vehicle; and $5 per pedestrian, bicycle, or motorcycle. Payable at gates, the admission is good for seven consecutive days at all park entrances. Annual passes are $25.

Admission Hours Open daily, year-round, both the main entrance near Florida City and Homestead, and the Gulf Coast entrance are open 24 hours a day. The Shark Valley entrance is open 8:30 am to 6 pm.

COE VISITOR CENTER TO FLAMINGO

About 30 miles from Miami.

The most utilized access to Everglades National Park is via the park headquarters entrance southwest of Homestead and Florida City. If you're coming to the Everglades from Miami, take Route 836 West to Route 826/874 South to the Homestead Extension of Florida's Turnpike, U.S. 1, and Krome Avenue (Route 997/old U.S. 27). To reach the Ernest F. Coe Visitor Center from Homestead, go right (west) from U.S. 1 or Krome Avenue onto Route 9336 (Florida's only four-digit route) in Florida City and follow signage to the park entrance.

Route 9336 travels 38 miles from the Ernest F. Coe Visitor Center southwest to the Florida Bay at Flamingo. It crosses a section of the park's eight distinct ecosystems: hardwood hammock, freshwater prairie, pinelands, freshwater slough, cypress, coastal prairie, mangrove, and marine-estuarine. Route highlights include a dwarf cypress forest, the transition zone between saw grass and mangrove forest, and a wealth of wading birds at Mrazek and Coot Bay ponds—where in early morning or late afternoon you can observe them feeding. Be forewarned, however, that flamingo sightings are extremely rare. Boardwalks, looped trails, several short spurs, and observation platforms help you stay dry. You may want to stop along the way to walk several short trails (each takes about 30 minutes): the wheelchair-accessible Anhinga Trail, which cuts through saw-grass marsh and allows you to see lots of wildlife (be on the lookout for alligators and the trail's namesake water birds: anhingas); the junglelike—yet, also wheelchair-accessible—Gumbo-Limbo Trail; the Pinelands Trail, where you can see the park's limestone bedrock; the Pahayokee Overlook Trail, ending at an observation tower; and the Mahogany Hammock Trail with its dense growth. ■TIP➔ Before heading out on the trails, inquire about insect and weather conditions to plan accordingly, stocking up on bug repellent, sunscreen, and water as necessary. Even on seemingly sunny days, it's smart to bring rain gear.

EXPLORING

To explore this section of the park, follow Route 9336 from the park entrance to Flamingo; you'll find plenty of opportunities to stop along the way, and assorted activities to pursue in the Flamingo area. Other than campgrounds, there are no lodging options within the national park at this writing.

Ernest F. Coe Visitor Center. Get your park map here, but don't just grab and go; this visitor center's numerous interactive exhibits and films are well worth your time. The 15-minute film *River of Life,* updated frequently, provides a succinct park overview. A movie on hurricanes and a 35-minute wildlife film for children are available upon request. A bank of telephones offers differing viewpoints on the Great Water Debate, detailing how the last century's gung ho draining of swampland for residential and agricultural development also cut off water-supply routes for precious wetlands in the Everglades ecosystem. You'll also find a schedule of daily ranger-led activities, mainly walks and talks; information on the popular Nike missile site tour (harking back to the Cuban missile crisis era); and details about canoe rentals and boat tours at Flamingo. The Everglades Discovery Shop stocks books, kids' stuff, and jewelry including bird-oriented earrings, plus insect repellent, sunscreen, and water. Coe Visitor Center, which has restrooms, is outside park gates, so you can stop in without paying park admission. ✉ *40001 State Rd. 9336, Homestead* ✚ *11 miles southwest of Homestead* ☏ *305/242–7700* ☉ *Daily 9–5, subject to change.*

Flamingo. At the far end of the main road to the Flamingo community along Florida Bay, you'll find a marina (with beverages, snacks, and a gift shop), visitor center, and campground, with nearby hiking and nature trails. Despite the name, what you are unlikely to find here are flamingos. To improve your luck for glimpsing these flamboyant pink birds with toothpick legs, check out Snake Bight Trail, starting about 5 miles from the Flamingo outpost, but they are a rare sight indeed. Before hurricanes Katrina and Wilma washed them away in 2005, a lodge, cabins, and restaurant facilities in Flamingo provided Everglades National Park's only accommodations. Rebuilding of Flamingo Lodge, long projected, has yet to materialize. For now, you can still pitch tents or bring RVs to the campground, where improvements include solar-heated showers and electricity for RV sites. A houseboat rental concession offers a pair of 35-footers each sleeping six and equipped with shower, toilet, bedding, kitchenware, stereo, and depth finder. The houseboats (thankfully air-conditioned) have 60-horsepower outboards and rent for $350 per night, plus a $200 fuel deposit. ⊠ *Flamingo* ⊕ *www.nps. gov/ever/planyourvisit/flamdirections.*

NEED A BREAK? Worthwhile spots to pull over for a picnic are **Paurotis Pond**, about 10 miles north of Florida Bay, or **Nine Mile Pond**, less than 30 miles from the main visitor center. Another option is along **Bear Lake**, 2 miles north of the Flamingo Visitor Center.

Flamingo Visitor Center. Check the schedule here for ranger-led activities, such as naturalist talks, trail hikes, and evening programs in the 100-seat campground amphitheater, replacing the old gathering spot destroyed by 2005 hurricanes. Mosquito repellent will be your favorite take-along here. If you're starving, the center's Buttonwood Cafe (closed in summer) serves sandwiches, salads, and pizza, but really only if there's no other option for you. You'll find natural history exhibits and pamphlets on canoe, hiking, and biking trails in the second-floor Florida Bay Flamingo Museum, accessible only by stairway and a steep ramp. You can get drinks and snacks at the marina store when the café is closed. ⊠ *1 Flamingo Lodge Hwy., Flamingo* ☎ *239/695–2945, 239/695–3101 marina* ⊙ *Exhibits always open, staffed mid-Nov.–mid-Apr., daily 8–4:30.*

Royal Palm Visitor Center. Ideal for when there's limited time to experience the Everglades, this small center with a bookstore and vending machines permits access to the **Anhinga Trail boardwalk,** where in winter spotting alligators congregating in watering holes is virtually guaranteed. Neighboring **Gumbo Limbo Trail** takes you through a hardwood hammock. Combining these short strolls (½ mile or so) allows you to experience two Everglades ecosystems. Rangers conduct daily Anhinga Ambles in season (call ahead for times). A Glades Glimpse program takes place afternoons daily in season, as do starlight walks and bike tours. As always, arm yourself with insect repellent. If you have a mind for history, ask about narrated Nike missile site tours, stemming from the '60s-era Cuban missile crisis. ⊠ *Rte. 9336, Everglades National Park* ✛ *4 miles west of Ernest F. Coe Visitor Center* ☎ *305/242–7700* ⊙ *Daily 8–4:15.*

SPORTS AND THE OUTDOORS
BIRD-WATCHING
Some of the park's best birding is in the Flamingo area.

BOATING

The 99-mile inland **Wilderness Trail** between Flamingo and Everglades City is open to motorboats as well as canoes, although, depending on water levels, powerboats may have trouble navigating above White-water Bay. Flat-water canoeing and kayaking are best in winter, when temperatures are moderate, rainfall diminishes, and mosquitoes back off—a little, anyway. You don't need a permit for day trips, although there's a seven-day, $5 launch fee for all motorized boats brought into the park. The Flamingo area has well-marked canoe trails, but be sure to tell someone where you're going and when you expect to return. Getting lost is easy, and spending the night without proper gear can be unpleasant, if not dangerous.

EVERGLADES BIRDING

Where birds of a feather flock, birders often do, too. Each January on Martin Luther King Weekend, the Everglades Birding Festival attracts enthusiasts from far and wide. Field workshops cover "birding by ear," habitat, behavior, advanced skills, photography, and other topics. Target species range from the peregrine falcon to the purple swamp hen and plenty of feathered wonders in between. For info, check out ⊕ *www.evergladesbirdingfestival.com*.

Flamingo Lodge, Marina, and Everglades National Park Tours. Everglades National Park's official concessionaire operates a marina, runs tours, and rents canoes, kayaks, and skiffs, secured by credit cards. A one-hour, 45-minute backcountry cruise aboard the 50-passenger *Pelican* ($32.50) winds under a heavy canopy of mangroves, revealing abundant wildlife—from alligators, crocodiles, and turtles to herons, hawks, and egrets. Renting a 17-foot, 40-hp skiff from 7 am runs $195 per day (eight hours, if returned by 4 pm), $150 per half day, or $80 for two hours; there is a $100 credit card deposit required. Canoes for up to three paddlers rent for $16 for two hours (minimum), $22 for four hours, $32 for eight hours, and $40 overnight. Family canoes for up to four go for $20 for two hours, $30 for four hours, $40 for eight hours, and $50 for 24 hours. The concessionaire also rents bikes, binoculars, rods, reels, and other equipment for up to a full day. Feeling sticky after a day in the 'Glades? Hot showers are $3. (Flamingo Lodge, a victim of massive hurricane damage in 2005, remains closed pending a fresh start.) ■TIP➔ An experimental Eco Tent of canvas and wood, unveiled in winter 2012–13, was booked solid for the season. Built by University of Miami architecture students, Eco Tent sleeps four, has a table and chairs, and wins rave reviews from designers, park officials, and campers. It's a prototype for up to 40 more units, once funding is secured. ⊠ *1 Flamingo Lodge Hwy., on Buttonwood Canal, Flamingo* ☎ *239/695–3101, 239/695–0124 Eco Tent reservations* ⊕ *www.evergladesnationalparkboattoursflamingo.com.*

GULF COAST ENTRANCE

To reach the park's western gateway, take U.S. 41 west from Miami for 77 miles, turn left (south) onto Route 29, and travel another 3 miles through Everglades City to the Gulf Coast Ranger Station. From

Naples on the Gulf Coast, take U.S. 41 east for 35 miles, and turn right onto Route 29.

Gulf Coast Visitor Center. The best place to bone up on Everglades National Park's watery western side is at this center just south of Everglades City (5 miles south of Tamiami Trail) where rangers can give you the park lowdown and address your inquiries. In winter, backcountry campers purchase permits here and canoeists check in for trips to the Ten Thousand Islands and 99-mile Wilderness Waterway Trail. Nature lovers view interpretive exhibits on local flora and fauna while waiting for naturalist-led boat trips. In season (Christmas through Easter), rangers lead bike tours and canoe trips. A selection of about 30 nature presentations and orientation films are available by request for view on a big screen. Admission is free only to this section, since no direct roads from here link to other parts of the park. ⊠ *815 Oyster Bar La., off Rte. 29, Everglades City* ☎ *239/695–3311* ☉ *Mid-Nov.–mid-Apr., daily 8–4:30; mid-Apr.–mid-Nov., daily 9–4:30.*

SPORTS AND THE OUTDOORS

BOATING AND KAYAKING

Everglades National Park Boat Tours. In conjunction with boat tours at Flamingo, this operation runs 1½-hour trips ($32) through the Ten Thousand Islands National Wildlife Refuge. Adventure-seekers often see dolphins, manatees, bald eagles, and roseate spoonbills. In peak season (November–April), 49-passenger boats run on the hour and half hour daily. Mangrove wilderness tours ($40) on smaller boats are for up to six passengers. These one-hour, 45-minute trips are the best option to see alligators. The outfitter also rents canoes ($24 per day) and kayaks (from $45 per day) plus tax. Ask about group discounts. ⊠ *Gulf Coast Visitor Center, 815 Oyster Bar La., Everglades City* ☎ *239/695–2591, 866/628–7275* ⊕ *www.evergladesnationalparkboattoursgulfcoast.com/ index.php.*

Fodor's Choice ★ **Everglades Rentals & Eco Adventures.** Ivey House Inn houses this established, year-round source for guided Everglades paddling tours and rentals. Canoes cost $35 the first day, $29 daily thereafter. Daylong kayak rentals are from $45. Shuttles deliver you to major launching areas such as Turner River ($25 for the first person, $5 for each additional person, round-trip). Highlights include bird and gator sightings, mangrove forests, no-man's-land beaches, and spectacular sunsets. Longer adventures include equipment rental, guide, and meals. ⊠ *Ivey House, 107 Camellia St., Everglades City* ☎ *877/567–0679, 239/695–3299* ⊕ *www.evergladesadventures.com.*

Much skill is required to navigate boats through the shallow, muddy waters of the Everglades.

SHARK VALLEY

23½ miles west of Florida's Turnpike, off Tamiami Trail. Approximately 45 mins west of Miami.

You won't see sharks at Shark Valley. The name comes from the Shark River, also called the River of Grass, flowing through the area. Several species of shark swim up this river from the coast (about 45 miles south of Shark Valley) to give birth, though not at this particular spot. Young sharks (called pups), vulnerable to being eaten by adult sharks and other predators, gain strength in waters of the slough before heading out to sea.

The Shark Valley entrance to the national park is on U.S. Hwy. 41 (Tamiami Trail), 25 miles west of Florida's turnpike (SR 821) or 39 miles east of SR 29. Some GPS units don't recognize it. If asked for a cross street, use U.S. Hwy. 41.

EXPLORING

Although Shark Valley is the national park's north entrance, no roads here lead directly to other parts of the park. However, it's still worth stopping to take the two-hour narrated bio-diesel tram tour from Shark Valley Tram Tours. Stop at the halfway point and ascend the Shark Valley Observation Tower via the ramp.

Prefer to do the trail on foot? It takes nerve to walk the paved 15-mile loop in Shark Valley, because in the winter months alligators lie alongside the road, basking in the sun—most, however, do move out of the way.

You also can ride a bicycle (the folks who operate the tram tours also rent one-speed, well-used bikes daily from 8:30 to 4 for $9 per hour with helmets available). Near the bike-rental area a short boardwalk trail meanders through saw grass, and another passes through a tropical hardwood hammock.

Shark Valley Observation Tower. At the Shark Valley trail's end (really, the halfway point of the 15-mile loop), you can pause to navigate this tower, first built in 1984, spiraling 50 feet upward. Once on top, you'll find the River of Grass gloriously spreads out as far as you can see. Observe waterbirds as well as alligators, and maybe even river otters crossing the road. The tower has a wheelchair-accessible ramp to the top. If you don't want to take the tram from the Shark Valley Visitor Center, you can either hike or bike in, but private cars are not allowed. ⊠ *Shark Valley Loop Rd., Miami.*

Shark Valley Visitor Center. The old ramshackle outpost has been razed altogether to make room for a nice picnic area, and a new white concrete-block building nearby is now in place with the bike rental concession and a bookstore (run by the Everglades Association) with hats, postcards, and other souvenirs. Park rangers are still there, ready for your questions. ⊠ *36000 S.W. 8th St., Miami* ✛ *23½ miles west of Florida's Tpke., off Tamiami Trail* ☎ *305/221–8776* ☉ *Daily 9:15–5:15.*

> ### THE EVERGLADES WITH KIDS
>
> Although kids of all ages can enjoy the park, those six and older typically get the most out of the experience. Consider how much you as a supervising adult will enjoy keeping tabs on tiny ones around so much water and so many teeth. Some children are frightened by sheer wilderness.

SPORTS AND THE OUTDOORS

BIKING

FAMILY **Shark Valley Bicycle Rentals.** You can gaze at gators while getting your exercise, too, by renting a bike at the Shark Valley Visitor Center. The same outfitter that operates the tram tours rents bikes as well. Pedal along 15 miles of paved, level roadway (no hills or dales) to the observation tower and back while keeping an eye on plentiful roadside reptiles. Bikes, rented at $9 per hour, are single gear, coaster-style two-wheelers with baskets and helmets available, along with some child seats for kids under 35 pounds. The well-used fleet also includes a few 20-inch junior models. You'll need a driver's license or other ID for a deposit. Arm yourself with water, insect repellent, and sunscreen. ⊠ *Shark Valley Visitor Center, Shark Valley Loop Rd., Shark Valley, Miami* ☎ *305/221–8776* ⊕ *www.sharkvalleytramtours.com/biking.*

BOATING

Many Everglades-area tours operate only in season, roughly November through April.

Buffalo Tiger's Airboat Tours. A former chief of Florida's Miccosukee tribe—Buffalo Tiger, who died in January 2015 at the age of 94—founded this Shark Valley–area tour operation, and his spirit carries on. Savvy guides narrate the trip to an old Indian camp on the north side of Tamiami Trail from the Native American perspective. Don't worry about airboat noise, since engines are shut down during informative talks. The 45-minute tours go 10–5 Saturday through Thursday at $27.50 per person. Look online for discount coupons. Reservations are not required, and credit cards are now accepted at this once cash-only outpost. ⊠ *29708 S.W. 8th St., 5 miles east of Shark Valley, 25 miles west of Florida's Tpke., Miami* ☎ *305/559–5250* ⊕ *www.buffalotigersairboattours.com.*

GUIDED TOURS

Shark Valley Tram Tours. Starting at the Shark Valley Visitor Center, these popular two-hour, narrated tours ($23) on bio-diesel trams follow a 15-mile loop road—great for viewing gators—into the interior, stopping at a 50-foot observation tower. Bring your own water. Reservations are strongly recommended December through April. ⊠ *Shark Valley Visitor Center, Shark Valley Loop Rd., Miami* ☎ *305/221–8455* ⊕ *www.sharkvalleytramtours.com* ☉ *Tours Dec.–Apr., daily hourly 9–4; May–Nov., daily hourly 9–3.*

BIG CYPRESS NATIONAL PRESERVE

Through the early 1960s the world's largest cypress-logging industry prospered in Big Cypress Swamp until nearly all the trees were cut down. With the demise of the industry, government entities began buying parcels. Now more than 729,000 acres, or nearly half of the swamp, form this national preserve. "Big" refers not to the new-growth trees but to the swamp, jutting into the north edge of Everglades National Park like a jigsaw-puzzle piece. Size and strategic location make Big Cypress an important link in the region's hydrological system, where rainwater first flows through the preserve, then south into the park, and eventually into Florida Bay. Its variegated pattern of wet prairies, ponds, marshes, sloughs, and strands provides a wildlife sanctuary, and thanks to a policy of balanced land use—"use without abuse"—the watery wilderness is devoted to recreation as well as to research and preservation. Bald cypress trees that may look dead are actually dormant, with green needles springing to life in spring. The preserve allows—in limited areas—hiking, hunting, and off-road vehicle use (airboat, swamp buggy, four-wheel drive) by permit. Compared with Everglades National Park, the preserve is less developed and hosts fewer visitors. That makes it ideal for naturalists, birders, and hikers preferring to see more wildlife than people.

Several scenic drives link from Tamiami Trail, some requiring four-wheel-drive vehicles, especially in wet summer months. A few lead to camping areas and roadside picnic spots. Apart from the Oasis Visitor Center, popular as a springboard for viewing alligators, the newer Big Cypress Swamp Welcome Center features a platform for watching manatees. Both centers, along Tamiami Trail between Miami and Naples, feature a top-notch 25-minute film on Big Cypress.

PARK ESSENTIALS

Admission Fees There's no admission fee to visit the preserve.

Admission Hours The park is open 24 hours daily, year-round. Accessible only by boat, Adams Key is for day use only.

Contacts **Big Cypress National Preserve.** Big Cypress, open year-round, has an allure all its own, especially for those who prefer few people and more wildlife roaming about. To avoid steam heat, try visiting in winter. ☎ *239/695–1201* ⊕ *www.nps.gov/bicy.*

EXPLORING

Big Cypress Swamp Welcome Center. As a sister to the Oasis Visitor Center, the newer Big Cypress Swamp Welcome Center on the preserve's western side has abundant information, as well as restrooms, picnic facilities, and a 70-seat auditorium. An outdoor breezeway showcases an interactive Big Cypress watershed exhibit, illustrating Florida water flow. It's a great place to stop when crossing from either coast. ■ TIP➔ Love manatees? A platform allows for viewing these intriguing mammals, attracted to warm water. (They were possibly once mistaken for mermaids by thirsty or love-starved ancient sailors.) ⊠ *33000 Tamiami Trail E, 5 miles east of SR29, Ochopee* ☎ *239/695–4758* ⊕ *www.nps. gov/bicy/planyourvisit/visitorcenters.htm* ✉ *Free* ⊗ *Daily 9–4:30.*

Clyde Butcher's Big Cypress Gallery. For taking swamp memories in stark black and white back home, you can't do better than picking up a postcard, calendar, or more serious piece of artwork by photographer Clyde Butcher at his namesake trailside gallery. Butcher, a big guy with an even bigger beard, is an affable personality renowned for his knowledge of the 'Glades and his ability to capture its magnetism through a large-format lens. Even if you can't afford his big stuff, you're warmly invited to gaze. Out back, Butcher and his wife Niki also rent a bungalow ($225 per night, October–April) and a cottage ($295 per night, year-round). ■ TIP➔ Ask about Clyde's muck-abouts or Saturday Swamp Walks ($50), September through March. You'll need a hat, long pants, old sneakers, and—because you will get wet—spare, dry clothing. ⊠ *MM 54.5, 52388 Tamiami Trail, Ochopee* ☎ *239/695–2428* ⊕ *www. clydebutchersbigcypressgallery.com* ⊗ *Daily 10–5.*

Oasis Visitor Center. The big attraction at Oasis Visitor Center, on the east side of Big Cypress Preserve, is the observation deck for viewing fish, birds, and other wildlife. A small butterfly garden's native plants seasonally attract winged wonders. Inside, you'll find an exhibit area, bookshop, and a theater showing an informative 25-minute film on Big Cypress Preserve swamplands. Leashed pets allowed, but not on boardwalk deck. ■ TIP➔ Get your gator watch on at the center's observation deck where big alligators congregate. ⊠ *52105 Tamiami Trail, Ochopee* ✛ *24 miles east of Everglades City, 50 miles west of Miami, 20 miles west of Shark Valley* ☎ *239/695–1201* ⊕ *www.nps.gov/bicy/ planyourvisit/visitorcenters* ✉ *Free* ⊗ *Daily 9–4:30.*

FAMILY **Ochopee Post Office.** North America's smallest post office is a former irrigation pipe shed on the Tamiami Trail's south side. Blink and you'll risk missing it. To support this picturesque outpost during an era of postal service cutbacks, why not buy a postcard of this one-room shack for mailing to whomever would appreciate it? Mail packages or buy money orders here, too. ✉ *38000 E. Tamiami Trail, 4 miles east of Rte. 29, Ochopee* ☎ *239/695–2099* ⏲ *Weekdays 8–10 and noon–4, Sat. 10–11:30.*

WHERE TO EAT

$ SEAFOOD 🍴 **Joanie's Blue Crab Cafe.** West of the nation's tiniest post office by a quarter mile or so, you'll find this red barn of a place dishing out catfish, frogs' legs, gator, grouper, burgers, salads, and (no surprise here) an abundance of soft-shell crabs, crab cakes, and she-crab soup. Entrées run from around $15 and up, and peanut butter pie makes for a solid finish. Grab an icy beer from the cooler or order wine by the glass and eat out front or on the back patio—keep an eye out for Gertrude, a neighborhood gator on the loose. Joanie's doors are open from 11 am to 5 pm, so don't be late for supper, and don't be surprised if there's some live entertainment. [$] *Average main: $13* ✉ *39395 Tamiami Trail, Ochopee* ✣ *About 3.5 miles east of Hwy. 29, less than a mile west of Ochopee post office* ☎ *239/695–2682* 🌐 *www.joaniesbluecrabcafe.com* ⏲ *Closed Mon. (varies seasonally; call to confirm).*

SPORTS AND THE OUTDOORS

There are three types of trails—walking (including part of the extensive Florida National Scenic Trail), canoeing, and bicycling. All three trail types are easily accessed from the Tamiami Trail near the preserve visitor center, and one boardwalk trail departs from the center. Canoe and bike equipment can be rented from outfitters in Everglades City, 24 miles west, and Naples, 40 miles west.

Hikers can tackle the Florida National Scenic Trail, which begins in the preserve and is divided into segments 6.5 to 28 miles each. Two 5-mile trails, Concho Billy and Fire Prairie, can be accessed off Turner River Road, a few miles east. Turner River Road and Birdon Road form a 17-mile gravel loop drive that's excellent for birding. Bear Island has about 32 miles of scenic, flat, looped trails that are ideal for bicycling. Most trails are hard-packed lime rock, but a few miles are gravel. Cyclists share the road with off-road vehicles, most plentiful from mid-November through December.

To see the best variety of wildlife from your vehicle, follow 26-mile Loop Road, south of U.S. 41 and west of Shark Valley, where alligators, raccoons, and soft-shell turtles crawl around beside the gravel road, often swooped upon by swallowtail kites and brown-shouldered hawks. Stop at H. P. Williams Roadside Park, west of the Oasis, and walk along the boardwalk to spy gators, turtles, and garfish in the river waters.

RANGER PROGRAMS

From the Oasis Visitor Center you can get in on the seasonal ranger-led or self-guided activities, such as campfire and wildlife talks, hikes, slough slogs, and canoe excursions. The 8-mile Turner River Canoe Trail begins nearby and crosses through Everglades National Park before ending in Chokoloskee Bay, near Everglades City. Rangers lead four-hour canoe trips and two-hour swamp walks in season; call for days and times. Bring shoes and long pants for swamp walks and be prepared to wade at least knee-deep in water. Ranger program reservations are accepted up to 14 days in advance.

BISCAYNE NATIONAL PARK

Occupying 172,000 acres along the southern portion of Biscayne Bay, south of Miami and north of the Florida Keys, Biscayne National Park is 95% submerged, its terrain ranging from 4 feet above sea level to 60 feet below. Contained within are four distinct zones: Biscayne Bay, undeveloped upper Florida Keys, coral reefs, and coastal mangrove forest. Mangroves line mainland shores much as they do elsewhere along South Florida's protected waters. Biscayne Bay serves as a lobster sanctuary and a nursery for fish, sponges, crabs, and other sea life. Manatees and sea turtles frequent its warm, shallow waters. The park hosts legions of boaters and landlubbers gazing in awe over the bay.

GETTING HERE

To reach Biscayne National Park from Homestead, take Krome Avenue to Route 9336 (Palm Drive) and turn east. Follow Palm Drive about 8 miles until it becomes Southwest 344th Street, and follow signs to park headquarters in Convoy Point. The entry is 9 miles east of Homestead and 9 miles south and east of Exit 6 (Speedway Boulevard/Southwest 137th Avenue) off Florida's Turnpike.

PARK ESSENTIALS

Admission Fees There's no fee to enter Biscayne National Park, and you don't pay a fee to access the islands, but there's a $20 overnight camping fee that includes a $5 dock charge to berth vessels at some island docks. The park concession charges for trips to the coral reefs and islands.

Admission Hours The park is open daily, year-round.

Contacts Biscayne National Park ⊠ *Dante Fascell Visitor Center, 9700 S.W. 328th St., Homestead* ☎ *305/230-7275* ⊕ *www.nps.gov/bisc.*

EXPLORING

Biscayne is a magnet for diving, snorkeling, canoeing, birding, and, to some extent (if you have a private boat), camping. Elliott Key is the best place to hike.

Biscayne's corals range from soft, flagellant fans, plumes, and whips found chiefly in shallow patch reefs to the hard brain corals, elkhorn, and staghorn forms that can withstand depths and heavier shoreline wave action.

To the east, about 8 miles off the coast, 44 tiny keys stretch 18 nautical miles north to south, and are reached only by boat. No mainland commercial transportation operates to the islands, and only a handful are accessible: Elliott, Boca Chita, Adams, and Sands keys, lying between Elliott and Boca Chita. The rest are wildlife refuges or have rocky shores or waters too shallow for boats. December through April, when

the mosquito population is less aggressive, is the best time to explore. Bring repellent, sunscreen, and water.

Adams Key. A stone's throw from the western tip of Elliott Key and 9 miles southeast of Convoy Point, the island is open for day use. It was the onetime site of the Cocolobo Club, a yachting retreat known for hosting presidents Harding, Hoover, Johnson, and Nixon as well as other famous and infamous luminaries. Hurricane Andrew blew away what remained of club facilities in 1992. Adams Key has picnic areas with grills, restrooms, dockage, and a short trail running along the shore and through a hardwood hammock. Rangers live on-island. Access is by private boat, with no pets or overnight docking allowed. ⊕ *www. nps.gov/bisc/planyourvisit/adamskey.*

Boca Chita Key. Ten miles northeast of Convoy Point and about 12 miles south of the Cape Florida Lighthouse on Key Biscayne, this key once was owned by the late Mark C. Honeywell, former president of Honeywell Company, and is on the National Register of Historic Places for its 10 historic structures. A half-mile hiking trail curves around the island's south side. Climb the 65-foot-high ornamental lighthouse (by ranger tour only) for a panoramic view of Miami or check out the cannon from the HMS *Fowey.* There's no freshwater, access is by private boat only, and no pets are allowed. Only portable toilets are on-site, with no sinks or showers. A $20 fee for overnight docking (6 pm to 6 am) covers a campsite; pay at the harbor's automated kiosk.

FAMILY **Dante Fascell Visitor Center.** Go outside on the wide veranda to soak up views across mangroves and Biscayne Bay at this Convoy Point visitor center. Inside the museum, artistic vignettes and on-request videos including the 11-minute *Spectrum of Life* explore the park's four ecosystems, while the Touch Table gives both kids and adults a feel for bones, feathers, and coral. Facilities include the park's canoe and tour concession, restrooms with showers, a ranger information area, gift shop with books, and vending machines. Various ranger programs take place daily during busy fall and winter seasons. Rangers give informal tours on Boca Chita key, but these must be arranged in advance. A short trail and boardwalk lead to a jetty, and there are picnic tables and grills. This is the only area of the park accessible without a boat. ⊠ *9700 S.W. 328th St., Homestead* ☎ *305/230–7275* ⊕ *www.nps.gov/ bisc* ⊠ *Free* ⊙ *Daily 9–5.*

Elliott Key. The largest of the islands, 9 miles east of Convoy Point, Elliott Key has a mile-long loop trail on the bay side at the north end of the campground. Boaters may dock at any of 36 slips (call ahead; Hurricane Sandy forced closure of the boardwalk and harbor in 2012, and at this writing docks remained closed). Head out on your own to hike the 6-mile trail along so-called Spite Highway, a 225-foot-wide swath of green that developers mowed down in hopes of linking this key to the mainland. Luckily the federal government stepped in, and now it's a hiking trail through tropical hardwood hammock. Facilities include restrooms, picnic tables, fresh drinking water, cold (occasionally lukewarm) showers, grills, and a campground. Leashed pets are allowed in developed areas only, not on trails. A 30-foot-wide sandy shoreline about a mile north of the harbor on the west (bay) side of the key is the only one in the national park, and boaters like to anchor off here to swim. You can fish (check on license requirements) from the maintenance dock south of the harbor. The beach, fun for families, is for day use only; it has picnic areas and a short trail that cuts through the hammock.

SPORTS AND THE OUTDOORS

BIRD-WATCHING

More than 170 species of birds have been identified in and around the park. Expect to see flocks of brown pelicans patrolling the bay—suddenly rising, then plunging beak first to capture prey in their baggy pouches. White ibis probe exposed mudflats for small fish and crustaceans. Although all the Keys are excellent for birding, Jones Lagoon (south of Adams Key, between Old Rhodes Key and Totten Key) is outstanding. It's approachable only by nonmotorized craft.

DIVING AND SNORKELING

Diving is great year-around but best in summer, when calmer winds and smaller seas result in clearer waters. Ocean waters, 3 miles east of the Keys, showcase the park's main attraction—the northernmost section of Florida's living tropical coral reefs. Some are the size of an office desk, others as large as a football field. Glass-bottom-boat rides, when operating, showcase this underwater wonderland, but you really should snorkel or scuba dive to fully appreciate it.

> **BISCAYNE IN ONE DAY**
>
> Most visitors come to snorkel or dive. Divers should plan to spend the morning on the water and the afternoon exploring the visitor center. The opposite is true for snorkelers, as snorkel trips (and one-tank shallow-dive trips) depart in the afternoon. If you want to hike as well, turn to the trails at Elliott Key—just be sure to apply insect repellent (and sunscreen, too, no matter what time of year).

A diverse population of colorful fish—angelfish, gobies, grunts, parrotfish, pork fish, wrasses, and many more—flits through the reefs. Shipwrecks from the 18th century are evidence of the area's international maritime heritage, and a Maritime Heritage Trail has been developed to link six of the major shipwreck and underwater cultural sites including the Fowey Rocks Lighthouse, built in 1878. Sites, including a 19th-century wooden sailing vessel, have been plotted with GPS coordinates and marked with mooring buoys.

WHAT'S NEARBY

EVERGLADES CITY

35 miles southeast of Naples and 83 miles west of Miami.

Aside from a chain gas station or two, Everglades City retains its Old Florida authenticity. No high-rises (other than an observation tower named for pioneer Ernest Hamilton) mar the landscape at this western gateway to Everglades National Park, just off the Tamiami Trail. Everglades City was developed in the late 19th century by Barron Collier, a wealthy advertising entrepreneur, who built it as a company town to house workers for his numerous projects, including construction of the Tamiami Trail. It grew and prospered until the Depression and World War II. Today this ramshackle town draws adventure seekers heading to the park for canoeing, fishing, and bird-watching excursions. Airboat tours, though popular, are banned within the park because of the environmental damage they cause to the mangroves. The Everglades Seafood Festival, launched in 1970 and held the first full weekend of February, draws huge crowds for delights from the sea, music, and craft displays. At quieter times, dining choices center on a handful of rustic eateries big on seafood. The town is small, fishing-oriented, and unhurried, making it excellent for boating, bicycling, or just strolling around. You can pedal along the waterfront on a 2-mile strand out to Chokoloskee Island.

VISITOR INFORMATION

Everglades Area Chamber of Commerce Welcome Center. Pick up brochures and pamphlets for area lodging, restaurants, and attractions here, and ask for additional information from friendly staffers. Open daily 9 to 4. ⊠ *32016 E. Tamiami Trail, at Rte. 29* ☎ *239/695–3941* ⊕ *www. evergladeschamber.net.*

EXPLORING

OFF THE
BEATEN
PATH

Collier-Seminole State Park. Opportunity to try biking, hiking, camping, and canoeing in Everglades territory makes this park a prime introduction to this often forbidding land. Of historical interest, a Seminole War blockhouse has been re-created to hold the interpretative center, and one of the "walking dredges"—a towering black machine invented to carve the Tamiami Trail out of the muck—stands silent on grounds amid tropical hardwood forest. Campsites (closed at this writing but planned to reopen with upgraded facilities by 2016, so call first). ⊠ *20200 E. Tamiami Trail, Naples* ☎ *239/394–3397* ⊕ *www.floridastateparks.org/ collier-seminole* ☞ *$5 per car, $4 with lone driver, $2 for pedestrians or bikers* ☉ *Daily 8–sunset.*

Fakahatchee Strand Preserve State Park. The half-mile Big Cypress Bend boardwalk through this linear swamp forest provides opportunity to see rare plants, nesting eagles, and Florida's largest stand of native royal palms co-existing—unique to Fakahatchee Strand—with bald cypress under the forest canopy. Fakahatchee Strand, about 20 miles long and 5 miles wide, is also the orchid and bromeliad capital of the continent with 44 native orchids and 14 native bromeliads, many blooming most extravagantly in hotter months. It's particularly famed for its ghost orchids (as featured in Susan Orlean's novel *The Orchid Thief*), visible on guided hikes. In your quest for ghost orchids, keep alert for white-tailed deer, black bears, bobcats, and the Florida panther. For park nature on parade, take the 12-mile-long (one-way) W. J. Janes Memorial Scenic Drive, (deposit your admission fee at the honor box; have exact change). Hike its spur trails if you have time. Rangers lead swamp walks and canoe trips November through April. ⊠ *Boardwalk on north*

Native plants along the Turner River Canoe Trail hem paddlers in on both sides, and alligators lurk nearby.

side of Tamiami Trail, 7 miles west of Rte. 29; W. J. Janes Scenic Dr., ¾ mile north of Tamiami Trail on Rte. 29; ranger station on W. J. Janes Scenic Dr., 137 Coastline Dr., Copeland ☎ 239/695–4593 ⊕ www. floridastateparks.org/fakahatcheestrand ✉ Free; W. J. Janes Memorial Scenic Drive $3 per car, $2 per motorcycle ☉ Daily 8 am–sunset.

Florida Panther National Wildlife Refuge. When this refuge opened in 1989, it was off-limits to the public to protect endangered cougar subspecies. In 2005, responding to public demand, the 26,400-acre refuge opened two short loop trails in a region lightly traveled by panthers so visitors could get tastes of wet prairies, tropical hammocks, and pine uplands where panthers roam and wild orchids thrive. The 1.3-mile trail is rugged and often thigh-high under water during summer and fall; it's closed when completely flooded. The shorter 0.3-mile Leslie M. Duncan Memorial Trail is wheelchair-accessible and open year-round. For either, bring drinking water and insect repellent. Sightings are rare, but you may spot deer, black bears, and the occasional panther—or their tracks. ⊠ Off Rte. 29, between U.S. 41 and I–75 ☎ 239/353–8442 ⊕ www.fws.gov/floridapanther ✉ Free ☉ Daily dawn–dusk; trails may be closed July–Nov. because of rain.

Museum of the Everglades. Through artifacts and photographs you can meet American Indians, pioneers, entrepreneurs, and anglers playing pivotal roles in southwest Florida development. Exhibits and a short film chronicle the tremendous feat of building the Tamiami Trail across mosquito-ridden, gator-infested Everglades wetlands. Permanent displays and monthly exhibits rotate works of local artists. The small museum is housed in the Laundry Building, completed in 1927 and once used for washing linens from the Rod and Gun Club and Everglades Inn. ✉ *105 W. Broadway* ☎ *239/695–0008* 🎟 *Free* 🕒 *Tues.–Sat. 9–4.*

WHERE TO EAT

$$ SEAFOOD 🍴 **Everglades Seafood Depot.** Count on tasty, affordable meals in a scenic setting at this storied 1928 Spanish-style stucco structure fronting Lake Placid. Beginning life as the original Everglades train depot, the building later was deeded to the University of Miami for marine research and appeared in the 1958 film *Winds across the Everglades* (starring Christopher Plummer, Peter Falk, Gypsy Rose Lee, and Burl Ives). Seafood is the only star here now, including lobster, frogs' legs, crab, and alligator. Steak, seafood, and combo entrées include salad or soup, or an extra-charge option for a salad bar with steamed shrimp. All-you-can-eat specials—fried chicken, a taco bar, or a seafood buffet—are staged on selected nights. Save room for "secret family recipe" coconut guava cake. If you'd like a view, ask for a back porch table or a lakeside window seat. The "you hook it, we cook it" is $9.99 [$] *Average main: $20* ✉ *102 Collier Ave.* ☎ *239/695–0075* 🌐 *www.evergladesseafooddepot.com.*

$ CUBAN 🍴 **Havana Cafe.** Cuban specialties are a tasty alternative from the seafood houses of Everglades City. This cheery eatery with a dozen or so tables inside, has more seating on the porch. Service is order-at-the-counter for breakfast and lunch (7 am–3 pm), with dinner in season on Friday and Saturday nights. Jump-start your day with *café con leche* and a pressed-egg sandwich, or try a Havana omelet. For lunch, you'll find the ubiquitous Cuban sandwich, burgers, shrimp, grouper, steak, and pork plates with rice and beans and yucca. For take-home zing, try Carlos' Havana Cafe Hot Sauce. [$] *Average main: $15* ✉ *191 Smallwood Dr., Chocoloskee* ☎ *239/695–2214* 🌐 *www.myhavanacafe.com* 💳 *No credit cards* 🕒 *No dinner Apr.–Oct.; no dinner Sun.–Thurs. Nov.–Mar.*

$$ SEAFOOD FAMILY 🍴 **Oyster House Restaurant.** One of the town's oldest fish houses, Oyster House serves all the local staples—shrimp, gator tail, frogs' legs, oysters, stone crab, and grouper—in a lodgelike setting with mounted wild game on walls and rafters. Deep-frying remains an art in these parts, so if you're going to indulge, do it here where you can create your own fried platter for under $30. Try to dine at sunset for golden rays with your watery view. Outside, the 75-foot observation tower named for the late pioneer Ernest Hamilton affords a terrific overview of the Ten Thousand Islands. [$] *Average main: $20* ✉ *901 S. Copeland Ave.* ☎ *239/695–2073* 🌐 *www.oysterhouserestaurant.com.*

$$$ SEAFOOD 🍴 **Rod and Gun Club.** Striking, polished pecky-cypress woodwork in this historic building dates from the 1920s, when wealthy hunters, anglers, and yachting parties arrived for the winter season. Presidents Hoover, Roosevelt, Truman, Eisenhower, and Nixon stopped by here, as have Ernest Hemingway, Burt Reynolds, and Mick Jagger. The main dining room holds overflow from the expansive screened porch overlooking the river. Like life in general here, friendly servers move slowly and upkeep is minimal. Fresh seafood dominates, from stone crab in season (October 15–May 15) to a surf-and-turf combo of steak and grouper or a swamp-and-turf duet of frogs' legs and steak (each around $30), or pasta pairings, from $20 or so. For $14.95 you can have your

own catch fried, broiled, or blackened, served with salad, veggies, and potato. Pie choices are key lime and chocolate–peanut butter. Separate checks are discouraged at this cash-only venue, and there's a $5 plate-sharing charge. Yesteryear's main lobby is well worth a look—even if you're eating elsewhere. Arrive by boat or land. $ *Average main: $25* ⊠ *200 Riverside Dr.* ☎ *239/695–2101* ⊕ *www.evergladesrodandgun. com* ▬ *No credit cards* ☺ *Sometimes shuts down in summer. Call ahead.*

$ ✕ **Triad Seafood.** Along the Barron River, seafood houses, fishing boats,
SEAFOOD and crab traps populate one shoreline; mangroves the other. Selling fresh off the boat, some seafood houses added picnic tables and eventually grew into restaurants. Family-owned Triad Seafood Market & Cafe is one, with a screened dining area and additional outdoor seating under a breezeway and on a deck (heated in winter) overhanging the river. Here you can savor fresh seafood at its finest, or have it shipped. It's nothing fancy (although smoked fish and oyster Caesar salad are on the menu), but you'd be hard-pressed to find a better grouper sandwich. Fried green tomatoes are tasty, too. An all-you-can-eat fresh stone crab feast with butter or mustard sauce (October 15 to May 15; market prices fluctuate wildly and can be over $100) can thin your wallet, especially for the jumbos. Lunch starts at 11 am with fried shrimp, oyster, crab cake, and soft-shell blue crab baskets, plus Reubens, Philly cheesesteaks, burgers, and inexpensive kid meals. $ *Average main: $15* ⊠ *401 School Dr.* ☎ *239/695–0722* ⊕ *www.triadseafoodmarketcafe. com* ☺ *Closed May 16–Oct. 15.*

WHERE TO STAY

$ ⚏ **Glades Haven Cozy Cabins.** Bob Miller wanted to build a Holiday Inn
HOTEL next to his Oyster House Restaurant on marina-channel shores, but when that didn't fly, he sent for cabin kits and set up mobile-home-size units around a pool on his property as part of "Miller's World." **Pros:** great nearby food options; convenient to ENP boating; free docking; marina. **Cons:** trailer-park crowded feel with a noisy bar nearby; no phones, no pets. $ *Rooms from: $99* ⊠ *801 Copeland Ave.* ☎ *239/695–2746, 888/956–6251* ⊕ *www.gladeshaven.com* ⏎ *24 cabins, 2 3-bedroom houses* ⦿ *No meals.*

$ ⚏ **Ivey House.** A remodeled 1928 boardinghouse built for crews work-
B&B/INN ing on the Tamiami Trail, Ivey House (originally operated by Mr. and
Fodor's Choice Mrs. Ivey) now fits adventurers on assorted budgets. **Pros:** historic;
★ pleasant; affordable. **Cons:** not on water; some small rooms. $ *Rooms from: $169* ⊠ *107 Camellia St.* ☎ *877/567–0679, 239/695–3299* ⊕ *www.iveyhouse.com* ⏎ *30 rooms, 18 with bath; 1 2-bedroom cottage* ⦿ *Breakfast.*

SPORTS AND THE OUTDOORS

AIR TOURS

Wings Ten Thousand Islands Aero Tours. These 20-minute to nearly two-hour flightseeing tours of the Ten Thousand Islands National Wildlife Refuge, Big Cypress National Preserve, Everglades National Park, and Gulf of Mexico operate November through April. Aboard an Alaskan Bush plane, you can see saw-grass prairies, American Indian shell mounds, alligators, and wading birds. Rates start at $50 and go up to

$120 for a two-hour Everglades tour (per person with groups of three or four). Flights also can be booked to the Keys, connecting to the Dry Tortugas. ⌧ *Everglades Airpark, 650 Everglades City Airpark Rd.* ☎ *239/695–3296.*

BOATING AND CANOEING

On the Gulf Coast explore the nooks, crannies, and mangrove islands of Chokoloskee Bay and Ten Thousand Islands National Wildlife Refuge, as well as rivers near Everglades City. The Turner River Canoe Trail, popular and populated even on Christmas as a pleasant day trip with almost guaranteed bird and alligator sightings, passes through mangrove tunnels, dwarf cypress, coastal prairie, and freshwater slough ecosystems of Everglades National Park and Big Cypress National Preserve.

Glades Haven Marina. Access Ten Thousand Islands waters in a 19-foot Sundance or a 17-foot Flicker fishing boat. Rates start at $200 a day, plus fuel, with half-day and hourly options. The outfitter also rents kayaks and canoes and has a 24-hour boat ramp and dockage for up to 24-foot vessels. Launch your own boat for $15, a canoe or kayak for $5. ⌧ *801 Copeland Ave. S* ☎ *239/695–2628* ⊕ *www.gladeshaven.com.*

FLORIDA CITY

3 miles southwest of Homestead on U.S. 1.

Florida's Turnpike ends in Florida City, the southernmost town on the Miami-Dade County mainland, spilling thousands of vehicles onto U.S. 1 and eventually west to Everglades National Park, east to Biscayne National Park, or south to the Florida Keys. Florida City and Homestead run into each other, but the difference couldn't be more noticeable. As the last outpost before 18 miles of mangroves and water, this stretch of U.S. 1 is lined with fast-food eateries, service stations, hotels, bars, dive shops, and restaurants. Hotel rates increase significantly during NASCAR races at the nearby Homestead-Miami Speedway. Like Homestead, Florida City is rooted in agriculture, with expanses of farmland west of Krome Avenue and a huge farmers' market that ships produce nationwide.

GETTING HERE AND AROUND

Super Shuttle. This 24-hour service runs air-conditioned vans between MIA and the Homestead-Florida City area; pickup is outside baggage claim and costs around $60 per person depending on your destination zip code. For a return to MIA, reserve 24 hours in advance and know your pickup zip code for a price quote. ☎ *305/871–2000* ⊕ *www. supershuttle.com.*

EXPLORING

Tropical Everglades Visitor Center. Run by the nonprofit Tropical Everglades Visitor Association, this pastel pink center with teal signage offers abundant printed material plus tips from volunteer experts on exploring South Florida, especially Homestead, Florida City, and the Florida Keys. ⌧ *160 U.S. 1* ☎ *305/245–9180, 800/388–9669* ⊕ *www. tropicaleverglades.com.*

WHERE TO EAT

$ SEAFOOD 🍴 **Farmers' Market Restaurant.** Although this eatery is within the farmers' market on the edge of town and is big on serving fresh vegetables, seafood figures prominently on the menu. A family of anglers runs the place, so fish and shellfish are only hours from the sea, and there's a fish fry on Friday nights. Catering to farmers, the restaurant opens at 5:30 am, serving pancakes and fluffy omelets with home fries or grits in a pleasant dining room with red and green checked tablecloths. For lunch or dinner, choose among fried shrimp or conch, seafood pasta, country-fried steak, and roast turkey, as well as salads, burgers, and sandwiches. [$] *Average main: $13* ✉ *300 N. Krome Ave.* ☎ *305/242–0008.*

$$ SEAFOOD 🍴 **Mutineer Wharf Restaurant.** Families and older couples flock to this kitschy roadside outpost with a fish-and-duck pond. Built in 1980 to look like a ship—back when Florida City barely got on maps—etched glass divides bi-level dining rooms, with velvet-upholstered chairs, an aquarium, and nautical antiques. Florida lobster tails, stuffed grouper, shrimp, and snapper top the menu, along with another half dozen daily seafood specials. Add to that steaks, ribs, and chicken. Yellowfin tuna wraps and grouper sandwiches are filling items for lunch, especially before heading to Everglades Park. You also can relax for dinner in the restaurant's Wharf Lounge, sometimes with live entertainment on Friday and Saturday nights. [$] *Average main: $20* ✉ *11 S.E. 1st Ave. (U.S. 1), at Palm Dr.* ☎ *305/245–3377* 🌐 *www.mutineerrestaurant.com.*

WHERE TO STAY

$ HOTEL 🏨 **Best Western Gateway to the Keys.** For easy access to Everglades and Biscayne national parks as well as the Keys, you'll be well situated at this sprawling, two-story motel two blocks off Florida's Turnpike. **Pros:** convenient to parks, outlet shopping, and dining; business services; attractive pool area. **Cons:** traffic noise; fills up fast in high season. [$] *Rooms from: $135* ✉ *411 S. Krome Ave.* ☎ *305/246–5100, 888/981–5100* 🌐 *www.bestwestern.com/gatewaytothekeys* 🛏 *114 rooms* 🍽 *Breakfast.*

$ HOTEL 🏨 **Econo Lodge.** Close to Florida's Turnpike and with access to the Keys, this is a serviceable overnight pullover spot with complimentary WiFi in public spaces and breakfast. **Pros:** laundry facility on property; pool; proximity to mall outlet shopping. **Cons:** urban-ugly location; noisy. [$] *Rooms from: $89* ✉ *553 N.E. 1st Ave.* ☎ *305/248–9300, 800/553–2666* 🌐 *www.econolodge.com* 🛏 *42 rooms* 🍽 *Breakfast.*

$ HOTEL 🏨 **Fairway Inn.** With a waterfall pool, this two-story motel with exterior room entry has some of the area's lowest chain rates, and it's next to the Chamber of Commerce visitor center so you'll have easy access to tourism brochures and other information. **Pros:** affordable; convenient to restaurants, parks, and raceway. **Cons:** plain, small rooms; no-pet policy. [$] *Rooms from: $89* ✉ *100 S.E. 1st Ave.* ☎ *305/248–4202, 888/340–4734* 🛏 *160 rooms* 🍽 *Breakfast.*

$ HOTEL 🏨 **Quality Inn.** Amid an asphalt complex of hotels, gas stations, and eateries just off U.S. 1, this two-story Quality Inn with exterior corridors has a friendly front desk staff offering tips on Everglades or Keys adventures, or race action at the nearby track. **Pros:** close to restaurants and services. **Cons:** no elevator; noisy location. Ⓢ *Rooms from: $90* ✉ *333 S. E. 1st Ave.* ☎ *305/248–4009, 888/352–2489* ⊕ *www.qualityinn.com* ⤴ *123 rooms* ⏐◯⏐ *Breakfast.*

$ ☷ **Ramada Inn.** If you're seeking an uptick from other chains, this prop-
HOTEL   erty offers more amenities and comfort, such as 32-inch flat-screen TVs, duvet-covered beds, closed closets, and stylish furnishings. **Pros:** extra room amenities; convenient location. **Cons:** chain anonymity. Ⓢ *Rooms from: $99* ✉ *124 E. Palm Dr.* ☎ *305/247–8833* ⊕ *www.hotelfloridacity. com* ⤴ *118 rooms* ⏐◯⏐ *Breakfast.*

SHOPPING

FAMILY   **Robert Is Here.** Want take-home gifts? This remarkable fruit stand sells more than 100 types of jams, jellies, honeys, and salad dressings along with its vegetables, juices, fabulous fresh-fruit milk shakes (try the papaya key lime or guanabana, under $6), and some 30 kinds of tropi-cal fruits, including (in season) carambola, lychee, egg fruit, monstera, sapodilla, dragonfruit, genipa, sugar apple, and tamarind. Back in 1960, the stand got started when pint-size Robert sat at this spot hawking his father's bumper cucumber crop. Now Robert (still on the scene daily with wife and kids), ships nationwide and donates seconds to needy area families. An assortment of animals out back—goats to iguanas and emus, along with a splash pool—creates entertainment value for youngsters. Picnic tables, benches, and a waterfall with a koi pond add serenity. On the way to Everglades National Park, Robert opens at 8 am, operating until at least 7, and shutting down from Labor Day until November. ✉ *19200 S. W. 344th St.* ☎ *305/246–1592.*

HOMESTEAD

30 miles southwest of Miami.

Since recovering from Hurricane Andrew in 1992, Homestead has rede-fined itself as a destination for tropical agro- and ecotourism. At a cross-roads between Miami and the Keys as well as Everglades and Biscayne national parks, the area has the added dimension of shopping cen-ters, residential development, hotel chains, and the Homestead-Miami Speedway—when car races are scheduled, hotels hike rates and require minimum stays. The historic downtown has become a preservation-driven Main Street. Krome Avenue, where it cuts through the city's heart, is lined with restaurants, an arts complex, antiques shops, and low-budget, sometimes undesirable, accommodations. West of north–south Krome Avenue, miles of fields grow fresh fruits and vegetables. Some are harvested commercially, and others beckon with "U-pick" signs. Stands selling farm-fresh produce and nurseries that grow and sell orchids and tropical plants abound. In addition to its agricultural legacy, the town has an eclectic flavor, attributable to its population mix: descendants of pioneer Crackers, Hispanic growers and farm workers, professionals escaping the Miami hubbub, and latter-day northern retirees.

EXPLORING

Fruit & Spice Park. Because it officially qualifies for tropical status, this 37-acre park in Homestead's Redland historic agricultural district is the only public botanical garden of its type in the United States. More than 500 varieties of fruit, nuts, and spices typically grow here, and there are 75 varieties of bananas alone, plus 160 of mango. Tram tours (included in admission) run three times daily, and you can sample fresh fruit at the gift shop, which also stocks canned and dried fruits plus cookbooks. The Mango Café, open daily, serves mango salsa, smoothies, and shakes along with salads, wraps, sandwiches, and a yummy Mango Passion Cheesecake. Picnic in the garden at provided tables or on your own blankets. Annual park events include January's Redland Heritage Festival and June's Summer Fruit Festival. Kids age six and under are free. ✉ *24801 S.W. 187th Ave.* ☎ *305/247–5727* 🌐 *www.fruitandspicepark.org* 🎟 *$8* 🕓 *Daily 9–5; guided tram tours at 11, 1:30, and 3.*

Schnebly Redland's Winery. Homestead's fruity bounty comes in liquid form at this growing enterprise that began producing wines of lychee, mango, guava, and other fruits as a way to avoid waste from family groves each year—bounty not perfect enough for shipping. Over the years, this grape-free winery (now with a beer brewery, too) has expanded with a reception/tasting indoor area serving snacks and a lush plaza picnic area landscaped in coral rock, tropical plants, and waterfalls—topped with an Indian thatched chickee roof. Tours and tastings are offered daily. The Ultimate Tasting includes five wines, and an etched Schnebly glass you can keep. On Sunday, there's yoga on the lawn. Count on a cover charge of $10 per person after 6 pm on Friday and Saturday nights. ✉ *30205 S.W. 217th Ave.* ☎ *305/242–1224, 888/717–9463* 🌐 *www.schneblywinery.com* 🎟 *Winery tours (weekends only) $7; tastings $11.95* 🕓 *Mon.–Thurs. 10–5, Fri. and Sat. 10–11, Sun. noon–5.*

WHERE TO EAT

$$ ITALIAN FAMILY

🍴 **The Big Cheese.** With ya-can't-miss cheesy yellow frontage beckoning for seating up to 185 folks inside, The Big Cheese of Homestead (an offshoot of the South Miami original) serves up a wide variety of Italian-style sustenance, from pizza, calzones, subs, and salads to pastas like baked ziti or spinach lasagna and pasta-seafood dishes like linguine with white clam sauce (or red), shrimp al forno, or mussels marinara. Dolly's Special (spaghetti with fresh mushrooms and grilled chicken) is named after a favored Homestead local. Dinners come in half- or full-size orders. There's beer and wine to slake your thirst, with handcrafted brews made in or near in the Redlands. Kid's menu meals (fingers, wings, pasta, shrimp, etc.) include a soda. Eat in at tables or booths seating six or so, or order for takeout or delivery. [$] *Average main: $18* ✉ *350 N. Homestead Dr.* ☎ *305/247–0657* 🌐 *www.bigcheesehomestead.com.*

$ SOUTHERN

🍴 **Momma D's Kountry Kitchen.** For Southern home-style cooking with breakfast all day, head to Momma D's Kountry Kitchen, previously known as Bobbie Jo's and as of early 2015 under new ownership. (The sign may still say "Bobbi Jo's" so don't be confused.) Dinners—including chicken livers, chicken and dumplings, and fried clams—come with

Are baby alligators more to your liking than their daddies? You can pet one at Gator Park.

fresh-baked corn bread and a daily selection of sides such as okra with tomatoes, turnip greens, pickled beets, or onion rings. Don't miss out on the changing lineup of homemade soups and desserts. All this goodness comes comparatively cheap, but at the expense of anything-but-glamorous dining environs at Formica tables and booths, with friendly service. $ *Average main: $10* ✉ *1320 N. Krome Ave.* ☎ *305/246–2990* ✆ *No dinner Sun.*

$ ✕ **Royal Palm Grill.** Don't feel bewildered if after passing Royal Palm Grill
AMERICAN   (within the Royal Palm Pharmacy) on Krome Avenue you have a deja vu moment when encountering another Royal Palm Grill just a hop-skip away. This popular "breakfast all day, every day" enterprise has two locations, only a few blocks apart, to accommodate a steady stream of customers for the aforementioned breakfast fare from omelets and pancakes to biscuits and gravy, plus salads, steaks, and seafood. A true throwback to yesteryear with booths and a counter near apothecary items, it's open seven days starting at 6:30 am but generally closes at either 4 (weekdays) or 3 (weekends). (Royal Palm's second location is at 436 North Krome Avenue, and it's open until 9 pm on weekdays.) $ *Average main: $10* ✉ *Royal Palm Pharmacy, 806 N. Krome Ave.* ☎ *305/246–5701* ⊕ *www.royalpalmgrill.com.*

$ ✕ **Shiver's BBQ.** Piggin' out since the 1960s, Shiver's ranks as a lip-
BARBECUE   smackin' must for lovers of hickory-smoked barbecued pork, beef and chicken in assorted forms from baby backs to briskets. Longtime owners Martha and Perry Curtis are typically on hand attending to traditions with original recipes, although Martha does offer her new, alternative "secret recipe" sauce. Be forewarned as you settle in at

picnic-style tables, Shiver's is no place to cut calories. BBQ cheese fries, BBQ potato skins, fried mac'n'cheese, fried mushrooms, and fried okra are for starters. You then can choose among platters, sandwiches, and sides, including the rib and chicken combo or BBQ short ribs and collard greens. The corn-bread soufflé draws raves, and there's also the hickory burger, Shiver burger, and what's known as the sausage bomb. For kids, fingers and bites await. A half dozen desserts include fried cheesecake. For feasting in the Everglades, you also can order takeout in bulk by the pound. $ *Average main: $15* ⊠ *28001 S. Dixie Hwy.* ☎ *305/248–2272* ⊕ *www.shiversbbq.com.*

WHERE TO STAY

$ 🏨 **Hotel Redland.** Of downtown Homestead's smattering of mom-and-
HOTEL   pop lodging options, this historic inn is by far the most desirable with its Victorian-style rooms done up in pastels and reproduction antique furniture. **Pros:** historic character; convenient to downtown and near antiques shops; well maintained; smoke-free. **Cons:** traffic noise; small rooms. $ *Rooms from: $120* ⊠ *5 S. Flagler Ave.* ☎ *305/246–1904, 800/595–1904* ⊕ *www.hotelredland.com* ⤴ *13 rooms* ❢◯❢ *No meals.*

SPORTS AND THE OUTDOORS

AUTO RACING

Homestead-Miami Speedway. Buzzing more than 280 days each year, the speedway hosts racing, manufacturer testing, car-club events, driving schools, and ride-along programs. The facility has 65,000 grandstand seats, club seating eight stories above racing action, and two tracks—a 2.21-mile continuous road course and a 1.5-mile oval. A packed schedule includes Grand-AM and NASCAR events. Two tunnels on the grounds are below sea level. ⊠ *1 Speedway Blvd.* ☎ *866/409–7223* ⊕ *www.homesteadmiamispeedway.com.*

WATER SPORTS

Homestead Bayfront Park. Boaters, anglers, and beachgoers give high ratings to facilities at this recreational area adjacent to Biscayne National Park. The 174-slip Herbert Hoover Marina, accommodating up to 50-foot vessels, has a ramp, dock, bait-and-tackle shop, fuel station, ice, and dry storage. The park also has a snack bar, tidal swimming area, a beach with lifeguards, playground, ramps for people with disabilities, and a picnic pavilion with grills, showers, and restrooms. ⊠ *9698 S.W. 328th St.* ☎ *305/230–3033* 🖙 *$7 per passenger vehicle; $12 per vehicle with boat Mon.–Thurs., $15 Fri.–Sun.; $15 per RV or bus* ☉ *Daily sunrise–sunset.*

TAMIAMI TRAIL

U.S. 41, between Naples and Miami.

An 80-mile stretch of U.S. 41 (known as the Tamiami Trail) traverses the Everglades, Big Cypress National Preserve, and Fakahatchee Strand Preserve State Park. The road was conceived in 1915 to link Miami to Fort Myers and Tampa. When it finally became a reality in 1928, it cut through the Everglades and altered the natural flow of water as well as the lives of the Miccosukee Indians who were trying mightily to eke out a living fishing, hunting, farming, and frogging here. The landscape is surprisingly varied, changing from hardwood hammocks to pinelands, then abruptly to tall cypress trees dripping with Spanish moss and back to saw-grass marsh. Slow down to take in the scenery and you'll likely be rewarded with glimpses of alligators sunning themselves along the banks of roadside canals and hundreds of waterbirds, especially in the dry winter season. The man-made landscape includes Native American villages, chickee huts, and airboats parked at roadside enterprises. Between Miami and Naples the road goes by several names, including Tamiami Trail, U.S. 41, 9th Street in Naples, and, at the Miami end, Southwest 8th Street. ■TIP➜ Businesses along the trail give their addresses based on either their distance from Krome Avenue, Florida's Turnpike, or Miami on the east coast or Naples on the west coast.

> ## CROCS OR GATORS?
>
> You can tell you're looking at a crocodile, not an alligator, if you can see its lower teeth protruding when those powerful jaws are shut. Gators are much darker in color—a grayish black—compared with the lighter tan shades of crocodiles. Alligator snouts—sort of U-shape—are also much broader than their long, thin A-shape crocodilian counterparts. South Florida is the world's only place where the two coexist in the wild. Alligators are primarily found in freshwater habitats, whereas crocodiles (better at expelling salt from water) are typically in coastal estuaries.

EXPLORING

Everglades Safari Park. A perennial favorite with tour-bus operators, this family-run park open 365 days has an arena, seating up to 300 for shows with alligator wrestling. Before and after, get a closer look at both alligators and crocodiles on Gator Island, follow a jungle trail, walk through a small wildlife museum, or board an airboat for a 35-minute ride on the River of Grass (included in admission). There's also a restaurant, gift shop, and an observation platform looking out over the Glades. Smaller, private airboats can be chartered for tours lasting 40 minutes to two hours. Check online for coupons and count on free parking. ⊠ *26700 S.W. 8th St., Miami* ✛ *15 miles west of Florida's Tpke.* ☎ *305/226–6923, 305/223–3804* ⊕ *www.evergladessafaripark. com* ☜ *$23* ⊗ *Daily 9–5, last tour departs 3:30.*

FAMILY **Gator Park.** Here you can get face-to-face with and even touch an alligator—albeit a baby one—during the park's Wildlife Show. You also can squirm in a "reptilium" of some 30 different venomous and nonpoisonous native snakes or learn about American Indians of the Everglades through a reproduction of a Miccosukee village. The park, open rain or shine, also has 35-minute airboat tours as well as a gift shop and restaurant serving fare from burgers to gator tail. ⊠ *24050 Tamiami Trail, Miami* ✛ *12 miles west of Florida's Tpke.* ☎ *305/559–2255, 800/559–2205* ⊕ *www.gatorpark.com* ☜ *Tours, wildlife show, airboat ride $22.99* ⊗ *Daily 9–5.*

FAMILY **Miccosukee Indian Village and Gift Shop.** Showcasing the skills and lifestyle of the Miccosukee Tribe of Florida, this cultural center offers craft demonstrations and insight into interaction with alligators. Narrated 30-minute airboat rides take you into the wilderness where natives hid after the Seminole Wars and Indian Removal Act of the mid-1800s. In modern times, many of the Miccosukee have relocated to this village along Tamiami Trail, but most still maintain their hammock farming and hunting camps. The museum shows two new films on tribal culture and displays chickee structures and artifacts. Guided tours run throughout the day, and a gift shop stocks dolls, apparel, silver jewelry, beadwork, and other handcrafts. The Miccosukee Everglades Music and Craft Festival, going strong for four decades, falls on a July weekend, and the 10-day Miccosukee Indian Arts Festival is in late December. ✉ *U.S. 41, just west of Shark Valley entrance, 25 miles west of Florida's Turnpike at MM 70, Miami* ☎ *305/552–8365* 🌐 *www.miccosukee.com* 🎟 *Village $10, airboat rides $16* 🕒 *Daily 9–5.*

3

WHERE TO EAT

$ AMERICAN 🍴 **Coopertown Restaurant.** Make this a pit stop for local color and cuisine fished straight from the swamp. Started in the early 1960s as a sandwich stand, this eatery inside an airboat concession storefront has long attracted the famous and the humbly hungry. New, improved washrooms are outside. Besides catfish and shrimp, house specialties are frogs' legs and alligator tail breaded in cornmeal and deep-fried, served with lemon wedges and Tabasco. Sandwich options include burgers, hot dogs, and grilled cheese. [$] *Average main: $14* ✉ *22700 S.W. 8th St., Miami* ✢ *11 miles west of Florida's Tpke.* ☎ *305/226–6048* 🌐 *www.coopertownairboats.com* 🕒 *No dinner.*

$ SOUTHWESTERN 🍴 **Miccosukee Restaurant.** For breakfast or lunch (or dinner until 9 pm, November–April), this roadside cafeteria a quarter mile from the Miccosukee Indian Village provides the best menu variety along Tamiami Trail in Everglades territory. Atmosphere comes from the view overlooking the River of Grass, friendly servers wearing traditional Miccosukee patchwork vests, and a mural depicting American Indian women cooking while men powwow. Catfish and frogs' legs are breaded and deep-fried. Besides pumpkin and Indian fry bread, you'll also find burgers, salads, and south-of-the-border dishes. The Miccosukee Platter (the most expensive thing on the menu) includes gator bites. [$] *Average main: $15* ✉ *U.S. 41, 18 miles west of Miccosukee Resort & Gaming; 25 miles west of Florida's Tpke., Miami* ☎ *305/894–2374* 🕒 *No dinner May–Oct.*

$ BARBECUE FAMILY 🍴 **Pit Bar-B-Q.** This old-fashioned roadside eatery along Tamiami Trail near Krome Avenue was launched in 1965 by the late Tommy Little, who wanted to provide easy access to cold drinks and rib-sticking fare for folks heading into or out of the Everglades. This recently spiffed up backwood heritage vision remains a popular, affordable family option. Order at the counter, grab your food, and eat at picnic tables on the screened porch or outdoors. Specialties include barbecued chicken and ribs with a tangy sauce, fries, coleslaw, and a fried biscuit, plus burgers, fish sandwiches, and wings of fire. The whopping double-decker beef or pork sandwich with slaw requires multiple napkins. Latin specialties include deep-fried pork and fried green plantains. Beer is by the bottle or pitcher. Locals flock here with kids on weekends for pony rides.

[$] *Average main: $12* ✉ *16400 S.W. 8th St., 5 miles west of Florida's Tpke., Miami* ☎ *305/226–2272* 🌐 *www.thepitbarbq.com.*

WHERE TO STAY

$ RESORT 🏨 **Miccosukee Resort & Gaming.** Like an oasis on the horizon of endless saw grass, this nine-story resort at the southeastern edge of the Everglades can't help but attract attention, even if you're not on the lookout for 24-hour gaming action. **Pros:** casino; most modern resort in these parts; golf. **Cons:** smoky lobby; hotel guests find parking lot fills with gamblers; feels incompatible with the Everglades. [$] *Rooms from: $149* ✉ *500 S.W. 177th Ave., Miami* ✢ *6 miles west of Florida's Tpke.* ☎ *305/925–2555, 877/242–6464* 🌐 *www.miccosukee.com* 🛏 *256 rooms, 46 suites* 🍴 *No meals.*

SPORTS AND THE OUTDOORS

BOAT TOURS

Many Everglades-area tours operate only in season, roughly November through April.

Coopertown Airboats. In business since 1945, the oldest airboat operator in the Everglades offers 35- to 40-minute tours ($23) that take you 9 miles to hammocks and alligator holes to see red-shouldered hawks or turtles. You also can book private charters of up to two hours. ✉ *22700 S.W. 8th St., Miami* ✢ *11 miles west of Florida's Tpke.* ☎ *305/226–6048* 🌐 *www.coopertownairboats.com.*

Everglades Alligator Farm. Open daily near the entrance to Everglades National Park, this working farm—home of the late 14-foot "Grandpa" gator (now mounted for display)—runs a 4-mile, 30-minute airboat tour with departures 25 minutes after the hour. The tour ($23) includes free hourly alligator, snake, and wildlife shows; or see only the gator farm and show ($15.50). Alligator feedings are at noon and 3 pm. Look for online coupons. ✉ *40351 S.W. 192nd Ave., Homestead* ☎ *305/247–2628* 🌐 *www.everglades.com.*

FAMILY **Wooten's Everglades Airboat Tours.** This classic Florida roadside attraction, now under new ownership, runs airboat tours (starting at $28 per person) through the Everglades for up to 22 people and swamp-buggy rides ($24 per person) through the Big Cypress Swamp for up to 25 passengers. Each lasts approximately 30 minutes. (Swamp-buggies are giant tractorlike vehicles with huge rubber wheels.) More personalized airboat tours on smaller boats, seating six to eight, last about an hour. An on-site animal sanctuary with a live gator show ($8) shelters the typical Everglades array of alligators, snakes, and other creatures. Some packages include an airboat ride, swamp-buggy adventure, and sanctuary access. Rates change frequently, but check out the website for combo packages. ✉ *32330 Tamiami Trail E, Ochopee* ✢ *1½ miles east of Rte. 29* ☎ *239/695–2781, 800/282–2781* 🌐 *www.wootenseverglades.com* 🕒 *Daily 8:30–5; last ride departs at 4:30.*

THE FLORIDA KEYS

4

Visit Fodors.com for advice, updates, and bookings

WELCOME TO THE FLORIDA KEYS

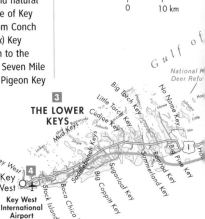

TOP REASONS TO GO

★ **John Pennekamp Coral Reef State Park:** A perfect introduction to the Florida Keys, this nature reserve offers snorkeling, diving, camping, and kayaking. An underwater highlight is the massive *Christ of the Deep* statue.

★ **Under the sea:** Whether you scuba dive, snorkel, or ride a glass-bottom boat, don't miss gazing at the coral reef and its colorful denizens.

★ **Sunset at Mallory Square:** Sure, it's touristy, but just once while you're here, you've got to witness the circuslike atmosphere of this nightly celebration.

★ **Duval crawl:** Shop, eat, drink, repeat. Key West's Duval Street and the nearby streets make a good day's worth of window-shopping and people-watching.

★ **Get on the water:** From angling for trophy-size fish to zipping out to the Dry Tortugas, a boat trip is in your future. It's really the whole point of the Keys.

1 The Upper Keys. As the doorstep to the islands' coral reefs and blithe spirit, the Upper Keys introduce all that's sporting and sea-oriented about the Keys. They stretch from Key Largo to the Long Key Channel (MM 105–65).

2 The Middle Keys. Centered on the town of Marathon, the Middle Keys hold most of the chain's historic and natural attractions outside of Key West. They go from Conch (pronounced *konk*) Key through Marathon to the south side of the Seven Mile Bridge, including Pigeon Key (MM 65–40).

3 The Lower Keys. Pressure drops another notch in this laid-back part of the region, where key-deer viewing and fishing reign supreme. The Lower Keys go from Little Duck Key west through Big Coppitt Key (MM 40–9).

4 Key West. The ultimate in Florida Keys craziness, this party town isn't for the closed-minded or those seeking a quiet retreat. The Key West area encompasses MM 9–0.

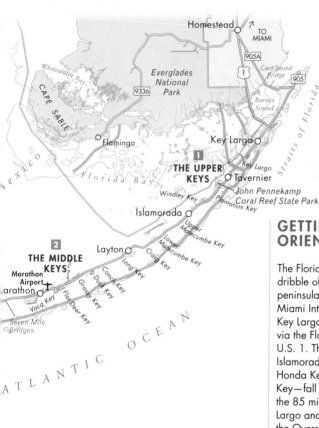

Homestead

TO MIAMI

905A

Card Sound Bridge

905

1

Everglades National Park

9336

Barnes Sound

Whitewater Bay

CAPE SABLE

Key Largo

Straits of Florida

Flamingo

1
THE UPPER KEYS

Key Largo

Tavernier

Windley Key

John Pennekamp Coral Reef State Park

Plantation Key

Islamorada

Upper Matecumbe Key

Lignumvitae

Lower Matecumbe Key

2
THE MIDDLE KEYS

Layton

Craig Key

Long Key

Conch Key

Duck Key

Grassy Key

Marathon Airport

arathon

Vaca Key

Fla. Deer Key

Seven Mile Bridges

ATLANTIC OCEAN

exico

Florida Bay

GETTING ORIENTED

The Florida Keys are the dribble of islands off the peninsula's southern tip. From Miami International Airport, Key Largo is a 56-mile drive via the Florida Turnpike and U.S. 1. The rest of the Keys— Islamorada, Marathon, Bahia Honda Key, and Big Pine Key—fall in succession for the 85 miles between Key Largo and Key West along the Overseas Highway. At their north end, the Florida Keys front Florida Bay, part of Everglades National Park. The Middle and Lower Keys front the Gulf of Mexico; the Atlantic Ocean borders the length of the chain on its eastern shores.

4

SEAFOOD IN THE FLORIDA KEYS

Fish. It's what's for dinner in the Florida Keys. The Keys' runway between the Gulf of Mexico or Florida Bay and Atlantic warm waters means fish of many fin. Restaurants take full advantage by serving it fresh, whether you caught it or a local fisherman did.

Menus at a number of colorful waterfront shacks such as **Snapper's** (⊠ *139 Seaside Ave., Key Largo* ☎ *305/852–5956*) in Key Largo and **Half Shell Raw Bar** (⊠ *231 Margaret St., Key West* ☎ *305/294–7496*) range from basic raw, steamed, broiled, grilled, or blackened fish to some Bahamian and New Orleans–style interpretations. Other seafood houses dress up their fish in creative haute cuisine styles, such as **Pierre's** (⊠ *MM 81.5 BS, Islamorada* ☎ *305/664–3225* ⊕ *www.pierres-restaurant.com*) hogfish meunière, or yellowtail snapper with pear-ricotta pasta purses with caponata and red pepper coulis at **Café Marquesa** (⊠ *600 Fleming St., Key West* ☎ *305/292–1244* ⊕ *www.marquesa.com*). Try a Keys-style breakfast of "grits and grunts"—fried fish and grits—at the **Stuffed Pig** (⊠ *3520 Overseas Hwy., Marathon* ☎ *305/743–4059*).

BUILT-IN FISH

You know it's fresh when you see a fish market as soon as you open the door to the restaurant where you're dining. It happens frequently in the Keys. You can even peruse the seafood showcases and pick the fish fillet or lobster tail you want.

Many of the Keys' best restaurants are found in marina complexes, where the commercial fishermen bring their catches straight from the sea. Those in **Stock Island** (one island north of Key West) and at **Keys Fisheries Market & Marina** (⊠ *MM 49 BS, end of 35th St., Marathon* ☎ *305/743-4353, 866/743-4353*) take some finding.

CONCH

One of the tastiest legacies of the Keys' Bahamian heritage (and most mispronounced), conch (pronounced *konk*) shows up on nearly every menu in some shape or form. It's so prevalent in local diets that natives refer to themselves as Conchs. Conch fritters are the most popular culinary manifestations, followed by cracked (pounded, breaded, and fried) conch, and conch salad, a ceviche-style refresher. Since the harvesting of queen conch is now illegal, most of the islands' conch comes from the Bahamas.

FLORIDA LOBSTER

Where are the claws? Stop looking for them: Florida spiny lobsters don't have 'em, never did. The sweet tail meat, however, makes up for the loss. Commercial and sport divers harvest these glorious crustaceans from late July through March. Check with local dive shops on restrictions, and then get ready for a fresh feast. Restaurants serve them broiled with drawn butter or in creative dishes such as lobster Benedict, lobster spring rolls, lobster Reuben, and lobster tacos.

GROUPER

Once central to Florida's trademark seafood dish—fried grouper sandwich—its populations have been overfished in recent years, meaning that the state has exerted more control over

bag regulations and occasionally closes grouper fishing on a temporary basis during the winter season. Some restaurants have gone antigrouper to try to bring back the abundance, but most grab it when they can. Black grouper is the most highly prized of the several varieties.

STONE CRAB

In season October 15 through May 15, it gets its name from its rock-hard shell. Fishermen take only one claw, which can regenerate in a sustainable manner. Connoisseurs prefer them chilled with tangy mustard sauce. Some restaurants give you a choice of hot claws and drawn butter, but this means the meat will be cooked twice, because it's usually boiled or steamed as soon as it's taken from its crab trap.

YELLOWTAIL SNAPPER

The preferred species of snappers, it's more plentiful in the Keys than in any other Florida waters. As pretty as it is tasty, it's a favorite of divers and snorkelers. Mild, sweet, and delicate, its meat lends itself to any number of preparations. It's available pretty much year-round, and many restaurants will give you a choice of broiled, baked, fried, or blackened. Chefs top it with everything from key lime beurre blanc to mango chutney. **Ballyhoo's** in Key Largo (⊠ *MM 97.8, in median* ☎ *305/852–0822*) serves it 10 different ways.

Updated by Jill
Martin

Your Keys experience begins on your 18-mile drive south on "The Stretch," a portion of U.S. 1 with a specially colored blue median that takes you from Florida City to Key Largo. The real magic begins at mile marker 113, where the Florida Keys Scenic Highway begins. As the only All-American Road in Florida, it is a destination unto itself, one that crosses 42 bridges over water, including the Seven Mile Bridge—with its stunning vistas—and ends in Key West. Look for crocodiles, alligators, and bald eagles along the way.

Key West has a Mardi Gras mood with Fantasy Festival, a Hemingway look-alike contest, and the occasional threat to secede from the Union. It's an island whose eclectic natives, known as "Conchs," mingle well with visitors (of the spring-break variety as well as those seeking to escape reality for a while) on this scenic, sometimes raucous 4x2-mile island paradise.

Although life elsewhere in the island chain isn't near as offbeat, it is as diverse. Overflowing bursts of bougainvillea, shimmering waters, and mangrove-lined islands can be admired throughout. The one thing most visitors don't admire much in the Keys are their beaches. They're not many, and they're not what you'd expect. The reason? The coral reef. It breaks up the waves and prevents sand from being dumped on the shores. That's why the beaches are mostly rough sand, as it's crushed coral. Think of it as a trade-off: the Keys have the only living coral reef in the United States, but that reef prevents miles of shimmering sands from ever arriving.

In season, a river of traffic gushes southwest on this highway. But that doesn't mean you can't enjoy the ride as you cruise along the islands. Gaze over the silvery blue-and-green Atlantic and its living coral reef, with Florida Bay, the Gulf of Mexico, and the backcountry on your right (the Keys extend southwest from the mainland). At a few points the ocean and gulf are as much as 10 miles apart; in most places, however, they're from 1 to 4 miles apart, and on the narrowest landfill islands they're separated only by the road.

While the views can be mesmerizing, to appreciate the Keys you need to get off the highway, especially in more developed regions like Key Largo, Islamorada, and Marathon. Once you do, rent a boat, anchor, and then fish, swim, or marvel at the sun, sea, and sky. Or visit one of the many sandbars, which are popular places to float the day away. Ocean side, dive or snorkel spectacular coral reefs or pursue grouper, blue marlin, mahimahi, and other deepwater game fish. Along Florida Bay's coastline, kayak to secluded islands through mangrove forests, or seek out the bonefish, snapper, snook, and tarpon that lurk in the shallow grass flats and mangrove roots of the backcountry.

PLANNING

WHEN TO GO

High season in the Keys falls between Christmas and Easter. November to mid-December crowds are thinner, the weather is wonderful, and hotels and shops drastically reduce their prices. Summer, which is hot and humid, is becoming a second high season, especially among Floridians, families, and European travelers. If you plan to attend the wild Fantasy Fest in October, book your room at least six months in advance. Accommodations are also scarce during the last consecutive Wednesday and Thursday in July (lobster sport season) and starting the first weekend in August, when the commercial lobster season begins.

Winter is typically 10°F warmer than on the mainland; summer is usually a few degrees cooler. The Keys also get substantially less rain, around 40 inches annually, compared with an average 55–60 inches in Miami and the Everglades. In the summertime, "thunder boomers" (quick-moving thunderstorms) pass through most afternoons, although tropical storms can dump rain for two or more days. Winter cold fronts occasionally stall over the Keys, dragging overnight temperatures down to the low 50s.

GETTING HERE AND AROUND

AIR TRAVEL

About 450,000 passengers use the **Key West International Airport (EYW)** each year; its most recent renovation includes a beach where travelers can catch their last blast of rays after clearing security. Because flights are few, many prefer flying into Miami International Airport (MIA) and driving the 110-mile Overseas Highway (aka U.S. 1).

Contact Key West International Airport *(EYW). ⊠ 3491 S. Roosevelt Blvd., Key West ☎ 305/296–5439 ⊕ www.monroecounty-fl.gov/index.aspx?NID=105.*

BOAT AND FERRY TRAVEL

Key West can be reached by high-speed catamaran ferry from Fort Myers and Marco Island through Key West Express.

Boaters can travel to and along the Keys either along the Intracoastal Waterway through Card, Barnes, and Blackwater sounds and into

Florida Bay or along the deeper Atlantic Ocean route through Hawk Channel. The Keys are full of marinas that welcome transient visitors, but there aren't enough slips for all the boats heading to these waters. Make reservations far in advance and ask about channel and dockage depth—many marinas are quite shallow.

Contact Key West Express ⊠ *100 Grinnell St., Key West* ☎ *888/539–2628* ⊕ *www.seakeywestexpress.com.*

BUS TRAVEL

Those unwilling to tackle the route's 42 bridges and peak-time traffic can take **Greyhound's** Keys Shuttle, which has multiple daily departures from Miami International Airport.

Contacts Greyhound ☎ *800/231–2222* ⊕ *www.greyhound.com.* **Keys Shuttle** ⊠ *1333 Overseas Hwy., Marathon* ☎ *888/765–9997* ⊕ *www.keysshuttle.com.*

CAR TRAVEL

By car, from Miami International Airport, follow signs to Coral Gables and Key West, which puts you on LeJeune Road, then Route 836 west. Take the Homestead Extension of Florida's Turnpike south (toll road), which ends at Florida City and connects to the Overseas Highway (U.S. 1). Tolls from the airport run approximately $3. Payment is collected via SunPass, a prepaid toll program, or with Toll-By-Plate, a system that photographs each vehicle's license plate and mails a monthly bill for tolls, plus a $2.50 administrative fee, to the vehicle's registered owner.

Vacationers traveling in their own cars can obtain a mini-SunPass sticker via mail before their trip for $4.99 and receive the cost back in toll credits and discounts. The pass also is available at many major Florida retailers and turnpike service plazas. It works on all Florida toll roads and many bridges. For details on purchasing a mini-SunPass, call or visit the website.

For visitors renting cars in Florida, most major rental companies have programs allowing customers to use the Toll-By-Plate system. Tolls, plus varying service fees, are automatically charged to the credit card used to rent the vehicle (along with a hefty service charge in most cases). For details, including pricing options at participating rental-car agencies, check the program website. Under no circumstances should motorists attempt to stop in high-speed electronic tolling lanes. Travelers can contact Florida's Turnpike Enterprise for more information about the all-electronic tolling on Florida's Turnpike.

The alternative from Florida City is Card Sound Road (Route 905A), which has a (cash-only) bridge toll of $1. SunPass isn't accepted. Continue to the only stop sign and turn right on Route 905, which rejoins the Overseas Highway 31 miles south of Florida City. The best Keys road map, published by the Homestead–Florida City Chamber of Commerce, can be obtained for $5.50 from the Tropical Everglades Visitor Center.

Contacts Florida's Turnpike Enterprise ☎ *800/749–7453* ⊕ *www. floridasturnpike.com.* **SunPass** ☎ *888/865–5352* ⊕ *www.sunpass.com.*

THE MILE MARKER SYSTEM

Getting lost in the Keys is almost impossible once you understand the unique address system. **Many addresses are simply given as a mile marker (MM) number.** The markers are small, green, rectangular signs along the side of the Overseas Highway (U.S. 1). They begin with MM 126, 1 mile south of Florida City, and end with MM 0, in Key West. **Keys residents use the abbreviation BS for the bay side of Overseas Highway and OS for the ocean side.** From Marathon to Key West, residents may refer to the bay side as the gulf side.

HOTELS

Throughout the Keys, the types of accommodations are remarkably varied, from 1950s-style motels to cozy inns to luxurious resorts. Most are on or near the ocean, so water sports are popular. Key West's lodging portfolio includes historic cottages, restored Conch houses, and large resorts. Some larger properties throughout the Keys charge a mandatory daily resort fee of $15 or more, which can cover equipment rental, fitness-center use, and other services. You can expect another 12.5% (or more) in state and county taxes. Some guesthouses and inns don't welcome children, and many don't permit smoking. *Hotel reviews have been shortened. For full information, visit Fodors.com.*

RESTAURANTS

Seafood rules in the Keys, which is full of chef-owned restaurants with not-too-fancy food. Many restaurants serve cuisine that reflects the proximity of the Bahamas and Caribbean (you'll see the term "Floribbean" on many menus). Tropical fruits figure prominently—especially on the beverage side of the menu. Florida spiny lobster should be local and fresh from August to March, and stone crabs from mid-October to mid-May. And don't dare leave the islands without sampling conch, be it in a fritter or in ceviche. Keep an eye out for authentic key lime pie— yellow custard in a graham-cracker crust. If it's green, just say "no." Note: Particularly in Key West and particularly during spring break, the more affordable and casual restaurants can get loud and downright rowdy, with young visitors often more interested in drinking than eating. Live music contributes to the decibel levels. If you're more of the quiet, intimate-dining type, avoid such overly exuberant scenes by eating early or choosing a restaurant where the bar isn't the main focus.

WHAT IT COSTS				
	$	$$	$$$	$$$$
RESTAURANTS	under $16	$16–$20	$21–$30	over $30
HOTELS	under $201	$201–$300	$301–$400	over $400

Restaurant prices are the average cost of a main course at dinner or, if dinner is not served, at lunch. Hotel prices are the lowest cost of a standard double room in high season.

VISITOR INFORMATION

In addition to traditional tourist information, many divers will be interested in the Florida Keys National Marine Sanctuary, which has its headquarters in Key West and has another office in Key Largo.

Contact Florida Keys National Marine Sanctuary ☏ *305/809–4700* ⊕ *floridakeys.noaa.gov.* **Monroe County Tourist Development Council** ☏ *800/352–5397* ⊕ *www.Fla-Keys.com.* **Tropical Everglades Visitor Association** ☏ *305/245–9180, 800/388–9669* ⊕ *www.tropicaleverglades.com.*

THE UPPER KEYS

Diving and snorkeling are the primary draws in the Upper Keys, thanks to the tropical coral reef that runs a few miles off the seaward coast. Divers of all skill levels benefit from accessible dive sites and an established tourism infrastructure. Fishing is another huge draw, especially around Islamorada, known for its sportfishing in both deep offshore waters and in the backcountry. Offshore islands accessible only by boat are popular destinations for kayakers. In short, if you don't like the water, you might get bored here.

Other nature lovers won't feel shortchanged. Within 1½ miles of the bay coast lie the mangrove trees and sandy shores of Everglades National Park, where naturalists lead tours of one of the world's few saltwater forests. Here you'll see endangered manatees, curious dolphins, and other underwater creatures. Although the number of birds has dwindled since John James Audubon captured their beauty on canvas, the rare Everglades snail kite, bald eagles, ospreys, and a colorful array of egrets and herons delight bird-watchers. At sunset, flocks take to the skies as they gather to find their night's roost, adding a swirl of activity to an otherwise quiet time of day.

The Upper Keys are full of low-key eateries where the owner is also the chef and the food is tasty and never too fussy. The one exception is Islamorada, where you'll find more upscale restaurants. Places to eat may close for a two- to four-week vacation during the slow season between mid-September and late October.

In the Upper Keys the accommodations are as varied as they are plentiful. The majority of lodgings are in small waterfront complexes with furnished one- or two-bedroom units. These places offer dockage and often arrange boating, diving, and fishing excursions. There are also larger resorts with every type of activity imaginable and smaller boutique hotels where the attraction is personalized service.

Depending on which way the wind blows and how close the property is to the highway, there may be some noise from Overseas Highway. If this is an annoyance for you, ask for a room as far from the traffic as possible. Some properties require two- or three-day minimum stays during holiday and high-season weekends. Conversely, discounts may apply for midweek, weekly, and monthly stays.

GETTING HERE AND AROUND

Airporter operates scheduled van and bus pickup service from all Miami International Airport (MIA) baggage areas to wherever you want to go in Key Largo ($50) and Islamorada ($55). Groups of three or more passengers receive discounts. There are three departures daily; reservations are required 48 hours in advance. The SuperShuttle charges $165 to $185 for two passengers for trips from Miami International Airport to Key Largo; reservations are required. For a trip to the airport, place your request 24 hours in advance.

Contacts Airporter ☎ *305/852–3413, 800/830–3413.* **SuperShuttle** ☎ *305/871–2000* ⊕ *www.supershuttle.com.*

KEY LARGO

56 miles south of Miami International Airport.

The first of the Upper Keys reachable by car, 30-mile-long Key Largo is also the largest island in the chain. Key Largo—named Cayo Largo ("Long Key") by the Spanish—makes a great introduction to the region.

The history of Largo is similar to that of the rest of the Keys, with its succession of native people, pirates, wreckers, and developers. The first settlement on Key Largo was named Planter, back in the days of pineapple, and later, key lime plantations. For a time it was a convenient shipping port, but when the railroad arrived, Planter died on the vine. Today three communities—North Key Largo, Key Largo, and Tavernier—make up the whole of Key Largo.

If you've never tried diving, Key Largo is the perfect place to learn. Dozens of companies will be more than happy to show you the ropes. Nobody comes to Key Largo without visiting John Pennekamp Coral Reef State Park, one of the jewels of the state-park system. Also popular is the adjacent Key Largo National Marine Sanctuary, which encompasses about 190 square miles of coral reefs, sea grass beds, and mangrove estuaries. Both are good for underwater exploration.

Fishing is the other big draw, and world records are broken regularly. There are plenty of charter operations to help you find the big ones and teach you how to hook the elusive (but inedible) bonefish, sometimes known as the ghost fish. On land, restaurants will cook your catch or dish up their own offerings with inimitable style.

Key Largo offers all the conveniences of a major resort town, with most businesses lined up along Overseas Highway (U.S. 1), the four-lane highway that runs down the middle of the island. Cars whiz past at all hours—something to remember when you're booking a room. Most lodgings are on the highway, so you'll want to be as far from the road as possible.

GETTING HERE AND AROUND

Key Largo is 56 miles south of Miami International Airport, with the mile markers going from 105 to 91. The island runs northeast–southwest, with Overseas Highway running down the center. If the highway is your only glimpse of the island, you're likely to feel barraged by its tacky commercial side. Make a point of driving Route 905 in North Key Largo and down side streets to the marinas to get a better feel for it.

VISITOR INFORMATION

Contact Key Largo Chamber of Commerce. Stop in for brochures, directions, recommendations, or some colorful Key Largo T-shirts and gifts. ✉ *MM 106 BS, 10600 Overseas Hwy.* ☎ *305/451–4747, 800/822–1088* ⊕ *www.keylargochamber.org.*

EXPLORING

Dagny Johnson Key Largo Hammock Botanical State Park. American crocodiles, mangrove cuckoos, white-crowned pigeons, Schaus swallowtail butterflies, mahogany mistletoe, wild cotton, and 100 other rare critters and plants inhabit these 2,400 acres, sandwiched between Crocodile Lake National Wildlife Refuge and Pennekamp Coral Reef State Park. The park is also a user-friendly place to explore the largest remaining stand of the vast West Indian tropical hardwood hammock and mangrove wetland that once covered most of the Keys' upland areas. Interpretive signs describe many of the tropical tree species along a wide 1-mile paved road (2 miles round-trip) that invites walking and biking. There are also more than 6 miles of nature trails accessible to bikes and wheelchairs. Pets are welcome if on a leash no longer than 6 feet. You'll also find restrooms, information kiosks, and picnic tables. ■TIP→ Rangers recommend not visiting when it's raining as the trees can drip poisonous sap. ⊠ *Rte. 905 OS, 0.5 mile north of Overseas Hwy.* ☎ *305/451–1202* ⊕ *www.floridastateparks.org/keylargohammock* 🖃 *$2.50 (exact change needed)* ⊗ *Daily 8–sundown.*

FAMILY **Dolphins Plus Oceanside.** A sister property to Dolphins Plus Bayside, Dolphins Plus offers some of the same programs and the age requirement is lower. The cheapest option, a Natural Swim program, begins with a one-hour briefing; then you enter the water to become totally immersed in the dolphins' world. In this visual orientation, participants snorkel but are not allowed to touch the dolphins. For tactile interaction (kissing, fin tows, etc.), sign up for the Structured Swim program, which is more expensive. ⊠ *MM 99, 31 Corrine Pl.* ☎ *305/451–1993, 866/860–7946* ⊕ *www.dolphinsplus.com* 🖃 *Programs from $165* ⊗ *Daily 8–5.*

FAMILY **Jacobs Aquatic Center.** Take the plunge at one of three swimming pools: an eight-lane, 25-meter lap pool with two diving boards; a 3- to 4-foot-deep pool accessible to people with mobility challenges; and an interactive children's play pool with a waterslide, pirate ship, waterfall, and sloping zero entry instead of steps. Because so few of the motels in Key Largo have pools, it remains a popular destination for visiting families. ⊠ *Key Largo Community Park, 320 Laguna Ave., at St. Croix Pl.* ☎ *305/453–7946* ⊕ *www.jacobsaquaticcenter.org* 🖃 *$12 ($2 discount weekdays)* ⊗ *Daily 10–6 (10–7 in summer).*

BEACHES

FAMILY
Fodor's Choice
★

John Pennekamp Coral Reef State Park. This state park is on everyone's list for easy access to the best diving and snorkeling in Florida. The underwater treasure encompasses 78 square miles of coral reefs and sea-grass beds. It lies adjacent to the Florida Keys National Marine Sanctuary, which contains 40 of the 52 species of coral in the Atlantic Reef System and nearly 600 varieties of fish, from the colorful parrot fish to the demure cocoa damselfish. Whatever you do, get in the water. Snorkeling and diving trips ($30 and $55, respectively, equipment extra) and glass-bottom-boat rides to the reef ($24) are available, weather permitting. One of the most popular snorkel trips is to see *Christ of the Deep,* the 2-ton underwater statue of Jesus. The park also has nature trails, two man-made beaches, picnic shelters, a snack bar, and a campground. **Amenities:** food and drink; parking (fee); showers;

toilets; water sports. **Best for:** snorkeling; swimming. ✉ *MM 102.5 OS, 102601 Overseas Hwy.* ☎ *305/451–1202 for park, 305/451–6300 for excursions* 🌐 *www.pennekamppark.com, www.floridastateparks.org/pennekamp* 🎟 *$4.50 for 1 person in vehicle, $8 for 2–8 people, $2 for pedestrians and cyclists or extra people (plus a 50¢ per-person county surcharge)* 🕒 *Daily 8–sunset.*

WHERE TO EAT

$$$ SEAFOOD Fodor's Choice ★

🍴 **Buzzard's Roost Grill and Pub.** The views are nice at this waterfront restaurant but the food is what gets your attention. Burgers, fish tacos, and seafood baskets are lunch faves. Dinner is about seafood and steaks, any way you like them. Try the smoked-fish dip, served with Armenian heart-shape lavash crackers. Look for the big signs on U.S. 1 that direct you where to turn—it's worth finding. [$] *Average main: $21* ✉ *Garden Cove Marina, 21 Garden Cove Dr., Northernmost Key Largo* ☎ *305/453–3746* 🌐 *www.buzzardsroostkeylargo.com.*

$$$ SEAFOOD

🍴 **The Fish House.** Restaurants not on the water have to produce the highest quality food to survive in the Keys. That's how the Fish House has succeeded since the 1980s—so much so that it built the Fish House Encore (a fancier version) next door to accommodate fans. The pan-sautéed catch of the day is a long-standing favorite, as is the "Matecumbe-style" preparation—baked with tomatoes, capers, olive oil, and lemon juice, it will make you moan with pleasure. Prefer shellfish? Choose from shrimp, lobster, and (mid-October to mid-May) stone crab. The smoked fish chunks are the best in the Keys. The only things bland are their side dishes: simple boiled red potatoes, a hunk of corn on the cob, or black beans and rice. For a sweet ending, the homemade key lime pie is award-winning. [$] *Average main: $21* ✉ *MM 102.4 OS, 102341 Overseas Hwy.* ☎ *305/451–4665* 🌐 *www.fishhouse.com* ✍ *Reservations not accepted* 🕒 *Closed Sept.* ☞ *American Express not accepted.*

$ AMERICAN

🍴 **Harriette's Restaurant.** If you're looking for comfort food—like melt-in-your-mouth biscuits the size of a salad plate—try this refreshing throwback. The kitchen makes muffins daily in 13 different flavors like mango, coconut, and key lime. Since the early 1980s, owner Harriette Mattson has been here to personally greet guests who come for the to-die-for omelets and old-fashioned hotcakes with sausage or bacon. For something unique, try the conch burger and eggs. At lunch, Harriette shines in the burger department, and her soups—from garlic tomato to chili—are homemade. No wonder there's always a wait. [$] *Average main: $8* ✉ *MM 95.7 BS, 95710 Overseas Hwy.* ☎ *305/852–8689* ✍ *Reservations not accepted* 🕒 *No dinner* ☞ *American Express not accepted.*

$$ SEAFOOD

🍴 **Jimmy Johnson's Big Chill.** Owned by former NFL coach, Jimmy Johnson, this waterfront establishment offers three entertaining experiences, and all are big winners. You'll find the best sports bar in the Upper Keys complete with the coach's Super Bowl trophies, a main restaurant with all-glass indoor seating and a waterfront deck, and an enormous outdoor tiki bar with entertainment seven nights a week. There's even a pool and cabana club where (for an entrance fee) you can spend the day sunning. Menu favorites are the Parmesan-crusted snapper and brick-oven roasted chicken wings, but don't miss the tuna nachos—as delicious as they are artfully presented. As the sun sets over the bay, enjoy the views and a slice of key lime pie. $ *Average main: $16* ⊠ *MM104 BS, 104000 Overseas Hwy.* ☎ *305/453–9066* ⊕ *www. jjsbigchill.com.*

$ ✗ **Mrs. Mac's Kitchen.** Townies pack the counters and booths at this tiny
SEAFOOD eatery, where license plates are stuck on the walls and made into chandeliers, for everything from blackened prime rib to crab cakes. Every night is themed including Meatloaf Monday, Italian Wednesday, and Seafood Sensation (offered Friday and Saturday). There's also a Champagne breakfast (at this original location) and an assortment of tasty Angus beef burgers, sandwiches, a famous chili, and key lime freeze (a tangy concoction somewhere between a shake and a float). In season, ask about the hogfish special du jour. A second location, Mrs. Mac's Kitchen 2, is half a mile south on the Overseas Highway (99020 Overseas Hwy., MM99 Center), also in Key Largo. The newer location offers a similar menu, a full bar, and double the seating, but the original rules supreme on food. $ *Average main: $15* ⊠ *MM 99.4 BS, 99336 Overseas Hwy.* ☎ *305/451–3722, 305/451–6227* ⊕ *www.mrsmacskitchen. com* ☉ *Closed Sun.*

$$$ ✗ **Sundowners.** The name doesn't lie. If it's a clear night and you can
AMERICAN snag a reservation, this restaurant will treat you to a sherbet-hue sunset over Florida Bay. If you're here in mild weather—anytime other than the dog days of summer or the rare winter cold snap—the best seats are on the patio. The food is excellent: try the key lime seafood, a happy combo of sautéed shrimp, lobster, and lump crabmeat swimming in a tangy sauce spiked with Tabasco served over penne or rice. Wednesday and Saturday are all about prime rib, and Friday draws the crowds with an all-you-can-eat fish fry. Vegetarian and gluten-free options are available. To beat the crowds, stop in for lunch, which offers the same great food, minus the hassle. $ *Average main: $22* ⊠ *MM 104 BS, 103900 Overseas Hwy.* ☎ *305/451–4502* ⊕ *sundownerskeylargo.com* ☖ *Reservations essential.*

WHERE TO STAY

$$ ⛱ **Azul del Mar.** The dock points the way to many beautiful sunsets
B&B/INN at this no-smoking, adults-only boutique hotel, which Karol Marsden (an ad exec) and her husband Dominic (a travel photographer) have transformed from a run-down mom-and-pop place into a waterfront gem. **Pros:** great garden; good location; sophisticated design. **Cons:** small beach; high-priced; minimum stays during holidays. $ *Rooms from: $299* ⊠ *MM 104.3 BS, 104300 Overseas Hwy.* ☎ *305/451–0337, 888/253–2985* ⊕ *www.azulkeylargo.com* ⤳ *2 studios, 3 1-bedroom suites, 1 2-bedroom suite* ⛆ *No meals.*

$ ⛱ **Coconut Bay Resort & Bay Harbor Lodge.** Some 200 feet of waterfront
RESORT is the main attraction at these side-by-side sister properties that offer a choice between smaller rooms and larger separate cottages. **Pros:** bay front; neatly kept gardens; walking distance to restaurants; free use of kayaks, paddleboat, and paddleboards. **Cons:** a bit dated; small sea-walled sand beach. $ *Rooms from: $175* ⊠ *MM 97.7 BS, 97702 Overseas Hwy.* ☎ *305/852–1625, 800/385–0986* ⊕ *www.*

coconutbaykeylargo.com ⇗ 7 rooms, 5 efficiencies, 2 suites, 1 2-bedroom villa, 6 1-bedroom cottages ❍| *Breakfast.*

$$
B&B/INN
❄ **Coconut Palm Inn.** You'd never find this waterfront haven unless someone told you it was there, as it's tucked into a residential neighborhood beneath towering palms and native gumbo limbos. **Pros:** secluded; quiet; sophisticated feel. **Cons:** front desk closes early each evening; no access to ice machine when staff leaves; breakfast is ho-hum. $ *Rooms from: $299 ⊠ MM 92 BS, 198 Harborview Dr., via Jo-Jean Way off Overseas Hwy., Tavernier* ☎ *305/852–3017* ⊕ *www.coconutpalminn.com* ⇗ *13 rooms, 7 suites* ❍| *Breakfast.*

$$
B&B/INN
❄ **Dove Creek Lodge.** With its sherbet-hue rooms and plantation-style furnishings, these tropical-style units (19 in all) range in size from simple lodge rooms to luxury two-bedroom suites. **Pros:** luxurious rooms; walk to Snapper's restaurant; complimentary kayaks and Wi-Fi. **Cons:** no beach; some find the music from next door bothersome. $ *Rooms from: $269 ⊠ MM 94.5 OS, 147 Seaside Ave.* ☎ *305/852–6200, 800/401–0057* ⊕ *www.dovecreeklodge.com* ⇗ *11 rooms, 8 suites* ❍| *Breakfast.*

$$
RESORT
Fodor'sChoice
★
❄ **Hilton Key Largo Resort.** Nestled within a hardwood hammock (localese for uplands habitat where hardwood trees such as live oak grow) near the southern border of Everglades National Park, this sprawling resort had a $12-million renovation in 2012 and offers a full slate of amenities in a woodsy setting. **Pros:** nice nature trail on bay side; pretty pools with waterfalls; awesome trees; bicycles available for rent. **Cons:** some rooms overlook the parking lot; pools near the highway; expensive per-night resort fee. $ *Rooms from: $259 ⊠ MM 97 BS, 97000 Overseas Hwy.* ☎ *305/852–5553, 888/871–3437* ⊕ *www.keylargoresort.com* ⇗ *190 rooms, 10 suites* ❍| *No meals.*

$$
RENTAL
❄ **Island Bay Resort.** When Mike and Carol Shipley took over this off-the-beaten-path resort in 2000, they revamped the 10 bay-side cottages, improved the landscaping, and added touches such as hammocks and Adirondack chairs that make you feel like this is your own personal tropical playground. **Pros:** on the water; sunset views. **Cons:** most units are small; no pool; lacks on-site amenities. $ *Rooms from: $249 ⊠ 92530, Overseas Hwy.* ☎ *305/852-4087* ⊕ *www.islandbayresort.com* ⇗ *10 units* ❍| *No meals.*

$$
RESORT
Fodor'sChoice
★
❄ **Kona Kai Resort, Gallery & Botanic Gardens.** Brilliantly colored bougainvillea, coconut palm, and guava trees—and a botanical garden of other rare species—make this 2-acre adult hideaway one of the prettiest places to stay in the Keys. **Pros:** free custom tours of botanical gardens for guests; free use of sports equipment; knowledgeable staff. **Cons:** expensive; some rooms are very close together. $ *Rooms from: $289 ⊠ MM 97.8 BS, 97802 Overseas Hwy.* ☎ *305/852–7200, 800/365–7829* ⊕ *www.konakairesort.com* ⇗ *8 suites, 5 rooms* ❍| *No meals.*

$$$
RESORT
FAMILY
❄ **Marriott's Key Largo Bay Beach Resort.** This 17-acre bayside resort has plenty of diversions, from diving to parasailing to a day spa. **Pros:** lots of activities; free covered parking; dive shop on property; free Wi-Fi. **Cons:** rooms facing highway can be noisy; thin walls. $ *Rooms from: $359 ⊠ MM 103.8 BS, 103800 Overseas Hwy.* ☎ *305/453–0000, 866/849–3753* ⊕ *www.marriottkeylargo.com* ⇗ *132 rooms, 20 2-bedroom suites, 1 penthouse suite* ❍| *No meals.*

$ HOTEL **The Pelican.** This 1950s throwback is reminiscent of the days when parents packed the kids into the station wagon and headed to no-frills seaside motels, complete with old-fashioned fishing off the dock. **Pros:** free use of kayaks and a canoe; well-maintained dock; reasonable rates. **Cons:** some small rooms; basic accommodations and amenities. [$] *Rooms from: $150* ✉ *MM 99.3, 99340 Overseas Hwy.* ☎ *305/451–3576, 877/451–3576* 🌐 *www.hungrypelican.com* 🛏 *13 rooms, 4 efficiencies, 4 suites* 🍴 *Breakfast.*

NIGHTLIFE

The semiweekly *Keynoter* (Wednesday and Saturday), weekly *Reporter* (Thursday), and Friday through Sunday editions of the *Miami Herald* are the best sources of information on entertainment and nightlife.

Breezers Tiki Bar & Grille. Mingle with locals over cocktails and sunsets at Marriott's Key Largo Bay Beach Resort. ✉ *Marriott Key Largo Bay Beach Resort, 103800 Overseas Hwy.* ☎ *305/453–0000.*

Caribbean Club. Walls plastered with Bogart memorabilia remind customers that the classic 1948 Bogart–Bacall flick *Key Largo* has a connection with this worn watering hole. Although no food is served and the floors are bare concrete, this landmark draws boaters, curious visitors, and local barflies to its humble bar stools and pool tables. But the real magic is around back, where you can grab a seat on the deck and catch a postcard-perfect sunset. Live music draws revelers Thursday through Sunday. ✉ *MM 104 BS, 10404 Overseas Hwy.* ☎ *305/451–4466.*

SHOPPING

For the most part, shopping is sporadic in Key Largo, with a couple of shopping centers and fewer galleries than you find on the other big islands. If you're looking to buy scuba or snorkeling equipment, you'll have plenty of places from which to choose.

Gumbo Limbo Pottery. Here you'll find functional and decorative ceramics ranging from signature lanterns and porcelain kitchenware to one-of-a-kind high-fire sculptures where the owners' creative talent at the wheel blazes. It's no coincidence that their creations will remind you of the sky, land, and sea of the Florida Keys. ✉ *MM 102.9 OS, 102991 Overseas Hwy.* ☎ *305/741–7108* 🌐 *www.gumbolimbopottery.com* ⏲ *Closed Tues.*

Fodor's Choice ★ **Key Largo Chocolates.** Specializing in key lime truffles made with quality Belgian chocolate, this is the only chocolate factory in the entire Florida Keys. But you'll find much more than just the finest white, milk, and dark chocolate truffles; try their cupcakes, ice cream, and famous "chocodiles." Another fan favorite is the salted turtles, which are worth every calorie. Chocolate classes are also available for kids and adults, and a small gift area showcases local art, jewelry, hot sauces, and other goodies. Look for the bright green-and-pink building. ✉ *MM100 BS, 100471 Overseas Hwy.* ☎ *305/453–6613* 🌐 *www.keylargochocolates.com.*

Randy's Florida Keys Gift Co. Since 1989, Randy's has been "the" place for unique gifts. Owner Randy and his wife Lisa aren't only fantastic at stocking the store with a plethora of items, they're well respected in the community for their generosity and dedication. Stop in and say hello then browse the tight aisles and loaded shelves filled with key lime candles, books, wood carvings, jewelry, clothing, T-shirts, and eclectic, tropical decor items. This friendly shop prides itself on carrying wares from local craftsmen and there's something for every budget. ✉ *102421 Overseas Hwy.* ✛ *Right on U.S. 1, next to Sandal Factory Outlet* ☎ *305/453–9229* ⊕ *www.keysmermaid.com.*

SPORTS AND THE OUTDOORS

BOATING

Everglades Eco-Tours. Captain Sterling operates Everglades and Florida Bay ecology tours and more expensive sunset cruises. You can see dolphins, manatees, and birds from the casual comfort of his pontoon boat, equipped with PVC chairs. Bring your own food and drinks. ✉ *MM 104 BS, Sundowners Restaurant, 103900 Overseas Hwy.* ☎ *305/853–5161, 888/224–6044* ⊕ *www.captainsterling.com* ✍ *From $59.*

M.V. Key Largo Princess. Two-hour glass-bottom-boat trips and sunset cruises on a luxury 70-foot motor yacht with a 280-square-foot glass viewing area depart from the Holiday Inn docks three times a day. ✉ *Holiday Inn, MM 100 OS, 99701 Overseas Hwy.* ☎ *305/451–4655, 877/648–8129* ⊕ *www.keylargoprincess.com* ✍ *$35.*

CANOEING AND KAYAKING

Sea kayaking continues to gain popularity in the Keys. You can paddle for a few hours or the whole day, on your own or with a guide. Some outfitters even offer overnight trips. The **Florida Keys Paddling Trail,** part of a statewide system, runs from Key Largo to Key West. You can paddle the entire distance, 110 miles on the Atlantic side, which takes 9–10 days. The trail also runs the chain's length on the bay side, which is a longer route.

Coral Reef Park Co. At John Pennekamp Coral Reef State Park, this operator has a fleet of canoes and kayaks for gliding around the 2½-mile mangrove trail or along the coast. Powerboat rentals are also available. ✉ *MM 102.5 OS, 102601 Overseas Hwy.* ☎ *305/451–6300* ⊕ *www.pennekamppark.com* ✍ *Rentals from $12 per hr.*

Florida Bay Outfitters. Rent canoes or sea kayaks from this company, which sets up self-guided trips on the Florida Keys Paddling Trail, helps with trip planning, and matches equipment to your skill level. It also runs myriad guided tours around Key Largo. Take a full-moon paddle or a one- to seven-day kayak tour to the Everglades, Lignumvitae Key, or Indian Key. ✉ *MM 104 BS, 104050 Overseas Hwy.* ☎ *305/451–3018* ⊕ *www.paddleflipidakeys.com* ✍ *From $15.*

FISHING

Private charters and big head boats (so named because they charge "by the head") are great for anglers who don't have their own vessel.

Sailors Choice. Fishing excursions depart twice-daily (half-day trips are cash-only), but the company also does private charters. The 65-foot boat leaves from the Holiday Inn docks. Rods, bait, and license are included. ✉ *Holiday Inn Resort & Marina, MM 100 OS, 99701 Overseas Hwy.* ☎ *305/451–1802, 305/451–0041* ⊕ *www.sailorschoicefishingboat.com* ✍ *From $40.*

SCUBA DIVING AND SNORKELING

Much of what makes the Upper Keys a singular dive destination is variety. Places like Molasses Reef, which begins 3 feet below the surface and descends to 55 feet, have something for everyone, from novice snorkelers to experienced divers. The *Spiegel Grove,* a 510-foot vessel, lies in 130 feet of water, but its upper regions are only 60 feet below the surface. On rough days, Key Largo Undersea Park's Emerald Lagoon is a popular spot. Expect to pay about $80 for a two-tank, two-site dive trip with tanks and weights, or $35–$40 for a two-site snorkel outing. Get big discounts by booking multiple trips.

Amy Slate's Amoray Dive Resort. This outfit makes diving easy. Stroll down to the full-service dive shop (NAUI, PADI, TDI, and BSAC certified), then onto a 45-foot catamaran. Certification courses are also offered. ✉ *MM 104.2 BS, 104250 Overseas Hwy.* ☎ *305/451–3595, 800/426–6729* ⊕ *www.amoray.com* ⌨ *From $85.*

Conch Republic Divers. Book diving instruction as well as scuba and snorkeling tours of all the wrecks and reefs of the Upper Keys. Two-location dives are the standard, and you'll pay an extra $15 for tank and weights. ✉ *MM 90.8 BS, 90800 Overseas Hwy.* ☎ *305/852–1655, 800/274–3483* ⊕ *www.conchrepublicdivers.com* ⌨ *From $70.*

Coral Reef Park Co. At John Pennekamp Coral Reef State Park, this company gives 3½-hour scuba and 2½-hour snorkeling tours of the park. In addition to the great location and the dependability it's also suited for water adventurers of all levels. ✉ *MM 102.5 OS, 102601 Overseas Hwy.* ☎ *305/451–6300* ⊕ *www.pennekamppark.com* ⌨ *From $30.*

Ocean Divers. The PADI five-star facility has been around since 1975 and offers day and night dives, a range of courses, and dive-lodging packages. Two-tank reef dives include tank and weight rental. There are also organized snorkeling trips with equipment. ✉ *MM 100 OS, 522 Caribbean Dr.* ☎ *305/451–1113, 800/451–1113* ⊕ *www.oceandivers. com* ⌨ *Snorkel trips from $35, diving from $85.*

Fodor's Choice ★ **Quiescence Diving Services.** This operator sets itself apart in two ways: it limits groups to six to ensure personal attention and offers both two-dive day and night dives, as well as twilight dives when sea creatures are most active. There are also organized snorkeling excursions. ✉ *MM 103.5 BS, 103680 Overseas Hwy.* ☎ *305/451–2440* ⊕ *www.quiescence. com* ⌨ *Snorkel trips $49, diving from $69.*

ISLAMORADA

Islamorada is between mile markers 90.5 and 70.

Early settlers named this key after their schooner, *Island Home,* but to make it sound more romantic they translated it into Spanish: *Isla Morada.* The chamber of commerce prefers to use its literal translation "Purple Island," which refers either to a purple-shelled snail that once inhabited these shores or to the brilliantly colored orchids and bougainvilleas.

Early maps show Islamorada as encompassing only Upper Matecumbe Key. But the incorporated "Village of Islands" is made up of a string of

Islamorada's warm waters attract large fish and the anglers and charter captains who want to catch them.

islands that the Overseas Highway crosses, including Plantation Key, Windley Key, Upper Matecumbe Key, Lower Matecumbe Key, Craig Key, and Fiesta Key. In addition, two state-park islands accessible only by boat—Indian Key and Lignumvitae Key—belong to the group.

Islamorada (locals pronounce it *eye*-la-mor-*ah*-da) is one of the world's top sportfishing destinations. For nearly 100 years, seasoned anglers have fished these clear, warm waters teeming with trophy-worthy fish. There are numerous options for those in search of the big ones, including chartering a boat with its own crew or heading out on a vessel rented from one of the plethora of marinas along this 20-mile stretch of the Overseas Highway.

ESSENTIALS

Visitor Information Islamorada Chamber of Commerce & Visitors Center ✉ *MM 87.1 BS, 87100 Overseas Hwy.* ☎ *305/664–4503, 800/322–5397* ⊕ *www. islamoradachamber.com.*

EXPLORING

Florida Keys Memorial / Hurricane Monument. On Monday, September 2, 1935, more than 400 people perished when the most intense hurricane to make landfall in the United States swept through this area of the Keys. Two years later, the Florida Keys Memorial was dedicated in their honor. Native coral rock, known as keystone, covers the 18-foot obelisk monument that marks the remains of more than 300 storm victims. A sculpted plaque of bending palms and waves graces the front (although many are bothered that the palms are bending in the wrong direction). In 1995, the memorial was placed on the National Register of Historic Places. ✉ *MM 81.5, OS, 81000 Overseas Hwy.* ✉ *Free.*

History of Diving Museum. Adding to the region's reputation for world-class diving, this museum plunges into the history of man's thirst for undersea exploration. Among its 13 galleries of interactive and other interesting displays are a submarine and helmet re-created from the film *20,000 Leagues Under the Sea*. Vintage U.S. Navy equipment, diving helmets from around the world, and early scuba gear explore 4,000 years of diving history. For the grand finale, spend $3 for a mouthpiece and sing your favorite tune at the helium bar. There are extended hours (until 7 pm) on the third Wednesday of every month. ⊠ *MM 83 BS, 82990 Overseas Hwy., Upper Matecumbe Key* ☎ *305/664–9737* ⊕ *www.divingmuseum.org* 🖅 *$12* ⊙ *Daily 10–5.*

Islamorada Founder's Park. This public park is the gem of Islamorada and boasts a palm-shaded beach, swimming pool, marina, skate park, tennis, and plenty of other facilities. If you want to rent a boat or learn to sail, businesses here can help you. If you're staying in Islamorada, admission is free. Those staying elsewhere pay $8 to enter the park. Either way, you pay an additional $3 to use the Olympic-size pool. A spiffy amphitheater hosts concerts, plays, and shows. The shallow water beach is ideal for swimming and families with little ones. Showers and bathrooms are beachside. ⊠ *MM 87 BS, 87000 Overseas Hwy.* ☎ *305/853–1685.*

FAMILY **Robbie's Marina.** Huge, prehistoric-looking denizens of the not-so-deep, silver-sided tarpon congregate around the docks at this marina on Lower Matecumbe Key. Children—and lots of adults—pay $3 for a bucket of sardines to feed them and $1 each for dock admission. Spend some time hanging out at this authentic Keys community, where you can grab a bite to eat indoors or out, shop at a slew of artisans' booths, or charter a boat, kayak, or other watercraft. ⊠ *MM 77.5 BS, 77522 Overseas Hwy., Lower Matecumbe Key* ☎ *305/664–9814, 877/664–8498* ⊕ *www.robbies.com* 🖅 *Dock access $1* ⊙ *Daily sunrise–sunset.*

FAMILY **Theater of the Sea.** The second-oldest marine-mammal center in the world doesn't attempt to compete with more modern, more expensive parks. Even so, it's among the better attractions north of Key West, especially if you have kids in tow. In addition to marine life exhibits and shows, you can make reservations for up-close-and-personal encounters like a swim with a dolphin or sea lion, or stingray and turtle feedings (which include general admission; reservations required). These are popular, so reserve in advance. Ride a "bottomless" boat to see what's below the waves and take a guided tour of the marine-life exhibits. Nonstop animal shows highlight conservation issues. You can stop for lunch at the grill, shop in the extensive gift shop, or sunbathe and swim at their private beach. This easily could be an all-day attraction. ⊠ *MM 84.5 OS, 84721 Overseas Hwy., Windley Key* ☎ *305/664–2431* ⊕ *www.theaterofthesea. com* 🖅 *$31.95; interaction programs $35–$185* ⊙ *Daily 9:30–5 (last ticket sold at 3:30).*

Upper Matecumbe Key. This was one of the first of the Upper Keys to be permanently settled. Early homesteaders were so successful at growing pineapples in the rocky soil that at one time the island yielded the country's largest annual crop. However, foreign competition and the hurricane of 1935 killed the industry. Today, life centers on fishing and tourism, and the island is filled with everything from bait shops and charter boats to eclectic galleries and fusion restaurants. ⊠ *MM 84–79.*

OFF THE BEATEN PATH

Indian Key Historic State Park. Mystery surrounds 10-acre Indian Key, on the ocean side of the Matecumbe islands. Before it became one of the first European settlements outside of Key West, it was inhabited by American Indians for several thousand years. The islet served as a base for 19th-century shipwreck salvagers until an Indian attack wiped out the settlement in 1840. Dr. Henry Perrine, a noted botanist, was killed in the raid. Today his plants grow in the town's ruins. Most people kayak or canoe here from Indian Key Fill or take a boat from Robbie's Marina to tour the nature trails and the town ruins or to snorkel. There are no restrooms or picnic facilities on Indian Key. ⊠ *Islamorada* ☎ *305/664–2540 park* ⊕ *www.floridastateparks.org/indiankey* ☜ *Free* ☉ *Daily 8–5.*

OFF THE BEATEN PATH

Lignumvitae Key Botanical State Park. On the National Register of Historic Places, this 280-acre bay-side island is the site of a virgin hardwood forest and the 1919 home of chemical magnate William Matheson. His caretaker's cottage serves as the park's visitor center. Access is by boat—your own, a rented vessel, or a tour operated from Robbie's Marina. The tour leaves at 8:30 am Friday through Sunday and takes in both Lignumvitae and Indian keys (reservations required). Paddling here from Indian Key Fill, at MM 78.5, is a popular pastime. The only way to do the trails is by a guided ranger walk, offered at 10 am and 2 pm Friday to Sunday. Wear long sleeves and pants, and bring mosquito repellent. On the first Saturday in December is the Lignumvitae Christmas Celebration, when the historic home is decorated 1930s-style. ⊠ *Islamorada* ☎ *305/664–2540 park, 305/664–8070 boat tours* ⊕ *www.floridastateparks.org/lignumvitaekey* ☜ *$2.50; $35 for boat tours* ☉ *Park Thurs.–Mon. 8–5; house tours Fri.–Sun. at 10 and 2.*

Windley Key Fossil Reef Geological State Park. The fossilized-coral reef, dating back about 125,000 years, demonstrates that the Florida Keys were once beneath the ocean. Excavation of Windley Key's limestone bed by the Florida East Coast Railway exposed the petrified reef, full of beautifully fossilized brain coral and sea ferns. Visitors can see the fossils along a 300-foot quarry wall when hiking the park's three trails. There are guided (Friday, Saturday, and Sunday only) and self-guided tours along the trails, which lead to the railway's old quarrying equipment and cutting pits, where you can make rubbings of the quarry walls. The **Alison Fahrer Environmental Education Center** holds historic, biological, and geological displays about the area, including videos. The first Saturday in March is Windley Key Day, when the park sells native plants and hosts environmental exhibits. ⊠ *MM 84.9 BS, Windley Key* ☎ *305/664–2540* ⊕ *www.floridastateparks.org/windleykey* ☜ *$2.50; additional $2 for guided tours (self-guided is free)* ☉ *Education center Fri.–Sun. 9–5 (tours at 10 and 2).*

BEACHES

Anne's Beach Park. On Lower Matecumbe Key this popular village park is named for a local environmental activist. Its "beach" (really a typical Keys-style sand flat with a gentle slope) is best enjoyed at low tide. The nicest feature here is an elevated, wooden half-mile boardwalk that meanders through a natural wetland hammock. Covered picnic areas along the way give you places to linger and enjoy the view. Restrooms are at the north end. Weekends are packed with Miami day-trippers as it's the only public beach until you reach Marathon. **Amenities:** parking (no fee); toilets. **Best for:** partiers; snorkeling; swimming; windsurfing. ⊠ *MM 73.5 OS, Lower Matecumbe Key* ☎ *305/853–1685.*

WHERE TO EAT

$$$
SEAFOOD
Fodor's Choice
★

✕ **Chef Michael's.** Peace. Love. Hogfish. That's the motto of this local favorite that's been making big waves since its opening in 2011 with Chef Michael Ledwith at the helm. Sit outdoors on the covered wood deck and tap your toes to the live music, or dine inside amid dark wood floors and white linens. Seafood is selected fresh daily, then elegantly prepared with a splash of tropical flair. Try hogfish with mango sauce, or the catch "Juliette" with shrimp, scallops, Chardonnay butter, and toasted almonds. Carnivores can feast on prime-grade beef, carved in-house—with the kind of marbling that just melts in your mouth. Chef Michael even grows his own herbs, right outside the kitchen door. How about a watermelon mint sangria? Just say yes. Gluten-free and vegetarian dishes are available. $ *Average main: $29* ⊠ *MM81.7, 81671 Overseas Hwy, Upper Matecumbe Key* ☎ *305/664–0640* ⊕ *www.foodtotalkabout.com* ⌂ *Reservations essential* ☾ *No lunch Mon.–Sat.*

$$
SEAFOOD

✕ **Hungry Tarpon.** As part of the colorful, bustling Old Florida scene at Robbie's Marina, you know that the seafood here is fresh and top quality. The extensive menu seems as if it's bigger than the dining space, which consists of a few tables and counter-seating indoors, plus tables out back under the mangrove trees, close to where tourists pay to feed the tarpon in the marina. While tarpon are snacking on sardines, diners enjoy quite the impressive smattering of dishes for breakfast, lunch, and dinner. Specialties include biscuits and gravy, cracked conch, a Matecumbe fish sandwich with provolone and bacon on grilled sourdough, and a shrimp burrito. $ *Average main: $19* ⊠ *MM 77.5 BS, 77522 Overseas Hwy., Lower Matecumbe Key* ☎ *305/664–0535* ⊕ *www.hungrytarpon.com* ⌂ *Reservations not accepted.*

$$
SEAFOOD
FAMILY

✕ **Islamorada Fish Company.** When a restaurant is owned by Bass Pro Shops, you know the seafood should be as fresh as you can get it. The fun begins in the parking lot with painted white fish marking the parking spaces. The restaurant is housed in an open-air, oversized tiki hut right on Florida Bay, making this the quintessential Keys experience. There's a small, low-key tiki bar area if you prefer a stool to a table. Menu highlights include cracked conch beaten 'til tender and fried crispy, and Grouper Portofino, which will keep you coming back for more. Each afternoon, the staff feed the fish in the bay. Jump out of your seat and walk over for a close-up view of snapper, large tarpon, and even sharks. $ *Average main: $18* ⊠ *MM 81.5 BS, 81532*

Overseas Hwy., Windley Key ☎ *305/664–9271* ⊕ *restaurants.basspro. com/fishcompany/Islamorada/* ☾ *Daily 11–10.*

$ ✕**Lorelei Restaurant & Cabana Bar.** Local anglers gather here for breakfast.
AMERICAN Lunch and dinner bring a mix of islanders and visitors for straightforward food and front row seats to the sunset. Live music seven nights a week ensures a lively nighttime scene, and the menu staves off inebriation with burgers, barbecued baby back ribs, and Parmesan-crusted snapper. Key lime pie comes frozen with mango sauce. Service can be less than stellar and the gathering at sunset is always crowded. $ *Average main: $15* ⊠ *MM 82 BS, 81924 Overseas Hwy., Upper Matecumbe Key* ☎ *305/664–2692* ⊕ *www.loreleicabanabar.com* ⚑ *Reservations not accepted.*

$$$$ ✕**Marker 88.** A few yards from Florida Bay, this seafood restaurant
SEAFOOD has been popular since the late '60s. Large picture windows offer great sunset views, but the bay is lovely no matter what time of day you visit. Outdoor dining is popular, too. Chef Bobby Stoky serves such irresistible entrées as onion-crusted mahimahi, crispy yellowtail snapper, and house-smoked seasalt-and-black-pepper-encrusted rib eye. In addition, there are a half dozen burgers and sandwiches, and you can't miss the restaurant's famous key lime baked Alaska dessert. The extensive wine list is an oenophile's delight. $ *Average main: $34* ⊠ *MM 88 BS, 88000 Overseas Hwy., Plantation Key* ☎ *305/852–9315* ⊕ *www.marker88. info* ⚑ *Reservations essential.*

$$$ ✕**Morada Bay Beach Café.** This bay-front restaurant wins high marks for
ECLECTIC its surprisingly stellar cuisine, tables planted in the sand, and tiki torches
FAMILY that bathe the evening in romance. Entrées feature alluring combinations like fresh fish of the day sautéed with Meyer lemon butter and whole fried snapper with coconut rice. Seafood takes center stage, but you can always get roasted organic chicken or prime rib. Tapas and raw bar menus cater to smaller appetites or those who can't decide, with offerings like fried calamari, conch fritters, and Wagyu beef sliders. Lunch adds interesting sandwiches to the mix. Sit in a dining room outfitted with surfboards, or outdoors on a beach, where the sunset puts on a mighty show and kids (and your feet) play in the sand. $ *Average main: $27* ⊠ *MM 81 BS, 81600 Overseas Hwy., Upper Matecumbe Key* ☎ *305/664–0604* ⊕ *www.moradabay-restaurant.com.*

$$$$ ✕**Pierre's.** One of the Keys' most elegant restaurants, Pierre's marries
FRENCH colonial style with modern food trends. Full of interesting architec-
Fodor's Choice tural artifacts, the place oozes style, especially the wicker chair–strewn
★ veranda overlooking the bay. Save your best "tropical chic" duds for dinner here, so you don't stand out from your surroundings. The food, drawn from French and Floridian influences, is multilayered and beautifully presented. Among the seasonally changing appetizer choices, you might find smoked hogfish chowder and foie gras sliders with a butternut squash milk shake. A changing list of entrées might include hogfish meunière and scallops with pork belly tortellini. The downstairs bar is a perfect spot for catching sunsets, sipping martinis, and enjoying light eats. $ *Average main: $40* ⊠ *MM 81.5 BS, 81600 Overseas Hwy., Upper Matecumbe Key* ☎ *305/664–3225* ⊕ *www.moradabay. com* ⚑ *Reservations essential* ☾ *No lunch.*

WHERE TO STAY

$$ B&B/INN Fodor's Choice ★ **Casa Morada.** This relic from the 1950s has been restyled into a suave, design-forward, all-suites property with outdoor showers and Jacuzzis in some of the suites. **Pros:** cool design; complimentary snacks and bottled water; complimentary use of bikes, kayaks, and snorkel gear. **Cons:** trailer park across the street; beach is small and inconsequential. [$] *Rooms from: $299* ✉ *MM 82 BS, 136 Madeira Rd., Upper Matecumbe Key* ☎ *305/664–0044, 888/881–3030* 🌐 *www.casamorada.com* 🛏 *16 suites* 🍴 *Breakfast.*

$$ RESORT Fodor's Choice ★ **Cheeca Lodge & Spa.** At 27 acres, this may be the largest resort in the Keys, and it's also big on included amenities. **Pros:** beautifully landscaped grounds; new designer rooms; water-sports center on property. **Cons:** expensive rates; expensive resort fee; very busy. [$] *Rooms from: $299* ✉ *MM 82 OS, Upper Matecumbe Key* ☎ *305/664–4651, 800/327–2888* 🌐 *www.cheeca.com* 🛏 *60 1-bedroom suites, 64 junior suites* 🍴 *No meals.*

$ HOTEL **Drop Anchor Resort and Marina.** Immaculately maintained, this place has the feel of an old friend's beach house. **Pros:** bright and colorful; attention to detail; laid-back charm. **Cons:** noise from the highway; beach is better for fishing than swimming. [$] *Rooms from: $149* ✉ *MM 85 OS, 84959 Overseas Hwy., Windley Key* ☎ *305/664–4863, 888/664–4863* 🌐 *www.dropanchorresort.com* 🛏 *18 suites* 🍴 *No meals.*

$$ RESORT **The Islander, A Guy Harvey Outpost Resort.** Guests here get to choose between a self-sufficient town home on the bay with room for a boat, or an oceanfront resort with on-site restaurants and oodles of amenities. **Pros:** spacious rooms; nice kitchens; eye-popping views. **Cons:** pricey for what you get; beach has rough sand. [$] *Rooms from: $249* ✉ *MM 82.1 OS, 82200 Overseas Hwy., Upper Matecumbe Key* ☎ *305/664–2031, 800/753–6002* 🌐 *www.guyharveyoutpostislamorada.com* 🛏 *114 rooms, 12 suites, 25 townhomes* 🍴 *Breakfast.*

$$$$ HOTEL Fodor's Choice ★ **The Moorings Village.** This tropical retreat is everything you imagine when you think of the Keys—from hammocks swaying between towering trees to sugar-white sand (arguably the Keys' best resort beach) lapped by aqua-green waves. **Pros:** romantic setting; good dining options with room-charging privileges; beautiful beach. **Cons:** no room service; $20 daily resort fee for activities. [$] *Rooms from: $529* ✉ *MM 81.6 OS, 123 Beach Rd., Upper Matecumbe Key* ☎ *305/664–4708* 🌐 *www.themooringsvillage.com* 🛏 *18 cottages* 🍴 *No meals.*

$$$ HOTEL Fodor's Choice ★ **Ocean House.** Islamorada's newest adult boutique hotel is situated right on the Atlantic, yet it's hidden from passersby amid lush gardens. **Pros:** complimentary use of kayaks, snorkel equipment and bicycles; luxurious facilities and amenities. **Cons:** limited number of units means they're often booked solid; luxury comes at a price. [$] *Rooms from: $319* ✉ *MM 82 OS, 82885 Old Hwy., Windley Key* ☎ *866/540–5520* 🌐 *www.oceanhousefloridakeys.com* 🛏 *8 suites* 🍴 *Some meals.*

$$ RESORT **Postcard Inn Beach Resort & Marina at Holiday Isle.** After an $11-million renovation that encompassed updating everything from the rooms to the public spaces, this iconic property (formerly known as the Holiday Isle Beach Resort) has found new life. **Pros:** large private beach; heated

pools; on-site restaurants including Shula's 2. **Cons:** rooms near tiki bar are noisy; minimum stay required during peak times; bathrooms need updating. [$] *Rooms from: $215* ✉ *MM 84 OS, 84001 Overseas Hwy., Plantation Key* ☎ *305/664–2321* 🌐 *www.holidayisle.com* 🛏 *143 rooms* 🍴 *No meals.*

$ HOTEL FAMILY 🏨 **Ragged Edge Resort.** Nicely tucked away in a residential area at the ocean's edge, this family-owned hotel draws returning guests who'd rather fish off the dock and grill up dinner than loll around in Egyptian cotton sheets. **Pros:** oceanfront; boat docks and ramp; cheap rates. **Cons:** dated decor; off the beaten path. [$] *Rooms from: $169* ✉ *MM 86.5 OS, 243 Treasure Harbor Rd., Plantation Key* ☎ *305/852–5389, 800/436–2023* 🌐 *www.ragged-edge.com* 🛏 *6 studios, 1 efficiency, 3 2-bedroom suites* 🍴 *No meals.*

SHOPPING

Art galleries, upscale gift shops, and the mammoth World Wide Sportsman (if you want to look the part of a local fisherman, you must wear a shirt from here) make up the variety and superior style of Islamorada shopping.

Banyan Tree. Stroll and shop among the colorful orchids and lush plants at this outdoor garden and indoor boutique known for its tropical splendor, unique gifts and free-spirited clothing. There is nothing quite like it in the area. ✉ *MM 81.2 OS, 81197 Overseas Hwy., Upper Matecumbe Key* ☎ *305/664–3433* 🌐 *www.banyantreegarden.com* ⏲ *Closed Sun.*

Casa Mar Village. Change is good, and in this case, it's fantastic. What was once a row of worn-down buildings is now a merry blend of gift shops and galleries with the added bonus of a place selling fresh-roasted coffee. By day, these colorful shops glisten at their canalfront location, by nightfall, they're lit up like a lovely Christmas town. The offerings include the Jolly Pelican, Casa Mar Seafood, and the Fresh Press Cafe. ✉ *MM90 OS, 90775 Old Hwy., Upper Matecumbe Key* ☎ *305/522–0330* 🌐 *www.casamarvillage.com.*

Gallery Morada. This gallery is a go-to destination for one-of-a-kind gifts, beautifully displayed blown glass, original sculptures, paintings, and jewelry by 200 artists. Its location, front and center, makes it the gateway to the Morada Way Arts and Cultural District, an area with artist galleries, shops, potters, gardens, and culinary classes. ✉ *MM 81.6 OS, 81611 Old Hwy., Upper Matecumbe Key* ☎ *305/664–3650* 🌐 *www.gallerymorada.com.*

Hooked on Books. Among the best buys in town are the used best sellers at this bookstore, which also sells new titles, audiobooks, and CDs. Their Florida book collection is noteworthy. ✉ *MM 81.9 OS, 81909 Overseas Hwy., Upper Matecumbe Key* ☎ *305/517–2602* 🌐 *www.hookedonbooksfloridakeys.com.*

Rain Barrel Artisan Village. This is a natural and unhurried shopping showplace. Set in a tropical garden of shady trees, native shrubs, and orchids, the crafts village has shops selling the work of local and national artists as well as resident artists who sell work from their own studios. Have your photo taken with "Betsy," the giant Florida lobster, roadside. ⊠ *MM 86.7 BS, 86700 Overseas Hwy., Plantation Key* ☎ *305/852–3084* ⊕ *www.seefloridaonline.com/rainbarrel/index. html.*

Redbone Gallery. One of the largest sportfishing–art galleries in Florida stocks hand-stitched clothing and giftware, in addition to work by wood and bronze sculptors such as Kendall van Sant; watercolorist C.D. Clarke; and painters Daniel Caldwell, David Hall, Steven Left, and Stacie Krupa. Proceeds benefit cystic fibrosis research. Find them in the Morada Way Arts & Cultural District. ⊠ *MM 81.5 OS, 200 Morada Way, Upper Matecumbe Key* ☎ *305/664–2002* ⊕ *www.redbone.org.*

World Wide Sportsman. This two-level retail center sells upscale and everyday fishing equipment, resort clothing, sportfishing art, and other gifts. When you're tired of shopping, relax at the Zane Grey Long Key Lounge, located above the store—but not before you step up and into *Pilar*, a replica of Hemingway's boat. ⊠ *MM 81.5 BS, 81576 Overseas Hwy., Upper Matecumbe Key* ☎ *305/664–4615, 800/327–2880.*

SPORTS AND THE OUTDOORS
BOATING

Marinas pop up every mile or so in the Islamorada area, so finding a rental or tour is no problem. Robbie's Boat Rentals & Charters is a prime example of a salty spot where you can find it all—from fishing charters and kayaking rentals to lunch and tarpon feeding.

Bump & Jump. You can rent both fishing and deck boats here (from 15 to 29 feet) by the day or the week. Free local delivery with seven-day rentals from each of their locations. ⊠ *MM 85.9 BS, 85920 Overseas Hwy., Upper Matecumbe Key* ☎ *305/664–9404, 877/453–9463* ⊕ *www.keysboatrental.com* ⧉ *Rentals from $165 per day.*

Houseboat Vacations of the Florida Keys. See the islands from the comfort of your own boat (captain's cap optional). The company maintains a fleet of 44- to 55-foot boats that accommodate up to 10 people and come outfitted with everything you need besides food. (You may provision yourself at a nearby grocery store.) There's a three-day minimum; weekly rates are available. Kayaks, paddleboards, and dinghys suitable for bay side use also available. ⊠ *MM 85.9 BS, 85944 Overseas Hwy.* ☎ *305/664–4009* ⊕ *www.baysidetikiboats.com* ⧉ *From $1,350.*

Robbie's Boat Rentals & Charters. This full-service company will even give you a crash course on how not to crash your boat. The rental fleet includes an 18-foot skiff with a 90-horsepower outboard to a 21-foot deck boat with a 130-horsepower engine. Robbie's also rents snorkeling gear (there's good snorkeling nearby) and sells bait, drinks, and snacks. Want to hire a guide who knows the local waters and where the fish lurk? Robbie's offers offshore-fishing trips, patch-reef trips, and party-boat fishing. Backcountry flats trips are a specialty. ⊠ *MM 77.5 BS, 77522 Overseas Hwy., Lower Matecumbe Key* ☎ *305/664–9814, 877/664–8498* ⊕ *www.robbies.com* ⧉ *From $185 per day.*

Treasure Harbor Marine. The Anderson family will provide everything you need for a bareboat sailing vacation at sea. They also give excellent advice on where to find the best anchorages, snorkeling spots, or

Kayak ready to be used on the beach in the Florida Keys

lobstering sites. Vessels range from a 23.5-foot Hunter to a 41-foot Morgan Out Island. Boats can be rented by the day or week. Marina facilities include water, electric, laundry, picnic tables, and restrooms with showers. Transient and long-term dockage available. ⊠ *MM 86.5 OS, 200 Treasure Harbor Dr., Plantation Key* ☎ *305/852–2458, 800/352–2628* ⊕ *www.treasureharbor.com* ⊒ *From $175 per day.*

FISHING

Here in the self-proclaimed "sportfishing capital of the world," sailfish is the prime catch in the winter and dolphinfish (mahimahi) in the summer. Buchanan Bank just south of Islamorada is a good spot to try for tarpon in the spring. Blackfin tuna and amberjack are generally plentiful in the area, too. ■TIP→ The Hump at Islamorada ranks highest among anglers' favorite fishing spots in Florida because of the incredible offshore marine life.

Captain Ted Wilson. Go into the backcountry for bonefish, tarpon, redfish, snook, and shark aboard a 17-foot boat that accommodates up to three anglers. Two people can choose three-quarter or full-day trips, two-hour sunset bonefishing excursions, or evening fishing excursions. There's an extra $100 charge for each additional person. ⊠ *MM 79.9 OS, 79851 Overseas Hwy., Upper Matecumbe Key* ☎ *305/942–5224, 305/664–9463* ⊕ *www.captaintedwilson.com* ⊒ *Bonefishing from $250, 3/4-day trips from $500.*

Florida Keys Fly Fish. Like other top fly-fishing and light-tackle guides, Captain Geoff Colmes helps his clients land trophy fish in the waters around the Keys. ⊠ *105 Palm La., Upper Matecumbe Key* ☎ *305/853–0741* ⊕ *www.floridakeysflyfish.com* ⊒ *From $550.*

Florida Keys Outfitters. Long before fly-fishing became popular, Sandy Moret was fishing the Keys for bonefish, tarpon, and redfish. Now he attracts anglers from around the world on a quest for the big catch. His weekend fly-fishing classes include classroom instruction, equipment, and daily lunch. Guided fishing trips can be done for a half day or full day. Packages combining fishing and accommodations at Islander Resort are available. ⊠ *MM 81.2, Green Turtle, 81219 Overseas Hwy., Upper Matecumbe Key* ☎ *305/664–5423* ⊕ *www.floridakeysoutfitters. com* ☞ *Half-day trips from $495.*

Hubba Hubba Charters. Captain Ken Knudsen has fished the Keys waters since the 1970s. A licensed backcountry guide, he's ranked among Florida's top 10 by national fishing magazines. He offers four-hour sunset trips for tarpon and two-hour sunset trips for bonefish, as well as half- and full-day outings. Prices are for one or two anglers, and tackle and bait are included. ⊠ *MM 79.8 OS, Upper Matecumbe Key* ☎ *305/664–9281* ☞ *From $200.*

SCUBA DIVING AND SNORKELING

Florida Keys Dive Center. Dive from John Pennekamp Coral Reef State Park to Alligator Light with this outfitter. The center has two 46-foot Coast Guard–approved dive boats, offers scuba training, and is one of the few Keys dive centers to offer Nitrox and Trimix (mixed gas) diving. ⊠ *MM 90.5 OS, 90451 Overseas Hwy., Plantation Key* ☎ *305/852–4599, 800/433–8946* ⊕ *www.floridakeysdivectr.com* ☞ *Snorkeling from $38, diving from $65.*

Islamorada Dive Center. This one-stop dive shop has a resort, pool, restaurant, lessons, and twice-daily dive and snorkel trips. You can take a day trip with a two-tank dive or a one-tank night trip with their equipment or yours. Snorkel and spearfishing trips are also available. ⊠ *MM 84 OS, 84001 Overseas Hwy., Windley Key* ☎ *305/664–3483, 800/327–7070* ⊕ *www.islamoradadivecenter.com* ☞ *Snorkel trips from $45, diving from $80.*

WATER SPORTS

The Kayak Shack. You can rent kayaks for trips to Indian (about 20 minutes one-way) and Lignumvitae (about 45 minutes one way) keys, two favorite destinations for paddlers. Kayaks can be rented for a half day (and you'll need plenty of time to explore those mangrove canopies). Pedal kayaks are also available and are a bit more expensive. The company also offers guided three-hour tours, including a snorkel trip to Indian Key. It also rents stand-up paddleboards, including instruction, and canoes. ⊠ *Robbie's Marina, MM 77.5 BS, 77522 Overseas Hwy., Lower Matecumbe Key* ☎ *305/664–4878* ⊕ *www.kayakthefloridakeys. com* ☞ *From $40 for single, $55 for double; guided trips from $45.*

THE MIDDLE KEYS

Most of the activity in this part of the Florida Keys centers on the town of Marathon—the region's third-largest metropolitan area. On either end of it, smaller keys hold resorts, wildlife research and rehab facilities, a historic village, and a state park. The Middle Keys make

Continued on page 200

DID YOU KNOW?

The coral making up the Barrier Reef is living and provides an ecosystem for small marine creatures. Bumping against or touching the coral can kill these creatures as well as damage the reef itself.

UNDER THE SEA
SNORKELING AND DIVING
IN THE FLORIDA KEYS by Lynne Helm

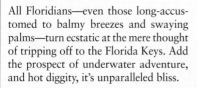

Up on the shore they work all day...

> While we devotin',
>
> Full time to floatin',
>
> Under the sea ...

—"Under the Sea,"
from Disney's *Little Mermaid*

All Floridians—even those long-accustomed to balmy breezes and swaying palms—turn ecstatic at the mere thought of tripping off to the Florida Keys. Add the prospect of underwater adventure, and hot diggity, it's unparalleled bliss.

Perennially laid back, the Keys annually attract nearly 800,000 snorkeling and scuba diving aficionados, and why not? There's arguably no better destination to learn these sports that put you up close to the wonders of life under the sea.

THE BARRIER REEF
The continental United States' only living coral barrier reef stretches 5 mi offshore of the Keys and is a teeming backbone of marine life, ranging from brilliant corals to neon-colored fish from blue-striped grunts to green moray eels. This is the prime reason why the Keys are where you descend upon intricate natural coral formations and encrusted shipwrecks, some historic, others sunk by design to create artificial reefs that attract divers

and provide protection for marine life. Most diving sites have mooring buoys (nautical floats away from shore, sometimes marking specific sites); these let you tie up your boat so you don't need to drop anchor, which could damage the reef. Most of these sites also are near individual keys, where dozens of dive operators can cater to your needs.

Reef areas thrive in waters as shallow as 5 feet and as deep as 50 feet. Shallow reefs attract snorkelers, while deeper reefs suit divers of varying experience levels. The Keys' shallow diving offers two benefits: longer time safely spent on the bottom exploring, and more vibrant colors because of sunlight penetration. Most divers log maximum depths of 20 to 30 feet.

(left) Shallow-water coral reef, (top) Nine Foot Stake is a popular site for underwater photography.

WHERE TO SNORKEL AND DIVE

KEY WEST
Mile Marker 0–4

You can soak up a mesmerizing overview of submerged watery wonders at the **Florida Keys Eco-Discovery Center**, opened in 2007 on Key West's Truman

Nine Foot Stake

Annex waterfront. Both admission and parking are free at the 6,000 square–foot center (☉ 9–4 Tues.–Sat. ☎ 305/809–4750); interactive exhibits here focus on Keys marine life and habitats. Key West's offshore reefs are best accessed via professional charters, but it's easy to snorkel from shore at **Key West Marine Park**. Marked by a lighthouse, **Sand Key Reef** attracts snorkelers and scuba divers. **Joe's Tug**, at 65-foot depths, sets up encounters with Goliath grouper. **Ten-Fathom Ledge**, with coral caves and dramatic overhangs, shelters lobster. The **Cayman Salvor**, a buoy tender sunk as an artificial reef in 1985, shelters baitfish. Patch reef **Nine Foot Stake**, submerged 10 to 25 feet, has soft corals and juvenile marine life. **Kedge Ledge** features a pair of coral-encrusted anchors from 18th-century sailing vessels. 🚩 *Florida Keys main visitor line at ☎ 800/FLA-KEYS (352-5397).*

BIG PINE KEY/LOWER KEYS
Mile Marker 4–47

Many devotees feel a Florida dive adventure would not be complete without heading 5 mi from Big Pine Key to **Looe Key National Marine Sanctuary**, an underwater preserve named for the HMS Looe running aground in 1744. If you time your visit for July, you might hit the one-day free underwater music festival for snorkelers

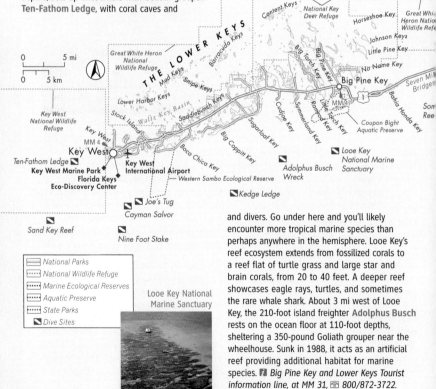

Looe Key National Marine Sanctuary

and divers. Go under here and you'll likely encounter more tropical marine species than perhaps anywhere in the hemisphere. Looe Key's reef ecosystem extends from fossilized corals to a reef flat of turtle grass and large star and brain corals, from 20 to 40 feet. A deeper reef showcases eagle rays, turtles, and sometimes the rare whale shark. About 3 mi west of Looe Key, the 210-foot island freighter **Adolphus Busch** rests on the ocean floor at 110-foot depths, sheltering a 350-pound Goliath grouper near the wheelhouse. Sunk in 1988, it acts as an artificial reef providing additional habitat for marine species. 🚩 *Big Pine Key and Lower Keys Tourist information line, at MM 31, ☎ 800/872-3722.*

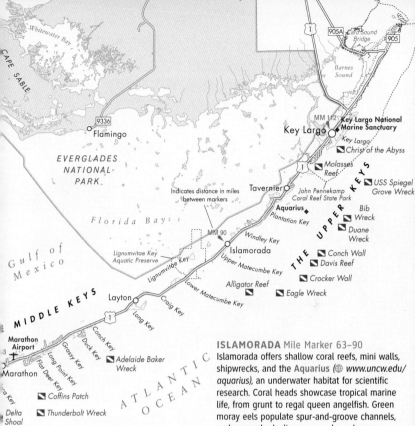

Whitewater Bay

CAPE SABLE

905A Card Sound Bridge 905

1

Barnes Sound

9336
Flamingo

MM 112 Key Largo National Marine Sanctuary
Key Largo

Key Largo
Christ of the Abyss

EVERGLADES NATIONAL PARK

Molasses Reef

1

USS Spiegel Grove Wreck

Indicates distance in miles between markers

Tavernier
John Pennekamp Coral Reef State Park

THE UPPER KEYS

Florida Bay

Aquarius
Plantation Key

Bib Wreck

Duane Wreck

Gulf of Mexico

MM 90
Windley Key

Islamorada
Upper Matecumbe Key

Conch Wall

Davis Reef

Lignumvitae Key Aquatic Preserve

Lignumvitae Key

Crocker Wall

Alligator Reef

Eagle Wreck

Layton
Craig Key
Lower Matecumbe Key

MIDDLE KEYS

1

Long Key

Conch Key

Marathon Airport

Duck Key

Grassy Key

Adelaide Baker Wreck

Long Point Key

ATLANTIC OCEAN

Hat Deer Key

Marathon

Coffins Patch

Delta Shoal

Thunderbolt Wreck

MARATHON/MIDDLE KEYS
Mile Marker 47–63

The Middle Keys yield a marine wilderness of a spur-and-groove coral and patch reefs. The **Adelaide Baker** historic shipwreck has a pair of stacks in 25 feet of water.

Sombrero Reef

Popular **Sombrero Reef**, with coral canyons and archways, is marked by a 140-foot lighted tower. Six distinct patch reefs known as **Coffin's Patch** have shallow elkhorn forests. **Delta Shoals**, a network of coral canyons fanning seaward from a sandy shoal, attracts divers to its elkhorn, brain, and star coral heads. Marathon's **Thunderbolt**, a 188-foot ship sunk in 1986, sits upright at 115-foot depths, coated with sponge, coral, and hydroid, and attracting angelfish, jacks, and deep-water pelagic creatures. 🚹 *Greater Marathon Chamber and visitors center at MM 53.5,* ☎ *800/262-7284.*

ISLAMORADA Mile Marker 63–90

Islamorada offers shallow coral reefs, mini walls, shipwrecks, and the **Aquarius** (🌐 www.uncw.edu/aquarius), an underwater habitat for scientific research. Coral heads showcase tropical marine life, from grunt to regal queen angelfish. Green moray eels populate spur-and-groove channels, and nurse sharks linger around overhangs. Submerged attractions include the **Eagle**, a 287-foot ship in 110 feet of water; **Davis Reef**, with gorgonian coral; **Alligator Reef**, where the *USS Alligator* sank while fighting pirates; the sloping **Conch Wall**, with barrel sponges and gorgonian; and **Crocker Wall**, featuring spur-and-groove and block corals. 🚹 *Islamorada Chamber and visitor center at MM 83.2,* ☎ *800/322-5397.*

KEY LARGO Mile Marker 90–112

Key Largo marine conservation got a big leg up with creation of **John Pennekamp Coral Reef State Park** in 1960, the nation's first undersea preserve, followed by 1975's designation of the **Key Largo National Marine Sanctuary**. A popular underwater attraction is the bronze statue of **Christ of the Abyss** between coral formations. Explorers with a "lust for rust" can dive down to 60 to 90 feet and farther to see the murky cemetery for two twin 327-foot U.S. Coast Guard cutters, *Duane* and *Bibb*, used during World War II; *USS Spiegel Grove*, a 510-foot Navy transport ship sunk in 2002 to create an artificial reef; and **Molasses Reef**, showcasing coral heads. 🚹 *Key Largo Chamber at MM 106,* ☎ *800/822-1088.*

SCUBA DIVING

A diver explores the coral reef in the Florida Keys National Marine Sanctuary off Key Largo.

Florida offers wonderful opportunities to spend your vacation in the sun and become a certified diver at the same time. In the Keys, count on setting aside three to five days for entry-level or so-called "Open Water" certification offered by many dive shops. Basic certification (covering depths to about 60 feet) involves classroom work and pool training, followed by one or more open-water dives at the reef. After passing a knowledge test and completing the required water training (often starting in a pool), you become a certified recreational scuba diver, eligible to rent dive gear and book dive trips with most operations worldwide. Learning through video or online computer programs can enable you to complete classroom work at home, so you can more efficiently schedule time in the Keys for completing water skills and getting out to the reef for exploration.

Many would-be divers opt to take the classroom instruction and pool training at home at a local dive shop and then spend only two days in the Keys completing four dives. It's not necessarily cheaper, but it can be far more relaxing to commit to only two days of diving.

Questions you should ask: Not all dive shops are created equal, and it may be worthwhile to spend extra money for a better diving experience. Some of the larger dive shops take out large catamarans that can carry as many as 24 to 40 people. Many people prefer the intimacy of a smaller boat.

4

Good to know: Divers can become certified through PADI *(www.padi.com)*, NAUI *(www.naui.org)*, or SSI *(www. divessi.com)*. The requirements for all three are similar, and if you do the classroom instruction and pool training with a dive shop associated with one organization, the referral for the open water dives will be honored by most dive shops. Note that you are not allowed to fly for at least 24 hours after a dive, because residual nitrogen in the body can pose health risks upon decompression. While there are no rigid rules on diving after flying, make sure you're well-hydrated before hitting the water.

Cost: The four-day cost can range from $300 to $475, but be sure to ask if equipment, instruction manuals, and log books are extra. Some dive shops have relationships with hotels, so check for dive/stay packages. Referral dives (a collaborative effort among training agencies) run from $285 to $300 and discover scuba runs around $175 to $200.

SNUBA

Beyond snorkeling or the requirements of scuba, you also have the option of "Snuba." The word is a trademarked portmanteau or combo of snorkel and scuba. Marketed as easy-to-learn family fun, Snuba lets you breathe underwater via tubes from an air-supplied vessel above, with no prior diving or snorkel experience required.

NOT CERTIFIED?

Not sure if you want to commit the time and money to become certified? Not a problem. Most dive shops and many resorts will offer a discover scuba day-long course. In the morning, the instructor will teach you the basics of scuba diving: how to clear your mask, how to come to the surface in the unlikely event you lose your air supply, etc. In the afternoon, instructors will take you out for a dive in relatively shallow water—less than 30 feet. Be sure to ask where the dive will take place. Jumping into the water off a shallow beach may not be as fun as actually going out to the coral. If you decide that diving is something you want to pursue, the open dive may count toward your certification.

■ TIP→ You can often book the discover dives at the last minute. It may not be worth it to go out on a windy day when the currents are stronger. Also the underwater world looks a whole lot brighter on sunny days.

(top) Scuba divers; (bottom) Diver ascending line.

SNORKELING

Snorkling lets you see the wonders of the sea from a new perspective.

The basics: Sure, you can take a deep breath, hold your nose, squint your eyes, and stick your face in the water in an attempt to view submerged habitats . . . but why not protect your eyes, retain your ability to breathe, and keep your hands free to paddle about when exploring underwater? That's what snorkeling is all about.

Equipment needed: A mask, snorkel (the tube attached to the mask), and fins. In deeper waters (any depth over your head), life jackets are advised.

Steps to success: If you've never snorkeled before, it's natural to feel a bit awkward at first, so don't sweat it. Breathing through a mask and tube, and wearing a pair of fins take getting used to. Like any activity, you build confidence and comfort through practice.

If you're new to snorkeling, begin by submerging your face in shallow water or a swimming pool and breathing calmly through the snorkel while gazing through the mask.

Next you need to learn how to clear water out of your mask and snorkel, an essential skill since splashes can send water into tube openings and masks can leak. Some snorkels have built-in drainage valves, but if a tube clogs, you can force water up and out by exhaling through your mouth. Clearing a mask is similar: lift your head from water while pulling forward on mask to drain. Some masks have built-in purge valves, but those without can be cleared underwater by pressing the top to the forehead and blowing out your nose (charming, isn't it?), allowing air to bubble into the mask, pushing water out the bottom. If it sounds hard, it really isn't. Just try it a few times and you'll soon feel like a pro.

Now your goal is to get friendly with fins—you want them to be snug but not too tight—and learn how to propel yourself with them. Fins won't help you float, but they will give you a leg up, so to speak, on smoothly moving through the water or treading water (even when upright) with less effort.

Flutter stroking is the most efficient underwater kick, and the farther your foot bends forward the more leg power you'll be able to transfer to the water and the farther you'll travel with each stroke. Flutter kicking movements involve alternately separating the legs and then drawing them back together. When your legs separate, the leg surface encounters drag from the water, slowing you down. When your legs are drawn back together, they produce a force pushing you forward. If your kick creates more forward force than it causes drag, you'll move ahead.

Submerge your fins to avoid fatigue rather than having them flailing above the water when you kick, and keep your arms at your side to reduce drag. You are in the water—stretched out, face down, and snorkeling happily away—but that doesn't mean you can't hold your breath and go deeper in the water for a closer look at some fish or whatever catches your attention. Just remember that when you do this, your snorkel will be submerged, too, so you won't be breathing (you'll be holding your breath). You can dive head-first, but going feet-first is easier and less scary for most folks, taking less momentum. Before full immersion, take several long, deep breaths to clear carbon dioxide from your lungs.

If your legs tire, flip onto your back and tread water with inverted fin motions while resting. If your mask fogs, wash condensation from lens and clear water from mask.

TIPS FOR SAFE SNORKELING

- Snorkel with a buddy and stay together.
- Plan your entry and exit points prior to getting in the water.
- Swim into the current on entering and then ride the current back to your exit point.
- Carry your flippers into the water and then put them on, as it's difficult to walk in them.
- Make sure your mask fits properly and is not too loose.
- Pop your head above the water periodically to ensure you aren't drifting too far out, or too close to rocks.
- Think of the water as someone else's home—don't take anything that doesn't belong to you, or leave any trash behind.
- Don't touch any sea creatures; they may sting.
- Wear a T-shirt over your swimsuit to help protect you from being fried by the sun.
- When in doubt, don't go without a snorkeling professional; try a guided tour.

Cayman Salvor

4

IN FOCUS UNDER THE SEA

a fitting transition from the Upper Keys to the Lower Keys not only geographically but mentally. Crossing Seven Mile Bridge prepares you for the slow pace and don't-give-a-damn attitude you'll find a little farther down the highway. Fishing is one of the main attractions—in fact, the region's commercial-fishing industry was founded here in the early 1800s. Diving is another popular pastime. There are many natural areas to enjoy in the Middle Keys, where mainland stress becomes an ever more distant memory.

If you get bridge fever—the heebie-jeebies when driving over long stretches of water—you may need a pair of blinders (or a couple of tranquilizers) before tackling the Middle Keys. Stretching from Conch Key to the far side of the Seven Mile Bridge, this zone is home to the region's two longest bridges: Long Key Viaduct and Seven Mile Bridge, both historic landmarks.

DUCK KEY

Duck Key is at mile marker 61.

Duck Key holds one of the region's nicest marina resorts, Hawks Cay, plus a boating-oriented residential community.

EXPLORING

Dolphin Connection. Hawk's Cay Resort's Dolphin Connection offers three programs, including Dockside Dolphins, a 30-minute encounter from the dry training docks; Dolphin Discovery, an in-water program that lasts about 45 minutes and lets you kiss, touch, and feed the dolphins; and Trainer for a Day, a three-hour session with the animal training team. ✉ *Hawk's Cay Resort, MM 61 OS, 61 Hawks Cay Blvd.* ☎ *305/743–7000* 🌐 *www.dolphinconnection.com* 🎟 *From $60.*

WHERE TO EAT AND STAY

$$$ LATIN AMERICAN 🍴 **Alma.** A refreshing escape from the Middle Keys' same-old menus, Alma serves expertly prepared Florida and Latin-Caribbean dishes in an elegant setting. Nightly changing menus might include a trio of ceviche, ahi tuna with a wonderful garbanzo bean tomato sauce, gnocchi and exotic mushroom ragout, or pan-seared Wagyu steak. Finish your meal with the silky, smooth, passion fruit crème brûlée, which has just the right amount of tartness to balance the delicate caramelized crust. [$] *Average main: $28* ✉ *Hawks Cay Resort, 61 Hawks Cay Blvd.* ☎ *305/743–7000, 888/432–2242* 🌐 *www.hawkscay.com* 🕒 *No lunch.*

$$$ RESORT FAMILY Fodor's Choice ★ 🏨 **Hawks Cay Resort.** The 60-acre, Caribbean-style retreat with a full-service spa and restaurants has plenty to keep the kids occupied (and adults happy). **Pros:** huge rooms; restful spa; full-service marina and dive shop. **Cons:** no real beach; far from Marathon's attractions. [$] *Rooms from: $315* ✉ *MM 61 OS, 61 Hawks Cay Blvd.* ☎ *305/743–7000, 888/432–2242* 🌐 *www.hawkscay.com* 🛏 *161 rooms, 16 suites, 254 2- and 3-bedroom villas* 🍽 *No meals.*

DID YOU KNOW?

Dolphins in Florida are predominantly of the Atlantic bottlenose variety. These playful and smart creatures love to leap out of the water and synchronize their movements with others. By swimming next to boats, dolphins can conserve energy.

GRASSY KEY

Grassy Key is between mile markers 60 and 57.

Local lore has it that this sleepy little key was named not for its vegetation—mostly native trees and shrubs—but for an early settler by the name of Grassy. The key is inhabited primarily by a few families operating small fishing camps and roadside motels. There's no marked definition between it and Marathon, so it feels sort of like a suburb of its much larger neighbor to the south. Grassy Key's sights tend toward the natural, including a worthwhile dolphin attraction and a small state park.

GETTING HERE AND AROUND

Most visitors arriving by air drive to this destination either from Miami International Airport or Key West International Airport. Rental cars are readily available at both, and in the long run, are the most convenient means of transportation for getting here and touring around the Keys.

EXPLORING

Curry Hammock State Park. Looking for a slice of the Keys that's far removed from tiki bars? On the ocean and bay sides of Overseas Highway are 260 acres of upland hammock, wetlands, and mangroves. On the bay side, there's a trail through thick hardwoods to a rocky shoreline. The ocean side is more developed, with a sandy beach, a clean bathhouse, picnic tables, a playground, grills, and a 28-site campground. Locals consider the paddling trails under canopies of arching mangroves one of the best kayaking spots in the Keys. Manatees frequent the area, and it's a great spot for bird-watching. Herons, egrets, ibis, plovers, and sanderlings are commonly spotted. Raptors are often seen in the park, especially during migration periods. ⊠ *MM 57 OS, 56200 Overseas Hwy., Little Crawl Key* ☎ *305/289–2690* ⊕ *www.floridastateparks.org/curryhammock* ✉ *$4.50 for 1 person, $6 for 2, 50¢ per additional person* ⊙ *Daily 8–sunset.*

FAMILY   **Dolphin Research Center.** The 1963 movie *Flipper* popularized the notion of humans interacting with dolphins, and Milton Santini, the film's creator, also opened this center, which is home to a colony of dolphins and sea lions. The nonprofit center has educational sessions and programs that allow you to greet the dolphins from dry land or play with them in their watery habitat. You can even paint a T-shirt with a dolphin—you pick the paint, the dolphin "designs" your shirt. The center also offers five-day programs for children and adults with disabilities. ⊠ *MM 59 BS, 58901 Overseas Hwy.* ☎ *305/289–1121 information, 305/289–0002 reservations* ⊕ *www.dolphins.org* ✉ *$25* ⊙ *Daily 9–4:30.*

WHERE TO EAT

$$$ ✕ **Hideaway Café.** The name says it all. Tucked between Grassy Key and
AMERICAN   Marathon, it's easy to miss if you're barnstorming through the middle islands. When you find it (upstairs at Rainbow Bend Resort), you'll discover a favorite of locals who appreciate a well-planned menu, lovely ocean view, and quiet evening away from the crowds—fancy with white tablecloths, but homey with worn carpeting. For starters, dig into escargots à la Edison (sautéed with vegetables, pepper, cognac, and cream).

Then feast on several specialties, such as a rarely found chateaubriand for one, a whole roasted duck, or the seafood medley combining the catch of the day with scallops and shrimp in a savory sauce. $ *Average main: $30* ⊠ *Rainbow Bend Resort, MM 58 OS, 57784 Overseas Hwy.* ☎ *305/289–1554* ⊕ *www.hideawaycafe.com* ⌣ *Reservations essential* ⊗ *No lunch.*

MARATHON

Marathon is between mile markers 53 and 47.5.

Marathon is a bustling town, at least compared with other Keys communities. If you get off the main drag, you'll find the few oceanfront hotels, but there are a number of good dining options right on Overseas Highway, so you'll definitely want to stop for a bite even if you're just passing through on the way to Key West.

If you stop a while, you'll find Marathon has the most historic attractions outside of Key West, and the well-worth-visiting Sombrero Beach—though fishing, diving, and boating are the main events here. The town throws tarpon tournaments in April and May, more fishing tournaments in June and September, a seafood festival in March, and lighted boat parades around the winter holidays.

New Englanders founded this former fishing village in the early 1800s. The community on Vaca Key subsequently served as a base for pirates, salvagers (also known as "wreckers"), spongers, and, later, Bahamian farmers who eked out a living growing cotton and other crops. More Bahamians arrived in hopes of finding work building the railroad. According to local lore, Marathon was renamed when a worker commented that it was a marathon task to position the tracks across the 6-mile-long island. During the building of the railroad, Marathon developed a reputation for lawlessness that rivaled that of the Old West. It's said that to keep the rowdy workers from descending on Key West for their off-hours endeavors, residents would send boatloads of liquor up to Marathon. Needless to say, things have quieted down considerably since then. Grassy Key segues into Marathon with little more than a slight increase in traffic and higher concentration of commercial establishments. Marathon's roots are anchored to fishing and boating, so look for marinas to find local color, fishing charters, and good restaurants. At its north end, Key Colony Beach is an old-fashioned island neighborhood worth a visit for its shops and restaurants. Just be warned the police are plentiful and love to catch speeders. Nature lovers shouldn't miss the attractions on Crane Point. Other good places to leave the main road are at Sombrero Beach Road (MM 50), which leads to the beach, and 35th Street (MM 49), which takes you to a funky little marina and restaurant. Overseas Highway hightails through Hog Key and Knight Key before the big leap over Florida Bay and Hawk's Channel via the Seven Mile Bridge.

GETTING HERE AND AROUND

The SuperShuttle charges $65 to $185 per passenger for trips from Miami International Airport to Key Largo. To go farther into the Keys, you must book an entire 11-person van, which costs about $250 to

Marathon. For a trip to or from the airport, place your request 24 hours in advance.

Miami Dade Transit provides daily bus service from MM 50 in Marathon to the Florida City Walmart Supercenter on the mainland. The bus stops at major shopping centers as well as on-demand anywhere along the route during daily round-trips on the hour from 6 am to 10 pm. The cost is $2 one-way, exact change required. The Lower Keys Shuttle bus runs from Marathon to Key West ($4 one way), with scheduled stops along the way.

ESSENTIALS

Transportation Contacts Lower Keys Shuttle ☎ *305/809–3910* ⊕ *www. kwtransit.com.* **Miami Dade Transit** ☎ *305/770–3131* ⊕ *www.miamidade.gov/ transit.*

Visitor Information Greater Marathon Chamber of Commerce and Visitor Center ✉ *MM 53.5 BS, 12222 Overseas Hwy.* ☎ *305/743–5417, 800/262–7284* ⊕ *www.floridakeysmarathon.com.*

EXPLORING

FAMILY **Crane Point Museum, Nature Center, and Historic Site.** Tucked away from the highway behind a stand of trees, Crane Point—part of a 63-acre tract that contains the last-known undisturbed thatch-palm hammock—is delightfully undeveloped. This multiuse facility includes the **Museum of Natural History of the Florida Keys,** which has displays about local wildlife, a seashell exhibit, and a marine-life display that makes you feel you're at the bottom of the sea. Kids love the replica 17th-century galleon and pirate dress-up room where they can play, and the re-created **Cracker House** filled with insects, sea-turtle exhibits, and children's activities. On the 1-mile indigenous loop trail, visit the **Laura Quinn Wild Bird Center** and the remnants of a Bahamian village, site of the restored **George Adderly House.** It is the oldest surviving example of Bahamian tabby (a concretelike material created from sand and seashells) construction outside of Key West. A boardwalk crosses wetlands, rivers, and mangroves before ending at Adderly Village. From November to Easter, docent-led tours are available; bring good walking shoes and bug repellent during warm weather. ✉ *MM 50.5 BS, 5550 Overseas Hwy.* ☎ *305/743–9100* ⊕ *www.cranepoint.net* 🎫 *$12.50* ⊘ *Mon.–Sat. 9–5, Sun. noon–5; call to arrange trail tours.*

Pigeon Key. There's much to like about this 5-acre island under the Old Seven Mile Bridge. You might even recognize it from one season finale of the TV show *The Amazing Race.* You can reach it via a ferry that departs from behind the visitors center (look for the old red railroad car on Knight's Key, MM 47 OS). Once there, tour the island on your own or join a guided tour to explore the buildings that formed the early-20th-century work camp for the Overseas Railroad that linked the mainland to Key West in 1912. Later the island became a fish camp, a state park, and then government-administration headquarters. Exhibits in a small museum recall the history of the Keys, the railroad, and railroad baron Henry M. Flagler. The ferry ride with tour lasts two hours; visitors can self-tour and catch the ferry back in a half hour. ✉ *MM 45*

OS, 1 Knights Key Blvd., Pigeon Key ☎ *305/743–5999* ⊕ *pigeonkey. net* ✉ *$12* ⊘ *Daily 9:30–2:30; ferry departures at 10, noon, and 2.*

Seven Mile Bridge. This is one of the most photographed images in the Keys. Actually measuring slightly less than 7 miles, it connects the Middle and Lower Keys and is believed to be the world's longest segmental bridge. It has 39 expansion joints separating its various concrete sections. Each April runners gather in Marathon for the annual Seven Mile Bridge Run. The expanse running parallel to Seven Mile Bridge is what remains of the **Old Seven Mile Bridge,** an engineering and architectural marvel in its day that's now on the National Register of Historic Places. Once proclaimed the Eighth Wonder of the World, it rested on a record 546 concrete piers. No cars are allowed on the old bridge today. ⊠ *Marathon.*

FAMILY **The Turtle Hospital.** More than 100 injured sea turtles check in here every year. The 90-minute guided tours take you into recovery and surgical areas at the world's only state-certified veterinary hospital for sea turtles. In the "hospital bed" tanks, you can see recovering patients and others that are permanent residents due to their injuries. After the tour, you can feed some of the "residents." Call ahead—space is limited and tours are sometimes canceled due to medical emergencies. The turtle ambulance out front makes for a memorable souvenir photo. ⊠ *MM 48.5 BS, 2396 Overseas Hwy.* ☎ *305/743–2552* ⊕ *www.turtlehospital. org* ✉ *$18* ⊘ *Daily 9–5.*

BEACHES

FAMILY **Sombrero Beach.** No doubt one of the best beaches in the Keys, here you'll find pleasant, shaded picnic areas that overlook a coconut palm–lined grassy stretch and the Atlantic Ocean. Roped-off areas allow swimmers, boaters, and windsurfers to share the narrow cove. Facilities include barbecue grills, a large playground, a pier, a volleyball court, and a paved, lighted bike path off Overseas Highway. Sunday afternoons draw lots of local families toting coolers. The park is accessible for those with disabilities and allows leashed pets. Turn east at the traffic light in Marathon and follow signs to the end. **Amenities:** showers; toilets. **Best for:** families; swimming; windsurfing. ⊠ *MM 50 OS, Sombrero Beach Rd.* ☎ *305/743–0033* ✉ *Free* ⊘ *Daily 8–sunset.*

WHERE TO EAT

$ SEAFOOD ✕ **Fish Tales Market and Eatery.** This roadside eatery with its own seafood market serves signature dishes such as snapper on grilled rye with coleslaw and melted Muenster cheese and a fried fish burrito. You also can slurp luscious lobster bisque or tomato-based conch chowder. There are burgers, chicken, and dogs for those who don't do seafood. Plan to dine early; it's only open until 6:30 pm (4 pm on Saturday).This is a no-frills kind of place with a loyal local following, unfussy ambience, a couple of outside picnic tables, and friendly service. $ *Average main: $9* ⊠ *MM 52.5 OS, 11711 Overseas Hwy.* ☎ *305/743–9196, 888/662–4822* ⊕ *www.floridalobster.com* ⚞ *Reservations not accepted* ⊘ *Closed Sun. No dinner Sat.*

$$ ITALIAN ✕ **Key Colony Inn.** The inviting aroma of an Italian kitchen pervades this family-owned favorite with a supper-club atmosphere. As you'd expect,

the service is friendly and attentive. For lunch there are fish and steak entrées served with fries, salad, and bread in addition to Italian specialties. At dinner you can't miss with traditional dishes like veal Oscar and New York strip, or such specialties as seafood *Italiano*, a dish of scallops and shrimp sautéed in garlic butter and served with marinara sauce over a bed of linguine. The place is renowned for its Sunday brunch, served from November to April. $ *Average main: $19* ⊠ *MM 54 OS, 700 W. Ocean Dr.* ☎ *305/743–0100* ⊕ *www.kcinn.com.*

$$
SEAFOOD
FAMILY
✕ **Keys Fisheries Market & Marina.** From the parking lot, you can't miss the enormous tiki bar on stilts, but the walk-up window on the ground floor is the heart of this warehouse-turned-restaurant. Order at the window, pick up your food, then dine at one of the waterfront tables outfitted with rolls of paper towels. The menu is comprised of fresh seafood and a token hamburger and chicken sandwich. A huge lobster Reuben ($16.95) served on thick slices of toasted bread is the signature dish. Other delights include the shrimp burger, very rich whiskey-peppercorn snapper, and the Keys Kombo (grilled lobster, shrimp, scallops, and mahimahi for $33). The adults-only upstairs tiki bar offers a sushi and raw bar for eat-in only. Bring quarters for fish food—you can feed the tarpon while you wait for your food. $ *Average main: $16* ⊠ *MM 49 BS, 3390 Gulfview Ave., at end of 35th St.* ⊹ *Turn right on 35th St. off Gulfview Ave.* ☎ *305/743–4353, 866/743–4353* ⊕ *www.keysfisheries. com* ⌦ *Reservations not accepted.*

$$$
SEAFOOD
Fodor'sChoice
★
✕ **Lazy Days South.** Tucked into Marathon Marina a half mile north of the Seven Mile Bridge, this restaurant offers views just as spectacular as its highly lauded food. A spin-off of an Islamorada favorite, here you'll find a wide range of daily offerings from fried- or sautéed conch and a coconut-fried fish du jour sandwich to seafood pastas and beef tips over rice. Choose a table on the outdoor deck, or inside underneath paddle fans and surrounded by local art. $ *Average main: $22* ⊠ *MM 47.3 OS, 725 11th St.* ☎ *305/289–0839* ⊕ *www.lazydayssouth.com.*

$
DINER
✕ **The Stuffed Pig.** With only nine tables and a counter inside, this breakfast-and-lunch place is always hopping. When the weather's right, grab a table out back. The kitchen whips up daily lunch specials like burgers, seafood platters, or pulled pork with hand-cut fries, but a quick glance around the room reveals that the all-day breakfast is the main draw. You can get the usual breakfast plates, but most newcomers opt for oddities like the lobster omelet, alligator tail and eggs, or "grits and grunts" (that's fish, to the rest of us). $ *Average main: $9* ⊠ *MM 49 BS, 3520 Overseas Hwy.* ☎ *305/743–4059* ⊕ *www.thestuffedpig.com* ⌦ *Reservations not accepted* ⊟ *No credit cards* ⊗ *No dinner.*

WHERE TO STAY

$$
RENTAL
🏠 **Glunz Ocean Beach Hotel & Resort.** The Glunz family got it right when they purchased this former time-share property and put a whole lot of love into renovating it to its full oceanfront potential. **Pros:** oceanfront; convenient amenities; excellent free Wi-Fi. **Cons:** neighbor noise; small elevator; no interior corridors; not cheap. $ *Rooms from: $260* ⊠ *MM 53.5 OS, 351 E. Ocean Dr.* ☎ *305/289–0525* ⊕ *www. GlunzOceanBeachHotel.com* ⤴ *22 rooms, 16 suites, 8 3-bed/3-bath villas* ⭘ *No meals.*

$$$ RESORT FAMILY Fodor's Choice ★ **Tranquility Bay.** Ralph Lauren could have designed the rooms at this stylish, luxurious resort on a nice beach. **Pros:** secluded setting; gorgeous design; lovely crescent beach. **Cons:** a bit sterile; no real Keys atmosphere; cramped building layout. [$] *Rooms from: $399* ✉ *MM 48.5 BS, 2600 Overseas Hwy.* ☎ *305/289–0888, 866/643–5397* 🌐 *www.tranquilitybay.com* 🛏 *16 rooms, 45 2-bedroom suites, 41 3-bedroom suites* 🍴 *No meals.*

SPORTS AND THE OUTDOORS

BIKING

Bike Marathon Bike Rentals. "Have bikes, will deliver" could be the motto of this company, which gets beach cruisers to your hotel door, including a helmet and basket. They also rent kayaks. Note that there's no physical location, but services are available Monday through Saturday 9–4 and Sunday 9–2. ✉ *Marathon* ☎ *305/743–3204* 🌐 *www.bikemarathonbikerentals.com* 🎟 *$45 per wk.*

Overseas Outfitters. Aluminum cruisers and hybrid bikes are available for rent at this outfitter. It's open weekdays 9–5:30 and Saturday 9–3. All rentals include a helmet and lock. ✉ *MM 48 BS, 1700 Overseas Hwy.* ☎ *305/289–1670* 🌐 *www.overseasoutfitters.com* 🎟 *Rentals from $15 per day.*

BOATING

Sail, motor, or paddle—whatever your choice of modes, boating is what the Keys are all about. Brave the Atlantic waves and reefs or explore the backcountry islands on the calmer gulf side. If you don't have a lot of boating and chart-reading experience, it's a good idea to tap into local knowledge on a charter.

Captain Pip's. This operator rents 19- to 24-foot outboards as well as tackle and snorkeling gear. Fishing charters are also available with a captain and a mate (full-day charters are also available). Ask about multiday deals, or try one of their accommodation packages and walk right from your bay-front room to your boat. ✉ *MM 47.5 BS, 1410 Overseas Hwy.* ☎ *305/743–4403, 800/707–1692* 🌐 *www.captainpips.com* 🎟 *Rentals from $195 per day; half-day charters from $650.*

Fish 'n Fun. Get out on the water on 19- to 26-foot powerboats. Rentals can be for a half or full day. The company also offers free delivery in the Middle Keys. ✉ *MM 49.5 OS, 4590 Overseas Hwy., at Banana Bay Resort & Marina* ☎ *305/743–2275, 800/471–3440* 🌐 *www.fishnfunrentals.com* 🎟 *From $175.*

FISHING

For recreational anglers, the deepwater fishing is superb in the ocean. Marathon West Hump, one good spot, has depths ranging from 500 to more than 1,000 feet. Locals fish from a half dozen bridges, including Long Key Bridge, the Old Seven Mile Bridge, and both ends of Tom's Harbor. Barracuda, bonefish, mahimahi, and tarpon all frequent local waters. Party boats and private charters are available.

Marathon Lady. Morning, afternoon, and night, fish for mahimahi, grouper, and other tasty catch aboard this 73-footer, which departs on half-day excursions from the Vaca Cut Bridge (MM53), north of Marathon.

Join the crew for night fishing ($55) from 6:30 to midnight from Memorial Day to Labor Day; it's especially beautiful on a full-moon night. ✉ *MM 53 OS., 11711 Overseas Hwy., at 117th St.* ☎ *305/743–5580* ⊕ *www.marathonlady.net* ⌨ *From $50.*

Sea Dog Charters. Captain Jim Purcell, a deep-sea specialist for ESPN's *The American Outdoorsman,* provides one of the best values in Keys fishing. Next to the Seven Mile Grill, his company offers half- and full-day offshore, reef and wreck, and backcountry fishing trips, as well as fishing and snorkeling trips aboard 30- to 37-foot boats. The per-person for a half-day trip is the same regardless of whether your group fills the boat, and includes bait, light tackle, ice, coolers, and fishing licenses. If you prefer an all-day private charter on a 37-foot boat, he offers those, too, for up to six people. A fuel surcharge may apply. ✉ *MM 47.5 BS, 1248 Overseas Hwy.* ☎ *305/743–8255* ⊕ *www. seadogcharters.net* ⌨ *From $60.*

SCUBA DIVING AND SNORKELING

Local dive operations take you to Sombrero Reef and Lighthouse, the most popular down-under destination in these parts. For a shallow dive and some lobster nabbing, Coffins Patch, off Key Colony Beach, is a good choice. A number of wrecks such as *Thunderbolt* serve as artificial reefs. Many operations out of this area will also take you to Looe Key Reef.

Hall's Diving Center & Career Institute. The institute has been training divers for more than 40 years. Along with conventional twice-a-day snorkel and two-tank dive trips to the reefs at Sombrero Lighthouse and wrecks like the *Thunderbolt,* the company has more unusual offerings like rebreather, photography, and nitrox courses. ✉ *MM 48.5 BS, 1994 Overseas Hwy.* ☎ *305/743–5929, 800/331–4255* ⊕ *www.hallsdiving. com* ⌨ *From $45.*

Spirit Snorkeling. Join regularly scheduled snorkeling excursions to Sombrero Reef and Lighthouse Reef on this company's comfortable catamaran. They also offer sunset cruises, private charters, and new-age yoga cruises. ✉ *MM 47.5 BS, 1410 Overseas Hwy., Slip No. 1* ☎ *305/289–0614* ⊕ *www.spiritsnorkeling.net* ⌨ *From $30.*

THE LOWER KEYS

Beginning at Bahia Honda Key, the islands of the Florida Keys become smaller, more clustered, and more numerous—a result of ancient tidal water flowing between the Florida Straits and the gulf. Here you're likely to see more birds and mangroves than other tourists, and more refuges, beaches, and campgrounds than museums, restaurants, and hotels. The islands are made up of two types of limestone, both denser than the highly permeable Key Largo limestone of the Upper Keys. As a result, freshwater forms in pools rather than percolating through the rock, creating watering holes that support alligators, snakes, deer, rabbits, raccoons, and migratory ducks. Many of these animals can be seen in the National Key Deer Refuge on Big Pine Key. Nature was generous with her beauty in the Lower Keys, which have both Looe

Key Reef, arguably the Keys' most beautiful tract of coral, and Bahia Honda State Park, considered one of the best beaches in the world for its fine-sand dunes, clear warm waters, and panoramic vista of a historic bridge, hammocks, and azure sky and sea. Big Pine Key is fishing headquarters for a laid-back community that swells with retirees in the winter. South of it, the dribble of islands can flash by in a blink of an eye if you don't take the time to stop at a roadside eatery or check out tours and charters at the little marinas.

GETTING HERE AND AROUND

The Lower Keys in this section include the keys between MM 37 and MM 9. The Seven Mile Bridge drops you into the lap of this homey, quiet part of the Keys.

Heed speed limits in these parts. They may seem incredibly strict given that the traffic is lightest of anywhere in the Keys, but the purpose is to protect the resident Key deer population, and officers of the law pay strict attention and will readily issue speeding tickets.

BAHIA HONDA KEY

Bahia Honda Key is between mile markers 38 and 36.

All of Bahia Honda Key is devoted to its eponymous state park, which keeps it in a pristine state. Besides the park's outdoor activities, it offers an up-close look at the original railroad bridge.

EXPLORING

FAMILY

Fodor's Choice

★

Bahia Honda State Park. Most first-time visitors to the region are dismayed by the lack of beaches—but then they discover Bahia Honda Key. The 524-acre park sprawls across both sides of the highway, giving it 2½ miles of fabulous sandy coastline. The snorkeling isn't bad, either; there's underwater life (soft coral, queen conchs, random little fish) just a few hundred feet offshore. Although swimming, kayaking, fishing, and boating are the main reasons to visit, you shouldn't miss biking along the 2½ miles of flat roads or hiking the Silver Palm Trail, with rare West Indies plants and several species found nowhere else in the nation. Along the way you'll be treated to a variety of butterflies. Seasonal ranger-led nature programs take place at or depart from the Sand and Sea Nature Center. There are rental cabins, a campground, snack bar, gift shop, 19-slip marina, nature center, and facilities for renting kayaks and arranging snorkeling tours. Get a panoramic view of the island from what's left of the railroad—the Bahia Honda Bridge. ⊠ *MM 37 OS, 36850 Overseas Hwy.* ☎ *305/872–2353* ⊕ *www.floridastateparks. org/bahiahonda* 🖻 *$4.50 for single occupant vehicle, $8 for vehicle with 2–8 people, plus 50¢ per person up to 8* ⊗ *Daily 8–sunset.*

BEACHES

Sandspur Beach. Bahia Honda Key State Beach contains three beaches in all—on both the Atlantic Ocean and the Gulf of Mexico. Sandspur Beach, the largest, is regularly declared the best beach in the Florida Keys, and you'll be hard-pressed to argue. The sand is baby-powder soft, and the aqua water is warm, clear, and shallow. With their mild currents, the beaches are great for swimming, even with

DID YOU KNOW?

An old railroad bridge connected Bahia Honda Key with Key West until a hurricane destroyed it in 1935. The bridge is no longer in operation, yet it's standing, barely. Falling debris prevents snorkeling below or exploring, but it makes for pretty photos, especially at sunrise and sunset.

small fry. **Amenities:** food and drink; showers; toilets; water sports. **Best for:** snorkeling; swimming. ✉ *MM 37 OS, 36850 Overseas Hwy.* ☎ *305/872–2353* 🌐 *www.floridastateparks.org/bahiahonda* 🎫 *$4.50 for single-occupant vehicle, $9 for vehicle with 2–8 people* 🕒 *Daily 8–sunset.*

WHERE TO STAY

$ RENTAL 🏨 **Bahia Honda State Park Cabins.** Elsewhere you'd pay big bucks for the wonderful water views available at these cabins on Florida Bay. **Pros:** great bay-front views; beachfront camping; affordable rates. **Cons:** books up fast; area can be buggy. [$] *Rooms from: $163* ✉ *MM 37 OS, 36850 Overseas Hwy.* ☎ *305/872–2353, 800/326–3521* 🌐 *www.reserveamerica.com* 🛏 *6 cabins* 🍴 *No meals.*

SPORTS AND THE OUTDOORS

SCUBA DIVING AND SNORKELING

Bahia Honda Dive Shop. The concessionaire at Bahia Honda State Park manages a 19-slip marina; rents wet suits, snorkel equipment, and corrective masks; and operates twice-a-day offshore-reef snorkel trips. Park visitors looking for other fun can rent kayaks and beach chairs. ✉ *MM 37 OS, 36850 Overseas Hwy.* ☎ *305/872–3210* 🌐 *www.bahiahondapark.com* 🕒 *Kayak rentals from $10 per hr; snorkel tours from $30.*

BIG PINE KEY

Big Pine Key runs from mile marker 32 to 30.

Welcome to the Keys' most natural holdout, where wildlife refuges protect rare and endangered animals. Here you've left behind the commercialism of the Upper Keys for an authentic backcountry atmosphere.

How could things get more casual than Key Largo? Find out by exiting Overseas Highway to explore the habitat of the charmingly diminutive Key deer or cast a line from No Name Bridge. Tours explore the expansive waters of National Key Deer Refuge and Great White Heron National Wildlife Refuge, one of the first such refuges in the country. Along with Key West National Wildlife Refuge, it encompasses more than 200,000 acres of water and more than 8,000 acres of land on 49 small islands. Besides its namesake bird, the Great White Heron National Wildlife Refuge provides habitat for uncounted species of birds and three species of sea turtles. It's the only U.S. breeding site for the endangered hawksbill turtle.

ESSENTIALS

Visitor Information Big Pine and the Lower Keys Chamber of Commerce ☎ *305/872–2411, 800/872–3722* 🌐 *www.lowerkeyschamber.com.*

EXPLORING

National Key Deer Refuge. This 84,824-acre refuge was established in 1957 to protect the dwindling population of the Key deer, one of more than 22 animals and plants federally classified as endangered or threatened, including five that are found nowhere else on Earth. The Key deer, which stands about 30 inches at the shoulders and is a subspecies of

4

the Virginia white-tailed deer, once roamed throughout the Lower and Middle Keys, but hunting, destruction of their habitat, and a growing human population caused their numbers to decline to 27 by 1957. The deer have made a comeback, increasing their numbers to approximately 750. The best place to see Key deer in the refuge is at the end of Key Deer Boulevard and on No Name Key, a sparsely populated island just east of Big Pine Key. Mornings and evenings are the best time to spot them. Deer may turn up along the road at any time of day, so drive slowly. They wander into nearby yards to nibble tender grass and bougainvillea blossom, but locals do not appreciate tourists driving into their neighborhoods after them. Feeding them is against the law and puts them in danger.

A quarry left over from railroad days, the **Blue Hole** is the largest body of freshwater in the Keys. From the observation platform and nearby walking trail, you might see the resident alligator, turtles, and other wildlife. There are two well-marked trails, recently revamped: the Jack Watson Nature Trail (0.6 mile), named after an environmentalist and the refuge's first warden; and the Fred Mannillo Nature Trail (0.2 mile), one of the most wheelchair-accessible places to see an unspoiled pine-rockland forest and wetlands. The visitor center has exhibits on Keys biology and ecology. The refuge also provides information on the Key West National Wildlife Refuge and the Great White Heron National Wildlife Refuge. Accessible only by water, both are popular with kayak outfitters. ✉ *MM 30.5 BS, Visitor Center–Headquarters, Big Pine Shopping Center, 28950 Watson Blvd.* ☎ *305/872–2239* 🌐 *www.fws.gov/nationalkeydeer* 🎟 *Free* 🕒 *Daily sunrise–sunset; headquarters weekdays 8–5.*

WHERE TO EAT

$ VEGETARIAN

🍴 **Good Food Conspiracy.** Like good wine, this small natural-foods eatery and market surrenders its pleasures a little at a time. Step inside to the aroma of brewing coffee, and then pick up the scent of fresh strawberries or carrots blending into a smoothie, the green aroma of wheatgrass juice, followed by the earthy odor of hummus. Order raw or cooked vegetarian and vegan dishes, organic soups and salads, and organic coffees and teas. Bountiful sandwiches include the popular tuna melt or hummus and avocado. Sit at the counter or in the back garden and mingle with the locals as folks have been doing since the early 1980s. Then stock up on healthful snacks like dried fruits, raw nuts, and carob-covered almonds. Gluten-free items, too. [$] *Average main: $10* ✉ *MM 30.2 OS, 30150 Overseas Hwy.* ☎ *305/872–3945* 🌐 *www.goodfoodconspiracy.com* ✍ *Reservations not accepted* 🕒 *No dinner Sun.*

$ AMERICAN

🍴 **No Name Pub.** This no-frills honky-tonk has been around since 1936, delighting inveterate locals and intrepid vacationers who come for the excellent pizza, cold beer, and *interesting* companionship. The decor, such as it is, amounts to the autographed dollar bills that cover every inch of the place. The full menu printed on place mats includes a tasty conch chowder, a half-pound fried-grouper sandwich, spaghetti and meatballs, and seafood baskets. The lighting is poor, the furnishings are rough, and the music is oldies. This former brothel and bait shop is just before the No Name Key Bridge in the midst of a residential neighborhood. It's a bit hard to find, but worth the trouble if you want a singular Keys experience. $ *Average main: $15* ⊠ *MM 30 BS, 30813 Watson Blvd.* ✛ *From U.S. 1, turn west on Wilder Rd., left on South St., right on Ave. B, right on Watson Blvd.* ☎ *305/872–9115* ⊕ *www. nonamepub.com* ⚄ *Reservations not accepted.*

WHERE TO STAY

$

HOTEL

Big Pine Key Fishing Lodge. There's a congenial atmosphere at this lively family-owned lodge-campground-marina—a happy mix of tent campers (who have the fabulous waterfront real estate), RVers (who look pretty permanent), and motel dwellers who like to mingle at the rooftop pool and challenge each other to a game of poker. **Pros:** local fishing crowd; nice pool; great price. **Cons:** RV park is too close to motel; deer will eat your food if you're camping. $ *Rooms from: $114* ⊠ *MM 33 OS, 33000 Overseas Hwy.* ☎ *305/872–2351* ⊕ *www.big-pine-key.com/fishinglodge.php* ⤳ *16 rooms* ⦿ *No meals* ⚄ *To protect Key deer, no dogs allowed.*

$$$

B&B/INN

Deer Run Bed & Breakfast. Innkeepers Jen DeMaria and Harry Appel were way ahead of the green-lodging game when they opened in 2004, and guests love how Key deer wander the grounds of this beachfront B&B on a residential street lined with mangroves. **Pros:** quiet location; vegan, organic breakfasts; complimentary bikes, kayaks, and state park passes. **Cons:** price is a bit high; hard to find. $ *Rooms from: $355* ⊠ *MM 33 OS, 1997 Long Beach Dr.* ☎ *305/872–2015* ⊕ *www. deerrunfloridabb.com* ⤳ *4 rooms* ⦿ *Breakfast.*

SPORTS AND THE OUTDOORS

BIKING

A good 10 miles of paved roads run from MM 30.3 BS, along Wilder Road, across the bridge to No Name Key, and along Key Deer Boulevard into the National Key Deer Refuge. Along the way you might see some Key deer. Stay off the trails that lead into wetlands, where fat tires can do damage to the environment.

Big Pine Bicycle Center. Owner Marty Baird is an avid cyclist and enjoys sharing his knowledge of great places to ride. He's also skilled at selecting the right bike for the journey, and he knows his repairs, too. His old-fashioned single-speed, fat-tire cruisers rent by the half or full day. Helmets, baskets, and locks are included. ⊠ *MM 30.9 BS, 31 County Rd.* ☎ *305/872–0130* ⊕ *www.bigpinebikes.com* ⛛ *From $8.*

BOATING AND FISHING EXCURSIONS

Those looking to fish can cast from No Name Key Bridge or hire a charter to take them into backcountry or deep waters for fishing year-round. If you're looking for a good snorkeling spot, stay close to Looe Key Reef, which is prime scuba and snorkeling territory. One resort caters to divers with dive boats that depart from their own dock. Others can make arrangements for you.

Strike Zone Charters. Glass-bottom-boat excursions venture into the backcountry and Atlantic Ocean. The five-hour Island Excursion emphasizes nature and Keys history; besides close encounters with birds, sea life, and vegetation, there's a fish cookout on an island. Snorkel and fishing equipment, food, and drinks are included. This is one of the few nature outings in the Keys with wheelchair access. Deep-sea charter rates for up to six people can be arranged for a half or full day. It also offers flats fishing in the Gulf of Mexico. Dive excursions head to the wreck of the 110-foot *Adolphus Busch*, and scuba and snorkel trips to Looe Key Reef, prime scuba and snorkeling territory, aboard glass-bottom boats. ⊠ *MM 29.6 BS, 29675 Overseas Hwy.* ☎ *305/872–9863, 800/654–9560* ⊕ *www.strikezonecharter.com* ⊟ *From $38.*

KAYAKING

There's nothing like the vast expanse of pristine waters and mangrove islands preserved by national refuges from here to Key West. The maze-like terrain can be confusing, so it's wise to hire a guide at least the first time out.

Big Pine Kayak Adventures. There's no excuse to skip a water adventure with this convenient kayak rental service, which delivers them to your lodging or anywhere between Seven Mile Bridge and Stock Island. The company, headed by *The Florida Keys Paddling Guide* author Bill Keogh, will rent you a kayak and then ferry you—called taxi-yakking—to remote islands with clear instructions on how to paddle back on your own. Rentals are by the half day or full day. Three-hour group kayak tours are the cheapest option and explore the mangrove forests of Great White Heron and Key Deer National Wildlife Refuges. More expensive four-hour custom tours transport you to exquisite backcountry areas teeming with wildlife. Kayak fishing charters are also popular. ⊠ *Old Wooden Bridge Fishing Camp* ⊕ *From MM 30, turn right at traffic light, continue on Wilder Rd. toward No Name Key; fishing camp is just before bridge with big yellow kayak on sign out front* ☎ *305/872–7474* ⊕ *www.keyskayaktours.com* ⊟ *From $50.*

LITTLE TORCH KEY

Little Torch Key is between mile markers 29 and 10.

Little Torch Key and its neighbor islands, Ramrod Key and Summerland Key, are good jumping-off points for divers headed for Looe Key Reef. The islands also serve as a refuge for those who want to make forays into Key West but not stay in the thick of things.

The undeveloped backcountry at your door makes Little Torch Key an ideal location for fishing and kayaking. Nearby Ramrod Key, which also caters to divers bound for Looe Key, derives its name from a ship that wrecked on nearby reefs in the early 1800s.

NEED A BREAK?

Baby's Coffee. The aroma of rich roasting coffee beans arrests you at the door of "the Southernmost Coffee Roaster." Buy it by the pound or by the cup along with sandwiches and sweets. ⊠ *MM 15 OS, 3180 Overseas Hwy.* ☎ *305/744–9866, 800/523–2326* ⊕ *www.babyscoffee.com.*

WHERE TO EAT

$$

AMERICAN

✕ Geiger Key Smokehouse Bar & Grill. There's a strong hint of the Old Keys at this oceanside marina restaurant, which came under new management in 2010 by the same folks who own Hogfish Grill on Stock Island.

"On the backside of paradise," as the sign says, its tiki structures overlook quiet mangroves at an RV park marina. Locals usually outnumber tourists. The all-day menu spans an ambitious array of sandwiches, tacos, and seafood. Local fishermen stop here for breakfast before heading out in search of the big one. Don't miss the Sunday barbecue from 4 to 9. $ *Average main: $16* ⊠ *MM 10, 5 Geiger Key Rd., off Boca Chica Rd., Bay Point, Geiger Key* ☎ *305/296–3553, 305/294–1230* ⊕ *www.geigerkeymarina.com.*

$$
SEAFOOD

✕ **Mangrove Mama's Restaurant.** This could be the prototype for a Keys restaurant, given its shanty appearance, lattice trim, and roving sort of indoor-outdoor floor plan. Then there's the seafood, from the ubiquitous fish sandwich (fried, grilled, broiled, or blackened) to lobster reubens, crab cakes, and coconut shrimp. Burgers, steaks, and ribs round out the menu. Hidden in a grove of banana and palm trees, the place opens for lunch, Sunday brunch, and dinner. $ *Average main: $20* ⊠ *MM 20 BS, Sugarloaf Key* ☎ *305/745–3030* ⊕ *www.mangrovemamasrestaurant.com.*

$$$
SEAFOOD
Fodor's Choice
★

✕ **Square Grouper.** In an unassuming warehouse-looking building right off U.S. 1, chef and owner Lynn Bell is creating seafood magic. Just ask the locals, who wait in line for a table along with visitors in the know. But don't let the exterior fool you: the dining room is surprisingly suave, with butcher paper–lined tables, mandarin-color walls, and textural components throughout. While the restaurant earns rave reviews, its name still earns snickers. (A "square grouper" is slang for bales of marijuana dropped into the ocean during the drug-running 1970s.) The dishes here not only taste close-your-eyes-and-grin good, their presentation is lovely. For starters, try the flash-fried conch with wasabi drizzle or home-smoked fish dip. Then perhaps order the seafood pasta with key lime butter sauce. It's okay to drool. Upstairs, Chef Lynn has just opened a beatnik-style tapas bar. $ *Average main: $25* ⊠ *MM 22.5 OS, Cudjoe Key* ☎ *305/745–8880* ⊕ *www.squaregrouperbarandgrill.com* ⊗ *Closed Sun.; Mon. May–Dec.; and Sept.*

WHERE TO STAY

$$$$
RESORT
Fodor's Choice
★

⊞ **Little Palm Island Resort & Spa.** *Haute tropicale* best describes this luxury retreat, and "second mortgage" might explain how some can afford the extravagant prices. **Pros:** secluded setting; heavenly spa; easy wildlife viewing. **Cons:** expensive; might be too quiet for some; only accessible by boat or seaplane. $ *Rooms from: $1590* ⊠ *MM 28.5 OS, 28500 Overseas Hwy.* ☎ *305/872–2524, 800/343–8567* ⊕ *www.littlepalmisland.com* ⇆ *30 suites* ⦿ *Some meals* ↝ *No one under 16 allowed on island.*

$
HOTEL

⊞ **Parmer's Resort.** Almost every room at this budget-friendly option has a view of South Pine Channel, with the lovely curl of Big Pine Key in the foreground. **Pros:** bright rooms; pretty setting; good value. **Cons:** a bit out of the way; housekeeping costs extra; little shade around the pool. $ *Rooms from: $159* ⊠ *MM 28.7 BS, 565 Barry Ave.* ☎ *305/872–2157* ⊕ *www.parmersresort.com* ⇆ *18 rooms, 12 efficiencies, 15 apartments, 2 2-bedroom cottages* ⦿ *Breakfast.*

SPORTS AND THE OUTDOORS

BOATING AND KAYAKING

Dolphin Marina. Dolphin Marina rents 19- and 22-foot boats with 150 horsepower for up to eight people by the half day and full day. ✉ *28530 Overseas Hwy.* ☎ *305/872–2685* ⊕ *www.dolphinmarina.net* ⬛ *From $200 half day, from $250 full day.*

Sugarloaf Marina. Rates for one-person kayaks are based on an hourly or daily rental. Two-person kayaks are also available. Delivery is free for rentals of three days or more. The folks at the marina can also hook you up with an outfitter for a day of offshore or backcountry fishing. There's also a well-stocked ship store. ✉ *MM 17 BS, 17015 Overseas Hwy., Sugarloaf Key* ☎ *305/745–3135* ⊕ *www.sugarloafkeymarina. com* ⬛ *From $15 per hr.*

SCUBA DIVING AND SNORKELING

In 1744 the HMS *Looe*, a British warship, ran aground and sank on one of the most beautiful coral reefs in the Keys, 5 nautical miles off the coast of Little Torch Key. Today the key owes its name to the ill-fated ship. The 5.3-square-nautical-mile reef, part of the Florida Keys National Marine Sanctuary, has strands of elkhorn coral on its eastern margin, purple sea fans, and abundant sponges and sea urchins. On its seaward side, it drops almost vertically 50 to 90 feet. In its midst, Shipwreck Trail plots the location of nine historic wreck sites in 14 to 120 feet of water. Buoys mark the sites, and underwater signs tell the history of each site and what marine life to expect. Snorkelers and divers will find the sanctuary a quiet place to observe reef life—except in July, when the annual Underwater Music Festival pays homage to Looe Key's beauty and promotes reef awareness with six hours of music broadcast via underwater speakers. Dive shops, charters, and private boats transport about 500 divers and snorkelers to hear the spectacle, which includes classical, jazz, new age, and Caribbean music, as well as a little Jimmy Buffett. There are even underwater Elvis impersonators.

Looe Key Reef Resort & Dive Center. This center, the closest dive shop to Looe Key Reef, offers two affordable trips daily, 7:30 am or 12:15 pm (for divers, snorkelers, or bubble watchers). The maximum depth is 30 feet, so snorkelers and divers go on the same boat. Call to check for availability for wreck and night dives. The dive boat, a 45-foot catamaran, is docked at the full-service Looe Key Reef Resort. ✉ *Looe Key Reef Resort, MM 27.5 OS, 27340 Overseas Hwy., Ramrod Key* ☎ *305/872–2215, 877/816–3483* ⊕ *www.diveflakeys.com* ⬛ *From $39.*

EN ROUTE The huge object that looks like a white whale floating over Cudjoe Key (MM 23–21) isn't a figment of your imagination. It's Fat Albert, a radar balloon that monitors local air and water traffic.

KEY WEST

Situated 150 miles from Miami, 90 miles from Havana, and an immeasurable distance from sanity, this end-of-the-line community has never been like anywhere else. Even after it was connected to the rest of the country—by the railroad in 1912 and by the highway in 1938—it maintained a strong sense of detachment.

Key West reflects a diverse population: Conchs (natives, many of whom trace their ancestry to the Bahamas), freshwater Conchs (longtime residents who migrated from somewhere else years ago), Hispanics (primarily descendants of Cuban immigrants), recent refugees from the urban sprawl of mainland Florida, military personnel, and an assortment of vagabonds, drifters, and dropouts in search of refuge. The island was once a gay vacation hot spot, and it remains a decidedly gay-friendly destination. Some of the most renowned gay guesthouses, however, no longer cater to an exclusively gay clientele. Key Westers pride themselves on their tolerance of all peoples, all sexual orientations, and even all animals. Most restaurants allow pets, and it's not surprising to see stray cats, dogs, and chickens roaming freely through the dining rooms. The chicken issue is one that government officials periodically try to bring to an end, but the colorful iconic fowl continue to strut and crow, particularly in the vicinity of Old Town's Bahamian Village.

Although the rest of the Keys are known for outdoor activities, Key West has something of a city feel. Few open spaces remain, as promoters continue to churn out restaurants, galleries, shops, and museums to interpret the city's intriguing past. As a tourist destination, Key West has a lot to sell—an average temperature of 79°F, 19th-century architecture, and a laid-back lifestyle. Yet much has been lost to those eager for a buck. Duval Street looks like a miniature Las Vegas lined with garish signs for T-shirt shops and tour-company offices. Cruise ships dwarf the town's skyline and fill the streets with day-trippers gawking at the hippies with dogs in their bike baskets, gay couples walking down the street holding hands, and the oddball lot of locals, some of whom bark louder than the dogs.

GETTING HERE AND AROUND
BOAT TRAVEL
Key West Express operates air-conditioned ferries between the Key West Terminal (Caroline and Grinnell streets) and Marco Island and Fort Myers Beach. The trip from Fort Myers Beach takes at least four hours each way and costs $86 one-way, $146 round-trip. Ferries depart from Fort Myers Beach at 8:30 am and from Key West at 6 pm. The Marco Island ferry costs $86 one-way and $146 round-trip, and departs at 8:30 am (the return trip leaves Key West at 5 pm). A photo ID is required for each passenger. Advance reservations are recommended. The SuperShuttle charges $165 to $185 per passenger for trips from Miami International Airport to Key Largo. To go farther into the Keys, you must book an entire 11-person van, which costs about $350 to Key West. You need to place your request for transportation back to the airport 24 hours in advance.

Contact **Key West Express** ⊠ *100 Grinnell St.* ☎ *888/539–2628* ⊕ *www. seakeywestexpress.com.*

KEY WEST'S COLORFUL HISTORY

The United States acquired Key West from Spain in 1821, along with the rest of Florida. The Spanish had named the island Cayo Hueso, or Bone Key, after the Native American skeletons they found on its shores. In 1823 President James Monroe sent Commodore David S. Porter to chase pirates away. For three decades the primary industry in Key West was wrecking—rescuing people and salvaging cargo from ships that foundered on the nearby reefs. According to some reports, when pickings were lean, the wreckers hung out lights to lure ships aground. Their business declined after 1849, when the federal government began building lighthouses.

In 1845 the army began construction on Fort Taylor, which kept Key West on the Union side during the Civil War, even though most of Florida seceded. After the fighting ended, an influx of Cubans unhappy with Spain's rule brought the cigar industry here. Fishing, shrimping, and sponge gathering became important industries, as did pineapple canning. Through much of the 19th century and into the 20th, Key West was Florida's wealthiest city in per-capita terms. But in 1929 the local economy began to unravel. Cigar making moved to Tampa, Hawaii dominated the pineapple industry, and the sponges succumbed to blight. Then the Depression hit, and within a few years half the population was on relief.

Tourism began to revive Key West, but that came to a halt when a hurricane knocked out the railroad bridge in 1935. To help the tourism industry recover from that crushing blow, the government offered incentives for islanders to turn their charming homes—many of them built by shipwrights—into guesthouses and inns. The wise foresight has left the town with more than 100 such lodgings, a hallmark of Key West vacationing today. In the 1950s the discovery of "pink gold" in the Dry Tortugas boosted the economy of the entire region. Harvesting Key West shrimp required a fleet of up to 500 boats and flooded local restaurants with sweet, luscious shrimp. The town's artistic community found inspiration in the colorful fishing boats.

BUS TRAVEL

Greyhound Lines runs a special Keys shuttle two times a day (depending on the day of the week) from Miami International Airport (departing from Concourse E, lower level) and stops throughout the Keys. Fares run about $45 for Key West (⌧ 3535 S. Roosevelt, Key West International Airport). Keys Shuttle runs scheduled service six times a day in 15-passenger vans between Miami Airport and Key West with stops throughout the Keys for $70 to $90 per person.

The City of Key West Department of Transportation has six color-coded bus routes traversing the island from 6:30 am to 11:30 pm. Stops have signs with the international bus symbol. Schedules are available on buses and at hotels, visitor centers, and shops. The fare is $2 one-way. The Lower Keys Shuttle bus runs from Marathon to Key West ($4 one-way), with scheduled stops along the way.

Contacts **City of Key West Department of Transportation** ☎ *305/809–3910* ⊕ *www.kwtransit.com.* **Greyhound Lines** ☎ *305/296–9072 local information,* *800/231–2222* ⊕ *www.greyhound.com.* **Keys Shuttle** ☎ *305/289–9997,* *888/765–9997* ⊕ *www.keysshuttle.com.*

CAR TRAVEL

Between mile markers 4 and 0, Key West is the one place in the Keys where you could conceivably do without a car, especially if you plan on staying around Old Town. If you've driven the 106 miles down the chain, you're probably ready to abandon your car in the hotel parking lot anyway. Trolleys, buses, bikes, scooters, and feet are more suitable alternatives. To explore the beaches, New Town, and Stock Island, you'll probably need a car.

Old Town Key West is the only place in the Keys where parking is a problem. There are public parking lots that charge by the hour or day (some hotels and bed-and-breakfasts provide parking or discounts at municipal lots). If you arrive early, you can sometimes find a spot on side streets off Duval and Whitehead, where you can park for free—just be sure it's not marked for residential parking only. Your best bet is to bike or take the trolley around town if you don't want to walk. You can disembark and reboard the trolley at will.

VISITOR INFORMATION

Contact **Greater Key West Chamber of Commerce** ☎ *305/294–2587,* *800/527–8539* ⊕ *www.keywestchamber.org.*

EXPLORING

OLD TOWN

The heart of Key West, the historic Old Town area runs from White Street to the waterfront. Beginning in 1822, wharves, warehouses, chandleries, ship-repair facilities, and eventually, in 1891, the U.S. Custom House sprang up around the deep harbor to accommodate the navy's large ships and other sailing vessels. Wreckers, merchants, and sea captains built lavish houses near the bustling waterfront. A remarkable number of these fine Victorian and pre-Victorian structures have been restored to their original grandeur and now serve as homes, guesthouses, shops, restaurants, and museums. These, along with the dwellings of famous writers, artists, and politicians who've come to Key West over the past 175 years, are among the area's approximately 3,000 historic structures. Old Town also has the city's finest restaurants and hotels, lively street life, and popular nightspots.

TOP ATTRACTIONS

Audubon House and Tropical Gardens. If you've ever seen an engraving by ornithologist John James Audubon, you'll understand why his name is synonymous with birds. See his works in this three-story house, which was built in the 1840s for Captain John Geiger and filled with period furniture. It now commemorates Audubon's 1832 stop in Key West while he was traveling through Florida to study birds. After an introduction by a docent, you can do a self-guided tour of the house and gardens (or just the gardens). An art gallery sells lithographs of the artist's

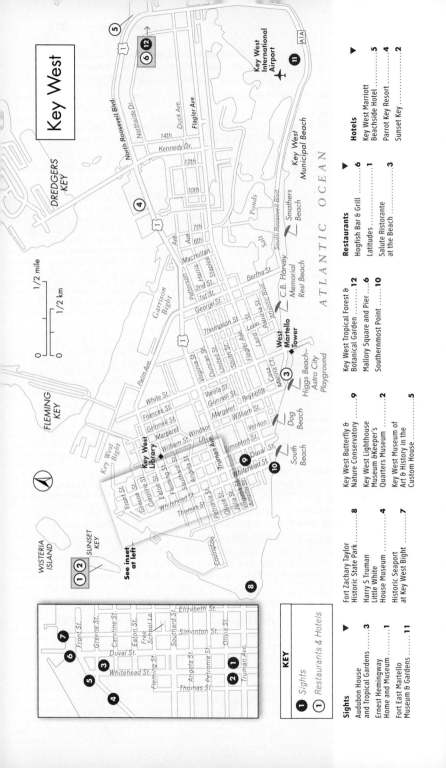

Key West

1/2 mile

1/2 km

ATLANTIC OCEAN

DREDGERS KEY

FLEMING KEY

WISTERIA ISLAND

SUNSET KEY

DVD

Key West International Airport

Key West Municipal Beach

Smathers Beach

C.B. Harvey Memorial Rest Beach

Higgs Beach– Astro City Playground

South Beach

Dog Beach

KEY

Sights

1 Restaurants & Hotels

Sights

Audubon House and Tropical Gardens 3

Ernest Hemingway Home and Museum 1

Fort East Martello Museum & Gardens 11

Fort Zachary Taylor Historic State Park 8

Harry S Truman Little White House Museum 4

Historic Seaport at Key West Bight 7

Key West Butterfly & Nature Conservatory 9

Key West Lighthouse Museum &Keeper's Quarters Museum 2

Key West Museum of Art & History in the Custom House 5

Key West Tropical Forest & Botanical Garden 12

Mallory Square and Pier 6

Southernmost Point 10

Restaurants

Hogfish Bar & Grill 6

Latitudes 1

Salute Ristorante at the Beach 3

Hotels

Key West Marriott Beachside Hotel 5

Parrot Key Resort 4

Sunset Key 2

See inset at left

Key West Library

West Martello Tower

famed portraits. ⊠ *205 Whitehead St.* ☎ *305/294–2116, 877/294–2470* ⊕ *www.audubonhouse.com* ⏄ *$7.50 gardens only; $12 house and gardens* ⊙ *Daily 9:30–5 (last tour at 4:15).*

Fodor's Choice
★

Ernest Hemingway Home and Museum. Amusing anecdotes spice up the guided tours of Ernest Hemingway's home, built in 1801 by the town's most successful wrecker. While living here between 1931 and 1942, Hemingway wrote about 70% of his life's work, including classics like *For Whom the Bell Tolls.* Few of his belongings remain aside from some books, and there's little about his actual work, but photographs help you visualize his day-to-day life. The famous six-toed descendants of Hemingway's cats—many named for actors, artists, authors, and even a hurricane—have free rein of the property. Tours begin every 10 minutes and take 30 minutes; then you're free to explore on your own. Be sure to find out why there is a urinal in the garden! ⊠ *907 Whitehead St.* ☎ *305/294–1136* ⊕ *www.hemingwayhome.com* ⏄ *$13* ⊙ *Daily 9–5.*

Fort Zachary Taylor Historic State Park. Construction of the fort began in 1845 but was halted during the Civil War. Even though Florida seceded from the Union, Yankee forces used the fort as a base to block Confederate shipping. More than 1,500 Confederate vessels were detained in Key West's harbor. The fort, finally completed in 1866, was also used in the Spanish-American War. Take a 30-minute guided walking tour of the redbrick fort, a National Historic Landmark, at noon and 2, or self-tour anytime between 8 and 5. In February a celebration called Civil War Heritage Days includes costumed reenactments and demonstrations. From mid-January to mid-April the park serves as an open-air gallery for pieces created for Sculpture Key West. One of its most popular features is its man-made beach, a rest stop for migrating birds in the spring and fall; there are also picnic areas, hiking and biking trails, and a kayak launch. ⊠ *Southard St., at end of street, through Truman Annex* ☎ *305/292–6713* ⊕ *www.floridastateparks.org/forttaylor* ⏄ *$4 for single-occupant vehicles, $6 for 2–8 people in vehicle, plus 50¢ per person county surcharge* ⊙ *Daily 8–sunset.*

NEED A BREAK?

Key West Library. Check out the pretty palm garden next to the Key West Library at 700 Fleming Street, just off Duval. This leafy, outdoor reading area, with shaded benches, is the perfect place to escape the frenzy and crowds of downtown Key West. There's free Internet access in the library, too. ⊠ *700 Fleming St.* ☎ *305/292–3595* ⊕ *www.keyslibraries.org.*

Harry S Truman Little White House Museum. Renovations to this circa-1890 landmark have restored the home and gardens to the Truman era, down to the wallpaper pattern. A free photographic review of visiting dignitaries and presidents—John F. Kennedy, Jimmy Carter, and Bill Clinton are among the chief executives who passed through here—is on display in the back of the gift shop. Engaging 45-minute tours begin every 20 minutes until 4:30. They start with an excellent 10-minute video on the history of the property and Truman's visits. On the grounds of **Truman Annex,** a 103-acre former military parade grounds and barracks, the home served as a winter White House for presidents Truman, Eisenhower, and Kennedy. ■TIP➜ **The house**

See the typewriter Hemingway used at his home office in Key West. He lived here from 1931 to 1942.

tour does require climbing steps. Visitors can do a free self-guided botanical tour of the grounds with a brochure from the museum store. ⊠ *111 Front St.* ☎ *305/294–9911* ⊕ *www.trumanlittlewhitehouse.com* ✉ *$16.13* ⏱ *Daily 9–5; grounds 7–6.*

Historic Seaport at Key West Bight. What was once a funky—in some places even seedy—part of town is now an 8½-acre historic restoration of 100 businesses, including waterfront restaurants, open-air bars, museums, clothing stores, bait shops, dive shops, docks, a marina, and water-sports concessions. It's all linked by the 2-mile waterfront **Harborwalk,** which runs between Front and Grinnell streets, passing big ships, schooners, sunset cruises, fishing charters, and glass-bottom boats. ⊠ *100 Grinnell St.* ☎ *305/293–8309* ⊕ *www.keywestseaport.com.*

NEED A BREAK?

Coffee Plantation. Get your morning (or afternoon) buzz, and hook up to the Internet in the comfort of a homelike setting in a circa-1890 Conch house. Munch on sandwiches, wraps, and pastries, and sip a hot or cold espresso beverage. ⊠ **713 Caroline St.** ☎ **305/295–9808** ⊕ **www. coffeeplantationkeywest.com.**

FAMILY **Key West Butterfly & Nature Conservatory.** This air-conditioned refuge for butterflies, birds, and the human spirit gladdens the soul with hundreds of colorful wings—more than 45 species of butterflies alone—in a lovely glass-encased bubble. Waterfalls, artistic benches, paved pathways, birds, and lush, flowering vegetation elevate this above most butterfly attractions. The gift shop and gallery are worth a visit on their own. ⊠ *1316 Duval St.* ☎ *305/296–2988, 800/839–4647* ⊕ *www.*

CLOSE UP

Hemingway Was Here

In a town where Pulitzer Prize–winning writers are almost as common as coconuts, Ernest Hemingway stands out. Bars and restaurants around the island claim that he ate or drank there (except Bagatelle, where a sign in the bar reads, "Hemingway never liked this place").

Hemingway came to Key West in 1928 at the urging of writer John dos Passos and rented a house with wife number two, Pauline Pfeiffer. They spent winters in the Keys and summers in Europe and Wyoming, occasionally taking African safaris. Along the way they had two sons, Patrick and Gregory. In 1931 Pauline's wealthy uncle Gus gave the couple the house at 907 Whitehead Street. Now known as the Ernest Hemingway Home & Museum, it's Key West's number-one tourist attraction. Renovations included the addition of a pool and a tropical garden.

In 1935, when the visitor bureau included the house in a tourist brochure, Hemingway promptly built the brick wall that surrounds it today. He wrote of the visitor bureau's offense in a 1935 essay for *Esquire,* saying, "The house at present occupied by your correspondent is listed as number eighteen in a compilation of the forty-eight things for a tourist to see in Key West. So there will be no difficulty in a tourist finding it or any other of the sights of the city, a map has been prepared by the local F.E.R.A. authorities to be presented to each arriving visitor. This is all very flattering to the easily bloated ego of your correspondent but very hard on production."

During his time in Key West, Hemingway penned some of his most important works, including *A Farewell to Arms, To Have and Have Not, Green Hills of Africa,* and *Death in the Afternoon.* His rigorous schedule consisted of writing almost every morning in his second-story studio above the pool, and then promptly descending the stairs at midday. By afternoon and evening he was ready for drinking, fishing, swimming, boxing, and hanging around with the boys.

One close friend was Joe Russell, a craggy fisherman and owner of the rugged bar Sloppy Joe's, originally at 428 Greene Street but now at 201 Duval Street. Russell was the only one in town who would cash Hemingway's $1,000 royalty check. Russell and Charles Thompson introduced Hemingway to deep-sea fishing, which became fodder for his writing. Another of Hemingway's loves was boxing. He set up a ring in his yard and paid local fighters to box with him, and he refereed matches at Blue Heaven, then a saloon at 729 Thomas Street.

Hemingway honed his macho image, dressed in cutoffs and old shirts, and took on the name Papa. In turn, he gave his friends new names and used them as characters in his stories. Joe Russell became Freddy, captain of the *Queen Conch* charter boat in *To Have and Have Not.*

Hemingway stayed in Key West for 11 years before leaving Pauline for wife number three. Pauline and the boys stayed on in the house, which sold in 1951 for $80,000, 10 times its original cost.

—Jim and Cynthia Tunstall

Divers examine the intentionally scuttled 327-foot former U.S. Coast Guard cutter *Duane* in 120 feet of water off Key Largo.

keywestbutterfly.com ✉ *$12* ⊙ *Daily 9–5; gallery and shop open until 5:30.*

Key West Lighthouse Museum & Keeper's Quarters Museum. For the best view in town, climb the 88 steps to the top of this 1847 lighthouse. The 92-foot structure has a Fresnel lens, which was installed in the 1860s at a cost of $1 million. The keeper lived in the adjacent 1887 clapboard house, which now exhibits vintage photographs, ship models, nautical charts, and lighthouse artifacts from all along the Key reefs. A kids' room is stocked with books and toys. ✉ *938 Whitehead St.* ☎ *305/295–6616* ⊕ *www.kwahs.com* ✉ *$10* ⊙ *Daily 9:30–4:30.*

Fodor's Choice
★

Key West Museum of Art & History in the Custom House. When Key West was designated a U.S. port of entry in the early 1820s, a customhouse was established. Salvaged cargoes from ships wrecked on the reefs were brought here, setting the stage for Key West to become—for a time—the richest city in Florida. The imposing redbrick-and-terra-cotta Richardsonian Romanesque–style building reopened as a museum and art gallery in 1999. Smaller galleries have long-term and changing exhibits about the history of Key West, including a Hemingway room and a fine collection of folk artist Mario Sanchez's wood paintings. In 2011, to commemorate the 100th anniversary of the railroad's arrival to Key West in 1912, a new permanent Flagler exhibit opened. ✉ *281 Front St.* ☎ *305/295–6616* ⊕ *www.kwahs.com* ✉ *$9* ⊙ *Daily 9:30–4:30.*

Mallory Square and Pier. For cruise-ship passengers, this is the disembarkation point for an attack on Key West. For practically every visitor, it's the requisite venue for a nightly sunset celebration that includes street performers—human statues, sword swallowers, tightrope walkers,

THE CONCH REPUBLIC

Beginning in the 1970s, pot smuggling became a source of income for islanders who knew how to dodge detection in the maze of waterways in the Keys. In 1982 the U.S. Border Patrol threw a roadblock across the Overseas Highway just south of Florida City to catch drug runners and undocumented aliens. Traffic backed up for miles as Border Patrol agents searched vehicles and demanded that the occupants prove U.S. citizenship. Officials in Key West, outraged at being treated like foreigners by the federal government, staged a protest and formed their own "nation": the so-called Conch Republic. They hoisted a flag and distributed mock border passes, visas, and Conch currency. The embarrassed Border Patrol dismantled its roadblock, and now an annual festival recalls the city's victory. You can even "apply" for a Conch Republic passport (for entertainment purposes, not travel!). It'll set you back $100, but those who hold one think it's priceless. Begin your journey online at ⊕ *www. conchrepublic.com.*

musicians, and more—plus craft vendors, conch fritter fryers, and other regulars who defy classification. (Wanna picture with my pet iguana?) With all the activity, don't forget to watch the main show: a dazzling tropical sunset. ⊠ *Mallory Sq.*

The Southernmost Point. Possibly the most photographed site in Key West (even though the actual geographic southernmost point in the continental United States lies across the bay on a naval base, where you see a satellite dish), this is a must-see. Who wouldn't want his picture taken next to the big striped buoy that marks the southernmost point in the continental United States? A plaque next to it honors Cubans who lost their lives trying to escape to America and other signs tell Key West history. ⊠ *Whitehead and South Sts.*

NEW TOWN

The Overseas Highway splits as it enters Key West, the two forks rejoining to encircle New Town, the area east of White Street to Cow Key Channel. The southern fork runs along the shore as South Roosevelt Boulevard (Route A1A), skirting Key West International Airport. Along the north shore, North Roosevelt Boulevard (U.S. 1) leads to Old Town. Part of New Town was created with dredged fill. The island would have continued growing this way had the Army Corps of Engineers not determined in the early 1970s that it was detrimental to the nearby reef.

Fort East Martello Museum & Gardens. This redbrick Civil War fort never saw a lick of action during the war. Today it serves as a museum, with historical exhibits about the 19th and 20th centuries. Among the latter are relics of the USS *Maine*, cigar factory and shipwrecking exhibits, and the citadel tower you can climb to the top. The museum, operated by the Key West Art and Historical Society, also has a collection of Stanley Papio's "junk art" sculptures inside and out, and a gallery of Cuban folk artist Mario Sanchez's chiseled and painted wooden carvings of historic Key West street scenes. ⊠ *3501 S. Roosevelt Blvd.* ☎ *305/296–3913* ⊕ *www.kwahs.com* ✉ *$9* ☉ *Daily 9:30–4:30.*

Key West Tropical Forest & Botanical Garden. Established in 1935, this unique habitat is the only frost-free botanical garden in the continental United States. You won't see fancy topiaries and exotic plants, but you'll see a unique ecosystem that naturally occurs in this area and the Caribbean. There are paved walkways that take you past butterfly gardens, mangroves, Cuban palms, lots of birds like herons and ibis, and ponds where you can spy turtles and fish. It's a nice respite from the sidewalks and shops, and offers a natural slice of Keys paradise. ⊠ *5210 College Rd.* ☎ *305/296–1504* ⊕ *www.kwbgs.org* ✍ *$7* ⊙ *Daily 10–4.*

BEACHES

OLD TOWN

Dog Beach. Next to Louie's Backyard, this tiny beach—the only one in Key West where dogs are allowed unleashed—has a shore that's a mix of sand and rocks. **Amenities:** none. **Best for:** walking. ⊠ *Vernon and Waddell Sts.* ✍ *Free* ⊙ *Daily sunrise–sunset.*

FAMILY **Fort Zachary Taylor Beach.** The park's beach is the best and safest place to swim in Key West. There's an adjoining picnic area with barbecue grills and shade trees, a snack bar, and rental equipment, including snorkeling gear. A café serves sandwiches and other munchies. **Amenities:** food and drink; showers; toilets; water sports. **Best for:** swimming; snorkeling. ⊠ *Southard St., at end of street, through Truman Annex* ☎ *305/292–6713* ⊕ *www.floridastateparks.org/forttaylor* ✍ *$4 for 1-occupant vehicles, $6 for 2–8 people in vehicle, plus 50¢ per person county surcharge* ⊙ *Daily 8–sunset; tours at noon and 2.*

FAMILY **Higgs Beach–Astro City Playground.** This Monroe County park with its groomed pebbly sand is a popular sunbathing spot. A nearby grove of Australian pines provides shade, and the West Martello Tower provides shelter should a storm suddenly sweep in. Kayak and beach-chair rentals are available, as is a volleyball net. The beach also has a marker and cultural exhibit commemorating the grave site of 295 enslaved Africans who died after being rescued from three South America–bound slave ships in 1860. Across the street, **Astro City Playground** is popular with young children. **Amenities:** parking; toilets; water sports. **Best for:** swimming; snorkeling. ⊠ *Atlantic Blvd., between White and Reynolds Sts.* ✍ *Free* ⊙ *Daily 6 am–11 pm.*

NEW TOWN

C.B. Harvey Memorial Rest Beach. This beach and park were named after Cornelius Bradford Harvey, former Key West mayor and commissioner. Adjacent to Higgs Beach, it has half a dozen picnic areas across the street, dunes, a pier, and a wheelchair and bike path. **Amenities:** none. **Best for:** walking. ⊠ *Atlantic Blvd., east side of White St. Pier* ✍ *Free* ⊙ *Daily 6 am–11 pm.*

Smathers Beach. This wide beach has nearly 1 mile of nice white sand, plus beautiful coconut palms, picnic areas, and volleyball courts, all of which make it popular with the spring-break crowd. Trucks along the road rent rafts, Windsurfers, and other beach "toys." **Amenities:**

food and drink; parking; toilets; water sports. **Best for:** partiers. ✉ *S. Roosevelt Blvd.* 🎟 *Free* 🕒 *Daily 7 am–11 pm.*

WHERE TO EAT

Bring your appetite, a sense of daring, and a lack of preconceived notions about propriety. A meal in Key West can mean overlooking the crazies along Duval Street, watching roosters and pigeons battle for a scrap of food that may have escaped your fork, relishing the finest in what used to be the dining room of some 19th-century Victorian home, or gazing out at boats jockeying for position in the marina. And that's just the diversity of the setting. Seafood dominates local menus, but the treatment afforded that fish or crustacean can range from Cuban and American to Asian and Continental.

$$ JAPANESE 🍴 **Ambrosia.** Ask any savvy local where to get the best sushi on the island and you'll undoubtedly be pointed to this bright and airy dining room with a modern indoor waterfall literally steps from the Atlantic. Grab a seat at the sleek bar, where the back wall glows from purple to blue, or sit at the sushi bar and watch owner and head sushi chef Masa (albeit not the famous chef of the eponymous restaurants in New York and Las Vegas) prepare an impressive array of super fresh sashimi delicacies. Sushi lovers can't go wrong with the Ambrosia special: miso soup served with a sampler of 15 kinds of sashimi, seven pieces of sushi, and sushi rolls. There's an assortment of lightly fried tempura and teriyaki dishes and a killer bento box at lunch. Enjoy it all with a glass of premium sake or a cold glass of Sapporo beer. [$] *Average main: $20* ✉ *Santa Maria Resort, 1401 Simonton St.* ☎ *305/293–0304* 🌐 *www.ambrosiasushi.com* 🕒 *Closed 2 wks after Labor Day. No lunch weekends.*

$$$ ECLECTIC 🍴 **Azur Restaurant.** Fuel up on the finest fare at this former gas station, now part of the Eden House complex. In a contemporary setting with indoor and outdoor seating, welcoming staff serves breakfast, lunch, and dinner that stand out from the hordes of Key West restaurants by virtue of originality. For instance, key lime–stuffed French toast and yellowtail snapper Benedict make breakfast a pleasant wake-up call. The crab cake BLT, duck Cubano with fontina cheese, and charred marinated octopus command notice on the lunch menu. Four varieties of homemade gnocchi are a dinner-time specialty, along with tasting plates, "almost entrées" like braised lamb over Moroccan-spiced chickpeas, and main courses that include branzino, veal, and steak. Sunday brunch served. [$] *Average main: $26* ✉ *425 Grinnell St.* ☎ *305/292–2987* 🌐 *www.azurkeywest.com* ✍ *Reservations essential.*

$ SEAFOOD 🍴 **B.O.'s Fish Wagon.** What started out as a fish house on wheels appears to have broken down on the corner of Caroline and William streets and is today the cornerstone for one of Key West's junkyard-chic dining institutions. Step up to the wood-plank counter window and order the specialty: a grouper sandwich fried or grilled and topped with key lime sauce. Other choices include fish nuts (don't be scared, they're just fried nuggets), hot dogs, cracked conch sandwich, and shrimp or soft-shell-crab sandwich. Talk sass with your host and find a picnic table or take a seat at the plank. Grab some paper towels off one of the rolls hanging around and busy yourself reading graffiti, license plates, and irreverent signs. It's a must-do Key West experience. [$] *Average main: $12* ✉ *801 Caroline St.* ☎ *305/294–9272* 🌐 *www.bosfishwagon.com* 💳 *No credit cards.*

$$$ CARIBBEAN 🍴 **Blue Heaven.** The outdoor dining area here is often referred to as "the quintessential Keys experience," and it's hard to argue. There's much to like about this historic restaurant where Hemingway refereed boxing matches and customers cheered for cockfights. Although these events are no more, the free-roaming chickens and cats add that "what-a-hoot" factor. Nightly specials include black bean soup, Caribbean BBQ shrimp, bison strip steak with blackberry salad, and jerk chicken. Desserts and breads are baked on the premises. The banana bread and shrimp and grits are hits during breakfast, but the signature meal here is the lobster Benedict with key lime hollandaise. Bring patience as there is always a wait. [$] *Average main: $24* ✉ *729 Thomas St.* ☎ *305/296–8666* 🌐 *www.blueheavenkw.com* ✍ *Reservations not accepted* 🕑 *Closed after Labor Day for 6 wks.*

4

$ VEGETARIAN 🍴 **The Café.** You don't have to be a vegetarian to love this new-age café decorated with bright artwork and a corrugated tin–fronted counter. Local favorites include homemade soup, veggie sandwiches and burgers (order them with a side of sweet potato fries), grilled portobello mushroom salad, seafood, vegan specialties, stir-fry dinners, and grilled Gorgonzola pizza. There's also a nice selection of draft beer and wines by the glass, plus daily desserts (including vegan selections). [$] *Average main: $11* ✉ *509 Southard St.* ☎ *305/296–5515* 🌐 *www.thecafekw.com* ✍ *Reservations not accepted.*

$$$ EUROPEAN Fodor's Choice ★ 🍴 **Café Marquesa.** Chef Susan Ferry presents seven or more inspired entrées on her changing menu each night; delicious dishes can include yellowtail snapper with pear, ricotta pasta purses with caponata, and Australian rack of lamb crusted with goat cheese and a port-fig sauce. End your meal on a sweet note with key lime napoleon with tropical fruits and berries. There's also a fine selection of wines and custom martinis such as the key limetini and the Irish martini. Adjoining the intimate Marquesa Hotel, the dining room is equally relaxed and elegant. [$] *Average main: $29* ✉ *600 Fleming St.* ☎ *305/292–1244* 🌐 *www.marquesa.com* ✍ *Reservations essential* 🕑 *No lunch.*

$$$ FRENCH 🍴 **Café Solé.** This little corner of France hides behind a high wall in a residential neighborhood. Inside, French training intertwines with local ingredients, creating delicious takes on classics, including a must-try conch carpaccio, yellowtail snapper with mango salsa, and some of the best bouillabaisse that you'll find outside of Marseilles. Hog snapper, aka hogfish, is a house specialty here, prepared several ways by Chef John Correa, including with beurre blanc or red pepper custard sauce. From the land, there is filet mignon with a wild-mushroom demi-glaze. [$] *Average main: $27* ✉ *1029 Southard St.* ☎ *305/294–0230* 🌐 *www.cafesole.com* ✍ *Reservations essential.*

$$$ MODERN AMERICAN 🍴 **Camille's Restaurant.** Break out the stretchy pants because everything on the menu at this affordable hot spot not only sounds scrumptious, it is. Start your day with a shrimp, lobster, or crab-cake Benedict—the latter was voted best in the Florida Keys. Lunch brings dishes like

hand-pulled chicken salad or a mahimahi wrap. Evenings will have you swooning for the famous grilled stone-crab cakes with an addictive Captain Morgan spiced-rum mango sauce. Locals have tried to keep this place a secret for over 20 years, but the word is out. Line up beneath the bright pink awning and happily wait for your seat. Be sure to ask your server about the Barbie dolls—they have a most unique collection, many with a Key West flair. $ *Average main: $21* ✉ *1202 Simonton St., at Catherine St.* ☎ *305/296–4811* ⊕ *www.camilleskeywest.com* ⚑ *Reservations essential.*

$$$
MODERN AMERICAN

✕ **Deuce's Off the Hook Grill.** It's a tight fit with only six tables (and six counter seats), but if you don't mind sitting close to fellow diners, you will be rewarded with a made-from-scratch meal almost anytime of day. Battered chicken tenders with waffles and *huevos rancheros* will rev up your morning. Coconut-crusted mahi with mango salsa is the signature lunch dish, but the lobster pie (pizza with poached lobster, goat cheese, arugula, and shaved fig) is a close second. Dinners run the gamut with the likes of "The Gobbler" (freshly roasted turkey with bacon smashed potatoes on a sage-stuffed waffle) to grouper in bouillabaisse with fennel. A specials board lists plenty of tempting options, too, but be sure to ask the price since seafood risotto might *sound* great, but when the reality hits your bill, your wallet won't be happy. $ *Average main: $21* ✉ *728 Simonton St.* ☎ *305/414–8428* ⊕ *www.offthehookkeywest.com* ⚑ *Reservations essential* ☯ *Closed Tues.*

$$
CUBAN

✕ **El Meson de Pepe.** If you want to get a taste of the island's Cuban heritage, this is the place. Perfect for after watching a Mallory Square sunset, you can dine alfresco or in the dining room on refined versions of Cuban classics. Begin with a megasized mojito while you enjoy the basket of bread and savory sauces. The expansive menu offers *tostones rellenos* (green plantains with different traditional fillings), ceviche (raw fish "cooked" in lemon juice), and more. Choose from Cuban specialties such as roasted pork in a cumin mojo sauce and *ropa vieja* (shredded beef stew). At lunch, the local Cuban population and cruise-ship passengers enjoy Cuban sandwiches and smaller versions of dinner's most popular entrées. A Latin band performs outside at the bar during the sunset celebration. $ *Average main: $19* ✉ *Mallory Sq., 410 Wall St.* ☎ *305/295–2620* ⊕ *www.elmesondepepe.com.*

$
CUBAN

✕ **El Siboney.** Dining at this family-style restaurant is like going to Mom's for Sunday dinner—if your mother is Cuban. The dining room is noisy, and the food is traditional *cubano.* There are well-seasoned black beans, a memorable paella, traditional ropa vieja (shredded beef), and local seafood served grilled, stuffed, and breaded. Dishes come with plantains and beans and rice or salad and fries. To make a good thing even better, the prices are very reasonable and the homemade sangria is *muy bueno.* $ *Average main: $10* ✉ *900 Catherine St.* ☎ *305/296–4184* ⊕ *www. elsiboneyrestaurant.com* ⚑ *Reservations not accepted.*

$$
SEAFOOD
FAMILY

✕ **Half Shell Raw Bar.** Smack-dab on the docks, this legendary institution gets its name from the oysters, clams, and peel-and-eat shrimp that are a departure point for its seafood-based diet. It's not clever recipes or fine dining (or even air-conditioning) that packs 'em in; it's fried fish, po'boy sandwiches, and seafood combos. For a break from the deep

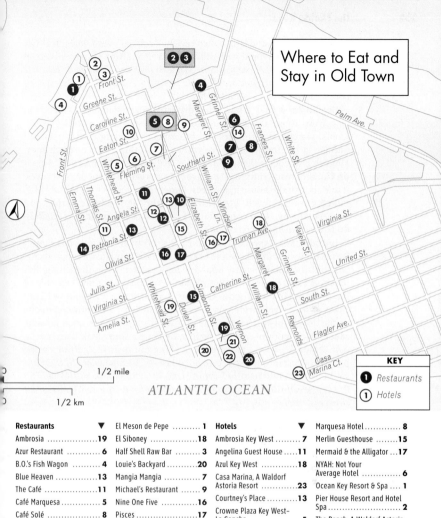

Where to Eat and Stay in Old Town

ATLANTIC OCEAN

KEY

🍽 *Restaurants*

① *Hotels*

fryer, try the fresh and light conch ceviche "cooked" with lime juice. The potato salad is flavored with dill, and the "PamaRita" is a new twist in Margaritaville. $ *Average main: $16* ⊠ *Lands End Village at Historic Seaport, 231 Margaret St.* ☎ *305/294–7496* ⊕ *www.halfshellrawbar. com* ⌒ *Reservations not accepted.*

$

SEAFOOD

✕ **Hogfish Bar & Grill.** It's worth a drive to Stock Island, just outside of Key West, to sit along one of Florida's last surviving working waterfronts, watch the shrimpers and fishermen unloading their catch, and indulge in the freshness you're witnessing at this down-to-earth spot. Hogfish is of course the specialty. The "Killer Hogfish Sandwich" comes on Cuban bread (you can also have it as a breakfast Benedict); sprinkle it with one of the house hot sauces. Other favorites include lobster BLT, pulled pork sandwich, hogfish tacos, gator bites, lobster potpie, and barbecued ribs. $ *Average main: $13* ⊠ *6810 Front St.* ☎ *305/293–4041* ⊕ *www.hogfishbar.com.*

$$$

ECLECTIC

✕ **Latitudes.** For a special treat, take the short boat ride to lovely Sunset Key for lunch or dinner on the beach. Creativity and quality ingredients combine for dishes that are bound to impress as much as the setting. For lunch, the fish tacos with chipotle aioli and salsa are a fine example of the chef's use of local foods. At dinner, start with the crispy lobster-crab cakes or seared yellowfin tuna stacked with mango, then move on to one of the delightful entrées, such as yellowtail snapper with coconut-lime sauce, sweet potato–crusted grouper, or Wagyu skirt steak with mocha demi-glace. Choose a table inside looking out over the gulf or on the patio. The restaurant also serves breakfast. $ *Average main: $28* ⊠ *Sunset Key Guest Cottages, 245 Front St.* ☎ *305/292–5300, 888/477–7786* ⊕ *www.westinsunsetkeycottages.com/latitudes-restaurant* ⌒ *Reservations essential.*

$$$$

ECLECTIC

✕ **Louie's Backyard.** Feast your eyes on a steal-your-breath-away view and beautifully presented dishes prepared by executive Chef Doug Shook. Once you get over sticker shock on the seasonally changing menu, settle in on the outside deck and enjoy dishes like grilled scallops with portobello relish, grilled king salmon with fried risotto, and mint-rubbed pork chop with salsa verde. A more affordable option upstairs is the Upper Deck, which serves tapas such as flaming ouzo shrimp, roasted olives with onion and feta, and Gruyère and duck confit pizza. If you come for lunch, the menu is less expensive but the view is just as fantastic. For night owls, the tin-roofed Afterdeck Bar serves cocktails on the water until the wee hours. $ *Average main: $36* ⊠ *700 Waddell Ave.* ☎ *305/294–1061* ⊕ *www.louiesbackyard.com* ⌒ *Reservations essential* ⊙ *Closed Labor Day–mid-Sept. Upper Deck closed Sun. and Mon. No lunch at Upper Deck.*

$$

ITALIAN

✕ **Mangia Mangia.** This longtime favorite serves large portions of homemade pastas that can be matched with any of their homemade sauces. Tables are arranged in a brick garden hung with twinkling lights and in a cozy, casual dining room in an old house. Everything out of the open kitchen is outstanding, including the *bollito misto di mare* (fresh seafood sautéed with garlic, shallots, white wine, and pasta) or the memorable spaghettini "schmappellini," homemade pasta with asparagus, tomatoes, pine nuts, and Parmesan. The wine list—with more than 350 offerings—includes old and rare vintages, and also has a good by-the-glass selection. $ *Average main: $16* ⊠ *900 Southard St.* ☎ *305/294–2469* ⊕ *www.mangia-mangia.com* ⌂ *Reservations not accepted* ⊙ *No lunch.*

$$$ ✕ **Michaels Restaurant.** White tablecloths, subdued lighting, and romantic
AMERICAN music give Michaels the feel of an urban eatery. Garden seating reminds you that you are in the Keys. Chef-owner Michael Wilson flies in prime rib, cowboy steaks, and rib eyes from Allen Brothers in Chicago, which has supplied top-ranked steak houses for more than a century. Also on the menu is a melt-in-your-mouth grouper stuffed with jumbo lump crab, Kobe and tenderloin meat loaf, veal saltimbocca, and a variety of made-to-order fondue dishes (try the pesto pot, spiked with hot pepper and basil). To lighten up, smaller portions of many of the favorites are available until 7:30 Sunday through Thursday. The Hemingway (mojito-style) and the Third Degree (raspberry vodka and white crème de cacao) top the cocktail menu. $ *Average main: $25* ⊠ *532 Margaret St.* ☎ *305/295–1300* ⊕ *www.michaelskeywest.com* ⌂ *Reservations essential* ⊙ *No lunch.*

$$$ ✕ **Nine One Five.** Twinkling lights draped along the lower- and upper-
ECLECTIC level outdoor porches of a 100-year-old Victorian home set an unstuffy and comfortable stage here. If you like to sample and sip, you'll appreciate the variety of smaller-plate selections and wines by the glass. Starters include a cheese platter, crispy duck confit, a tapas platter, and the signature "tuna dome" with fresh crab, lemon-miso dressing, and an ahi tuna–sashimi wrapping. There are also larger plates if you're craving something like Soul Mama Seafood Soup or Roasted Hogfish with chorizo. Dine outdoors and people-watch along upper Duval, or sit at a table inside while listening to light jazz. $ *Average main: $28* ⊠ *915 Duval St.* ☎ *305/296–0669* ⊕ *www.915duval.com* ⌂ *Reservations essential* ⊙ *No lunch.*

$$$$ ✕ **Pisces.** In a circa-1892 former store and home, Chef William Arnel
EUROPEAN and staff create a contemporary setting with a stylish granite bar, Andy Warhol originals, and glass oil lamps. Favorites include "lobster tango mango," flambéed in cognac and served with saffron butter sauce and sliced mangoes; filet mignon with bordelaise sauce; and yellow tail Atocha with lemon brown butter, shrimp, and scallops. Their wine collection is just as impressive. $ *Average main: $35* ⊠ *1007 Simonton St.* ☎ *305/294–7100* ⊕ *www.pisceskeywest.com* ⌂ *Reservations essential* ⊙ *No lunch.*

$$ ✕ **Salute Ristorante at the Beach.** Sister restaurant to Blue Heaven, this
ITALIAN colorful establishment sits on Higgs Beach, giving it one of the island's best lunch views—and a bit of sand and salt spray on a windy day. The intriguing menu is Italian with a Caribbean flair and will not disappoint. For dinner, popular dishes include linguine with mussels, lasagna, and white bean soup. At lunch the gazpacho refreshes with great flavor and texture, and the calamari marinara, antipasti sandwich, and yellowtail sandwich will having you singing, *amore.* $ *Average main: $20* ⊠ *1000 Atlantic Blvd., Higgs Beach* ☎ *305/292–1117* ⊕ *www. saluteonthebeach.com* ⌂ *Reservations not accepted.*

$ TAPAS Fodor's Choice ★ 🍴 **Santiago's Bodega.** If you've ever wondered where chefs go for a great meal in the lower Keys, this is their secret spot. Picky palates will be satisfied at this funky, dark, and sensuous corner house, which is well off the main drag. Dine on the front porch surrounded by fuchsia bougainvillea or inside amid eclectic paintings and mismatched chandeliers. Waiters recommend choosing three of the small plates per person, then sharing. That number works. Cold tapas include dishes like yellowfin tuna ceviche with large hunks of avocado and mango, and shaved beef carpaccio with smoked sea salt and truffle oil. Favorite hot tapas are filet mignon with creamy Gogonzola butter and cherry-hoisin glazed beef short ribs. Dessert? The bread pudding is legendary. Reward yourself for finding this place with a fruit-filled glass of homemade red or white sangria. All bets say you'll eat here over and over again. [$] *Average main: $13* ✉ *Bahama Village, 207 Petronia St.* ☎ *305/296–7691* 🌐 *www.santiagosbodega.com* ✍ *Reservations essential.*

$$$ SEAFOOD 🍴 **Seven Fish.** A local hot spot, this intimate, off-the-beaten-track eatery is good for an eclectic mix of dishes like tropical shrimp salsa, wild-mushroom quesadilla, seafood marinara, and old-fashioned meat loaf with real mashed potatoes. For dessert, the sweet potato pie provides an added measure of down-home comfort. Those in the know reserve for dinner early to snag one of the 20 or so tables clustered in the bare-bones dining room. [$] *Average main: $26* ✉ *632 Olivia St.* ☎ *305/296–2777* 🌐 *www.7fish.com* ✍ *Reservations essential* 🕒 *Closed Tues. No lunch.*

$$ SEAFOOD FAMILY 🍴 **Turtle Kraals.** Named for the kraals, or corrals, where sea turtles were once kept until they went to the cannery, this place calls to mind the island's history. The lunch–dinner menu offers an assortment of marine cuisine that includes seafood enchiladas, mesquite-grilled fish of the day, and mango crab cakes. The slow-cook wood smoker results in wonderfully tender ribs, brisket, mesquite-grilled oysters with Parmesan and cilantro, and mesquite grilled chicken sandwich. The open restaurant overlooks the marina at the Historic Seaport. Turtle races entertain during happy hour on Monday and Friday at 6 pm. [$] *Average main: $16* ✉ *231 Margaret St.* ☎ *305/294–2640* 🌐 *www.turtlekraals.com.*

WHERE TO STAY

Historic cottages, restored century-old Conch houses, and large resorts are among the offerings in Key West, the majority charging from $100 to $300 a night. In high season, Christmas through Easter, you'll be hard-pressed to find a decent room for less than $200, and most places raise prices considerably during holidays and festivals. Many guesthouses and inns don't welcome children under 16, and most don't permit smoking indoors. Rates often include an expanded continental breakfast and afternoon wine or snack.

$$$ B&B/INN 🏨 **Ambrosia Key West.** If you desire personal attention, a casual atmosphere, and a dollop of style, stay at these twin inns spread out on nearly 2 acres. **Pros:** spacious rooms; poolside breakfast; friendly staff. **Cons:** on-street parking can be tough to come by; a little too spread out. [$] *Rooms from: $325* ✉ *615, 618, 622 Fleming St.* ☎ *305/296–9838,*

800/535–9838 🌐 www.ambrosiakeywest.com 🛏 6 rooms, 3 town houses, 1 cottage, 10 suites 🍴 Breakfast.

$ B&B/INN 🏨 **Angelina Guest House.** In the heart of Old Town, this home away from home offers simple, clean, attractively priced accommodations. **Pros:** good value; nice garden; friendly staff. **Cons:** thin walls; basic rooms; shared balcony. [$] *Rooms from: $124 ✉ 302 Angela St. ☎ 305/294–4480, 888/303–4480 🌐 www.angelinaguesthouse.com 🛏 13 rooms 🍴 Breakfast.*

$$ B&B/INN 🏨 **Azul Key West.** The ultramodern—nearly minimalistic—redo of this classic circa-1903 Queen Anne mansion is a break from the sensory overload of Key West's other abundant Victorian guesthouses. **Pros:** lovely building; marble-floored baths; luxurious linens. **Cons:** on a busy street. [$] *Rooms from: $269 ✉ 907 Truman Ave. ☎ 305/296–5152, 888/253–2985 🌐 www.azulhotels.us 🛏 10 rooms, 1 suite 🍴 Breakfast.*

$$$ RESORT FAMILY 🏨 **Casa Marina, A Waldorf-Astoria Resort.** At any moment, you expect the landed gentry to walk across the oceanfront lawn of this luxurious resort, just as they did when this 13-acre resort was built back in the 1920s. **Pros:** nice beach; historic setting; away from the crowds. **Cons:** long walk to central Old Town; expensive resort fee. [$] *Rooms from: $359 ✉ 1500 Reynolds St. ☎ 305/296–3535, 866/203–6392 🌐 www.casamarinaresort.com 🛏 241 rooms, 70 suites 🍴 No meals.*

$$ B&B/INN 🏨 **Courtney's Place.** If you like kids, cats, and dogs, you'll feel right at home in this collection of accommodations ranging from cigar-maker cottages to shotgun houses. **Pros:** near Duval Street; fairly priced. **Cons:** small parking lot; small pool, minimum-stay requirements. [$] *Rooms from: $249 ✉ 720 Whitmarsh La., off Petronia St. ☎ 305/294–3480, 800/869–4639 🌐 www.courtneysplacekeywest.com 🛏 6 rooms, 2 suites, 2 efficiencies, 8 cottages 🍴 Breakfast.*

$$$ HOTEL 🏨 **Crowne Plaza Key West–La Concha.** History and franchises can mix, as this 1920s-vintage hotel proves with its handsome atrium lobby and sleep-conducive rooms. **Pros:** restaurant and Starbucks in-house; close to downtown attractions; free Wi-Fi. **Cons:** high-traffic area; confusing layout; expensive valet-only parking. [$] *Rooms from: $339 ✉ 430 Duval St. ☎ 305/296–2991 🌐 www.laconchakeywest.com 🛏 160 rooms, 8 rooms with balconies, 10 suites 🍴 No meals.*

$ HOTEL 🏨 **Eden House.** From the vintage metal rockers on the street-side porch to the old neon hotel sign in the lobby, this 1920s rambling Key West mainstay hotel is high on character, low on gloss. **Pros:** free parking; hot tub is actually hot; daily happy hour around the pool; discount at excellent Azur restaurant. **Cons:** pricey; a bit of a musty smell in some rooms; no TV in some rooms. [$] *Rooms from: $200 ✉ 1015 Fleming St. ☎ 305/296–6868, 800/533–5397 🌐 www.edenhouse.com 🛏 36 rooms, 8 suites 🍴 No meals.*

$$$$ HOTEL Fodor's Choice ★ 🏨 **The Gardens Hotel.** Built in 1875, this gloriously shaded, award-winning property was a labor of love from the get-go, and it covers a third of a city block in Old Town. **Pros:** luxurious bathrooms; secluded garden seating; free Wi-Fi. **Cons:** hard to get reservations; expensive; nightly secure parking fee. [$] *Rooms from: $415 ✉ 526 Angela St. ☎ 305/294–2661, 800/526–2664 🌐 www.gardenshotel.com 🛏 23 rooms 🍴 Breakfast.*

$$$$
RESORT
FAMILY
Hyatt Key West Resort and Spa. With its own man-made beach, the Hyatt Key West is one of few resorts where you can dig your toes in the sand, then walk a short distance away to the streets of Old Town. **Pros:** a little bit away from the bustle of Old Town; plenty of activities. **Cons:** beach is small; cramped-feeling property. $ *Rooms from: $419* ✉ *601 Front St.* ☎ *305/809–1234* ⊕ *www.keywest.hyatt.com* ⇆ *118 rooms* ⏐○⏐ *No meals.*

$$
B&B/INN
Key Lime Inn. This 1854 Grand Bahama–style house on the National Register of Historic Places succeeds by offering amiable service, a great location, and simple rooms with natural-wood furnishings. **Pros:** free parking; some rooms have private outdoor spaces; free Wi-Fi. **Cons:** standard rooms are pricey; pool faces a busy street; mulch-covered paths. $ *Rooms from: $259* ✉ *725 Truman Ave.* ☎ *305/294–5229, 800/549–4430* ⊕ *www.keylimeinn.com* ⇆ *37 rooms* ⏐○⏐ *Breakfast.*

$
B&B/INN
Key West Bed and Breakfast/The Popular House. There are accommodations for every budget, but the owners reason that budget travelers deserve as pleasant an experience (and lavish a tropical continental breakfast) as their well-heeled counterparts. **Pros:** lots of art; tiled outdoor shower; hot tub and sauna area is a welcome hangout. **Cons:** some rooms are small. $ *Rooms from: $125* ✉ *415 William St.* ☎ *305/296–7274, 800/438–6155* ⊕ *www.keywestbandb.com* ⇆ *10 rooms, 6 with bath* ⏐○⏐ *Breakfast.*

$$$$
HOTEL
Key West Marriott Beachside Hotel. This hotel vies for convention business with the biggest ballroom in Key West, but it also appeals to families with its spacious condo units decorated with impeccable good taste. **Pros:** private beach; poolside cabanas. **Cons:** small beach; long walk to Old Town; cookie-cutter facade. $ *Rooms from: $409* ✉ *3841 N. Roosevelt Blvd., New Town* ☎ *305/296–8100, 800/546–0885* ⊕ *www. keywestmarriottbeachside.com* ⇆ *93 rooms, 93 1-bedroom suites, 10 2-bedroom suites, 26 3-bedroom suites* ⏐○⏐ *No meals.*

$$$
HOTEL
Fodor's Choice
★
Marquesa Hotel. In a town that prides itself on its laid-back luxury, this complex of four restored 1884 houses stands out. **Pros:** room service; romantic atmosphere; turndown service. **Cons:** street-facing rooms can be noisy; expensive rates. $ *Rooms from: $395* ✉ *600 Fleming St.* ☎ *305/292–1919, 800/869–4631* ⊕ *www.marquesa.com* ⇆ *27 rooms* ⏐○⏐ *No meals.*

$$
B&B/INN
Merlin Guesthouse. Key West guesthouses don't usually welcome families, but this laid-back jumble of rooms and suites is an exception. **Pros:** good location near Duval Street; good rates. **Cons:** neighbor noise; street parking. $ *Rooms from: $279* ✉ *811 Simonton St.* ☎ *305/296–3336, 800/642–4753* ⊕ *www.merlinguesthouse.com* ⇆ *10 rooms, 6 suites, 4 cottages* ⏐○⏐ *Breakfast.*

$$
B&B/INN
Mermaid & the Alligator. An enchanting combination of flora and fauna makes this 1904 Victorian house a welcoming retreat. **Pros:** hot plunge pool; massage pavilion; island-getaway feel. **Cons:** minimum stay required (length depends on season); dark public areas; plastic lawn chairs. $ *Rooms from: $278* ✉ *729 Truman Ave.* ☎ *305/294–1894, 800/773–1894* ⊕ *www.kwmermaid.com* ⇆ *9 rooms* ⏐○⏐ *Breakfast.*

$$$
B&B/INN
NYAH: Not Your Average Hotel. From its charming white picket fence, it may look similar to other Victorian-style, Key West B&Bs, but that's

Sunset Key cottages are right on the water's edge, far away from the action of Old Town.

where the similarities end. **Pros:** central location; expert staff; free daily happy hour. **Cons:** small rooms; even smaller closets; no toiletries provided. [$] *Rooms from: $349* ✉ *420 Margaret St.* ☎ *305/296-2131* 🌐 *www.nyahotels.com* 🛏 *36 rooms* 🍴 *Breakfast* ☞ *18 and over only.*

$$$$ RESORT Fodor's Choice ★ 🏨 **Ocean Key Resort & Spa.** A pool and lively open-air bar and restaurant sit on Sunset Pier, a popular place to watch the sun sink into the horizon. **Pros:** well-trained staff; lively pool scene; best spa on the island. **Cons:** $20 per night valet parking; too bustling for some; pricey. [$] *Rooms from: $495* ✉ *Zero Duval St.* ☎ *305/296–7701, 800/328–9815* 🌐 *www.oceankey.com* 🛏 *64 rooms, 36 suites* 🍴 *No meals.*

$$$ HOTEL 🏨 **Parrot Key Resort.** This revamped destination resort feels like an old-fashioned beach community with picket fences and rocking-chair porches. **Pros:** four pools; finely appointed units; access to marina and other facilities at three sister properties in Marathon. **Cons:** outside of walking distance to Old Town; no transportation provided; hefty resort fee. [$] *Rooms from: $329* ✉ *2801 N. Roosevelt Blvd., New Town* ☎ *305/809–2200* 🌐 *www.parrotkeyresort.com* 🛏 *74 rooms, 74 suites, 74 3-bedroom villas* 🍴 *No meals.*

$$$$ RESORT 🏨 **Pier House Resort and Spa.** The location—on a quiet stretch of beach at the foot of Duval—is ideal as a buffer from and gateway to the action. **Pros:** beautiful beach; good location; nice spa. **Cons:** lots of conventions; poolside rooms are small; not really suitable for children under 16. [$] *Rooms from: $460* ✉ *1 Duval St.* ☎ *305/296–4600, 800/327–8340* 🌐 *www.pierhouse.com* 🛏 *116 rooms, 26 suites* 🍴 *No meals.*

$$$ RESORT 🏨 **The Reach, A Waldorf Astoria Resort.** Embracing Key West's only natural beach, this full-service, luxury resort offers sleek rooms, all with balconies and modern amenities as well as shared access to its sister Casa

Marina resort nearby. **Pros:** removed from Duval hubbub; great sunrise views; pullout sofas in most rooms. **Cons:** expensive resort fee; high rates; some say it lacks the grandeur of a Waldorf property. [$] *Rooms from: $300* ✉ *1435 Simonton St.* ☎ *305/296–5000, 888/318–4316* 🌐 *www.reachresort.com* ⇨ *72 rooms, 78 suites* 🍴 *No meals.*

$$$$ RENTAL Fodor's Choice ★ 🏨 **Santa Maria Suites.** It's odd to call this a hidden gem when it sits on a prominent corner just one block off Duval, but you'd never know the luxury that awaits behind its concrete facade. **Pros:** amenities galore; front desk concierge services; private parking lot. **Cons:** daily resort fee; beds low to the ground. [$] *Rooms from: $549* ✉ *1401 Simonton St.* ☎ *866/726–8259, 305/296–5678* 🌐 *www.santamariasuites.com* ⇨ *35 suites* 🍴 *No meals.*

$$ B&B/INN 🏨 **Simonton Court.** A small world all its own, this adult lodging makes you feel deliciously sequestered from Key West's crasser side, but close enough to get there on foot. **Pros:** lots of privacy; well-appointed accommodations; friendly staff. **Cons:** minimum stays required in high season. $25 a night off-street parking. [$] *Rooms from: $299* ✉ *320 Simonton St.* ☎ *305/294–6386, 800/944–2687* 🌐 *www.simontoncourt.com* ⇨ *17 rooms, 6 suites, 6 cottages* 🍴 *Breakfast.*

$$$ HOTEL 🏨 **Southernmost Hotel.** This hotel's location on the quiet end of Duval means you don't have to deal with the hustle and bustle of downtown unless you want to—it's within a 20-minute walk (but around sunset, this end of town gets its share of car and foot traffic). **Pros:** pool attracts a lively crowd; access to nearby properties and beach; free parking and Wi-Fi. **Cons:** can get crowded around the pool and public areas; expensive nightly resort fee. [$] *Rooms from: $359* ✉ *1319 Duval St.* ☎ *305/296–6577, 800/354–4455* 🌐 *www.southernmostresorts.com* ⇨ *118 rooms* 🍴 *No meals.*

$ B&B/INN 🏨 **Speakeasy Inn.** During Prohibition, Raul Vasquez made this place popular by smuggling in rum from Cuba; today its reputation is for having reasonably priced rooms within walking distance of the beach. **Pros:** good location; reasonable rates; kitchenettes. **Cons:** no pool; on busy Duval. [$] *Rooms from: $189* ✉ *1117 Duval St.* ☎ *305/296–2680* 🌐 *www.speakeasyinn.com* ⇨ *4 suites* 🍴 *Breakfast.*

$$$$ RESORT Fodor's Choice ★ 🏨 **Sunset Key.** This private island retreat with its own sandy beach feels completely cut off from the world, yet you're just minutes away from the action. **Pros:** peace and quiet; roomy verandas; free 24-hour shuttle; free Wi-Fi. **Cons:** luxury doesn't come cheap. [$] *Rooms from: $780* ✉ *245 Front St.* ☎ *305/292–5300, 888/477–7786* 🌐 *www.westinsunsetkeycottages.com* ⇨ *40 cottages* 🍴 *Breakfast.*

$$$$ RESORT 🏨 **Westin Key West Resort & Marina.** This waterfront resort's two three-story, Keys-style buildings huddle around its 37-slip marina in the middle of Old Town. **Pros:** good location; bar and restaurant overlook Mallory Square; access to Sunset Key; free Wi-Fi. **Cons:** feels too big for Key West; often crowded; conference clientele. [$] *Rooms from: $409* ✉ *245 Front St.* ☎ *305/294–4000* 🌐 *www.westin.com/keywest* ⇨ *146 rooms, 32 suites* 🍴 *No meals.*

NIGHTLIFE

Rest up: Much of what happens in Key West does so after dark. Open your mind and have a stroll. Scruffy street performers strum next to dogs in sunglasses. Brawls tumble out the doors of Sloppy Joe's. Drag queens strut across stages in Joan Rivers garb. Tattooed men lick whipped cream off women's body parts. And margaritas flow like a Jimmy Buffett tune.

BARS AND LOUNGES

Capt. Tony's Saloon. When it was the original Sloppy Joe's in the mid-1930s, Hemingway was a regular. Later, a young Jimmy Buffett sang here and made this watering hole famous in his song "Last Mango in Paris." Captain Tony was even voted mayor of Key West. Yes, this place is a beloved landmark. Stop in and take a look at the "hanging tree" that grows through the roof, listen to live music seven nights a week, and play some pool. ⊠ *428 Greene St.* ☎ *305/294–1838* ⊕ *www. capttonyssaloon.com.*

Durty Harry's. This megasize entertainment complex is home to eight different bars and clubs, both indoor and outdoor. Their motto is, "Eight Famous Bars, One Awesome Night," and they're right. You'll find pizza, dancing, live music, Rick's Key West, and the infamous Red Garter strip club. ⊠ *208 Duval St.* ☎ *305/296–5513* ⊕ *www.ricksbarkeywest.com.*

Green Parrot Bar. Pause for a libation in the open-air and breathe in the spirit of Key West. Built in 1890 as a grocery store, this property has been many things to many people over the years It's touted as the oldest bar in Key West and the sometimes-rowdy saloon has locals outnumbering out-of-towners, especially on nights when bands play. ⊠ *601 White-head St., at Southard St.* ☎ *305/294–6133* ⊕ *www.greenparrot.com.*

Hog's Breath Saloon. Belly up to the bar for a cold mug of the signature Hog's Breath Lager at this infamous joint, a must-stop on the Key West bar crawl. Live bands play daily 1 pm–2 am (except when the game's on TV). You never know who'll stop by and perhaps even jump on stage for an impromptu concert (can you say Kenny Chesney?). ⊠ *400 Front St.* ☎ *305/296–4222* ⊕ *www.hogsbreath.com.*

Margaritaville Café. A youngish, touristy crowd mixes with aging Parrot Heads. It's owned by former Key West resident and recording star Jimmy Buffett, who has been known to perform here. The drink of choice is, of course, a margarita, made with Jimmy's own brand of Margaritaville tequila. There's live music nightly, as well as lunch and dinner. ⊠ *500 Duval St.* ☎ *305/292–1435* ⊕ *www.margaritaville.com.*

Pier House. The party here begins at the Beach Bar with live entertainment daily to celebrate the sunset on the beach, then moves to the funky Chart Room. It's small and odd but there's free hotdogs and peanuts and its history is worth learning. ⊠ *1 Duval St.* ☎ *305/296–4600, 800/327–8340* ⊕ *www.pierhouse.com.*

Schooner Wharf Bar. This open-air waterfront bar and grill in the historic seaport district retains its funky Key West charm and hosts live entertainment daily. Its margaritas rank among Key West's best, as does the bar itself, voted Best Local's Bar six years in a row. For great

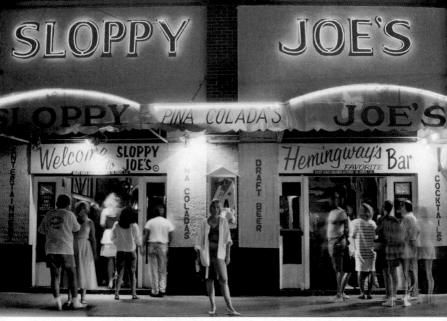

Sloppy Joe's is one must-stop on most Key West visitors' bar-hop stroll, also known as the Duval Crawl.

views, head up to the second floor and be sure to order up some fresh seafood and fritters and Dark and Stormy cocktails. ✉ *202 William St.* ☎ *305/292–3302* ⊕ *www.schoonerwharf.com.*

Sloppy Joe's. There's history and good times at the successor to a famous 1937 speakeasy named for its founder, Captain Joe Russell. Decorated with Hemingway memorabilia and marine flags, the bar is popular with travelers and is full and noisy all the time. A Sloppy Joe's T-shirt is a de rigueur Key West souvenir, and the gift shop sells them like crazy. Grab a seat (if you can) and be entertained by the bands and by the parade of people in constant motion. ✉ *201 Duval St.* ☎ *305/294–5717* ⊕ *www.sloppyjoes.com.*

Two Friends Patio Lounge. Love karaoke? Get it out of your system at Two Friends Patio Lounge, where your performance gets a live Internet feed via the bar's Karaoke Cam. The singing starts at 8:30 pm most nights. ✉ *512 Front St.* ☎ *305/296–3124* ⊕ *www.twofriendskeywest.com.*

SHOPPING

On these streets you'll find colorful local art of widely varying quality, key limes made into everything imaginable, and the raunchiest T-shirts in the civilized world.

MALLS AND SHOPPING CENTERS

Bahama Village. Where to start your shopping adventure? This cluster of spruced-up shops, restaurants, and vendors is responsible for the restoration of the colorful historic district where Bahamians settled in the 19th century. The village lies roughly between Whitehead and Fort streets and Angela and Catherine streets. Hemingway frequented the bars, restaurants, and boxing rings in this part of town. ⊠ *Between Whitehead and Fort Sts. and Angela and Catherine Sts.*

ARTS AND CRAFTS

Alan S. Maltz Gallery. The owner, declared the state's official wildlife photographer by the Wildlife Foundation of Florida, captures the state's nature and character in stunning portraits. Spend four figures for large-format images on canvas or save on small prints and closeouts. ⊠ *1210 Duval St.* ☎ *305/294–0005* ⊕ *www.alanmaltz.com.*

Art@830. This inviting gallery carries a little bit of everything, from pottery to paintings and jewelry to sculptures. Most outstanding is its selection of glass art, particularly the jellyfish lamps. Take time to admire all that is here. ⊠ *830 Caroline St., Historic Seaport* ☎ *305/295–9595* ⊕ *www.art830.com.*

Gallery on Greene. This is the largest gallery–exhibition space in Key West and it showcases 37 museum-quality artists. They pride themselves on being the leader in the field of representational fine art, painting, sculptures, and reproductions from the Florida Keys and Key West. You can see the love immediately from gallery curator Nancy Frank, who aims to please everyone, from the casual buyer to the established collector. ⊠ *606 Greene St.* ☎ *305/294–1669* ⊕ *www.galleryongreene.com.*

Gingerbread Square Gallery. The oldest private art gallery in Key West represents local and internationally acclaimed artists on an annually changing basis, in mediums ranging from graphics to art glass. ⊠ *1207 Duval St.* ☎ *305/296–8900* ⊕ *www.gingerbreadsquaregallery.com.*

Glass Reunions. Find a collection of wild and impressive fine-art glass here. It's worth a stop in just to see the imaginative and over-the-top glass chandeliers, jewelry, dishes, and platters. ⊠ *825 Duval St.* ☎ *305/294–1720* ⊕ *www.glassreunions.com.*

Key West Pottery. You won't find any painted coconuts here, but you will find a collection of contemporary tropical ceramics. Wife and husband owners Kelly Lever and Adam Russell take real pride in this working studio that, in addition to their own creations, features artists from around the country. This is one of the island's few specialty galleries. ⊠ *1203 Duval St.* ☎ *305/900–8303* ⊕ *www.keywestpottery.com.*

KW Light Gallery at Island Arts. Historian, photographer, and painter Sharon Wells opened this gallery to showcase her own fine-art photography, painted tiles and canvases. She also offers private tours of Key West, including historic walking tours at the Custom House Museum. ⊠ *1128 Duval St.* ☎ *305/923–5133* ⊕ *www.keywesttiles.com.*

Lucky Street Gallery. High-end contemporary paintings are the focus at this gallery with more than 30 years of experience and a passionate staff. There are also a few pieces of jewelry by internationally recognized Key West–based artists. Changing exhibits, artist receptions, and special events make this a lively venue. ⊠ *1130 Duval St.* ☎ *305/294–3973* ⊕ *www.luckystreetgallery.com.*

Nightlife, shops, and some interesting street art can all be found on Key West's Duval Street.

BOOKS

Key West Island Bookstore. This home away from home for the large Key West writers' community carries new, used, and rare titles. It specializes in Hemingway, Tennessee Williams, and South Florida mystery writers. ⊠ *513 Fleming St.* ☎ *305/294–2904* ⊕ *www.keywestislandbooks.com.*

CLOTHING AND FABRICS

Fairvilla Megastore. Don't leave town without a browse through the legendary shop, where you'll find an astonishing array of fantasy wear, outlandish costumes (check out the pirate section), and other "adult" toys. ⊠ *520 Front St.* ☎ *305/292–0448* ⊕ *www.fairvilla.com.*

Kino Sandals. A pair of Kino Sandals was once a public declaration that you'd been to Key West. The attraction? You can watch these inexpensive items being made. The factory has been churning out several styles since 1966. Walk up to the counter, grab a pair, try them on, and lay down some cash. It's that simple. ⊠ *107 Fitzpatrick St.* ☎ *305/294–5044* ⊕ *www.kinosandalfactory.com* ⊘ *Closed Sun. in off-season.*

FOOD AND DRINK

Fausto's Food Palace. Since 1926 Fausto's has been the spot to catch up on the week's gossip and to chill out in summer—it has groceries, organic foods, marvelous wines, a sushi chef on duty 8 am–3 pm, and box lunches to go. There are two locations you can shop at in Key West (the other is at 1105 White Street) plus a recently opened online store. ⊠ *522 Fleming St.* ☎ *305/296–5663* ⊕ *www.faustos.com.*

Fodor's Choice
★

Kermit's Key West Lime Shoppe. You'll see Kermit himself standing on the corner every time a trolley passes, pie in hand. Besides pie, his shop carries a multitude of key lime products from barbecue sauce to jellybeans.

His prefrozen pies, dressed with a special long-lasting whipped cream instead of meringue, travels well. This is a must-stop shop while in Key West. The key lime pie is the best on the island; once you try it frozen on a stick, dipped in chocolate, you may consider quitting your job and moving here. Savor every bite on their outdoor patio/garden area. Heaven. ⊠ *200 Elizabeth St., Historic Seaport* ☎ *305/296–0806, 800/376–0806* ⊕ *www.keylimeshop.com.*

GIFTS AND SOUVENIRS

Cayo Hueso y Habana. Part museum, part shopping center, this circa-1879 warehouse includes a hand-rolled cigar shop, one-of-a-kind souvenirs, a Cuban restaurant, and exhibits that tell of the island's Cuban heritage. Outside, a memorial garden pays homage to the island's Cuban ancestors. ⊠ *410 Wall St., Mallory Sq.* ☎ *305/293–7260.*

Cocktails! Key West. Could there possibly be a better location to celebrate the art of the drink than Key West? This celebratory shop carries everything you need for cocktails including beautiful hand-painted stemware, hi-ball, martini, and shot glasses, mugs, accessories, and art that blends perfectly. Most of the designs are made on the island. ⊠ *808 Duval St.* ☎ *305/292–1190* ⊕ *www.cocktailskeywest.com.*

Montage. For that unique (but slightly overpriced) souvenir of your trip to Key West head here, where you'll discover hundreds of handcrafted signs of popular Key West guesthouses, inns, hotels, restaurants, bars, and streets. If you can't find what you're looking for, they'll make it for you. ⊠ *291 Front St.* ☎ *305/395–9101, 877/396–4278* ⊕ *www. montagekeywest.com.*

SPORTS AND THE OUTDOORS

Unlike the rest of the region, Key West isn't known primarily for outdoor pursuits. But everyone should devote at least half a day to relaxing on a boat tour, heading out on a fishing expedition, or pursuing some other adventure at sea. The ultimate excursion is a boat trip to Dry Tortugas National Park for snorkeling and exploring Fort Jefferson. Other excursions cater to nature lovers, scuba divers and snorkelers, anglers, and those who would just like to get out in the water and enjoy the scenery and sunset. For those who prefer their recreation land-based, biking is the way to go.

BIKING

Key West was practically made for bicycles, but don't let that lull you into a false sense of security. Narrow and one-way streets along with car traffic result in several bike accidents a year. Some hotels rent or lend bikes to guests; others will refer you to a nearby shop and reserve a bike for you. Rentals usually start at about $10 a day, but some places also rent by the half day. ■ TIP→ Lock up! Bikes—and porch chairs—are favorite targets for local thieves.

A&M Rentals. Rent beach cruisers with large baskets or scooters. Look for the huge American flag on the roof, or call for free airport, ferry, or cruise ship pickup. ⊠ *523 Truman Ave.* ☎ *305/294–0399* ⊕ *www. amscooterskeywest.com* ⌨ *Bicycles from $15, scooters from $35.*

Eaton Bikes. Tandem, three-wheel, and children's bikes are available in addition to the standard beach cruisers and hybrid bikes. Delivery is free for all Key West rentals. ⊠ *830 Eaton St.* ☎ *305/294–8188* ⊕ *www. eatonbikes.com* ✉ *From $18 per day.*

Lloyd's Original Tropical Bike Tour. Explore the natural, noncommercial side of Key West at a leisurely pace, stopping on backstreets and in backyards of private homes to sample native fruits and view indigenous plants and trees with a 30-year Key West veteran. The behind-the-scenes tours run two hours and include a bike rental. ⊠ *Truman Ave. and Simonton St.* ☎ *305/304–4700, 305/294–1882* ⊕ *www. lloydstropicalbiketour.com* ✉ *$39.*

Moped Hospital. This outfit supplies balloon-tire bikes with yellow safety baskets for adults and kids, as well as scooters and even double-seater scooters. ⊠ *601 Truman Ave.* ☎ *305/296–3344, 866/296–1625* ⊕ *www. mopedhospital.com* ✉ *Bicycles from $12 per day, scooters from $35 per day.*

BOAT TOURS

Dancing Dolphin Spirit Charters. Victoria Impallomeni, a wilderness guide and environmental marine science expert, invites up to six nature lovers—especially children—aboard the *Imp II,* a 25-foot Aquasport, for four-hour and seven-hour ecotours that frequently include encounters with wild dolphins. While island-hopping, you visit underwater gardens, natural shoreline, and mangrove habitats. For her Dolphin Day for Humans tour, Impallomeni pulls you through the water, equipped with mask and snorkel, on a specially designed "dolphin water massage board" that simulates dolphin swimming motions. Sometimes dolphins follow the boat and swim among participants. All equipment is supplied. ⊠ *MM 5 OS, Murray's Marina, 5710 Overseas Hwy.* ☎ *305/304–7562, 888/822–7366* ⊕ *www.captainvictoria.com* ✉ *From $500.*

Sunset Culinaire Tours. Owner/operator Chef Brian, serves a full menu of gourmet meals with fine wine and beer aboard a sleek cruising yacht every evening at sunset. They cruise when they have six or more guests so bring friends or join others who want to experience this magical evening. ⊠ *5555 College Rd.* ☎ *305/296–0982* ⊕ *www.sunsetculinaire. com* ✉ *$85.*

BUS AND TROLLEY TOURS

City View Trolley Tours. In 2010, City View Trolley Tours began service, offering a little competition to the Conch Train and Old Town Trolley, which are owned by the same company. Purchase your tickets online or with your smartphone, but you pay double if you pay in person. Tours depart every 30 minutes from 9:30 to 4:30. Passengers can board and disembark at any of nine stops, and can reboard at will. ☎ *305/294–0644* ⊕ *www.cityviewtrolleys.com* ✉ *From $19.*

Conch Tour Train. The Conch Tour Train is a 90-minute narrated tour of Key West, traveling 14 miles through Old Town and around the island. Board at Mallory Square or Angela Street and Duval Street depot every half hour (9–4:30 from Mallory Square). Discount tickets are available online. ☎ *305/294–5161, 888/916–8687* ⊕ *www.conchtourtrain.com* ✉ *$30.45.*

Gay & Lesbian Trolley Tour. Decorated with a rainbow, the Gay and Lesbian Trolley Tour rumbles around the town beginning at 11 am every Saturday morning. The 70-minute tour highlights Key West's influential gay history. ⊠ *513 Truman Ave.* ☎ *305/294–4603* ⊕ *www.keywestsites. com* ✄ *$20.*

Old Town Trolley. Old Town Trolley operates trolley-style buses, departing from the Mallory Square every 30 minutes from 9 to 4:30, for 90-minute narrated tours of Key West. The smaller trolleys go places the larger Conch Tour Train won't fit and you can ride a second consecutive day for free. You may disembark at any of 13 stops and reboard a later trolley. You can save $3 by booking online. It also offers package deals with Old Town attractions. ⊠ *201 Front St.* ☎ *305/296–6688, 888/910–8687* ⊕ *www.trolleytours.com* ✄ *$30.45.*

FISHING

Key West Bait & Tackle. Prepare to catch a big one with the live bait, frozen bait, and fishing equipment provided here. They even offer rod and reel rentals (starting at $15 for 24 hours). Stop by their on-site Live Bait Lounge where you can sip $2.50 ice-cold beer while telling fish tales. ⊠ *241 Margaret St.* ☎ *305/292–1961* ⊕ *www. keywestbaitandtackle.com.*

Key West Pro Guides. This outfitter offers private charters, and you can choose 4, 5, 6, or 8 hour trips. Choose from flats, backcountry, reef, offshore fishing, and even specialty trips to the Dry Tortugas. Whatever your fishing (even spearfishing) pleasure, their captains will hook you up. ⊠ *G-31 Miriam St.* ☎ *866/259–4205* ⊕ *www.keywestproguides. com* ✄ *From $400.*

GOLF

Key West Golf Club. Key West isn't a major golf destination, but there is one course on Stock Island designed by Rees Jones that will downright surprise you with its water challenges and tropical beauty. It's also the only "Caribbean" golf course in the United States, boasting 200 acres of unique Florida foliage and wildlife. Hole 8 is the famous "Mangrove Hole," which will give you stories to tell. It's a 143-yard, par 3 that is played completely over a mass of mangroves with their gnarly roots and branches completely intertwined. Bring extra balls and book your tee time early in season. Nike rental clubs available. ⊠ *6450 E. College Rd.* ☎ *305/294–5232* ⊕ *www.keywestgolf.com* ✄ *$52–$97* ⛳ *18 holes, 6500 yards, par 70.*

KAYAKING

Key West Eco-Tours. Key West is surrounded by marinas, so it's easy to find a water-based activity or tour, whether it's sailing with dolphins or paddling in the mangroves. These sail-kayak-snorkel excursions take you into backcountry flats and mangrove forests without the crowds. The 4½-hour trip includes lunch. Private sunset sails, kayak, and paddleboard tours are available, too. ⊠ *Historic Seaport, 100 Grinnell St.* ☎ *305/294–7245* ⊕ *www.keywestecotours.com* ✄ *From $115.*

Lazy Dog Adventures. Take a two- or four-hour guided sea kayak–snorkel tour around the mangrove islands just east of Key West. Costs include transportation, bottled water, a snack, and supplies, including snorkeling gear. Paddleboard tours are also available, as are rentals for self-touring. Paddleboard yoga and PaddleFit are exciting new classes. ✉ *5114 Overseas Hwy.* ☎ *305/295–9898* ⊕ *www.lazydog.com* 🎫 *From $40.*

SUP Key West. This ancient sport from Hawaii involves a surfboard and a paddle and has quickly become a favorite Florida water sport known as SUP (stand-up paddleboarding). SUP Key West gives lessons and morning, afternoon, or sunset tours of the estuaries. What's more, your tour guides are experts (one's even a PhD) in marine biology and ecology. Call ahead to make arrangements. ✉ *110 Grinnell St.* ☎ *305/240–1426* ⊕ *www.supkeywest.com* 🎫 *From $45.*

SCUBA DIVING AND SNORKELING

The Florida Keys National Marine Sanctuary extends along Key West and beyond to the Dry Tortugas. Key West National Wildlife Refuge further protects the pristine waters. Most divers don't make it this far out in the Keys, but if you're looking for a day of diving as a break from the nonstop party in Old Town, expect to pay about $65 and upward for a two-tank dive. Serious divers can book dive trips to the Dry Tortugas.

Captain's Corner. This PADI–certified dive shop has classes in several languages and twice-daily snorkel and dive trips to reefs and wrecks aboard the 60-foot dive boat *Sea Eagle*. Use of weights, belts, masks, and fins is included. ✉ *125 Ann St.* ☎ *305/296–8865* ⊕ *www.captainscorner. com* 🎫 *From $40.*

Dive Key West. Operating over 40 years, Dive Key West is a full-service dive center that has charters, instruction, gear rental, sales, and repair. You can take either snorkel excursions or scuba trips with this outfit that is dedicated to coral reef education and preservation. ✉ *3128 N. Roosevelt Blvd.* ☎ *305/296–3823* ⊕ *www.divekeywest.com* 🎫 *Snorkeling from $59, scuba from $75.*

Snuba of Key West. Safely dive the coral reefs without getting a scuba certification. Ride out to the reef on a catamaran, then follow your guide underwater for a one-hour tour of the coral reefs. You wear a regulator with a breathing hose that is attached to a floating air tank on the surface. No prior diving or snorkeling experience is necessary, but you must know how to swim and be at least eight years old. The price includes beverages. ✉ *Garrison Bight Marina, Palm Ave., between Eaton St. and N. Roosevelt Blvd.* ☎ *305/292–4616* ⊕ *www. snubakeywest.com* 🎫 *From $99.*

WALKING TOURS

Key West Garden Club at West Martello Tower. For more than 65 years, the Key West Garden Club has maintained lush gardens among the arches and ruins of this redbrick Civil War–era fort. In addition to the impressive collection of native and tropical plants, you can meander past fountains, sculptures and a picture-perfect gazebo on your self-guided tour. These volunteers hold art, orchid, and flower shows February through April and lead private garden tours one weekend in March. ✉ *1100 Atlantic Blvd, where White St. and the Atlantic Ocean* meet ☎ 305/294–3210 ⊕ *www.keywestgardenclub.com* ✉ *Donation welcome* ⊗ *Daily 9:30–5.*

DRY TORTUGAS NATIONAL PARK

70 miles southwest of Key West.

History buffs might remember long-deactivated Fort Jefferson as the prison that held Dr. Samuel Mudd for his role in the Lincoln assassination. But today's "guests" are much more captivated by this sanctuary's thousands of birds and marine life.

GETTING HERE AND AROUND

At this writing, the ferryboat *Yankee Freedom II* departs from a marina in Old Town and does day trips to Garden Key. Key West Seaplane Adventures has half- and full-day trips to the Dry Tortugas, where you can explore Fort Jefferson, built in 1846, and snorkel on the beautiful protected reef. Departing from the Key West airport, the flights include soft drinks and snorkeling equipment for $280 (half day) and $495 (full day), plus there's a $5 (cash only) park fee. If you want to explore the park's other keys, look into renting a boat or hiring a private charter. ⇨ *For more information on the two ferries and the seaplane, see Exploring.*

EXPLORING

Dry Tortugas National Park. This park, 70 miles off the shores of Key West, consists of seven small islands. Tour the fort; then lay out your blanket on the sunny beach for a picnic before you head out to snorkel on the protected reef. Many people like to camp here ($3 per person per night, eight sites plus group site and overflow area; first come, first served), but note that there's no freshwater supply and you must carry off whatever you bring onto the island.

The typical visitor from Key West, however, makes it no farther than the waters of Garden Key. Home to 19th-century Fort Jefferson, it is the destination for seaplane and fast ferry tours out of Key West. With 2½ to 6½ hours to spend on the island, visitors have time to tour the mammoth fort-prison and then cool off with mask and snorkel along the fort's moat wall.

History buffs might remember long-deactivated Fort Jefferson, the largest brick building in the western hemisphere, as the prison that held Dr. Samuel Mudd, who unwittingly set John Wilkes Booth's leg after the assassination of Abraham Lincoln. Three other men were also held there for complicity in the assassination. Original construction on the fort began in 1846 and continued for 30 years, but was never completed because the invention of the rifled cannon made it obsolete. That's when it became a Civil War prison and later a wildlife refuge. In 1935 President Franklin Roosevelt declared it a national monument for its historic and natural value.

The brick fort acts as a gigantic, almost 16-acre reef. Around its moat walls, coral grows and schools of snapper, grouper, and wrasses hang out. To reach the offshore coral heads requires about 15 minutes of swimming over sea-grass beds. The reef formations blaze with the color and majesty of brain coral, swaying sea fans, and flitting tropical fish. It takes a bit of energy to swim the distance, but the water depth pretty much measures under 7 feet all the way, allowing for sandy spots to stop and rest. (Standing in sea-grass meadows and on coral is detrimental to marine life.)

Serious snorkelers and divers head out farther offshore to epic formations, including Palmata Patch, one of the few surviving concentrations of elkhorn coral in the Keys. Day-trippers congregate on the sandy beach to relax in the sun and enjoy picnics. Overnight tent campers have use of restroom facilities and achieve a total getaway from noise, lights, and civilization in general. Remember that no matter how you get here, the park's $5 admission fee must be paid in cash.

The park has set up with signage a self-guided tour that takes about 45 minutes. You should budget more time if you're into photography, because the scenic shots are hard to pass up. Ranger-guided tours are also available at certain times. Check in at the visitor center for a schedule. The small office also shows an orientation video, sells books and other educational materials, and, most importantly, provides a blast of air-conditioning on hot days.

Birders in the know bring binoculars to watch some 100,000 nesting sooty terns at their only U.S. nesting site, Bush Key, adjacent to Garden Key. Noddy terns also nest in the spring. During winter migrations, birds fill the airspace so thickly they literally fall from the sky to make their pit stops, birders say. Nearly 300 species have been spotted in the park's seven islands, including frigatebirds, boobies, cormorants, and broad-winged hawks. Bush Key is closed to foot traffic during nesting season, January through September. ⊠ *Key West* ⊕ *www.nps.gov/drto* ⌨ *$5.*

Yankee Freedom III. The fast, sleek, 110-foot catamaran *Yankee Freedom III* travels to the Dry Tortugas in 2¼ hours. The time passes quickly on the roomy vessel equipped with four restrooms, three warm freshwater showers, and two bars. Stretch out on two decks that are both air-conditioned, with cushioned seating. There is also an open sundeck with sunny and shaded seating. Continental breakfast and lunch are included. On arrival, a naturalist leads a 45-minute guided tour, which is followed by lunch and a free afternoon for swimming, snorkeling (gear included), and exploring. The vessel is ADA–certified for visitors using wheelchairs. ■TIP➡ **The Dry Tortugas lies in the central time zone.** ⊠ *Lands End Marina, 240 Margaret St.* ☎ *305/294–7009, 800/634–0939* ⊕ *www.yankeefreedom.com* ⌨ *$170; parking $13 in city garage* ⊙ *Trips daily at 8 am; check-in 7:15 am.*

FORT LAUDERDALE

With Broward County

WELCOME TO FORT LAUDERDALE

TOP REASONS TO GO

★ **Blue waves:** Sparkling Lauderdale beaches spanning Broward County's entire coast were Florida's first to capture Blue Wave Beach status from the Clean Beaches Council.

★ **Inland waterways:** More than 300 miles of inland waterways, including downtown Fort Lauderdale's historic New River, create what's known as the Venice of America.

★ **Everglades access:** Just minutes from luxury hotels and golf courses, the rugged Everglades tantalize with alligators, colorful birds, and other wildlife.

★ **Vegas-style gaming:** Since slots and blackjack tables hit Hollywood's glittering Seminole Hard Rock Hotel & Casino in 2008, smaller competitors have followed this lucrative trend on every square inch of Indian Territory.

★ **Cruise gateway:** Port Everglades—home port for *Allure* and *Oasis of the Seas,* the world's largest cruise vessels—hosts ships from major cruise lines.

1 **Fort Lauderdale.** Anchored by the fast-flowing New River and its attractive Riverwalk, Fort Lauderdale embraces high-rise condos along with single-family homes, museums, parks, and attractions. Las Olas Boulevard, lined with boutiques, sidewalk cafés, and restaurants, links downtown with 20 miles of sparkling beaches.

2 **North on Scenic A1A.** Stretching north on Route A1A, old-school seaside charm abounds, from high-rise Galt Ocean Mile to quiet, low-rise resort communities farther north.

3 **Hollywood.** From its beachside Boardwalk to historic Young Circle (the latter transformed into an Arts Park), South Broward's main destination provides grit, glitter, and diversity in attractions.

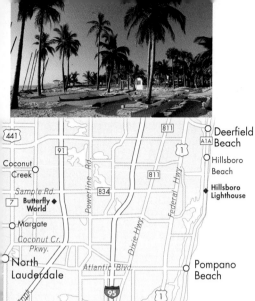

GETTING ORIENTED

Along the southeast's Gold Coast, Fort Lauderdale and Broward County anchor a delightfully chic middle ground between the posh and elite Palm Beaches and the international hubbub of Miami. From downtown Fort Lauderdale, it's about a four-hour drive to either Orlando or Key West, but there's plenty to keep you in Broward. All told, Broward boasts 31 communities from Deerfield Beach to Hallandale Beach along the coast, and from Coral Springs to Southwest Ranches closer to the Everglades. Big—in fact, huge—shopping options await in the western suburbs, home of Sawgrass Mills, the upscale Colonnade Outlets at Sawgrass, and IKEA Sunrise.

5

Map labels:
441, 811, Deerfield Beach, A1A, Coconut Creek, 91, Hillsboro Beach, 811, Sample Rd., 834, Hillsboro Lighthouse, Butterfly World, 7, Powerline Rd., Margate, Coconut Cr. Pkwy., North Lauderdale, Atlantic Blvd., Federal Hwy., Dixie Hwy., Pompano Beach, 95, Cypress Creek Rd., Commercial Blvd., N. Andrews Ave., Lauderdale-by-the-Sea, 2, Oakland Park Blvd., Lauderdale Lakes, A1A, 41, Sunrise Blvd., Fort Lauderdale, Seminole Dr., S.W. 31st Ave., Broward Blvd., Las Olas Blvd., 1, ATLANTIC OCEAN, Davie Blvd., Melrose Park, 84, S.E. 17th St. Causeway, 7, 595, Port Everglades, Fort Lauderdale-Hollywood International Airport, Griffin Rd., 1, Stirling Rd., Dania Beach Blvd., Dania Beach, Sheridan St., A1A, 822, 95, Hollywood Blvd., Dixie Hwy., Hollywood, 3, Pembroke Rd., Hallandale, Hallandale Blvd., 0 3 mi, 0 3 km

By Paul Rubio   Collegians of the 1960s returning to Fort Lauderdale would be hard-pressed to recognize the onetime "Sun and Suds Spring Break Capital of the Universe." Back then, Fort Lauderdale's beachfront was lined with T-shirt shops, and downtown consisted of a lone office tower and dilapidated buildings waiting to be razed. Not anymore!

The beach and downtown have since exploded with upscale shops, restaurants, and luxury resort hotels equipped with enough high-octane amenities to light up skies all the way to western Broward's Alligator Alley. At risk of losing small-town 45-rpm magic in iPod times—when hotel parking fees alone eclipse room rates of old—Greater Fort Lauderdale somehow seems to meld disparate eras into nouveau nirvana, seasoned with a lot of Gold Coast sand.

The city was named for Major William Lauderdale, who built a fort at the river's mouth in 1838 during the Seminole Indian wars. It wasn't until 1911 that the city was incorporated, with only 175 residents, but it grew quickly during the Florida boom of the 1920s. Today's population hovers around 165,000, and suburbs keep growing—1.75 million live in Broward County's 31 municipalities and unincorporated areas.

As elsewhere, many speculators busily flipping property here got caught when the sun-drenched real-estate bubble burst, leaving Broward's foreclosure rate to skyrocket. But the worst is far behind us. By the time the city began celebrating its centennial in 2011, it had resumed the renaissance that began before the economic crisis. The 20-mile shoreline—with wide ribbons of golden sand for beachcombing and sunbathing—remains the anchor draw for Fort Lauderdale and Broward County, but amazing beaches are now complemented by show-stopping hotels, an exploding foodie scene, and burgeoning cultural scene.

PLANNING

WHEN TO GO

Peak season runs Thanksgiving through April, when concert, art, and entertainment seasons go full-throttle. Expect heat and humidity and some rain in summer. Hurricane winds come most notably in August and September. Golfing tee-time waits are longer on weekends year-round. Regardless of season, remember that Fort Lauderdale sunshine can burn even in cloudy weather.

GETTING HERE AND AROUND

AIR TRAVEL

Serving more than 23 million travelers a year, **Fort Lauderdale–Hollywood International Airport** is 3 miles south of downtown Fort Lauderdale, just off U.S. 1 between Fort Lauderdale and Hollywood, and near Port Everglades and Fort Lauderdale Beach. Other options include **Miami International Airport,** about 32 miles to the southwest, and the far less chaotic **Palm Beach International Airport,** about 50 miles to the north. All three airports link to **Tri-Rail,** a commuter train operating seven days through Palm Beach, Broward, and Miami-Dade counties.

Airport Information Fort Lauderdale–Hollywood International Airport *(FLL).* ✉ *Fort Lauderdale* ☎ *866/435–9355* ⊕ *www.broward.org/airport.* **Miami International Airport** *(MIA).* ✉ *Miami* ☎ *305/876–7000* ⊕ *www.miami-airport. com.* **Palm Beach International Airport** *(PBI).* ✉ *Palm Beach* ☎ *561/471–7400* ⊕ *www.pbia.org.* **Tri-Rail** ☎ *800/874–7245* ⊕ *www.tri-rail.com.*

BUS TRAVEL

Broward County Transit operates bus route No. 1 between the airport and its main terminal at Broward Boulevard and Northwest 1st Avenue, near downtown Fort Lauderdale. Service from the airport is every 20 minutes and begins at 5:22 am on weekdays, 5:37 am Saturday, and 8:41 am Sunday; the last bus leaves the airport at 11:38 pm Monday–Saturday and 9:41 pm Sunday. The fare is $1.75 (coins only). △ **The Northwest 1st Avenue stop is in a crime-prone part of town. Exercise special caution there, day or night. Better yet, take a taxi to and from the airport.** Broward County Transit (BCT) also covers the county on 303 fixed routes. The fare is $1.75 (cash only). Service starts around 5 am and continues to 11:30 pm, except on Sunday.

Bus Contact Broward County Transit ☎ *954/357–8400* ⊕ *www.broward.org/ BCT.*

CAR TRAVEL

Renting a car to get around Broward County is highly recommended. Taxis are scarce and costly. Public transportation is rarely used.

By car, access to Broward County from north or south is via Florida's Turnpike, Interstate 95, U.S. 1, or U.S. 441. Interstate 75 (Alligator Alley, requiring a toll despite being part of the nation's interstate-highway system) connects Broward with Florida's west coast and runs parallel to State Road 84 within the county. East–west Interstate 595 runs from westernmost Broward County and links Interstate 75 with Interstate 95 and U.S. 1, providing handy access to the airport and seaport.

Route A1A, designated a Florida Scenic Highway by the state's Department of Transportation, parallels the beach.

TRAIN TRAVEL
Amtrak provides daily service to Fort Lauderdale and stops at Deerfield Beach and Hollywood.

HOTELS
Back-to-back openings of luxury beachfront hotels have created Fort Lauderdale's upscale "hotel row"—with the Atlantic Resort & Spa, the Hilton Beach Resort, the Ritz-Carlton, the W, and the Westin all less than a decade old. More upscale places to hang your hat are on the horizon, whereas smaller family-run lodging spots are disappearing. You can also find chain hotels along the Intracoastal Waterway. If you want to be *on* the beach, be sure to ask specifically when booking your room, since many hotels advertise "waterfront" accommodations that are along inland waterways or overlooking the beach from across Route A1A. *Hotel reviews have been shortened. For full information, visit Fodors.com.*

RESTAURANTS
References to "Fort Liquordale" from spring-break days of old have given way to au courant allusions for the decidedly cuisine-oriented "Fork Lauderdale." Greater Fort Lauderdale offers some of the finest, most varied dining of any U.S. city its size, spawned in part by the advent of new luxury hotels and upgrades all around. From among more than 4,000 wining-and-dining establishments in Broward, choose from basic Americana or cuisines of Asia, Europe, or Central and South America, and enjoy more than just food in an atmosphere with subtropical twists.

WHAT IT COSTS			
$	**$$**	**$$$**	**$$$$**
RESTAURANTS under $16	$16–$20	$21–$30	over $30
HOTELS under $201	$201–$300	$301–$400	over $400

Restaurant prices are the average cost of a main course at dinner or, if dinner is not served, at lunch. Hotel prices are the lowest cost of a standard double room in high season.

FORT LAUDERDALE

Like many southeast Florida neighbors, Fort Lauderdale has long been revitalizing. In a state where gaudy tourist zones often stand aloof from workaday downtowns, Fort Lauderdale exhibits consistency at both ends of the 2-mile Las Olas corridor. The sparkling look results from upgrades both downtown and on the beachfront. Matching the downtown's innovative arts district, cafés, and boutiques is an equally inventive beach area, with hotels, cafés, and shops facing an undeveloped shoreline, and new resort-style hotels replacing faded icons of yesteryear. Despite wariness of pretentious overdevelopment, city leaders have allowed a striking number of glittering high-rises. Nostalgic locals and frequent visitors fret over the diminishing vision of sailboats bobbing in waters near downtown; however, Fort Lauderdale remains the yachting capital of the world, and the water toys don't seem to be going anywhere. Sharp demographic changes are also altering the faces of Greater Fort Lauderdale communities, increasingly cosmopolitan with more minorities, including Hispanics and people of Caribbean descent, as well as gays and lesbians. In Fort Lauderdale, especially, a younger populace is growing, whereas longtime residents are heading north, to a point where one former city commissioner likens the change to that of historic New River—moving with the tide and sometimes appearing at a standstill: "The river of our population is at still point, old and new in equipoise, one pushing against the other."

GETTING HERE AND AROUND

The Fort Lauderdale metro area is laid out in a grid system, and only myriad canals and waterways interrupt the mostly straight-line path of streets and roads. Nomenclature is important here. Streets, roads, courts, and drives run east–west. Avenues, terraces, and ways run north–south. Boulevards can (and do) run any which way. For visitors, boutique-lined Las Olas Boulevard is one of the most important east–west thoroughfares from the beach to downtown, whereas Route A1A—referred to as Atlantic Boulevard, Ocean Boulevard, and Fort Lauderdale Beach along some stretches—runs along the north–south oceanfront. These names can confuse visitors, since there are separate streets called Atlantic and Ocean in Hollywood and Pompano Beach. Boulevards, composed of either pavement or water, give Fort Lauderdale its distinct "Venice of America" character.

The city's transportation system, though less congested than elsewhere in South Florida, suffers from traffic overload. Interstate 595 connects the city and suburbs and provides a direct route to the Fort Lauderdale–Hollywood International Airport and Port Everglades, but lanes slow to a crawl during rush hours. The Intracoastal Waterway, paralleling Route A1A, is the nautical equivalent of an interstate highway. It runs north–south between downtown Fort Lauderdale and the beach and provides easy boating access to neighboring beach communities.

To hop around Fort Lauderdale for free, catch an orange-bottomed, yellow-topped Sun Trolley, running every 15 minutes. Sun Trolley has expanded its presence with several routes, covering downtown, Las Olas, the beaches, and Galt Ocean Mile. Sun Trolley's popular Las Olas and Beaches route passes from downtown through Las Olas and then north on A1A. Wave at trolley drivers—yes, they'll stop—for pickups anywhere along the route. It's best to review the Sun Trolley map online, and identify the designated stops to be sure they stop where you are going, before using this as your means of transportation.

Meters in Yellow Cab taxis run at rates of $4.50 for the first mile and $2.40 for each additional mile; waiting time is $0.40 per minute. There's a $10-fare minimum to or from seaport or airport, and an additional $2 service charge when you are collected from the airport. All Yellow Cab vehicles accept major credit cards. Uber has a large presence in Fort

Lauderdale much to taxi drivers' chagrin. Though there's constant talk of eliminating Uber in Broward County, it is still going strong.

Transportation Contacts Sun Trolley ☎ 954/761–3543 ⊕ www.suntrolley. com. **Yellow Cab** ☎ 954/777–7777 ⊕ www.yellowcabbroward.com.

TOURS

Honeycombed with some 300 miles of navigable waterways, Fort Lauderdale is the home port for about 44,000 privately owned vessels, but you don't need to be a boat owner to ply the waters. For a scenic way to really see this canal-laced city, take a relaxing boat tour or simply hop on a Water Taxi, part of Fort Lauderdale's water-transportation system. See why the city is called the "Venice of America."

Carrie B Harbor Tours. Board a 300-passenger day cruiser for a 90-minute sightseeing tour on the New River and Intracoastal Waterway. Cruises depart at 11, 1, and 3 daily November through May and Thursday–Monday between June and October. The cost is $22.95. ■TIP→ **Book ahead online for discounts.** ⊠ 440 N. New River Dr. E, off Las Olas Blvd. ☎ 954/642–1601 ⊕ www.carriebcruises.com.

Jungle Queen Riverboat. The kitsch Jungle Queen riverboat seats more than 550 and cruises up the New River through the heart of Fort Lauderdale, as it has since 1935. It's old school and totally touristy but that's half the fun! The daily sightseeing cruises at 11:30 and 1:30 cost $21.95, and the 6 pm all-you-can-eat BBQ dinner cruise, which runs Wednesday to Sunday evenings, costs $44.95. ⊠ Bahia Mar Yachting Centre, 801 Seabreeze Blvd. ☎ 954/462–5596 ⊕ www.junglequeen. com.

FAMILY

Fodor's Choice

★

Water Taxi. A great way to experience the multimillion-dollar homes, hotels, and seafood restaurants along Fort Lauderdale's waterways is via the public Water Taxi, which runs every 30 minutes beginning at 10 am and ending at midnight. There are more than a dozen regularly scheduled pickup stations in Fort Lauderdale, including Las Olas Riverfront, the Shops of Las Olas, Bahia Mar, Hugh Taylor Birch State Park, and Gallery ONE near the Galleria Mall. An unlimited day pass serves for both a tour and a means of transportation between Fort Lauderdale's hotels and hot spots, though Water Taxi is most useful when viewed as a tour. It's possible to cruise all afternoon while taking in the waterfront sights. Captains and helpers indulge guests in fun factoids about Fort Lauderdale, white lies about the city's history, and bizarre tales about the celebrity homes along the Intracoastal. A day pass is $26. Water Taxi also connects Fort Lauderdale to Hollywood, where there are seven scheduled stops. ☎ 954/467–6677 ⊕ www.watertaxi.com.

VISITOR INFORMATION

Greater Fort Lauderdale Convention and Visitors Bureau ⊠ 101 NE 3rd Ave., #100 ☎ 954/765–4466 ⊕ www.sunny.org.

EXPLORING

DOWNTOWN AND LAS OLAS

The jewel of downtown along New River is the small Arts and Entertainment District, with Broadway shows, ballet, and theater at the riverfront Broward Center for the Performing Arts. Clustered within a five-minute walk are the Museum of Discovery & Science, the Fort Lauderdale Historical Museum, and the Museum of Art—home to stellar touring exhibits. Restaurants, sidewalk cafés, bars, and dance clubs flourish along Las Olas and its downtown extension. Tying these areas together is the Riverwalk, extending 2 miles along the New River's north and south banks. Tropical gardens with benches and interpretive displays fringe the walk on the north, boat landings on the south.

TOP ATTRACTIONS

FATVillage. Inspired by the Wynwood Arts District in Miami, The Flagler Arts and Technology Village or FATVillage comprises several square blocks of a former downtrodden neighborhood in downtown Fort Lauderdale, now inhabited by a number of production studios, art studios, loft-style apartments, and a fabulous coffee shop. Similar to Wynwood, on the last Saturday of every month, FATVillage hosts an evening art walk, where businesses display eclectic art from local talent and serve libations, and the village erupts into one giant, culture-infused street party. Most tourists come simply for this monthly affair, but if visiting by day, check out Fort Lauderdale's coolest coffee shop—Next Door Cafe at C&I Studios—adorned with antique nods to the literary world, tufted couches, and an eerie 1972 Airstream trailer and serving Black Cat Classic Espresso from Intelligentsia Coffee. ✉ *17 N.W. 5th St.* ☎ *954/760–5900* ⊕ *www.fatvillage.com.*

Historic Stranahan House Museum. The city's oldest residence, on the National Register of Historic Places, and increasingly dwarfed by high-rise development, was once home to businessman Frank Stranahan, who arrived in 1892. With his wife, Ivy, the city's first schoolteacher, he befriended and traded with Seminole Indians, and taught them "new ways." In 1901 he built a store that would later become his home after serving as a post office, a general store, and a restaurant. Frank and Ivy's former residence is now a museum, with many period furnishings, and tours. The historic home remains Fort Lauderdale's principal link to its brief history. Note that self-guided tours are not allowed. ✉ *335 S.E. 6th Ave., at Las Olas Blvd.* ☎ *954/524–4736* ⊕ *www.stranahanhouse. org* 🎟 *$12* ⊙ *Tours Oct.–Aug., daily at 1, 2, and 3.*

Fodor's Choice ★ **Las Olas Boulevard.** What Lincoln Road is to South Beach, Las Olas Boulevard is to Fort Lauderdale. The terrestrial heart and soul of Broward County, Las Olas is the premier street for restaurants, art galleries, shopping, and people-watching. From west to east the landscape of Las Olas transforms from modern downtown high-rises to original boutiques and ethnic eateries. Beautiful mansions and traditional Floridian homes line the Intracoastal and define Fort Lauderdale. The streets of Las Olas connect to the pedestrian-friendly Riverwalk, which continues to the edge of the New River on Avenue of the Arts. ✉ *E. Las Olas Blvd.* ⊕ *www. lasolasboulevard.com.*

FAMILY **Museum of Discovery & Science/AutoNation IMAX Theater.** With more than
Fodor's Choice   200 interactive exhibits, the aim here is to entertain children—*and*
★   adults—with the wonders of science and the wonders of Florida. Exhibits include the Ecodiscovery Center with an Everglades Airboat Adventure ride, resident otters, and an interactive Florida storm center. Florida Ecoscapes has a living coral reef, plus sharks, rays, and eels. Runways to Rockets offers stimulating trips to Mars and the moon while nine different cockpit simulators let you try out your pilot skills. The AutoNation IMAX theater, part of the complex, was renovated in 2014 and shows mainstream and educational films, some in 3-D. Off-property and during summer, the museum hosts sea turtle night walks along Fort Lauderdale beach with high chances of witnessing an enormous female loggerhead turtle laying eggs. These walks require reservations weeks, if not months, in advance. ✉ *401 S.W. 2nd St.* ☎ *954/467–6637 museum, 954/463–4629 IMAX, 954/713–0930 sea turtle walks* ⊕ *www.mods. org* ✉ *Museum $14, $19 with 1 IMAX educational screening* ⊙ *Mon.– Sat. 10–5, Sun. noon–6.*

NSU Museum of Art Fort Lauderdale. Currently in an Edward Larrabee Barnes–designed building that's considered an architectural masterpiece, activists started this museum in a nearby storefront more than 50 years ago. Now part of Nova Southeastern University and under the leadership of Chief Curator Bonnie Clearwater of MOCA (Museum of Contemporary Art Miami) fame, the museum hosts world-class touring exhibits and has an impressive permanent collection of 6,000 works of 20th-century European and American art, including pieces by Picasso, Calder, Dalí, Mapplethorpe, Warhol, and Stella, as well as works by celebrated Ashcan School artist William Glackens. ■TIP→ The lobby-level store and café combo, Museum Café, is a cool, local hangout. ✉ *1 E. Las Olas Blvd.* ☎ *954/525–5500* ⊕ *www.moafl.org* ✉ *$10* ⊙ *Tues., Wed., Fri., and Sat. 11–5, Thurs. 11–8, Sun. noon–5* ⊙ *Closed Mon.*

Riverwalk. Some lovely views prevail on this paved promenade on the New River's north bank. On the first Sunday of every month a free jazz festival attracts visitors; other days, you'll be sharing the Riverwalk with Fort Lauderdale's prolific homeless population. From west to east, the Riverwalk begins at the residential New River Sound, passes through the Arts and Science District, then the historic center of Fort Lauderdale, and wraps around the New River until it meets with Las Olas Boulevard's shopping district. ⊕ *www.goriverwalk.com.*

ALONG THE BEACH

Fodor's Choice   **Bonnet House Museum & Gardens.** A 35-acre oasis in the heart of the beach
★   area, this subtropical estate on the National Register of Historic Places stands as a tribute to the history of Old South Florida. This charming home, built in the 1920s, was the winter residence of the late Frederic and Evelyn Bartlett, artists whose personal touches and small surprises are evident throughout. If you're interested in architecture, artwork, or the natural environment, this place is worth a visit. After admiring the fabulous gardens, be on the lookout for playful monkeys swinging from trees. Interesting factoid: The Bonnet House was the final stop in the 2005 season of CBS's *Amazing Race* hit television show. ✉ *900 N.*

THE GHOSTS OF STRANAHAN HOUSE

These days the historic Stranahan House is as famous for its night-time ghost tours as it is for its daytime history tour. Originally built as a trading post in 1901 and later expanded into a town hall, a post office, a bank, and the personal residence of Frank Stranahan and his wife, Ivy Cromartie, the historic Stranahan House was more than plagued by a number of tragic events and violent deaths, including Frank's suicide. After financial turmoil, Stranahan tied himself to a concrete sewer grate and jumped into New River, leaving his widow to carry on. Sunday night at 7:30, house staff reveal the multiple tragic tales from the Stranahan crypt during the River House Ghost Tour ($25) and help visitors communicate with "the other side." Using special tools and snapping photos to search for orbs, guests are encouraged to field energy from the supposed five ghosts in the house. Given the high success rate of reaching out to the paranormal, the Stranahan House has become a favorite campground for global ghost hunters and television shows. Advance reservations are required.

Birch Rd. ☎ *954/563–5393* ⊕ *www.bonnethouse.org* ✉ *$20 for house tours, $10 for gardens only* ⊗ *Tues.–Sun. 9–4; tours hourly 9:30–3:30.*

NEED A BREAK?

Casablanca Café. For respite from the sun, duck in for a nice glass of chardonnay or a light bite while still enjoying ocean views. ✉ *3049 Alhambra St.* ☎ *954/764–3500* ⊕ *www.casablancacafeonline.com.*

Steak 954. Recover from a long day in the sun with a much-deserved, refreshing cocktail on the covered oceanfront terrace of this Fort Lauderdale favorite. ✉ *West Fort Lauderdale, 401 N. Fort Lauderdale Beach Blvd.* ☎ *954/414–8333* ⊕ *www.steak954.com.*

WILTON MANORS AND OAKLAND PARK

Eucalyptus Gardens. In the heart of Wilton Manors, this small, eucalyptus-laced urban oasis houses fewer than a dozen storefronts and functions as a cool place to simply hang out, sip coffee or wine, people-watch, and gather inspiration for your green thumb. Stores include Chateau D'Vine Wine Tapas and Cheese; The Alchemist Coffee Shop; Seed Of Life Bistro; and the Outdoor Design & Living Center. ✉ *2430 N.E. 13th Ave., Wilton Manors and Oakland Park, Wilton Manors* ☎ *954/394–4322* ⊕ *www.eucalyptus-gardens.com.*

WESTERN SUBURBS AND BEYOND

West of Fort Lauderdale is ever-growing suburbia, with most of Broward's golf courses, shopping, casinos, and chain restaurants. As you head farther west, the terrain takes on more characteristics of the Everglades, and you'll occasionally see alligators sunning on canal banks. Eventually, you reach the Everglades themselves after hitting the airboat outfitters on the park's periphery. Tourists flock to these airboats, but the best way of seeing the Everglades is to visit the Everglades National Park itself.

FAMILY **Ah-Tah-Thi-Ki Museum.** A couple of miles from Billie Swamp Safari is Ah-Tah-Thi-Ki Museum, whose name means "a place to learn, a place to remember." This museum documents the traditions and culture of the Seminole Tribe of Florida through artifacts, exhibits, and reenactments of rituals and ceremonies. The 60-acre site includes a living-history Seminole village, nature trails, and a wheelchair-accessible boardwalk through a cypress swamp. ■TIP➡ Guided tours are available daily, but call for exact times. Self-guided audio tours are available anytime. There are also children's programs. ⊠ *34725 W. Boundary Rd., Western Suburbs and Beyond, Clewiston* ☎ *877/902–1113* ⊕ *www.ahtahthiki. com* ⊑ *$10* ⊗ *Daily 9–5.*

FAMILY **Billie Swamp Safari.** At the Billie Swamp Safari, experience life in the Everglades firsthand albeit in a somewhat touristy setting. Daily tours of wildlife-filled wetlands and hammocks yield sightings of deer, water buffalo, raccoons, wild hogs, hawks, eagles, and alligators. Animal and reptile shows entertain audiences. Sixty-minute ecotours are conducted aboard motorized swamp buggies, and 20-minute airboat rides are available, too. The on-site Swamp Water Café serves gator nuggets, frogs' legs, catfish, and Indian fry bread with honey. ⊠ *Big Cypress Seminole Indian Reservation, 30000 Gator Tail Trail, Western Suburbs and Beyond, Clewiston* ☎ *863/983–6101, 800/949–6101* ⊕ *www. swampsafari.com* ⊑ *Swamp Safari Day Package (ecotour, shows, exhibits, and airboat ride) $50* ⊗ *Daily 9–6.*

FAMILY
Fodor's Choice
★
Butterfly World. As many as 80 butterfly species from South and Central America, the Philippines, Malaysia, Taiwan, and other Asian nations are typically found within the serene 3-acre site inside Tradewinds Park in the northwest reaches of Broward County. A screened aviary called North American Butterflies is reserved for native species. The Tropical Rain Forest Aviary is a 30-foot-high construction, with observation decks, waterfalls, ponds, and tunnels filled with thousands of colorful butterflies. There are lots of birds, too; and kids love going in the lorikeet aviary, where the colorful birds land on every limb! ⊠ *Tradewinds Park, 3600 W. Sample Rd., Western Suburbs and Beyond, Coconut Creek* ☎ *954/977–4400* ⊕ *www.butterflyworld.com* ⊑ *$26.95* ⊗ *Mon.–Sat. 9–5, Sun. 11–5.*

FAMILY **Everglades Holiday Park.** Most episodes of Animal Planet's *Gator Boys* have been filmed here, making this 30-acre "park" an extremely popular tourist attraction. The park provides a decent glimpse of the Everglades and Florida's wild west circa 1950. Take an hour-long airboat tour, look at an 18th-century-style American Indian village, or catch the alligator wrestling. The airboats tend to be supersize and the experience very commercialized. ⊠ *21940 Griffin Rd.* ☎ *954/434–8111* ⊕ *www.evergladesholidaypark.com* ⊑ *Airboat tour and gator show $26* ⊗ *Daily 9–5.*

FAMILY **Sawgrass Recreation Park.** A half-hour airboat ride through the Everglades allows you to view a good variety of plants and wildlife, from ospreys and alligators to turtles, snakes, and fish. Besides the ride, your entrance fee covers admission to an Everglades nature exhibit; a native Seminole village; and exhibits on alligators, other reptiles, and birds of

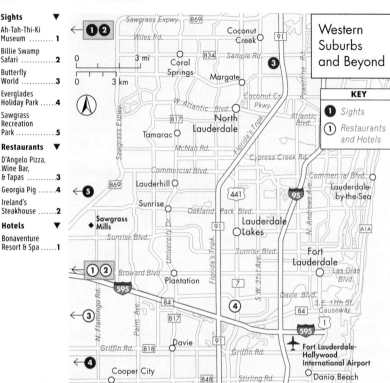

prey. ■TIP→ The Everglades truly come to life at night. Sawgrass Recreation Park offers airboat night tours on Wednesday and Saturday at 8:30 pm. Reservations required. ⊠ *1006 N. U.S. Hwy. 27, Western Suburbs and Beyond, Weston* ☎ *954/389–0202* ⊕ *www.evergladestours. com* ⊠ *$19.50; $40 night tours* ☉ *Airboat rides daily 9–5.*

BEACHES

Fodor'sChoice
★

Fort Lauderdale Beach. The same downy sands that once welcomed America's youth-gone-wild (aka wild spring breakers) now frame a multimile shoreline of beachside sophistication. Alone among Florida's major beachfront communities, Fort Lauderdale's principal beach remains gloriously open and uncluttered. Walkways line both sides of the beach roadway, and traffic has been trimmed to two gently curving northbound lanes. Fort Lauderdale Beach unofficially begins between the B Ocean Resort (formerly the Sheraton Yankee Clipper) and the DoubleTree Bahia Mar Resort, starting with the quiet **South Beach Park**, where picnic tables and palm trees rule. Going north, the younger, barely legal crowd gravitates toward the section of sand at the mouth of Las Olas Boulevard. The beach is actually most crowded between Las Olas and Sunrise boulevards, directly in front of the major hotels and condominiums, namely in front of **Beach Place**, home to the Marriott time-share building and touristy places like Hooters and Fat Tuesday (and a beach-themed CVS Pharmacy). Gay men and women get their fix of vitamin D along **Sebastian Beach**, on Sebastian Street, just north of The Ritz-Carlton, Fort Lauderdale. Families with children enjoy hanging out between Seville Street and Vistamar Street, between the Westin Fort Lauderdale Beach and the Atlantic Resort and Spa. **Amenities:** food and drink; lifeguards; parking (fee). **Best for:** sunrise; swimming; walking. ⊠ *A1A from Holiday Dr. to Sunrise Blvd.*

Harbor Beach. The posh neighborhood of Harbor Beach boasts Fort Lauderdale's most opulent homes along the Intracoastal Waterway. Due east of this community, and just south of Fort Lauderdale's South Beach Park, a stunning swath of beach has adopted the name of its neighborhood—Harbor Beach. This section offers some of the few private beaches in Fort Lauderdale, most of which belong to big hotel names like the Marriott Harbor Beach Resort and the Lago Mar Resort and Club. (Only hotel guests can access these beaches since they are considered private.) Such status permits the hotels to offer full-service amenities and eating and drinking outlets on their bespoke slices of sugarloafed heaven. **Amenities:** water sports. **Best for:** solitude; swimming; walking. ⊠ *South Ocean La. and southern tip of Holiday Dr.*

Hugh Taylor Birch State Park. North of Fort Lauderdale's bustling beachfront, past Sunrise Boulevard, the quieter sands of Fort Lauderdale beach run parallel to Hugh Taylor Birch State Park, a nicely preserved patch of primeval Florida. The 180-acre tropical park sports lush mangrove areas along the Intracoastal Waterway, and lovely nature trails. Visit the Birch House Museum, enjoy a picnic, play volleyball, or paddle a rented canoe. Since parking is limited on Route A1A, park here and take a walkway underpass to the beach (which can be accessed 9–5, daily). In July and August, the park teams up with the Sea Turtle Oversight Protection organization to conduct turtle walks on Tuesday and Wednesday nights, helping to release sea turtle hatchlings into the ocean. **Amenities:** toilets. **Best for:** solitude; walking. ⊠ *3109 E. Sunrise Blvd.* ☎ *954/564–4521, 954/770–2344 sea turtle walks* ⊕ *www.floridastateparks.org/HughTaylorBirch* ⊒ *$6 per vehicle, $2 per pedestrian; $25 turtle walks* ☉ *Daily 8–sunset.*

WHERE TO EAT

DOWNTOWN AND LAS OLAS

$$

MODERN
AMERICAN

Fodor's Choice

★

✕ **American Social.** A charming slice of Americana in the heart of Las Olas Boulevard, American Social flaunts a sexy nerd vibe, packing the house nightly with Fort Lauderdale's hottest twenty- and thirtysomethings. The intimate restaurant and bar are adorned with framed *Life* magazine covers and library books, fostering an ambience that is oh-so-Boston. The drinks here rock, and the modern American cuisine is equally awesome. Choose from 16 beers on tap or some tantalizing mixology (e.g., the Strawberry Honey Smash—vodka, strawberries, simple syrup, honey liqueur, and fresh lemon juice). Feast on the seafood mac-and-cheese skillet, shrimp pesto flatbread, and the full gamut of gourmet burgers with sides of Parmesan and truffle fries or

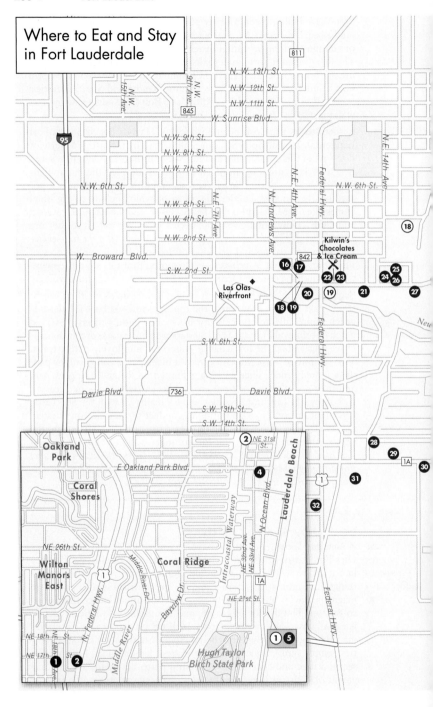

Where to Eat and Stay in Fort Lauderdale

Restaurants ▼

American Social **23**

Anthony's Coal Fired
Pizza **32**

Beauty & the Feast **8**

Big City Tavern **22**

Canyon Southwest Cafe **6**

Casablanca Cafe **10**

Casa D'Angelo
Ristorante **3**

Coco Asian Bistro & Bar ...**31**

15th Street Fisheries &
Dockside Cafe **12**

The Floridian **27**

Fork & Balls **24**

Georgio's 17th Street **29**

Gran Forno Cafe **21**

Grille 401 ....**19**

Lobster Bar Sea Grille **20**

Luigi's Coal Oven Pizza **25**

Market 17 ....**30**

Oasis Cafe **11**

Ocean 2000 .... **5**

Old Fort Lauderdale
Breakfast House **17**

Pelican Landing **13**

Rocco's Tacos &
Tequila Bar **26**

Royal Pig Pub **18**

S3 .... **7**

Sea Level **14**

Southport Raw Bar **28**

Steak 954 .... **9**

Sublime **1**

Thasos Greek Taverna **4**

3030 Ocean **15**

YOLO **16**

Zona Fresca **2**

Hotels ▼

The Atlantic
Resort & Spa **5**

B Ocean Resort **13**

Bahia Mar Fort Lauderdale
Beach Hotel **12**

GALLERYone
by DoubleTree **3**

Hilton Fort Lauderdale
Beach Resort **7**

Hilton Fort Lauderdale
Marina **17**

Hyatt Regency
Pier Sixty-Six
Resort & Spa **16**

Lago Mar
Resort and Club **15**

Marriott Harbor
Beach Resort **14**

Pelican Grand
Beach Resort **1**

The Pillars Hotel **10**

Pineapple Point **18**

Residence Inn by Marriott
Fort Lauderdale
Intracoastal **2**

The Ritz-Carlton
Fort Lauderdale **11**

Riverside Hotel **19**

Sonesta
Fort Lauderdale **4**

The Westin Fort Lauderdale
Beach Resort **9**

W Fort Lauderdale **8**

The Worthington
Guest House **6**

5

sweet-potato fries. ■ **TIP→ Arrive early on weekends as the restaurant quickly reaches capacity.** [$] *Average main: $20* ✉ *721 E. Las Olas Blvd.* ☎ *954/764–7005* 🌐 *www.americansocialbar.com.*

$$$ MODERN AMERICAN FAMILY 🍴 **Big City Tavern.** A Las Olas landmark, Big City Tavern is a consistent spot for good food, good spirits, and good times. The diverse menu commingles Asian entrées like pad thai, Italian options like homemade meatballs and cheese ravioli in a toasted garlic marinara, and American dishes like the grilled skirt-steak Cobb salad. Don't forget to ask about the crispy flatbread of the day, and make sure to save room for the homemade desserts. The pistachio brown-butter bundt cake with honey-roasted spiced peaches and pistachio gelato, the caramelized banana sundae in a mason jar, and the devil's-food-cake ice-cream sandwich are all heaven on Earth. ■ **TIP→ Big City is open late into the night for drinks, desserts, and even offers a special late-night menu.** [$] *Average main: $25* ✉ *609 E. Las Olas Blvd.* ☎ *954/727–0307* 🌐 *www.bigtimerestaurants.com.*

$ DINER FAMILY 🍴 **The Floridian.** This classic diner is plastered with photos of Monroe, Nixon, and local notables past and present in a succession of brightly painted rooms with funky chandeliers. The kitchen dishes up typical grease-pit breakfast favorites (no matter the hour), with oversize omelets that come with biscuits, toast, or English muffins, plus a choice of grits or tomatoes. The restaurant also has good hangover eats, but don't expect anything exceptional (besides the location and the rock-bottom prices). It's open 24 hours—even during hurricanes, as long as the power holds out—and still maintains an old school "cash-only" policy. [$] *Average main: $13* ✉ *1410 E. Las Olas Blvd.* ☎ *954/463–4041* 🌐 *www.thefloridiandiner.com* 💳 *No credit cards.*

$$ MODERN AMERICAN 🍴 **Fork & Balls.** It's all about the balls at this metro-chic, meatball-centric eatery. And the libations, too. True, the restaurant's name and signage had quite a few heads turning when it first opened in late summer 2014, but locals soon developed a new appreciation for meatballs of all flavors, shapes, and sizes. The menu centers around six different types—-beef, chicken, veggie, spicy pork, the house blend, and a daily special—and these round hunks of protein are served atop salad, pasta, as sliders, as subs, or simply alone with one of several savory sauces (from roasted tomato to Parmesan cream). There are appetizer salads and veggie sides to create somewhat of a healthy balance. In addition, the restaurant offers 20 wines on tap and some awesome craft cocktails, creating a bar scene beyond the regular dining scene. [$] *Average main: $18* ✉ *1301 E. Las Olas Blvd.* ☎ *954/771–2257* 🌐 *www.forkandballs.com.*

$ CAFÉ Fodor's Choice ★ 🍴 **Gran Forno Cafe.** The gamble of importing an entire Italian bakery direct from Brescia, Italy, definitely paid off. Most days, the sandwiches, fresh baked breads, and pastries sell out even before lunchtime. All products are made fresh daily (except Monday), beginning at 4 am, by a team of bakers who can be seen hard at work through the café's glass windows. Customers line up at the door early in the morning to get their piping-hot artisanal breads, later returning for the scrumptious paninis and decadent desserts. A second branch, five blocks east on Las Olas at 704 East Las Olas Boulevard, called Gran Forno Pronto, offers full service and a more extensive menu seven days a week and stays open until 11 pm. [$] *Average main: $14* ✉ *1235 E. Las Olas Blvd.* ☎ *954/467–2244* 🌐 *www.granforno.com* ⏲ *Closed Mon.*

$$$ STEAKHOUSE 🍴 **Grille 401.** Enveloped in panes of wine bottles, floor-to-ceiling glass windows, and masculine wood panels, seductive Grille 401 is part avante-garde steak house, part pan-Asian eatery, part chic lounge—all together 100% fabulous. With a diverse menu that includes Osaka-style pressed sushi, classic filet mignon, crispy crab fritters, wood-grilled lobster, as well as a "light and healthy" menu for the lithe and calorie-conscious, there's something special for just about everyone. For the not-so-calorie-conscious, the homemade desserts, including a white-chocolate brioche bread pudding and a sublime carrot cake, are must-tries. By day, Grille 401 caters to a power-lunch crowd escaping the ordinary in the Las Olas financial district; by night, Grille 401 is all about sophisticated dining and excellent cocktails. [$] *Average main: $30* ✉ *401 E. Las Olas Blvd.* ☎ *954/767–0222* 🌐 *www.grille401.com.*

$$$$ SEAFOOD Fodor's Choice ★ 🍴 **Lobster Bar Sea Grille.** A spectacular, high-design restaurant at the crossroads of Las Olas's financial and shopping districts, Lobster Bar Sea Grille brings a much-needed infusion of sophisticated dining to the Fort Lauderdale scene. The intricately tiled archways and high ceilings of the restaurant recall New York's Grand Central station while the nautical-inspired decor is meant to evoke an ambience of fine dining on a yacht. Mission accomplished. The seafood and fish selections here are sublime, specializing in simply prepared, fresh, whole fish and flash-fried lobster tails. There's also a range of custom-aged prime steaks with the full gamut of sides from Parmesan-baked asparagus to cauliflower gratin. [$] *Average main: $49* ✉ *450 E. Las Olas Blvd.* ☎ *954/772–2675* 🌐 *www.buckheadrestaurants.com/lobster-bar-sea-grille* ✍ *Reservations essential.*

$ PIZZA FAMILY Fodor's Choice ★ 🍴 **Luigi's Coal Oven Pizza.** Hands down the best little pizza joint in South Florida, Luigi's Coal Oven Pizza wows with every dish on the one-page menu, including of course the full gamut of pizzas served up by Italian native Chef Luigi DiMeo, but also phenomenal salads with homemade dressings, classics like eggplant parmigiana, and oven-baked, daily fish specials. There's no substitutions or toppings allowed on the best seller—the Margherita Napoletana—a testament to the quality and flavors of the crust, cheese, and sauce of Luigi's century-old Napoli recipe. The petite eatery only has about a dozen tables, contributing to a cozy and familial vibe. [$] *Average main: $15* ✉ *1415 E. Las Olas Blvd.* ☎ *954/522–9888* 🌐 *www.luigiscoalovenpizza.com.*

$$ AMERICAN Fodor's Choice ★ 🍴 **Old Fort Lauderdale Breakfast House.** Undoubtedly the best breakfast/brunch joint in Fort Lauderdale, the O-B House has revolutionized South Florida mornings with its crave-worthy delights, exclusively using fresh and organic ingredients. An adaptive reuse of the old downtown Fort Lauderdale post office, this intimate eatery packs the house daily. Locals can't get enough of the cheesy grits, the mega-pancakes with real Vermont maple syrup, the free-range omelets overflowing with day-caught mahimahi, and the incredibly fresh salads with Florida's finest corn and house-made buttermilk ranch dressing. A handful of outdoor tables accommodate folks with pets in tow as well as those

looking to simply enjoy a sun-kissed Fort Lauderdale morning/early afternoon. Service runs until about 2 pm. $ *Average main: $19* ✉ *333 Himmarshee St.* ☎ *954/530–7520* ⊕ *www.o-bhouse.com* ⌣ *Reservations not accepted* ⊘ *No dinner.*

$$
MODERN
MEXICAN
Fodor's Choice
★

✕ **Rocco's Tacos & Tequila Bar.** The busiest spot on the Las Olas strip, Rocco's is more of a scene than just a restaurant. With pitchers of margaritas a-flowin', the middle-age crowd is boisterous and fun, recounting (and reliving) the days of spring break debauchery from their preprofessional years. In fact, Rocco's drink menu is even larger than its sizable food menu. Guacamole is made table-side, and Mexican dishes such as chimichangas and enchiladas have been reinvented (and made far less spicy) for the American palate. Expect a wild night and lots of fun. All-you-can-eat Tuesday Taco nights are particularly crazy! $ *Average main: $19* ✉ *1313 E. Las Olas Blvd.* ☎ *954/524–9550* ⊕ *www.roccostacos.com.*

$$$
CAJUN

✕ **Royal Pig Pub.** Fort Lauderdale's coolest gastro-pub revels in doling out hefty portions of Cajun comfort cuisine and potent, creative libations. As the name implies, this is indeed the place to be a pig and unapologetically pig out on the beer and butter-soaked New Orleans–style BBQ shrimp; grilled fish-of-the-day atop cheese grits and mussel étouffée; sweet-potato fries with honey-cider drizzle; and grilled free-range turkey burgers loaded with exotic condiments. Plenty of folks come here just for the awesome drinks. In fact, it's one of Fort Lauderdale's busiest watering holes. The pub's arched ceilings are lined with flat-screen TVs, and the bar occupies nearly half the restaurant. Rub elbows with Fort Lauderdale's yuppies and hotties over dragon-fruit cosmos and spiked, cucumber, and mint-berry lemonades. $ *Average main: $22* ✉ *350 E. Las Olas Blvd.* ☎ *954/617–7447* ⊕ *www.royalpigpub.com.*

$$$
AMERICAN

✕ **YOLO.** The now-overused term YOLO stands for "You Only Live Once," but you will definitely want to eat here more than once. For Fort Lauderdale's bourgeoisie, this is the place to see and be seen and to show off your hottest wheels in the driveway. For others, it's an upscale restaurant with affordable prices and a great ambience. The restaurant, renovated in 2014, serves the full gamut of new American favorites like tuna tartar, fire-roasted corn dip, Tuscan kale salad, and crispy whole yellowtail snapper. Don't miss the Szechuan calamari—flash-fried and then covered in garlic-chili sauce, chopped peanuts, and sesame seeds— or the blistered shishito peppers starter. $ *Average main: $26* ✉ *333 E. Las Olas Blvd.* ☎ *954/523–1000* ⊕ *www.yolorestaurant.com.*

ALONG THE BEACH

$$$
MODERN
AMERICAN

✕ **Beauty & the Feast.** Don't let the gimmicky name fool you. There's nothing *Disney* or cheesy about this eclectic, oceanfront restaurant flanking the lobby of the sleek Atlantic Resort & Spa, serving up a diverse array of Southern-inspired, tapas-style small plates and hefty "feast" plates. The name of the game here is sharing, so expect family-style dining and ordering a little of a lot. Chow down on the divine sea scallops in porcini butter, scrape the bowl for the final spoon of the sherry-kissed Florida Crab Bisque, and feast on the short rib with a side of jalapeño-rich, grilled cream of corn. Wash it all down with some house-made sangria, made table-side with fresh fruits. Beauty also offers a fabulous weekend brunch menu, as well as a breakfast and lunch menu weekdays. Diners are entitled to complimentary valet parking, a rarity in South Florida. [$] *Average main: $26* ✉ *The Atlantic Resort & Spa, 601 N. Fort Lauderdale Beach Blvd.* ☎ *954/567–8070* 🌐 *www.society8.com.*

$$ ECLECTIC 🍴 **Casablanca Cafe.** Located along A1A in the heart of Fort Lauderdale's hotel row, Casablanca Cafe offers alfresco and indoor dining with a fabulous ocean view. The historic two-story Moroccan-style villa was built in the 1920s by local architect Francis Abreu. The menu at this piano bar and restaurant showcases a global potpourri of American, Mediterranean, and Asian flavors; however, the recommended "house favorites" focus on eclectic preparations of Florida fish. The food isn't particularly delicious, but the location and ambience are excellent. Prepare for long waits to eat in the outdoor section; it's incredibly popular morning, noon, and night with tourists and locals alike. [$] *Average main: $18* ✉ *3049 Alhambra St.* ☎ *954/764–3500* 🌐 *www.casablancacafeonline.com.*

$$ AMERICAN 🍴 **Oasis Cafe.** On a spit of land near Route A1A, this outdoor-only spot has swing-glide tables covered by green-striped awnings affording plenty of shade. The swinging tables are enticing, but the food you'll get is just okay even for cheap, bar-style food (except the delicious key lime pie). Drinks are great though! Friendly staffers serve up libations and casual fare from burgers and wraps to salads and steak. Be aware that a gratuity is tacked on no matter what your party size. A free valet assists with cramped parking. [$] *Average main: $18* ✉ *600 Seabreeze Blvd.* ☎ *954/463–3130* 🌐 *www.oasiscafefortlauderdalebeach.com.*

$$$$ SEAFOOD 🍴 **Ocean 2000.** This waterfront restaurant and lounge at the Pelican Grand Beach Resort is a favorite of locals in the know, renowned for its stunning Atlantic Ocean views and excellent fish and seafood (prepared with a Latin flair). Expect succulent and savory dishes that include local fish ceviche, tuna "Poke" tacos, and Florida yellowtail snapper *á la plancha* (skillet-grilled). If indulging in the wildly popular Sunday brunch or a casual seaside lunch, make sure to request seating on the oceanfront patio, arguably the best seats in any house in Fort Lauderdale. Come nightfall, the slick dining room comes to life, illuminated by futuristic chandeliers, ubiquitous candles, and the moonlight over the ocean through oversize windows. [$] *Average main: $32* ✉ *Pelican Grand Beach Resort, 2000 N. Ocean Blvd.* ☎ *954/556–7667* 🌐 *www.pelicanbeach.com/ocean2000.*

$$$ SEAFOOD 🍴 **S3.** S3 stands for the fabulous trio of sun, surf, and sand, paying homage to its prime beachfront location. Located on the ground floor of the Hilton Fort Lauderdale Beach Resort, S3 flaunts a fun, fresh, sophisticated, beachside swagger. On any given night, you'll have an even mix of locals and tourists loving life, taking Twitter pics of their S3 cocktail sampler—a tray of adorable miniature versions of the signature libations. The menu features a variety of Japanese-inspired raw dishes, sushi rolls, and small plates, all meant for sharing and delivered as soon as they're ready. A few must-tries: the spicy Kamikaze roll, the crunchy mac and cheese with smoked Gouda and crispy prosciutto, and the shrimp toast from the wood-fired oven. [$] *Average main: $29*

Sand can sometimes be forgiving if you fall, and bicyclists also appreciate the ocean views.

⊠ *Hilton Fort Lauderdale Beach Resort, 505 N. Fort Lauderdale Beach Blvd.* ⊕ *www.s3restaurant.com.*

$$$
SEAFOOD
FAMILY
Fodor'sChoice
★

✕ **Sea Level.** Finding this seafood-centric restaurant takes a bit a work, but there are handsome rewards for those taking the road less traveled. Nestling prime beachfront on the southern perimeter of Marriott's Harbor Beach Resort & Spa, the indoor-outdoor Sea Level wows with its sublime farm-to-table and ocean-to-table menu that includes an ever-changing chalkboard of daily specials. Chef Jason Connelly is the brains behind this waterfront locale, where ingredients are sourced regionally from the docks of Miami to the farms of Orlando, and plates arrive artistically presented, leaving minutes later with nary a crumb in sight. Experience seafoodie fantasia savoring the day boat scallops with edamame risotto, the seafood paella, or Connelly's crab cakes (he worked in Baltimore for years and does his former hometown proud). Even the libations uphold Connelly's house-made-everything mantra, with vodkas infused in house and mixers like the sours made on the premises. Oh, and did we mention the killer views of the ocean? $ *Average main: $27* ⊠ *Marriott's Harbor Beach Resort & Spa, 3030 Holiday Dr.* ☎ *954/765–3041* ⊕ *www.sealevelharborbeach.com.*

$$$$
STEAKHOUSE

✕ **Steak 954.** It's not just the steaks that impress at Stephen Starr's superstar restaurant. The lobster and crab-coconut ceviche and the red snapper *tiradito* are divine; the butter-poached Maine lobster is perfection; the raw bar showcases only the best and freshest seafood on the market; and the ice cream sandwiches are pure foodie fantasia. Located on the first floor of the swanky W Fort Lauderdale, Steak 954 offers spectacular views of the ocean for those choosing outdoor seating; inside, there's a sexy, sophisticated ambience for those choosing to dine in the main dining room, with bright tropical colors balanced with dark woods and an enormous jellyfish tank spanning the width of the restaurant. Sunday brunch is very popular, so arrive early for the best views. [$] *Average main: $55* ✉ *W Fort Lauderdale, 401 N. Fort Lauderdale Beach Blvd.* ☎ *954/414–8333* 🌐 *www.steak954.com.*

$$$$ SEAFOOD Fodor's Choice ★ 🍴 **3030 Ocean.** 3030 Ocean has been the talk of the town for decades. Previously under the direction of celebrity Chef Dean Max, Fort Lauderdale's most legendary fish-and-seafood restaurant is now helmed by two other top chefs—local celebrity Chef Paula DaSilva and season 13 *Hell's Kitchen* winner Chef La Tasha McCutchen. Constantly evolving with new flavors and fusions, 3030 Ocean gives plenty of great reasons to return time and time again. The ahi tuna ceviche—bathed in cilantro, jalapeño, aji amarillo, red onion, lime, olive oil—is so fresh, it melts in your mouth. The pan-seared roasted local corvina and sautéed Maine scallops over white corn grits are nothing short of experiential. The martini menu is also heaven sent, advancing mixology with its ever-changing list of martinis. [$] *Average main: $39* ✉ *Marriott's Harbor Beach Resort & Spa, 3030 Holiday Dr.* ☎ *954/765–3030* 🌐 *www.3030ocean.com* ✍ *Reservations essential.*

5

INTRACOASTAL AND INLAND

$$ PIZZA FAMILY 🍴 **Anthony's Coal Fired Pizza.** Before this legendary "pizza well done" spread to more than 50 outposts across six states, Anthony's original coal-fired oven was heating up Fort Lauderdale in a big way. The petite first location of the wildly popular pizza joint still packs the house nightly, serving a simple menu of coal-fired pizza, chicken wings, and salad. Vegetarians and nonvegetarians alike love the cheeseless Eggplant Marino pizza and the Roasted Cauliflower pizza, with olive oil and whole garlic cloves, bread crumbs, and Romano and mozzarella cheeses. [$] *Average main: $17* ✉ *2203 S. Federal Hwy.* ☎ *954/462–5555* 🌐 *www.acfp.com.*

$$$$ SOUTHWESTERN 🍴 **Canyon Southwest Cafe.** Southwestern fusion fare helps you escape the ordinary at this small, magical enclave, managed hands-on by executive Chef Chris Wilber. Order, for example, bison medallions with scotch bonnets, a tequila-jalapeño smoked-salmon tostada, coriander-crusted tuna, or blue-corn fried oysters. Chipotle, wasabi, mango, and red chilies accent fresh seafood and wild game. Cocktail lovers should start off with a signature prickly pear margarita or choose from a well-rounded wine list or beer selection. **■ TIP→ On every night but Saturday, eat at the bar and ladies get the special price of $6 margaritas while both sexes enjoy half off small plates.** [$] *Average main: $31* ✉ *1818 E. Sunrise Blvd.* ☎ *954/765–1950* 🌐 *www.canyonfl.com* ✍ *Reservations not accepted* ⊗ *No lunch.*

$$$$ ITALIAN Fodor's Choice ★ 🍴 **Casa D'Angelo Ristorante.** Casa D'Angelo is packed year-round and for excellent reason. Owner-chef Angelo Elia has created a gem of a Tuscan-style white-tablecloth restaurant in Fort Lauderdale, and the city can't get enough. All meals begin with the hearty plates of bruschetta, green olives, and Parmesan cheese. Next, choose from the myriad daily appetizer specials, but don't miss the antipasto "Angelo," an assortment of seasonal grilled vegetables, and the mouthwatering burrata. For the main course, Casa D'Angelo's oak oven turns out plenty of sublime

seafood and beef dishes, but it's the ever-changing "fish of the day" that impresses most, simply yet exquisitely prepared. The pastas are also prepared to perfection. ⓢ *Average main: $38* ✉ *1201 N. Federal Hwy., No. 5A* ☎ *954/564–1234* ⊕ *www.casa-d-angelo.com* ⊗ *No lunch.*

$$$
ASIAN
Fodor's Choice
★

✕ **Coco Asian Bistro & Bar.** The best of Thai and Japanese cuisine unite under one roof at Coco Asian Bistro & Bar, a locally famous gastronomic gem in a jazzy Fort Lauderdale strip mall. Chef Mike Ponluang's expansive menu spans authentic Asian to pan-Asian flavors more suited to the American palate to downright avant-garde interpretations of Asian cuisine. You'll never go wrong with the traditional pad thai or the variety of classic curries; but there are also dishes like the Emerald Scallops, a decadent marriage of diver scallops, asparagus, and portobello mushrooms in a green curry, as well as the off-the-menu lobster pad thai served in the shell. The oversize sushi rolls are beautifully crafted, often mingling at least five flavors, fostering utter sushitopia. Try, for example, Mike's Roll, a taste explosion of tuna, spinach, avocado, tempura flakes, and kampyo rolled in sweet, black, sticky rice and served with sweet chili sauce for dipping. The artisan cocktails are also excellent; don't leave without having a lycheetini or two! ⓢ *Average main: $27* ✉ *1841 Cordova Rd.* ☎ *954/525–3541* ⊕ *www.cocoasianbistro. com* ⊗ *No lunch weekends.*

$$$$
SEAFOOD
FAMILY

✕ **15th Street Fisheries & Dockside Cafe.** A prime Intracoastal Waterway view is a big part of the allure at this two-story seafood landmark; the fresh seafood is the other. The old 15th carries on solidly with spicy conch chowder, grilled fish dishes, and homemade breads. There are two separate menus: a pricey dinner menu for more formal upstairs dining and a casual dockside menu served day and night. Kids love feeding the families of giant tarpon circling around the dock. ⓢ *Average main: $37* ✉ *1900 S.E. 15th St.* ☎ *954/763–2777* ⊕ *www.15streetfisheries.com.*

$$$$
MODERN
AMERICAN
Fodor's Choice
★

✕ **Market 17.** Using only the best ingredients from regional farmers and local fishermen, Market 17 leads the organic farm-to-table revolution in South Florida. The menu at this chic restaurant shifts daily, lending to an ever-changing kaleidoscope of mouthwatering creations. The daily "Market Ceviche" and fresh-catch preparations are always popular. The desserts, too, are outstanding and include homemade ice creams. For something awesome and different with a small group, Market 17 offers "dining in the dark," where dinner is served in a blacked-out room, forcing you to rely on your senses of touch, taste, and smell to figure out what you're eating and drinking. ⓢ *Average main: $31* ✉ *1850 S.E. 17th St., Suite 109* ☎ *954/835–5507* ⊕ *www.market17.net* ⌱ *Reservations essential* ⊗ *No lunch.*

$
SEAFOOD
Fodor's Choice
★

✕ **Pelican Landing.** In this age of globalization and instant information, it's nearly impossible to remain the city's "best-kept secret," but somehow Pelican Landing has managed to do exactly that. Located on a second-story terrace in the Pier Sixty-Six Marina and renovated in 2014, the serene outdoor restaurant serves mouthwatering beach-shack-style eats surrounded by picturesque panoramas of boats, sea, and sunset. The fish is caught daily, served simply blackened or grilled, and presented with sides. There's also more modern ocean eats like fish tacos and ceviches; and the conch fritters are outstanding. Match these mouthwatering fruits of the sea with the innovative cocktail menu, and you'll quickly reach a state of "paradise found!" $ *Average main: $15* ✉ *Hyatt Regency Pier Sixty Six, 2301 S.E. 17th St. Causeway, at end of main dock* ☎ *954/525–6666* ⊕ *www.pier66.hyatt.com.*

$$
SEAFOOD ✕ **Southport Raw Bar.** You can't go wrong at this unpretentious spot where the motto, on bumper stickers for miles around, proclaims, "Eat fish, live longer, eat oysters, love longer, eat clams, last longer." Raw or steamed clams, raw oysters, and peel-and-eat shrimp are market priced. Sides range from Bimini bread to key lime pie, with conch fritters, beer-battered onion rings, and corn on the cob in between. Order wine by the bottle or glass, and beer by the pitcher, bottle, or can. Avoid the dimly-lit restaurant proper, and eat outside overlooking the Intracoastal. $ *Average main: $16* ✉ *1536 Cordova Rd.* ☎ *954/525–2526* ⊕ *www.southportrawbar.com.*

$$
VEGETARIAN ✕ **Sublime.** Paul McCartney, Alec Baldwin, Bob Barker, Alicia Silverstone, and their celebrity pals are not the only vegetarians that love this vegan powerhouse. The innovative pizzas, pastas, and meat-substitute products surprisingly can satisfy even carnivore cravings. All dishes are organic and void of any animal by-products, showing the world how vegan eating does not compromise flavor or taste. Standout items include: mushroom ravioli, Thai red curry, Florentine flatbread, and the chocolate nirvana. $ *Average main: $18* ✉ *1431 N. Federal Hwy.* ☎ *954/539–9000* ⊕ *www.sublimerestaurant.com* ⊗ *Closed Mon.*

$$$
GREEK ✕ **Thasos Greek Taverna.** A small, heavenly slice of the Greek Isles has floated ashore between Fort Lauderdale's beach and the Intracoastal Waterway. Upon entering the Taverna, you'll immediately think Greek chic, with the whitewashed walls, blue trim, streaming images of Greece on the walls, and the easy-on-the-eyes crowd. Plan on eating family style. Start with a variety of *pikilia* (Greek spreads), which include spicy whipped feta, divine *tzatziki* (a garlicky yogurt-cucumber dip), and melt-in-your-mouth *taramosalata* (whitefish caviar). Then move onto the *mezedes* (hot shared plates) that include shrimp *Saganaki* (fried with tomatoes, olives, and feta), stuffed grape leaves, and the oh-so-tender fire-grilled octopus. Finally, expand your waistline with a main course, including specialties like the traditional *moussaka* (souffle of ground lamb and eggplant). $ *Average main: $29* ✉ *3330 E. Oakland Park Blvd., between N. Ocean Blvd. and N.E. 33rd Ave.* ☎ *954/200–6006* ⊕ *www.thasostaverna.com* ⌂ *Reservations essential.*

$
MEXICAN
Fodor's Choice
★ ✕ **Zona Fresca.** A local favorite on the cheap, Zona Fresca serves healthful Mexican fast food with the best chips, salsas, burritos, and quesadillas in town. Everything is made fresh on the premises, including the authentic salsas, presented in a grand salsa bar. Zona is busy seven days a week for both lunch and dinner and offers both indoor and outdoor seating. It's likely to be your best (and cheapest) lunch in Fort Lauderdale. $ *Average main: $10* ✉ *1635 N. Federal Hwy.* ☎ *954/566–1777* ⊕ *www.zonafresca.com.*

WESTERN SUBURBS AND BEYOND

$$
PIZZA
FAMILY ✕ **D'Angelo: Pizza, Wine Bar, and Tapas.** Florida's famous restaurateur and Tuscan chef Angelo Elia has opened an outpost of his casual pizza, tapas, and wine bar in the western suburbs of Fort Lauderdale to great

fanfare. D'Angelo serves affordable small plates, salads, ceviches, and pizzas (based with either red or white sauce) and has quickly become a neighborhood favorite. Both kids and adults love the rotating selections of homemade gelatos. Don't miss the zucchini flowers stuffed with mozzarella, the spinach gnocchi with four cheeses and pine nuts, and the sorrentina pizza with eggplant, mozzarella, fresh tomato, and basil oil. This is superb Italian comfort food! [$] *Average main: $20* ✉ *Country Isle Shopping Center, 1370 Weston Rd., Weston* ☎ *954/306–0037* 🌐 *www.dangelopizza.com.*

$ SOUTHERN FAMILY 🍴 **Georgia Pig.** When heading out to the area's western reaches, this postage-stamp-size outpost can add down-home zing to your day—if you can find it, that is (signage has been known to disappear), and if you don't mind the somewhat gritty atmosphere. Breakfast, which includes sausage gravy and biscuits, is served 6–11 am, but the big attraction is barbecue beef, pork, or chicken, on platters or in sandwiches for lunch through dinner until about 8 pm. Alternatives include a spicy Brunswick stew and fried jumbo shrimp. There's apple, peach, cherry, and pecan pie, and a small-fry menu. Order takeout or eat at the counter, at wooden tables, or at a half dozen or so booths. [$] *Average main: $12* ✉ *1285 S. State Rd. 7, U.S. 441, just south of Davie Blvd.* ☎ *954/587–4420* 💳 *No credit cards* 🕓 *Closed Sun. No dinner Sat.*

$$$$ STEAKHOUSE 🍴 **Ireland's Steakhouse.** Don't let the name fool you. Ireland's Steakhouse is not particularly Irish nor is it just a steak house. In fact, this restaurant is most popular for its sustainable-seafood menu. Promoting a holistic philosophy of green eating, the restaurant meticulously chooses its ingredients and the purveyors that supply them, while staying true to the international "Seafood Watch" guide. The restaurant is a warm and woodsy enclave in the back corner of the Bonaventure Resort & Spa. In keeping with trends of other steak houses, hearty mains (like the mustard-glazed king salmon and the 22-ounce bone-in rib eye) are paired with loads of decadent sides made for sharing (like lobster mac and cheese and lobster fries). [$] *Average main: $45* ✉ *Bonaventure Resort & Spa, 250 Racquet Club Rd., Weston* ☎ *800/327–8090* 🌐 *www.bonaventureresortandspa.com* ✍ *Reservations essential* 🕓 *Closed Sun. and Mon. No lunch.*

WILTON MANORS AND OAKLAND PARK

$$ AMERICAN 🍴 **Lips.** The 1990s trend of drag dining is still alive and well in Fort Lauderdale. The hit restaurant and show bar Lips is a favorite for large groups celebrating birthdays, bachelorette parties, and other milestones. Expect some showstopping entertainment while you eat, peppered with quite a few embarrassing moments as the queens love to drag guests up on stage. ■ **TIP→ Locals tend to visit Lips on Sunday for Sunday Gospel Brunch, the only "church" service with unlimited sparkling wine.** Besides the meal, there's a show charge that ranges from $5 to $10. [$] *Average main: $20* ✉ *1421 E. Oakland Park Blvd., Oakland Park* ☎ *954/567–0987* 🌐 *www.floridalips.com* 🕓 *Closed Mon.*

$$$$ SOUTH PACIFIC FAMILY 🍴 **Mai-Kai.** Touristy to some yet exciting to others, the South Pacific meets South Florida at this torch-lit landmark. It's undeniably gimmicky, but droves arrive for the popular Polynesian dance review and fire shows, Peking duck, and umbrella-garnished exotic tropical drinks. The Pacific

allure is maintained with freshly planted palms, thatch, and bamboo, and a wood-planked bridge rebuilt to make arriving cars sound like rumbling thunder. An expanded wine list embraces boutique vintages from around the world. Valet parking is available. [$] *Average main: $39* ✉ *3599 N. Federal Hwy.* ☎ *954/563–3272* 🌐 *www.maikai.com.*

$$$$ SEAFOOD 🍴 **Sunfish Grill.** The former Pompano Beach institution migrated south in 2009 and hasn't looked back since. Quickly establishing itself in the Oakland Park area (albeit in a quiet strip mall), Sunfish Grill doles out beautifully presented contemporary American cuisine, namely well-executed, outside-the-box seafood and fish dishes. The spaghetti Bolognese is made with ground tuna instead of beef; the Sunfish Caesar with Maytag Blue Cheese instead of Parmesan; the "not the usual" key lime pie with coconut sorbet instead of whipped cream. The results of this ingenuity are fantastic. [$] *Average main: $36* ✉ *2775 E. Oakland Park Blvd.* ☎ *954/561–2004* 🌐 *www.sunfishgrill.com* 🕒 *Closed Sun. and Mon. No lunch.*

5

WHERE TO STAY

DOWNTOWN AND LAS OLAS

$$ B&B/INN 🏨 **Pineapple Point.** Tucked a few blocks behind Las Olas Boulevard in the residential neighborhood of Victoria Park, clothing-optional Pineapple Point is a magnificent maze of posh tropical cottages and dense foliage catering to the gay community and is nationally renowned for its stellar service. **Pros:** superior service; tropical setting. **Cons:** difficult to find at first; need a vehicle for beach jaunts. [$] *Rooms from: $298* ✉ *315 N.E. 16th Terr.* ☎ *954/527–0094, 888/844–7295* 🌐 *www.pineapplepoint.com* 🛏 *25 rooms* 🍽 *Breakfast.*

$$ HOTEL 🏨 **Riverside Hotel.** On Las Olas Boulevard, just steps from boutiques, restaurants, and art galleries, Fort Lauderdale's oldest hotel (circa 1936) evokes a time bygone with historical photos gracing hallways, and guest rooms outfitted with antique oak furnishings, ornamental palm trees, and a bold tropical color palate with a Tommy Bahamas throwback flair. **Pros:** historic appeal; in the thick of Las Olas action; nice views. **Cons:** questionable room decor; dated lobby; small bathrooms. [$] *Rooms from: $229* ✉ *620 E. Las Olas Blvd.* ☎ *954/467–0671, 800/325–3280* 🌐 *www.riversidehotel.com* 🛏 *208 rooms, 6 suites* 🍽 *No meals.*

ALONG THE BEACH

$$$ HOTEL 🏨 **The Atlantic Resort & Spa.** The hotel that catalyzed Fort Lauderdale's luxe revolution circa 2000 continues to be a beautiful and well-run gem, and the skyscraping, oceanfront beauty seems well positioned to stay at the top of her contemporary game for years to come. **Pros:** sophisticated lodging option; en suite kitchenettes; hotel received full renovation in 2011. **Cons:** no complimentary water bottles in room; expensive parking. [$] *Rooms from: $350* ✉ *601 N. Fort Lauderdale Beach Blvd.* ☎ *954/567–8020* 🌐 *www.atlantichotelfl.com* 🛏 *61 rooms, 58 suites, 4 penthouses* 🍽 *No meals.*

$ HOTEL 🏨 **Bahia Mar Fort Lauderdale Beach Hotel, A DoubleTree by Hilton.** This nicely situated Fort Lauderdale beachfront classic received a long-overdue nip/tuck in 2011–12 that included cheery, refreshed guest rooms and rebranding as a DoubleTree hotel. **Pros:** crosswalk from hotel to beach; on-site yacht center; easy to navigate Fort Laud with on-site water taxi stop. **Cons:** dated exteriors; small bathrooms; popcorn ceilings. *[$] Rooms from: $189 ✉ 801 Seabreeze Blvd. ☎ 954/764–2233 🌐 www.bahiamarhotel.com 🛏 296 rooms 🍴 No meals.*

$$ HOTEL **B Ocean Resort.** Formerly the Sheraton Yankee Clipper Hotel, this Fort Lauderdale riverboat-shape beachfront landmark has been rechristened B Ocean Resort, the young "B" brand's sophomore endeavor on Fort Lauderdale Beach (its first has now been rebranded a Sonesta—talk about hotel mambo!). **Pros:** Friday-night retro mermaid show in swimming pool; proximity to beach; excellent gym. **Cons:** small rooms; low ceilings in lobby; faded exteriors. *[$] Rooms from: $239 ✉ 1140 Seabreeze Blvd. ☎ 954/564–1000 🌐 www.boceanfortlauderdale.com 🛏 486 rooms 🍴 No meals.*

$$$ RESORT FAMILY Fodor's Choice ★ **Hilton Fort Lauderdale Beach Resort.** This 26-story oceanfront sparkler features 374 tastefully appointed guest rooms and a fabulous sixth-floor pool deck, colorfully and whimsically decorated. **Pros:** excellent gym; most rooms have balconies; great location. **Cons:** charge for Wi-Fi; no outdoor bar; expensive valet parking. *[$] Rooms from: $329 ✉ 505 N. Fort Lauderdale Beach Blvd. ☎ 954/760–7177 🌐 www.fortlauderdalebeachresort.hilton.com 🛏 374 rooms 🍴 No meals.*

$$$ RESORT FAMILY **Lago Mar Resort and Club.** The sprawling, kid-friendly Lago Mar, owned by the Banks family since the early 1950s, retains its sparkle and a refreshed old Florida feel thanks to frequent renovations. **Pros:** secluded setting; plenty of activities; on the very private Harbor beach. **Cons:** not easy to find; far from restaurants and beach action. *[$] Rooms from: $325 ✉ 1700 S. Ocean La. ☎ 855/209–5677 🌐 www.lagomar.com 🛏 52 rooms, 160 suites 🍴 No meals.*

$$$ RESORT FAMILY Fodor's Choice ★ **Marriott Harbor Beach Resort.** Bill Marriott's personal choice for his annual four-week family vacation, the Marriott Harbor Beach Resort sits on a quarter-mile swath of private beach and bursts with the luxe beachfront personality of an upscale Caribbean resort. **Pros:** excellent gym; all rooms have balconies; great eating outlets; no resort fees. **Cons:** Wi-Fi isn't free; expensive parking; interiors are new but feel a little cookie-cutter. *[$] Rooms from: $379 ✉ 3030 Holiday Dr. ☎ 954/525–4000 🌐 www.marriottharborbeach.com 🛏 650 rooms, 31 suites 🍴 No meals.*

$$$ RESORT FAMILY **Pelican Grand Beach Resort.** Smack on Fort Lauderdale beach, this yellow spired, Key West–style, Noble House property fuses a heritage of Old Florida seaside charm with understated luxury; there's renovated rooms upstairs, an amazing beachfront, an old-fashioned emporium, and Fort Lauderdale's only lazy river. **Pros:** free popcorn in the Postcard Lounge; directly on the beach; Ocean 2000 restaurant. **Cons:** high tide can swallow most of beach area; small fitness center. *[$] Rooms from: $323 ✉ 2000 N. Atlantic Blvd. ☎ 954/568–9431, 800/525–6232 🌐 www.pelicanbeach.com 🛏 156 rooms 🍴 No meals.*

$$$ B&B/INN Fodor's Choice ★ **The Pillars Hotel.** Once a "small secret" kept by locals in the know, this elegant boutique gem, sandwiched between Fort Lauderdale beach and the Intracoastal Waterway, rarely falls below capacity since it invariably lands on reader's choice lists year after year. **Pros:** attentive staff; lovely

decor; idyllic pool area. **Cons:** small rooms; not for families with young kids given proximity to dock and water with no lifeguard on duty. [$] *Rooms from: $325* ✉ *111 N. Birch Rd.* ☎ *954/467–9639* 🌐 *www.pillarshotel.com* 🛏 *13 rooms, 5 suites* 🍴 *No meals.*

$$$$ HOTEL Fodor's Choice ★ 🏨 **The Ritz-Carlton, Fort Lauderdale.** Inspired by the design of an opulent luxury liner, 24 dramatically tiered, glass-walled stories rise from the sea, forming a sumptuous Ritz-Carlton hotel with guest rooms that reinvent a golden era of luxury travel, a lavish tropical sundeck and infinity-edge pool peering over the ocean, and a Club Lounge that spans an entire floor. **Pros:** prime beach location; modern seaside elegance deviates dramatically from traditional Ritz-Carlton decor; views from Club Lounge. **Cons:** no complimentary Wi-Fi; expensive valet parking. [$] *Rooms from: $649* ✉ *1 N. Fort Lauderdale Beach Blvd.* ☎ *954/465–2300* 🌐 *www.ritzcarlton.com/FortLauderdale* 🛏 *138 rooms, 54 suites* 🍴 *No meals.*

$$ HOTEL 🏨 **Sonesta Fort Lauderdale.** The Sonesta Fort Lauderdale merges trendiness with affordability in a 13-story U-shape tower overlooking the ocean, making it a smart choice for chic, clean, linear style guest rooms with pops of tropical colors and all the amenities you'd want in a youthful, beachfront hotel (though the exterior still harbors its original 1970s Holiday Inn architecture). **Pros:** all rooms have ocean views; trendy but affordable; nighttime fire pits. **Cons:** small pool area; lackluster exterior; small driveway. [$] *Rooms from: $279* ✉ *999 N. Fort Lauderdale Beach Blvd.* ☎ *954/315–1460* 🌐 *www.sonesta.com/FortLauderdale* 🛏 *240 rooms* 🍴 *No meals.*

$$$ RESORT FAMILY 🏨 **The Westin Fort Lauderdale Beach Resort.** Smack dab in the center of Fort Lauderdale Beach and connected directly to the beach through a private overpass, the hotel once known as the Sheraton Yankee Trader has been transformed into a modern convention-centric Westin. **Pros:** direct beach access; heavenly beds and spa. **Cons:** lengthy walks to get to some rooms; fee for Wi-Fi; lot of conventioneers. [$] *Rooms from: $319* ✉ *321 N. Fort Lauderdale Beach Blvd.* ☎ *954/467–1111* 🌐 *www.westin.com/fortlauderdalebeach* 🛏 *433 rooms* 🍴 *No meals.*

$$$$ HOTEL 🏨 **W Fort Lauderdale.** Fort Lauderdale's trendiest hotel—equipped with a rooftop see-through swimming pool, a wide range of contemporary rooms and suites, and an easy-on-the-eyes youthful crowd—boasts a vibe highly reminiscent of South Beach. **Pros:** trendy and flashy; amazing pool; great spa. **Cons:** party atmosphere not for everyone; 2008 furniture looking a bit worn. [$] *Rooms from: $439* ✉ *435 N. Fort Lauderdale Beach Blvd.* ☎ *954/462–1633* 🌐 *www.wfortlauderdalehotel.com* 🛏 *346 rooms, 171 condominiums* 🍴 *No meals.*

$ B&B/INN 🏨 **Worthington Guest House.** Located five minutes from gay Sebastian Beach, this hotel is one of Fort Lauderdale Beach's 27 clothing-optional guesthouses for gay men. **Pros:** fresh-squeezed orange juice in the morning; nice pool area; ability to also hang out at sister properties Alcazar and Villa Venice. **Cons:** not on the beach; windows open towards fence or other buildings. [$] *Rooms from: $175* ✉ *543 N. Birch Rd.* ☎ *954/563–6819* 🌐 *www.theworthington.com* 🛏 *14 rooms* 🍴 *Breakfast.*

INTRACOASTAL AND INLAND

$$ ⊞ **GALLERYone—A DoubleTree Suites by Hilton Hotel.** A condo hotel favored
HOTEL by vacationers preferring longer stays, and named after its lobby art
gallery, the residential-style GALLERYone rises over the Intracoastal,
within short walking distance of both Fort Lauderdale Beach and the
city's popular Galleria Mall. **Pros:** walking distance to both beach
and supermarket; easy water taxi access; good for longer stays. **Cons:**
pool area needs refurbishment; kitchens don't have stoves; no bath-
tubs. $ *Rooms from: $239* ⊠ *2670 E. Sunrise Blvd.* ☎ *954/565–3800*
⊕ *www.doubletree.com* ⇴ *231 rooms* ﹖⃝*No meals.*

$ ⊞ **Hilton Fort Lauderdale Marina.** Since its $72-million renovation in
RESORT 2011, the mammoth, 589-room, 20-boat-slip Hilton Fort Lauderdale
FAMILY Marina has maintained its modern edge without compromising its
Fodor'sChoice charming, old school Key West style. **Pros:** sexy fire pit; outdoor bar
★ popular with locals; easy water taxi access. **Cons:** no bathtubs in tower
rooms; small fitness center. $ *Rooms from: $169* ⊠ *1881 S.E. 17th St.*
☎ *954/463–4000* ⊕ *www.fortlauderdalemarinahotel.com* ⇴ *589 rooms*
﹖⃝*No meals.*

$$ ⊞ **Hyatt Regency Pier Sixty-Six Resort & Spa.** Don't let the 1970s exterior
RESORT of the iconic 17-story tower fool you; this lovely 22-acre resort teems
with contemporary interior-design sophistication and remains one of
Florida's few hotels where a rental car isn't necessary. **Pros:** great views;
plenty of activities; free shuttle to beach; easy water taxi access. **Cons:**
tower rooms are far less stylish than Lanai rooms; totally retro rotating rooftop is used exclusively for private events. $ *Rooms from: $219*
⊠ *2301 S.E. 17th St. Causeway* ☎ *954/525–6666* ⊕ *www.pier66.hyatt.*
com ⇴ *384 rooms* ﹖⃝*No meals.*

$$ ⊞ **Residence Inn By Marriott Fort Lauderdale Intracoastal.** Formerly the Il
HOTEL Lugano hotel, this all-suites condo hotel on Fort Lauderdale's northern
FAMILY Intracoastal Waterway offers all the comforts of home (washer, dryer,
kitchenette, fridge, sleeper sofa, huge terraces) with all the glamour of
a hypermodern trendsetting hotel. **Pros:** 800-square-foot rooms; easy
water taxi access; good for longer stays. **Cons:** limited sunlight in pool
area; need wheels to reach main beach and downtown area. $ *Rooms*
from: $289 ⊠ *3333 N.E. 32nd Ave.* ☎ *954/564–4400* ⊕ *www.marriott.*
com/hotels/travel/fllne-residence-inn-fort-lauderdale-intracoastal ⇴ *28*
suites ﹖⃝*No meals.*

WESTERN SUBURBS AND BEYOND

$$ ⊞ **Bonaventure Resort & Spa.** This massive suburban enclave—formerly
RESORT a Hyatt Regency–flagged resort—targets conventioneers and business
FAMILY executives as well as international vacationers who value golf, the Everglades, and shopping over beach proximity; factor in the allure of the
huge and soothing ALaya Spa and the "Choose Your Journey" package
that includes a spa treatment with the room and you'll see why. **Pros:**
lush landscaping; pampering spa; great in-house restaurant, Ireland's
Steakhouse. **Cons:** difficult to find; in the suburbs; poor views from
some rooms; rental car necessary. $ *Rooms from: $259* ⊠ *250 Racquet*
Club Rd., Westin ☎ *954/389–3300* ⊕ *www.bonaventureresortandspa.*
com ⇴ *501 rooms* ﹖⃝*No meals.*

Lago Mar Resort and Club in Fort Lauderdale has its own private beach on the Atlantic Ocean.

NIGHTLIFE AND PERFORMING ARTS

For the most complete weekly listing of events, check "Showtime!," the *South Florida Sun-Sentinel*'s tabloid-size entertainment section and events calendar published on Friday. "Weekend," in the Friday Broward edition of the *Herald*, also lists area happenings. The weekly *City Link* and *New Times Broward* are free alternative newspapers, detailing plenty of entertainment and nightlife options. For the latest happenings in GLBT nightlife, visit **Mark's List** (⊕ *www.jumponmarkslist.com*), the online authority of all things GLBT in South Florida or pick up one of the weekly gay rags, *GUY Magazine* or *Hot Spots*.

NIGHTLIFE

DOWNTOWN AND LAS OLAS

The majority of Fort Lauderdale nightlife takes place near downtown, beginning on Himmarshee Street (2nd Street) and continuing on to the Riverfront, and then to Las Olas Boulevard. The downtown Riverfront tends to draw a younger demographic somewhere between underage teens and late twenties. On Himmarshee Street, a dozen rowdy bars and clubs, ranging from the seedy to the sophisticated, entice a wide range of partygoers. Toward East Las Olas Boulevard, near the financial towers and boutique shops, bars cater to the yuppie crowd.

Fodor's Choice ★ **Laser Wolf.** Far from the main drag of Fort Lauderdale's nightlife district, Laser Wolf celebrates the urban grit that is downtown's other side of the tracks as a hipster and hippie infused, indoor-outdoor craft beer bar randomly located in an adaptive reuse building, bordering the railroad tracks. It's actually one of—if not *the*—most popular watering holes for locals, consistently delivering great drinks, great music, and a great vibe. ■TIP→ Drive or cab it here. It's not recommended to walk from the other bars off Las Olas and Himmarshee Street due to distance and safety. ⊠ *901 Progresso Dr., No. 101* ☎ *954/667–9373* ⊕ *www.laserwolf.com.*

Maguire's Hill 16. With the requisite lineup of libations and pub-style food, this classic Irish pub is good for no-frills fun, fried eats, and daily live music. It's famous locally as the oldest award-winning traditional Irish pub and restaurant in Fort Lauderdale. Live music is on tap every Wednesday, Friday, and Saturday night. ⊠ *535 N. Andrews Ave.* ☎ *954/764–4453* ⊕ *www.maguireshill16.com.*

O Lounge. This lounge and two adjacent establishments, **Yolo** and **Vibe**, on Las Olas and under the same ownership, cater to Fort Lauderdale's sexy yuppies during happy hour and on the weekends. Crowds alternate between Yolo's outdoor fire pit, O Lounge's chilled atmosphere and lounge music, and Vibe's more intense beats. Expect flashy cars in the driveway and a bit of plastic surgery. ⊠ *333 E. Las Olas Blvd.* ☎ *954/523–1000* ⊕ *www.yolorestaurant.com.*

ROK: BRG. Downtown Fort Lauderdale loves this personality-driven burger bar and gastro-pub as it gives the grown-ups something to enjoy in the teenage-infested nightlife district. The long and narrow venue, adorned with exposed-brick walls and flat-screen TVs is great for watching sports and for mingling on weekends. Locals come here for the great cocktails and beer selection. Their burgers are also locally famous. ⊠ *208 S.W. 2nd St.* ☎ *954/525–7656* ⊕ *www.rokbrgr.com.*

Fodor'sChoice ★ **Stache, 1920's Drinking Den.** Inspired by the Roaring Twenties, this speakeasy style drinking den and nightclub infuses party-hard downtown Fort Lauderdale with some class and pizzazz. Expect awesome craft cocktails, inclusive of bespoke ice cubes, especially for old-school drinks like Manhattans and Side Cars. Most Friday nights offer a live burlesque show (check website for details). Late night on Friday and Saturday anticipate great house music and a fun, easy-on-the-eyes, young sophisticate crowd. ⊠ *109 S.W. 2nd Ave.* ☎ *954/449–1044* ⊕ *www.stacheftl.com.*

Fodor'sChoice ★ **Tap 42 Bar and Kitchen.** With 42 rotating draft beers from around the United States, 50-plus bourbons, a few dozen original cocktails (including beer cocktails), and 66 bottled craft beers, awesome drinks and good times headline a typical evening at classy cool Tap 42. Although the indoor/outdoor gastro pub is a bit off the beaten path, it's well worth the detour. The 42 drafts protrude from a stylish wall constructed of pennies, surfacing more like a work of art than a beer-filling station. The venue attracts large crowds of young professionals for nights of heavy drinking and highly caloric new-age bar eats. ⊠ *1411 S. Andrews Ave.* ☎ *954/463–4900* ⊕ *www.tap42.com.*

Tarpon Bend. This casual two-story restaurant transforms into a jovial resto-bar in the early evening, ideal for enjoying a few beers, mojitos, and some great bar food. It's consistently busy, day, night, and late night with young professionals, couples, and large groups of friends. It's one place that has survived all the ups and downs of downtown Fort Lauderdale. ⊠ *200 S.W. 2nd St.* ☎ *954/523–3233* ⊕ *www.tarponbend.com.*

ALONG THE BEACH

Given its roots as a beachside party town, it's hard to believe that Fort Lauderdale Beach offers very few options in terms of nightlife. A few dive bars are at opposite ends of the main strip, near Sunrise Boulevard and Route A1A, as well as Las Olas Boulevard and A1A. On the main thoroughfare between Las Olas and Sunrise, a few high-end bars at the beach's show-stopping hotels have become popular, namely those at the W Fort Lauderdale.

Elbo Room. You can't go wrong wallowing in the past, lifting a drink, and exercising your elbow at the Elbo, a noisy, suds-drenched hot spot since 1938. It seems like nothing has changed here since Fort Lauderdale's spring break heyday. The watering hole phased out food (except for light nibbles) ages ago, but kept a hokey sense of humor: upstairs a sign proclaims "We don't serve women here. You have to bring your own." ⊠ *241 S. Fort Lauderdale Blvd.* ☎ *954/463–4615* ⊕ *www.elboroom.com.*

Living Room at the W. The large living-room-like space next to the lobby of the W Fort Lauderdale transforms into a major house-party-style event, mainly on weekends. There are plenty of plush couches, but it's usually standing-room-only early for this South Beach–style throwdown, with great DJs, awesome libations, and an easy-on-the-eyes crowd. A breezy and beautiful outdoor area is idyllic for the overflow, as is the less popular downstairs lounge, Whiskey Blue (which is only open Thursday–Saturday). ⊠ *W Fort Lauderdale, 401 N. Fort Lauderdale Beach Blvd.* ☎ *954/414–8300* ⊕ *www.wfortlauderdalehotel. com/living-room.*

McSorley's. This classic Irish pub offers standard pub fun—from a jukebox to 35 beers on tap to bar games—but remains wildly popular thanks to its location right across from Fort Lauderdale beach. Indeed it's one of the few places on the beach to get an affordable drink and attracts its fair share of both tourists and locals. Upstairs, the pub has a second lounge that's far more clubby and busiest on weekends. ⊠ *837 N. Fort Lauderdale Beach Blvd.* ☎ *954/565–4446* ⊕ *www.mcsorleysftl.com.*

Parrot Lounge. An old-school Fort Lauderdale hangout, this dive bar/ sports bar is particularly popular with Philadelphia Eagles fans, those longing to recall *Where the Boys Are,* and folks reminiscing about Fort Lauderdale's big-hair, sprayed-tan, Sun-In-bright 1980s heyday. This place is stuck in the past, but it's got great libations, wings, fingers, poppers, and skins. 'Nuff said. ⊠ *911 Sunrise La.* ☎ *954/563–1493* ⊕ *www.parrotlounge.com.*

The Wreck Bar. Like something out of an H.G. Wells novel, travel back in time to the 1950s at this nautical-inspired "under the sea" dive bar, enveloped in huge aquariums and a porthole view into the principal swimming pool, where live mermaids perform for your entertainment every Friday and Saturday at 6:30 pm. ⊠ *B Ocean Resort, 1140 Seabreeze Blvd.* ☎ *954/564–1000* ⊕ *www.boceanfortlauderdale.com.*

INTRACOASTAL AND INLAND

Bars and pubs along Fort Lauderdale's Intracoastal cater to the city's large, transient boating community. Heading inland along Sunrise Boulevard, the bars around Galleria Mall target thirty- and fortysomething singles.

Blue Martini Fort Lauderdale. A hot spot for thirtysomething-plus adults gone wild, Blue Martini's menu is filled with tons of innovative martini creations (42 to be exact!) The drinks are great and the scene is fun for everyone, even those who aren't single and looking to mingle. ⊠ *Galleria Fort Lauderdale, 2432 E. Sunrise Blvd.* ☎ *954/653–2583* ⊕ *www. bluemartinilounge.com.*

Kim's Alley Bar. Around since 1948, Kim's Alley Bar is the ultimate no-frills South Florida dive bar, a neighborhood spot in a strip mall near the Intracoastal. It has two smoke-filled bar areas, a jukebox, and pool tables that provide endless entertainment (if the patrons aren't providing enough diversion). ⊠ *The Gateway, 1920 E. Sunrise Blvd.* ☎ *954/763–7886.*

WILTON MANORS AND OAKLAND PARK

Fort Lauderdale's gay nightlife is most prevalent in Wilton Manors, affectionately termed Fort Lauderdale's "gayborhood." Wilton Drive, known as "the Drive," has dozens of bars, clubs, and lounges that cater to all types of GLBT subcultures.

Georgie's Alibi. A Fort Lauderdale LGBT institution, Georgie's Alibi is an anchor for the Wilton Manors gay community. The gargantuan pub fills to capacity for $3, 32-ounce Long Island Iced Tea Thursday, both the regular and blue varieties (from 9 pm 'til close). Any night of the week, Alibi stands out as a kind of gay Cheers of Fort Lauderdale—a neighborhood bar with darts, pool, libations, offering a no-frills, laid-back attitude. ⊠ *2266 Wilton Dr.* ☎ *954/565–2526* ⊕ *www. alibiwiltonmanors.com.*

The Manor. Inspired by The Abbey in West Hollywood, The Manor sought to offer a one-stop gay party shop in the heart of the Wilton Manors gayborhood. It didn't quite work out that way, but the multi-faceted two-story enclave is still open for the campy pop night Bubble Gum Friday and the circuit-party-style Saturday. ⊠ *2345 Wilton Dr.* ☎ *954/626–0082* ⊕ *www.themanorcomplex.com.*

Fodor's Choice ★ **Rosie's Bar and Grill.** Rosie's is consistently lively, pumping out tons of pop tunes and volumes of joyous laughter to surrounding streets. The former Hamburger Mary's has become an institution in South Florida as the go-to gay-friendly place for cheap drinks, decent bar food, and great times. Most of the fun at Rosie's is meeting new friends and engaging in conversation with the person seated next to you. Drink specials change daily. Sunday brunch with alternating DJs is wildly popular. ⊠ *2449 Wilton Dr.* ☎ *954/563–0123* ⊕ *www.rosiesbng.com.*

Sidelines. One of the most popular and consistently busy joints on the Wilton Manors "Drive" is this spacious sports and video bar that taps into the butch side of gay culture. The bar is often locally awarded the "Best Gay Bar in South Florida," and its all-welcoming vibe draws crowds both young and old, men and women. Expect large crowds during major football and basketball games. ⊠ *2031-A Wilton Dr., Wilton Manors* ☎ *954/563–8001* ⊕ *www.sidelinessports.com.*

Village Pub. Arguably the most consistently busy spot on "The Drive" in Wilton Manors, this gay pub delivers good times and cheap drinks nightly. Regardless of where you start or end your gay pub crawl in Wilton Manors, you'll invariably end up here at some point. There's a drink special or theme each night, like Show Tune Tuesday and 2-4-1 Saturday. ⊠ *2283 Wilton Dr., Wilton Manors and Oakland Park, Wilton Manors* ☎ *754/200–5244* ⊕ *www.villagepubwm.com.*

WESTERN SUBURBS AND BEYOND
Florida's cowboy country, Davie, offers country-western fun out in the 'burbs. In addition, South Florida's Native American tribes have long offered gambling on Indian Territory near Broward's western suburbs. With new laws, Broward's casinos offer Vegas-style slot machines and even blackjack. Hollywood's Seminole Hard Rock Hotel & Casino offers the most elegant of Broward's casino experiences. ⇨ *See Nightlife in Hollywood.*

5

SHOPPING

FOOD

Chef Jean-Pierre Cooking School. Catering to locals, seasonal snowbirds, and folks winging in for even shorter stays, Jean-Pierre Brehier (former owner of the Left Bank Restaurant on Las Olas) teaches the basics, from boiling water onward. The enthusiastic Gallic transplant has appeared on NBC's *Today,* among other shows. Choose from demonstration classes, hands-on classes, and a full series of cooking classes. Book ahead as classes often fill up. For souvenir hunters, this fun cooking facility also sells nifty pots, pastas, oils, and other great items. ⊠ *1436 N. Federal Hwy., Intracoastal and Inland* ☎ *954/563–2700* ⊕ *www. chefjp.com* ▨ *Starting at $65 per demonstration class, $125 hands-on class; "Cooking 101" and "Cooking 102" series $350 each* ⊙ *Store Mon.–Sat. 10–7; class schedules vary.*

MALLS

Galleria Fort Lauderdale. Fort Lauderdale's most upscale mall is just west of the Intracoastal Waterway. The split-level emporium entices with Neiman Marcus, Dillard's, Macy's, an Apple Store, plus 150 specialty shops for anything from cookware to exquisite jewelry. Chow down at Capital Grille, Truluck's, P.F. Chang's, or Seasons 52, or head for the food court, which will defy expectations with its international food-market feel. The mall itself is open Monday through Saturday 10–9, Sunday noon–6. The stand-alone restaurants and bars, like Capital Grille and Blue Martini Fort Lauderdale, are open later. ⊠ *2414 E. Sunrise Blvd., Intracoastal and Inland* ☎ *954/564–1036* ⊕ *www. galleriamall-fl.com.*

FAMILY

Fodor'sChoice

★

Sawgrass Mills. This alligator-shape megamall draws 26 million shoppers a year to its collection of 400 outlet stores and name-brand discounters. The mall claims to be the second-largest attraction in Florida—second only to Disney World. Though that claim is probably an exaggeration, you should prepare for insane crowds even during nonpeak hours and seasons. ⊠ *12801 W. Sunrise Blvd., at Flamingo Rd., Western Suburbs and Beyond, Sunrise* ⊕ *www.sawgrassmills.com.*

SHOPPING DISTRICTS

The Gallery at Beach Place. Just north of Las Olas Boulevard on Route A1A, this shopping gallery is attached to the mammoth Marriot Beach Place time-share. Spaces are occupied by touristy shops that sell everything from sarongs to alligator heads, chain restaurants like Hooter's, bars serving frozen drinks, and a supersize CVS pharmacy, which sells everything you need for the beach. ■TIP➡ **Beach Place has covered parking, and usually has plenty of spaces, but you can pinch pennies by using a nearby municipal lot that's metered.** ⊠ *17 S. Fort Lauderdale Beach Blvd., Along the beach* ⊕ *www.galleryatbeachplace.com.*

Fodor'sChoice   **Las Olas Boulevard.** Las Olas Boulevard is the heart and soul of Fort
★   Lauderdale. Not only are 50 of the city's best boutiques, 30 top restaurants, and a dozen art galleries found along this beautifully landscaped street, but Las Olas links Fort Lauderdale's growing downtown with its superlative beaches. Though you'll find a Cheesecake Factory on the boulevard, the thoroughfare tends to shun chains and welcomes one-of-a-kind clothing boutiques, chocolatiers, and ethnic eateries. Window shopping allowed. ⊠ *E. Las Olas Blvd., Downtown and Las Olas* ⊕ *www.lasolasboulevard.com.*

SPORTS AND THE OUTDOORS

BIKING

Among the most popular routes are Route A1A and Bayview Drive, especially in early morning before traffic builds, and a 7-mile bike path that parallels State Road 84 and New River and leads to Markham Park, which has mountain-bike trails. ■TIP➡ **Alligator alert: Do not dangle your legs from seawalls.**

Broward B–cycle. The big-city trend of "pay and ride" bicycles is alive and well in Broward County. With 40 station locations over 20 scenic miles, from as far south as Hallandale to as far north as Pompano Beach and Coconut Creek, bikes can be rented for as little as 30 minutes or as long as a week, and can be picked up and dropped off at any and all stations in Broward County. Most stations are found downtown and along the beach. This is an excellent green and health-conscious way to explore Fort Lauderdale. Please note, however, that helmets are not provided at the kiosks. ⊕ *www.broward.bcycle.com.*

FISHING

Bahia Mar Marina. If you're interested in a saltwater charter, check out the offerings at the marina of the Bahia Mar Fort Lauderdale Beach Hotel, A DoubleTree by Hilton. Sportfishing and drift-fishing bookings can be arranged. Snorkeling and diving outfitter Sea Experience also leaves from here, as does the famous *Jungle Queen* steamboat. In addition, the water taxi makes regular stops here. ⊠ *Bahia Mar Fort Lauderdale Beach Hotel, A DoubleTree by Hilton, 801 Seabreeze Blvd., Along the beach* ☎ *954/627–6309.*

RODEOS

Davie Pro Rodeo. It may sound strange, but South Florida has a rather large cowboy scene, concentrated in the western suburb of Davie. And for over four decades, the Bergeron Rodeo Grounds has surfaced as Davie's biggest tourist attraction. Throughout the year, the rodeo hosts national tours and festivals as well as the annual Southeaster Circuit Finals. Check the website for the exact dates of these rodeos. ⊠ *Davie Pro Rodeo Arena, 4271 Davie Rd., Western Suburbs and Beyond, Davie* ☎ *954/680–8005* ⊕ *www.davieprorodeo.com.*

SCUBA DIVING AND SNORKELING

Lauderdale Diver. A PADI 5-Star Certification Agency, this dive center facilitates daily day trips on a variety of dive boats up and down Broward's shoreline (they don't have their own boat but work with a handful of preferred outfitters). A variety of snorkeling, reef diving, and wreck diving trips are offered daily as well as scuba diving lessons. ⊠ *1334 S.E. 17th St., Intracoastal and Inland* ☎ *954/467–2822* ⊕ *www. lauderdalediver.com.*

FAMILY

Fodor'sChoice

★

Sea Experience. The *Sea Experience I* leaves daily at 10:15 am and 2:15 pm for two-hour glass-bottom-boat and snorkeling combination trips that explore Fort Lauderdale's offshore reefs. The tour costs $28; $7 more to snorkel, equipment provided. They also offer beginner and more advanced scuba diving experiences. ⊠ *Bahia Mar Fort Lauderdale Beach Hotel, A DoubleTree by Hilton, 801 Seabreeze Blvd., Along the beach* ☎ *954/770–3483* ⊕ *www.seaxp.com.*

SEGWAY TOURS

FAMILY

Fodor'sChoice

★

M.Cruz Rentals. M.Cruz Rentals rents out just about everything pertaining to Fort Lauderdale fun-in-the-sun—Jet-Skis, kayaks, bicycle rentals by the hour—as well as offers guided Segway Tours of Fort Lauderdale Beach four times per day. The rental facility is at the beach entrance of Hugh Taylor Birch State Park, just north of hotel row. The Segway Tours leave from here as well. Staff are exceptionally friendly and accommodating. ⊠ *Hugh Taylor Birch State Park, 3109 E. Sunrise Blvd., Along the beach* ☎ *954/235–5082* ⊕ *www.mcruzrentals.com.*

TENNIS

Jimmy Evert Tennis Center. With 22 courts (18 lighted clay courts, 3 hard courts, and a low-compression sand "beach" court), this is the crown jewel of Fort Lauderdale's public tennis facilities. Legendary champ Chris Evert learned her two-handed backhand here under the watchful eye of her now-retired father, Jimmy, the center's tennis pro for 37 years. ⊠ *Holiday Park, 701 N.E. 12th Ave., Intracoastal and Inland* ☎ *954/828–5378* ⊕ *www.fortlauderdale.gov/tennis/jetc.htm* 🎟 *$18 day pass (for Broward nonresidents)* ⊙ *Weekdays 7:45 am–9 pm, weekends 7:45 am–6 pm.*

NORTH ON SCENIC A1A

North of Fort Lauderdale's Birch Recreation Area, Route A1A edges away from the beach through a stretch known as Galt Ocean Mile, and a succession of oceanside communities line up against the sea. Traffic can line up, too, as it passes through a changing pattern of beach-blocking high-rises and modest family vacation towns and back again. As far as tourism goes, these communities tend to cater to a different demographic than Fort Lauderdale. Europeans and cost-conscious families head to Lauderdale-by-the-Sea, Pompano, and Deerfield for fewer frills and longer stays.

Towns are shown on the Broward County map.

LAUDERDALE-BY-THE-SEA

Lauderdale-by-the-Sea is 5 miles north of Fort Lauderdale.

Just north of Fort Lauderdale's northern boundary, this low-rise family resort town traditionally digs in its heels at the mere mention of high-rises. The result is choice shoreline access that's rapidly disappearing in nearby communities. Without a doubt, Lauderdale-by-the-Sea takes delight in embracing its small beach-town feel and welcoming guests to a different world of years gone by.

GETTING HERE AND AROUND

Lauderdale-by-the-Sea is just north of Fort Lauderdale. If you're driving from Interstate 95, exit east onto Commercial Boulevard and head over the Intracoastal Waterway. From U.S. 1 (aka Federal Highway), turn east on Commercial Boulevard. If coming from A1A, just continue north from Fort Lauderdale Beach.

ESSENTIALS

Visitor Information Lauderdale-by-the-Sea Chamber of Commerce ⊠ *4201 N Ocean Dr.* ☎ *954/776–1000* ⊕ *www.lbts.com.*

BEACHES

FAMILY   **Lauderdale-by-the-Sea Beach.** Especially popular with divers and snorkelers, this laid-back stretch of sand provides great access to lovely coral reefs. When you're not underwater, look up and you'll likely see a pelican flying by. Gentle trade winds make this an utterly relaxing retreat from the hubbub of Fort Lauderdale's busier beaches. That said, the southern part of the beach at Commercial Boulevard. and A1A is often busy due to a concentrated number of restaurants at the intersection, including the wildly popular Aruba Beach Cafe. Going north from Commercial Boulevard, the beach is lined with no-frills hotels and small inns for families and vacationers visiting Fort Lauderdale for longer periods of time, mainly Europeans. Look for metered parking around Commercial Boulevard and A1A. **Amenities:** food and drink; lifeguards; parking (fee). **Best for:** snorkeling; swimming. ⊠ *Commercial Blvd. at Hwy. A1A.*

WHERE TO EAT

$$$ ✕ **Aruba Beach Café.** This casual beachfront eatery is always crowded
CAFÉ   and always fun. One of Lauderdale-by-the-Sea's most famous restau-
FAMILY rants, Aruba Beach serves a wide range of American and Caribbean cuisine, including Caribbean conch chowder and conch fritters. There are also fresh tropical salads, sandwiches, and seafood. The café is famous for its divine fresh-baked Bimini bread with Aruba glaze (think challah with donut glaze). A band performs day and night, so head for

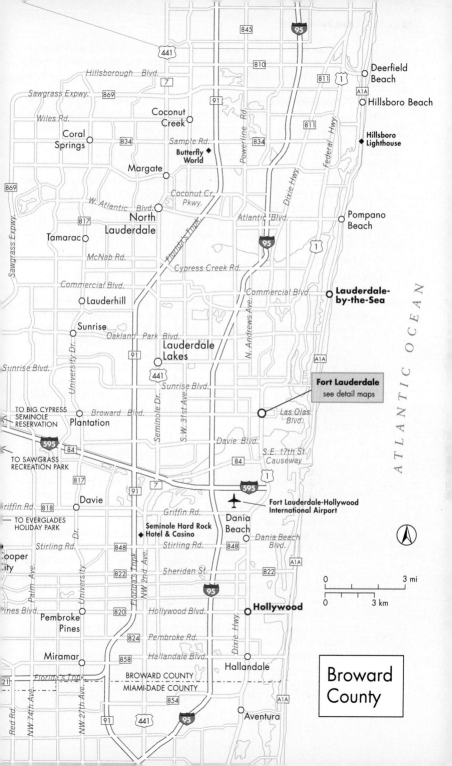

the back corner with excellent views of the beach if you want conversation while you eat and drink. Sunday breakfast buffet starts at 9 am. Ⓢ *Average main: $21* ✉ *1 Commercial Blvd.* ☎ *954/776–0001* ⊕ *www.arubabeachcafe.com.*

$$$$
SEAFOOD
✕ **Blue Moon Fish Company.** Since the late 1990s, Blue Moon Fish Company has never faltered on the magic that comes from the seafood-centric kitchen, where chefs create moon-and-stars-worthy dishes. Though the restaurant was completely renovated in 2014, the menu remains true to its ocean-to-table core with incredibly fresh local catch and stellar New England seafood. Start with whole roasted garlic and bread and continue on to the mussels, the rosemary roasted golden beets salad, and the pan-roasted yellowtail snapper. For Sunday's Champagne brunch extravaganza ($58.95) book early, even in the off-season. Ask to sit outside to enjoy the vistas of the Intracoastal Waterway. Ⓢ *Average main: $42* ✉ *4405 W. Tradewinds Ave.* ☎ *954/267–9888* ⊕ *www.bluemoonfishco.com.*

$
MODERN
MEXICAN
Fodor's Choice
★
✕ **JoJo's Tacos.** Following 20 years in the world of white-glove dining, Chef Joseph Parsons returned home to Fort Lauderdale to open this intimate, no-frills yet fabulous taco joint that mixes authentic Mexican flavors with hefty portions of innovation to produce some pretty amazing fusion eats. This place is true foodie fantasia with an adventurous menu of $6 tacos, including the blow-your-mind delish vegetarian "Shrooms & Asp" taco and the sweet-and-sour "Peachy Pollo" taco (two to three tacos usually is big enough for a meal). The resto's motto "We Rock The Guac!" is a testament to just how darn good the guacamole is; the savory fire-roasted street corn and the coconut and macadamia nut-crusted fried ice cream ain't bad either! Ⓢ *Average main: $14* ✉ *216 Commercial Blvd.* ☎ *954/835–5561* ⊕ *www.jojostacos.com.*

WHERE TO STAY

$
B&B/INN
▦ **Blue Seas Courtyard.** Husband-and-wife team Cristie and Marc Furth run this quaint Mexican-themed motel across the street from Lauderdale-by-the-Sea's family-friendly beaches. **Pros:** south-of-the-border vibe; friendly owners; vintage stoves from 1972; memory-foam mattress toppers. **Cons:** rooms lack ocean views; old bathtubs in some rooms. Ⓢ *Rooms from: $168* ✉ *4525 El Mar Dr.* ☎ *954/772–3336* ⊕ *www.blueseascourtyard.com* ↝ *12 rooms* ⦿*Breakfast.*

$$
HOTEL
▦ **High Noon Beach Resort.** Family-run since 1961, this hotel sits on 300 feet of beautiful beach, with plenty of cozy spots and an old-school homey ambience that keeps repeat visitors coming back for more. **Pros:** smack on the beach; friendly vibe; great staff. **Cons:** early booking required; not on happening part of beach. Ⓢ *Rooms from: $201* ✉ *4424 El Mar Dr.* ☎ *954/776–1121, 800/382–1265* ⊕ *www.highnoonresort.com* ↝ *40 rooms* ⦿*Breakfast.*

$
HOTEL
▦ **Sea Lord Hotel & Suites.** This ocean-side hotel received major upgrades back in 2010, including a new pool deck, restaurant, lobby, sundeck, entranceway, small fitness center, and room enhancements, making it one of the nicest in Lauderdale-by-the-Sea. **Pros:** terrific beach location; void of the moldy smell in nearby older hotels. **Cons:** shaky elevators; limited parking. Ⓢ *Rooms from: $170* ✉ *4140 El Mar Dr.*

☎ *954/776–1505, 800/344–4451* 🌐 *www.sealordhotel.com* 🛏 *47 rooms* 🍴 *Breakfast.*

$$ HOTEL FAMILY 🏨 **Tropic Seas Resort Motel.** This two-story property has an unbeatable location—directly on the beach, flanking 150 feet of pristine sands and sparkling blues—and is a favorite of annual European vacationers looking for longer stays. **Pros:** family-owned friendliness; great lawn furniture. **Cons:** must reserve far ahead; dated bathrooms. [$] *Rooms from: $220* ✉ *4616 El Mar Dr.* ☎ *954/491–3733 reservations, 954/772–2555 hotel direct line* 🌐 *www.tropicseasresort.com* 🛏 *16 rooms* 🍴 *Breakfast.*

SPORTS AND THE OUTDOORS

Anglin's Fishing Pier. This longtime favorite for 24-hour fishing has a fresh, renovated appearance after shaking off repeated storm damage that closed the pier at intervals during the past decade. ✉ *2 Commercial Blvd.* ☎ *954/491–9403* 🌐 *www.boatlessfishing.com/anglins.htm.*

HOLLYWOOD

Hollywood has had several face-lifts to shed its old-school image, but there's still something delightfully retro about the city. Young Circle, once down-at-heel, is now Broward's first Arts Park. On Hollywood's western outskirts, the flamboyant Seminole Hard Rock Hotel & Casino has enlivened this previously downtrodden section of the State Road 7/U.S. 441 corridor, drawing local weekenders, architecture buffs, partiers, and gamblers. But Hollywood's redevelopment efforts don't end there: new shops, restaurants, and art galleries open at a persistent clip, and the city has continually spiffed up its boardwalk—a wide pedestrian walkway along the beach—where local joggers are as commonplace as sun-seeking snowbirds from the north. On the coast of Hallandale, the beach is backed by older, towering condominiums. Inland, Hallandale has been trying to get some business from neighboring Aventura and Sunny Isles in Dade County with the development of the high-end Village at Gulfstream Park, a luxury retail arcade anchored by a reinvented casino and racetrack.

GETTING HERE AND AROUND

From Interstate 95, exit east on Sheridan Street or Hollywood Boulevard for Hollywood or Hallandale Beach Boulevard for either Hollywood or Hallandale.

ESSENTIALS

Visitor Information Hollywood Community Redevelopment Agency ☎ *954/924–2980* 🌐 *www.visithollywoodfl.org.*

EXPLORING

FAMILY **Arts Park at Young Circle.** This 10-acre urban park has completely transformed the run-down traffic circle linking downtown Hollywood with its beaches into a beautiful, lively public space. There's no shortage of things to do here: a huge playground beckons for the little ones, a state-of-the-art amphitheater hosts regular concerts, and educational workshop spaces host regular events, like Friday glassblowing workshops and jewelry-making classes. ✉ *1 Young Circle, Hollywood Blvd. and U.S. 1* ☎ *954/921–3500* ⊕ *www.visithollywoodfl.org/artspark.aspx.*

DCOTA. Though access is typically reserved strictly to those in the design biz, The Design Center of the Americas (DCOTA) still permits visitors to browse the myriad showrooms, parading the latest and greatest in home furnishings and interior design. Note, however, that this is purely "window-shopping" as direct consumer sales do not take place here, but amazing window-shopping (and inspiration) it is! ✉ *1855 Griffin Rd., Dania Beach* ☎ *954/920–7997* ⊕ *www.dcota.com* ⊙ *Weekdays 9–5.*

IGFA Fishing Hall of Fame and Museum. This creation of the International Game Fishing Association is a shrine to the sport. It has an extensive museum and research library where seven galleries feature fantasy fishing and other interactive displays. At the Catch Gallery, you can cast off virtually to reel in a marlin, sailfish, trout, tarpon, or bass. (If you suddenly get an urge to gear up for your own adventures, a Bass Pro Shops Outdoor World is next door.) ✉ *300 Gulf Stream Way, Dania Beach* ☎ *954/922–4212* ⊕ *www.igfa.org* 🎟 *$10* ⊙ *Mon.–Sat. 10–6, Sun. noon–6.*

FAMILY **West Lake Park.** Rent a canoe, kayak, or take the 40-minute boat tour at this park bordering the Intracoastal Waterway. At 1,500 acres, it is one of Florida's largest urban nature facilities. Extensive boardwalks traverse mangrove forests that shelter endangered and threatened species. A 65-foot observation tower showcases the entire park. At the free **Anne Kolb Nature Center,** named after Broward's late environmental advocate, there's a 3,500-gallon aquarium. The center's exhibit hall has 27 interactive displays. ✉ *1200 Sheridan St.* ☎ *954/357–5161* ⊕ *www. broward.org/parks/WestLakePark* 🎟 *Weekends $1.50, weekdays free* ⊙ *Park daily 9–6:30; Nature Center daily 9–5.*

BEACHES

FAMILY **Hollywood Beach and Broadwalk.** The name might be Hollywood, but Fodor's Choice there's nothing hip or chic about **Hollywood North Beach Park,** which ★ sits at the north end of Hollywood (Route A1A and Sheridan Street), before the pedestrian Broadwalk begins. And that's a good thing. It's just a laid-back, old-fashioned place to enjoy the sun, sand, and sea. The film *Marley & Me,* starring Jennifer Aniston and Owen Wilson and filmed in Greater Fort Lauderdale, spurred a comeback for dog beaches in South Florida, and ever since then, the year-round **Dog Beach of Hollywood** in North Beach Park has allowed dogs to enjoy fun in the sun from 3 pm to 7 pm Friday–Sunday (4 pm to 8 pm during Daylight Savings Time). Farther south on Hollywood beach, the 2.5-mile **Broadwalk** is a delightful throwback to the '50s, with mom-and-pop stores, ice-cream parlors, elderly couples going for long strolls, and families building sand castles on the beach. Thanks to millions in investment, this popular stretch of beach has spiffy features like a pristine pedestrian walkway, a concrete bike path, a crushed-shell jogging path, an 18-inch decorative wall separating the broadwalk from the sand, and places to shower off after a dip. Expect to hear French spoken throughout

5

Hollywood, since its beaches have long been a favorite getaway for Quebecois. **Amenities:** food and drink; lifeguards; parking (fee); toilets. **Best for:** sunrise; swimming; walking. ⊠ *Rte. A1A from Dania Beach Blvd. to Halladale Beach Blvd.* ▤ *Parking in public lots $1.50 per hr weekdays, $2 per hr weekends.*

John U. Lloyd Beach State Park. The once-pine-dotted natural area was restored to its natural state, thanks to government-driven efforts to pull out all but indigenous plants. Now native sea grape, gumbo-limbo, and other native plants offer shaded ambience. Nature trails and a marina are large draws as is canoeing on Whiskey Creek. The beaches are also excellent, but beware of mosquitoes in summer! On Wednesday and Friday in June and July, park rangers lead sea turtle awareness programs that include an educational presentation and a beach patrol to search for nesting loggerhead turtles. Advance reservations are required. **Amenities:** parking (fee); toilets. **Best for:** solitude; sunrise. ⊠ *6503 N. Ocean Dr.* ☎ *954/923–2833* ⊕ *www.floridastateparks.org/lloydbeach* ▤ *$6 per vehicle for 2–8 passengers, $4 for lone driver* ☉ *Daily 8–sunset.*

WHERE TO EAT

$$$ ✕ **Café Martorano.** Located within Seminole Hard Rock's entertainment-
ITALIAN   and-restaurant zone, this Italian-American institution pays homage to anything and everything that has to do with the *Godfather* and impresses with humungous family-style portions. Dishes run the full Italian-American gamut, from the classic parmigianas to the lobster and snapper francaise. The homemade mozzarella and fried calamari are excellent choices for starters. It's easy to gorge here since each dish is so succulent and savory. The ever-present *Godfather* motif is taken to the extreme—dinner is interrupted hourly with clips from the movie played on the surrounding flat screens. There's an undeniable nightclub vibe to the joint, especially later into the night. Ⓢ *Average main: $27* ⊠ *5751 Seminole Way* ☎ *954/584–4450* ⊕ *www.cafemartorano.com* ☉ *No lunch.*

$$$$ ✕ **Diplomat Prime.** Hollywood's superlative choice for fine dining, the
STEAKHOUSE   intimate 15-table Diplomat Prime is a classic American steak house
Fodor'sChoice   done right. A living slice of golden age glamour, the restaurant's ambi-
★   ence recalls a bygone era of dress-up dining in South Florida, where decked-out patrons are rightfully treated as VIPs. Perfected steak-house classics headline the menu: jumbo shrimp cocktail, lobster bisque, onion soup gratinée, Caesar salad, 21-day dry-aged prime steaks including a 28-ounce prime porterhouse and an 18-ounce prime rib eye as well as a 3½-pound Maine lobster (yes, you read correctly!). All this is complemented by a wine list with more than 600 fine wines. It doesn't get much better than this. Oh wait, it does! The key lime pie is a divine intervention of creamy tart pie, buttery crust, fresh whipped cream, and white chocolate. Ⓢ *Average main: $67* ⊠ *Diplomat Resort & Spa Hollywood, 3555 S. Ocean Dr.* ☎ *954/602–8347* ⊕ *www.hollywoodprime. com* ⌱ *Reservations essential* ☉ *No lunch.*

$ ✕ **Jaxson's Ice Cream Parlour & Restaurant.** This 1950s landmark whips
AMERICAN up malts, shakes, and jumbo sundaes from ice creams prepared daily
FAMILY on premises, plus sandwiches and salads, amid an antique-license-plate
Fodor's Choice decor. Owner Monroe Udell's trademarked Kitchen Sink—a small sink
★ full of ice cream, topped by sparklers—for parties of four or more goes
for $12.95 per person (no sharing). Those wanting a sample before
committing to a flavor, think again. The oh-so-popular Jaxson's doesn't
give samples! $ *Average main: $15* ✉ *128 S. Federal Hwy., Dania
Beach* ☎ *954/923–4445* ⊕ *www.jaxsonsicecream.com.*

$ ✕ **LeTub.** Once a Sunoco gas station, this quirky waterside saloon has an
AMERICAN enduring affection for claw-foot bathtubs. Hand-painted porcelain is
everywhere—under ficus, sea grape, and palm trees. If a potty doesn't
appeal, there's a secluded swing facing the water north of the main
dining area. Despite molasses-slow service and an abundance of flies
at sundown, this eatery is favored by locals, and management seemed
genuinely appalled when hordes of trend-seeking city slickers started
jamming bar stools and tables after Oprah declared its thick, juicy
Angus burgers the best around. A 13-ounce sirloin burger and small
fries will run you around $15 (burger $11; small fries $3.50). ⚠ **There's
no children's menu and no children allowed after 8 pm.** $ *Average main:
$15* ✉ *1100 N. Ocean Dr.* ☎ *954/921–9425* ⊕ *www.theletub.com.*

WHERE TO STAY

$$$ 🏨 **Diplomat Resort & Spa Hollywood.** This colossal 39-story, contempo-
RESORT rary, triple-tower property—formerly a Westin and now part of Hilton's
FAMILY "Curio Collection"—effectively brings style, sophistication, and pizzazz
Fodor's Choice to Hollywood Beach with its massive, 60-foot-high atrium, casual-chic
★ guest rooms, a 120-foot bridged infinity pool (extending from lobby to
oceanfront), one of South Florida's largest and most high-design spas,
and a handful of excellent restaurants. **Pros:** superbly comfortable beds;
excellent gym; eye-popping architecture. **Cons:** large complex; numer-
ous conventioneers; expensive parking. $ *Rooms from: $319* ✉ *3555 S.
Ocean Dr.* ☎ *954/602–6000* ⊕ *www.diplomatresort.com* ⤳ *902 rooms,
96 suites* ❍ *No meals.*

$ 🏨 **Sea Downs.** Facing the boardwalk and ocean, this no-frills, three-
RENTAL story lodging is a good choice for families looking for budget accom-
FAMILY modation, as one-bedroom units can be joined to create two-bedroom
apartments. **Pros:** facing ocean; reasonable rates; great location for Hol-
lywood. **Cons:** minimum stay often required; outdated decor; cash only.
$ *Rooms from: $140* ✉ *2900 N. Surf Rd.* ☎ *954/923–4968* ⊕ *www.
seadowns.com* ⤳ *4 efficiencies, 8 1-bedroom apartments* ⊟ *No credit
cards* ❍ *No meals.*

$$ 🏨 **Seminole Hard Rock Hotel & Casino.** On the industrial flatlands of west-
HOTEL ern Hollywood, the Seminole Hard Rock Hotel & Casino serves as
a magnet for pulsating Vegas-style entertainment and folks looking
for 24 hours of casino, clubbing, and hedonism. **Pros:** nonstop entertainment; plenty of activities; rooms renovated in 2012. **Cons:** in an
unsavory neighborhood; no tourist sights in close proximity; rental car
necessary. $ *Rooms from: $269* ✉ *1 Seminole Way* ☎ *866/502–7529,*

800/937–0010   ⊕ *www.seminolehardrockhollywood.com*   ⤳395
rooms, 86 suites ✝◎∣*No meals.*

NIGHTLIFE

Fodor's Choice
★

Seminole Hard Rock Casino. The glitzy, Vegas-style Seminole Hard Rock Casino is the superlative gaming and entertainment complex in Florida. Though located in a somewhat downtrodden area of inland Hollywood, once inside the Hard Rock enclave, you'll be mesmerized by the excitement radiating from the 145,000-square-foot casino, the 5,500-seat arena (Hard Rock Live), a dozen restaurants, and near dozen bars and nightclubs. The casino has blackjack, baccarat, three-card poker, more than 2,500 gaming machines, and just under 100 tables. It's open 24/7 and is connected to a hotel tower and entertainment complex, including great nightlife options such as an Improv Comedy Club, the multi-level Passion nightclub, a classic piano bar, and Bongo's Cuban Cafe. While weekends are guaranteed party-hard mayhem, not all clubs are open on weekdays so check Hard Rock's detailed, user-friendly website for schedules. ■TIP➔ The Seminole Hard Rock is not to be confused with its neighbor, the smoky and seedy Seminole Casino of Hollywood. ✉ *1 Seminole Way* ☎ *866/502–7529* ⊕ *www.seminolehardrockhollywood.com.*

PALM BEACH AND THE TREASURE COAST

WELCOME TO PALM BEACH

TOP REASONS TO GO

★ **Exquisite resorts:** Two grandes dames, The Breakers and the Boca Raton Resort & Club, perpetually draw the rich, the famous, and anyone else who can afford the luxury. The Eau Palm Beach and Four Seasons sparkle with service fit for royalty.

★ **Beautiful beaches:** From Jupiter, where dogs run free, to Stuart's tubular waves, to the broad stretches of sand in Delray Beach and Boca Raton, swimmers, surfers, sunbathers—and sea turtles looking for a place to hatch their eggs—all find happiness.

★ **Top-notch golf:** The Champion Course and re-envisioned Fazio Course at PGA National Resort & Spa are world-renowned; pros sharpen up at PGA Village.

★ **Horse around:** Wellington, with its popular polo season, is often called the winter equestrian capital of the world.

★ **Excellent fishing:** The Atlantic Ocean, teeming with kingfish, sailfish, and wahoo, is a treasure chest for anglers.

1 **Palm Beach.** With Gatsby-era architecture, stone-and-stucco estates, and extravagant dining, Palm Beach is a must-see for travelers to the area. Plan to spend time on Worth Avenue, a collection of more than 200 chic shops, and at Whitehall, the palatial retreat for Palm Beach's founder, Henry Flagler. West Palm Beach and its environs, including Lake Worth, are bustling with their own identities. Culture fans have plenty to cheer about with the Kravis Center and Norton Museum of Art; sports enthusiasts will have a ball golfing or boating; and kids love Lion Country Safari.

2 **Delray Beach.** Its lively downtown, with galleries, independent boutiques, and trendy restaurants blocks from the ocean, is perfect for strolling.

3 **Boca Raton.** An abundance of modern shopping plazas mix with historic buildings from the 1920s, masterpieces by renowned architect Addison Mizner.

4 **North County.** Palm Beach Gardens, Jupiter, quaint Juno Beach, and Tequesta are more laid-back cousins to the areas south. It's a golfer's paradise with PGA courses that make the pros.

5 **Treasure Coast.** The area north of Palm Beach county remains blissfully low-key, with fishing towns, spring-training stadiums, and ecotourism attractions until you hit the cosmopolitan— yet understated—Vero Beach.

GETTING ORIENTED

This diverse region extends 120 miles from laid-back Sebastian to tony Boca Raton. The area's glitzy epicenter, Palm Beach, attracts socialites, the well-heeled, and interested onlookers. The northernmost cities are only about 100 miles from Orlando, making that area an ideal choice for families wanting some beach time to go with their visit to Mickey Mouse. Delightfully funky Delray Beach is only an hour north of Miami. The Intracoastal Waterway runs parallel to the ocean and transforms from a canal to a tidal lagoon separating islands from the mainland, starting with Palm Beach and moving northward to Singer Island (Palm Beach Shores and Riviera Beach), Jupiter Island, Hutchinson Island (Stuart, Jensen Beach, and Fort Pierce), and Orchid Island (Vero Beach and Sebastian).

6

ATLANTIC OCEAN

be Sound
Jupiter Island

1

Tequesta
Jupiter

1A

Juno Beach
Singer Island

Palm Beach Gardens

Palm Beach Shores

Riviera Beach

1

Palm Beach

1

1A

Lake Worth

South Palm Beach

Manalapan

Boynton Beach

95

Gulf Stream

Delray Beach

Highland Beach

1A

Boca Raton

1

Updated by
Jan Norris

A golden stretch of the Atlantic shore, the Palm Beach area resists categorization, and for good reason: the territory stretching south to Boca Raton, appropriately coined the Gold Coast, defines old-world glamour and new-age sophistication.

To the north you'll uncover the comparatively undeveloped Treasure Coast—liberally sprinkled with seaside gems and wide-open spaces along the road awaiting your discovery. Speaking of discovery, its moniker came from the 1715 sinking of a Spanish fleet that dumped gold, jewels, and silver in the waters; today the *Urca de Lima*, one of the original 11 ships and now an undersea "museum," can be explored by scuba divers.

Altogether, there's a delightful disparity between Palm Beach, pulsing with old-money wealth, and under-the-radar Hutchinson Island. Seductive as the gorgeous beaches, eclectic dining, and leisurely pursuits can be, you should also take advantage of flourishing commitments to historic preservation and the arts, as town after town yields intriguing museums, galleries, theaters, and gardens.

Palm Beach, proud of its status as America's first luxe resort destination and still glimmering with its trademark Mediterranean-revival mansions, manicured hedges, and highbrow shops, can rule supreme as the focal point for your sojourn any time of year. From there, head off in one of two directions: south toward Delray Beach and Boca Raton along an especially scenic estate-dotted route known as A1A, or back north to the beautiful barrier islands of the Treasure Coast. For rustic inland activities such as bass fishing and biking atop the dike around Lake Okeechobee, head west.

PLANNING

WHEN TO GO
The weather is optimal from November through May, but the trade-off is that roads, hotels, and restaurants are more crowded and prices higher. If the scene is what you're after, try the early weeks of December

when the "season" isn't yet in full swing. However, be warned that after Easter, the crowd relocates to the Hamptons, and Palm Beach feels like another universe. For some, that's a blessing—and a great time to take advantage of lower summer lodging rates and dining deals, but you'll need to bring your tolerance for heat, humidity, and afternoon downpours.

GETTING HERE AND AROUND

AIR TRAVEL

Palm Beach International Airport is in West Palm, but it's possible (and sometimes cheaper) to fly to Fort Lauderdale, Miami, or Orlando. Do rent a car if you plan on exploring. Scenic Route A1A, also called Ocean Boulevard or Ocean Drive, depending on where you are, ventures out onto the barrier islands. I–95 runs parallel to U.S. 1, but a few miles inland.

From the airport, call Southeastern Florida Transportation Group, a local hotline for cabs, airport shuttles, and private sedans.

Airport Palm Beach International Airport (*PBI*). ⊠ *1000 Turnage Blvd., West Palm Beach* ☎ *561/471–7420* ⊕ *www.pbia.org.*

Airport Transfers Southeastern Florida Transportation Group ☎ *561/777–7777* ⊕ *www.yellowcabflorida.com.*

BUS TRAVEL

The county's bus service, Palm Tran, runs two routes (nos. 44 and 40) that offer daily service connecting the airport, the Tri-Rail stop near it, and locations in central West Palm Beach. A network of 34 routes joins towns all across the area; it's $5 for a day pass. The free Downtown Trolley connects the West Palm Beach Amtrak station and the Tri-Rail stop in West Palm on its Green Line. Its Yellow Line makes continuous loops down Clematis Street, the city's main stretch of restaurants and watering holes interspersed with stores, and through CityPlace, a shopping-dining-theater district. Hop on and off at any of the seven stops. The trolley's Yellow Line runs Sunday to Wednesday 11–9 and Thursday to Saturday 11–11. The trolley's Green Line, which stretches farther east, west, and south, and connects to Tri-Rail and Amtrak, runs weekdays 7–6, Saturday 9–6, and Sunday 11–6. A seasonal Orange Line, operating from fall to spring, takes in museums and gardens in downtown West Palm Beach and on the island.

Contacts Downtown Trolley ☎ *561/833-8873* ⊕ *www.westpalmbeachdda. com/transportation.* **Palm Tran** ☎ *561/841-4287* ⊕ *www.pbcgov.com/palmtran.*

TRAIN TRAVEL

Amtrak stops daily in West Palm Beach. The station is at the same location as the Tri-Rail stop, so the same free shuttle, the Downtown Trolley, is available (via the trolley's Green Line).

Tri-Rail Commuter Service is a rail system with 18 stops altogether between West Palm Beach and Miami; tickets can be purchased at each stop, and a one-way trip from the first to the last point is $6.90 weekdays, $5 weekends. Three stations—West Palm Beach, Lake Worth, and Boca—have free shuttles to their downtowns, and taxis are on call at others.

Contacts Amtrak ☎ 800/872–7245 ⊕ www.amtrak.com. **Tri-Rail** ☎ 800/874–7245 ⊕ www.tri-rail.com.

HOTELS

Palm Beach has a number of smaller hotels in addition to the famous Breakers. Lower-priced hotels and bed-and-breakfasts can be found in West Palm Beach, Palm Beach Gardens. and Lake Worth. Heading south, the oceanside town of Manalapan has the Eau Palm Beach Resort & Spa. The Seagate Hotel & Spa sparkles in Delray Beach, and the posh Boca Beach Club lines the superlative swathe of shoreline in Boca Raton. In the opposite direction there's the PGA National Resort & Spa, and across from it by the water is the Marriott on Singer Island, a well-kept secret for spacious, sleek suites. Even farther north, Vero Beach has a collection of luxury boutique hotels, as well as more modest options along the Treasure Coast. To the west, towns close to Lake Okeechobee offer country-inn accommodations geared to bass-fishing pros. *Hotel reviews have been shortened. For full information, visit Fodors.com.*

RESTAURANTS

Numerous elegant establishments offer upscale American, Continental, and international cuisine, but the area also is chock-full of casual waterfront spots serving affordable burgers and fresh seafood feasts. Snapper and grouper are especially popular here, along with the ubiquitous shrimp. Happy hours and early-bird menus, Florida hallmarks, typically entice the budget-minded with several dinner entrées at reduced prices offered during certain hours, usually before 5 or 6.

WHAT IT COSTS				
	$	**$$**	**$$$**	**$$$$**
Restaurants	under $16	$16–$20	$21–$30	over $30
Hotels	under $201	$201–$300	$301–$400	over $400

Restaurant prices are the average cost of a main course at dinner or, if dinner is not served, at lunch. Hotel prices are the lowest cost of a standard double room in high season.

VISITOR INFORMATION

Contacts Palm Beach County Convention and Visitors Bureau ✉ 1555 *Palm Beach Lakes Blvd., Suite 800, West Palm Beach* ☎ 561/233–3000 ⊕ www.palmbeachfl.com.

PALM BEACH

70 miles north of Miami, off I–95.

Long reigning as the place where the crème de la crème go to shake off winter's chill, Palm Beach, which is actually on a barrier island, continues to be a seasonal hotbed of platinum-grade consumption. The town celebrated its 100th birthday in 2011, and there's no competing with its historic social supremacy. It's been the winter address for heirs of the iconic Rockefeller, Vanderbilt, Colgate, Post, Kellogg, and Kennedy families. Even newer power brokers, with names like Kravis, Peltz, and Trump, are made to understand that strict laws govern everything from building to landscaping, and not so much as a pool awning gets added without a town council nod. Only three bridges allow entry, and huge tour buses are a no-no.

All this fabled ambience started with Henry Morrison Flagler, Florida's premier developer, and cofounder, along with John D. Rockefeller, of Standard Oil. No sooner did Flagler bring the railroad to Florida in the 1890s than he erected the famed Royal Poinciana and Breakers hotels. Rail access sent real-estate prices soaring, and ever since, princely sums have been forked over for personal stationery engraved with 33480, the zip code of Palm Beach (which didn't actually get its status as an independent municipality until 1911). Setting the tone in this town of unparalleled Florida opulence is the ornate architectural work of Addison Mizner, who began designing homes and public buildings here in the 1920s and whose Moorish-Gothic Mediterranean-revival style has influenced virtually all landmarks.

But the greater Palm Beach area is much larger and encompasses several communities on the mainland and to the north and south. To provide Palm Beach with servants and other workers, Flagler created an off-island community across the Intracoastal Waterway (also referred to as Lake Worth in these parts). West Palm Beach, now cosmopolitan and noteworthy in its own right, evolved into an economically vibrant business hub and a sprawling playground with some of the best nightlife and cultural attractions around, including the glittering Kravis Center for the Performing Arts, the region's principal entertainment venue. The mammoth Palm Beach County Judicial Center and Courthouse and the State Administrative Building underscore the breadth of the city's governmental and corporate activity.

The burgeoning equestrian development of Wellington, with its horse shows and polo matches, lies a little more than 10 miles west of downtown, and is the site of much of the county's growth.

Spreading southward from the Palm Beach/West Palm Beach nucleus set between the two bridges that flow from Royal Poinciana Way and Royal Palm Way into Flagler Drive on the mainland are small cities like Lake Worth, with its charming artsy center, Lantana, and Manalapan (home to the fabulous Eau Palm Beach resort, formerly the Ritz-Carlton Palm Beach). All three have turf that's technically on the same island as Palm Beach, and at its bottom edge across the inlet is Boynton Beach, a 20-minute drive from Worth Avenue.

GETTING HERE AND AROUND

Palm Beach is 70 miles north of Miami (a 90-minute trip with traffic). To access Palm Beach off I–95, exit east at Southern Boulevard, Belvedere Road, or Okeechobee Boulevard. To drive from Palm Beach to Lake Worth, Lantana, Manalapan, and Boynton Beach, head south on Ocean Boulevard/Route A1A; Lake Worth is roughly 6 miles south, and Boynton is another 6. Similarly, to reach them from West Palm Beach, take U.S. 1 or I–95. To travel between Palm Beach and Singer Island, you must cross over to West Palm before returning to the beach. Once there, go north on U.S. 1 and then cut over on Blue Heron Boulevard/ Route 708. If coming straight from the airport or somewhere farther west, take I–95 up to the same exit and proceed east. The main drag in Palm Beach Gardens is PGA Boulevard/Route 786, which is 4 miles north on U.S. 1 and I–95; A1A merges with it as it exits the top part of Singer Island. Continue on A1A to reach Juno Beach and Jupiter.

TOURS

FAMILY **DivaDuck Amphibious Tours.** Running 75 minutes, these duck tours go in and out of the water on USCG-inspected amphibious vessels around West Palm Beach and Palm Beach. The tours depart two or three times most days for $25 per person (adults); there are discounts for seniors and kids. ⊠ *CityPlace, 600 S. Rosemary Ave., corner of Hibiscus St. and Rosemary Ave., West Palm Beach* ☎ *877/844–4188* ⊕ *www.divaduck. com.*

Island Living Tours. Book a private mansion-viewing excursion around Palm Beach, and hear the storied past of the island's upper crust. Owner Leslie Diver also hosts an Antique Row Tour and a Worth Avenue Shopping Tour. All vehicle tours are 3 hours and from $60 per person to $150 per person, depending on the vehicle used. Leslie also runs 90-minute bicycle tours through Palm Beach ($35, not including bike rental). One bicycle tour explores the Estate Section and historic Worth Avenue; another explores the island's lesser known North End. Call in advance for location and to reserve. ☎ *561/868–7944* ⊕ *www. islandlivingpb.com.*

EXPLORING

PALM BEACH

Most streets around major attractions and commercial zones have free parking as well as metered spaces. If you can stake out a place between a Rolls Royce and a Bentley, do so, but beware of the "Parking by Permit Only" signs, as a $50 ticket might take the shine off your spot. Better yet, if you plan to spend an entire afternoon strolling Worth Avenue, park in the Apollo lot behind Tiffany's midway off Worth on Hibiscus; some stores will validate your parking ticket.

TOP ATTRACTIONS

Fodor's Choice **The Breakers.** Built by Henry Flagler in 1896 and rebuilt by his descen-
★ dants after a 1925 fire, this magnificent Italian Renaissance–style resort helped launch Florida tourism with its Gilded Age opulence, attracting influential wealthy Northerners to the state. The hotel, still owned by Flagler's heirs, is a must-see even if you aren't staying there. Walk through the 200-foot-long lobby, which has soaring arched ceilings painted by 72 Italian artisans and hung with crystal chandeliers. Meet for a drink at the HMF, one of the most beautiful bars in the state. ■TIP➔ Book a pampering spa treatment or dine on top of the Seafood Bar's whimsical aquarium counter, where leggy green starfish prance below your plate, and the $25 parking is waived; it's actually waived if you spend at least $25 anywhere in the hotel (just have your ticket validated). ⊠ *1 S. County Rd.* ☎ *561/655–6611* ⊕ *www.thebreakers.com.*

Draped in European elegance, the Breakers in Palm Beach sits on 140 acres along the oceanfront.

Fodor's Choice **Henry Morrison Flagler Museum.** The worldly sophistication of Florida's
★ Gilded Age lives on at Whitehall, the plush 55-room "marble palace"
Henry Flagler commissioned in 1901 for his third wife, Mary Lily
Kenan. Architects John Carrère and Thomas Hastings were instructed
to create the finest home imaginable—and they outdid themselves.
Whitehall rivals the grandeur of European palaces and has an entrance
hall with a baroque ceiling similar to Louis XIV's Versailles. Here you'll
see original furnishings; a hidden staircase Flagler used to sneak from
his bedroom to the billiards room; an art collection; a 1,200-pipe organ;
and Florida East Coast Railway exhibits, along with Flagler's personal
railcar, No. 91, showcased in an 8,000-square-foot beaux arts–style
pavilion behind the mansion. Docent-led tours and audio tours are
included with admission. The museum's Café des Beaux-Arts, open
from Thanksgiving through mid-April, offers a Gilded Age–style early
afternoon tea for $40 (11:30–2:30); the price includes museum admis-
sion. ⊠ *1 Whitehall Way* ☎ *561/655–2833* ⊕ *www.flaglermuseum.us*
⌦ *$18* ⊗ *Tues.–Sat. 10–5, Sun. noon–5.*

Fodor's Choice **Worth Avenue.** Called "the Avenue" by Palm Beachers, this half-mile-
★ long street is synonymous with exclusive shopping. Nostalgia lovers
recall an era when faces or names served as charge cards, purchases
were delivered home before customers returned from lunch, and bills
were sent directly to private accountants. Times have changed, but a
stroll amid the Spanish-accented buildings, many designed by Addison Mizner, offers a tantalizing taste of the island's ongoing commitment to elegant consumerism. Explore the labyrinth of nine pedestrian
"vias" off of each side that wind past boutiques, tiny plazas, bubbling

Palm Beach and West Palm Beach

fountains, and bougainvillea-festooned balconies; this is where the smaller, unique shops are. The Worth Avenue Association holds historic walking tours on Wednesdays at 11 am during "season" (after Thanksgiving to late April). The $10 fee benefits local nonprofit organizations. ⊠ *Worth Ave., between Cocoanut Row and S. Ocean Blvd.* ☎ *561/659–6909* ⊕ *www.worth-avenue.com.*

WORTH NOTING

Mar-a-Lago. Breakfast-food heiress Marjorie Merriweather Post commissioned a Hollywood set designer to create Ocean Boulevard's famed Mar-a-Lago, a 114-room, 110,000-square-foot Mediterranean-revival palace. Its 75-foot Italianate tower is visible from many areas of Palm Beach and from across the Intracoastal Waterway in West Palm Beach. Owner Donald Trump has turned it into a private membership club. So you'll have to enjoy the view from the car window unless you have a membership, but even the gates are impressive. ⊠ *1100 S. Ocean Blvd.* ☎ *561/832–2600* ⊕ *www.maralagoclub.com.*

FAMILY **Society of the Four Arts.** Despite widespread misconceptions of its members-only exclusivity, this privately endowed institution—founded in 1936 to encourage appreciation of art, music, drama, and literature—is funded for public enjoyment. The Esther B. O'Keeffe gallery building artfully melds an exhibition hall that houses traveling exhibits with a 700-seat theater. A library designed by prominent Mizner-peer Maurice Fatio, a children's library, a botanical garden, and the Philip Hulitar Sculpture Garden round out the facilities and are open daily. A complete schedule of programming is available on the society's website. ⊠ *2 Four Arts Plaza* ☎ *561/655–7227* ⊕ *www.fourarts.org* 🎫 *$5 gallery; special program costs vary* ☉ *Gallery, Dec.–Apr., Mon.–Sat. 10–5, Sun. 1–5; gardens, daily 10–5; children's library, weekdays 10–4:45, also Sat. 10–12:45 Nov.–Apr. Closed Aug.*

WEST PALM BEACH

Long considered Palm Beach's less privileged stepsister, West Palm Beach has come into its own over the past 35 years, and just in this millennium the $30 million Centennial Square waterfront complex at the eastern end of Clematis Street, with piers, a pavilion, and an amphitheater, has transformed West Palm into an attractive, easy-to-walk downtown area—not to mention there's the Downtown Trolley that connects the shopping-and-entertainment mecca CityPlace with restaurant-and-lounge-lined Clematis Street. The recently opened Palm Beach Outlet Mall gives options to those looking for tony bargains. West Palm is especially well regarded for its arts scene, with unique museums and performance venues.

The city's outskirts, vast flat stretches with fast-food outlets and car dealerships, may not inspire, but are worth driving through to reach attractions scattered around the southern and western reaches. Several sites are especially rewarding for children and other animal and nature lovers.

CLOSE UP

The Mansions of Palm Beach

Whether you aspire to be a Kennedy, Donald Trump, or Rod Stewart—all onetime or current Palm Beach residents—no trip to the island is complete without gawking at the megamansions lining its perfectly manicured streets.

No one is more associated with how the island took shape than Addison Mizner, architect extraordinaire and society darling of the 1920s. But what people may not know is that a "fab four" was really the force behind the residential streets as they appear today: Mizner, of course, plus Maurice Fatio, Marion Sims Wyeth, and John Volk.

The four architects dabbled in different genres, some more so than others, but the unmissable style is Mediterranean revival, a Palm Beach hallmark mix of stucco walls, Spanish red-tile roofs, Italianate towers, Moorish-Gothic carvings, and the uniquely Floridian use of coquina, a grayish porous limestone made of coral rock with fossil-like imprints of shells. As for Mizner himself, he had quite the repertoire of signature elements, including using differently sized and shaped windows on one facade, blue tile work inside and out, and tiered roof lines (instead of one straight-sloping panel across, having several sections overlap like scales on a fish).

The majority of preserved estates are clustered in three sections: along Worth Avenue; the few blocks of South County Road after crossing Worth and the streets shooting off it; and the 5-mile stretch of South Ocean Boulevard from Barton Avenue to near Phipps Ocean Park, where the condos begin cropping up.

If 10 miles of riding on a bike while cars zip around you isn't intimidating, the two-wheeled trip may be the best way to fully take in the beauty of the mansions and surrounding scenery. Many hotels have bicycles for guest use. Another option is the dependable Palm Beach Bicycle Trail Shop (☎ 561/659–4583 ⊕ www. palmbeachbicycle.com). Otherwise, driving is a good alternative. Just be mindful that Ocean Boulevard is a one-lane road and the only route on the island to cities like Lake Worth and Manalapan, so you can't go too slowly, especially at peak travel times.

If gossip is more your speed, in-the-know concierges rely on Leslie Diver's "Island Living Tours" (☎ 561/868–7944 ⊕ www.islandlivingpb.com); she's one of the town's leading experts on architecture *and* dish, both past and present.

Top 10 Self-Guided Stops: (1) Casa de Leoni, 450 Worth Avenue (Addison Mizner); (2) Villa des Cygnes, 456 Worth Avenue (Addison Mizner and Marion Sims Wyeth); (3) 17 Golfview Road (Marion Sims Wyeth); (4) 220 and 252 El Bravo Way (John Volk); (5) 126 South Ocean Boulevard (Marion Sims Wyeth); (6) El Solano, 720 South Ocean Boulevard (Addison Mizner); (7) Casa Nana, 780 South Ocean Boulevard (Addison Mizner); (8) 920 and 930 South Ocean Boulevard (Maurice Fatio); (9) Mar-a-Lago, 1100 South Ocean Boulevard (Joseph Urban); (10) Il Palmetto, 1500 South Ocean Boulevard (Maurice Fatio).

—Dorothea Hunter Sönne

The Armory Art Center in West Palm Beach helps students of all ages create works of art in various mediums.

TOP ATTRACTIONS

Ann Norton Sculpture Gardens. This landmarked complex is a testament to the creative genius of the late American sculptor Ann Weaver Norton (1905–1982), who was the second wife of Norton Museum founder, industrialist Ralph H. Norton. A set of art galleries in the studio and main house where she lived is surrounded by 2 acres of gardens with 300 species of rare palm trees, eight brick megaliths, a monumental figure in Norwegian granite, and plantings designed to attract native birds. ✉ *253 Barcelona Rd.* ☎ *561/832–5328* ⊕ *www.ansg.org* 🎫 *$10* ⏱ *Wed.–Sun. 10–4* ⏱ *Closed Aug.*

FAMILY **Lion Country Safari.** Drive your own vehicle along four miles of paved roads through a cageless zoo with free-roaming animals (chances are you'll have a giraffe nudging at your window) and then let loose in a 55-acre fun-land with camel rides, bird feedings, and a pontoon-boat cruise past islands with monkeys. A CD included with admission narrates the winding trek past white rhinos, zebras, and ostriches grouped into exhibits like Gir Forest that's modeled after a sanctuary in India and has native twisted-horned blackbuck antelope and water buffalo. (For obvious reasons, lions are fenced off, and no convertibles or pets are allowed.) ✉ *2003 Lion Country Safari Rd., at Southern Blvd.* W ☎ *561/793–1084* ⊕ *www.lioncountrysafari.com* 🎫 *$31.50, $7 parking* ⏱ *Mid-Dec.–Aug., daily 9:30–5:30 (last entry 4:30); Sept.–mid-Dec., daily 10–5 (last entry 4).*

Mounts Botanical Garden. The oldest public green space in the county is, unbelievably, across the road from the West Palm Beach airport; but the planes are the last thing you notice while walking around and relaxing amid the nearly 14 acres of exotic trees, rain-forest flora, and butterfly and water gardens. The gift shop contains a selection of rare gardening books on tropical climes. Frequent plant sales are held here, and numerous plant societies with international ties hold meetings open to the public in the auditorium. Experts in tropical edible and ornamental plants are on staff. ☒ *531 N. Military Trail* ☎ *561/233–1757* ⊕ *www.mounts.org* ☒ *$5 (suggested donation)* ⊘ *Mon.–Sat. 8:30–4, Sun. noon–4.*

Fodor's Choice **Norton Museum of Art.** Constructed in 1941 by steel magnate Ralph H.
★ Norton and his wife, Elizabeth, it has grown to become one of the most impressive museums in South Florida with an extensive collection of 19th- and 20th-century American and European paintings—including works by Picasso, Monet, Matisse, Pollock, Cassatt, and O'Keeffe—plus Chinese art, earlier European art, and photography. There is a sublime outdoor sculpture garden, a glass ceiling by Dale Chihuly, a gift shop, and a schedule of lectures, programs, and concerts for adults and children. Galleries showcase traveling exhibits, too. Art After Dark on Thursday (free with museum admission) includes live music, films, or culinary demos. ■TIP➔ **One of the city's best-kept secrets is the gourmet restaurant Fratelli Lyon in the West Courtyard of the Museum. Lunch is served Tuesday–Sunday; an à la carte dinner menu is available on Thursday evenings.** ☒ *1451 S. Olive Ave.* ☎ *561/832–5196* ⊕ *www.norton.org* ☒ *$12* ⊘ *Tues., Wed., Fri., and Sat. 10–5, Thurs. 10–9, Sun. 11–5.*

WORTH NOTING

Armory Art Center. Built by the Work Progress Administration (WPA) in 1939, this art deco facility is now a nonprofit art school hosting rotating exhibitions and art classes throughout the year. The Armory Art Center became an institution for art instruction, when the Norton Museum Gallery and School of Art dropped the latter part of its name in 1986 and discontinued art instruction classes. ☒ *1700 Parker Ave.* ☎ *561/832–1776* ⊕ *www.armoryart.org* ☒ *Free* ⊘ *Weekdays 9–4:30, Sat. 9–4.*

Richard and Pat Johnson Palm Beach County History Museum. A beautifully restored 1916 courthouse in downtown opened its doors in 2008 as the permanent home of the Historical Society of Palm Beach County's collection of artifacts and records dating back before the town's start—a highlight is furniture and decorative objects from Mizner Industries (a real treat since many of his mansions are not open to the public). ☒ *300 N. Dixie Hwy.* ☎ *561/832–4164* ⊕ *www.historicalsocietypbc. org* ☒ *Free* ⊘ *Tues.–Sat. 10–5.*

FAMILY **South Florida Science Museum.** Aside from permanent exhibits with outta-this-world finds like moon and Mars rocks and a 232-pound meteorite, there are fresh- and saltwater aquariums, daily planetarium shows, and even 9 holes of mini-golf. On the second Saturday of each month, the planetarium offers three separate laser shows (6:30, 7:30, and 8:30 pm) incorporating music from the likes of Dave Matthews, Pink Floyd, and Michael Jackson. ☒ *4801 Dreher Trail N* ☎ *561/832–1988* ⊕ *www.*

The posh Palm Beach area has its share of luxury villas on the water; many are Mediterranean in style.

sfsciencecenter.org 🎟 *$15 adults, laser show $10* 🕙 *Weekdays 9–5, weekends 10–6.*

LAKE WORTH

For years, tourists looked here mainly for inexpensive lodging and easy access to Palm Beach, since a bridge leads from the mainland to a barrier island with Lake Worth's beach. Now Lake Worth has grown into an arts community, with several blocks of restaurants, nightclubs, shops, and galleries, making this a worthy destination on its own.

Museum of Polo and Hall of Fame. Start here in Lake Worth for an introduction to polo. See memorabilia, art, and a film on the history of the sport. Then, treat yourself to a Sunday match; polo season is January– April. ✉ *9011 Lake Worth Rd.* ☎ *561/969–3210* ⊕ *www.polomuseum. com* 🎟 *Free (donations accepted)* 🕙 *Jan.–Apr., weekdays 10–4, Sat. 10–2; May–Dec., weekdays 10–4 (subject to change).*

LANTANA

Lantana—just a bit farther south from Palm Beach than Lake Worth— has inexpensive lodging and a bridge connecting the town to its own beach on a barrier island. Tucked between Lantana and Boynton Beach is **Manalapan,** a tiny but posh residential community.

BOYNTON BEACH

In 1884, when fewer than 50 settlers lived in the area, Nathan Boynton, a Civil War veteran from Michigan, paid $25 for 500 acres with a mile-long stretch of beachfront thrown in. How things have changed, with today's population at about 118,000 and property values still on an upswing. Far enough from Palm Beach to remain low-key, Boynton

Beach has two parts, the mainland and the barrier island—the town of Ocean Ridge—connected by two bridges.

FAMILY   **Arthur R. Marshall Loxahatchee National Wildlife Refuge.** The most robust part of the northern Everglades, this 221-square-mile refuge is one of two huge water-retention areas accounting for much of the 'River of Grass' outside the national park near Miami. Start at the visitor center, which has fantastic interactive exhibits and videos like Night Sounds of the Everglades and an airboat simulator. From there, you can take a marsh trail to a 20-foot-high observation tower, or stroll a ½-mile boardwalk lined with educational signage through a dense cypress swamp. There are also guided nature walks (including some specifically for bird-watching), and there's great bass fishing (bring your own poles and bait) and a 5½-mile canoe and kayak trail loop (both can be rented from a kiosk by the fishing pier). ⊠ *10216 Lee Rd., off U.S. 441 between Rte. 804 and Rte. 806* ☎ *561/734–8303* ⊕ *www. loxahatcheefriends.com* ⊠ *$5 per vehicle; $1 per pedestrian or bicyclist* ☉ *Daily 5 am–10 pm; visitor center daily 9–4.*

BEACHES

PALM BEACH

Phipps Ocean Park. About 2 miles south of "Billionaire's Row" on Ocean Boulevard sits this public oceanside park, with two metered parking lots separated by a fire station. There are four entry points to the beach, but the north side is better for beachgoers. At the southern entrance, there is a six-court tennis facility. The beach is narrow and has natural rock formations dotting the shoreline, making it ideal for snorkelers. Parking is metered, and time limits strictly enforced. There's a two-hour time limit for free parking—but read the meter carefully, it's valid only during certain hours at some spots. **Amenities:** parking (free); toilets; showers; lifeguards. **Best for:** walking; solitude. ⊠ *2201 S. Ocean Blvd.* ☎ *561/838–5400, 561/227–6450 Tennis reservations* ⊠ *Free* ☉ *Daily 8–8.*

Town of Palm Beach Municipal Beach. You know you're here if you see Palm Beach's younger generation frolicking on the sands and nonxenophobic locals setting up chairs as the sun reflects off their gleaming white veneers. The Worth Avenue clock tower is within sight, but the gateways to the sand are actually on Chilean Avenue, Brazilian Avenue, and Gulfstream Road. It's definitely the most central and longest lifeguarded strip open to everyone and a popular choice for hotel guests from the Colony, Chesterfield, and Brazilian Court. Lifeguards are present from Brazilian Avenue down to Chilean Avenue. It's also BYOC (bring your own chair). You'll find no water-sport or food vendors here; however, casual eateries are a quick walk away. Metered spots line A1A. **Amenities:** lifeguards; showers. **Best for:** swimming; sunsets. ⊠ *S. Ocean Blvd. from Brazilian Ave. to Gulfstream Rd.* ☎ *561/838–5483 Beach patrol* ☉ *Daily 8–8.*

LAKE WORTH

FAMILY **Lake Worth Beach.** This public beach bustles with beachgoers of all ages thanks to the prolific family offerings. The waterfront retail promenade—the old fashioned nongambling Lake Worth "casino"—has a Mulligan's Beach House Bar & Grill, a T-shirt store, a pizzeria, and a Kilwin's ice cream shop. The beach also has a municipal Olympic-size public swimming pool, a playground, a fishing pier—not to mention the pier's wildly popular daytime eatery, Benny's on the Beach (open for dinner weekends in season). Tideline Ocean Resort and Four Seasons guests are steps away from the action; Eau Palm Beach guests are a short bike ride away. **Amenities:** food and drink; lifeguards; parking (fee); showers; toilets; water sports. **Best for:** sunsets; swimming. ✉ *10 S. Ocean Blvd., at A1A and Lake Ave.* 🌐 *www.lakeworth.org/visitors/casino-building-and-beach-complex/* 🎫 *$1 to enter pier, $3 to enter and fish, $2 per hr for parking.*

LANTANA

Town of Lantana Public Beach. Ideal for quiet ambles, this sandy stretch is also noteworthy for a casual restaurant, the no-frills breezy Dune Deck Café, which is perched above the waterline and offers great views for an oceanfront breakfast or lunch. The beach's huge parking lot is directly adjacent to the Eau Palm Beach (meters take credit cards), and diagonally across the street is a sizeable strip mall with all sorts of conveniences, including boutiques and more eateries. Note: the beach is very narrow and large rocks loom in the water. However, these are some of the clearest waters along the Florida coastline, and they make an idyllic background for long walks and great photos. **Amenities:** food and drink; lifeguards; parking (fee); showers; toilets. **Best for:** walking. ✉ *100 E. Ocean Ave.* 🎫 *$1.50 per hr for parking.*

WHERE TO EAT

PALM BEACH

$$$$ ECLECTIC Fodor's Choice ★

🍴 **bûccan.** Lanterns cast a soft glow as young bluebloods rocking D&G jeans slip into tightly packed copper-topped tables alongside groups of silver-haired oil scions. It's island casual in its trendiest, most boisterous, yet still refined incarnation, with a menu to match. Chef-owner Clay Conley's small plates to share (wood-fired wild mushroom pizza with black truffle vinaigrette) with unfussy presentations (house-made squid-ink orecchiette stewed with sausage, conch, and chilies in a mini–Le Creuset cocotte) and inventive, sophisticated flavor combinations and textures (hamachi sashimi with yuzu and crisped lotus root (from next door's Imoto, also Conley's, connected via a hallway) make this the place to see and be seen—and the best-tasting meal at a price more expected of the mainland. The chef's sandwich shop, also on the premises just next door, draws beachgoers who want to pack a picnic lunch. [$] *Average main: $32* ✉ *350 S. County Rd.* ☎ *561/833–3450* 🌐 *www.buccanpalmbeach.com* ✍ *Reservations essential* 🕑 *No lunch.*

$$$$ FRENCH Fodor's Choice ★

🍴 **Café Boulud.** Palm Beach socialites just can't get enough of this prized restaurant by celebrated chef Daniel Boulud. This posh French-American venue in the Brazilian Court hotel is casual yet elegant, with a palette of honey, gold, and citron. Plenty of natural light spills through arched glass doors opening to a lush courtyard that's just the place to

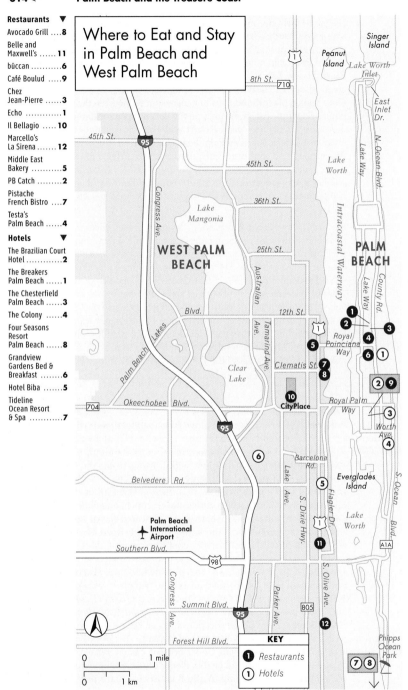

Where to Eat and Stay
in Palm Beach and
West Palm Beach

KEY

❶ Restaurants

① Hotels

be on a warm evening. Lunch and dinner entrées on the restaurant's signature four-section menu include classic French, seasonal, vegetarian, and a rotating roster of international dishes. A special Mediterranean menu is offered in summer, dubbed Boulud Sud. The lounge, with its illuminated amber glass bar, is the perfect perch to take in the jet-set crowd that comes for a hint of the south of France in South Florida. [$] *Average main: $38* ✉ *The Brazilian Court Hotel & Beach Club, 301 Australian Ave.* ☎ *561/655–6060* 🌐 *www.cafeboulud.com* ✍ *Reservations essential.*

$$$$ FRENCH 🍴 **Chez Jean-Pierre.** With walls adorned with avant-garde Dalí- and Picasso-like art, this bistro is where the Palm Beach old guard likes to let down its hair, all the while partaking of sumptuous northern French cuisine along with an impressive wine selection. Forget calorie or cholesterol concerns, and indulge in scrambled eggs with caviar or homemade foie gras, or the best-selling Dover sole. Duck lovers rave about the braised half-duck with a thyme-honey glaze. Desserts like frozen hazelnut soufflé or profiteroles au chocolat are equally impressive. Jackets are not required, although many men wear them. The main entrance is through a courtyard in the back. [$] *Average main: $39* ✉ *132 N. County Rd.* ☎ *561/833–1171* 🌐 *www.chezjean-pierre.com* ✍ *Reservations essential* 🕓 *Closed mid-July–Aug. Closed Sun. No lunch.*

$$$ ASIAN 🍴 **Echo.** Palm Beach's window on Asia has a sleek sushi bar and floor-to-ceiling glass doors separating the interior from the popular terrace dining area. Chinese, Japanese, Thai, and Vietnamese selections are neatly categorized: Wind (small plates starting your journey), Water (seafood mains), Fire (open-flame wok creations), Earth (meat dishes), and Flavor (desserts, sweets). Pick from dim sum to sashimi, pad thai to Szechuan beef, steamed sea bass to shrimp lo mein. On weekdays, come for the early shift (5–6:30 pm) for half-priced sushi and cocktails in the restaurant's Dragonfly Lounge. [$] *Average main: $30* ✉ *230-A Sunrise Ave.* ☎ *561/802–4222* 🌐 *www.echopalmbeach.com* 🕓 *Closed Mon. No lunch.*

$$$$ SEAFOOD 🍴 **PB Catch.** As the name implies, it's all about fins and shells here, including the live ones that entertain diners in their tanks in the modern dining room. The menu includes a raw bar with a good selection of raw (or grilled) oysters, clams, and the chef's "seacuterie" platter, a build-your-own sampler of such choices as salmon pastrami, citrus-cured fluke, cured seabass, or octopus torchon. Local fish—grouper, snapper, and yellowfin tuna—are best bets as entrees. Hipsters point up the craft cocktails, and the happy hour discounts include certain foods. That's a good thing since Palm Beach prices apply. [$] *Average main: $35* ✉ *251 Sunrise Blvd.* ☎ *561/655–5558* 🌐 *www.pbcatch.com* 🕓 *Closed Sun.*

$$$ AMERICAN FAMILY 🍴 **Testa's Palm Beach.** Attracting a loyal clientele since 1921, this restaurant is still owned by the Testa family. Lunches range from burgers to crab salad, and dinner specialties include snapper Florentine and jumbo lump-crab cakes. You can dine inside in an intimate pine-paneled room with cozy bar, out back in a gazebo-style room for large groups, or outside at tables that are pet-friendly. Don't miss the signature strawberry pie made with fresh Florida berries. At this writing, the restaurant was expected to close at the end of 2016 and be rebuilt.

$ *Average main: $27* ✉ *221 Royal Poinciana Way* ☎ *561/832–0992* ⊕ *www.testasrestaurants.com.*

WEST PALM BEACH

$$ ✕ **Avocado Grill.** In downtown West Palm Beach's waterfront district,
ECLECTIC this newcomer (opened 2014) is an alternative to the bar food, tacos, and burgers more common in the area. "Green" cuisine—seasonal salads, vegetarian dishes, and sustainably produced meats and seafood—is making waves at the avocado-themed restaurant. Small plates of stuffed zucchini blossoms, octopus with chorizo and fingerling potatoes, or a mushroom fricassee with grits and truffle oil are examples of plates designed for sharing. A raw bar, specialty sushi, a vegetarian list, and inspired sandwiches are included among the pastas, salads, meats, and fish also listed. A brunch here with an extensive menu is very popular. Craft cocktails, a nice wine selection, and beers are served at the long bar in the bistrolike eatery with casual-chic decor. Dine inside or out. $ *Average main: $19* ✉ *125 Datura St.* ☎ *561/623–0822* ⊕ *www. avocadogrillwpb.com* ⌂ *Reservations essential.*

$$ ✕ **Belle and Maxwell's.** Palm Beach ladies who lunch leave the island for
AMERICAN an afternoon at Belle and Maxwell's, while young professionals loosen up after work at the wine bar, part of the bistro's recently expanded dining area. Tucked along Antique Row, it looks like a storybook tea party at lunch, with eclectic furnishings and decor. Expect colorful luncheonette dresses and great soups, salads, and sandwiches at affordable prices mid-day; at night, it becomes a fun, twinkling bistro setting, offering creative comfort fare such as house-made orecchiette with squid and sausage, and classic chicken marsala, along with filets, and a risotto of the day. The large appetizer list and many dishes offered in half-portions make it a fun stop for those who like several nibbles. The garden is romantic—and a choice spot for a slice of cake and espresso. Dessert lovers know the sweets are all made in-house; call ahead to get whole cakes, pies, and tarts to take to grateful hosts. $ *Average main: $18* ✉ *3700 S. Dixie Hwy.* ☎ *561/832–4449* ⊕ *www.belleandmaxwells. net* ⊗ *Closed Sun. No dinner Mon.*

$$$ ✕ **Il Bellagio.** In the heart of CityPlace, this European-style eatery offers
ITALIAN Italian specialties and a wide variety of fine wines. The menu includes
FAMILY classics like chicken parmigiana, risotto, and fettuccine alfredo. Pizzas from the wood-burning oven are especially good. Service is friendly and efficient, but the overall noise level tends to be high. Sit at the outdoor tables next to the main plaza's dancing fountains if you can. $ *Average main: $23* ✉ *CityPlace, 600 S. Rosemary Ave.* ☎ *561/659–6160* ⊕ *www.ilbellagiocityplace.com.*

$$$$ ✕ **Marcello's La Sirena.** A longtime favorite of locals, this sophisticated
ITALIAN Italian restaurant is in an unexpected, nondescript location on Dixie Highway away from downtown and central hubs. But warm hospitality from a husband-and-wife team, along with smart service and delectable dishes await. Portraits of the chef's parents overlook the relaxed, formal dining room set with linens starched like the chef's jacket. A stellar wine list, including a popular "50 under $50" draws from international vineyards and complements the traditional foods: *pepperoni e acciughe* (oven-roasted peppers with white anchovies, extra virgin

olive oil), rigatoni ala vodka (said to be invented by the chef's father); veal chops, and scaloppini prepared several ways. Desserts alone are worth an after-dinner stop. $ *Average main: $31* ⊠ *6316 S. Dixie Hwy.* ☎ *561/585–3128* ⊕ *www.lasirenaonline.com* ⌦ *Reservations essential* ⊘ *Closed Sun.*

$ ✕ **Middle East Bakery.** This hole-in-the-wall Middle Eastern bakery, deli,
MIDDLE EASTERN and market is packed at lunchtime with regulars who are on a first-name
Fodor's Choice basis with the gang behind the counter. From the nondescript parking
★ lot the place doesn't look like much, but inside, delicious hot and cold Mediterranean treats await. Choose from traditional gyro sandwiches and lamb salads with sides of grape leaves, tabbouleh, and couscous. There's a big take-out business, as seating is limited, and it closes shop at 6 pm (4:30 pm on Saturday). $ *Average main: $10* ⊠ *327 5th St.* ☎ *561/659–7322* ⊘ *Closed Sun.*

$$$ ✕ **Pistache French Bistro.** Although "the island" is no doubt a bastion of
FRENCH French cuisine, this cozy bistro across the bridge on the Clematis Street waterfront entices a lively crowd looking for a good meal with pretention checked at the door. The outdoor terrace can't be beat, and the fabulous modern French menu such as roasted sliced duck with truffled polenta rather than the ubiquitous *à l'orange*, are a delight. Save room for dessert: the house-made pudding Breton, a fluffy, raisin-accented brioche bread pudding paired with Crème Anglaise, could be straight out of a Parisian café. $ *Average main: $27* ⊠ *101 N. Clematis St.* ☎ *561/833–5090* ⊕ *www.pistachewpb.com.*

LAKE WORTH

$ ✕ **Benny's on the Beach.** Perched on the Lake Worth Pier, Benny's has a
AMERICAN walk-up bar, a take-out window, and a full-service beach-themed restaurant serving casual fare with a twist: "Beach Bread" is a take on a waffle sandwich; the fresh seafood is from Florida waters. All are served up at bargain prices. Eat-in diners come here for long afternoons of beer and cocktails, enjoying prolific alfresco seating and a spectacular view of the sun glistening on the water and the waves crashing directly below. There's no free parking here, just meters. ■ TIP➔ **Though officially open for just breakfast and lunch, on weekends Benny's usually serves until sunset all year and serves dinner during the season.** $ *Average main: $12* ⊠ *Lake Worth Beach, 10 S. Ocean Blvd.* ☎ *561/582–9001* ⊕ *www. bennysonthebeach.com* ⊘ *No dinner.*

LANTANA

$$ ✕ **Old Key Lime House.** An informal seafood spot—serving crab cakes,
SEAFOOD fish sandwiches, and fillets—is covered by a chickee-hut roof built by Seminole Indians, it's perched on the Intracoastal Waterway and is open and airy. Observation decks with separate bars wrap around the back. In 1889, the Lyman family, some of the earliest settlers in Lantana, built this as their house, and it has grown over the years into the popular island-style eatery it is today. Kids love feeding the fish below, but families should dine inside. Live music is on the deck most nights, where you can arrive by boat. Of course, order the namesake key lime pie—the house specialty has been featured in *Bon Appétit*. $ *Average main: $20* ⊠ *300 E. Ocean Ave.* ☎ *561/582–1889* ⊕ *www.oldkeylimehouse.com.*

6

$$ PIZZA 🍴 **Pizzeria Oceano.** Take cash and your patience along if you're going for what some call the best pizza in the county. It's made in a tiny, old, nondescript house where the chef puts together fresh pies one by one. The small menu changes daily, depending on what's on the farm truck that day. Maybe it's mozzarella (made in-house) and tomatoes. Or cheese and spinach. Or sopressatta and smoked buffalo mozzarella. There are only six stools at the counter indoors by the oven, so expect a wait for one of the outdoor deck tables, especially on weekends and in season. Wait your turn with a craft brew or glass of vino, order one of the daily salads to tide you over until your pie arrives, and follow the rules: no credit cards, no substitutions, no takeout, no perfume. And don't even think about rushing the chef. Really good food takes time. [$] *Average main: $16* ✉ *210 E. Ocean Ave.* ☎ *561/429–5550* 🌐 *www.pizzeriaoceano.com* ✍ *Reservations not accepted* 💳 *No credit cards* ⏲ *Closed Sun.*

WHERE TO STAY

PALM BEACH

$$$$ HOTEL Fodor's Choice ★ 🏨 **The Brazilian Court Hotel.** This posh boutique hotel, stomping ground of Florida's well-heeled, is full of historic touches and creature comforts—from its yellow facade with dramatic white-draped entry, to modern draws like the renowned spa and Daniel Boulud restaurant. **Pros:** stylish and hip local crowd; charming courtyard; free beach shuttle; award-winning restaurant; plush spa. **Cons:** small fitness center; nondescript pool; 10-minute ride to ocean and suggested 24-hour advance reservation for shuttle. [$] *Rooms from: $409* ✉ *301 Australian Ave.* ☎ *561/655–7740* 🌐 *www.thebraziliancourt.com* 🛏 *80 rooms* 🍽 *No meals.*

$$$$ RESORT FAMILY Fodor's Choice ★ 🏨 **The Breakers Palm Beach.** More than an opulent hotel, The Breakers is a legendary 140-acre self-contained jewel of a resort built in a Mediterranean style and loaded with amenities, from a 20,000-square-foot luxury spa and grandiose beach club to 10 tennis courts and two 18-hole golf courses—not to mention Henry Flagler's descendants still run the place and invest $25 million a year to keep it at the cutting edge. **Pros:** impeccable attention to detail; fantastic service; beautiful room views; extensive activities for families. **Cons:** big price tag; short drive to reach off-property attractions. [$] *Rooms from: $649* ✉ *1 S. County Rd.* ☎ *561/655–6611, 888/273–2537* 🌐 *www.thebreakers.com* 🛏 *540 rooms* 🍽 *No meals.*

$$$ HOTEL 🏨 **The Chesterfield Palm Beach.** A distinctly upper-crust northern European feel pervades the peach stucco walls and elegant rooms here; the hotel sits just north of the western end of Worth Avenue, and high tea, a cigar parlor, and daily turndown service recall a bygone, more refined era. **Pros:** gracious, attentive staff; Leopard Lounge entertainment; free valet parking. **Cons:** long walk to beach; only one elevator; to some, can come off as a bit stuffy. [$] *Rooms from: $375* ✉ *363 Cocoanut Row* ☎ *561/659–5800, 800/243–7871* 🌐 *www.chesterfieldpb.com* 🛏 *41 rooms, 11 suites* 🍽 *No meals.*

$$$$ HOTEL **The Colony.** In 2014, nearly $10 million was spent to redecorate and refurbish every room at the island's legendary British colonial-style hotel. **Pros:** unbeatable location; famous polo bar; pillow-top mattresses; full English breakfast included. **Cons:** lobby is small; elevators are tight. [$] *Rooms from: $500* ✉ *155 Hammon Ave.* ☎ *561/655–5430, 800/521–5525* 🌐 *www.thecolonypalmbeach.com* 🛏 *83 rooms, 7 villas* 🍴 *Breakfast.*

$$$$ RESORT FAMILY Fodor's Choice ★ **Four Seasons Resort Palm Beach.** Couples and families seeking relaxed seaside elegance in a ritzy, yet understated, setting will love this manicured 6-acre oceanfront escape at the south end of Palm Beach, with serene, bright, airy rooms in a cream-color palette and spacious marble-lined baths. **Pros:** accommodating service; all rooms have balconies; outstanding complimentary kids' program. **Cons:** 10-minute drive to downtown Palm Beach (but can walk to Lake Worth); pricey. [$] *Rooms from: $499* ✉ *2800 S. Ocean Blvd.* ☎ *561/582–2800, 800/432–2335* 🌐 *www.fourseasons.com/palmbeach* 🛏 *210 rooms* 🍴 *No meals.*

$$$$ RESORT **Tideline Ocean Resort & Spa.** The former Omphoy is now affiliated with the Kimpton boutique resort company, putting it in new hands, but the Zen-like boutique hotel has retained its loyal following of young, hip travelers. **Pros:** most rooms have beautiful views of the private beach; ultra-contemporary vibe; luxury setting. **Cons:** a hike from shopping and nightlife; the infinity pool is across the driveway. [$] *Rooms from: $459* ✉ *2842 S. Ocean Blvd.* ☎ *561/540–6440, 888/344–4321* 🌐 *www.tidelineresort.com* 🛏 *144 rooms* 🍴 *No meals.*

WEST PALM BEACH

$$ B&B/INN **Grandview Gardens Bed & Breakfast.** Defining the Florida B&B experience, this 1925 Mediterranean Revival home overlooks a serene courtyard pool and oozes charm and personality, while the owners provide heavy doses of bespoke service. **Pros:** multilingual owners; outside private entrances to rooms; free bicycle use; innkeepers offer historic city tours. **Cons:** not close to the beach; in a residential area; rental car needed. [$] *Rooms from: $219* ✉ *1608 Lake Ave.* ☎ *561/833–9023* 🌐 *www.grandview-gardens.com* 🛏 *5 rooms, 2 cottages* 🍴 *Breakfast.*

$ HOTEL **Hotel Biba.** In the El Cid historic district, this 1940s-era motel has gotten a fun stylish revamp from designer Barbara Hulanicki: each room has a vibrant mélange of colors, along with handcrafted mirrors, mosaic bathroom floors, and custom mahogany furnishings. **Pros:** cool, punchy design and luxe fixtures; popular wine bar; free continental breakfast with Cuban pastries. **Cons:** water pressure is weak; bathrooms are tiny; noisy when the bar is open late and trains run nearby; not all rooms have central a/c. [$] *Rooms from: $129* ✉ *320 Belvedere Rd.* ☎ *561/832–0094* 🌐 *www.hotelbiba.com* 🛏 *43 rooms* 🍴 *Breakfast.*

LAKE WORTH

$ B&B/INN **Sabal Palm House.** Built in 1936, this romantic, two-story B&B is a short walk from Lake Worth's downtown shops, eateries, and the Intracoastal Waterway, and each room is decorated with antiques and inspired by a different artist, including Renoir, Dalí, Norman Rockwell, and Chagall. **Pros:** on quiet street; hands-on owners; chairs and totes with towels provided for use at nearby beach. **Cons:** no pool; peak times require a two-night minimum stay; no parking lot. $ *Rooms from:* $179 ⊠ *109 N. Golfview Rd.* ☎ *561/582–1090, 888/722–2572* ⊕ *www. sabalpalmhouse.com* ⤳ *5 rooms, 2 suites* ⭙ *Breakfast.*

SOUTH PALM BEACH AND MANALAPAN

$$$$
RESORT
FAMILY
Fodor'sChoice
★

🏠 **Eau Palm Beach.** In the coastal town of Manalapan (just south of Palm Beach), this sublime, glamorous destination resort (formerly the Ritz-Carlton) showcases a newer, younger face of luxury, including a 3,000-square-foot oceanfront terrace, two sleek pools, a huge fitness center, and a deluxe spa. **Pros:** magnificent aesthetic details throughout; indulgent pampering services; excellent on-site dining; kids love the cool cyber-lounge just for them. **Cons:** golf course is off property; 15-minute drive to Palm Beach. $ *Rooms from: $499* ⊠ *100 S. Ocean Blvd., Manalapan* ☎ *561/533–6000, 800/241–3333* ⊕ *www.eaupalmbeach. com* ⤳ *309 rooms* ⭙ *No meals.*

NIGHTLIFE AND PERFORMING ARTS

PALM BEACH

NIGHTLIFE

Palm Beach is teeming with restaurants that turn into late-night hot spots, plus hotel lobby bars perfect for tête-à-têtes.

Fodor'sChoice
★

bûccan. A hip Hamptons-esque scene with society darlings crowds the lounge, throwing back killer cocktails like the Basil Rathbone (gin, orange juice, mint, basil, strawberry) and Buccan T (vodka, black tea, cranberry, citrus, basil, and agave nectar). ⊠ *350 S. County Rd.* ☎ *561/833–3450* ⊕ *www.buccanpalmbeach.com.*

Cucina Dell' Arte. Though this spot is popular for lunch and dinner, it's even more popular later in the night. The younger, trendier set comes late to party, mingle, and dance into the wee hours. ⊠ *257 Royal Poinciana Way* ☎ *561/655–0770* ⊕ *www.cucinadellarte.com/palmbeach.*

The Leopard Lounge. In the Chesterfield hotel, this enclave feels like an exclusive club. The trademark ceiling and spotted floors of the renovated lounge are a nod to this hotel's historic roots, but the rest of the decor is new age Palm Beach glam. Though it starts each evening as a restaurant, as the night progresses the Leopard is transformed into an old-fashioned club with live music for Palm Beach's old guard. The bartenders know how to pour a cocktail here. ⊠ *The Chesterfield Palm Beach, 363 Cocoanut Row* ☎ *561/659–5800* ⊕ *www.chesterfieldpb. com.*

WEST PALM BEACH

NIGHTLIFE

West Palm is known for its exuberant nightlife—Clematis Street and CityPlace are the prime party destinations. In fact, downtown rocks every Thursday from 6 pm on with Clematis by Night (⊕ *www.wpb. org/clematis-by-night*), a celebration of music, dance, art, and food at Centennial Square.

Blue Martini. The CityPlace outpost of this South Florida hot spot for thirty, forty, and fiftysomething adults gone wild has a menu filled with tons of innovative martini creations (42 to be exact), tasty tapas, and lots of cougars on the prowl, searching for a first, second, or even third husband. And the guys aren't complaining! The drinks are great and the scene is fun for everyone, even those who aren't single and looking to mingle. Expect DJs some nights, live music others. ⊠ *CityPlace, 550 S. Rosemary Ave., #244* ☎ *561/835–8601* ⊕ *www.bluemartinilounge. com.*

ER Bradley's Saloon. People of all ages congregate to hang out and socialize at this kitschy open-air restaurant and bar to gaze at the Intracoastal Waterway; the mechanical bull is a hit on Saturdays. Live music's on tap five to seven nights a week. ⊠ *104 Clematis St.* ☎ *561/833–3520* ⊕ *www.erbradleys.com.*

Fodor's Choice ★ **Rocco's Tacos and Tequila Bar.** In the last few years, Rocco's has taken root in numerous South Florida downtowns and become synonymous with wild nights of chips 'n' guac, margaritas, and intoxicating fun. This is more of a scene than just a restaurant, and when Rocco's in the house and pouring shots, get ready to party hearty. There's another branch at 5250 Town Center Circle in Boca Raton, and one in Palm Beach Gardens in PGA Commons at 5090 PGA Boulevard. ⊠ *224 Clematis St.* ☎ *561/650–1001* ⊕ *www.roccostacos.com.*

PERFORMING ARTS

Palm Beach Dramaworks *(pbd)*. Housed in an intimate venue with only 218 seats in downtown West Palm Beach, their modus operandi is "theater to think about" with plays by Pulitzer Prize-winners on rotation. ⊠ *201 Clematis St.* ☎ *561/514–4042* ⊕ *www.palmbeachdramaworks. org.*

Fodor's Choice ★ **Raymond F. Kravis Center for the Performing Arts.** This is the crown jewel amid a treasury of local arts attractions, and its marquee star is the 2,195-seat Dreyfoos Hall, a glass, copper, and marble showcase just steps from the restaurants and shops of CityPlace. The center also boasts the 289-seat Rinker Playhouse, 170-seat Persson Hall, and the Gosman Amphitheatre, which holds 1,400 total in seats and on the lawn. A packed year-round schedule features a blockbuster lineup of Broadway's biggest touring productions, concerts, dance, dramas, and musicals; the Miami City Ballet, Palm Beach Opera, and the Palm Beach Pops perform here. ⊠ *701 Okeechobee Blvd.* ☎ *561/832–7469 box office* ⊕ *www.kravis.org.*

SHOPPING

As is the case throughout South Florida, many of the smaller boutiques in Palm Beach close in the summer, and most stores are closed on Sunday. Consignment stores in Palm Beach are definitely worth a look; you'll often find high-end designer clothing in impeccable condition.

PALM BEACH

SHOPPING AREAS

Royal Poinciana Way. Cute shops dot the north side of Royal Poinciana Way between Bradley Place and North County Road. Wind through the courtyards past upscale consignment stores to Sunset Avenue, then stroll down Sunrise Avenue: this is the place for specialty items like out-of-town newspapers, health foods, and rare books. ⊠ *Worth Ave., between Bradley Pl. and N. County Rd.*

Fodor'sChoice ★ **Worth Avenue.** One of the world's premier showcases for high-quality shopping runs half a mile from east to west across Palm Beach, from the beach to Lake Worth. The street has more than 200 shops (more than 40 of them sell jewelry), and many upscale chain stores (Gucci, Hermès, Pucci, Saks Fifth Avenue, Neiman Marcus, Louis Vuitton, Chanel, Cartier, Tiffany & Co., and Tourneau) are represented—their merchandise appealing to the discerning tastes of the Palm Beach clientele. Don't miss walking around the vias, little courtyards lined with smaller boutiques; historic tours are available each month during "season" from the Worth Avenue Association. ■TIP➔ **For those looking to go a little lighter on the pocket book, just north of Worth Avenue, the six blocks of South County Road have interesting and somewhat less expensive stores.** ⊠ *Worth Ave., between Cocoanut Row and S. Ocean Blvd.* ⊕ *www.worth-avenue.com.*

WEST PALM BEACH
SHOPPING AREAS

Fodor'sChoice ★ **Antique Row.** West Palm's U.S. 1, "South Dixie Highway," is the destination for those who are interested in interesting home decor. From thrift shops to the most exclusive stores, it is all here within 40 stores—museum-quality furniture, lighting, art, junk, fabric, frames, tile, and rugs. So if you're looking for an art deco, French-provincial, or Mizner pièce de résistance, big or small, schedule a few hours for an Antique Row stroll. You'll find bargains during the off-season (May to November). Antique Row runs north–south from Belvedere Road to Forest Hill Boulevard, although most stores are bunched between Belvedere Road and Southern Boulevard. ⊠ *U.S. 1, between Belvedere Rd. and Forest Hill Blvd.* ⊕ *www.westpalmbeachantiques.com.*

CityPlace. The 72-acre, four-block-by-four-block commercial and residential complex centered on Rosemary Avenue attracts people of all ages to with restaurants like Italian-inspired Il Bellagio, bars like Blue Martini, a 20-screen Muvico and IMAX, the Harriet Himmel Theater, and a 36,000-gallon water fountain and light show. The dining, shopping, and entertainment are all family-friendly; at night a lively crowd likes to hit the outdoor bars. Among CityPlace's stores are such popular national retailers as Macy's, H & M, Banana Republic, and Restoration Hardware. There are also shops unique to Florida: Behind the punchy, brightly colored clothing in the front window of **C. Orrico** (☎ 561/832–9203) are family fashions and accessories by Lily Pulitzer—the originals. ⊠ *700 S. Rosemary Ave.* ☎ *561/366–1000* ⊕ *www. cityplace.com.*

FAMILY **Clematis Street.** If lunching is just as important as window-shopping, the renewed downtown West Palm around Clematis Street that runs west to east from South Rosemary Avenue to Flagler Drive is the spot for you. Centennial Park by the waterfront has an attractive design—and fountains where kids can cool off—which adds to the pleasure of browsing and resting at one of the many outdoor cafés. Hip national retailers such as Design Within Reach (⊕ *www.dwr.com*) mix with local boutiques like third-generation Pioneer Linens, and both blend in with restaurants and bars. ⊠ *Clematis St., between S. Rosemary Ave. and Flagler Dr.* ⊕ *www.westpalmbeach.com/clematis.*

Palm Beach Outlets. An outlet mall worthy of Palm Beach finally opened in 2014. In West Palm Beach it features more than 130 retailers, with big names among the usual suspects. Off Fifth (Saks Fifth Avenue's store), Giorgio's of Palm Beach (its original is on Worth Avenue), Nordstrom's Rack, White House ⏐ Black Market, Brooks Brothers, DKNY, and Malo are interspersed with stores selling discounted home decor, sports gear, kids fashions, and more. The mall has several restaurants as well as coffee shops and a food court. And it continues to expand, so check the website for an updated list of shops. ■TIP➔ The wine bar in Whole Foods Market is the "see and be seen" scene at this outdoor mall. ⊠ *1751 Palm Beach Lakes Blvd.* ☎ *561/515–4400* ⊕ *www. palmbeachoutlets.com.*

SPORTS AND THE OUTDOORS

PALM BEACH

Palm Beach Island has two good golf courses—the Breakers and the Palm Beach Par 3 Golf Course, but only the latter is open to the public. Not to worry, there are more on the mainland, as well as myriad other outdoor sports opportunities.

BIKING

Bicycling is a great way to get a closer look at Palm Beach. Only 14 miles long, half a mile wide, flat as the top of a billiard table, and just as green, it's a perfect biking place.

Fodor's Choice ★ **Palm Beach Bicycle Trail Shop.** Open daily year-round, the shop rents bikes by the hour or day, and it's about a block from the north Lake Trail entrance. The shop has maps to help you navigate your way around the island, or you can download the main map from the shop's website. They are experts on the nearby, palm-fringed, 4-mile Lake Trail. ⊠ *223 Sunrise Ave.* ☎ *561/659–4583* ⊕ *www.palmbeachbicycle.com.*

GOLF

Fodor's Choice ★ **Palm Beach Par 3 Golf Course.** This course has been named the best par-3 golf course in the United States by *Golf Digest* magazine. The 18-hole course—originally designed by Dick Wilson and Joe Lee in 1961—was redesigned in 2009 by Hall of Famer Raymond Floyd. The par-3 course includes six holes directly on the Atlantic Ocean, with some holes over 200 yards. The grounds are exquisitely landscaped, as one would expect in Palm Beach. A lavish clubhouse houses Al Fresco, an Italian restaurant. A cart is an extra $15, but walking is encouraged. Summer rates are greatly discounted. ⊠ *2345 S. Ocean Blvd.* ☎ *561/547–0598* ⊕ *www.golfontheocean.com* ✎ *$40 for 18 holes* 🏌 *18 holes, 2458 yards, par 58.*

Worth Avenue is the place in Palm Beach for high-end shopping, from international boutiques to independent jewelers.

WEST PALM BEACH
POLO

International Polo Club Palm Beach. Attend matches and rub elbows with celebrities who make the pilgrimage out to Palm Beach polo country (the western suburb of Wellington) during the January-through-April season. The competition is not just among polo players. High society dresses in their best polo couture week after week, each outfit more fabulous than the next; they tailgate out of their Bentleys and Rolls. An annual highlight at the polo club is the U.S. Open Polo Championship at the end of season. ■TIP→ One of the best ways to experience the polo scene is by enjoying a gourmet brunch on the veranda of the International Polo Club Pavilion; it'll cost you $100–$120 per person depending on the month, but it's well worth it. ✉ 3667 120th Ave. S ☎ 561/204–5687 ⊕ www.internationalpoloclub.com.

LAKE WORTH
GOLF

Palm Beach National Golf and Country Club. Despite the name, this classic 18-hole course resides in Lake Worth, not in Palm Beach. It is, however, in Palm Beach County and prides itself on being "the most fun and friendly golf course" in Palm Beach County. The championship layout was designed by Joe Lee in the 1970s and is famous for its 3rd and 18th holes. The 3rd: a par-3 island hole with a sand bunker. The 18th: a short par-4 of 358 yards sandwiched between a wildlife preserve and water. Due to the challenging nature of the course, it's more popular with seasoned golfers. The Steve Haggerty Golf Academy is also based here. Summer rates are significantly discounted. ✉ 7500 St. Andrews

Rd. ☎ 561/965–0044 ⊕ www.palmbeachnational.com ✍ $89 for 18 holes ⚑ 18 holes, 6734 yards, par 72.

DELRAY BEACH

15 miles south of West Palm Beach.

A onetime artists' retreat with a small settlement of Japanese farmers, Delray has grown into a sophisticated beach town. Delray's current popularity is caused in large part by the fact that it has the feel of an organic city rather than a planned development or subdivision—and it's completely walkable. Atlantic Avenue, which fell from a tony downtown to a dilapidated main drag, has been reinvented into a mile-plus-long stretch of palm-dotted sidewalks lined with stores, art galleries, and restaurants. Running east–west and ending at the beach, it's a happening place for a stroll, day or night. Another active pedestrian area, the Pineapple Grove Arts District, begins at Atlantic and stretches northward on Northeast 2nd Avenue about half a mile, and yet another active pedestrian way begins at the eastern edge of Atlantic Avenue and runs along the big, broad swimming beach that extends north to George Bush Boulevard and south to Casuarina Road. Renovations and buildings in progress in adjoining areas both south and north of the Avenue will offer more shops and restaurants, as well as condos.

GETTING HERE AND AROUND

To reach Delray Beach from Boynton Beach, drive 2 miles south on I–95, U.S. 1, or Route A1A.

ESSENTIALS

VISITOR INFORMATION

Contacts **Palm Beach County Convention and Visitors Bureau** ✉ *1555 Palm Beach Lakes Blvd., Suite 800, West Palm Beach* ☎ *561/233–3000* ⊕ *www. palmbeachfl.com.*

EXPLORING

Colony Hotel. The chief landmark along Atlantic Avenue since 1926 is this sunny Mediterranean revival–style building, which is a member of the National Trust's Historic Hotels of America. Walk through the lobby to the parking lot where original garages still stand—relics of the days when hotel guests would arrive via chauffeured cars and stay there the whole season. ✉ *525 E. Atlantic Ave.* ☎ *561/276–4123* ⊕ *www.thecolonyhotel.com.*

FAMILY **Delray Beach Center for the Arts at Old School Square.** Instrumental in the revitalization of Delray Beach circa 1995, this cluster of galleries and event spaces were established in restored school buildings dating from 1913 and 1925. The **Cornell Museum of Art & American Culture** offers ever-changing exhibits on fine arts, crafts, and pop culture, plus a hands-on children's gallery. From November to April, the 323-seat **Crest Theatre** showcases national-touring Broadway musicals, cabaret concerts, dance performances, and lectures. The area is being renovated at this writing. ✉ *51 N. Swinton Ave.* ☎ *561/243–7922* ⊕ *www.oldschool.org* ✍ *$10 for museum* ☉ *Museum Tues.–Sat. 10:30–4:30, Sun. 1–4:30.*

Morikami Museum and Japanese Gardens gives a taste of the Orient through its exhibits and tea ceremonies.

FAMILY

Fodor's Choice

★

Morikami Museum and Japanese Gardens. The boonies west of Delray Beach seems an odd place to encounter one of the region's most important cultural centers, but this is exactly where you can find a 200-acre cultural and recreational facility heralding the Yamato Colony of Japanese farmers that settled here in the early 20th century. A permanent exhibit details their history, and all together the museum's collection has more than 7,000 artifacts and works of art on rotating display. Traditional tea ceremonies are conducted monthly from October to June, along with educational classes on topics like calligraphy and sushi-making (these require advance registration and come with a fee). The six main gardens are inspired by famous historic periods in Japanese garden design and have South Florida accents (think tropical bonsai), and the on-site Cornell Café serves light Asian fare at affordable prices and was recognized by the Food Network as being one of the country's best museum eateries. ⊠ *4000 Morikami Park Rd.* ☎ *561/495–0233* ⊕ *www.morikami.org* ☑ *$15* ☯ *Tues.–Sun. 10–5.*

BEACHES

Fodor's Choice

★

Delray Municipal Beach. If you're looking for a place to see and be seen, head for this wide expanse of sand, the heart of which is where Atlantic Avenue meets A1A, close to restaurants, bars, and quick-serve eateries. Singles, families, and water sports enthusiasts alike love it here. Lounge chairs and umbrellas can be rented every day, and lifeguards man stations half a mile out in each direction. The most popular section of beach is south of Atlantic Ave. on A1A, where the street parking is found. There are also two metered lots with restrooms across from A1A at Sandoway Park and Anchor Park (bring quarters if parking here!). On the beach by Anchor Park, north of Casuarina Rd., are six volleyball nets and a kiosk that offers Hobie Wave rentals, surfing lessons, and snorkeling excursions to the 1903 SS *Inchulva* shipwreck half a mile offshore. The beach itself is open 24 hours, if you're at a nearby hotel and fancy a moonlight stroll. **Amenities:** water sports; food and drink; lifeguards; parking (fee); toilets; showers. **Best for:** windsurfing; partiers; swimming. ⊠ *Rte. A1A and E. Atlantic Ave.* 🚗 *$1.50 per 1 hr parking* ⊙ *Daily 24 hrs.*

WHERE TO EAT

$$ ✕ **Blue Anchor.** Yes, this pub was actually shipped from England, where
BRITISH it had stood for 150 years in London's historic Chancery Lane. There it was a watering hole for famed Englishmen, including Winston Churchill; here you may hear stories of lingering ghosts told over some suds. Chow down on a ploughman's lunch (a chunk of Stilton cheese, a piece of bread, English pork pie, and pickled onions), fish-and-chips, and bangers and mash (sausages with mashed potatoes). This is a pub's pub—nothing fancy, very hearty. English beers and ales are on tap and by the bottle. It's also a late-night place and has live music on weekends. $ *Average main: $18* ⊠ *804 E. Atlantic Ave.* ☎ *561/272–7272* ⊕ *www.theblueanchor.com.*

$$$ ✕ **City Oyster & Sushi Bar.** This trendy restaurant mingles the personali-
SEAFOOD ties and flavors of a New England oyster bar, a modern sushi eatery,
Fodor's Choice an eclectic seafood grill, and an award-winning dessert bakery to cre-
★ ate a can't-miss foodie haven in the heart of Delray's bustling Atlantic Avenue. Dishes like the oyster bisque, New Orleans–style shrimp and crab gumbo, tuna crudo, and lobster fried rice are simply sublime. The restaurant's colossal bakery adds an unexpected element of carb bliss with a full roster of house-made breads and desserts, including seasonal pies and an insanely divine pecan pie in a glass. Pastas, too, are made in-house. On the downside, the place can be so busy and noisy that you can't hear your dining companions, especially in high season. $ *Average main: $26* ⊠ *213 E. Atlantic Ave.* ☎ *561/272–0220* ⊕ *www. cityoysterdelray.com.*

$$$ ✕ **Max's Harvest.** A few blocks off Atlantic Avenue in the artsy Pine-
MODERN apple Grove neighborhood, a tree-shaded, fenced-in courtyard wel-
AMERICAN comes foodies eager to dig into its "farm-to-fork" offerings. The menu
Fodor's Choice encourages people to experiment with "to share," "start small," and
★ "think big" plates. An ideal sampling: organic deviled eggs with chives and truffle sea salt; tequila-cured salmon; ricotta gnocchi, boiled then sautéed with porcini mushrooms and truffle tremor (goat cheese with truffles); and a pork chop over mustard spaetzle. Sunday brunch is wildly popular and includes an unlimited interactive Bloody Mary bar and champagne cocktails. $ *Average main: $27* ⊠ *169 N.E. 2nd Ave.* ☎ *561/381–9970* ⊕ *www.maxsharvest.com* ⊙ *No lunch Mon.–Sat.*

$$$ ✕ **The Office.** Scenesters line the massive indoor-outdoor bar from noon
AMERICAN 'til the wee hours at this cooler-than-thou retro library restaurant, but
Fodor's Choice it's worth your time to stop here for the best burger in town. There's a
★ whole selection, but the Prime CEO steals the show: Maytag bleu cheese and Gruyere with tomato-onion confit, arugula, and bacon. It's so juicy,

6

you'll quickly forget the mess you're making. Other upscale renditions of comforting classics like nachos (a delicate puff of whipped crab per chip served with jicama slaw), fried green tomatoes (panko-and-cornmeal crusted with crisped bits of Serrano ham), and "naughty" alcoholic shakes are worth every indulgent calorie. $ *Average main: $24* ✉ *201 E. Atlantic Ave.* ☎ *561/276–3600* ⊕ *www.theofficedelray.com.*

$$$$
AMERICAN
Fodor'sChoice
★

✕ **32 East.** Although restaurants come and go every year on Atlantic Avenue, 32 East remains one of the best—if not the best—in Delray Beach. An ever-changing daily menu defines modern American cuisine. Depending on what is fresh and plentiful, you might indulge in oak-fired organic dates and pears wrapped in bacon or perfectly prepared cumin-chile spiced cobia over black bean-tomato salad. Medium-tone wood accents and dim lighting make this brasserie seem cozy. There's a packed bar in front, an open kitchen in back, and patio seating on the sidewalk. ■TIP➔ **If you splurge on one dinner in Delray, make it 32 East.** $ *Average main: $36* ✉ *32 E. Atlantic Ave.* ☎ *561/276–7868* ⊕ *www.32east.com* ⌂ *Reservations essential* ☾ *No lunch.*

WHERE TO STAY

$$
HOTEL

🏨 **Colony Hotel & Cabaña Club.** Not to be confused with the luxurious Colony in Palm Beach, this charming hotel in the heart of downtown Delray dates back to 1926; and although it's landlocked, it does have a cabana club 2 miles away for hotel guests only. **Pros:** pet-friendly; full breakfast buffet included with rooms; free use of cabanas, umbrellas, and hammocks. **Cons:** no pool at main hotel building; must walk to public beach for water sport rentals. $ *Rooms from: $219* ✉ *525 E. Atlantic Ave.* ☎ *561/276–4123, 800/552–2363* ⊕ *www.thecolonyhotel. com* ⇱ *48 rooms, 22 suites* ⧉ *Breakfast.*

$$$
HOTEL

🏨 **Crane's Beach House Boutique Hotel & Luxury Villas.** A tropical oasis, this boutique hotel last renovated in 2014 is a hidden jungle of lush exotic and tropical plants, only a block from the beach. **Pros:** private location within the city setting; short walk to the beach; free parking; property is smoke-free. **Cons:** pricey; no restaurants on-site; no fitness or spa facilities. $ *Rooms from: $329* ✉ *82 Gleason St.* ☎ *866/372–7263, 561/278–1700* ⊕ *www.cranesbeachhouse.com* ⇱ *28 rooms: 4 villas* ⧉ *No meals.*

$$$$
HOTEL
FAMILY

🏨 **Delray Beach Marriott.** By far the largest hotel in Delray Beach, the Marriott has two towers on a stellar plot of land at the east end of Atlantic Avenue—it's the only hotel that directly overlooks the water, yet it is still within walking distance of restaurants, shopping, and nightlife. **Pros:** fantastic ocean views; pampering spa; two pools. **Cons:** chain-hotel feel; charge for parking; must rent beach chairs. $ *Rooms from: $499* ✉ *10 N. Ocean Blvd.* ☎ *561/274–3200* ⊕ *www.delraybeachmarriott. com* ⇱ *181 rooms, 88 suites* ⧉ *No meals.*

$$$$
RESORT
FAMILY
Fodor'sChoice
★

🏨 **The Seagate Hotel & Spa.** Those who crave 21st-century luxury in its full glory (ultraswank tilework and fixtures, marble vanities, seamless shower doors) will love this LEED-certified hotel that offers a subtle Zen coastal motif throughout. **Pros:** two swimming pools; fabulous beach club; exceptionally knowledgeable concierge team. **Cons:** main building not directly on beach; daily resort fee; separate charge for parking. [$] *Rooms from: $489* ✉ *1000 E. Atlantic Ave.* ☎ *561/665–4800, 877/577–3242* 🌐 *www.theseagatehotel.com* 🛏 *154 rooms* 🍴 *No meals.*

$$ B&B/INN Fodor's Choice ★ 🏨 **Sundy House.** Just about everything in this bungalow-style B&B is executed to perfection—especially its tropical, verdant grounds, which are actually a nonprofit botanical garden (something anyone can check out during free weekday tours) with a natural, freshwater swimming pool where your feet glide along limestone rocks and mingle with fish. **Pros:** charming eclectic decor; each room is unique; renowned restaurant with popular indoor-outdoor bar and free breakfast; in quiet area off Atlantic Avenue. **Cons:** need to walk through garden to reach rooms (i.e., no covered walkways); beach shuttle requires roughly half-hour advance notice; no private beach facilities. [$] *Rooms from: $209* ✉ *106 Swinton Ave.* ☎ *561/272–5678, 877/434–9601* 🌐 *www.sundyhouse.com* 🛏 *11 rooms* 🍴 *Breakfast.*

NIGHTLIFE

Boston's on the Beach. You'll find beer flowing and the ocean breeze blowing at this beach bar and eatery, a local watering hole since 1983. The walls are laden with paraphernalia from the Boston Bruins, New England Patriots, and Boston Red Sox, including a shrine to Ted Williams. Boston's can get loud and rowdy (or lively, depending on your taste) later at night. Groove to reggae on Monday, live blues music on Tuesday, and other live music from rock to country on Friday, Saturday, and Sunday. ✉ *40 S. Ocean Blvd.* ☎ *561/278–3364* 🌐 *www.bostonsonthebeach.com.*

Dada. Bands play in the living room of this historic house, though much of the action is outdoors on the lawn in fair weather, where huge trees and lanterns make it a fun stop for drinks or a group night out. It's a place where those who don't drink will also feel comfortable, however, and excellent gourmet nibbles are a huge bonus (a full dinner menu is available, too). A bohemian, younger crowd gathers later into the night. ✉ *52 N. Swinton Ave.* ☎ *561/330–3232* 🌐 *www.sub-culture.org/dada.*

Jellies Bar at the Atlantic Grille. Within the Seagate Hotel, the fun and fabulous bar at the Atlantic Grille is known locally as Jellies Bar. The over-30 set consistently floats over to this stunning bar to shimmy to live music Tuesdays to Saturdays; the namesake jellyfish tank never fails to entertain as well. ✉ *The Seagate Hotel & Spa, 1000 E. Atlantic Ave.* ☎ *561/665–4900* 🌐 *www.theatlanticgrille.com.*

SHOPPING

Atlantic Avenue and Pineapple Grove, both charming neighborhoods for shoppers, have maintained Delray Beach's small-town integrity. Atlantic Avenue is the main street, with art galleries, boutiques, restaurants, and bars lining it from just west of Swinton Avenue all the way east to the ocean. The now established Pineapple Grove Arts District is centered on the half-mile strip of Northeast 2nd Avenue that goes

6

north from Atlantic; these areas are broadening as the downtown area expands south and east.

SPORTS AND THE OUTDOORS

BIKING

There's a bicycle path in Barwick Park, but the most popular place to ride is up and down the special oceanfront bike lane along Route A1A. The city also has an illustrated and annotated map on key downtown sights available through the Palm Beach Convention and Visitors Bureau.

Richwagen's Bike & Sport. Rent bikes by the hour, day, or week (they come with locks, baskets, and helmets); Richwagen's also has copies of city maps on hand. A 7-Speed Cruiser rents for $60 per week, or $30 a day. They also rent bike trailers, child seats and electric carts. The shop is closed both Sunday and Monday. ⌂ *298 N.E. 6th Ave.* ☎ *561/276–4234* ⊕ *www.delraybeachbicycles.com.*

TENNIS

Delray Beach Tennis Center. Each year this complex hosts simultaneous professional tournaments where current stars like Ivo Karlovic and Marin Cilic along with legends like Andy Roddick, Ivan Lendl and Michael Chang duke it out (⊕ *www.yellowtennisball.com*). Florida's own Chris Evert hosts the Pro-Celebrity Tennis Classic charity event here (⊕ *www.chrisevert.org*). The rest of the time, you can practice or learn on 14 clay courts and 7 hard courts; private lessons and clinics are available, and it's open from 7:30 am to 9 pm weekdays and until 6 pm weekends. Since most hotels in the area do not have courts, tennis players visiting Delray Beach often come here to play. ⌂ *201 W. Atlantic Ave.* ☎ *561/243–7360* ⊕ *www.delraytennis.com.*

BOCA RATON

6 miles south of Delray Beach.

Less than an hour south of Palm Beach and anchoring the county's south end, upscale Boca Raton has much in common with its fabled cousin. Both reflect the unmistakable architectural influence of Addison Mizner, their principal developer in the mid-1920s. The meaning of the name Boca Raton (pronounced boca rah-*tone*) often arouses curiosity, with many folks mistakenly assuming it means "rat's mouth." Historians say the probable origin is Boca Ratones, an ancient Spanish geographical term for an inlet filled with jagged rocks or coral. Miami's Biscayne Bay had such an inlet, and in 1823 a mapmaker copying Miami terrain confused the more northern inlet, thus mistakenly labeling this area Boca Ratones. No matter what, you'll know you've arrived in the heart of downtown when you spot the historic town hall's gold dome on the main street, Federal Highway. Much of the Boca landscape was heavily planned, and many of the bigger sights are clustered in the area around town hall and Lake Boca, a wide stretch of the Intracoastal

Waterway between Palmetto Park Road and Camino Real (two main east–west streets at the southern end of town).

GETTING HERE AND AROUND
To get to Boca Raton from Delray Beach, drive south 6 miles on Interstate 95, Federal Highway (U.S. 1), or Route A1A.

ESSENTIALS
VISITOR INFORMATION
Contacts **Palm Beach County Convention and Visitors Bureau** ✉ *1555 Palm Beach Lakes Blvd., Suite 800, West Palm Beach* ☎ *561/233–3000* ⊕ *www. palmbeachfl.com.*

EXPLORING

FAMILY **Boca Raton Museum of Art.** Changing-exhibition galleries on the first floor showcase internationally known artists—both past and present—at this museum in a spectacular building that's part of the Mizner Park shopping center; the permanent collection upstairs includes works by Picasso, Degas, Matisse, Klee, Modigliani, and Warhol, as well as notable African and pre-Columbian art. Daily tours are included with admission. In addition to the treasure hunts and sketchbooks you can pick up from the front desk, there's a roster of special programs that cater to kids, including studio workshops and gallery walks. Another fun feature is the cell phone audio guide—certain pieces of art have a corresponding number you dial to hear a detailed narration. ✉ *501 Plaza Real, Mizner Park* ☎ *561/392–2500* ⊕ *www.bocamuseum.org* 🖙 *$12* ☉ *Tues., Thurs., and Fri. 10–5, Wed. 10–9; weekends noon–5.*

FAMILY **Gumbo Limbo Nature Center.** A big draw for kids, this stellar spot has four huge saltwater tanks brimming with sea life, from coral to stingrays to spiny lobsters, plus a sea turtle rehabilitation center. Nocturnal walks in spring and early summer, when staffers lead a quest to find nesting female turtles coming ashore to lay eggs, are popular; so are the hatching releases in August and September. (Call to purchase tickets in advance as there are very limited spaces.) This is one of only a handful of centers that offer this. There is also a nature trail and butterfly garden, a ¼-mile boardwalk, and a 40-foot observation tower, where you're likely to see brown pelicans and osprey. ✉ *1801 N. Ocean Blvd.* ☎ *561/544–8605* ⊕ *www.gumbolimbo.org* 🖙 *Free ($5 suggested donation); turtle walks $15* ☉ *Mon.–Sat. 9–4, Sun. noon–4.*

BEACHES

Boca's three city beaches (South Beach, Red Reef Park, and Spanish River Park, south to north, respectively) are beautiful and hugely popular; but unless you're a resident or enter via bicycle, parking can be very expensive. Save your receipt if you care to go in and out, or park hop—most guards at the front gate will honor a same-day ticket from another location if you ask nicely. Another option is the county-run South Inlet Park that's walking distance from the Boca Raton Bridge Hotel at the southern end of Lake Boca; it has a metered lot for a fraction of the cost, but not quite the same charm as the others.

FAMILY **Red Reef Park.** The ocean with its namesake reef that you can wade up to is just one draw: a fishing zone on the Intracoastal Waterway across the street, a 9-hole golf course next door, and the Gumbo Limbo Environmental Education Center at the northern end of the park can easily make a day at the beach into so much more. Pack snorkels and explore the reef at high tide when fish are most abundant. Swimmers, be warned: once lifeguards leave at 5, anglers flock to the shores and stay well past dark. **Amenities:** lifeguards; parking (fee); showers; toilets. **Best for:** snorkeling; swimming; walking. ⌂ *1400 N. Rte. A1A* ☎ *561/393-7974, 561/393-7989 for beach conditions* ⊕ *www.ci.boca-raton.fl.us/rec/parks/redreef.shtm* ⌸ *$16 parking (weekdays), $18 parking (weekends)* ☉ *Daily 8 am–10 pm.*

South Beach Park. Perched high up on a dune, a large open-air pavilion at the east end of Palmetto Park Road offers a panoramic view of what's in store below on the sand that stretches up the coast. Serious beachgoers need to pull into the main lot ¼ mile north on the east side of A1A, but if a short-but-sweet visit is what you're after, the 15 or so one-hour spots with meters in the circle driveway will do (and not cost you the normal $15 parking fee). During the day, pretty young things blanket the shore, and windsurfers practice tricks in the waves. Quiet quarters are farther north. **Amenities:** lifeguards; parking (fee); toilets; showers. **Best for:** sunsets; windsurfing; walking; swimming. ⌂ *400 N. Rte A1A* ⊕ *www.ci.boca-raton.fl.us/rec/parks/southbeach.shtm* ⌸ *$15 parking (weekdays), $17 parking (weekends)* ☉ *Daily 8–sunset.*

Spanish River Park. At 76 acres and including extensive nature trails, this is by far one of the largest ocean parks in the southern half of Palm Beach County and a great pick for people who want more space and fewer crowds. Big groups, including family reunions, favor it because of the number of covered picnic areas for rent, but anyone can snag a free table (there are plenty!) under the thick canopy of banyan trees. Even though the vast majority of the park is separated from the surf, you never actually have to cross A1A to reach the beach, because tunnels run under it at several locations. **Amenities:** lifeguards; parking (fee); showers; toilets. **Best for:** swimming; walking; solitude. ⌂ *3001 N. Rte. A1A* ☎ *561/393-7815* ⊕ *www.ci.boca-raton.fl.us/rec/parks/spanishriver.shtm* ⌸ *$16 parking (weekdays), $18 parking (weekends)* ☉ *Daily 8–sunset.*

WHERE TO EAT

$$$$ ✕ **Casa D'Angelo Ristorante.** The lines are deservedly long at Chef Angelo
TUSCAN   Elia's upscale Tuscan restaurant in tony Boca Raton. The third outpost
Fodor'sChoice   of his renowned Casa D'Angelo chain impresses with an outstanding
★   selection of antipasti, carpaccios, pastas, and specialties from the wood-burning oven. From staples like the antipasto *angelo* (grilled vegetables and buffalo mozzarella), osso buco, and linguine with white-water clams and garlic, to the ever-changing gnocchi, risotto, veal scallopine, and fish specials of the day, Angelo's dishes deliver pure perfection in every bite. The wine list is also exceptional with hundreds of Italian and American wines to choose from. Servers are experienced and top-notch.

$ *Average main: $38* ✉ *171 East Palmetto Park Rd.* ☎ *561/996–1234* ⊕ *www.casa-d-angelo.com* ⌦ *Reservations essential* ⊘ *No lunch.*

$$ ✕ **Farmer's Table.** Taking up the local food mantle, chefs here create
MODERN inventive dishes following the seasons using locally sourced meats,
AMERICAN seafood, and vegetables. Whenever possible, the foods are organic or sustainable. Bison meatloaf, a Buddha bowl, and "Spasta" (pasta made from squash) with chicken meatballs are some of the popular entrees. Dishes such as the chicken chop tagine or zahtar-spiced salmon are preparations that let foods work with flavors rather than be disguised by them. Vegan and vegetarian dishes, including juices, "mocktails," and desserts, are on the menu, and dietary requests are accommodated with the same creativity. The wine list includes many organic and sustainable varietals. Mixologists apply the same philosophy of fresh, local foods to their craft cocktails. $ *Average main: $22* ✉ *Wyndham Boca Raton, 1901 N. Military Trail* ☎ *561/417–5836* ⊕ *www.farmerstableboca.com* ⌦ *Reservations essential.*

$$$$ ✕ **Truluck's.** This popular Florida and Texas seafood chain is so serious
SEAFOOD about its fruits of the sea that it supports its own fleet of 16 fishing
Fodor's Choice boats. Stone crabs are the signature dish, and you can have all you can
★ eat on Monday night from October to May. Other recommended dishes include salmon topped with blue crab and shrimp, hot-and-crunchy trout, crab cakes, and blackened Florida grouper. Portions are huge, so you might want to make a meal of appetizers. And don't miss the warm carrot cake—it's heaven on a plate! The place comes alive each night with its popular piano bar. $ *Average main: $35* ✉ *351 Plaza Real, Mizner Park* ☎ *561/391–0755* ⊕ *www.trulucks.com.*

$$$ ✕ **Uncle Tai's.** The draw at this upscale eatery is some of the best Hunan
CHINESE cuisine on Florida's east coast. Specialties include sliced duck with snow peas and water chestnuts in a tangy plum sauce, and orange beef delight—flank steak stir-fried until crispy and then sautéed with pepper sauce, garlic, and orange peel. They'll go easy on the heat on request. The service is quietly efficient. The early-bird crowd will appreciate the very filling Sunset Dinner specials (5–6:15 pm), which come with a starter, a dessert, and a main dish. $ *Average main: $21* ✉ *5250 Town Center Circle* ☎ *561/368–8806* ⊕ *www.uncletais.com.*

WHERE TO STAY

$$$ ⛱ **Boca Beach Club.** Dotted with turquoise lounge chairs, ruffled umbrel-
RESORT las, and white-sand beaches, this newly reconceived and rebranded hotel
FAMILY is now part of the Waldorf-Astoria collection and looks as if it was
Fodor's Choice carefully replicated from a retro-chic postcard. **Pros:** great location on
★ the beach; kids' activity center. **Cons:** pricey; shuttle ride away from the main building. $ *Rooms from: $449* ✉ *900 S. Ocean Blvd.* ☎ *888/564–1312* ⊕ *www.bocabeachclub.com* ⇗ *212 rooms* ⊙ *No meals.*

$$$ ⛱ **Boca Raton Resort & Club.** Addison Mizner built this Mediterranean-
RESORT style hotel in 1926, and additions over time have created a sprawling,
FAMILY sparkling resort, one of the most luxurious in all of South Florida and
Fodor's Choice part of the Waldorf-Astoria collection. **Pros:** super-exclusive—grounds
★ are closed to the public; decor strikes the right balance between his-toric roots and modern comforts; plenty of activities. **Cons:** daily resort

charge; conventions often crowd common areas. [$] *Rooms from: $309* ✉ *501 E. Camino Real* ☎ *561/447–3000, 888/543–1277* 🌐 *www.bocaresort.com* 🛏 *635 rooms* 🍴 *No meals.*

$$ HOTEL 🏨 **Waterstone Resort & Marina.** The former Bridge Hotel was transformed into a sleek, modern resort with a $20-million restoration in 2014. **Pros:** short walk to beach; pet friendly; waterfront views throughout. **Cons:** parking fee; no quiet common space; some rooms noisy from nearby bridge traffic. [$] *Rooms from: $179* ✉ *999 E. Camino Real* ☎ *561/368–9500* 🌐 *www.waterstoneboca.com* 🛏 *139 rooms* 🍴 *No meals.*

NIGHTLIFE

Jazziz. A smart, sexy, and intimate jazz dinner club in Mizner Park attracts a variety of top musical talent. David Sanborn, Kevin Eubanks, Lee Ritenour, Nestor Torres, and Jon Secada are a few of the names that have played in the 12,000-square-feet space. It has several dining rooms and an indoor-outdoor bar that swings late into the night with or without entertainment. An "out back" cigar bar is always smokin'. The Sunday Jazz Brunch is a local favorite. ✉ *Mizner Park, 201 Plaza Blvd.* ☎ *561/300–0730* 🌐 *www.jazziz.com.*

SHOPPING

Mizner Park. This distinctive 30-acre shopping center off Federal Highway, one block north of Palmetto Park Road, intersperses apartments and town houses among its gardenlike commercial areas. Some three dozen retailers—including Lord and Taylor, which moved in as the only national department store east of I–95 in Boca—line the central axis. It's peppered with fountains and green space, restaurants, galleries, a jazz club, a movie theater, the Boca Raton Museum of Art, and an amphitheater that hosts major concerts as well as community events. ✉ *327 Plaza Real* ☎ *561/362–0606* 🌐 *www.miznerpark.com.*

Royal Palm Place. The retail enclave of Royal Palm is filled with independent boutiques selling fine jewelry and apparel. By day, stroll the walkable streets and have your pick of sidewalk cafés for lunch alongside Boca's ladies who lunch. Royal Palm Place assumes a different personality come nightfall, as its numerous restaurants and lounges attract throngs of patrons for great dining and fabulous libations. ✉ *101 Plaza Real S* ☎ *561/392–8920* 🌐 *www.royalpalmplace.com.*

Town Center at Boca Raton. Over on the west side of the interstate in Boca, this indoor megamall has more than 220 stores, with anchor stores including Saks and Neiman Marcus and just about every major high-end designer, including Bulgari and Anne Fontaine. But not every shop here requires deep pockets. The Town Center at Boca Raton is also firmly rooted with a variety of more affordable national brands like Gap and Guess. ✉ *6000 Glades Rd.* ☎ *561/368–6000* 🌐 *www.simon.com/mall/town-center-at-boca-raton.*

SPORTS AND THE OUTDOORS

GOLF

Red Reef Park Executive Golf Course. This executive golf course offers 9 holes with varying views of the Intracoastal and the Atlantic Ocean. The Joe Palloka and Charles Ankrom designed course dates back to 1957. It was refreshed in 2001 through a multimillion-dollar renovation. The scenic holes are between 54 and 227 yards each—great for a quick round. Fees range from $11 to walk in the off-season to $19 in season. Carts are available, but the short course begs to be walked. Park in the lot across the street from the main beach entrance, and put the greens fees receipt on the dash; that covers parking. ⊠ *1221 N. Ocean Blvd.* ☎ *561/391–5014* ⊕ *www.bocacitygolf.com* ⏢ *$19* ⟟ *9 holes, 1357 yards, par 32.*

SCUBA AND SNORKELING

Force-E. This company, in business since the late 1970s, rents, sells, and repairs scuba and snorkeling equipment—and organizes about 80 dive trips a week from the Palm Beach Inlet to Port Everglades in Broward County. The PADI–affiliated five-star center has instruction for all levels and offers private charters, too. They have two other outposts besides this Boca Raton location—one north in Riviera Beach and one south in Pompano Beach. ⊠ *2181 N. Federal Hwy.* ☎ *561/368–0555, 866/307–3483* ⊕ *www.force-e.com.*

NORTH COUNTY

Just over the bridge at the Port of Palm Beach are the more laid-back towns of North County, where families and golf pros, not to mention the celebs on Jupiter Island, call home. On **Singer Island,** visible from Palm Beach across the Palm Beach Inlet, and a mere 20 minutes by land, are the towns of **Palm Beach Shores** and **Riviera Beach.** With good beach access and waterfront parks, surf- and sun-seekers have several options, including the nearby Peanut Island. On the mainland north and west, suburban **Palm Beach Gardens** is the golf capital of the county, with PGA courses and country club greens making for greenspace throughout, along with a shopper's paradise (malls abound). The tiny seaside **Juno Beach,** with turtle-rich beaches, melds quickly into Jupiter, where the beach is the star—for both two- and four-legged sun-worshippers—with parks and public pavilions providing gathering sites for groups.

PALM BEACH GARDENS

13.5 miles north of West Palm Beach.

About 15 minutes northwest of Palm Beach is this relaxed, upscale residential community known for its high-profile golf complex, the **PGA National Resort & Spa.** Although not on the beach, the town is less than a 15-minute drive from the ocean. Malls and dining are centered on the main street, PGA Boulevard, running east from the resort to U.S. 1.

WHERE TO EAT

$$$$ AMERICAN

🍴 **Café Chardonnay.** At the end of a strip mall, Café Chardonnay is surprisingly elegant and has some of the most refined food in the suburban town of Palm Beach Gardens. Soft lighting, warm woods, white tablecloths, and cozy banquettes set the scene for a quiet lunch or romantic dinner. The place receives consistent praise for its innovative, continually changing menu and outstanding wine list. Starters can include wild-mushroom strudel and pancetta-wrapped diver scallops. Entrées might be grilled filet mignon or a pan-roasted veal chop with Parmesan risotto and brandy morel sauce. A wine bar off to the side with knowledgeable servers is an attraction for oenophiles. [$] *Average main: $34* ✉ *The Gardens Square Shoppes, 4533 PGA Blvd.* ☎ *561/627–2662* 🌐 *www.cafechardonnay.com* 🕒 *No lunch weekends.*

$$ AMERICAN

🍴 **Coolinary Cafe.** It's tucked away in a strip mall and has only 50 seats inside (counting the bar) and a handful out on the sidewalk, but everything down to the condiments is made in-house here. Rabbit sausage and noodles or lamb meatball risotto are examples on the seasonal one-page menus the chef puts together daily. When there's fish on the menu from local waters, go for it. At the open kitchen in the spare but modern space, you can banter with the chefs if you sit at the bar. ⚠ **No reservations are accepted, and in season the wait can be over an hour—lunch is a best bet.** [$] *Average main: $20* ✉ *Donald Ross Village Plaza, 4650 Donald Ross Rd., Suite 110* ☎ *561/249–6760* 🌐 *www.coolinarycafe.com* ✍ *Reservations not accepted* 🕒 *Closed Sun.*

$$$ AMERICAN

🍴 **The Cooper.** With a contemporary farm-to-table menu, and spacious dining rooms and bars, this spot in PGA Commons has plenty of local fans. Happy hour crowds fill the patio bar-lounge area to sip the craft cocktails and nibble from a cheese or salumi board. The fare includes such contemporary farm-fresh dishes as a double-cut Duroc pork chop with borlotti beans, rainbow Swiss chard and crispy sunchokes, and chophouse steaks, including a daily butcher's cut. Comfort dishes like Jerry's bacon-wrapped meat loaf satisfy those missing their mom's cooking. A separate children's menu is available. [$] *Average main: $23* ✉ *PGA Commons, 4610 PGA Blvd.* ☎ *561/622–0032* 🌐 *www.thecooperrestaurant.com.*

$$$$ STEAKHOUSE

🍴 **Ironwood Steak & Seafood.** Located in the PGA National Resort & Spa, this eatery draws guests, locals, and tourists alike eager for a taste of its fired-up Vulcan-cooked steaks (Vulcan to meat-eaters is like Titleist to golfers—the best equipment around). Wagyu and Angus beef cuts are featured. The she-crab soup with sherry and locally fished wahoo are seafood favorites, as are the raw bar items, like the truly jumbo shrimp cocktail and tuna tartare. Impressive for its sexy decor—bright red banquettes, slate-tile walls, private rooms, and a glass-walled, award-winning wine cellar—it all comes together to create a relaxed, contemporary setting that spills out onto the equally chic adjoining lobby I-bar, which becomes a high-energy scene on weekend nights when a DJ spins. [$] *Average main: $38* ✉ *PGA National Resort & Spa, 400 Ave. of the Champions* ☎ *561/627–4852* 🌐 *www.pgaresort.com/restaurants/ironwood-grille.*

$$$ SEAFOOD 🍴 **Spoto's Oyster Bar.** If you love oysters and other raw bar nibbles, head here, where black-and-white photographs of oyster fisherman adorn the walls. The polished tables give the eatery a clubby look. Spoto's serves up a delightful bowl of New England clam chowder and a truly impressive variety of oysters and clams. The Caesar salad with crispy croutons and anchovies never disappoints. Sit outside on the patio to take advantage of the area's perfect weather, or in the Blue Point Lounge off the main room, where live music is often booked. [$] *Average main: $26* ✉ *PGA Commons, 4560 PGA Blvd.* ☎ *561/776–9448* 🌐 *www.spotosoysterbar.com.*

WHERE TO STAY

$ HOTEL 🏨 **Hilton Garden Inn Palm Beach Gardens.** A hidden find in Palm Beach Gardens, this hotel sits on a small lake next to a residential area, but near two shopping malls and close to PGA golf courses. **Pros:** 24-hour free business center; walk to two different malls with shops, restaurants, and movie theaters. **Cons:** outdoor self-parking; no bell service; pool closes at dusk; 15 minutes from the beach. [$] *Rooms from: $164* ✉ *3505 Kyoto Gardens Dr.* ☎ *561/694–5833* 📠 *561/694–5829* 🌐 *hiltongardeninn3.hilton.com* 🛏 *180 rooms* 🍽 *No meals.*

$$ RESORT Fodor's Choice ★ 🏨 **PGA National Resort & Spa.** This golfer's paradise (five championship courses and the site of the yearly Honda Classic pro-tour tournament) is a sleek modern playground with a gorgeous zero-entry lagoon pool, seven different places to eat, and a full-service spa with unique mineral-salt therapy pools. **Pros:** dream golf facilities; affordable rates for top-notch amenities; close to shopping malls. **Cons:** no beach shuttle; difficult to get around if you don't have a car; long drive to Palm Beach proper. [$] *Rooms from: $279* ✉ *400 Ave. of the Champions* ☎ *561/627–2000, 800/633–9150* 🌐 *www.pgaresort.com* 🛏 *280 rooms, 59 suites* 🍽 *No meals.*

SHOPPING

FAMILY **Downtown at The Gardens.** This open-air pavilion down the street from The Gardens Mall has boutiques, chain stores, day spas, a 16-screen movie theater, and a lively restaurant and nighttime bar scene that includes the Dirty Martini and Cabo Flats, which both feature live music. A carousel, children's barbershop, boutiques, and Cool Beans (an indoor playground), make this a family-friendly mall. ✉ *11701 Lake Victoria Gardens Ave.* ☎ *561/340–1600* 🌐 *www.downtownatthegardens.com.*

Fodor's Choice ★ **The Gardens Mall.** One of the most refined big shopping malls in America, the 160-store Gardens Mall in northern Palm Beach County has stores like Burberry, Chanel, Gucci, Louis Vuitton, and David Yurman, along with Saks 5th Avenue and Nordstrom. There are also plenty of reasonably priced national retailers like H&M and Abercrombie & Fitch, Bloomingdale's, and Macy's. This beautiful mall has prolific seating pavilions, making it a great place to spend a humid summer afternoon. ✉ *3101 PGA Blvd.* ☎ *561/775–7750* 🌐 *www.thegardensmall.com.*

SPORTS AND THE OUTDOORS

Spring training fans travel to the area to see the Cardinals and Marlins tune up for their seasons at Roger Dean Stadium in Palm Beach Gardens, and to watch their AAA feeder teams in summer. Port St. Lucie and Vero Beach stadiums and more teams are only a short drive up I–95.

GOLF

Fodor'sChoice ★ **PGA National Resort & Spa.** If you're the kind of traveler who takes along a set of clubs, you'll achieve nirvana on the greens of PGA National Resort & Spa. The five championship courses are open only to hotel guests and club members, which means you'll have to stay to play, but packages that include a room and a round of golf are reasonably priced. The Champion Course, redesigned by Jack Nicklaus and famous for its Bear Trap holes, is the site of the yearly Honda Classic pro tournament. The four other challenging courses are also legends in the golfing world: the Palmer, named for its architect, the legendary Arnold Palmer; the Fazio (formerly the "Haig," the resort's first course re-opened in November 2012 after a major renovation) and the Squire, both from Tom and George Fazio; and the Karl Litten–designed Estates, the sole course not on the property (it is located five miles west of the PGA resort). Lessons are available at the David Leadbetter Golf Academy, and they also run a summertime kids' golf camp. ⊠ *PGA National Resort & Spa, 1000 Ave. of the Champions* ☎ *561/627–1800* ⊕ *www.pgaresort.com/golf/pga-national-golf* ✉ *$349 for 18 holes for Champion Course, Fazio Course, and Squire Course. $319 for 18 holes for Palmer Course and Estates Course.* 🏌 *Champion Course: 18 holes, 7048 yards, par 72. Palmer Course: 18 holes, 7079 yards, par 72. Fazio Course: 18 holes, 6806 yards, par 72. Squire Course: 18 holes, 6465 yards, par 72. Estates Course: 18 holes, 6694 yards, par 72.*

SINGER ISLAND

6.2 miles north of West Palm Beach.

Across the inlet from the northern end of Palm Beach is Singer Island, which is actually a peninsula that's big enough to pass for a barrier island, rimmed with mom-and-pop motels and high-rises. Palm Beach Shores occupies its southern tip (where tiny Peanut Island is a stone's throw away); farther north are Riviera Beach and North Palm Beach, which also straddle the inlet and continue on the mainland.

EXPLORING

Palm Beach Maritime Museum. Though the main building of the Palm Beach Maritime Museum is found in Currie Park in West Palm Beach, its chief treasure—the restored "Kennedy Bunker," a bomb shelter built for President John F. Kennedy, and a historic Coast Guard station—is located on Peanut Island. You can take a guided tour of the bunker through the museum's Peanut Island outpost. The museum also has a nice little gift shop, an outdoor deck on the water, and a lawn where you can play games including horseshoes. To get there, catch a water taxi from Riviera Beach Municipal Marina (⊕ *www.peanutislandwatertaxi.com*) but call ahead as the boats won't run in choppy waters. ⊠ *Peanut*

Island, Riviera Beach ☎ *561/848–2960* 🌐 *www.pbmm.org* 🎟 *$14 (not including water transportation)* 🕒 *Thurs.–Sun. 11–4.*

BEACHES

FAMILY Fodor's Choice ★ **John D. MacArthur Beach State Park.** If getting far from rowdy crowds is your goal, this spot on the north end of Singer Island is a good choice. Encompassing 2 miles of beach and a lush subtropical coastal habitat, inside you'll find a great place for kayaking, snorkeling at natural reefs, bird-watching, fishing, and hiking. You might even get to see a few manatees! A 4,000-square-foot nature center has aquariums and displays on local flora and fauna, and there's a long roster of monthly activities, such as surfing clinics, art lessons, and live bluegrass music. Guided sea turtle walks are available at night in season, and daily nature walks depart at 10 am. Check the website for times and costs of activities. **Amenities:** water sports; parking (fee); toilets; showers. **Best for:** swimming; walking; solitude; surfing. ✉ *10900 Jack Nicklaus Dr., North Palm Beach* ☎ *561/624–6950* 🌐 *www.macarthurbeach.org* 🎟 *Parking $5, bicyclists and pedestrians $2* 🕒 *Park daily 8–sunset; nature center and gift shop daily 9–5.*

Peanut Island Park. Partiers, families, and overnight campers all have a place to go on the 79 acres here. The island, in a wide section of the Intracoastal between Palm Beach Island and Singer Island with an open channel to the sea, is accessible only by private boat or water taxi, two of which set sail regularly from the Riviera Beach Municipal Marina (🌐 *www.peanutislandwatertaxi.com*) and the Sailfish. Fun-loving seafarers looking for an afternoon of Jimmy Buffett and picnics aboard pull up to the day docks or the huge sandbar on the north—float around in an inner tube, and it's spring break déjà vu. Walk along the 20-foot-wide paver-lined path encircling the island, and you'll hit a 170-foot fishing pier, a campground, the lifeguarded section to the south that is particularly popular with families because of its artificial reef, and last but not least, the Palm Beach Maritime Museum's "Kennedy Bunker" (a bomb shelter prepared for President John F. Kennedy that was restored and opened to the public in 1999). There are picnic tables and grills, but no concessions. ⚠ **A new ordinance means alcohol possession and consumption is restricted to permit areas.** **Amenities:** lifeguards (summer only); toilets; showers. **Best for:** partiers; walking; swimming; sunrise. ✉ *6500 Peanut Island Rd., Riviera Beach* ☎ *561/845–4445* 🌐 *www.pbcgov.com/parks/peanutisland* 🎟 *Beach free; water taxi $10* 🕒 *Sunrise–sunset.*

WHERE TO STAY

$$$$ RESORT FAMILY 🏨 **Palm Beach Marriott Singer Island Beach Resort & Spa.** Families with a yen for the cosmopolitan but requiring the square footage and comforts of home revel in these one- and two-bedroom suites with spacious, marble-tiled, granite-topped kitchens. **Pros:** wide beach; genuinely warm service; plenty of kids' activities; sleek spa. **Cons:** no upscale dining nearby; unspectacular room views for an ocean-side hotel. [$] *Rooms from: $429* ✉ *3800 N. Ocean Dr., Singer Island, Riviera Beach* ☎ *561/340–1700, 877/239–5610* 🌐 *www.marriott.com* 🛏 *202 suites* 🍴 *No meals.*

6

SPORTS AND THE OUTDOORS

FISHING

Sailfish Marina. Book a full or half day of deep-sea fishing for up to six people with the seasoned captains and large fleet of 28- to 65-foot boats. A ship's store and restaurant are also on-site. ⊠ *Sailfish Marina Resort, 98 Lake Dr., Palm Beach Shores* ☎ *561/844–1724* ⊕ *www. sailfishmarina.com.*

JUNO BEACH

11.8 miles north of West Palm Beach.

This small town east of Palm Beach Gardens has 2 miles of shoreline that becomes home to thousands of sea turtle hatchlings each year, making it one of the world's densest nesting sites. A 990-foot-long pier lures fishermen and beachgoers seeking a spectacular sunrise.

EXPLORING

Fodor's Choice ★ **Loggerhead Park Marine Life Center of Juno Beach.** Located in a certified green building in Loggerhead Park—and established by Eleanor N. Fletcher, the "turtle lady of Juno Beach"—the center focuses on the conservation of sea turtles, using education, research, and rehabilitation. The education center houses displays of coastal natural history, detailing Florida's marine ecosystems and the life and plight of the various species of sea turtles found on Florida's shores. You can visit recovering turtles in their outdoor hospital tanks; volunteers are happy to tell you the turtles' heroic tales of survival. The center has regularly scheduled activities, such as Kid's Story Time and Junior Vet Lab, and most are free of charge. During peak nesting season, the center hosts night walks to experience turtle nesting in action. Given that the adjacent beach is part of the second biggest nesting ground for loggerhead turtles in the world, your chances of seeing this natural phenomenon is pretty high (over 10,000 loggerheads nested here in 2014). ⊠ *14200 U.S. Hwy. 1* ☎ *561/627–8280* ⊕ *www.marinelife.org* ⊠ *Free* ☉ *Mon.– Sat. 10–5, Sun. 11–5.*

BEACHES

FAMILY **Juno Beach Ocean Park.** An angler's dream, this beach has a 990-foot pier that's open daily, like the beach, from sunrise to sunset—but from November through February, pier gates open at 6 am and don't close until 10 pm on weeknights and midnight on weekends, making it an awesome place to catch sunrise and sunset (that is, if you don't mind paying the small admission fee). A concession stand on the pier sells fish food as well as such human favorites as burgers, sandwiches, and ice cream. Rods and tackle are rented here. Families adore this shoreline because of the amenities and vibrant atmosphere. There are plenty of kids building castles but also plenty of teens having socials and hanging out along the beach. Pets are not allowed here, but they are allowed on the adjacent Jupiter Beach. **Amenities:** lifeguards; food and drink; parking (free); showers; toilets. **Best for:** sunrise; sunset; swimming. ⊠ *14775 U.S. 1* ☎ *561/799–0185 for pier* ⊕ *www.pbcgov.com/ parks/locations/junobeach.htm* ⊠ *$4 to fish, $1 to enter pier; beach free* ☉ *Daily sunrise–sunset.*

Away from developed shorelines, Blowing Rocks Preserve on Jupiter Island lets you wander the dunes.

JUPITER AND VICINITY

12 miles north of West Palm Beach.

Jupiter is one of the few towns in the region not fronted by an island but still quite close to the fantastic hotels, shopping, and dining of the Palm Beach area. The beaches here are on the mainland, and Route A1A runs for almost 4 miles along the beachfront dunes and beautiful homes.

Northeast across the Jupiter Inlet from Jupiter is the southern tip of Jupiter Island, which stretches about 15 miles to the St. Lucie Inlet. Here expansive and expensive estates often retreat from the road behind screens of vegetation, and the population dwindles the farther north you go. At the very north end, which adjoins tiny Hobe Sound in Martin County on the mainland, sea turtles come to nest.

GETTING HERE AND AROUND

If you're coming from the airport in West Palm Beach, take I–95 to Route 706. Otherwise, Federal Highway (U.S. 1) and Route A1A are usually more convenient.

Contacts Palm Beach County Convention and Visitors Bureau ✉ *1555 Palm Beach Lakes Blvd., Suite 800, West Palm Beach* ☎ *561/233–3000* ⊕ *www. palmbeachfl.com.*

EXPLORING

Fodor'sChoice
★

Blowing Rocks Preserve. Managed by the Nature Conservancy, this pro-tected area on Jupiter Island is headlined by an almost other-worldly looking limestone shelf that fringes South Florida's most turquoise waters. Also protected within its 73 acres are plants native to beach-front dunes, coastal strand (the landward side of the dunes), mangrove swamps, and tropical hardwood forests. There are two short walking trails on the Intracoastal side of the preserve, as well as an education center and a butterfly garden. The best time to come and seeing the "blowing rocks" is when a storm is brewing: If high tides and strong offshore winds coincide, the sea blows spectacularly through the holes in the eroded outcropping. During a calm summer day, you can swim in crystal clear waters on the mile-long beach and climb around the rock formations at low tide. Park in one of the two lots because police ticket cars on the road. ⊠ *574 S. Beach Rd., CR 707, Hobe Sound* ☎ *561/744–6668* ⊕ *www.nature.org/blowingrocks* ⊡ *$2* ⊗ *Daily 9–4:30.*

FAMILY | **Hobe Sound Nature Center.** Though located in the Hobe Sound National
Fodor'sChoice | Wildlife Refuge, this nature center is an independent organization. The
★ | exhibit hall houses live baby alligators, crocodiles, a scary-looking tarantula, and more—and is a child's delight. ■ **TIP→ Among the center's more popular events are the annual nighttime sea turtle walks, held between May and June; reservations are accepted as early as April 1.** Just off the center's entrance is a mile-long nature trail loop that snakes through three different kinds of habitats: coastal hammock, estuary beach, and sand pine scrub, which is one of Florida's most unusual and endangered plant communities and what composes much of the refuge's nearly 250 acres. ⊠ *13640 S.E. U.S. 1, Hobe Sound* ☎ *772/546–2067* ⊕ *www.hobesoundnaturecenter.com* ⊡ *Free (donation requested)* ⊗ *Mon.–Sat. 9–3.*

FAMILY | **Jonathan Dickinson State Park.** This serene state park provides a glimpse of
Fodor'sChoice | predevelopment "real" Florida. A beautiful showcase of Florida inland
★ | habitat, the park teems with endangered gopher tortoises and manatees. From Hobe Mountain, an ancient dune topped with a tower, you are treated to a panoramic view of this park's more than 11,000 acres of varied terrain and the Intracoastal Waterway. The Loxahatchee River, named a National Wild and Scenic River, cuts through the park, and is home to plenty of charismatic manatees in winter and alligators year-round. Two-hour boat tours of the river depart daily *(see* ⇨ *Jonathan Dickinson State Park River Tours).* Kayak rentals are available, as is horseback riding (it was reintroduced after a 30-year absence). Among the amenities are a dozen newly redone cabins for rent, tent sites, bicycle and hiking trails, two established campgrounds and some primitive campgrounds, and a snack bar. Palmettos on the Loxahatchee is a new food and beverage garden with wine, beer, and local foods featured. Don't skip the Elsa Kimbell Environmental Education and Research Center, which has interactive displays, exhibits, and a short film on the natural history of the area. The park is also a fantastic birding location, with about 150 species to spot. ⊠ *16450 S.E. U.S. 1, Hobe Sound* ☎ *772/546–2771* ⊕ *www.floridastateparks.org/jonathandickinson* ⊡ *Vehicles $6, bicyclists and pedestrians $2* ⊗ *Daily 8–sunset; Elsa Kimbell Environmental Education and Research Center daily 9–5.*

Fodor'sChoice | **Jupiter Inlet Lighthouse & Museum.** Designed by Civil War hero Lieutenant
★ | George Gordon Meade, this working brick lighthouse has been under the Coast Guard's purview since 1860. Tours of the 108-foot-tall landmark are held approximately every half-hour and are included with admission. (Children must be at least 4 feet tall to go to the top.) The

museum tells about efforts to restore this graceful spire to the way it looked from 1860 to 1918; its galleries and outdoor structures, including a pioneer home, also showcase local history dating back 5,000 years. ✉ *Lighthouse Park, 500 Capt. Armour's Way* ☎ *561/747–8380* ⊕ *www.jupiterlighthouse.org* ✉ *$10* ☾ *Jan.–Apr., daily 10–5; May–Dec., Tues.–Sun., 10–5. Last tour at 4.*

BEACHES

Carlin Park. About ½ mile south of the Jupiter Beach Resort and Indiantown Road, the quiet beach here is just one draw; otherwise, the manicured park, which straddles A1A, is chock-full of activities and amenities, and it has the most free parking of any beach park in the area. Several picnic pavilions, including a few beachside, two bocce ball courts, six lighted tennis courts, a baseball diamond, a wood-chip-lined running path, and an amphitheater that hosts free concerts and Shakespeare productions are just some of the highlights. Locals also swear by the Lazy Loggerhead Café that's right off the seaside parking lot for a great casual breakfast and lunch. **Amenities:** lifeguards; food and drink; parking (free); toilets; showers. **Best for:** swimming; walking; picnics. ✉ *400 S. Rte. A1A* ⊕ *www.pbcgov.com/parks/locations/carlin.htm.*

Hobe Sound National Wildlife Refuge. Nature lovers seeking to get as far as possible from the madding crowds will feel at peace at this refuge managed by the U.S. Fish & Wildlife service. It's a haven for people who want some quiet while they walk around and photograph the gorgeous coastal sand dunes, where turtles nest and shells often wash ashore. The beach has been severely eroded by high tides and strong winds (surprisingly, surfing is allowed and many do partake). You can't actually venture within most of the 735 protected acres, so if hiking piques your interest, head to the refuge's main entrance a few miles away on Hobe Sound (✉ *13640 S.E. U.S. 1 in Hobe Sound*) for a mile-long trek close to the nature center, or to nearby Jonathan Dickinson State Park (✉ *16450 S.E. U.S. 1 in Hobe Sound*). **Amenities:** parking (fee); toilets. **Best for:** solitude; surfing; walking. ✉ *198 N. Beach Rd., at end of N. Beach Rd., Jupiter Island* ☎ *772/546–6141* ⊕ *www.fws. gov/hobesound* ✉ *$5.*

Fodor's Choice ★ **Jupiter Beach.** Famous throughout all of Florida for a unique pooch-loving stance, the town of Jupiter's beach welcomes Yorkies, Labs, pugs—you name it—along its 2½-mile oceanfront. Dogs can frolic unleashed (once they're on the beach) or join you for a dip. Free parking spots line A1A in front of the sandy stretch, and there are multiple access points and continuously refilled dog-bag boxes (29 to be exact). The dog beach starts on Marcinski Rd. (Beach Marker #25) and continues north until Beach Marker #59. Before going, read through the guidelines posted on the Friends of Jupiter Beach website; the biggest things to note are be sure to clean up after your dog and to steer clear of lifeguarded areas to the north and south. ■TIP➔ **Dogs fare best early morning and late afternoon, when the sand isn't too hot for their paws.** **Amenities:** toilets; showers. **Best for:** walking; dog play dates. ✉ *2188 Marcinski Rd., across street from parking lot* ☎ *561/748–8140* ⊕ *www. friendsofjupiterbeach.com.*

6

WHERE TO EAT

$$ SEAFOOD 🍴 **Guanabanas.** Expect a wait for dinner, which is not necessarily a bad thing at this island paradise of a waterfront restaurant and bar. Take the wait time to explore the bridges and trails of the open-air tropical oasis, or grab a chair by the river to watch the sunset, or nibble on some conch fritters at the large tiki bar until your table is ready. Try the lemon-butter hogfish for dinner and stick around for the live music (a full concert calendar is on the website). Breakfast, offered only on weekends, is good, too. That said, it's more about the view and vibe than the food here. ⚠ **There's only valet parking on site; a free lot is about a block away but fills up fast in season.** [$] *Average main: $18* ✉ *960 N. Rte. A1A* ☎ *561/747–8878* 🌐 *www.guanabanas.com* ✍ *Reservations not accepted.*

$$ SEAFOOD 🍴 **Little Moir's Food Shack.** This local favorite is not much to look at and a bit tricky to find, but well worth the search. The fried-food standards you might expect at such a casual, small place that uses plastic utensils are not found on the menu; instead there are fried tuna rolls with basil, and panko-crusted fried oysters with spicy fruit salad. A variety of beers are fun to pair with the creatively prepared seafood dishes that include wahoo, mahimahi, and snapper, all of which is locally sourced. Wait for your table next door at Maxi's Lineup—also under Moir's ownership—during the busy winter season when lines are long. [$] *Average main: $17* ✉ *103 S. U.S. 1* ☎ *561/741–3626* 🌐 *www.littlemoirs.com/food-shack* ✍ *Reservations not accepted* 🕒 *Closed Sun.*

$$$$ SEAFOOD 🍴 **Sinclair's Ocean Grill.** Remodeled in late 2012 to give it a slick, contemporary look, this upscale restaurant at the Jupiter Beach Resort & Spa is a favorite of locals in the know. The menu has a daily selection of fresh fish, such as Atlantic black grouper over lemon crab salad, sesame-seared tuna, and mahimahi with fruit salsa. There are also thick, juicy cuts of meat, including New York strip steak and beef tenderloin, as well as mouth-watering chicken and lamb dishes. The new Sinclair's Lounge is idyllic for a predinner aperitif. For something more casual, dine outside on the terrace to hear the waves lapping and take in the beachscape. [$] *Average main: $31* ✉ *Jupiter Beach Resort, 5 N. Rte. A1A* ☎ *561/746–2511* 🌐 *www.jupiterbeachresort.com.*

$$ AMERICAN 🍴 **Taste Casual Dining.** Located in the center of historic Hobe Sound, this cozy dining spot with a pleasant, screened-in patio offers piano dinner music on Friday. Locals like to hang out at the old, English-style wine bar; however, the food itself is the biggest draw here. Try a lobster roll and the signature Gorgonzola salad for lunch, and any fish dish for dinner. On weekend nights, order the excellent, slow-cooked prime rib, another specialty. [$] *Average main: $18* ✉ *11750 S.E. Dixie Hwy., Hobe Sound* ☎ *772/546–1129* 🌐 *www.tastehobesound.com* 🕒 *May–Oct., closed Sun.*

WHERE TO STAY

$$$ RESORT FAMILY Fodor's Choice ★ 🏨 **Jupiter Beach Resort & Spa.** Families love this nine-story hotel filled with rich Caribbean-style rooms containing mahogany sleigh beds and armoires; all rooms have balconies, and many have stunning views of the ocean and local landmarks like the Jupiter Lighthouse and Juno Pier. **Pros:** fantastic beachside pool area with hammocks and a fire

pit; marble showers; great restaurant. **Cons:** $25 nightly resort fee; no covered parking; bathtubs only in suites. [$] *Rooms from: $360* ✉ *5 N. Rte. A1A* ☎ *561/746–2511, 800/228–8810* 🌐 *www.jupiterbeachresort.com* 🛏 *134 rooms, 34 suites* 🍴 *No meals.*

$$$ HOTEL **Wyndham Grand Jupiter at Harbourside Place.** Open since 2014, this luxury waterfront hotel is in an upscale complex of business and retail development just minutes from the beach. **Pros:** convenient to plaza shops and restaurants; only minutes from the beach; boat docks and fitness center available. **Cons:** no covered walkway to restaurant; no green spaces; pricey. [$] *Rooms from: $309* ✉ *Harbourside Place, 122 Soundings Ave.* ☎ *561/273–6600* 🌐 *www.wyndhamgrandjupiter.com* 🛏 *179 rooms* 🍴 *No meals.*

SPORTS AND THE OUTDOORS

BASEBALL

Roger Dean Stadium. It's a spring training doubleheader! Both the St. Louis Cardinals and the Miami Marlins call this 6,600-seat facility home base from February to April. The rest of the year two minor league teams (Jupiter Hammerheads and Palm Beach Cardinals) share its turf. In the Abacoa area of Jupiter, the grounds are surrounded by a mix of restaurants and sports bars for pre- and post-game action. ✉ *4751 Main St.* ☎ *561/775–1818* 🌐 *www.rogerdeanstadium.com.*

BOATING AND CANOEING

Fodor's Choice ★ **Canoe Outfitters of Florida.** See animals, from otters to eagles, along 8 miles of the Loxahatchee River in Riverbend County Park daily except Tuesday and Wednesday. Canoe and two-person kayak rentals are $35 for four hours. Bike rentals are available, too. ✉ *Riverbend County Park, 9060 W. Indiantown Rd.* ☎ *561/746–7053* 🌐 *www.canoeoutfittersofflorida.com* ⏲ *Closed Tues. and Wed.*

FAMILY Fodor's Choice ★ **Jonathan Dickinson State Park River Tours.** Boat tours of the Loxahatchee River and guided horseback rides, along with canoe, kayak, bicycle, and boat rentals are offered daily. The popular Wilderness Guided Boat Tour leaves four times daily at 9, 11, 1, and 3 pm and costs $18.87 (for best wildlife photos take the 11 or 1 tour). The pontoon cruises up the Loxahatchee in search of manatees, herons, osprey, alligators, and more. The skipper details the region's natural and cultural history; and from Thursday to Monday the boat also stops at the Trapper Nelson Interpretive Site for a tour of the home of a local legend, the so-called "Wildman" of the Loxahatchee. ✉ *Jonathan Dickinson State Park, 16450 S.E. U.S. 1, Hobe Sound* ☎ *561/746–1466* 🌐 *www.floridaparktours.com.*

GOLF

Abacoa Golf Club. Built in 1999, the tag line for this Joe Lee–designed 18-hole course in Jupiter is "public golf at its finest." Most of the courses in this golfing community are private, but the range at Abacoa is on par with them and membership (nor deep pockets) *isn't* required. $1 million has been spent since 2013 to renovate the facilities throughout the course and clubhouse. One of the course's more interesting features includes the several elevation changes throughout, which is a rarity in flat Florida. The course caters to golfers at all skill levels. The greens fee ranges from $30 to $115 (including cart), depending on time of year, time of day, and weekday versus weekend. ✉ *105 Barbados Dr.* ☎ *561/622–0036* ⊕ *www.abacoagolfclub.com* ✉ *$89 for 18 holes* ⌘. *18 holes, 7200 yards, par 72.*

Golf Club of Jupiter. Locally owned and operated since 1981, this Lamar Smith–designed golf club features a public, championship golf course— the "Jupiter" course—with 18 holes of varying difficulty. It has a course rating of 69.9 and a slope rating of 117 on Bermuda grass. There's a full-time golf pro on staff and an on-site bar and restaurant. ✉ *1800 S. Central Blvd.* ☎ *561/747–6262* ⊕ *www.golfclubofjupiter.com* ✉ *$70 for 18 holes.* ⌘. *18 holes, 6275 yards, par 70.*

OFF THE BEATEN PATH

Forty miles west of West Palm Beach, amid the farms and cattle pastures rimming the western edges of Palm Beach and Martin counties, is **Lake Okeechobee,** the second-largest freshwater lake completely within the United States. It's girdled by 120 miles of road yet remains shielded from sight for almost its entire circumference. Lake Okeechobee— the Seminole's "Big Water" and the gateway of the great Everglades watershed—measures 730 square miles, at its longest roughly 33 miles north–south and 30 miles east–west, with an average natural depth of only 10 feet (flood control brings the figure up to 12 feet and deeper). Six major lock systems and 32 separate water-control structures manage the water and allow boaters to cross the state through its channels from the Atlantic Ocean to the Gulf of Mexico. Encircling the lake is a 34-foot-high grassy levee that locals call "the dike," and atop it, the Lake Okeechobee Scenic Trail, a segment of the Florida National Scenic Trail that's an easy, flat ride for bikers. Anglers have a field day here as well, with great bass and perch catches. ■TIP→ There's no shade, so wear a hat, sunscreen, and bug repellent. Be sure to bring lots of bottled water, too, because restaurants and stores are few and far between.

TREASURE COAST

In contrast to the glitzy, überplanned Gold Coast that includes Greater Palm Beach and Boca Raton, the more bucolic Treasure Coast stretches from south Martin County into St. Lucie and Indian River counties. Along the east are barrier islands all the way to Sebastian and beyond, starting with Jupiter Island, then Hutchinson Island, and finally Orchid Island—and reefs, too. Those reefs are responsible for the region's nickname: they've caused ships carrying riches dating back as far as 1715 to fall asunder and cast their treasures ashore. The Intracoastal Waterway here is called the Indian River starting at the St. Lucie Inlet in Stuart and morphs into a broad tidal lagoon with tiny uninhabited islands and wildlife galore. Inland, there's cattle ranching and tracts of pine and palmetto scrub, along with sugar and citrus production.

Despite a growing number of malls and beachfront condominiums, much of the Treasure Coast remains untouched, something not lost on ecotourists, game fishers, and people who want a break from the over-saturated digital age. Consequently, there are fewer lodging options in this region of Florida, but if 30 minutes in the car sounds like a breeze, culture vultures can live in the lap of luxury in Vero Beach and detour south to Fort Pierce's galleries and botanical gardens. Likewise, families will revel in every amenity imaginable at the Hutchinson Island Marriott and be able to swing northwest to hit up the Mets spring-training stadium in Port St. Lucie or down to Jupiter for the Cardinals and the Marlins.

STUART AND JENSEN BEACH

10 miles north of Hobe Sound.

The compact town of Stuart lies on a peninsula that juts out into the St. Lucie River off the Indian River and has a remarkable amount of shoreline for its size. It scores huge points for its charming historic district and is the self-described "Sailfish Capital of the World." On the southern end, you'll find Port Salerno and its waterfront area, the Manatee Pocket, which are a skip away from the St. Lucie Inlet.

Immediately north of Stuart is down-to-earth Jensen Beach. Both Stuart and Jensen Beach straddle the Indian River and occupy Hutchinson Island, the barrier island that continues into the town of Fort Pierce. Between late April and August, hundreds, even thousands, of turtles come here to nest along the Atlantic beaches. Residents have taken pains to curb the runaway development that has created commercial crowding to the north and south, although some high-rises have popped up along the shore.

GETTING HERE AND AROUND
To get to Stuart and Jensen Beach from Jupiter and Hobe Sound, drive north on Federal Highway (U.S. 1). Route A1A crosses through downtown Stuart and is the sole main road throughout Hutchinson Island. Route 707 runs parallel on the mainland directly across the tidal lagoon.

EXPLORING
Strict architectural and zoning standards guide civic-renewal projects in the heart of Stuart. Antiques stores, restaurants, and more than 50 specialty shops are rooted within the two-block area of Flagler Avenue and Osceola Street north of where A1A cuts across the peninsula (visit ⊕ *www.stuartmainstreet.org* for more information). A self-guided walking-tour pamphlet is available at assorted locations to clue you in on this once-small fishing village's early days.

Elliott Museum. Opened in March 2013, the museum's glittering, green-certified 48,000-square-foot facility is double its previous size and houses a permanent collection along with traveling exhibits pertaining to art, history, and technology. The original museum was founded in 1961 in honor of Sterling Elliott, an inventor of an early automated-addressing machine, the egg crate, and a four-wheel bicycle, and it celebrates history, art, and technology, much of it viewed through the lens of the automobile's effect on American society. There's an impressive array of antique cars, plus paintings, historic artifacts, and nostalgic goods like vintage baseball cards and toys. ⊠ *825 N.E. Ocean Blvd., Jensen Beach* ☎ *772/225–1961* ⊕ *www.elliottmuseumfl.org* ⊠ *$14* ☺ *Mon.–Sun. 10–5.*

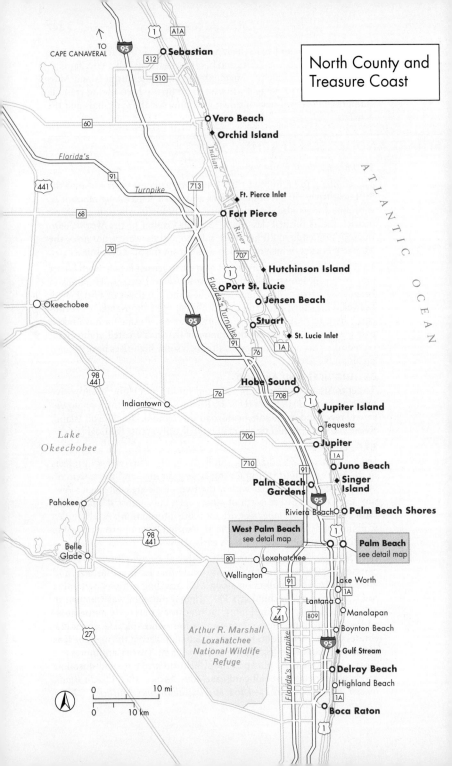

North County and Treasure Coast

TO CAPE CANAVERAL

Sebastian

Vero Beach
Orchid Island

Florida's
Turnpike

Ft. Pierce Inlet
Fort Pierce

Indian River

Hutchinson Island

Okeechobee

Port St. Lucie
Jensen Beach

Florida's Turnpike

Stuart
St. Lucie Inlet

Hobe Sound

Indiantown

Jupiter Island

Tequesta

Lake Okeechobee

Jupiter

Juno Beach

Palm Beach Gardens

Singer Island

Pahokee

Riviera Beach
Palm Beach Shores

Belle Glade

West Palm Beach
see detail map

Palm Beach
see detail map

Loxahatchee

Wellington

Lake Worth

Lantana

Manalapan

Arthur R. Marshall
Loxahatchee
National Wildlife
Refuge

Boynton Beach

Gulf Stream

Delray Beach

Highland Beach

Boca Raton

ATLANTIC OCEAN

0   10 mi

0   10 km

CLOSE UP

Florida's Sea Turtles: The Nesting Season

From May to October, turtles nest all along the Florida coast. Female loggerhead, Kemp's ridley, and other species living in the Atlantic Ocean or Gulf of Mexico swim as much as 2,000 miles to the Florida shore. By night they drag their 100- to 400-pound bodies onto the beach to the dune line. Then each digs a hole with her flippers, drops in 100 or so eggs, covers them up, and returns to sea.

The babies hatch about 60 days later. Once they burst out of the sand, the hatchlings must get to sea rapidly or risk becoming dehydrated from the sun or being caught by crabs, birds, or other predators.

Instinctively, baby turtles head toward bright light, probably because for millions of years starlight or moonlight reflected on the waves was the brightest light around, serving to guide hatchlings to water. Many coastal towns enforce light restrictions during nesting months. Florida homeowners are asked to dim their lights on behalf of baby sea turtles.

At night, volunteers walk the beaches, searching for signs of turtle nests. Upon finding telltale scratches in the sand, they cordon off the sites, so beachgoers will leave the spots undisturbed. (It is illegal to disturb turtle nests.) Volunteers also keep watch over nests when babies are about to hatch, and assist disoriented hatchlings.

Several local organizations offer nightly turtle walks during nesting season. Most are in June and July, starting around 8 pm and sometimes lasting until midnight. Expect a $10 to $15 fee. Call in advance to confirm times and to reserve a spot—places usually take reservations as early as April. If you're in southern Palm Beach County, contact Boca Raton's **Gumbo Limbo Nature Center** (☎ 561/338–1473 ⊕ www.gumbolimbo.org). The **John D. MacArthur Beach State Park** (☎ 561/624–6952 ⊕ www.macarthurbeach.org) is convenient for Palm Beach–area visitors at the northern end of Singer Island. **Hobe Sound Nature Center** (☎ 772/546–2067 ⊕ www.hobesoundnaturecenter.com) is farther up. Treasure Coasters in or near Vero Beach can go to **Sebastian Inlet State Park** (☎ 321/984–4852 ⊕ www.floridastateparks.org/sebastianinlet).

6

FAMILY **Florida Oceanographic Coastal Center.** This hydroland is the place to go for an interactive marine experience and live the center's mission "to inspire environmental stewardship of Florida's coastal ecosystems through education and research." Petting and feeding stingrays can be done at various times; in the morning, a sea turtle program introduces you to three full-time residents. Make sure to catch the "feeding frenzy" when keepers toss food into the 750,000-gallon lagoon tank and sharks, tarpon, and snook swarm the surface. Join a 1-mile guided walk through the coastal hardwood hammock and mangrove swamp habitats, or explore the trails on your own—you may see a dolphin or manatee swim by. ✉ 890 N.E. Ocean Blvd. ☎ 772/225–0505 ⊕ www.floridaocean.org 🎟 $12 ⊙ Mon.–Sat. 10–5, Sun. noon–4. Nature trails close at 4.

BEACHES

FAMILY **Bathtub Reef Beach.** Rough tides are often the norm in this stretch of the Atlantic Ocean, but a charming enclave at the southern end of Hutchinson Island—after the Marriott's beach and right by the Indian River Plantation luxury development—provides a perfect escape for families with young children and anyone who likes to snorkel. The waters are shallow and usually calm, and youngsters can walk up to the reef and see a dazzling assortment of fish. The parking lot is small, so get there early. Erosion is a problem, and sometimes lifeguards can't pull their hefty chairs out, leaving the beach unguarded (but it shouldn't deter you, because the sea isn't rough). **Amenities:** toilets; parking (free); lifeguards. **Best for:** swimming; snorkeling. ⊠ *1585 S.E. MacArthur Blvd.* ☉ *Daily 24 hrs.*

FAMILY **Stuart Beach.** When the waves robustly roll in, the surfers are rolling in, too. Beginning surfers are especially keen on Stuart Beach because of its ever-vigilant lifeguards, and pros to the sport like the challenges that the choppy waters here bring. But the beach is equally popular with surf fishers. Families enjoy the snack bar known for its chicken fingers, the basketball courts, the large canopy-covered playground, and the three walkways interspersed throughout the area for easy ocean access. **Amenities:** lifeguards; food and drink; parking (free); showers; toilets. **Best for:** surfing; swimming. ⊠ *889 N.E. Ocean Blvd.* ☉ *Daily 24 hrs.*

WHERE TO EAT

$$ ✕ **District Table and Bar.** Farm-fresh foods with a Southern accent are
SOUTHERN served up at this chef-owned restaurant with a theater kitchen, where comfort foods are taken to new levels. (Slow Foods, a group that celebrates local foods and artisans, has given the restaurant a "Snail of Approval.") The vibe is both hipster and rustic melded into an open (and often noisy) space; the chefs provide entertainment, and the bar is lively. On an ever-changing menu (check the website for current list), find house-made condiments and jams served with crab hushpuppies, sweet tea fried chicken, or a Key West hogfish. Look for unusual meat dishes as well: a U.S. Prime teres major is a seldom-seen shoulder cut served here with asparagus, warm potato salad, and garlic butter—creative fare in a convivial setting. If listed, don't miss the Grand Marnier soufflé for dessert. Ⓢ *Average main: $23* ⊠ *900 S.E. Indian St.* ☎ *772/324–8357* ⊕ *www.districttableandbar.com* ☉ *Closed Mon.*

$$$$ ✕ **11 Maple Street.** This cozy spot is as good as it gets on the Treasure
ECLECTIC Coast. Soft music and a friendly staff set the mood in the antiques-filled dining room of this old house, which holds only 21 tables. An extensive list of small plates can be ordered as starters or mains and include tasty treats like black-rice and calamari fritters with Thai sauce and Wagyu hanger steak with onion rings and salsa verde. Many of the vegetables are grown by the chef. The limited but superb selection of entrées include wood-grilled elk with roasted faro and Wagyu ribeye with port wine. All desserts are made from scratch and are also seductive, including white-chocolate custard with blackberry sauce. Ⓢ *Average main: $42* ⊠ *3224 N.E. Maple Ave., Jensen Beach* ☎ *772/334–7714* ⊕ *www.elevenmaple.com* ⚟ *Reservations essential* ☉ *Closed Sun. and Mon. No lunch.*

$$ SEAFOOD 🍴 **Ian's Tropical Grill.** Tucked inside a small plaza, the restaurant has a small, cozy dining room and covered alfresco patio. Start with cocktails—the mixologist here wins critics' approval. The chef finds ways to rescue food that might otherwise be discarded. An appetizer of fish ribs (the remains of a fish carcass) roasted with spices and served with a dipping sauce is one example, and a good ice-breaker with a group. Scallops and yellowfin tuna dishes are most popular, but Florida-inspired fare like mango-shrimp ceviche and cobia crudo, as well as a good conch salad with citrus offer visitors a taste of the tropics. The menu changes often, depending on what's fresh in the markets and from local farms, which are named. [$] *Average main: $25* ✉ *2875 S.E. Ocean Blvd.* ☎ *772/334–4563* 🌐 *www.ianstropicalgrille.com* 🕒 *Closed Sun.*

WHERE TO STAY

$ RESORT FAMILY 🏨 **Hutchinson Island Marriott Beach Resort & Marina.** With a 77-slip marina, a full water sports program, a golf course, two pools, tons of tennis courts, and children's activities, this self-contained resort is excellent for families, most of whom prefer to stay in the tower directly on the ocean. **Pros:** attentive, warm staff; rooms are comfortable and casually chic; all rooms have balconies. **Cons:** only one sit-down indoor restaurant; common areas are a bit dated; no spa; daily resort fee. [$] *Rooms from: $150* ✉ *555 N.E. Ocean Blvd., Hutchinson Island* ☎ *772/225–3700, 800/775–5936* 🌐 *www.marriott.com/pbiir* 🛏 *204 rooms, 70 suites* 🍽 *No meals.*

$ RESORT 🏨 **Pirate's Cove Resort & Marina.** This cozy enclave on the banks of the Manatee Pocket with ocean access at the southern end of Stuart is the perfect place to set forth on a day at sea or wind down after one—it's relaxing and casual, and has amenities like a swimming pool courtyard, restaurant, and fitness center. **Pros:** spacious tropical-themed rooms; great for boaters, with a 50-slip full-service, deepwater marina; each room has a balcony overlooking the water; free Wi-Fi and parking. **Cons:** lounge gets noisy at night; decor and furnishings are pretty but not luxurious; pool is on the small side. [$] *Rooms from: $165* ✉ *4307 S.E. Bayview St., Port Salerno* ☎ *772/287–2500* 🌐 *www.piratescoveresort.com* 🛏 *50 rooms* 🍽 *No meals.*

SHOPPING

More than 60 restaurants and shops with antiques, art, and fashion draw visitors downtown along Osceola Street.

B&A Flea Market. A short drive from downtown and operating for more than two decades, the oldest and largest flea market on the Treasure Coast has a street-bazaar feel, with shoppers happily scouting the 500 vendors for the practical and unusual. A produce market carries local tropical fruits and vegetables. ✉ *2885 S.E. U.S. 1* ☎ *772/288–4915* 🌐 *www.bafleamarket.com* 🎟 *Free* 🕒 *Weekends 8–3.*

SPORTS AND THE OUTDOORS

BOAT TOURS

Island Princess Cruises. Cruise the Indian River and St. Lucie River as well as Jupiter Sound aboard the Island Princess, an 82-footer that docks at the Sailfish Marina in Stuart. In season, there are nature cruises and "locks" cruises, going through the St. Lucie River locks. Have lunch

or during their Jupiter Island cruise, embarking Tuesdays and weekends year-round. The schedule, which changes often, is posted on the company's website. All ages are welcome, and advance reservations are required. ⊠ *Sailfish Marina, 3585 S.E. St. Lucie Blvd.* ☎ *772/225–2100* ⊕ *www.islandprincesscruises.com.*

FISHING

Sailfish Marina of Stuart. Nab a deep-sea charter here to land a sailfish, a popular sport fish that is prolific off the St. Lucie Inlet. This is the closest public marina to the St. Lucie Inlet. Recently expanded, it is home to Island Princess Cruises, which takes visitors to Vero Beach or Jupiter via the Intracoastal Waterway. ⊠ *3565 S.E. St. Lucie Blvd.* ☎ *772/283–1122* ⊕ *www.sailfishmarinastuart.com.*

FORT PIERCE AND PORT ST. LUCIE

11 miles north of Jensen Beach.

About an hour north of Palm Beach, Fort Pierce has a distinctive rural feel—but it has a surprising number of worthwhile attractions for a town of its size, including those easily seen while following Route 707 on the mainland (A1A on Hutchinson Island). A big draw is an inlet that offers fabulous fishing and excellent surfing. Nearby Port St. Lucie is largely landlocked southwest of Fort Pierce and is almost equidistant from there and Jensen Beach. It's not a big tourist area except for two sports facilities near I–95: the St. Lucie Mets' training grounds, Tradition Field, and the PGA Village. If you want a hotel directly on the sand or crave more than simple, motel-like accommodations, stay elsewhere and drive up for the day.

GETTING HERE AND AROUND

You can reach Fort Pierce from Jensen Beach by driving 11 miles north on Federal Highway (U.S. 1), Route 707, or Route A1A. To get to Port St. Lucie, continue north on U.S. 1 and take Prima Vista Boulevard west. From Fort Pierce, Route 709 goes diagonally southwest to Port St. Lucie, and I–95 is another choice.

ESSENTIALS

Visitor Information St. Lucie County Tourist Development Council ⊠ *2300 Virginia Ave.* ☎ *800/344-8443* ⊕ *www.visitstluciefla.com.*

EXPLORING

National Navy UDT-SEAL Museum. Commemorating the more than 3,000 troops who trained on these shores during World War II when this elite military unit got its start, there are weapons, vehicles, and equipment on view. Exhibits honor all frogmen and underwater demolition teams and depict their history. The museum houses the lifeboat from which SEALs saved the *Maersk Alabama* captain from Somali pirates in 2009. Kids get a thrill out of the helicopters and aircraft on the grounds. ⊠ *3300 N. Rte. A1A* ☎ *772/595–5845* ⊕ *www.navysealmuseum.com* ☞ *$8* ☉ *Tues.–Sat. 10–4, Sun. noon–4.*

FAMILY **Savannas Recreation Area.** Once a reservoir, the 550 acres have been returned to their natural wetlands state. Today the wilderness area has campgrounds, interpretive trails, and a boat ramp, and the recreation area is open year-round. Canoe and kayak rentals are available Thursday through Monday. A dog park (open daily) is also on-site. Amenities include showers, toilets, and free Wi-Fi for campers. ⊠ *1400 E. Midway Rd.* ☎ *772/464–7855* ⊕ *www.stlucieco.gov/parks/savannas.htm* ⊠ *Free* ⊗ *Daily 6:30–6:30.*

BEACHES

Fort Pierce Inlet State Park. Across the inlet at the northern side of Hutchinson Island, a fishing oasis lures beachgoers who can't wait to reel in snook, flounder, and bluefish, among others. The park is also known as a prime wave-riding locale, thanks to a reef that lies just outside the jetty. Summer is the busiest season by a long shot, but don't be fooled: it's a laid-back place to sun and surf. There are covered picnic tables but no concessions; however, from where anglers perch, a bunch of casual restaurants can be spotted on the other side of the inlet that are a quick drive away. Note that the area of Jack Island Preserve has been closed indefinitely. **Amenities:** toilets; showers; parking (fee); lifeguards (summer only). **Best for:** surfing; walking; solitude. ⊠ *905 Shorewinds Dr.* ☎ *772/468–3985* ⊕ *www.floridastateparks.org/fortpierceinlet* ⊠ *Vehicle $6, bicyclists and pedestrians $2* ⊗ *Daily 8–sunset.*

WHERE TO STAY

$ **Dockside Inn.** This hotel is the best of the lodgings lining the scenic Fort
HOTEL Pierce Inlet on Seaway Drive (and that's not saying much); it's a practical base for fishing enthusiasts with nice touches like two pools and a waterfront restaurant. **Pros:** good value; overnight boat docking available; reasonable rates at marina; parking included. **Cons:** basic decor; some steps to climb; grounds are nothing too fancy but have great views. $ *Rooms from: $139* ⊠ *1160 Seaway Dr.* ☎ *772/468–3555, 800/286–1745* ⊕ *www.docksideinn.com* ⇴ *36 rooms* ⊠ *No meals.*

SPORTS AND THE OUTDOORS

BASEBALL

Tradition Field. Out west by I–95, this Port St. Lucie baseball stadium, formerly known as Digital Domain Park as well as Thomas J. White Stadium, is where the New York Mets train; it's also the home of the St. Lucie Mets minor league team. ⊠ *525 N.W. Peacock Blvd., Port St. Lucie* ☎ *772/871–2115* ⊕ *www.stluciemets.com.*

GOLF

PGA Village. Owned and operated by the PGA of America, the national association of teaching pros, PGA Village is the winter home to many Northern instructors, along with permanent staff. The facility is a little off the beaten path and the clubhouse is basic, but serious golfers will appreciate the three championship courses by Pete Dye and Tom Fazio and the chance to sharpen their skills at the 35-acre PGA Center for Golf Learning and Performance, which has nine practice bunkers mimicking sands and slopes from around the globe. Between the Fazio-designed Wanamaker Course, the Ryder Course, and the Dye-designed Dye Course, there are 54 holes of championship golf at PGA Village. Also affiliated is the nearby St. Lucie Trail Golf Club. Beginners can start out on the lesser known (and easier) 6-hole PGA Short Course. Holes are 35 to 60 yards each, and course play is free. ⊠ *1916 Perfect*

6

Dr., Port St. Lucie ☎ *772/467–1300, 800/800–4653* ⊕ *www.pgavillage. com* ✉ *Wanamaker Course: 18 holes for $129; Ryder Course: 18 holes for $59; Dye Course: 18 holes for $44. St. Lucie Trail Golf Club: 18 holes for $49* ⚲ *Wanamaker Course: 18 holes, 7123 yards, par 72; Ryder Course: 18 holes, 7037 yards, par 72; Dye Course: 18 holes, 7279 yards, par 72; St. Lucie Golf Club Trail Course: 18 holes, 6901 yards, par 72.*

SCUBA DIVING

The region's premier dive site is actually on the National Register of Historic Places. The *Urca de Lima* was part of the storied treasure fleet bound for Spain that was destroyed by a hurricane in 1715. It's now part of an underwater archaeological preserve about 200 yards from shore, just north of the National Navy UDT-SEAL Museum and under 10 to 15 feet of water. The remains contain a flat-bottom, round-bellied ship and cannons that can be visited on an organized dive trip.

Dive Odyssea. This full-service dive shop offers kayak rentals, tank rentals, and scuba lessons. The shop can arrange a scuba charter in Jupiter or Palm Beach (two-tank dive trips typically start at $65), but Dive Odyssea no longer offers dive trips of its own. ⊠ *Fort Pierce Inlet, 621 N. 2nd St.* ☎ *772/460–1771* ⊕ *www.diveodyssea.com.*

VERO BEACH AND SEBASTIAN

12 miles north of Fort Pierce.

Tranquil and picturesque, these Indian River County towns have a strong commitment to the environment and culture, particularly to the upscale yet low-key Vero Beach, which is home to eclectic galleries and even trendy restaurants. Sebastian, a coastal fishing village that feels as remote as possible between Jacksonville and Miami Beach, has plenty of outdoor activities—including those at the Sebastian Inlet State Park, one of Florida's biggest and best recreation areas (and a paradise for surfers). It's actually within the boundaries of the federal government's massive protected Archie Carr National Wildlife Refuge, which encompasses several smaller parks within its boundaries. Downtown Vero is centered on the historic district on 14th Avenue, but much of the fun takes place across the Indian River (aka the Intracoastal Waterway) around Orchid Island's beaches.

GETTING HERE AND AROUND

To get here, you have two basic options: Route A1A along the coast (not to be confused with Ocean Drive, an offshoot on Orchid Island), or either U.S. 1 or Route 605 (also called Old Dixie Highway) on the mainland. As you approach Vero on the latter, you pass through an ungussied-up landscape of small farms and residential areas. On the beach route, part of the drive bisects an unusually undeveloped section of the Florida coast. If flying in, consider Orlando International Airport, which is larger and a smidge closer than Palm Beach International Airport.

ESSENTIALS

Visitor Information Indian River County Chamber of Commerce ✉ *1216 21st St.* ☎ *772/567–3491* ⊕ *www.indianriverchamber.com.* **Sebastian River Area Chamber of Commerce** ✉ *700 Main St., Sebastian* ☎ *772/589–5969* ⊕ *www.sebastianchamber.com.*

EXPLORING

Fodor'sChoice
★
McKee Botanical Garden. On the National Register of Historic Places, the 18-acre plot is a tropical jungle garden—one of the most lush and serene around. This is *the* place to see spectacular water lilies, and the property's original 1932 Hall of Giants, a rustic wooden structure that has stained-glass and bronze bells, contains the world's largest single-plank mahogany table at 35 feet long. There's a Seminole bamboo pavilion, a gift shop, and café (open for lunch Tuesday through Saturday—and Sunday in season), which serves especially tasty snacks and sandwiches. ✉ *350 U.S. 1* ☎ *772/794–0601* ⊕ *www.mckeegarden.org* 🎟 *$12* ⊙ *Tues.–Sat. 10–5, Sun. noon–5.*

McLarty Treasure Museum. On a National Historic Landmark site on the southern boundary of Sebastian Inlet State Park, this museum underscores the credo: "Wherever gold glitters or silver beckons, man will move mountains." On display are coins, weapons, and tools salvaged from the fleet of Spanish treasure ships that sank here in the 1715 storm, leaving some 1,500 survivors struggling to shore between Sebastian and Fort Pierce. The museum sits on the site of the survivors' camp. The museum's last video showing of "The Queen's Jewels and the 1715 Fleet" begins at 3:15. ✉ *Sebastian Inlet State Park, 13180 Rte. A1A, Sebastian* ☎ *772/589–2147* ⊕ *www.floridastateparks.org/ sebastianinlet/activities.cfm* 🎟 *$2* ⊙ *Daily 10–4.*

Mel Fisher's Treasure Museum. You'll really come upon hidden loot when you enter this place operated by the family of late treasure hunter Mel Fisher. See some of what he recovered in 1985 from the Spanish *Atocha* that sank in 1622 and dumped 100,000 gold coins, Colombian emeralds, and 1,000 silver bars into Florida's high seas—and what his team still salvages each year off the Treasure Coast. The museum certainly piques one's curiosity about what is still buried, and the website is all about the quest for more booty. ✉ *1322 U.S. 1, Sebastian* ☎ *772/589–9875* ⊕ *www.melfisher.com* 🎟 *$6.50* ⊙ *Mon.–Sat. 10–5, Sun. noon–5* ⊙ *Closed Sept.*

Pelican Island National Wildlife Refuge. Founded in 1903 by President Theodore Roosevelt as the country's first national wildlife refuge, the park encompasses the historic Pelican Island rookery itself—a small island in the Indian River Lagoon and important nesting place for 16 species of birds such as endangered wood storks and, of course, brown pelicans—and the land surrounding it overlooking Sebastian. The rookery is a closed wilderness area, so there's no roaming alongside animal kingdom friends; however, there is an 18-foot observation tower across from it with direct views and more than 6 miles of nature trails in the refuge. Another way to explore is via guided kayak tours from the Florida Outdoor Center *(⇨ see listing below).* Make sure to bring a camera—it's a photographer's dream. ✉ *Rte. A1A, 1 mile north of Treasure Shores*

Park ⚓ Take A1A and turn on Historic Jungle Trail ☎ *772/581–5557* ⊕ *www.fws.gov/pelicanisland* ✉ *Free* ☉ *Daily 7:30–sunset.*

BEACHES

Most of the hotels in the Vero Beach area are clustered around South Beach Park or line Ocean Drive around Beachland Boulevard just north of Humiston Park. Both parks have lifeguards daily. South Beach, at the end of East Causeway Boulevard, is one of the widest, quietest shores on the island, and has plenty of hammock shade before the dunes to picnic in, plus volleyball nets on the beach. Humiston Park is smack-dab in the main commercial zone with restaurants galore, including the lauded Citrus Grillhouse at its southern tip.

Humiston Park. Just south of the Driftwood Resort on Ocean Drive sits Humiston Park, one of the best beaches in town. Parking is free and plentiful, as there's a large lot on Easter Lily Lane and there are spots all over the surrounding business district. The shore is somewhat narrow and there isn't much shade, but the vibrant scene and other amenities make it a great choice for people who crave lots of activity. With lifeguards on call daily, there's a children's playground, plus several hotels, restaurants, bars, and shops within walking distance. **Amenities:** lifeguards; food and drink; toilets; showers. **Best for:** swimming; partiers; sunsets; walking. ✉ *3000 Ocean Dr., at Easter Lily La.* ☎ *772/231–5790.*

FAMILY
Fodor's Choice
★

Sebastian Inlet State Park. The 1000-acre park, which spans from the tip of Orchid Island across the passage to the barrier island just north, is one of the Florida park system's biggest draws, especially because of the inlet's highly productive fishing waters. Views from either side of the tall bridge are spectacular, and a unique hallmark is that the gates never close. Two jetties are usually packed with fishers and spectators alike. The park has two entrances, the entrance in Vero Beach and the main entrance in Melbourne (✉ *9700 Rte. A1A*). Within its grounds, you'll discover a wonderful two-story restaurant that overlooks the ocean, a fish and surfing shop (by the way, this place has some of the best waves in the state, but there are also calmer zones for relaxing swims), two museums, guided sea turtle walks in season, 51 campsites with water and electricity, and a marina with powerboat, kayak, and canoe rentals. **Amenities:** food and drink; parking (fee); showers; toilets; water sports. **Best for:** surfing; sunrise; sunset; walking. ✉ *14251 N. Rte. A1A* ☎ *321/984–4852* ⊕ *www.floridastateparks.org/sebastianinlet* ✉ *$8 vehicles with up to 8 people, $4 single drivers, $2 bicyclists and pedestrians* ☉ *Daily 24 hrs (gates never close).*

FAMILY
Wabasso Beach Park. A favorite for local surfboarding teens and the families at the nearby Disney's Vero Beach Resort, the park is nestled in a residential area at the end of Wabasso Road, about 8 miles up from the action on Ocean Drive and 8 miles below the Sebastian Inlet. Aside from regular amenities like picnic tables, restrooms, and a dedicated parking lot (which really is the "park" here—there's not much green space—and it's quite small, so arrive early), the Disney crowd walks there for its lifeguards (the strip directly in front of the hotel is unguarded) and the local crowd appreciates its conveniences, like a pizzeria and a store that

sells sundries, snacks, and beach supplies. **Amenities:** food and drink; lifeguards; parking (free); toilets; showers. **Best for:** swimming; surfing. ✉ *1820 Wabasso Rd.* 🕑 *Daily 7–sunset.*

WHERE TO EAT

$$$ MODERN AMERICAN Fodor's Choice ★

🍴 **Citrus Grillhouse.** There are rooms with a view, and then there's this view: uninterrupted sea from a wraparound veranda at the southern end of Humiston Park. Even better, the food here is a straightforward, delicious celebration of fresh and fabulous. One such dish—the fire-roasted baby squid with grilled lemon, garlic, toasted crouton—is an exercise in restraint that you can't help but gobble up. Speaking of gobble-gobble, the herb-roasted breast of turkey sandwich with arugula, tomato, red onion, and red-wine vinaigrette on a toasted sesame roll is the idyllic light lunch on the beach. Sunset lovers (and bargain hunters) rejoice over the three-course prix-fixe menu Monday through Thursday from 5 to 6 pm. [$] *Average main: $24* ✉ *Humiston Park, 1050 Easter Lily La.* ☎ *772/234–4114* 🌐 *www.citrusgrillhouse.com* 🕑 *No lunch Sun.*

$$ DINER FAMILY

🍴 **The Lemon Tree.** If Italy had old school luncheonettes, this is what they'd look like: a storefront of yellow walls, dark-green booths, white linoleum tables, and cascading sconces of faux ivy leaves and hand-painted Tuscan serving pieces for artwork. It's self-described by the husband-wife owners (who are always at the front) as an "upscale diner," and locals swear by it for breakfast (served all day) and lunch. Expect a short wait any day in season at peak hours. There's always a treat on the house, like a glass of sorbet to finish lunch; and don't miss the shrimp scampi—the sauce is so good, you'll want to dip every bit of the fresh focaccia in it. [$] *Average main: $20* ✉ *3125 Ocean Dr.* 🌐 *www.lemontreevero.com* 🕑 *No lunch or dinner Sun. No dinner June–Sept.*

$$$ ECLECTIC Fodor's Choice ★

🍴 **The Tides.** A charming cottage restaurant west of Ocean Drive prepares some of the best food around—not just in Vero Beach, but all of South Florida. The chefs, classically trained, give a nod to international fare with disparate dishes such as tuna tataki, Asian-inspired carpaccio with satay, penne quattro formaggi, and classic lobster bisque. The setting is effortlessly elegant and service top-notch. An appetizer's two jumbo crab cakes have scarcely anything but sweet, fresh flesh; a Southern-inspired corn-and-pepper sauce naps them. Floridian fish are a focus, testament to the chef's commitment to local sourcing. Adventurous eaters may want to book the Chef's Table, where the chef's choice menu is paired with wines from an impressive list. [$] *Average main: $27* ✉ *3103 Cardinal Dr.* ☎ *772/234–3966* 🌐 *www.tidesofvero.com* ✍ *Reservations essential* 🕑 *No lunch.*

WHERE TO STAY

$ HOTEL

🏨 **Capt Hiram's Resort.** Popular with boaters, this Key West–style inn on Sebastian's Riverfront has a lobby embellished with a classic surfboard collection and renovated (but still no-frills) guest rooms, all of which have private balconies (and most, oak furnishings). **Pros:** great location for fishing; good price; plenty of amenities; pet friendly. **Cons:** eastern rooms can be noisy; simple decor. [$] *Rooms from: $125* ✉ *1580 U.S. 1, Sebastian* ☎ *772/388–8588* 🌐 *www.hirams.com* 🔑 *67 rooms* 🍽 *No meals.*

$$ RESORT Fodor's Choice ★ **Costa d'Este Beach Resort.** This stylish, contemporary boutique hotel in the heart of Vero's bustling Ocean Drive area has a gorgeous infinity pool overlooking the ocean and a distinctly Miami Beach vibe—just like its famous owners, singer Gloria Estefan and producer Emilio Estefan, who bought the property in 2004. **Pros:** all rooms have balconies or secluded patios; huge Italian marble showers; complimentary signature mojitos on arrival. **Cons:** spa is on small side; rooms have only blackout shades; daily resort fee. [$] *Rooms from: $239* ✉ *3244 Ocean Dr.* ☎ *772/562–9919* 🌐 *www.costadeste.com* *94 rooms* 🍴 *No meals.*

$ RESORT FAMILY **The Driftwood Resort.** On the National Register of Historic Places, the two original buildings of this 1935 inn were built entirely from ocean-washed timbers with no blueprints; over time more buildings were added, and all are now decorated with such artifacts as ship's bells, Spanish tiles, and a cannon from a 16th-century Spanish galleon, and plenty of wrought iron, which create a quirky, utterly charming landscape. **Pros:** central location and right on the beach; free Wi-Fi; laundry facilities; weekly treasure hunt is a blast. **Cons:** older property; rooms can be musty; no-frills furnishings. [$] *Rooms from: $150* ✉ *3150 Ocean Dr.* ☎ *772/231–0550* 🌐 *www.verobeachdriftwood.com* *100 rooms* 🍴 *No meals.*

$$ RESORT FAMILY Fodor's Choice ★ **Vero Beach Hotel & Spa.** With a sophisticated, relaxed British West Indies feel, this luxurious five-story beachfront hotel at the north end of Ocean Drive is an inviting getaway and, arguably, the best on the Treasure Coast. **Pros:** beautiful pool; complimentary daily wine hour with hors d'oeuvres. **Cons:** separate charge for valet parking; some rooms overlook parking lot. [$] *Rooms from: $279* ✉ *3500 Ocean Dr.* ☎ *772/231–5666* 🌐 *www.verobeachhotelandspa.com* *102 rooms* 🍴 *No meals.*

SHOPPING

The place to go when in Vero Beach is **Ocean Drive.** Crossing over to Orchid Island from the mainland, the Merrill P. Barber Bridge turns into Beachland Boulevard; its intersection with Ocean Drive is the heart of a commercial zone with a lively mix of upscale clothing stores, specialty shops, restaurants, and art galleries.

Just under 3 miles north of that roughly eight-block stretch on A1A is a charming outdoor plaza, the **Village Shops.** It's a delight to stroll between the brightly painted cottages that have more unique, high-end offerings.

Back on the mainland, take 21st Street westward and you'll come across a small, modern shopping plaza with some independent shops and national chains. Keep going west on 21st Street, and then park around 14th Avenue to explore a collection of art galleries and eateries in the historic downtown.

SHOPPING CENTERS AND MALLS

Vero Beach Outlets. Need some retail therapy? Just west of I–95 off Route 60 is a discount shopping destination with 50 high-end brand-name stores, including Ann Taylor, Calvin Klein, Christopher & Banks, Dooney & Bourke, Polo Ralph Lauren, Restoration Hardware, White House/Black Market, and Jones New York. ✉ *1824 94th Dr.* ✣ *On Rte.*

6

60, West of I–95 at Exit 147 ☎ *772/770–6097* ⊕ *www.verobeachoutlets.com.*

SPORTS AND THE OUTDOORS
BOATING AND FISHING
Most of the region's fishing outfitters are based at the Capt. Hiram's Resort marina in Sebastian, though fly-fishing is popular here in the river, and there are a few guides available.

Big Easy Fishing Charters. For more than 40 years, Big Easy has offered Sebastian off-shore fishing, including guided backwater and deep-sea excursions. The boat is a 37-foot custom sport fisherman, originally built for the U.S. Navy, and is captained by Terry Wildey. Charters cost $650 for five hours, $750 for seven hours, and $859 for nine hours; the boat holds up to six people. ⊠ *Capt Hiram's Resort, 1606 N. Indian River Dr., Sebastian* ☎ *772/538–1072* ⊕ *www.bigeasyfishingcharter.com.*

Sebastian Watercraft Rentals. Based at Capt Hiram's Resort, this rental company has a fleet that ranges from 16-passenger pontoons and 18-foot sport boats to Waverunners. The company also organizes fishing charters on the Indian River and rents fishing gear. ⊠ *Capt Hiram's Resort, 1606 N. Indian River Dr., Sebastian* ☎ *772/589–5560* ⊕ *www.floridawatercraftrentals.com.*

Skipper Sportfishing Charters. Based at the marina at Capt. Hiram's Resort, Captain Eric Olsen offers full- and half-day ocean and river fishing trips aboard a 23-foot Mako for one to three anglers at $500 and $300, respectively. ⊠ *Capt. Hiram's Resort, 1606 N. Indian River Dr., Sebastian* ☎ *772/589–8505* ⊕ *www.skipperfish.com.*

GOLF
Sandridge Golf Club. The Sandridge Golf Club features two public 18-hole courses designed by Ron Garl: the Dunes course, with six holes located on a sand ridge; and the Lakes course, named for—you guessed it—the ubiquitous lakes around the course. The Dunes course, opened in 1987, follows a history-steeped pathway once used during mining operations. The Lakes course, opened in 1992, is renowned for the very challenging, par-4 14th hole with an island green. There's a pro shop on site offering lessons and clinics. Florida and Indian River County residents can get membership cards to book tee times eight days out—and get discounts for play. ⊠ *5300 73rd St.* ☎ *772/770–5000* ⊕ *www.sandridgegc.com* ⌂ *$53.50 for 18 holes* ⚑ *Dunes course: 18 holes, 6817 yards, par 72; Lakes course: 18 holes, 6181 yards, par 72.*

GUIDED TOURS
Florida Outdoor Center. Guided tours explore the area's natural wonders like the Pelican Island National Wildlife Refuge and begin at only $45 per adult. Tours include the Adventure Walk, a Bird Biking Safari, or Wildlife Watching Paddling Excursion. The company is mobile, launching from numerous sites, and, therefore, flexible. A van is available for pick-up at hotels, and they accommodate trekkers ages two and older. ☎ *772/202–0220* ⊕ *www.floridaoutdoorcenter.com.*

THE TAMPA
BAY AREA

WELCOME TO THE TAMPA BAY AREA

TOP REASONS TO GO

★ **Art gone wild:** Whether you take the guided tour or chart your own course, experience the one-of-a-kind collection at the Salvador Dalí Museum, which has relocated to a gorgeous waterfront building in downtown St. Petersburg.

★ **Cuban roots:** You'll find great food and vibrant nightlife in historic Ybor City, just east of downtown Tampa.

★ **Beachcomber bonanza:** Caladesi Island State Park has some of the best shelling on the Gulf Coast, and its five-star sunsets are a great way to end the day.

★ **Culture fix:** If you love the arts, there's no finer offering in the Bay Area than at the Florida State University Ringling Center for the Cultural Arts in Sarasota.

1 Tampa. Situated on a large bay of the same name, Tampa is a growing waterfront metropolis that's packed with state-of-the-art zoos, plenty of museums, and inviting shopping districts. Among the main draws is Busch Gardens, which doubles as a theme park and a zoo.

2 St. Petersburg. Although downtown St. Petersburg can be rowdy, there are also pockets of culture. The mellow but pricey Pinellas County beach towns include St. Pete Beach and Treasure Island.

3 Clearwater and Vicinity. Quiet during the winter, the beach areas north of St. Petersburg buzz all spring and summer. In addition to Clearwater, the area includes Dunedin and Tarpon Springs.

4 Citrus County. North of the Tampa/St. Petersburg area, the area known as the "Nature Coast" is filled with protected natural areas inhabited by manatees.

5 Sarasota and Vicinity. Sarasota County's barrier islands lure travelers to a battery of white-sand beaches, but Sarasota's cultural treasures are the true draw for many of its visitors.

GETTING ORIENTED

On the east side of the bay, Tampa is a sprawling cosmopolitan city offering attractions like Busch Gardens and Ybor City. To the west, St. Petersburg and Clearwater boast lovely barrier island beaches. Moving to the south, Sarasota's arts scene is among the finest in Florida.

7

Cosme

598

41 275 75

Gunn Hwy.

597

Fletcher   Ave.

41

Fowler   Ave.

Temple Terrace

Busch Blvd.

586

580

Carrollwood

Waters

Sheldon   Rd.

Oldsmar

Nebraska   Ave.

Dale Mabry   Hwy.

583

afety rbor

Hillsborough   Ave.

92

Tampa International Airport   ✈

574

Courtney Campbell Causeway

Old Tampa Bay

Rocky Point

60

Ybor City

Adamo   St.

St Petersburg-Clearwater International Airport   ✈

275

Howard Frankland Bridge

Kennedy Blvd.

92

BUS 41

TAMPA

Selmon Crosstown Expwy.

BIG ISLAND

West Shore   Blvd.

Gandy Bridge

92

Hillsborough Bay

41

1

East Tampa

WEEDON I.

62nd   Ave. N.

ROSS I.

MacDill Air Force Base

Gibsonton

92

38th   St. N.

2

Gadsden Point

Adamsville

Ave. M

19

ST. PETERSBURG

Ave. S

T a m p a   B a y

Apollo Beach

Boyd Hill Nature Park

Mangrove Point

Tamiami   Trail

54th   Ave. S

COQUINA KEY

Ruskin

Pinellas Point

Golf City

Little   Manatee   River

75

Sun City

41

Valroy

Sunshine Skyway   (toll)

Piney Point

301

TO SARASOTA ↓

5

Gillette

275

275

Parrish

19

75

Updated
by Kate
Bradshaw

If you seek a destination that's no one-trick pony, the Tampa Bay region is a spot you can't miss. Encompassing an area from Tarpon Springs to Tampa proper and all the way south to Sarasota, it's one of those unsung places as dynamic as it is appealing—and word has definitely started to spread about its charms. With its long list of attractions—from pristine beaches to world-class museums—it's easy to see why.

First and foremost, Tampa Bay's beaches are some of the best in the country. Whether you want coarse or fine sand, and whether you seek a mellow day of shelling or a raucous romp on a crowded stretch of waterfront, this place has it all. Of course, you can choose from a range of water activities, including charter fishing, parasailing, sunset cruises, kayaking, and more.

The region has its share of boutique districts spotted with shops and sidewalk cafés. Tampa's Hyde Park Village and downtown St. Petersburg's Beach Drive are among the top picks if you're looking to check out some upscale shops and dine alfresco while getting the most of the area's pleasant climate. Vibrant nightlife tops off Tampa Bay's list of assets. Ybor City attracts the club set, and barrier islands like St. Pete Beach offer loads of live music and barefoot dancing into the wee hours.

Tampa Bay has lots of family-friendly attractions, too. You can check out Busch Gardens, Adventure Island, and the Clearwater Marine Aquarium, to name a few. And art fanatics will find an astonishing array of attractions, including Sarasota's Ringling Museum of Art, St. Petersburg's enrapturing Salvador Dalí and Dale Chihuly collections (both permanent and housed in exquisite new digs), and Tampa's Museum of Art. Come prepared to explore and see for yourself what a compelling, unforgettable place the Tampa Bay area really is.

PLANNING

WHEN TO GO

Winter and spring are high season, and the amount of activity during this time is double that of the off-season. Beaches do stay pretty packed throughout the sweltering summer, which is known for massive, almost-daily afternoon thunderstorms. Summer daytime temperatures hover around or above 90°F. Luckily the mercury drops to the mid-70s at night, and the beaches have a consistent onshore breeze that starts just before sundown, which enabled civilization to survive here before air-conditioning arrived.

GETTING HERE AND AROUND

AIR TRAVEL

Tampa International Airport, the area's largest and busiest airport, with 19 million passengers per year, is served by most major carriers and offers ground transportation to surrounding cities. Many of the large U.S. carriers also fly into and out of Sarasota–Bradenton International Airport. St. Petersburg–Clearwater International Airport, 9 miles west of downtown St. Petersburg, is much smaller than Tampa International and has limited service.

Airport Transfers: SuperShuttle is one of the easiest ways to get to and from the airport if you forgo a rental car. All you need to do is call or visit the SuperShuttle website to book travel—they'll pick you up and drop you off wherever you're staying at any hour. Basic service costs around $28.

Blue One Transportation provides service to and from Tampa International Airport for areas including Hillsborough (Tampa, Plant City), Pinellas (St. Petersburg, St. Pete Beach, Clearwater), and Polk (Lakeland) counties. Rates vary by pickup location, destination, and fuel costs.

Airport Sarasota–Bradenton International Airport ✉ *Sarasota* ☎ *941/359-2777* ⊕ *www.srq-airport.com.* **St. Petersburg–Clearwater International Airport** ✉ *Clearwater* ☎ *727/453-7800* ⊕ *www.fly2pie.com.* **Tampa International Airport** ✉ *Tampa* ☎ *813/870-8700* ⊕ *www.tampaairport.com.*

Airport Transfers Blue One Transportation ☎ *813/282-7351* ⊕ *www.blueonetransportation.com.* **SuperShuttle** ☎ *800/258-3826* ⊕ *www.supershuttle.com.*

BUS TRAVEL

Several transit lines serve Hillsborough (Tampa), Pinellas (St. Petersburg and Clearwater), Sarasota, and Manatee (Bradenton) counties, and if you are staying in a resort, they may meet your needs, but none is as convenient as a car.

CAR TRAVEL

Interstates 75 and 275 span the Bay Area from north to south. Coming from Orlando, you're likely to drive west into Tampa on Interstate 4. Along with Interstate 75, U.S. 41 (the Tamiami Trail) stretches the length of the region and links the business districts of many communities; avoid this route during rush hours (7–9 am and 4–6 pm).

HOTELS

Many convention hotels in the Tampa Bay area double as family-friendly resorts—taking advantage of nearby beaches, marinas, spas, tennis courts, and golf links. However, unlike Orlando and some other parts of Florida, the area has been bustling for more than a century, and its accommodations often reflect a sense of its history.

You'll find a turn-of-the-20th-century beachfront resort where Zelda and F. Scott Fitzgerald stayed, a massive all-wood building from the 1920s, plenty of art deco, and Spanish-style villas. But one thing they all have in common is a certain Gulf Coast charm. *Hotel reviews have been shortened. For full information, visit Fodors.com.*

RESTAURANTS

Fresh gulf seafood is plentiful—raw bars serving oysters, clams, and mussels are everywhere. Tampa's many Cuban and Spanish restaurants serve paella with seafood and chicken, *boliche criollo* (sausage-stuffed eye-round roast) with black beans and rice, *ropa vieja* (shredded flank steak in tomato sauce), and other treats. Tarpon Springs adds classic Greek specialties. In Sarasota the emphasis is on ritzier dining, though many restaurants offer extra-cheap early-bird menus.

WHAT IT COSTS				
	$	$$	$$$	$$$$
RESTAURANTS	under $16	$16–$20	$21–$30	over $30
HOTELS	under $201	$201–$300	$301–$400	over $400

Restaurant prices are the average cost of a main course at dinner or, if dinner is not served, at lunch. Hotel prices are the lowest cost of a standard double room in high season.

TAMPA

84 miles southwest of Orlando via I–4.

Tampa, the west coast's business-and-commercial hub, has a sprinkling of high-rises and heavy traffic. A concentration of restaurants, nightlife, stores, and cultural events is amid the bustle. The city has really come into its own in recent years. The downtown Tampa waterfront features stunning views and excellent museums. Animal lovers flock here for attractions like Lowry Park Zoo, Busch Gardens, Big Cat Rescue, and Giraffe Ranch. Revelers will enjoy the strip of bars and clubs that constitutes Ybor City, a historic area with a heavy Cuban influence. The city also abounds with art museums, shops, and a wide array of restaurants. Downtown and Ybor City are both excellent spots to look for live music. Not too far out of town are some great golf courses and nature trails. Tampa is also a short drive from a long stretch of gorgeous Gulf Coast beaches.

GETTING AROUND

Downtown Tampa's Riverwalk, on Ashley Drive at the Hillsborough River, connects waterside entities such as the Florida Aquarium, the Channelside shopping-and-entertainment complex, and Marriott Waterside. The landscaped park is 6 acres and extends along the Garrison cruise-ship channel and along the Hillsborough River downtown. The walkway is being expanded as waterside development continues.

Hillsborough Area Regional Transit and TECO Line Street Cars replicate Tampa's first electric streetcars, transporting cruise-ship passengers to Ybor City and downtown Tampa.

Although downtown Tampa, the Channelside District, and Ybor City are easy to navigate without a car, you'll want to rent one if you plan on hitting the beaches or heading to Busch Gardens, Hyde Park, International Plaza, or any of the zoos.

Bus and Trolley Contacts Hillsborough Area Regional Transit ☎ *813/254–4278* ⊕ *www.gohart.org.* **TECO Line Street Cars** ☎ *813/254–4278* ⊕ *www.tecolinestreetcar.org.*

VISITOR INFORMATION

Contacts Tampa Bay & Company ✉ *401 E. Jackson St., Suite 2100* ☎ *800/448–2672, 813/223–1111* ⊕ *www.visittampabay.com.* **Tampa Bay Beaches Chamber of Commerce.** The staff here will give you the lowdown on the Pinellas County beaches. ✉ *6990 Gulf Blvd., St. Pete Beach* ☎ *727/360–6957* ⊕ *www.tampabaybeaches.com.* **Ybor City Chamber Visitor Bureau** ✉ *1800 E. 9th St.* ☎ *813/248–3712* ⊕ *www.ybor.org.*

7

EXPLORING

TOP ATTRACTIONS

Fodor'sChoice
★

Big Cat Rescue. Suburban Citrus Park in North Tampa is probably the last place you'd expect to be able to get face-to-face with an 800-pound tiger. Yet at the end of a shaded road just yards off the Veterans' Expressway, you can do just that. This nonprofit, accredited sanctuary rescues and provides a permanent home for lions, tigers, ocelots, bobcats, cougars, and members of any other large-cat species you can imagine. Each and every one of these marvelous creatures has a unique story. Some arrived here after narrowly avoiding becoming an expensive coat. Others were kept as pets until the owners realized how pricey 15 pounds of meat per day (what it takes to feed some of these creatures) can be. They're all kept in large enclosures. A volunteer guide will lead you around the property and tell you the story of every cat you see. You'll also get an earful of little-known facts about these big cats, from the true origin of the white tiger to why some cats have white spots on the backs of their ears. Tours (no unescorted visits are allowed) are every day but Thursday, and special tours for children under 10 accompanied by an adult are offered on weekends. Night tours, feeding tours, and appointment-only private tours are also available. ✉ *12802 Easy St., Citrus Park* ☎ *813/920–4130* ⊕ *bigcatrescue.org* 🎫 *$29* ☉ *Mon.–Wed. and Fri. at 3 pm; weekends at 10 am and 1 pm; kids' tour weekends at 9 am. Other special tours available by reservation only, at varying costs.*

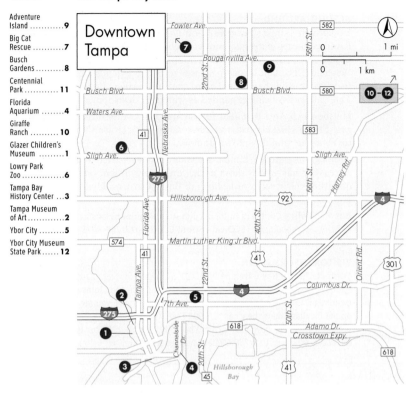

FAMILY

Fodor'sChoice

★

Busch Gardens. The Jungala exhibit at Busch Gardens brings Bengal tigers to center stage and puts them at eye level—allowing you to view them from underground caves and underwater windows. The big cats are just one of the reasons the theme park attracts some 4.5 million visitors each year. This is a world-class zoo, with more than 2,000 animals, and a live-entertainment venue that provides a full day (or more) of fun for the whole family. If you want to beat the crowds, start in the back of the park and work your way around clockwise.

The 335-acre adventure park's habitats offer views of some of the world's most endangered and exotic animals. For the best animal sightings, go to their habitats early, when it's cooler. You can experience up-close animal encounters on the Serengeti Plain, a 65-acre free-roaming habitat, home to reticulated giraffes, Grevy's zebras, white rhinos, bongos, impalas, and more. Myombe Reserve allows you to view lowland gorillas and chimpanzees in a lush, tropical-rain-forest environment. Down Under–themed Walkabout Way offers those ages five and up an opportunity to hand-feed kangaroos and wallabies (a cup of vittles is $5).

Interested in watching a tiger get a dental checkup? Then head over to the Animal Care & Nutrition Center, where you can observe veterinary care for many of the park's animals.

The park's newest thrill ride is Falcon's Fury, a 335-foot drop that is reportedly the tallest freestanding drop ride on the continent. It's the centerpiece of a the park's newest "land," Pantopia, a colorful collection of rides, cafés, and retail space that replaces its Timbuktu section.

Many consider the seven roller coasters to be the biggest lure. On the wings of an African hawk, SheiKra—North America's first dive coaster—takes riders on a three-minute journey 200 feet up, then (gulp!) plunges 90 degrees straight down at 70 mph. The park's coaster lineup also includes steel giants Kumba, Scorpion, and Montu; a double, and Sand Serpent, a five-story family coaster full of hairpin turns and breathtaking dips. When it's running, the Cheetah Hunt is an absolutely exhilarating 4,429-foot-high launch coaster. With three different launch points, this coaster takes you through the Serengeti and into a rocky gorge with a top speed of 60 mph.

The off-road-safari Rhino Rally brings you face-to-face with zebras, elephants, and white rhinos. Catering to the shorter set, the Sesame Street Safari of Fun is a 5-acre kids' playground with Sesame-themed rides, shows, and water adventures. The Air Grover Rollercoaster takes kids (and parents) on minidives and twisty turns over the Sahara, while Jungle Flyers gets them swinging and screeching. If you're looking to cool off, your best bets are Congo River Rapids, Tanganyika Tidal Wave, Stanleyville Falls (a flume ride), or Bert & Ernie's Water Hole—complete with bubblers, geysers, water jets, and dumping buckets. Character lunches are available (but you might want to wait until after your rides). ⌧ *10165 N. Malcolm McKinley Dr., Central Tampa* 🕾 *813/987–5000, 888/800–5447* ⊕ *www.buschgardens.com* 🖅 *$95; parking $15* ⊘ *Daily 9:30–6.*

FAMILY **Florida Aquarium.** Although eels, sharks, and stingrays are the headliners, the Florida Aquarium is much more than a giant fishbowl. This architectural landmark features an 83-foot-high, multitier, glass dome; 250,000 square feet of air-conditioned exhibit space; and more than 20,000 aquatic plants and animals representing species native to Florida and the rest of the world—from black-tip sharks to leafy sea dragons.

Floor-to-ceiling interactive displays, behind-the-scenes tours, and in-water adventures allow kids to really get hands-on—and even get their feet wet. Adventurous types (certified divers age 15 and up) can dive with mild-mannered sharks and sea turtles, participate in shark-feeding programs (age 12 and up), or shallow-water swim with reef fish such as eels and grouper (age 6 and up).

However, you don't have to get wet to have an interactive experience: the Ocean Commotion exhibit offers virtual dolphins and whales and multimedia displays and presentations. The Coral Reef Gallery is a 500,000-gallon tank with viewing windows, an awesome 43-foot-wide panoramic opening, and a walk-through tunnel that gives the illusion of venturing into underwater depths. There you see a thicket of elkhorn coral teeming with tropical fish, and a dark cave reveals sea life you would normally see only on night dives. The new Journey to Madagascar exhibit features ring-tailed lemurs, hissing cockroaches, and an

DID YOU KNOW?

One of six roller coasters at Busch Gardens, the steel, 60-foot-tall Scorpion twists and turns at speeds near 50 mph and then throws you into a 360-degree vertical loop. During the two-minute ride you'll experience a 3.5 g-force.

Indian Ocean coral reef to showcase the nation's vast diversity of creatures and ecosystems.

If you have an extra 90 minutes, try the Wild Dolphin Adventure Cruise, which takes up to 130 passengers onto Tampa Bay in a 72-foot catamaran for an up-close look at bottlenose dolphins and other wildlife. The outdoor Explore a Shore exhibit, which gives younger kids a chance to release some energy, is an aquatic playground with a waterslide, water-jet sprays, and a climbable replica pirate ship. Last but not least, two black-footed South African penguins make daily appearances in the Coral Reef Gallery. For an extra cost, you can get an up-close look at the daily lives of these penguins during the half-hour-long Penguins: Backstage Pass demonstration. ⊠ *701 Channelside Dr., Downtown* ☎ *813/273–4000* ⊕ *www.flaquarium.org* ⏢ *Aquarium $23.95; Aquarium/Adventure Cruise combo $49.90; Penguins Backstage Pass combo $53.95; Behind the Scenes Combo $35.95; Stingray feeding tour combo $37.95; Dive with the Sharks $175; Swim with the Fishes $75; parking $6* ⊗ *Daily 9:30–5.*

FAMILY
Fodor's Choice
★
Giraffe Ranch. Rural Dade City is known mostly for its strawberries, but word is quickly spreading about something else that makes people flock here: giraffes. These graceful creatures are the headliners at this nearly 50-acre ranch. You can view them as part of a tour in a safari-style vehicle, on the back of a camel, or on a Segway; on any tour, you get to hand-feed them cabbage leaves. You'll also see tons of zebras, a pair of pygmy hippos, a couple of rhinos, ostriches, and many other animal species roaming the grounds. Near the ranch's welcome center and gift shop is a corral of enclosures where you can watch guinea pigs chomp on sweet-potato chunks, hold a baby goat, (for a little extra cash) feed a flock of resident lemurs, watch a group of otters (the ranch's newest residents), or bathe a pair of rhinos. The ranch's proprietors have encyclopedic knowledge of the animal kingdom, and the overall experience is meant to impart a sense of connection to the animal world—and the environment—on those who visit. Tours take about two hours, and reservations are required. Credit cards are not accepted. ⊠ *38650 Mickler Rd., Dade City* ☎ *813/482–3400* ⊕ *www.girafferanch.com* ⏢ *$75 for tour in safari van; $150 for tour by camelback; $150 by Segway* ⊗ *Tues.–Sun. at 11 am and 2 pm, by reservation only.*

FAMILY
Glazer Children's Museum. It's all about play here, and, with 53,000 square feet, more than a dozen themed areas, and 175 "interactives," there's plenty of opportunity for it. Areas designed to nurture imagination and strengthen confidence allow children and families to experience everything from flying an airplane to shopping for groceries. Kids can also create art, control the weather, navigate a mini–shipping channel, and "drive" a miniature (stationary) fire truck through Tampa. The Water's Journey Tree lets kids climb the tree to the second floor and mimics the water cycle. ⊠ *110 W. Gasparilla Plaza, Downtown* ☎ *813/443–3861* ⊕ *wwww.glazermuseum.org* ⏢ *$15 adult; $9.50 children* ⊗ *Weekdays 10–5, Sat. 10–6, Sun. 1–6.*

FAMILY
Lowry Park Zoo. Natural-habitat exhibits include Safari Africa, where a herd of African elephants (including two calves) is free to roam, make

the 56-acre Lowry Park Zoo one of the best midsize zoos in the country. Asia gardens features two clouded leopards, and residents of Ituri Forest include a cheetah and lovably plump pygmy hippos. As you stroll through, keep an eye out for okapis, a rare forest giraffe from Central Africa. The stars at Primate World range from cat-size lemurs to a family of heavyweight Bornean orangutans that love to ham for the camera.

For hands-on experiences, Lowry has more options than most large parks, including chances to feed a giraffe, hold a colorful lorikeet, or touch a slippery stingray. Majestic red-tailed hawks and other raptors put on a show at the Birds of Prey Center, and a flock of majestic macaws soars through the zoo in a one-of-a-kind free-flight experience each day at 10:15 and 2. You can come face-to-face with Florida manatees at the Manatee Aquatic Center, the only nonprofit manatee hospital on the planet.

Dwindling native species like Florida panthers, black bears, and red wolves may be tough to find in the wild, but you can easily find them at the Florida Wildlife Center. Adorable koalas, wallabies, and emus populate the Wallaroo Station children's zoo. There are also water-play areas, rides (all of which are included with zoo admission), shows, and restaurants. ⊠ *1101 W. Sligh Ave., Central Tampa* ☎ *813/935–8552* ⊕ *www.lowryparkzoo.com* ⊡ *$24.95* ⊙ *Daily 9:30–5.*

FAMILY **Tampa Bay History Center.** From the early civilizations that once flourished on its shores to the 2000 presidential vote recount, the Tampa Bay region has long had an integral role in Florida history and that of the country as a whole. The interactive exhibits here let you peer back in time at the people and events that helped shape the area. You'll learn about the Tocobaga and other people who lived in coastal areas and the Spanish explorers who encountered them. You'll find a wealth of information and artifacts from the Seminole Wars, Ybor City's once-thriving cigar industry, and Florida crackers who, believe it or not, once drove their cattle in areas now saturated with busy roads and shopping centers. Exhibits also cover the sports teams that have called Tampa Bay home, not to mention the war heroes and politicians of the 20th and 21st centuries. Museumgoers looking for a bite to eat are in for a treat: the café here is branch of none other than the Columbia, Tampa's most famous and historic restaurant. ⊠ *801 Old Water St., Channelside* ☎ *813/228–0097* ⊕ *tampabayhistorycenter.org* ⊡ *$12.95* ⊙ *Daily 10–5.*

Fodor'sChoice **Ybor City.** Tampa's lively Latin quarter is one of only a few National
★ Historic Landmark districts in Florida. Bordered by Interstate 4 to the north, 22nd Street to the east, Adamo Drive to the south, and Nebraska Avenue to the West, it has antique-brick streets and wrought-iron balconies. Cubans brought their cigar-making industry to Ybor (pronounced *ee*-bore) City in 1886, and the smell of cigars—hand-rolled by Cuban immigrants—still wafts through the heart of this east Tampa area, along with the strong aroma of roasting coffee. These days the neighborhood is one of Tampa's hot spots, if at times a rowdy one, as empty cigar factories and historic social clubs have been transformed into trendy boutiques, art galleries, restaurants, and nightclubs. ⊠ *Ybor City.*

WORTH NOTING

FAMILY **Adventure Island.** From spring until fall, rides named Everglides, Gulf Scream, and Key West Rapids promise heat relief at Busch Gardens' water park. Tampa's most popular "wet" park features waterslides and artificial wave pools, along with tranquil "beaches" in a 30-acre package. The most recent addition is Colossal Curl, a massive thrill ride that's the tallest waterslide in the park. One of the attraction's headliners, Riptide, challenges you to race three other riders on a sliding mat through twisting tubes and hairpin turns. Planners of this park also took the younger kids into account, with offerings such as Fabian's Funport, which has a scaled-down pool and interactive water gym. Along with a volleyball complex and a rambling river, there are cafés, snack bars, picnic and sunbathing areas, changing rooms, and private cabanas. Good discounts are sometimes offered on the park's website. ⊠ *10001 N. McKinley Dr., less than 1 mile north of Busch Gardens, Central Tampa* ☎ *813/987–5660, 888/800–5447* ⊕ *www.adventureisland.com* ⌨ *$47; parking $12* ⊙ *Mid-Mar.–Aug., daily 10–5; Sept. and Oct., weekends only 10–5.*

Centennial Park. You can step back into the past at Centennial Park, which re-creates a period streetscape and hosts a farmers' market called the "Fresh Market" every Saturday, among a host of other events like festivals and pottery classes. ⊠ *1800 E. 8th Ave., Ybor City.*

Tampa Museum of Art. Housed in an exquisitely designed new building, the Tampa Museum of Art is emblematic of the city's efforts to revitalize the downtown riverfront. The facility overlooks Curtis Hixon Park, the towering minarets of the University of Tampa, and the Hillsborough River. The museum's 66,000 square feet of gallery space displays an impressive permanent collection of 20th- and 21st-century sculpture as well as Greek and Roman antiquities. Five additional galleries host traveling exhibits ranging from the classics to some of the most prominent artists working today. The building's external walls are lit at night with colorful LED lights, which are best viewed from Curtis Hixon Waterfront Park. Also notable is Sono, the museum's café, which is operated by Mise en Place, one of Tampa's top restaurants. ⊠ *120 W. Gasparilla Plaza, Downtown* ☎ *813/274–8130* ⊕ *www.tampamuseum.org* ⌨ *$10* ⊙ *Mon.–Thurs. 11–7, Fri. 11–8, weekends 11–5.*

Ybor City Museum State Park. This park provides a look at the history of the cigar industry. Admission includes a tour of La Casita, one of the shotgun houses occupied by cigar workers and their families in the late 1890s, held every half hour between 10 am and 3 pm. ⊠ *1818 E. 9th Ave., between Nuccio Pkwy. and 22nd St. from 7th to 9th Aves., Ybor City* ☎ *813/247–6323* ⊕ *www.ybormuseum.org* ⌨ *$4* ⊙ *Daily 9–5.*

WHERE TO EAT

$$ ✕ **Bella's Italian Café.** Carnivores are not slighted here, but it is often more
ITALIAN delicious to go meatless at this SoHo (South Howard Avenue) eatery. The lasagna *napoletana* is bursting with four kinds of cheese, and the garlicky basil-tomato sauce gives it just the right bite. The grouper *alla calabrese* (lightly battered and sautéed with red wine, capers, olives,

and onions) is another memory maker. Bella's is not too highbrow to ignore pizza and calzones—there are dozens of options. Offerings like these have kept the restaurant popular since 1986. If you're in a rush, there's curbside pickup. [$] *Average main: $20* ✉ *1413 S. Howard Ave., Hyde Park* ☎ *813/254–3355* 🌐 *www.bellasitaliancafe.com.*

$$$$ STEAKHOUSE Fodor's Choice ★

🍴 **Bern's Steak House.** With the air of an exclusive club, this is one of Florida's finest steak houses. Rich mahogany paneling and ornate chandeliers define the legendary Bern's, where the chef ages his own beef, grows much of his own produce, and roasts his own coffee. There's also a Cave Du Fromage, housing a discriminating selection of artisanal cheeses from around the world. Cuts of prime beef are sold by weight and thickness. There's a 60-ounce strip steak that's big enough to feed your pride (of lions), but for most appetites the veal loin chop or 8-ounce chateaubriand is more than enough. The wine list includes approximately 7,000 selections (with 1,000 dessert wines). After dinner, tour the kitchen and wine cellar before having dessert upstairs in a cozy booth. The dessert room is a hit. For a real jolt, try the Turkish coffee with an order of Mississippi mud pie. Casual business attire is recommended. Those looking for the Bern's touch but aren't up for donning a jacket and tie should opt for SideBern's, the steak house's more low-key sister property a few blocks up the road. [$] *Average main: $32* ✉ *1208 S. Howard Ave., Hyde Park* ☎ *813/251–2421* 🌐 *www.bernssteakhouse.com* ✍ *Reservations essential* 👔 *Jacket and tie.*

$$$ ASIAN FUSION

🍴 **BT.** Local restaurateur B. T. Nguyen has earned quite a following since opening her first eatery in the early 1990s. Her modern take on conscientiously sourced local ingredients fits well within its upscale South Tampa surroundings, and the high-style Vietnamese cuisine features fresh herbs grown on-site and a drink list that includes organic sake martinis—some flavored with herbs from that same garden. With a motto like "Eat local, think global," the menu is inevitably sophisticated yet simple, with creative offerings like Shaken beef, a go-to dish for regulars, consisting of cubed filet mignon flavored with cognac and shallots. Vegetarians and vegans can rest easy here, with options such as Food Karma (braised tofu, edamame, eggplant, and ginger in coconut broth over black rice). Casual dress is acceptable, but patrons tend to dress up. [$] *Average main: $28* ✉ *2507 S. MacDill Ave., Suite B, SoHo* ☎ *813/258–1916* 🌐 *www.restaurantbt.com.*

$$ ECLECTIC

🍴 **Café Dufrain.** Dogs can tag along if you dine on the front patio at pet-friendly Café Dufrain, an eatery right on the Hillsborough River across from the Amalie Arena. Creative menu items, which vary by season, include apple cider-braised chicken breast and short rib mac and cheese. The bar menu has a nice selection of craft beers and cocktails. In mild weather, opt for the waterfront view of downtown Tampa. [$] *Average main: $20* ✉ *707 Harbour Post Dr., Downtown* ☎ *813/275–9701* 🌐 *cafedufrain.com.*

$ PIZZA

🍴 **Cappy's Pizza.** Chicago may be the first place you think of when you hear the words "deep-dish pizza," which is why the high-quality pies this local chain offers may surprise (and please) you. The menu at this family-friendly spot is pretty simple: choose either a Chicago- or New York–style crust, and select your toppings. The "Cappy" features a blend of pepperoni, ham, onions, green pepper, sausage, and mushrooms. You can also go with a calzone. There's no hostess here, so put your name on the (usually long) list you see when you first walk in. If it's not too packed, try to get garden seating. The feel inside is very nostalgic—vintage signs and an old toy train set adorn the walls. You'll find a lengthy list of craft brews, and the kids might enjoy an IBC root beer. This location is cash-only, but there is an ATM on-site. [$] *Average main: $12* ✉ *4910 N. Florida Ave., Seminole Heights* ☎ *813/238–1516* 🌐 *cappyspizzaonline.com* ✍ *Reservations not accepted* 💳 *No credit cards* ⏲ *No lunch.*

$$ SPANISH Fodor's Choice ★ 🍴 **Columbia.** Make a date for some of the best Latin cuisine in Tampa. A fixture since 1905, this magnificent structure with an old-world air and spacious dining rooms takes up an entire city block and seems to feed the entire city—locals as well as visitors—throughout the week, but especially on weekends. The paella, bursting with seafood, chicken, and pork, is arguably the best in Florida, and the 1905 salad—with ham, olives, cheese, and garlic—is legendary. The menu has Cuban classics such as *boliche criollo* (tender eye of round stuffed with chorizo), *ropa vieja* (shredded beef with onions, peppers, and tomatoes), and *arroz con pollo* (chicken with yellow rice). Don't miss the flamenco dancing show every night but Sunday. This place is also known for its sangria. If you can, walk around the building and check out the elaborate, antique decor along every inch of the interior. [$] *Average main: $19* ✉ *2117 E. 7th Ave., Ybor City* ☎ *813/248–4961* 🌐 *www.columbiarestaurant.com.*

7

$ ECLECTIC 🍴 **Datz.** Fans of a hearty meal will not be slighted here; the eclectic menu is mostly massive sandwiches and hefty plates (and printed on tabloid paper, an indication of how much it changes). Ty's two-fister, for example, combines corned beef and pastrami with Swiss and Muenster cheese and honeycup mustard on house-baked sauerkraut rye. The *banh mi* tacos, made with braised short ribs, pickled daikon, carrots, and Asian BBQ sauce are a favorite. But the story doesn't end with the entrées here. For starters, when you walk into this spot, the first thing you'll probably notice (aside from the vintage decor) is the chocolate counter. If you mosey over to the bar, you'll find some very special craft cocktail concoctions. If you happen to stop in during the breakfast hour, check out the amazing offerings at the adjacent bakery, Datz Dough, where the donuts (caramel curry, for example) are worth the stop. [$] *Average main: $15* ✉ *2616 S. MacDill Ave., SoHo* ☎ *813/831–7000* 🌐 *datztampa.com.*

$$$$ ECLECTIC 🍴 **Edison Food + Drink Lab.** In the relatively short time this gastro pub has been around, it has handily earned a spot at the table of Tampa culinary musts. The creative menu changes almost every day as chef/owner Jeannie Pierola experiments with a revolving list of intriguing ingredients. Choices include pomegranate and blood orange–braised short ribs (served with butternut squash polenta and roasted baby beets and tops) and spicy Jamaican fried organic chicken (served with a banana bacon waffle). And the list goes on. The kitchen happily makes substitutions or changes recipes if you have any dietary restrictions. The bar has a great list of craft cocktails. [$] *Average main: $32* ✉ *912 W. Kennedy Blvd., Downtown* ☎ *813/254–7111* 🌐 *edison-tampa.com.*

$ ✕ **Kojak's House of Ribs.** Few barbecue joints can boast the staying power
SOUTHERN   of this family-owned and -operated pit stop. Located along a shaded
stretch in South Tampa, it debuted in 1978 and has since earned a following of sticky-fingered regulars who have turned it into one of the
most popular barbecue stops in central Florida. It's located in a 1927
house complete with veranda, pillars supporting the overhanging roof,
and brick steps. Day and night, three indoor dining rooms and an outdoor dining porch have a steady stream of hungry patrons digging into
tender pork spareribs that are dry-rubbed and tanned overnight before
visiting the smoker for a couple of hours. Then they're bathed in the
sauce of your choice. Kojak's also has a nice selection of sandwiches,
including chopped barbecue chicken and country-style sausage. This is
definitely not the kind of place you'd want to bring a vegan. $ *Average
main: $11* ⌧ *2808 W. Gandy Blvd., South Tampa* ☎ *813/837–3774*
⊕ *kojaksbbq.net* ⊘ *Closed Mon.*

$ ✕ **Mel's Hot Dogs.** This is a must after a long day of riding roller coasters
HOT DOG   and scoping out zebras at Busch Gardens. Visitors as well as passersby
usually are greeted by a red wiener-mobile parked on the north side of
the highway near Busch Gardens. Venture inside to find walls dotted
with photos from fans and a hot-diggity menu that's heaven for tube-
steak fans. You can order a traditional dog, but try something with a
little more pizzazz, such as a bacon-cheddar Reuben-style bowwow on
a poppy-seed bun, or the Mighty Mel, a quarter-pounder decked out
with relish, mustard, and pickles. Herbivores, fear not: there's a vegan
option on the menu, and it's mighty tasty. To avoid lunch crowds, arrive
before 11:30 or after 1:30. $ *Average main: $8* ⌧ *4136 E. Busch Blvd.,
Central Tampa* ☎ *813/985–8000* ⊕ *www.melshotdogs.com* ▭ *No credit
cards* ⊘ *Closed Sun.*

$$$ ✕ **Mise en Place.** Known to locals as "Mise" (pronounced *meez*), this
MODERN   upscale, modern downtown space is a popular lunch spot for Tam-
AMERICAN   pa's political and social elite. At night, it transforms into an elegant,
understated dining destination with a menu that offers adventurous
yet meticulously crafted modern American cuisine. The menu changes
every week, save for staples like the chicken liver pâté and the rack of
lamb. Another thing that doesn't change is the intricacy of every item
listed—whether it's tandoori-crusted tofu or pumpkin-spiced rubbed
scallops. The long list of boutique wines and specialty cocktails further
demonstrate the intelligence and imagination that go into the crafting of
the menu. This place is on the western edge of downtown, just across
the street from University of Tampa's shining minarets. Parking and
entry are behind the building. $ *Average main: $29* ⌧ *442 W. Kennedy
Blvd., Suite 110, Downtown* ☎ *813/254–5373* ⊕ *www.miseonline.com*
⊘ *Closed Sun.–Mon.*

$ ✕ **Taco Bus.** It's a Mexican joint with a simple name in a less-than-mag-
MEXICAN   nificent location, but that matters not to anyone who's ever eaten to
this legendary late-night establishment. Its popularity has turned what
was little more than a food truck into a small local chain. You have a
long list of meat, seafood, and vegetarian/vegan options, which employ-
ees will stuff into the casing of your choice and hand to you through
the window of a stationary bus. Don't let the low-key nature of this

establishment fool you—the menu features classier items like ceviche, butternut-squash tostadas, and chicken mole among the quesadillas and carne asada. There is also a downtown Tampa location (✉ *505 Franklin St.*) as well as one in St. Petersburg's Grand Central District (✉ *2324 Central Ave.*). Ⓢ *Average main: $11* ✉ *913 E. Hillsborough Ave., Central Tampa* ☎ *813/232–5889.*

$$$ ⨯ **Ulele.** Named after a 16th-century Tocobagan princess, this hot spot
ECLECTIC from the same family behind the historic Columbia restaurant in Ybor
Fodor's Choice City has become the go-to spot for Tampa diners in the know. The
★ diverse menu focuses on locally available ingredients but has an easy-to-detect Southern accent. Favorites include gator bites, okra fries, pan-seared Florida pompano fillet (served with sun-dried-tomato shallot cream and fried carrot ribbons), and a deconstructed seafood potpie (featuring Gulf seafood chowder shrimp, pulpo, grouper, smoked oysters, vegetables, and white wine cream) with a side of puff pastry. In the refurbished old Tampa Waterworks building, its location high on the bank of the Hillsborough River offers spectacular views of the water, especially at dusk, and it's an easy walk from downtown and the Straz Center. Beer is brewed on-site, and the creative cocktail menu (go for the Ring of Fire, a spicy creation of vodka, gin, and lychee liqueur) is supplemented with wines from domestic, family-owned vineyards like Silver Oak Winery. Ⓢ *Average main: $25* ✉ *1810 N. Highland Ave., Tampa Heights* ☎ *813/999–4952* ⊕ *ulele.com* ⌦ *Reservations essential.*

WHERE TO STAY

$$ ⌂ **Epicurean.** Brought to you in part by the people at Bern's Steak House
HOTEL (which happens to be across the street), this vibrant, cuisine-centric
Fodor's Choice installment of Marriott's Autograph Collection is an absolute must
★ for foodies, but it doesn't make nonfoodies feel left out. **Pros:** excellent service; great location; tons of amenities. **Cons:** can get pricey; exclusive vibe. Ⓢ *Rooms from: $240* ✉ *1207 S. Howard Ave., SoHo* ☎ *813/999–8701, 855/829–2536* ⊕ *epicureanhotel.com* ⌦ *142 rooms, 5 suites* ⧢ *No meals.*

$ ⌂ **Grand Hyatt Tampa Bay.** On the southwestern edge of Tampa, near the
RESORT airport and overlooking the Courtney Campbell Causeway, the Grand Hyatt has a lot to offer—both in its guest rooms and on the property. **Pros:** extensive amenities; amazing views; world-class dining. **Cons:** far from beach; getting here can be tough due to traffic and awkward road layout. Ⓢ *Rooms from: $169* ✉ *2900 Bayport Dr., West Tampa* ☎ *813/874–1234* ⊕ *www.grandtampabay.hyatt.com* ⌦ *442 rooms* ⧢ *No meals.*

$ ⌂ **Hilton Garden Inn Tampa Ybor Historic District.** Although its modern
HOTEL architecture makes it seem out of place in this historic district, this chain hotel's location across from Centro Ybor is a plus. **Pros:** located in top cultural and nightlife district; reasonable rates. **Cons:** neighborhood can be rowdy on weekends; chain-hotel feel. Ⓢ *Rooms from: $199* ✉ *1700 E. 9th Ave., Ybor City* ☎ *813/769–9267* ⊕ *www.hiltongardeninn.com* ⌦ *81 rooms, 14 suites* ⧢ *No meals.*

$$ ⌂ **Le Méridien Tampa.** A meticulous renovation transformed this historic,
HOTEL marble-lined former federal courthouse into Tampa's most talked-about

7

Where to Eat and Stay in Tampa

Restaurants ▼

Hotels ▼

KEY

● 1 *Restaurants*

① 1 *Hotels*

1/2 mi

1/2 km

boutique hotel. **Pros:** close to downtown attractions; fascinating for history buffs; lots of amenities. **Cons:** traffic in surrounding area can be a nightmare; all that marble makes for loud echoes in the hallways. [$] *Rooms from: $269* ✉ *601 N. Florida Ave., Downtown* ☎ *813/221–9555* 🌐 *lemeridientampa.com* 🛏 *126 rooms, 4 suites* 🍴 *No meals.*

$$ RESORT 🏨 **Saddlebrook Resort Tampa.** If you can't get enough golf and tennis, here's your fix. **Pros:** away from urban sprawl; great choice for the fitness minded. **Cons:** a bit isolated. [$] *Rooms from: $249* ✉ *5700 Saddlebrook Way, Wesley Chapel* ☎ *813/973–1111, 800/729–8383* 🌐 *www.saddlebrookresort.com* 🛏 *540 rooms, 407 suites* 🍴 *No meals.*

$ HOTEL 🏨 **Tampa Marriott Waterside Hotel & Marina.** Across from the Tampa Convention Center, this downtown hotel was built for conventioneers but is also convenient to tourist spots such as the Florida Aquarium and the Ybor City and Hyde Park shopping and nightlife districts. **Pros:** great downtown location; near sights, dining, nightlife. **Cons:** gridlock during rush hour; streets tough to maneuver. [$] *Rooms from: $190* ✉ *700 S. Florida Ave., Downtown* ☎ *888/268–1616, 813/221–4900* 🌐 *www.marriott.com* 🛏 *683 rooms, 36 suites* 🍴 *No meals.*

$ HOTEL 🏨 **Westin Tampa Harbour Island.** Few folks think of the islands when visiting Tampa, but this 12-story hotel on a 177-acre man-made islet is a short drive from downtown Tampa and even closer to the cruise terminal. **Pros:** close to downtown; nice views; on the TECO streetcar line. **Cons:** lots of traffic in immediate area; chain-hotel feel. [$] *Rooms from: $199* ✉ *725 S. Harbour Island Blvd., Harbour Island* ☎ *813/229–5000* 🌐 *westintampaharbourisland.com* 🛏 *299 rooms, 19 suites* 🍴 *No meals.*

NIGHTLIFE

When it comes to entertainment, there's never a dull moment in Tampa. Colorful Ybor City, a heavily Cuban-influenced area minutes from downtown, is a case in point. It has by far the biggest concentration of nightclubs (too many to list here), all situated along 7th and 8th avenues. Ybor comes alive at night and on weekends, when a diverse array of bars and clubs open their doors to throngs of partygoers. Whether it's bumping house music or some live rock and roll you seek, you'll find it here. Downtown Tampa is also becoming a formidable nightlife destination. When it comes to the arts—visual, musical, performing, or otherwise—Tampa is one of the South's leading spots.

BARS

Blue Martini Lounge. This spot in International Plaza has live entertainment nightly, except Sunday, and a menu of killer martinis. ✉ *2223 N. West Shore Blvd., Suite B203, West Tampa* ☎ *813/873–2583* 🌐 *bluemartinilounge.com.*

Centro Cantina. There are lots of draws here: a balcony overlooking the crowds on Seventh Avenue, live music Thursday through Sunday nights, a large selection of margaritas, and more than 30 brands of tequila. Food is served until 2 am. ✉ *1600 E. 8th Ave., Ybor City* ☎ *813/241–8588* 🌐 *centrocantina.comm.*

Cigar City Brewing Tasting Room. Offering the fruits of the adjacent Cigar City brewery, the large tasting room here puts Tampa on the map for craft beer enthusiasts. On tap, it offers mainstay brews like Jai Alai IPA and Maduro Brown Ale as well as an interesting rotation of seasonal beers. It's a spot with friendly staff and generally good music. But beware: happy hour can be packed. Brewery tours are available on the hour Wednesday through Sunday between 11 and 3 during the week (11 to 4 on weekends) for a nominal fee. ⊠ *3924 W. Spruce St., Suite A, Central Tampa* ☎ *813/348–6363* ⊕ *cigarcitybrewing.com* ⊗ *Sun.– Thurs. 11–11, Fri. and Sat. 11 am–1 am.*

Fly Bar. A happy hour mecca for hip young professionals, Fly Bar and Restaurant offers an intriguing selection of creative cocktails with ingredients like violets, walnut bitters, and salted celery-apple puree. The list goes on. If you're hungry, you'll find a food menu to match. There's live music on weekends and occasionally during the week. A huge draw—in fair weather, anyway—is the rooftop deck, which offers killer views of surrounding downtown Tampa. ⊠ *1202 N. Franklin St., Downtown* ☎ *813/275–5000* ⊕ *www.flybarandrestaurant.com.*

Gaspar's Grotto. Spanish pirate Jose Gaspar was known for swashbuckling up and down Florida's west coast in the late 18th and early 19th century. His legend has inspired a massive, raucous street festival each winter. This Ybor City drinkery has adopted his name, and rightly so. Decked out in tons of pirate memorabilia, it's the cornerstone to any night spent barhopping on the Ybor strip. The sangria is a good choice, but the aged rums may be a better fit here. You'll also find a food menu that goes well beyond standard bar fare. ⊠ *1805 E. 7th Ave., Ybor City* ☎ *813/248–5900* ⊕ *www.gasparsgrotto.com.*

Hub. Considered something of a dive—but a lovable one—by a loyal and young local following that ranges from esteemed jurists to nose-ring-wearing night owls, the Hub is known for strong drinks and a jukebox that goes well beyond the usual. ⊠ *719 N. Franklin St., Downtown* ☎ *813/229–1553* ⊕ *thehubbartampa.com.*

CASINO

Seminole Hard Rock Hotel & Casino. In addition to playing one of the hundreds of Vegas-style slot machines, gamers can get their kicks at the casino's poker tables and video-gaming machines. The lounge serves drinks 24 hours a day. Hard Rock Cafe, of course, has live music, dinner, and nightlife. There is a heavy smell of cigarette smoke here, as with most casinos. ⊠ *5223 N. Orient Rd., off I–4 at N. Orient Rd. exit, East Tampa* ☎ *813/627–7625* ⊕ *www.seminolehardrock.com.*

MUSIC CLUB

Skippers Smokehouse. A junkyard-style restaurant and oyster bar, Skippers has live reggae on Wednesday, Uncle John's Band (a long-running Grateful Dead cover act) on Thursday, and great smoked fish every night. Check their calendar for exceptional musical lineups on the weekends. ⊠ *910 Skipper Rd., Northeast Tampa* ☎ *813/971–0666* ⊕ *www. skipperssmokehouse.com.*

SHOPPING

MALLS

Centro Ybor. Ybor City's destination within a destination is this dining-and-entertainment palace. It has shops, trendy bars and restaurants, and a 20-screen movie theater. ✉ *1600 E. 8th Ave., Ybor City* ⊕ *www.centroybor.com.*

Channelside Bay Plaza. Right next to Tampa's cruise-ship terminal, this outdoor mall offers a vast array of shopping and dining options, as well as live music in a large courtyard. Look out for Qachbals Chocolatier, inventive fusion restaurant Flambe, and Splitsville, a 21-and-up bowling alley and restaurant chain targeting a younger crowd. ✉ *615 Channelside Dr., Downtown* ⊕ *www.channelsidebayplaza.com.*

International Plaza. If you want to grab something at Neiman Marcus or Nordstrom, this is the place. You'll also find Juicy Couture, Burberry, Michael Kors, Louis Vuitton, and many other upscale shops. Stick around after hours, when watering holes in the mall's courtyard become a high-end club scene. ✉ *2223 N. West Shore Blvd., Airport Area* ⊕ *www.shopinternationalplaza.com.*

Old Hyde Park Village. It's a typical upscale shopping district in a quiet, shaded neighborhood near the water. Boutiques and upscale chains like Restoration Hardware and Anthropologie are mixed in with bistros and sidewalk cafés. ✉ *1602 W. Swann Ave., Hyde Park* ⊕ *www.hydeparkvillage.net.*

SPORTS AND THE OUTDOORS

GOLF

The Claw at USF. Named for its many dog-legged fairways, this University of South Florida course is one of the most challenging public courses in the area. Live oaks as well as cypress and pine trees line the tight twists and turns of the fairways. This is one of the few places in Tampa Bay where you'll find deer grazing along the fairway (especially early in the morning) and gators sunning themselves next to the course's ponds. You'll also find a driving range and a golf shop. After you play, grab a beer at Rocky's Sports Grill, where you'll be able to catch the game on one of several flat- or plasma-screen TVs. ✉ *13801 N. 46th St., North Tampa* ☎ *813/632–6893* ⊕ *www.theclawatusfgolf.com* ✉ *$20–$45* ⛳ *18 holes, 6863 yards, par 71.*

Saddlebrook Golf Club. This expansive complex half an hour northeast of Tampa offers not one but two courses designed by Arnold Palmer. The Palmer Golf Course's hilly terrain contrasts with Tampa Bay's generally flat landscape, and it make you think you're playing on a course somewhere in New England. With its Spanish moss–draped cypress hammocks, the Saddlebrook Golf Course has more of an Old Florida feel to it. As you make your way past this course's green ponds, keep an eye out for turtles—and gators. There's also a golf shop, driving range, on-site pros, and, if you're aching from a grueling day on the course, a luxury spa on the resort property. ✉ *Saddlebrook Resort, 5700 Saddlebrook Way, Wesley Chapel* ☎ *813/973–1111* ⊕ *www.saddlebrook.*

com ✉ *$50–$145 (varies seasonally)* 🏌 *Palmer Course: 18 holes, 6243 yards, par 71; Saddlebrook Course: 18 holes, 6480 yards, par 70.*

Tournament Players Club of Tampa Bay. A stop along the PGA Champion's Tour, this public course sits about 15 miles north of Tampa. It was designed by Bobby Weed with consultation from Chi Chi Rodriguez and is laid out along natural wetlands, which means you can spot plenty of local wildlife as you play. The course was designed to be challenging while still giving novices a fair shake. Practice ahead of time at the driving, chipping, or putting range. There's a golf shop on-site as well as the TPC Grille Room, where you can grab a cold one after your game. ✉ *5300 W. Lutz Lake Fern Rd., Lutz* ☎ *813/949–0090* ⊕ *www. tpctampabay.com* ✉ *$85–$165* 🏌 *18 holes, 6898 yards, par 71.*

WALKING

Bayshore Boulevard Trail. Considered the world's longest continuous sidewalk, this 4.5-mile trail is a good spot for just standing still and taking it all in, with its spectacular views of downtown Tampa and the Hillsborough Bay area. Of course, you can also walk, talk, jog, bike, and in-line skate with locals. The trail is open from dawn to dusk daily. ✉ *Bayshore Blvd.* ☎ *813/274–8615.*

ST. PETERSBURG

21 miles west of Tampa.

Nicknamed the Sunshine City, St. Pete is much more than a mass of land between the airport and the beaches. In recent years it's seen a fierce arts and cultural revival, which you can plainly see as you stroll through the city's lively downtown area. The Salvador Dalí Museum building is a testament to the great pride residents of the 'Burg take in their waterfront city. But the city has other arts-oriented attractions, including the Dale Chihuly Collection, the Fine Arts Museum, and the burgeoning young artist hub known as the 600 Block, where eateries and bars attract crowds in the evening. Beach Drive offers some upscale options, whereas Central Avenue appeals more to night owls. The Grand Central District offers some unique vintage and antiques shopping. Gulfport is a stylishly low-key suburb southwest of St. Petersburg. The long strip of barrier islands lining St. Pete's west coast offer miles of gorgeous white beaches as well as dining, nightlife, and phenomenal sunsets. Nearby beach towns include St. Pete Beach, Treasure Island, Madeira Beach, and Redington Shores. No trip to this area is complete without a visit to the remote, pristine beaches of Fort De Soto.

GETTING HERE AND AROUND

Interstate 275 heads west from Tampa across Tampa Bay to St. Petersburg, swings south, and crosses the bay again on its way to Terra Ceia, near Bradenton. U.S. 19 is St. Petersburg's major north–south artery; traffic can be heavy, and there are many lights, so try to avoid it. Alternatives include 66th and 4th streets. One key thing to remember about St. Pete is that the roads form an easy-to-navigate grid: streets run north to south; avenues run east to west. Central Avenue connects downtown to the beaches.

7

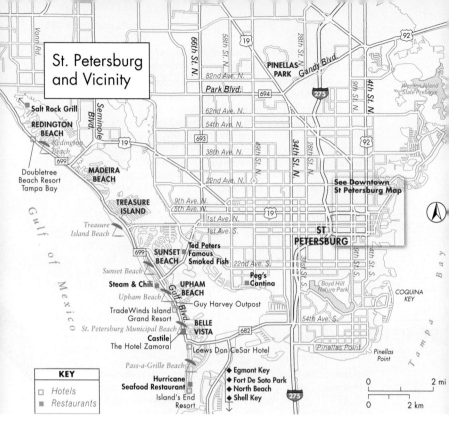

Around St. Petersburg, Pinellas Suncoast Transit Authority serves Pinellas County. Look for buses that cover the beaches and downtown exclusively.

St. Petersburg Trolley will get you to key destinations throughout downtown St. Pete, and even offers free service between the Chamber of Commerce Visitor's Bureau and certain destinations.

Contacts Pinellas Suncoast Transit Authority ☎ 727/540–1800 ⊕ www.psta. net. **St. Petersburg Trolley** ☎ 727/821–5166 ⊕ www.stpetetrolley.com.

TOURS

All About Fun Tours. What sets this tour apart from others is you are not going by bus or boat—your self-guided chariot is a motorized Segway. Each tour starts with an easy 15- to 20-minute training session. Tours are 60 or 90 minutes and are offered up to three times daily. It's a carefree way to see downtown St. Petersburg, the park system, and the waterfront while learning about local history. Reservations are required. ⊠ 335 N.E. 2nd Ave. ☎ 727/896–3640 ⊕ www.gyroglides. com ☎ Tours $35–$50 ⊗ Tues.–Sat. 10:30 and 2, Sun. 12:30 and 2:30, Mon. call for availability.

Dolphin Landings Tours. This operation runs a four-hour shelling trip, a two-hour dolphin-sighting excursion powered mostly by sail, back-bay or party-boat fishing, and other outings to Egmont Key and Shell Key. It's not easy to spot from the road: the boats are docked behind a strip mall. ⊠ *4737 Gulf Blvd., St. Pete Beach* ☎ *727/360–7411* ⊕ *www. dolphinlandings.com.*

VISITOR INFORMATION

Contacts St. Petersburg Area Chamber of Commerce ☎ 727/821–4069 ⊕ www.stpete.com. **St. Petersburg/Clearwater Area Convention and Visitors Bureau** ☎ 727/464–7200, 877/352–3224 ⊕ www.visitstpeteclearwater.com.

EXPLORING

TOP ATTRACTIONS

Fodor'sChoice ★ **Chihuly Collection.** For the uninitiated, those passing this collection's polished exterior may think it's a gallery like any other. Yet what's contained inside is an experience akin to *Alice in Wonderland.* This, the first permanent collection of world-renowned glass sculptor Dale Chihuly's work, has such impossibly vibrant, larger-than-life pieces as "Float Boat" and "Ruby Red Icicle." You can tour the museum independently or with one of its volunteer docents (no added cost; tours are given hourly on the half-hour during the week). Each display is perfectly lit, which adds to the drama of Chihuly's designs. After passing under a hallway with a semi-transparent ceiling through which a brilliant array of smaller glass pieces shine, you'll wind up at the breathtaking finale, "Mille Fiore" ("Thousand Flowers"), a spectacular, whimsical glass montage mimicking a wildflower patch, critters and all. Check out the gift shop at the end if you'd like to take some of the magic home with you. A combination ticket gets you a glimpse into Morean Arts Center's off-site glass-blowing studio, where you can watch resident artisans create a unique glass piece before your eyes. ⊠ *400 Beach Dr., Downtown* ☎ *727/822–7872* ⊕ *www.moreanartscenter.com.* ⌑ *$15* ⏱ *Mon.–Sat. 10–5, Sun. noon–5.*

Fodor'sChoice ★ **The Dalí Museum.** Inside and out, the waterfront Dalí Museum, which opened on 1/11/11 (Dali is said to have been into numerology), is almost as remarkable as the Spanish surrealist's work. The state-of-the-art building has a surreal geodesic-like glass structure called the Dalí Enigma, as well as an outdoor labyrinth and a DNA-inspired spiral staircase leading up to the collection. All this, before you've even seen the collection, which is one of the most comprehensive of its kind—courtesy of Ohio magnate A. Reynolds Morse, a friend of Dalí's.

Here, you can scope out his early impressionistic works and see how the painter evolved into the visionary he's now seen to be. The mind-expanding paintings in this downtown headliner include *Eggs on a Plate Without a Plate, The Hallucinogenic Toreador,* and more than 90 other oils. You'll also discover more than 2,000 additional works including watercolors, drawings, sculptures, photographs, and objets d'art. The museum also hosts temporary collections from the likes of Pablo Picasso and Andy Warhol. Free hour-long tours are led by well-informed docents. ⊠ *1 Dali Blvd.* ☎ *727/823–3767* ⊕ *www.thedali. org* ⌑ *$24* ⏱ *Mon.–Wed., Fri., and Sat. 10–5:30, Thurs. 10–8, Sun. noon–5:30.*

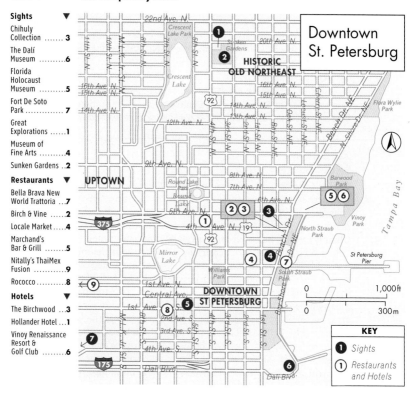

FAMILY **Sunken Gardens.** A cool oasis amid St. Pete's urban clutter, this lush 4-acre plot was created from a lake that was drained in 1903. Explore the cascading waterfalls and koi ponds, and walk through the butterfly house and exotic gardens where more than 50,000 tropical plants and flowers from across the globe thrive amid groves of some of the area's most spectacular palm trees. The on-site restaurant and hands-on kids' museum make this place a family favorite. ⊠ *1825 4th St. N* ☎ *727/551–3102* ⊕ *www.sunkengardens.org* ⊠ *$8* ☉ *Mon.–Sat. 10–4:30, Sun. noon–4:30.*

WORTH NOTING

Florida Holocaust Museum. The downtown Florida Holocaust Museum is one of the largest of its kind in the United States. It has the permanent History, Heritage, and Hope exhibit, an original boxcar, and an extensive collection of photographs, art, and artifacts. One compelling display includes portraits and biographies of Holocaust survivors. The museum, which also has a series of rotating exhibits, was conceived as a learning center for children, so many of the exhibits avoid overly graphic content; signs are posted outside galleries if the subject matter might be too intense for kids. ⊠ *55 5th St. S* ☎ *727/820–0100* ⊕ *www. flholocaustmuseum.org* ⊠ *$16* ☉ *Daily 10–5.*

FAMILY **Fort De Soto Park.** Spread over five small islands, 1,136-acre Fort De Soto Park lies at the mouth of Tampa Bay. It has 7 miles of waterfront (much of it beach), two fishing piers, a 4-mile hiking and skating trail, picnic-and-camping grounds, and a historic fort that kids of any age can explore. The fort for which it's named was built on the southern end of Mullet Key to protect sea lanes in the gulf during the Spanish-American War. Roam the fort or wander the beaches of any of the islands within the park. Kayaks and beach cruisers are available for rental. While most of Tampa Bay's beaches don't allow dogs, Fort De Soto has a somewhat lengthy dog beach for those who can't bear to hit the sand without their best buddy. ⊠ *3500 Pinellas Bayway St., Tierra Verde* 🕾 *727/582–2267* ⊕ *www.pinellascounty.org/park/05_ft_desoto.htm* 🎫 *$5* ☉ *Beaches, daily sunrise–sunset; fishing and boat ramp, 24 hrs.*

FAMILY **Great Explorations.** "Don't touch" are words never spoken here. The museum is hands-on through and through, with an art studio, replica vet's office and grocery store, a "beach" with real sand, a touch tunnel, and other interactive play areas. Kids and grown-ups alike will marvel at Reefscape, a brilliantly colorful fabric and yarn interpretation of the underwater ecosystems surrounding Florida. ⊠ *1925 4th St. N* 🕾 *727/821–8992* ⊕ *greatex.org* 🎫 *$10* ☉ *Mon.–Sat. 10–4:30, Sun. noon–4:30.*

Museum of Fine Arts. One of the city's cornerstones, this museum is a gorgeous Mediterranean-revival structure that houses outstanding collections of Asian, African, Native American, European, and American art. Major works here by American artists range from Hassam to O'Keeffe to Bellows and Morisot, but the museum is known for its collection of French artists, including Cézanne, Monet, Rodin, Gauguin, and Renoir. There are also photography exhibits that draw from a permanent collection of more than 14,000 works. Docents give narrated gallery tours. Special events abound on Thursday nights. A café offers visitors a lunch respite and a beautiful view of the bay. ⊠ *255 Beach Dr. NE* 🕾 *727/896–2667* ⊕ *www.fine-arts.org* 🎫 *$17* ☉ *Mon.–Wed., Fri., and Sat. 10–5, Sun. noon–5, Thurs. 10–8.*

BEACHES

Egmont Beach. An undeveloped island teeming with birds, shells, and native plants is a short ferry ride away. You'll find serene lengths of beach, abandoned former military buildings, a lighthouse and a herd of gopher tortoises patrolling nearby hiking paths. You can grab a ferry here from Dolphin Landings, John's Pass, or Fort De Soto for as little as $15. **Amenities:** none. **Best for:** solitude; walking. ⊠ *Egmont Key National Wildlife Refuge, accessible by boat only, Tierra Verde* 🕾 *727/867–6569* ⊕ *floridastateparks.org/egmontkey.*

Madeira Beach. Known to locals as "Mad Beach," this lively barrier island town occupies the southern tip of Shell Key. The beachfront consists of a long stretch of soft, shell-strewn sand, and it's often crowded with families as well as clusters of twentysomething beachgoers. You can get to the beach via numerous public access points, but your best bet is to park at the municipal beach parking lot and head to the sand from there. It's easily accessible from Treasure Island, northern St. Petersburg, and Clearwater Beach. **Amenities:** food and drink; parking; showers; toilets. **Best for:** partiers; swimming; walking. ⊠ *14400 Gulf Blvd., Madeira Beach.*

North Beach, Fort De Soto. Pretty much anywhere you go in this county park can make you feel like you're hundreds of miles from civilization, but the beach on the northern tip of this island chain has perhaps the most remote feel. Sure, it gets pretty packed with weekend revelers and family reunions, but you can easily find your own space on this award-winning beach. It starts out wide at the entrance, and narrows as you go north, so it's perfect for those who enjoy a good stroll. There are some striking panoramic views of the park's undeveloped wetlands. Be warned that once you get past a certain point, the beach becomes clothing optional. **Amenities:** food and drink; parking; showers; toilets. **Best for:** solitude; sunset; swimming; walking. ⊠ *3500 Pinellas Bayway, head right at flag, Tierra Verde.*

FAMILY

Fodor's Choice
★

Pass-a-Grille Beach. At the southern tip of St. Pete Beach (past the Don Cesar), this is the epitome of Old Florida. One of the most popular beaches in the area, it skirts the west end of charming, historic Pass-a-Grille, a neighborhood that draws tourists and locals alike with its stylish yet low-key mom-and-pop motels and restaurants. There's a sunset celebration each night. On weekends, check out the Art Mart, an open-air market off the boulevard between 9th and 10th avenues that showcases the work of local artisans. **Amenities:** food and drink; parking; showers; toilets. **Best for:** sunset; windsurfing. ⊠ *1000 Pass-a-Grille Way, St. Pete Beach.*

Redington Beach. Sand Key, the landmass that is home to Madeira Beach at the south end and Belleaire Beach in the north, is spotted with public beach access points. This particular spot has a bigger parking area than the others, though it's not free. It's also within walking distance of the Redington Pier, one of the most popular areas for fishing. **Amenities:** food and drink; parking; toilets. **Best for:** solitude; swimming; walking. ⊠ *160th Ave. at Gulf Blvd., Redington Beach.*

Shell Key. If you want to find the most pristine beach possible without heading to some remote outpost, this is your best bet. Shuttles to this seemingly remote paradise run out of Pass-A-Grille and Dolphin Landings. You can catch them in the morning and early afternoon most days. If you do, expect some amazing snorkeling, shelling, and bird-watching. (You can also kayak or canoe here from a launch near Fort DeSoto.) Rustic overnight camping is allowed here in the part of the island not designated as a bird sanctuary. Watch for rip currents when swimming, as they can be pretty strong. **Amenities:** none. **Best for:** solitude; swimming; walking. ⊠ *Shell Key Shuttle, 801 Pass-A-Grille Way, Pass-A-Grille, St. Pete Beach* ☎ *727/360–1348* ⊕ *shellkeyshuttle.com* ✉ *$25.*

FAMILY

St. Petersburg Municipal Beach. Though the beach is technically in the city of Treasure Island, the city of St. Pete Beach owns and maintains this stretch. Due in part to a concession stand and playground, it's excellent for families. The beach here is very, very wide, near hotels, and great for beach volleyball. **Amenities:** food and drink; parking; showers; toilets.

A St. Petersburg pelican stares down passersby on the wharf; photo by Seymour Levy, Fodors.com member.

Best for: solitude; partiers; sunset; swimming. ✉ *11260 Gulf Blvd., Treasure Island.*

FAMILY **Sunset Beach.** Technically part of Treasure Island, this 2-mile-long out-crop is one of Tampa Bay's best-kept secrets. The northern end has a mixed crowd—from bikers to spring breakers—the middle portion is good for families (there's a pavilion and playground at around 78th and West Gulf Boulevard), and the southern tip attracts the LGBT crowd. Surfers hit up Sunset Beach on the rare occasion that the gulf has some swells to offer. Once you turn onto West Gulf, you can find parking on the side streets, but make sure you park legally—it's all too easy to unwittingly get a barrage of parking tickets here. There are several pay lots starting to your right just south of 82nd Ave. **Amenities:** parking; toilets. **Best for:** solitude; partiers; sunset. ✉ *West Gulf Blvd., Treasure Island.*

Treasure Island. Large, wide swaths of sand that are sans crowd abound, but you can also find some good crowds, especially on weekends. The Sunday-evening drum circle, which happens around sunset just south-west of the Bilmar, makes for some interesting people-watching, as do the many festivals occurring here each month. It's also the only beach that allows alcohol, as long as it's not contained in glass. Plus, getting here is super easy—just head west on St. Petersburg's Central Avenue, which dead-ends smack-dab in the middle of T.I. (that's what the locals call it), where the iconic Thunderbird Beach Resort sign towers over the boulevard. Hang a left at the light. There's a Publix right across the street if you're up for an impromptu picnic or don't want to pay beach-bar prices for a beer. **Amenities:** food and drink; parking; showers;

toilets. **Best for:** solitude; partiers; sunsets. ✉ *10400 Gulf Blvd., Treasure Island.*

Upham Beach. One of the most notable things about this popular beach is the series of large objects that look like yellow school buses buried in the sand. These are actually designed to stabilize the shoreline (this beach is known for rapid erosion). The structures, called T-groins, may not please the eye, but that doesn't keep locals from flocking here. Upham is a wide beach with tons of natural landscaping, and it's near Postcard Inn and the TradeWinds. **Amenities:** food and drink; showers; toilets. **Best for:** partiers; sunset; swimming; walking. ✉ *900 Gulf Way, St. Pete Beach.*

WHERE TO EAT

$$ ITALIAN

🍴 **Bella Brava New World Trattoria.** This trendy eatery is one of the more sought-after places on equally trendy Beach Drive. It offers a fresh, imaginative approach to Italian fare. Dishes like ravioli Genovese, stuffed with fresh goat cheese and toasted pine nuts, and the trattoria burger, loaded with Gorgonzola and garlic aioli, are some of the more decadent menu items; a spate of colorful salads and flatbreads make up the lighter side of things. Specials often feature fresh, local seafood. There's almost always a lengthy wait for a table, even on a weeknight, so reservations are really a must. However, sitting at the bar, which has an equally creative beer, wine, and cocktail menu, is also an option. [$] *Average main: $18* ✉ *204 Beach Dr. NE, Downtown* ☎ *727/895–5515* 🌐 *bellabrava.com* ✍ *Reservations essential.*

$$$ MODERN AMERICAN

🍴 **Birch & Vine.** Seasonal, locally sourced ingredients work equally well in both the surf and the turf columns at Birch & Vine, which has turned The Birchwood hotel lobby and patio into an evening dining destination for hunger diners in downtown St. Petersburg. Take particular note of the orange miso sous vide scallops, and the hoison-chili brined maple duck breast, contemporary preparations that complement the reimagined 1920s property. Umbrella-covered patio tables face Beach Drive and North Straub Park to provide the best people watching. The lively weekend scene can create conversational challenges at the interior tables and banquettes; for a quiet dinner, reserve on Monday or Tuesday, or arrange to rent one of the private dining rooms for up to 12 guests. [$] *Average main: $28* ✉ *The Birchwood, 340 Beach Dr., NE, Downtown* ☎ *727/896–1080* 🌐 *thebirchwood.com/birch-vine.html.*

$$$ SPANISH

🍴 **Castile.** Within the chic Hotel Zamora, this popular dining spot has been getting much praise from local and national press since it opened in summer 2014. As the name suggests, much of the menu's inspiration comes from Spain, but many items—all the creations of executive chef Ted Dorsey—have other influences. Take the coconut curry–braised short ribs, or flounder served on a bed of grits (keep in mind the menu does change a lot). One particularly brilliant creation, especially for vegetarians, is the roasted vegetable endive poppers, which feature lightly cooked endive leaves stuffed with a flavorful ratatouille and topped with black truffle pearls, which bear an odd resemblance to caviar. The bar here offers an extensive wine list, plenty of craft beers on tap, and handmade cocktails bursting with fresh fruit and muddled spices. $ *Average main: $28* ⊠ *Hotel Zamora, 3701 Gulf Blvd., St. Pete Beach* ☎ *727/456–8660* ⊕ *www.castilerestaurant.com* ⬧ *Reservations essential.*

$$$ ✕ **Ceviche.** A choice romantic destination as well as an excellent launch-
TAPAS pad for a night out, this tapas bar offers an astonishing spate of pleasant sensations for those with savvy taste buds. You can't go wrong with a huge order of seafood or chicken paella. The ceviche, *solomillo a la parilla* (prime fillet with wild mushrooms and brandy cream sauce), and super-garlicky spinach (sautéed with figs) are good bets for tapas. In the catacomb-like bar downstairs, there's jazz, salsa, and flamenco every night but Monday. While you're here, the sangria is a must. $ *Average main: $25* ⊠ *10 Beach Dr., Downtown* ☎ *727/209–2299* ⊕ *www. ceviche.com.*

$ ✕ **Hurricane Seafood Restaurant.** Sunsets and gulf views are the bait that
SEAFOOD hooks regulars as well as travelers who find their way to this somewhat
Fodor's Choice hidden pit stop in historic Pass-A-Grille. Dating to 1977, it's mainly
★ heralded as a watering hole where you can hoist a cold one while munching on one of the area's better grouper sandwiches. (Speaking of this sweet white fish, it's the real deal here, which—be warned—isn't always a guarantee in some restaurants.) There's also a range of sea-food and steak entrées, and the crab cakes are legendary. The afore-mentioned sunsets are best seen from the rooftop sundeck. $ *Average main: $15* ⊠ *809 Gulf Way, St. Pete Beach* ☎ *727/360–9558* ⊕ *www. thehurricane.com.*

$ ✕ **Locale Market.** The brainchild of celebrity chefs Michael Mina and
CONTEMPORARY Don Pintabona, this unconventional farm-to-table food court in the new upscale Sundial St. Pete shopping and dining complex allows you to choose your own culinary adventure. Multiple stations are scattered throughout the two-story culinary fortress. You can order a burger at one, sushi and seafood at another, gourmet olives at another, and fresh baked goods at yet another. There's a butcher as well as seafood and cheese counters, among others, if you want to buy ingredients to cook at home. Downstairs the walls are lined with gourmet grocery items you'd typically find at a health food store. Upstairs is the wine bar, which also features craft beer and innovative cocktails made from wine, aperitifs, and fresh herbs (there's no hard liquor here as yet). As for seating, if it's nice out you can opt for outdoor seating, or there are a limited number of tables inside. $ *Average main: $15* ⊠ *179 2nd Ave. N, Downtown* ☎ *727/523–6300* ⊕ *localegourmetmarket.com.*

$$$ ✕ **Marchand's Bar & Grill.** Opened in 1925, this wonderful restaurant in
ECLECTIC the posh Renaissance Vinoy Resort has frescoed ceilings and a spectacu-lar view of Tampa Bay. Upscale and special-occasion diners are drawn to Marchand's dynamic menu, which changes often and embraces a farm-to-table approach. You'll always see salmon and a multitude of other seafood options on the menu amid items like wild boar ribs and farm-fresh vegetable potpie. There are also gluten-free and veggie options, such as a squash-and-corn taco. For early birds, the 1925 menu (named for the year the hotel originally opened) offers a four-course meal for just—as you may have guessed—$19.25. Sushi is available Tuesday

7

through Saturday. The wine list is extensive, including a number of by-the-glass selections. [$] *Average main: $28* ✉ *Renaissance Vinoy Resort, 501 5th Ave. NE* ☎ *727/824–8072* 🌐 *www.marchandsbarandgrill.com.*

$$ ECLECTIC 🍴 **Nitally's ThaiMex Fusion.** For those who take pride in their ability to handle the heat, this casual yet acclaimed fusion eatery is a must. It's run by a married couple, one of whom is from Thailand and the other from, as you may have guessed, Mexico. The resulting menu consists of many a match made in heaven by melding the spice and nuances of either cuisine into a spate of tasty options—think panang-mole curry or chorizo pad thai. (Some of these are even suitable for spice-phobes.) The bravest of souls can try the "inferno soup," which is less of a dish than a double dare, featuring a giant bowl of Thai chicken soup flavored with ghost peppers (finish it in a half hour and you win a cash prize). Regardless of what you order, go for a shade less spicy than you normally would: their idea of medium is what most restaurants consider hot. Portions are massive; if you order a burrito, you may actually receive two. Finally, keep in mind that this place can get packed at dinnertime, especially on weekends, so call ahead. [$] *Average main: $18* ✉ *2462 Central Ave.* ☎ *727/321–8424* 🌐 *nitallys.com* ⏲ *Closed Sun.*

$ MODERN MEXICAN 🍴 **Peg's Cantina.** A favorite watering hole for Tampa Bay's craft beer enthusiasts, Peg's also offers a variety of specialty pizzas and healthy Mexican options. Housed in an old bungalow along Gulfport's famed Beach Boulevard, it features excellent outdoor seating, and, in perfect Gulfport form, hospitable service for the canine set. Cyclists enjoy cruising here from the Pinellas Trail. Tap beers include house-brand brews as well as options from regional and national breweries. [$] *Average main: $15* ✉ *3038 Beach Blvd. S, Gulfport* ☎ *727/328–2720* 🌐 *www.pegscantina.com* ⏲ *Closed Mon. No lunch Tues.–Thurs.*

$$$ STEAKHOUSE 🍴 **Rococo.** Yet another spot inspired by the St. Pete of yesteryear, this happening steak house sits in what was once an historic YWCA building. Possibly the only independent steakhouse in St. Petersburg, it gets its name from the late-baroque art movement (but displays the work of local artists on its walls). Steak is obviously the main draw—corn-fed, aged, you name it—but the menu goes well beyond the normal bounds. On a given night, you can find elk, swordfish, or any number of less typical denizens of the land and sea, for those who are not enamored of beef. The chef is also attentive to special diets here, including the needs of gluten-free, vegetarian, and vegan diners. Craft cocktails have a local flair, and the beer and wine selection is expansive. It's really one of the best options in town for a romantic night out in St. Pete. [$] *Average main: $30* ✉ *655 2nd Ave. S* ☎ *727/822–0999* 🌐 *rococosteak.com* ✍ *Reservations essential* ⏲ *No lunch.*

$ CAFÉ 🍴 **Steam & Chill.** This gem on St. Pete Beach, offers creative breakfast options that tend to be a bit healthier—and more worldly—than their greasy-spoon counterparts (think: vegan hash and berry-and-Brie crepes). It's also pretty much the only neighborhood spot in St. Pete Beach where you'll find proper espresso drinks, not to mention formidable brunch and tapas menus. At night, the dining room transforms into a tapas bar with live music and flowing sangria. [$] *Average main:*

$12 ✉ 7400 Gulf Blvd., St. Pete Beach ☎ 727/360–8080 🌐 chillstpetebeach.com.

$ SEAFOOD Fodor's Choice ★ 🍴 **Ted Peters Famous Smoked Fish.** Picture this: flip-flop-wearing anglers and beach-towel-clad bathers lolling on picnic benches, sipping a beer, and devouring oak-smoked salmon, mullet, mahimahi, and mackerel. Dinner comes to the table with heaped helpings of potato salad and coleslaw. If you're industrious enough to have hooked your own fish, the crew will smoke it for about $1.50 per pound. If not, there's always what many consider to be the best burger in the region. The popular smoked fish spread and Manhattan clam chowder are available to go. There's also indoor seating at Ted's, which has been a south-side fixture for more than six decades. Closing time is 7:30 pm, so dinner is only for early diners. [$] *Average main: $13 ✉ 1350 Pasadena Ave. S, South Pasadena ☎ 727/381–7931 🌐 tedpetersfish.com ✍ Reservations not accepted ▭ No credit cards ⏲ Closed Tues.*

WHERE TO STAY

$$ B&B/INN 🏨 **The Birchwood.** Few things are as emblematic of Beach Drive's renaissance as this boutique hotel, which like many of downtown St. Pete's best attractions, seamlessly blends old and new. **Pros:** highly sought-after location; exquisite furnishings; close to downtown attractions. **Cons:** service seems more like a B&B than a hotel and is often MIA; not the best choice for families with kids; 20 minutes from the beach. [$] *Rooms from: $220 ✉ 340 Beach Dr. NE, Downtown ☎ 727/896–1080 🌐 thebirchwood.com 🛏 18 rooms 🍴 No meals.*

$$$ RESORT FAMILY 🏨 **Guy Harvey Outpost.** The namesake artist's trademark vibrantly painted swordfish, mahimahi, and other sea creatures adorn the walls of this high-rise beachfront hotel that offers good options for both dining and exploring. **Pros:** large rooms; lots of amenities; close to other beach attractions. **Cons:** layout can be confusing; $35 nightly resort fee. [$] *Rooms from: $315 ✉ 6000 Gulf Blvd., St. Pete Beach ☎ 727/360–5551 🌐 www.tradewindsresorts.com 🛏 52 rooms, 159 suites 🍴 No meals.*

$ HOTEL Fodor's Choice ★ 🏨 **Hollander Hotel.** This chicly renovated 1933 hotel and restaurant on the edge of downtown has become a hub for visitors and local alike and offers a less pricey alternative to the Vinoy. **Pros:** charming; close to action; good for nightlife. **Cons:** smaller rooms; some blight nearby. [$] *Rooms from: $109 ✉ 421 4th Ave. N, Downtown ☎ 727/873–7900 🌐 hollanderhotel.com 🛏 72 rooms, 28 suites 🍴 No meals.*

$$$ HOTEL 🏨 **The Hotel Zamora.** An excellent choice for a romantic getaway, this new hotel offers modern rooms with a flamenco twist—you may think you've been swept away to a luxurious Spanish villa. **Pros:** stylish and trendy; great restaurant; beautiful views. **Cons:** beach is across busy street. [$] *Rooms from: $319 ✉ 3701 Gulf Blvd., St. Pete Beach ☎ 877/798–2434 🌐 thehotelzamora.com 🛏 36 rooms 36 suites 🍴 No meals.*

$$ HOTEL 🏨 **Island's End Resort.** This converted 1950s-vintage motel has some of the area's best sunrise and sunset views and, like the rest of historic Pass-A-Grille, is totally friendly and totally Old Florida. **Pros:** good value; nice views; near restaurants and shops. **Cons:** access via a traffic-clogged road, parking can be tricky. [$] *Rooms from: $229 ✉ 1 Pass-A-Grille*

Way, St. Pete Beach ☎ *727/360–5023* ⊕ *www.islandsend.com* ⤴ *6 cottages* ⏹ *Breakfast.*

$$ 🏨 **Loews Don CeSar Hotel.** Today the "Pink Palace," as it's called thanks
RESORT to its paint job, is a storied resort and gulf-coast architectural land-
Fodor's Choice mark, with exterior and public areas oozing turn-of-the-20th-century
★ elegance. **Pros:** romantic destination; great beach; tasty dining options.
Cons: small rooms, can be quite pricey. $ *Rooms from: $269* ⊠ *3400
Gulf Blvd., St. Pete Beach* ☎ *727/367–6952, 800/282–1116* ⊕ *www.
doncesar.com* ⤴ *277 rooms, 40 suites* ⏹ *No meals.*

$$ 🏨 **TradeWinds Island Grand Resort.** The only resort on the beach offer-
RESORT ing up its own fireworks display, the island-chic TradeWinds is very
FAMILY popular with foreign travelers and the go-to place for beach weddings;
it's also one of the few pet-friendly resorts in the area, with a play area
and a room-service menu for dogs and cats. **Pros:** great beachfront
location; close to restaurants. **Cons:** large, sprawling complex; lots of
conventions; pesky resort fee. $ *Rooms from: $219* ⊠ *5500 Gulf Blvd.,
St. Pete Beach* ☎ *727/363–2212* ⊕ *www.tradewindsresort.com* ⤴ *584
rooms, 103 suites* ⏹ *No meals.*

$$$ 🏨 **Vinoy Renaissance Resort & Golf Club.** Built in 1925 (making it roughly
RESORT the same vintage as the Don CeSar), the Vinoy is a luxury resort in
Fodor's Choice St. Petersburg's gorgeous Old Northeast. **Pros:** charming property;
★ friendly service; close to downtown museums. **Cons:** pricey; small
rooms; drive to the beach. $ *Rooms from: $319* ⊠ *501 5th Ave. NE*
☎ *727/894–1000* ⊕ *www.vinoyrenaissanceresort.com* ⤴ *346 rooms,
15 suites* ⏹ *No meals.*

NIGHTLIFE

BARS AND PUBS

Ale and the Witch. Situated in the courtyard of an office building just off
trendy Beach Drive, this establishment is a live-music hub—mostly jam
bands—as well as the cornerstone of St. Petersburg's exploding craft-
beer scene. Fans of IPAs, saisons, stouts, you name it, will find their
beer of choice somewhere amid the lengthy list of brews on tap. There's
some seating inside, but all the action happens outside in the courtyard,
where there are plenty of tables and a makeshift band shell. Patrons are
welcome to grab food from one of the complex's several restaurants
to go along with their brews. Although it's a late-night draw, kids and
dogs are welcome. ⊠ *111 2nd Ave. NE, Downtown* ☎ *727/821–2533*
⊕ *thealeandthewitch.com.*

Daiquiri Shak. If frozen DayGlo concoctions spinning around in washing
machine–like mechanisms are your thing, this place should certainly
be on your list. If not, this is still a good go-to weekend watering hole
on Madeira Beach (technically, it's across the street from the beach). In
addition to selections like the Grape Ape and the Voodoo Loveshake,
there's a respectable selection of beer on tap and a full bar. Entertain-
ment includes some excellent funk and rock bands Thursday through
Sunday. The menu includes loads of seafood, of course (oysters are
a winner), and the late-night menu is served until 1:30 am. ⊠ *14995
Gulf Blvd., Madeira Beach* ☎ *727/393–2706* ⊕ *www.daiquirishak.com.*

Green Bench Brewing Company. The name of this bar is a nod to the green benches that once lined Central Avenue, which retirees occupied in a bygone era. St. Pete has shaken its rap as a sleepy retirement town, and this brewery embodies the Sunshine City's recent emergence as a craft-beer town. Barkeeps here serve up brews made on-site as well as a few guest kegs. The interior has a lodgelike feel (as much as a bar can in Florida), but the real ambience lies outside, where Adirondack chairs and badminton sets are scattered across the lawn. It's also conveniently located a couple of blocks from Tropicana Field, so the place can get packed before and after the Rays play. ⊠ *1133 Baum Ave., Downtown* ☎ *727/800–9836* ⊕ *greenbenchbrewing.com.*

Jimmy B's Beach Bar. This is a default stop for tourists and locals alike. The newly-renovated, open-air beach bar has seating for all as well as three full bars. It overlooks the vast dunes leading down to the beach. There's live music virtually every afternoon and each night on one of two stages. The beer selection isn't too exotic here, but they make a mean mai-tai. Sports fans can catch the game at Player's, a bar located on the same property ⊠ *6200 Gulf Blvd., behind the Beachcomber Resort, St. Pete Beach* ☎ *727/367–1902.*

Mad Beach Craft Brewing Company. Until very recently, Tampa Bay's beach towns were something of a craft beer dead zone, even as the rest of the region teemed with such establishments. This spot, located in John's Pass, is a shining example of how things are changing. Most of the beers on tap are brewed on-site, though there are a few guest taps. While there is plenty of space at the bar, the barroom is massive and styled after a German beer hall, large tables and all. There's foosball and indoor beanbag tossing if you're feeling competitive. ⊠ *12945 Village Blvd., Madeira Beach* ☎ *727/362–0008* ⊕ *madbeachbrewing.com.*

The Mandarin Hide. Perhaps the epitome of downtown St. Pete's bold transformation into a stylish nightlife destination, this place exudes a classy yet jubilant speakeasy vibe. A claw-foot bathtub is one of the first things you see when you walk in the door. Just as vintage as the decor is the drinks menu, which features numerous classic cocktails (made the old-fashioned way), tasty concoctions you'll find nowhere else, and craft beers. You'll find either live music or a DJ most nights. On weekends you can get a mean bloody Mary when the bar opens early. ⊠ *231 Central Ave., Downtown* ☎ *727/231–4007* ⊕ *www.mandarinhide.com* ⊗ *Closed Mon.*

St. Pete Brewing Company. A welcoming spot just off the main drag in downtown, this tasting room offers tons of craft beer options (the St. Pete Orange Wheat is a longtime local favorite). There's plenty of outdoor and indoor seating, and the clientele tends to be friendly. It's not far from St. Pete's dining and other nightlife. If you are looking to bring your dog, this is one of the best places to have a beer. ⊠ *544 1st Ave. N, Downtown* ☎ *727/623–4837* ⊕ *stpetebrewingcompany.com.*

3 Daughters Brewing. This local craft brewery and tasting room is something of an oasis within the Warehouse Arts District, but it's close enough to Central Avenue to be within easy walking distance from Tropicana Field and the restaurants of the Grand Central District (or drive/trolley ride from downtown). On tap in this converted industrial space is a spate of excellent creations made in-house (their Bimini Twist IPA is a favorite). There's live music some nights as well as a few game options. ✉ *222 22nd St. S, Warehouse Arts District* ☎ *727/495–6002* ⊕ *3dbrewing.com.*

World of Beer. The name says it all. This local chain is less than a decade old, but it's caught on beyond Tampa Bay. There are now locations throughout the state, including outlets in Tampa and West Palm Beach, but this one fits right in with the downtown St. Pete vibe and locals' endless thirst for craft brew. A new and improved version of the neighborhood pub, WOB offers bottle and draft beers from as far away as New Zealand and as nearby as St. Pete and Tarpon Springs. There's live music most nights. ✉ *100 4th St. S, Downtown* ☎ *727/823–2337* ⊕ *wobusa.com.*

SHOPPING

There's no need for a trip to the mall here. Few places in the Tampa Bay area offer so many eclectic shopping options as the St. Petersburg area. Downtown St. Petersburg's Beach Drive is sprinkled with tons of smart yet pricey boutiques. The Grand Central district has plenty of antiques and vintage clothing shops. Beach shopping hubs John's Pass Village and 8th Avenue offer souvenir shopping that goes well beyond the norm. Each of these is also packed with a range of enticing eateries, many with outdoor seating and live entertainment.

Epitomizing St. Petersburg's cultural rebirth, the block-long stretch of Central Avenue between 6th and 7th streets has loads of art galleries and indie shops, as well as dive bars frequented by tattooed hipsters. The central point is Crislip Arcade, where you'll find a vintage clothing shop (Ramblin' Rose), local art galleries (eve-N-odd and Olio, to name a couple), and a unique jewelry shop (Kathryn Cole). Local businesses line the street, including one that specializes in Moroccan imports (Treasures of Morocco), one that hawks a colorful array of vintage clothing and campy memorabilia (Star Booty), and a smoky bar specializing in craft beer and punk rock (Fubar). Local 662 and the State Theater are two music venues on this block that attract national indie music acts.

ARTpool Gallery. This local gallery/boutique offers scores of works by local artists and so much more. With one of the flashier storefronts in St. Pete's bustling Grand Central District, this sprawling store is a must for lovers of real-deal vintage clothing and accessories, not to mention furnishings and handmade crafts. There's a courtyard connecting the two buildings that constitute this creative megaplex. In the second building, where you can score everything from record albums to antique ashtrays and typewriters, there's a café with a diverse menu as well as wine and craft beer. Occasionally, owner Marina Williams opens her doors up for after-hours art-centric special events. ✉ *2030 Central Ave., Grand Central District, Gulfport* ☎ *727/324–3878* ⊕ *www.artpoolrules.com* ☾ *Closed Sun.*

Charlie Parker Pottery. For those who like to look beyond the well-worn paths when they shop, this spot in St. Pete's growing Warehouse

Arts District offers the pottery of Charlie Parker, a true master of his craft, as well as those of his apprentices. Some of what's created here belongs more rightly on a wall rather than on a table filled with fruit. But many of the works are useful, too; and there's even a $5 rack for those not looking to spend a fortune on a colorful platter. Parker himself offers pottery classes daily; they're worth it for his witty repartee. ⊠ *2724 6th Ave. S, Warehouse Arts District* ☎ *727/321–2071* ⊕ *www. charlieparkerpottery.com.*

Craftsman House Gallery. In a lovingly renovated historic Craftsman-style bungalow, this spot offers a variety of wares, mostly from both local national artists and craftspeople. The jewelry counter has some particularly intriguing finds. You'll also come across art made from glass, wood, and other media. Toward the back is a small café where you can order a wrap or bowl of soup and a craft beer or espresso drink, which you can take onto the large front porch as you watch the action along bustling Central Avenue. Occasionally, owner Jeff Schorr opens the gallery up for house concerts by touring musicians. ⊠ *2955 Central Ave., Grand Central District, Gulfport* ☎ *727/323–2787* ⊕ *craftsmanhousegallery.com.*

Downtown Gulfport. It's hard to believe that the low-key yet vibrant artist enclave of Gulfport was once a blighted fishing village. Now, it's a colorful waterfront community and popular with the LGBT community. It's pretty much in between St. Pete Beach and St. Petersburg proper, and the area's main thoroughfare, Beach Boulevard, is home to a large number of locally owned boutiques, galleries, and eclectic eateries. Highlights include Hula Hula, a shop dealing in vintage tropical attire and decor, and Domain, where you can find items—Floridiana or otherwise—you'll find nowhere else, given that much of it was forged at the hands of local artisans. An Art Walk occurs every first Friday and third Saturday of the month, and there's a farmers' market every Tuesday. Keep an eye out for cool local events, as there are many here. ⊠ *Beach Blvd. at Shore Dr., Gulfport.*

Florida CraftArt. Downtown St. Pete's bursting art revival is epitomized at this nonprofit, formerly known as Florida Craftsmen Gallery, that gives 125 artisans from throughout the state a chance to exhibit glassware, jewelry, furniture, and more. (Think: a vivid coral reef seascape made entirely out of yarn. Stuff like that.) While you're here, take a stroll along Central Avenue's 600 block for a real glimpse into downtown St. Pete's fresh, burgeoning art scene. The gallery is open Monday through Saturday, from 10 to 5:30 but stays open late for the famed Second Saturday Art Walk. ⊠ *501 Central Ave.* ☎ *727/821–7391* ⊕ *www. floridacraftsmen.net.*

Haslam's. One of the state's most notable bookstores, this family-owned emporium has been doing business in St. Petersburg's Grand Central District since the 1930s. Rumored to be haunted by the ghost of *On the Road* author Jack Kerouac (indeed the renowned Beat Generation author used to frequent Haslam's before he died in St. Pete in 1969), the store carries some 300,000 volumes, from cutting-edge best-sellers to ancient tomes. If you value a good book or simply like to browse, you could easily spend an afternoon here. ⌧ *2025 Central Ave.* ☎ *727/822–8616* ⊕ *www.haslams.com.*

Sundial St. Pete. With a gigantic (and functional) sundial in the middle of the plaza, this open-air collection of upscale shops occupies the space of former shopping and dining hub Baywalk. The renovation of the space created a more open atmosphere that has attracted a Ruth's Chris Steakhouse, a St. Pete branch of the restaurant Sea Salt, and celebrity Chef Michael Mina's Locale. The shopping here is equally high-end, and retail here includes Diamonds Direct, lululemon, Tracy Negoshian, as well as local retailers like Florida Jean Company. If that's not enough, there's the Shave Cave, something of a masculine take on a salon, and its feminine counterpart Marilyn Monroe Glamour Room. At the back of the complex is a 19-screen Muvico theater with an IMAX theater. ⌧ *153 2nd Ave. N, Downtown* ☎ *727/800–3201* ⊕ *sundialstpete.com.*

Zen Glass Studio. Glass art is pretty big in St. Pete, and this place showcases all the ways in which it can be done. There's a gallery here with some thoroughly intriguing pieces as well as a retail shop where you can find glassware, jewelry, decor items, and much more. Those not afraid of the flame can even take part in the glassblowing process themselves in the on-site hot shop. Classes offer amateur glassblowers the opportunity to make everything from beads to beer- and wineglasses. ⌧ *600 27th St. S, Warehouse Arts District, Gulfport* ☎ *727/323–3141* ⊕ *www.zenglass.com.*

SPORTS AND THE OUTDOORS

BASEBALL

Tampa Bay Rays. Major League Baseball's Tampa Bay Rays completed an improbable worst-to-first turnaround when they topped the American League Eastern Division in 2008, and again in 2010. Then there was that dramatic end-of-season comeback in 2011. Tickets are available at the box office for most games, but you may have to rely on the classifieds sections of the *Tampa Tribune* and *Tampa Bay Times* for popular games. Get here early; parking is often at a premium (pregaming at Ferg's is always a safe bet). ⌧ *Tropicana Field, 1 Tropicana Dr., off I–175* ☎ *727/825–3137* ⊕ *www.tampabay.rays.mlb.com.*

CLEARWATER AND VICINITY

12 miles north of St. Petersburg via U.S. 19.

In Clearwater itself, residential areas are a buffer between the commercial zone that centers on U.S. 19 and the beach, which is moderately quiet during winter but buzzing with life during spring break and in the busy summer season. There's a quaint downtown area on the mainland, just east of the beach, with a theater and a couple of small eateries.

On the beach itself, which is part of the city of Clearwater, you'll find a nightly sunset celebration at Pier 60 and tons of options for dining and entertainment, not to mention the beautiful sand. Among this area's celebrity residents is Winter, the dolphin who was fitted with a

Continued on page 404

SPRING TRAINING, FLORIDA-STYLE

by Jim Tunstall and Connie Sharpe

Sunshine, railroads, and land bargains were Florida's first tourist magnets, but baseball had a hand in things, too. The Chicago Cubs led the charge when they opened spring training in Tampa in 1913 — the same year the Cleveland Indians set up camp in Pensacola.

Over the next couple of decades, World War I and the Great Depression interrupted normal lives, but the Sunshine State became a great fit for the national pastime. Soon, big-league teams were flocking south to work off the winter rust.

At one point, the Florida "Grapefruit League" held a monopoly on spring training, but in 1947 Arizona's "Cactus League" started cutting into the action.

Today, roughly half of Major League Baseball's 30 teams arrive in Florida in February for six weeks of calisthenics, tryouts, and practice games. The clubs range from the Detroit Tigers, who have been in the same city (Lakeland) longer than any other team (since 1934), to the Tampa Bay Rays, who moved to a new spring home (Port Charlotte) in 2009.

The Los Angeles Dodgers play the Washington Nationals in Viera during a spring training game.

HERE COME THE FANS

Fan appreciate the relative intimacy of Spring Training stadiums.

Florida's spring training teams play 25 or 30 home and away games, to the delight of 1.68 million annual ticker buyers. Diehards land as soon as the first troops—pitchers and catchers—come to practice around the third week of February. Intersquad games start in the fourth week, while the real training schedule begins by the end of February or first of March and lasts until the end of the month or early April. These games don't count in the regular season, but they give managers and fans a good idea of which players will be on the opening-day rosters, and who will be traded, sent to the teams' minor leagues, or told it's time to find a regular day job.

Spring training games provide a great excuse for local baseball fans to cut out of work early, while visitors from the North can leave ice, snow, and sleet behind. And who doesn't want a few chili dogs,

brats, burgers, and brews on a March day? Spring training's draw is more than just a change of venue with an early sample of concession-stand staples. There is also the ample choice of game sites. Teams are scattered around most of the major tourist areas of central and southern Florida, so those coming to watch the games can try a different destination each spring—or even make a road trip to several. Baseball fans also like that it's a melting pot—teams from more than a dozen cities are represented here.

Finally, you can't beat the price—tickets are usually cheaper than during the regular season—nor the access you have to baseball celebrities. In fact, the relaxed atmosphere of spring training makes most players more willing to sign your ball, glove, or whatever. You can get autographs during pregame workouts (practice sessions), which are free, as well as after the game.

4 TIPS

■ **Have a game plan.** Don't just show up. Most teams only have about 15 home games, and those involving popular teams often sell out weeks in advance. Consider buying tickets ahead of time, and if needed, make hotel room reservations at the same time.

■ **Beat the crowds.** The best chance to do this is to go to a weekday game. You'll still encounter lots of fans, but weekday games generally aren't as well attended as weekenders. Also, each team only has a few night games.

■ **Pack a picnic.** Some stadiums let you bring coolers through the turnstiles. Many game attendees also gather for a tailgate party, grilling burgers and sipping a lemonade or beer while jawing with fellow fans (have a chair in tow).

■ West coast games get a lot of sun. Seats in the shade are premium.

(above) Hammond Stadium in Ft. Myers is where the Minnesota Twins practice.
(right) St. Louis Cardinals Chris Duncan is tagged out at Roger Dean Stadium in Jupiter.

Atlanta Braves **2**
Baltimore Orioles **7**
Boston Red Sox **14**
Detroit Tigers **9**
Houston Astros **11**
Minnesota Twins **8**
New York Mets **6**
New York Yankees **4**
Philadelphia Phillies **1**
Pittsburgh Pirates **10**
St. Louis Cardinals/
Florida Marlins **12**
Tampa Bay Rays **3**
Toronto Blue Jays **5**
Washington Nationals **13**

PLAY BALL!

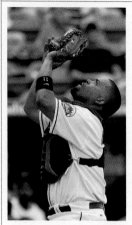

Spring training schedules are determined around Thanksgiving. Ticket prices change each year. For all of these teams, you also can order spring training tickets through Ticketmaster (☎ 866/448–7849 ⊕ www.ticketmaster.com) or through the respective team's box office or team Web site. For more information about any of the teams, visit ⊕ www.florida-grapefruitleague.com.

SPRING TRAINING GUIDE
Order a free Guide to *Florida Spring Training* from the **Florida Sports Foundation** (✉ 2930 Kerry Forest Parkway, Tallahassee, FL ☎ 850/488–8347 ⊕ www.flasports.com). Published in February each year, it's packed with information about teams, sites, tickets, and more.

New York Mets catcher Ramon Castro.

ATLANTA BRAVES
Home Field: Champion Stadium, ESPN Wide World of Sports, 700 S. Victory Way, Kissimmee. **Tickets:** $10–$49 ☎ 407/939–4263 ⊕ www.braves.mlb.com

BALTIMORE ORIOLES
Home Field: Ed Smith Stadium, 2700 12th St., Sarasota.
Tickets: $8–$32
☎ 941/893–6300 ⊕ www.orioles.mlb.com

BOSTON RED SOX
Home Field: JetBlue Park, 11500 Fenway South Dr., Fort Myers. **Tickets:** $10–$46
☎ 239/334–4700, 888/733–7696 ⊕ www.redsox.mlb.com

DETROIT TIGERS
Home Field: Joker Marchant Stadium, 2301 Lakeland Hills Blvd., Lakeland. **Tickets:** $10–$32
☎ 863/686–8075 ⊕ www.tigers.mlb.com

HOUSTON ASTROS
Home Field: Osceola County Stadium, 631 Heritage Parkway, Kissimmee. **Tickets:** $15–$27
☎ 321/697–3200 ⊕ www.astros.mlb.com

MIAMI MARLINS
Home Field: Roger Dean Stadium (shared with St. Louis Cardinals), 4751 Main St., Jupiter. **Tickets:** $15–$28
☎ 561/630–1828 ⊕ www.marlins.mlb.com

MINNESOTA TWINS
Home Field: Hammond Stadium, CenturyLink Sports Complex, 14100 Six Mile Cypress Parkway, Fort Myers. **Tickets:** $13–$29
☎ 800/338-9467 ⊕ www.twins.mlb.com

NEW YORK METS
Home Field: Mets Field, 525 NW Peacock Blvd., Port St. Lucie. **Tickets:** $8–$25
☎ 772/712-4300 ⊕ www.mets.mlb.com

NEW YORK YANKEES
Home Field: George M. Steinbrenner Field, 1 Steinbrenner Dr., Tampa. **Tickets:** $17–$33
☎ 813/879-2244 ⊕ www.yankees.mlb.com

PHILADELPHIA PHILLIES
Home Field: Bright House Networks Field, 601 N. Old Coachman Rd., Clearwater. **Tickets:** $14–$39
☎ 727/467-4457 ⊕ www.phillies.mlb.com

PITTSBURGH PIRATES
Home Field: McKechnie Field, 1611 9th St. W, Bradenton. **Tickets:** $12–$22
☎ 941/747-3031 ⊕ www.pirates.mlb.com

ST. LOUIS CARDINALS
Home Field: Roger Dean Stadium (shared with Miami Marlins), 4751 Main St., Jupiter. **Tickets:** $15–$28
☎ 561/630-1828 ⊕ www.cardinals.mlb.com

TAMPA BAY RAYS
Home Field: Charlotte County Sports Park, 2300 El Jobean Rd., Port Charlotte. **Tickets:** $10–$27
☎ 888/326-7297 ⊕ www.rays.mlb.com

TORONTO BLUE JAYS
Home Field: Florida Auto Exchange Park, 373 Douglas Ave., Dunedin. **Tickets:** $15–$30
☎ 727/733-0429 ⊕ www.bluejays.mlb.com

WASHINGTON NATIONALS
Home Field: Space Coast Stadium, 5800 Stadium Parkway, Viera. **Tickets:** $12–$26
☎ 321/633-4487 ⊕ www.nationals.mlb.com

prosthetic tail and depicted in the 2011 film *Dolphin Tale*, along with her friend Hope, her costar in the 2014 sequel.

The smaller towns surrounding Clearwater are generally more low-key. To the southwest, Indian Rocks Beach and its neighboring towns are less crowded alternatives to their busy neighbor to the north. To the north on U.S. 19 is Dunedin, a Scottish settlement that's packed with cute shops, restaurants, and craft beer bars, as well as the Toronto Blue Jays' spring training facility. Farther north is Palm Harbor, a key destination for cyclists and craft beer enthusiasts. Charming Tarpon Springs has a highly Greek-influenced downtown; you'll find historic sponge docks, a Greek restaurant or two, and some great beaches for watching the sunset.

GETTING HERE AND AROUND

Clearwater is due west from Tampa International Airport via State Road 60, and it's about 45 minutes north of St. Petersburg. If you want to fly directly to Clearwater instead of Tampa, though, St. Pete/Clearwater International Airport is another option. From St. Pete you can get here via U.S. 19, which is notorious for its congestion, Alternate U.S. 19, or County Road 1. If you're up for a scenic yet slower drive, Gulf Boulevard takes you all the way to Clearwater from St. Pete Beach—as does a beach trolley that runs along that route.

VISITOR INFORMATION

Contacts Clearwater Regional Chamber of Commerce ☎ 727/461–0011 ⊕ *clearwaterflorida.org.* **Greater Dunedin Chamber of Commerce** ☎ 727/733–3197 ⊕ *www.dunedin-fl.com.* **Tarpon Springs Chamber of Commerce** ☎ 727/937–6109 ⊕ *tarponspringschamber.com.*

EXPLORING

CLEARWATER

Clearwater Marine Aquarium. This aquarium gives you the opportunity to participate in the work of saving and caring for endangered marine species. Many of the sea turtles, dolphins, and other animals living at the aquarium were brought here to be rehabilitated from an injury or saved from danger. The dolphin exhibit has an open-air arena giving the dolphins plenty of room to jump during their shows. This aquarium is also home to Winter, a dolphin fitted with a prosthetic tail that was the subject of the 2011 film *Dolphin Tale* (and its 2014 sequel), as well as her friend Hope. The aquarium conducts tours of the bays and islands around Clearwater, including a daily cruise on a pontoon boat (you might just see a wild dolphin or two), and kayak tours of Clearwater Harbor and St. Joseph Sound. ✉ 249 *Windward Passage* ☎ 727/441–1790 ⊕ *seewinter.com* 💲$21.95 ⊙ *Daily 9–6.*

FAMILY **Pier 60.** This spot is the terminus of State Road 60 (hence the name), which runs under various names between Vero Beach on the east coast and Clearwater Beach on the west coast. Around 3:30 pm each day, weather permitting, the area surrounding the pier starts to liven up. Local artists and craftspeople populate their folding tables with beaded jewelry, handmade skin-care products, and beach landscape paintings.

Jugglers, musicians, break-dancers, and fire breathers put on some lively shows for those in attendance. And the grand finale is the sun setting over the Gulf of Mexico. On weekends when the weather is mild, there are also free, family-friendly movie screenings. ✉ *10 Pier 60 Dr., Clearwater Beach* ☎ *727/449–1036* ⊕ *www.sunsetsatpier60.com.*

TARPON SPRINGS

FAMILY **Konger Tarpon Springs Aquarium.** Although it's not on par with larger facilities in Tampa and Clearwater, this is certainly an entertaining attraction. There are some good exhibits, including a 120,000-gallon shark tank complete with a coral reef. (Divers feed the sharks several times daily.) Also look for tropical fish exhibits and a tank where you can touch baby sharks and stingrays. ✉ *850 Dodecanese Blvd., off U.S. 19, Tarpon Springs* ☎ *727/938–5378* ⊕ *www.tarponspringsaquarium. com* ✉ *$7.75* ⊙ *Mon.–Sat. 10–5, Sun. noon–5.*

The Sponge Docks. Paralleled by a busy boulevard lined with sponge shops and Greek restaurants, this several blocks-long waterfront spot showcase's Tarpon Spring's Greek roots as well as the industry that first made the town thrive over a century ago. Stroll along the docks and you'll find an aquarium, tons of small boutiques, bakeries specializing in baklava and the like and several boat tours of the surrounding waters. Pop into the Sponge Docks Museum to see a film about the much-sought-after creatures from the phylum *porifera* and how they helped the town prosper in the early 1900s. You'll come away converted to (and loaded up with) natural sponges. ✉ *Dodecanese Blvd., off Alt. U.S. 19, Tarpon Springs* ☎ *727/938–5366* ⊕ *www.spongedocks. net* ✉ *Free* ⊙ *Daily 9–6.*

BEACHES

CLEARWATER

Fodor's Choice ★ **Clearwater Beach.** On a narrow island between Clearwater Harbor and the gulf is a stretch of sand with a widespread reputation for beach volleyball. Pier 60, which extends from shore here, is the site of a nightly sunset celebration, complete with musicians and artisans. It's one of the area's nicest and busiest beaches, especially on weekends and during spring break, but it's also one of the costliest in terms of parking fees, which can reach $2 per hour. **Amenities:** food and drink; showers; toilets. **Best for:** partiers; sunset; walking. ✉ *Western end of Rte. 60, 2 miles west of downtown Clearwater.*

Sand Key Park. This is a mellow counterpart to often-crowded Clearwater Beach to the north. It has a lovely beach, plenty of green space, a playground, and a picnic area in an otherwise congested area. Parking is a flat $5. **Amenities:** food and drink; lifeguards; showers; toilets. **Best for:** solitude; sunset; swimming. ✉ *1060 Gulf Blvd.* ☎ *727/588–4852.*

DUNEDIN

Caladesi Island State Park. Quiet, secluded, and still wild, this 3½-mile-long barrier island is one of the best shelling beaches on the Gulf Coast, second only to Sanibel. The park also has plenty of sights for birders—from common sandpipers to majestic blue herons to rare black

Clearwater's Bait House lures in those heading to the pier to fish. —photo by watland, Fodors.com member.

skimmers—and miles of trails through scrub oaks, saw palmettos, and cacti (with tenants such as armadillos, rabbits, and raccoons). The landscape also features mangroves and dunes, and the gradual slope of the sea bottom makes this a good spot for novice swimmers and kids. You have to get to Caladesi Island by private boat (there's a 108-slip marina) or through its sister park, Honeymoon Island State Recreation Area, where you take the hourly ferry ride across to Caladesi; ferry rides cost $14 per person. You can also paddle yourself over in a kayak. **Amenities:** food and drink; showers; toilets. **Best for:** solitude; swimming. ⊠ *Dunedin Causeway, Dunedin* ☎ *727/469–5918* ⊕ *floridastateparks. org/caladesiisland* ⊟ *$6 per boat; $2 per kayaker* ☉ *Daily 8–sunset.*

Honeymoon Island State Park. If you're seeking an almost completely undeveloped beach that's still easily accessible by car, this is one of your best bets. Northwest of Clearwater, this large state park offers some of the best shell hunting you'll find, as well as thousands of feet of serene beachfront. If you head north along the park road, you find extensive hiking trails, along which you'll see an astonishing array of birds. **Amenities:** food and drink; showers; toilets. **Best for:** solitude; swimming; walking. ⊠ *1 Causeway Blvd., Dunedin* ⊕ *floridastateparks. org/honeymoonisland* ⊟ *$8 per vehicle; $4 per single occupant vehicle* ☉ *Daily 8 am–sunset.*

INDIAN ROCKS BEACH

Indian Rocks Beach. This beach community is a mellow alternative to the oft-crowded shorelines of Clearwater and St. Pete Beach along the gulf coast. This is a town in which the road narrows to two lanes and is lined with upscale residential condos instead of busy hotels. There are quite a few beach access points, though your best bet is a landscaped facility offering ample parking, nearby food and drink, and an occasional event. **Amenities:** food and drink; parking; showers; toilets. **Best for:** solitude; swimming; walking. ⊠ *Indian Rocks Beach Nature Preserve, 1700 Gulf Blvd., Indian Rocks Beach* ⊕ *indian-rocks-beach.com.*

TARPON SPRINGS

Fred Howard Park Beach. It comes in two parts: a shady mainland picnic area with barbecues and a white-sand beach island. The causeway is a popular hangout for windsurfers, and the entire area is great for birding. The beach itself is very relaxed and family-friendly, and you can find kayak rentals on the island's eastern side. **Amenities:** showers; toilets. **Best for:** sunset; swimming; windsurfing. ⊠ *1700 Sunset Dr., Tarpon Springs* ⏍ *$5 flat fee to park.*

Sunset Beach. As the name suggests, this beach park is known as one of the best places in North Pinellas County to watch the sunset. It's a small beach but a great place to barbecue. From April through November there's a weekly concert. **Amenities:** toilets. **Best for:** sunset; swimming. ⊠ *1800 Gulf Rd., Tarpon Springs.*

WHERE TO EAT

CLEARWATER

$$$
AMERICAN
✕ **Bob Heilman's Beachcomber.** The Heilman family has fed hungry diners since 1920. Although it's very popular with tourists, you'll also rub shoulders with devoted locals. Despite the frequent crowds, the service is fast and friendly. The sautéed chicken is an American classic—arriving with mashed spuds, gravy, veggie du jour, and fresh baked bread. Or try some Gulf shrimp prepared in nearly any way you can imagine, including lightly breaded and fried, tossed with pasta primavera and sautéed vegetables, or served Rockefeller-style. ⏍ *Average main: $25* ⊠ *447 Mandalay Ave., Clearwater Beach* ☎ *727/442–4144* ⊕ *www.bobheilmans.com.*

$
SEAFOOD
✕ **Frenchy's Rockaway Grill.** Quebec native Mike "Frenchy" Preston runs four eateries in the area, including the fabulous Rockaway Grill. Visitors and locals alike keep coming back for the grouper sandwiches that are moist and not battered into submission. (It's also real grouper, something that's not a given these days.) Frenchy also gets a big thumbs-up for the she-crab soup, and, on the march-to-a-different-drummer front, the grouper eggrolls. In mild weather, eat on the deck, though the screaming yellow awning can be nearly as blinding as the sun. ⏍ *Average main: $15* ⊠ *7 Rockaway St.* ☎ *727/446–4844* ⊕ *www.frenchysonline.com.*

$
SEAFOOD
✕ **Palm Pavilion Beachside Grill & Bar.** Long heralded as one of the best spots for watching sunsets, this place also gets high marks for its fresh seafood offerings. The grouper cheeks and avocado shrimp in particular are among more intriguing menu items. Healthier fare includes an array of wraps. The restaurant is casual but not too casual. It's got a bit of a Tommy Bahama feel to it, so you may want to ditch the beach attire if you plan to dine here. Be advised that it gets pretty packed around sunset, when a live band plays island music and the margaritas

flow. [$] *Average main: $15* ✉ *10 Bay Esplande, Clearwater Beach* ☎ *727/446–2642* 🌐 *www.palmpavilion.com.*

DUNEDIN

$$$ EUROPEAN 🍴 **Bon Appétit.** Known for its creative fare, this waterfront restaurant has a menu that changes frequently, offering such entrées as broiled rack of lamb in herbed pecan crust, and red snapper on a bed of lobster hash. The creative grouper options, that is, grouper medallions, get well-deserved plaudits from many patrons. Bon Appétit has staying power, having served at the same location for more than three decades. It's a great place to catch a sunset over the Gulf of Mexico. There's live music every night, and a pianist plays Wednesday through Sunday evenings and at Sunday brunch. [$] *Average main: $25* ✉ *148 Marina Plaza, Dunedin* ☎ *727/733–2151* 🌐 *www.bonappetitrestaurant.com.*

$ MEXICAN Fodor's Choice ★ 🍴 **Casa Tina.** At this colorful Dunedin institution, vegetarians can veg out on roasted chiles rellenos (cheese-stuffed peppers), enchiladas with vegetables, and a cactus salad that won't prick your tongue but will tickle your taste buds with the tantalizing flavors of tender pieces of cactus, cilantro, tomatoes, onions, lime, and queso fresco. The stuffed sapote squash also makes the grade. Tamales, tacos, and tortillas are prepared in dozens of ways. The place is often crowded, and service can be slow as a result, but there's a reason everyone's eating here. [$] *Average main: $15* ✉ *365 Main St., Dunedin* ☎ *727/734–9226.*

WHERE TO STAY

CLEARWATER

$$$$ RESORT 🏨 **Hyatt Regency Clearwater Beach.** One of the more recent additions to the Clearwater Beach skyline, this upscale resort towers above almost everything else in the immediate area, both in terms of height and luxury. **Pros:** gorgeous facility; plenty of amenities; near the action. **Cons:** beach is across busy street; some floors are residential; expensive. [$] *Rooms from: $450* ✉ *301 S. Gulfview Blvd.* ☎ *727/373–1234* 🌐 *www.clearwaterbeach.hyatt.com* 🛏 *250 suites* 🍴 *No meals.*

$$$$ RESORT 🏨 **Sandpearl Resort.** Two things set this expansive, luxurious Clearwater Beach resort apart from other upscale accommodations in the vicinity: it's not part of a major chain, and the property has deep local ties. **Pros:** on the beach; tons of amenities and dining options. **Cons:** resort fee; lots of conventions. [$] *Rooms from: $499* ✉ *500 Mandalay Ave.* ☎ *727/441–2425* 🌐 *sandpearl.com* 🛏 *203 rooms, 50 suites* 🍴 *No meals.*

$$ RESORT 🏨 **Sheraton Sand Key Resort.** Expect something special when you stay here, including a modern property and one of the few uncluttered beaches in the area. **Pros:** private beach; great views; no resort fee and parking is also free. **Cons:** near crowded Clearwater Beach; views come with a high price tag. [$] *Rooms from: $275* ✉ *1160 Gulf Blvd., Clearwater Beach* ☎ *727/595–1611* 🌐 *www.sheratonsandkey.com* 🛏 *375 rooms, 15 suites* 🍴 *No meals.*

PALM HARBOR

$ RESORT 🏨 **Innisbrook Resort & Golf Club.** A massive pool complex with a 15-foot waterfall, two winding waterslides, and a sandy waterfront are part of the allure of this sprawling resort, but it may be the 72 holes of golf, including the challenging Copperhead course, that are the real draw. **Pros:** great for serious golfers; varied dining options. **Cons:** far from attractions. [$] *Rooms from: $179* ✉ *36750 U.S. 19 N, Palm Harbor* ☎ *727/942–2000, 888/794–8627* 🌐 *www.innisbrookgolfresort.com* 🛏 *50 rooms, 550 suites* 🍴 *No meals.*

SAFETY HARBOR

$$ RESORT 🏨 **Safety Harbor Resort & Spa.** Those who enjoy old-school pampering love this hotel's exceptional 50,000-square-foot spa, which has the latest in therapies and treatments. **Pros:** charm to spare; good choice for pampering. **Cons:** far from beach; not ideal for families with children. [$] *Rooms from: $219* ✉ *105 N. Bayshore Dr., Safety Harbor* ☎ *727/726–1161, 877/237–8772* 🌐 *www.safetyharborspa.com* 🛏 *175 rooms, 16 suites* 🍴 *No meals.*

NIGHTLIFE

PALM HARBOR

Stilt House Brewery. If you happen to be riding on the Pinellas Trail between Clearwater and Tarpon Springs, this place is right on the trail. It's also right on Alternate U.S. 19, though it can be hard to spot from the road since it's in a small strip mall. Beers are brewed on-site (like the Norbert's Valkyrie Belgian Tripel or the Soul Candy Milk Stout), though there are also some guest taps. There's always a friendly crowd. Off to the side you'll notice a small room packed with vintage video games. ✉ *625 U.S. 19 Alternate, Palm Harbor* ☎ *727/271–6958* 🌐 *www.stilthousebrewery.com.*

DUNEDIN

Dunedin Brewery. Tampa Bay is seen by many as a flourishing craft-beer hub. If it weren't for Dunedin Brewery, that might not be the case. It was the first of its kind in the area and continues to offer delicious brews to throngs of patrons. It doesn't hurt that it offers live music many nights of the week, either. ✉ *937 Douglas Ave., Dunedin* ☎ *727/736–0606* 🌐 *dunedinbrewery.com.*

7venth Sun Brewery. Northern Pinellas County is a hotbed for craft brewing. This small tasting room features this brewery's offerings, largely Belgian-style, spirit barrel-aged sour beer as well as IPAs, and a handful of others. It's near downtown Dunedin's shopping, dining, and nightlife and isn't too far from the Pinellas Trail. ✉ *1012 Broadway, Dunedin* ☎ *727/733–3013* 🌐 *www.7venthsun.com.*

SPORTS AND THE OUTDOORS

BASEBALL

Philadelphia Phillies. The Phillies get ready for the season with spring training here (late February to early April). The stadium also hosts the Phillies' farm team. Check out their minor league team, the Clearwater

Threshers, at Bright House Field during the summer months. ⊠ *Bright House Networks Field, 601 N. Old Coachman Rd.* ☎ *727/712–4300* ⊕ *philadelphia.phillies.mlb.com.*

Toronto Blue Jays. The Jays play around 15 to 20 spring training games here, starting in February, which is why Dunedin is packed with Canadians this time of year. The team has trained here since its 1977 inception—and this consistency is not common for a major league team. A farm team plays here in the summer. The training fields are located several miles away, at 1700 Solon Avenue. ⊠ *Florida Auto Exchange Stadium, 373 Douglas Ave., north of Hwy. 580, Dunedin* ☎ *727/733–0429* ⊕ *toronto.bluejays.mlb.com.*

BIKING

Pinellas Trail. This 42-mile paved route spans Pinellas County, from near the southernmost point all the way north to Tarpon Springs. Along a former railway line, the trail runs adjacent to major thoroughfares, no more than 10 feet from the roadway, so you can access it from almost any point. The trail, also popular with in-line skaters, has spawned trailside businesses such as repair shops and health-food cafés. There are also many lovely rural areas to bike through and plenty of places to rent bikes. Be wary of traffic in downtown Clearwater and on the congested areas of the Pinellas Trail, which still needs more bridges for crossing over busy streets, and avoid the trail at night. To start riding from the route's south end, park at Trailhead Park (⊠ *37th Str. S at 8th Ave. S*) in St. Petersburg. To ride south from the north end, park your car in downtown Tarpon Springs (⊠ *E. Tarpon Ave. at N. Stafford Ave.*). ☎ *727/549–6099* ⊕ *www.pinellascounty.org/trailgd.*

GOLF

Dunedin Golf Club. Dunedin is Tampa Bay's little Scotland, the birthplace of golf, so it's only natural that one of the area's better courses is here. Designed by influential golf-course architect Donald Ross, this semiprivate, recently restored facility also has a driving range, a pro shop, and a clubhouse. The course itself offers numerous challenging holes with names like "Isn't Easy," "Calamity Jane," and "Devil's Kick," with the twists and turns to match. Water hazards aren't too overwhelming here, except on the 14th hole, known as "Round the Lake." ⊠ *1050 Palm Blvd., Dunedin* ☎ *727/733–7836* ⊕ *www.dunedingolfclub.com* 🖢 *$50* 🏌 *18 holes, 6625 yards, par 72.*

Innisbrook. Considered one of the top 100 golf destinations in Florida, this resort is home to Larry Packard–designed Copperhead Course, which hosts the annual PGA Tour Valspar Championship. Open to resort guests as well as the public, the four courses here take full advantage of the fact that they're on the coast, with plenty of ponds and sand traps adding to the scenery as well as the challenge. Fairways here on the Copperhead Course consist of rolling hills lined with trees, which are prime for spotting blue herons, squirrels, and even an alligator or two. The Island Course offers narrow fairways, some of which are lined by Lake Innisbrook, others by tall stands of pine and cypress trees. The North Course features tight fairways, numerous bunkers, and 11 water hazards, while the South Course has more of a links course–like layout. The Fox Squirrel Course is a quick 9-hole course available to guests only. ⊠ *36750 U.S. Hwy. 19 N, Palm Harbor* ☎ *888/794–8627, 727/942–2000* ⊕ *innisbrookgolfresort.com* ⌦ *Copperhead Course, $280; Island Course, $240; North and South Courses, $190.* ⅃ *Copperhead Course: 18 holes, 7430 yards, par 71; Island Course: 18 holes, 7310 yards, par 70; North Course: 18 holes, 6325 yards, par 70; South Course, 18 holes, 6620 yards, par 71; Fox Squirrel Course: 9 holes, 1236 yards, par 36 (resort guests only, closed during high season).*

Saddlebrook. The courses of this golf-centric resort 30 minutes northeast of Tampa are open to the public, and offer a remoteness that's hard to find in such a densely populated metro area. The star here is the Palmer Course, which, as one might expect, is named for Arnold Palmer, who designed it. It's characterized by a hilly terrain uncharacteristic of Florida as well as island-dotted ponds and plenty of troublesome bunkers. The Saddlebrook Course is more scenic than it is challenging (but is very much both), with long fairways lined with rows of pine trees. There's a pro on-site Tuesday, Thursday, and Saturday to help you perfect your game, not to mention a full-fledged golf academy. ⊠ *5700 Saddlebrook Way, Wesley Chapel* ☎ *813/907–4401* ⊕ *saddlebrook.com* ⌦ *$96 for 9 holes, $145 for 18 holes* ⅃ *Palmer Course: 18 holes, 6243 yards, par 71; Saddlebrook Course: 18 holes, 6480 yards, par 70.*

SURFING

FlowRider at Surf Style. Surf Style, in the towering Hyatt, is a chain store that sells beach essentials like sarongs, sunblock, and souvenirs. But what sets this particularly enormous store apart is the FlowRider, an indoor pool that generates artificial waves suitable for surfing; for $20 per half-hour, you and the kids can surf or learn to surf, something you can't usually do out in the gulf. An instructor is on hand to show you the ropes. ⊠ *Hyatt Regency Clearwater Beach, 311 S. Gulfview Blvd.* ☎ *888/787–3789* ⊕ *www.surfstyle.com.*

CITRUS COUNTY

The coastal and western inland areas of Citrus County north of Tampa and St. Petersburg are sometimes called the Nature Coast, and aptly so. Flora and fauna have been well preserved in this area, and West Indian manatees are showstoppers. These gentle vegetarian marine mammals, distantly related to elephants, remain an endangered species, though their numbers have grown to 3,500 or more today. Many manatees have massive scars on their backs from run-ins with boat propellers. Extensive nature preserves and parks have been created to protect them and other wildlife indigenous to the area, and these are among the best spots to view manatees in the wild. Although they're far from mythical beauties, it's believed that manatees inspired ancient mariners' tales of mermaids. This is one of the few spots in the world where you can legally swim with—and even touch—these gentle creatures.

GETTING HERE AND AROUND

U.S. 19 and the Suncoast Parkway, a toll road, are the prime north–south routes through this rural region, and traffic flows freely once you've left the congestion of St. Petersburg, Clearwater, and Port Richey. In most cases, the Suncoast Parkway is a far quicker drive than U.S. 19, though you'll have to pay several dollars in tolls. If you're planning a day trip from the Bay Area, pack a picnic lunch before leaving, since most of the sights are outdoors.

WEEKI WACHEE

Weeki Wachee Springs. At Weeki Wachee Springs, the spring flows at the remarkable rate of 170 million gallons a day with a constant temperature of 74°F. The spring has long been famous for its live "mermaids," clearly not the work of Mother Nature, as they wear bright costumes and put on an Esther Williams–like underwater choreography show that's been virtually unchanged since the park opened in 1947. The park is considered a classic piece of Florida history and culture, also features snorkel tours and canoe trips on the river, and a wilderness boat ride gives an up-close look at raccoons, otters, egrets, and other semitropical Florida wetlands wildlife. In summer, Buccaneer Bay water park opens for swimming, beaching, and riding its thrilling slides and flumes. ✉ *6131 Commercial Way, at U.S. 19 and Rte. 50* ☎ *352/592–5656* ⊕ *weekiwachee.com* ✍ *$13* ⏱ *Daily 9–5:30.*

HOMOSASSA SPRINGS

65 miles north of St. Petersburg on U.S. 19.

A little more than an hour north of Clearwater, you'll come upon this small and friendly hub for water lovers. Along with a phenomenal manatee-centric state park, you'll find more than a handful of charming restaurants, some featuring live music in the evening. This and Crystal River provide you with the once-in-a-lifetime chance to swim with manatees, something best done in winter. Summer's scallop season is also a massive draw.

EXPLORING

FAMILY **Ellie Schiller Homosassa Springs Wildlife State Park.** Here you can see many manatees and several species of fish through a floating glass observatory known as the Fish Bowl—except in this case the fish are outside the bowl and you are inside it. The park's wildlife walk trails lead you to excellent manatee, alligator, and other animal programs. Among the species are bobcats, a western cougar, white-tailed deer, a black bear, pelicans, herons, snowy egrets, river otters, whooping cranes, and even a hippopotamus named Lu, a keepsake from the park's days as an exotic-animal attraction. Boat cruises on Pepper Creek lead you to the Homosassa wildlife park (which takes its name from a Creek Indian word meaning "place where wild peppers grow"). ✉ *4150 S. Suncoast Blvd., U.S. 19* ☎ *352/628–5343* ⊕ *floridastateparks.org/ homosassasprings* ✍ *$13* ⏱ *Daily 9–5:30; last boat departs at 3:15.*

Yulee Sugar Mill Ruins Historic State Park. This state park has the remains of a circa-1851 sugar mill and other remnants of a 5,100-acre sugar plantation owned by Florida's first U.S. senator, David Levy Yulee. It makes for pleasant picnicking and dog-walking, although it is somewhat lacking visually. ✉ *Rte. 490 (Yulee Dr.), 3 miles off U.S. 19/98* ☎ *352/795–3817* 🌐 *floridastateparks.org/yuleesugarmill* 🎟 *Free* 🕒 *Daily 8 am–sunset.*

WHERE TO EAT

$ SEAFOOD 🍴 **Dan's Clam Stand.** Four reasons to go: the fried grouper sandwich, the clam "chowda," anything else seafood, and the beef burgers. The original location is about 2 miles east of Homosassa Springs State Wildlife Park. It's very popular among locals—just check out the packed parking lot at lunch and dinner. New England–style seafood is a house specialty, including whole-belly clams and lobster, but the grouper and mahimahi are fresh from local waters. Best of all, Dan's won't bust your budget. There's another branch in Crystal River. [$] *Average main: $10* ✉ *7364 Grover Cleveland Blvd.* ☎ *352/628–9588* 🕒 *Closed Sun.*

$ CUBAN 🍴 **Museum Cafe.** A short trip west of Homosassa Springs State Wildlife Refuge, this tiny eatery housed in the Olde Mill House Printing Museum is known for its Cuban sandwiches and occasional blues shows. It's only open for lunch, but it's well worth making room for a visit here in your itinerary. You can sit at a table within the museum itself or one of the tables in the very casual main dining room. Another option is to get your lunch to go and picnic at nearby Yulee Sugar Mill Ruins State Park. [$] *Average main: $10* ✉ *10466 W. Yulee Dr.* ☎ *352/628–1081* 🕒 *No dinner.*

$$ SEAFOOD 🍴 **Neon Leon's Zydeco Steakhouse.** If you couldn't already tell, the Nature Coast is about as Southern as you can get. This place is a case in point. This roadhouse-style eatery is co-owned by family members of former Lynyrd Skynyrd bassist Leon Wilkeson. Legend has it that Wilkeson had long dreamed of opening a restaurant serving Southern and Cajun food like fried okra and gator tail, with live music to match. You'll hear nightly live zydeco here, and the menu offers Dixieland staples like jambalaya (a favorite here), frog legs, and catfish. It may have a roadhouse feel and plenty of musical memorabilia, but it's also smoke-free and pretty family-friendly. A word of caution: the music can get loud. [$] *Average main: $15* ✉ *10350 W. Yulee Dr.* ☎ *352/621–3663* 🌐 *www.neonleonszydecosteakhouse.com* 🕒 *Closed Mon.*

CRYSTAL RIVER

6 miles north of Homosassa Springs on U.S. 19.

Situated along the peaceful Nature Coast, this area is *the* low-key getaway spot in one of the most pristine and beautiful areas in the state. It's also one of the few places on the planet where you can legally swim with manatees. The river's fed by a spring that's a constant 72°F, which is why manatees enjoy spending their winters here. Boating and snorkeling are popular, as is scalloping in the summer. This is a true paradise for nature lovers, and absolutely worth making room for in your vacation itinerary.

EXPLORING

Crystal River National Wildlife Refuge. This is a U.S. Fish and Wildlife Service sanctuary for the endangered manatee. Kings Bay, around which manatees congregate in winter (generally from November to March), feeds crystal-clear water into the river at 72°F year-round. This is one of the sure-bet places to see manatees in winter since hundreds congregate near this 90-acre refuge. The small visitor center has displays about the manatee and other refuge inhabitants. If you want to get an even closer look at these gentle giants, several dive companies provide opportunities for you to swim among them—if you don't mind shelling out some extra cash, donning a wetsuit, and adhering to some strict interaction guidelines. In warmer months, when most manatees scatter, the main spring is fun for a swim or scuba diving. ⊠ *1502 S.E. Kings Bay Dr.* ☎ *352/563–2088* ⊕ *www.fws.gov/crystalriver* ⌦ *Free* ☉ *Daily 8–4.*

BEACHES

Fort Island Gulf Beach. This is one of the most remote beaches you will find north of Fort De Soto, the isolated beach south of St. Petersburg. One of the best parts of coming here is the drive. The beach sits as the terminus of Fort Island Trail, the same road where you'll find the Plantation Inn & Golf Resort. A 9-mile drive through the wetlands gets you here, offering sweeping views along the way (though the Crystal River nuclear plant looms to the north). The beach itself is raw and subdued, though there are picnic shelters, barbecues and a fishing pier. Don't expect many frills, but if you need to relax after a long day of playing in the water, this is your place. **Amenities:** showers; toilets. **Best for:** solitude; sunset. ⊠ *16000 W. Fort Island Trail* ⊕ *www.bocc.citrus.fl.us/ commserv/parksrec/parks_recreation.htm.*

SPORTS AND THE OUTDOORS

MANATEE DIVES

American Pro Diving Center. This is one of several local operators in the area conducting manatee tours of Crystal River National Wildlife Refuge or Homosassa River, something you can't legally do pretty much anywhere else in the country. Tours start at around $30. ⊠ *821 S.E. U.S. 19* ☎ *352/563–0041* ⊕ *www.americanprodiving.com.*

Crystal Lodge Dive Center. This dive center is one of the more popular operators offering dives, swims, and snorkel trips to see manatees, with rates starting as low as $25. ⊠ *525 N.W. 7th Ave.* ☎ *352/795–6798* ⊕ *www.manatee-central.com.*

Plantation Adventure Center. An obvious choice if you're staying at the Plantation on Crystal River, this dive tour company stands on its own as a manatee tour operator. The guides bring you out to various spots along the river to interact with manatees, and tend to be long-time residents who know their subject well. If the weather is warm, that means no manatees, so opt for a sunset cruise instead. ⊠ *Plantation on Crystal River, 9301 Fort Island Tr.* ☎ *352/795–5797* ⊕ *www.crystalriverdivers. com* ⌦ *$30 plus equipment.*

7

SARASOTA AND VICINITY

Widely thought of as one of the best places in Florida to live, Sarasota County anchors the southern end of Tampa Bay. A string of barrier islands borders it with 35 miles of gulf and bay beaches. Sarasota County has something for everyone, from the athletic to the artistic. Thirteen public beaches, two state parks, 22 municipal parks, plus more than 60 public and private golf courses will help keep the active in motion. Spring training was an original destination attraction that now shares the stage with international rowing, swimming, and sailing events. Add to that a plentiful cultural scene dating to the era of circus magnate John Ringling, who chose this area for the winter home of his circus and his family.

BRADENTON

49 miles south of Tampa.

In 1539 Hernando de Soto landed near this Manatee River city, which has some 20 miles of beaches. Bradenton is well situated for access to fishing, both fresh- and saltwater, and it also has its share of golf courses and historic sites dating to the mid-1800s. Orange groves and cattle ranches mix with farmlands between Bradenton's beaches and Interstate 75.

GETTING HERE AND AROUND

You can get to Bradenton via Interstate 75, Interstate 275, and U.S. 41/301. West Manatee Avenue gets you out to the beaches. Manatee County Area Transit (MCAT) has buses throughout Bradenton and the nearby towns of Palmetto and Ellenton, as well as connections to Sarasota attractions. Fares for local bus service range from $1.25 to $3 (for an all-day pass); exact change is required. A $30 monthly "M-Card" is available for unlimited rides on all MCAT routes. However, if you want to get around efficiently—and want access to more places—you're best off renting a car.

Contacts **Manatee County Area Transit** ☎ 941/749–7116 ⊕ www.mymanatee.org.

VISITOR INFORMATION

Contacts **Bradenton Area Convention and Visitors Bureau.** This organization has all you need to know about everything Bradenton, Anna Maria Island, Palmetto, and Ellenton have to offer. ☎ 941/729–9177 ⊕ www.bradentongulfislands.com.

EXPLORING

De Soto National Memorial. One of the first Spanish explorers to land in North America, Hernando de Soto came ashore with his men and 200 horses near what is now Bradenton in 1539; this federal park commemorates De Soto's expedition and the Native Americans he and his crew encountered. During the height of tourist season, from mid-December to late April, park staff and volunteers dress in period costumes at Camp Uzita, demonstrate the use of 16th-century weapons, and show how European explorers prepared and preserved food for their overland journeys. The season ends with a reenactment of the explorer's landing. The site also offers a film and short nature trail through the mangroves. ✉ *8300 De Soto Memorial Hwy.* ☎ *941/792–0458* ⊕ *www.nps.gov/ deso* 🗐 *Free (donations accepted)* ⊘ *Visitor center daily 9–5, grounds daily dawn–dusk.*

Gamble Plantation Historic State Park. Built in the 1840s, this antebellum mansion five miles northeast of Bradenton was home to Major Robert Gamble and is the headquarters of an extensive sugar plantation. It is the only surviving plantation house in South Florida. The Confederate secretary of state took refuge here when the Confederacy fell to Union forces. Picnic tables are available. Guided tours of the house are available six times a day. ✉ *3708 Patten Ave., Ellenton* ☎ *941/723–4536* ⊕ *floridastateparks.org/gambleplantation* 🗐 *Free, tours $6* ⊘ *Daily 8– sunset. Tours Thurs.–Mon. 8–5:40.*

Pine Avenue. Anna Maria Island's newly restored "Main Street" features numerous upscale mom-and-pop boutiques, including beach-appropriate clothiers, beach-inspired home decor stores, and antique furniture shops. You can also find shops offering items such as quality jewelry and infused olive oil. The Anna Maria City Pier, which overlooks the southern end of Tampa Bay, sits at the end of the street. If you're here in the morning, check out Anna Maria Donuts, which offers made-to-order custom donuts, some having sriracha sauce among their ingredients. ✉ *Pine Ave., Anna Maria* ☎ *941/592–6642* ⊕ *www.pineavenueinfo. com.*

Robinson Preserve. With miles of trails that wind through wetlands and mangroves to lookout towers and peaceful waterfront spots, this Manatee County park is a must for anyone who likes a quiet walk (or run) and sweeping views of the landscape and the wildlife that inhabit it. There's also a kayak launch here, which links into a network of trails for small watercraft. Toward the front of the property the historic Valentine House, which was moved from its original site in Palmetto and restored, now serves as a visitor center and offers a few wonders of its own, including reptiles and shells the kids will dig. ✉ *1704 99th St. NW* ☎ *941/742–5923* ⊕ *mymanatee.org.*

OFF THE BEATEN PATH **Solomon's Castle.** For a visit to the wild and weird side, particularly fun for children, head to this "castle" about 45 minutes east of Bradenton through orange groves and cattle farms. Artist and Renaissance man Howard Solomon began building the 12,000-square-foot always-in-progress work out of thousands of aluminum offset printing plates. Inside, you'll find tons of intrigues—everything from a knight assembled with Volkswagen parts to a chair fashioned out of 86 beer cans to an elephant made from seven oil drums. A restaurant serves sit-down lunches in a full-scale model of a Spanish galleon. It closes for the summer (July through September). ✉ *4585 Solomon Rd., Ona* ☎ *863/494– 6077* ⊕ *www.solomonscastle.org* 🗐 *$10* ⊘ *Oct.–June, Tues.–Sun 11–4.*

FAMILY **South Florida Museum and Parker Manatee Aquarium.** Snooty, the oldest manatee in captivity, is the headliner here. Programs about the endangered marine mammals run four times daily. View changing exhibits such as digital images of water and other natural resources in the East

Gallery; glass cases and roll-out drawers on the second floor allow you to look at exhibits normally out of public view. At the Bishop Planetarium (with a domed theater screen), programs presented range from black holes to the origin of life itself. ✉ *201 10th St. W* ☎ *941/746–4131* ⊕ *www.southfloridamuseum.org* ✉ *$19* ⊙ *Mon.–Sat. 10–5, Sun. noon–5. May and June, Aug.–Dec., closed Mon.*

Fodor's Choice ★ **TreeUmph! Adventure Course.** Daredevils of all ages will love this collection of aerial ropes courses and zip lines. Those who partake will traverse swinging bridges, Tarzan ropes, treacherous hanging nets, and other obstacles suspended high in the air between the tall trees here, not to mention the many zip lines at the end of each set of obstacles. Adrenaline will flow more than once during this half-day adventure, but cautious parents need not worry; everyone is secured in a harness, and staff require everyone to demonstrate that they understand the park's many rules by watching a safety video and traversing a small demo course. There's a course that's just for small kids aged 7–12, but most can test their bravery on the five main courses, which get progressively more difficult (culminating in the ultratough Summit Course; most people don't get that far). At the end, everyone, regardless of whether they finished, can partake in a 650 foot-long zip line that starts at 60 feet high and offers spectacular views (the only way to get there is to climb a series of ladders). ■TIP➔ Check the weather before you go. If there's lightning within a small radius, staff has to ground you for at least half an hour, and the clock gets set back every time there's a nearby strike. ✉ *21805 State Rd. 70 E* ☎ *941/322–2130, 855/322–2130* ⊕ *treeumph. com* ✉ *$49.95.*

BEACHES

Anna Maria Island, Bradenton's 7-mile barrier island to the west, has a number of worthwhile beaches, as does Longboat Key. Manatee Avenue connects the mainland to the island via the Palma Sola Causeway, adjacent to which is a long, sandy beach fronting Palma Sola Bay. There are boat ramps, a dock, and picnic tables.

Coquina Beach. Singles and families flock to Coquina Beach, a wider swath of sand is at the southern end of Anna Maria Island. Beach walkers love this stretch since it's Anna Maria's longest beach, and it also attracts crowds of young revelers. **Amenities:** food and drink; lifeguards; showers; toilets. **Best for:** solitude; swimming; walking. ✉ *1800 Gulf Dr. S, Anna Maria Island.*

Cortez Beach. Towering Australian pines greet you at the entrance of this popular beach park, a favorite among locals and visitors alike. **Amenities:** lifeguards; showers; toilets. **Best for:** solitude; swimming; walking. ✉ *Gulf Blvd., between 5th and 13th Aves., Bradenton Beach.*

Greer Island Beach. Just across the inlet on the northern tip of Longboat Key, Greer Island Beach is accessible by boat or by car via North Shore Boulevard (you can walk here at low tide, but be sure to leave before the tide comes in. You'll also hear this place referred to as Beer Can Island. The secluded peninsula has a wide beach and excellent shelling, but no facilities. **Amenities:** none. **Best for:** solitude; walking. ✉ *7500 Gulf of Mexico Dr., Longboat Key.*

DID YOU KNOW?

Sometimes called "sea cows," manatees are aquatic relatives of elephants. They can weigh more than 1,500 pounds and live 50-plus years. There are more than 3,000 in Florida's coastal waters.

Manatee Beach Park. In the middle of Anna Maria Island, Manatee County Beach is popular with beachgoers of all ages. Paid parking is in the gravel lot next to the beach. **Amenities:** food and drink; parking; showers; toilets. **Best for:** solitude; swimming; walking. ⊠ *4000 S.R. 64, at Gulf Dr., Holmes Beach.*

WHERE TO EAT

$$$$
STEAKHOUSE
Fodor's Choice
★

✕ **Euphemia Haye.** A lush tropical setting on the barrier island of Long-boat Key, this is one of the most romantic restaurants around. The staff is friendly and gracious, the food delightful, and the atmosphere contagious. Its popular dessert display is a sweet ending to the pricey menu items that feature signature dishes such as crisp roast duckling with bread stuffing, and flambéed prime peppered steak. The upstairs Haye Loft, once the home of the original owner's grandson, has been converted into a more casual bistro and lounge. $ *Average main: $40* ⊠ *5540 Gulf of Mexico Dr., Longboat Key* ☎ *941/383–3633* ⊕ *www. euphemiahaye.com* ⌆ *Reservations essential* ⊘ *No lunch.*

$
AMERICAN

✕ **Gulf Drive Café & Tiki.** Especially popular for breakfast (served all day), this unassuming landmark squats on the beach and serves cheap sit-down eats: mostly sandwiches, but also a wide array of entrées after 4 pm. $ *Average main: $14* ⊠ *900 N. Gulf Dr. N, Bradenton Beach* ☎ *941/778–1919.*

$$$
AMERICAN

✕ **Sandbar Restaurant.** While their ever-evolving menu features cutting-edge fare for the most sophisticated of palates, the margarita-and-coco-nut-shrimp crowd will thoroughly enjoy it here as well. Much of what you'll find on the menu at this beachfront spot is harvested nearby, whether it's herbs and vegetables from one of the gardens along Pine Avenue or fresh fish from nearby Cortez. If the grouper is not fresh, it is not on the menu. You can find grouper blackened or in taco form, or you can venture from the norm and order crab bellies and caviar or wild boar served with sauerkraut salsa verde. The vision here is quint-essentially local and sustainable. If you opt for wine, the restaurant's private-label bottles, produced in California, are a good option. $ *Average main: $22* ⊠ *100 Spring Ave., Anna Maria Island* ☎ *941/778–0444* ⊕ *www.groupersandwich.com.*

WHERE TO STAY

$$
RENTAL

🛏 **BridgeWalk.** This circa-1947 Caribbean colonial-style property is across from the beach and a community within itself. **Pros:** great location; variety of lodging and dining experiences. **Cons:** can be pricey. $ *Rooms from: $219* ⊠ *100 Bridge St., Bradenton Beach* ☎ *941/779–2545, 866/779–2545* ⊕ *www.silverresorts.com* ⇱ *28 apartments* ⏹ *No meals.*

$$$$
RESORT

🛏 **Longboat Key Club & Resort.** This spectacularly landscaped property is one of the best places to play golf in the state, and among the top tennis resorts in the country. **Pros:** upscale vibe; lovely grounds; most rooms have private balcony. **Cons:** service can feel snooty. $ *Rooms from: $569* ⊠ *220 Sands Point Rd., Longboat Key* ☎ *941/383–8821, 855/314–2619* ⊕ *www.longboatkeyclub.com* ⇱ *218 rooms and suites* ⏹ *No meals.*

$$$$
RENTAL

🛏 **Mainsail Beach Inn.** If you're looking for upscale digs on low-key Anna Maria Island, you'll find them at this small, amenity-laden complex on

Ringling Mansion Sarasota

the beach. **Pros:** on beach; upscale apartments; full of amenities. **Cons:** not for the thrifty; early (10 am) checkout. $ *Rooms from: $534* ✉ *101 66th St., Holmes Beach* ☎ *888/849–2642* ⊕ *mainsailbeachinn.com* ⇴ *6 2-bedroom condos, 6 3-bedroom condos* ⦿ *No meals.*

$$
RESORT
⛱ **Silver Surf Gulf Beach Resort.** A sister to BridgeWalk, the Silver Surf has the air of a well-maintained 1960s motel with a modern twist, thanks to recent renovations to all of the studios and full apartments. **Pros:** location; freshly renovated rooms and exterior; good value for your money. **Cons:** while nice, the rooms are still pretty basic (this is not luxury). $ *Rooms from: $219* ✉ *1301 Gulf Dr. N, Anna Maria Island, Bradenton Beach* ☎ *941/778–6626, 800/441–7873* ⊕ *www.silverresorts.com* ⇴ *10 rooms, 14 suites, 2 townhomes* ⦿ *No meals.*

SARASOTA

30 miles south of Tampa and St. Petersburg.

Sarasota is a year-round destination and home to some of Florida's most affluent residents. Circus magnate John Ringling and his wife, Mable, started the city on the road to becoming one of the state's hotbeds for the arts. Today sporting and cultural events can be enjoyed anytime of the year, and there's a higher concentration of upscale shops, restaurants, and hotels here than in other parts of the Tampa Bay area. Across the water from Sarasota lie the barrier islands of Siesta Key and Lido Key, with myriad beaches, shops, hotels, condominiums, and houses.

GETTING HERE AND AROUND

Sarasota is accessible from Interstate 75, Interstate 275, and U.S. 41. The town's public transit company is Sarasota County Area Transit (SCAT). Fares for local bus service range from $0.75 to $3 (for an all-day pass); exact change is required. A $60 monthly "R-Card" is available for unlimited rides on all SCAT and Manatee County Area Transit (MCAT) routes. If you want to make it to the farther reaches of the area, though, renting a car is probably your best bet.

Contacts **Sarasota County Area Transit (SCAT)** ☎ 941/861–5000 ⊕ www. scgov.net/scat.

VISITOR INFORMATION

Contacts **Sarasota Convention and Visitors Bureau.** This organization has the skinny on South Tampa Bay. ✉ 701 N. Tamiami Trail ☎ 941/957–1877 ⊕ www.sarasotafl.org.

EXPLORING

TOP ATTRACTIONS

FAMILY

Fodor's Choice

★

John and Mable Ringling Museum of Art. Administered by Florida State University, the museum encompasses the entire Ringling estate, far more than just the art museum; there's also the Tibbals Learning Center and Circus Museums as well as Ca' d'Zan Mansion, the original Ringling home, and its expansive gardens. The entire compound covers 20 waterfront acres and also has the Historic Asolo Theater, restaurants, and a research library.

The **Art Museum** was a dream long in the making for John Ringling (of Ringling Brothers fame). Finally finished in 1931 after setbacks including a land bust and the death of his wife Mable, this enormous museum was originally built to house Ringling's mindblowingly expansive art collection. You'll find works ranging from Indian doorways elaborately carved with Jain deities to opalescent Baroque paintings from the likes of Rubens. There seems to be an endless number of rooms, themselves decorated in an appropriately gorgeous manner, housing these masterpieces. A wing that features traveling exhibits serves as a temporary home to many thought-provoking pieces throughout the year. The museum's exit opens out into an enormous courtyard, over which a towering statue of David replica presides, flanked by royal palms.

Circus magnate John Ringling's grand home, **Ca' d'Zan,** which was built along Sarasota Bay, was patterned after Doge's Palace in Venice. This exquisite mansion of 32 rooms, 15 bathrooms, and a 61-foot Belvedere Tower was completed in 1925, and today is the crowning jewel at the site of the Ringling Estate. Its 8,000-square-foot terrace overlooks the dock where Ringling's wife, Mable, moored her gondola. Mansion tours occur on the hour, and last half an hour. If you don't want a guided tour, show up on the half-hour for a self-guided tour.

Allot some extra time to wander around in the Mable Ringling's **Rose Garden,** a lush labyrinth surrounded by towering banyans and full of rare roses and haunting statues.

Don't let the name **Tibbals Learning Center** fool you. This Ringling estate attraction offers a colorful glimpse into a most wondrous element

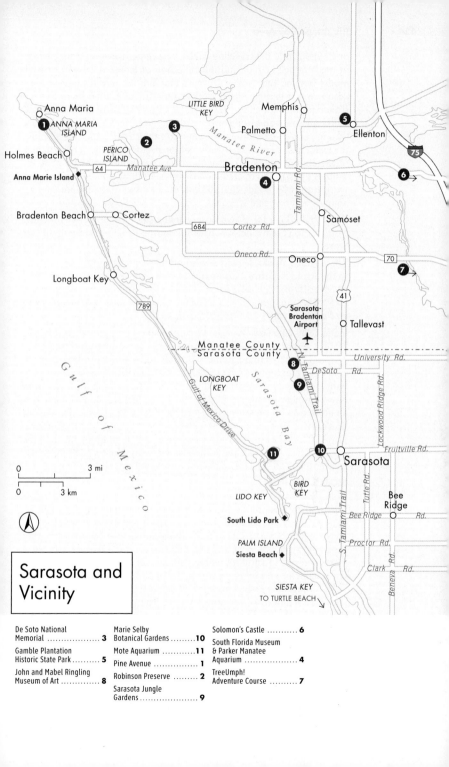

Sarasota and Vicinity

of a bygone era: the traveling circus. The center focuses on the history of the American circus and the collection of Howard Tibbals, master model builder, who spent 40 years building the world's largest miniature circus. Perhaps the center's main attraction, this impressive to-scale replica of the circa 1920s and '30s Ringling Bros. and Barnum & Bailey Circus is an astonishingly accurate portrayal of a circus coming through town—the number of pancakes the circus cooks are flipping, the exact likenesses and costumes of the performers, the correct names of the animals marked on the miniature mess buckets—you name it. Tibbals's passion to re-create every exact detail continues in his on-site workshop, where kids can ask him questions and watch him carving animals and intricate wagons.

If you're looking for clown noses, ringmaster hats, and circus-themed T-shirts, don't leave before checking out the **Ringling Museum of Art Store.**

The **Historic Asolo Theater** is also on the estate grounds and is home to the Asolo Repertory Company. ⊠ *5401 Bay Shore Rd., ½ mile west of Sarasota-Bradenton Airport* ☎ *941/359–5700* ⊕ *www.ringling.org* 🖅 *$25 (art museum only free Mon.)* ⊗ *Grounds daily 9:30–6; museums and mansion daily 10–5 (until 8 Thurs.).*

Marie Selby Botanical Gardens. Orchids make up nearly a third of the 20,000 species of flowers and plants here. You can stroll through the Tropical Display House, home of orchids and colorful bromeliads gathered from rain forests, and wander the garden pathway past plantings of bamboo, ancient banyans, and mangrove forests along Little Sarasota Bay. Although spring sees the best blooms, the greenhouses make this an attraction for all seasons. The added bonus is a spectacular view of downtown. There are rotating exhibits of botanical art and photography in a 1934 restored Southern Colonial mansion. Enjoy lunch at the Local Coffee + Tea, a cafe in the historic Selby House. ⊠ *811 S. Palm Ave.* ☎ *941/366–5731* ⊕ *www.selby.org* 🖅 *$19* ⊗ *Daily 10–5.*

WORTH NOTING

FAMILY   **Mote Aquarium.** A renowned research facility, the Mote is also a popular tourist attraction that draws families and others interested in its international array of ocean creatures. A 135,000-gallon shark tank lets you view various types of sharks from above and below the surface. Other tanks show off eels, rays, and other marine creatures native to the area. There's also a touch tank where you can get friendly with horseshoe crabs, conchs, and other creatures. Fossil Creek offers aspiring marine paleontologists a chance to sift through a bucket of sand for ancient shark teeth and fossilized stingray tails. The expanded Seahorse Conservation Lab offers a glimpse into the unusual creatures' lives and how the aquarium is working to help them survive and thrive. Hugh and Buffett are the resident manatees and, though not as venerable as Snooty at the Parker Manatee Aquarium, they have lived here since 1996 as part of a research program. There's also a permanent sea-turtle exhibit. For an extra fee, Sarasota Bay Explorers *(⇨ see the separate listing under Boat Tours in Sports and the Outdoors)* offers boat tours from the museum's dock (reservations required), guided kayak tours through the mangroves, private tours and a "Nature Safari." ✉ *1600 Ken Thompson Pkwy., City Island* ☎ *941/388–4441* ⊕ *www.mote.org* 🖹 *$19.75* ⊙ *Aquarium daily 10–5; boat tours daily at varying times.*

FAMILY **Sarasota Jungle Gardens.** One of Old Florida's charming, family-owned and -operated attractions, Sarasota Jungle Gardens fills 10 acres with native and exotic animals as well as tropical plants. The lush gardens date to 1939, and still have the small-world feel of yesterday's Florida. You'll find red-tailed hawks and great horned owls in the birds of prey show, American alligators and a variety of snakes in the reptile encounter, and bugs of many varieties in a show called Critters and Things. Among more cuddly residents here are lemurs, monkeys, and prairie dogs. You can talk to trainers and get to know such plants as the rare Australian nut tree and the Peruvian apple cactus in the gardens. Also on-site are flocks of flamingos that guests can hand-feed, plus reptiles and a butterfly garden. ✉ *3701 Bay Shore Rd.* ☎ *941/355–5305* ⊕ *www.sarasotajunglegardens.com* 🖹 *$15.99* ⊙ *Daily 10–5.*

BEACHES

Fodor's Choice ★ **Siesta Beach.** With 40 acres of nature trails, this park is popular; you'll find tons of amenities. This beach has fine, powdery quartz sand that squeaks under your feet, very much like the sand along the state's northwestern coast. Don't forget to bring a volleyball—or a tennis racket. **Amenities:** food and drink; lifeguards; toilets. **Best for:** partiers; sunset; swimming; walking. ✉ *948 Beach Rd., Siesta Key.*

South Lido Park. At the southern tip of the island, South Lido Park has one of the best beaches in the region, but there are no lifeguards. The 100-acre park interacts with four significant bodies of water: the Gulf of Mexico, Big Pass, Sarasota Bay, and Brushy Bayou. The sugar-sand beach has plenty of early morning sand dollars and is a popular place to fish. Picnic as the sun sets through the Australian pines into the water. Facilities include nature trails, canoe and kayak trails, restrooms, and picnic grounds. This park was purchased by John Ringling in 1920 as part of his ambitious plan to develop island properties. His plan collapsed with the great Florida Land bust of 1926. Because of swift rip currents, swimming here is not recommended. **Amenities:** showers; toilets. **Best for:** solitude; walking. ✉ *2201 Ben Franklin Dr., Lido Key.*

Turtle Beach. A 14-acre beach-park that's popular with families, Turtle has 2,600 linear feet of beach frontage and is more secluded than most gulf beaches. Though narrower than most of the region's beaches, it's also much less crowded, so it doesn't feel so narrow. It's known for abundant sea turtles. It has covered picnic shelters, grills, and a volleyball court. Locals like the 40-site campground that is also open to visitors with advance reservations. Fittingly enough, this beach is near the über-mellow Turtle Beach Resort. **Amenities:** toilets. **Best for:** solitude; sunset; swimming; walking. ✉ *8918 Midnight Pass Rd., Siesta Key* ☎ *941/349–3839.*

WHERE TO EAT

$$$$ STEAKHOUSE ✕ **Beach Bistro.** The menu at this cozy beachfront spot features "One Helluva Soup" made of plum tomatoes with sweet cream and blue cheese—it can be "goosed" with a half-shot of Grey Goose if ordered.

Standards here include a melt-in-your-mouth, herb-rubbed rack of lamb, a seafood bouillabaisse, and duckling confit with a peppercorn-and-cognac demi-glace. There also are five or six nightly specials such as nut-and-coconut-crusted grouper. Smaller appetites can save some pesos by ordering from the menu of smaller plates that features the likes of lobster, duckling, and a single lamb chop. Outside seating at new tables that are directly on the beach offers amazing sunset views, and a special beachfront menu features more casual fare. $ *Average main: $45* ⊠ *6600 Gulf Dr., Holmes Beach* ☎ *941/778–6444* ⊕ *www. beachbistro.com* ⊗ *No lunch.*

$$$
CAFÉ
Fodor's Choice
★

✕ **Bijou Café.** Once a 50-seat 1920 gas station–turned-restaurant, the Bijou is now a 140-seat restaurant with the type of enchanting decor you might expect in a quaint, modern European café—think French windows and doors, sparkling glassware, bouquets of freshly picked flowers, and the soft glow of candlelight. Lunches begin with an inspired soup, salads, or sandwiches such as the pesto chicken salad croissant. Dinners emphasize fresh local produce and sustainable seafood. Opera season—typically February and March—is the only time Sunday dinner is served. $ *Average main: $30* ⊠ *1287 1st St.* ☎ *941/366–8111* ⊕ *www.bijoucafe.net* ⊗ *Apr.–Jan., closed Sun. No lunch weekends.*

$$$
ITALIAN

✕ **Café Baci.** Specializing in Tuscan and Roman cuisine, Café Baci appeals to loyal locals and savvy travelers alike. Its menu highlights original family recipes; specialties range from fresh, succulent seafood dishes and homemade pastas to traditional veal recipes such as *piccata de vitella* simmered with white wine, lemon, and capers or grilled salmon served on spinach pesto risotto. From the moment you walk through the door, you'll enjoy the peaceful, elegant, Italian-inspired atmosphere. $ *Average main: $23* ⊠ *4001 S. Tamiami Trail* ☎ *941/921–4848* ⊕ *www. cafebacisarasota.com* ⊗ *No lunch weekends*

$$$
AMERICAN

✕ **Michael's on East.** Not only do the lounge and piano bar, with their extensive wines and vintage cocktails, lure the after-theater set, but inspired cuisine and superior service also entice. Inside its Midtown Plaza shopping center location, you'll find a decor similar to New York's better bistros of the 1930s and '40s, but there is plenty of veranda seating for enjoying Sarasota's balmy weather. The fare ranges from pan-roasted cobia to Manchester Farm grilled quail with anise-scented sweet potato puree. The ever-evolving dessert menu features creative combinations for concluding your cuisine adventure. $ *Average main: $26* ⊠ *1212 East Ave. S* ☎ *941/366–0007* ⊕ *www.michaelsoneast.com* ⊗ *Closed Sun. No lunch Sat.*

$$
AMERICAN

✕ **The Old Salty Dog.** A menu of steamer and raw-bar options has been added to the much-enjoyed old favorites, including quarter-pound hot dogs, fish-and-chips, wings, and burgers. With views of New Pass between Longboat and Lido Keys, this is a popular stop for locals and visitors en route from Mote Aquarium and the adjoining bayfront park. Open-air dining area is comfortable even in summer, thanks to a pleasant breeze. Its bar is shaped from the hull of an old boat. There's another branch on Siesta Key (*5023 Ocean Blvd., 941/349–0158*). $ *Average main: $15* ⊠ *1601 Ken Thompson Pkwy., City Island* ☎ *941/388–4311* ⊕ *www.theoldsaltydog.com* ⚑ *Reservations not accepted.*

$$$$ ✕ **Ophelia's on the Bay.** Florida the way it should be: you can watch as
AMERICAN dolphins swim past while blue herons lounge on the dock. Enjoy the
flowering gardens while dining alfresco on the outdoor patio on its
dock at Market #48 or in one of two casually elegant dining rooms.
An ever-evolving menu highlights the Florida surroundings with selections such as Gulf mangrove snapper served with a side of truffle gratin dauphinoise. A popular dish is the "lazy" Maine lobster, served
without a shell with stewed San Marzano tomatoes and crushed chilis.
The tuna (bigeye, yellowfin, and more) is flown in from Hawaii thanks
to owner Jane Ferro, who is also the grandniece of the restaurant's
namesake. ⓢ *Average main: $32* ✉ *9105 Midnight Pass Rd., Siesta Key*
☎ *941/349–2212* ⊕ *www.opheliasonthebay.net* ⊘ *No lunch Mon.–Sat.*

$$ ✕ **Owen's Fish Camp.** Nestled in a banyan-shaded corner of the hip Burns
SOUTHERN Court district of downtown Sarasota, this spot dishes out quintessen-
tially Southern fare (though the menu is not geographically limited) that
is particularly heavy on the seafood options—everything from an oyster
po' boy with bacon to grilled giant prawns with chili, a popular appe-
tizer. The restaurant is a converted cottage built in 1923, and the setting
gives an additional layer of charm to a casual eatery that's already won
the hearts of tourists and locals alike. Takeaway "jars" offered include
smoked fish spread with saltines, fried pickles, and boiled peanuts.
Note: there can often be a wait, so get here early because you can't
reserve a table. ⓢ *Average main: $16* ✉ *516 Burns Ct.* ☎ *941/951–6936*
⊕ *owensfishcamp.com* ⌦ *Reservations not accepted* ⊘ *No lunch.*

$ ✕ **Yoder's.** Lines for meals stretch well beyond the hostess podium here.
AMERICAN Pies—key lime, egg custard, banana cream, peanut butter, strawberry
rhubarb, and others—are the main event at this family restaurant in the
heart of Sarasota's Amish community. Daily specials typically include
zesty goulash, chicken and dumplings, and pulled smoked pork. For
breakfast, choose from French toast stuffed with cream cheese (or
Oreos) or perhaps a hearty stack of pancakes. Sandwiches include
Manhattans (roast beef, turkey, or meat loaf on homemade bread with
mashed potatoes and gravy). The entire village is always crowded, but
there's plenty of waitstaff who keep tables clean and cleared, so the
flow is steady. The decor retains its Old Florida efficiency appearance.
ⓢ *Average main: $10* ✉ *3434 Bahia Vista* ☎ *941/955–7771* ⊕ *www.*
yodersrestaurant.com ⌦ *Reservations not accepted* ⊘ *Closed Sun.*

WHERE TO STAY

$$ ⛱ **Gulf Beach Resort.** Lido Key's first motel, this beachfront condo com-
RENTAL plex has been designated a historic property. **Pros:** near shopping; well
maintained; lots of beach; free Wi-Fi. **Cons:** basic rooms; motel feel.
ⓢ *Rooms from: $205* ✉ *930 Ben Franklin Dr., Lido Key* ☎ *941/388–*
2127, 800/232–2489 ⊕ *www.gulfbeachsarasota.com* ⇥ *8 rooms, 41*
suites ⦶ *No meals.*

$$$ ⛱ **Hyatt Regency Sarasota.** Popular among business travelers, the Hyatt
HOTEL Regency is contemporary in design and sits in the heart of the city across
from the Van Wezel Performing Arts Hall. **Pros:** great location; stellar
views. **Cons:** chain-hotel feel. ⓢ *Rooms from: $369* ✉ *1000 Blvd. of*
the Arts ☎ *941/953–1234, 800/233–1234* ⊕ *www.sarasota.hyatt.com*
⇥ *294 rooms, 12 suites* ⦶ *Multiple meal plans.*

7

$$$ ⊞ **Lido Beach Resort.** Superb gulf views can be found at this stylish beach-
RENTAL front resort. **Pros:** beachfront location; many rooms have kitchens.
Cons: bland, somewhat dated furnishings. $ *Rooms from: $369* ⊠ *700*
Ben Franklin Dr., Lido Key ☎ *941/388–2161, 800/441–2113* ⊕ *www.*
lidobeachresort.com ⤳ *158 rooms, 64 suites* ⋔❍⋔ *No meals.*

$$$$ ⊞ **Ritz-Carlton, Sarasota.** With a style that developers like to say is cir-
HOTEL cus magnate John Ringling's realized dream, The Ritz is appointed
with fine artwork and fresh-cut flowers. **Pros:** Ritz-style glitz; lots of
amenities; attentive staff. **Cons:** long distance to golf course; not on
the beach. $ *Rooms from: $559* ⊠ *1111 Ritz-Carlton Dr.* ☎ *941/309–*
2000, 800/241–3333 ⊕ *www.ritzcarlton.com/sarasota* ⤳ *266 rooms,*
30 suites ⋔❍⋔ *No meals.*

$$ ⊞ **Turtle Beach Resort.** Reminiscent of a quieter time, many of the cot-
HOTEL tages at this friendly, affordable, family- and pet-friendly resort date
Fodor's Choice to the 1940s, a romantic plus for yesteryear lovers. **Pros:** nice location;
★ romantic setting; self-serve laundry and Wi-Fi included. **Cons:** far from
the area's cultural attractions. $ *Rooms from: $299* ⊠ *9049 Midnight*
Pass Rd., Siesta Key ☎ *941/349–4554* ⊕ *www.turtlebeachresort.com*
⤳ *7 rooms, 3 suites, 10 cottages* ⋔❍⋔ *No meals.*

NIGHTLIFE AND PERFORMING ARTS

NIGHTLIFE

5 O'clock Club. If you find yourself in Southside Village after dinner and
are looking for a watering hole that offers live music, look no further.
This spot has been one of Sarasota's key music venues for years. Musical offerings differ by night, but you can expect to hear blues, jazz, or
rock covers on a given night. If you're looking for a more upscale club,
look elsewhere; this is a no-frills kind of place. ⊠ *1930 Hillview St.*
☎ *941/366–5555* ⊕ *www.5oclockclub.net.*

Gator Club. A famous nightclub located in a beautifully restored, brick
historic cornerstone building downtown, the Gator Club has live
music and dancing 365 days a year. ⊠ *1490 Main St.* ☎ *941/366–5969*
⊕ *www.thegatorclub.com.*

Straight Up Night Club @ 15 South. St. Armand's Circle is a pretty bustling
place in the daytime, but the action continues into the wee hours—if
you know where to find it. This bar, which is upstairs from the popular
upscale Italian restaurant of the same name, has an excellent martini list
and plenty of live music, namely salsa on weekends. ⊠ *15 S. Blvd. of the*
Presidents, Lido Key ☎ *877/708–8312* ⊕ *www.15southristorante.com.*

PERFORMING ARTS

Asolo Repertory Theatre. One of the best theaters in Sarasota stages productions from November to June in varying venues, which include the
Historic Asolo Theater in the Ringling Estate. ⊠ *5555 Tamiami Trail*
☎ *941/351–8000* ⊕ *www.asolorep.org.*

Burns Court Cinema. There aren't many places in the Tampa Bay area
where you can catch indie and foreign films. Since it first opened on
the edge of downtown Sarasota in 1993, this old-timey four-screen
movie house has been one of the few. It's less than a block from Burns
Square's many stylish yet low-key dining offerings, and, unlike your
average corporate movie theater, admission doesn't cost an arm and a

leg. Beer and wine are also available. ✉ *506 Burns Ct.* ☎ *941/955–3456* ⊕ *filmsociety.org.*

The Players Theatre. A long-established community theater, having launched such actors as Montgomery Clift and Paul Reubens, this troupe performs comedies, special events, live concerts, and musicals. ✉ *838 N. Tamiami Trail, U.S. 41 and 9th St.* ☎ *941/365–2494* ⊕ *www. theplayers.org.*

Sarasota Opera. Performing in a historic 1,122-seat downtown theater, the Sarasota Opera features internationally known artists singing the principal roles, supported by a professional chorus of young apprentices. ✉ *The Edwards Theater, 61 N. Pineapple Ave.* ☎ *941/328–1300* ⊕ *sarasotaopera.org.*

SHOPPING

St. Armand's Circle. No visit to Sarasota is complete without a visit to this busy yet laid-back shopping and dining hub. One can literally refer to it as a hub because it's arranged around a large traffic circle in the middle of Lido Key. You'll find a sprinkling of upscale retail chains, including White House Black Market, but the area's small, imaginative boutiques are the real draw. Among them is Foxy Lady, which sells trendy women's clothing. The Met is also a good option for women's fashion. St. Armand's Circle also offers plenty of dining/desert (especially ice cream) options, nightlife, and just plain people watching. Some days you can even spot a busker or two performing on one of the area's many street corners. ✉ *300 Madison Dr.* ☎ *941/388–1554* ⊕ *www.starmandscircleassoc.com.*

Siesta Key Village. Not too far from Siesta Key's wildly popular beaches is a cluster of shops, restaurants, and watering holes you won't want to miss. This is a great place to shop and grab a bite after the beach—or earlier if it's not a beach day. Park in the municipal lot at the end of Avenida Madera, then stroll down Ocean Boulevard, where you'll find clusters of upscale shops and a range of restaurants and bars. ✉ *Ocean Blvd., between Beach Rd. and Av. Madera, Siesta Key* ⊕ *www. siestakeyvillage.org.*

Southside Village. This is one of Sarasota's newer spots, with tons of sidewalk cafés, hip boutiques, jewelry stores, and an excellent gourmet market. This place hasn't gotten as much attention as St. Armand's Circle, but it's also got a much shorter history. It's popular among locals and is now starting to get on the radar for visitors. ✉ *Osprey Ave. at Hillview St.* ☎ *941/366–0771.*

SPORTS AND THE OUTDOORS
BOAT TOURS
Sarasota Bay Explorers. Many visitors to the Mote Aquarium take the 105-minute boat trip onto Sarasota Bay. Conducted by Sarasota Bay Explorers, all boat trips are done in conjunction with the aquarium and leave from the aquarium's dock. The crew brings marine life on board, explains what it is, and throws it back to swim away. You are almost guaranteed to see bottlenose dolphins. Reservations are recommended. You can also charter the *Miss Explorer,* a 24-foot Sea Ray Sundeck, or take a guided kayak or nature tour. ✉ *Mote Aquarium, 1600 Ken*

Thompson Pkwy. ☎ *941/388–4200* ⊕ *www.sarasotabayexplorers.com* ⌦ *Boat tour $27, kayak tour $55, nature tour $45, charters $295–$445* ⊙ *Tours daily at 11, 1:30, and 4 (reservations required).*

FISHING

Flying Fish Fleet. Several boats can be chartered for deep-sea fishing, and there are daily group trips on a "party" fishing boat. ⊠ *2 Marina Plaza, U.S. 41, on bay front at Marina Jack* ☎ *941/366–3373* ⊕ *www. flyingfishfleet.com.*

GOLF

Bobby Jones Golf Course. This public 45-hole course is over a century old and caters to a range of golfers. The setting is lush and green, with plenty of live oak trees and water. The grounds here are so pleasant that many choose to walk their chosen course, of which there are three. The American Course is best for less experienced golfers or those who want to practice their short shot, and features a range of lakes and varied terrain. The British Course is slightly more challenging, offering longer fairways dotted with water hazards and sand bunkers. The Gillespie Executive Course is recommended for beginners or those lacking the time needed for a full 18 holes. A large ravine divides much of the course from several of its greens approaches. ⊠ *1000 Circus Blvd.* ☎ *941/365–2200* ⊕ *www.bobbyjonesgolfclub.com* ⌦ *$25 for 9 holes, $35 for 18 holes* ⚑ *American Course: 18 holes, 6032 yards, par 71; British Course: 18 holes, 6710 yards, par 72; Gillespie Executive Course: 9 holes, 1716 yards, par 30.*

KAYAKING

Sarasota Bay Explorers, which operates from the Mote Aquarium, also offers guided kayaking trips *(see* ⇨ *Boat Tours).*

Siesta Sports Rentals. Up for rent here are kayaks, bikes, beach chairs, scooters, and beach wheelchairs and strollers. Guided kayaking trips are also available. ⊠ *6551 Midnight Pass Rd., Siesta Key* ☎ *941/346–1797* ⊕ *www.siestasportsrentals.com.*

8

THE LOWER GULF COAST

With Fort Myers, Naples, and the Coastal Islands

Visit Fodors.com for advice, updates, and bookings

WELCOME TO THE LOWER GULF COAST

TOP REASONS TO GO

★ **Heavenly beaches:**
Whether you go to the beach to sun, swim, gather shells, or watch the sunset, the region's Gulf of Mexico beaches rank among the best.

★ **Edison & Ford Winter Estates:** A rare complex of two famous inventors' winter homes comes complete with botanical-research gardens, Edison's lab, and a museum.

★ **Island hopping:** Rent a boat or jump aboard a charter for lunch, picnicking, beaching, or shelling on a subtropical island adrift from the mainland.

★ **Naples shopping:**
Flex your buying power in downtown Naples's charming shopping districts or in lush outdoor centers around town.

★ **Watch for wildlife:** On the edge of Everglades National Park, the region protects vast tracts of fragile land and water where you can see alligators, manatees, dolphins, roseate spoonbills, and hundreds of other birds.

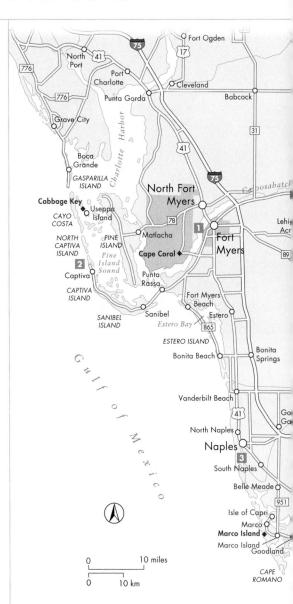

1 Fort Myers and Vicinity.
Don't miss the Edison & Ford Winter Estates along royal palm–lined McGregor Boulevard. For museums, theater, and art, the up-and-coming downtown River District rules.

2 The Coastal Islands.
Shells and wildlife refuges bring nature lovers to Sanibel and Captiva islands. Fort Myers Beach is known for its lively clubs and shrimp fleet. For true seclusion, head to the area's unbridged island beaches.

3 Naples and Vicinity.
Some of the region's best shopping and dining take up residence in historic buildings trimmed with blossoms and street sculptures in Old Naples. Hit Marco Island for the boating lifestyle and funky fishing-village character.

GETTING ORIENTED

The Lower Gulf Coast of Florida, as its name suggests, occupies a stretch of coastline along southernmost west Florida, bordered by the Gulf of Mexico. It lies south of Tampa and Sarasota, directly on the other side of the state from West Palm Beach and Fort Lauderdale. In between the two coasts stretch heartland agricultural areas and Everglades wilderness. The region encompasses the major resort towns of Fort Myers, Fort Myers Beach, Sanibel Island, Naples, and Marco Island, along with a medley of suburban communities and smaller islands.

8

Updated by
Jill Martin

With its subtropical climate and beckoning family-friendly beaches known for their powdery sand, calm surf, and nary a freighter in sight, the Lower Gulf Coast, also referred to as the state's southwestern region, is a favorite vacation spot of Florida residents as well as visitors. Vacationers tend to spend most of their time outdoors—swimming, sunning, shelling, fishing, boating, and playing tennis or golf.

The region has several distinct travel destinations. Small and historic downtown Fort Myers rises inland along the Caloosahatchee River, and the rest of the town sprawls in all directions. It got its nickname, the City of Palms, from the hundreds of towering royal palms that inventor Thomas Edison planted between 1900 and 1917 along McGregor Boulevard, a historic residential street and site of his winter estate. Edison's idea caught on, and more than 2,000 royal palms now line 14-mile-long McGregor Boulevard. Museums and educational attractions are the draw here. Across the river, Cape Coral has evolved from a mostly residential community to a resort destination for water sports enthusiasts.

Off the coast west of Fort Myers are more than 100 coastal islands in all shapes and sizes. Connected to the mainland by a 3-mile causeway, Sanibel is known for its superb shelling, fine fishing, beachfront resorts, and wildlife refuge. Here and on Captiva, to which it is connected by a short bridge, multimillion-dollar homes line both waterfronts. Just southwest of Fort Myers is Estero Island, home of busy Fort Myers Beach, and farther south, Lovers Key State Park and Bonita Beach.

Farther down the coast lies Naples, once a small fishing village and now a thriving and sophisticated enclave. It's like a smaller, more understated version of Palm Beach, with fine restaurants, chichi shopping areas, luxury resorts, and—locals will tell you—more golf holes per capita than anywhere else in the world. A half hour south basks Marco Island, best known for its beaches and fishing. See a maze of pristine miniature mangrove islands when you take a boat tour from the island's marinas into Ten Thousand Islands National Wildlife Refuge. Although high-rises line much of Marco's waterfront, the tiny fishing village of Goodland, an outpost of Old Florida, tries valiantly to stave off new development.

PLANNING

WHEN TO GO
In winter this is one of the warmest areas of the United States. Occasionally temperatures drop in December or January, but rarely below freezing. From February through April you may find it next to impossible to find a hotel room.

Numbers drop the rest of the year, but visitors within driving range, European tourists, and convention clientele still keep things busy. Temperatures and humidity spike, but discounted room rates make summer attractive. Summer is also rainy season, but most storms occur in the afternoon and last for a flash. Hurricane season runs from June through November.

GETTING HERE AND AROUND
AIR TRAVEL
The area's primary airport is in Fort Myers, where many airlines offer flights; private pilots land at both RSW and Page Field, also in Fort Myers. Gulf Coast Airways to Key West and a couple of private charter services also land at Naples Municipal Airport, and North Captiva Island has a private airstrip.

Airport Transfer Contacts Aaron Airport Transportation ☎ 239/768–1898 ⊕ www.aarontaxi.com. **Sanibel Taxi** ☎ 239/472–4160, 888/527–7806 ⊕ www.sanibeltaxi.com.

Contacts Naples Municipal Airport ✉ 160 Aviation Dr. N, Naples ☎ 239/643–0733 ⊕ www.flynaples.com. **Southwest Florida International Airport** (RSW). ✉ 11000 Terminal Access Rd., Fort Myers ☎ 239/590–4800 ⊕ www.flylcpa.com.

CAR TRAVEL
If you're driving, U.S. 41 (the Tamiami Trail) runs the length of the region. Sanibel Island is accessible from the mainland via the Sanibel Causeway (toll $6 round-trip). Captiva Island lies across a small pass from Sanibel's north end, accessible by bridge.

Be aware that the destination's popularity, especially during winter, means traffic congestion at peak times of day. Avoid driving when the locals are getting to and from work and visitors to and from the beach.

HOTELS
Lodging in Fort Myers, the islands, and Naples can be pricey, but there are affordable options even during the busy winter season. If these destinations are too rich for your pocket, consider visiting in the off-season, when rates drop drastically, or look to Fort Myers Beach and Cape Coral for better rates. Beachfront properties tend to be more expensive; to spend less, look for properties away from the water. In high season—Christmastime and Presidents' Day through Easter—always reserve ahead for the top properties. Fall is the slowest season: rates are low and availability is high, but this is also hurricane season

8

(June–November). *Hotel reviews have been shortened. For full information, visit Fodors.com.*

RESTAURANTS

In this part of Florida, fresh seafood reigns supreme. Succulent native stone-crab claws, a particularly tasty treat, in season from mid-October through mid-May, are usually served hot with drawn butter or chilled with tangy mustard sauce. Supplies are typically steady, since claws regenerate in time for the next season. Other seafood specialties include fried grouper sandwiches and Sanibel pink shrimp. In Naples's highly hailed restaurants and sidewalk cafés, mingle with locals, winter visitors, and other travelers, and catch up on the latest culinary trends.

WHAT IT COSTS				
	$	$$	$$$	$$$$
RESTAURANTS	under $16	$16–$20	$21–$30	over $30
HOTELS	under $201	$201–$300	$301–$400	over $400

Restaurant prices are the average cost of a main course at dinner or, if dinner is not served, at lunch. Hotel prices are the lowest cost of a standard double room in high season.

TOURS

Captiva Cruises. Shelling, dolphin, luncheon, beach, sunset, and history cruises run to and around the out islands of Cabbage Key, Useppa Island, Cayo Costa, and Gasparilla Island. Night sky cruises and excursions also go to historic Tarpon Lodge and Calusa Indian Mound Trail on Pine Island. Excursions from $27. ⊠ *McCarthy's Marina, 11401 Andy Rosse La., Captiva* ☎ *239/472–5300* ⊕ *www.captivacruises.com.*

Manatee Sightseeing Adventure. You are guaranteed to see manatees or you don't pay. Tours depart at Port of the Islands. Discount tickets are available online. ⊠ *525 Newport Dr., Naples* ☎ *239/642–8818* ⊕ *www. see-manatees.com.*

Tarpon Bay Explorers. One of the best ways to see the J.N. "Ding" Darling National Wildlife Refuge is by taking one of these guided or self-guided nature tours. There are many options to choose depending on your activity level and desire—including a sea life cruise, open-air tram tours, and nature cruises, to name a few. Rentals of kayaks, canoes, stand-up paddleboards, bikes, and pontoon boats are right on-site. Charter boats are also available. ⊠ *900 Tarpon Bay Rd., Sanibel* ☎ *239/472–8900* ⊕ *www.tarponbayexplorers.com.*

FORT MYERS AND VICINITY

In parts of Fort Myers, old Southern mansions and their modern-day counterparts peek out from behind stately palms and blossomy foliage. Views over the broad Caloosahatchee River, which borders the city's small but businesslike cluster of office buildings downtown, soften the look of the area. These days it's showing the effects of age and urban sprawl, but planners work at reviving what has been termed the River

District at the heart of downtown. North of Fort Myers are small fishing communities and new retirement towns, including Boca Grande on Gasparilla Island; Englewood Beach on Manasota Key; and Port Charlotte, north of the Peace River.

FORT MYERS

80 miles southeast of Sarasota, 125 miles west of Palm Beach.

The city core lies inland along the banks of the Caloosahatchee River, a half hour from the nearest beach. The town is best known as the winter home of inventors Thomas A. Edison and Henry Ford.

GETTING HERE AND AROUND

The closest airport to Fort Myers is Southwest Florida International Airport (RSW), about 15 miles southeast of town. A taxi for up to three passengers costs about $20–$40. Extra people are charged $10 each. LeeTran bus service serves most of the Fort Myers area.

If you're driving here from Florida's East Coast, consider Alligator Alley, a toll section of Interstate 75 that runs from Fort Lauderdale to Naples. Interstate 75 then runs north–south the length of the region. U.S. 41 (the Tamiami Trail, also called South Cleveland Avenue in Fort Myers) runs parallel to the interstate to the west and goes through downtown Naples and Fort Myers. McGregor Boulevard (Route 867) and Summerlin Road (Route 869), Fort Myers's main north–south city streets, head toward Sanibel and Captiva islands. San Carlos Boulevard (Route 865) runs southwest from Summerlin Road to Fort Myers Beach, and Pine Island–Bayshore Road (Route 78) leads from North Fort Myers through northern Cape Coral onto Pine Island.

Key West Express operates a ferry from Fort Myers Beach (year-round) to Key West.

Bus Contacts LeeTran ☎ 239/275–8726, 239/533–8726 ⊕ www.rideleetran. com.

Ferry Contacts Key West Express ✉ 1200 Main St., Fort Myers Beach ☎ 239/394–9700, 888/539–2628 ⊕ www.keywestexpress.us.

VISITOR INFORMATION

Contacts Lee County Visitor & Convention Bureau ✉ 2201 2nd St., Suite 600 ☎ 239/338–3500, 800/237–6444 ⊕ www.fortmyers-sanibel.com.

EXPLORING

TOP ATTRACTIONS

Fodor's Choice ★ **Edison & Ford Winter Estates.** Fort Myers's premier attraction pays homage to two of America's most ingenious inventors: Thomas A. Edison, who gave the world the stock ticker, the incandescent lamp, and the phonograph, among other inventions; and his friend and neighbor, automaker Henry Ford. Donated to the city by Edison's widow, his once 12-acre estate has been expanded into a remarkable 25 acres, with three homes, two caretaker cottages, a laboratory, botanical gardens, and a museum. The laboratory contains the same gadgets and gizmos as when Edison last stepped foot into it. Visitors can see many of his inventions, along with historic photographs and memorabilia, in the museum. Edison

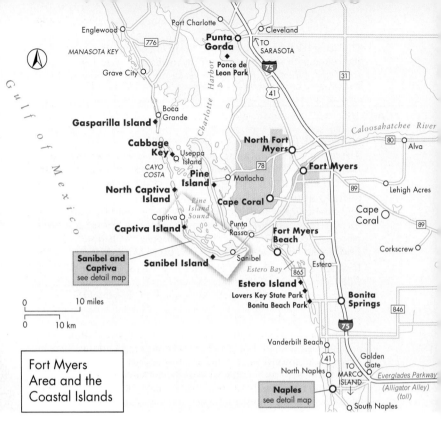

Sanibel and
Captiva
see detail map

Naples
see detail map

Fort Myers
Area and the
Coastal Islands

traveled south from New Jersey and devoted much of his time here to inventing things (there are 1,093 patents to his name), experimenting with rubber for friend and frequent visitor Harvey Firestone, and planting hundreds of plant species collected around the world. Next door to Edison's two identical homes is Ford's "Mangoes," the more modest seasonal home of Edison's fellow inventor. The property's oldest building, the Edison Caretaker's House, dates to 1860. Tours are guided or audio self-guided. One admission covers homes of both men; museum and laboratory-only tickets and botanical-garden tour tickets are also available. ⊠ 2350 McGregor Blvd. ☎ 239/334–7419 ⊕ www. edisonfordwinterestates.org 🎫 Complete Estate Tour $20; other tours available ⊗ Daily 9–5:30, tours hourly 10–4.

FAMILY

Fodor's Choice

★

Imaginarium Science Center. Kids can't wait to get their hands on the wonderful interactive exhibits at this lively museum–aquarium combo that explores technology, physics, weather, and other science topics. Check out the stingrays and other marine life in the aquariums, touch tanks, and the living-reef tank; feed the fish, turtles, and swans in the outdoor lagoon; visit a tarantula, python, hissing cockroach, juvenile alligator, and other live critters in the Animal Lab; dig for dinosaur bones; score in the Sporty Science sports simulator; watch a 3-D movie in the theater; take part in a hands-on Animal Encounter demonstration, and touch a cloud. Other highlights include the Tiny Town early childhood area, Backyard Nature, Discovery Lab exploration station, Idea Lab engineering design center, as well as Build-Your-Own-Coaster and Science of Motion. ✉ *2000 Cranford Ave.* ☎ *239/321–7420* ⊕ *www. imaginariumfortmyers.com* ✍ *$12* ☉ *Tues.–Sat. 10–5, Sun. noon–5.*

FAMILY **Manatee Park.** Here you may glimpse Florida's most famous, yet often hard to spot, marine mammal. When gulf waters drop to 68 degrees F or below—usually from November to March—the sea cows congregate in these waters, which are warmed by the outflow of a towering nearby power plant. Pause at any of the three observation decks (the first nearest the outflow and last at the lagoon usually yield the most sightings, as does the fishing pier) and watch for bubbles. Hydrophones on the last deck allow you to eavesdrop on their songs. Periodically, one of these gentle giants—mature adults weigh an average of 1,000 pounds—will surface. Calusa Blueway Outfitters *(see ⇨ Kayaking in Sports and the Outdoors)* run the visitor center/gift shop and offer kayak and canoe rentals, as well as clinics and tours to paddle the canals and get a closer look. ✉ *10901 Palm Beach Blvd., 1¼ miles east of I–75 Exit 141* ☎ *239/690–5030* ⊕ *www.leeparks.org* ✍ *Free. Parking May–Nov. $1 per hr, $5 daily; Dec.–Apr. $2 per hr, $5 daily* ☉ *Park daily 8–sunset; concession 9 am–4 pm Dec.–Mar.*

WORTH NOTING

FAMILY **Calusa Nature Center & Planetarium.** Get a look at Florida's native animals and habitats. Boardwalks and trails lead through subtropical wetlands, a birds-of-prey aviary, and a screened-in butterfly house. There are snake, alligator, butterfly, and other live-animal demonstrations several times daily. Museum exhibits include an Exotic Species room and the Insectarium. The domed, state-of-the-art, 90-seat planetarium hosts astronomy shows daily and special laser shows. ✉ *3450 Ortiz Ave.* ☎ *239/275–3435* ⊕ *www.calusanature.org* ✍ *$10* ☉ *Mon.–Sat. 10–5, Sun. 11–5.*

Sidney & Berne Davis Art Center. The River District has become a haven for independent galleries, and in 2003 Florida Arts, Inc., a nonprofit organization, stepped in to turn an abandoned post office from 1933 into a space for edgy, up-and-coming visual artists, musical acts, films, and theater. Even if your taste runs more to Broadway and Monet than M-Pact and Marcus Jansen, a visit is worthwhile for the neoclassical revival facade: eight towering coral-rock Ionic columns give way to swaths of intricately detailed window screens. The friendly staff is happy to answer questions about the building's history. Renovations of the upper floors have recently been completed. ■TIP➔ **Plan a trip around the first or third Friday every month for Art Walk or Music Walk; the center stays open late for the throngs of passersby.** ✉ *2301 1st St.* ☎ *239/333–1933* ⊕ *www.sbdac.com* ✍ *$5 suggested donation* ☉ *Weekdays 9–5; performances most weekend nights.*

Southwest Florida Museum of History. A restored railroad depot serves as a showcase for the area's history dating to 800 BC. Displays include prehistoric animals and Calusa artifacts, a reconstructed *chickee* hut, a dugout canoe, clothing and photos from Seminole settlements, historical

View 200 phonographs, an invention Thomas Edison patented in 1878, at his Fort Myers winter estate.

vignettes, changing exhibits, and a replicated Florida Cracker house. A favorite attraction is the *Esperanza,* a private, restored 1929 Pullman rail car. ✉ *2031 Jackson St.* ☎ *239/321–7430* 🌐 *www.swflmuseumofhistory.com* 🎟 *$9.50* 🕒 *Tues.–Sat. 10–5.*

WHERE TO EAT

$$$ AMERICAN 🍴 **Bistro 41.** Shoppers and businesspeople meet in the newly remodeled dining room for some of the town's most dependable and inventive cuisine. Amid brightly painted, textured walls and a display kitchen, the menus roam from "41 Prime Dip" sandwich and the popular bistro salad with portobellos and a pesto drizzle to a delicious pork pot roast. To experience the kitchen at its imaginative best, check the night's specials, which often include daringly done seafood (crabmeat-crusted triple-tail fish with caramelized plantains and passion-fruit beurre blanc, for instance). When weather permits, ask for a table on the patio. [$] *Average main: $23* ✉ *13499 S. Cleveland Ave.* ☎ *239/466–4141* 🌐 *www.bistro41.com* ✍ *Reservations essential.*

$ MEXICAN 🍴 **Chile Ranchero.** Latinos and gringos alike converge on this authentic little corner of Mexicana in a strip mall along busy Tamiami Trail. The decor is humble, but you can't beat the prices or the portions. The warm and inviting staff speaks Spanish and so does the menu, with English subtitles. The intensely flavorful dishes appeal to American and Latin palates, with a range from fajitas and steak ranchero to seafood soup and excellent nachos con ceviche. [$] *Average main: $12* ✉ *11751 S. Cleveland Ave., No. 18* ☎ *239/275–0505.*

$$$ ITALIAN 🍴 **Cibo.** Its flavor-bursting Italian food and its propensity for fresh, quality ingredients keep Cibo (pronounced *chee-bo*) at the head of the class

for local Italian restaurants. In contrast to the sophisticated black-and-white setting, the menu comes in colors from the classic Caesar salad with shaved Grana Padano and spaghetti and meatballs to salmon piccata and veal porterhouse with porcini risotto. The lasagna Napoletana is typical of the standards set here—a generous square of pasta layered with fluffy ricotta, meat ragu, mozzarella, and the totally fresh-tasting, garlicky pomodoro sauce. $ *Average main: $24* ✉ *12901 McGregor Blvd.* ☎ *239/454–3700* ⊕ *www.cibofortmyers.com* ⌦ *Reservations essential* ⊗ *No lunch.*

$$$
VIETNAMESE

✕ **Saigon Paris Bistro.** Irish omelets, Belgian waffles, crêpes, steak au poivre, Vietnamese sea bass, Waldorf chicken salad: this eatery's extensive menu clearly travels farther abroad than its name implies. And it does so with utmost taste and flavor, as its faithful local clientele will attest. The best deals are the lunchtime Vietnamese entrées and chicken egg-drop soup. The restaurant is known for its gigantic bowls of *pho* (traditional soup), which can be ordered any time of day (some people have them for breakfast). It also offers three-course Vietnamese or Parisian dinners for $30. Leave room for crêpes à la Grand Marnier, prepared tableside. The interior is pleasant, if a bit old-fashioned, but provides a soothing surprise in this busy part of town with its fireplace, floral motif, and classic columns. $ *Average main: $21* ✉ *12995 S. Cleveland. Ave., No. 118* ☎ *239/936–2233* ⊕ *www.saigonparisbistro. com* ⊗ *Closed Mon. June–Sept.*

$
SEAFOOD
FAMILY

✕ **Shrimp Shack.** Seafood lovers, families, and retired snowbirds flock to this venue with its vivacious staff, bustle, and colorful, cartoonish wall murals. There's a wait for lunch in winter season and a brisk take-out business with drive-through. Southern-style deep frying prevails—whole-belly clams, grouper, shrimp, onion rings, hush puppies, and fried pork loins—though you can get certain selections broiled or blackened, and there's some New England flavor with seafood rolls at lunch. Create your own combo by selecting two or three fried, broiled, or blackened choices. Kids love this place for the buzzing atmosphere and parents love the inexpensive kids meals. For more savings, print out the restaurant's "Kids Eat Free" coupon from the web site. This is your place if you like your seafood simple. $ *Average main: $13* ✉ *13361 Metro Pkwy.* ☎ *239/561–6817* ⊕ *www.shrimpshackusa.com.*

$$$$
SOUTHERN

✕ **The Veranda.** Restaurants come and go quickly as downtown reinvents itself, but this one has endured since 1978. A favorite of business and government bigwigs at lunch (the fried-green-tomato salad is signature), it serves imaginative Continental fare with a trace of a Southern accent for dinner. Notable are tournedos with smoky sour-mash-whiskey sauce, rack of lamb with rosemary-merlot sauce, herb-crusted honey-grilled salmon, and a grilled seafood sampler with prosciutto cream fettuccine, all served with homemade honey-drizzled bread and corn muffins with pepper jelly. The restaurant is a combination of two turn-of-the-20th-century homes, with a two-sided central brick fireplace, and sconces and antique oil paintings on its pale-yellow walls. Ask for an outdoor courtyard table when weather permits. $ *Average main: $34* ✉ *2122 2nd St.* ☎ *239/332–2065* ⊕ *www.verandarestaurant.com* ⊗ *Closed Sun. No lunch Sat.*

8

WHERE TO STAY

$$$ ⌂ **Crowne Plaza Hotel Fort Myers at the Bell Tower Shops.** Baseball fans often
HOTEL   make this hotel home base since spring training and other sports parks
are just a few miles away, while singles love the sports bar downstairs
and being a stroll from the Bell Tower Shops, and families appreciate
the mini-refrigerators and microwaves in the rooms. **Pros:** free airport
shuttle; complimentary transportation within a 3-mile radius; laundry
facilities. **Cons:** showing signs of age; rooms a bit tight; meeting traf-
fic crowds the lobby. $ *Rooms from: $210* ⌂ *13051 Bell Tower Dr.*
☎ *239/482–2900* ⊕ *www.cpfortmyers.com* ⇗ *225 rooms* ❍| *No meals.*

$$$ ⌂ **Hilton Garden Inn Fort Myers.** This compact, prettily landscaped low-
HOTEL   rise is near Fort Myers's cultural and commercial areas, and a business
clientele favors it for its convenience. **Pros:** near performing-arts center;
enjoyable restaurant; large rooms. **Cons:** chain feel; small pool; at busy
intersection. $ *Rooms from: $199* ⌂ *12600 University Dr.* ☎ *239/790–*
3500 ⊕ *www.fortmyers.stayhgi.com* ⇗ *126 rooms* ❍| *Breakfast.*

$$$ ⌂ **Hotel Indigo, Ft. Myers Downtown River District.** The only modern bou-
HOTEL   tique hotel downtown, it attracts a cosmopolitan set that wants to be in
the center of the River District's art, dining, and shopping scene—and
just minutes from other attractions. **Pros:** sleek design; walking distance
to restaurants and nightlife; tower built in 2009 and lobby part of his-
toric arcade; rooftop bar. **Cons:** must drive to beach; no suites have full
kitchens. $ *Rooms from: $199* ⌂ *1520 Broadway* ☎ *239/337–3446*
⊕ *www.hotelindigo.com* ⇗ *60 rooms, 7 suites* ❍| *No meals.*

$$$ ⌂ **Sanibel Harbour Marriott Resort & Spa.** Vacationing families and busi-
RESORT   nesspeople who want luxury pick this sprawling resort complex that
FAMILY   towers over the island-studded San Carlos Bay at the last mainland
Fodor'sChoice   exit before the Sanibel Causeway. **Pros:** top-notch accommodations;
★   full amenities; updated spa. **Cons:** daily parking fee as well as resort
fee added to rate; unspectacular beach. $ *Rooms from: $369* ⌂ *17260*
Harbour Pointe Dr. ☎ *239/466–4000, 800/767–7777* ⊕ *www.sanibel-*
resort.com ⇗ *283 rooms, 64 suites* ❍| *No meals.*

NIGHTLIFE

Crü. Trendsters in the mood for a drink and excellent global tapas crowd
the lounge area of this cutting-edge restaurant. The lounge serves food
until midnight on weekends. ⌂ *13499 S. Cleveland Ave., Suite 241*
☎ *239/466–3663* ⊕ *www.eatcru.com.*

Groove Street Grille & Discotheque. Dance to those fabulous songs of the
1970s and hot hits from today. Happy hour, ladies' night, and good
food add to the fun atmosphere. Comedy shows play regularly in the
Laugh-In Comedy Cafe, which is in the same building. ⌂ *College Plaza,*
8595 College Pkwy., #300 ☎ *239/437–2743* ⊕ *www.groovestreet.com*
🕐 *Thurs. 9 pm–2 am, Fri. 5 pm–2 am, Sat. 8 pm–2 am.*

The Happy Buddha. A giant gold statue of his Zen-ness out front greets
fans—a fun mix of frat boys, retirees, and young professionals—who
crowd the casual, smoky bar and groove to hits from live bands and DJs.
This is a local favorite. ⌂ *12701 McGregor Blvd.* ☎ *239/482–8565.*

Laugh-In Comedy Cafe. For more than 20 years, this is the place to watch
top comedians perform every Friday and Saturday, in a no-smoking

atmosphere. ⊠ *College Plaza, 8595 College Pkwy., No. 300* ☎ *239/479–5233* ⊕ *www.laughincomedycafe.com.*

Stevie Tomato's Sports Page. Five miles up on Interstate 75 from the buzzing Gulf Coast Town Center bars, this is a low-key spot to catch a game and feast on good food; earlier in the evening it's very family-friendly. Best bets are their baby back ribs, Chicago-style pizza, and Italian beef. ⊠ *9510 Market Place Rd.* ☎ *239/939–7211* ⊕ *www.stevietomatossportspage.com.*

SHOPPING

Bell Tower Shops. This open-air shopping center has about 40 stylish boutiques and specialty shops, a Saks 5th Avenue, some of Fort Myers's best restaurants and bars, as well as 20 movie screens. ⊠ *S. Cleveland Ave. at Daniels Pkwy.* ☎ *239/489–1221* ⊕ *www.thebelltowershops.com.*

Edison Mall. The largest air-conditioned indoor mall in Fort Myers houses several major department stores and some 160 specialty shops. ⊠ *4125 Cleveland Ave.* ☎ *239/939–1933* ⊕ *www.simon.com/mall/edison-mall.*

Fleamasters Fleamarket. Just east of downtown, more than 900 vendors sell new and used goods Friday through Sunday 9–5. Its music hall hosts live entertainment. ⊠ *4135 Dr. Martin Luther King Jr. Blvd., 1.7 miles west of I–75 Exit 138* ☎ *239/334–7001* ⊕ *www.fleamall.com.*

Fort Myers Tanger Factory Outlets. Its boardwalks are lined with outlets for Nike, Van Heusen, Maidenform, Coach, Under Armour, Bath & Body Works, and Samsonite, among others. ⊠ *20350 Summerlin Rd.* ☎ *888/471–3939* ⊕ *www.tangeroutlet.com/fortmyers.*

Gulf Coast Town Center. This megamall of stores and chain restaurants includes a 130,000-square-foot Bass Pro Shops, Ron Jon Surf Shop, Best Buy, Costco, Golf Galaxy, and movie theaters. ⊠ *9903 Gulf Coast Main St.* ☎ *239/267–0783* ⊕ *www.gulfcoasttowncenter.com.*

8

SPORTS AND THE OUTDOORS

BASEBALL

The region is a popular outpost for spring training teams, with two in Fort Myers.

Boston Red Sox. The Sox settled into new digs in 2012 at JetBlue Park at Fenway South, a new $77 million, 10,823-capacity stadium and 106-acre training facility. The field itself is an exact duplicate of their famous home turf, with a Green Monster wall and manual scoreboard. ⊠ *JetBlue Park, 11581 Daniels Pkwy.* ☎ *239/334–4700, 888/733–7696* ⊕ *boston.redsox.mlb.com.*

Minnesota Twins. The team plays exhibition games in town during March and early April. From April through September, the Miracle (⊕ *www.miraclebaseball.com*), a Twins single-A affiliate, plays home games at Hammond Stadium. ⊠ *Lee County Sports Complex, 14100 6 Mile Cypress Pkwy.* ☎ *800/338–9467* ⊕ *minnesota.twins.mlb.com.*

BIKING

One of the longest bike paths in Fort Myers is along Summerlin Road. It passes commercial areas and gets close to Sanibel through dwindling wide-open spaces. Linear Park, which runs parallel to Six Mile Cypress Parkway, offers more natural, less congested views. Trailhead Park is linked to the new John Yarbrough Linear Park to create a 30-mile pathway, the longest in Lee County.

Bike Route. Since 1974, this is the place to come for a good selection of rentals. ⊠ *8595 College Pkwy., Suite 200* ☎ *239/481–3376* ⊕ *www.thebikeroute.com* ⊗ *Closed Sun.*

BOATING AND SAILING

Southwest Florida Yachts. Charter a sailboat or powerboat, or take lessons. With 30 years in the business, they can help you explore Southwest Florida like a native. ⊠ *6095 Silver King Blvd., Cape Coral* ☎ *239/656-1339, 800/257-2788* ⊕ *www.swfyachts.com.*

GOLF

Eastwood Golf Course. Golfers love how this Robert von Hagge– and Bruce Devlin–designed course is in an area where there is little development, meaning no homes around the course, just plenty of water, trees, and wildlife (aka gators). The driving range and course are affordable, too, especially if you don't mind playing at unfavorable times (midday in summer, for example). Test your skills on the short par 4 on hole 7, where your second shot is over water. The 10th hole will have you shooting over water, too. ⊠ *4600 Bruce Herd La.* ☎ *239/321–7487* ⊕ *www.cityftmyers.com/eastwood* ▨ *From $45; rentals clubs $15* ⚑ *18 holes, 6772 yards, par 72.*

Fort Myers Country Club. Walk in the footsteps of Thomas Edison and Henry Ford when you play this course known as "The Fort" to its huge fan base. Located less than a mile from the winter estates of these famous inventors, this course is one of the oldest on Florida's west coast. In fact, it was designed in 1916 by Donald Ross and opened in 1917. Number 10 is a par 3 where you can hit anything from a 7 iron to a hybrid as the hole stretches out 203 yards. The Coors Light Open is held here early each year. Next door is a lively restaurant and bar, The Edison. ⊠ *3591 McGregor Blvd.* ☎ *239/321–7488* ⊕ *www.cityftmyers.com/countryclub* ▨ *$45–$65* ⚑ *18 holes, 6400 yards, par 72.*

Shell Point Golf Club. Newbies to heavy hitters enjoy the layout of this Gordon Lewis–designed course with its challenging fairways and share of water hazards—eight tees on every hole. The front nine play like a symphony, but the back nine can be rough and slow with the wind and their somewhat compacted layouts. If you're looking for a 19th hole where you can toast your one-under-par score, you won't find it here as no alcohol is served. One nice feature at "The Shell" is that they offer Laser Link for accurate yardage to the pin. ⊠ *17401 On Par Blvd.* ☎ *239/433–9790* ⊕ *www.shellpointgolf.com* ▨ *$85* ⚑ *18 holes, 6880 yards, par 71.*

KAYAKING

Calusa Blueway Outfitters. Paddling enthusiasts can rent kayaks to explore the Manatee Park environs daily from Thanksgiving to Easter and on weekends in the summer; clinics and guided tours are also available, but go in winter if spotting sea cows is your aim. ⊠ *Manatee Park, 10901 Palm Beach Blvd., 1¼ mile east of I–75 Exit 141* ☎ *239/481–4600* ⊕ *www.calusabluewayoutfitters.com.*

CAPE CORAL, PINE ISLAND, AND NORTH FORT MYERS

13 miles from downtown Fort Myers.

Cape Coral is determinedly trying to move from its pigeonhole as a residential community by attracting tourism with its downtown reconfiguration, the Resort at Marina Village, and destination restaurants at the Cape Harbour residential marina development.

GETTING HERE AND AROUND

Four bridges cross from Fort Myers to Cape Coral and North Fort Myers. Pine Island–Bayshore Road (Route 78) leads from North Fort Myers through northern Cape Coral onto off-the-beaten path Pine Island, known for its art galleries, fishing, and exotic fruit farms.

EXPLORING

Calusa Heritage Trail. Affiliated with the University of Florida's natural history museum in Gainesville, this 7/10-mile interpretive walkway explores the site of an ancient Amerindian village—more than 1,500 years old—with excellent signage, two intact shell mounds you can climb, the remains of a complex canal system, and ongoing archaeological research. Guided tours are given 3 times a week from January to April. Check the website for special tours and lecture events. ⊠ *Randell Research Center, 13810 Waterfront Dr., Bokeelia, Pine Island, Pineland* ☎ *239/283–2157* ⊕ *www.flmnh.ufl.edu/rrc* ☜ *$7 (suggested donation)* ⊙ *Open daily sunrise–sunset. Restrooms and gift shop open Mon.–Sat. 10–4.*

FAMILY **Shell Factory & Nature Park.** This entertainment complex, once just a quirky shopping destination and a survivor from Florida's roadside-attraction era, now contains eateries, an arcade, bumper boats, miniature golf, and a mining sluice where kids can pan for shells, fossils, and gemstones. Strolling the grounds is free, including seeing over $6 million worth of exhibits and displays, but some activities carry individual fees, and a separate admission is required to enter the Nature Park, which has the feel of a small zoo. There you can find llamas; a petting farm with sheep, pigs, and goats; a walk-through aviary; an EcoLab; a touch center; and a gator slough. The Shell Factory hosts family-friendly events throughout the year, such as the Gumbo Fest in January. It's newest addition is the Soaring Eagle Zipline. ⊠ *2787 N. Tamiami Trail, North Fort Myers* ☎ *239/995–2141* ⊕ *www.shellfactory.com* ☜ *Shell Factory free; attractions starting at $2 each; Nature Park $12* ⊙ *Shell Factory daily 9–7; Nature Park daily 10–5.*

FAMILY
Fodor's Choice
★
Sun Splash Family Waterpark. Head here to cool off when summer swelters. Nearly two dozen wet and dry attractions include 10 thrill waterslides; the Sand Dollar Walk, where you step from one floating "sand dollar" to another; pint-size Pro Racer flumes; a professional sand volleyball court; a family pool and Tot Spot; and a river-tube ride. Rates go down after 2 pm, plus the park offers Family Fun Night specials. ⊠ *400 Santa Barbara Blvd.* ☎ *239/574–0558* ⊕ *www.sunsplashwaterpark.com* ☜ *$17.95* ⊙ *Mar.–Sept., weekends and some weekdays 10–5; call or visit website for specific open hrs.*

8

PUNTA GORDA DAY TRIP

A half hour (23 miles) north of Fort Myers, the small, old town of Punta Gorda merits a day trip for its restaurants and historic sites. If you're driving to Boca Grande via U.S. 41, it also makes a nice stop along the way. On the mouth of the Peace River, where it empties into Charlotte Harbor, a new riverfront park, water views, and murals enliven the compact downtown historic district. Away from the downtown area, a classic-car museum, wildlife rehabilitation center, and waterfront shopping complex built into an old fish-packing plant fills out a day of sightseeing. Fishing and nature-watching tours also depart from the Fishermen's Village complex.

OFF THE
BEATEN
PATH

Babcock Wilderness Adventures. To see what Florida looked like centuries ago, visit Babcock's Crescent B Ranch, northeast of Fort Myers. During the 90-minute swamp-buggy-style excursion you ride in a converted school bus through several ecosystems, including the unusual and fascinating Telegraph Cypress Swamp. Along the way an informative and typically amusing guide describes the area's social and natural history while you keep an eye peeled for alligators, wild pigs, all sorts of birds, Florida panthers, and other denizens of the wild. The tour also takes in the ranch's resident cattle and cougar in captivity. Reservations are needed for tours. An on-site restaurant serves "Cracker" chow in season. ⊠ *8000 Rte. 31, Punta Gorda* ☎ *800/500–5583* ⊕ *www. babcockwilderness.com* ✉ *Eco-tour $24; cost for other specialty tours varies* ⌚ *Reservations essential* ☉ *Oct.–May, tours daily; June–Sept., tours Tues.–Sat. All tours by reservation only; some specialty tours offered only monthly or seasonally.*

WHERE TO EAT

$

AMERICAN

✕ Bert's Bar & Grill. Looking to hang out with the locals of Pine Island? Here you'll find cheap eats, live entertainment, a pool table, and a water view to boot. Speaking of boots, you're likely to see some of the clientele wearing white rubber fishing boots, known here as Pine Island Reeboks. Order fried oysters, a burger, pizza, or a grouper Reuben melt from the no-nonsense menu, and enjoy live music most days. $ *Average main: $9* ⊠ *4271 Pine Island Rd., Matlacha* ☎ *239/282–3232* ⊕ *www. bertsbar.com* ⌚ *Reservations not accepted.*

$

AMERICAN

✕ Rumrunners. Cape Coral's best casual cuisine is surprisingly affordable, considering the luxury condo development that rises around it and the size of the yachts that pull up to the docks. Caribbean in spirit, with lots of indoor and outdoor views of a mangrove-fringed waterway, it serves bistro specialties such as conch fritters, seafood potpie, bronzed salmon, and a warm chocolate bread pudding that is addictive. Bar staff is affable and welcoming. $ *Average main: $13* ⊠ *Cape Harbour Marina, 5848 Cape Harbour Dr., off Chiquita Blvd.* ☎ *239/542–0200* ⊕ *www.rumrunnersrestaurant.com.*

$

THAI

✕ Siam Hut. Lunch and dinner menus at this Cape Coral fixture let you design your own stir-fry, noodle, or fried-rice dish. Dinner specialties

include fried crispy frogs' legs with garlic and black pepper, a sizzling shrimp platter, fried whole tilapia with curry sauce, salads, and pad thai (rice noodles, egg, ground peanuts, vegetables, and choice of protein). Get your food fiery hot or extra mild. Two traditional Thai tables allow you to sit on floor pillows (conveniently with backs), or you can opt for a more conventional table or booth. [$] *Average main: $14* ✉ *4521 Del Prado Blvd.* ☎ *239/945–4247* 🌐 *www.siamhutcapecoral.com* 🕒 *Closed Sun. No lunch Sat.*

WHERE TO STAY

$$ HOTEL 🏨 **Casa Loma Motel.** Stay at this pretty little motel, 15 minutes from Fort Myers at the end of the Croton Canal, to be close to Cape Coral's attractions and escape the sticker shock of beachfront lodgings. **Pros:** kitchen facilities in rooms; free Wi-Fi; large sundeck with canal access. **Cons:** must drive to beach; on a busy street; decor a bit dated; no restaurant. [$] *Rooms from: $119* ✉ *3608 Del Prado Blvd.* ☎ *239/549–6000, 877/227–2566* 🌐 *www.casalomamotel.com* 🛏 *48 efficiencies, 1 suite* 🍴 *No meals.*

$$$ RESORT 🏨 **The Westin Cape Coral Resort at Marina Village.** Cape Coral's only luxury resort, this modern 19-story tower sits alongside a marina fringed with mangroves and caters to families and water-ports enthusiasts. **Pros:** designer touches; kids club; great kayaking. **Cons:** 45-minute ferry to beach; high-rise. [$] *Rooms from: $309* ✉ *5951 Silver King Blvd.* ☎ *239/541–5000, 888/372–9256* 🌐 *www.westincapecoral.com* 🛏 *83 studios, 83 1-bedroom condos, 82 2-bedroom condos, 16 3-bedroom condos* 🍴 *No meals.*

THE COASTAL ISLANDS

A maze of islands in various stages of habitation fronts Fort Myers mainland, separated by the Intracoastal Waterway. Some are accessible via a causeway; to reach others, you need a boat. If you cut through bay waters, you have a good chance of being escorted by bottlenose dolphins. Mostly birds and other wild creatures inhabit some islands, which are given over to state parks. Traveler-pampering hotels on Sanibel, Captiva, and Fort Myers Beach give way to rustic cottages, old inns, and cabins on quiet Cabbage Key and Pine Island, which have no beaches because they lie between the barrier islands and mainland. Others are devoted to resorts. When exploring barrier island beaches, keep one eye on the sand: collecting seashells is a major pursuit in these parts.

GASPARILLA ISLAND (BOCA GRANDE)

43 miles northwest of Fort Myers.

Before roads to the Lower Gulf Coast were even talked about, wealthy Northerners came by train to spend the winter at the Gasparilla Inn. The inn was completed in 1913 in Boca Grande on Gasparilla Island, named, legend has it, for a Spanish pirate who set up headquarters in these waters. Although condominiums and modern mansions occupy the rest of Gasparilla, much of the town of Boca Grande evokes another era. The mood is set by the Old Florida homes and tree-framed

roadways. The island's calm is disrupted in the spring when anglers descend with a vengeance on Boca Grande Pass, considered among the best tarpon-fishing spots in the world.

GETTING HERE AND AROUND

Boca Grande is more than an hour's drive northwest of Fort Myers. Day-trippers can catch a charter boat or rent a boat, dock at a marina, and rent a bike or golf cart for a day of exploring and lunching. North of it stretches a long island, home to Don Pedro Island State Park and Palm Island Resort, both accessible only by boat. Also nearby is the off-the-beaten-path but car-accessible island of Manasota Key and its fishing resort community of Englewood Beach.

EXPLORING

Gasparilla Island State Park and Port Boca Grande Lighthouse Museum. The island's beaches are its greatest prize and lie within the state park at the south end. The long, narrow beach ends at Boca Grande Pass, famous for its deep waters and tarpon fishing. The pretty, two-story, circa-1890 lighthouse once marked the pass for mariners. In recent years it has been restored as a museum that explores the island's fishing and railroad heritage. The lighthouse is closed in August. ✉ *880 Belcher Rd., Boca Grande* ☎ *941/964–0060* 🌐 *www.floridastateparks.org/gasparillaisland* 🎟 *$3 per vehicle; $3 suggested donation to lighthouse (exact change only)* 🕓 *Park daily 8–sunset. Lighthouse Nov.–Apr., Mon.–Sat. 10–4, Sun. noon–4; May–July, Sept., and Oct., Wed.–Sat. 10–4, Sun. noon–4.*

WHERE TO EAT

$$$ AMERICAN

🍴 **The Loose Caboose.** Revered by many—including Katharine Hepburn in her time—for its homemade ice cream, this is also a good spot for solid, affordable fare, from burgers and a Thanksgiving wrap (turkey and cranberry sauce) to chicken potpie and crispy duck with orange-teriyaki sauce. Housed in the town's historic depot, it offers indoor and patio seating in an all-American setting. Expect slow service in season, and paper plates with plastic utensils. [$] *Average main: $24* ✉ *433 W. 4th St., Boca Grande* ☎ *941/964–0440* 🌐 *www.loosecaboose.biz* 🕓 *No dinner Wed. or Apr.–Dec.*

WHERE TO STAY

$$$ HOTEL

🏨 **Gasparilla Inn & Club.** Once the playground of social-register members such as the Vanderbilts and DuPonts, the gracious pale-yellow wooden hotel was built by shipping industrialists in the early 1900s. **Pros:** historic property; nicely renovated. **Cons:** expensive rates; the quirks of a very old building. [$] *Rooms from: $385* ✉ *500 Palm Ave., Boca Grande* ☎ *941/964–2201, 800/996–1913* 🌐 *www.gasparillainn.com* 🛏 *137 rooms, 18 cottages, 5 homes* 🍽 *Multiple meal plans.*

CABBAGE KEY

5 miles south of Boca Grande.

Cabbage Key is the ultimate island-hopping escape in these parts. Some say Jimmy Buffett was inspired to write "Cheeseburger in Paradise" after a visit to its popular restaurant.

GETTING HERE AND AROUND

You'll need to take a boat—from Bokeelia or Pineland, on Pine Island, or from Captiva Island—to get to this island, which sits at mile marker 60 on the Intracoastal Waterway. Local operators offer day trips and luncheon cruises.

WHERE TO STAY

$ ⊞ **Cabbage Key Inn.** Atop an ancient Calusa Indian shell mound and
HOTEL   accessible only by boat, the friendly, somewhat quirky inn built by novelist and playwright Mary Roberts Rinehart in 1938 welcomes guests seeking quiet and isolation. **Pros:** plenty of solitude; Old Florida character. **Cons:** two-night minimum stay; accessible only by boat or seaplane; limited amenities, some rooms have no TV; in season the restaurant is busy. $ *Rooms from: $175* ☎ *239/283–2278* ⊕ *www.cabbagekey.com* ⌂ *6 rooms, 8 cottages* †○† *No meals.*

SANIBEL AND CAPTIVA ISLANDS

23 miles southwest of downtown Fort Myers.

Sanibel Island is famous as one of the world's best shelling grounds, a function of the unusual east–west orientation of the island's south end. Just as the tide is going out and after storms, the pickings can be superb, and shell seekers performing the telltale "Sanibel stoop" patrol every beach carrying bags of conchs, whelks, cockles, and other bivalves and gastropods. (Remember, it's unlawful to pick up live shells.) Away from the beach, flowery vegetation decorates small shopping complexes, pleasant resorts and condo complexes, mom-and-pop motels, and casual restaurants. But much of the two-lane road down the spine of the island is bordered by nature reserves that have made Sanibel as well known among bird-watchers as it is among seashell collectors.

Captiva Island, connected to the northern end of Sanibel by a bridge, is quirky and engaging. At the end of a twisty road lined with million-dollar mansions lies a delightful village of shops, eateries, and beaches.

GETTING HERE AND AROUND

Sanibel Island is approximately 23 miles southwest of downtown Fort Myers, and Captiva lies north of 12-mile-long Sanibel. If you're flying into Southwest Florida International Airport, an on-demand taxi for up to three passengers to Sanibel or Captiva costs about $60–$68; additional passengers are charged $10 each. Sanibel Island is accessible from the mainland via the Sanibel Causeway (toll $6 round-trip). Captiva Island lies across a small pass from Sanibel's north end, accessible by bridge.

ESSENTIALS

Visitor Information Sanibel and Captiva Islands Chamber of Commerce ⊠ *1159 Causeway Rd., Sanibel* ☎ *239/472–1080* ⊕ *www.sanibel-captiva.org.*

EXPLORING

FAMILY   **Bailey-Matthews National Shell Museum.** There have been big changes here
Fodor's Choice   at the museum and it all starts before you even enter, with giant shell
★   photos on the exterior of the building by nature photographer Henry Domke. Once inside, there are more than 30 permanent and short-term

exhibits. See a life-size display of native Calusa and how they used shells. From tiny to enormous, view local specimens and a variety from around the world. Play in the colorful kids' lab. Watch movies about how shells are formed and where to find them. Get a close-up look at mollusks in the 8-foot-long, live-viewing tank. The museum has also added two full-time marine biologists who lead daily tank talks (at 11:30 and 3), host daily guided beach walks, and lead a weekly marine naturalist cruise (Thursday). From colossal squids to Shelling 101, make this your first stop and you'll be giving your own talks on the beach. Don't miss the museum store, filled with upscale nautical gifts. ⊠ *3075 Sanibel–Captiva Rd., Sanibel* ☎ *239/395–2233, 888/679–6450* ⊕ *www. shellmuseum.org* 🖙 *$11* ⊙ *Daily 10–5.*

Clinic for the Rehabilitation of Wildlife (C.R.O.W.). In existence for more than 40 years, the clinic currently cares for more than 4,000 wildlife patients each year. The center offers a look inside the world of wildlife medicine through exhibits, videos, interactive displays, touch screens, and critter cams that feed live footage from four different animal spaces. Wildlife walks give a behind-the-scenes look and can be reserved for $20 per person. This is an excellent facility, but the displays may be too graphic for young visitors. ⊠ *3883 Sanibel–Captiva Rd., Sanibel* ☎ *239/472–3644* ⊕ *www.crowclinic.org* 🖙 *$5* ⊙ *Tues.–Sat. 10–4.*

FAMILY

Fodor'sChoice

★

J.N. "Ding" Darling National Wildlife Refuge. More than half of Sanibel is occupied by the subtly beautiful 6,300 acres of wetlands and jungly mangrove forests named after a conservation-minded Pulitzer prize–winning political cartoonist. The masses of roseate spoonbills and ibis and the winter flock of white pelicans here make for a good show even if you're not a die-hard bird-watcher. Birders have counted some 230 species, including herons, ospreys, and the timid mangrove cuckoo. Raccoons, otters, alligators, and a lone American crocodile also may be spotted. The 4-mile Wildlife Drive is the main way to explore the preserve; drive, walk, or bicycle along it, or ride a specially designed open-air tram with an onboard naturalist. QR-coded signs link to interactive YouTube videos and a new "Discover Ding" app combines social media, GPS, and trivia to make learning on-site fun. There are also a couple of short walking trails, including one to a Calusa shell mound. Or explore from the water via canoe or kayak (guided tours are available). The best time for bird-watching is in the early morning and about an hour before or after low tide; the observation tower along the road offers prime viewing. Interactive exhibits in the free visitor center, at the entrance to the refuge, demonstrate the refuge's various ecosystems and explain its status as a rest stop along a major bird-migration route. A new hands-on manatee exhibit was recently unveiled, too. Wildlife Drive is closed to vehicular traffic on Friday, but you can still kayak and do tours from the Tarpon Bay Recreation Area. ⊠ *1 Wildlife Dr., off Sanibel–Captiva Rd. at MM 2, Sanibel* ☎ *239/472–1100 for refuge, 239/472–8900 for kayaking and tours* ⊕ *www.fws.gov/dingdarling* 🖙 *$5 per car, $1 for pedestrians and bicyclists, tram $13* ⊙ *Education Center Jan.–Apr., daily 9–5; May–Dec., daily 9–4. Wildlife Drive Sat.–Thurs. 7:30–½ hr before sunset.*

Continued on page 456

SHELL-BENT ON SANIBEL ISLAND

by Chelle Koster Walton

Sanibel Island beachgoers are an unusual breed: they pray for storms; they muck around tidal pools rather than play in the waves; and instead of lifting their faces to the sun, they have their heads in the sand—almost literally—as they engage in the so-called "Sanibel Stoop."

Odd? Not when you consider that this is Florida's prime shelling location, thanks to the island's east-west bend (rather than the usual north-south orientation of most beaches along the coastline). The lay of the land means a treasure trove of shells—more than 400 species—wash up from the Caribbean.

These gifts from the sea draw collectors of all levels. Come winter, when the cold and storms kill the shellfish and push them ashore, a parade of stoopers forms on Sanibel's shores.

The reasons people shell are as varied as the shellers themselves. The hardcore compete and sell, whereas others collect simply for the fun of discovery, for displaying, for use in gardens, or for crafts. The typical Sanibel tourist who comes seeking shells is usually looking for souvenirs and gifts to take home.

WHERE TO SHELL

Shelling is good anywhere along Sanibel's gulf-front. Remote **Bowman's Beach** (*off Sanibel-Captiva Road at Bowman's Beach Rd.*) offers the least competition. Other public accesses include **Lighthouse Beach** (Periwinkle Way), **Tarpon Bay Beach** (Tarpon Bay Rd.), and **Turner Beach** (Sanibel-Captiva Rd.). If you want to ditch your car (and crowds), walk or bike using **resident access beaches** (along the Gulf drives). If you want to search with others and get a little guidance, you can join shelling cruises from Sanibel and Captiva islands to the unbridged island of Cayo Costa. Cruises leave from both islands and usually include pickup from your hotel or condo. Most are done on a covered catamaran.

Captiva
Island

Captiva

Turner
Beach

Bowman's
Beach

SANIBEL ISLAND

Lighthouse
Beach

Sanibel

Tarpon Bay
Beach

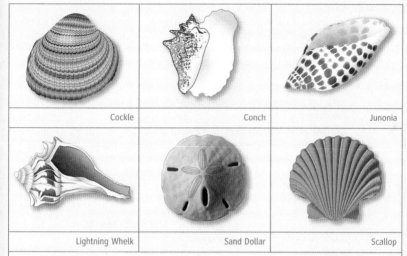

| Cockle | Conch | Junonia |
| Lightning Whelk | Sand Dollar | Scallop |

TYPES OF SHELLS

Cockles: The common Sanibel bivalve (hinged two-shelled mollusk), the heart cockle (named for its Valentine shape) is larger and more bowl-like than the scallop, which makes it a popular, colorful find for soap dishes, ashtrays, and catch-alls.

Conchs: Of the large family of conchs, fighting conchs are most commonly found on Sanibel. Contrary to its macho name, the fighting conch is one of the few vegetarian gastropods. While alive, the shell flames brilliant orange; it fades under tropical sunshine.

Junonias: These olive-shaped, spotted gastropods (single-shell mollusks) are Sanibel's signature, though somewhat rare, finds. People who hit upon one get their picture in the local paper. Resorts have been accused of planting them on their beaches for publicity.

Lightning Whelks: The lightning variety of whelk is "left-handed"—opening on the opposite side from most gastropods. Early islanders used them for tools. The animals lay their miniature shell eggs in papery egg-case chains on the beach.

Sand Dollars: Classified as an echinoderm not a mollusk, the thin sand dollar is brown and fuzzy while alive, studded with tiny tubes for breathing and moving. Unoccupied shells bleach to a beautiful white textured pattern, ideal for hanging on Christmas trees.

Scallops: No surprise that these pretty little bivalves have "scalloped" edges. They invented the word. Plentiful on Sanibel beaches, they come in a variety of colors and sizes.

SHELLING LIKE A PRO

Veteran shell-seekers go out before the sun rises so they can be the first on the beach after a storm or night of high tides. (Storms and cold fronts bring in the best catches.)

Most shellers use a bag to collect their finds. But once you're ready to pack shells for transit, wash them thoroughly to remove sand and debris. Then wrap fragile species such as sand dollars and sea urchins in tissue paper or cotton, then newspaper. Last, place your shells in a cardboard or plastic box. To display them, restore the shell's luster by brushing it with baby oil.

Sanibel shops sell books and supplies for identifying your finds and turning them into craft projects.

FAMILY **Sanibel–Captiva Conservation Foundation.** For a quiet walk to watch for inhabitants of Sanibel's interior wetlands, follow some or all of the 4½ miles of interlocking walking trails here and climb the observation tower. View information about wildlife research projects, a butterfly house, live turtles, snakes, and a marine touch tank at the nature center. In winter, guided walks and programs are available on and off property. ✉ *3333 Sanibel–Captiva Rd., Sanibel* ☎ *239/472–2329* ⊕ *www.sccf.org* 💲 *$5; 17 and under free* ⊙ *Oct.–May, weekdays 8:30–4; June–Sept., weekdays 8:30–3.*

Sanibel Historical Museum & Village. Charming buildings from the island's past include a general store, a one-room schoolhouse, 1927 post office, a tearoom, a 1925 winter-vacation cottage, a 1898 fishing cottage, and the 1913 Rutland House Museum, containing old documents and photographs, artifacts, and period furnishings. All buildings are authentic and have been moved from their original locations to the museum grounds. ✉ *950 Dunlop Rd., Sanibel* ☎ *239/472–4648* ⊕ *www.sanibelmuseum.org* 💲 *$10* ⊙ *Mid-Oct.–Apr., Wed.–Sat. 10–4; May–July, Wed.–Sat. 10–1; closed Aug.–mid-Oct.*

BEACHES

Red tide, an occasional natural beach occurrence that kills fish, also has negative effects on the human respiratory system. It causes scratchy throats, runny eyes and noses, and coughing. Although the effects aren't long-term, it's a good idea to avoid the beach when red tide is in the vicinity (look for posted signs).

SANIBEL

FAMILY **Bowman's Beach.** This long, wide beach on Sanibel's northwest end is the island's most secluded strand, but it also has the most amenities. Park facilities include a playground, picnic tables, grills, bathrooms, and bike racks. It is famed for its shell collecting and spectacular sunsets at the north end—try to spot the green flash, said to occur just as the sun sinks below the horizon. For utmost seclusion, walk north from the two main access points where bridges cross an estuary to reach the beach. It's a long walk from the parking lot over the estuary to the beach, so pack accordingly and plan on a long stay. Tall Australian pines provide shade behind the white sands. Typically gentle waves are conducive to swimming and wading with kids. **Amenities:** parking (fee); showers; toilets. **Best for:** sunsets; swimming; walking. ✉ *Bowman Beach Rd., at Blind Pass* ☎ *239/472–3700* 💲 *Parking $3 per hr.*

FAMILY **Gulfside Park Preserve.** The beach is quiet, safe from strong currents, and good for solitude, bird-watching, and shell-finding. There are restrooms, and long stretches to stroll. The white sand is slightly coarse and borders a park with shade, picnic tables, and a loop nature trail. Low-rise resorts and homes lie to the east and west of the parking lot accesses. **Amenities:** parking (fee); toilets. **Best for:** swimming; walking. ✉ *Algiers La., off Casa Ybel Rd.* ☎ *239/472–3700* 💲 *Parking $3 per hr.*

Lighthouse Beach. At Sanibel's eastern tip, the beach is guarded by the frequently photographed Sanibel Lighthouse, built in 1884, before the island was settled. The lighthouse is not currently open to the public, but there's talk of refurbishing the tower so visitors can climb to the top. The park rounds the island's east end for waterfront on both the gulf and bay, where a fishing pier draws avid anglers. Shaded nature trails connect the two shores; the park is listed on the Great Florida Birding Trail because of its fall and spring migration fall-outs. A pair of ospreys frequently perch on the lighthouse railing; look and listen for these local residents while you're there. **Amenities:** parking (fee); toilets. **Best for:** sunrise; walking; windsurfing. ⊠ *East end of Periwinkle Way* ☎ *239/472–3700* ✉ *Parking $3 per hr.*

Tarpon Bay Beach. This centrally located beach is safer for swimming than beaches at the passes, where waters move swiftly. It is, however, one of the more populated beaches, lined with low-rise condos and resorts set back behind vegetation. Casa Ybel Resort lies east of the public access; other smaller resorts can be found along the stretch to the west. The parking lot is a five-minute walk from the beach, so drop off your gang and gear before you park (the lot is open daily from 7 am to 7 pm). At the beach, you can walk for miles in either direction on soft white sand studded with shells. **Amenities:** parking (fee); toilets. **Best for:** swimming; walking. ⊠ *Off Sanibel–Captiva Rd., Tarpon Bay Rd. at Gulf Dr.* ✛ *Drive to end of West Gulf Dr. and east to Casa Ybel Rd.* ☎ *239/472–3700* ✉ *Parking $3 per hr.*

CAPTIVA

FAMILY **Alison Hagerup Beach Park.** This park, once called Captiva Beach, is acclaimed as one of the nation's most romantic beaches for its fabulous sunsets—the best view on Sanibel and Captiva. Shells stud the white, wide sands. The parking lot is filled with potholes and is small, so arrive early, watch where you're driving, and bring an umbrella if you need shade. The beach can get crowded, especially in the busy winter and spring seasons. Facilities are limited to portable restrooms and a volleyball net, but stores and restaurants are nearby. South Seas Island Resort lines the north end of the beach. **Amenities:** parking (fee); toilets. **Best for:** sunsets; swimming; walking. ⊠ *Captiva Dr., at north end* ✉ *Parking 2 hrs $5, 5 hrs $10.*

Turner Beach. Looking for some romance? This is a prime sunset-watching spot on the southern point of Captiva. Strong currents through Blind Pass make swimming tricky but shelling amazing, and parking is limited. Surfers head here when winds whip up the waves. The beach is narrower than in other parts of the island. No buildings sit on the beach, but 'Tween Waters Resort is across the road to the north of the public access, and Castaways Beach & Bay Cottages is beachfront across the bridge on the Sanibel side of Blind Pass. Restaurants are nearby. **Amenities:** parking (fee); toilets. **Best for:** sunsets; surfing; walking. ⊠ *Captiva Dr. at Blind Pass* ✉ *Parking $3 per hr.*

WHERE TO EAT

SANIBEL

$ ✕ **Lazy Flamingo.** At two Sanibel locations, plus two more in neighboring Fort Myers and Pine Island Sound, this is a friendly neighborhood hangout enjoyed by locals and visitors alike. All of these restaurants have a funky nautical look à la Key West and a popular following for their Dead Parrot Wings (buffalo wings coated with tongue-scorching

AMERICAN
FAMILY

8

hot sauce), mesquite-grilled grouper sandwiches, burgers, and steamer pots. The Flamingo garlic bread is always a hit, and the grouper Caesar salad is cheesy and award-winning. Kids' meals are served on a Frisbee that makes not only a great souvenir but also a cool new beach toy. The second Sanibel location is at 1036 Periwinkle Way, 239/472–6939. [$] *Average main: $12* ✉ *6520C Pine Ave.* ☎ *239/472–5353* 🌐 *www.lazyflamingo.com* ✍ *Reservations not accepted.*

$$ AMERICAN

🍴 **Over Easy Café.** Locals head to this chicken-theme eatery mainly for breakfast and lunch, although it also serves dinner in season. Kick-start the day with the egg Reuben sandwich, veggie Benedict, pancakes, or omelets such as crab and asparagus or "meat-lovers." Breakfast is available until 3 pm. The lunch and dinner menu includes a vast variety of salads, sandwiches, wraps, and seafood. Indoor dining is cheerful; outdoors is pet-friendly. While waiting for a table, you can shop for gifts next door. [$] *Average main: $16* ✉ *630-1 Tarpon Bay Rd.* ☎ *239/472–2625* 🌐 *www.overeasycafesanibel.com* ✍ *Reservations not accepted* ⏲ *No dinner.*

$$$ MODERN AMERICAN Fodor's Choice ★

🍴 **Sweet Melissa's Cafe.** You've seen them before, those people who take photos of their food: you'll become one of them when you eat here. Choose from full portions or small plates, but the latter are recommended so that you can savor more outstanding dishes in one sitting. Lunch offers simpler dishes like sandwiches (smoked chicken with avocado aioli) and salads (grilled romaine with truffle drizzle). Dinner truly brings out Melissa's magic. Even if you don't like duck, you'll love it here. Fish stew, grilled smoked beef tenderloin, fresh mahi: they all are good choices for people who don't mind sharing. Chef Melissa also makes her own sorbet. Dine indoors, on the patio, at the bar, or at the chef's bar overlooking the exhibition kitchen. Live guitar music adds to the experience. [$] *Average main: $25* ✉ *1625 Periwinkle Way* ☎ *239/472–1956* 🌐 *www.sweetmelissascafe.com* ✍ *Reservations essential* ⏲ *No lunch weekends.*

$$$$ CONTEMPORARY Fodor's Choice ★

🍴 **Thistle Lodge Restaurant.** Now this is romance: the lodge was built as a wedding gift from a husband to his wife and is now a gift to those lucky enough to dine here. Lush green grounds are right outside the window, then just beyond is the Gulf of Mexico and Sanibel's seashell-laden shores. But it's more than the views that will lull you into a dreamy mood. The food is fresh, elegant, and flavorful. Entrées span everything from Parmesan-and-herb-crusted black grouper to Asian braised beef short ribs. Frequent patrons back in the day included Thomas Edison and Henry Ford. [$] *Average main: $35* ✉ *Casa Ybel Resort, 2255 W. Gulf Dr.* ☎ *239/472–9200* 🌐 *www.thistlelodge.com.*

$$$ SEAFOOD

🍴 **Timbers Restaurant & Fish Market.** One of Sanibel's longest-running restaurants successfully satisfies visitors and residents with consistent quality and a full net of nightly catches and specials. The fish market inside the door is a sure sign of freshness, and most of the dishes showcase seafood simply and flavorfully. The oysters Romanoff with caviar, shallots, and sour cream are a nice twist on oyster "sliders." Corn flakes grant the crunchy grouper and shrimp rights to their names. Choose to have your fresh catch blackened, fried, or broiled, or go for a sirloin or beef filet. House salad or soup du jour comes with each entrée, or you can

Where to Eat and Stay on Sanibel and Captiva

KEY

□ *Hotels*
■ *Restaurants*
■ *Restaurants in Hotels*

Gulf of Mexico

CAPTIVA ISLAND

Alison Hagerup Beach

The Mucky Duck

South Seas Island Resort

■ **Bubble Room**

Green Flash

'Tween Waters Inn
Captiva House

Captiva Dr.

BUCK KEY

Turner Beach

Lazy Flamingo

Blind Pass Beach

Pine Island Sound

Bowman's Beach

SANIBEL ISLAND

Sanibel-Captiva Rd.

J. N. Darling National Wildlife Refuge

PINE ISLAND

Stringfellow Rd.

St. James City

Tarpon Bay

West Wind Inn
Island Inn
Waterside Inn

Over Easy Café

Timbers Restaurant & Fish Market

Tarpon Bay Rd.

Tarpon Bay Beach

Periwinkle Wy.

Sanibel-C. R.

San Carlos Bay

Thistle Lodge Restaurant
Casa Ybel Resort

Casa Ybel Rd.

Sweet Melissa's Cafe

Traders Store & Café

Gulfside City Park

Middle Gulf Dr.

Sundial Beach Resort and Spa

Sanibel Siesta on the Beach

Lazy Flamingo

Sanibel Causeway

E. Gulf Dr.

Seaside Inn

Lighthouse Beach

0 ___ 1 mi
0 ___ 1 km

8

upgrade to the crab bisque, which just might be the best on the island. For lighter fare and a sports bar vibe, Sanibel Grill shares the same space. $ *Average main: $21* ⊠ *703 Tarpon Bay Rd.* ☎ *239/472–3128* ⊕ *www.prawnbroker.com* ⌘ *Reservations not accepted.*

$$$
AMERICAN
Fodor'sChoice
★

✕ **Traders Store & Café.** In the midst of a warehouse-size store, this bistro, accented with stunning Florida photography from Alan Maltz, is a favorite of locals. The marvelous sesame-seared tuna lunch salad with Asian slaw and wasabi vinaigrette exemplifies the creative fare. For dinner, try the barbecued baby back ribs, macadamia-crusted grouper, or any of the day's finely crafted specials. A local band entertains two nights a week. The bar serves light nibbles and happy-hour twofers. While waiting for your food, visit the attached shop filled with everything from affordable trinkets to pricey island wear. $ *Average main: $26* ⊠ *1551 Periwinkle Way* ☎ *239/472–7242* ⊕ *www.traderssanibel. com* ⌘ *Reservations not accepted.*

CAPTIVA

$$$
AMERICAN
FAMILY

✕ **Bubble Room.** This lively, kitschy visitors' favorite is fun for families and nostalgic types with fat wallets. Servers wear scout uniforms and funny headgear. Electric trains circle overhead, glossies of Hollywood stars past and present line the walls, and glass tabletops showcase old-time toys. There's so much going on that you might not notice your food is not quite as happening, and somehow that's okay. After grazing your basket of cheesy bubble bread and sweet, yeasty sticky buns, go for slow-cooked prime rib or shrimp sautéed in spicy tequila garlic butter. The homemade triple-layer cakes, delivered in hefty wedges, are notorious, and the gooey orange crunch cake is a signature favorite. Kids are welcome and will love to gawk at the Christmas Room before or after they gobble up the hand-breaded chicken fingers. Be prepared to wait for a table in season. $ *Average main: $25* ⊠ *15001 Captiva Dr.* ☎ *239/472–5558* ⊕ *www.bubbleroomrestaurant.com* ⌘ *Reservations not accepted.*

$$$$
SEAFOOD
Fodor'sChoice
★

✕ **Captiva House.** This wonderfully romantic restaurant is casual, comfortable, and considered by many to be the best fine-dining restaurant on Captiva Island. Executive Chef Jason Miller adds a fresh, Florida flair to seafood dishes like the island snapper wrap (moist snapper wrapped in crispy phyllo then drizzled with an aged balsamic glaze). Tempting appetizers, creative salads, juicy steaks, and tantalizing desserts round out the menu. The restaurant has its own baker on-site for sweet and savory breads and cakes. No need to dress up; island casual is welcome. Make time to enjoy the fantastic sunsets just across the street at the beach. $ *Average main: $32* ⊠ *'Tween Waters Inn, 15951 Captiva Dr.* ☎ *239/472–5161* ⊕ *www.tween-waters.com/dining.php* ⌘ *Reservations essential.*

$$$
SEAFOOD

✕ **Green Flash.** Good food and sweeping views of quiet waters and a mangrove island keep boaters and others coming back to this casual indoor-outdoor restaurant. Seafood dominates, but there's a bit of everything on the menu, from barbecued shrimp and bacon to grilled swordfish to pork tenderloin wrapped in prosciutto and puff pastry. For lunch, try the Green Flash sandwich (smoked turkey and prosciutto or vegetables, both with cheese on grilled focaccia). Grouper tacos are filling and dripping with freshness. On cool, sunny days, grab a table out back, dockside. $ *Average main: $23* ⊠ *15183 Captiva Dr.* ☎ *239/472–3337* ⊕ *www.greenflashcaptiva.com.*

$$$ ✕**The Mucky Duck.** A longtime fixture on Captiva's beach, it parodies
SEAFOOD British pubs with its name and sense of humor. Since 1975, it has consistently drawn crowds that occupy themselves with walking the beach and watching sunset while waiting for their name to be called for a table indoors or out. A little Brit, a lot Florida, the revamped menu has kept some favored specialties such as barbecued shrimp wrapped in bacon appetizer, crab cakes, fish-and-chips, and frozen key lime pie. $ *Average main: $24* ⊠ *11546 Andy Rosse La.* ☎ *239/472–3434* ⊕ *www.muckyduck.com* ⚋ *Reservations not accepted.*

WHERE TO STAY

SANIBEL

$$$$ 🖳 **Casa Ybel Resort.** Palm trees, quiet ponds, and gazebos set the mood at
RESORT this resort on 23 acres of gulf-facing grounds. **Pros:** on the beach; good
FAMILY restaurants; lots of recreational opportunities. **Cons:** spa treatments in-
Fodor'sChoice room only; minimum-stay requirement in some units. $ *Rooms from:*
★ *$599* ⊠ *2255 W. Gulf Dr.* ☎ *239/472–3145, 800/276–4753* ⊕ *www.
casaybelresort.com* ⟿ *40 1-bedroom units, 74 2-bedroom units* ⧖ *No meals.*

$$$ 🖳 **Island Inn.** Choose from your own cottage on the beach, or take
RESORT your pick from six different styles of modernized hotel rooms at the most established inn on Sanibel. **Pros:** right on the beach; free breakfast; laundry facilities. **Cons:** minimum stays in season; furniture and bathrooms are dated in some units. $ *Rooms from: $360* ⊠ *3111 West Gulf Dr.* ☎ *239/472–1561* ⊕ *www.islandinn.com* ⟿ *42 rooms; 7 cottages* ⧖ *Breakfast.*

$$$ 🖳 **Sanibel Siesta on the Beach.** You might want to move right in and never
RENTAL leave once you discover these luxurious two-bedroom/two-bath con-
FAMILY dos right on the sand. **Pros:** on the beach; swimming pool; free Wi-Fi.
Fodor'sChoice **Cons:** minimum stays; office closes early. $ *Rooms from: $330* ⊠ *1246*
★ *Fulgur St.* ☎ *239/472–4117* ⊕ *www.sanibelsiesta.com* ⟿ *67 2-bedroom condos* ⧖ *No meals.*

$$ 🖳 **Seaside Inn.** Tucked among the tropical greenery, this beachfront inn is
HOTEL a pleasant alternative to the area's larger resorts. **Pros:** intimate feel; lots of character; beautiful beachfront. **Cons:** no on-site restaurant; cramped parking lot. $ *Rooms from: $289* ⊠ *541 E. Gulf Dr.* ☎ *239/472–1400, 866/565–5092* ⊕ *www.seasideinn.com* ⟿ *32 rooms, 6 cottages, 4 suites* ⧖ *Breakfast.*

$$ 🖳 **Sundial Beach Resort and Spa.** With multimillion-dollar renovations
RESORT completed in 2015, Sanibel's largest resort encompasses 400 privately
FAMILY owned studio, one-, two-, and three-bedroom low-rise condo units, about half of which are in its rental program. **Pros:** great beach; plenty of amenities; no charge for beach chairs. **Cons:** conference crowds; packed pool area, $30 per night resort fee. $ *Rooms from: $279* ⊠ *1451 Middle Gulf Dr.* ☎ *239/472–4151, 866/565–5093* ⊕ *www.sundialresort.com* ⟿ *184 1-, 2-, and 3-bedroom units (varies according to rental program participants)* ⧖ *No meals.*

8

$$ HOTEL **Waterside Inn.** Palm trees, sea-grape trees, pastel cottages, and a tiki on the Gulf set the scene at this quiet beachside vacation spot. **Pros:** beachfront location; intimate feel; small pets allowed in most cottages. **Cons:** office closes at night; cottage interiors are worn; parking for only one car per unit. [$] *Rooms from: $291* ✉ *3033 W. Gulf Dr.* ☎ *239/472–1345, 800/741–6166* 🌐 *www.watersideinn.net* *4 rooms, 10 efficiencies, 13 cottages* 🍴 *No meals.*

$$$ HOTEL **West Wind Inn.** Families and couples flock to this resort for its upscale, West Gulf Drive location on the residential side of the island. **Pros:** on the beach; quiet side of the island; laundry facilities on-site. **Cons:** Wi-Fi can be sporadic; pool towels are small and wafer thin. [$] *Rooms from: $340* ✉ *3345 W. Gulf Dr.* ☎ *239/472–1541* 🌐 *www.westwindinn.com* *103 rooms* 🍴 *No meals.*

CAPTIVA

$$$ RESORT FAMILY Fodor's Choice ★ **South Seas Island Resort.** This full-service 330-acre resort feels as lush as its name suggests, and with 18 swimming pools (one with two tubular slides), private restaurants including Doc Ford's, shops, a full-service spa, a nature center stocked with live animals, a family interactive center, and a 9-hole beachfront golf course, it won't disappoint. **Pros:** full range of amenities; exclusive feel; car-free transportation. **Cons:** high rates in season; a bit isolated; spread out. [$] *Rooms from: $339* ✉ *5400 Plantation Rd.* ☎ *239/472–5111, 888/222–7848* 🌐 *www.southseas.com* *106 rooms, 365 suites* 🍴 *No meals.*

$$ B&B/INN **'Tween Waters Inn.** Besides its great beach-to-bay location, this inn has historic value and in 2011 was listed in the National Register of Historic Places. **Pros:** great views; lots of water-sports options; free Wi-Fi. **Cons:** beach is across the road. [$] *Rooms from: $250* ✉ *Captiva Dr.* ☎ *239/472–5161, 800/223–5865* 🌐 *www.tween-waters.com* *48 rooms, 24 studios, 41 1-bedroom suites, 4 2-bedroom suites, 2 3-bedroom suites, 19 cottages* 🍴 *Breakfast.*

SHOPPING

Sanibel is known for its art galleries, shell shops, and one-of-a-kind boutiques; the several small open-air shopping complexes are inviting, with their tropical flowers and shady ficus trees.

SANIBEL

Periwinkle Place. The largest complex of outdoor Sanibel shopping has 26 shops in a parklike setting on 7 acres. Fountains, gazebos, and a playground make it even more family friendly. ✉ *2075 Periwinkle Way* ☎ *734/769–2289* 🌐 *www.periwinkleplace.com.*

Seashells.com. Among the island's cache of shell shops, this one is favored by serious collectors and crafters because of its reasonable prices and the knowledgeable family that runs it. For shell gifts, the family operates another little shop right behind the warehouse-size one. It's super easy to find, located right on the main drag. ✉ *905 Fitzhugh St.* ☎ *239/472–1603* 🌐 *www.seashells.com.*

She Sells Sea Shells. At She Sells Sea Shells, everything imaginable is made from shells, from mirrors to lamps to Christmas ornaments. The owner wrote the book on shell art, and you can buy it here. You can also purchase local shells, like the prized junonia and pick up a T-shirt at a fair price. A second location is on the same road at 2422 Periwinkle. ✉ *1157 Periwinkle Way* ☎ *239/472–6991* ⊕ *www.sanibelshellcrafts.com.*

CAPTIVA

Fodor'sChoice **Jungle Drums.** Expect the unexpected in wildlife art, where fish, sea tur-
★ tles, and other creatures are depicted with utmost creativity and touches of whimsy. If you're looking for souvenirs above and beyond the usual, or unique jewelry, paintings, sculptures, and pottery—this is the place. ✉ *11532 Andy Rosse La.* ☎ *239/395–2266* ⊕ *www.jungledrumsgallery. com* ☾ *Closed Sun.*

SPORTS AND THE OUTDOORS

BIKING

Everyone bikes around flat-as-a-pancake Sanibel and Captiva—on bikeways that edge the main highway in places, on the road through the wildlife refuge, and along side streets. Free maps are available at bicycle liveries.

Billy's Bikes. Rent by the hour or the day from this Sanibel outfitter, which also rents motorized scooters and leads Segway tours. They even have beach gear like chairs, umbrellas, and boogie boards. ✉ *1470 Periwinkle Way, Sanibel* ☎ *239/472–5248* ⊕ *www.billysrentals.com.*

Yolo Watersports. Bikes and water-sports recreation rentals of all kinds (sailboats, wave runners, paddle boards) are available at this Cap-tiva operator. Gear is also for sale. ✉ *11534 Andy Rosse La., Captiva* ☎ *239/472–1296* ⊕ *www.yolowatersports.com.*

CANOEING AND KAYAKING

Tarpon Bay Explorers. One of the best ways to scout out the wildlife refuge is by paddle. Rent a canoe or kayak from the refuge's official conces-sionaire and explore at your leisure. The kayak water trail is easy to follow, simply paddle your way along 17 markers and see a bevy of birds and other wildlife. Guided tours by kayak or pontoon boat are also offered and worthwhile for visitors unfamiliar with the ecosystem. Their on-site touch tank gives a hands-on learning experience about local sea life. ✉ *900 Tarpon Bay Rd., Sanibel* ☎ *239/472–8900* ⊕ *www. tarponbayexplorers.com.*

FISHING

Local anglers head out to catch mackerel, pompano, grouper, snook, snapper, tarpon, and shark.

Sanibel Marina. To find a charter captain on Sanibel, visit their on-site Ship Store or give them a call. ✉ *634 N. Yachtsman Dr., Sanibel* ☎ *239/472–2723* ⊕ *www.sanibelmarina.com.*

'Tween Waters Marina. On Captiva, this is the place to look for guides. You can also rent kayaks, canoes, stand-up paddleboards, and other recreational watercrafts. ✉ *'Tween Waters Inn, 15951 Captiva Dr., Captiva* ☎ *239/472–5161* ⊕ *www.tween-waters.com/marina.php.*

GOLF

Dunes Golf & Tennis Club. When your back nine are sanctioned as a wild-life preserve by the Audubon Cooperative Society—even if you play poorly—you're rewarded with lusher than lush fairways and more wild-life than you can shake a stick at. Bring your camera if you golf here,

8

as it's not every day that bald eagles watch you play. Water hazards at every hole will have you losing more balls than usual, so bring plenty. Hole 10 is the toughest, which explains why most wish it were a par 5 instead of a par 4. Go for a long, straight tee shot and watch out for the water (and the gators). ⊠ *949 Sandcastle Rd., Sanibel* ☎ *239/472–2535* ⊕ *www.dunesgolfsanibel.com* ⊠ *$110* ⚑ *18 holes, 5583 yards, par 70.*

FORT MYERS BEACH (ESTERO ISLAND)

18 miles southwest of Fort Myers.

Crammed with motels, hotels, and restaurants, Estero Island is one of Fort Myers's more frenetic gulf playgrounds. Dolphins frequently frolic in Estero Bay, part of the Intracoastal Waterway, and marinas provide a starting point for boating adventures, including sunset cruises, sightseeing cruises, and deep-sea fishing. At the southern tip, a bridge leads to Lovers Key State Park.

GETTING HERE AND AROUND

San Carlos Boulevard in Fort Myers leads to Fort Myers Beach's high bridge, Times Square, and Estero Boulevard, the island's main drag. Estero Island is 18 miles southwest of Fort Myers.

BEACHES

Lovers Key State Park. Once a little-known secret, this out-of-the-way park encompassing 1,616 acres on four barrier islands and several uninhabited islets is popular among beachgoers and birders. Bike, hike, walk, or paddle the park's trails (rentals available); go shelling on its 2½ miles of white-sand beach; take a boat tour; or have a beach picnic under the trees. Trams run regularly from 9 to 4:30 to deliver you and your gear to South Beach. The ride is short but often dusty. North Beach is a five-minute walk from the concession area and parking lot. Watch for osprey, bald eagles, herons, ibis, pelicans, and roseate spoonbills, or sign up for a free excursion to learn fishing and nature photography. On the park's bay side, across the road from the beach entrance, playgrounds and a picnic area cater to families, plus there are boat ramps, kayak rentals, and a bait shop. **Amenities:** food and drink; parking (fee); showers; toilets; water sports. **Best for:** swimming; walking. ⊠ *8700 Estero Blvd.* ☎ *239/463–4588* ⊕ *www.floridastateparks. org/loverskey* ⊠ *$4–$8 per vehicle, $2 for pedestrians and bicyclists* ☉ *Daily 8–sunset.*

FAMILY **Lynn Hall Memorial Park.** At the 17-acre park in the commercial northern part of Estero Island, the wide, sandy shore slopes gradually into the usually tranquil and warm gulf waters, providing safe swimming for children. And since houses, restaurants, condominiums, and hotels (including the Best Western Beach Resort and Pink Shell Resort north of the parking lot) line most of the beach, you're never far from civilization. There are picnic pavilions and barbecue grills, as well as playground equipment and a free fishing pier. The park is part of a pedestrian mall with a number of beach shops and restaurants steps away. The parking lot fills early on sunny days. **Amenities:** food and drink; parking (fee); showers; toilets; water sports. **Best for:** partiers; sunsets; walking. ⊠ *Estero Blvd. at San Carlos Blvd., to Bowditch*

Point Park ☎ *239/463–1116* ⊕ *www.leeparks.org* 🚗 *Parking $2 per hr* ⊙ *Daily 7 am–11 pm.*

WHERE TO EAT

$$ ✕ **Doc Ford's Rum Bar & Grille.** For dependably well-prepared food with
MODERN   a water view, Doc Ford's is the top choice in Fort Myers Beach. A
AMERICAN   spinoff of a Sanibel Island original, its name and theme come from a
murder-mystery series by local celebrity author Randy Wayne White.
Diners rave about the Yucatan shrimp—steamed in the shell with spicy
key lime butter. Other choice picks include the beach bread, pulled-
pork sandwich, banana leaf–wrapped snapper, shrimp and grits with
tomatillo sauce, and penne with rock shrimp. Live bands play Wednes-
day through Sunday. Ⓢ *Average main: $20* ⊠ *708 Fisherman's Wharf*
☎ *239/765–9660* ⊕ *www.docfordsfortmyersbeach.com* 🍽 *Reservations
not accepted.*

$$ ✕ **Matanzas Inn.** Watch boats coming and going whether you sit inside
SEAFOOD   or out at this rustic Old Florida–style restaurant right on the docks
alongside the Intracoastal Waterway. When the weather cooperates,
enjoy the view from the shaded outdoor tables. Inside, a rustic shack
gives way to a more formal dining area in the back; there's a bar upstairs
with sweeping views, pizza, and live music nightly. You can't miss with
grouper or shrimp from the local fleets—delicately cornmeal-breaded,
stuffed, or dipped in rum and coconut. Landlubbers can choose from
ribs and steak. This is true Fort Myers Beach style, meaning service
can be a bit gruff—and slow. Ⓢ *Average main: $18* ⊠ *416 Crescent St.*
☎ *239/463–3838* ⊕ *www.matanzas.com* 🍽 *Reservations not accepted.*

$$ ✕ **Parrot Key Caribbean Grill.** For something more contemporary than
SEAFOOD   Fort Myers Beach's traditional shrimp and seafood houses, head to
San Carlos Island on the east side of the high bridge where the shrimp
boats dock. Parrot Key sits marina-side near the shrimp docks and
exudes merriment with its Floribbean cuisine and island music. Lunch
menu goes from 11 to 4 and includes such dishes as the crab, avocado,
and mango stack or Gorda Grouper fish-and-chips. For dinner, choose
the Crabby New Yorker, a N.Y. strip topped with blue crab meat,
au poivre, or the Creole shrimp and grits. There's live entertainment
most nights. Ⓢ *Average main: $20* ⊠ *2500 Main St.* ☎ *239/463–3257*
⊕ *www.myparrotkey.com* 🍽 *Reservations not accepted.*

$ ✕ **The Plaka.** A casual longtimer and a favorite for a quick breakfast,
GREEK   lunch breaks, and sunset dinners, Plaka—Greek for "fun"—has typical
Greek fare such as moussaka, pastitsio, gyros, and roast lamb, as well
as burgers, sandwiches, fried seafood, and strip steak. It lies along a
row of casual sidewalk restaurants in a pedestrian mall near the beach.
There's indoor dining, but grab a seat on the porch or under an umbrella
on the patio for the best people-watching and sunset view. Ⓢ *Average
main: $13* ⊠ *1001 Estero Blvd.* ☎ *239/463–4707* 🍽 *Reservations not
accepted.*

WHERE TO STAY

$$$$ 🏨 **DiamondHead.** This 12-story resort sits on the beach, and many of the
RESORT   suites, especially those on higher floors, have stunning views. **Pros:** on
FAMILY   the beach; nice views; kitchen facilities. **Cons:** heavy foot and car traffic;

8

tiny fitness center; not the best value on the beach. [$] *Rooms from: $429* ✉ *2000 Estero Blvd.* ☎ *239/765–7654, 888/765–5002* 🌐 *www.diamondheadfl.com* 🛏 *121 suites* 🍴 *No meals.*

$$ RENTAL 🏨 **Harbour House.** This condo-hotel adds a degree of beach luxury with brightly painted and sea-motif studios and one- and two-bedroom condos, all privately owned. **Pros:** close to lots of restaurants; roomy units; all have private balconies or lanais; free covered parking. **Cons:** a walk to the beach; not great views from most rooms. [$] *Rooms from: $239* ✉ *450 Old San Carlos Blvd.* ☎ *239/463–0700, 866/998–9250* 🌐 *www.harbourhouseattheinn.com* 🛏 *6 studios, 15 1-bedroom condos, 13 2-bedroom condos* 🍴 *No meals.*

$ HOTEL 🏨 **Lighthouse Resort Inn & Suites.** These pastel-painted buildings hold fairly basic but spacious rooms, standing tall and welcoming at the foot of the Fort Myers bridge, an ideal location for exploring. **Pros:** location; on-site laundry; views of the area from balconies. **Cons:** can be noisy; may have to park across the street if under-building parking is full. [$] *Rooms from: $175* ✉ *1051 5th Ave.* ☎ *239/463–9392* 🌐 *www.lighthouseislandresort.com* 🛏 *79 units* 🍴 *No meals.*

$$ RENTAL 🏨 **Lovers Key Resort.** Views can be stupendous from upper floors in this 14-story tower just north of Lovers Key State Park. **Pros:** excellent views; off the beaten path; spacious accommodations. **Cons:** not a true beach; far from shopping and restaurants; limited amenities. [$] *Rooms from: $280* ✉ *8771 Estero Blvd.* ☎ *239/765–1040, 877/798–4879* 🌐 *www.loverskey.com* 🛏 *100 condominiums* 🍴 *No meals.*

$ RESORT FAMILY 🏨 **Outrigger Beach Resort.** On a wide gulf beach, this casual resort has rooms and efficiencies with configurations to suit different guests' needs. **Pros:** beautiful beach; water-sports rentals; family-friendly vibe. **Cons:** can be noisy; crowded pool area; old-school feel. [$] *Rooms from: $199* ✉ *6200 Estero Blvd.* ☎ *239/463–3131, 800/657–5659* 🌐 *www.outriggerfmb.com* 🛏 *76 rooms, 68 efficiencies* 🍴 *No meals.*

SPORTS AND THE OUTDOORS

BIKING

Fort Myers Beach has no designated trails, so most cyclists ride along the road.

Fun Rentals. Bike rentals are available from anywhere between two hours and a week. Not your speed? Rent a Harley or a scooter instead. ✉ *1901 Estero Blvd.* ☎ *239/463–8844* 🌐 *www.funrentals.org.*

Lover's Key Adventures and Events. This company rents one-speed bikes, kayaks, canoes, paddleboards, and concessions in Lovers Key State Park. Fees for adult bikes are $20 for a half day, $25 for a full day. ✉ *8700 Estero Blvd.* ☎ *239/765–7788* 🌐 *www.loverskeyadventures.com.*

CANOEING

Lover's Key Adventures and Events. Lovers Key State Park offers kayak, canoe, and paddleboard rentals and guided kayaking tours of its bird-filled estuary. Guided tours cost $55 (call for dates and times). Rentals begin at $38 for a half day. ✉ *8700 Estero Blvd.* ☎ *239/765–7788* 🌐 *www.loverskeyadventures.com.*

FISHING

Getaway Deep Sea Fishing. Arrange anything from half-day party-boat charters to full-day excursions, fishing equipment included. Rates start at $65 for a half-day trip. ⊠ *18400 San Carlos Blvd.* ☎ *800/641–3088, 239/466–3600* ⊕ *www.getawaymarina.com.*

FAMILY   **SoulMate Charters.** Local "REEL Talk" radio host Captain Rob Modys

Fodor's Choice   takes care of everything from the fishing license to the rods and bait on

★   the half-, three-quarter-, and full-day fishing charters he offers around the scenic back bays and tiny islands near Fort Myers Beach. He's a local guide who knows every "honey hole" and will no doubt find fish for you to catch. As a father himself (and now grandfather), he's great with kids and has the patience to teach budding anglers. He is based out of Fish Tale Marina. ⊠ *7225 Estero Blvd.* ☎ *239/851–1242* ⊕ *www.soulmatecharters.com.*

NAPLES AND VICINITY

As you head south from Fort Myers on U.S. 41, you soon come to Estero and Bonita Springs, followed by the Naples and Marco Island areas, which are sandwiched between Big Cypress Swamp and the Gulf of Mexico. East of Naples the land is largely undeveloped and mostly wetlands, all the way to Fort Lauderdale. Naples itself is a major vacation destination that has sprouted pricey high-rise condominiums and golfing developments, plus a spate of restaurants and shops to match. A similar but not as thorough evolution has occurred on Marco Island, the largest of the Ten Thousand Islands.

8

ESTERO/BONITA SPRINGS

10 miles south of Fort Myers via U.S. 41.

Towns below Fort Myers have started to flow seamlessly into one another since the opening of Florida Gulf Coast University in San Carlos Park and as a result of the growth of Estero and Bonita Springs, which were agricultural communities until the 1990s. In recent years the area has become a shopping mecca of mega–outdoor malls mixing big-box stores, smaller chains, and restaurants. Bonita Beach, the closest beach to Interstate 75, has evolved from a fishing community into a strip of upscale homes and beach clubs built to provide access for residents of inland golf developments.

GETTING HERE AND AROUND

U.S. 41 (Tamiami Trail) runs right through the heart of these two adjacent communities. You can also reach them by exits 123 and 116 off Interstate 75.

EXPLORING

FAMILY   **Everglades Wonder Gardens.** Opened in 1936 by two retired moonshiners from Detroit, the Everglades Wonder Gardens was one of the first roadside attractions in the state and remained little changed until 2013, when the family decided to close its doors—and thus a rich chapter of Florida tourism history—forever. In stepped Florida landscape photographer John Brady, who negotiated a lease with the founding family and transformed the old-style cramped zoological gardens (that once featured Florida panthers, black bears, crocodiles, alligators, and tame Florida deer) into a botanical garden by conserving the flora and fauna following contemporary standards. Now in focus are diverse gardens that include old-growth trees like kapok, banyan, candle nut, egg fruit, plumeria, jaboticaba, mahogany, cashew, avocado, and mango, as well as integrated animal exhibits with tortoises, turtles, smaller alligators, flamingos, and a butterfly garden. The original buildings have been preserved and made into a modern gallery that showcases Brady's photography. ⊠ *27180 Old 41 Rd.* ☎ *239/992–2591* ⊕ *www. evergladeswondergardens.com* ⌦ *$12.95* ⊗ *Daily 9–5.*

Koreshan State Historic Site. Tour one of Florida's quirkier chapters from the past. Named for a religious cult that was active at the turn of the 20th century, Koreshan preserves a dozen structures where the group practiced arts, worshipped a male-female divinity, and created its own branch of science called cosmogony, which claimed the universe existed within a giant hollow sphere. The cult floundered when leader Cyrus Reed Teed died in 1908, and in 1961 the four remaining members deeded the property to the state. Rangers and volunteers lead tours and demonstrations, and the grounds are lovely for picnicking and camping. Canoeists paddle the Estero River, fringed by a forest of exotic vegetation the Koreshans planted. ⊠ *3800 Corkscrew Rd., at U.S. 41 (Tamiami Trail), Estero* ☎ *239/992–0311* ⊕ *www.floridastateparks. org/park/Koreshan* ⌦ *$5 per vehicle with up to 8 passengers; $4 for single motorist; $2 per bicyclist, pedestrian, or extra passenger* ⊗ *Daily 8–sunset.*

BEACHES

Barefoot Beach Preserve. This one isn't exactly easy to find since it's accessible only by a quiet neighborhood road around the corner from buzzing Bonita Beach Park, but it's well worth the effort if you appreciate natural coastal habitats with fun interpretive programs. Shells here are bountiful, as are gopher tortoises that may park in shade of your car. Stop by the nature center to join a ranger-led walk through the trails and gardens, or take up a paddle and go kayaking. There's no towel-jockeying here along the wide-open space (the preserve as a whole is 342 acres), and refreshments and beach rentals provide ample comfort while you unwind in the pristine sands. **Amenities:** parking (fee); food and drink; showers; toilets; water sports. **Best for:** solitude; walking. ⊠ *5901 Bonita Beach Rd., at Barefoot Beach Rd.* ☎ *239/591–8596* ⊕ *www.collierparks.com* ⌦ *Parking $8.*

Bonita Beach Park. The joint is always jumping on this rowdy stretch of coast, the easiest by far to reach from the inland areas south of Fort Myers. Local favorite hangout Doc's Beach House, open from breakfast until the wee hours of the night, keeps bellies full and libations flowing. Other food and sports vendors camp out here, too, making it nearly impossible to resist an ice cream or a ride on a Jet Ski. Shaded pavilions between the parking lot and dunes are a great way to cool off from the sweltering heat—just don't sit too close to the picnickers barbecuing. **Amenities:** showers; toilets; parking (fee); food and drink; water sports.

Best for: partiers; windsurfing. ✉ *27954 Hickory Blvd., at Bonita Beach Rd.* ☎ *239/949–4615* 🌐 *www.leeparks.org* 🅿 *Parking $2 per hr.*

WHERE TO EAT

$$$ ITALIAN Fodor's Choice ★ 🍴 **Angelina's Ristorante.** Here it's all about the experience—one of the most indulgent, pampered meals you'll ever eat. Formally trained waitstaff attend to your every need in this temple of traditional Italian cuisine. A dramatic wine tower hovers over the main room; the plush private booths surrounding it are the best tables (call early to snag one). The taste circus begins with an amuse bouche. Pick between antipasti, crispy flatbreads, and wholesome soups before moving on to homemade pastas and grilled meats. Absolutely try the butternut squash ravioli, an inventive version with citrus-tomato butter and truffled almonds. The evening ends with a complimentary nightcap. There is also a great prix-fixe menu. ■ **TIP→ This is an upscale restaurant. Don't show up in flip-flops, jeans, or shorts; the staff may be too polite to turn you away, but you will be uncomfortable.** [$] *Average main: $25* ✉ *24041 U.S. 41* ☎ *239/390–3187* 🌐 *www.angelinasofbonitasprings.com* ✍ *Reservations essential* ⏲ *No lunch.*

$$$ SEAFOOD 🍴 **Blue Water Bistro.** For the convenience of shoppers at Coconut Point, several excellent restaurants cluster in the midst of the shopping center. Most are hooked to a chain. This one, although part of a Naples-Bonita Springs dining dynasty, has a personality all its own with a suave indoor-outdoor bar scene and seafood that's anything but timid. Its specialty is grilled fish from around the globe that you can mix and match with a choice of sauces and sides. For instance, try swordfish with a sweet-and-sour mango sauce and coconut sticky rice. Other specialties include lobster bomb sushi, potato-chip-encrusted tilapia, and the crispy crunchy crab-stuffed grouper. [$] *Average main: $22* ✉ *Coconut Point Mall, 23151 Village Shops Way, Suite 109, Estero* ☎ *239/949–2583* 🌐 *www.bluewaterbistro.net* ⏲ *No lunch.*

$ AMERICAN FAMILY 🍴 **Doc's Beach House.** Right next door to the public access point for Barefoot Beach, Doc's has fed hungry beachgoers for decades. Come barefoot and grab a quick libation or meal downstairs, outside on the beach, or in the courtyard. When the thermometer reaches "searing," take refuge on the air-conditioned second floor, with its great view of beach action. Basic fare on the breakfast and all-day menu includes a popular Angus burger, Chicago-style pizza, and seafood plates. The conch chowder is some of the best in these parts, with just the right amount of fire. [$] *Average main: $10* ✉ *27908 Hickory Blvd.* ☎ *239/992–6444* 🌐 *www.docsbeachhouse.com* ✍ *Reservations not accepted* 💳 *No credit cards.*

$ AMERICAN 🍴 **Old 41 Restaurant.** Locals vote this "best breakfast," "best lunch," and "best Philly cheesesteak," and mostly locals populate its cheery dining room with its Philadelphia allegiance. For breakfast, don't miss the incredible Texas French toast with homemade caramel and pecans, Carbon's malted Belgian waffles, or eggs and homemade hash with Boar's Head meat. Besides cheesesteak, lunch specialties include Boar's Head hoagies, burgers, in-house-roasted beef or turkey sandwiches, and other comfort food—all served until 3 pm. ■ **TIP→ Though you can't make a reservation here, you can call ahead (weekends) to get your name on the waiting list.** [$] *Average main: $7* ✉ *25091 Bernwood*

8

Dr. ☎ *239/948–4123* 🌐 *www.old41.com* ✍ *Reservations not accepted* ⏲ *No dinner.*

WHERE TO STAY

$$$$ RESORT FAMILY Fodor's Choice ★ 🏨 **Hyatt Regency Coconut Point Resort & Spa.** This secluded luxury resort, with its marble-and-mahogany lobby and championship golf course, makes a lovely sanctuary for families who want a refined atmosphere, plus fun features like a 140-foot waterslide, a rock climbing wall, and a s'mores fire pit. **Pros:** pampering spa; great ceviche bar; championship golf; water activities galore. **Cons:** need water shuttle to reach the beach; expensive restaurants. [$] *Rooms from: $649* ✉ *5001 Coconut Rd.* ☎ *239/444–1234, 800/554–9288* 🌐 *www.coconutpoint.hyatt.com* 🛏 *454 rooms and suites* 🍴 *No meals.*

$$ HOTEL 🏨 **Trianon Bonita Bay.** Convenient to Bonita Springs's best shopping and dining, this branch of a refined downtown Naples favorite has a peaceful, sophisticated feel and a poolside–lakeside alfresco bar and grill. **Pros:** spacious rooms; intimate atmosphere. **Cons:** sometimes less-than-friendly staff; far from beach; slightly stuffy. [$] *Rooms from: $229* ✉ *3401 Bay Commons Dr.* ☎ *239/948–4400, 800/859–3939* 🌐 *www.trianon.com* 🛏 *100 rooms.*

SHOPPING

FAMILY **Coconut Point.** A 500-acre planned community is host to one of the area's largest shopping complexes with more than 140 stores including upscale boutiques, big-box retailers, and plenty of big-name restaurants. There's a boardwalk for a breather between impulse purchases, and a castle-themed kids' play area. ✉ *23106 Fashion Dr., Estero* ☎ *239/992–9966* 🌐 *www.shopcoconutpoint.com.*

Miromar Outlets. The complex includes Adidas, Coach, Michael Kors, Nike, Nautica, and more than 140 other stores and eateries, plus a free Playland for kids. ✉ *10801 Corkscrew Rd., at I–75 Exit 123, near Germain Arena, Estero* ☎ *239/948–3766* 🌐 *www.miromaroutlets.com.*

SPORTS AND THE OUTDOORS

BIRDING

The last leg of the Great Florida Birding Trail has more than 20 stops in the Lower Gulf Coast. Go to 🌐 *www.floridabirdingtrail.com* for a complete list.

CANOEING

The meandering Estero River is pleasant for canoeing as it passes through Koreshan State Historic Site to the bay.

Estero River Outfitters. Since 1977, this is the place to rent canoes, kayaks, paddleboards, and equipment. They're also a full-service tackle shop. ✉ *20991 Tamiami Trail S, Estero* ☎ *239/992–4050* 🌐 *www.esteroriveroutfitters.com.*

NAPLES

21 miles south of Bonita Springs, on U.S. 41.

Poised between the Gulf of Mexico and the Everglades, Naples belies its wild setting and Indian past with the trappings of wealth—neo-Mediterranean-style mansions, neatly manicured golfing developments, revitalized downtown streets lined with galleries and one-of-a-kind shops, and a reputation for lively and eclectic dining. Visitors come for its luxury hotels—including two Ritz-Carltons—its fabulous white-sand beaches, fishing, shopping, theater and arts, and a lofty reputation for golf. Yet with all the highfalutin living, Naples still appeals to families, especially with its water park and the Golisano Children's Museum of Naples that opened in 2012.

Old Naples, the historic downtown section, has two main commercial areas, 5th Avenue South and 3rd Street South, and there's also a small cluster of restaurants right by City Dock on Naples Bay. Farther north on U.S. 41 (the Tamiami Trail, or 9th Street here), hotels, shopping centers, and developments have fast been filling in the area around and south of Vanderbilt Beach, including the dining and shopping meccas Waterside Shops, and the Village on Venetian Bay.

GETTING HERE AND AROUND

The Naples Municipal Airport is a small facility east of downtown principally serving private planes, commuter flights, and charters. A taxi for up to three passengers is about $60–$90 from Southwest Florida International Airport (RSW) in Fort Myers to Naples; each additional person is charged $10. You don't need to reserve in advance; simply go to the ground-transportation booth. If you prefer to book a car or limo pickup in advance, three major companies are Aaron Airport Transportation, Naples Taxi & Limo Services, and Naples Airport Shuttle. In Naples and Marco Island, Collier Area Transit runs regular routes.

Downtown Naples is 15 miles south of Bonita Springs, on U.S. 41. If you're driving here from Florida's east coast, consider Alligator Alley, a toll section of Interstate 75 that's a straight shot from Fort Lauderdale to Naples. In Naples, east–west county highways exiting off Interstate 75 include, from north to south, Immokalee Road (Route 846), Pine Ridge Road (Route 896), and Collier Boulevard (Route 951), which actually goes north–south and takes you also to Marco Island.

Contacts Aaron Airport Transportation ☎ 239/768–1898 ⊕ www.aarontaxi. com. **Collier Area Transit (CAT)** ☎ 239/252–7777 ⊕ www.colliergov.net/ CAT. **Naples Airport Shuttle** ☎ 239/430–4747, 888/569–2227 ⊕ www. naplesairportshuttle.com. **Naples Taxi & Limo Services** ☎ 239/435-0000, 800/472–1371 ⊕ www.naplestaxiflorida.com.

TOURS

If you want someone to be your guide as you go about town, Naples Trolley Tours offers eight narrated tours daily, covering more than 100 points of interest in town. The tour ($27) lasts about two hours, but you can get off and on at no extra cost.

Contacts Naples Trolley Tours ✉ 1010 6th Ave. S ☎ 239/262–7300, 800/592–0848 ⊕ www.naplestrolleytours.com ⌚ Daily 8:30–5:30.

VISITOR INFORMATION

Contacts Naples, Marco Island, Everglades Convention and Visitors Bureau ☎ 800/688–3600, 239/225–1013 ⊕ www.paradisecoast.com.

EXPLORING
TOP ATTRACTIONS

Fodor'sChoice ★ **The Baker Museum.** This cool, contemporary museum at Artis–Naples displays provocative, innovative pieces, including renowned miniatures, antique walking sticks, modern and contemporary American and Mexican masters, and traveling exhibits. Dazzling installations by glass artist Dale Chihuly include a fiery cascade of a chandelier and an illuminated ceiling layered with many-hued glass bubbles, glass corkscrews, and other shapes that suggest the sea; alone, this warrants a visit, but with three floors and 15 galleries, your cultural curiosity is sure to pique, perhaps in the glass-domed conservatory. Reward your visual arts adventure with lunch at the on-site Cafe Intermezzo. ⊠ *5833 Pelican Bay Blvd.* 🕿 *239/597–1900, 800/597–1900* ⊕ *www.artisnaples.org* 🖃 *$10* ⊙ *Tues.–Sat. 10–4, Sun. noon–4* ⊙ *Closed Mon.*

FAMILY **Collier County Museum.** To get a feel for local history, stroll the nicely presented indoor vignettes and traveling exhibits and outdoor parklike displays at this museum. A Seminole *chickee* village, native plant garden, swamp buggy, reconstructed 19th-century fort, steam logging locomotive, and more capture important Naples-area developments from prehistoric times to the World War II era. ⊠ *3331 Tamiami Trail E* 🕿 *239/252–8476* ⊕ *www.colliermuseums.com* 🖃 *Free* ⊙ *Mon.–Sat. 9–4.*

FAMILY **Conservancy of Southwest Florida Nature Center.** If you're looking to connect with nature, this is the place, regardless of age. Take a 45-minute electric boat tour (ages 2-plus) along the Gordon River, rent a kayak, or go on a guided nature walk. The Dalton Discovery Center features interactive exhibits on six Florida ecosystems including a touch tank where you can learn about many of the same animals you find on the local beaches, and meet the area's only loggerhead sea turtle living in a spectacular aquarium. Preschoolers can have hands-on fun at the new Little Explorer Play Zone. The onsite wildlife hospital's viewing area gives you a peek at staff working on any number of animals. Check out Cinema Sunday and other events in their Nature Center. ■ TIP→ **The electric boat tours are free, and you don't have to pay the admission fee for the center to ride.** ⊠ *1495 Smith Preserve Way* 🕿 *239/262–0304* ⊕ *www.conservancy.org* 🖃 *$12.95* ⊙ *Mon.–Sat. 9:30–4:30.*

Fodor'sChoice ★ **Corkscrew Swamp Sanctuary.** To get a feel for what this part of Florida was like before civil engineers began draining the swamps, drive 17 miles east of North Naples to these 13,000 acres of pine flatwood and cypress, grass-and-sedge "wet prairie," saw-grass marshland, and lakes and sloughs filled with water lettuce. Managed by the National Audubon Society, the sanctuary protects North America's largest remaining stand of ancient bald cypress, 600-year-old trees as tall as 130 feet, as well as endangered birds, such as wood storks, which often nest here. This is a favorite destination for serious birders and is the gateway to the Great Florida Birding and Wildlife Trail. If you spend a couple of hours to take the 2¼-mile self-guided tour along the boardwalk, you'll spot ferns, orchids, and air plants, as well as wading birds and possibly alligators and river otters. A nature center educates you about this precious, unusual habitat with a dramatic re-creation of the preserve and its creatures in the Swamp Theater. ⊠ *375 Sanctuary Rd. W, 17 miles*

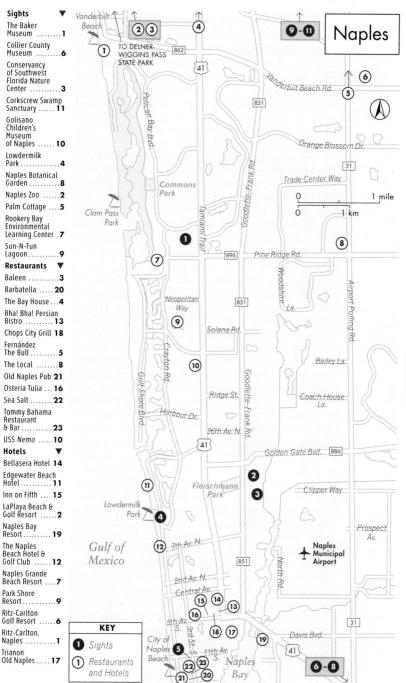

Sights ▼

The Baker Museum **1**

Collier County Museum **6**

Conservancy of Southwest Florida Nature Center **3**

Corkscrew Swamp Sanctuary ...**11**

Golisano Children's Museum of Naples **10**

Lowdermilk Park **4**

Naples Botanical Garden **8**

Naples Zoo **2**

Palm Cottage **5**

Rookery Bay Environmental Learning Center **.7**

Sun-N-Fun Lagoon...........**9**

Restaurants ▼

Baleen **3**

Barbatella **20**

The Bay House ...**4**

Bha! Bha! Persian Bistro **13**

Chops City Grill **18**

Fernández The Bull **5**

The Local **8**

Old Naples Pub **21**

Osteria Tulia ...**16**

Sea Salt **22**

Tommy Bahama Restaurant & Bar **23**

USS *Nemo* **10**

Hotels ▼

Bellasera Hotel **14**

Edgewater Beach Hotel **11**

Inn on Fifth **15**

LaPlaya Beach & Golf Resort **2**

Naples Bay Resort **19**

The Naples Beach Hotel & Golf Club **12**

Naples Grande Beach Resort **7**

Park Shore Resort............**9**

Ritz-Carlton Golf Resort **6**

Ritz-Carlton, Naples **1**

Trianon Old Naples **17**

KEY

1 *Sights*

① *Restaurants and Hotels*

east of I–75 on Rte. 846 ☎ *239/348–9151* ⊕ *www.corkscrew.audubon.org* 🔊 *$12* ⊙ *Daily 7–5:30* ☞ *Entirely wheelchair accessible.*

FAMILY **Golisano Children's Museum of Naples.** This bright, cheery 30,000-square-foot ode to playful learning burst onto Naples's cultural scene in 2012 after a decade of much-anticipated planning, and its 12 state-of-the-art permanent galleries do not disappoint. Kids of many ages and abilities (exhibits were designed to be accessible for children with special needs, too) will love the gigantic Banyan Tree, a focal point at 45 feet tall and a climbing obstacle of sorts; the Farm & Market, a cooperative playground where roles are assigned (a harvester or cashier, for example) to subtly enforce team building and math skills; and the Green Construction zone, where hard hats and ecofriendly building materials will inspire future architects. ■TIP➔ It's in the same park as Sun-n-Fun Lagoon, and it's possible to do both in one day. ⊠ *North Collier Regional Park, 15080 Livingston Rd.* ☎ *239/514–0084* ⊕ *www.cmon.org* 🔊 *$10* ⊙ *Mon., Tues., and Thurs.–Sat. 10–5, Sun. 11–4* ⊙ *Closed Wed.*

Naples Botanical Garden. An expansion and renovation of the botanical gardens that finished in 2010 elevated this attraction to one of Naples's most culturally and botanically exciting. Its "gardens with latitude" flourish with plants and architectural and decorative elements from Florida and other subtropical locales including Asia, Brazil, and the Caribbean. Highlights of the 170 acres include a Children's Garden with a butterfly house, tree house, waterfall, cave, Florida Cracker house, and hidden garden; an infinity water lily pool; an aromatic Enabling Garden with a how-to theme; and a dramatic waterfall feature. A new visitor center, café, and restaurant opened in the fall of 2014. At the visitor center, they've added three gardens including an orchid garden with more than 1,000 species and cultivars. ⊠ *4820 Bayshore Dr.* ☎ *239/643–7275* ⊕ *www.naplesgarden.org* 🔊 *$14.95* ⊙ *Fri.–Wed. 9–5, Tues. 8–5* ☞ *Complimentary wheelchairs; fee for scooters.*

FAMILY **Naples Zoo at Caribbean Gardens.** The lush 44-acre zoo got its start as a botanical garden in 1919 and has since drawn visitors curious to see lions, tigers, bears, leopards, gazelles—and a wildly popular giraffe herd added in 2011. For an extra fee you can feed the gentle, eyelash-batting giants or, in the winter season only, ride aboard dromedary camels. Other exhibits include the cult-favorite honey badgers (only four U.S. zoos have them), whose innocuous-sounding name belies their ferocious ways; a "Snakes Live" show; a pair of endangered Madagascar fossas; a giant ant eater in the South American exhibit; and the "Primate Expedition Cruise" that sails past islands populated with monkeys and lemurs. Youngsters can amuse themselves in three play zones, and there are daily meet-the-keeper times, alligator feedings, and live animal shows. New exhibits added in 2015 include an endangered Florida panther and a 19-foot reticulated python. ■TIP➔ Purchase tickets online for a $3 discount per ticket. ⊠ *1590 Goodlette-Frank Rd.* ☎ *239/262–5409* ⊕ *www.napleszoo.org* 🔊 *$19.95; giraffe feeding and camel rides (seasonal) $5 each* ⊙ *Daily 9–5; gates close at 4.*

FAMILY **Rookery Bay Environmental Learning Center.** In the midst of 110,000-acre Rookery Bay National Marine Estuary, the center dramatically interprets the Everglades environment and local history with interactive models, aquariums, an art gallery, a film, tours, and "coastal connections" programs (45 minutes, at 11 and 2 daily). It's on the edge of the estuary, about five minutes east of Marco's north bridge on Collier Boulevard. Take a walk along Observation Bridge, a 440-foot pedestrian bridge that spans the reserve's creek from the center's second floor, and connects with 1.5 miles of nature trails and leads to a creekside viewing platform. Guided and self-guided walks available. Kayak and boat tours are also available through advance registration. Exhibits include an interactive research boat, a display on the importance of the Gulf of Mexico to coastal communities, and another on global climate change. Geocaches can be found on the trail and parking area. ■TIP→ Kids go free on Friday in June and July. Also, visit the website for a printable coupon for admission. ⊠ *300 Tower Rd.* ☎ *239/530–5940* ⊕ *www. rookerybay.org* 🎫 *$5* ⊗ *May–Oct., weekdays 9–4; Nov.–Apr., Mon.– Sat. 9–4.*

WORTH NOTING

Palm Cottage. Houses in 19th-century South Florida were often built of a concrete-like material made of sand and seashells called tabby mortar. For a fine example of such construction, stop by Palm Cottage, built in 1895 and one of the Lower Gulf Coast's few surviving tabby homes. The historically accurate interior contains simple furnishings typical of the period. Next door to the cottage, Norris Gardens was designed to reflect turn-of-the-last-century garden trends. Docent tours of the home are included with admission; for an extra $6, join the weekly two-hour walking tour of the garden and historic district on Wednesday mornings (reservations required). ⊠ *137 12th Ave. S* ☎ *239/261–8164, 800/979– 3370 historic district reservations* ⊕ *www.napleshistoricalsociety.org* 🎫 *$10* ⊗ *Tues.–Sat. 1–4.*

FAMILY **Sun-N-Fun Lagoon.** This is a splashy water park across from the children's museum along the eastern edge of town. Interactive water features throughout such as dumping buckets and spray guns will delight younger kids, and there's a Tadpole Pool geared to those age six and under. The whole family will go for the diving pool, a Sunny's Lazy River, and five waterslides. The park is generally closed from October to President's Day weekend (except during some local school breaks). ⊠ *North Collier Regional Park, 15000 Livingston Rd.* ☎ *239/252–4021* ⊕ *www.napleswaterpark.com* 🎫 *$12* ⊗ *Memorial Day–late Aug., daily 10–5; weekends 10–5 in fall and spring (check website for specific schedules).*

BEACHES

FAMILY **City of Naples Beach.** There's something here for everyone just west of the Third Street South shopping area, but what gets the most attention by far is the historic pier that extends deep into the gulf and has the best free dolphin-viewing seats around. Sunsets are a nightly ritual, and dodging anglers' poles is par for the course. The concession stand sells food for humans as well as for fishy friends, and on the sand below, teenagers hold court at the volleyball nets and families picnic

8

on blankets, while a handful of people can always be seen swooping up cockles, fighting conchs, and coquinas. For a charming landscape away from the commotion, head south on Gulf Shore Boulevard and take your pick of the public access points. They may not have the amenities of the pier—or amenities, period—but the solitude can't be beat. **Amenities:** showers; toilets; parking (fee); food and drink. **Best for:** sunsets; swimming. ⊠ *12th Ave. S at Gulf Shore Blvd.* ☎ *239/213–3062* 🖻 *Parking 25¢ per 10 min* ☉ *Daily 7–sunset.*

Clam Pass Beach Park. A quiet day at the beach gets an adventurous start when you board a tram and career down a ¾-mile boardwalk through shaded mangroves and a network of canals. At the end is a pretty, secluded patch of sand that still has notable activities because of the family-vacation-magnet Naples Grande Beach Resort just a few steps from the public parking lot. The surf is calm, perfect for swimming, and aside from the usual lying out, shelling, and sand-castle building, you can spring for a kayak and meander around the marsh for a different kind of water experience. **Amenities:** food and drink; showers; toilets; water sports; parking (fee). **Best for:** solitude; swimming. ⊠ *465 Seagate Dr.* ☎ *239/252–4000* ⊕ *www.collierparks.com* 🖻 *Parking $8* ☉ *Daily 8–sunset.*

Fodor'sChoice
★
Delnor-Wiggins Pass State Park. This wide, virtually untouched expanse—about 166 acres—of open beach makes visitors feel transported from the bustling high-rises and resorts just a few blocks south. A full roster of eco-inclined features, like a designated fishing zone, hard-bottom reef (one of the few in the region and close enough to swim up to), boat dock, and observation tower hooks anglers, nature lovers, and water-sports enthusiasts drawn to the peaceful, laid-back vibe. Moms and dads love the educational displays on the local environment and the ranger-led sea turtle and birding programs, not to mention the picnic tables, grills, and plenty of shade offshore. A new concession stand was added in 2013, making food, drinks, and beach gear easily accessible to those less inclined to self-catering. **Amenities:** food and drink; parking (fee); showers; toilets; water sports. **Best for:** solitude; snorkeling; walking. ⊠ *11135 Gulf Shore Dr. N* ☎ *239/597–6196* ⊕ *www. floridastateparks.org/park/Delnor-Wiggins* 🖻 *$6 per vehicle with up to 8 people, $4 for single drivers, $2 for pedestrians and bicyclists* ☉ *Daily 8–sunset.*

FAMILY
Lowdermilk Park. Do you prefer your beach loud and active with a big dose of good old-fashioned fun? Kids running around in the surf, volleyballers hitting the sand, and tykes getting up close and personal with the park's most colorful residents, the red-throated Muscovy ducks, are all part of the Lowdermilk experience. Shallow waters and little-to-no wave action beg for a dip from even the most hesitant swimmer, and thatched umbrellas dotting the shoreline complete the happy tiki vibe and are yours for the taking—assuming you can snag one (they are strictly first come, first served). Even more, a food stand, two playgrounds, and some casual eateries down the strand at the Naples Beach Hotel make digging your feet into the sand a no-brainer. **Amenities:** food and drink; parking (fee); showers; toilets. **Best for:** swimming; walking.

✉ *1301 Gulf Shore Blvd. N* ☎ *239/213–3029* ⊕ *www.naplesgov.com* 🅿 *Parking 25¢ per 10 min* ☉ *Daily 8–sunset.*

Vanderbilt Beach. If a day at the shore just doesn't seem quite complete without a piña colada and serious people-watching, this place is for you. The white powdery sand often looks like a kaleidoscope, with multihued towels and umbrellas dotting the landscape in front of the nearly 3 miles of tony north Naples condos and luxe resorts, including the Ritz-Carlton and LaPlaya. If you walk far enough—which many people do—you come across eye candy of a different kind: the architecturally stunning megamansions of Bay Colony perched up on the dunes. A covered public parking garage gives easy access, and the beach really comes alive at sunset with onlookers. **Amenities:** water sports; food and drink; parking (fee); toilets; showers. **Best for:** partiers; sunsets; walking. ■TIP➜ Stroll up to Gumbo Limbo at the Ritz for the best Floribbean, yet surprisingly not wallet-busting, lunches and panoramic views from a shaded deck. ✉ *100 Vanderbilt Beach Rd.* ☎ *239/252–4000* ⊕ *www. collierparks.com* 🅿 *Parking $8* ☉ *Daily 8–sunset.*

WHERE TO EAT

$$$$
SEAFOOD
✕ **Baleen.** The mood cast in this well-appointed dining room and the romantic gulf-view patio that spills onto the sand feels like the perfect Florida restaurant experience. There's only one small problem: lighting is so low at dinner that you can't read the menu, even with its built-in flashlight. Too bad, because that means you also miss the effect of the beautifully presented dishes: Asian pear–and-arugula salad, black grouper with tamarind glaze, grilled scallops paired with polenta and serrano chilies, Grand Marnier crème brûlée, and the like. (Thankfully, there's a great prix-fixe option.) At breakfast, the house-made corned beef hash is divine. For lunch, the lobster Cobb salad is a popular choice. Ⓢ *Average main: $37* ✉ *La Playa Beach & Golf Resort, 9891 Gulf Shore Dr.* ☎ *239/598–5707, 800/237–6883* ⊕ *www.laplayaresort. com* ⌂ *Reservations essential.*

$$
ITALIAN
✕ **Barbatella.** This trattoria with an edge was the most buzzed-about opening in 2012; it's still just as popular. The restaurant has three dining spaces to suit any whim: the wine bar, with sleek eclectic decor, has a communal table, green ceiling medallions, crystal chandeliers wrapped in birdcages, and a wine dispenser that allows guests to sip their way through 32 bottles (Italian, of course) by the 1-, 3-, or 6-ounce glass. The brick room, with 150-year-old recycled floors, is more casual and open to the kitchen; and the central patio is shaded and relaxed. The menu, straight-up Italian and expertly done, stars refined versions of classics, including bruschetta, fried calamari, lasagna, and wood-fired pizza. Don't miss the house's sweetest treat: a gelateria that's open to passersby on 3rd Street South, a partnership with artisan-chocolate king Norman Love. Ⓢ *Average main: $20* ✉ *1290 3rd St. S* ☎ *239/263–1955* ⊕ *www.barbatellanaples.com.*

$$$$
SEAFOOD
✕ **The Bay House.** Nestled in a hidden expanse of twisted mangrove trees and flowing canals is one of the area's best restaurants for casual fine dining—and beautifully natural scenery. Restored wooden rowboats and modern chandeliers hang from the ceiling of the main dining room, which is packed almost every night in season. The food is a serious

8

DID YOU KNOW?

Beaches are for so much more than sunning and sandcastle building. Many are used for fishing, weddings, and horseback riding. And come July 4, some, like the city of Naples Beach (shown here), draw people at night for viewing fireworks over the water.

celebration of the sea with Southern accents, like their signature coastal pan roast with fresh gulf fish and shellfish with a red wine butter sauce. Adjacent Tierney's Tavern & Claw Bar shares the same kitchen but focuses on chilled shellfish and other Southern delights with nightly live music and a more casual vibe. ■TIP➔ Saturday lunches are surprisingly quiet and a perfect time to snag one of the coveted tables closest to the windows. $ *Average main: $32* ⊠ *799 Walkerbilt Rd.* ☎ *239/591–3837* ⊕ *www.bayhousenaples.com* ⌣ *Reservations essential* ☾ *No lunch May–Nov.*

$$$ ✕ **Bha! Bha! Persian Bistro.** Long considered one of Naples's best ethnic
MIDDLE EASTERN restaurants, loyal fans of Bha! Bha! have flocked to a tiny north Naples strip mall year in and year out to indulge in the restaurant's chic Persian atmosphere and cuisine. On the eve of its 15th birthday came a well-deserved present: a brand-new location on bustling Fifth Avenue South. But the move didn't spoil the cooking or the following. All of the old favorites still garner loyal reviews, including plum lamb with tomato-pomegranate sauce, mango-garlic shrimp (which was featured in *Bon Appétit*), and spicy beef in saffron sauce with cucumber yogurt— all made completely from scratch on premises. $ *Average main: $25* ⊠ *865 5th Ave. S* ☎ *239/594–5557* ⊕ *www.bhabhapersianbistro.com* ⌣ *Reservations essential.*

$$$$ ✕ **Chops City Grill.** Count on high-quality cuisine that fuses, as its name
ECLECTIC suggests, chopstick cuisine and steak-house mainstays. Sophisticated yet resort-wear casual, it draws everyone from young businesspeople to local retirees. Sushi and Pacific Rim inspirations such as shrimp spring rolls rub elbows with beef carpaccio and watermelon salad with goat cheese and pecans. Grilled seafood and fine cuts of meat like dry-aged rib eyes and strip steaks come with side options such as "wild" sherry-laced mushrooms and four-cheese mac. For dessert, sip a Special K Express martini, made with a full shot of espresso. Dine alfresco or inside with a view of the kitchen. There's a second location at Brooks Grand Plaza, U.S. 41 at Coconut Road, in Bonita Springs (239/992–4677). $ *Average main: $32* ⊠ *837 5th Ave. S* ☎ *239/262– 4677* ⊕ *www.chopscitygrill.com* ⌣ *Reservations essential* ☾ *No lunch.*

$$ ✕ **Fernández The Bull.** Intrepid palates venture several miles inland to
CUBAN get a taste of the "Best Cuban Food in Naples," as voted by readers of *Gulfshore Life* magazine. You'll get authentic, home-cooked specialties, without pretension, at this simple storefront café. Stick to the basics, and don't miss the lemony *lechon asado* (slow-roasted pork that's grilled and basted with garlic) or *ropa vieja* (shreds of flank steak simmered in tomato sauce with heaps of peppers and onions). In chichi Naples, the prices are good, and the portions are better: one entrée is enough for dinner and lunch the next day, as all are served with salads, big slabs of toasted garlic bread, and two sides. The bar is wine-and-beer only; the mojitos are *faux*-jitos but still pretty tasty. $ *Average main: $17* ⊠ *1201 Piper Blvd., No. 10* ☎ *239/254–9855* ⊕ *www.fernandezthebull.com.*

$$ ✕ **The Local.** You'll find an epicurean take on healthy eating at this farm-
CONTEMPORARY and-sea-to-table bistro that, as the name declares, looks almost exclu-
Fodor's Choice sively to local suppliers to stock its kitchen. Though in a strip mall a
★ few blocks inland, the setting is hip and polished with an interior that

8

evokes both the beach and the farm, no doubt a reflection of the young and stylish owners' passion for nourishment. Foodies, the health-conscious, hipsters, and retirees mix equally at The Local, where ingredient origins are proudly traced: microgreens come from Herban Gardens in Fort Myers, dairy and cheese from Winter Park, and organic produce from any number of Florida growers. Choose from healthy options like a super-food salad to more savory indulgences like pork shoulder in natural jus with mango mustard. [$] *Average main: $18* ✉ *5323 Airport Pulling Rd. N* ☎ *239/596–3276* 🌐 *www.thelocalnaples.com.*

$ AMERICAN

🍴 **Old Naples Pub.** Local blue- and white-collar workers gather with shoppers for affordable sandwiches and seafood in the vaulted, vine-twisted courtyard of this traditional pub, which has been tucked away from shopping traffic off upscale 3rd Street since 1990. It strikes one as an everybody-knows-your-name kind of place, with jars of pickles on the tables and friendly bartenders. Taste any of 25 kinds of beer and order fried "ungrouper" sandwiches (made with "mild flaky white fillet" as grouper numbers wait to make a comeback), burgers, crispy chicken salad, and nachos, as well as such not-so-traditional pub grub as grilled fresh catch-of-the-day and fried gator tail. There's musical entertainment Wednesday through Sunday year-round. [$] *Average main: $15* ✉ *255 13th Ave. S* ☎ *239/649–8200* 🌐 *www.naplespubs.com* ✍ *Reservations not accepted.*

$$$ ITALIAN Fodor's Choice ★

🍴 **Osteria Tulia.** An ancestral air pervades at this intimate yet lively restaurant on 5th Avenue, where the Sicilian-born chef (and part owner) drives an authentic celebration of the Italian table. Opened in 2013, the concept is a refreshing departure from long, ornate menus and focuses on simple, finely produced, house-made Italian cuisine in a rustic, refined setting. Everything wooden was crafted from a dilapidated barn in north Florida, and the 1940s-era bricks came from a reclaimed Chicago firehouse. The signature fennel sausage is homemade from a family recipe, and the kitchen cures its own pancetta, makes its own mozzarella and ricotta cheeses, and makes and extrudes all pastas on-site. Peasant recipes for things like rabbit and wild boar shine when they're offered seasonally, but the tortelloni with braised short ribs pleases nightly. [$] *Average main: $25* ✉ *466 5th Ave. S* ☎ *239/213–2073* 🌐 *www.tulianaples.com.*

$$$$ MEDITERRANEAN Fodor's Choice ★

🍴 **Sea Salt.** Naples's hottest upscale restaurant draws a crowd of connoisseurs to its modern coral-rock dining room that spills out onto the sidewalk. Venetian-born Chef Fabrizio Aielli puts a New World spin on traditional Italian on his nightly changing menu often incorporating local and organic ingredients. Everyone gets a sea-salt sampler. The best way to start is to dabble in charcuterie and European cheese. The finest quality meats and seafood go into dishes including Wagyu beef and Kurobuta pork, grilled local black grouper, and dry-packed scallops with lemon-caper oil. At lunch, choose between creative sandwiches and salads. [$] *Average main: $35* ✉ *1186 3rd St. S* ☎ *239/434–7258* 🌐 *www.seasaltnaples.com* ✍ *Reservations essential.*

$$$
SEAFOOD
Fodor's Choice
★

✕ **USS Nemo.** Don't be fooled by the tacky glowing sign from the highway: most Neapolitans swear this is *the* place for seafood in town, which is why you should still make a reservation even in the heat of summer. The food is in the vein of fine dining but served in a whimsical setting with portholes, antique bronze diving gear, and colorful sculptures of fish. Speaking of fish, almost all are locally caught and reach new depths of deliciousness with eclectic, often Asian-inspired preparations. The house signature miso-broiled sea bass with citrus-ginger butter strikes the right balance between sweet and savory; the ginger-steamed halibut with soy-lime dressing and the herb-grilled tuna with warm goat cheese and seared diver scallops are also winners. $ *Average main: $24* ✉ *3745 Tamiami Trail N* ☎ *239/261–6366* ⊕ *www.ussnemorestaurant. com* ⌂ *Reservations essential* ⊗ *No lunch weekends.*

WHERE TO STAY

$$$$
HOTEL

⊞ **Bellasera Hotel.** This downtown hotel is just far enough "off Fifth" to be away from the dining-and-shopping foot traffic but close enough for convenience, and it feels like a lovely Italian villa with its red tile roofs and burnt-ocher stucco. **Pros:** spacious accommodations with full home amenities (kitchens, living areas, porches, and balconies); on-site restaurant and near downtown restaurants; free bikes for guests; first-come, first-served private cabanas at pool. **Cons:** must take shuttle to beach; on a busy highway (though surprisingly quiet). $ *Rooms from: $489* ✉ *221 9th St. S* ☎ *239/649–7333, 888/612–1115* ⊕ *www. bellaseranaples.com* ⇥ *10 studios, 30 1-bedroom suites, 46 2-bedroom suites, 9 3-bedroom suites* ⏹ *No meals.*

$$$$
HOTEL

⊞ **Edgewater Beach Hotel.** At this all-suite, beachfront property at the north end of scenic Gulf Shore Boulevard, the rooms are large and refreshing, exuding a relaxed, contemporary vibe. **Pros:** beautiful beach; quiet; exquisite views. **Cons:** far from shopping; surrounded closely by high-rises; no tubs in some rooms. $ *Rooms from: $479* ✉ *1901 Gulf Shore Blvd. N* ☎ *239/403–2000, 888/564–1308* ⊕ *www. edgewaternaples.com* ⇥ *97 1-bedroom suites, 28 2-bedroom suites* ⏹ *No meals.*

$$$
HOTEL

⊞ **Inn on Fifth.** You can't top this luxe hotel if you want to plant yourself in the heart of Naples nightlife and shopping, and its $22-million expansion across the street in 2012 added 32 new club-level suites with perks galore like a private concierge lounge with 24/7 Champagne, a full bar and hors d'oeuvres each night, and a roof deck. **Pros:** central location; metro vibe; spa has free sauna for guests. **Cons:** pool is eye-level with power lines; beach is a long stroll or shuttle ride away. $ *Rooms from: $385* ✉ *699 5th Ave. S* ☎ *239/403–8777, 888/403–8778* ⊕ *www. innonfifth.com* ⇥ *117 rooms, 2 suites* ⏹ *No meals.*

$$$$
RESORT
Fodor's Choice
★

⊞ **LaPlaya Beach & Golf Resort.** LaPlaya bespeaks posh and panache down to the smallest detail—note the Balinese-style spa, marble bathrooms, and a stuffed sea turtle toy to cuddle during your stay. **Pros:** right on the beach; high-end amenities; beautiful rooms, which were renovated in 2012. **Cons:** golf course is off property; no locker rooms in spa. $ *Rooms from: $619* ✉ *9891 Gulf Shore Dr.* ☎ *239/597–3123, 800/237–6883* ⊕ *www.laplayaresort.com* ⇥ *180 rooms, 9 suites* ⏹ *No meals.*

8

$$$
RESORT
FAMILY

Naples Bay Resort. Dual personalities are at work in this sprawling resort, and both are upscale and polished at every turn: at one end, a 97-slip marina with a luxury hotel (a boater's dream), and at the other a cottage resort with a busy, water-oriented recreation park. **Pros:** walk to downtown; $5 water taxi to other bay-side hot spots. **Cons:** no beach; some highway noise. $ *Rooms from: $369* ⊠ *1500 5th Ave. S* ☎ *239/530–1199, 866/605–1199* ⊕ *www.naplesbayresort.com* ⤴ *20 rooms, 29 1-bedroom suites, 36 2-bedroom suites, 108 cottages (minimum 6-night stay in cottages)* ⦿*No meals.*

$$$$
RESORT
FAMILY

The Naples Beach Hotel & Golf Club. Family-owned and managed since 1946, this art-deco resort is a piece of Naples history—and its stretch of powdery sand has lots of action at all times. **Pros:** terrific beach scene; golf course and driving range on property; complimentary kids' program. **Cons:** expensive nightly rates; have to cross street to reach spa and breakfast dining; though interiors are freshly renovated, signature old-school exterior may not appeal to sleek tastes. $ *Rooms from: $459* ⊠ *851 Gulf Shore Blvd. N* ☎ *239/261–2222, 800/237–7600* ⊕ *www.naplesbeachhotel.com* ⤴ *267 rooms, 42 suites, 10 efficiencies* ⦿*No meals.*

$$$$
RESORT
FAMILY
Fodor's Choice
★

Naples Grande Beach Resort. Beach access, a golf club, and top-shelf luxury are all yours at this ultramodern high-rise formerly known as the Waldorf Astoria Naples. **Pros:** indulgent spa; great tennis; golf; beach service with cabanas; attentive service; seven bars and restaurants; family and adult pool areas. **Cons:** not directly on the beach; golf facility is 6 miles away with no shuttle. $ *Rooms from: $729* ⊠ *475 Seagate Dr.* ☎ *239/597–3232, 888/722–1267* ⊕ *www.naplesgrande.com* ⤴ *474 rooms, 29 suites, 50 bungalows* ⦿*No meals.*

$$$
RENTAL

Park Shore Resort. Well situated near the beaches and shopping off Gulf Shore Boulevard, this hidden retreat is practical and comfortable, offering spacious suites (all with kitchens and screened balconies), a tropical pool and grounds (with upscale gas grills), and a casual calm. **Pros:** good value; tropical pool and shaded grounds; quiet. **Cons:** no restaurant; long walk to beach; no shuttle service. $ *Rooms from: $349* ⊠ *600 Neoplitan Way* ☎ *800/548-2077* ⊕ *www.parkshorefl.com* ⤴ *156 rooms* ⦿*No meals.*

$$$$
RESORT
Fodor's Choice
★

Ritz-Carlton Golf Resort, Naples. Ardent golfers with a yen for luxury will find their dream vacation at Naples's most elegant golf resort where Ritz style prevails and service exceeds your wildest expectations. **Pros:** best golf academy in area; two championship courses at the front door; plush setting; access to Ritz spa and beach via shuttle; service par excellence. **Cons:** 10-minute drive to beaches; expensive rates; farther inland than most properties. $ *Rooms from: $649* ⊠ *2600 Tiburón Dr.* ☎ *239/593-2000* ⊕ *www.ritzcarlton.com* ⤴ *295 rooms* ⦿*No meals.*

$$$$
RESORT
FAMILY
Fodor's Choice
★

Ritz-Carlton, Naples. This is a regal Ritz-Carlton, with marble statues and antique furnishings blended with artistic modernity in the rooms, and restaurants that now breathe airy light-blue and natural tones. **Pros:** flawless service; fun tiki bar and water-sport options; near north Naples shopping and restaurants; private, ultra-indulgent spa (guests and members only). **Cons:** high price tag; hike to downtown; valet parking only; extra charge for beach umbrellas annoying at this nice a place.

[$] *Rooms from: $999* ✉ *280 Vanderbilt Beach Rd.* ☎ *239/598–3300* 🌐 *www.ritzcarlton.com* 🛏 *450 rooms* 🍴 *No meals.*

$$$ HOTEL 🏨 **Trianon Old Naples.** Refined ladies and gents will feel at home in this classy boutique hotel that's right smack in the central historic district, yet enrobed in an aura of privacy two quiet residential blocks south of 5th Avenue's bustle. **Pros:** can't-beat location for urbanites; large rooms. **Cons:** limited facilities; long walk (or short drive) to beach. [$] *Rooms from: $319* ✉ *955 7th Ave. S* ☎ *239/435–9600, 877/482–5228* 🌐 *www.trianon.com* 🛏 *55 rooms, 3 suites.*

NIGHTLIFE AND PERFORMING ARTS

NIGHTLIFE

The heart of Old Naples, 5th Avenue South, already known for its scene of lively bars and sidewalk cafés, has undergone a renaissance of sorts.

Avenue Wine Café. Young, casual oenophiles camp out here; there's also an impressive craft beer list (that includes brews from the new Naples Beach Brewery) as well as cigars. ✉ *483 5th Ave. S* ☎ *239/403–9463* 🌐 *www.avenuewinecafe.com.*

Burn by Rocky Patel. At this part cigar bar, part dance club, you can expect pretty young things grooving to a house DJ. ✉ *9110 Strada Pl.* ☎ *239/653–9013* 🌐 *www.burnbyrockypatel.com.*

Naples Beach Brewery. With the opening of Naples Beach Brewery in 2013, the Naples scene isn't only about fine wine anymore. This microbrewery's concoctions can be found in almost 50 local bars and restaurants including some of Naples' finest dining establishments. Eight brews range from the straw colored Weizen to the Naples Beach Stout. Look for a palm tree logo on bottles and taps signifying the local craft beers, or head directly to the brewery on Friday and Saturday afternoons for guided tours and tastings. But don't expect to be wowed by a big gleaming factory, as this brewery is small and authentic, located in an industrial neighborhood sandwiched between hardware manufacturers—the real deal. ✉ *4110 Enterprise Ave, Suite 217* ☎ *239/304–8795* 🌐 *www.naplesbeachbrewery.com* 🎟 *$15* ⏲ *Fri. 3 pm–8 pm, Sat. noon–8 pm.*

Osetra. A hint of SoBe on the Gulf Coast serves sushi, Champagne, and caviar in a sleek setting on 5th Avenue South. ✉ *469 5th Ave. S* ☎ *239/776–7938* 🌐 *www.osetranaples.com.*

The Pub. Long lists of brews, flat-screens, and fun British decor attract a lively crowd to this popular outpost of a small, family-run chain. ✉ *9118 Strada Pl.* ☎ *239/594–2748* 🌐 *www.experiencethepub.com.*

Vergina. The mature crowd hits the dance floor for Gloria Gaynor and the Bee Gees. ✉ *700 5th Ave. S* ☎ *239/659–7008* 🌐 *www.verginarestaurant.com.*

PERFORMING ARTS

Naples is the cultural capital of this stretch of coast.

Naples Philharmonic. See the 85-piece Naples Philharmonic Orchestra perform more than 140 plays, ballets, orchestral, and chamber concerts each year at the Hayes Hall at Artis–Naples from September to June. The Miami City Ballet performs here during its winter season.

✉ *Artis–Naples, 5833 Pelican Bay Blvd.* ☎ *239/597–1900, 800/597–1900* ⊕ *www.artisnaples.org.*

Naples Players. Musicals and dramas are performed year-round; winter shows often sell out well in advance. ✉ *Sugden Community Theatre, 701 5th Ave. S* ☎ *239/263–7990* ⊕ *www.naplesplayers.org.*

SHOPPING
SHOPPING AREAS

Tin City. Near 5th Avenue South, a collection of tin-roof former boat docks along Naples Bay has more than 30 boutiques, eateries, and souvenir shops, with everything from jewelry and T-shirts to Jet Ski rentals and seafood. ✉ *1200 5th Ave. S* ⊕ *www.tincity.com.*

Village on Venetian Bay. Stroll along the classy boutiques that line the water's edge, and grab a bite at one of the excellent restaurants, all with fantastic views. ✉ *4200 Gulf Shore Blvd. N* ⊕ *www.venetianvillage. com.*

Waterside Shops. Only in South Florida can you find more than four dozen upscale stores plus eateries wrapped around a series of waterfalls, waterways, and shaded open-air promenades. Saks 5th Avenue and Nordstrom are the main anchors; Burberry, De Beers, Ralph Lauren, and St. John are in the mix. ✉ *5415 Tamiami Trail N* ☎ *239/598–1605* ⊕ *www.watersideshops.com.*

SPORTS AND THE OUTDOORS
BIKING

Naples Cyclery. For daily rentals, rates range from $6 to $32 for two hours and selections include two- and four-passenger surreys, tandems, and more; weekly rentals are also available. ■ TIP➔ **If you need a little boost, have breakfast, lunch, or an espresso at the store's Fit & Fuel Café, where there's a serious fitting room if you're in the market for a custom-fit bike.** ✉ *Pavilion Shopping Center, 813 Vanderbilt Beach Rd.* ☎ *239/566–0600* ⊕ *www.naplescyclery.com.*

BOATING AND FISHING

Mangrove Outfitters. Take a guided boat and learn to cast and tie flies. ✉ *4111 Tamiami Trail E* ☎ *239/793–3370, 888/319–9848* ⊕ *www. mangroveoutfitters.com.*

Port Of Naples Marina. All new boats makes this the youngest fleet to rent. Choose pontoon or deck boats, starting at $169 for two hours. ✉ *550 Port-O-Call Way* ☎ *239/774–0479* ⊕ *www.portofnaplesmarina.com.*

FAMILY   **Pure Naples.** Half-day deep-sea and backwater fishing trips depart twice daily. Sightseeing cruises and thrilling jet tours are also available, along with jet ski and boat rentals and private charters. ✉ *Tin City, 1200 5th Ave. S* ☎ *239/263–4949* ⊕ *www.purenaples.com.*

GOLF

Lely Resort Golf and Country Club. Flamingo Island (designed by Robert Trent Jones) and The Mustang (designed by Lee Trevino) are the two championship courses open to the public at Lely Resort. Flamingo Island features white-sand bunkers, hourglass fairways, and large greens, along with its signature 3200-yard hole 5 with a water-rimmed rolling fairway, bunkers, and two bridges providing the only access to the mainland. The Mustang features 12 lakes and rolling fairways. There's also a John Jacobs' golf school on premises. ⊠ *8004 Grand Lely Blvd.* ☏ *239/793–2600* ⊕ *www.lelyresortgolfandcountryclub.com/* ✉ *$169* ⚑ *Flamingo Island: 18 holes, 7171 yards, par 72; The Mustang: 18 holes, 7217 yards, par 72.*

The Naples Beach Hotel & Golf Club. This historic club has weekly clinics, a driving range, and a putting green and is replete with nostalgia as the region's oldest course, built in 1929. It was last redesigned in 1998 by golf architect Ron Garl, and refurbished in 2011. ■TIP➔ It has been voted "Top 50 Women Friendly Golf Courses in the U.S." by the magazine *Golf for Women.* ⊠ *851 Gulf Shore Blvd. N* ☏ *239/435–2475* ⊕ *www. naplesbeachhotel.com* ✉ *$55 for 9 holes, $99 for 18 holes* ⚑ *18 holes, 6488 yards, par 72.*

Tiburón Golf Club. There are two 18-hole Greg Norman–designed courses, the Gold and the Black—an especially difficult course carved right out of a cypress preserve. Challenging and environmentally pristine, the links include narrow fairways, stacked sod wall bunkers, coquina sand, and no roughs. New this year is the PGA Experience's TOURAcademy. ■TIP➔ You cannot books months in advance unless you're staying at one of the Ritz-Carlton hotels. Nonguests can book 10 days out. ⊠ *Ritz-Carlton Golf Resort, 2620 Tiburón Dr.* ☏ *239/593–2201* ⊕ *www. tiburongcnaples.com* ✉ *$225* ⚑ *Tiburón Gold: 18 holes, 7271 yards, par 74.9; Tiburón Black: 18 holes, 6949 yards, par 75.01.*

MARCO ISLAND

20 miles south of Naples via Rte. 951.

High-rises dominate part of the shores of Marco Island, which is connected to the mainland by two bridges. Yet because of its distance from downtown Naples, it retains an isolated feeling much appreciated by those who love this corner of the world. Some natural areas have been preserved, and the down-home fishing village of Goodland, a 20-minute drive from historic Old Marco, resists change. Fishing, boating, sunning, swimming, and tennis are the primary activities here.

GETTING HERE AND AROUND

From Naples, Collier Boulevard (Route 951) takes you to Marco Island. If you're not renting a car, taxi rides cost about $100 from the regional airport in Fort Myers, and Collier Area Transit (CAT) runs regular buses through the area. Key West Express operates a ferry from Marco Island (from Christmas through Easter) and Fort Myers Beach (year-round) to Key West. The cost for the round-trip (less than four hours each way) is $147 from either Fort Myers Beach or Marco Island.

Contacts Collier Area Transit (CAT) ☏ *239/252–7777* ⊕ *www.colliergov.net/ CAT.* **Key West Express** ⊠ *951 Bald Eagle Dr.* ☏ *239/394–9700, 888/539–2628* ⊕ *www.keywestexpress.us.*

VISITOR INFORMATION

Contacts **Marco Island Area Chamber of Commerce** ✉ *1102 N. Collier Blvd.* ☎ *239/394–7549, 888/330–1422* 🌐 *www.marcoislandchamber.org.* **Naples, Marco Island, Everglades Convention and Visitors Bureau** ☎ *800/688–3600, 239/225–1013* 🌐 *www.paradisecoast.com.*

EXPLORING

Marco Island Historical Museum. Marco Island was once part of the ancient Calusa kingdom. The Key Marco Cat, a statue found in 1896 excavations, has become symbolic of the island's prehistoric significance. The original is part of the Smithsonian Institution's collection, but a replica of the Key Marco Cat is among displays illuminating the ancient past at this museum, which opened in January 2011. Three rooms examine the island's history with dioramas, artifacts, and signage: the Calusa Room, Pioneer Room, and Modern Marco Room. A fourth hosts traveling exhibits focusing on the settlement history of the island. Outside, the yard was built to look like a Calusa village atop a shell mound with a water feature and *chickee* structure. ✉ *180 S. Heathwood Dr.* ☎ *239/642–1440* 🌐 *www.colliermuseums.com* 🎫 *Free* 🕒 *Tues.–Sat. 9–4.*

BEACHES

FAMILY **Tigertail Beach.** On the northwest side of the island is 2,500 feet of both developed and undeveloped areas. Once gulf front, in recent years a sand spit known as Sand Dollar Island has formed, which means the stretch especially at the north end has become mud flats—great for birding. There's plenty of powdery sand further south and across the lagoon that draws a broad base of fans flocking there for its playgrounds, butterfly garden, volleyball nets, and kayak and umbrella rentals. Beach wheelchairs are also available for free use. **■ TIP→ The Conservancy of Southwest Florida conducts free educational beach walks at Tigertail Beach every weekday from 8:30 to 9:30 from January to mid-April.** **Amenities:** food and drink; showers; toilets; water sports; parking (paid). **Best for:** sunset; walking; swimming. ✉ *490 Hernando Dr.* ☎ *239/252–4000* 🌐 *www.collierparks.com* 🎫 *Parking $8* 🕒 *Daily 8–sunset.*

WHERE TO EAT

$$ ITALIAN Fodor's Choice ★ 🍴 **Arturo's.** This place is huge, with expansive Romanesque dining rooms and more seating on the patio. Still, it fills up year-round with a strong well-dressed following that appreciates a fun attitude and serious Italian cuisine done comprehensively and traditionally. Start with the plump mussels marinara, then choose from a lengthy list of classic Italian entrées, including homemade pasta. The stuffed pork chop, a nightly special, is a winner, as is the New York–style cheesecake. [$] *Average main: $20* ✉ *844 Bald Eagle Dr.* ☎ *239/642–0550* 🌐 *www.arturosmarcoisland.com* ✍ *Reservations essential* 🕒 *No lunch.*

$$$ ECLECTIC 🍴 **Café de Marco.** This cozy little bistro with cheery yellow walls and stained-glass windows has served expertly prepared local fish since 1983. The jumbo prawns—an entire pound butterflied and broiled in their shell—are the signature dish, but grilled filet mignon on phyllo pastry proves the kitchen also knows how to do meat. Try stuffed Florida lobster, sautéed frogs' legs, or the broiled seafood platter. For a taste of the café without the sticker shock, dine from 5 to 5:45 for a

reduced-price early-bird menu. $ *Average main: $29* ✉ *244 Palm St.* ☎ *239/394–6262* ⊕ *www.cafedemarco.com* ⚄ *Reservations essential* ⊗ *Closed Sun. May–Dec. No lunch.*

$ ✕ **Crazy Flamingo.** Burgers, conch fritters, and chicken wings draw
AMERICAN mostly locals to this neighborhood bar, where there's counter service only and seating indoors and outdoors on the sidewalk. Try the peel-and-eat shrimp, sushi, mussels marinara, chicken bistro salad, or fried grouper basket. $ *Average main: $11* ✉ *Marco Island Town Center, 1035 N. Collier Blvd.* ☎ *239/642–9600* ⊕ *www.thecrazyflamingo.com.*

$$$ ✕ **Old Marco Lodge Crab House.** Built in 1869, this waterfront restaurant
SEAFOOD is Goodland's oldest landmark. Boaters often cruise in and tie up dockside to sit on the veranda and dine on local seafood and pasta entrées. The crab-cake sandwich is a popular lunch option. For dinner, start with a wholesome bowl of vegetable crab soup and then a trip to the salad bar (included in the price of entrées). The menu has all manner of seafood dishes, including a teriyaki shrimp wrap, a basket of fried oysters, and a soft-shell crab sandwich. There's also steak and chicken dishes for landlubbers. Save room for the authentic key lime pie. $ *Average main: $25* ✉ *401 Papaya St., Goodland* ☎ *239/642–7227* ⊕ *www. oldmarcolodge.com* ▬ *No credit cards* ⊗ *Closed Aug.–Sept.*

$$$ ✕ **Sale e Pepe.** Marco's best dining view comes also with some of its
ITALIAN finest cuisine. The name means "salt and pepper," an indication that this palatial restaurant with terrace seating overlooking the beach adheres to the basics of Southern Italian cuisine. Pastas, sausages, and ice cream are made right here in the kitchen. Simple, artfully presented dishes—butternut squash ravioli, Cornish hen with grilled oyster mushrooms, yellow-pepper-and-shrimp soup, baked salmon with lobster sauce, Chianti-braised short ribs, and tomato-crusted Atlantic salmon—explode with home-cooked, long-simmered flavors. With the exception of a handful of pizzas, lunch is more traditional, less Italian. $ *Average main: $25* ✉ *Marco Beach Ocean Resort, 480 S. Collier Blvd.* ☎ *239/393–1400* ⊕ *www.sale-e-pepe.com.*

$$$ ✕ **Snook Inn.** Situated on the water with live entertainment in the tiki bar
SEAFOOD and a loaded salad bar, it's no wonder this place has been a casual favorite for locals and visitors for decades. Signature items include the spicy conch chowder, beer-battered grouper, Caribbean BBQ baby back ribs, and grouper in a bag with mushroom crab sauce. $ *Average main: $21* ✉ *1215 Bald Eagle Dr., Old Marco* ☎ *239/394–3313* ⊕ *www.snookinn. com* ⚄ *Reservations not accepted.*

$$$ ✕ **Verdi's American Bistro.** There's a Zen feel to this intimate bistro built
ECLECTIC on creative American-Italian-Asian fusion cuisine. You might start with steamed littleneck clams in garlic butter or duck potstickers, then move on to entrées such as grilled swordfish with pumpkin seeds, miso-glazed shrimp, pasta pomodoro, or the New Zealand rack of lamb. Cuban coffee crème brûlée and deep-dish apple strudel are among the tempting desserts. $ *Average main: $28* ✉ *Sand Dollar Plaza, 241 N. Collier Blvd.* ☎ *239/394–5533* ⊕ *www.verdisbistro.com* ⊗ *Closed Sept. No lunch.*

WHERE TO STAY

$
HOTEL
The Boat House Motel. For a great location at a good price, check into this modest, but appealing, two-story motel at the north end of the island on the Marco River, close to the Gulf. **Pros:** away from busy beach traffic; affordable; boating docks and access. **Cons:** no beach; hard to find; tight parking area. *$ Rooms from: $177 ⊠ 1180 Edington Pl. ☎ 239/642–2400, 800/528–6345 ⊕ www.theboathousemotel.com ⇄ 20 rooms ⏇ No meals.*

$$$$
RESORT
Fodor's Choice
★
Marco Beach Ocean Resort. One of the island's first condo hotels, this 12-story class act has luxurious one- and two-bedroom suites decorated in elegant neutral tones with the finest fixtures; all rooms face the water and look down onto the crescent-shape rooftop pool (on the fifth floor). **Pros:** gourmet dining; intimate; on beach; sophisticated crowd. **Cons:** steep prices; squeezed between high-rises; near a busy resort. *$ Rooms from: $609 ⊠ 480 S. Collier Blvd. ☎ 239/393–1400, 800/715–8517 ⊕ www.marcoresort.com ⇄ 83 1-bedroom and 15 2-bedroom suites ⏇ No meals.*

$$$$
RESORT
FAMILY
Marco Island Marriott Beach Resort. A grandiose circular drive with rock waterfalls front this hilltop, beachfront resort that's undergoing a $250 million makeover on its rebranding journey (that will be unveiled in 2017). **Pros:** great spa; eight on-site restaurants; appeals to children and adults; two private golf courses. **Cons:** huge size; lots of convention business; paid parking across the street in an uncovered lot; $25 daily resort fee but at least it includes a bevy of freebies like Wi-Fi and range balls. *$ Rooms from: $569 ⊠ 400 S. Collier Blvd. ☎ 239/394–2511, 800/438–4373 ⊕ www.marcoislandmarriott.com ⇄ 664 rooms, 62 suites ⏇ No meals.*

$$$
RENTAL
Olde Marco Island Inn & Suites. This Victorian with tin roofs and royal-blue shutters and awnings used to be the only place to stay on the island when lodging back then was in the circa-1883 historic building that now holds the restaurant; today guests check into newer hotel sections with comfortable condo suites. **Pros:** quiet part of the island; full kitchen in every room; free Wi-Fi; laundry facilities; free covered parking. **Cons:** must drive to beach; annexed to a shopping center; office closes at night. *$ Rooms from: $306 ⊠ 100 Palm St. ☎ 239/394–3131, 877/475–3466 ⊕ www.oldemarcoinn.com ⇄ 50 suites, 1 penthouse ⏇ No meals.*

SPORTS AND THE OUTDOORS
FISHING
Sunshine Tours. Try a deep-sea ($135 per person for half day) or back-country ($65 per person for three hours) fishing charter with this out-fitter. *⊠ Rose Marina, 951 Bald Eagle Dr. ☎ 239/642–5415 ⊕ www.sunshinetoursmarcoisland.com.*

ORLANDO AND ENVIRONS

WELCOME TO ORLANDO AND ENVIRONS

TOP REASONS TO GO

★ **Magic and Fantasy:** Unleash your inner child, in the glow of Cinderella Castle, at WDW's Magic Kingdom. Fireworks transform the night skies—and you—at this park and at Epcot. And, over at Universal Orlando we have just, two words: Harry Potter.

★ **Around:** Visit Epcot's 11 countries, complete with perfect replicas of foreign monuments, unique crafts, and traditional cuisine.

★ **Amazing Animals:** Safari through Africa in Disney's Animal Kingdom, get splashed by Shamu at SeaWorld, kiss a dolphin at Discovery Cove, and watch gators wrestle at Gatorland.

★ **Shopping Ops:** Hit the national chains at Orlando's upscale malls, or browse Winter Park's unique Park Avenue boutiques. Don't forget the mouse ears: Main Street U.S.A. and Downtown Disney are filled with the best classic souvenirs and some quirkier items as well.

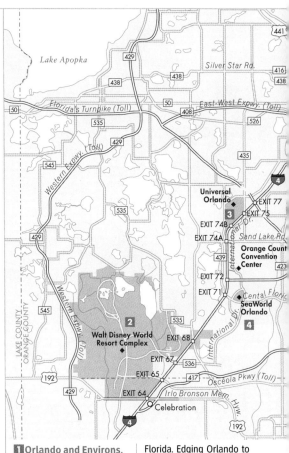

1 Orlando and Environs. Once you've exhausted the theme parks, or have been exhausted by them, turn your attention to a wealth of offerings, including museums, parks, and gardens, in Winter Park, Kissimmee, and elsewhere. Thanks to Disney World, Orlando is the gateway for many visitors to central Florida. Edging Orlando to the south is Kissimmee, with home-grown attractions like Gatorland. Looking for more laid-back local flavor? You'll find it just 20 miles northeast of Orlando in the charming Winter Park suburb.

CENTRAL FLORIDA

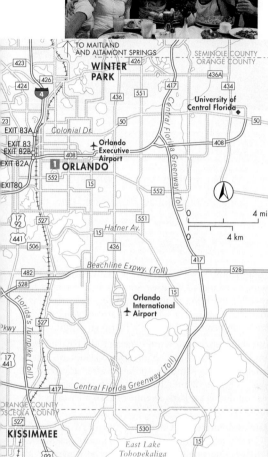

GETTING ORIENTED

Central Florida runs from Tampa/St. Petersburg in the west through Orlando to the coastal attractions of Daytona Beach and Cape Canaveral on the east coast. Orlando is more or less equidistant, about 90 minutes by car to the Gulf of Mexico. Walt Disney World is not, contrary to advertising, in Orlando, but lies about 25 miles southwest of the city.

9

2 Walt Disney World.
Walt Disney's original decree that his parks be ever-changing, along with some healthy competition from Universal Studios and SeaWorld, has kept the Disney Imagineers dreaming up new entertainment and installing higher-tech thrills and attractions.

3 Universal Orlando.
While Disney creates a fantasy world for those who love fairy tales, Universal Orlando is geared to older kids, adults, and anyone who enjoys pop culture. Movie and TV fans love this place. Two other parks—Islands of Adventure (IOA) and Wet 'n Wild—add to the fun.

4 SeaWorld and Discovery Cove. Less glitzy than Walt Disney World or Universal, SeaWorld and Discovery Cove are worth a visit for a low-key, relaxing, ocean-theme experience. If you want to get more keyed up, pay a call on SeaWorld's Aquatica water park.

Updated by
Rona Grindin,
Joseph Hayes,
Jennifer Green-
hill-Taylor, and
Jennie Hess

Most Orlando locals look at the theme parks as they would an unruly neighbor: it's big and loud, but it keeps a nice lawn. Central Florida's many theme parks can become overpowering for even the most enthusiastic visitor, and that's when an excursion into the "other" Orlando—the one the locals know and love—is in order.

There are ample opportunities for day trips. If the outdoors is your thing, you can swim or canoe at Wekiwa Springs State Park or one of the area's many other sparkling springs, where the water remains a refreshing 72°F no matter how hot the day. Alternatively, you can hike, horseback ride, canoe, and camp in the Ocala National Forest.

If museums are your thing, charming Winter Park has the Charles Hosmer Morse Museum of American Art with its huge collection of Tiffany glass, and the Cornell Fine Arts Museum on the oak-tree-covered Rollins College campus. While in Winter Park, you can indulge in some high-end shopping and dining on Park Avenue or take a leisurely boat tour of the lakefront homes.

Got kids to educate and entertain? Check out WonderWorks or the Orlando Science Center, where you can view live gators and turtles. Even more live gators (some as long as 14 feet) can be viewed or fed (or even eaten) at Gatorland, just south of Orlando.

Do the kids prefer rockets and astronauts? Don't miss a day trip to Kennedy Space Center, where you can tour a rocket forest, sit in a space capsule, or see a space shuttle up close.

Kissimmee is a 19th-century cattle town south of Orlando that proudly hangs on to its roots with a twice-yearly rodeo where real cowboys ride bulls and rope cattle. The town sits on Lake Tohopekaliga, a favorite spot for airboat rides or fishing trips.

EXPLORING

Updated by
Joseph Hayes

Orlando is a diverse town. The Downtown area, though small, is dynamic, thanks to an ever-changing skyline of high-rises, sports venues, museums, restaurants, nightspots, a history museum, and several annual cultural events—including film festivals and a world-renowned theater fest. Downtown also has a central green, Lake Eola Park, which offers a respite from otherwise frantic touring.

Neighborhoods such as Thornton Park (great for dining) and College Park (an outpost of great dining) are fun to wander. Not too far to the north, you can come in contact with natural Florida—its manatees, gators, and crystal clear waters in spring-fed lakes.

Closer to the theme-park action, International Drive, the hub of resort and conference hotels, offers big restaurants and even bigger outlet-mall bargains. Sand Lake Road, between the two, is Orlando's Restaurant Row, with plenty of exciting dining prospects.

GETTING HERE AND AROUND

Orlando is spread out. During rush hour, car traffic crawls along the often-crowded Interstate 4 (particularly now that the multibillion-dollar upgrade, expected to end in 2021, has begun), which runs to both coasts. If you're heading east, you can also take Route 528 (aka the Beachline), a toll road that heads directly for Cape Canaveral and points along the Space Coast; no such option leads west.

If you avoid rush-hour traffic, traveling to points of interest shouldn't take too much time out of your vacation. Winter Park is no more than 20 minutes from Downtown; International Drive and the theme parks are about 30 minutes away in heavier traffic. Orlando International Airport is only 9 miles south of Downtown, but it will take about 30 minutes via a circuitous network of highways (Interstate 4 west to Florida's Turnpike south to Route 528 east).

VISITOR INFORMATION

Contacts **Orlando Visitors Bureau** ✉ *8723 International Dr., Suite 101* ☎ *407/363–5872, 800/972–3304* ⊕ *www.visitorlando.com.*

9

CENTRAL ORLANDO

Fodor'sChoice
★

Harry P. Leu Gardens. A few miles outside of downtown—on the former lakefront estate of a citrus entrepreneur—is this 50-acre garden. Among the highlights are a collection of historical blooms (many varieties of which were established before 1900), ancient oaks, a 50-foot floral clock, and one of the largest camellia collections in eastern North America (in bloom November–March). Mary Jane's Rose Garden, named after Leu's wife, is filled with more than 1,000 bushes; it's the largest formal rose garden south of Atlanta. The simple 19th-century Leu House Museum, once the Leu family home, preserves the furnishings and appointments of a well-to-do, turn-of-the-20th-century Florida family. ✉ *1920 N. Forest Ave., Audubon Park* ☎ *407/246–2620* ⊕ *www.leugardens.org* 🎟 *$10, free 1st Mon. of month* ☺ *Garden daily 9–5; guided house tours daily on hr and ½ hr 10–3:30; closed Dec. 25.*

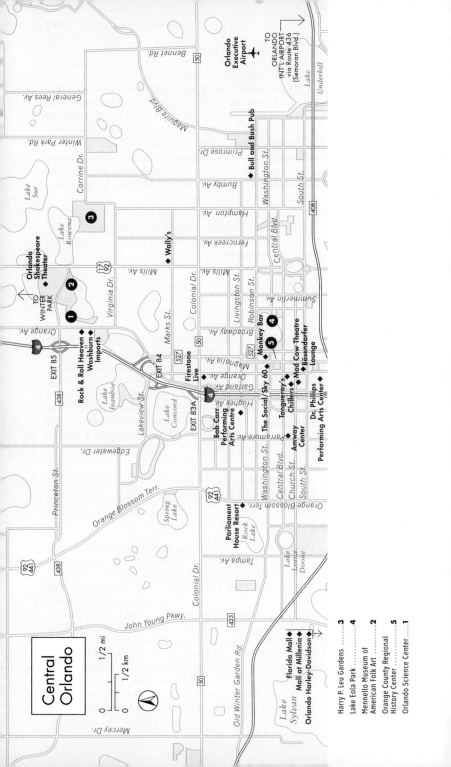

Central Orlando

0   1/2 mi

0   1/2 km

Harry P. Leu Gardens **3**
Lake Eola Park **4**
Mennello Museum of
American Folk Art **2**
Orange County Regional
History Center **5**
Orlando Science Center ...**1**

Florida Mall ◆
Mall at Millenia ◆
Orlando Harley-Davidson ◆

Parliament
House Resort ◆

Bob Carr
Performing
Arts Centre ◆

Firestone
Live ◆

Rock & Roll Heaven ◆
Washburn
Imports ◆

Orlando
Shakespeare
Theater ◆

Wally's ◆

Bull and Bush Pub ◆

The Social/Sky 60 ◆
Tanqueray's ◆
Chillers ◆
Amway
Center ◆
Dr. Phillips
Performing Arts Center ◆

Monkey Bar ◆
Mad Cow Theatre ◆
Bösendorfer
Lounge ◆

Orlando
Executive
Airport

TO
ORLANDO
INT'L AIRPORT
via Route 436
(Semoran Blvd.)

TO
WINTER
PARK

TO WINTER PARK

FAMILY **Lake Eola Park.** This beautifully landscaped 43-acre park is the verdant heart of downtown Orlando, its mile-long walking path a gathering place for families, health enthusiasts out for a run, and culture mavens exploring area offerings. The well-lighted playground is alive with children, and ducks, swans, and native Florida birds call the lake home. A popular and expanded farmers' market takes up residence on Sunday afternoon.

The lakeside Walt Disney Amphitheater is a dramatic site for concerts, ethnic festivals, and spectacular Fourth of July fireworks. Don't resist the park's biggest draw: a ride in a swan-shape pedal boat. Up to five adults can fit comfortably into each. (Children under 16 must be accompanied by an adult.)

The Relax Grill, by the swan-boat launch, is a great place for a snack. There are also several good restaurants in the upscale Thornton Park neighborhood along the park's eastern border. The ever-expanding skyline rings the lake with modern high-rises, making the peace of the park even more welcome. The landmark fountain features an LED light and music show on summer evenings at 9:30. ⊠ *195 N. Rosalind Ave., Downtown Orlando* ☎ *407/246–4485 park, 407/246–4485 swan boats* 🖅 *Swan boat rental $15 per ½ hr* ☯ *Park daily 6 am–midnight; swan boats Sun.–Tues. 10–7, Wed.–Sat. 10–10.*

Mennello Museum of American Folk Art. One of the few museums in the United States devoted to folk art has intimate galleries, some with lovely lakefront views. Look for the nation's most extensive permanent collection of Earl Cunningham paintings as well as works by many other self-taught artists. There's a wonderful video about Cunningham and his "curio shop" in St. Augustine, Florida. Temporary exhibitions have included the works of Wyeth, Cassatt, and Michael Eastman. At the museum shop you can purchase folk-art books, toys, and unusual gifts. The Mennello is the site of the annual Orlando Folk Festival, held the second weekend of February. ⊠ *900 E. Princeton St., Lake Ivanhoe* ☎ *407/246–4278* ⊕ *www.mennellomuseum.org* 🖅 *$5* ☯ *Tues.–Sat. 10:30–4:30, Sun. noon–4:30.*

FAMILY **Orange County Regional History Center.** Exhibits here take you on a journey back in time to discover how Florida's Paleo-Indians hunted and fished the land, what the Sunshine State was like when the Spaniards first arrived, and how life in Florida was different when citrus was king. Visit a cabin from the late 1800s, complete with Spanish moss–stuffed mattresses and mosquito netting over the beds. Seminole Indian displays include interactive activities, and the Tourism Before Disney exhibit previews Florida's destiny as a future vacation mecca. Traveling exhibits bring modern technology and art to the Museum. ⊠ *65 E. Central Blvd., Downtown Orlando* ☎ *407/836–8500, 800/965–2030* ⊕ *www. thehistorycenter.org* 🖅 *$15; seniors, students $13; 5–12 $12; under 4 free* ☯ *Mon.–Sat. 10–5, Sun. noon–5.*

FAMILY

Fodor's Choice

★

Orlando Science Center. With all the high-tech glitz and imagined worlds of the theme parks, is it worth visiting Orlando's reality-based science center? If you're a kid crazy about science, the answer is an overwhelming "yes." With exhibits about the human body, mechanics, computers,

9

The 300-seat Dr. Phillips CineDome, a movie theater with an eight-story screen at the Orlando Science Center, offers large-format iWERKS films.

math, nature, the solar system, and optics, the science center has something for every child's inner geek.

The four-story internal atrium is home to live gators and turtles and is a great spot for simply gazing at what Old Florida once looked like. The 300-seat Dr. Phillips CineDome, a movie theater with a giant eight-story screen, offers large-format iWERKS films and planetarium programs. The Crosby Observatory and Florida's largest publicly accessible refractor telescope are here, as are several smaller telescopes; some weekends you can safely view spots and flares on the sun's surface.

Adults like the science center, too, thanks to events like the annual Science of Wine and Cosmic Golf Challenge; evenings of stargazing in the Crosby Observatory, live music, art, and film; and Otronicon, the annual interactive technology expo. ⊠ *777 E. Princeton St., Lake Ivanhoe* ☎ *407/514–2000* ⊕ *www.osc.org* ✉ *$19; senior, student $17; 3–11 $13; under 2 free; parking $5; tickets include all permanent and special exhibits, films, live science presentations, and planetarium shows* ⊘ *Daily 10–5; closed Wed., Easter Sun., Thanksgiving Day, Christmas Eve, and Christmas Day.*

INTERNATIONAL DRIVE

FAMILY **Fun Spot America.** Four go-kart tracks offer a variety of driving experiences. Though drivers must be at least 10 years old and meet height requirements, parents can drive younger children in two-seater cars on several of the tracks, including the Conquest Track. Nineteen rides range from the dizzying Paratrooper to an old-fashioned Revolver Ferris

Wheel to the twirling toddler Teacups. Fun Spot recently expanded from five to 15 acres and now features Central Florida's only wooden roller coaster as well as the Freedom Flyer steel suspension family coaster, a kiddie coaster, and what's billed as the world's second-tallest (250 feet) SkyCoaster—part skydive, part hang-glide. The tallest, at 300 feet, is located at sister park Fun Spot USA, in Kissimmee. There's also an arcade. From Exit 75A, turn left onto International Drive, then left on Fun Spot Way. ✉ *5700 Fun Spot Way, I-Drive area* ☎ *407/363–3867* ⊕ *www.funspotattractions.com* ✉ *$39.95 for all rides (online discounts available) or pay per ride; admission for nonriders free; arcade extra; parking free* ☾ *Apr.–Oct., daily 10 am–midnight; Nov.–Mar., weekdays noon–11, weekends 10 am–midnight.*

Ripley's Believe It or Not! Odditorium. A 10-foot-square section of the Berlin Wall. A pain and torture chamber. Two African fertility statues that women swear have helped them conceive. These and almost 200 other oddities (shrunken heads included) speak for themselves in this museum-cum-attraction in the heart of tourist territory on International Drive. The building itself is designed to appear as if it's sliding into one of Florida's notorious sinkholes. Give yourself an hour or two to soak up the weirdness, but remember: this is a looking, not touching, experience; it might drive antsy youngsters—and their parents—crazy. ■ TIP→ Buy tickets online ahead of time, and you can get discounts. ✉ *8201 International Dr., I-Drive area* ☎ *407/351–5803* ⊕ *www. ripleysorlando.com* ✉ *$19.99; 4–12 $12.99; parking free* ☾ *Daily 9 am–midnight; last admission at 11 pm.*

FAMILY **WonderWorks.** The building seems to be sinking into the ground . . . at a precarious angle and upside down. Many people stop to take pictures in front of the topsy-turvy facade, complete with upended palm trees and broken skyward-facing sidewalks. Inside, the upside-down theme continues only as far as the lobby. After that, it's a playground of 100 interactive experiences—some incorporating virtual reality, others educational (similar to those at a science museum), and still others pure entertainment. You can experience an earthquake or a hurricane, land a space shuttle using simulator controls, make giant bubbles in the Bubble Lab, play laser tag in the enormous laser-tag arena and arcade, design and ride your own roller coaster, lie on a bed of real nails, and play baseball with a virtual Major League batter. ✉ *9067 International Dr., I-Drive area* ☎ *407/351–8800* ⊕ *www.wonderworksonline.com/ orlando* ✉ *$26.99; seniors, 4–12 $20.99; laser tag and Outta Control Magic Comedy Dinner Show extra (online discounts available); parking $3–$9* ☾ *Daily 9 am–midnight.*

9

KISSIMMEE

18 miles south of Orlando, 10 miles southeast of Walt Disney World (WDW).

Although Kissimmee is primarily known as the gateway to Disney (technically, the vast Disney property of theme parks and resorts lies in both Osceola and Orange counties), its non-WDW attractions just might tickle your fancy. They range from throwbacks to old-time Florida to

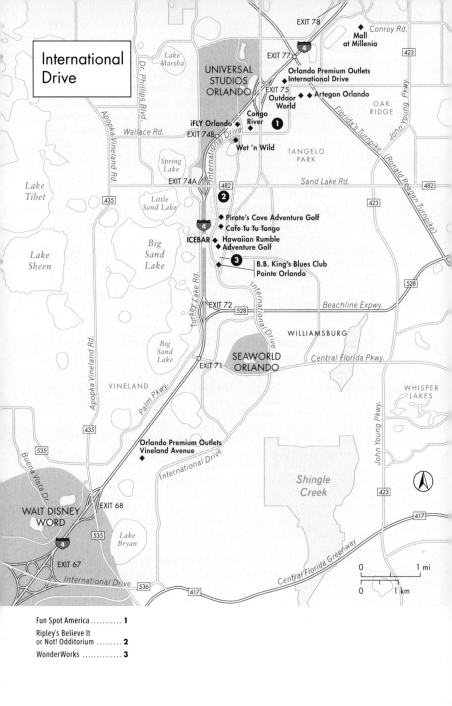

International Drive

EXIT 78

Conroy Rd.

Mall at Millenia

423

EXIT 77

Orlando Premium Outlets
International Drive

EXIT 75
Outdoor World

Artegon Orlando

OAK RIDGE

UNIVERSAL STUDIOS ORLANDO

Congo River

1

iFLY Orlando

EXIT 74B

Wet 'n Wild

TANGELO PARK

Sand Lake Rd.

482

482

423

EXIT 74A

Little Sand Lake

2

435

Pirate's Cove Adventure Golf

Cafe Tu Tu Tango

ICEBAR

Hawaiian Rumble

Adventure Golf

3

B.B. King's Blues Club

Pointe Orlando

Big Sand Lake

Lake Tibet

Lake Sheen

528

EXIT 72

528

Beachline Expwy.

WILLIAMSBURG

Big Sand Lake

EXIT 71

SEAWORLD ORLANDO

Central Florida Pkwy.

VINELAND

WHISPER LAKES

435

Orlando Premium Outlets
Vineland Avenue

International Drive

Shingle Creek

423

535

WALT DISNEY WORD

EXIT 68

417

Lake Bryan

535

4

EXIT 67

International Drive

536

417

Central Florida Greenway

0   1 mi

0   1 km

Dr. Phillips Blvd.

Lake Marsha

Apopka Vineland Rd.

Wallace Rd.

Spring Lake

International Drive

Florida's Turnpike (Ronald Reagan Turnpike)

John Young Pkwy.

Turkey Lake Rd.

Palm Pkwy.

Apopka Vineland Rd.

Buena Vista Dr.

John Young Pkwy.

dinner shows for you and 2,000 of your closest friends. Orlando used to be prime cattle country, and the best sampling of what life was like is here during the Silver Springs Rodeo in February and June.

With at least 100,000 acres of freshwater lakes, the Kissimmee area brings anglers and boaters to national fishing tournaments and speed-boat races. A 50-mile-long series of lakes, the Kissimmee Waterway, connects Lake Tohopekaliga—a Native American name that means "Sleeping Tiger"—with huge Lake Okeechobee in South Florida, and from there, to both the Atlantic Ocean and the Gulf of Mexico.

FAMILY **Gatorland.** This campy attraction near the Orlando–Kissimmee border on U.S. 441 has endured since 1949 without much change, despite competition from the major parks. Over the years, the theme park and registered conservancy has gone through some changes while retaining its gator-rasslin' spirit. Kids get a kick out of this unmanufactured, old-timey thrill ride.

The Gator Gulley Splash Park is complete with giant "egrets" spilling water from their beaks, dueling water guns mounted atop giant gators, and other water-park splash areas. There's also a small petting zoo and an aviary. A free train ride is a high point, taking you through an alligator breeding marsh and a natural swamp setting where you can spot gators, birds, and turtles. A three-story observation tower overlooks the breeding marsh, swamped with gator grunts, especially come sundown during mating season.

For a glimpse of 37 giant, rare, and deadly crocodiles, check out the Jungle Crocs of the World exhibit. To see eager gators leaping out of the water to catch their food, come on cool days for the Gator Jumparoo Show (summer heat just puts them to sleep). The most thrilling is the first one in the morning, when the gators are hungriest. There's also a Gator Wrestlin' Show, and although there's no doubt who's going to win the match, it's still fun to see the handlers take on those tough guys with the beady eyes. In the educational Upclose Encounters show, the show's host handles a variety of snakes. Recent park additions include Panther Springs, featuring brother-and-sister endangered panthers, and the Screamin' Gator Zip Line (additional cost). This is a real Florida experience, and you leave knowing the difference between a gator and a croc. ✉ *14501 S. Orange Blossom Trail, between Orlando and Kissimmee* ☎ *407/855–5496, 800/393–5297* ⊕ *www.gatorland. com* 🎟 *$26.99; 3–12 $18.99; discount coupons online* ⊙ *Daily 10–5.*

LEGOLAND

50 miles southwest of Orlando.

LEGOLAND Florida. The quiet town of Winter Haven is home to numerous lakes and a waterskiing school. From 1936 to 2009, it was also home to the Sunshine State's first theme park, Cypress Gardens. Today the spot holds the world's largest LEGOLAND, set on 150 acres and built using nearly 56 million LEGOs. In addition to its 1:20-scale miniature reproductions of U.S. cities, the park features more than 50 rides, shows, and attractions throughout 10 different zones, as well as

Kissimmee's Lake Tohopekaliga (affectionately known as Lake Toho) is famous with fishers the world over. It's also great for wildlife spotting—an especially exhilarating experience when done from an airboat.

the marvelous botanical gardens from the original park. Just opened mid-2013, the World of Chima presented by Cartoon Network invites guests into a fantastical world of animal tribal habitats anchored by an interactive water ride, the Quest for CHI. In Chima's new Speedorz Arena, participants compete to win a supply of the mystical CHI energy source. A 4-D movie and Chima-character meet and greets round out the experience.

The Danish toy company's philosophy is to help children "play well." And play they do, as LEGOLAND attractions are very hands-on. Kids can hoist themselves to the top of a tower, power a fire truck, or navigate a LEGO robot. Sights include huge LEGO dragons, wizards, knights, pirates, castles, roller coasters, racetracks, villages, and cities.

The cityscapes in Miniland USA fascinate children and adults, who delight in discovering what's possible when you have enough bricks. Miniland opens with Kennedy Space Center, where a 6-foot shuttle waits on the launch pad. Miami Beach features bikini-clad bathers and art deco hotels; St. Augustine and its ancient fort play into LEGO's pirate theme; Key West's Mallory Square is accurate right down to the trained cats leaping through rings of fire. The rest of the United States is not ignored: New York City, Las Vegas, San Francisco, and Washington, D.C., appear in intricate detail. Visitors spend hours looking for amusing details hidden in each city, like New York's purse snatcher.

Among other highlights are LEGO Kingdoms, whose castle towers over a jousting area and a roller coaster where knights, damsels, dragons, and ogres are found; Land of Adventure, where you can explore hidden tombs and hunt for treasure; and the Imagination Zone, showcasing

LEGO Mindstorms robots, where a giant head of Albert Einstein invites kids to explore and invent. Things get wild in LEGO Technic, the most active of the park's zones, where Test Track, Aquazone Wave Racers, and Technicycle let the family expend some energy. And Pirates' Cove provides a chance to sit in the shade and watch a full-size pirate battle, with actors wearing LEGO suits defending the huge ship from attacking pirates on water skis.

LEGOLAND Water Park features a wave pool; Build-a-Raft, where families construct a LEGO vessel and float down a lazy river; a 375-foot pair of intertwined waterslides that plunge riders into a pool; and a DUPLO toddler water play area. Not to be forgotten, Cypress Gardens, at the heart of the park, preserves one of Florida's treasures. Families can wander the lush, tropical foliage and gasp at one of the world's largest banyan trees.

The trip to Winter Haven is worth it. The rides, interactive games, gardens, water park, and other attractions will amuse and engage. Round-trip transportation from Orlando Premium Outlets, on Vineland Avenue, leaves at 9 and costs $5. ⊠ *One Legoland Way, Winter Haven* ☎ *877/350–5346* ⊕ *www.legoland.com* ✉ *$84; seniors, 3–12 $77; parking $14* ☉ *Hrs vary seasonally.*

BOK TOWER GARDENS

57 miles southwest of Orlando, 42 miles southwest of WDW.

Fodor'sChoice ★ **Bok Tower Gardens.** You'll see citrus groves as you ride south along U.S. 27 to the small town of Lake Wales and the Bok Tower Gardens. This appealing sanctuary of plants, flowers, trees, and wildlife has been something of a local secret for years. Shady paths meander through pine forests with silvery moats, mockingbirds and swans, blooming thickets, and hidden sundials. The majestic, 200-foot Bok Tower is constructed of coquina—from seashells—and pink, white, and gray marble. The tower houses a carillon with 60 bronze bells that ring out each day at 1 and 3 pm during 30-minute recitals that might include early-American folk songs, Appalachian tunes, Irish ballads, or Latin hymns. The bells are also featured in recordings every half hour after 10 am, and sometimes even moonlight recitals.

The landscape was designed in 1928 by Frederick Law Olmsted Jr., son of the planner of New York's Central Park. The grounds include the 20-room, Mediterranean-style Pinewood Estate, built in 1930 and open for self-guided touring. January through April, guides lead you on a 60-minute tour of the gardens (included in the admission price); tours of the inside of the tower are a benefit of membership ($100 and up).

Take Interstate 4 to Exit 55 and head south on U.S. 27 for about 23 miles. Proceed past Eagle Ridge Mall, then turn left after two traffic lights onto Mountain Lake Cut Off Road, and follow the signs. ⊠ *1151 Tower Blvd., Lake Wales* ☎ *863/676–1408* ⊕ *www.boktower. org* ✉ *$12–18; 5–12 $3–$8* ☉ *Daily 8–6.*

Wildlife-rich Wekiwa Springs State Park is a great place to camp, hike, picnic, canoe, fish, swim, or snorkel.

WEKIWA SPRINGS STATE PARK

13 miles northwest of Orlando, 28 miles north of WDW.

FAMILY

Fodor's Choice

★

Wekiwa Springs State Park. *Wekiva* is a Creek Indian word meaning "flowing water"; *wekiwa* means "spring of water." The river, springs, and surrounding 6,400-acre Wekiwa Springs State Park are well suited to camping, hiking, picnicking, swimming, canoeing, and fishing. The area is also full of Florida wildlife: otters, raccoons, alligators, bobcats, deer, turtles, and birds.

Canoe trips can range from a simple hour-long paddle around the lagoon to observe a colony of water turtles to a full-day excursion through the less congested parts of the river, which haven't changed much since the area was inhabited by the Timacuan Indians. You can rent canoes ($16.98 for two hours and $3 per hour after that) in the town of Apopka, near the park's southern entrance.

The park has 60 campsites: some are "canoe sites" that you can reach only via the river, and others are "trail sites," meaning you must hike a good bit of the park's 13½-mile trail to reach them. Most, however, are for the less hardy—you can drive right up to them. Sites go for $60 a night with electric and water hookups.

To get here, take Interstate 4 Exit 94 (Longwood) and turn left on Route 434. Go 1¼ miles to Wekiwa Springs Road; turn right and go 4½ miles to the entrance, on the right. ⊠ *1800 Wekiva Circle* ☎ *407/884–2008, 800/326–3521 campsites, 407/884–4311 canoe rentals* ⊕ *www.floridastateparks.org/wekiwasprings/default.cfm* ✉ *$2 per pedestrian or bicycle; $6 per vehicle* ☉ *Daily 8–dusk.*

WINTER PARK

6 miles northeast of Orlando, 20 miles northeast of WDW.

This peaceful, upscale community may be just outside the hustle and bustle of Orlando, but it feels like a different country. The town's name reflects its early role as a warm-weather haven for those escaping the frigid blasts of Northeast winters. From the late 1880s until the early 1930s, wealthy industrialists and their families would travel to Florida by rail on vacation, and many stayed, establishing grand homes and cultural institutions. The lovely, 8-square-mile village retains its charm with brick-paved streets, historic buildings, and well-maintained lakes and parkland. Even the town's bucolic 9-hole golf course is on the National Register of Historic Places.

On Park Avenue you can spend a few hours sightseeing, shopping, or both. The street is lined with small boutiques and fine restaurants and bookended by world-class museums: the Charles Hosmer Morse Museum of American Art, with the world's largest collection of artwork by Louis Comfort Tiffany, and the Cornell Fine Arts Museum, on the campus of Rollins College (the oldest college in Florida).

TOURS

Scenic Boat Tour. Head east from Park Avenue and, at the end of Morse Boulevard, you'll find the launching point for this tour, a Winter Park tradition since 1938. The one-hour cruise takes in 12 miles of waterways, including three lakes and narrow, oak- and cypress-shaded canals built in the 1800s as a transportation system for the logging industry. A well-schooled skipper shares stories about the moguls who built their mansions along the shore and points out wildlife and remnants of natural Florida still surrounding the expensive houses. Cash or check only is accepted. ⊠ *312 E. Morse Blvd.* ☎ *407/644–4056* ⊕ *www. scenicboattours.com* 🎫 *$12; 2–11 $6* ⊙ *Daily 10–4.*

EXPLORING

Fodor'sChoice **Charles Hosmer Morse Museum of American Art.** The world's most com-
★ prehensive collection of work by Louis Comfort Tiffany—including immense stained-glass windows, lamps, watercolors, and desk sets—is in this museum, which also contains American decorative art and paintings from the mid-19th to the early 20th centuries.

Among the draws is the 1,082-square-foot Tiffany Chapel, originally built for the 1893 World's Fair in Chicago. It took craftsmen 2½ years to painstakingly reassemble the chapel here. Many of the works were rescued from Tiffany's Long Island estate, Laurelton Hall, after a 1957 fire destroyed much of the property. The 12,000-square-foot Laurelton Hall wing, opened in 2011, allows for much more of the estate's collection to be displayed at one time. Exhibits in the wing include architectural and decorative elements from Laurelton's dining room, living room, and Fountain Court reception hall. There's also a re-creation of the striking Daffodil Terrace, so named for the glass daffodils that serve as the capitals for the terrace's marble columns. ⊠ *445 N. Park Ave.* ☎ *407/645–5311* ⊕ *www.morsemuseum.org* 🎫 *$5; free Nov.–Apr., Fri. 4–8* ⊙ *Tues.–Sat. 9:30–4, Sun. 1–4; Nov.–Apr., Fri. until 8.*

9

WHERE TO EAT

Updated by
Rona Gindin

You'll find burger-and-fries combos everywhere in Orlando, yet the ambitious chefs behind Orlando's theme-park and independent restaurants provide loads of better options—much better. Locally sourced foods, creative preparations, and clever international influences are all the rage here. Theme-park complexes have some of the best restaurants in town, although you may opt for a rental car to seek out the local treasures.

The signs of Orlando's dining progress is most evident in the last place one would look: Disney's fast-food outlets. Every eatery on Disney property offers a tempting vegetarian option, and kiddie meals come with healthful sides and drinks unless you specifically request otherwise. Chefs at Disney's table-service restaurants consult face-to-face with guests about food allergies.

Around town, locals flock to the Ravenous Pig, the Rusty Spoon, the Smiling Bison, and other gastropubs where the menu changes regularly; Luma on Park, a suave home of thoughtfully created cutting-edge meals; and any number of dining establishments competing to serve the very finest steak. Orlando's culinary blossoming began in 1995, when Disney's signature California Grill debuted, featuring farm-to-table cuisine and wonderful wines by the glass. Soon after, celebrity chefs started opening up shop. And in 2013, Disney completely revamped California Grill so it's a trendsetter once again.

Orlando's destination restaurants can be found in the theme parks, as well as in the outlying towns. Sand Lake Road is now known as Restaurant Row for its eclectic collection of worthwhile tables. Here you'll find fashionable outlets for sushi and seafood, Italian and chops, Hawaiian fusion and upscale Lebanese. Heading into the residential areas, the neighborhoods of Winter Park (actually its own city), Thornton Park, and College Park are prime locales for chow. Scattered throughout Central Florida, low-key ethnic restaurants specialize in the fare of Turkey, India, Peru, Thailand, Vietnam—you name it. Prices in these family-owned finds are usually delightfully low.

MAPS

Throughout the chapter, you'll see mapping symbols and coordinates (✚ 1:F2) after property names or reviews. Maps are within the chapter. The first number after the ✚ symbol indicates the map number. After that is the property's coordinate on the map grid.

MEAL PLANS

Disney Magic Your Way Plus Dining Plan allows you one table-service meal, one counter-service meal, and one snack per day of your trip at more than 100 theme-park and resort restaurants, provided you stay in a Disney hotel. You'll also receive a refillable drink mug for use at your hotel's fast fooderies. For more money, you can upgrade the plan to include more; to save, you can downgrade to a counter-service-only plan. Used wisely, a Disney dining plan is a steal, but be careful to buy only the number of meals you'll want to eat. Moderate eaters can end up turning away appetizers and desserts to which they're entitled. Plan ahead, and use "extra" meals to your advantage by swapping two table-service meals for a Disney dinner show, say, or an evening at a high-end restaurant like California Grill.

Universal Meal Deal offers one sit-down and one quick-service meal at participating walk-up eateries inside Universal Studios and Islands of Adventure, plus a snack and soft drink. Daily prices are $52 and $18 (both parks) and must be purchased with a resort stay. A quick-service-only arrangement, with one meal a day, is $20 and $13. All-you-can-drink soft drinks are $12 daily for all.

WHAT IT COSTS				
	$	$$	$$$	$$$$
AT DINNER	under $15	$15–$21	$22–$30	over $30

Prices are per person for a median main course, at dinner, excluding tip and tax of 6.5%.

RESERVATIONS

Reservations are strongly recommended throughout the theme parks. Indeed, make reservations for Disney restaurants and character meals at both Universal and Disney at least 90 (and up to 180) days out. And be sure to ask about the cancellation policy—at a handful of Disney restaurants, for instance, you may be charged penalties if you don't give 24 to 48 hours' notice.

For restaurant reservations within Walt Disney World, call ☎ *407/939–3463* (*WDW–DINE*) or book online at ⊕ *www.disneyworld.com/dining.* You can also get plenty of information on the website, including the meal periods served, price range, and specialties of all Disney eateries. Menus for all restaurants are posted online and tend to be up to date. For Universal Orlando reservations, call ☎ *407/224–9255* (theme parks and CityWalk) or ☎ *407/503–3463* (hotels). Learn about the complex's 50-plus restaurants at ⊕ *www.universalorlando.com/dining.*

In our reviews, reservations are mentioned only when they're essential or not accepted. Unless otherwise noted, the restaurants listed are open daily for lunch and dinner.

WALT DISNEY WORLD

MAGIC KINGDOM

$$$
BRASSERIE
Fodor'sChoice
★

✕**Be Our Guest.** Traverse a bridge flanked by gargoyles and gas lamps to reach the Beast's castle, home of this massive new restaurant with a *Beauty and the Beast* theme, French flair, and the Magic Kingdom's first and only wine and beer served at dinner. The 500-seat restaurant has three rooms: a gilded ballroom, whose ceiling sports cherubs with the faces of Imagineers' children; the tattered West Wing, with a slashed painting that changes from prince to beast during faux storms; and the Rose Gallery. Decor comprises French provincial furniture, suits of armor, and heavy drapes. Food, scratch-prepared on-site, includes pan-seared salmon, grilled steak, and maybe a pork rack with red wine au jus. The signature kids' soft drink comes in a light-up castle cup, and

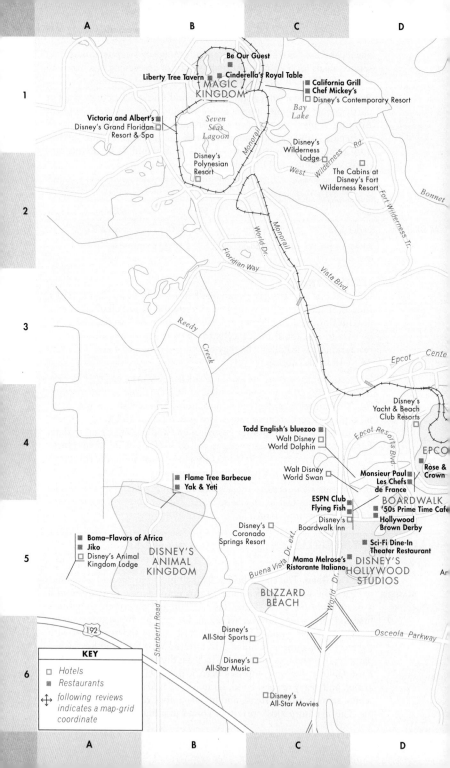

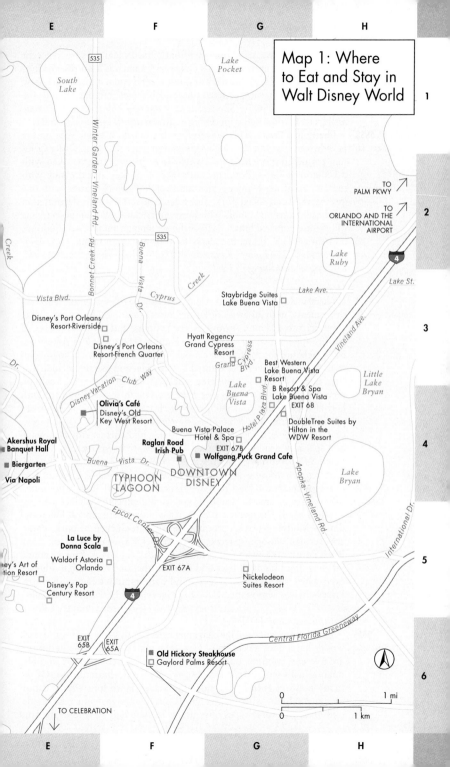

Map 1: Where to Eat and Stay in Walt Disney World

E   F   G   H

1

South
Lake

Lake
Pocket

535

TO
PALM PKWY

TO
ORLANDO AND THE
INTERNATIONAL
AIRPORT

2

535

Lake
Ruby

Lake St.

Winter Garden - Vineland Rd.

Creek

Bonnet Creek Rd.

Buena Vista Dr.

Cyprus   Creek

Vista Blvd.

Lake Ave.

Vineland Ave.

3

Staybridge Suites
Lake Buena Vista

Disney's Port Orleans
Resort-Riverside

Hyatt Regency
Grand Cypress
Resort

Grand Cypress Blvd.

Best Western
Lake Buena Vista
Resort

Little
Lake
Bryan

Disney's Port Orleans
Resort-French Quarter

Dr.

Disney Vacation Club Way

Lake
Buena
Vista

Hotel Plaza Blvd.

B Resort & Spa
Lake Buena Vista
EXIT 68

Olivia's Café
Disney's Old
Key West Resort

DoubleTree Suites by
Hilton in the
WDW Resort

4

Akershus Royal
Banquet Hall

Buena   Vista   Dr.

Buena Vista Palace
Hotel & Spa

Apopka - Vineland Rd.

Lake
Bryan

Biergarten

Raglan Road
Irish Pub

EXIT 67B

Via Napoli

TYPHOON
LAGOON

DOWNTOWN
DISNEY

Wolfgang Puck Grand Cafe

International Dr.

Epcot Center

5

La Luce by
Donna Scala

Waldorf Astoria
Orlando

EXIT 67A

Nickelodeon
Suites Resort

ney's Art of
tion Resort

Disney's Pop
Century Resort

4

Central Florida Greeneway

EXIT
65B

EXIT
65A

Old Hickory Steakhouse
Gaylord Palms Resort

6

0   1 mi

0   1 km

TO CELEBRATION

E   F   G   H

desserts, while sweet, are made without refined sugar. Be sure to accept a dollop of "the grey stuff—it's delicious." Lunch is a no-reservations fast-casual affair with the likes of quinoa salad and a braised pork stew with mashed potatoes, ordered on a touch screen and delivered to the table. $ *Average main: $26* ⊠ *Fantasyland* ☎ *407/939–3463* ⊕ *www. disneyworld.disney.go.com/dining* ⏦ *Reservations essential* ⊹ *1:B1.*

$$$$ ✕ **Liberty Tree Tavern.** This "tavern" is dry, but it's a prime spot on the
AMERICAN parade route, so you can catch a good meal while you wait. Order Colonial-period comfort food for lunch like hearty pot roast cooked with a Cabernet wine–and–mushroom sauce, or turkey and dressing with mashed potatoes. Dinner is the family-style Patriot's Platter, with turkey, carved beef, sliced pork, and sides. The restaurant is decorated in lovely Williamsburg colors with Early American–style antiques and lots of brightly polished brass. Each of the six dining rooms commemorates a historical U.S. figure, like Betsy Ross or Benjamin Franklin. $ *Average main: $32* ⊠ *Liberty Square* ☎ *407/939–3463* ⊕ *www.disneyworld. disney.go.com/dining* ⊹ *1:B1.*

EPCOT

$$$$ ✕ **Akershus Royal Banquet Hall.** This restaurant has character buffets at all
SCANDINAVIAN three meals, with an array of Disney princesses, including Ariel, Belle, Jasmine, Snow White, Aurora, Mary Poppins, and even an occasional cameo appearance by Cinderella. The breakfast menu is American, but lunch and dinner find an ever-changing assortment of Norwegian specialties. Appetizers are offered buffet style, and usually include herring, goat-milk cheese, peppered mackerel, and gravlax (cured salmon served with mustard sauce) or *fiskepudding* (a seafood mousse with herb dressing). For your main course, chosen à la carte, you might try traditional ground pork and beef *kjottkake* (dumplings), venison stew, or a grilled pork chop with Jarlsberg mac and cheese. Aquavit, wine, and specialty drinks are offered. All meals are fixed price. $ *Average main: $48* ⊠ *Norway Pavilion* ☎ *407/939–3463* ⊕ *www.disneyworld. disney.go.com/dining* ⏦ *Reservations essential* ⊹ *1:D4.*

$$$$ ✕ **Biergarten.** Oktoberfest runs 365 days a year here. The cheerful, some-
GERMAN times raucous, crowds are what you would expect in a place with an oompah band. The menu and level of frivolity are the same at lunch and dinner. Mountains of sauerbraten, bratwurst, chicken or pork schnitzel, German sausage, spaetzle, apple strudel, Bavarian cheesecake, and Black Forest cake await you at the all-you-can-eat buffet. Patrons pound pitchers of all kinds of beer and wine on the long communal tables— even when the yodelers, singers, and dancers aren't egging them on. Prices change seasonally. $ *Average main: $40* ⊠ *Germany Pavilion* ☎ *407/939–3463* ⊕ *www.disneyworld.disney.go.com/dining* ⏦ *Reservations essential* ⊹ *1:D4.*

$$$$ ✕ **Le Cellier Steakhouse.** This charming eatery with stone arches and dark
CANADIAN woods has a good selection of Canadian wine and beer. Menu options are à la carte and include the signature cheddar cheese soup and filet mignon with wild-mushroom risotto and truffle–butter sauce. Of the many nonbeef entrées, consider the seared lamb loin with mustard jus, and salmon with beluga lentils and bacon gastrique. As a side, add on any of three types of poutine. Desserts pay tribute to the land

up north with crème brûlée made with maple sugar. [$] *Average main: $40* ✉ *Canada Pavilion* ☎ *407/939–3463* 🌐 *www.disneyworld.disney.go.com/dining* ✣ *1:D4.*

$$$$ FRENCH Fodor's Choice ★ 🍴 **Monsieur Paul.** A mere staircase away from Epcot's busy World Showcase, Monsieur Paul is a subdued and sophisticated fine dinery. It's owned by Chef Jerome Bocuse and named for his world-famous father, the Culinary Institute of America's Chef of the Century, Paul Bocuse. The restaurant is expensive and sophisticated—in odd juxtaposition to the rumpled clothing and sneakers of most diners—and a delightful diversion from the theme park's bustle. The menu is overtly French while incorporating the best of America. For example, the signature fish dish, which has "scales" of potato, braised fennel, and rosemary sauce, is made with Florida red snapper instead of the original's red mullet. Escargot is presented in large ravioli and a parsley cream. The seared scallops and roasted duck breast are especially interesting entrées. A three-course prix-fixe menu is often available. Although the service isn't as polished as the menu, it is heartening to hear the waitstaff converse in French. [$] *Average main: $42* ✉ *France Pavilion* ☎ *407/939–3463* 🌐 *www.disneyworld.disney.go.com/dining* ⏲ *No lunch* ✣ *1:D4.*

$$$ BRITISH 🍴 **Rose & Crown Pub & Dining Room.** If you're an Anglophile and you love a beer so thick you could stand a spoon up in your mug, this is the place to soak up both the suds and British street culture. "Wenches" serve up traditional English fare—fish-and-chips, cottage or shepherd's pie (ground lamb with onions, carrots, and peas, topped with mashed potatoes and cheddar cheese), and, at times, the ever-popular bangers and mash (sausage over mashed potatoes). Scotch egg makes a good appetizer. Vegetarians can always find one item adapted for them, such as vegetable cottage pie. For dessert, try the sticky toffee pudding. The terrace has a splendid view of IllumiNations. [$] *Average main: $24* ✉ *United Kingdom Pavilion* ☎ *407/939–3463* 🌐 *www.disneyworld.disney.go.com/dining* ✣ *1:D4.*

$$$ PIZZA 🍴 **Via Napoli Ristorante e Pizzeria.** When the Patina Restaurant Group decided to open a second Italian eatery in Epcot (the first was Tutto Italia Ristorante), they opted to specialize in authentic Neapolitan wood-fired pizza, importing the mozzarella from Italy and using only San Marzano tomatoes. The result is crusty, thin pies topped with your choice of pepperoni; portobello and crimini mushrooms; or eggplant, artichokes, cotto ham, and mushrooms. The eggplant parmigiana is an outstanding alternative. [$] *Average main: $24* ✉ *Italy Pavilion* ☎ *407/939–3463* 🌐 *www.disneyworld.disney.go.com/dining* ✣ *1:D4.*

DISNEY'S HOLLYWOOD STUDIOS

$$ AMERICAN FAMILY 🍴 **50's Prime Time Café.** Who says you can't go home again? If you grew up in middle America in the 1950s, just step inside. While *I Love Lucy* and *The Donna Reed Show* clips play on a television screen, you can feast on meat loaf, pot roast, or fried chicken, all served on a Formica tabletop. At $17, the meat loaf is one of the best inexpensive, filling dinners in any local theme park. Enjoy it with a malted-milk shake or root-beer float (or a bottle of wine). The place offers some fancier dishes, like grilled salmon with maple bourbon butter sauce, which is a good choice for lightish eaters. If you're not feeling totally wholesome,

go for Dad's Electric Lemonade (rum, vodka, blue curaçao, sweet-and-sour mix, and Sprite), which is worth every bit of the $11.25 price tag. Just like Mother, the menu admonishes, "Keep your elbows off the table." $ *Average main: $18 ⊠ Echo Lake* ☎ *407/939–3463 ⊕ www.disneyworld.disney.go.com/dining* ✛ *1:C5.*

$$$$ ✕ **Hollywood Brown Derby.** At this reproduction of the famous 1940s
AMERICAN   Hollywood restaurant, the walls are lined with movie-star caricatures, just as in Tinseltown. The specialty is the Cobb salad, which by legend was invented by Brown Derby founder Robert Cobb; the salad consists of finely chopped lettuce enlivened by loads of tomato, bacon, turkey, blue cheese, chopped egg, and avocado, all tossed table-side. Other menu choices include grilled salmon with golden lentils, applewood-smoked bacon, and green onions topped with fennel and citrus salad, and herb-crusted grilled loin of lamb. Dining with an Imagineer is a special option; you will have lunch or dinner with one of Disney's creative engineers while enjoying a set-price four-course meal including soup, salad, entrée, and dessert. If you request the Fantasmic! dinner package, make a reservation for no later than two hours before the start of the show. $ *Average main: $31 ⊠ Hollywood Blvd.* ☎ *407/939–3463 ⊕ www.disneyworld.disney.go.com/dining* ✛ *1:C5.*

$$$ ✕ **Sci-Fi Dine-In Theater Restaurant.** If you don't mind zombies leering at
AMERICAN   you while you eat, then head to this enclosed faux drive-in, where you can sit in a fake candy-color '50s convertible and watch trailers from classics like *Attack of the Fifty-Foot Woman* and *Teenagers from Outer Space.* The menu includes choices like steak and garlic-mashed potatoes, an Angus or veggie burger, shrimp with whole-grain pasta, and a huge Reuben sandwich with fries or cucumber salad. End with a hot-fudge sundae. $ *Average main: $23 ⊠ Commissary La.* ☎ *407/939–3463 ⊕ www.disneyworld.disney.go.com/dining* ✛ *1:D5.*

DISNEY'S ANIMAL KINGDOM

$ ✕ **Flame Tree Barbecue.** This counter-service eatery is one of the rela-
FAST FOOD   tively undiscovered gems of Disney's culinary offerings. There's nothing fancy here, but you can dig into ribs and pulled pork sandwiches. For something with a lower calorie count, try the smoked turkey sandwich served with cranberry mayo or a great barbecued chicken served with baked beans and coleslaw. The outdoor tables, set beneath intricately carved wood pavilions, make great spots for a picnic, and they're not usually crowded. $ *Average main: $12 ⊠ Discovery Island ⊕ www.disneyworld.disney.go.com/dining* ⌦ *Reservations not accepted* ✛ *1:A4.*

$$$ ✕ **Yak & Yeti.** The location of this pan-Asian cuisine, sit-down eatery—
ASIAN   the only full-service restaurant inside Disney's Animal Kingdom—certainly makes sense. It's just at the entrance to the Asia section, in a two-story, 250-seat building that is pleasantly faux-Asian, with cracked plaster walls, wood carvings, and tile mosaic tabletops. Standout entrées include seared miso salmon, roasted duck with orange-wasabi glaze, and tempura shrimp with jasmine rice and chili-plum sauce. Also tasty, if not authentically Asian, are the baby back ribs with a hoisin barbecue sauce and sweet chili slaw. $ *Average main: $22 ⊠ Asia* ☎ *407/939–3463 ⊕ www.disneyworld.disney.go.com/dining* ✛ *1:A4.*

DOWNTOWN DISNEY/DISNEY SPRINGS

$$$
IRISH

✕ **Raglan Road Irish Pub.** An authentic Irish pub in Downtown Disney seems oxymoronic, particularly when that pub seats 600 people. But if Irish grub's your thing, Raglan's is the place to go. The shepherd's pie served here is of higher quality than the usual version, prepared with beef and lamb and jazzed up with house spices. And you don't have to settle for plain fish-and-chips (though you can for $19); there's also baked salmon with smoked salmon and maple glaze; shiitake risotto; and lamb shanks braised with rosemary jus. Massive and ornate bars, imported from Ireland and more than a century old, help anchor the pub. The entertainment alone makes this place worth the visit. The house bands play nightly, and a troupe of Irish dancers performs every evening and during Rollicking Raglan Sunday Brunch. Another band plays outside for guests dining alfresco. A store called Shop for Ireland sells Irish merchandise. $ *Average main: $23* ✉ *Downtown Disney, 1640 E. Buena Vista Dr.* ☎ *407/938–0300* ⊕ *www.raglanroadirishpub. com* ✛ *1:F4.*

$$$$
AMERICAN

✕ **Wolfgang Puck Grand Cafe.** There are lots of choices here, from wood-oven pizza at the informal Puck Express to fine-dining meals in the upstairs formal dining room. There's also a sushi bar and an informal café; the café is quite literally a happy medium, and may be the best bet for families hoping for a bit of elegance without the pressure of a formal dinner. At Express try the butternut squash soup or the Margherita pizza. At the café, midprice entrées like rosemary chicken and bacon-wrapped meat loaf are winners, and you can always have a personal pizza, such as barbecued chicken with smoked mozzarella. The dining room offers creative entrées like smoked pork chop with maple brown butter. $ *Average main: $32* ✉ *1482 E. Buena Vista Dr., West Side* ☎ *407/938–9653* ⊕ *www.wolfgangpuckcafeorlando.com* ✛ *1:F4.*

WDW RESORTS

$$$$
AFRICAN
Fodor'sChoice
★

✕ **Boma—Flavors of Africa.** Boma takes Western-style ingredients and prepares them with an African twist—then invites guests to walk through an African marketplace–style dining room to help themselves at the extraordinary buffet. The dozen or so serving stations have entrées such as roasted pork, Durban-style chicken, spice-crusted beef, and fish served with tamarind and other robust sauces; intriguing salads; and some of the best hummus this side of the Atlantic. Don't pass up the soups, as the coconut-curry seafood stew is excellent. The zebra dome dessert is chocolate mousse covered with white chocolate and striped with dark chocolate. All meals are prix fixe, and prices change seasonally. The South African wine list is outstanding. $ *Average main: $40* ✉ *Animal Kingdom Lodge, 2901 Osceola Pkwy.* ☎ *407/939–3463* ⊕ *www.disneyworld.disney.go.com/dining* ⌂ *Reservations essential* ☾ *No lunch* ✛ *1:A5.*

$$$$
AMERICAN
Fodor'sChoice
★

✕ **California Grill.** The view from the surrounding Disney parks from this 15th-floor restaurant—the World's signature dining establishment since 1995—is as stunning as the food, especially after dark, when you can watch the nightly Magic Kingdom fireworks. The space has stylish midcentury modern furnishings and chandeliers, while the exhibition kitchen is so well equipped that it has a cast-iron flat grill designed

9

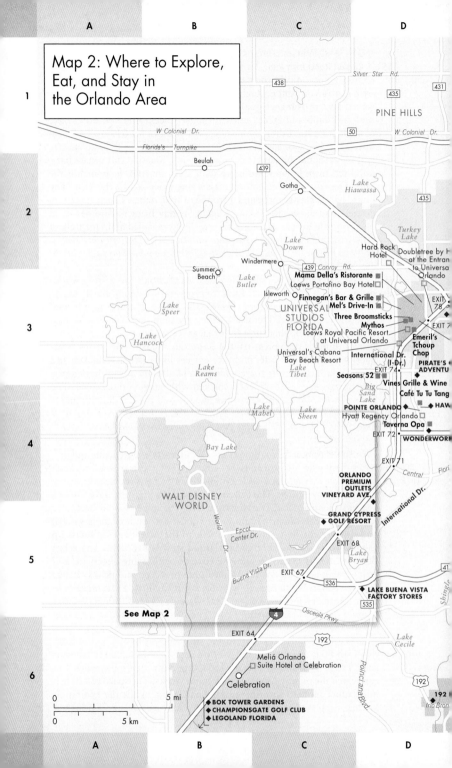

Map 2: Where to Explore, Eat, and Stay in the Orlando Area

A   B   C   D

1

438

Silver Star Rd.

435   431

PINE HILLS

W Colonial Dr.

50   W Colonial Dr.

Florida's Turnpike

Beulah

439

Gotha

Lake Hiawassa

435

2

Lake Down

Turkey Lake

Hard Rock Hotel

Doubletree by H at the Entran to Universa Orlando

Windermere

439   Conray Rd.

Mama Della's Ristorante

Summer Beach

Lake Butler

Loews Portofino Bay Hotel

Isleworth

Finnegan's Bar & Grille

Mel's Drive-In

EXIT 78

Lake Speer

UNIVERSAL STUDIOS FLORIDA

Three Broomsticks

Mythos

EXIT 7

3

Lake Hancock

Loews Royal Pacific Resort at Universal Orlando

Emeril's Tchoup Chop

Universal's Cabana Bay Beach Resort

International Dr. (I-Dr.)

PIRATE'S ADVENTU

Lake Reams

Lake Tibet

EXIT 74

Seasons 52

Big Sand Lake

Vines Grille & Wine

Café Tu Tu Tang

Lake Mabel

Lake Sheen

POINTE ORLANDO

HAW

Hyatt Regency Orlando

Taverna Opa

EXIT 72

WONDERWOR

4

Bay Lake

EXIT 71

Central   Flori

WALT DISNEY WORLD

World Dr.

ORLANDO PREMIUM OUTLETS VINEYARD AVE.

International Dr.

Epcot Center Dr.

GRAND CYPRESS GOLF RESORT

EXIT 68

Lake Bryan

5

Buena Vista Dr.

EXIT 67

536

41

LAKE BUENA VISTA FACTORY STORES

535

See Map 2

4

Osceola Pkwy.

Shingle

EXIT 64

Lake Cecile

192

6

Meliá Orlando Suite Hotel at Celebration

Celebration

Poinciana Blvd.

192

0   5 mi

192

0   5 km

BOK TOWER GARDENS

CHAMPIONSGATE GOLF CLUB

LEGOLAND FLORIDA

Irlo Bron

A   B   C   D

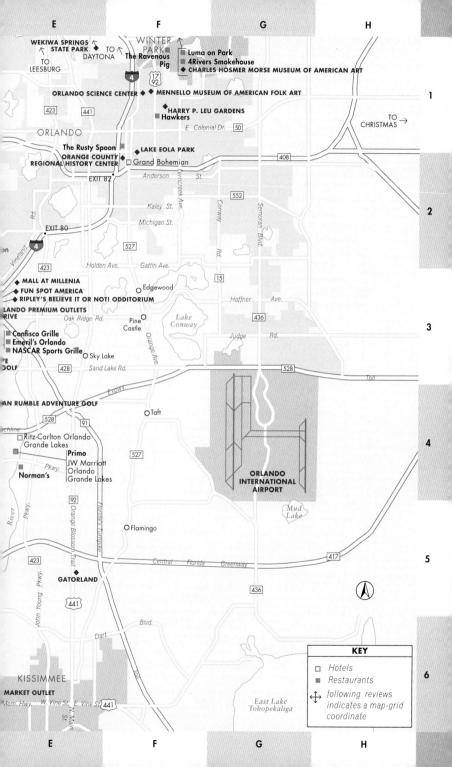

specifically for cooking fish. Expect locally sourced foods where possible, made-from-scratch items such as the house-made charcuterie sampler appetizer, and many items cooked in the wood-fired oven. Sushi is a highlight, alongside creative, globally inspired entrées. Specialties include oak-fired fillet of beef with heirloom tomato risotto, and scallops with piquillo pepper rouille. $ *Average main: $42* ⊠ *Contemporary Resort, 4600 N. World Dr.* ☎ *407/939–3463* ⊕ *www.disneyworld. disney.go.com/dining* ⚏ *Reservations essential* ⊙ *No lunch* ✛ *1:C1.*

$$$$ ✕ **Chef Mickey's.** This is the holy shrine for character meals, with Mickey,
AMERICAN   Minnie, or Goofy around for breakfast and dinner. Folks come here for entertainment and comfort food, not a quiet spot to read the *Orlando Sentinel*. The breakfast buffet includes "pixie-dusted" challah French toast, mountains of pancakes, and even a breakfast pizza. The dinner buffet doesn't disappoint with Thai-curry-chipotle barbecue chicken, roasted ham, and spice-rubbed beef sirloin. Finish off your meal at the all-you-can-eat dessert bar of sundaes. $ *Average main: $47* ⊠ *Contemporary Resort, 4600 N. World Dr.* ☎ *407/939–3463* ⊕ *www. disneyworld.disney.go.com/dining* ⊙ *No lunch* ✛ *1:C1.*

$$ ✕ **ESPN Club.** Not only can you watch sports on a big-screen TV here
AMERICAN   (the restaurant has about 100 monitors), but you can also periodically see ESPN programs being taped in the club itself and be part of the audience of sports-radio talk shows. Food ranges from a variety of half-pound burgers, made with Angus chuck (and one topped with Cajun crawfish salad), to Philly cheesesteaks and *char siu* sliders. If you want an appetizer, try the Pub Nachos, crispy corn tortilla chips piled high with barbecued pulled pork, spicy chili, shredded cheddar cheese, cheddar cheese sauce, sour cream, pico de gallo, and sliced jalapeños. This place is open quite late by Disney standards—until 1 am daily. Beware, the place can be pretty loud during any broadcast sports event, especially football games. $ *Average main: $17* ⊠ *BoardWalk Inn, 2101 Epcot Resorts Blvd.* ☎ *407/939–3463* ⊕ *www.disneyworld. disney.go.com/dining* ✛ *1:C4.*

$$$$ ✕ **Flying Fish.** One of Disney's best restaurants, Flying Fish is whimsi-
SEAFOOD   cally decorated with murals along the upper portion of the walls that
Fodor's Choice   pay tribute to Atlantic seaboard spots of the early 1900s. This is a place
★   where you put on your "resort casual" duds to "dine," as opposed to putting on your flip-flops and shorts to "chow down." The chefs take the food so seriously that the entire culinary team takes day trips to local farms to learn their foodstuffs' origins. Flying Fish's best dishes include potato-wrapped red snapper, which is so popular it has been on the menu for several years, and oak-grilled salmon. Groups of up to six can sit at the counter that directly faces the exhibition kitchen for a five-course wine-tasting menu. The restaurant serves breakfast during the busiest tourist seasons only. $ *Average main: $36* ⊠ *BoardWalk Inn, 2101 Epcot Resorts Blvd.* ☎ *407/939–2359* ⊕ *www.disneyworld. disney.go.com/dining* ⊙ *No lunch* ✛ *1:C4.*

$$$$ ✕ **Jiko.** The name of this restaurant means "the cooking place" in
AFRICAN   Swahili, and it is certainly that. The dining area surrounds two big,
Fodor's Choice   wood-burning ovens and a grill area where you can watch cooks in
★   North African–style caps working on your meal. The menu here is

more African-inspired than purely African, but it does include authentic flavors in appetizers like peri-peri chicken flatbread and wild boar tenderloin with mealie pap and chakalaka. Menu items often change, but entrées might include scallops with Senegal black-eyed pea salad, or spicy Botswana-style beef short ribs with cassava-potato puree. The restaurant offers dozens of wines by the glass, including a large selection of South African vintages. Ask about the Wednesday wine tastings. [$] *Average main: $40* ✉ *Animal Kingdom Lodge, 2901 Osceola Pkwy.* ☎ *407/939–3463* 🌐 *www.disneyworld.disney.go.com/dining* ✍ *Reservations essential* ⏲ *No lunch* ✣ *1:A5.*

$$$ AMERICAN 🍴 **Olivia's Café.** This is like a meal at Grandma's—provided she lives in Key West and likes to gussy up her grub with trendy twists. The menu ranges from a shrimp pasta with vegetables in a tomato broth to pork chops with smoked Gouda fondue and a side of multigrain rice and Broccolini. Desserts are indulgent, such as the banana-bread-pudding sundae with bananas Foster topping and vanilla ice cream. The outdoor seating, which overlooks a waterway, is a nice place to dine anytime the midsummer heat is not bearing down. [$] *Average main: $25* ✉ *Old Key West Resort, 1510 N. Cove Rd.* ☎ *407/939–3463* 🌐 *www.disneyworld.disney.go.com/dining* ✣ *1:E3.*

$$$$ SEAFOOD Fodor's Choice ★ 🍴 **Todd English's bluezoo.** Celebrity chef Todd English oversees this cutting-edge seafood eatery, a sleek, modern restaurant that resembles an underwater dining hall, with blue walls and carpeting, aluminum fish along the wall behind the bar, and bubblelike lighting fixtures. The menu is creative and pricey, with entrées like the 2-pound Maine "Cantonese lobster," fried and tossed in a sticky soy glaze, and the daily "dancing fish," cooked on an upright rotisserie with an apple-soy marinade. If you don't care for fish, you can opt for seasonal chicken or steak preparations. The children's menu is especially good. [$] *Average main: $44* ✉ *Walt Disney World Dolphin, 1500 Epcot Resorts Blvd.* ☎ *407/934–1111* 🌐 *www.thebluezoo.com* ⏲ *No lunch* ✣ *1:C4.*

$$$$ MODERN AMERICAN Fodor's Choice ★ 🍴 **Victoria & Albert's.** At this ultraposh award-winning Disney restaurant, a well-polished service team will anticipate your every need during a gourmet extravaganza. This is one of the plushest fine-dining experiences in Florida, with an ambience so sophisticated that children under 10 aren't on the guest list. The seven-course, prix-fixe menu changes daily, and you'd do well to supplement the $150 tab with a $65 wine pairing. Appetizer choices may include wild turbot with toasted capers and preserved lemon, and masago-crusted scallop with coconut-curry broth. Entrées may feature veal with chanterelles or Australian Kobe-style beef with oxtail ravioli. For most of the year, there are two seatings, at 5:45 and 9 pm. In July and August, however, there's generally just one seating at 6:30 pm. For a more luxe experience, reserve a table in the intimate Queen Victoria Room or at the Chef's Table, which have more courses (10 to 12) and a bigger bill ($250, wine pairing $105). [$] *Average main: $200* ✉ *Grand Floridian, 4401 Floridian Way* ☎ *407/939–3862* 🌐 *www.victoria-alberts.com* ✍ *Reservations essential* 👔 *Jacket required* ⏲ *No lunch* ✣ *1:A1.*

UNIVERSAL ORLANDO

UNIVERSAL STUDIOS

$$
IRISH

✕ **Finnegan's Bar & Grill.** In an Irish pub that would look just right in downtown New York during the Ellis Island era, Finnegan's offers classic Irish comfort food like shepherd's pie, corned beef and cabbage, bangers and mash (sausage and mashed potatoes), and fish-and-chips, plus Guinness on tap and a five-beer sampler. If shepherd's pie isn't your thing, opt instead for a steak, burger, entrée salad, or sandwich. Irish folk music, sometimes live, completes the theme. $ *Average main: $16* ✉ *New York* ☎ *407/363–8757* ⊕ *www.universalorlando.com* ✛ *2:D3.*

$
BRITISH

✕ **Leaky Cauldron.** British pub staples are fitting fare for Diagon Alley's restaurant, which complements those hearty meals with kooky-sounding beverages from the Harry Potter books like Tongue-Tying Lemon Squash, Otter's Fizzy Orange Juice, and Fishy Green Ale (it's minty, with blueberry-flavored filled boba). Order at the counter, then be seated; a microchip in your "candlestick" will tell servers where to bring the grub. The Ploughman's Platter, with its cheeses, Scotch eggs, and apple-beet salad is food enough for two average eaters. English sausages can be had in toad-in-the-hole, bangers and mash, or a sandwich with three-mustard mayo. The fish-and-chips has an excellent flaky crust; the cod is flown in daily. End with the indulgent sticky toffee pudding. $ *Average main: $14* ✉ *Diagon Alley* ☎ *407/224–9716* ⊕ *https://www. universalorlando.com* ⌾ *Reservations not accepted* ✛ *2:D3.*

$
AMERICAN

✕ **Mel's Drive-In.** At the corner of Hollywood and Vine is a flashy '50s eatery with a pink-and-white 1956 Ford Crown Victoria parked out in front. For burgers and fries, this is one of the best choices in the park, and it comes complete with a roving doo-wop group during peak seasons. You're on vacation, so go ahead and have that extra-thick shake or the decadent chili-cheese fries. Mel's is also a great place to meet up, in case you decide to go your separate ways in the park. $ *Average main: $11* ✉ *Hollywood* ☎ *407/363–8766* ⊕ *www.universalorlando. com* ⌾ *Reservations not accepted* ✛ *2:D3.*

ISLANDS OF ADVENTURE

$
AMERICAN

✕ **Confisco Grille.** You could walk right past this full-service restaurant without noticing it, but if you want a good meal and sit-down service, don't pass by too quickly. The menu is American with international influences. Entrées include pad thai, grilled or blackened fresh fish of the day with mashed potatoes and sautéed spinach in a lemon-butter-cilantro sauce, and penne puttanesca—the vodka-cream tomato sauce is enhanced with sausage, Kalamata olives, fried pepperoncini, and roasted garlic. Wash it all down with refreshing sangria, available by glass, pitcher, and half pitcher. $ *Average main: $13* ✉ *Port of Entry* ☎ *407/224–4404* ⊕ *www.universalorlando.com* ✛ *2:D3.*

$$
ECLECTIC

✕ **Mythos.** The name may be Greek, but the dishes are eclectic. The menu includes such mainstays as pad thai and pan-seared salmon with lemon-basil butter. The building itself—which looks like a giant rock formation from the outside and a huge cave (albeit one with plush upholstered seating) from the inside—is enough to grab your attention, but so do sandwiches like crab-cake sliders and roast beef panini with caramelized yellow onions, roasted red peppers, and pepperocini. Mythos also has a waterfront view of the big lagoon in the center of the theme park. Except during the busiest weeks, the restaurant is open only for lunch. *$ Average main: $15* ⊠ *The Lost Continent* ☎ *407/224–4533* ⊕ *www. universalorlando.com* ☾ *No dinner* ✛ *2:D3.*

$
BRITISH ✕ **Three Broomsticks.** Now Harry Potter fans can taste pumpkin juice (with hints of honey and vanilla) and butterbeer (sort of like bubbly butterscotch cream soda, or maybe shortbread cookies). They're on the menu along with barbecue and British foodstuffs at this Hogsmeade restaurant modeled after the fantasy books. Rickety staircases and gaslit chandeliers set the tone for the counter-service restaurant, where families gobble down ample portions of shepherd's pie, fish-and-chips, turkey legs, and Cornish pasty. In the adjacent Hog's Head pub, a faux hog's head sneers now and then. The breakfast menu has American and British staples. *$ Average main: $12* ⊠ *Wizarding World of Harry Potter* ☎ *407/224–4233* ⊕ *www.universalorlando.com* ☖ *Reservations not accepted* ✛ *2:D3.*

CITYWALK

$$$$
CAJUN
Fodor's Choice
★
✕ **Emeril's Orlando.** The popular eatery is a culinary shrine to Emeril Lagasse, the famous TV chef who occasionally makes an appearance. And although the modern interior of the restaurant with its 30-foot ceilings, blond woods, second-story wine loft, and lots of galvanized steel looks nothing like the French Quarter, the hardwood floors and linen tablecloths create an environment befitting the stellar nature of the cuisine. Entrées, which change frequently, may include andouille-crusted pan-roasted redfish with creole meunière sauce, apple cider–glazed pork "ham" chop with mascarpone grits, and mango barbecue swordfish with andouille-potato hash. Reservations are usually essential, but there's a chance of getting a walk-in seating if you show up for lunch (11:30 am) or early for dinner (5:30 pm). *$ Average main: $33* ⊠ *6000 Universal Blvd.* ☎ *407/224–2424* ⊕ *www.emerils.com* ☖ *Reservations essential* ✛ *2:D3.*

UNIVERSAL HOTELS

$$$
SOUTH PACIFIC
✕ **Emeril's Tchoup Chop.** The bold interior decor—with lots of bamboo, bright glazed tile, an exposition kitchen, and a long zero-edge pool with porcelain lily pads running the length of the dining room—is just as ambitious as the food at Emeril Lagasse's Pacific-influenced restaurant. Following the theme of the Royal Pacific Resort, Lagasse melds his signature bold flavors with Asian- and Polynesian-fusion tastes. A *robata* (charcoal) grill that heats to 1,000°F churns out appetizers and side dishes; try the pork belly. Entrées change regularly, but representative dishes include Hawaiian-style snapper with ginger, cilantro, and sesame soy sauce; and a grilled pork chop with apple cider ginger butter. Sushi varieties are offered. For dessert, get the Hawaiian-style *malasadas* doughnuts. They're served with three sauces in plastic bottles; you insert the tip into the donuts and squirt in the fillings yourself. *$ Average main: $29* ⊠ *Loews Royal Pacific Resort, 6300 Hollywood Way* ☎ *407/503–2467* ⊕ *www.emerils.com* ☖ *Reservations essential* ✛ *2:D3.*

9

$$$ ITALIAN 🍴 **Mama Della's Ristorante.** This playfully themed Italian restaurant happens to have excellent food. The premise is that you're eating at a home-turned-restaurant owned by an Italian woman. That woman, Mama Della, is played by an actress, whose warmth enhances the experience (as does the serenade by an accordionist, guitar player, and vocalist). The menu features Italian classics like chicken parmigiana and lasagna as well as more ambitious dishes like salmon with fennel sofrito and braised lamb with eggplant caponata. Outdoor seating on the patio provides a view of the hotel's nightly *Musica Della Notte* (Music of the Night) opera show. [$] *Average main: $30* ✉ *Loews Portofino Bay Hotel, 5601 Universal Blvd.* ☎ *407/503–3463* 🌐 *www.loewshotels.com* 🕒 *No lunch* ✥ *2:D3.*

ORLANDO METRO AREA

KISSIMMEE

$$$$ STEAKHOUSE 🍴 **Old Hickory Steakhouse.** This upscale steak house is designed to look like rustic cabins in the Everglades. Beyond the playful facade is a polished restaurant with a classic steak-house menu—cowboy rib eye, porterhouse, and center-cut fillet, supplemented by rack of lamb, veal porterhouse, and wild salmon, all priced for the hotel's convention-goers. The chef gets creative with appetizers like braised pork belly with black-eyed pea succotash, but most are standards such as onion soup, shrimp cocktail, and wedge salad. Artisanal cheese plates are on the menu, and desserts are interesting, such as fudge-dipped derby pie. [$] *Average main: $47* ✉ *Gaylord Palms Resort, 6000 W. Osceola Pkwy., I–4 Exit 65* ☎ *407/586–1600* 🌐 *www.gaylordpalms.com* 🕒 *No lunch* ✥ *1:F6.*

INTERNATIONAL DRIVE

$$$ ECLECTIC 🍴 **Café Tu Tu Tango.** The food here is served tapas-style—everything is appetizer size but plentiful, and relatively inexpensive. If you want a compendium of cuisines at one go, try the black-bean soup with cilantro sour cream, guava barbecue-glazed pork ribs, hazelnut-lemongrass fish, and spiced alligator bites. The wine list includes more than 35 wines from several countries, with all but a handful by the bottle and the glass, and 50-plus craft beers. The restaurant is designed to resemble an artist's loft; artists paint at easels while diners take a culinary trip around the world. Belly dancers, flamenco dancers, Bolivian dancers, and African drummers are among the entertainers who perform in the evening. Thanks to a patio, diners can also share their small plates alfresco. [$] *Average main: $23* ✉ *8625 International Dr.* ☎ *407/248–2222* 🌐 *www.cafetututango.com* ✥ *2:D4.*

$$$ GREEK 🍴 **Taverna Opa.** This high-energy Greek restaurant bills itself as offering "fun with a capital F—Not Just Dining, It's an Experience!" Here the ouzo flows like a mountain stream, the Greek (and global) music almost reaches the level of a rock concert, and the roaming belly dancers actively encourage diners to take part in the mass Zorba dancing, which often happens on the tops of dining tables. The only thing missing is the Greek restaurant tradition of throwing dinner plates, made up in part by the throwing of small paper napkins, which sometimes

reaches near-blizzard level. The food, by the way, is also excellent. Standouts include traditional staples like spanakopita, *saganaki* (the traditional flaming cheese appetizer), *avgolemono* (lemony chicken-rice soup), and perhaps the most famous Greek entrée, moussaka. Family-style meals for groups of four and up are available at $33 and $44 per person. The best dessert is the baklava. [$] *Average main: $27* ✉ *Pointe Orlando, 9101 International Dr.* ☎ *407/351–8660* 🌐 *www.opaorlando.com* ✣ *2:D4.*

SOUTH ORLANDO

$$$$ ECLECTIC Fodor's Choice ★

🍴 **Norman's.** Celebrity-chef Norman Van Aken brings impressive credentials to the restaurant that bears his name, as you might expect from the headline eatery in the Ritz-Carlton Orlando Grande Lakes. Van Aken's culinary roots go back to the Florida Keys, where he's credited with creating "Floribbean" cuisine, a blend that is part Key West and part Caribbean—although he now weaves in flavors from all continents. The Orlando operation is a formal, sleek restaurant with marble floors, starched tablecloths, servers in ties and vests, eight certified sommeliers, and a creative, if expensive, menu. In addition to exceptional ceviches and a signature appetizer called Down Island French toast made with Curacao-marinated foie gras, favorites include a Mongolian-marinated veal chop, pan-cooked Florida snapper with citrus butter, and pork Havana with "21st-century mole sauce." A six-course tasting menu is $99, $49 more with beverage pairings. Covered terrace seating is also available. [$] *Average main: $49* ✉ *Ritz-Carlton Orlando Grande Lakes, 4000 Central Florida Pkwy.* ☎ *407/393–4333* 🌐 *www.normans.com* ⏲ *No lunch* ✣ *2:E4.*

$$$$ ITALIAN Fodor's Choice ★

🍴 **Primo.** James Beard Award winner Melissa Kelly cloned her Italian-organic Maine restaurant in an upscale Orlando hotel and brought her farm-to-table sensibilities with her. Here the daily dinner menu pays tribute to Sicily's lighter foods, made with produce grown in the hotel garden. Homemade pasta is served with spicy lamb sausage or all-natural beef-pork Bolognese; if the butternut-squash ravioli with butter-poached Maine lobster is available, order it. Dry-aged prime New York strip steak is enhanced with Taleggio "tater tots" and pancetta-wrapped baby leeks. Fish plays prominently, such as a whole roasted sea bass with black salsify, petite kalettes, and pistachio salsa. Desserts are just as special, with the likes of warm Belgian chocolate *budino* (pudding) cake or hot zeppole tossed in cinnamon and sugar. [$] *Average main: $43* ✉ *JW Marriott Orlando Grande Lakes, 4040 Central Florida Pkwy.* ☎ *407/393–4444* 🌐 *www.primorestaurant.com* ⏲ *No lunch* ✣ *2:E4.*

LAKE BUENA VISTA

$$$ ITALIAN

🍴 **La Luce by Donna Scala.** Having made a name for herself at California's Bistro Don Giovanni, Donna Scala brought the same Italian cuisine with a Napa Valley farm-fresh flair to this upscale Hilton at the edge of Disney World. Scala has since passed, but the restaurant remains as she designed it. The walls are decorated with chalk art, which changes at least twice a year. Equal effort goes into the menu, where pastas are made fresh. Try the gnocchetti with wild porcini and sausage ragu, the grilled rib eye with gremolata butter, or a simple seared salmon fillet with a tomato-chive-butter sauce. $ *Average main: $30* ⊠ *Hilton Orlando Bonnet Creek, 14100 Bonnet Creek Resort La., Bonnet Creek* ☎ *407/597–3600* ⊕ *www.laluceorlando.com* ⊘ *No lunch* ✛ *1:E5.*

SAND LAKE ROAD

$$ ✕ **Seasons 52.** Parts of the menu change every week at this innovative

AMERICAN restaurant that serves different foods at different times of year, depending on what's in season. Meals here tend to be healthful yet hearty and very flavorful. The flatbreads starters are on nearly every table. For an entrée, you might have wood-roasted pork tenderloin with sweet potato mash plus French green beans tossed with a dot of bacon, or caramelized grilled sea scallops with butternut squash and leek risotto, broccolini, and lemon butter. An impressive wine list with dozens of selections by the glass complements the menu. For dessert, have mini-indulgence classics like pecan pie, rocky road, carrot cake, and key lime pie served in petite portions. Although the cuisine is haute, the prices are modest—not bad for a snazzy, urbane bistro and wine bar. It has live music nightly to boot. Another Seasons is located in Altamonte Springs. $ *Average main: $21* ⊠ *Plaza Venezia, 7700 Sand Lake Rd., I–4 Exit 75A* ☎ *407/354–5212* ⊕ *www.seasons52.com* ✛ *2:D3.*

$$$$ ✕ **Vines Grille & Wine Bar.** Live jazz and blues music fills the night at

STEAKHOUSE the bar section of this dramatically designed restaurant, but the food and drink in the snazzy main dining room are headliners in their own right. The kitchen bills itself as a steak house, but it really is far more than that. Entrées range from Prime steaks (alas, no longer dry-aged) to pan-seared Chilean sea bass with lobster risotto and basil *beurre blanc,* from a one-pound Wagyu burger with truffle fries to pork osso bucco. Be sure to start with the grilled octopus, which is simply prepared with red onions, capers, and roasted fennel. The wine list here is extensive, and the cocktails are serious business, too. The crowd tends to dress up, but jackets and ties are not required. $ *Average main: $62* ⊠ *The Fountains, 7533 W. Sand Lake Rd.* ☎ *407/351–1227* ⊕ *www. vinesgrille.com* ⊘ *No lunch* ✛ *2:D3.*

CENTRAL ORLANDO

$$ ✕ **Hawkers.** Hipsters, families, and business groups dine side by side at

ASIAN this popular restaurant, a laid-back spot that specializes in serving Asian

Fodor's Choice street food. Travel the continent with $3.50 to $8.50 appetizer-size

★ portions of scratch-made specialties from Malaysia, Singapore, Thailand, China, Japan, Korea, and Vietnam. Musts for adventurous diners include *roti canai,* a flaky bread with a chicken-curry dip; curry *laksa,* a noodle soup with exotic flavors; and stir-fried udon noodles. More timid eaters adore the marinated beef skewers with Malaysian satay sauce, peanut-y chilled sesame noodles, duck tacos, and any of the Americanized (but flavorful) lettuce wraps. $ *Average main: $16* ⊠ *1103 Mills Ave., Mills 50 District* ☎ *407/237–0606* ⊕ *www.facebook.com/ hawkersstreetfare* ✛ *2:F1.*

$$$$ ✕ **K Restaurant & Wine Bar.** A vibrant restaurant down the road from Col-

AMERICAN lege Park's restaurant hub, K is a hot spot for locals, serving upscale,

Fodor's Choice eclectic, American and Italian cuisine in an intimate setting. Besides

★ lunch and dinner, K hosts flip-flop-friendly wine tastings in the garden

or on the patio and popular wine dinners—generally four courses for $50. Menus change daily and feature appetizers such as fried green tomatoes with sweet corn and crab salad and grain mustard dressing, and country-fried chicken livers with caramelized onion marmalade. For entrées, check out the mushroom-dusted filet mignon with red wine sauce, the mac and cheese gussied up with lobster, or homemade sausage. [$] *Average main: $34* ✉ *1710 Edgewater Dr., College Park* ☎ *407/872–2332* 🌐 *www.kwinebar.com* 🕒 *Closed Sun. No lunch Sat.* ✥ *2:E2.*

$$$ SOUTHERN Fodor's Choice ★

🍴 **The Rusty Spoon.** Lovingly raised animals and locally grown produce are the menu foundation at this Downtown gastropub, an ideal spot for a business lunch or a pre–basketball game, -theater, or -concert dinner. The wood-and-brick dining room is a comfortable backdrop to hearty, seasonal American meals with Italian and Southern elements. Creatively stuffed eggs and buttermilk-soaked Vidalia onion rings are top starters. The salads—with ultrafresh greens—are always sensational. All pastas are made from scratch, whether a "remodeled" ravioli with roasted organic Seminole pumpkin, radicchio, and cremini mushrooms, or hand-cut wide noodles with a beef tenderloin/pork ragu with chili oil. The Dirty South seafood stew is a signature take on bouillabaisse. End with a very grown-up version of s'mores. [$] *Average main: $22* ✉ *55 W. Church St., Downtown Orlando* ☎ *407/401–8811* 🌐 *www.therustyspoon.com* 🕒 *No lunch weekends.* ✥ *2:F1.*

WINTER PARK

$ BARBECUE Fodor's Choice ★

🍴 **4 Rivers Smokehouse.** Obsessed with Texas-style barbecue brisket, John Rivers decided to turn his passion into a business upon retiring from the corporate world. The result is the über-popular 4 Rivers, which turns out barbecue standards like pulled pork and cornbread, plus more unusual items like the addicting bacon-wrapped smoked jalapeño peppers, the Six Shooter with cheese grits, and a sausage-filled pastry called *kolache*. Old-time soft drinks such as Frostie Root Beer and Cheerwine are for sale, along with desserts like the kiddie favorite Chocolate Awesomeness, an indulgent layering of chocolate cake, chocolate pudding, Heath Bar, whipped cream, and chocolate and caramel sauces. Some units have a Sweet Shop that sells whole oversize cakes. Additional 4 Rivers are scattered throughout Central Florida. [$] *Average main: $13* ✉ *1600 W. Fairbanks Ave.* ☎ *855/368–7748* 🌐 *www.4rsmokehouse.com* ✍ *Reservations not accepted* 🕒 *Closed Sun.* ✥ *2:F1.*

$$$ MODERN AMERICAN Fodor's Choice ★

🍴 **Luma on Park.** Indisputably one of the Orlando area's best restaurants, Luma on Park is a popular spot for progressive American cuisine served in a fashionable setting. Every ingredient is carefully sourced from local producers when possible, and scratch preparation—from pastas to sausages to pickled rhubarb—is the mantra among its dedicated clique of chefs. The menu changes daily. You might discover chestnut agnolotti with Maine lobster or a cauliflower-onion tart as starters, followed by tilefish with tangerine-fennel broth or duck breast with kale, toasted pine nuts, parsnip puree, and pickled white asparagus. The wine cellar is a high point, holding 7,000 bottles—80 varieties, all available by the half glass, glass, and bottle. The restaurant offers a three-course, prix-fixe dinner Sunday through Tuesday for $35 per person, $45 with wine pairings. $ *Average main: $30* ⊠ *290 S. Park Ave.* ☎ *407/599–4111* ⊕ *www.lumaonpark.com* ⊗ *No lunch Mon.–Thurs.* ✛ *2:F1.*

$$$$
MODERN
AMERICAN
Fodor's Choice
★

✕ **The Ravenous Pig.** A trendy, vibrant gastropub in one of Orlando's most affluent enclaves, the Pig is arguably Orlando's most popular foodie destination. Run by husband-and-wife chefs James and Julie Petrakis, the restaurant dispenses delicacies such as pork porterhouse with mustard glaze and pear relish, and speckle trout with romesco sauce. The menu changes daily and always includes less expensive pub fare like rock shrimp tacos and homemade pretzels with a taleggio-porter fondue. All charcuterie is made in house, from spiced orange salami to game-bird terrine. The signature dessert is the Pig Tails, essentially a basket full of piping hot, pig tail–shaped doughnuts with a chocolate-espresso dipping sauce. $ *Average main: $31* ⊠ *1234 N. Orange Ave.* ☎ *407/628–2333* ⊕ *www.theravenouspig.com* ⌦ *Reservations essential* ⊗ *Closed Sun. and Mon.* ✛ *2:F1.*

WHERE TO STAY

Updated
by Jennifer
Greenhill-Taylor

With tens of thousands of lodging choices available in the Orlando area, from tents to deluxe villas, there is no lack of variety in price or amenities. In fact, narrowing down the possibilities is part of the fun.

More than 50 million visitors come to the Orlando area each year, making it the most popular tourism destination on the planet. More upscale hotels are opening as visitors demand more luxurious surroundings, such as luxe linens, tasteful and refined decor, organic toiletries, or ergonomic chairs and work desks. But no matter what your budget or desires, lodging comes in such a wide range of prices, themes, color schemes, brands, meal plans, and guest-room amenities, you will have no problem finding something that fits.

Resorts on and off Disney property combine function with fantasy, as befits visitor expectations. Characters in costume perform for the kids, pools are pirates' caves with waterfalls, and some, like the Gaylord Palms, go so far as to re-create Florida landmarks under a gargantuan glass roof, giving visitors the illusion of having visited more of the state than they expected.

International Drive's expanding attractions, including The Orlando Eye, Madame Tussauds, and a widening array of eateries are drawing more savvy conventioneers who bring their families along for the fun.

Many hotels have joined the trend toward green lodging, bringing recycling, water conservation, and other environmentally conscious practices to the table. Best of all, the sheer number and variety of hotel rooms means you can still find relative bargains throughout the Orlando area, even on Disney property, by researching your trip well, calling the lodgings directly, negotiating packages and prices, and shopping wisely.

RESERVATIONS

Always book your lodging months in advance in Orlando, regardless of where you stay.

Walt Disney Travel Co. Packages can be arranged through the Walt Disney Travel Co. Guests can find planning tools on the website that allow them to customize vacation itineraries based on interests as well as age, height restrictions, and medical needs. ☎ *407/939–5277* ⊕ *www. disneyworld.com.*

WDW Central Reservations Office. You can book many accommodations—Disney-owned hotels and some non-Disney-owned hotels—through the WDW Central Reservations Office. The website allows you to compare prices at the various on-site resorts. ☎ *407/934–7639* ⊕ *www. disneyworld.com.*

WDW Special Request Reservations. People with disabilities can call the regular WDW reservations number, as the representatives are all knowledgeable about services available at resorts and parks for guests with disabilities. All representatives have TTY ability. The website is also a valuable source for specific needs. Go to Guest Services and search the word "Disabilities." ☎ *407/394–5277 Reservations, 407/939–7838 Parks* ⊕ *www.disneyworld.com.*

WHAT IT COSTS				
	$	$$	$$$	$$$$
FOR TWO PEOPLE	under $175	$175–$249	$250–$350	over $350

ABOUT OUR REVIEWS

Prices: Prices in the hotel reviews are the lowest cost of a standard double room in high season, excluding taxes, service charges, resort fees, and meal plans (except at all-inclusives). Prices for rentals are the lowest per-night cost for a one-bedroom unit in high season. Note that taxes in Central Florida can be as high as 12.5%.

Maps: *Throughout the chapter, you'll see mapping symbols and coordinates (✛ 1:F2) after property names or reviews. Maps are within the chapter. The first number after the ✛ symbol indicates the map number. After that is the property's coordinate on the map grid.*

Hotel reviews have been shortened. For full information, visit Fodors. com.

WALT DISNEY WORLD

Disney-operated hotels are fantasies unto themselves. Each is designed according to a theme (quaint New England, the relaxed culture of the Polynesian Islands, an African safari village, and so on), and each offers the same perks: free transportation from the airport and to the parks, the option to charge all of your purchases to your room, special guest-only park-visiting times, and much more. If you stay on-site, you'll have better access to the parks and be more immersed in the Disney experience.

ON-SITE NON-DISNEY HOTELS

Although not operated by the Disney organization, the Swan and the Dolphin, just outside Epcot; Shades of Green, near the Magic Kingdom; and the hotels along Hotel Plaza Boulevard near Downtown Disney call themselves "official" Walt Disney World hotels. Whereas the Swan, Dolphin, and Shades of Green have the special privileges of on-site Disney hotels, such as free transportation to and from the parks and early park entry, the Downtown Disney resorts may use Disney transportation, but don't have all the same perks.

MAGIC KINGDOM RESORT AREA

$$$$
RESORT
Disney's Contemporary Resort. You're paying for location at this sleek, modern, luxury resort next to the Magic Kingdom, as the monorail runs right through the lobby, making park hopping a breeze, and offering quick respite for families seeking relief from the midday heat. **Pros:** monorail access; Chef Mickey's, the epicenter of character-meal world; health and wellness suites. **Cons:** a mix of conventioneers and vacationers means it can be too frenzied for the former and too staid for the latter. $ *Rooms from: $571* ✉ *4600 N. World Dr.* ☎ *407/824–1000* ⊕ *www.disneyworld.com* ✈ *1,013 rooms, 25 suites* ⏹ *No meals* ✛ *1:C1.*

$$$$
RESORT
Fodor's Choice
★
Disney's Grand Floridian Resort & Spa. On the shores of the Seven Seas Lagoon, so close to the Magic Kingdom that you can see the colors change on the Cinderella Castle, this red-roofed Victorian emulates the style of the great railroad resorts of the past with beautifully appointed rooms, rambling verandas, delicate, white-painted woodwork, and brick chimneys. **Pros:** old-Florida ambience; on the monorail route; Victoria & Albert's offers an evening-long experience in dining; if you're a couple with no kids, this is definitely the most romantic on-property hotel; right next to Disney's Wedding Pavilion. **Cons:** pricey; convention clientele and vacationing couples may be more comfortable than families with young children. $ *Rooms from: $655* ✉ *4401 Floridian Way* ☎ *407/824–3000* ⊕ *www.disneyworld.com* ✈ *867 rooms, 90 suites* ⏹ *No meals* ✛ *1:B1.*

$$$$
RESORT
Disney's Polynesian Village Resort. This South Pacific–themed resort with its tropical backdrop of orchids, ferns, and palms, lies directly across the lagoon from the Magic Kingdom, on the monorail and water taxi routes, and has lots of kids activities, making it a good family choice. **Pros:** kids activities; on the monorail; great atmosphere; free Wi-Fi. **Cons:** pricey; lots of loud children. $ *Rooms from: $493* ✉ *1600 Seven Seas Dr.* ☎ *407/824–2000* ⊕ *www.disneyworld.disney.go.com/resorts* ✈ *844 rooms, 366 suites, 20 bungalows* ⏹ *No meals* ✛ *1:B2.*

$$$$
RESORT
Disney's Wilderness Lodge. The architects outdid themselves in designing this seven-story hotel modeled after majestic turn-of-the-20th-century lodges in the American Northwest, with a cavernous lobby, supported by towering tree trunks, an 82-foot-high fireplace made of rocks from the Grand Canyon, two 55-foot-tall hand-carved totem poles that pay homage to the region's Native American culture, all lighted by enormous tepee-shaped chandeliers. **Pros:** impressive architecture; boarding point for romantic cruises or free water taxi to Magic Kingdom; elegant dining options; children's activity center, free Wi-Fi. **Cons:** no direct bus to Magic Kingdom, no monorail. $ *Rooms from: $431* ✉ *901 Timberline Dr.* ☎ *407/824–3200* ⊕ *www.disneyworld.disney.go.com/resorts* ✈ *727 rooms, 31 suites* ⏹ *No meals* ✛ *1:B2.*

WHERE SHOULD WE STAY?

	VIBE	PROS	CONS
Disney	Thousands of rooms at every price; convenient to Disney parks; free transportation all over WDW complex.	Perks like early park entry, MyMagic+ and Magical Express, which lets you circumvent airport bag checks.	Without a rental car, you likely won't leave Disney. On-site buses, although free, can take a big bite out of your entertainment day; convenience comes at a price.
Universal	On-site hotels offer luxury, convenience, and value. There are less expensive options just outside the gates.	Central to Disney, Universal, SeaWorld, malls, and I–4; free water taxis to parks from on-site hotels.	Most on-site hotels are pricey; the Cabana Bay Beach Resort, however, is reasonable; expect heavy rush-hour traffic during drives to and from other parks.
I-Drive	A hotel, convention center, and activities bonanza. A trolley runs from one end to the other.	Outlet malls provide bargains; world-class restaurants; the Orlando Eye lifts visitors up for a bird's-eye view; many hotels offer free park shuttles.	Transportation can be pricey, in cash and in time, as traffic is often heavy. Crime is up, especially after dark, although area hotels and businesses have increased security.
Kissimmee	It offers mom-and-pop motels and upscale choices, restaurants, and places to buy saltwater taffy.	It's just outside Disney, very close to Magic Kingdom. Lots of Old Florida charm and low prices.	Some of the older motels here are a little seedy. Petty crime in which tourists are victims is rare—but not unheard of.
Lake Buena Vista	Many hotel and restaurant chains here. Adjacent to WDW, which is where almost every guest in your hotel is headed.	Really close to WDW; plenty of dining and shopping options; easy access to I–4.	Heavy peak-hour traffic. As in all neighborhoods near Disney, a gallon of gas will cost 10%–15% more than elsewhere.
Central Orlando	Parts of town have the modern high-rises you'd expect. Other areas have oak tree–lined brick streets winding among small, cypress-ringed lakes.	Locally owned restaurants, trendy hotels, vibrant nightlife, and some quaint B&Bs. City buses serve the parks. There's good access to I–4.	You'll need to rent a car. And you will be part of the traffic headed to WDW. Expect the 25-mile drive to take at least 45 minutes.
Orlando International Airport	Mostly business and flight-crew hotels and car-rental outlets.	Great if you have an early flight or just want to shop in a mall. There's even a Hyatt on-site.	Watching planes, buses, taxis, and cars arrive and depart is all the entertainment you'll get.

EPCOT RESORT AREA

$$ **Disney's Art of Animation Resort.** This brightly colored, three-story
RESORT   resort is a kid's version of paradise: each of its four wings features
FAMILY   images from *Finding Nemo*, *Cars*, *The Lion King*, or *The Little Mermaid*, and in-room linens and carpeting match the wing's theme. **Pros:**

direct transportation to airport; free parking; images that kids adore; free Wi-Fi. **Cons:** can be crowded; standard rooms fill up fast. $ *Rooms from: $197* ✉ *1850 Animation Way* ☎ *407/938–7000* ⊕ *www. disneyworld.disney.go.com/resorts* ↝ *1,984 rooms, 1,120 suites* ⓘ *No meals* ✚ *1:E5.*

$$$$
RESORT

⌂ **Disney's Yacht Club and Beach Club Resorts.** These big Crescent Lake inns next door to Epcot seem straight out of a Cape Cod summer, with their nautical decor, waterfront locale, airy, light-filled rooms, rocking-chair porches, and family-friendly water-based activities. **Pros:** location, location, location—it's easy to walk or hop a ferry to Epcot, the BoardWalk, or Hollywood Studios; free Wi-Fi. **Cons:** distances within the hotel—like from your room to the front desk—can seem vast; remote from other parks. $ *Rooms from: $560* ✉ *1700 Epcot Resorts Blvd.* ☎ *407/934–8000 Beach Club, 407/934–7000 Yacht Club* ⊕ *www.disneyworld.disney.go.com/resorts* ↝ *1,213 rooms, 112 suites* ⓘ *No meals* ✚ *1:D4.*

$$$$
RESORT

⌂ **Four Seasons Orlando at Walt Disney World Resort.** The award-winning Four Seasons presides majestically over Disney's exclusive Golden Oak community, and its amenities and dedication to service are clear from the moment you step into the marble, flower-bedecked lobby and head for your room, which offers the option of separate quarters for nannies and/or grannies, and twice-daily housekeeping service. **Pros:** free Wi-Fi; free transportation to Disney parks; lots of on-site kids' entertainment; no resort fee. **Cons:** Pricey, but then, it is the Four Seasons; long way from Universal or SeaWorld. $ *Rooms from: $479* ✉ *10100 Dream Tree Blvd.* ☎ *407/313–7777* ⊕ *www.fourseasons.com/orlando* ↝ *443* ⓘ *No meals* ✚ *1:E2.*

$$$
RESORT

⌂ **Walt Disney World Dolphin.** A pair of 56-foot-tall sea creatures book-ends this 25-story glass pyramid, a luxe resort designed, like the adjoining Swan, by world-renowned architect Michael Graves, and close enough to the parks that you can escape the midday heat for a dip in the pool. **Pros:** character meals available; access to all facilities at the Swan; free boat to BoardWalk, Epcot and Hollywood Studios, buses to other parks; excellent on-site restaurants; MyMagic+ benefits available. **Cons:** daily self-parking fee; a daily resort fee; no charging to room key at parks. $ *Rooms from: $335* ✉ *1500 Epcot Resorts Blvd.* ☎ *407/934–4000, 800/227–1500* ⊕ *www.swandolphin.com* ↝ *1,509 rooms, 114 suites* ⓘ *No meals* ✚ *1:C4.*

$$$
RESORT

⌂ **Walt Disney World Swan.** With Epcot and Hollywood Studios close by, guests here can hit the parks in the morning, return for a swim or nap on a hot afternoon, and go back to the parks refreshed and ready to play until the fireworks. **Pros:** easy walk to BoardWalk; free boats to BoardWalk, Epcot, and Hollywood Studios; good on-site restaurants; MyMagic+ available. **Cons:** long bus ride to Magic Kingdom; daily resort and parking fee. $ *Rooms from: $315* ✉ *1200 Epcot Resorts Blvd.* ☎ *407/934–3000, 800/325–3535* ⊕ *www.swandolphin.com* ↝ *758 rooms, 55 suites* ⓘ *No meals* ✚ *1:C4.*

DISNEY AND UNIVERSAL RESORT PERKS

DISNEY PERKS

Extra Magic Hours. You get special early and late-night admission to certain Disney parks on specified days. Call ahead for details so you can plan your early- and late-visit strategies.

Free Parking. Parking is free for Disney hotel guests at Disney hotel and theme-park lots.

Magical Express. If you're staying at a select Disney hotel, this free airport service means you don't need to rent a car or think about finding a shuttle or taxi or worry about baggage handling.

At your hometown airport, you check your bags in and won't see them again till you get to your Disney hotel. At Orlando International Airport you're met by a Disney rep, who leads you to a coach that takes you to your hotel. Your luggage is delivered separately and usually arrives in your room an hour or two after you do. If your flight arrives before 5 am or after 10 pm, you will have to pick up your luggage and deliver it to the coach.

On departure, the process works in reverse (though only on some participating airlines, so check in advance). You get your boarding pass and check your bags at the hotel. At the airport you go directly to your gate, skipping check-in. You won't see your bags until you're in your hometown airport. Participating airlines include American, Delta, JetBlue, Southwest, and United.

Charging Privileges. You can charge most meals and purchases throughout Disney to your hotel room, using your MyMagic+ bands or cards.

Package Delivery. Anything you purchase at Disney—at a park, a hotel, or in Downtown Disney—can be delivered to the gift shop of your Disney hotel for free.

Priority Reservations. Disney hotel guests get priority reservations at Disney restaurants and choice tee times at Disney golf courses up to 30 days in advance, using MyMagic+.

Guaranteed Entry. Disney theme parks sometimes reach capacity, but on-site guests can enter even when others would be turned away.

UNIVERSAL PERKS

Head-of-the-Line Access. Your hotel key (except Cabana Bay) lets you go directly to the head of the line for most Universal Orlando attractions. Unlike Disney's FastPass+ program, you don't need to use this at a specific time; it's always good. Hotel guests also get early admission to the often-crowded Harry Potter attractions.

Priority Seating. Many of Universal's restaurants offer priority seating to those staying at on-site hotels.

Charging Privileges. You can charge most meals and purchases throughout Universal to your hotel room.

Delivery Services. If you buy something in the theme parks, you can have it sent directly to your room, so you don't have to carry it around.

Free Loaners. Some on-site hotels have a "Did You Forget?" closet that offers everything from kids' strollers to dog leashes to computer accessories. There's no fee for using this service.

9

ANIMAL KINGDOM RESORT AREA

$

RESORT

FAMILY

Fodor's Choice

★

Disney's All-Star Sports Resort. Stay here if you want the All-American, sports-mad, quintessential Disney-with-your-kids experience, or if you're a couple to whom all that pitter-pattering of little feet is a reasonable tradeoff for a good deal on a room. **Pros:** unbeatable price for a Disney property; free Wi-Fi. **Cons:** no kids clubs or programs, because this is among the least expensive Disney resorts; distances between rooms and on-site amenities can seem vast; farthest resort from Magic Kingdom means you'll spend time on the bus. $ *Rooms from: $170* ✉ *1701 W. Buena Vista Dr.* ☎ *407/939–5000 Sports* ⊕ *www.disneyworld.disney. go.com/resorts* ⇥ *1,920 rooms* ⦿ *No meals* ✛ *1:B6.*

$$$$

RESORT

FAMILY

Fodor's Choice

★

Disney's Animal Kingdom Lodge. Giraffes, zebras, and other wildlife roam three 11-acre savannas separated by the encircling arms of this grand hotel, designed to resemble a *kraal,* or animal enclosure, in Africa. **Pros:** extraordinary wildlife and cultural experiences; excellent on-site restaurants: Jiko, Boma, and Sanaa; breakfast buffet in Boma is a bargain. **Cons:** shuttle to parks other than Animal Kingdom can take more than an hour; guided savanna tours available only to guests on the concierge level, where the least expensive room is $100 a night higher than the least expensive rooms in other parts of the hotel. $ *Rooms from: $467* ✉ *2901 Osceola Pkwy.* ☎ *407/938–3000* ⊕ *www. disneyworld.disney.go.com/resorts* ⇥ *972 rooms, 499 suites and villas* ⦿ *No meals* ✛ *1:A5.*

$$$

RESORT

Fodor's Choice

★

Disney's Coronado Springs Resort. Popular with convention-goers who need huge meeting spaces, and with families who appreciate its casual Southwestern architecture; lively, Mexican-style food court; and elaborate swimming pool, colorful Coronado Springs Resort also offers a moderate price. **Pros:** great pool with a play-area arcade for kids and a bar for adults; lots of outdoor activities, free Wi-Fi. **Cons:** some accommodations are a long trek from the restaurants; standard rooms are on the small side; as in many Disney lakefront properties, the lake is for looking at and boating on, not for swimming in. $ *Rooms from: $251* ✉ *1000 W. Buena Vista Dr.* ☎ *407/939–1000* ⊕ *www.disneyworld. disney.go.com/resorts* ⇥ *1,917 rooms* ⦿ *No meals* ✛ *1:C5.*

DOWNTOWN DISNEY RESORT AREA

$

RESORT

B Resort & Spa Lake Buena Vista. The white and blue tower of the B Resort on Hotel Plaza Boulevard, formerly the Royal Plaza, is the most recent addition to the cluster of hotels just outside Disney Springs, and a stay there combines an excellent location with a reasonable price. **Pros:** walk to Disney Springs; kids' activities; park shuttles. **Cons:** resort fee; parking fee; need a car to get to Universal or Downtown Orlando. $ *Rooms from: $152* ✉ *1905 Hotel Plaza Blvd.* ☎ *407/828–2828* ⊕ *www.bhotelsandresorts.com/b-walt-disney-world/* ⇥ *394 rooms, 12 suites* ⦿ *No meals* ✛ *1:G4.*

$

RESORT

Fodor's Choice

★

Best Western Lake Buena Vista Resort. Only a few minutes' walk from Disney Springs' growing number of shops and restaurants, this towering resort with its airy lobby offers luxury linens, flat-screen TVs, and, in many rooms, a bird's-eye view of the fireworks, all for a bargain price. **Pros:** a quick walk to shopping and restaurants; free transportation to parks, discount shops. **Cons:** inconvenient to Universal and Downtown

Orlando; transportation to the parks can eat up time. $ *Rooms from: $119* ✉ *2000 Hotel Plaza Blvd.* ☎ *407/828–2424, 800/348–3765* ⊕ *www.lakebuenavistaresorthotel.com* ⇥ *325 rooms; 8 suites* ⦿ *No meals* ✛ *1:G3.*

$ 📶 **Buena Vista Palace Hotel & Spa.** This towering hotel, just yards from
RESORT Disney Springs, caters to business and leisure guests and gets kudos as much for its on-site amenities as for its location. **Pros:** easy walk to Disney Springs; good restaurants and bars on-site; kids' activities; pool is heated; spa is large and luxurious. **Cons:** inconvenient to Universal and Downtown Orlando; daily resort fee for Wi-Fi and fitness center. $ *Rooms from: $164* ✉ *1900 E. Buena Vista Dr.* ☎ *407/827–2727* ⊕ *www.buenavistapalace.com* ⇥ *1,014 rooms* ⦿ *No meals* ✛ *1:G4.*

$$ 📶 **Disney's Port Orleans Resort–French Quarter.** Ornate, Big Easy–style row
HOTEL houses with wrought-iron balconies cluster around magnolia- and oak-shaded squares in this relatively quiet resort, which appeals to couples more than families. **Pros:** authentic—or as authentic as Disney can make it—fun, New Orleans–style; moderate price; lots of water recreation options, including boat rentals; free Wi-Fi. **Cons:** even though there are fewer kids here, public areas can still be quite noisy; shuttle service is slow; food court is the only on-site dining option. $ *Rooms from: $246* ✉ *1251 Riverside Dr.* ☎ *407/934–5000* ⊕ *www.disneyworld.disney. go.com/resorts* ⇥ *1,008 rooms* ⦿ *No meals* ✛ *1:E3.*

$$ 📶 **DoubleTree Suites by Hilton in the WDW Resort.** Price and location make
HOTEL this all-suites, Hilton-owned hotel a good choice for families and business travelers, as there are amenities for both, and it's a quick, free bus ride to any of the Disney parks. **Pros:** family and business traveler amenities; restaurants on-site; adult pool and splash pad for kids, adults; free shuttle to Disney attractions; quick access to I-4. **Cons:** of the properties on Hotel Plaza Boulevard, this is the farthest away from Downtown Disney; inconvenient to Universal and Downtown Orlando; daily fee for parking, Wi-Fi. $ *Rooms from: $199* ✉ *2305 Hotel Plaza Blvd.* ☎ *407/934–1000, 800/222–8733* ⊕ *www.doubletreeguestsuites. com* ⇥ *229 units* ⦿ *No meals* ✛ *1:G3.*

UNIVERSAL ORLANDO AREA

Universal Orlando's on-site hotels were built in a little luxury enclave that has everything you need, so you never have to leave Universal property. In minutes, you can walk from any hotel to CityWalk, Universal's dining and entertainment district, or take a ferry that cruises the adjacent artificial river.

The newest Universal lodging, Cabana Bay Beach Resort, with 900 family suites and 900 standard rooms, is so close to Islands of Adventure, you may see the spires of Hogwarts Castle from your room. This more affordable, motor court–style resort is designed to evoke 20th-century driving vacations with a hip, retro look.

A burgeoning hotel district across Kirkman Road and down to Sand Lake Road offers convenient accommodations and some even less expensive rates. Although these off-property hotels don't have the perks of the on-site places, you'll probably be smiling when you see your hotel bill.

$ ⛆ **Drury Inn & Suites Orlando.** This reasonably priced, centrally located
HOTEL   hotel is really shaking up the competition in Orlando with free Wi-Fi,
Fodor's Choice   free parking, free hot breakfast, free long-distance and local phone
★   calls, and free hot food and cold beverages in the late afternoon. **Pros:**
free everything; central location; reasonable price. **Cons:** if Disney is
your destination, this might be a little far afield. $ *Rooms from: $129*
✉ *7301 W. Sand Lake Rd., at I–4* ☎ *407/354–1101* ⊕ *www.druryhotels.
com* ⤢ *238* ⑩ *Some meals* ✛ *2:D3.*

$$$$ ⛆ **Hard Rock Hotel.** Music rules in this mission-style building, from the
HOTEL   darkly amusing *Hotel California* quote above the entrance, "You can
check out any time you like. **Pros:** shuttle, water taxi, or short walk
to Universal Parks and CityWalk; preferential treatment at Universal
rides; charge privileges extend to the other on-property Universal hotels.
Cons: rooms and meals are pricey; resort fee for parking, gym, and in-
room Wi-Fi; loud rock music in public areas, even the pool, but that's
why you're here, right? $ *Rooms from: $464* ✉ *5800 Universal Blvd.*
☎ *407/503–7625, 800/232–7827* ⊕ *www.hardrockhotelorlando.com*
⤢ *650 rooms, 29 suites* ⑩ *No meals* ✛ *2:D3.*

$$$$ ⛆ **Loews Portofino Bay Hotel at Universal Orlando.** The charm and romance
HOTEL   of Portofino, Italy—destination of Europe's rich and famous—are con-
Fodor's Choice   jured up at this lovely luxury resort, where part of the fun is exploring
★   the waterfront "village" from end to end and not knowing what you'll
find around a corner or down some steps. **Pros:** Italian villa atmosphere;
large spa; restaurants on-site; short walk or ferry ride to CityWalk,
Universal; guests skip lines at Universal rides; kids' activities; shuttles
to SeaWorld. **Cons:** rooms and meals are pricey; daily fee for parking. $ *Rooms from: $479* ✉ *5601 Universal Blvd.* ☎ *407/503–1000,
800/232–7827* ⊕ *www.loewshotels.com/Portofino-Bay-Hotel* ⤢ *750
rooms, 49 suites* ⑩ *Breakfast* ✛ *2:D3.*

$$$$ ⛆ **Loews Royal Pacific Resort at Universal Orlando.** The entrance—a broad,
RESORT   covered footbridge high above a tropical stream—sets the tone for the
Fodor's Choice   Pacific Rim theme of this hotel, which lies amid 53 acres of lush shrubs,
★   soaring bamboo, orchids, and palms. **Pros:** preferential treatment and
early admission to Universal; character dining; shuttle to CityWalk
and parks; free Wi-Fi; serene, Zen-garden vibe. **Cons:** rooms can feel
smallish; fees for parking. $ *Rooms from: $404* ✉ *6300 Hollywood
Way* ☎ *407/503–3000, 800/232–7827* ⊕ *www.universalorlando.com*
⤢ *1,000 rooms, 51 suites* ⑩ *No meals* ✛ *2:D3.*

$$ ⛆ **Universal's Cabana Bay Beach Resort.** Universal's Cabana Bay Beach
RESORT   Resort takes guests back in time to a 1950s Florida beach town with
FAMILY   a modern, ironic twist, and offers families a less expensive option to
Fodor's Choice   staying on-site at Universal. **Pros:** early and easy access to Universal
★   parks; food court on property; two swimming pools. **Cons:** parking fee;
access to Disney or Downtown Orlando requires a car or taxi journey
via busy I–4. $ *Rooms from: $199* ✉ *6550 Adventure Way* ☎ *407/503–
4000* ⊕ *www.loewshotels.com/Cabana-Bay* ⤢ *1,800 rooms, 900 suites*
⑩ *No meals* ✛ *2:C2.*

ORLANDO METRO AREA

KISSIMMEE, CELEBRATION, AND POINTS SOUTH

$$ RESORT **Gaylord Palms Resort and Convention Center.** Built in the style of a grand turn-of-the-20th-century Florida resort, this huge building is meant to inspire awe: inside its enormous atrium, covered by a 4-acre glass roof, are re-creations of Florida destination icons such as the Everglades, Key West, and old St. Augustine. **Pros:** you could have a great vacation without ever leaving the grounds; free shuttle to Disney. **Cons:** daily resort and parking fee; rooms can be pricey; not much within walking distance (although the hotel is so big that you can take quite a hike inside the building); shuttles to Universal and SeaWorld are available for a fee. [$] *Rooms from: $249* ✉ *6000 W. Osceola Pkwy., I–4 Exit 65, Kissimmee* ☎ *407/586–0000* 🌐 *www.gaylordpalms.com* 🛏 *1,406 rooms, 86 suites* 🍴 *No meals* ⊕ *1:F6.*

$$ HOTEL **Meliá Orlando Suite Hotel at Celebration.** Much like a European boutique hotel in style, the Meliá Orlando is very human in scale, minimalist in decor, and is only minutes from Disney. **Pros:** shuttle to Celebration, Disney parks, Universal, and SeaWorld; golf privileges at Celebration Golf; spa privileges at Celebration Day Spa. **Cons:** busy U.S. 192 is close by; daily resort fee; need a car to go anywhere besides Celebration and the parks. [$] *Rooms from: $199* ✉ *225 Celebration Pl., Celebration* ☎ *866/404–6662, 407/964–7000* 🌐 *www.solmelia.com* 🛏 *240 suites* 🍴 *Breakfast* ⊕ *2:B6.*

INTERNATIONAL DRIVE

$$$ RESORT **Hyatt Regency Orlando.** This deluxe high-rise conference hotel, formerly the Peabody, offers anything a full-service resort customer could want, with richly appointed rooms, two pools with cabanas, a full-service spa and fitness center the size of your local Y, two large restaurants, and a 360-seat, glass-walled lounge overlooking the pool. **Pros:** good spa; close to shops and more restaurants, on I-Drive Trolley route. **Cons:** check-in can take a while if a convention is arriving; long walk from end to end; daily resort and parking fees. [$] *Rooms from: $299* ✉ *9801 International Dr.* ☎ *407/284–1234* 🌐 *www.orlando.regency.hyatt.com* 🛏 *1,639 rooms, 192 suites, 5 penthouse suites* 🍴 *No meals* ⊕ *2:D4.*

SOUTH ORLANDO

$$$ RESORT **JW Marriott Orlando Grande Lakes.** This lush resort, set in 500 acres of natural beauty, certainly caters to a convention clientele, but leisure-seekers and families are given equal attention: a European-style spa, a Greg Norman–designed golf course, and a lazy river–style pool complex offer plenty of family fun. **Pros:** pool is great for kids and adults; shares amenities with the Ritz, including huge spa; golf course; free shuttle to SeaWorld and Universal. **Cons:** daily resort fees for parking and in-room Wi-Fi; the resort is huge and spread out; need a car to reach Disney or shopping. [$] *Rooms from: $319* ✉ *4040 Central Florida Pkwy.* ☎ *407/206–2300, 800/576–5750* 🌐 *www.grandelakes.com* 🛏 *1,000 rooms, 64 suites* 🍴 *Multiple meal plans* ⊕ *2:E4.*

9

$$$$ RESORT Fodor's Choice ★ **Ritz-Carlton Orlando, Grande Lakes.** Orlando's only Ritz-Carlton is a particularly extravagant link in the luxury chain, which shares a lush 500-acre campus with the JW Marriott, and offers exemplary service that extends from the porte-cochere entrance to the 18-hole golf course, restaurants, children's programs, and 40-room spa. **Pros:** truly luxurious; impeccable service; great spa; golf course; award-winning restaurants; transportation to theme parks. **Cons:** pricey; remote from theme parks, attractions; lots of convention and meeting traffic; resort fee. [$] *Rooms from: $579* ✉ *4012 Central Florida Pkwy.* ☎ *407/206–2400, 800/576–5760* 🌐 *www.ritzcarlton.com* 🛏 *582 rooms, 63 suites* 🍴 *Multiple meal plans* ✣ *2:E4.*

LAKE BUENA VISTA

$$ RESORT Fodor's Choice ★ **Hyatt Regency Grand Cypress Resort.** Sitting amid 1,500 palm-filled acres just outside Disney's back gate, this huge luxury resort hotel has a private lake with watercraft, three golf courses, and miles of trails for strolling, bicycling, jogging, and horseback riding. **Pros:** Marilyn Monroe spa, huge pool; lots of recreation options, for kids and adults, including nearby equestrian center; free Wi-Fi. **Cons:** need a car or taxi to get to Downtown Orlando or Universal; steep resort fee. [$] *Rooms from: $249* ✉ *1 Grand Cypress Blvd.* ☎ *407/239–1234, 800/233–1234* 🌐 *www.hyattgrandcypress.com* 🛏 *815 rooms* 🍴 *No meals* ✣ *1:G3.*

$$ RESORT FAMILY Fodor's Choice ★ **Nickelodeon Suites Resort.** This 24-acre Nickelodeon-themed resort is so kid-friendly that you can barely take a step without bumping into images of SpongeBob, Dora the Explorer, Jimmy Neutron, or other Nick characters. **Pros:** extremely kid-friendly; Disney shuttles included in resort fee; mini-golf course. **Cons:** daily resort fee of $35; not within walking distance of Disney parks or Disney Springs; way too frenetic for folks without kids. [$] *Rooms from: $199* ✉ *14500 Continental Gateway* ☎ *407/387–5437, 866/462–6425* 🌐 *www.nickhotel.com* 🛏 *777 suites* 🍴 *No meals* ✣ *1:G5.*

$$ HOTEL **Staybridge Suites Lake Buena Vista.** Just minutes from a Disney entrance, this pleasant all-suites (one- and two-bedroom, two-bath) accommodation is perfect for a big family on a small budget who want a home away from home. **Pros:** free scheduled shuttle service to Disney; free hot breakfast; free Wi-Fi and parking. **Cons:** no restaurant; no shuttles to other parks. [$] *Rooms from: $189* ✉ *8751 Suiteside Dr.* ☎ *407/238–0777* 🌐 *www.staybridge.com* 🛏 *150 suites* 🍴 *Multiple meal plans* ✣ *1:G3.*

$$$$ RESORT Fodor's Choice ★ **Waldorf Astoria Orlando.** While it can't duplicate the famed Waldorf Astoria Hotel in New York, this Waldorf echoes the original with imagination and flair, from the iconic clock in the center of the circular lobby to tiny, black-and-white accent tiles on guest room floors. **Pros:** lavish and luxurious hotel with spa and golf, next to Disney; free transportation to Disney parks. **Cons:** pricey, but you knew that; if you can bear to leave your cabana, you'll need a car to see anything else in the area; steep daily resort fee. [$] *Rooms from: $559* ✉ *14200 Bonnet Creek Resort La., Bonnet Creek* ☎ *407/597–5500* 🌐 *www.waldorfastoriaorlando.com* 🛏 *328 rooms, 169 suites* 🍴 *Breakfast* ✣ *1:F5.*

NIGHTLIFE

Updated by
Joseph Hayes

Outside of Downtown Disney and Universal's CityWalk, the focal point of adult Orlando nightlife is Downtown. If you stand on the corner of Orange Avenue and Church Street long enough, you can watch all types of gussied-up revelers walk by. The bars and music clubs here hop even after the 2 am last call.

CENTRAL ORLANDO

BARS

AERO. You have to head up to the roof using the side staircase of The Social nightclub to reach the former Sky60 rooftop bar. Revamped and updated, it offers a hip and social view of downtown Orlando. ⊠ *60 N. Orange Ave.* ☎ *407/246–1599* ⊕ *www.skysixty.com/* ☾ *Thurs.–Sat. 10 pm–2 am, Sun. 5 pm–11 pm.*

Wally's. One of Orlando's oldest bars (circa 1954), this longtime local favorite is a hangout for a cross section of cultures and ages. Some would say it's a dive, but that doesn't matter to the students, bikers, lawyers, and barflies who land here to drink surrounded by the go-go-dancer wallpaper and '60s-era interior. Just grab a stool at the bar to take in the scene and down a cold one. ⊠ *1001 N. Mills Ave.* ☎ *407/896–6975* ⊕ *www.wallysonmills.com* ☾ *Mon.–Sat. 7:30 am–2 am.*

MUSIC CLUBS

Fodor'sChoice
★

The Social. Beloved by locals, The Social is a great place to see touring and area musicians. Up to seven nights a week you can sip trademark martinis while listening to anything from indie rock to rockabilly to undiluted jazz. Several now-national acts got their start here, including Matchbox Twenty, Seven Mary Three, and other groups that don't have numbers in their names. Hours vary. ⊠ *54 N. Orange Ave.* ☎ *407/246–1419* ⊕ *www.thesocial.org* ✏ *$5–$30, depending on entertainment.*

Venue 578. Originally an old automotive repair shop, this multilevel, high-energy club, the former Firestone Live, went through a very costly renovation to attract international music acts. Something's always going on to make the crowd hop: DJ mixes, big band, jazz, hip-hop, rock. Often the dance floor is more like semicontrolled chaos than a place to just listen, so be prepared. Hours and prices vary by event; check the website. ⊠ *578 N. Orange Ave.* ☎ *407/872–0066* ⊕ *www.venue578.com/.*

INTERNATIONAL DRIVE AREA

MUSIC CLUBS

B.B. King's Blues Club. The blues great was doing quite well as a musician before becoming a successful entrepreneur, with blues clubs in Memphis, Nashville, Las Vegas, and West Palm Beach as well as Orlando. Like the others, this club has music at its heart. There's a dance floor and stage for live performances by the B.B. King All-Star Band or visiting musicians seven nights a week. You can't really experience Delta blues without Delta dining, so the club doubles as a restaurant with

9

fried dill pickles, catfish bites, po' boys, ribs, and other comfort foods. Oh, yeah, and there's a full bar. ⊠ *Pointe Orlando, 9101 International Dr.* ☎ *407/370–4550* ⊕ *www.bbkingclubs.com/orlando/* ⊗ *Fri. and Sat. noon–2 am, Sun.–Thurs. 12–midnight.*

NIGHTCLUBS

ICEBAR. Thanks to the miracle of refrigeration, this is Orlando's coolest bar—literally and figuratively. Fifty tons of pure ice is kept at a constant 27°F and has been cut and sculpted by world-class carvers into a cozy (or as cozy as ice can be) sanctuary of tables, sofas, chairs, and a bar. The staff loans you a thermal cape and gloves (upgrade to a fur coat for $10), and when you enter the frozen hall your drink is served in a glass made of crystal-clear ice. There's no cover charge if you just want to hang out in the Fire Lounge or outdoor Polar Patio, but you will pay $19.95 to spend as much time as you can handle in the subfreezing ICEBAR. There's no beer or wine inside; it's simply too cold. ⊠ *Pointe Orlando, 8967 International Dr.* ☎ *407/426–7555* ⊕ *www. icebarorlando.com* ⊗ *Fri. and Sat. 7 pm–2 am, Sun.–Wed. 7–midnight, Thurs. 7–1.*

SPORTS AND THE OUTDOORS

Updated by Gary McKechnie

There are many ways to enjoy the outdoors here, but a few activities stand out. You can keep your feet planted firmly on the ground and play golf (or miniature golf), or you can take to the "skies."

BALLOONING

Fodor's Choice ★

Bob's Balloons. Bob's offers one-hour rides over protected marshland and even flies over the Disney area if wind and weather conditions are right. You meet at Champions Gate, near Disney World, at dawn, where Bob and his assistant take you by van to the launch site. It takes about 15 minutes to get the balloon in the air, and then you're off on an adventure that definitely surpasses Peter Pan's Flight in the Magic Kingdom.

You'll see farm and forest land for miles, along with horses, deer, wild boar, cattle, and birds flying *below* you. Bob may take you as high as 1,000 feet, and you may be able to see such landmarks as the Animal Kingdom's Expedition Everest mountain and Epcot's Spaceship Earth sphere. Several other balloons are likely to go up near you—there's a tight-knit community of ballooners in the Orlando area—so you'll view these colorful sky ornaments from an unparalleled sightline. There are seats in the basket, but you'll probably be too thrilled to sit down. Check the website for specials and call Bob to reserve. ⊠ *Orlando* ☎ *407/466–6380, 877/824–4606* ⊕ *www.bobsballoons.com* 🖳 *$175 per person.*

GOLF

If golf is your passion, you already know that Arnold Palmer and Gary Player—in fact, almost half of the PGA tour—make Orlando their off-road home. It's not by accident that the Golf Channel originates from

here. The Bay Hill Invitational and several LPGA tourneys (the head-quarters is in Daytona) come to Orlando every year. And with more than 170 public and private courses, there's ample opportunity for you to play on world-class courses such as Grand Cypress or Champions Gate.

MINIATURE GOLF

FAMILY

Fodor'sChoice

★

Hawaiian Rumble Adventure Golf. Who can resist miniature golfing around an erupting volcano? Hawaiian Rumble combines a tropical setting with waterfalls, tunnels, tiki gods, and flame-belching mountains. There's also a location in the Lake Buena Vista area. Enjoyed your first round? It's only a few bucks to play an additional 18 holes. ✉ *8969 International Dr.* ☎ *407/351–7733* ⊕ *www.hawaiianrumbleorlando. com* ✆ *$9.95 (18 holes), $12.95 (36 holes)* ⊙ *Sun.–Thurs. 9 am–11 pm, Fri. and Sat. 9 am–11:30 pm.*

FAMILY

Pirate's Cove Adventure Golf. Two 18-hole miniature golf courses wind around artificial mountains, through caves, beside waterfalls, and into lush foliage. The beginner's course is called Captain Kidd's Adventure; the more advanced course is Blackbeard's Challenge. There's another Pirate's Cove on International Drive. ✉ *12545 State Rd. 535, Lake Buena Vista* ☎ *407/827–1242* ⊕ *www.piratescove.net* ✆ *$9.45 (under 10), $10.45 (18 holes), $14.95 (36 holes)* ⊙ *Daily 9 am–11 pm.*

SKYDIVING

Fodor'sChoice

★

iFLY Orlando. OK, so technically you aren't really skydiving, but you come pretty close in this 12-foot-high, 1,000-horsepower wind tunnel that lets you experience everything skydivers do, but closer to the ground.

The experience starts with instruction, after which you suit up and hit the wind tunnel, where you soar like a bird (or try to) under your instructor's watchful eye. It's all so realistic that skydiving clubs come to hone their skills. It's also pretty surreal as you look through the window and see people floating in mid-air. The attraction is safe for anyone under 250 pounds and older than three. The 90-minute intro-ductory experience includes two flights. You can purchase a video of your "jump" for $24.95. ✉ *6805 Visitors Circle* ☎ *407/903–1150* ⊕ *www.skyventureorlando.com* ✆ *$59.95 and up, depending on pack-age* ⊙ *Daily 10–10:30.*

SHOPPING

Updated by
Joseph Hayes

Visitors from as far away as Britain and Brazil often arrive in Orlando with empty suitcases for their purchases. Although shopping has all but disappeared from Downtown, the metro area is filled with options. There really is something for everyone—from high-end fashion to out-let-mall chic, from the world's largest flea market to a boutique-filled town, from an antique treasure to a hand-hewn Florida find.

The College Park area, once an antiques-hunter's dream, still has some treasures to be found along North Orange Avenue and Edgewater Drive, including the largest vinyl-record shop in Florida.

The simultaneously glitzy and kitschy International Drive has almost 500 designer outlet stores and odd, off-brand electronics shops. The factory outlets on the north end of I-Drive once consisted of shops with merchandise piled on tables; today the shops here are equal to their higher-priced first-run cousins. The strip also has plenty of massive restaurants and, for those in your group who don't feel like shopping, movie theaters.

CENTRAL ORLANDO

MALLS

Florida Mall. With 250-plus stores and 1.8 million square feet of shopping, it's big enough for you to vacation here—in fact, there's even an attached hotel. Only 7 miles from the airport, the mall attracts crowds of international visitors eager for American bargains. Anchor stores include Sears, JCPenney, Dillard's, and Macy's. An expanded food court adds a total of almost 50 casual eateries and sit-down restaurants to the shopping mix. Stroller and wheelchair rentals are available; there are even concierge services and a currency exchange. The mall is 4½ miles east of Interstate 4 and International Drive at the corner of Sand Lake Road and South Orange Blossom Trail. ⊠ *8001 S. Orange Blossom Trail, South Orlando* ☎ *407/851–7234* ⊕ *www.simon.com/mall/the-florida-mall* ⊘ *Weekdays 10–9, Sat. 10–10, Sun. noon–8.*

INTERNATIONAL DRIVE AREA

FACTORY OUTLETS

Orlando International Premium Outlets. This is a prime destination for international shoppers, who can find shoes, clothing, cosmetics, electronics, and household goods at a fraction of their home-country prices. The massive complex at the north tip of International Drive includes Saks Fifth Avenue OFF 5TH, Coach, Kate Spade New York, Victoria's Secret Outlet, and a Disney outlet. Searching for bargains works up an appetite, and there are plenty of places to eat here, either in the well-lit food court or in one of several sit-down and highly regarded restaurants. ⊠ *4951 International Dr.* ☎ *407/352–9600* ⊕ *www.premiumoutlets.com* ⊘ *Mon.–Sat. 10 am–11 pm, Sun. 10–9.*

Orlando Vineland Premium Outlets. This outlet capitalizes on its proximity to Disney (it's at the confluence of Interstate 4, State Road 535, and International Drive). It's easier to see from the highway than to enter, and parking is tedious and scarce, but smart shoppers have lunch on International Drive and take the I-Ride Trolley right to the front entrance (it runs every 15 minutes). The center's design makes this almost an open-air market, so walking can be pleasant on a nice day. You'll find Prada, Gap, Nike, Adidas, Tory Burch, Polo Ralph Lauren, Giorgio Armani, Burberry, Tommy Hilfiger, Reebok, and about

9

100 other stores. ✉ *8200 Vineland Ave.* ☎ *407/238–7787* ⊕ *www. premiumoutlets.com* ⊗ *Mon.–Sat. 10 am–11 pm, Sun. 10–9.*

MALLS

Pointe Orlando. What was once an enclosed shopping center is now a dining, shopping, and entertainment hot spot—one that's within walking distance of five top hotels and the Orange County Convention Center. In addition to WonderWorks and the enormous Regal IMAX theater, the complex has specialty shops such as Armani Exchange, Tommy Bahama, Chico's, Tommy Hilfiger, Hollister, Charming Charlie, and Victoria's Secret. Restaurants have become a reason to visit, with the very high-end Capital Grille, the Oceanaire Seafood Room, Cuba Libre Restaurant and Rum Bar, The Pub, Marlow's Tavern, the popular Funky Monkey Bistro & Bar, B.B. King's Blues Club, and Taverna Opa. Blue Martini and Lafayette's provide after-hours entertainment and adult beverages. Check the website for a list of happy hour specials. ✉ *9101 International Dr.* ☎ *407/248–2838* ⊕ *www.pointeorlando.com* ⊗ *Oct.–May, Mon.–Sat. noon–10, Sun. noon–8; June–Sept., Fri. and Sat. noon–9, Sun.–Thurs. noon–8.*

WALT DISNEY WORLD

WELCOME TO WALT DISNEY WORLD

TOP REASONS TO GO

★ **Nostalgia:** Face it— Mickey and Company are old friends. And you probably have childhood pictures of yourself in front of Cinderella Castle. Even if you don't, nobody does yesteryear better: head to Main Street, U.S.A or Hollywood Boulevard and see.

★ **Memories in the Making:** Who doesn't want to snap selfies on the Dumbo ride or of Junior after his Splash Mountain experience? The urge to pass that Disney nostalgia on to the next generation is strong.

★ **The Thrills:** For some this means roller coasting to an Aerosmith soundtrack or simulating space flight; for others it's about cascading down a waterslide or going on safari.

★ **The Chills:** If the Pirates of the Caribbean cave doesn't give you goose bumps, try the Haunted Mansion or Twilight Zone Tower of Terror.

★ **The Spectacle:** The list is long—fireworks, laser-light displays, arcade games, parades. . . .

1 **Magic Kingdom.** Disney's emblematic park is home to Space Mountain, Pirates of the Caribbean, and an expanded Fantasyland full of new experiences.

2 **Epcot.** Future World's focus is science, technology, and hands-on experiences. In the World Showcase, you can tour 11 countries without getting jet-lagged.

3 **Disney's Hollywood Studios.** Attractions at this re-creation of old-time Hollywood include Rock 'n' Roller Coaster Starring Aerosmith and Twilight Zone Tower of Terror.

4 **Disney's Animal Kingdom.** Amid a 403-acre wildlife preserve are an Asian-themed water ride, an African safari ride, a runaway-train coaster, and shows.

5 **Blizzard Beach.** Water thrills range from steep flume rides to tubing expeditions in the midst of a park that you'd swear is a slowly melting ski resort. There's plenty for little ones, too.

CENTRAL FLORIDA

Orlando

GETTING ORIENTED

Walt Disney World straddles Orange and Osceola counties to the west of Interstate 4. Four exits will get you to the parks and resort areas: 64B, 65, 67, and 68. To reach hotels along I-Drive, use Exit 72, 74A, or 75A.

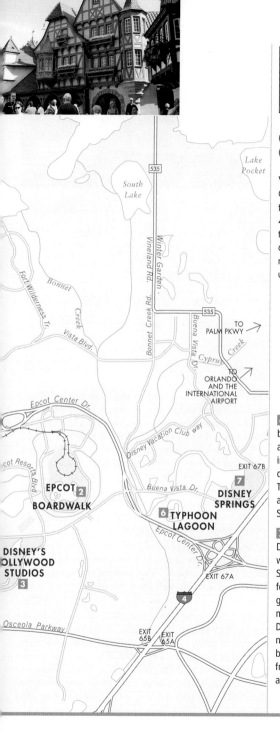

6 Typhoon Lagoon. Sandy beaches, oceanlike waves, and a themed water coaster invite castaways to enjoy a day of fun and relaxation. Take the kids on Bay Slides and don snorkels to explore Shark Reef.

7 Disney's Other Worlds. Downtown Disney, which will be renamed Disney Springs, is the place to go for shopping, dining, and great entertainment from morning through late night. Disney's BoardWalk is a nostalgia trip, with bicycles built for two, surreys with fringe on top, pizza, bars, and a dance hall.

Updated by
Jennie Hess
and Joseph
Hayes

Mickey Mouse. Tinker Bell. Cinderella. What would child-hood be like without the magic of Disney? When kids and adults want to go to *the* theme park, they're heading to Disney. Here you're walking amid people from around the world and meeting characters like Snow White and Donald Duck while rides whirl nonstop and the irrepressible "it's a small world" tune and lyrics run through your head. You can't help but believe dreams really do come true here.

The **Magic Kingdom** is the heart and soul of the Walt Disney World empire. It was the first Disney outpost in Florida when it opened in 1971, and it's the park that launched Disney's presence in France, Japan, Hong Kong, and Shanghai. For a landmark that wields such world-wide influence, the 142-acre Magic Kingdom may seem small—indeed, Epcot is more than double the size of the Magic Kingdom, and Animal Kingdom is almost triple the size when including the park's expansive animal habitats. But looks can be deceiving. Packed into six different "lands" are nearly 50 major crowd-pleasers, and that's not counting all the ancillary attractions: shops, eateries, live entertainment, character meet-and-greet spots, fireworks shows, and parades.

Nowhere but at **Epcot** can you explore and experience the native food, entertainment, culture, and arts and crafts of countries in Europe, Asia, North Africa, and the Americas. What's more, employees at the World Showcase pavilions actually hail from the countries the pavilions represent.

Epcot, or "Experimental Prototype Community of Tomorrow," was the original inspiration for Walt Disney World. Walt envisioned a future in which nations coexisted in peace and harmony, reaping the miraculous harvest of technological achievement. The Epcot of today is both more and less than his original dream. Less, because the World Showcase presents views of its countries that are, as an Epcot guide once put it, "as Americans perceive them"—highly idealized. But this is a minor quibble in the face of the major achievement: Epcot is that rare paradox—a successful educational theme park that excels at entertainment, too.

Disney's Hollywood Studios were designed to be a trip back to Tinseltown's golden age, when Hedda Hopper, not tabloids, spread celebrity gossip and when the girl off the bus from Ohio could be the next Judy Garland.

The result is a theme park that blends movie-themed shows and attractions and high-tech wonders with breathtaking rides and Hollywood nostalgia. The park's old-time Hollywood atmosphere begins with a rosy-hued view of the moviemaking business presented in a dreamy stage set from the 1930s and '40s, amid sleek art-moderne buildings in pastel colors, funky diners, kitschy decorations, and sculptured gardens populated by roving actors playing, well, roving actors. There are also casting directors, gossip columnists, and other colorful characters.

Thanks to a rich library of film scores, the park is permeated with music, all familiar, all evoking the magic of the movies, and all constantly streaming from the camouflaged loudspeakers at a volume just right for humming along. The park icon for many years, a 122-foot-high Sorcerer Mickey Hat that served as a gift shop and Disney pin-trading station, towered over Hollywood Boulevard until it was removed in 2015.

Disney's Animal Kingdom explores the stories of all animals—real, imaginary, and extinct. Enter through the Oasis, where you hear exotic background music and find yourself surrounded by gentle waterfalls and gardens alive with exotic birds, reptiles, and mammals.

At 403 acres and several times the size of the Magic Kingdom, Animal Kingdom is the largest in area of all Disney theme parks. Animal habitats take up much of that acreage. Creatures here thrive in careful re-creations of landscapes from Asia and Africa. Throughout the park, you'll also learn about conservation in a low-key way.

Amid all the nature are thrill rides, a 3-D show (housed in the "root system" of the iconic Tree of Life), two first-rate musicals, and character meet and greets. Cast members are as likely to hail from Kenya or South Africa as they are from Kentucky or South Carolina. It's all part of the charm. New park areas based on the movie *Avatar* are expected to open in 2017, a fitting addition, since the film's theme of living in harmony with nature reflects the park's eco-philosophy.

10

Typhoon Lagoon and **Blizzard Beach** are two of the world's best water parks. What sets them apart? It's the same thing that differentiates all Disney parks—the detailed themes. Whether you're cast away on a balmy island at Typhoon Lagoon or washed up on a ski-resort-turned-seaside-playground at Blizzard Beach, the landscaping and clever architecture will add to the fun of flume and raft rides, wave pools, and splash areas. Another plus: the vegetation has matured enough to create shade. The Disney water parks give you that lost-in-paradise feeling on top of all those high-speed, wedgie-inducing waterslides. They're so popular that crowds often reach overflow capacity in summer. If you're going to Disney for four days or more between April and October, add the Water Park Fun & More option to your Magic Your Way ticket.

PLANNING

ADMISSION

At the gate, the per-person, per-day price for Magic Kingdom guests is $99 for adults (ages 10 and older) and $93 for children (ages 3–9). At Disney's other three parks, Epcot, Hollywood Studios and Animal Kingdom, the per-person, per-day price is $94 for adults (ages 10 and older) and $88 for children (ages 3–9). You can buy tickets at the Ticket and Transportation Center (TTC) in the Magic Kingdom, from booths at other park entrances, in all on-site resorts if you're a guest, at the Disney store in the airport, and at various other sites around Orlando. You can also buy them in advance online—the best way to save time and money.

If you opt for a multiday ticket, you'll be issued a nontransferable pass that uses your fingerprint for ID. Hold your pass up to the reader, just like people with single-day tickets, and also slip your finger into the V-shaped reader. A new option, the MagicBand wristband, serves as park ticket, attraction FastPass+ ticket, and even hotel room key.

OPERATING HOURS

Walt Disney World operates 365 days a year. Opening and closing times vary by park and by season, with the longest hours during prime summer months and year-end holidays. The parking lots open at least an hour before the parks do.

In general, openings hover around 9 am, though certain attractions might not start up till 10 or 11. Closings range between 5 and 8 pm in the off-season and between 8 and 10, 11, or even midnight in high season. Downtown Disney/Disney Springs and BoardWalk shops stay open as late as 11 pm.

EXTRA MAGIC HOURS

The Extra Magic Hours program gives Disney resort guests free early and late-night admission to certain parks on specified days—check ahead (⊕ *www.disneyworld.disney.go.com/calendars*) for information about each park's "magic hours" days to plan your early- and late-visit strategies.

PARKING AND IN-PARK TRANSPORT

Parking at Disney parks is free to resort guests; all others pay $17 for cars and $18 for RVs and campers. Parking is free for everyone at Typhoon Lagoon, Blizzard Beach, Downtown Disney, and the BoardWalk. Trams take you between the theme-park lots (*note your parking location!*) and turnstiles. Disney's buses, boats, and monorails whisk you from resort to park and park to park. If you're staying on Disney property, you can use this system exclusively. Either take a Disney bus or drive to Typhoon Lagoon and Blizzard Beach. Once inside the water parks, you can walk, swim, slide, or chill out. Allow up to an hour for travel between parks and hotels on Disney transportation.

FASTPASS+

FastPass+ helps you avoid lines, and it's included in regular park admission. Using the new My Disney Experience app or FastPass+ kiosks in each park, you can select up to three attractions at one time; each appointment will give you a one-hour window within which you can experience each attraction. The FastPass+ appointments are loaded directly to your plastic theme-park ticket or your new MagicBand. It's best to make appointments only for the most popular attractions and to stick with the standby queue for attractions that aren't in such demand. Strategy is everything.

Guests can get FastPass+ reservations for some designated character greetings, parades, and shows. These "experience" FastPass+ reservations count just the same as those for the rides. You get three to start with (in a single park) and can add as many more as you have time for (and these can be in a different park if you have the Park Hopper option). Best FastPass+ practices are explained by the program. It will direct you to the attractions where FastPass+ is most helpful. If these attractions don't meet your family's specific needs—your kids are too young to ride coasters, for example—the program will also help you customize your FastPass+ selections.

DISNEY STRATEGIES

Keep in mind these essential strategies, tried and tested by generations of Disney fans.

■ **Buy tickets before leaving home.** It saves money and gives you time to look into all the ticket options. It also offers an opportunity for you to consider vacation packages and meal plans and to register with the My Disney Experience program and mobile app for vacation planning.

■ **Make dining reservations before leaving home.** If you don't, you might find yourself eating fast food (again) or leaving Disney for dinner. On-site restaurants, especially those featuring character appearances, book up months ahead, and you can reserve 180 days before you arrive.

■ **Arrive at least 30 minutes before the parks open.** We know, it's your vacation and you want to sleep in. But you probably want to make the most of your time and money, too. Plan to be up by 7:30 am each day to get the most out of your park visits. After transit time, it'll take you 15–20 minutes to park, get to the gates, and pick up your park guide maps and *Times Guide*.

■ **See top attractions in the morning.** And we mean *first thing*. Decide in advance on your can't-miss attractions, find their locations, and hotfoot it to them before 10 am.

■ **Use FastPass+.** The system is free, easy, more streamlined than ever with the new FastPass+ online prebooking system, and it's your ticket to the top attractions with little or no waiting in line. Even if you wait to book once you're in the park, you can now schedule up to three Fastpasses at one time; paper Fastpass tickets are obsolete. Instead, your attraction appointments are loaded onto your MagicBand or plastic ticket, whichever you choose to use.

■ **Use Baby Swap.** Disney has a theme-park "rider switch" policy that works like this: one parent waits with the baby or toddler while the other parent rides the attraction. When the ride ends, they switch places with minimal wait.

■ **Build in rest time.** Start early and then leave the parks around 3 or 4 pm, thus avoiding the hottest and often most crowded period. After a

10

couple of hours' rest at your hotel, head back for a nighttime spectacle or to ride a big-ticket ride (lines often are shorter around closing time).

■ **Create an itinerary, but leave room for spontaneity.** Don't try to plot your trip hour by hour. If you're staying at a Disney resort, find out which parks have Extra Magic Hours on which days.

■ **Eat at off hours.** To avoid the mealtime rush hours, have a quick, light breakfast at 7 or 8 am, lunch at 11, and dinner at 5 or 6.

OTHER DISNEY SERVICES

If you can shell out $360–$500 an hour (with a six-hour minimum), you can take a customized **VIP Tour** with guides who help you park hop and get good seats at parades and shows. These tours don't help you skip lines, but they make navigating easy. Groups can have up to 10 people; book up to three months ahead.

WDW Tours. Reserve with WDW Tours up to 180 days in advance for behind-the-scenes tours. Participant age requirements vary, so be sure to check before you book. ☎ *407/939–8687 ⊕ www.disneyworld.com.*

DISNEY CONTACTS

Cruise Line: ☎ *800/370–0097 ⊕ www.disneycruise.com*

Dining Reservations: ☎ *407/939–3463*

Extra Magic Hours: ⊕ *www.disneyworld.disney.go.com/calendars*

Fairy-Tale Weddings: ☎ *321/939–4610 ⊕ www.disneyweddings.disney. go.com*

Golf Reservations: ☎ *407/939–4653*

Guest Info: ☎ *407/824–4321*

VIP Tours: ☎ *407/560–4033*

WDW Travel Company: ☎ *407/828–8101*

Web: ⊕ *www.disneyworld.disney.go.com*

THE MAGIC KINGDOM

Whether you arrive at the Magic Kingdom via monorail, boat, or bus, it's hard to escape that surge of excitement or suppress that smile upon sighting the towers of Cinderella Castle or the spires of Space Mountain. So what if it's a cliché by now? There's magic beyond the turnstiles, and you aren't going to miss one memorable moment.

Most visitors have some idea of what they'd like to see and do during their day in the Magic Kingdom. Popular attractions like Space Mountain and Splash Mountain are on the lists of any thrill seeker, and the recently expanded Fantasyland is Destination One for parents of small children and seekers of moderate thrills like the new Seven Dwarfs Mine Train. Visitors who steer away from wilder rides are first in line at the Jungle Cruise or Pirates of the Caribbean in Adventureland.

It's great to have a strategy for seeing the park's attractions, grabbing a bite to eat, or scouring the shops for souvenir gold. But don't forget that Disney Imagineers—the creative pros behind every themed land and attraction—are famous for their attention to detail. Your experience

TOP ATTRACTIONS

FOR AGES 7 AND UP	FOR AGES 6 AND UNDER
Big Thunder Mountain Railroad	Dumbo the Flying Elephant
Buzz Lightyear's Space Ranger Spin	Enchanted Tales with Belle
	The Magic Carpets of Aladdin
Haunted Mansion	The Many Adventures of Winnie the Pooh
Pirates of the Caribbean	
Seven Dwarfs Mine Train	Under the Sea: Journey of the Little Mermaid
Space Mountain	

will be richer if you take time to notice the extra touches—from the architecture to the music and the costumes. The same genius is evident even in the landscape, from the tropical setting of Adventureland to the red-stone slopes of Frontierland's Big Thunder Mountain Railroad.

Wherever you go, watch for hidden Mickeys—silhouettes and abstract images of Mickey Mouse—tucked by Imagineers into every corner of the Kingdom. For instance, at the Haunted Mansion, look for him in the place settings in the banquet scene.

Much of the Magic Kingdom's pixie dust is spread by the people who work here, the costumed cast members who do their part to create fond memories for each guest who crosses their path. Maybe the grim ghoul who greets you solemnly at the Haunted Mansion will cause you to break down and giggle. Or the sunny shop assistant will help your daughter find the perfect sparkly shoes to match her princess dress. You get the feeling that everyone's in on the fun; in fact, you wonder if they ever go home!

PLANNING

10

GETTING ORIENTED

The park is laid out on a north–south axis, with Cinderella Castle at the center and the various lands surrounding it in a broad circle.

As you pass underneath the railroad tracks, symbolically leaving behind the world of reality and entering a world of fantasy, you'll immediately notice the charming buildings lining Town Square and Main Street, U.S.A, which runs due north and ends at the Hub (also called Central Plaza), in front of Cinderella Castle. If you're lost or have questions, cast members are available at almost every turn to help you.

PARK AMENITIES

Guest Relations. To the left in Town Square as you face Main Street, **City Hall** houses Guest Relations (aka Guest Services), the Magic Kingdom's principal information center (☎ *407/824–4521*). Here you can search for misplaced belongings or companions, ask questions of staffers, and pick up a guide map and a *Times Guide* with schedules of events and

Adventure Number 1: Being shipwrecked with the Swiss Family Robinson and exploring their treehouse.

character-greeting information. ■TIP→ **If you're trying for a last-minute lunch or dinner reservation, you may be able to book it at City Hall.**

Lockers: Lockers ($7 or $9 plus $5 deposit) are in an arcade under the Main Street railroad station. If you're park hopping, use your locker receipt to get a free locker at the next park.

Lost People and Things: Instruct your kids to talk to anyone with a Disney name tag if they lose you. **City Hall** also has a lost and found and a computerized message center, where you can leave notes for your companions in the Magic Kingdom and other parks.

VISITING TIPS

■ Try to come toward the end of the week, because most families hit the Magic Kingdom early in a visit.

■ Ride a star attraction during a parade; lines ease considerably. (But be careful not to get stuck on the wrong side of the parade route when it starts, or you may never get across.)

■ At City Hall, near the park's Town Square entrance, pick up a map and a *Times Guide,* which lists showtimes, character-greeting times, and hours for attractions and restaurants.

■ Book character meals early. Main Street, U.S.A.'s The Crystal Palace, A Buffet with Character has breakfast, lunch, and dinner with Winnie the Pooh, Tigger, and friends. All three meals at the Fairy Tale Dining experience in Cinderella Castle are extremely popular—so much so that you should reserve your spot six months out. The same advice goes for booking the full-service dinner at the new Be Our Guest Restaurant in the Beast's Castle in Fantasyland.

EXPLORING THE MAGIC KINGDOM

MAIN STREET, U.S.A.

With its pastel Victorian-style buildings, antique automobiles ahoohga-oohga-ing, sparkling sidewalks, and an atmosphere of what one writer has called "almost hysterical joy," Main Street is more than a mere conduit to the other enchantments of the Magic Kingdom. It's where the spell is first cast.

You emerge from beneath the Walt Disney World Railroad Station into a realization of one of the most tenacious American dreams. The perfect street in the perfect small town in a perfect moment of time is burnished to jewel-like quality, thanks to a four-fifths-scale reduction, nightly cleanings with high-pressure hoses, and constant repainting. And it's a very sunny world, thanks to an outpouring of welcoming entertainment: live bands, barbershop quartets, and background music from Disney films and American musicals played over loudspeakers. Horse-drawn trolleys and omnibuses with their horns tooting chug along the street. Vendors in Victorian costumes sell balloons and popcorn. And Cinderella's famous castle floats whimsically in the distance where Main Street disappears.

Although attractions with a capital A are minimal on Main Street, there are plenty of inducements—namely, shops and eateries—to while away your time and part you from your money. The largest of these, the Emporium, is often the last stop for souvenir hunters at day's end. At the Main Street Bakery, you can find your favorite Starbucks latte and a sandwich or baked treats like cupcakes and brownies. If you can't resist an interactive challenge while making your way through the park, head first to the Firehouse, next to City Hall, to join the legendary wizard Merlin in the Sorcerers of the Magic Kingdom role-playing game. For no extra charge, you can take ownership of special cards with "magic spells" that help you search for symbols and bring down Disney villains like Yzma and Kronk from the Disney film *The Emperor's New Groove*. Don't worry—you'll have time between fireball battles and cyclone spells to ride Space Mountain.

The Harmony Barber Shop lets you step back in time for a haircut ($15 for children 12 and under, $19 for anyone older). Babies or tots get free Mickey Ears, a souvenir lock of hair, and a certificate if it's their first haircut ever, but you pay $19 for the experience. At the Town Square Theater (formerly Exposition Hall), presented by Kodak, Mickey Mouse meets you for photos and autographs. And, for the first time in Disney history, you can pick up a FastPass+ appointment for such meet and greets. While you're here, stock up on batteries and memory cards or disposable cameras.

ADVENTURELAND

From the scrubbed brick, manicured lawns, and meticulously pruned trees of the Central Plaza, an artfully dilapidated wooden bridge leads to the jungles of Adventureland. Here, South African cape honeysuckle droops, Brazilian bougainvillea drapes, Mexican flame vines cling, spider plants clone, and three varieties of palm trees sway. The bright, all-American sing-along tunes that fill the air along Main Street and Central

10

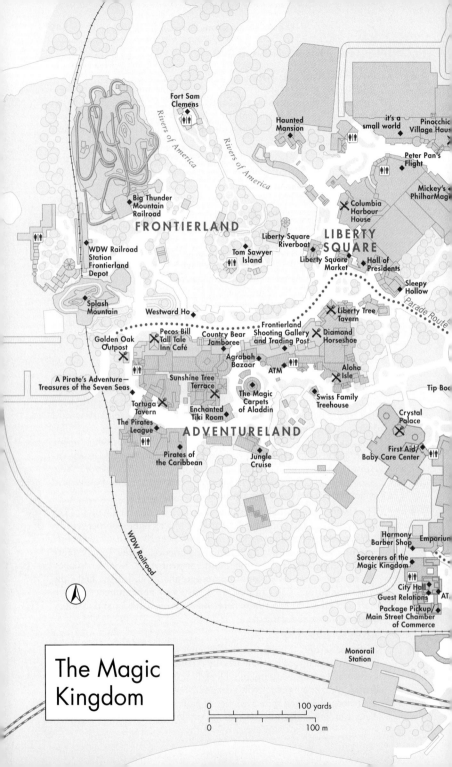

The Magic Kingdom

FRONTIERLAND

LIBERTY SQUARE

ADVENTURELAND

Rivers of America

Rivers of America

Parade Route

WDW Railroad

Fort Sam Clemens

Haunted Mansion

it's a small world

Pinocchio Village Haus

Peter Pan's Flight

Mickey's PhilharMagic

Big Thunder Mountain Railroad

Columbia Harbour House

WDW Railroad Station Frontierland Depot

Liberty Square Riverboat

Tom Sawyer Island

Liberty Square Market

Hall of Presidents

Sleepy Hollow

Splash Mountain

Westward Ho

Liberty Tree Tavern

Golden Oak Outpost

Pecos Bill Tall Tale Inn Café

Country Bear Jamboree

Frontierland Shooting Gallery and Trading Post

Diamond Horseshoe

Agrabah Bazaar

ATM

Aloha Isle

Tip Boa

A Pirate's Adventure— Treasures of the Seven Seas

Sunshine Tree Terrace

The Magic Carpets of Aladdin

Swiss Family Treehouse

Crystal Palace

Tortuga Tavern

Enchanted Tiki Room

First Aid/ Baby Care Center

The Pirates League

Pirates of the Caribbean

Jungle Cruise

Harmony Barber Shop

Emporium

Sorcerers of the Magic Kingdom

City Hall

Guest Relations

AT

Package Pickup/ Main Street Chamber of Commerce

Monorail Station

0		100 yards
0		100 m

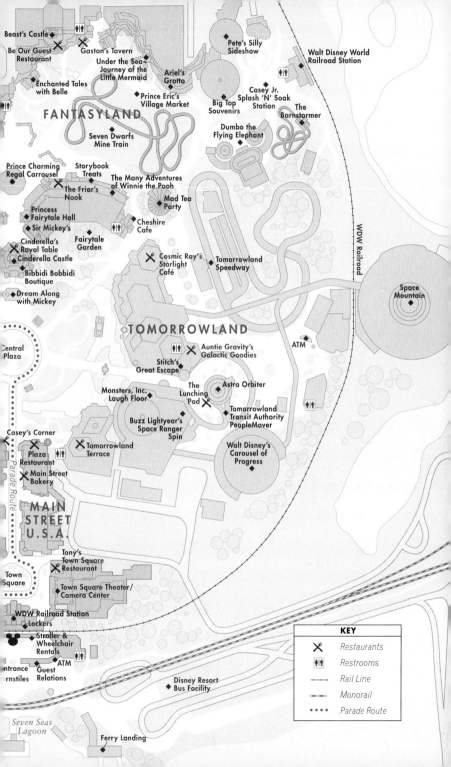

ANIMAL KINGDOM

	NAME	Height Req.	Type of Entertainment	Duration	Crowds	Audience	Tips
	Africa						
★	Festival of the Lion King	n/a	Show	30 mins.	Moderate	All Ages	Book a FastPass+ or arrive 30–40 mins. before showtime. Sit in one of the front rows to increase your kid's chance of being chosen to participate in a show number.
★	Kilimanjaro Safaris	n/a	Riding Tour	22 mins.	Moderate to Heavy	All Ages	Do this first thing in the morning or use FastPass+. If you arrive at the park late morning, save it for day's end, when animals may be more active.
	Pangani Forest Exploration Trail	n/a	Zoo/Aviary	Up to you	Light to Moderate	All Ages	Come while waiting for your safari FastPass+; try to avoid coming in the hottest time of day, when the gorillas like to nap.
	Asia						
★	Expedition Everest	At least 44"	Thrill Ride	2½ mins.	Huge	All but Young Kids	Arrive early or use FastPass+. This is the park's biggest thrill ride.
	Flights of Wonder	n/a	Show	25 mins.	Light	All Ages	Arrive 15 mins. before showtime, and find a shaded seat beneath one of the awnings—the sun can be brutal.
	Kali River Rapids	At least 38"	Thrill Ride	7 mins.	Heavy	All but Young Kids	Use your FastPass+ or come during the parade. You'll get wet.
	Maharajah Jungle Trek	n/a	Zoo/Aviary	Up to you	Light to Moderate	All Ages	Come anytime.
	DinoLand U.S.A.						
	Boneyard	n/a	Playground	Up to you	Moderate to Heavy	Young Kids	Play here while waiting for DINOSAUR FastPass+, or come late in the day.

DINOSAUR	At least 40"	Thrill Ride	4 mins.	Heavy	All but Young Kids	Come first thing in the morning or at the end of the day, or use FastPass+.
★ Finding Nemo—The Musical	n/a	Show	40 mins.	Heavy	All Ages	Arrive 40 mins. before showtime or book a FastPass+. Take young kids here while older kids wait for Expedition Everest.
Fossil Fun Games	n/a	Arcade/Fair	Up to you	Light	All Ages	Bring a stash of ones to buy play tickets.
Primeval Whirl	At least 48"	Thrill Ride	2½ mins.	Heavy	All but Young Kids	Kids may want to ride twice. Take your first spin early, then use FastPass+ if the wait is more than 20 mins.
TriceraTop Spin	n/a	Thrill Ride for Young Kids	2 mins.	Heavy	Young Kids	Ride early while everyone else heads for the safari or while waiting for your FastPass+ appointment for DINOSAUR.
Discovery Island						
★ Tree of Life—It's Tough to Be a Bug!	n/a	3-D film	20 mins.	Moderate to Heavy	All but Young Kids	Do this after Kilimanjaro Safaris or Expedition Everest. Small children may be frightened at creepy crawly moments in the dark.
Rafiki's Planet Watch						
Affection Section	n/a	Petting Yard	Up to you	Light	All Ages	Pet exotic goats and other rare domesticated animals.
Conservation Station	n/a	Walk-Through	Up to you	Light to Moderate	All Ages	Wait for the critter encounter and learn how to protect endangered species.
Habitat Habit!	n/a	Trail Walk	Up to you	Light	All Ages	Watch cotton-top tamarins along this discovery trail.
Wildlife Express Train	n/a	Train Ride	5 mins.	Moderate	All Ages	Head straight to Affection Section with little kids to come face-to-face with domesticated critters.

★ Fodor'sChoice

Coasting down Splash Mountain in Frontierland will put some zip in your doo-dah and some water on your clothes.

Plaza are replaced by the recorded repetitions of trumpeting elephants, pounding drums, and squawking parrots. The architecture is a mishmash of the best of Thailand, the Middle East, the Caribbean, Africa, and Polynesia, arranged in an inspired disorder that recalls comic-book fantasies of far-off places.

Once contained within the Pirates of the Caribbean attraction, Captain Jack Sparrow and the crew of the Black Pearl are brazenly recruiting new hearties at the Pirates League, adjacent to the ride entrance. You can get pirate and mermaid makeovers (for lots of doubloons) here. On a nearby stage furnished with pirate booty, the captain instructs scurvy dog recruits on brandishing a sword at Captain Jack Sparrow's Pirate Tutorial (several shows a day). And that's not all! At "A Pirate's Adventure: Treasures of the Seven Seas" park guests embark on an interactive quest with a pirate map and talisman to complete "raids" through Adventureland as they fight off pirate enemies along the way. Shiver me timbers—it's a pirate's life for ye!

FRONTIERLAND

Frontierland evokes the American frontier and is planted with mesquite, twisted Peruvian pepper trees, slash pines, and cacti. The period seems to be the latter half of the 19th century, and the West is being won by Disney cast members dressed in checked shirts, leather vests, cowboy hats, and brightly colored neckerchiefs. Banjo and fiddle music twangs from tree to tree, and snackers walk around munching turkey drumsticks so large that you could best an outlaw single-handedly with one. (Beware of hovering seagulls that migrate to the parks during cooler months—they've been known to snatch snacks.)

The screams that drown out the string music aren't the result of a cowboy surprising an Indian. They come from two of the Magic Kingdom's more thrilling rides: Splash Mountain, an elaborate flume ride, and Big Thunder Mountain Railroad, a roller coaster. The Walt Disney World Railroad tunnels past a colorful scene in Splash Mountain and drops you off between it and Thunder Mountain.

LIBERTY SQUARE

The rough-and-tumble Western frontier gently folds into Colonial America as Liberty Square picks up where Frontierland leaves off. The weathered siding gives way to solid brick and neat clapboard. The mesquite and cactus are replaced by stately oaks and masses of azaleas. The theme is Colonial history, which Northerners will be happy to learn is portrayed here as solid Yankee. The buildings, topped with weather vanes and exuding prosperity, are pure New England.

A replica of the Liberty Bell, crack and all, seems an appropriate prop to separate Liberty Square from Frontierland. There's even a Liberty Tree, a more than 150-year-old live oak, transported here from elsewhere on Disney property. Just as the Sons of Liberty hung lanterns on trees as a signal of solidarity after the Boston Tea Party, the Liberty Tree's branches are decorated with 13 lanterns representing the 13 original colonies. Around the square are tree-shaded tables for an alfresco lunch and plenty of carts and fast-food eateries to supply the goods.

FANTASYLAND

Walt Disney called this "a timeless land of enchantment," and Fantasyland does conjure pixie dust. Perhaps that's because the fanciful gingerbread houses, gleaming gold turrets, and, of course, the rides are based on Disney-animated movies.

Many of these rides, which could ostensibly be classified as rides for children, are packed with enough delightful detail to engage the adults who accompany them. Fantasyland has always been the most heavily trafficked area in the park, and its rides and shows are almost always crowded.

The good news is that Fantasyland has undergone the largest expansion in the park's history to offer several new attractions and experiences. Dumbo the Flying Elephant now is double the size, flying above circus-themed grounds that also include the Great Goofini coaster, starring Goofy as stuntman. There's also a Walt Disney World Railroad station in Fantasyland. And a circus-themed Casey Jr. Splash 'N' Soak Station provides water-play respite for kids. Ariel of *The Little Mermaid* invites you to her own state-of-the-art attraction, Under the Sea: Journey of the Little Mermaid. Disney princesses welcome you for a photo op in the glittering Princess Fairytale Hall. You can be part of the show when you join Belle, Lumiere, and Madame Wardrobe of *Beauty and the Beast* at the Enchanted Tales with Belle attraction for a story performance. Meanwhile, Beast may be brooding in his castle, where the Be Our Guest dining room beckons to lunch and dinner guests. And the musical Seven Dwarfs Mine Train family coaster opened in 2014 to complete the expansion.

You can enter Fantasyland on foot from Liberty Square, Tomorrowland, or via the Walt Disney World Railroad, but the classic introduction is through Cinderella Castle. As you exit the castle's archway, look left to discover a charming and often overlooked touch: Cinderella Fountain, a lovely brass casting of the castle's namesake, who's dressed in her peasant togs and surrounded by her beloved mice and bird friends.

From the southern end of Liberty Square, head toward the park hub and stop at the Disney PhotoPass picture spot for one of the park's best, unobstructed ground-level views of Cinderella Castle. It's a great spot for that family photo.

TOMORROWLAND

The "future that never was" spins boldly into view as you enter Tomorrowland, where Disney Imagineers paint the landscape with whirling spaceships, flashy neon lights, and gleaming robots. This is the future as envisioned by sci-fi writers and moviemakers in the 1920s and '30s, when space flight, laser beams, and home computers were fiction, not fact. Retro Jetsonesque styling lends the area lasting chic.

Gamers who want a break from the crowds can find their favorite video challenges in the arcade attached to Space Mountain. SEGA race car, NASCAR, and Fast and Furious Super Bikes games draw tweens and teens; Lil' Hoops give young kids a manageable basketball challenge. Though Tomorrowland Transit Authority (TTA) PeopleMover isn't a big-ticket ride, it's a great way to check out the landscape from above as it zooms in and out of Space Mountain and curves around the entire land.

TOP MAGIC KINGDOM SPECTACLES

Fodor's Choice ★ **Disney Festival of Fantasy Parade.** Who'd want to miss a parade that delivers in 12 entertainment-packed minutes a lineup of Disney characters and royalty, a Steampunk-inspired, fire-breathing dragon, elaborate towering floats, and handsome pairs of dancers twirling to some of Disney's best tunes? This newest daily 3 pm parade celebrates Walt's legacy with vignettes featuring the glamour, drama, and fun of classic films like *Sleeping Beauty* and *Peter Pan* while also catering to fans of contemporary box-office hits like *Brave* and *Frozen*. The colorful pageant of nine floats outperforms its predecessors with über-creative costuming, inventive float technology, a cast of nearly 100 gung-ho performers, and a musical score that invites singing along with familiar medleys. From the 50-foot-long topiary garden float of Disney royal couples led by dancers in swan-neck-collared ball gowns with iridescent feathers to the 32-foot-tall Airship float finale with Mickey and Minnie, the parade energizes spectators as it rolls past. A Lost Boy from *Peter Pan* may grab your hand and kiss it. A stilt-walker might lean into your camera for a snapshot. You'll hear viewers gasp or shout when the towering 53-foot-long, green-eyed Maleficent Dragon, created with help from Tony-award-winning designer Michael Curry, rears its head and spews flames. **For people with disabilities:** There are viewing areas for guests in wheelchairs along the route; ask any cast member for guidance. A sign-language schedule is available at Guest Relations. ■ TIP→ The parade runs from Frontierland to Town Square. Check your guide map for the complete route. Disney now distributes a limited number of Fast-Pass+ reservations, but book as far ahead as possible. Otherwise, find shade beneath a Frontierland porch at least an hour before showtime. If you've seen the parade, this is a good time to head for popular rides while crowds gather along the route. ⊠ *Magic Kingdom* ⌛ *Duration: 12 mins. Crowds: Heavy. Audience: All Ages.*

Fodor's Choice ★ **Main Street Electrical Parade.** The Main Street parade, with 23 illuminated floats, 80 performers, and a half-million lights in all, first debuted at Disneyland in California in 1972. It lights up Magic Kingdom nights with plenty of power and its distinctive synthesizer-infused "Baroque Hoedown" musical theme. The lead float features Tinker Bell showering guests with 25,000 pixie-dusted points of light, and a finale float with a patriotic tribute that includes a majestic bald eagle shining with golden lights. Check *Times Guide;* the parade sometimes runs twice in one night and occasionally not at all. **For guests with disabilities:** Ask a cast member for best wheelchair viewing. ■TIP→ Use MyDisneyExperience.com to sign up before your visit for FastPass+ viewing, or take your place on the curb at least 40 minutes before the parade begins. ⊠ *Magic Kingdom* ⌛ *Duration: 20 mins. Crowds: Heavy. Audience: All Ages.*

Fodor's Choice ★ **Wishes.** When the lights dim on Main Street and orchestral music fills the air, you know this fireworks extravaganza is about to begin. In Wishes, Jiminy Cricket's voice comes to life and tries to convince you that your wishes really can come true. He gets plenty of support from the Disney stars of classic films such as *Pinocchio, Fantasia, Cinderella,* and *The Little Mermaid.* Portions of famous film songs play over loudspeakers, and you hear the voices of film characters like Peter Pan and Aladdin as more than 680 individual fireworks paint the night sky. Oh, and don't worry that Tinker Bell may have been sealed in her jar for the night—she comes back to fly above the crowd in grand pixie-dust style. Check the *Times Guide* for performance time, which varies seasonally. ■TIP→ You can book a FastPass+ ahead of your visit for best viewing. The Castle forecourt and surrounding bridges offer great views; or find a place near the front of the park for a quick post-show exit. ⊠ *Magic Kingdom* ⌛ *Duration: 12 mins. Crowds: Heavy. Audience: All Ages.*

10

EPCOT

Walt Disney said that Epcot would "take its cue from the new ideas and new technologies that are now emerging from the creative centers of American industry." He wrote that Epcot—never completed, always improving—"will never cease to be a living blueprint of the future, a showcase to the world for the ingenuity of American free enterprise."

But the permanent settlement that Disney envisioned wasn't to be. Epcot opened in 1982—16 years after his death—as a showcase, ostensibly, for the concepts that would be incorporated into the real-life Epcots of the future. (Disney's vision *has* taken an altered shape in the self-contained city of Celebration, an urban-planner's dream opened in 1996 on Disney property near Kissimmee.)

TOP ATTRACTIONS

The American Adventure

IllumiNations

Mission: SPACE

Soarin'

Test Track

Epcot, the theme park, has two key areas: Future World, where most pavilions are collaborations between Walt Disney Imagineering and U.S. corporations and are designed to demonstrate technological advances through innovative shows and attractions; and the World Showcase, where shops, restaurants, attractions, and live entertainment create microcosms of 11 countries from four continents.

For years, Epcot was considered the more staid park, a place geared toward adults. But after its 10th anniversary, Epcot began to evolve into a livelier, more child-friendly park, with interactive fun at Innoventions and such "wow" attractions as Future World's Test Track, Mission: SPACE, and Soarin'.

There's something for everyone here. The World Showcase appeals to younger children with the Kidcot Fun Stop craft stations and the Norway pavilion's Princess Storybook Dining. Soarin', in the Land Pavilion, is a family favorite. And the Seas with Nemo & Friends—with one of the world's largest saltwater aquariums and a Nemo-themed ride—is a must-see for all. Adrenaline junkie? Don't miss Test Track presented by Chevrolet, where you can design your own custom concept car, then put it through its high-speed paces.

Wear comfortable shoes—there's *a lot* of territory to cover here. Arrive early, and try to stay all day, squeezing in extras like high-tech games at Innoventions and a relaxing meal. If you enter through International Gateway before 11 am, cast members will direct you to Future World, which usually opens two hours before World Showcase, or you can indulge in a latte and éclair at the France bakery, the sole quick-service eatery open early in World Showcase.

PLANNING

GETTING ORIENTED

Epcot is composed of two areas: Future World and the World Showcase. The inner core of Future World's pavilions has the Spaceship Earth geosphere and a plaza anchored by the computer-animated Fountain of Nations. Also at the core is Innoventions, popular for its hands-on, high-tech exhibits, and immersion entertainment.

Six pavilions compose Future World's outer ring. Each of the three east pavilions has a ride and the occasional postride showcase; a visit rarely takes more than 30 minutes. The blockbuster exhibits on the west side contain rides and interactive displays; each exhibit can take up to 90 minutes for the complete experience.

World Showcase pavilions are on the promenade that circles the World Showcase Lagoon. Each houses shops, restaurants, and friendly international staffers; some have films or displays. Mexico offers a tame ride. Live entertainment is scheduled at every pavilion except Norway. Disney's monorail and buses drop you off at the main entrance in front of Future World. But if you're staying at one of the Epcot resorts (the BoardWalk, Yacht Club, Beach Club, Dolphin, or Swan), you can use the International Gateway entrance between World Showcase's France and U.K. pavilions.

PARK AMENITIES

Guest Relations: To the right of the ticket windows at the park entrance and to the left of Spaceship Earth inside the park, this is the place to pick up schedules and maps. You also can get maps at the park's International Gateway entrance and most shops. Guest Relations will also assist with dining reservations, ticket upgrades, and services for guests with disabilities.

Lockers: Lockers ($7 and $9, with $5 refundable deposit) are at the International Gateway and to the west of Spaceship Earth. Coin-operated lockers also are at the bus information center by the bus parking lot.

Lost People and Things: Instruct children to speak to someone with a Disney name tag if you become separated. Guest Relations has a computerized message center for contacting companions in any of the parks.

Stroller Rentals: You can rent strollers on the east side of the Entrance Plaza and at the International Gateway. Singles are $15 daily, $13 for multiday rental; doubles cost $31 daily, $27 for multiple days. Even preschoolers will be glad for a stroller in this large park.

VISITING TIPS

■ Epcot is so vast and varied that you really need two days to explore. With just one day, you'll have to be highly selective.

■ Go early in the week, when others are at Magic Kingdom.

■ If you like a good festival, visit during the International Flower & Garden Festival (early March through mid-May) or the International Food & Wine Festival (late September through mid-November).

■ Once through the turnstiles at either the main Future World entrance or the back World Showcase entrance, make a beeline for the popular Mission: SPACE and Test Track (for fast-paced thrills) or the Seas with Nemo & Friends and Soarin' (for family fun). Or get a FastPass+ and return later.

EXPLORING EPCOT

FUTURE WORLD

Future World's inner core is composed of the iconic Spaceship Earth geosphere and, beyond it, a plaza anchored by the awe-inspiring computer-animated Fountain of Nations, which shoots water 150 feet skyward. Don't miss interactive fun at Innoventions.

Six pavilions compose Future World's outer ring. On the east side, they are the Ellen's Energy Adventure, Mission: SPACE, and Test Track. Each

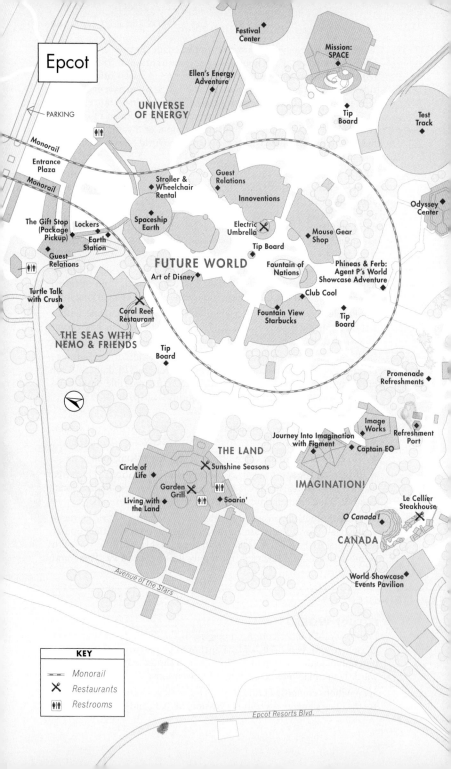

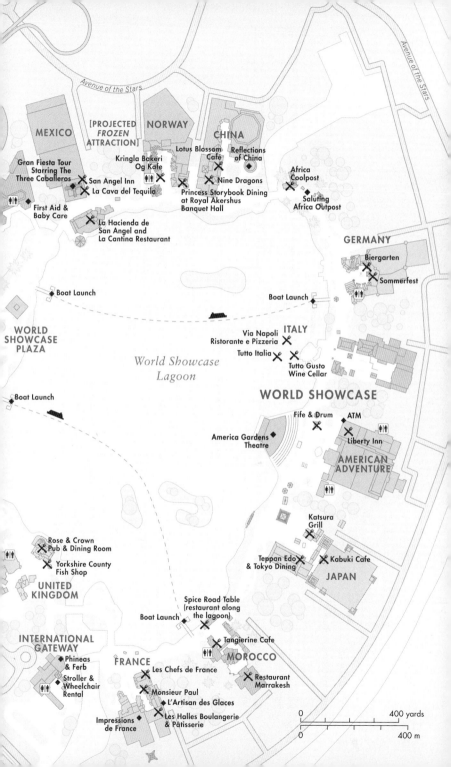

Avenue of the Stars

Avenue of the Stars

MEXICO

[PROJECTED *FROZEN* ATTRACTION]

NORWAY

CHINA

Gran Fiesta Tour Starring The Three Caballeros

Kringla Bakeri Og Kafe

Lotus Blossom Café

Reflections of China

San Angel Inn
La Cava del Tequila

Nine Dragons

Africa Coolpost

First Aid & Baby Care

Princess Storybook Dining at Royal Akershus Banquet Hall

Saluting Africa Outpost

La Hacienda de San Angel and La Cantina Restaurant

GERMANY

Biergarten

Sommerfest

Boat Launch

Boat Launch

WORLD SHOWCASE PLAZA

World Showcase Lagoon

Via Napoli Ristorante e Pizzeria

ITALY

Tutto Italia

Tutto Gusto Wine Cellar

WORLD SHOWCASE

Boat Launch

Fife & Drum

ATM

America Gardens Theatre

Liberty Inn

AMERICAN ADVENTURE

Katsura Grill

Rose & Crown Pub & Dining Room

Yorkshire County Fish Shop

Teppan Edo & Tokyo Dining

Kabuki Cafe

JAPAN

UNITED KINGDOM

Spice Road Table (restaurant along the lagoon)

Boat Launch

INTERNATIONAL GATEWAY

Phineas & Ferb

Tangierine Cafe

Stroller & Wheelchair Rental

FRANCE

Les Chefs de France

MOROCCO

Restaurant Marrakesh

Monsieur Paul

L'Artisan des Glaces

Impressions de France

Les Halles Boulangerie & Pâtisserie

0   400 yards

0   400 m

EPCOT

NAME	Height Req.	Type of Entertainment	Duration	Crowds	Audience	Tips
Future World						
Captain EO (Imagination!)	n/a	3-D Film	18 mins.	Moderate to Heavy	All but Young Kids	Come in the early morning or just before closing. Take off the 3-D glasses if little kids get scared.
Journey into Imagination with Figment (Imagination!)	n/a	Ride-Through	8 mins.	Light	Young Kids	Ride after Captain EO. Warn toddlers about darkness at the end of the ride.
Ellen's Energy Adventure (Universe of Energy)	n/a	Ride-Through	45 mins.	Moderate	All but very Young Kids	Best seats are to the far left and front of the theater.
Innoventions	n/a	Walk-Through	Up to you	Moderate to Heavy	All Ages	Come anytime.
The Circle of Life (The Land)	n/a	Film	20 mins.	Moderate to Heavy	All Ages	Come early or for your toddler's afternoon nap.
Living with the Land (The Land)	n/a	Cruise	14 mins.	Moderate	All	The line moves quickly, so come anytime.
★ Soarin' (The Land)	At least 40"	Simulator Ride	5 mins.	Heavy	All but very Young Kids	Use FastPass+, or come early, or just before closing.
The Seas with Nemo & Friends	n/a	Ride- and Walk-Through	Up to you	Moderate to Heavy	All Ages	Get Nemo fans here early in the morning.
Turtle Talk with Crush (The Seas with Nemo & Friends)	n/a	Animated Show	15 mins.	Moderate to Heavy	Young Kids and Families	Line up here after "clamobile" ride.

				You Bet!		Comments
★	Mission: SPACE	At least 44"	Thrill Ride	4 mins.	You Bet!	All but Young Kids	Come before 10 am or use FastPass+. Don't ride on a full stomach. A milder misson available for simulator-phobes.
	Spaceship Earth	n/a	Ride-Through	15 mins.	Moderate to Heavy	All Ages	Ride while waiting for Mission: SPACE or Soarin' FastPass+ appointment or just before closing.
★	Test Track	At least 40"	Thrill Ride	5 mins.	Heavy	All but Young Kids	Come early or use FastPass+. The ride can't function on wet tracks, so don't come after a downpour.
	World Showcase						
★	The American Adventure	n/a	Show/Film	30 mins.	Heavy	All Ages	Arrive 10 mins. before the Voices of Liberty are slated to perform.
	America Gardens Theatre	n/a	Live Show	Varies	Varies	Varies	Arrive more than an hour or so ahead of time for holiday and celebrity performances.
	Gran Fiesta Tour Starring the Three Caballeros	n/a	Cruise	9 mins.	Light to Moderate	All Ages	Especially good if you have young children.
	Impressions de France	n/a	Film	20 mins.	Moderate	All Ages	Come anytime.
	O Canada!	n/a	Film	14 mins.	Moderate to Heavy	All Ages	Stop in any time. Be prepared to stand for the film. No strollers permitted.
	Reflections of China	n/a	Film	14 mins.	Moderate	All Ages	Come anytime. Be prepared to stand during the film. No strollers permitted.

★ **Fodor's**Choice

pavilion presents a single, self-contained ride and an occasional postride showcase; a visit rarely takes more than 30 minutes, but it depends on how long you spend in the postride area. On the west side are the Seas with Nemo & Friends, The Land, and Imagination! These blockbuster exhibits contain both rides and interactive displays; you could spend at least 1½ hours at each of these pavilions, but there aren't enough hours in the day, so prioritize.

■TIP→ Before setting out, look into the Disney PhotoPass at the Camera Center in the Entrance Plaza. It tracks photos of your group shot by Disney photographers, which you can view and purchase later at the center or online.

WORLD SHOWCASE

Nowhere but at Epcot can you explore a little corner of nearly a dozen countries in one day. As you stroll the 1⅓ miles around the 40-acre World Showcase Lagoon, you circumnavigate the globe-according-to-Disney by experiencing native food, entertainment, culture, and arts and crafts at pavilions representing countries in Europe, Asia, North Africa, and the Americas. Pavilion employees are from the countries they represent—Disney hires them as part of its international college program.

Instead of rides, you have solid film attractions at the Canada, China, and France pavilions; several art exhibitions; and the chance to try your foreign language skills with the staff. Each pavilion also has a designated Kidcot Fun Stop, open daily from 11 or noon until about 8 or 9, where youngsters can try a cultural crafts project. Live entertainment is an integral part of the experience, and you'll enjoy watching the incredibly talented Jeweled Dragon Acrobats in China and the Matsuriza Taiko drummers in Japan or laughing along with the mime and juggler in the Italy courtyard.

Dining is another favorite pastime at Epcot, and the World Showcase offers tempting tastes of the authentic cuisines of the countries here.

TOP EPCOT SPECTACLES

Fodor's Choice ★ **IllumiNations: Reflections of Earth.** This marvelous nighttime spectacular takes place over the World Showcase Lagoon every night before closing. Be sure to stick around for the lasers, lights, flames, fireworks, fountains, and music that fill the air over the water. The show's Earth Globe—a gigantic, spherical, video-display system rotating on a 350-ton floating island—is three stories tall with 180,000 light-emitting diodes. It houses six computer processors and 258 strobe lights and projects images celebrating the diversity and unified spirit of humankind. The globe opens like a lotus flower in the grand finale, revealing a huge torch that rises 40 feet into the air as additional flames spread light across the lagoon. Nearly 2,800 fireworks shells paint colorful displays across the night sky.

Although there's generally good viewing from all around the lagoon, some of the best spots are in front of the Italy pavilion, on the bridge between France and the United Kingdom, on the promenade in front of Canada, at the World Showcase Plaza, and at La Hacienda de San Angel

The Temple of Quetzalcoatl (ket-zel-co-WAH-tal) at Teotihuacán (tay-o-tee-wah-CON), just outside Mexico City, is the model for the pyramid at the Mexico pavilion.

and La Cantina de San Angel in Mexico. **For people with disabilities:** During the show, certain areas along the lagoon's edge at Showcase Plaza, Canada, and Germany are reserved for guests using wheelchairs. ■ **TIP→** Limited FastPass+ reservations are offered; otherwise, for best views, find your place 45 minutes in advance and send someone in your group for ice cream or other treats. ⊠ *World Showcase* ☞ *Duration: 12 mins. Crowds: Heavy. Audience: All Ages.*

NIGHTLIFE

BARS

Cava del Tequila. Set inside the Mexico pavilion, this intimate bar serves tasty tapas, tequila flights, and some of the best margaritas anywhere, including the Cava Organic Skinny Lime Margarita. ⊠ *World Showcase, Mexico, Epcot.*

Rose & Crown Pub. Great piano sets by the Hat Lady and, on busy nights, four-to-six-deep at the bar guarantees good times at this United Kingdom watering hole. The fish-and-chips are first rate, and the Trio of United Kingdom Cheeses includes aged Irish cheddar and Stilton. (If you don't want to wait, the Yorkshire County Fish Shop next door serves the same goodies.) Grab a beer and let the fun begin! ⊠ *World Showcase, United Kingdom, Epcot.*

Tutto Gusto. This cool, cozy wine cellar adjoining Tutto Italia is a slice of Naples and the ideal place to kick back and sip a bubbly Prosecco or a glass of Italian wine while noshing on antipasto or tapas-size pastas.

For quicker service, head straight for the bar. ✉ *World Showcase Italy pavilion, Epcot.*

DISNEY'S HOLLYWOOD STUDIOS

The first thing you notice when you pass through the Hollywood Studios turnstiles is the laid-back California attitude. Palm-lined Hollywood Boulevard oozes glamour—but in a casual way that makes you feel as if you belong, even without your slinky Michael Kors jersey and Jimmy Choos.

When the park opened in May 1989 its name was Disney-MGM Studios. Disney changed the name in 2008 to broaden its appeal. Unlike the first movie theme park—Universal Studios in California—Hollywood Studios combined Disney detail with MGM's motion-picture legacy and Walt Disney's own animated classics. Imagineers built the park with real film and television production in mind, and during its first decade, the Studios welcomed films like *Ernest Saves Christmas* and TV shows like *Wheel of Fortune* to its soundstages.

The Animation Studios, too, were busy. Stories such as *Aladdin* and *Lilo & Stitch* came to life on the easels and computers of Disney's Florida animators. Though production has mostly halted at the park, you can enjoy plenty of attractions that showcase how filmmakers practice their craft. If you're wowed by action-film stunts, you can learn the tricks of the trade at the Indiana Jones Epic Stunt Spectacular! or the Lights, Motors, Action! Extreme Stunt Show. No trip to the Studios would be complete without a tour of the Magic of Disney Animation, where you can sit down and draw a character like Mickey or Donald.

In a savvy effort to grab a big piece of the pop-culture pie, Disney replaced its American Idol attraction with a Frozen singalong show in 2015. But big-hit attractions such as Toy Story Midway Mania! and new twists on old favorites like the 3-D Star Wars–themed simulator ride, Star Tours—The Adventures Continue keep the crowds happy.

PLANNING

10

GETTING ORIENTED

The park is divided into sightseeing clusters. **Hollywood Boulevard** is the main artery to the heart of the park, and is where you find the glistening replica of Graumann's Chinese Theater.

Encircling it are **Sunset Boulevard,** the **Animation Courtyard, Mickey Avenue, Pixar Place, Commissary Lane, the Streets of America area,** and **Echo Lake.**

The entire park is 135 acres, and has fewer than 20 attractions (compared with Magic Kingdom's 40-plus). It's small enough to cover in a day and even repeat a favorite ride or two.

If you're staying at one of the Epcot resorts (BoardWalk, Yacht or Beach Club, Swan, or Dolphin), getting to the Entrance Plaza on a motor launch is part of the fun. Disney resort buses also drop you at the entrance.

TOP ATTRACTIONS

FOR AGES 8 AND UP
Indiana Jones Epic Stunt Spectacular!

The Magic of Disney Animation

Rock 'n' Roller Coaster Starring Aerosmith

Star Tours—The Adventures Continue

Toy Story Midway Mania!

Twilight Zone Tower of Terror

FOR AGES 7 AND UNDER
Beauty and the Beast—Live on Stage

Disney Junior—Live on Stage!

Honey, I Shrunk the Kids Movie Set Adventure

Muppet*Vision 3-D

If you're staying off-property and driving, your parking ticket will remain valid for parking at another Disney park later in the day—provided, of course, you have the stamina.

PARK AMENITIES

Guest Relations: You'll find it just inside the turnstiles on the left side of the Entrance Plaza. **A FastPass+ kiosk** is at the corner of Hollywood and Sunset boulevards.

Lockers: You can rent lockers at the Crossroads of the World kiosk in the center of the Entrance Plaza. The cost is $7 or $9 with a $5 refundable key deposit. The lockers themselves are at Oscar's Super Service.

Lost People and Things: Instruct your kids to go to a Disney staffer with a name tag if they can't find you. If you lose them, ask any cast member for assistance; logbooks of lost children's names are kept at Guest Relations, which also has a computerized message center where you can leave notes for companions.

Disney's Hollywood Studios Lost and Found. Report lost or found articles at Guest Relations. ✉ *Hollywood Blvd.* ☎ *407/560–4666.*

Stroller Rentals: Oscar's Super Service rents strollers. Single strollers are $15 daily, $13 for more than one day; doubles are $31 daily, $27 multiday.

VISITING TIPS

■ Visit early in the week, when most people are at Magic Kingdom and Animal Kingdom.

■ Check the Tip Board periodically for attractions with short wait times to visit between FastPass+ appointments.

■ Be at the Fantasmic! amphitheater at least an hour before showtime if you didn't book the lunch or dinner package.

■ Need a burst of energy? On-the-run hunger pangs? Grab a slice at **Pizza Planet** at Streets of America. Alternatively, **Hollywood Scoops ice cream** on Sunset is the place to be on a hot day.

EXPLORING DISNEY'S HOLLYWOOD STUDIOS

HOLLYWOOD BOULEVARD

With its palm trees, pastel buildings, and flashy neon, Hollywood Boulevard paints a rosy picture of 1930s Tinseltown. There's a sense of having walked right onto a movie set of old, with art-deco storefronts and roving starlets and nefarious agents—actually costumed actors known as the Citizens of Hollywood. Throughout the park, characters from Disney movies new and old—from *Mickey Mouse* to *Toy Story* friends—pose for photos and sign autographs.

SUNSET BOULEVARD

This avenue honors Hollywood with facades derived from the Carthay Circle, the Beverly Wilshire Theatre, and other City of Angels landmarks.

ANIMATION COURTYARD

As you exit Sunset Boulevard, veer right through the high-arched gateway to the Animation Courtyard. Straight ahead are *Disney Junior—Live on Stage!*, the Magic of Disney Animation, and *Voyage of the Little Mermaid*.

PIXAR PLACE

Pixar Place is home to one of the park's biggest attractions, Toy Story Midway Mania! Where TV- and film-production soundstages once stood, warm brick facades welcome you to the land of Woody and Buzz. Open-air kiosks invite you to browse for themed toys and souvenirs. The brick building featuring Toy Story Friends is the place to mix and mingle with characters from the blockbuster movie *Toy Story*. Check schedules on your *Times Guide*.

STREETS OF AMERICA

It's fun to tour the New York and San Francisco sets here on foot so that you can check out the windows of shops and apartments, the taxicabs, and other details. If you're lucky (or smart enough to check the *Times Guide* show schedule), you'll join the street party for a performance by Mulch, Sweat & Shears—Live in Concert, as they play a 30-minute set of rock classics or rockin' seasonal tunes during holidays.

10

ECHO LAKE

In the center of an idealized slice of Southern California is a cool, blue lake—an oasis fringed with trees, benches, and things like pink-and-aqua, chrome-trimmed restaurants with sassy waitresses and black-and-white TVs at the tables; the shipshape Min & Bill's Dockside Diner; and Tatooine Traders, where kids can build their own Lightsabers and browse a trove of Star Wars–inspired goods. You'll also find two of the park's longest-running attractions, the Indiana Jones Epic Stunt Spectacular! and Star Tours—The Adventures Continue, where a 3-D attraction transformation jazzes up the galaxy.

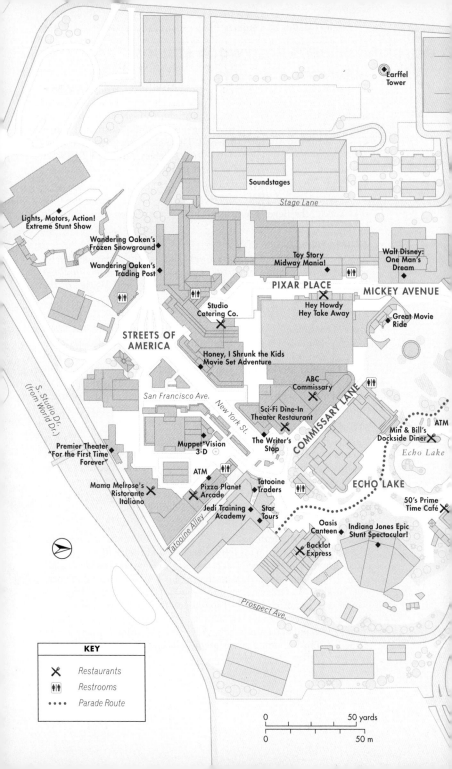

Earffel
Tower

Soundstages

Stage Lane

Lights, Motors, Action!
Extreme Stunt Show

Wandering Oaken's
Frozen Snowground

Toy Story
Midway Mania!

Walt Disney:
One Man's
Dream

Wandering Oaken's
Trading Post

PIXAR PLACE

Hey Howdy
Hey Take Away

MICKEY AVENUE

Studio
Catering Co.

Great Movie
Ride

**STREETS OF
AMERICA**

Honey, I Shrunk the Kids
Movie Set Adventure

ABC
Commissary

San Francisco Ave.

Sci-Fi Dine-In
Theater Restaurant

COMMISSARY LANE

Min & Bill's
Dockside Diner

ATM

Premier Theater
"For the First Time
Forever"

New York St.

The Writer's
Stop

Echo Lake

Muppet*Vision
3-D

S. Studio Dr.
(from World Dr.)

Mama Melrose's
Ristorante
Italiano

ATM

Pizza Planet
Arcade

Tatooine
Traders

ECHO LAKE

50's Prime
Time Café

Jedi Training
Academy

Star
Tours

Tatooine Alley

Oasis
Canteen

Indiana Jones Epic
Stunt Spectacular!

Backlot
Express

Prospect Ave.

KEY

✕	*Restaurants*
🚻	*Restrooms*
••••	*Parade Route*

0   50 yards

0   50 m

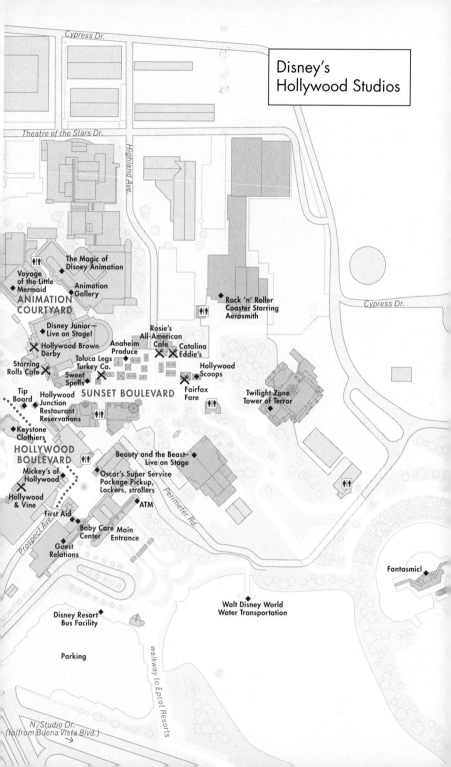

Cypress Dr.

Theatre of the Stars Dr.

Highland Ave.

Disney's Hollywood Studios

Cypress Dr.

The Magic of
Disney Animation

Voyage
of the Little
Mermaid

Animation
Gallery

**ANIMATION
COURTYARD**

Rock 'n' Roller
Coaster Starring
Aerosmith

Disney Junior—
Live on Stage!

Rosie's
All-American
Cafe

Hollywood Brown
Derby

Anaheim
Produce

Catalina
Eddie's

Toluca Legs
Turkey Co.

Starring
Rolls Cafe

Sweet
Spells

Hollywood
Scoops

SUNSET BOULEVARD

Tip
Board

Hollywood
Junction
Restaurant
Reservations

Fairfax
Fare

Twilight Zone
Tower of Terror

Keystone
Clothiers

**HOLLYWOOD
BOULEVARD**

Beauty and the Beast—
Live on Stage

Mickey's of
Hollywood

Oscar's Super Service
Package Pickup,
Lockers, strollers

Hollywood
& Vine

First Aid

ATM

Perimeter Rd.

Baby Care
Center

Main
Entrance

Prospect Ave.

Guest
Relations

Fantasmic!

Walt Disney World
Water Transportation

Disney Resort
Bus Facility

Parking

walkway to Epcot Resorts

N. Studio Dr.
(to/from Buena Vista Blvd.)

DISNEY'S HOLLYWOOD STUDIOS

NAME	Height Req.	Type of Entertainment	Duration	Crowds	Audience	Tips
Animation Courtyard						
Disney Junior—Live on Stage!	n/a	Show	24 mins.	Moderate to Heavy	Young Kids	Come first thing in the morning, when your child is most alert and lines are shorter.
The Magic of Disney Animation	n/a	Tour	15+ mins.	Moderate	All Ages	Come in the morning or late afternoon. Toddlers may get bored.
Voyage of the Little Mermaid	n/a	Show	15 mins.	Heavy	All Ages	Come first thing in the morning. Otherwise, wait until after 5.
Echo Lake						
Indiana Jones Epic Stunt Spectacular!	n/a	Show	30 mins.	Moderate to Heavy	All but Young Kids	Come at night, when the idol's eyes glow. Sit up front to feel the heat of a truck on fire.
★ Star Tours 3-D—The Adventure Continues	At least 40"	Simulator Exp.	6 mins.	Heavy	All but Young Kids	Get a FastPass+. Sit in rear for wildest ride.
Hollywood Boulevard						
Great Movie Ride	n/a	Ride/Tour	22 mins.	Moderate	All but Young Kids	Come while waiting for FastPass+ appointment. Lines out the door mean 25-min. wait—or longer.
Mickey Avenue						
Walt Disney: One Man's Dream	n/a	Walk-Through/ Film	15+ mins.	Light to Moderate	All but Young Kids	See this attraction while waiting for a FastPass+ appointment.

Pixar Place

Toy Story Midway Mania!	n/a	Interactive Ride	7 mins.	Heavy	All Ages	Come early; use FastPass+.

Streets of America

Honey, I Shrunk the Kids Movie Set Adventure	n/a	Playground	Up to you	Moderate	Young Kids	Come after you've done several shows and your kids need to cut loose. Keep an eye on toddlers who can quickly get lost in the caves and slides.
Lights, Motors, Action! Extreme Stunt Show	n/a	Show	38 mins.	Heavy	All but Young Kids	For the best seats, line up for the show while others are lining up for the parade.
Muppet*Vision 3-D	n/a	3-D Film	25 mins.	Moderate	All Ages	Arrive 10 mins. early. And don't worry—there are no bad seats.
For the First Time in Forever A "Frozen" Singalong Celebration*	n/a	Actors, film, music	30 mins.	Heavy	All Ages	Check showtimes in Studio Times Guide.

Sunset Boulevard

Beauty and the Beast—Live on Stage!	n/a	Show	30 mins.	Moderate to Heavy	All Ages	Come 30 mins. before showtime for good seats. Performance times vary, so check ahead. FastPass+ available for show fans.
★ Rock 'n' Roller Coaster Starring Aerosmith	At least 48"	Thrill Ride	1 min., 22 secs.	Huge	All but Young Kids	Ride early, then use FastPass+ for another go later.
★ Twilight Zone Tower of Terror	At least 40"	Thrill Ride	10 mins.	You Bet!	All but Young Kids	Use FastPass+. Come early or late evening.

*This new show is expected eventually to move to Echo Lake area in old American Idol Theater. But no word on when.

★ Fodor's Choice

ANIMAL KINGDOM

If you're thinking, "Oh, it's just another zoo, let's skip it," think again. Walt Disney World's fourth theme park, opened in 1998, takes its inspiration from humankind's enduring love for animals and pulls out all the stops. Your day will be packed with unusual animal encounters, enchanting entertainment, and themed rides that'll leave you breathless.

A large chunk of the park is devoted to animal habitats, especially the forest and savanna of Africa's Kilimanjaro Safaris. Towering acacia trees and tall grasses sweep across the land where antelopes, giraffes, and wildebeests roam. A lion kopje, warthog burrows, a zebra habitat, and an elephant watering hole provide ample space for inhabitants.

About 94 acres contain foliage like hibiscus and mulberry, perfect for antelope and many other species. The largest groups of Nile hippos and African elephants in North America live along the winding waterway that leads to the savanna. The generously landscaped Pangani Forest Exploration Trail provides roaming grounds for troops of gorillas and authentic habitats for meerkats, birds, fish, and other creatures.

Beyond the park's Africa territory, similar large spaces are set aside for the homes of Asian animals like tigers and giant fruit bats, as well as for creatures such as Galápagos tortoises and a giant anteater.

Disney Imagineers didn't forget to include their trademark thrills, from the Kali River Rapids ride in Asia to the fast-paced DINOSAUR journey in DinoLand U.S.A. Expedition Everest, the park's biggest thrill attraction, is a "runaway" train ride on a faux rugged mountain complete with icy ledges, dark caves, and a yeti legend. Next up: Imagineers are building a new land in the former Camp Minnie-Mickey location based on the blockbuster film *Avatar* and expected sequels.

Although you won't find a parade or a fireworks show, several live entertainment ensembles perform, including the popular Tam Tam Drummers of Harambe.

The only downside to the Animal Kingdom layout is that walking paths and spaces can get very crowded and hot in the warmest months. Your best bet is to arrive very early and see the animals first before the heat makes them (and you) woozy.

Just before the park opens, Minnie Mouse, Pluto, and Goofy arrive at the iconic Tree of Life in a safari vehicle to welcome the first guests into the heart of the park. Let the adventure begin!

PLANNING

GETTING ORIENTED

Animal Kingdom's hub is the Tree of Life, in the middle of Discovery Island. The park's lands, each with a distinct personality, radiate from Discovery Island. To the southwest, home of the former Camp Minnie-Mickey, Disney Imagineers are creating the new land of Pandora based on the *Avatar* film and upcoming sequels. The new area is expected to open in 2017. North of the hub is Africa, where Kilimanjaro Safaris travel across extensive savanna. In the northeast corner is Rafiki's Planet Watch with conservation activities.

Asia, with thrills like Expedition Everest and Kali River Rapids, is east of the hub, and DinoLand U.S.A brings *T. rex* and other prehistoric creatures to life in the park's southeast corner.

If you're staying on-site, you can take a Disney bus to the Entrance Plaza. If you drive, the $17 parking fee allows you to park at other Disney lots throughout the day.

Although this is technically Disney's largest theme park, most of the land is reserved for the animals. Pedestrian areas are actually quite compact, with relatively narrow passageways. The only way to get around is on foot or in a wheelchair or electronic convenience vehicle (ECV).

TOP ATTRACTIONS

Africa

Festival of the Lion King

Kilimanjaro Safaris

Asia

Expedition Everest

DinoLand U.S.A.

DINOSAUR.

Finding Nemo: The Musical

Discovery Island

Tree of Life: It's Tough to Be a Bug!

Tour

Wild Africa Trek

PARK AMENITIES

Guest Relations: This office will help with tickets at a window to the left just before you pass through the turnstile. Once you've entered, Guest Relations staffers in the Oasis can provide park maps, schedules, and answers to questions. They can also assist with dining reservations, ticket upgrades, and services for guests with disabilities.

Lockers: Lockers are in Guest Relations in the Oasis. Rental fees are $7 to $9 (depending on size) for a day plus a $5 key deposit.

Lost People and Things: Instruct your kids to speak to someone with a Disney name tag if you become separated. Lost children are taken to the baby-care center, where they can watch Disney movies, or to Guest Relations, whichever is closer. If you do lose your child, contact any cast member immediately and Disney security personnel will be notified.

Animal Kingdom Lost and Found. To retrieve lost articles on the same day, visit or call Lost and Found, which is at Guest Relations. ⊠ *Oasis* ☎ *407/938–2785.*

Stroller Rentals: Garden Gate Gifts in the Oasis rents strollers. Singles are $15 daily, $13 multiday; doubles run $31 daily, $27 multiday.

VISITING TIPS

■ Try to visit during the week. Pedestrian areas are compact, and the park can feel uncomfortably packed on weekends.

■ Plan on a full day here. That way, while exploring Africa's Pangani Forest Exploration Trail, say, you can spend 10 minutes (rather than just two) watching vigilant meerkats stand sentry or tracking a mama gorilla as she cares for her youngster.

10

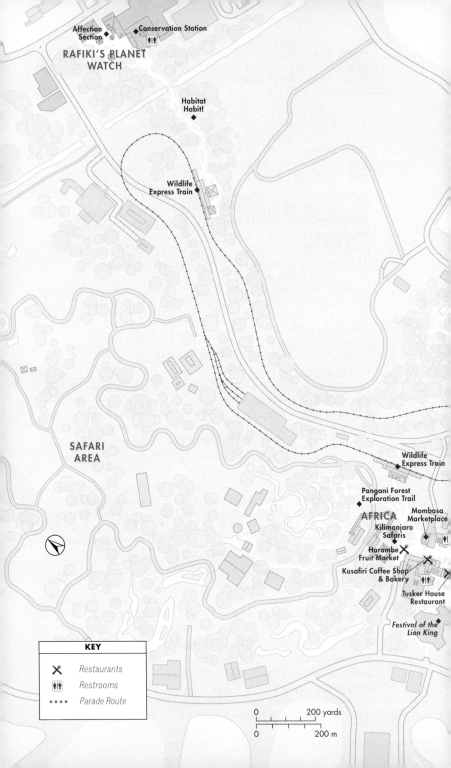

RAFIKI'S PLANET WATCH

Affection Section

Conservation Station

Habitat Habit!

Wildlife Express Train

SAFARI AREA

Wildlife Express Train

Pangani Forest Exploration Trail

AFRICA

Mombasa Marketplace

Kilimanjaro Safaris

Harambe Fruit Market

Kusafiri Coffee Shop & Bakery

Tusker House Restaurant

Festival of the Lion King

KEY	
✕	Restaurants
🚻	Restrooms
••••	Parade Route

0   200 yards

0   200 m

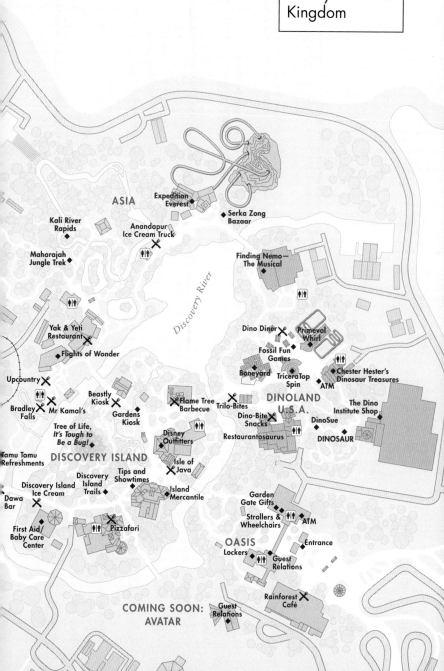

Disney's Animal Kingdom

ASIA

Expedition Everest

Kali River Rapids

Serka Zong Bazaar

Anandapur Ice Cream Truck

Maharajah Jungle Trek

Finding Nemo— The Musical

Discovery River

Yak & Yeti Restaurant

Flights of Wonder

Dino Diner

Primeval Whirl

Fossil Fun Games

Boneyard

TriceraTop Spin

ATM

Chester Hester's Dinosaur Treasures

Upcountry

Beastly Kiosk

Flame Tree Barbecue

Trilo-Bites

DINOLAND U.S.A.

The Dino Institute Shop

Bradley Falls

Mr Kamal's

Gardens Kiosk

Dino-Bite Snacks

DinoSue

Tree of Life, It's Tough to Be a Bug!

Disney Outfitters

Restaurantosaurus

DINOSAUR

Tamu Tamu Refreshments

DISCOVERY ISLAND

Isle of Java

Discovery Island Ice Cream

Discovery Island Trails

Tips and Showtimes

Island Mercantile

Garden Gate Gifts

Dawa Bar

Strollers & Wheelchairs

ATM

First Aid/ Baby Care Center

Pizzafari

OASIS

Entrance

Lockers

Guest Relations

Rainforest Café

COMING SOON: AVATAR

Guest Relations

ANIMAL KINGDOM

NAME	Height Req.	Type of Entertainment	Duration	Crowds	Audience	Tips
Africa						
★ Festival of the Lion King	n/a	Show	30 mins.	Moderate	All Ages	Book a FastPass+ or arrive 30–40 mins. before showtime. Sit in one of the front rows to increase your kid's chance of being chosen to participate in a show number.
★ Kilimanjaro Safaris	n/a	Riding Tour	22 mins.	Moderate to Heavy	All Ages	Do this first thing in the morning or use FastPass+. If you arrive at the park late morning, save it for day's end, when animals may be more active.
Pangani Forest Exploration Trail	n/a	Zoo/Aviary	Up to you	Light to Moderate	All Ages	Come while waiting for your safari FastPass+; try to avoid coming in at the hottest time of day, when the gorillas like to nap.
Asia						
★ Expedition Everest	At least 44″	Thrill Ride	2½ mins.	Huge	All but Young Kids	Arrive early or use FastPass+. This is the park's biggest thrill ride.
Flights of Wonder	n/a	Show	25 mins.	Light	All Ages	Arrive 15 mins. before showtime, and find a shaded seat beneath one of the awnings—the sun can be brutal.
Kali River Rapids	At least 38″	Thrill Ride	7 mins.	Heavy	All but Young Kids	Use your FastPass+ or come during the parade. You'll get wet.
Maharajah Jungle Trek	n/a	Zoo/Aviary	Up to you	Light to Moderate	All Ages	Come anytime.
DinoLand U.S.A.						
Boneyard	n/a	Playground	Up to you	Moderate to Heavy	Young Kids	Play here while waiting for DINOSAUR FastPass+, or come late in the day.

	Name		Type	Duration	Crowds	Ages	Tips
★	DINOSAUR	At least 40"	Thrill Ride	4 mins.	Heavy	All but Young Kids	Come first thing in the morning or at the end of the day, or use FastPass+.
	Finding Nemo—The Musical	n/a	Show	40 mins.	Heavy	All Ages	Arrive 40 mins. before showtime or book a FastPass+. Take young kids here while older kids wait for Expedition Everest.
	Fossil Fun Games	n/a	Arcade/Fair	Up to you	Light	All Ages	Bring a stash of ones to buy play tickets.
	Primeval Whirl	At least 48"	Thrill Ride	2½ mins.	Heavy	All but Young Kids	Kids may want to ride twice. Take your first spin early, then use FastPass+ if the wait is more than 20 mins.
	TriceraTop Spin	n/a	Thrill Ride for Young Kids	2 mins.	Heavy	Young Kids	Ride early while everyone else heads for the safari or while waiting for your FastPass+ appointment for DINOSAUR.
	Discovery Island						
★	Tree of Life—It's Tough to Be a Bug!	n/a	3-D film	20 mins.	Moderate to Heavy	All but Young Kids	Do this after Kilimanjaro Safaris or Expedition Everest. Small children may be frightened at creepy crawly moments in the dark.
	Rafiki's Planet Watch						
	Affection Section	n/a	Petting Yard	Up to you	Light	All Ages	Pet exotic goats and other rare domesticated animals.
	Conservation Station	n/a	Walk-Through	Up to you	Light to Moderate	All Ages	Wait for the critter encounter and learn how to protect endangered species.
	Habitat Habit!	n/a	Trail Walk	Up to you	Light	All Ages	Watch cotton-top tamarins along this discovery trail.
	Wildlife Express Train	n/a	Train Ride	5 mins.	Moderate	All Ages	Head straight to Affection Section with little kids to come face-to-face with domesticated critters.

★ **Fodor's**Choice

■ Arrive a half hour before the park opens as much to see the wild animals at their friskiest (morning is a good time to do the safari ride) as to get a jump on the crowds.

■ For updates on line lengths, check the Tip Board, just after crossing the bridge into Discovery Island.

■ Good places to rendezvous include the outdoor Dawa Bar or Tamu Tamu Refreshments areas in Africa, in front of DinoLand U.S.A.'s Boneyard, or on one of the benches outside Expedition Everest in Asia.

EXPLORING ANIMAL KINGDOM

THE OASIS

This entrance makes you feel as if you've been plunked down in the middle of a rain forest. Cool mist, the aroma of flowers, playful animals, and colorful birds enliven a miniature landscape of streams and grottoes, waterfalls, and glades fringed with banana leaves and jacaranda. It's also where you can take care of essentials before entering. Here you'll find guide maps, stroller and wheelchair rentals, Guest Relations, and an ATM.

DISCOVERY ISLAND

The park hub and site of the Tree of Life, this island is encircled by Discovery River, which isn't an actual attraction but makes for attractive views from the bridge to Harambe and another between Asia and DinoLand U.S.A. The island's whimsical architecture, with wood carvings from Bali, lends charm and a touch of fantasy. The Discovery Island Trails that lead to the Tree of Life provide habitats for African crested porcupines, lemurs, Galápagos tortoises, and other creatures you won't want to miss.

You'll discover some great shops and good counter-service eateries here. Visitor services that aren't in the Oasis are here, on the border with Harambe, including the baby-care center and the first-aid center.

DINOLAND U.S.A.

Just as it sounds, this is the place to come in contact with re-created prehistoric creatures, including the fear-inspiring carnotaurus and the gentle iguanodon. The landscaping includes live plants that have evolved over the last 65 million years. In collaboration with Chicago's Field Museum, Disney displays a complete, full-scale skeleton cast of Dino-Sue—also known as "Sue"—the 65-million-year-old *Tyrannosaurus rex* discovered near the Black Hills of South Dakota.

After admiring Sue, you can go on the thrilling DINOSAUR ride, play in the Boneyard, or take in the Finding Nemo: The Musical show at the Theater in the Wild. Kids will want to try the TriceraTop Spin and the Primeval Whirl family coaster, which has spinning "time machines." There's no need to dig for souvenirs at Chester and Hester's Dinosaur Treasures gift shop—all you need is your wallet.

ASIA

Meant to resemble an Asian village, this land is full of remarkable rain-forest scenery and ruins. Groupings of trees grow from a crumbling tiger shrine, and massive towers—representing Thailand and Nepal—are the habitat for gibbons, whose hooting fills the air.

AFRICA

The largest of the lands is an area of forests and grasslands, predominantly an enclave for wildlife from the continent. Harambe, on the northern bank of Discovery River, is Africa's starting point. Inspired by several East African villages, this Disney town has so much detail that it's mind-boggling to try to soak it all up. Signs on the apparently peeling stucco walls are faded, as if bleached by the sun, and everything has a hot, dusty look. For souvenirs with Disney and African themes, browse through the Mombasa Marketplace and Ziwani Traders.

RAFIKI'S PLANET WATCH

While in the Harambe, Africa, section, board the 250-passenger rustic Wildlife Express steam train for a ride to a unique center of eco-awareness named for the wise baboon from *The Lion King*. Young children especially enjoy the chance to explore these three animal-friendly areas.

TYPHOON LAGOON AND BLIZZARD BEACH

The beauty of Disney's water parks is that you can make either experience fit your mood. Like crowds? Head for the lounge chairs along the Surf Pool at Typhoon Lagoon or Melt-Away Bay at Blizzard Beach. Prefer peace? Walk past lush foliage along each park's circular path until you spot a secluded lean-to or tree-shaded patch of sand.

TYPHOON LAGOON

According to Disney legend, Typhoon Lagoon was created when the lush Placid Palms Resort was struck by a cataclysmic storm. It left a different world in its wake: surfboard-sundered trees, once-upright palms imitated the Leaning Tower of Pisa, and part of the original lagoon was cut off, trapping thousands of tropical fish—and a few sharks. Nothing, however, topped the fate of *Miss Tilly,* a shrimp boat from "Safen Sound, Florida," which was hurled high in the air and became impaled on Mt. Mayday, a magical volcano that periodically tries to dislodge *Miss Tilly* with huge geysers.

Ordinary folks, the legend continues, would have been crushed by such devastation. But the resourceful residents of Placid Palms were made of hardier stuff—and from the wreckage they created 56-acre Typhoon Lagoon, the self-proclaimed "world's ultimate water park."

GETTING ORIENTED

The layout is so simple. The wave and swimming lagoon is at the park's center. Note that the waves are born in the Mt. Mayday side and break on the beaches closest to the entrance. Any attraction requiring a gravitational plunge starts around the summit of Mt. Mayday. Shark Reef and Ketchakiddee Creek flank the head of the lagoon, to Mt. Mayday's

10

right and left, respectively, as you enter. The Crush 'n' Gusher water coaster is due right of Singapore Sal's.

You can take WDW bus transportation or drive to Typhoon Lagoon. There's no parking charge. Once inside, your options are to walk, swim, or slide.

WDW Information. Call WDW Information or check www.disney-world.com's park calendars for days of operation. ✉ *Blizzard Beach* ☎ *407/824–4321.*

WHAT TO EXPECT

You can speed down waterslides with names like Crush 'n' Gusher and Humunga Kowabunga or bump through rapids and falls at Mt. May-day. You can also bob along in 5-foot waves in a surf pool the size of two football fields or, for a mellow break, float in inner tubes along the 2,100-foot Castaway Creek. Go snorkeling in Shark Reef, rubberneck as fellow human cannonballs are ejected from the Storm Slides, or hunker down in a hammock or lounge chair and read a book. Ketchakiddee Creek, for young children, replicates adult rides on a smaller scale. It's Disney's version of a day at the beach—complete with friendly Disney lifeguards. Most people agree that kids under 7 and older adults prefer Typhoon Lagoon. Bigger kids and teens like Blizzard Beach.

During the off-season between October and April, Typhoon Lagoon closes for several weeks for routine maintenance and refurbishment.

PARK AMENITIES

Dressing Rooms and Lockers: There are thatched-roof dressing rooms and lockers to the right on your way into the park. It costs $8 a day to rent a small locker and $10 for a large one; there's also a $5 deposit. There are restrooms in every nook and cranny. Most have showers and are much less crowded than the dressing rooms. If you forgot your towel, rent ($2) or buy one at Singapore Sal's.

BLIZZARD BEACH

With its oxymoronic name, Blizzard Beach promises the seemingly impossible—a seaside playground with an alpine theme. As with its older cousin, Typhoon Lagoon, Disney Imagineers have created a legend to explain the park's origin.

The story goes that after a freak winter storm dropped snow over the western side of Walt Disney World, entrepreneurs created Florida's first downhill ski resort. Saunalike temperatures soon returned. But as the 66-acre resort's operators were ready to close up shop, they spotted a playful alligator sliding down the 120-foot-tall "liquid ice" slopes. The realization that the melting snow had created the world's tallest, fastest, and most exhilarating water-filled ski and toboggan runs gave birth to the ski resort–water park.

From its imposing ski-jump tower to its 1,200-foot series of rushing waterfalls, Blizzard Beach delivers cool fun even in the hot summertime. Where else can you wear your swimsuit on the slopes?

On Asia's Expedition Everest, you'll chug, twist, turn, and plunge up, through, and down Mt. Everest on nearly a mile of track. Oh, yeah, and beware of the yeti!

GETTING ORIENTED

The park layout makes it fairly simple to navigate. Once you enter and rent a locker, you'll cross a small bridge over Cross Country Creek before choosing a spot to park your towels and cooler. To the left is the Melt-Away Bay wave pool. Dead ahead you can see Mt. Gushmore, a chairlift to the top, and the park's many slopes and slides.

If thrills are your game, come early and line up for Summit Plummet, Slush Gusher, and Downhill Double Dipper before wait times go from light to moderate (or heavy). Anytime is a good time for a dip in Melt-Away Bay or a tube trip around Cross Country Creek. Parents with young children should claim their spot early at Tike's Peak, to the park's right even before you cross the bridge.

You can take WDW bus transportation or drive to Blizzard Beach. There's no charge for parking. Once inside, your options are to walk, swim, or slide.

WHAT TO EXPECT

Disney Imagineers have gone all out here to create the paradox of a ski resort in the midst of a tropical lagoon. Lots of verbal puns and sight gags play with the snow-in-Florida motif. The centerpiece is Mt. Gushmore, with its 120-foot-high Summit Plummet. Attractions have names like Teamboat Springs, a white-water raft ride. Themed speed slides include Toboggan Racers, Slush Gusher, and Snow Stormers. Between Mt. Gushmore's base and its summit, swim-skiers can also ride a chairlift converted from ski-resort to beach-resort use—with multihued umbrellas and snow skis on their undersides. Older kids and devoted waterslide enthusiasts generally prefer Blizzard Beach to other water parks.

PARK AMENITIES

Dressing Rooms and Lockers: Dressing rooms, showers, and restrooms are in the village area, just inside the main entrance. There are other restrooms in Lottawatta Lodge, at the Ski Patrol Training Camp, and just past the Melt-Away Bay beach area. Lockers are near the entrance, next to Snowless Joe's Rentals, and near Tike's Peak (the children's area and the most convenient if you have little swim-skiers in tow). It costs $8 to rent a small locker and $10 for a large one, and there's a $5 deposit. Note that there are only small lockers at Tike's Peak. The towels for rent ($2) at Snowless Joe's are tiny. If you forgot yours, you're better off buying a proper one at the Beach Haus.

TOP ATTRACTIONS
Typhoon Lagoon
Crush 'n' Gusher
Storm Slides
Typhoon Lagoon Surf Pool
Blizzard Beach
Slush Gusher
Summit Plummet
Tike's Peak

DISNEY'S OTHER WORLDS

Budget a few hours to explore Disney's "other" places. Several are no-admission-required charmers; one is a high-tech, high-cover-charge gaming wonderland.

DOWNTOWN DISNEY/DISNEY SPRINGS

EXPLORING

Epcot and close to Interstate 4 along a large lake, this shopping, dining, and entertainment complex called Downtown Disney (that will be renamed Disney Springs) now has four areas: the Marketplace, West Side, The Landing, and Town Center. Major changes are under way for the build-out expected by sometime in 2016 as new shops, restaurants, and promenades are completed. A much-needed, huge parking garage has opened, and another is under construction. You can rent lockers, strollers, or wheelchairs, and there are two Guest Relations centers.

DisneyQuest. In a five-story virtual-reality mini-theme park at Disney Springs West Side, DisneyQuest lets you pay a hefty cover to participate in high-tech virtual adventures and play video games. To be fair, you can play all day, and there are cutting-edge games and interactive adventures that make the admission worthwhile. It's also a great place for teens and older tweens (children under 14 must be accompanied by a guest age 14 or older).

In **Explore Zone,** fly through the streets of Agrabah with the help of a virtual-reality helmet on Aladdin's Magic Carpet Ride. Take a Virtual Jungle Cruise down the roiling rapids of a prehistoric world, and paddle (yes, *really* paddle) to adventure amid volcanoes, dinosaurs, and other

From the wreckage—like that shown here—in the wake of a storm, Placid Palms Resort residents created 56-acre Typhoon Lagoon. Or so the story goes....

cretaceous threats. At Pirates of the Caribbean: Battle for Buccaneer Gold, you and the gang must brave the high seas and sink pirate ships to acquire treasure.

In the **Score Zone,** battle supervillains while flying, headset firmly intact, through a 3-D comic world in Ride the Comix. Escape evil aliens and rescue colonists during Invasion! An ExtraTERRORestrial Alien Encounter. Or hip-check your friends in a life-size Mighty Ducks Pinball Slam game.

In the **Create Zone** learn the secrets of Disney animation at the Animation Academy. Create your own twisted masterpiece at Sid's Create-A-Toy, based on the popular animated film *Toy Story.* Or, at Living Easels, make a *living* painting on a giant electronic screen. Thrills await at Cyberspace Mountain, where you can design your own roller coaster on a computer screen, then climb aboard a 360-degree pitch-and-roll simulator for the ride of your dreams. At Radio Disney SongMaker, produce your own hit.

Classic free-play machines like Pac Man reside in the **Replay Zone.** You can also sit with a partner in an asteroid cannon–equipped bumper car and blast others to make their cars do a 360-degree spin in Buzz Lightyear's AstroBlaster.

Lost and Found is at the Guest Relations window and cash is available at ATMs inside the House of Blues merchandise shop not far from the DisneyQuest entrance. ⊠ *West Side* ☎ *407/828–4600* ✉ *$45 adults, $39 children 3–9, excluding sales tax* ⊙ *Sun.–Thurs. 11:30 am–10 pm, Fri. and Sat. 11:30 am–11 pm.*

The Landing. When it was a hopping nightlife destination called Pleasure Island, this area offered a mix of bars, comedy clubs, and dance spots. But the nightclubs are long closed, and the Island, renamed The Landing as part of the Disney Springs redevelopment, is more of a family-oriented dining and entertainment district. Raglan Road Irish Pub & Restaurant celebrates more than a decade in this location offering great food by Raglan Road's Irish celebrity chef Kevin Dundon, indoor and patio dining, live Irish music, and traditional Irish step-dance performances every night and during weekend brunch. Paradiso 37 also welcomes diners indoors and alfresco. New to this area are Morimoto Asia, The BOATHOUSE, and other dining experiences. ⊠ *Downtwon Disney.*

Marketplace. In the Marketplace, the easternmost Disney Springs area, you can meander along winding sidewalks and explore hidden alcoves. Children love to splash in fountains that spring from the pavement and ride the miniature train and old-time carousel ($2). Toy stores entice with creation-stations and too many treasures to comprehend. There are plenty of spots to grab a bite or sip a cappuccino along the lakefront. Most Marketplace shops, boutiques, and eateries begin opening at 9:30 am and stay open through 11 pm to midnight. ⊠ *Downtwon Disney.*

West Side. The main attractions in the hip West Side are the House of Blues music hall, Cirque du Soleil, Splitsville Luxury Lanes, Disney-Quest virtual indoor theme park and arcade, and a new Starbucks with covered patio overlooking the waterfront. You can also take a ride in the Characters in Flight helium balloon tethered here ($18 ages 10 and up, $12 ages 3–9), shop in boutiques, or dine in such restaurants as the Wolfgang Puck Café and Planet Hollywood. Shops open at 9:30 or 10:30 am, and closing time is between 11 pm and 2 am. The Splitsville entertainment center offers plenty of fresh fun with 30 bowling lanes on two floors, weekend DJs, and upscale eats like filet sliders and sushi at indoor and outdoor tables. ⊠ *Downtwon Disney.*

NIGHTLIFE

Bongos Cuban Café. Latin rhythms provide the beat at this restaurant and bar with a pre-Castro theme owned by pop singer Gloria Estefan. Four bars are especially busy on weekends, when a Latin band kicks it up a notch with *muy caliente* music. Samba, tango, salsa, and merengue rhythms roll throughout the week. ⊠ *West Side, Downtwon Disney*☏ *407/828–0999* ☾ *Sun.–Thurs. 11–10:30; Fri. and Sat. 11 am–2 am.*

House of Blues. The restaurant serves up live blues performances and rib-sticking Mississippi Delta cooking all week long. The attached concert hall has showcased such artists as Aretha Franklin, David Byrne, Steve Miller, Willie Nelson, and Journey. Many swear by the "World Famous Gospel Brunch" each Sunday. ⊠ *West Side, Downtwon Disney* ☏ *407/934–2583* 🍽 *Covers vary* ☾ *Restaurant open 11:30–11 Sun.–Thurs; 11:30–1 am Fri. and Sat. Concert times vary.*

La Nouba. If you've seen rave media reviews of this production, believe them. The surreal show by the world-famous Cirque du Soleil company starts at 100 mph and accelerates through 90 mesmerizing minutes of acrobatics, avant-garde costumes and staging, and captivating choreography. So much happens that even those who've seen the show once return to see what they missed last time.

The story of La Nouba—derived from the French phrase *faire la nouba* (live it up)—is alternately mysterious, dreamlike, comical, and sensual. A cast of 67 international performers—including two vocalists and six musicians who play 22 instruments from tower platforms—takes the stage in a 1,671-seat showroom of a big-top-style theater.

World-renowned jugglers manipulate balls, hoops, and clubs with breathtaking precision and speed. Another fresh act—Skipping Ropes—combines dance and acrobatics to elevate child's play to a seemingly impossible level.

The interplay is charming as the Cleaning Lady sweeps her way into a dreamworld of Technicolor characters who dance, tumble, and fly through the air on ribbons of red silk. Two silly clowns provide comic relief at intervals, and four adorable Chinese girls steal applause with their astonishing diabolo (Chinese yo-yo) performance. The jaw-dropping last act is a masterpiece of acrobatics and gymnastics synched to uplifting music.

Call ahead for good seats (there are three categories of seating), and hire a babysitter if necessary—you wouldn't want to miss one minute of this class act. ⊠ *West Side, Downtwon Disney* ☎ *407/939–7600 reservations* ⊕ *www.cirquedusoleil.com* ✉ *$63–$150 adults, $52–$125 children 3–9; higher holiday rates* ☺ *Performances Tues.–Sat. 6 and 9.*

DISNEY'S BOARDWALK

In the good ol' days, Americans escaped their city routines for breezy seaside boardwalks. Disney's BoardWalk is within walking distance of Epcot, across Crescent Lake from Disney's Yacht and Beach Club Resorts, and fronting a hotel of the same name. You may be drawn to its good restaurants, bars, shops, surreys, and performers. After sunset, the mood is festive. ■TIP➡ If you're here when Epcot is ready to close, you can watch the park fireworks from the bridge that connects BoardWalk to the Yacht and Beach Club Resorts.

10

NIGHTLIFE

Atlantic Dance Hall. This high-energy dance club plays music from the '80s onward, with a huge screen showing videos requested by the crowd. The parquet dance floor is set off by furnishings of deep blue, maroon, and gold, and the ceiling glows with gold stars and twinkling lights. Signature cocktails are in demand, and you can sip a cognac or choose from a selection of popular beers to inspire your dance floor moves. ⊠ *BoardWalk, Epcot Resort Area* ☎ *407/939–2444* ✉ *No cover* ☺ *Tues.–Sat. 9 pm–1:45 am.*

Big River Grille & Brewing Works. Disney World's only brewpub has intimate tables where brew masters tend to their potions. You can order an $8 sampler with five to seven 3-ounce pours of whatever's on tap that day, usually including Red Rocket, Southern Flyer Light Lager, Gadzooks Pilsner, and Steamboat Pale Ale. Upscale pub grub and sandwiches pair well. There's also a sidewalk café. ⊠ *BoardWalk, Epcot Resort Area* ☎ *407/560–0253* ⌨ *No cover* ⊙ *Daily 11–11.*

ESPN Club. The sports motif here is carried into every nook and cranny—the main dining area looks like a sports arena, with a basketball-court hardwood floor and a giant scoreboard that projects the day's big game. While you watch, you can munch on wings, nachos, and linebacker-size burgers. There are more than 100 TVs throughout (even in the restrooms). The place is packed for big games; call ahead to see if special seating rules are in effect. ⊠ *BoardWalk, Epcot Resort Area* ☎ *407/939–1177* ⌨ *No cover* ⊙ *Daily 11:30 am–1 am.*

Jellyrolls. In this rockin', boisterous piano bar, comedians act as emcees and play dueling grand pianos nonstop. The steady stream of conventions at Disney makes this the place to catch CEOs doing the conga to Barry Manilow's "Copacabana"—if that's your idea of a good time. ⊠ *BoardWalk, Epcot Resort Area* ☎ *407/560–8770* ⌨ *$12 cover* ⊙ *Daily 7 pm–2 am.*

11

UNIVERSAL ORLANDO

With Wet 'n Wild

WELCOME TO UNIVERSAL ORLANDO

TOP REASONS TO GO

★ **The Variety:** Universal Orlando is much more than just a single Hollywood-themed amusement park. It's also the fantasy-driven Islands of Adventure (IOA) theme park; the clubs and restaurants of the CityWalk entertainment complex; and the upscale, on-site Hard Rock Hotel, Portofino Bay, and Royal Pacific resorts. Nearby Wet 'n Wild water park is also affiliated with Universal.

★ **Theme-Park Powerhouse:** Neither SeaWorld nor any of Disney's four theme parks can match the collective energy at Universal Studios and Islands of Adventure. Wild rides, clever shows, constantly updated attractions, and an edgy attitude all push the envelope here.

★ **Party Central:** Throughout the year, Universal hosts festive park-wide events such as Mardi Gras, Halloween Horror Nights, Grinchmas, the Summer Concert Series, and the Rock the Universe Christian-music celebration.

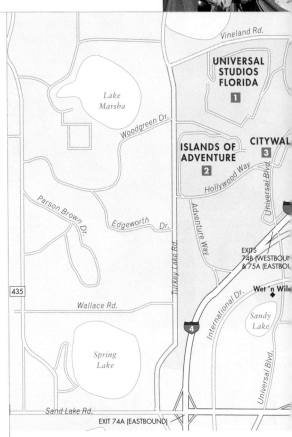

1 **Universal Studios Florida.** The centerpiece of Universal Orlando is a creative and quirky tribute to Hollywood past, present, and future. Overall, the collection of wild rides, quiet retreats, live shows, street characters, and clever movies (both 3-D and 4-D) are as entertaining as the motion pictures

Orlando

CENTRAL FLORIDA

GETTING ORIENTED

Universal Orlando is tucked into a corner created by the intersection of Interstate 4 and Kirkman Road (Highway 435), midway between Downtown Orlando and the Walt Disney World Resort. Here you'll be about 15 minutes from each and just 10 minutes from SeaWorld.

they celebrate. Another plus, they're always adding something new—like the Wizarding World of Harry Potter: Diagon Alley.

2 Islands of Adven-ture. Certainly the most significant addition to any Orlando theme park came when IOA introduced an entire land dedicated to

Harry Potter, which, in turn, sparked a s0ubstantial surge in attendance. Also at IOA are Spider-Man, the Hulk, velociraptors, the Cat in the Hat, and dozens of other characters that give guests every reason to head to the islands.

3 CityWalk. Even when the parks are closed (especially

when the parks are closed), locals and visitors come to this sprawling entertain-ment and retail complex to watch movies; dine at theme restaurants; shop for everything from cigars to surf wear; and stay up late at nightclubs celebrating the French Quarter, Jamaica, and the coolest clubs of NYC.

By Gary
McKechnie
and Joseph
Hayes

Universal Orlando's personality is revealed the moment you arrive on property. Mood music, cartoonish architecture, abundant eye candy, subtle and overt sound effects, whirling and whizzing rides, plus a throng of fellow travelers will follow you to nearly every corner of the park. For peace and quiet, seek out a sanctuary at one of the resort hotels.

At a breathless pace, there's a chance you could visit both Universal parks in a single day, but to do that you'll have to invest in an Express Pass. Without it, you'll spend a good portion of that day waiting in line at the premium attractions. So allow two days, perhaps three; a day for each park and a "pick-up" day to return to your favorites at a leisurely pace. Which attractions are the main attractions? At both IOA and Universal Studios, it's definitely the Wizarding World of Harry Potter. That pairing along with The Mummy and The Simpsons attractions are always popular.

Universal Studios appeals primarily to those who like loud, fast, high-energy attractions—generally teens and adults. Covering 444 acres, it's a rambling montage of sets, shops, and soundstages housing themed attractions, reproductions of New York and San Francisco and London, and some genuine moviemaking paraphernalia.

When Islands of Adventure (IOA) first opened in 1999, it took attractions to a new level. Most—from Marvel Super Hero Island and Toon Lagoon to Seuss Landing and the Lost Continent—are impressive; some even out-Disney Disney. In 2010, IOA received well-deserved worldwide attention when it opened the 20-acre Wizarding World of Harry Potter. And in 2014 Universal Studios made another huge leap forward when it opened a full-scale version of Diagon Alley, complete with Gringotts Bank and a magical train that departs for IOA from Platform 9¾.

PLANNING

GETTING HERE AND AROUND

East on Interstate 4 (from WDW and Tampa), exit at Universal Boulevard (75A); take a left into Universal Orlando, and follow the signs. Heading west on Interstate 4 (from Downtown or Daytona), exit at Universal Boulevard (74B), turn right, and follow Hollywood Way.

Both Universal Studios and IOA require a lot of walking—a whole lot of walking. Start off by using the parking area's moving walkways as much as possible. Arrive early at either park, and you may be able to complete a single lap that will get you to the main attractions.

OPERATING HOURS

Universal Studios and IOA are open 365 days a year, from 9 am to 7 pm, with hours as late as 10 pm in summer and at holidays. Wet 'n Wild is also open 365 days a year, weather permitting, but with widely varying hours. Usually it's open from 9 to 6, with summer hours from 9:30 am until 9 pm. Call for exact hours.

PARKING

Universal's two garages total 3.4 million square feet, so *note your parking space.* The cost is $17 for cars and motorcycles ($5 after 6 pm and free after 10), $22 for RVs & buses, and $25 for preferred parking. Although moving walkways get you partway, you could walk up to a half mile to reach the gates. Valet parking ($15 for up to two hours, $35 for more than two hours) is much closer.

ADMISSION

The at-the-gate, per-person, per-day rate for either Universal Studios Florida or IOA is $96 (ages 10 and up) and $90 for children (ages 3–9). Far less expensive are multiday passes.

EXPRESS PASSES

The Express Pass ranges in price from about $35 off-season to around $80 in peak season. This pass gets you to the front of most lines and saves a tremendous amount of time. Keep in mind, the pass is for one use only at each attraction—a more expensive "unlimited" pass takes you to the head of the line again and again and again. If you're a guest at a Universal hotel, this perk is free; your room key serves as the pass.

UNIVERSAL DINING PLAN

If you prefer to pay in advance, Quick Service meals include one meal, two snacks, and a nonalcoholic beverage ($20). The kids' version covers a kids meal, one snack, and a beverage ($13). Universal Studios locations include Mel's Drive-In, Louie's Italian, Beverly Hills Boulangerie, and the Classic Monsters Café. At Islands of Adventure, your choices are the Comic Strip Café, Croissant Moon, the Burger Digs, and Café 4.

UNIVERSAL STRATEGIES

Arrive early. Come as early as 8 am if the parks open at 9. Seriously. Better to share them with hundreds of people than with thousands.

Visit on a weekday. Crowds are lighter, especially fall through spring, when kids are in school.

Don't forget anything in your car. Universal's parking areas are at least a half mile from park entrances, and a round-trip hike will eat up valuable time. Consider valet parking. It costs $35 for longer than two hours before 6 pm (twice as much as regular parking), but it puts you much closer to Universal's park entrances and just steps from CityWalk.

Know the restrictions. A few things aren't allowed in the parks: alcohol and glass containers; hard-sided coolers; soft-sided coolers larger than 8½ inches wide by 6 inches high by 6 inches deep; and coolers, suitcases, and other bags with wheels. But if your flight's leaving later, you can check your luggage at the parks (unless you just leave them in your car).

Look into the Express Pass. Jumping to the front of the line with this pass really is worth the extra cost on busy days—unless you stay at a resort hotel, in which case front-of-line access is one of the perks.

Ride solo. At Universal some rides have a single-rider line that moves much faster than regular lines.

Get expert advice. The folks at Guest Services (aka Guest Relations) have great insight. The reps can even create a custom itinerary free of charge.

Check out Child Swap. At certain Universal attractions, one parent can enter the attraction, take a spin, and then return to take care of the baby while the other parent rides without having to wait in line again.

TOURS

VIP Tours. Universal has several VIP tours that are worthwhile if you're in a hurry, if crowds are heavy, if you're with a large group—and if you have the money to burn (prices leapt in 2014). The tours include extras like front-of-the-line access (that is, the right to jump to the head of the line). You can also arrange for extras like priority restaurant seating, bilingual guides, gift bags, refreshments at check-in, wheelchairs and strollers, and valet parking. Prices cited here do not include sales tax or park admission, and may edge up in peak seasons (or may not be available in peak season, so call ahead).

Here's what you'll pay in off-peak/peak seasons: Nonexclusive one-day tours (i.e., you'll tour with other park guests) cost $299/$369 per person for one park (five hours) and $329/$389 for two parks (seven hours). Then there are exclusive tours for your group only. If you're traveling with up to 10 people, consider splitting the cost of an eight-hour tour customized to your interests, which includes a sit-down lunch at the park of your choice. The eight-hour one-park exclusive price is $2,599/$2,899; two parks in eight hours will cost you $2,899/$3,199. What does $4,799/$4,999 get you? How about a two-day tour of both parks with backstage access and discussions on park history, decorating, and landscaping? And lunch. ☎ 407/363–8295 ⊕ www. universalorlando.com.

CONTACTS

Universal ☎ 407/363–8000 ⊕ www.universalorlando.com

Universal Dining and Tickets ☎ 407/224–7840

Universal (Loews Resorts) Room Reservations ☎ 877/819–7884

Universal Vacation Packages ☎ 800/407–4275

Wet 'n Wild ☎ 407/351–1800 or 800/992–9453 ⊕ www.wetnwild.com

UNIVERSAL STUDIOS

11

Inspired by the California original and opened in Orlando in 1990 (when the city assumed it would become "Hollywood East"), Universal Studios celebrates the movies. The park is a jumble of areas and attractions. But the same is true of back-lot sets at a film studio. Suspend any disbelief you might have, and just enjoy the motion-picture magic.

At Production Central large soundstages house attractions based on TV programs and films like *Shrek, Despicable Me,* and *Twister.* Because it's right near the entrance it can be the park's most crowded area.

Here you see firsthand that not every film or program based in New York is actually shot in New York. Cleverly constructed sets mean that nearly every studio can own its own Big Apple. Universal is no exception. As you explore Production Central, a collection of sparkling public buildings, well-worn neighborhoods, and back alleys are the next-best thing to Manhattan itself.

As you enter the area known as San Francisco, you're roughly one-third of the way through the park. The crowds spread out, and the pace seems to slow. You can stop to see a show starring Beetlejuice or dine at the waterfront Lombard's Seafood Grille.

After passing scenes from San Francisco, you'll reach the land everyone is talking about: the Wizarding World of Harry Potter: Diagon Alley. What the books suggest and what filmmakers created, Universal has replicated right here—putting you in the middle of a fantastic fantasyland. Just ahead, World Expo features two large attractions—MEN IN BLACK: Alien Attack and the Simpsons Ride. The scarcity of rides here is, however, offset by the colorful spectacle surrounding the Simpson's hometown of Springfield and the abundant attractions at Woody Woodpecker's KidZone. It matches the energy of toddlers and the under-10 crowd with diversions that include a junior-size roller coaster, a mini–water park, and a chance to meet E.T. and Barney the dinosaur. In Hollywood, quiet parks and flashy Rodeo Drive really do make you think you've stepped into vintage Tinseltown.

All in all, Universal Studios fulfills its promise: to put you in the movies.

PLANNING

GETTING ORIENTED

On a map, the park appears neatly divided into seven areas positioned around a huge lagoon. There's Production Central, which covers the entire left side of the Plaza of the Stars; New York, with street performances at 70 Delancey; San Francisco; the Wizarding World of Harry Potter: Diagon Alley; the futuristic World Expo; Woody Woodpecker's KidZone; and Hollywood.

What's tricky is that—because it's designed like a series of movie sets—there's no straightforward way to tackle the park. You'll probably make some detours and do some backtracking. To save time and shoe leather,

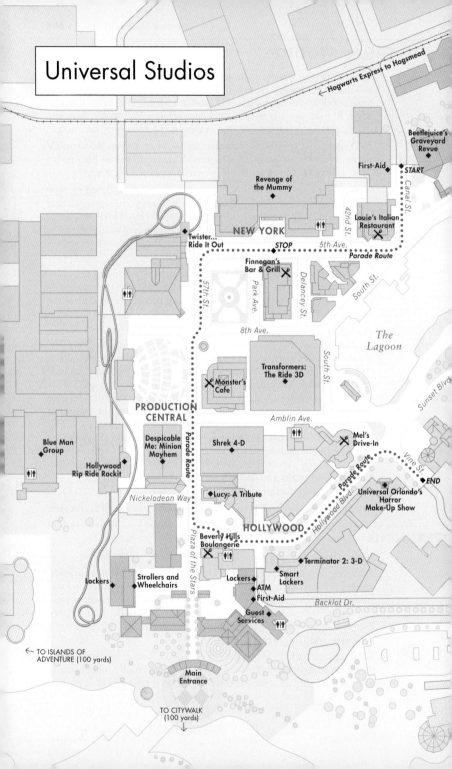

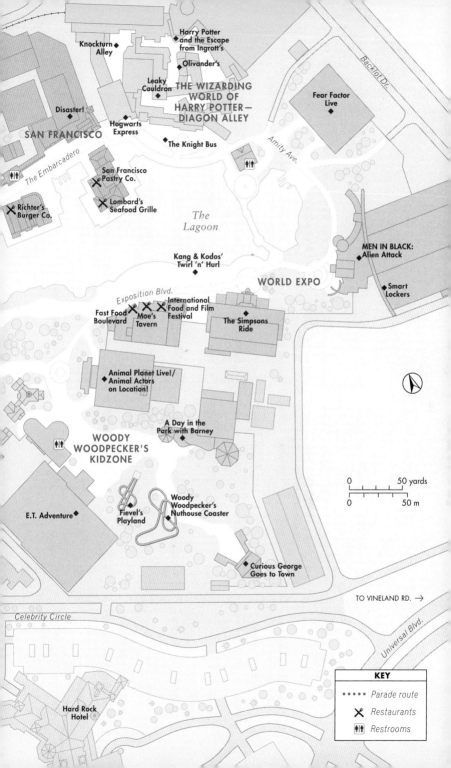

Knockturn Alley ◆

Harry Potter and the Escape from Ingrott's ◆

Olivander's ◆

Leaky Cauldron ◆

THE WIZARDING WORLD OF HARRY POTTER— DIAGON ALLEY

Fear Factor Live ◆

Disaster! ◆

Hogwarts Express ◆

SAN FRANCISCO

The Knight Bus ◆

Amity Ave.

Backlot Dr.

The Embarcadero

San Francisco Pastry Co. ✕

Lombard's Seafood Grille ✕

Richter's Burger Co. ✕

The Lagoon

Kang & Kodos' Twirl 'n' Hurl ◆

WORLD EXPO

MEN IN BLACK: Alien Attack ◆

Smart Lockers ◆

Exposition Blvd.

Fast Food Boulevard ✕ ✕ ✕

Moe's Tavern

International Food and Film Festival

The Simpsons Ride ◆

Animal Planet Live!/ Animal Actors on Location! ◆

A Day in the Park with Barney ◆

WOODY WOODPECKER'S KIDZONE

E.T. Adventure ◆

Fievel's Playland

Woody Woodpecker's Nuthouse Coaster

Curious George Goes to Town ◆

0   50 yards
0   50 m

TO VINELAND RD. →

Celebrity Circle

Universal Blvd.

Hard Rock Hotel

KEY	
•••••	*Parade route*
✕	*Restaurants*
�♀	*Restrooms*

UNIVERSAL STUDIOS

NAME	Height Req.	Type of Entertainment	Duration	Crowds	Audience	Tips
Hollywood						
Lucy: A Tribute	n/a	Walk-Through	15 mins.	Light	Adults	Save this for a hot afternoon or for on your way out.
Terminator 2 3-D	n/a	3-D Film/Simulator Exp.	21 mins.	Heavy	All but Young Kids	Come first thing in the morning or use Express Pass.
★ Universal Orlando's Horror Make-Up Show	n/a	Show	25 mins.	Moderate	All but Young Kids	Come in the afternoon or evening. Young children may be frightened; older children eat up the blood-and-guts comedy.
Production Central						
★ Hollywood Rip Ride Rockit!	At least 51"	Thrill Ride	2 mins.	You Bet!	All but Young Kids	Come early, late, or use a Express Pass. Be patient.
Shrek 4-D	n/a	3-D Film	12 mins.	Heavy	All Ages	Come early or late, or use Express Pass.
New York						
Revenge of the Mummy	At least 48"	Thrill Ride	3 mins.	Heavy	All but Young Kids	Use Express Pass, or come first thing in the morning.
Twister…Ride It Out	n/a	Show/Simulator Exp.	3 mins.	Heavy	All but Young Kids	Come first thing in morning or at closing. This "ride" involves standing and watching the action unfold.
San Francisco/Amity						
Beetlejuice's Graveyard Revue	n/a	Show	25 mins.	Light to Moderate	All but Young Kids	You can use Express Pass here, but there's really no need as there's little chance of a wait.
Disaster!	n/a	Thrill Ride	20 mins.	Heavy	All but Young Kids	Come early, before closing, or use Universal Express Pass. This is loud.
TRANSFORMERS	40"	3-D Thrill Ride	5 mins.	Heavy	All but Young Kids	No Express Pass. Come early.

Woody Woodpecker's KidZone

A Day in the Park with Barney	n/a	Show	20 mins.	Light	Young Kids	Arrive 10–15 mins. early on crowded days for a good seat—up close and in the center. Can use Express Pass.
Animal Actors on Location!	n/a	Show	20 mins.	Moderate to Heavy	All Ages	Stadium seating, but come early for a good seat. Express Pass accepted.
Curious George Goes to Town	n/a	Playground with Water	Up to you	Moderate	Young Kids	Come in late afternoon or early evening. Bring a towel.
E.T. Adventure	At least 34"	Thrill Ride for Kids	5 mins.	Moderate to Heavy	All Ages	Come early morning or use Express Pass.
Fievel's Playland	n/a	Playground with Water	Up to you	Light to Moderate	Young Kids	Generally light crowds, but there are waits for the waterslide. On hot days come late.
Woody Woodpecker's Nuthouse Coaster	At least 36"	Thrill Ride for Kids	1½ mins.	Moderate to Heavy	Young Kids	Come at park closing, when most little ones have gone home. Try Express Pass.

World Expo

★ MEN IN BLACK: Alien Attack	At least 42"	Thrill Ride	4½ mins.	Heavy	All but Young Kids	Solo riders can take a faster line, so split up. This ride spins. Use Express Pass.
The Simpsons Ride	40"	Thrill Ride/ Simulator Exp.	6 mins.	Heavy	All but Young Kids	Use Express Pass.

The Wizarding World of Harry Potter: Diagon Alley

Harry Potter and the Escape from Gringotts	42"	Simulator Exp.	5 mins.	Heavy	All but Young Kids	The single rider line moves fairly quickly.
Hogwarts Express–King's Cross Station	n/a	Railroad	10 mins.	Heavy	All Ages	You must have a Park-to-Park ticket

★ Fodor'sChoice

TOP ATTRACTIONS

AGES 7 AND UP

Hollywood Rip Ride Rockit. On this super-wild coaster, you select the soundtrack.

MEN IN BLACK: Alien Attack. The "world's first ride-through video game" gives you a chance to compete for points by plugging away at an endless swarm of aliens.

Revenge of the Mummy. It's a jarring, rocketing indoor coaster that takes you past scary mummies and billowing balls of fire (really).

Shrek 4-D. The 3-D film with sensory effects picks up where the original film left off—and adds some creepy extras in the process.

The Simpsons Ride. It puts you in the heart of Springfield on a wild-and-crazy virtual-reality experience.

Transformers: The Ride 3-D. Universal Studios' version of IOA's fantastic Spider-Man experience, but this one features a rough-and-tumble encounter with the mechanical stars of the film franchise.

Harry Potter and the Escape from Gringotts. Getting into the vault at Gringotts Bank can be a challenge, but it's also a first-class adventure thanks to technology similar to that of The Transformers and IOA's Spider-Man and Harry Potter and the Forbidden Journey.

Universal Orlando's Horror Make-Up Show. This sometimes gross, often raunchy, but always entertaining demonstration merges the best of stand-up comedy with creepy effects.

AGES 6 AND UNDER

Animal Actors on Location! It's a perfect family show starring a menagerie of animals whose unusually high IQs are surpassed only by their cuteness and cuddle-ability.

Curious George Goes to Town. The celebrated simian visits the Man with the Yellow Hat in a small-scale water park.

A Day in the Park with Barney. Young children love the big purple dinosaur and the chance to sing along.

ask theme park hosts for itinerary suggestions and time-saving tips. Here are a few of our own suggestions.

TOURING TIPS

We highly recommend you purchase your tickets online because it gives you plenty of time to consider your many options and includes a discount. Entering Universal Studios can be overwhelming as you and thousands of others flood through the turnstiles at once. Pick up a map in the entryway to CityWalk or by the park turnstiles and spend a few minutes reviewing it. Map out a route, find show schedules, and select restaurants. If a host is nearby, ask for insider advice on what to see first.

The "right" way. Upon entering, avoid the temptation to go left toward the towering soundstages, looping the park clockwise. Instead, head right—bypassing shops, restaurants, and some crowds to primary attractions like the Simpsons Ride and MEN IN BLACK: Alien Attack.

Photo ops. Universal Studios posts signs that indicate photo spots and show how best to frame your shot.

Rendezvous. Good meeting spots include Lucy: A Tribute, near the entrance; Mel's Drive-In, midway through the park on the right; and Beetlejuice's Graveyard Revue midway through the park on the left.

PARK AMENITIES

Guest Services: Get strategy advice *before* visiting by calling Guest Services at ☎ *407/224–4233.*

Lockers: Daily rates for lockers near the park entrance are $8 for a small unit and $10 for a larger one. There are free lockers near the entrances of some high-speed attractions (such as MEN IN BLACK: Alien Attack and Revenge of the Mummy), where you can stash your stuff before your ride; they're available to you for up to 90 minutes total.

Lost People and Things: If you plan to split up, be sure everyone knows where and when to reconnect. Staffers take lost children to Guest Services near the main entrance. This is also where you might find lost personal items.

Stroller Rentals: Just inside the main entrance, there are strollers for $15 (single) and $25 (double) a day. You can also rent small kiddie cars ($18) or large ones ($28) by the day.

EXPLORING

PRODUCTION CENTRAL

Expect plenty of loud, flashy, rollicking rides that appeal to tweens, teens, and adults. Clear the turnstiles and go straight. You can use Express Pass at all attractions.

NEW YORK

Universal has gone all out to re-create New York's skyscrapers, commercial districts, ethnic neighborhoods, and back alleys—right down to the cracked concrete. Hidden within these structures are restaurants, arcades, gift shops, and key attractions. And, although they're from Chicago, the Blues Brothers drive from the Second City to New York City in their Bluesmobile for free performances at 70 Delancey. Here you can use Express Pass at Revenge of the Mummy and Twister.

SAN FRANCISCO

This area celebrates the West Coast with the wharves and warehouses of San Francisco's Embarcadero and Fisherman's Wharf districts. *Use your Express Pass at both attractions.*

WORLD EXPO

At the far end of the park is a futuristic set of buildings containing a few of Universal Studios' most popular attractions, MEN IN BLACK: Alien Attack, the Simpsons Ride, and Kang & Kodos' Twirl 'n' Hurl, which offer fast admission with Express Pass.

WOODY WOODPECKER'S KIDZONE

With its colorful compilation of rides, shows, and play areas, this entire section caters to preschoolers. It's a pint-size Promised Land, where kids can try out a roller coaster and get sprayed, splashed, and soaked in a water-park area. It's also a great place for parents, since it gives them a

needed break after nearly circling the park. All shows and attractions except Curious George and Fievel accept Universal Express Pass.

HOLLYWOOD

The quintessential tribute to the golden age of the silver screen, this area to the right of the park entrance celebrates icons like the Brown Derby, Schwab's Pharmacy, and art deco Hollywood. There are only a few attractions here, and all except Lucy accept Universal Express Pass.

THE WIZARDING WORLD OF HARRY POTTER: DIAGON ALLEY

Hidden by a facade of London row homes, you may not think there's much to see. But when you spy an opening through a broken brick wall and step into Diagon Alley, you'll realize what an incredible blueprint J.K. Rowling created through her words. You can literally spend hours in this one district looking at the complete range of Potter-centric places: Universal Studios' version of Ollivanders wand shop; Weasleys' Wizard Wheezes (magical jokes and novelty items); the Magical Menagerie (all creatures furry, feathered, or scaly); Madam Malkin's Robes for All Occasions (wizard wear); Wiseacre's Wizarding Equipment; and Quality Quidditch Supplies. For practitioners of the Dark Arts, venture down Knockturn Alley and step inside Borgin and Burkes. For an appetizing break, stop at the Leaky Cauldron, the land's signature restaurant, or cool off at Florean Fortescue's Ice-Cream Parlour.

And when you're ready to head to Hogsmeade (conveniently located at the neighboring Islands of Adventure), make sure you have a park-to-park pass before stepping aboard the wonderful, magical Hogwarts Express—now departing to Islands of Adventure from Platform 9¾.

ISLANDS OF ADVENTURE

More so than just about any other theme park, Islands of Adventure has gone all out to create settings and attractions that transport you from reality into the surreal. What's more, no one island here has much in common with any other, so in a way, a visit here is almost like a visit to half a dozen different parks.

IOA's unique nature is first revealed when you arrive at the Port of Entry and are greeted by a kaleidoscope of sights and a cacophony of sounds. It's all designed to put you in the frame of mind for adventure.

When you reach the central lagoon, your clockwise journey commences with Marvel Super Hero Island and its tightly packed concentration of roller coasters and thrill rides. Of special note is the amazingly high-tech and dazzling Amazing Adventures of Spider-Man. In just minutes you'll have experienced a day's worth of sensations—and you've only just begun.

Stepping into Toon Lagoon is like stepping into the pages of a comic book, just as entering the upcoming island, Jurassic Park, is like entering a research center where reconstructed dinosaur DNA is being used to create a new breed of *brontosaurus*.

You move from the world of science into the world of magic when you segue into the Wizarding World of Harry Potter. For the first time anywhere, you—and not just a few fortunate actors—can wander through the magnificently fictional, yet now very realistic, realm of the young wizard and his Hogwarts classmates and tutors. Beyond belief.

But that's not the end of it. In the Lost Continent the mood is that of a Renaissance fair, where crafters work inside colorful tents. It's as pronounced an atmosphere as that of the final island, Seuss Landing, which presents the incredible, topsy-turvy world of Dr. Seuss. It's a riot of colors and shapes and fantastic wildlife that pay tribute to the good doctor's vivid imagination.

TOP ATTRACTIONS

Ages 7 and Up

Amazing Adventures of Spider-Man

Dudley Do-Right's Ripsaw Falls

Harry Potter and the Forbidden Journey

Incredible Hulk Coaster

Ages 6 and Under

The Cat in the Hat

Flight of the Hippogriff

Popeye & Bluto's Bilge-Rat Barges

PLANNING

GETTING ORIENTED

Getting your bearings at IOA is far easier than at its sister park, Universal Studios. Brochures in a multitude of languages are in a rack a few steps beyond the turnstiles. The brochures include a foldout map that will acquaint you with the park's simple layout (it's a circle). And, ahead by the lagoon, boards are posted with up-to-the-minute ride and show information—including the length of lines at the major attractions.

You pass through the turnstiles and into the Port of Entry plaza, a bazaar that brings together bits and pieces of architecture, landscaping, music, and wares from many lands—Dutch windmills, Indonesian pedicabs, African masks, restrooms marked "Loo's Landing," and Egyptian figurines that adorn a massive archway inscribed with the notice "The Adventure Begins." From here, themed islands—arranged around a large lagoon—are connected by walkways that make navigation easy. When you've done the full circuit, you'll recall the fantastic range of sights, sounds, and experiences and realize there can be truth in advertising. This park really *is* an adventure.

TOURING TIPS

Hosts. Just about any employee is a host, whether they're at a kiosk or attraction or turnstile. Ask them about their favorite experiences—and for suggestions for saving time.

Photo Ops. Islands of Adventure posts signs that indicate picture spots and show how best to frame your shot.

Retreat. Explore little-used sidewalks and quiet alcoves to counter IOA's manic energy.

In the Jurassic Park Discovery Center, your kids might just learn something about dinosaurs that they didn't already know.

Split the difference. If the park's open late, split the day in half. See part of it in the morning, head off-site to a restaurant for lunch (your parking ticket is good all day) then head to your hotel for a swim or a nap (or both). Return in the cooler, less crowded evening.

ISLANDS OF ADVENTURES PLANNER

PARK AMENITIES

Guest Services: Guest Services is right near the turnstiles, both before and after you enter Islands of Adventure (IOA). ☎ *407/224–6350* ⊕ *www. universalorlando.com.*

Lockers: There are $8-a-day lockers across from Guest Services at the entrance; for $10 a day you can rent a family-size model. You have unlimited access to both types throughout the day—although it's a hike back to retrieve things. Scattered strategically throughout the park— notably at the Incredible Hulk Coaster, Jurassic Park River Adventure, and Forbidden Journey—are so-called Smart Lockers. These are free for the first 45 to 75 minutes, $2 per hour afterward, and max out at $14 per day. Stash backpacks and cameras here while you're being drenched on a watery ride or going through the spin cycle on a twisty one.

Lost People and Things: If you've misplaced something, head to Guest Services in the Port of Entry. This is also where park staffers take lost children.

Stroller Rentals: You can rent strollers ($15 per day for singles, $25 for doubles) at the Port of Entry to your left after the turnstiles. You can also rent kiddie cars—small ones for $18, and large ones for $28.

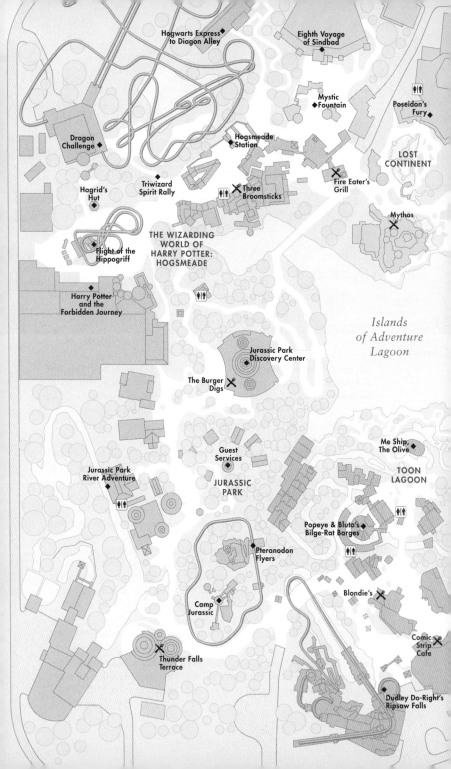

Hogwarts Express◆
to Diagon Alley

Eighth Voyage
◆of Sindbad

Mystic
◆Fountain

Poseidon's
Fury◆

Dragon
Challenge◆

Hogsmeade
◆Station

LOST
CONTINENT

Fire Eater's
✕ Grill

Hagrid's
Hut◆

Triwizard
Spirit Rally◆

✕ Three
Broomsticks

Mythos
✕

Flight of the◆
Hippogriff

THE WIZARDING
WORLD OF
HARRY POTTER:
HOGSMEADE

Harry Potter◆
and the
Forbidden Journey

Islands
of Adventure
Lagoon

Jurassic Park
Discovery Center◆

The Burger✕
Digs

Me Ship,◆
The Olive

Guest
Services◆

TOON
LAGOON

Jurassic Park
River Adventure◆

JURASSIC
PARK

Popeye & Bluto's◆
Bilge-Rat Barges

Pteranodon◆
Flyers

Blondie's✕

Camp◆
Jurassic

Comic
Strip✕
Cafe

Thunder Falls✕
Terrace

Dudley Do-Right's◆
Ripsaw Falls

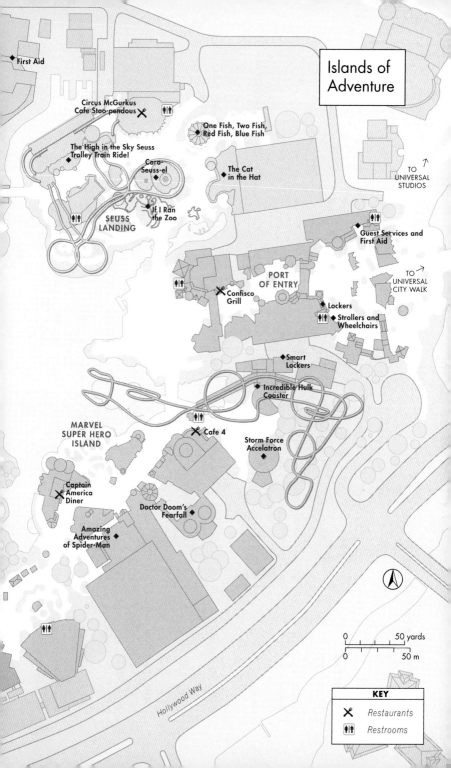

Islands of Adventure

◆ First Aid

Circus McGurkus
Cafe Stoo-pendous ✕   🚹🚺

One Fish, Two Fish,
Red Fish, Blue Fish

The High in the Sky Seuss
Trolley Train Ride!
Caro-
Seuss-el

◆ The Cat
in the Hat

TO
UNIVERSAL
STUDIOS

🚹🚺

SEUSS
LANDING

◆ If I Ran
the Zoo

🚹🚺 Guest Services and
First Aid

PORT
OF ENTRY

TO
UNIVERSAL
CITY WALK

🚹🚺

✕ Confisco
Grill

◆ Lockers

🚹🚺 ◆ Strollers and
Wheelchairs

◆ Smart
Lockers

◆ Incredible Hulk
Coaster

🚹🚺

MARVEL
SUPER HERO
ISLAND

✕ Cafe 4

Storm Force
Accelatron

✕ Captain
America
Diner

Doctor Doom's ◆
Fearfall

Amazing
Adventures ◆
of Spider-Man

🚹🚺

0 _____ 50 yards
0 _____ 50 m

Hollywood Way

KEY	
✕	*Restaurants*
🚹🚺	*Restrooms*

ISLANDS OF ADVENTURE

NAME	Height Req.	Type of Entertainment	Duration	Crowds	Audience	Tips
Jurassic Park						
Camp Jurassic	n/a	Playground	Up to you	Light to Moderate	All Ages	Come anytime.
Jurassic Park Discovery Center	n/a	Walk-Through	Up to you	Light	Young Kids to Teens	Come anytime.
Jurassic Park River Adventure	At least 42"	Thrill Ride with Water	6 mins.	Heavy	All but Young Kids	Use Express Pass. Come early or late.
Pteranodon Flyers	36" to 56"	Thrill Ride for Kids	2 mins.	Heavy	All Ages	Skip this on your first visit. 36" to 48" can ride but must do so with an adult.
Lost Continent						
Eighth Voyage of Sindbad	n/a	Show	25 mins.	Heavy	All but Young Kids	Stadium seating for everyone, but arrive at least 15 mins. early. Don't sit too far up front. Use Express Pass.
Poseidon's Fury	n/a	Walk-through Simulator Exp.	20 mins.	Heavy	All but Young Kids	Come at the end of the day. Stay to the left for best spot. Get in first row each time. Express Pass accepted.
Marvel Super Hero Island						
★ The Amazing Adventures of Spider-Man	At least 40"	Simulator Exp.	4½ mins.	Absolutely	All but Young Kids	Use Express Pass, or come early or late in day. Don't miss the bad guys in the wanted posters. Try it twice if you can.
Doctor Doom's Fearfall	At least 52"	Thrill Ride	1 min.	Light to Moderate	All but Young Kids	Use Express Pass, or come later in the day. Regardless, come with an empty stomach.
Incredible Hulk Coaster	At least 54"	Thrill Ride	2¼ mins.	Yes!	All but Young Kids	Come here first. Effects are best in the morning. The front row is best.
Storm Force Accelatron	n/a	Thrill Ride	2 mins.	Light	All but Young Kids	Come whenever—except right after eating.
Seuss Landing						

Attraction	Height	Type	Duration	Crowds	Ages	Notes
Caro-Seuss-el	n/a	Thrill Ride for Kids	2 mins.	Moderate	All Ages	Use Express Pass, or end your day here.
The Cat in the Hat	n/a	Thrill Ride for Kids	4½ mins.	Heavy	All Ages	Use Express Pass here, or come early or at the end of the day.
High in the Sky Seuss Trolley Train Ride!	At least 34"	Railroad	3 mins.	Heavy	All Ages	Kids love trains, so plan to get in line! 34" to 48" can ride but must do so with an adult. Express Pass accepted.
If I Ran the Zoo	n/a	Playground with Water	Up to you	Heavy	Young Kids	Come toward the end of your visit.
One Fish, Two Fish, Red Fish, Blue Fish	n/a	Thrill Ride for Kids	2+ mins.	Heavy	Young Kids	Use Express Pass, or come early or late in day. Skip it on your first visit.
Toon Lagoon						
Dudley Do-Right's Ripsaw Falls	At least 44"	Thrill Ride with Water	5½ mins.	Heavy	All but Young Kids	Ride the flume in late afternoon to cool down, or at day's end. There's no seat where you can stay dry. Express Pass accepted.
Me Ship, The Olive	n/a	Playground	Up to you	Heavy	Young Kids	Come in the morning or at dinnertime.
Popeye and Bluto's Bilge-Rat Barges	At least 42 "	Thrill Ride with Water	5 mins.	Heavy	All but Young Kids	Come early in the morning or before closing. You will get wet. Express Pass accepted.
The Wizarding World of Harry Potter						
Dragon Challenge	At least 54"	Thrill Ride	3 mins.	Heavy	All but Young Kids	Use Express Pass. Avoid if you're prone to motion sickness.
Flight of the Hippogriff	At least 36"	Thrill Ride for Kids	1 min.	Moderate	Young Kids	Keep an eye on the line, and come when there's an opening. Express Pass accepted.
★ Harry Potter and the Forbidden Journey	At least 48"	Walk-Through/Ride-Through/Thrill Ride	50 mins.	Yes!	All but Young Kids	Come early. Steer clear if you have a queasy stomach.
Hogwarts Express–Hogsmeade Station	n/a	Railroad	10 mins.	Heavy	All Ages	You must have a Park-to-Park ticket.

EXPLORING

MARVEL SUPER HERO ISLAND

The facades on Stanley Boulevard (named for Marvel's famed editor and co-creator Stan Lee) put you smack in the middle of an alternatively pleasant and apocalyptic comic-book world—complete with heroes, villains, and cartoony colors and flourishes. Although the spiky, horrific towers of Doctor Doom's Fearfall and the vivid green of the Hulk's coaster are focal points, the Amazing Adventures of Spider-Man is the must-see attraction. At various times Doctor Doom, Spider-Man, and the Incredible Hulk are available for photos, and sidewalk artists are on hand to paint your face like your favorite hero (or villain). All rides here accept Universal Express Pass.

TOON LAGOON

The main street, Comic Strip Lane, makes use of cartoon characters that are recognizable to anyone—anyone born before 1940, that is. Pert little Betty Boop, gangly Olive Oyl, muscle-bound Popeye, Krazy Kat, Mark Trail, Flash Gordon, Pogo, and Alley Oop are all here, as are the relatively more contemporary Dudley Do-Right, Rocky, Bullwinkle, Beetle Bailey, Cathy, and Hagar the Horrible. With its colorful backdrops, chirpy music, hidden alcoves, squirting fountains, and highly animated scenery, Toon Town is a natural for younger kids (even if they don't know who these characters are). All attractions here accept Universal Express Pass except Me Ship, The Olive.

JURASSIC PARK

Pass through the towering gates of Jurassic Park and the music becomes slightly ominous, the vegetation tropical and junglelike. All of this, plus the high-tension wires and warning signs, does a great job of re-creating the Jurassic Park of Steven Spielberg's blockbuster movie (and its insipid sequels). The half-fun, half-frightening Jurassic Park River Adventure (the only attraction here that uses Universal Express Pass) is the standout, bringing to life key segments of the movie's climax.

THE WIZARDING WORLD OF HARRY POTTER: HOGSMEADE

In mid-2010, Islands of Adventure fulfilled the fantasy of Harry Potter devotees when it unveiled the biggest theme-park addition since the arrival of Disney's Animal Kingdom in 1998. At the highly publicized premiere, even the actors from the Potter film franchise were amazed. Having performed their roles largely before a green screen, they had never seen anything like this. Neither have you. It's fantastic and unbelievable. The movie-magic-perfect re-creations of mythical locales such as Hogwarts and Hogsmeade Village are here, while playing supporting roles are a handful of candy shops, souvenir stores, and restaurants expertly and exquisitely themed to make you believe you've actually arrived in the incredible fantasy world of J.K. Rowling. Wands, candy, novelties, and more are unique to this magical land. Expect to be impressed—and to wait in line. Even if you owned a wand and were a real wizard, the only attractions in this land that accept the Universal Express Pass are Flight of the Hippogriff and Dragon Challenge. In fact, the land is so popular that in peak season it sometimes reaches capacity, and you have to wait for others to leave before you can enter. If you have a two-park pass, you can board the Hogwarts Express for a delightful train journey to Diagon Alley at Universal Studios.

LOST CONTINENT

Just beyond a wooden bridge, huge mythical birds guard the entrance to a land where trees are hung with weathered metal lanterns, and booming thunder mixes with chimes and vaguely Celtic melodies. Farther along the path, the scene looks similar to a Renaissance fair. Seers and fortune-tellers practice their trade in tents, and in a huge theater, Sindbad leaps and bounces all over Arabia. This stunt show and Poseidon let you bypass lines using Universal Express Pass.

SEUSS LANDING

This 10-acre tribute to Dr. Seuss puts you in the midst of his classic children's books. This means spending quality time with the Cat, Things 1 and 2, Horton, the Lorax, and the Grinch. From topiary sculptures to lurching lampposts to curvy fences (there was never a straight line in any of the books) to buildings that glow in lavenders, pinks, peaches, and oranges, everything seems surreal. It's a wonderful place to wrap up a day. Even the Cat would approve. All rides here except If I Ran the Zoo accept Express Pass.

CITYWALK

With an attitude that's distinctly non-Disney, Universal has created nightlife for adults who want to party. The epicenter is CityWalk, a 30-acre entertainment and retail complex at the hub of promenades that lead to both Universal parks.

When it comes to retail, much of the merchandise includes things you can find elsewhere—and most likely for less. But when you're swept up in the energy of CityWalk and dazzled by the degree of window-shopping (not to mention the fact that you're on vacation and you're more inclined to spend), chances are you'll want to drop into stores selling everything from surf wear and cigars to tattoos and timepieces.

In addition to stores, the open and airy gathering place includes an over-the-top discotheque, a theater for the fabulous and extremely popular Blue Man Group, and a huge hall where karaoke's king. There's a New Orleans bar, a Jamaican reggae lounge, a casual Key West hangout, and, as of 2012, Hollywood Drive-In Golf, a pair of fun-filled 1950s sci-fi movie–themed miniature golf courses. On weeknights you find families and conventioneers; weekends a decidedly younger crowd parties until the wee hours.

Clubs have individual cover charges, but it's far more economical to pay for the whole kit and much of the caboodle. Choose a Party Pass (a one-price-all-clubs admission) for $11.99, or upgrade to a Party Pass-and-a-Movie for $15; a Party Pass-and-a-Meal for $21; a Movie-and-a-Meal for $21.95; or a Meal and a Mini-Golf Deal for $23.95.

At AMC Universal Cineplex, with its 20 screens (including IMAX), there's certain to be something you like—including nightly midnight

movies. Meals (tax and gratuity included) are served at Jimmy Buffett's Margaritaville, the Hard Rock Cafe, and others. And as if these deals weren't sweet enough, after 6 the $15 parking fee drops to $5. Nevertheless, it's a long haul from the garage to CityWalk—if you prefer, simply call a cab. They run at all hours. ☎ *407/354–3374, 407/363–8000 Universal main line ⊕ www.citywalkorlando.com.*

NIGHTLIFE

With the wide range of nightlife you'll find at Universal, you may get the feeling that you're vacationing not in Orlando but in New York City. CityWalk's stores open by midmorning, and its restaurants come to life between lunchtime and late afternoon. Eateries that double as nightclubs (such as Pat O'Brien's, Bob Marley's, and the Red Coconut Club) start charging a cover before dusk and apply age restrictions (usually 21) around 9. For details on a particular establishment, check with Guest Services.

BARS AND CLUBS

Bob Marley—A Tribute to Freedom. Modeled after the King of Reggae's home in Kingston, Jamaica (even down to the a/c window units), in a way this nightclub is also part museum, with more than 100 photographs and paintings showing pivotal moments in Marley's life. Though the place does serve meals, most patrons are at the cozy bar or by the patio, where they can be jammin' to a (loud) live band that plays nightly. For a nice souvenir, pose by the wonderful Marley statue outside the club. Legendary Thursdays feature drink specials for everyone, and Sunday is ladies' night from 9 pm until closing. ■ **TIP→ Often on Monday and Tuesday, CityWalk's pace is slow enough where some clubs will offer free admission. Ask before you pay.** ⊠ *CityWalk* ☎ *407/224–2692* ⊕ *www.universalorlando.com* ⌚ *$7 after 9 pm* ☉ *Daily 4 pm–2 am.*

CityWalk's Rising Star. Here you and other hopeful (and hopeless) singers can really let loose. Instead of singing to recorded music, you're accompanied by a band complete with backup singers—in front of a live audience. Backup singers are on hand every night, while the live band plugs in Tuesday through Saturday, and a full bar is always on tap. ⊠ *6000 Universal Blvd., #717, CityWalk* ☎ *407/224–2961* ⊕ *www.universalorlando.com* ⌚ *$7, no charge to sing* ☉ *Nightly 8 pm–2 am.*

the groove. In this cavernous hall images flicker rapidly on several screens, and the lights, music, and mayhem appeal to a mostly under-thirty crowd. Prepare for lots of fog, swirling lights, and sweaty bodies. The '70s-style Green Room is filled with beanbag chairs and everything you threw out when Duran Duran hit the charts. The Blue Room is sci-fi Jetson-y, and the Red Room is hot and romantic in a bordello sort of way. The music is equally diverse: Top 40, hip-hop, R&B, techno, and the occasional live band. ⊠ *6000 Universal Blvd., CityWalk* ☎ *407/224–2692* ⊕ *www.universalorlando.com* ⌚ *$7* ☉ *Daily 9 pm–2 am.*

Jimmy Buffett's Margaritaville. Buffett tunes fill the air at the restaurant here and at the Volcano, Land Shark, and 12 Volt bars. Inside there's a miniature Pan Am Clipper suspended from the ceiling, music videos

The Cat and his Hat, McGurkus and the Circus, and fish both red and blue are among the attractions geared to the under-7 set at Seuss Landing.

projected onto sails, limbo and hula-hoop contests, a huge margarita blender that erupts "when the volcano blows," and live music nightly—everything that Parrotheads need to roost. Across the promenade, another full-size seaplane (emblazoned with "Jimmy Buffett, Captain") is the setting for the Lone Palm Airport, a pleasing and surprisingly popular outdoor waterfront bar. ⊠ *6000 Universal Studios Plaza, #704, CityWalk* ☎ *407/224–2692* ⊕ *www.margaritavilleorlando.com* ☒ *$7 after 10 pm* ☾ *Daily 11:30 am–2 am.*

Pat O'Brien's. An exact reproduction of the legendary New Orleans original, this comes complete with flaming fountain and dueling pianists who are playing for highly entertained regulars and visitors—even on weekday afternoons. Outside, the cozy and welcoming Patio Bar has a wealth of tables and chairs, allowing you to do nothing but enjoy the outdoors and your potent, rum-based Hurricanes in Orlando's version of the Big Easy. ⊠ *6000 Universal Blvd., CityWalk* ☎ *407/224–2692* ⊕ *www.patobriens.com* ☒ *$7 after 9 pm* ☾ *Patio Bar daily 4 pm–2 am; piano bar daily 5 pm–2 am, 21 and up after 9 pm.*

Red Coconut Club. Paying tribute to kitsch design of the 1950s, the interior here is part Vegas lounge, part Cuban club, and part Polynesian tiki bar. It's "where tropical meets trendy." There are three full bars on two levels, signature martinis, an extensive wine list, and VIP bottle service. Hang out in the lounge, on the balcony, or at the bar. On a budget? Take advantage of the daily happy hours and gourmet appetizer menu. A DJ (Sunday–Wednesday) or live music (Thursday–Saturday) pushes the energy with tunes ranging from Sinatra to rock. Thursday is ladies' night. ⊠ *6000 Universal Blvd., CityWalk* ☎ *407/224–2425*

⊕ www.universalorlando.com ✉ $7 after 9 pm ☉ Sun.–Wed. 8 pm–2 am, Thurs.–Sat. 6 pm–2 am.

SHOWS

Blue Man Group. At their own venue, the Sharp-Aquos Theatre, the ever-innovative Blue Men continue to pound out new music, sketches, and audience interaction that is nothing like you've ever seen. Attempting to understand the apps on a GiPad (a gigantic iPad), they may appear clueless and perplexed about cutting-edge technology (which for them can be as basic as a can of paint), but they're always excited when they can drum out rhythms on lengths of PVC pipes and throw a rave party finale for all in attendance. The show is a surreal comic masterpiece, so if you have the time and a little extra in your vacation budget, this is a must. Three levels of admission (Poncho, Tier 1, and Tier 2) hint at how messy things can get when the Blue Men cut loose. *⊠ CityWalk ☎ 407/258–3626 ⊕ www.universalorlando.com ✉ Adults start at $70 advance purchase, $85 at box office; children 9 and under from $30 ☉ Daily showtimes vary; call for schedule.*

SHOPPING

This 30-acre entertainment and retail complex is at the hub of promenades that lead to Universal Studios and Islands of Adventure. Shops here sell fine jewelry, cool beachwear, fashionable clothing, and stylish accessories. The best stores are near the entrance/exit of the complex.

Fresh Produce. Featuring fashions that look right at home in sunny Florida, this boutique showcases comfortable and colorful swimwear, blouses, Capri slacks, dresses, footwear, beach gear, and accessories designed for coastal comfort. *⊠ CityWalk ⊕ www.universalorlando. com/Shopping/shopping.aspx.*

Quiet Flight. Granted the closest beach is about 60 miles east, you can still get outfitted like a surfer at this shop, which sports an inventory featuring brand names such as Billabong, Quicksilver, Hurley, and Oakley. In addition to shorts and shirts, Quiet Flight also sells sandals, watches, sunglasses (Ray-Ban, Prada, and D&G among the featured names), and surfboards! *⊠ CityWalk ⊕ www.universalorlando.com/Shopping/ shopping.aspx.*

WET 'N WILD

When you were a kid, chances are all you needed for unlimited summer fun was a simple inflatable pool and a garden hose or sprinkler. Well, about the same time that you were growing up, so were water parks. They started with a few simple slides and are now the aquatic equivalents of megamalls.

It all began in 1977 with Wet 'n Wild, created by George Millay, who was also one of the founders of SeaWorld. Although it's now far from alone, Wet 'n Wild remains extremely popular thanks to its quality, service, and ability to create more heart-stopping waterslides, rides, and tubing adventures than its competitors. Indeed, new rides seem

Brain Wash is one of Wet 'n Wild's most thrilling slides.

to be added like clockwork, old ones improved, and settings developed for the comfort of guests. There's a complete water playground for kids, numerous high-energy slides for adults, a lazy-river ride, and some quiet, sandy beaches on which you can stretch out and get a tan.

Speaking of high energy, this is a park that requires a lot of it. A day here is often a marathon of climbing steps, sliding, swimming, and splashing, though you may not notice just how much your stamina is being drained as you scamper from slide to slide. Plan to take breaks: laze in a beach chair and eat high-protein meals and snacks to maintain your strength. You can bring in a cooler for a picnic or eat at a restaurant in one of several food courts.

If you're not a strong swimmer, don't worry. There are plenty of low-key attractions, and all of the ride entrances are marked with warnings to let you know which ones are safe for you. Plus, during peak season, there are as many as 200 lifeguards on duty daily. Also note that all the pools (if not the rides) are ADA-compliant and are heated in cooler weather. This, combined with Orlando's temperate climate, means that Wet 'n Wild is one of the few water parks in the country to stay open year-round.

Surf's up!

PLANNING

PARK AMENITIES

Guest Services: Get maps and other information at Guest Services (aka Guest Relations), to the left as you enter.

11

Lockers: There are dressing rooms with lockers in three different sizes (personal $6/$3 deposit, standard $9/$3 deposit, family $11/$3 deposit) as well as showers and restrooms to the left of the entrance gates. Additional restrooms are on the island inside the lazy river and near the First-Aid Stand and the Surge.

Lost People and Things: The Lost and Found is at Guest Services, to the left just after you enter the park. This is also where lifeguards and other staffers take lost children.

ESSENTIALS

Admission: Basic admission is about $56 for adults (ages 10 and up) and $51 for children. Often you can find discounts in tourist magazines throughout the I-Drive area, but you may have better luck ordering your tickets online—and more time to consider the multiple ticket options. Different discounts apply to different ticket choices, that is, 10% off, 14 consecutive days free, and so on, but for Wet 'n Wild (as well as SeaWorld, Universal, and Disney) online purchases seem to be the best source for saving money and avoiding vacation time in line. Other money-saving options include military and college discounts and the FlexTicket, which bundles Wet 'n Wild with parks and attractions at Universal Orlando, SeaWorld, and Busch Gardens.

Parking: Costing $13 for cars, vans, and motorcycles and $17 for RVs and cars with trailers, parking is in a large lot along Universal Boulevard.

Wet 'n Wild: For general information, call Wet 'n Wild or visit online. ⊠ *Wet 'n Wild* ☎ *407/351–3200 recorded information, 407/351–1800 park operations* ⊕ *www.wetnwildorlando.com.*

TOURING TIPS

■ Want to save a bundle? Admission drops to half price during the afternoon; exactly when depends on closing time, but can be as late as 5 pm in the summer. Call ahead for the magic hour. Even better, if you pay for a full-price ticket, you can return for free for 14 consecutive days. It's a great deal for families in town for an extended stay. You can see the big three (Disney, Universal, SeaWorld) during the day and return here in the evening.

■ When you arrive, it's a good idea to pick up a map, scan the park layout, and stake out a spot on the beach before heading on or in. To claim a prime beach spot, arrive at least 15 minutes before the park opens, or visit on a cloudy day. If it looks like rain all day, though, head elsewhere.

■ Men should wear a true bathing suit, and women should opt for a one-piece rather than a bikini. Cutoff shorts and garments with rivets, metal buttons, buckles, or zippers aren't allowed.

■ Wading slippers are a good idea—hot sidewalks and sandpaper-like pool bottoms can do a number on your feet—but put them in a locker or carry them when taking a plunge, since they can catch on slides.

■ Items too large to carry should be stashed in a locker. Some picnic tables have lockable containers (secured to the umbrella stand) that are just large enough to hold smaller items such as keys, glasses, and cell phones.

■   For extra privacy, a quiet oasis in the middle of the lazy river features cabanas with a fan, chaise longues, and a fridge stocked with a dozen bottles of water. It's a nice base for stowing your things, but the privilege costs some bucks. Depending on the time of the year, cabanas can go for a modest $60 to a high of $280 in the peak summer season. Don't want to get up? Servers will bring food to you.

■   Be patient with the lines here. Just when you think you've arrived, you discover there's another level or two to go.

■   To bypass lines at the popular rides, get an Express Pass (available seasonally), accepted at most rides. Prices change based on park attendance and time of day, so call Park Operations at ☎ *407/351–1800* for details. A limited number of passes are sold each day—all the more reason to get here early.

■   Okay. So you remembered your swimsuit and towel. But what about sunscreen? You can buy it and other necessities or souvenirs at the **Breakers Beach Shop**, near the park entrance. And if you did forget a towel, renting one here costs $4 with a $3 deposit. Rent a three-pack, though, and you save $2.

SEAWORLD

With Discovery Cove and Aquatica

WELCOME TO SEAWORLD, DISCOVERY COVE, AND AQUATICA

TOP REASONS TO GO

★ **Animal Magnetism:** If you love animals—slick, shiny, feathery, or furry—SeaWorld, Discovery Cove, and Aquatica are where you want to be. No robotic wildlife here; just well-cared-for and talented dolphins, whales, seals, otters, penguins, cats, dogs. . . .

★ **A Slower Pace:** The shows and natural settings of SeaWorld and Discovery Cove let you enjoy a theme-park vacation without racing from one attraction to the next. Living in the moment is the lesson here.

★ **Getting Smarter:** No one leaves these parks without learning a little something about nature through shows, backstage tours, instructional signage, and well-versed educators and naturalists who are always ready to answer questions.

★ **Memories in the Making:** Chances are SeaWorld and Discovery Cove will afford you the chance to pet a penguin, feed a dolphin, or watch a 5-ton whale leap out of the water. You can't forget things like that.

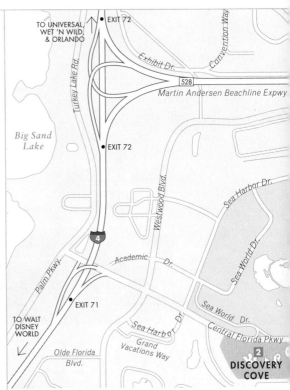

1 SeaWorld. With the exception of a handful of thrill rides, the original park (which opened in 1973 to reroute visitors heading to the then recently opened Walt Disney World) maintains a slow and easy pace. Here it's all about clever shows, shaded sidewalks, and plenty of opportunities to enjoy the natural grace and intriguing personalities of marine life and other animals.

Orlando

12

TO WET 'N WILD &
UNIVERSAL STUDIOS

Universal Blvd.

EXIT 2

528

EXIT 1

EXIT 3A
AND
EXIT 3B

3
AQUATICA

Gateway Ave.

Orangewood Blvd.

International Dr.

1
EAWORLD

423

0   1/4 mi

0   1/4 km

GETTING ORIENTED

SeaWorld is just off the intersection of Interstate 4 and the Beachline Expressway, equidistant from Universal Orlando and the Walt Disney World Resort, which are only about five minutes away. SeaWorld is also a mere 10 minutes from Downtown Orlando and 15 minutes from the airport. Discovery Cove is its own oasis across the street from SeaWorld. Aquatica, a little ways down the road from both, is the first of the three that you'll see after exiting the expressway.

2 Discovery Cove. SeaWorld spun off this park to give you the chance to enjoy a lot more time (and to spend a little more cash) with the animals. A trip to this aquatic oasis feels like a trip to the islands; a daylong, all-inclusive experience that includes breakfast and lunch, drinks, a private beach, snorkeling equipment, and—for approximately an extra $100—the chance to swim with dolphins. Paradise.

3 Aquatica. SeaWorld's water park offers the chance to slip and slide at adrenaline-rush speeds, relax in the current of two wave pools, laze on a wide beach, and take the wee ones to pint-size play areas of their very own. All in all, there's something for everyone, showcased in a tropical, tiki-themed setting.

By Gary
McKechnie

Just as Walt Disney World and Universal Orlando are much more than just a single park, the same is true of SeaWorld. The original park—which includes the Shamu shows as well as presentations featuring dolphins and seals—has expanded to include Discovery Cove (an immersive tropical retreat), and Aquatica (a water park loaded with aquatic excitement). So, as you plan your vacation, consider that SeaWorld can easily fill a single day or, if you're really eager to take to the waters, perhaps a day or two more.

There's a whole lot more to SeaWorld and Discovery Cove than being splashed by Shamu. You can see manatees face-to-snout, learn to love a shark, swim with dolphins, and be spat at by a walrus. These two parks celebrate all the mammals, birds, fish, and reptiles that live in and near the ocean.

Then there's Aquatica, a wild water park that takes its cues from SeaWorld and Discovery Cove in design and mood—marine-life motifs are everywhere. It also gives competitor water parks a run for their money with thrilling slides, broad beaches, calming rivers, and an area for small kids.

The park also takes some tips from the tropics. Right after you clear the parking lot, you see a tropical pastiche of buildings. Yup. That's definitely an island vibe you're detecting. Upon entering Aquatica, you feel as if you've left Central Florida for the Caribbean or Polynesia, even.

You might be drawn to the series of superfast waterslides (some of which conclude by sending you into serene streams), or you might feel the pull of the white-sand beaches beside the twin wave pools, where you can laze in the sun, venturing out every so often to try a ride or climb into an inner tube and float down a river. Whether you're spending the day at SeaWorld, Discovery Cove, or Aquatica, just go with it. Get into a groove, relax, and enjoy yourself at some of the most pleasant theme parks in Orlando.

PLANNING

GETTING HERE AND AROUND

Heading west on Interstate 4 (toward Disney) take Exit 72; heading east, take Exit 71. After that you'll be going east on the Beachline Expressway (aka Route 528), and the first right-hand exit leads you to International Drive. Turn left, and you'll soon see the entrance to Aquatica on your left. Sea Harbor Drive—leading to SeaWorld's entrance—will be on your right. To reach Discovery Cove, follow International Drive past Aquatica a half-mile to the Central Florida Parkway and turn right. The park's entrance will be on your left.

OPERATING HOURS

SeaWorld opens daily at 9 am and usually closes at 7 pm, with extended hours during the summer and holidays. Hours at Discovery Cove also vary seasonally, although it's generally open daily from 8 to 5:30, with check-in beginning 30 minutes earlier—which is not a bad idea considering Discovery Cove serves a complimentary breakfast until 10 am. Aquatica is open at 9 am, with closing times varying between 5 and 9 pm, depending on the season. Allow a full day to see each attraction.

ADMISSION

SeaWorld, Discovery Cove, Aquatica, and Busch Gardens Tampa Bay fall under the SeaWorld Parks & Entertainment umbrella, and you can save by buying combo tickets. Regular one-day tickets to **SeaWorld** cost $95 (adults) and $90 (children ages 3–9), excluding tax, but if you order in advance over the phone or online, you'll save as much as $20 per ticket—which just may be the best money-saving option you'll find. Combo-park admission prices, which include 14 days at each park, are as follows:

SeaWorld/Aquatica Online $89

SeaWorld/Busch Gardens Tampa Online $99

SeaWorld/Aquatica/Busch Gardens Tampa Online $109

Flex Ticket (14 days at SeaWorld/Aquatica/Busch Gardens Tampa) $345/$325

Aquatica Online $37 (at the gate $56)

Reserve **Discovery Cove** visits well in advance—attendance is limited to about 1,000 a day. Tickets (with a dolphin swim) start at about $229 (off-season, in January and February) but are generally around $289. Forgo the dolphin swim and save approximately $80. This park has what's called dynamic pricing (meaning prices change by season, and also at other times without notice). Admission is less expensive the earlier you book (so call well in advance) and includes access to all beach and snorkeling areas and the free-flight aviary; meals and snacks; use of a mask, snorkel, swim vest, towel, locker, and sunscreen; parking; and a pass for 14 days of unlimited admission to SeaWorld Orlando and Aquatica. Upgrade to an "ultimate" pass (about $20), which includes admission (and free transportation) to Busch Gardens Tampa.

Quick Queue Unlimited Passes. SeaWorld's Quick Queue passes (*$19– $35 per person, depending on season*) get you to the front of the line at major attractions and shows for one admission each. The higher price unlimited pass is good for unlimited admissions. Neither Discovery Cove nor Aquatica has such a pass.

All-Day Dining Deal. Available at select SeaWorld restaurants (Voyager's Smokehouse, Seaport Pizza, Terrace Garden Buffet, The Spice Mill, Seafire Inn, and Mango Joe's), adults will pay about $30 and kids from $15 to chow down on an entrée, side dish, drink, and dessert for each meal. Skip it if you plan on having just one meal in the park.

SEAWORLD STRATEGIES

Avoid weekend and school-holiday visits. These are the busiest times, so plan around them if you can.

Wear sneakers or water shoes—no heels or slip-on sandals. It may not seem like it, but there'll be a whole lot of walking as you roam from one end of the park to the other, stand in line, and walk through attractions.

Pack dry clothes. You can get wet just by being toward the front at the Shamu show or riding Journey to Atlantis. Alternatively, carry a rain poncho.

Budget for food for the animals. Participating in animal feedings is a major part of the SeaWorld experience, although it comes at a price: a small carton of fish costs $5.

Pick up a map-and-show schedule inside the entrance. SeaWorld has its show schedule down to a science. If you start by catching the show closest to the entrance, shortly after that one's over, guests are moving farther into the park to grab a seat at the next performance so you'll end up moving with the crowd. Instead, start off at a show farther inside the park so you are ahead of the crowds. Spend a few minutes planning so you can casually stroll from show to show and have time for learning, testing out thrill rides, *and* enjoying a leisurely meal.

Be open to learning. SeaWorld's trainers and educators are always at the ready to share information about the park's wildlife.

DISCOVERY COVE STRATEGIES

Make reservations well in advance. Prized June dates, for instance, can sell out in March. If there aren't openings when you call, though, don't despair. Call back often to inquire about cancellations.

Think about your eyewear. Park masks don't accommodate glasses, but there are a limited number of near- and far-sighted prescription masks (first-come, first-served) available. Just step into a booth and you'll be able to try on a few different pairs with different magnifications. If you don't mind risking lost contacts, just wear those beneath a non-prescription mask.

Don't bring your own wet suit or fins. Every guest must wear a Discovery Cove–issued wet suit or vest—not a bad idea, as the water can be cold.

Leave belongings in your locker. The plastic passes you're given are all you need to pick up your meals, soft drinks, and—if you're over 21—alcoholic drinks.

Be flexible when it comes to weather. If the weather on your reserved day looks like it'll be an all-day downpour, attempts will be made to

reschedule your visit while you're in town. If that's not possible, you'll have to settle for a refund.

Have a dolphin relay a message. The Special Occasion Package enlists the help of a bottlenose dolphin to deliver love notes, wedding proposals, birthday or anniversary greetings, and the like.

AQUATICA STRATEGIES

■ **Buy tickets in advance.** Tickets bought ahead of time online or at another SeaWorld park allow early entry (and discounts) to Aquatica, which, in turn, increases your chances of hitting all the big-deal flume and tube rides—possibly more than once.

■ **Be open to animal encounters.** The Commerson's dolphins of Dolphin Plunge have scheduled feeding times, and you can see macaws perched on tree limbs and small mammals on display in Conservation Cabanas—usually attended to by knowledgeable educators.

■ **Pack beach supplies.** You'll save a few bucks by having your own towels, lotion, water shoes, and snacks.

■ **Take care of yourself.** Fight fatigue by eating a good breakfast, drinking plenty of water, and nibbling on high-energy snacks. Avoid sunburn by reapplying sunscreen often—even the waterproof stuff washes off.

■ **Save your soles.** Water shoes protect your feet from hot sand and sidewalks and the rough surfaces in some pools.

CONTACTS
Aquatica ☎ 888/800–5447 ⊕ *www.aquaticabyseaworld.com*

Busch Gardens Tampa ☎ 888/800–5447 ⊕ *www.buschgardens.com/bgt*

Discovery Cove ☎ 877/557–7404 ⊕ *www.discoverycove.com*

SeaWorld ☎ 888/800–5447 ⊕ *www.seaworld.com*

Parking. Parking is $17 for a car or motorcycle, $20 for an RV or camper. For $22 you can pull into one of the six Preferred Parking rows closest to the front gate. At Aquatica, cars and motorcycles are charged $12, RVs $16—although if you already have your parking slip from that day at SeaWorld, it's free. Parking is free at Discovery Cove.

SEAWORLD

Just as you wouldn't expect to arrive at Disney and see nothing but Mickey Mouse, don't expect to arrive at SeaWorld and see only Shamu. Only a few steps into the park you'll find baby dolphins and their mothers, a pool filled with stingrays, colorful flamingos, rescued sea turtles, rescued pelicans, and even rescued manatees. SeaWorld's objective is to educate as well as entertain.

You'll see how lumbering manatees live and what they look like up close; watch otters and seals perform slapstick routines based on their natural behaviors; learn about the lives of giant tortoises and sea turtles; and be absolutely amazed at the scope of marine life celebrated throughout the park.

Then there are the attractions, each and every one designed not only to showcase the marine world but also to demonstrate ways in which humans can protect the earth's waters and wildlife. And, because there are more exhibits and shows than rides, the difference between Sea-World and other theme parks is that you can go at your own pace, without that hurry-up-and-wait feeling. It's also worth noting that because shows, attractions, and exhibits are based primarily on nature and animals, designers have created a natural layout as well, with winding lanes and plenty of places to relax by the waterfront or beside bouquets of flowers. There's never a nagging urge to race through anything; indeed, the entire park encourages you to slow down and move at a casual pace. That said, theme parks like SeaWorld have been criticized by animal welfare groups. They argue that the conditions and treatment of marine life kept in captivity are harmful for the animals, and that human interaction further exacerbates this.

PLANNING

GETTING ORIENTED

SeaWorld's performance venues, attractions, and activities surround a 17-acre lagoon, and the artful landscaping, curving paths, and concealing greenery sometimes lead to wrong turns. But armed with a map that lists showtimes, it's easy to plan an approach that lets you move fluidly from one show and attraction to the next and still have time for rest stops and meal breaks.

TOURING TIPS

Before investing in front-of-the-line Quick Queue passes (⌸ $19–$35), remember that there are only a handful of big-deal rides, and space is seldom a problem at shows.

If you bring your own food, remove all straws and lids before you arrive—they can harm fish and birds.

Arrive at least 30 minutes early for the Shamu show, which generally fills to capacity. Prepare to get wet in the "splash zone" down front.

In Discovery Cove make the aviary one of your first stops, since the 250-plus birds within will be more active in the morning. Check-in starts at around 7:30 am.

PARK AMENITIES

Guest Services: Ticket booths have become the new Guest Services (aka Guest Relations) center. If you ordered your tickets online, have questions about dining or attractions, or just need tickets to begin with, you can find it all here.

Information and Reservation Center: Right inside the entrance you can pick up the park map (which also has info on showtimes, services, and amenities); make dinner reservations; and buy tickets for Discovery Cove, Aquatica, and park tours.

Lockers: One-time-use, coin-op lockers ($1) are near flip-over coasters like Kraken and Manta, Journey to Atlantis, and Shamu's Happy Harbor as well as inside SeaWorld's main entrance. Also near the entrance, next to Shamu's Emporium, are day lockers ($8 small, $11 large per day). At Discovery Cove free lockers await you near the cabanas.

SeaWorld Orlando

TO AQUATICA →

Shark Encounter

Shark's Underwater Grill

Kraken

Pacific Point Preserve

Clyde and Seamore's Sea Lion High (Sea Lion & Otter Theater)

Spice Mill Café

Lockers

Antarctica: Empire of the Penguins

ATM

Lockers

Antarctic Market

Voyager Smokehouse

Pearl Dive

Journey to Atlantis

Seaport Pizza

Guest Services, Information

Reservations and Show Schedules

Seaport Theater/ Pets Ahoy

THE WATERFRONT

Blue Horizons (Dolphin Theater)

Manta

Seafire Inn

Turtle Trek

Lockers

Dolphin Nursery

Pelican Preserve

ATM Lockers

Dolphin Cove

ATM

Cypress Bakery

KEY WEST

Stingray Lagoon

First Aid

Captain Pete's Island Eats

Key West at SeaWorld

Information and Reservations

SeaWorld Rescue

Parking

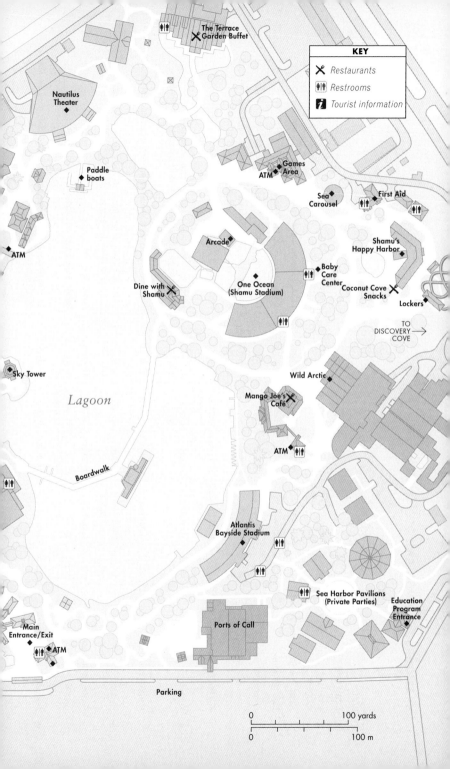

KEY

✕ *Restaurants*
🚻 *Restrooms*
🛈 *Tourist information*

The Terrace Garden Buffet

Nautilus Theater

Paddle boats

ATM

Games Area

Sea Carousel

First Aid

Arcade

Shamu's Happy Harbor

Dine with Shamu

One Ocean (Shamu Stadium)

Baby Care Center

Coconut Cove Snacks

Lockers

TO DISCOVERY COVE →

Sky Tower

Wild Arctic

Lagoon

Mango Joe's Café

ATM

Boardwalk

Atlantis Bayside Stadium

Sea Harbor Pavilions (Private Parties)

Education Program Entrance

Main Entrance/Exit

ATM

Ports of Call

Parking

0   100 yards

0   100 m

SEAWORLD ORLANDO AND DISCOVERY COVE

SeaWorld

NAME	Height Req.	Type of Entertainment	Duration	Crowds	Audience	Tips
Antarctica: Empire of the Penguins	48"	Tour/Thrill Ride	5 mins.	Heavy	All Ages	Come early.
A'Lure, the Call of the Ocean	n/a	Show	20 mins.	Heavy	All Ages	Plenty of seats, but arrive 15 mins. early for a wide selection.
Blue Horizons	n/a	Show	20 mins.	Heavy	All Ages	Arrive 20 mins. before showtime.
Dolphin Nursery	n/a	Aquarium	Up to you	Light	All Ages	Come during a Shamu show so the kids can be up front.
Journey to Atlantis	At least 42"	Thrill Ride with Water	6 mins.	Heavy	All but Young Kids	You can make a beeline here first thing or come about an hour before closing. But the best time for this is at night.
Key West at SeaWorld	n/a	Walk-Through/ Aquarium	Up to you	Light to Moderate	All Ages	If too crowded, wander until crowds disperse.
★ Kraken	At least 54"	Thrill Ride	6 mins.	Heavy	All but Young Kids	Get to the park when it opens and head straight to Kraken; otherwise, hit it near closing time or during a Blue Horizons show.
Manatees Rescue	n/a	Aquarium	Up to you	Light to Moderate	All Ages	Come during a Shamu show but *not right after* a dolphin show.
★ Manta	At least 54"	Thrill Ride with Water	6 mins.	You Bet!	All but Young Kids	Come first thing or late in the day, or purchase a Quick Queue pass for front-of-ride access.
Pacific Point Preserve	n/a	Aquarium	Up to you	Light	All Ages	Come anytime.
Pets Ahoy	n/a	Show	15–20 mins.	Moderate to Heavy	All Ages	Gauge the crowds, and come here early if necessary.
★ Sea Lion & Otter Stadium	n/a	Show	40 mins.	Heavy	All Ages	Sit toward the center for the best view, and don't miss the pre-show mime. Plenty of seats.

				Heavy	Young Kids	
Shamu's Happy Harbor	n/a	Playground with Water	Up to you	Light	All Ages	Don't come first thing in morning, or you'll never drag your child away. Bring a towel to dry them off.
★ Shamu Stadium (One Ocean)	n/a	Show	25 mins.	Moderate to Heavy	All Ages	Show itself lasts 25 minutes, but there's a 30-minute pre-show; plan accordingly.
Shark Encounter	n/a	Aquarium	Up to you	Light to Moderate	All Ages	Come during the sea lion show.
Sky Tower	48"	Tour/Thrill Ride	6 mins.	Light	All Ages	Come whenever there's no line. Note the extra $4 charge, though.
Stingray Lagoon	n/a	Aquarium	Up to you	Moderate to Heavy	All Ages	Walk by if it's crowded, but return before dusk.
Turtle Point	n/a	Zoo	Up to you	Light	All Ages	Come anytime.
Wild Arctic	At least 42"	Simulator Exp./Aquarium	5+ mins.	Moderate to Heavy	All Ages	Come during a Shamu show. You can skip the ride if you just want to see the mammals.
Discovery Cove						
Beaches	n/a	Beach Area	Up to you	Light	All Ages	Arrive early and head to the far side for a private spot.
★ Dolphin Lagoon	n/a	Pool	45–60 mins.	n/a	All but Young Kids	Be mindful of your appointment time.
Explorer's Aviary	n/a	Aviary	Up to you	Light to Moderate	All Ages	Come early, when the birds are most active.
Tropical Reef	n/a	Aquarium/Pool Area	Up to you	Light to Moderate	All Ages	Monitor crowds and come when they're lightest. Popular with teens.
Wind-Away River	n/a	Aquarium	Up to you	Light to Moderate	All Ages	When it gets hot, slip into the water. Popular with teens.

★ **Fodor's** Choice

632 <   **SeaWorld Orlando**

Lost People and Things: SeaWorld's Main Information Center operates as the park's Lost and Found. Lost children are brought here, and it's the place to report lost children. A park-wide paging system also helps reunite parents with kids. At Discovery Cove lost kids and items eventually find their way to the check-in lobby.

ANIMAL ENCOUNTERS AND TOURS

You can book tours up to three months in advance. For a list, check the SeaWorld website (⊕ *www. seaworld.com*) or call the park (☎ *407/351–3600*).

Behind the Scenes Tour. On this 90-minute program, you'll have a chance to see how SeaWorld's animal experts care for rescued manatees and sea turtles. Where else can you touch a shark, step inside a hidden polar bear den, and play with a penguin? From $29 adults, $9 children. ✉ *SeaWorld*.

> ### TOP SEAWORLD ATTRACTIONS
>
> Antarctica: Empire of the Penguin
>
> Clyde and Seamore Take Pirate Island
>
> Kraken
>
> Manta
>
> One Ocean
>
> Pets Ahoy

DISCOVERY COVE

If you were pleasantly surprised by the pace at SeaWorld, believe it or not, you'll find it's even slower at Discovery Cove. Here your mission is to spend an entire day doing nothing but savoring a 32-acre tropical oasis. It's a task made easier by an all-inclusive admission that covers all meals, towels, a wet suit, masks, sunscreen, and the option of springing for the highlight of the day: a unique swimming experience with a bottlenose dolphin.

Even without a dolphin encounter, you can have a great time splashing around coral reefs, swimming into a spacious aviary, floating down a quiet river, and lazing on a sandy beach beneath lovely palms. New in 2012, Freshwater Oasis is a tropical rain-forest environment of sparkling clear springs offering face-to-face encounters with playful otters and curious marmoset monkeys, while thanks to a special diving helmet, SeaVenture lets you walk underwater through a reef filled with tropical fish and rays that you can literally reach out and touch.

PLANNING

GETTING ORIENTED

Thanks to Discovery Cove's daily cap on crowds, it may seem as if you have the park to yourself. Navigating the grounds is simple; signs point to swimming areas, cabanas, or the free-flight aviary—aflutter with exotic birds and accessible via walkway or (even better) by swimming to it beneath a waterfall.

At Discovery Cove's Explorer's Aviary, you can attract exotic birds with fruit or feed. You might even get one (or two) to hop onto your shoulder. Get the camera ready.

TOURING TIP

In Discovery Cove make the aviary one of your first stops, since the 250-plus birds within will be more active in the morning. Remember that check-in starts at 7:30 am, and the waterways open around 9.

PARK AMENITIES

Guest Services: You can get information on meals, cabanas, lockers, dolphin swims, merchandise, souvenir photos, and other aspects of the park at the **Discovery Cove Check-In Lobby** when you arrive, or at Guest Services (**aka Guest Relations**) just after you enter.

Lost People and Things: Lost kids and items are usually turned over to Discovery Cove attendants, who bring them to the attendants at the Check-In Lobby.

ANIMAL ENCOUNTERS

Trainer for a Day. This opportunity (from $428, but often $500-plus) rivals SeaWorld's Marine Mammal Keeper Experience. General admission includes meals, wet suit, and diving gear; this tour adds a gift bag, waterproof camera, trainer T-shirt, 30-minute dolphin swim, a private photo session with two dolphins, feeding fish in the Grand Reef, a meet and greet with tropical birds and small animals, and an almost exclusive (only eight guests in the entire lagoon) interaction that includes a "double-foot push" (two dolphins propel you across the lagoon by the soles of your feet). Ready for more? Shadow a trainer all day: head to the dolphin back area for a private tour and talk to trainers about how they teach and care for these amazing animals. Like other Discovery Cove admissions, this includes unlimited access to SeaWorld and

DID YOU KNOW?

You can "swim" with the dolphins even if you didn't book a dolphin swim at Discovery Cove. Just take the Dolphin Plunge, a waterslide that jettisons you into a clear tube running through the pool inhabited by Commerson's dolphins.

Aquatica for 14 days. Call ahead to arrange a tour. ⊠ *Discovery Cove* ☎ *407/351–3600, 877/557–7404* ⊕ *www.discoverycove.com.*

AQUATICA

12

Just across International Drive from SeaWorld, Aquatica is the 60-acre water park that does a wonderful job angling water-park lovers away from Disney's Typhoon Lagoon and Blizzard Beach and Universal's Wet 'n Wild. And, sure, Aquatica has all the slides you'd expect, but it also has plenty of whimsical SeaWorld touches.

Aquatica takes cues from SeaWorld and Discovery Cove in design and mood. The park also takes its cues from the tropics. Right after you clear the parking lot, you see a tropical pastiche of buildings that may convince you your ship just sailed into the Caribbean. So go with it. Get into a groove, relax, and enjoy yourself. In addition to super-slippery waterslides, there are quiet coves, phenomenally creative kids' play areas, lazy streams, and an atmosphere that is guaranteed to relieve your pre-vacation stress.

Ideally you'll have arrived with some snacks and drinks to combat the fatigue you'll feel after scaling to the tops of all those watery thrill rides. If not, fear not—there are plenty of places to find food and drink.

You should also be toting beach towels, sunscreen, and water shoes. Again, if not, fear not—there are a number of shops and kiosks where you can buy (or rent) all of this stuff and more.

Many of the rides have height restrictions, so if you're traveling with kids, have their heights checked at the Information Center, which you'll see right when you enter the park. Each child will be issued a colored wristband that alerts attendants to which rides are appropriate for him or her (or just look for the height requirement signposted at the entrance to each attraction—and check our reviews). If anyone in your group isn't comfortable in the water, this is also a good place to inquire about the swimming lessons that are offered.

After stashing excess supplies in a locker and generally settling in, it's time to explore. Unless it's peak season, several hours should be enough to visit each ride and attraction once or twice, and will also allow for some downtime, lazing on the beach, or enjoying a leisurely meal.

PLANNING

GETTING ORIENTED

Initially, you might find it hard to get your bearings amid the towering slides, Caribbean palms, winding sidewalks, and the seemingly random layout of restaurants, rides, slides, and facilities. And there are no paper maps, only posted diagrams throughout the park. But in reality, the park is fairly easy to navigate—its layout forms a simple circle. The services (restaurants, changing rooms, shops) form a core around which the attractions are situated.

At the entrance, turn right and you'll be at the premier attraction, Dolphin Plunge; but after that you may want to do an about-face and head straight to the shores of the beach at Cutback Cove. This way, you can set up a base and then work your way to other attractions around the circle while remaining conveniently close to meals at Waterstone Grill and the Banana Beach Cookout.

TOURING TIPS

Be aware of the sun. Avoid sunburn by reapplying sunscreen (they suggest SPF 30) often—even waterproof sunblock washes off. For even more sun protection, rent a standard cabana (about $60) or go all out and splurge on the "ultimate cabana" for eight, which includes an all-day locker, bottled water, towels, and discount coupons for merchandise.

Be aware of your feet. Wear sandals or water shoes (or even socks) to protect your feet from hot sand, sidewalks, and rough pool surfaces. At the major thrill rides, a "sneaker keeper" offers a place to stash your footwear while you experience the ride.

Buy tickets in advance. Prepurchased tickets get you early entrance, and this head start will enable you to hit the major flume and tube rides more than once.

Commune with nature. You can catch Commerson's dolphins at feeding times; spot macaws on tree limbs; or see small mammals in the Conservation Cabanas, where docents answer questions. A variety of animals are on display around the park.

PARK AMENITIES

Information: The Main Information Center is at the park entrance, just past the ticket kiosks. Also at the entrance are an ATM, telephones, and restrooms. This is where you check out the posted park map and plan your approach. On the walkways outside the information center and leading into the park, attendants are stationed to help you get your bearings and point out where to find strollers and wheelchairs, help you with lost-and-found inquiries, and describe combination-ticket packages.

Lockers: There are three areas with unlimited-access lockers to rent for a day. One is near the splashdown area at Walhalla Wave and HooRoo Run; two others are at the center and far end of the park, where there are also nursing facilities. You pay $7 for a small locker (enough for one backpack) and $11 for a large one (for about two backpacks); there's also a $10 deposit, which is refunded when you leave. The central locker area also rents towels for $4 ($1 of which is refunded upon return).

Lost People and Things: Lost items and people are taken to a small tent called the Concierge Cabana, which is right by the entrance to the beach area.

NORTHEAST
FLORIDA

WELCOME TO NORTHEAST FLORIDA

TOP REASONS TO GO

★ **Get out and play:** Beautiful beaches and a wealth of state and national parks mean swimming, sunbathing, kayaking, fishing, hiking, bird-watching, and camping opportunities are all nearby.

★ **Golfer's paradise:** "Above par" describes the golf scene, from award-winning courses to THE PLAYERS Championship to the World Golf Hall of Fame.

★ **Start your engines:** Few things get racing fans as revved up as tours of Daytona International Speedway, home of the Daytona 500, Coke Zero 400, and Rolex 24 at Daytona.

★ **Be in the now:** Whether you want a yoga retreat or the ultimate in sybaritic pampering, the oceanfront spas at Amelia Island and Ponte Vedra Beach make this region the place to be.

★ **The rest is history:** The nation's oldest city, St. Augustine, is a must-see for anyone interested in history.

1 **Jacksonville.** With a metro-area population of 1.3 million, Jacksonville has the social and cultural appeal of a big city but the down-to-earth charm of a small town.

2 **Jacksonville Beaches.** The laid-back beach towns on the barrier islands east of Jacksonville are popular family destinations.

3 **Amelia Island/Fernandina Beach.** At the northeast edge of Florida you'll find a historic downtown, beautiful beaches, and two superlative resorts.

4 **St. Augustine.** You don't have to be a history buff to enjoy America's oldest city, founded in 1565.

5 **Daytona Beach and Inland Towns.** The Daytona 500, Bike Week, and spring break put it on the map, but the region is popular with vacationing families, too. Gainesville is home to the University of Florida and its Gators.

6 **The Space Coast.** This area includes Canaveral National Seashore; the Kennedy Space Center; Port Canaveral and its cruise ships; Cocoa, offering quiet appeal; and Cocoa Beach, the ultimate surf and bodyboard destination.

GETTING ORIENTED

13

Northeast Florida has historic port cities such as Fernandina Beach on Amelia Island and St. Augustine and inland towns such as Micanopy and Gainesville, as well as the urban hub of Jacksonville. About two hours south of Jacksonville, on Interstate 95, Titusville is the entry point for the Kennedy Space Center. It marks the northern perimeter of the Space Coast, which includes Cocoa and Melbourne. If you take U.S. 1, it lengthens the trip, but the scenery makes up for the inconvenience. Route A1A/Atlantic Avenue is the main road on all the barrier islands. In many places on A1A, you can see the area's beautiful beaches from your car window.

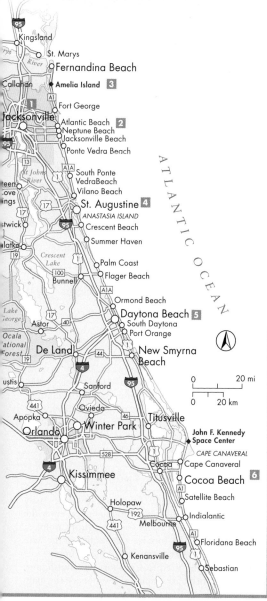

THE SPACE SHUTTLE ATLANTIS

Even if you have never had the inclination to strap into a rocket or live in zero gravity, no trip to Florida would be complete without a visit to the Kennedy Space Center's *Atlantis* Exhibit. A full day can be spent experiencing the educational and emotional life and history of the American space shuttle program.

Defying the term "exhibit," the Space Shuttle Atlantis defies stereotypes with a hands-on approach that enables you to not only see and hear, but also touch and feel, so that you *experience* rather than observe. There are no fingerprint-covered glass cases separating you from getting up close and personal with the symbolic passageways, 60-plus interactive displays, games, simulators, and even a slide to get you back to the ground level (adults are allowed). The Atlantis shuttle, complete with tile damage from the heat of re-entry, never fails to amaze visitors who see it as only astronauts have before. The walk-through replicas of the shuttle's living quarters give visitors the ability to more accurately understand life on the shuttle. The Atlantis exhibit has an open atmosphere with a friendly, enthusiastic, and knowledgeable staff that has a way of stoking curiosity and bringing out the inner-astronaut in everyone.

THE EXPERIENCE

The Shuttle Atlantis exhibit is easily located from the moment you enter the Kennedy Space Center Visitor Complex; the 184-foot life-size replica of the twin rocket boosters and massive orange fuel tank used to transport the shuttle into orbit are displayed just outside the main

13

entry. The Atlantis Experience begins with a dual-theater screening that showcases the history of the shuttle development. The motion-picturesque films provide a background and understanding of the necessity and evolution of the shuttle program. Passing through the theater and onto the upper level reveals Atlantis, with cargo doors open and robotic Canada arm extended.

Even for the space novice, it is easy to see the amount of thought, planning, and insight that went into the design and construction of the Atlantis facility, not to mention the engineering and transportation challenges overcome in order to display a real-life shuttle. Rotated 43.21 degrees and almost close enough to touch, this experience is the closest that many nonastronauts will ever come to something that has actually been into space—other than physically touching an astronaut (not recommended). The staff gladly answers any questions and provides an array of information regarding the facility, design, and interactive displays available for use. Touring Atlantis is an exploration in and of itself.

ACTIVITIES

The interactive games and displays are fun for children and parents alike, sometimes sparking fierce competition. Try your hand on the shuttle crane

simulator and experience the complex task of attaching the Shuttle Atlantis to the 58,500-pound fuel tank. Features like this are not only enjoyable, but also shed light on the often unheard engineering and physical obstacles encountered and conquered in order to prepare a shuttle for safe transport to the launch pad.

If you've ever wondered what it would be like to experience a shuttle liftoff, look no further. The Shuttle Launch Experience is the only place on Earth (and perhaps the galaxy) allowing nonastronauts to partake in a thrill only a select few Americans have known. After a series of informative videos, future astronauts are guided into the mock shuttle.

Once your safety belts have been fastened, the motion-based platform comes alive with specialized, interactive seating and high-fidelity video and audio to amaze the visitors with what astronauts call the most realistic simulation of a launch. After pushing through the high G-forces and separating from the rocket boosters and fuel tank, the simulation climaxes with a sense of weightlessness, along with a breathtaking view of the distant planet Earth. Be sure to secure belongings in the provided lockers to prevent inadvertent meteor showers of pocket debris during the launch.

Updated by
Steve Master
and Jennifer
Greenhill-Taylor

For many travelers, Florida is about fantasy, thanks in no small part to Central Florida's make-believe kingdoms. But the northeastern part of the state—you could call it "authentic Florida"—has its own allure, with unspoiled beaches and rivers, historic small towns, and urban arts and culture.

Northeastern Florida's beaches have wide, shell-strewn expanses of sand, in some places firm enough to ride bikes on, and breakers just the right height for kids to jump. Thanks to the temperate climate and waters warmed by the Gulf Stream, these beaches are a year-round playground—when it's too cold to swim, you can still enjoy surf-fishing or just riding on the beach, or strolling the shoreline looking for shells and sharks' teeth.

Sun and surf aren't the only reasons to explore northeastern Florida, though. There's historic St. Augustine and its horse-drawn carriages, Daytona and its classic spring-break flavor, and the Space Coast and its sense of discovery. Along the way is an array of little towns—from Fernandina and its shrimp fleets to Micanopy and its antiques stores— that invite quiet exploration.

There's city life in the northeast, too. In the last decade or so, Jacksonville has revitalized its institutions and infrastructure. And with the revitalization has come an arts renaissance—from virtuoso productions in the theaters of the Times-Union Center for the Performing Arts and the Florida Theatre, to world-class exhibitions in the Museum of Contemporary Art.

So, even if the ultimate reason for your Florida sojourn is Mickey and his friends, there's no reason to miss the northeast. Indeed, you'll find some authentic benefits—among them, a dearth of crowds and lines and an abundance of southern hospitality, plus good value for the money.

PLANNING

WHEN TO GO

It's not 90°F and sunny here every day. In winter the weather is fair, averaging in the low 50s in Jacksonville and low 60s in Cocoa Beach, but the temperature sometimes dips below freezing for a day or two. Summer temperatures hover around 90°F, but the humidity makes it seem hotter, and late-afternoon thunderstorms are frequent. April and May are good months to visit, because the ocean is beginning to warm up and the beaches aren't yet packed. Fall is usually pleasant, too, but September is still hurricane season.

13

GETTING HERE AND AROUND

AIR TRAVEL

Jacksonville International Airport (JAX) is the region's air hub. A welcome center with information on local attractions, including St. Augustine and Amelia Island, is on the ground floor at the foot of the escalator near baggage claim. It's open daily 9 am–10 pm.

Daytona Beach International (DAB) and Gainesville Regional (GNV) are smaller operations with fewer flights; that said, they may be more convenient in certain travel situations.

Although Orlando isn't part of the area, visitors to northeastern Florida often choose to arrive at Orlando International Airport (MCO), because cheaper flights are usually available. Driving east from Orlando on toll road 528 (aka the Beachline Expressway) brings you to Cocoa Beach in about an hour. To reach Daytona from Orlando, take Interstate 4 or the Beachline Expressway to Interstate 95 and drive north for an hour or so.

CAR TRAVEL

East–west traffic travels the northern part of the state on Interstate 10, a cross-country highway stretching from Jacksonville, Florida, to Santa Monica, California. Farther south, Interstate 4 connects Florida's west and east coasts. Signs on Interstate 4 designate it an east–west route, but actually the road rambles northeast from Tampa to Orlando, then heads north–northeast to Daytona. Two interstates head north–south on Florida's peninsula: Interstate 95 on the east coast and Interstate 75 on the west.

If you want to drive as close to the Atlantic as possible, choose Route A1A, but accept the fact that it will add considerably to your drive time. It runs along the barrier islands, changing its name several times along the way.

The Buccaneer Trail, which overlaps part of Route A1A, goes from St. Augustine north to Mayport, through marshlands and beaches, crosses the St. Johns via Ferry, and then proceeds north into Fort Clinch State Park. The extremely scenic Route 13, also known as the William Bartram Trail, runs from Jacksonville to East Palatka along the east side of St. Johns River through tiny hamlets. U.S. 17 travels the west side of the river, passing through Green Cove Springs and Palatka. Route 40 runs east–west through the Ocala National Forest, giving a nonstop view of stately pines and bold wildlife.

HOTELS

For the busy seasons—during summer in and around Jacksonville and during spring, summer, winter, and holiday weekends all over Florida—reserve well ahead for top properties. Jacksonville's beach hotels fill up quickly for PGA's THE PLAYERS Championship in mid-May. Daytona Beach presents similar problems during the Daytona 500 (late February), Bike Week (late February–early March), spring break (March), and the Coke Zero 400 (early July).

St. Augustine stays busy all year. In late summer and fall rates are low and availability is high, but it's also hurricane season. Although northeast Florida hasn't been hit directly since 1964, it's possible for threatening storms to disrupt plans. *Hotel reviews have been shortened. For full information, visit Fodors.com.*

RESTAURANTS

The ocean, St. Johns River, and numerous lakes and smaller rivers teem with fish, and so, naturally, seafood dominates local menus. Northeast Florida also has fine-dining restaurants, and its ethnic eateries include some excellent Middle Eastern places. And then there are the barbecue joints—more of them than you can shake a hickory chip at.

WHAT IT COSTS				
	$	$$	$$$	$$$$
RESTAURANTS	under $16	$16–$20	$21–$30	over $30
HOTELS	under $201	$201–$300	$301–$400	over $400

Restaurant prices are the average cost of a main course at dinner or, if dinner is not served, at lunch. Hotel prices are the lowest cost of a standard double room in high season.

TOURS

TourTime, Inc. This company offers custom group and individual motorcoach tours of Jacksonville, Amelia Island, Jekyll Island, and St. Augustine, as well as river cruises and trips to Silver Springs, Kennedy Space Center, Orlando, Okefenokee Swamp, and Savannah. Advance reservations are required. ☎ 904/282–8500 ⊕ *www.tourtimeinc.com.*

JACKSONVILLE

Updated by Jennifer Greenhill-Taylor

399 miles north of Miami, on I-95.

Jacksonville is an underrated vacation spot. It offers appealing downtown riverside areas, handsome residential neighborhoods, a thriving arts scene, spectacular beaches, and, for football fans, the NFL's Jaguars and the NCAA Gator Bowl.

Although the city has become the largest in area of the continental United States (841 square miles), its Old South flavor remains, especially in the Riverside/Avondale historic district. Here moss-draped oak trees frame prairie-style bungalows and Tudor Revival mansions, and palm trees, Spanish bayonet, and azaleas populate the landscape.

GETTING HERE AND AROUND

The main airport for the region is Jacksonville International Airport. Free shuttles run from the terminal to all parking lots (except the garage) around the clock, and transportation service into the city is available from numerous companies in vehicles that range from taxis to vans to elegant limousines. Check beforehand on prices, which vary widely, and on which credit cards are accepted. The average cost per person from airport to downtown is $35 to $45; it's $45 to $55 for trips to the beaches. The larger companies usually operate 24/7, but the smaller (and often less expensive ones) may be by appointment only.

Connecting the north and south banks of the St. Johns River, the Jacksonville Water Taxi runs between several locations, including Southbank Riverwalk at Friendship Fountain, the Wyndham Hotel, and the Jacksonville Landing. The one-way trip takes about five minutes. During football season the water taxi also makes trips to EverBank Field on game days and for special events. The water taxis run Sunday through Thursday, 11 to 9, and Friday and Saturday from 11 to 11 (except during rain or other bad weather), with special hours on game days and for special events. One-way fare is $3; special-event fare is $5.

Jacksonville Transportation Authority buses and shuttles serve the city and its beaches. The city also operates a small monorail system that links the convention center and a few downtown areas to several other stations across the river on the Southbank and San Marco. It is free and runs weekdays from 6 am to 9 pm and Saturday and Sunday during special events only.

Airport Jacksonville International Airport (*JAX*). ☎ *904/741–4902* ⊕ *www. flyjax.com.*

Airport Transfers Dana's Limousine & Transportation ☎ *904/744–3333.*

Public Transportation Jacksonville Transportation Authority (*JTA*). ☎ *904/630–3100* ⊕ *www.jtafla.com.*

Taxis Coastal Cab ☎ *904/246–9999* ⊕ *www.coastalcab-jax.com.* **Jacksonville Water Taxi** ☎ *904/834–4011.* **Yellow Cab-Jacksonville** ☎ *904/999–9999.*

VISITOR INFORMATION

Contact Visit Jacksonville ☎ *904/798–9111, 800/733–2668* ⊕ *www. visitjacksonville.com.*

EXPLORING

Jacksonville was settled along both sides of the twisting St. Johns River, and a number of attractions are on or near its banks. Both sides of the river, which is spanned by myriad bridges, have downtown areas and waterfront complexes of shops, restaurants, parks, and museums.

You can reach some attractions by water taxi or Skyway Express monorail system—scenic alternatives to driving back and forth across the bridges. That said, a car is generally necessary.

In addition to the visitor information center at the airport, there's one at the Jacksonville Landing marketplace and another in Jacksonville

Beach at the Beaches Historical Museum (⊠ *425 Beach Blvd.*) that is open Tuesday through Saturday 10–4 and Sunday noon–4.

TOP ATTRACTIONS

Cummer Museum of Art & Gardens. The Wark Collection of early-18th-century Meissen porcelain is just one reason to visit this former estate on the St. Johns River, which includes 13 permanent galleries with more than 5,500 items spanning more than 4,000 years, and 3 acres of riverfront gardens, including a sculpture garden and outdoor plaza, that form a showcase for northeast Florida's blooming seasons and indigenous fauna. Art Connections allows kids of all ages to experience art through hands-on, interactive exhibits. The Thomas H. Jacobsen Gallery of American Art focuses on works by American artists, including Max Weber, N.C. Wyeth, and Paul Manship. Complimentary tour guide brochures at front desk help visitors navigate the galleries, as do podcasts. ⊠ *829 Riverside Ave., Riverside* ☎ *904/356–6857* ⊕ *www.cummermuseum.org* 🔊 *$10, free Tues. 4–9* ⊙ *Tues. 10–9, Wed.–Sat. 10–4, Sun. noon–4.*

Jacksonville Landing. During the week, this riverfront market caters to locals (who sometimes arrive by boat) and tourists alike, with specialty shops, full-service restaurants—including a sushi bar, Italian bistro, Irish pub, and a steak house—and an internationally flavored food court, all of which look out over the boat traffic on the St. Johns River. Water taxis shuttle across the river between the Landing and the Southbank. The Landing hosts more than 250 weekend events each year, ranging from the good clean fun of the Lighted Boat Parade and Christmas Tree Lighting to the just plain obnoxious Florida/Georgia game afterparty, as well as live music (usually of the local cover-band variety) in the courtyard. ⊠ *2 W. Independent Dr., Downtown* ☎ *904/353–1188* ⊕ *www.jacksonvillelanding.com* 🔊 *Free* ⊙ *Mon.–Thurs. 10–8, Fri. and Sat. 10–9, Sun. noon–5:30; restaurant hrs vary.*

FAMILY
Fodor's Choice
★

Jacksonville Zoo and Gardens. The zoo offers visitors the chance to hop on a train and explore different countries through the animals that live there, from the Land of the Tiger, a 2½-acre Asian attraction featuring Sumatran and Malayan tigers, to the Tuxedo Coast, a controlled Antarctic-like environment for a group of Magellanic penguins, and the African Plains area, which houses elephants, white rhinos, and two highly endangered leopards, in addition to other species of African birds and mammals. The Range of the Jaguar, winner of the Association of Zoos and Aquarium's Exhibit of the Year, takes visitors to a 4-acre Central and South American exhibit, with exotic big cats as well as 20 other species native to the region. Among the other highlights are rare waterfowl and the African Reptile Building, which showcases some of the world's most venomous snakes. Wild Florida is a 2½-acre area with black bears, bald eagles, white-tailed deer, and other animals native to Florida, while RiverQuest reveals the ecology of the adjacent Trout River. Play Park contains a Splash Ground, forest play area, two mazes, and discovery building; Stingray Bay has a 17,000-gallon pool where visitors can pet and feed the mysterious creatures; and DinoTrek's life-size dinosaurs offer a glimpse into the past. Parking is free. ⊠ *370 Zoo*

Rainbox lorikeet might pop by and say hello while you're touring the Jacksonville Zoo.

Pkwy., off Heckscher Dr. E ☎ *904/757–4463* ⊕ *www.jacksonvillezoo. org* ✉ *$16.95* ⊙ *Daily 9–5.*

Fodor's Choice ★ **Museum of Contemporary Art Jacksonville.** In this loftlike, five-story, downtown building, the former headquarters of the Western Union Telegraph Company, a permanent collection of 20th-century art shares space with traveling exhibitions and a theater space. The museum encompasses five galleries and ArtExplorium, a highly interactive educational exhibit for kids, as well as a funky gift shop and Café Nola, open for lunch on weekdays and for dinner on Thursday. MOCA Jacksonville also hosts film series and workshops throughout the year, and packs a big art-wallop into a relatively small 14,000 square feet. A once-a-month Art Walk is free to all. ⊠ *Hemming Plaza, 333 N. Laura St., Downtown* ☎ *904/366–6911* ⊕ *www.mocajacksonville.org* ✉ *$8* ⊙ *Tues., Wed., Fri., and Sat. 11–5, Thurs. 11–9, Sun. noon–5; Art Walk 1st Wed. of month 5–9.*

WORTH NOTING

Anheuser-Busch Jacksonville Brewery Tour. Guided or self-guided tours give a behind-the-scenes look at how barley, malt, rice, hops, and water form the King of Beers. If you're 21 years or older, you'll receive a complimentary Budweiser at the beginning of the tour, and another beer of your choice in the Tap Room at the end of the tour. Soda or water is available for the under-21 set. Call ahead if you are interested in a guided tour. ⊠ *111 Busch Dr.* ☎ *904/696–8373* ⊕ *www.budweisertours. com* ✉ *Free self-guided; $10 guided* ⊙ *Mon., Tues., Thurs.–Sat. 10–4.*

Karpeles Manuscript Library Museum. File this one under "hidden treasure," given that even many residents have never visited Karpeles.

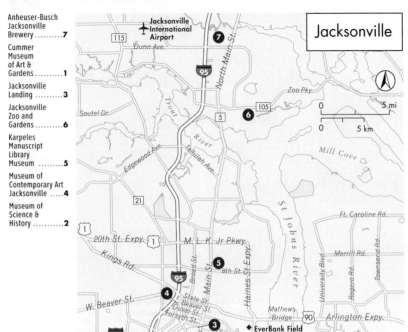

That's too bad, because this 1921 neoclassical building on the outskirts of downtown has displayed some priceless documents: the original draft of the Bill of Rights, the Emancipation Proclamation signed by Abraham Lincoln, handwritten manuscripts of Edgar Allan Poe and Charles Dickens, and musical scores by Beethoven and Mozart. Manuscript exhibitions change every four months or so and coincide with bi-monthly art exhibitions. Also on the premises is an antique-book library, with volumes dating from the late 1800s. ✉ *101 W. 1st St.* ☎ *904/356–2992* ⊕ *www.rain.org/~karpeles/jax.html* ✆ *Free* ☾ *Tues.– Fri. 10–3, Sat. 10–4.*

FAMILY   **Museum of Science & History.** Known locally as MOSH, this museum is home to the Bryan-Gooding Planetarium. As a next-generation planetarium, it can project 3-D laser shows that accompany the ever-popular weekend Cosmic Concerts. For those taking in the planetarium shows, the resolution is significantly sharper than that of the biggest HDTV on the market. Whether you're a kid taking in Sesame Street's *One World, One Sky,* or an adult star-gazing in the *Skies over Jacksonville* tour of the night sky, the experience is awesome. MOSH also has a wide variety of interactive exhibits and programs that include JEA Science Theater, where you can participate in live science experiments; JEA PowerPlay: Understanding our Energy Choices, where you can energize the future city of MOSHtopia as you learn about alternative energy resources and the science of energy; the Florida Naturalist's Center, where you can interact with northeast Florida wildlife; and the Currents of Time, where you'll navigate 12,000 years of Northeast Florida history, from the region's earliest Native American settlers to modern day events. Nationally acclaimed traveling exhibits are featured along with signature exhibits on regional history. ✉ *1025 Museum Circle* ☎ *904/396–6674* 🌐 *www.themosh.org* 🎟 *Museum $10, museum and planetarium $15, Cosmic Concerts $5; Fri. $5 all admissions* 🕒 *Mon.–Thurs. 10–5, Fri. 10–8, Sat. 10–6, Sun. noon–5.*

THE BIGGEST CITY?

It's nearly impossible to visit Jacksonville without hearing locals brag that their city is the largest in the United States. In fact, the River City's 841 square miles pale in comparison to the actual title holder: 4,710-square-mile Sitka, Alaska. More accurately, Jacksonville is the largest city in the continental United States, and that's due to the consolidation of Duval County and the city.

WHERE TO EAT

$$$ AMERICAN 🍴 **bb's.** Sleek yet cozy, this hip bistro is as popular with corporate types looking to close a deal as it is with young lovebirds seemingly on the verge of popping the question (though shouting the question might be more appropriate, considering how loud the dining room can get on weekends). The concrete floors and a stainless-steel wine bar provide an interesting backdrop for comfort-food-inspired entrées and daily specials that might include char-grilled beef tenderloin, pan-seared diver scallops with house-made parsnip pierogies, or linguini with catalan-style black angus meatballs. On the lighter side, grilled pizzas, sandwiches, and salads, especially the warm goat-cheese salad, are favorites. Although a wait is common, you can pass the time sizing up the display of diet-destroying desserts. [$] *Average main: $21* ✉ *1019 Hendricks Ave., San Marco, Southbank* ☎ *904/306–0100* 🌐 *www.bbsrestaurant.com* 🕒 *Closed Sun.*

$$$ AMERICAN 🍴 **Biscottis.** The local artwork on the redbrick walls is a mild distraction from the jovial yuppies, soccer moms, arty types, and well-heeled professionals—all of whom are among the crowd jockeying for tables in this midsize restaurant. Elbows almost touch, but no one seems to mind. The constantly changing dinner menu offers the unexpected: wild mushroom ravioli with a broth of corn, leek, and dried apricot; or curry-grilled swordfish with cucumber-fig bordelaise sauce. There are even gluten-free options. Be sure to sample from Biscottis's decadent desserts (courtesy of "b the bakery"). Brunch, a local favorite, is served until 3 on weekends. [$] *Average main: $21* ✉ *3556 St. Johns Ave.* ☎ *904/387–2060* 🌐 *www.biscottis.net* ✍ *Reservations not accepted.*

$$$ ECLECTIC 🍴 **Bistro Aix.** Named after the French city (and pronounced simply "X"), this sophisticated bistro-bar's leather booths, 1940s brickwork, olive drapes, and intricate marbled globes, provide a perfect home for well-prepared French food. Regulars can't get enough of the creamy onion soup or escargot appetizers, prosciutto and goat cheese salad, or entrées such as oak-grilled fish Aixoise, steak frites, or mushroom and fontina wood-fired pizza. Most items (salads included) come in full or lighter-appetite portions, and you'll definitely want to save room for dessert. Aix's in-house pastry team ensures no sweet tooth leaves unsatisfied, with offerings such as profiteroles (mini cream puffs filled with vanilla ice cream and topped with chocolate and caramel sauce) and warm chocolate banana walnut bread pudding. Call for preferred seating. $ *Average main: $25* ⊠ *1440 San Marco Blvd., San Marco* ☎ *904/398–1949* ⊕ *www.bistrox.com* ⌂ *Reservations essential* ⊘ *No lunch weekends.*

$$
SEAFOOD
✕ **Clark's Fish Camp.** It's out of the way, but every mile will be forgotten once you step inside this former bait shop overlooking Julington Creek. Clark's has more than 160 appetizers and entrées, including the usual—shrimp, catfish, and oysters—and the unusual—ostrich, rattlesnake, and kangaroo. In keeping with the more bizarre entrées is the decor, best described as early American taxidermy: hundreds of stuffed critters gaze upon you in the main dining room, and preserved lions, gazelles, baboons, even a rhino, keep a watchful eye in the bar. One person's kitschy may be another's creepy. Be careful not to park illegally—tickets are expensive. $ *Average main: $20* ⊠ *12903 Hood Landing Rd., Mandarin* ☎ *904/268–3474* ⊕ *www.clarksfishcamp.com* ⊘ *No lunch weekdays.*

$
AMERICAN
✕ **European Street Café.** Wicker baskets and lofty shelves brimming with European confections and groceries like Toblerone and Nutella fill practically every inch of space not occupied by café tables. The menu is similarly overloaded, with nearly 100 deli sandwiches and salads. Notable are raspberry-almond chicken salad and the Blue Max, with pastrami, corned beef, Swiss cheese, sauerkraut, hot mustard, and blue-cheese dressing. This quirky spot is favored by area professionals looking for a quick lunch, as well as the under-forty set doing 23-ounce curls with one of the restaurant's 20-plus beers on tap (plus more than 100 in bottles). Two other locations—at 1704 San Marco Boulevard and 5500 Beach Boulevard—offer live music several nights a week. $ *Average main: $9* ⊠ *2753 Park St.* ☎ *904/384–9999* ⊕ *www.europeanstreet. com* ⌂ *Reservations not accepted.*

$$$
ECLECTIC
Fodor's Choice
★
✕ **Matthew's.** No one can accuse chef Matthew Medure of resting on his laurels, of which there are many. Widely praised for culinary creativity and dazzling presentation at his signature San Marco restaurant, Medure's French- and Italian-inspired cuisine offers a wide range of choices, from caviar to sweets. Highlights include a create-your-own cheese-and-charcuterie spread "for the table"; house-made pasta with local fish and shrimp, shiitake mushrooms, and peas; seared duck breast with duck confit bread pudding; and espresso-smoked pork belly (an appetizer) are among many inventive menu items. Complement your meal with one of 450 wines (topping out at more than $1,000 per bottle). Or if you just can't choose, the Chef's Adventure Menu gives you a six-course tour of the menu. $ *Average main: $25* ⊠ *2107 Hendricks Ave., San Marco* ☎ *904/396–9922* ⊕ *www.matthewsrestaurant. com* ⌂ *Reservations essential* ⊘ *Closed Sun. No lunch.*

WHERE TO STAY

$ HOTEL **Hotel Indigo Jacksonville-Deerwood Park.** Bright, bold, and visually different from any other Jacksonville property, this contemporary boutique hotel—albeit a chain—makes you feel more like you're staying in a hip apartment rather than a by-the-night lodging. **Pros:** reasonable rates; free Wi-Fi throughout; 24-hour business center; loaner PC. **Cons:** wood floors can be noisy; convenient to business parks but not downtown and its sights; lots of traffic at rush hour. [$] *Rooms from: $178* ✉ *9840 Tapestry Park Circle, Southside* ☎ *904/996–7199, 877/270–1392* 🌐 *www.hotelindigo.com* 🛏 *96 rooms, 4 suites* 🍴 *No meals.*

$ HOTEL **Hyatt Regency Jacksonville Riverfront.** It doesn't get much more convenient than this gigantic 19-story, downtown, waterfront hotel within walking distance of Jacksonville Landing, EverBank Field, Florida Theatre, Times-Union Center, corporate office towers, and the county courthouse. **Pros:** riverfront location; rooftop pool and hot tub; free Wi-Fi; 24-hour gym and business center. **Cons:** not all rooms are riverfront; slow valet service. [$] *Rooms from: $159* ✉ *225 E. Coastline Dr., Downtown* ☎ *904/588–1234* 🌐 *www.jacksonville.hyatt.com* 🛏 *963 rooms, 21 suites* 🍴 *No meals.*

$ HOTEL FAMILY **Omni Jacksonville Hotel.** Jacksonville's most luxurious and glamorous downtown hotel underwent a major update in 2015—from lobby to spacious guest rooms—and offers across-the-street convenience to the big theatrical or musical shows at the Times-Union Center. **Pros:** award-winning on-site restaurant; downtown location; large rooms; rooftop pool; kids' offerings. **Cons:** fee for Wi-Fi and parking; congested valet area; restaurant pricey; can be chaotic when there's a show across the street. [$] *Rooms from: $189* ✉ *245 Water St.* ☎ *904/355–6664, 800/843–6664* 🌐 *www.omnijacksonville.com* 🛏 *354 rooms, 4 2-bedroom suites* 🍴 *No meals.*

$ B&B/INN **Riverdale Inn.** In the early 1900s, Jacksonville's wealthiest residents built mansions along Riverside Avenue—dubbed the Row—and the three-story Riverdale Inn is one of only two such homes remaining. **Pros:** close to area restaurants and shops; private baths. **Cons:** small rooms; limited parking; strict cancellation policy. [$] *Rooms from: $180* ✉ *1521 Riverside Ave., Riverside* ☎ *904/354–5080* 🌐 *www.riverdaleinn.com* 🛏 *10 rooms, 3 suites* 🍴 *Breakfast.*

$ B&B/INN **St. Johns House.** You can enjoy the grace and elegance of the past and all the modern amenities at this surprisingly inexpensive B&B. **Pros:** historic home; beautiful Riverside location near parks, restaurants, and river; elegant antique furnishings. **Cons:** only open six months a year. [$] *Rooms from: $99* ✉ *1718 Osceola St., Riverside* ☎ *904/384–3724* 🌐 *www.stjohnshouse.com* 🛏 *3 rooms* 🕒 *Closed Mar., June–Oct.* 🍴 *Breakfast.*

NIGHTLIFE

BARS

Mark's. This self-proclaimed "neighborhood lounge with a dash of dance club style" attracts beautiful people to a fairly classy bar with a small dance floor and a popular happy hour. ⊠ *315 E. Bay St., Downtown* ☎ *904/355–5099* ⊕ *www.marksjax.com.*

Metro. It's more than just a gay bar: it's like eight gay bars rolled into one, including a piano bar, dance club, lounge, and drag-show cabaret. ⊠ *859 Willow Branch Ave., Riverside* ☎ *904/388–8719* ⊕ *www.metrojax.com.*

COMEDY CLUBS

Comedy Zone. The area's premier comedy club is inside the Ramada Inn Mandarin, offering full food and bar service, in addition to laughs. ⊠ *Ramada Inn Mandarin, 3130 Hartley Rd.* ☎ *904/292–4242* ⊕ *www.comedyzone.com.*

DANCE CLUBS

Club TSI Discotheque. Billing itself as the city's premier dance club, TSI offers an outdoor hookah bar and a crowded indoor dance floor with a DJ and lights. ⊠ *333 E. Bay St., Downtown* ⊕ *www.clubtsi.com.*

FAMILY GATHERING SPOTS

Latitude 30. This place could be called a pleasure complex for the whole family, offering "luxury bowling," a game arcade, billiards, casual restaurants, sports bars, and "cinegrille" movie screening rooms, all at one 50,000-square-foot facility. On weekends it's open until 2 am. ⊠ *10370 Phillips Hwy., Southside* ☎ *904/365–5555* ⊕ *www.latitude360.com/jacksonville-fl/* 🎟 *Admission free; bowling $4–$5 game; others vary.*

LIVE MUSIC CLUBS

Jack Rabbits. It's the place to catch the latest and greatest indie bands and budding rock stars. ⊠ *1528 Hendricks Ave.* ☎ *904/398–7496.*

Murray Hill Theatre. Fans of Christian music flock to this no-smoking, no-alcohol club. ⊠ *932 Edgewood Ave. S, Westside* ☎ *904/388–3179* ⊕ *www.mhtrocks.com.*

Underbelly. In the heart of downtown Jacksonville, this cavernous brick bar and music venue hosts a wide variety of entertainment, from bands (national, international, and just local) to comedians. There's a full bar but no food. ⊠ *113 E. Bay St., Downtown* ☎ *904/699–8186* ⊕ *www.underbellylive.com.*

WINE BARS

The Grotto. Vinophiles, rejoice! Here you can enjoy more than 70 wines by the glass, along with small plates to share. ⊠ *2012 San Marco Blvd., San Marco* ☎ *904/398–0726* ⊕ *www.grottowine.com.*

DID YOU KNOW?

The Jacksonville Jazz Festival takes place in a five-block area centered on Laura Street in the heart of downtown. Highlights of the three-decade old festival include performances by renowned jazz musicians, and jazz piano and youth jazz talent competitions.

SHOPPING

SHOPPING AREAS

Five Points. This small but funky shopping district less than a mile southwest of downtown has new and vintage-clothing boutiques, shoe stores, and antiques shops. It also has a growing collection of inventive and off-beat eateries and bars, not to mention some of the city's most colorful characters. ⊠ *Intersection of Park, Margaret, and Lomax Sts., Riverside* ⊕ *www.5pointsjax.com.*

MALLS

San Marco Square. Dozens of interesting apparel, home, and jewelry stores and upscale restaurants surround the open square in 1920s Mediterranean revival–style buildings. ⊠ *San Marco and Atlantic Blvds., San Marco* ⊕ *www.mysanmarco.com.*

The Shoppes of Avondale. The highlights here include upscale clothing and accessories boutiques, art galleries, home-furnishings shops, a chocolatier, and trendy restaurants. ⊠ *St. Johns Ave., between Talbot Ave. and Dancy St., Avondale.*

St. Johns Town Center. Some of the shops at this huge outdoor "lifestyle center" aren't found anywhere else in northeast Florida, including Anthropologie, Apple, Lucky Brand Jeans, Lululemon, and Sephora, as well as the Cheesecake Factory, P.F. Chang's China Bistro, and Maggiano's Little Italy. ⊠ *4663 River City Dr., Southside* ☎ *904/998–7156* ⊕ *www.simon.com/mall/st-johns-town-center.*

MARKETS

Riverside Arts Market. The unique location—under the Fuller-Warren Bridge, a block from the Cummer Museum of Art & Gardens and a healthy walk along the RiverWalk from downtown—might be as much of a draw as the merchandise. Regardless, since its first Saturday in 2009, RAM has attracted larger and larger crowds of singles, couples, families, and their dogs. They all come to shop for locally created art and crafts, sample food from vendors that include some excellent area restaurants, and check out street performers or the live music shows on the riverfront stage. Quality is high in every aspect—artists and vendors all go through a fairly rigorous application/audition process—and what there is to see or hear or eat varies from week to week. Sometimes there's also a farmers' market, with licensed farmers and growers selling everything from just-laid eggs and local honey to salad greens that were still in the earth the day before. Inside the Children's Activity Center tent, several organizations offer free educational arts activities to kids. Because it's sheltered by the bridge, RAM goes on rain or shine. Free parking is available at EverBank and other adjacent businesses, and a "bike valet" service encourages people to travel on two wheels. ⊠ *715 Riverside Ave., Riverside* ☎ *904/349–2449* ⊕ *www.riversideartsmarket. com* ⬛ *Free* ☉ *Mar.–Dec., Sat. 10–4; Jan. and Feb., Sat. 10–1.*

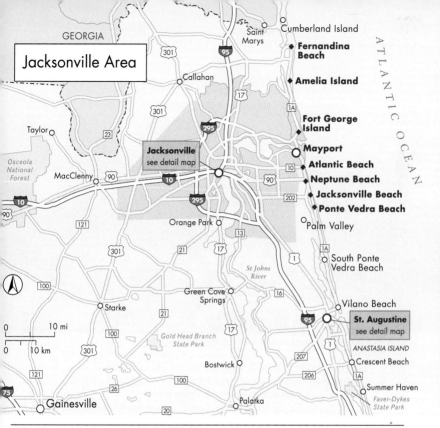

Jacksonville Area

GEORGIA

SPORTS AND THE OUTDOORS

BASEBALL

FAMILY **Jacksonville Suns.** The AA minor-league affiliate of the Miami Marlins plays at the $34-million Baseball Grounds of Jacksonville. The Suns were Southern League champions in 2009, 2010 and 2014. ☒ *Baseball Grounds of Jacksonville, 301 A. Philip Randolph Blvd., Downtown* ☎ *904/358–2846* ⊕ *www.jaxsuns.com.*

BOAT TOURS

River Cruises. Relaxing lunch and dinner-dancing cruises and private sightseeing charters are offered aboard this operation's *Annabelle Lee* paddleboat; schedules and prices vary but start at $45. ☒ *1501 Riverplace Blvd., Southbank* ☎ *904/306–2200* ⊕ *www.jaxrivercruises.com.*

JACKSONVILLE BEACHES

Updated
by Jennifer
Greenhill-Taylor

Atlantic Beach is 20 miles east of Jacksonville, on U.S. 90 (Beach Blvd.).

Perhaps because the Intracoastal Waterway isn't all that wide where it separates the mainland from the beaches, people here aren't likely to think of themselves as "islanders." But they are, indeed, living on a barrier island, functioning with its own rhythms and led by its own

Beaches make great places to drop a line and see if the fish are biting.

elected officials. And, although there's only one island, there are four beach communities, each with its own mayor and city officials, tax base, and local legislation. They are, from north to south, Atlantic Beach, Neptune Beach, Jacksonville Beach, and Ponte Vedra Beach. Technically, Ponte Vedra, which is home to the PGA Tour, crosses the border between Duval County and St. Johns County, but the four communities are all considered "Jacksonville's beaches." Further north are two other popular coastal destinations, Mayport and Fort George Island.

Oceanfront properties here can be worth millions, but a few blocks from the beach, things become more affordable. That means kids grow up and go to school together, and then stick around to live in and govern the towns together. Instead of pouring money into attractions designed to rake in tourism dollars, locals are likely to concentrate on subjects such as good schools and parks. Because of this, some visitors might find area beaches to be a little calmer and quieter than they expected.

But there's a real sense of community—and a laid-back pace. You might want to embrace it all. In fact, many vacationers like the easy pace so much that they decide to make the area their permanent home.

ATLANTIC BEACH

20 miles east of Jacksonville, on U.S. 90 (Beach Blvd.).

Beautiful sand and plentiful activities keep tourists coming back to this relatively tranquil beach community. You can even rejuvenate with some prime pampering at the One Ocean resort's spa. Hotel guests and those wandering in from the beach can both use this luxurious oceanfront hotel's beach rental services, which offer umbrellas, lounge chairs, Boogie boards, kayaks, and surfboards for a fee.

BEACHES

Atlantic Beach. If you're looking for sun-soaked relaxation, head for Atlantic Beach, where you can sink your feet into its white, sugary sands or catch some waves in the warm surf. Beachgoers with canine companions are welcome at Atlantic Beach during the day and evening as long as the dog is leashed. Atlantic Beach and next-door Neptune Beach share the trendy Town Center, which has lots of tempting dining and shopping within a block of the beach. **Amenities:** food and drink; lifeguards (seasonal); showers; water sports. **Best for:** sunrise; surfing; swimming; walking. ⊠ *Beach Ave., between 18th and 20th Sts.; Dewees Ave., between 1st and 16th Sts.; Ahern St. and Atlantic Blvd.* ☎ *904/247–5828* ⊕ *www.coab.us.*

WHERE TO EAT

$
ITALIAN

✕ **Al's Pizza.** The beach locations of this popular restaurant defy all expectations of a neighborhood pizza joint. Bright colors and geometric patterns accent the dining room, which manages to look retro (soda-fountain chairs) and modern (steel columns) at the same time. The menu is fairly predictable; there's pizza by the slice and by the pie, plus standbys like lasagna and ravioli. The clientele, too, is typical beachgoer, with lots of young surfer dudes and dudettes and sunburned families, as well as a fair representation of older Atlantic Beach couples, who come for the food more than the scene. Service is quick, but finding parking at peak hours can be a problem. Check behind the restaurant as well as out front. There's also a branch in Ponte Vedra Beach. $ *Average main: $10* ⊠ *303 Atlantic Blvd.* ☎ *904/249–0002* ⊕ *www.alspizza.com* ⌦ *Reservations not accepted.*

$$$
SEAFOOD

✕ **The Fish Company Restaurant and Oyster Bar.** If you want fresh fish, this is the place. Owners Bill and Ann Pinner have lots of street cred: among other area culinary achievements, Bill worked at Ragtime Tavern for years, helping establish it as an institution. Options include perfectly blended crab cakes, oh-so-lightly fried Mayport shrimp (never a heavy batter that might cover up the flavor), seafood salads, and delicious sides. And there are plenty of offerings for meat lovers in the family, too. The raw bar is the centerpiece, with happy hour prices for raw or steamed on Tuesday and Wednesday. The full drinks bar has happy-hour prices 2–7 Monday through Saturday and all day on Sunday. $ *Average main: $22* ⊠ *725-12 Atlantic Blvd.* ☎ *904/246–0123* ⊕ *www.thefishcojax.com* ⌦ *Reservations not accepted.*

$$$
ECLECTIC
Fodor's Choice
★

✕ **Ocean 60.** Despite being only a block from the Atlantic Ocean, this lively restaurant/wine bar/martini room has gone largely undiscovered by visitors, who might think fine dining and flip-flops don't mix. Those who do stumble upon it, however, are pleasantly surprised to find that despite its casual aura, Ocean 60's eclectic seasonal menu is quite sophisticated, with signature items including salmon gratin (seared salmon topped with a Parmesan and tomato gratin served over butternut squash risotto), rosemary grilled New York strip, and wild mushroom crepes. Things are anything but laid-back on Thursday, Friday, and Saturday nights, however, thanks to live music and potent cocktails. $ *Average* *main: $22* ✉ *60 Ocean Blvd.* ☎ *904/247–0060* 🌐 *www.ocean60.com* 🕐 *Closed Sun. No lunch.*

$$ CAJUN 🍴 **Ragtime Tavern Seafood & Grill.** A New Orleans theme prevails at this lively venue, a long-time favorite with locals and visitors alike. The restaurant attracts a crowd ranging in age from 21 to midlife-crisis, both to sample the craft beer and eat the seafood-based fare. Grouper oscar (seared and topped with crabmeat, asparagus, and Bernaise sauce) and Ragtime shrimp (deep-fried fresh shrimp rolled in coconut) are specialties (as are microbrews made on the premises), or try a po'boy sandwich or fish sizzled on the grill. Brunch is served Sunday only. [$] *Average main: $18* ✉ *207 Atlantic Blvd.* ☎ *904/241–7877* 🌐 *www.ragtimetavern.com.*

WHERE TO STAY

$ RESORT FAMILY 🏨 **One Ocean.** Atlantic Beach's only high-rise oceanfront hotel captures the serenity of the sea through a color palette of translucent green, sand, and sky blue, and reflective materials such as glass and marble. **Pros:** exceptional service; walking distance to restaurants, shops, and the beach; all rooms have ocean view; 24-hour room service. **Cons:** tiny bathrooms; no self-parking on property; steep resort fee and separate parking fee. [$] *Rooms from: $199* ✉ *1 Ocean Blvd.* ☎ *904/249–7402* 🌐 *www.oneoceanresort.com* 🛏 *190 rooms, 3 suites* 🍽 *No meals.*

NEPTUNE BEACH

1.7 miles south of Atlantic Beach.

One of the quieter and less crowded beach towns in the area is a great destination if you want to escape for the day from the more crowded sands to the north and south. Slider's Bar and Grill is a local favorite, or make a pit stop at the oldest bar at the beaches, Pete's Bar, just to say you were there.

BEACHES

Neptune Beach. Between Atlantic and Jacksonville beaches, this is a great family spot. It's an excellent destination for those wishing to combine a day at the beach with other activities. Because Neptune and Atlantic beaches share Atlantic Avenue's Town Center, with its assortment of restaurants, galleries, stores, and boutiques, beachgoers can escape the sun when they're ready for great food, shopping, and live entertainment. **Amenities:** food and drink; lifeguards (seasonal); showers. **Best for:** sunrise; swimming; walking. ✉ *Strand St., between Atlantic Blvd. and Gaillardia Pl., Oak St. and Rose Pl., North St. and 20th Ave.* 🌐 *www.ci.neptune-beach.fl.us.*

WHERE TO STAY

$ HOTEL 🏨 **Sea Horse Oceanfront Inn.** This bright-pink-and-aqua 1950s-era throwback caters to budget-minded guests seeking an ultracasual, laid-back oceanfront experience. **Pros:** beach access with private walk-over; popular bar on-site; walking distance to wide variety of restaurants and shops; free breakfast baskets available at front desk. **Cons:** no-frills; no room service; no elevator. [$] *Rooms from: $139* ✉ *120 Atlantic Blvd.*

☎ *904/246–2175, 800/881–2330* ⊕ *www.seahorseoceanfrontinn.com* ↩ *38 rooms, 1 suite* ○ *Breakfast.*

NIGHTLIFE

Pete's Bar. The oldest bar in the Jacksonville area is also notable for the cheapest drinks, cheapest pool tables, and most colorful clientele. Serving locals and tourists for more than seven decades, Pete's has been written about by authors like John Grisham and James W. Hall, probably because it's across from The BookMark, a great independent bookstore where writers love to give readings. ⊠ *117 1st St.* ☎ *904/249–9158.*

SHOPPING

The BookMark. It may be small in size, but this book shop is big in prestige. Thanks to its knowledgeable owners, many famous authors love this place and always include it on their publicity tours. Once you've bought books here a time or two, the staff will be able to recommend ones you'll like with amazing accuracy. ⊠ *220 1st St.* ☎ *904/241–9026* ⊕ *www.bookmarkbeach.com* ○ *Mon.–Wed. 10–7, Thurs.–Sat. 10–8, Sun. 11–5.*

JACKSONVILLE BEACH

2.2 miles south of Neptune Beach.

This family-friendly beach community has blossomed in recent years and remains busy during the spring and summer. The municipal Seawalk Pavilion hosts outdoor movies, concerts, and festivals, and the 2-acre Oceanfront Park (1st Street South, between 5th Avenue South and 6th Avenue South) has a small playground, volleyball court, and picnic areas. Anglers can fish without a license from the wheelchair-accessible 1,320-foot fishing pier ($4, $1 spectator; daily 6 am–10 pm), which also has free fish-cleaning stations, a bait-and-tackle shop, and free parking. The historic Casa Marina Hotel, which opened its doors here in 1925, has a popular Sunday brunch.

EXPLORING

FAMILY **Adventure Landing and Shipwreck Island Water Park.** With go-karts, two miniature-golf courses, laser tag, batting cages, kiddie rides, and an arcade, Adventure Landing is more like an old-time boardwalk than a high-tech amusement park. But when the closest theme park is more than two hours away, you make do. The largest indoor/outdoor family-entertainment center in northeast Florida also encompasses Shipwreck Island Water Park, which features a lazy river for tubing, a 500,000-gallon wave pool, and four extreme slides—the Rage, HydroHalfpipe, Eye of the Storm, and Undertow. ⊠ *1944 Beach Blvd.* ☎ *904/246–4386* ⊕ *www.adventurelanding.com* 🎟 *Adventure Landing free (fees for rides and games), Shipwreck Island $27.99* ○ *Adventure Landing: Sun.–Thurs. 10–10, Fri. and Sat. 10 am–2 am; Shipwreck Island: late Mar.–late Sept., hrs vary.*

Beaches Museum & History Park. This charming museum has exhibitions on the history of the beaches communities, the St. Johns River, the fishing and shrimping industry, and the area's early settlers. Its gift shop is a good place to find Florida souvenirs of every variety, from tasteful histories of the local area to pure kitsch. Admission includes a guided tour of the adjacent Historical Park with its 1911 steam locomotive, railroad foreman's house, and the Mayport Depot. ✉ *381 Beach Blvd.* ☎ *904/241–5657* 🌐 *www.beachesmuseum.org* 🎟 *Free (donations accepted)* 🕘 *Tues.–Sat. 10–4, Sun. noon–4.*

J. Johnson Gallery. Built by photographer and art collector Jennifer Johnson, this stunning Mediterranean building just a block from the ocean in Jacksonville Beach hosts contemporary art exhibits you'd expect to find only in the nation's largest and most sophisticated cities. Exhibits such as "Multiplicity" and "Contemporary Complexities" include work by emerging artists as well as established names. The gallery is also a sales gallery and, in addition, presents experimental and project work. ✉ *177 4th Ave. N* ☎ *904/435–3200* 🌐 *www.jjohnsongallery.com* 🎟 *Free* 🕘 *Tues.–Fri. 10–5, Sat. 1–5.*

BEACHES

Jacksonville Beach. Enjoy the waves at one of Jacksonville's busier beaches, which stretches along the coast for 4.1 miles. A boardwalk and a bevy of beachfront restaurants and shops are also draws, so expect moderate crowds during spring and summer school breaks. **Amenities:** toilets; showers; food and drink; lifeguards (seasonal); parking (free). **Best for:** partiers; sunrise; surfing; swimming. ✉ *1st St., between Seagate and S. 16th Aves.* ☎ *904/241–1515 fishing pier* 🌐 *www.jacksonvillebeach.org.*

WHERE TO EAT

$ AMERICAN FAMILY

🍴 **Ellen's Kitchen.** Once upon a time, Ellen's Kitchen was a breakfast and lunch place inside Silver's Drug Store at First and Atlantic, a longtime landmark where locals came to salve their hangovers. Silver's is no more, and Ellen's long ago relocated to a shopping strip, but it's still an institution, and probably will be for generations. It's also a great place to bring the kids, thanks to the kid-friendly menu, very reasonable prices, and relaxed atmosphere. Sure, you can get your eggs over easy and your bacon crisp, but if you want to be mistaken for a local, ask for a Hippie or a Surfer, two poached-egg-on-English-muffin creations. If it's hollandaise sauce you're craving, the crab cake Benedict is brunch perfection. Breakfast is served until the doors close at 2 pm, but the lunch menu is also fairly extensive. Don't expect too much chat from your server at "rush hour" on weekend mornings—everyone's usually working at warp speed. Regardless, though, the staffers do their best to please, no matter how crowded. [$] *Average main: $9* ✉ *1824 3rd St. S* ☎ *904/246–1572* ✍ *Reservations not accepted* 🕘 *No dinner.*

$ AMERICAN

🍴 **European Street Café.** This colorful, quirky, beer-hall inspired, family-owned eatery is part of a local chain and has a menu with an ambitious list of sandwiches, salads, and soups; an overflowing gourmet-food section; a mind-boggling beer list; cookies big enough to knock someone unconscious; and a range of other generous desserts. Thirsty locals belly up to the impressive, hand-carved bar for monthly beer tastings and daily happy hour (2–7 pm). More mature crowds prefer to sip their zinfandel in the bustling dining room. [$] *Average main: $9* ✉ *992 Beach Blvd.* ☎ *904/249–3001* 🌐 *www.europeanstreet.com* ✍ *Reservations not accepted.*

$ ✕ **Mojo Kitchen BBQ Pit & Blues Bar.** True barbecue aficionados know
BARBECUE that the country's really divided into four territories: North Carolina,
Memphis, Kansas City, and Texas, each renowned for its own barbecue
style. Owner Todd Lineberry did some serious research into each region
before deciding his restaurants would honor all four traditions—along
with some original flavor. In addition to great barbecue, you'll find Deep
South sides like cheese grits and fried green tomatoes as well as sweet
tea and banana pudding. The beach location attracts young and old,
blue collar and no-collar, all ready to chow down on generous portions,
with a backdrop of bright, bold-color walls and edgy portraits of blues
royalty. Mojo's appreciation for the blues doesn't end with the interior design. There's good recorded blues at all times, and on occasion,
some great live blues as well. $ *Average main: $14* ✉ *1500 Beach Blvd.*
☎ *904/247–6636* ⊕ *www.mojobbq.com* ⌛ *Reservations not accepted.*

WHERE TO STAY

$ ⛱ **Casa Marina Hotel.** Compared with nearby oceanfront inns, it's small,
HOTEL but Casa Marina's creature comforts and rich history—it opened in
1925 and hosted Franklin Delano Roosevelt and Al Capone in its early
days—make it a hit with those looking for a characterful retreat. **Pros:**
oceanfront location; comfortable beds; continental breakfast. **Cons:**
no pool; noise from lounge. $ *Rooms from: $159* ✉ *691 1st St. N*
☎ *904/270–0025* ⊕ *www.casamarinahotel.com* ↝ *7 rooms, 16 suites*
◎ *Breakfast.*

NIGHTLIFE

Free Bird Live. Named for local band Lynyrd Skynyrd's iconic song,
this medium-sized (it holds 700) concert venue is owned by Judy Van
Zant-Jenness (widow of Lynyrd Skynyrd's Ronnie Van Zant). While it
draws some complaints about its standing-room-only tickets and slow
bar service, it also gets raves for the chance to see great blues, rock,
funk, rockabilly, and jam bands in an intimate setting. However, the
club is only open when there's a show, so that often limits openings to
weekends. ✉ *200 1st St. N* ☎ *904/246–2473* ⊕ *www.freebirdlive.com*
⌛ *Admission varies by show.*

Lynch's Irish Pub. Hoist a pint o' Guinness and enjoy live local music.
This popular Irish eatery also offers traditional fare, along with pub
grub. ✉ *514 N. 1st St.* ☎ *904/249–5181* ⊕ *www.lynchsirishpub.com.*

Penthouse Lounge. If you'd rather gawk at sports stars in person than
on the tube, head to this oceanfront spot, perched atop the historic
Casa Marina Hotel, where local NFL and PGA stars have been known
to congregate. But they are not the only stellar objects on view; the
night sky or the moonrise over the ocean offer sights just as fabulous. ✉ *Casa Marina Hotel, 691 N. 1st St.* ☎ *904/270–0025* ⊕ *www.*
casamarinahotel.com.

Sneakers Sports Grille. With dozens of big screens and an impressive menu (by sports-bar standards anyway), this is the go-to sports
bar at the beach. ✉ *111 Beach Blvd.* ☎ *904/482–1000* ⊕ *www.*
sneakerssportsgrille.com.

13

SPORTS AND THE OUTDOORS
BIKING
Champion Cycling. You can rent beach cruisers by the hour or the day—or get your high-end racing bike repaired—at this full-service bike shop. ⊠ *1303 N. 3rd St.* ☎ *904/241–0900.*

PONTE VEDRA BEACH

3.9 miles south of Jacksonville Beach.

Although this upscale coastal community 18 miles southeast of downtown Jacksonville is primarily known for its golf courses and swanky homes, it also has beautiful beaches as well as a number of resorts: the Ponte Vedra Inn & Club, The Lodge & Club, and the Sawgrass Marriott.

BEACHES
Ponte Vedra Beach. Public beach access for nonresort guests is minimal in most areas because of heavily restricted parking. However, thanks to its free public parking, Mickler's Landing, south of most residences, is the most popular beach access point. It's also famous as a great place to find fossilized sharks' teeth. **Amenities:** showers; toilets; lifeguards (seasonal); parking (free). **Best for:** solitude; sunrise; walking. ⊠ *East of intersection of A1A S and Ponte Vedra Blvd.*

WHERE TO EAT

$$$ ⨉ **Aqua Grill.** Come hungry. That might be the best advice for visitors to
ECLECTIC this restaurant, whose menu covers all the bases—steaks, pasta, pork shank, burgers. But eclectic preparation of fresh seafood is what Aqua Grill does best. The constantly changing menu might include crispy red snapper Bangkok or pan-seared local triggerfish with pork belly confit and fried leeks. Portions are huge, so share an appetizer, several featuring local Mayport shrimp. The restaurant is a popular spot for locals celebrating special occasions, but it's more casual than formal and has a charming lakeside patio dining area surrounded by waterfalls. Kids—and adults—love observing the colorful saltwater aquarium in the dining room. There's a lively bar scene, with sports showing on seven HDTVs. The full menu is available at the bar, but there's bar food, too, such as the chef's El Presidente wings. Ⓢ *Average main: $25* ⊠ *950 Sawgrass Village* ☎ *904/285–3017* ⊕ *www.aquagrill.net.*

WHERE TO STAY

$$$ ▦ **The Lodge & Club.** This Mediterranean-revival oceanfront resort—
RESORT with its white-stucco exterior and Spanish roof tiles—is luxury lodging
FAMILY at its best. **Pros:** high-end accommodations; excellent service; pri-
Fodor'sChoice vate beach. **Cons:** most recreation facilities are a few blocks away at
★ Ponte Vedra Inn & Club; gratuity charge automatically added to bill nightly. Ⓢ *Rooms from: $319* ⊠ *607 Ponte Vedra Blvd.* ☎ *904/273–9500, 800/243–4304* ⊕ *www.pontevedra.com* ➦ *42 rooms, 24 suites* ⦿*No meals.*

$$$
RESORT
FAMILY
Fodor's Choice
★
Ponte Vedra Inn & Club. Considered northeast Florida's premier resort for decades, this award-winning 1928 landmark continues to wow guests with its stellar service and large guest rooms housed in white-brick, red-tile-roof buildings lining the beach. **Pros:** accommodating, friendly staff; private beach; adults-only pool. **Cons:** charge for umbrellas and chaises on the beach; crowded pools at some times of year. § *Rooms from: $399* ✉ *200 Ponte Vedra Blvd.* ☎ *904/285–1111, 800/234–7842* ⊕ *www.pontevedra.com* ⇗ *250 rooms, 33 suites* ¶◎¶ *No meals.*

$$
RESORT
FAMILY
Fodor's Choice
★
Sawgrass Marriott Golf Resort & Spa. Golf is at the heart of this luxurious resort, which underwent an extensive renovation in 2015, but there's no lack of opportunity for other recreation or for sheer indulgent relaxation, if that's what you're after. **Pros:** championship golf courses; beautiful surroundings; readily available shuttle; efficient staff. **Cons:** beach not within walking distance; steep resort fee for in-room Wi-Fi, parking, and shuttle. § *Rooms from: $219* ✉ *1000 PGA Tour Blvd.* ☎ *904/285–7777, 800/457–4653* ⊕ *www.sawgrassmarriott.com* ⇗ *489 rooms, 21 suites* ¶◎¶ *No meals.*

SPORTS AND THE OUTDOORS

BIKING

Ponte Vedra Bicycles. This outfitter includes free bike maps with your rental. ✉ *250 Solana Rd.* ☎ *904/273–0199.*

GOLF

Every May millions of golf fans watch golf's most elite competitors vie for the prestige of winning THE PLAYERS Championship. The event—considered by many to be the sport's "unofficial fifth major"—takes place each year at the Tournament Players Club (TPC) Sawgrass in Ponte Vedra Beach, 20 miles southeast of Jacksonville. Designed and built for major tournament golf, TPC has elevated seating areas that give more than 40,000 fans a great view of the action. And while you're in the area, be sure to visit the World Golf Hall of Fame a few miles down the road in St. Augustine.

Tournament Players Club Sawgrass. There are two golf courses here: the Stadium Course (with its world-renowned Island Green), which hosts THE PLAYERS Championship each year, and the Pete Dye–designed Valley Course. In conjunction with the Sawgrass Marriott, TPC offers packages like the Tour Player Experience, which not only provides access to the TPC's player area, but also gives you a caddie who wears your name on the back of his golf shirt just like he does when caddying for the pros. How cool is that? The Dye's Valley Course will be open throughout 2016. However, at this writing the Stadium Course was expected to close for a six-month renovation of the stadium greens from May to November 2016. Though not as lauded as the Stadium Course, the Valley Course has hosted its share of major golf events, such as the Senior Players Championship and the NFL Golf Classic. Though challenging, it has wider fairways and more expansive greens than the Stadium Course, which was designed to test the world's best players. If you want to play a round of golf and aren't staying at the Marriott, check out the Resort Day Passes. ✉ *110 Championship Way*

13

☎ *904/273–3235, 800/457–4653* ⊕ *www.tpc.com/sawgrass* ⌨ *Stadium Course, $400; Dye's Valley Course, $195* ⚑. *Stadium Course: 18 holes, 7215 yards, par 72; Dye's Valley Course: 18 holes, 6864 yards, par 72.*

MAYPORT

20 miles northeast of downtown Jacksonville, on Rte. A1A/105.

Dating back more than 300 years, this fishing village has several excellent and very casual seafood restaurants and markets, and a commercial shrimping fleet. It's also home to one of the largest naval facilities in the country, Naval Station Mayport.

GETTING HERE AND AROUND

St. Johns River Ferry. The arrival of the *Jean Ribault* ferry in 1948 made everyday life here more convenient—and fun. The 153-vessel continues to delight passengers young and old as they embark on the 10-minute cruise across the river between Mayport and Fort George Island. The cost is $5 per motorcycle, $6 per car. Pedestrians enjoy the ride for just $1 each way. Call for departure times. ☎ *904/241–9969* ⊕ *www. stjohnsriverferry.com.*

EXPLORING

Fodor's Choice ★ **Kathryn Abbey Hanna Park.** This 450-acre oceanfront park and campground just north of Atlantic Beach is beloved by surfers, swimmers, campers, hikers, and especially bikers, who regularly hit the many off-road bike trails from novice right up to those named Grunt and Misery. You can rent canoes, kayaks, or paddleboats to go out on the 60-acre freshwater lake. Younger kids delight in the lakefront playground and a water park with fountains and squirting hoses. There are restrooms, picnic areas, and grills throughout, and from Memorial Day to Labor Day lifeguards supervise all water activities. ✉ *500 Wonderwood Dr.* ☎ *904/249–4700* ⌨ *$5 per vehicle, cash only* ☉ *Apr.–Oct., daily 8–8; Nov.–Mar., daily 8–6.*

FORT GEORGE ISLAND

25 miles northeast of Jacksonville, on Rte. A1A/105.

One of the oldest inhabited areas of Florida, Fort George Island is lush with foliage, natural vegetation, and wildlife. A 4-mile nature and bike trail meanders across the island, revealing shell mounds dating as far back as 5,000 years.

EXPLORING

Kingsley Plantation. Built in 1792 by Zephaniah Kingsley, a landowner who produced Sea Island cotton, citrus, sugar cane, and corn with the aid of about 60 slaves, this is the oldest remaining cotton plantation in the state. The ruins of 23 tabby (a concretelike mixture of sand and crushed shells) slave houses, a barn, and the modest Kingsley home are open to the public via self-guided tours and reachable by bridge. ✉ *11676 Palmetto Ave.* ☎ *904/251–3537* ⊕ *www.nps.gov/ timu* ⌨ *Free* ☉ *Daily 9–5; plantation house weekends only; call ahead for reservations.*

Talbot Island State Parks. These parks, including Big and Little Talbot islands, have 17 miles of gorgeous beaches, sand dunes, and golden marshes that hum with birds and native waterfowl. Come to picnic, fish, swim, snorkel, or camp. Little Talbot Island, one of the few undeveloped barrier islands in Florida, has river otters, marsh rabbits, raccoons, alligators, and gopher tortoises. Canoe and kayak rentals are available, and the north area is considered the best surfing spot in northeast Florida. A 4-mile nature trail winds across Little Talbot, and there are several smaller trails on Big Talbot. ✉ *12157 Heckscher Dr.* ☎ *904/251–2320* ⊕ *www.floridastateparks.org/park/Big-Talbot-Island* 🖃 *$5 per vehicle, up to 8 people; $4 single occupant* ⊙ *Daily 8–sunset.*

13

AMELIA ISLAND AND FERNANDINA BEACH

Updated
by Jennifer
Greenhill-Taylor

35 miles northeast of Jacksonville.

At the northeasternmost reach of Florida, Amelia Island has beautiful beaches with enormous sand dunes along its eastern flank, a state park with a Civil War fort, sophisticated restaurants, interesting shops, and accommodations that range from bed-and-breakfasts to luxury resorts. The town of Fernandina Beach is on the island's northern end; a century ago casinos and brothels thrived here, but those are gone. Today there's little reminder of the town's wild days, though one event comes close: the Isle of Eight Flags Shrimp Festival, held during the first weekend of May.

TOURS

Amelia River Cruises and Charters. Narrated tours in shaded pontoon boats that glide near the area's marshes, rivers, and wilderness beaches, from American Beach and Fernandina on Amelia Island, to Cumberland Island in Georgia. ✉ *1 N. Front St.* ☎ *904/261–9972, 877/264–9972* ⊕ *www.ameliarivercruises.com.*

VISITOR INFORMATION

Contact Amelia Island Convention and Visitors Bureau ☎ *904/277–0717* ⊕ *www.ameliaisland.com.*

EXPLORING

Fernandina Historic District. This district in Fernandina Beach, which is home to Florida's oldest existing lighthouse, oldest bar, and oldest hotel, has more than 50 blocks of buildings listed on the National Register of Historic Places; 450 ornate structures built before 1927 offer some of the nation's finest examples of Queen Anne, Victorian, and Italianate homes. Many date from the haven's mid-19th-century glory days. Pick up a self-guided-tour map at the chamber of commerce, in the old train depot—once a stopping point on the first cross-state railroad—and take your time exploring the quaint shops, restaurants, and boutiques that populate the district, especially along Centre Street.

FAMILY

Fodor's Choice

★

Fort Clinch State Park. One of the country's best-preserved and most complete 19th-century brick forts, Fort Clinch was built to discourage further British intrusion after the War of 1812 and was occupied

in 1863 by the Confederacy; a year later it was retaken by the North. During the Spanish-American War it was reactivated for a brief time, but no battles were ever fought on its grounds (which explains why it's so well preserved). Wander through restored buildings, including furnished barracks, a kitchen, and a repair shop. Living-history reenactments of Civil War garrison life are scheduled throughout the year. The 1,086-acre park surrounding the fort has full-facility camping, nature trails, carriage rides, a swimming beach, and surf and pier fishing. Nature buffs enjoy the variety of flora and fauna, especially since Fort Clinch is the only state park in northeast Florida designated by the Florida Fish and Wildlife Conservation Commission as a viewing destination for the eastern brown pelican, green sea turtle, and loggerhead sea turtle. ✉ *2601 Atlantic Ave.* ☎ *904/277–7274* ⊕ *www. floridastateparks.org/fortclinch* ✍ *$6 per vehicle, up to 8 people; $4 motorcycles; $2 per person entry to fort* ☉ *Daily 8–sunset; fort 9–5.*

A BANNER BEACH

Fernandina Beach is also known as the "Isle of Eight Flags," derived from the fact that it's the only American site to have been under eight different flags (French, Spanish, British, Patriots, Green Cross of Florida, Mexican Revolutionary, National Flag of the Confederacy, and United States). Every May the Isle of Eight Flags Shrimp Festival celebrates another of Fernandina's claims to fame: birthplace of the modern shrimping industry.

13

BEACHES

There are a number of places on Amelia Island where driving on the beach is allowed in designated areas, including Seaside Park, Peters Point, Burney Park, and Amelia Island State Park. If you have a four-wheel-drive vehicle (and a lot of beach equipment to haul), you may want to try this. Be warned, though: it's easier to get stuck than you might think, and towing is expensive. You also need to watch the tides carefully if you don't want your car floating out to sea. And unless you're a county resident or disabled, you must buy a permit, which is available at the Nassau County Historic Courthouse (✉ *416 Centre St., Fernandina Beach* ☎ *904/491–6430*), Beach Rentals and More (✉ *2012 S. Fletcher Ave., Fernandina Beach* ☎ *904/310–6124*), and several other locations. All city beaches have free admission.

Huguenot Memorial Park. Though it's officially a Jacksonville city park, this popular spot on the northern side of the St. Johns River is usually grouped with Amelia's beaches. Among a handful of places where driving on the beach is permitted, it's unusual in that no special permit is required. Families with lots of beach equipment like the option of parking close to the water, but it takes vigilance to avoid soft sand and incoming tides. The ocean side offers good surfing, Boogie boarding, and surf fishing. On the western side is a shallow, sheltered lagoon that's a favorite with windsurfers, paddleboarders, and parents of small children. The eastern side offers views of the aircraft carriers and destroyers at Mayport Naval Station. The park is also an important stop for migrating birds, so at certain times of the year, some areas are closed to vehicles. **Amenities:** showers; toilets; lifeguards (seasonal); parking (free). **Best for:** surfing; swimming; windsurfing. ✉ *10980 Heckscher Dr., Jacksonville* ☎ *904/251–3335* 💰 *$3 per person 8–10 am, $4 per car after 10* ☉ *Apr.–Oct., daily 8–8; Nov.–Mar., daily 8–6.*

Main Beach Park. Of all Fernandina Beach access points, this is likely to be the most crowded—but also the most fun for kids and teens. Not only are there sand volleyball courts, a beachfront playground, picnic tables, and a multipurpose court, at the park itself, but there's old-school fun to be had at the adjacent skate park and vintage miniature-golf course, whose concession stand sells cold drinks, ice cream, and snow cones. A casual restaurant and bar are right on the beach. **Amenities:** showers; toilets; food and drink; lifeguards (seasonal); parking (free). **Best for:** swimming. ✉ *32 N. Fletcher Ave.*

Peters Point Beach. At the south end of the island, this beach allows you free access to the same gorgeous sands used by vacationers at the Ritz-Carlton. It has a large parking area, a picnic area, barbecue grills, and three lifeguard towers. **Amenities:** showers; toilets; lifeguards (seasonal); parking (free). **Best for:** sunrise; surfing; swimming; walking. ✉ *1974 S. Fletcher Ave.*

Seaside Park Beach. Like Main Beach to the north and Peters Point to the south, Seaside Park allows limited beach driving if you have a permit, but beware—vehicles here frequently get stuck and have to be towed. There are several pavilions with picnic tables and dune walkovers to the beach. It's a great place to fish or to ride bikes at low tide. Bikes and other beach equipment can be rented at Beach Rentals and More, right across from the park (✉ *2021 S. Fletcher Ave.*). Also nearby, Sliders Seaside Grill is a venerable oceanfront restaurant where you can enjoy food and drinks inside or at the tiki bar overlooking the beach, often with live music. **Amenities:** showers; toilets; food and drink; lifeguards (seasonal); parking (free). **Best for:** surfing; swimming; walking. ✉ *Sadler Rd. and S. Fletcher Ave.* ⊕ *www.fbfl.us.*

Talbot Islands State Parks Beaches. A few miles south of Fernandina Beach, the Talbot Islands State Parks system consists of seven parks, three of which have beach settings. All of the oceanfront parks have picnic areas and a small admission charge but free parking. **Little Talbot** is popular for swimming and beachcombing. Sand dollars are often found at the far north end. **Big Talbot,** with its Boneyard Beach of wind-twisted trees, is not recommended for swimming but is a photographer's paradise. **Amelia Island State Park** is best known for letting you horseback ride on the beach as well as for the adjacent George Crady fishing pier. Kayak and canoe tours can be booked through the parks system's vendor, Kayak Amelia. **Amenities:** showers; toilets; lifeguards (seasonal); parking (free). **Best for:** solitude; sunrise; swimming; walking. ✉ *Rte. A1A, south of Fernandina Beach* ⊕ *www.floridastateparks.org* 💰 *Little Talbot, $5 per vehicle; Big Talbot, $3 per vehicle for The Bluffs picnic area; Amelia Island, $2 per person.*

WHERE TO EAT

$$$$ ECLECTIC

🍴 **PLAE.** PLAE (People Laughing and Eating) has an extensive wine list and an upscale but eclectic menu with French, Asian, and Mediterranean influences. Adventurous diners love to order the Chef's Plate, not knowing exactly what delights the chef has prepared for the evening until they appear at the table. The atmosphere varies greatly depending on your seating choice. Indoors has a sleek, contemporary ambience with intimate, high-backed booths. The outdoor patio provides a view over the beautiful natural surroundings of the adjacent golf course. Although the location at the Spa & Shops at Omni Amelia Island Plantation makes it a favorite with Plantation visitors, it's an independently owned restaurant (the only one on property) and equally popular with locals. [$] *Average main: $35* ✉ *Omni Amelia Island Plantation, 80 Amelia Village Circle* ☎ *904/277–2132* ✍ *Reservations essential* ⏲ *Closed Sun.*

13

$$$$ ECLECTIC Fodor's Choice ★

🍴 **Salt.** The Ritz-Carlton's oceanfront restaurant serves inventive cuisine that utilizes seasonal ingredients such as golden tile fish with gnocchi, spinach, and grapefruit, or a Darling Downs Wagyu rib eye cooked on a wood-burning grill. The signature dish is beef tenderloin served on a block of Himalayan salt. The wine list has more than 300 bottles (24 by the glass), service is nothing short of impeccable, and there's that view of the Atlantic from every table. For a unique dining experience, reserve a seat in the private dining room within the kitchen to "Dine With the Chefs," watching them at work while you enjoy a personalized five-course meal. To learn the secrets of Salt's cuisine, consider taking one of the Salt cooking school sessions. They've proven so popular, the Ritz-Carlton has expanded the schedule to several a year. Long pants and collared shirts are recommended (for dining, we mean; cooking students get their own Ritz-Carlton aprons). [$] *Average main: $56* ✉ *The Ritz-Carlton, Amelia Island, 4750 Amelia Island Pkwy., Amelia Island* ☎ *904/277–1000* 🌐 *www.ritzcarlton.com* ✍ *Reservations essential* ⏲ *Closed Mon. No lunch.*

$$ SEAFOOD FAMILY

🍴 **Sliders Seaside Grill.** After the condo-building boom of the last decade or so, not many oceanfront restaurants remain, but thankfully this is one of them. Indeed there aren't many places where you can enjoy an ocean view like this—a surf break offshore makes it a good place to watch surfers do their thing—and even fewer with a moderately priced menu that allows for an affordable family outing. These are some of the reasons Sliders has evolved into a local favorite, but another is its award-winning Florida seafood dishes, including shrimp and grits, and Apalachicola oysters in season. Sliders also has three bars and live music every night during the summer, including the region's favorite reggae band, Pili Pili, on Wednesday. [$] *Average main: $18* ✉ *1998 S. Fletcher Ave.* ☎ *904/277–6652* 🌐 *www.slidersseaside.com.*

$$$$ SEAFOOD

🍴 **Verandah Restaurant.** Although it's at the Omni Amelia Island Plantation Resort, this family-friendly restaurant is open to nonresort guests, many of whom drive in from Jacksonville. The dining room has a casual vibe, with plush, roomy booths and tables overlooking the tennis facility, but the menu is all business, with a focus on Southern and local food. Start with the crab cake—nearly 100% blue crab—or deviled eggs topped with pecanwood smoked bacon. Fresh seafood entrées are a highlight, including the Florida fish muddle (fresh catch with Mayport shrimp and clams) and line-caught pink snapper with Cohen Farm's pecans and local strawberries. And if you luck out and find she-crab soup on the menu (it's seasonal and not always available), order yourself the biggest bowl or bucket they have. If it isn't she-crab season, go for the Low Country Oyster Chowder. $ *Average main: $39* ⊠ *Omni Amelia Island Plantation, 142 Raquet Park Dr., Amelia Island* ☎ *904/277–5958* ⊕ *www.omnihotels.com* ⚑ *Reservations essential* ☾ *No lunch.*

WHERE TO STAY

$
HOTEL
FAMILY
Amelia Hotel at the Beach. Across the street from the beach, this mid-size inn is not only convenient but an economical and family-friendly alternative to the area's luxury resorts and romantic and kid-unfriendly B&Bs. **Pros:** complimentary breakfast; free Wi-Fi; comfy beds. **Cons:** small pool; not all rooms have balconies. $ *Rooms from: $159* ⊠ *1997 S. Fletcher Ave.* ☎ *904/206–5200, 877/263–5428* ⊕ *www.ameliahotel. com* ⤳ *86 rooms* ⧉ *Breakfast.*

$$
B&B/INN
Elizabeth Pointe Lodge. Guests at this oceanfront inn, built to resemble an 1890s sea-captain's house, can't say enough about the impeccable personal service, legendary breakfasts, and enjoyable evening social hour. **Pros:** beachfront location; hospitable staff; 24-hour desk attendant; convenient to recreation possibilities; free Wi-Fi. **Cons:** pricey for a B&B; not all rooms are oceanfront; must reserve well in advance in high season. $ *Rooms from: $280* ⊠ *98 S. Fletcher Ave.* ☎ *904/277–4851, 800/772–3359* ⊕ *www.elizabethpointelodge.com* ⤳ *24 rooms, 1 2-bedroom cottage* ⧉ *Breakfast.*

$
B&B/INN
Florida House Inn. This charming, 150-year-old inn, once used by guests of the Vanderbilt, DuPont, and Carnegie families, whose "cottages" sat nearby on Cumberland and Jekyll islands, has been fully restored, with a rambling two-story clapboard main building full of character. **Pros:** breakfast included; outstanding service; walk to restaurants and shops; free Wi-Fi; bridal suite. **Cons:** bar can be noisy; rooms are small. $ *Rooms from: $160* ⊠ *22 S. 3rd St.* ☎ *904/491–3322, 800/258–3301* ⊕ *www.floridahouseinn.com* ⤳ *16 rooms* ⧉ *Breakfast.*

$$$
RESORT
FAMILY
Fodor'sChoice
★
Omni Amelia Island Plantation Resort and the Villas of Amelia Island Plantation. This huge resort (1,350 acres) was folded into the Omni hotel chain and transformed by an $85-million renovation and expansion in 2013, including 155 additional oceanfront rooms and stunning oceanfront Beach Club pools. **Pros:** family-friendly; variety of outdoor activities; shuttle service throughout property; kids' programs; "green" practices; largest poolscape in Northern Florida. **Cons:** some facilities require a golf cart or shuttle ride; quality of villas inconsistent. $ *Rooms from: $349* ⊠ *39 Beach Lagoon Rd., Amelia Island* ☎ *904/261–6161, 800/843–6664* ⊕ *www.omnihotels.com* ⤳ *404 rooms, more than 300 1-, 2-, and 3-bedroom villas* ⧉ *No meals.*

$
HOTEL
Residence Inn Amelia Island. Discerning, value-driven travelers love this newer all-suites property for its great location, modern design features, and family-friendly amenities. **Pros:** proximity to beach and

restaurants; complimentary breakfast; free Wi-Fi; bike rental on property; pet friendly (restrictions). **Cons:** no on-site restaurant or room service; historic district not within walking distance. $ *Rooms from: $199* ✉ *2301 Sadler Rd.* ☎ *904/277–2440* ⊕ *www.residenceinnameliaisland.com* ⤳ *133 suites* ⓘ*Breakfast.*

$$$$
RESORT
FAMILY
Fodor's Choice
★

📺 **The Ritz-Carlton, Amelia Island.** Guests know what to expect from the Ritz—elegance, superb comfort, excellent service—and the Amelia Island location is no exception. **Pros:** fine-dining restaurant; world-class spa; private beach access; accommodating staff; great programs, activities, and amenities for kids, teens, and families. **Cons:** resort fee; no self-parking ($20 per day valet); a drive to sites and other restaurants. $ *Rooms from: $519* ✉ *4750 Amelia Island Pkwy.* ☎ *904/277–1100* ⊕ *www.ritzcarlton.com/ameliaisland* ⤳ *446 rooms, 50 suites* ⓘ*No meals.*

13

NIGHTLIFE

Falcon's Nest. The 7,000-square-foot, aviation-themed club in Amelia Island Plantation has a dance floor and outdoor deck. ✉ *Omni Amelia Island Plantation, 36 Amelia Village Circle, Amelia Island* ☎ *904/277–5166* ⊕ *www.omnihotels.com/ameliaisland.*

Palace Saloon. Florida's oldest continuously operating saloon entertained the Rockefellers and Carnegies at the turn of the 20th century but now caters to common folk. When you enter the swinging doors and see the massive mahogany bar, tiled floors, and classic mural-adorned walls, you may feel as if you've gone back in time. The Palace also operates a package store, the only one in downtown Fernandina. ✉ *117 Centre St.* ☎ *904/491–3332* ⊕ *www.thepalacesaloon.com.*

The Surf Restaurant & Bar. Locals like to congregate on the outdoor deck here for drinks and good old-fashioned bar food (burgers, wings, nachos). The restaurant has an extensive menu. ✉ *3199 S. Fletcher Ave.* ☎ *904/261–5711* ⊕ *www.thesurfonline.com.*

SHOPPING

Amelia SanJon Gallery. One of a cluster of "Ash and Third" galleries, the Amelia SanJon offers watercolors, acrylic paintings, fused-glass art, and custom jewelry. ✉ *218-A Ash St.* ☎ *904/491–8040* ⊕ *www.ameliasanjongallery.com.*

Book Loft. Popular for its readings and book signings, this old-fashioned bookstore fits perfectly in an old-fashioned town. In keeping with Fernandina's emphasis on its pirate heritage, the store includes kid-friendly pirate volumes like *The Pirate of Kindergarten* and *Do Pirates Change Diapers?* ✉ *214 Centre St.* ☎ *904/261–8991* ⊕ *www.facebook.com/thebookloftamelia.*

Celtic Charm. In addition to the obvious coffee cup with shamrocks and Irish-blessing plaque, this shop carries wonderful clothing—such as colorful and artistic Bill Baber Scottish sweaters—as well as Galway Irish crystal and Donegal Town Hana Hats. ✉ *310 Centre St.* ☎ *904/277–8009* ⊕ *www.celticcharmamelia.com.*

Fantastic Fudge. Right there in the window, resting in splendor on several marble-topped tables, are huge blocks of fudge just calling your name— enough fudge to put every citizen of the town into a coma—not to mention ice cream (with house-made waffle cones), hand-dipped chocolates, caramel corn, and so on. Indeed, if you hang out at one of the tables in front of this confectionery/ice cream shop, you'll see just about every kind of person imaginable pause by the door, sigh, and give in to temptation. The service is fast and friendly, and the ice cream is excellent, too. ✉ *218 Centre St.* ☎ *904/277–4801* ⊕ *www.fantasticfudge.com.*

Gallery C. Up a wildly painted staircase, this gallery owned by artist Carol Winner (the "C" in the gallery's name) displays and sells one-of-a-kind semiprecious jewelry and mixed-media creations, as well as paintings of local nature scenes. ✉ *218-B Ash St.* ☎ *904/583–4676* ⊕ *www. carolwinnerart.com.*

Lindy's Jewelry. For tasteful jewelry that reflects beach life, Lindy's is a good place to shop. Those who wish to commemorate their vacations in jewelry may be charmed by the Fernandina Beach and Cumberland Island map charms or fossilized sharks teeth set into earrings and necklaces. ✉ *202 Centre St.* ☎ *904/277–4880* ⊕ *www.lindysjewelry.com.*

Sea Jade. Inside, it's funny T-shirts and cheap souvenirs; outside, it's fishnet floats and seashells in all their natural beauty, heaped up in old-fashioned wooden baskets. Whether you want to buy sand dollars or saltwater taffy, if it's beach related, there's a good chance you'll find it here. ✉ *208 Centre St.* ☎ *904/277–2977.*

Slightly Off Centre Gallery & Gifts. Just a block off the main drag, this store sells artistic ceramics as well as vivid photographs, paintings, pottery, and metalwork. ✉ *218-C Ash St.* ☎ *904/277–1147* ⊙ *Closed Tues.*

SPORTS AND THE OUTDOORS

HORSEBACK RIDING
Kelly Seahorse Ranch. At this concession within the Amelia Island State Park, you can arrange horseback rides on the beach. ✉ *Amelia Island State Park, 9500 1st Coast Hwy., Amelia Island* ☎ *904/491–5166* ⊕ *www.kellyranchinc.net* ⊙ *Closed Mon.*

KAYAKING
Kayak Amelia. This outfitter takes adventurous types on guided kayak tours of salt marshes and Fort George River and also rents equipment for those looking to create their own adventures. Reservations are required. ✉ *4 N. 2nd. St.* ☎ *904/251–0016* ⊕ *www.kayakamelia.com.*

ST. AUGUSTINE

Updated by
Steve Master

35 miles south of Jacksonville, on U.S. 1.

Along the banks of the shining Matanzas River lies St. Augustine, the nation's oldest city. It shows its age with charm, its history revealed in the narrow cobblestone streets, the horse-drawn carriages festooned with flowers, and the coquina bastions of the Spanish fort that guard the bay like sentinels. Founded in 1565 by Spanish explorers, St. Augustine is the site of the fabled Fountain of Youth, but travelers find additional treasures in the Historic District, which was built in the Spanish Renaissance Revival style. Terra-cotta roofs and narrow balconies overhang a wonderful hodgepodge of shops and eateries that can be happily explored for weeks.

St. Augustine also has miles of beaches on Anastasia Island to the east. From the idyllic, unspoiled beaches of Anastasia State Park to the more boisterous St. Augustine Beach, travelers have a full range of options when it comes to enjoying an ocean outing.

13

VISITOR INFORMATION

Centrally located between the south and north ends of St. Augustine's Historic District, the St. Augustine & St. Johns County Visitor Information Center is a smart place to start your day. You can park in the multistoried garage here ($1.25 per hour, $7.50 per day), as well as pick up maps, get information on and advice about attractions and restaurants, and hop aboard the sightseeing trolley.

Contacts St. Augustine, Ponte Vedra & the Beaches Visitors and Convention Bureau ☎ 904/829–1711, 800/418–7529 ⊕ www.floridashistoriccoast. com ⊗ Daily 8:30–5:30. **St. Augustine & St. Johns County Visitor Information Center** ✉ 10 W. Castillo Dr. ☎ 904/825–1000 ⊗ Daily 8:30–5:30.

TOURS

Old Town Trolley Tour. These fully narrated tours ($25) cover more than 100 points of interest and are, perhaps, the best way to take in the Historic District. Your pass is good for three days and, with parking at a premium and meters closely watched, it's nice to be able to park at one of the main stations (free) and get on and off at any of 23 stops throughout town. There are even shuttles to the beach. In the evening a macabre slant is added on the Ghosts and Graveyards Tour ($27), which includes visits to the Old Jail and Lighthouse. ✉ 167 San Marco Ave. ☎ 904/829–3800, 888/910-8687 ⊕ www.trolleytours.com/staugustine.

EXPLORING

St. Augustine's neighborhoods are fairly compact. Most include a stretch of waterfront—whether ocean, river, or creek—which, along with Mediterranean architectural details like curves, archways, and red-tile roofs, gives the city its relaxed semitropical aura. Neighborhoods range from centuries old to mere decades, but all have sights worthy of attention.

It can be confusing to see references to the "Old City," "Old Town," and "Historic District." The Old City, like the Big Apple, refers not to a neighborhood but to the entire city of St. Augustine. Old Town is a small neighborhood, with the Plaza de la Constitución at its northern border, a row of shops and restaurants along King Street, many award-winning B&Bs, and the Oldest House museum toward the south. Old Town is actually within a larger neighborhood, the Historic District, a 144-block area filled with many of the city's most popular attractions, including museums, parks, restaurants, nightspots, shops, and historic buildings.

Built to protect Spain's St. Augustine, the Castillo de San Marcos still stands along the shore.

St. Augustine's Uptown is filled with the shops, restaurants, and galleries along San Marco Boulevard, as well as museums, parks, and historic structures, all of which attract crowds. The narrow streets and hustle and bustle make for a vibrant atmosphere.

Heading east across the Bridge of Lions, you enter Anastasia Island, much of which is within city limits. In the 1920s, real estate developer D. P. Davis had big plans for a Mediterranean-style development here, but the Florida land boom went bust. Today Davis Shores has a mélange of styles and a casual beach vibe.

TOP ATTRACTIONS

FAMILY

Fodor's Choice

★

Castillo de San Marcos National Monument. The focal point of St. Augustine, this massive and commanding structure was completed by the Spaniards in 1695 (English pirates were handy with a torch back then), and it looks every day of its three centuries. The fort was constructed of coquina, a soft limestone made of broken shells and coral that, unexpectedly, could absorb the impact of British cannonballs. (Unlike solid stone, the softer coquina wouldn't shatter when hit by large munitions.) The fort was also used as a prison during the Revolutionary and Civil wars.

Park rangers provide an introductory narration, after which you're on your own to explore the moat, turrets, and 16-foot-thick walls. Garrison rooms depict the life of the era, and special cannon-firing demonstrations are held several times a day Friday through Sunday year-round. Children 15 and under are admitted free and must be accompanied by an adult. Save the receipt, since admission is valid for seven days. ✉ *11 S. Castillo Dr.* ☎ *904/829–6506* ⊕ *www.nps.gov/casa* 🎫 *$7* ⊗ *Daily 8:45–5:15, last ticket sold at 5.*

Cathedral Basilica of St. Augustine. This cathedral has the country's oldest written parish records, dating from 1594. The circa-1797 structure underwent changes after a fire in 1887 as well as restoration work in the mid 1960s. If you're around for the holidays, stop in for Christmas Eve's gorgeous midnight mass, conducted amid banks of flickering candles that reflect off gilded walls. Regular Sunday masses are held throughout the year at 7, 9, 11, and 5. ✉ *38 Cathedral Pl.* ☎ *904/824–2806* ⊕ *www. thefirstparish.org* 🎫 *Donations welcome* ⊗ *Daily 7–4:45.*

FAMILY **Colonial Quarter.** After being closed to the general public for yearlong renovations, the Colonial Quarter, formerly known as the Spanish Quarter, is now an even more appealing attraction. The 2-acre living history museum gives visitors a vivid sense of life in 16th-, 17th-, and 18th-century St. Augustine. The De Mesa–Sanchez House dates from the 1740s and the other buildings—including a soldier's home, print shop, blacksmith's shop, and gunsmith—are replicas, mostly built on the original foundations. Costumed reenactors help make the history come alive. New additions to the complex include a 35-foot watchtower from which you have a panoramic view of the city. You can also dig for replica artifacts, create a leather medallion, take part in a musket drill, watch a 16th-century ship being built, and more. Tours start 10:30, noon, 1:30, and 3. The complex also includes two restaurants: the Taberna del Caballo and the Bull and Crown British Publick House. ✉ *33 St. George St.* ☎ *904/342–2857* ⊕ *colonialquarter.com/* 🎫 *$12.99* ⊗ *Daily 10–5.*

NEED A BREAK?

St. George Tavern. Although they serve food (sandwiches, mostly), the appeal of this joint is that, in a city of historic recreations, this is the real deal: a noisy, packed, active bar where smokers smoke, drinkers drink, locals gather, and strangers blend right in. ✉ *116-A St. George St.* ☎ *904/824–4204* ⊕ *www.stgeorgetavern.com.*

Lightner Museum. In his quest to turn Florida into an American Riviera, Henry Flagler built two fancy hotels in 1888: the Ponce de León, which became Flagler College, and the Alcazar, which closed during the Great Depression, was purchased by publisher Otto Lightner in 1946, and was donated to the city in 1948. It's now a museum with three floors of furnishings, costumes, Victorian art glass, not-to-be-missed ornate antique music boxes, and even an early 20th-century-era shrunken head from the Jivaro Indians of Ecuador. The Lightner Antiques Mall is on three levels of what was once the hotel's indoor pool. City staff occupy other floors since, apparently, the guest rooms of a former grand hotel also make nice municipal-government offices. ✉ *75 King St.* ☎ *904/824–2874* ⊕ *www.lightnermuseum.org* 🎫 *$10* ⊗ *Museum daily 9–5, last admission at 4.*

Old Jail Museum. At this 19th-century prison, felons were detained and released or detained and hanged from the gallows in back. After learning the history of local crime and punishment and seeing displays of weapons and other artifacts, you can browse the surfeit of souvenirs

13

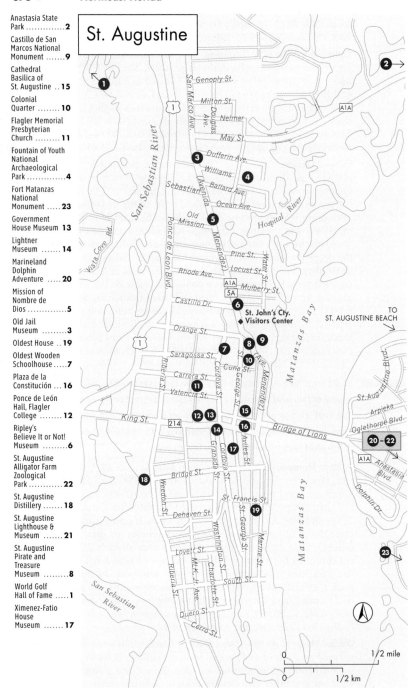

St. Augustine

in Cracker Bob's Trading Post and the adjacent Old Store Museum. Note that the museum is at the starting point for the Old Town Trolley Tour. ⌧ *167 San Marco Ave.* ☎ *904/829–3800* 🖙 *$9* 🕙 *Daily 9–4:30.*

Ponce de León Hall, Flagler College. Originally one of two posh hotels Henry Flagler built in the 1880s, this building—which is now part of a small liberal-arts college—is a riveting Spanish Renaissance–revival structure with towers, turrets, and stained glass by Louis Comfort Tiffany. The former Hotel Ponce de León is a National Historic Landmark, having hosted U.S. presidents Grover Cleveland, Theodore Roosevelt, and Warren Harding. Visitors can view the building free or take a guided tour offered daily through Flagler's Legacy Tours. ⌧ *74 King St.* ☎ *904/829–6481, 904/823–3378 tour information* ⊕ *legacy.flagler. edu* 🖙 *Tours $10* 🕙 *Tours daily at 10 and 2 when school's in session, on the hr 10–3 when school's out.*

FAMILY **St. Augustine Alligator Farm Zoological Park.** Founded in 1893, the Alligator Farm is one of Florida's oldest (and, at times, smelliest) zoological attractions and is credited with popularizing the alligator in the national consciousness and helping to fashion an image for the state. In addition to oddities like Maximo, a 15-foot, 1,250-pound saltwater crocodile, and a collection of rare albino alligators, the park is also home to Land of Crocodiles, the only place in the world to see all 23 species of living crocodilians. Traversing the treetops in Crocodile Crossing is an inventive, ambitious, and expensive ($65) zipline/rope course with more than 50 challenges and nine ziplines. In many places, a thin cable is all that keeps you from becoming croc cuisine. The shorter Sepik River course (three ziplines) is $35. Reptiles are the main attraction, but there's also a wading-bird rookery, an exotic-birds and mammals exhibit, and nature trails. Educational presentations are held throughout the day, and kids love the wild-animal shows. ⌧ *999 Anastasia Blvd.* ☎ *904/824–3337* ⊕ *www.alligatorfarm.com* 🖙 *$22.95* 🕙 *Daily 9–5.*

St. Augustine Lighthouse & Museum. It's unusual to find a lighthouse tucked into a residential neighborhood. This 1874 version replaced an earlier one built when the city was founded in 1565. Although its beacon no longer guides ships, it does draw thousands of visitors each year, in part because it has a reputation for being haunted. The visitor center has a museum with exhibits on the U.S. Coast Guard, historic boatbuilding, maritime archaeology, and the life of a lighthouse keeper—whose work involved far more than light housekeeping. You have to climb 219 steps to reach the peak, 140 feet up, but the wonderful view and fresh ocean breeze are well worth it. Children must be at least 44 inches tall to make the ascent. The museum also conducts evening "Dark of the Moon Paranormal" tours ($25) and "Sunset-Moonrise" tours ($30) that include a Champagne toast and light hors d'oeuvres. ⌧ *81 Lighthouse Ave.* ☎ *904/829–0745* ⊕ *www.staugustinelighthouse.org* 🖙 *$9.95* 🕙 *Daily 9–6.*

FAMILY **St. Augustine Pirate and Treasure Museum.** Inside this small museum established by entrepreneur and motivational speaker Pat Croce is a collection of more than 800 pirate artifacts, including one of only two Jolly Rogers (skull-and-crossbone flags) known to have actually flown above

The "Oldest Wooden Schoolhouse" is made of cedar and cypress wood and dates to the early 18th century.

a ship. Exhibits include a mock-up of a tavern, a captain's quarters, and a ship's deck. You'll learn about the lives of everyday and famous pirates, their navigation techniques, their weaponry, and the concoctions they drank (including something called Kill Devil, which is rum mixed with gunpowder). You'll get to touch an actual treasure chest; see piles of gold, jade, emeralds, and pearls; and leave knowing full well that there were pirates before Captain Jack Sparrow. ⊠ *12 S. Castillo Dr.* ☎ *877/467–5863, 904/819–1444* ⊕ *www.thepiratemuseum.com* ✉ *$12.99* ⊙ *Daily 10–8.*

WORTH NOTING

Anastasia State Park. This park draws families who like to hike, bike, swim, camp, and play on the beach to its 1,700 protected acres of bird sanctuary and 4 miles of secluded beachfront. ⊠ *1340-A Rte. A1A S* ☎ *904/461–2033* ⊕ *www.floridastateparks.org/anastasia* ✉ *$8 per vehicle; $2 pedestrians, bicyclists* ⊙ *Daily 8–sunset.*

Flagler Memorial Presbyterian Church. To look at a marvelous Venetian Renaissance–style structure, head to this church, built by Flagler in 1889 as a memorial to his daughter Jenny, who died during childbirth. In addition to Jenny, this is the final resting place for Flagler himself; his first wife, Mary; and their granddaughter Marjorie. The dome of this stunning sanctuary towers more than 100 feet and is topped by a 20-foot Greek cross. ⊠ *32 Sevilla St.* ☎ *904/829–6451* ⊕ *www. memorialpcusa.org* ⊙ *Sanctuary Mon.–Sat. 9–4; Sun. services, hrs vary.*

Fountain of Youth National Archaeological Park. This once-dated attraction continues to undergo a major rejuvenation. There are still fun elements from the original "Old Florida" (admittedly somewhat kitschy), but there's much that's new and exciting, too. The timing is appropriate—in 2013, the park celebrated the 500th anniversary of Ponce de León's arrival. The 15-acre waterfront site is also the location where Spanish explorer Pedro Menéndez de Avilés, in 1565, established the first and oldest continuous European settlement in what's now the United States. Excavations have also shown it was the site of a Franciscan mission to the Timucuan Indians. The park includes a replica of the mission, a Timucuan village and burial grounds, a boatyard in which a 16th-century-style boat is being constructed, and a three-story watchtower with broad, panoramic vistas of the bay, inlet, and Mendez Settlement field. Other highlights include cannon firings; Navigators Planetarium; a gift shop; a small, elegant café; and the springhouse where you can still quench your thirst from "the fountain of youth." ⊠ *11 Magnolia Ave.* ☎ *904/829–3168, 800/356–8222* ⊕ *www.fountainofyouthflorida. com* ⊠ *$15* ⊙ *Daily 9–6; last ticket sold at 5.*

OFF THE BEATEN PATH **Ft. Matanzas National Monument.** As you drive south on Anastasia Island, you head toward what was, in the 1700s, St. Augustine's farthest reaches. With Castillo de San Marcos guarding the town, in 1740 the Spanish created the relatively small Ft. Matanzas to defend their southern flank. A short ferry ride across the Matanzas River takes you to this national monument. Although it's only 15 miles from town, the fort feels eerily remote, and it takes little imagination to picture the demanding lives of the soldiers sent here to protect the young colony. Ferry shuttles are free and run every hour from 9:30 to 4:30, but you need to pick up a boarding pass from the visitor center. ⊠ *8635 Rte. A1A S* ☎ *904/471–0116* ⊕ *www.nps.gov/foma* ⊠ *Free* ⊙ *Daily 9–5:30.*

Government House Museum. This historical building has been a hospital, a courthouse, a customs house, a post office, and, during the American Revolution, the home of the British governors. And it was from here, in 1821, that the Spanish governor ceded control of East Florida to the United States to conclude 256 years of colonial control. After a major renovation, the building reopened in fall 2013 and features revolving exhibits. A shop on-site sells history-related souvenirs and a wide selection of books. ⊠ *48 King St.* ☎ *904/825–5034* ⊕ *www.staugustine.ufl. edu* ⊠ *Free; revolving exhibits may require fee* ⊙ *Daily 10–4.*

OFF THE BEATEN PATH **Marineland Dolphin Adventure.** The world's first oceanarium was constructed in 1938, 18 miles south of St. Augustine. This National Register of Historic Places designee, now part of the Georgia Aquarium, has come a long way from marine film studio to theme park to its current iteration as dolphin research, education, and entertainment center. The formal dolphin shows are history, but you can have a far more memorable experience with interactive programs that allow you to swim with and feed the animals or become a dolphin trainer for a day. Programs start at $32.95 a day (for the simple "touch-and-feed" option) and go as high as $475 (for "trainer for a day"). General admission allows you to observe the dolphins through 6-foot-by-10-foot acrylic windows. The 1.3-million-gallon facility is home to 13 dolphins, and until 2014 the park housed Nellie, the longest-lived dolphin in human care until her May 1, 2014, death at the age of 61. A new calf, Coquina, was born shortly after Nellie's death. Other exhibits feature native Florida marine life such as tarpon, sharks, spotted eagle rays, and giant sea turtles, as well as historical artifacts dating back to the park's inception as a nautical movie studio. ⊠ *9600 Ocean Shore Blvd.* ☎ *904/471–1111, 877/933–3402* ⊕ *www.marineland.net* ⊠ *$12.95* ☉ *Daily 9–4:30.*

Mission of Nombre de Dios. The site, north of the Historic District, commemorates where America's first mass was celebrated. A 208-foot-tall stainless-steel cross (purportedly the world's tallest) allegedly marks the spot where the mission's first cross was planted in 1565. Also on the property is the Shrine of Our Lady of La Leche, the first shrine devoted to Mary in the United States. The landscape is exquisitely maintained, and the mission is crisscrossed with paths. A museum and gift shop are also on the property. ⊠ *27 Ocean Ave.* ☎ *904/824–2809, 800/342–6529* ⊕ *www.missionandshrine.org* ⊠ *Donations welcome* ☉ *Site weekdays 9–5, weekends 10–5; museum Thurs.–Sat. 10–4, Sun. noon–4.*

Oldest House. Known as the Gonzalez-Alvarez House, Florida's oldest surviving Spanish-colonial dwelling is a National Historic Landmark. The current site dates from the early 1700s, but there's been a structure here since the early 1600s. Much of the city's history is seen in the building's modifications and additions, from the coquina blocks—which came into use to replace wood soon after the town burned in 1702—to the house's enlargement during the British occupation. The complex also includes the Manucy Museum; the Page L. Edwards Gallery and its rotating exhibits; a gift shop; and an ornamental garden. ⊠ *14 St. Francis St.* ☎ *904/824–2872* ⊕ *www.staugustinehistoricalsociety.org* ⊠ *$8* ☉ *Daily 9–5, tours every ½-hr (last tour 4:30).*

Oldest Wooden Schoolhouse. This tiny 18th-century building of cypress and cedar served not only as a schoolhouse but also as a tearoom, a farmhouse, and a guardhouse and sentry shelter during the Seminole Wars. In 1939, members of the Class of '64 (1864, that is) dressed out the school as they remembered it, and today automated mannequins instruct you on the education of 150 years ago. Apparently teachers had more leeway then because miscreants were given "time out" in a cubby beneath the stairs. And the heavy chain wrapped around the building? It was to hold the structure down during hurricanes. Kids will like the school bell and wishing well in the charming courtyard garden. ⊠ *14 St. George St.* ☎ *888/653–7245* ⊕ *www.oldestwoodenschoolhouse.com* ⊠ *$4.95* ☉ *Sun.–Thurs. 9–6, Fri. and Sat. 9–8.*

Plaza de la Constitución. At the foot of the Bridge of Lions, this central area of the original settlement was laid out in 1598 by decree of Spain's King Philip II. At its core is a monument to the Spanish constitution of 1812, and at its east end is a portico dating from early American days. This is where products and, regrettably, people were sold, earning the area the twin names of "public market" and "slave market." Today, it's the gathering spot for holiday events, art shows, and evening concerts. Toward the bridge, look for the life-size statue of Ponce de León. The man who "discovered" Florida in 1513 was, apparently, all of 4' 11". ⊠ *St. George St. and Cathedral Pl.*

FAMILY   **Ripley's Believe It or Not! Museum.** The nation's first Ripley's museum is, appropriately enough, in a historic structure—Castle Warden, an 1887

Moorish Revival–style mansion. Like its younger siblings, this odditorium is packed with plenty of unusual items including Robert Ripley's personal collections; a mummified cat; a death mask of Abraham Lincoln; a scale model of the original Ferris Wheel created from an Erector set; and life-size models of Robert Wadlow, the world's tallest man, and Robert Hughes, the world's fattest man. ✉ *19 San Marco Ave.* ☎ *904/824–1606* ⊕ *www.ripleys.com/staugustine* 🖅 *$12.99* ⊙ *Daily 9–8.*

St. Augustine Distillery. The first commercial block ice in Florida was made in this building more than 100 years ago. Today, the freshly restored, riverfront structure is full of barrels aging the first Florida-made bourbon. The small batch, craft distillery, opened in 2014, also makes "New World" gin and "Florida Cane" vodka using ingredients sourced from local farms. A free tour orients visitors to the building's rich history, partnerships with local farms, and the spirit-making process. Visitors are asked to punch a time card to enter the working distillery; they are "paid" at the end with samples of cocktails such as the Florida Mule and New World gin and tonic. A gift shop sells an assortment of bar gadgets and accessories, along with the vodka and gin. The first bourbon is scheduled for release in 2018. ✉ *112 Riberia St.* ☎ *904/825–4962* ⊕ *www. staugustinedistillery.com* 🖅 *Free tours* ⊙ *Mon.–Sat. 10–6, Sun. 11–6.*

World Golf Hall of Fame. This stunning tribute to the game of golf is the centerpiece of World Golf Village, an extraordinary complex that includes 36 holes of golf, a golf academy, several accommodations options, a convention center, spa, and a variety of restaurants, including Murray Bros. Caddyshack. The Hall of Fame features an adjacent IMAX theater and houses a variety of exhibits combining historical artifacts and personal memorabilia with the latest in interactive technology. Stand up to the pressures of the TV camera and crowd noise as you try to sink a final putt, take a swing on the museum's simulator, or snap a photo as you walk across a replica of St. Andrews's Swilcan Burn Bridge. Once you're sufficiently inspired, see how you fare on the 18-hole natural-grass putting course. Admission includes a chance to score a hole-in-one on a 132-yard hole. If you do, you win a prize, such as admission to THE PLAYERS Championship. ✉ *1 World Golf Pl.* ☎ *904/940–4123* ⊕ *www.worldgolfhalloffame.org* 🖅 *$19.50 (includes museum, round on 18-hole putting course, and shot at hole-in-one challenge); IMAX $13 features, $8.50 documentaries* ⊙ *Mon.–Sat. 10–6, Sun. noon–6.*

Ximenez-Fatio House Museum. Built as a merchant's house and store in 1798, the place became a boardinghouse in the 1800s and has been restored to look like it did during its inn days—romantic yet severe, with balconies that hearken back to Old Spain and sparely appointed rooms. Docents lead you around the property; be sure to look at the fascinating St. Augustine street scenes, painted in 1854 by an itinerant artist. Amazingly, much of what you see in the paintings is extant. ✉ *20 Aviles St.* ☎ *904/829–3575* ⊕ *www.ximenezfatiohouse.org* 🖅 *$7* ⊙ *Tues.–Sat. 11–4.*

13

BEACHES

Anastasia State Park Beach. If you don't mind paying a bit for beach access, this park offers some outstanding choices. At one end of the beach, there's a playground and snack bar, where you can order sandwiches and cold drinks or rent a beach chair, umbrella, surfboard, or other beach paraphernalia. If you walk north along the beach, however, all traces of civilization seem to vanish. An offshore break makes the park a good surfing spot, there's a boat launch, and canoes and kayaks can be rented. The campgrounds are very popular, too. **Amenities:** showers; toilets; food and drink; lifeguards (seasonal); parking (free); water sports. **Best for:** solitude; surfing; swimming; walking. ⊠ *1340-A Rte. A1A S* ☎ *904/461–2033* ⊕ *www.floridastateparks/anastasia* 💰 *$8 per vehicle; $2 pedestrians* ☉ *Daily 8–sundown.*

Butler Park Beach. In the days of racial segregation, Butler Beach, located south of St. Augustine and north of Crescent Beach, was an African-American beach. Today it is a county park that still provides access to the beachfront. **Amenities:** lifeguards (seasonal); parking (free); showers; toilets. **Best for:** swimming; walking. ⊠ *Rte. A1A, south of St. Augustine Beach, 5860 A1A S.*

Crescent Beach. A 15-minute drive beyond the area's big tourist destinations, this quieter, less crowded spot offers wide, white-sand beaches with good shelling, making it particularly popular with beachcombers. Adding to the laid-back atmosphere are some good restaurants, where visitors can enjoy the beach from a distance, glass in one hand and plate of fresh seafood in the other. **Amenities:** lifeguards (seasonal); parking (free); showers; toilets. **Best for:** solitude; swimming; walking. ⊠ *South of Rtes. A1A and 206, Crescent Beach.*

North Beach. Just five minutes from St. Augustine, this site (aka Usina Beach) includes boat ramps, two campsites, and a picnic area with grills. If you'd rather opt for a restaurant than a picnic, you're in the right spot—a variety of eateries overlook the ocean or the Intracoastal Waterway. **Amenities:** lifeguards (seasonal); parking (free); showers; toilets. **Best for:** solitude; walking. ⊠ *Rte. A1A, north of Vilano Beach.*

St. Augustine Beach. Just south of Anastasia State Park, this beach has a livelier setting, thanks to the restaurants, bars, and shops along Beachfront Avenue and the 4-acre St. Johns County Ocean Pier Park. The park includes a playground, small splash park, sand volleyball courts, and a covered pavilion, where from May to September a series of Music by the Sea concerts are offered free. Speaking of free, the beach doesn't charge a fee, but the popular fishing pier does ($3). In addition, there are some areas designated for driving on the beach. **Amenities:** lifeguards (seasonal); parking (free); showers; toilets. **Best for:** swimming. ⊠ *Old A1A/Beach Blvd., south of Rte. 312.*

Vilano Beach. This beach, 2 miles north of St. Augustine, is sandwiched between the Tolomato River and the Atlantic. In the 1920s it was home to the Grand Vilano Casino, but that was destroyed by a hurricane in 1937. Until recently, Vilano Beach had deteriorated into a small, somewhat run-down area, though with a nice, laid-back '60s surf vibe. That's changed rapidly, however. Now it's home to new stores and restaurants, the Vilano Beach Fishing Pier, and other community improvements. A Hampton Inn & Suites is within a few minutes' walk. The beach has some nice breakers for surfing—skimboarding is also popular—but strong currents sometimes make it dangerous for swimming. It's also one of the few beaches on which you can still drive a car. **Amenities:** lifeguards (seasonal); showers; toilets. **Best for:** solitude, surfing, walking. ✉ *3400 Coastal Hwy., Vilano Beach.*

WHERE TO EAT

$ CAFÉ 🍴 **The Bunnery Bakery & Café.** Hidden among the art galleries and trinket shops of St. George Street is this cozy little restaurant, which is very popular at breakfast and nearly as popular during lunch. There's nothing fancy—just high-back booths and a menu of pancakes, bacon, eggs, cinnamon buns, salads, and hot and cold sandwiches. It's the perfect spot when you want something familiar in a new place. [$] *Average main: $7* ✉ *121 St. George St.* ☎ *904/829–6166* 🌐 *www.bunnerybakeryandcafe.com* ✍ *Reservations not accepted* ⏲ *No dinner.*

$$ CAFÉ 🍴 **Café Alcazar.** Whether you browse the antiques shops and are drawn into having lunch or the other way around, there's plenty of temptation to go around here. Housed in the magnificent Lightner Museum—the luxurious Hotel Alcazar in its 1890s incarnation—this lovely little lunch spot sits where wealthy winter tourists once frolicked in the nation's largest indoor pool. The balconies that rise on all four sides are lined with intriguing stores, so it's easy for a relaxing lunch to expand into an entire afternoon of shopping pleasure. The food is good if slightly pricey, but it's beautifully presented in an atmosphere of elegance. Dinner is served on the first Friday of every month. [$] *Average main: $15* ✉ *25 Granada St.* ☎ *904/825–9948* 🌐 *www.thecafealcazar.com* ⏲ *No dinner.*

$ LATIN AMERICAN 🍴 **Casa Maya.** Latin-inspired cuisine abounds in the nation's oldest city, but Casa Maya has created a niche—and passionate following—with fresh, eclectic cuisine from Mexico's Yucatan Peninsula. Everything is made from scratch here—the sauces, marinades, even the mixers for unique cocktails such as the cucumber jalapeno margarita. The Mayan soup is a must—fresh vegetables, avocado chunks, and crispy tortillas in a light vegetable broth. Daily specials might include pork and chicken tamales (prepared at home by chef-owner Karla Barrera), or fresh local cobia with tequila-marinated shrimp, mango corn salsa, and chipotle sauce—a dish that looks as appealing as it tastes. The two-story restaurant has three seating areas—a shaded ground-level courtyard, a second-story deck overlooking the street, and a rustic indoor dining room. Weekend breakfasts are a special treat, offering items such as scrambled egg crepes with roasted poblanos and sweet-potato pancakes. [$] *Average main: $14* ✉ *22 Hypolita St.* ☎ *904/823–0787* ⏲ *Mon. 10:30–4:30, Wed.–Fri. 10:30–9:30, weekends 8:30–10* ⏲ *Closed Tues. No dinner Mon.*

$$$$ ECLECTIC Fodor's Choice ★ 🍴 **Collage.** Foodies seeking a new dining experience in the Oldest City head here for "artful global cuisine" in a warm and intimate setting. Tucked away on Hypolita Street in the Historic District, the 48-seat restaurant highlights local seafood, which, depending on the success of the fishermen, will include several fish entrées each day. The ever-changing menu also often has steak, lamb, or veal selections. For dessert, the bougainvillea, an original dessert inspired by the colorful flowering plants that frame the building, is made of strawberries, ice cream, and cabernet-vanilla sauce served in a leaf-shape phyllo cup. $ *Average main: $31* ⊠ *60 Hypolita St.* ☎ *904/829–0055* ⊕ *www.collagestaug. com* ☯ *No lunch.*

$$$
SPANISH
✕ **Columbia.** Arroz con pollo, fillet *salteado* (with a spicy sauce), an array of tapas, and a fragrant seafood paella (allow 30 minutes for preparation) are the time-honored Cuban and Spanish dishes served at this branch of the original Columbia, which was founded in Tampa in 1905. Befitting its cuisine, the restaurant is more like an airy Spanish villa, with many archival family photos; a white-stucco exterior; and an atrium dining room full of palm trees, hand-painted tiles, and decorative arches. Table not ready? Linger in the courtyard, listen to the fountains, and enjoy a glass of homemade sangria or a refreshing mojito. $ *Average main: $28* ⊠ *98 St. George St.* ☎ *904/824–3341* ⊕ *www.columbiarestaurant.com.*

$$
MODERN
AMERICAN
FAMILY
Fodor's Choice
★
✕ **The Floridian.** Although vegetarians flock to this artsy and inspired eatery for the veggie-centric menu, there's plenty to tantalize omnivores as well. Delicious Southern food with flair ranges from fried-green-tomato bruschetta to a choice of shrimp, fish, or tofu with polenta cakes (here called "grits"). Many dishes offer a choice of meat, tofu, or tempeh. Some gluten-free dishes are also available. The produce featured at this farm-to-table establishment is at the peak of freshness and plays a starring role in the Winter Salad and Florida Sunshine Salad. Attire is casual, and the oceanic hues and funky decor put you at ease. Kids' needs are handled with flexible good nature. It's a deservedly popular spot, especially on weekends. Reservations aren't accepted, but if you call ahead with a time and the number of diners in your party you move to the front of the line, essentially, upon arrival. $ *Average main: $17* ⊠ *39 Cordova St.* ☎ *904/829–0655* ⊕ *www.thefloridianstaug.com.*

$$$
MEDITERRANEAN
✕ **Michael's Tasting Room.** Chef Michael Lugo obviously learned the importance of execution during his career as a college football player. His execution at this bustling "Tasting Room"—from the cozy ambience to the creatively prepared Mediterranean-influenced cuisine—has created a winning formula, earning a devoted following among locals and tourists alike. Tapas are the specialty, highlighted by dishes such as *mejijiones con fritas* (steamed Maine mussels in garlic, white wine, and butter with truffle fries and saffron aioli), *conchinito frito* (crispy pork belly, pineapple cilantro pique, and white bean salad), and a goat cheese terrine layered with sun-dried tomatoes, olives, and pesto. Large plates include adobo braised short ribs and a lobster risotto with crispy leeks. The rustic, dimly lit dining room can get loud on busy weekend nights, as patrons—often celebrating special occasions—linger over their tapas and Spanish wines. There's a charming, more sedate courtyard for outdoor dining. $ *Average main: $21* ⊠ *25 Cuna St.* ☎ *904/810–2400* ⊕ *www.tastetapas.com* ☯ *Closed Mon. No lunch weekends.*

$$$$
ECLECTIC
✕ **95 Cordova.** On the first floor of the Casa Monica Hotel, this restaurant serves classic cuisine with an international flair. Sup in one of

three dining rooms, including the main room with intricate Moroccan-style chandeliers, wrought-iron chairs, and heavy wood columns, or the Sultan's Room, a gold-dipped space accented with potted palms and a silk-draped ceiling. Innovative dishes with New World, Middle Eastern, and Asian flavors change seasonally and highlight local seafood and produce. The jumbo lump crab cake is a popular lunch selection. Among the dinner items are several types of steak, duck two ways, braised pork osso bucco, Bahamian lobster tail with crab risotto, and coriander-crusted sea scallops. The tasting menu offers five courses paired with outstanding wines. [$] *Average main: $33* ✉ *95 Cordova St.* ☎ *904/810–6810* 🌐 *www.casamonica.com* ✍ *Reservations essential.*

13

$$$ 🍴 **O.C. White's Seafood & Spirits.** Dining outside is a treat at this bustling little spot across from the marina. Set in the circa-1791 General Worth house, it has a homelike feel with a balanced clientele of locals, students, and visitors. Favorites include coconut shrimp, blue-crab cakes, and fresh local grouper. Beef lovers may want to try the filet mignon or the New York strip. From upstairs, you have a great marina view; in the courtyard you might enjoy the perfume of blooming jasmine. Call ahead for "preferred seating." [$] *Average main: $21* ✉ *118 Ave. Menendez* ☎ *904/824–0808* 🌐 *www.ocwhitesrestaurant.com* ✍ *Reservations not accepted.*

$$ SEAFOOD 🍴 **O'Steen's.** Across the Bridge of Lions from downtown, this hole-in-the-wall restaurant is recognizable for the line of customers who wait patiently for fried shrimp (the specialty), oysters, scallops, hush puppies, fried chicken, coleslaw, biscuits and cornbread with gravy, and banana cream pie. Needless to say it's been a popular local eatery for generations. Bring cash; credit cards are not accepted. [$] *Average main: $16* ✉ *205 Anastasia Blvd.* ☎ *904/829–6974* 🌐 *www.osteensrestaurant.com* ✍ *Reservations not accepted* 💳 *No credit cards* ⏲ *Closed Sun. and Mon.*

WHERE TO STAY

$ B&B/INN FAMILY 🏨 **Bayfront Marin House Bed and Breakfast.** Children are rarely permitted at B&Bs, but this is a charming exception, thanks to separate entrances, several units large enough to accommodate families, and the warm welcome of the inn's owners, Mike and Sandy Wieber. **Pros:** personal service; child- and pet-friendly; waterfront location; porches and balconies with river views; moderate prices outside high season. **Cons:** parking a block away; dining area small if weather forces breakfast indoors. [$] *Rooms from: $169* ✉ *142 Ave. Menendez* ☎ *904/824–4301* 🌐 *www.bayfrontmarinhouse.com* 🛏 *15 units* 🍽 *Breakfast.*

$ B&B/INN 🏨 **Bayfront Westcott House.** A bit more elegant and formal than the average B&B, this inn wows guests with a combination of English and American antiques and a wealth of complimentary food, from extravagant breakfasts to wine and canapés in the early evening. **Pros:** great views, most from private balconies; romantic rooms; free Wi-Fi. **Cons:** parking a short distance away; carriage house rooms not as elegant as main house. [$] *Rooms from: $189* ✉ *146 Ave. Menendez* ☎ *904/825–4602, 800/513–9814* 🌐 *www.westcotthouse.com* 🛏 *16 rooms* 🍽 *Breakfast.*

$ B&B/INN **Carriage Way Bed and Breakfast.** When it comes to location, the Victorian-era Carriage Way has the best of both worlds; it's far enough from the Historic District to avoid tourist noise but close enough to have easy access to excellent restaurants (try the nearby Floridian) and shops. **Pros:** great location; free on-site parking; personal attention; excellent breakfasts. **Cons:** some small rooms; street can get loud with traffic. *$ Rooms from: $149 ✉ 70 Cuna St. ☎ 904/829–2467, 800/908–9832 🌐 www.carriageway.com 🛏 13 rooms, 1 cottage 🍴 Breakfast.*

$ B&B/INN **Casablanca Inn Bed & Breakfast on the Bay.** Breakfast comes with scenic views of the Matanzas Bay at this restored 1914 Mediterranean-revival stucco-and-stone house, just north of the Bridge of Lions in the Historic District. **Pros:** comfy beds; friendly staff; free early evening snacks and beverages. **Cons:** some rooms have no view; street noise in some rooms. *$ Rooms from: $139 ✉ 24 Ave. Menendez ☎ 904/829–0928, 800/826–2626 🌐 www.casablancainn.com 🛏 21 rooms, 2 suites 🍴 Breakfast.*

$ B&B/INN **Casa de Solana.** There's a reason you feel like you're stepping back in time when you enter this 1820s-era inn made of coquina and handmade bricks: It's on the oldest street in the oldest European-settled city in the country. **Pros:** excellent service; delicious breakfast; location. **Cons:** some small rooms; free parking is three blocks away; "forced" socialization. *$ Rooms from: $149 ✉ 21 Aviles St. ☎ 904/824–3555 🌐 www.casadesolana.com 🛏 10 rooms 🍴 Breakfast.*

$ HOTEL Fodor's Choice ★ **Casa Monica Hotel.** Hand-stenciled Moorish columns and arches, handcrafted chandeliers, and gilded iron tables decorate the lobby of this late-1800s Flagler-era masterpiece. **Pros:** location; affordable off-season rates; flat-screen TVs in all rooms. **Cons:** busy lobby; expensive ($24) parking; small rooms. *$ Rooms from: $188 ✉ 95 Cordova St. ☎ 904/827–1888, 800/648–1888 🌐 www.casamonica.com 🛏 127 rooms, 11 suites 🍴 No meals.*

$ HOTEL **DoubleTree by Hilton Historic District.** Opened in October 2014, this is the newest addition to the St. Augustine lodging scene, yet blends seamlessly into the city's old-world Spanish ethos. **Pros:** complimentary on-site parking; charming outdoor space with pool; comfortable beds. **Cons:** several-block walk to central tourist area; small lobby. *$ Rooms from: $169 ✉ 116 San Marco Ave. ☎ 904/825–1923 🌐 www.staugustinehistoricdistrict.DoubleTree.com 🛏 97 rooms 🍴 No meals.*

$ HOTEL FAMILY **Hilton St. Augustine Historic Bayfront.** In the heart of historic St. Augustine, this Spanish-colonial-inspired hotel overlooking Matanzas Bay has 19 separate buildings in a village setting. **Pros:** location; comfortable beds; great for families. **Cons:** expensive valet parking only ($21); late-night noise at street level. *$ Rooms from: $189 ✉ 32 Ave. Menendez ☎ 904/829–2277, 800/445–8667 🌐 www.hiltonhistoricstaugustine.com 🛏 72 rooms 🍴 No meals.*

$ B&B/INN **Inn on Charlotte Bed & Breakfast.** Innkeeper Rodney Holeman says guests comment that staying at his inn reminds them of visiting a friend or family member's home, assuming that person offers an elegant two-course breakfast and cozy rooms with whirlpool tubs. **Pros:** location; excellent service; free parking. **Cons:** strict cancellation policy; tight parking in compact lot; weekend street noise. *$ Rooms from:*

$149 ⊠ 52 Charlotte St. ☎ 904/829–3819, 800/355–5508 ⊕ www. innoncharlotte.com ⇄ 8 rooms †◯† Breakfast.

$ ⊞ **Old City House Inn & Restaurant.** Touches of Paris, Venice, and India
B&B/INN are just a few of the surprises within this small two-story inn's coquina walls, where the rooms are decorated to reflect international cities or themes. **Pros:** location; romantic; free Wi-Fi; on-site restaurant. **Cons:** thin walls; may have to share room with a ghost! $ Rooms from: $145 ⊠ 115 Cordova St. ☎ 904/826–0113 ⊕ www.oldcityhouse.com ⇄ 7 rooms, 2 suites †◯† Breakfast.

$ ⊞ **Renaissance Resort at World Golf Village.** If you want to be within
RESORT walking distance of all World Golf Village has to offer, this AAA
Fodor's Choice Four Diamond resort is an excellent choice. **Pros:** breakfast buffet;
★ large bathrooms; free shuttle to golf courses, spa, and downtown St. Augustine. **Cons:** small pool; daily fee for Internet/phone. $ Rooms from: $169 ⊠ 500 S. Legacy Trail ☎ 904/940–8000, 888/740–7020 ⊕ www.worldgolfrenaissance.com ⇄ 271 rooms, 30 suites †◯† Multiple meal plans.

$ ⊞ **St. Francis Inn Bed & Breakfast.** If the walls of this late-18th-century
B&B/INN house in the Historic District—and the oldest inn in the Oldest City— could talk, they would tell of slave uprisings, buried doubloons, and Confederate spies. **Pros:** warm hospitality; family-friendly cottage; Southern breakfast buffet; short walk to Historic District attractions. **Cons:** small rooms; small pool. $ Rooms from: $189 ⊠ 279 St. George St. ☎ 904/824–6068, 800/824–6062 ⊕ www.stfrancisinn.com ⇄ 12 rooms, 4 suites, 1 2-bedroom cottage †◯† Breakfast.

$ ⊞ **St. George Inn.** You can't be any closer to the St. George Street bustle
B&B/INN than this 25-room inn nestled in the City Gate Plaza. **Pros:** location; personal service; balconies with views; privacy; comfortable beds. **Cons:** some street noise; parking two blocks away. $ Rooms from: $169 ⊠ 4 St. George St. ☎ 904/827–5740, 888/827–5740 ⊕ www.stgeorge-inn. com ⇄ 25 rooms, 3 suites †◯† Breakfast.

NIGHTLIFE

A1A Aleworks. The Aleworks always seems to be filled with students and visitors taste-driving the microbrews and other selections from the full bar. Seats on the second-story balcony provide a great view of the marina and bay across the street. It's a little like being on Bourbon Street—but clean. ⊠ 1 King St. ☎ 904/829–2977 ⊕ www.A1Aaleworks.com.

Mill Top Tavern. The rustic Mill Top is famous for its live, local music. ⊠ 19½ St. George St. ☎ 904/829–2329 ⊕ www.milltoptavern.com.

The Original Cafe Eleven. This live music haven sets the stage for local groups, and tries to book national acts at least once a month. They also serve breakfast, lunch, and dinner seven days a week. ⊠ 501 Rte. A1A Beach Blvd. ☎ 904/460–9311 ⊕ www.originalcafe11.com.

Scarlett O'Hara's. It's a popular and convenient spot to stop for lunch or dinner (preferably enjoyed on the front porch); later in the evening it turns up the volume with blues, jazz, disco, Top 40, or karaoke. Whatever's playing, it's always packed. ⊠ 70 Hypolita St. ☎ 904/824–6535 ⊕ www.scarlettoharas.net.

Tini Martini Bar. The veranda overlooking Matanzas Bay at this Casablanca Inn bar is the perfect place to enjoy a cocktail, people-watch, and listen to live music. ✉ *Casablanca Inn, 24 Ave. Menendez* ☎ *904/829–0928* ⊕ *www.tini-martini-bar.com.*

Tradewinds. It's been showcasing bands—from country and western to rock and roll—since 1964. Thanks to the music, beer, and margaritas, you may feel as if you're in Key West. ✉ *124 Charlotte St.* ☎ *904/826–1590* ⊕ *www.tradewindslounge.com.*

The World Famous Oasis Deck and Restaurant. If you're staying on Anastasia Island, this is your best nightlife bet. It has a more than 20 draft beer selections, beach access, and what many locals consider the best burgers in town. ✉ *4000 Rte. A1A S, at Ocean Trace Rd.* ☎ *904/471–3424* ⊕ *www.worldfamousoasis.com.*

SHOPPING

One of the most pleasing pastimes in St. Augustine is a stroll along St. George Street, a pedestrian mall with shoulder-to-shoulder art galleries and one-of-a-kind shops selling candles, home accents, handmade jewelry, aromatherapy products, pottery, books, and clothing. There are also restaurants, clubs, and a veritable orchestra of street musicians.

Several blocks north of the Castillo and the popular St. George Street, a string of shops—galleries, antiques, a bookstore—line both sides of San Marco Avenue. Although this strip isn't as eclectic as it used to be, you'll still find some interesting independent stores.

MALLS

St. Augustine Outlets. Several miles outside the city, Prime Outlets has more than 60 name-brand stores including Gucci, Saks 5th Avenue's OFF 5TH, Kate Spade New York, and Michael Kors. ✉ *500 Belz Outlet Blvd.* ☎ *904/826–1311* ⊕ *www.staugoutlets.com.*

St. Augustine Premium Outlets. Just north of St. Augustine, off Interstate 95, is this collection of 85 designer and brand-name outlet stores. ✉ *2700 State Rd. 16* ☎ *904/825–1555* ⊕ *www.premiumoutlets.com.*

RECOMMENDED STORE

Whetstone Chocolate Factory. Chocolate fans won't want to miss a stop at Whetstone. Once upon a time the company operated a large factory in St. Augustine. They've scaled back to a small operation next door to their retail shop, but you can still take a quick-paced behind-the-scenes tour (reservations recommended). ✉ *139 King St., Vilano Beach* ☎ *904/217–0275* ⊕ *www.whetstonechocolates.com* 🎫 *$8* ⊙ *Tours: weekdays at 11, 1, 2:15, 3:30; Sat. at 10, 11:15, 1, 2:15, 3:30; Sun. at 1, 2:15, 3:30.*

SPORTS AND THE OUTDOORS

BIKING

Solano Cycle. Here you can rent bicycles, scooters, and "scoot coups," which look like the offspring of a scooter and a bumper car and are $49 for the first hour (one-hour minimum) and $69 for two. ⊠ *32 San Marco Ave.* ☎ *904/825–6766* ⊕ *www.solanocycle.com.*

BOAT TOURS

EcoTours. Amidst America's most enduring human history, EcoTours investigates St. Augustine's natural history. Scenic cruises, kayak tours, and catamaran excursions on Matanzas Bay offer a chance to see bottlenose dolphins, bird habitats, lakes, creeks, and saltwater marshes. Along the way are incredible photo ops of the city and the Castillo from the water. ⊠ *111 Ave. Menendez* ☎ *904/377–7245* ⊕ *www. staugustineecotours.com.*

FAMILY **The Pirate Ship Black Raven.** Whether you prefer Captain Hook or Captain Jack Sparrow, it's a pirate's life for everyone aboard the Black Raven, even if you're only sailing on the Mantanzas River. This "floating performance theater" hosts live pirate shows that include sea chanties, black powder cannon firings, sword-fighting lessons for kids (with harmless foam blades), and treasure hunts on weekends. This is just entertainment, not historical education, so expect the jokes to be cheap and cheesy. However, the atmosphere's lively and the river's lovely. Kids can trade their "letters of marque" to get a share of the booty— if, that is, the crew and the kids can manage to get their treasure back from Blackbeard. There are also adults-only evening cruises—the ship includes a fully licensed bar, so grown-ups can live out the fantasy of "yo-ho-ho and a bottle of rum." Cruises can be cancelled for inclement weather, so call to check before making final travel plans. ⊠ *St. Augustine Municipal Marina, 111 Ave. Menendez* ☎ *904/826–0000, 877/578–5050* ⊕ *www.blackravenadventures.com* 🎫 *$29.95.*

Schooner *Freedom.* Cutting a sharp profile, this 72-foot replica of a 19th-century blockade-runner sails from the marina for excursions across Matanzas Bay. You can relax and savor the breeze, or you can help the crew prepare to set sail. There are two-hour day ($35 per person) and sunset ($45) sails as well as a 75-minute twilight/after dark sail ($35). Precise times vary by season. Reservations are advised. ⊠ *St. Augustine Municipal Marina, 111 Ave. Menendez, Slip 86* ☎ *904/810–1010* ⊕ *www.schoonerfreedom.com.*

FISHING

Sea Love Charters. Tackle and bait are included on this outfit's half- or full-day deep-sea fishing trips. ⊠ *Cat's Paw Marina, 220 Nix Boat Yard Rd.* ☎ *904/824–3328* ⊕ *www.sealovefishing.com.*

GOLF

World Golf Village. The World Golf Hall of Fame complex has two 18-hole layouts named for and partially designed by golf legends Sam Snead, Gene Sarazen, Arnold Palmer, and Jack Nicklaus. The King & Bear course, a collaboration of Palmer and Nicklaus, features a design that symbolizes the styles of both golfing legends, including holes that especially reward outstanding power of the tees. Palmer chose the par-4 15th as one of his "Dream 18" in a *Sports Illustrated* report. It's the most picturesque hole on the course, with a dramatic rock wall surrounding the green. Snead and Sarazen consulted with designer Bobby Weed in creating The Slammer & Squire course, which features generous fairways and lots of water hazards. Amenities for both courses include complimentary range balls and fresh chilled apples on the 1st and 10th tees. ⊠ *1 World Golf Pl.* ☎ *904/940–6100 Slammer & Squire, 904/940–6200 King & Bear* ⊕ *www.worldgolfhalloffame.com* ⛳ *King & Bear, $179; Slammer & Squire, $139* 🏌 *King & Bear Course: 18 holes, 7279 yards, par 72; Slammer & Squite Course: 18 holes, 6939 yards, par 72.*

WATER SPORTS

Surf Station. Here you can rent surfboards, skimboards, and bodyboards. ⊠ *1020 Anastasia Blvd.* ☎ *904/471–9463, 800/460–6394* ⊕ *www.surfstation.com.*

DAYTONA BEACH AND INLAND TOWNS

Updated by
Steve Master

The section of the coast around Daytona Beach offers considerable variety, from the unassuming bedroom community of Ormond Beach to the auto-racing capital of Daytona Beach. (Go 75 miles to the south, and you've got speeding rockets instead of speeding cars.)

Peaceful little inland towns are separated by miles of two-lane roads, running through dense forest and flat pastureland and skirting one lake after another. There's not much to see but cattle and the state's few hills. Gentle and rolling, they're hardly worth noting to people from true hill country, but they're significant enough in Florida for much of this area to be called the "hill and lake region."

DAYTONA BEACH

65 miles south of St. Augustine.

Best known for the Daytona 500, Daytona has been the center of automobile racing since cars were first raced along the beach here in 1902. February is the biggest month for race enthusiasts, and there are weekly events at the International Speedway, which completed a $400 million renovation in 2016. During race weeks, bike weeks, spring-break periods, and summer holidays, expect extremely heavy traffic. On the mainland, near the inland waterway, several blocks of Beach Street have been "streetscaped," and shops and restaurants open onto an inviting, broad, brick sidewalk.

GETTING HERE AND AROUND

Several airlines have regular service to Daytona Beach International Airport, which is next to Daytona International Speedway on International Speedway Boulevard, an east–west artery that stretches from Interstate 95 to the beaches. The average drive time from the airport to beachside hotels is 20 minutes; Yellow Cab–Daytona Beach makes the trip for $12–$40.

DOTS Transit Service has scheduled service ($30 one-way, $55 round-trip) connecting Daytona Beach, DeLand, Deltona, and the Orlando International Airport, which serves more airlines and has more direct flights but is about a 70-mile commute via Interstate 4 and State Road 417 (allow at least 90 minutes). Note that DOTS doesn't serve the Daytona airport. Indeed, outside of a few hotel shuttles, there's no shuttle service between the Daytona airport and town.

Daytona Beach has an excellent bus network, Votran, which serves the beach area, airport, shopping malls, and major arteries, including service to DeLand and New Smyrna Beach and the Express Link to Orlando ($3.50). Exact fare is required for Votran ($1.75) if using cash.

13

Contacts Daytona Beach International Airport (*DAB*). ⊠ *700 Catalina Dr.* ☎ *386/248-8069* ⊕ *www.flydaytonafirst.com.* **DOTS Transit Service** ☎ *386/257-5411, 800/231-1965* ⊕ *www.dots-daytonabeach.com.* **Votran** ☎ *386/761-7700* ⊕ *www.votran.org.* **Yellow Cab–Daytona Beach** ☎ *386/255-5555, 888/333-3356* ⊕ *www.daytonataxi.com.*

VISITOR INFORMATION

Contact Daytona Beach Area Convention and Visitors Bureau ☎ *800/544-0415* ⊕ *www.daytonabeach.com.*

EXPLORING

The Casements. Built in 1912 for Reverend Harwood Huntington and named for its hand-crafted casement windows, the home was purchased by John D. Rockefeller Sr. in 1918 as a winter retreat. Once considered the richest man in the world, Rockefeller entertained famous friends such as Henry Ford, Will Rogers, and Henry Flagler at the home while remaining an active member of the Ormond Beach community. After Rockefeller's death in 1937, the property was bought and sold numerous times and is now a cultural center and museum. The waterfront estate and its formal gardens host daily tours and an annual lineup of events and exhibits; there's also a permanent exhibit of Hungarian folk art and Boy Scout memorabilia. ⊠ *25 Riverside Dr., Ormond Beach* ☎ *386/676-3216* ⊕ *www.thecasements.net/* ▣ *Donations accepted* ☉ *Weekdays 10–3:30, Sat. 10–11:30 am.*

Halifax Historical Museum. Memorabilia from the early days of beach automobile racing are on display here, as are historic photographs, Native American and Civil War artifacts, a postcard exhibit, and a video that details city history. There's a shop for gifts and antiques, too. Admission is by donation on Thursday and on Saturday, kids 12-and-under are free. ⊠ *252 S. Beach St.* ☎ *386/255-6976* ⊕ *www.halifaxhistorical.org* ▣ *$5* ☉ *Tues.–Fri. 10:30–4:30, Sat. 10–4.*

FAMILY **Museum of Arts & Sciences.** This behemoth museum has displays of Chinese art and an eye-popping complete skeleton of a giant ground sloth that's 130,000 years old. The museum also boasts a new Visible Storage Building, one of the most significant collections of Cuban art outside of Cuba, a large Coca-Cola and Americana collection, a rare Napoleonic exhibit, and one of the more expansive collections of American art in the Southeast. Kids love the Charles and Linda Williams Children's Museum, which features interactive science, engineering, and physics exhibits; a nature preserve with half a mile of boardwalks and nature trails; and a state-of-the-art planetarium with daily shows. Florida art dating back to the 18th century is featured in the recently opened Cici and Hyatt Brown Museum of Art, a freestanding, 26,000-square-foot Florida Cracker–style addition opened in early 2015. Artists represented include John James Audubon, Thomas Hart Benton, and N.C. Wyeth. ⊠ *352 S. Nova Rd.* 🕾 *386/255–0285* ⊕ *www.moas.org* 🖃 *$12.95 for science museum; $10.95 for art museum; $18.95 combo ticket for both museums* ⊘ *Mon.–Sat.10–5, Sun. 11–5.*

OFF THE BEATEN PATH

Ponce de León Inlet Light Station. At the southern tip of the barrier island that includes Daytona Beach is the sleepy town of Ponce Inlet, with a small marina, a few bars, and casual seafood restaurants. Boardwalks traverse delicate dunes and provide easy access to the beach, although storms have caused serious erosion. Marking this prime spot is the bright-red, century-old Ponce de León Inlet Light Station, a National Historic Monument and museum, the tallest lighthouse in the state and the third-tallest in the country. Climb to the top of the 175-foot-tall lighthouse tower for a bird's-eye view of Ponce Inlet. ⊠ *4931 S. Peninsula Dr., Ponce Inlet* 🕾 *386/761–1821* ⊕ *www.ponceinlet.org* 🖃 *$5* ⊘ *Sept.–May, daily 10–6; May–Sept., daily 10–9; last admission 1 hr before closing.*

BEACH

Daytona Beach. At the World's Most Famous Beach you can drive right onto the sand (at least from one hour after sunrise to one hour before sunset), spread out a blanket, and have all your belongings at hand (with the exception of alcohol, which is prohibited). All that said, heavy traffic during summer and holidays makes it dangerous for children, and families should be extra careful or stay in the designated car-free zones. The speed limit is 10 mph, and there's a $10 fee, collected at the beach ramps, for driving on the sands every month but December and January.

The wide, 23-mile-long beach can get crowded in the "strip" area (between International Speedway Boulevard and Seabreeze Boulevard) with its food vendors, beachfront bars, volleyball matches, and motorized-water-sports enthusiasts. Those seeking a quieter experience can head north or south in either direction toward car-free zones in more residential areas. The hard-packed sand that makes the beach suitable for driving is also perfect for running and cycling. There's also excellent surf fishing directly from the beach. **Amenities:** food and drink; lifeguards; parking (some with fee); showers; toilets; water sports. **Best for:** sunrise; surfing; swimming; walking. ■TIP➔ **Signs on Route A1A indicate car access via beach ramps. Sand traps aren't limited to the golf course, though—cars can get stuck.** ⊠ *Rte. A1A* ⊕ *www.daytonabeach.com.*

WHERE TO EAT

$$$
SEAFOOD

✕ Aunt Catfish's on the River. Don't be surprised if your server introduces herself as your cousin, though you've never seen her before in your life. You see, everybody is "cousin" at Aunt Catfish's (as in, "Can I get you another mason jar of sweet tea, Cousin?"). The silly Southern hospitality is only one of the draws at this wildly popular seafood restaurant just south of Daytona. The main lure, of course, is the food: mouth-watering plates of fresh seafood and other Southern favorites. Hot cinnamon rolls, hush puppies, baked beans, cheese grits, and slaw come with every entrée and can be a meal in themselves. Bring your appetite and your patience—a wait is practically guaranteed. Sunday brunch lures empty stomachs with made-to-order eggs and French toast, and a chocolate fountain. $ *Average main: $24* ⊠ *4009 Halifax Dr., Port Orange* ☎ *386/767–4768* ⊕ *www.auntcatfishontheriver.com* ⌂ *Reservations not accepted.*

$ ✕ **Daytona Brickyard.** It's not just the locals who swear that the Brick-
AMERICAN yard's charbroiled sirloin burgers are the best they've ever tasted—devotees have been known to drive from Georgia just for lunch. Given its name and location in the heart of NASCAR country, the popular bar and grill is covered in racing memorabilia. Dang, even the floor and the tablecloths are black-and-white checkered. But don't mistake the racing theme to mean the place merely serves greasy bar food to Joe Sixpacks. It also feeds T-bone and New York strip steaks to doctors. $ *Average main: $12* ⊠ *747 International Speedway Blvd.* ☎ *386/253–2270* ⊕ *www.brickyardlounge.com* ⌂ *Reservations not accepted.*

$$$$ ✕ **Hyde Park Prime Steakhouse.** This chophouse provides an upscale alter-
STEAKHOUSE native to Daytona's more prevalent shorts-and-flip-flop joints. The lively dining room—done in dark wood with soft lighting and splashes of colorful artwork—is complemented by dramatic ocean views. Attentive servers carry chalkboards detailing specials such as lobster mac and cheese. But steaks, especially the cuts named after race-car drivers, and mouthwatering sides (don't miss the potatoes Gruyère gratin) are the main attractions. The 22-ounce bone rib eye named after beefy Tony Stewart is, appropriately, the thickest, showing that these guys know their NASCAR. The popular Steak Earnhardt is a filet mignon over bordelaise crowned with lobster, béarnaise (yes, it has two sauces), asparagus, and mushroom caps. An expansive wine list includes more than 40 options by the glass. And don't let this restaurant chain's Ohio roots fool you—the key lime pie is absolutely Florida-worthy. $ *Average main: $38* ⊠ *Hilton Resort, 100 N. Atlantic Ave.* ☎ *386/226–9844* ⊕ *www.hydeparkrestaurants.com* ⊗ *No lunch.*

$$$ ✕ **Martini's Chophouse.** Local beautiful people seem to flock to this trendy
CONTEMPORARY South Daytona eatery and lounge as much for the scene as for the food.
Fodor's Choice The bar area, done in gray with splashes of lime green, is a modern
★ meeting place for the after-work crowd, and the outdoor deck and bar attract a livelier bunch. Those who do deign to dine appreciate the chef's use of homegrown herbs and creative sauces in dishes such as Bahamian lobster sautee and natural grass-fed filet mignon with Amish blue cheese au jus, frizzled leeks, and mashed potatoes, which can be enjoyed in the sleek dining room or in the garden, complete with a 20-foot lighted waterfall and fire pit. $ *Average main: $24* ⊠ *1815 S. Ridgewood Ave., South Daytona Beach* ☎ *386/763–1090* ⊕ *www.martinischophouse. com* ⊗ *Closed Sun. and Mon. No lunch.*

$ ✕ **Tia Cori's Tacos.** Mexican street food is the specialty at this tiny, coun-
MEXICAN ter-service eatery in the downtown riverfront shopping district. The namesake tacos come Mexican style (with onion, cilantro, and lime),

13

but for 50¢ more you can get an Americanized version with cheese. Fillings range from the familiar (chicken, steak, carnitas) to the less familiar (including beef tongue and spicy pork skin). Lines can get long during lunch hour, when surfers, college students, and the downtown business crowd converge for fresh, tasty, and cheap eats. The generously filled Mexican tacos are $1.50 apiece. Other favorites include fish tacos with pineapple and cabbage. The $9.99 steak dinner smothered with onions is another popular choice. Indoor and outdoor seating is available, and a mariachi band performs every Friday night. With a 3 am closing time on weekends, the restaurant is a late-night favorite for college students and the nightclub set. $ *Average main: $6* ⊠ *214 N. Beach St.* ☎ *386/947–4333* ⊕ *www.tiacoristacos.com* ⌂ *Reservations not accepted* ⊘ *Closed Sun.*

WHERE TO STAY

$ 🏨 **Courtyard Daytona Beach Speedway/Airport.** For those visiting Daytona
HOTEL   Beach for something other than surf and sand (a certain iconic racing facility comes to mind), this smartly located Marriott is the perfect base. **Pros:** proximity to speedway; welcoming indoor and outdoor public areas; friendly service. **Cons:** some noise from nearby airport; 15-minute drive to the beach. $ *Rooms from: $134* ⊠ *1605 Richard Petty Blvd.* ☎ *386/255–3388* ⊕ *www.marriott.com/hotels/travel/dabcy-courtyard-daytona-beach-speedway-airport/* ➹ *122 rooms* ⦿ *No meals.*

$ 🏨 **Hilton Daytona Beach Oceanfront Resort.** Perched on one of the few
RESORT   traffic-free strips of beach in Daytona, this high-rise is as popular with families as it is with couples. **Pros:** direct beach access; proximity to shops and restaurants. **Cons:** inconvenient self-parking; resort fee; not all rooms have balconies. $ *Rooms from: $139* ⊠ *100 N. Atlantic Ave.* ☎ *386/254–8200, 866/536–8477* ⊕ *www.daytonahilton.com* ➹ *744 rooms, 52 suites* ⦿ *No meals.*

$ 🏨 **Perry's Ocean Edge Resort.** Perhaps more than any other property in
RESORT   Daytona, Perry's has a die-hard fan base, many of whom started coming
FAMILY   to the oceanfront resort as children, then returned with their children and their children's children. **Pros:** spacious rooms; helpful staff; nice pools; family-friendly. **Cons:** small bathrooms; decor is dated. $ *Rooms from: $149* ⊠ *2209 S. Atlantic Ave.* ☎ *386/255–0581, 800/447–0002* ⊕ *www.perrysoceanedge.com* ➹ *183 rooms, 30 suites* ⦿ *Breakfast.*

$ 🏨 **The Shores Resort & Spa.** Rustic furniture and beds swathed in mos-
RESORT   quito netting are a nod to Old Florida at this 11-story beachfront resort,
Fodor'sChoice   but there's nothing rustic about the amenities, including a luxury four-
★   poster bed, doorless Italian marble showers and a 42-inch plasma TV in every room. **Pros:** beachfront; spa; friendly staff; 24-hour room service. **Cons:** expensive restaurant; not all rooms have balconies. $ *Rooms from: $159* ⊠ *2637 S. Atlantic Ave., Daytona Beach Shores* ☎ *386/767–7350, 866/934–7467* ⊕ *www.shoresresort.com* ➹ *212 rooms, 24 suites* ⦿ *No meals.*

$ 🏨 **Wyndham Ocean Walk Resort.** Kids definitely won't be bored at this
RESORT   all-suites high-rise beachfront resort with four swimming pools, a
FAMILY   waterslide, a lazy river, a game room, an indoor miniature-golf course,
Fodor'sChoice   an activities center, and the only traffic-free beach in Daytona Beach.
★   **Pros:** family-friendly; beachfront; great facilities; in-room washers

and dryers; spacious accommodations. **Cons:** no room service; dated decor; very slow elevators. [$] *Rooms from: $155* ✉ *300 N. Atlantic Ave.* ☎ *386/323–4800, 888/743–2323* 🌐 *www.oceanwalk.com* 🛏 *200 1-, 2-, and 3-bedroom suites* 🍴 *No meals.*

NIGHTLIFE

BARS

Boot Hill Saloon. Despite its reputation as a biker bar, this place welcomes nonbikers and even nonbiker tourists! ✉ *310 Main St.* ☎ *386/258–9506* 🌐 *www.boothillsaloon.com.*

Ocean Walk Village. Lively and always hopping, Ocean Walk is a cluster of shops, restaurants, and bars (the Mai Tai Bar is a good bet) stretching along Atlantic Avenue and the ocean. ✉ *250 N. Atlantic Ave.* ☎ *386/258–9544* 🌐 *www.oceanwalkshoppes.com.*

The Oyster Pub. Sports fans and oyster lovers congregate by the thousands here. ✉ *555 Seabreeze Blvd.* ☎ *386/255–6348* 🌐 *www.oysterpub.com.*

DANCE CLUBS

Razzle's Nightclub. DJs play high-energy dance music 8 pm–3 am. ✉ *611 Seabreeze Blvd.* ☎ *386/257–6236* 🌐 *www.razzlesnightclub.com.*

SHOPPING

Daytona Flea and Farmers' Market. One of the largest flea markets in the South draws residents from all over the state as well as visitors to the state. It's open weekends, including Friday, from 9 to 5. ✉ *2987 Bellevue Ave.* ☎ *386/253–3330* 🌐 *www.daytonafleamarket.com.*

Destination Daytona. This 100-acre biker enclave is complete with an expansive Harley-Davidson dealership; retail shops; a restaurant; bars; a tattoo parlor; a hotel; and a pavilion used for concerts, conventions—even biker-inspired weddings. ✉ *1635 N. U.S. 1, Ormond Beach* 🌐 *www.brucerossmeyer.com.*

The Pavilion at Port Orange. Just off Interstate 95 (Port Orange exit), this outdoor shopping complex houses a 14-screen Hollywood Theaters; numerous restaurants; and retailers like the Southern department store, Belk, and ULTA beauty and cosmetics. ✉ *5501 S. Williamson Blvd., Port Orange* 🌐 *www.thepavilionatportorange.com.*

Volusia Mall. This mall has more than 125 stores, including anchors like JCPenney, Macy's, and Dillard's. ✉ *1700 W. International Speedway Blvd.* ☎ *386/253–6783* 🌐 *www.volusiamall.net.*

SPORTS AND THE OUTDOORS

AUTO RACING

Daytona International Speedway. The massive Daytona International Speedway, on Daytona's major east–west artery, has year-round auto and motorcycle racing, including the Daytona 500 in February and the Coke Zero 400 in July. ✉ *1801 W. International Speedway Blvd.* ☎ *800/748–7467* 🌐 *www.daytonainternationalspeedway.com.*

BIRD-WATCHING

Tomoka State Park. With more than 160 species to see, this scenic park is perfect for bird-watching. It also has wooded campsites, bicycle and walking paths, and kayak and canoe rentals on the Tomoka and Halifax

Continued on page 700

by John Blodgett
and Steve Masler

THE RACE IS ON IN DAYTONA

It's morning on race day. Check the weather—rain or shine? The race won't run if it's raining, but bring a poncho just in case, and pack some sunscreen, too. Oh, and don't forget your binoculars and ear plugs. Fill your cooler with snacks and drinks—yes, it's allowed. Got your waterproof padded seat? Good. If you have a radio scanner, bring it to listen in on the pit crews; if you don't, you can rent one at the track for $50 ($30 for Sprint customers). This handheld device, in addition to its scanning capabilities, provides live video feeds, driver statistics, and auto replay.

You're here! Welcome to Daytona International Speedway—the storied race track that is home to one of America's most famous races, the Daytona 500. Hope you like crowds, because you'll be jostling with upward of 150,000 fellow race fanatics. The gate generally opens at 8 AM, with the race starting at 1 PM. The hours in between are one of the best times to seek autographs from your favorite racers in their garages near the Sprint FANZONE (drivers also can be approached throughout race weekend as they hang out at their respective souvenir haulers).

Watching the race is a sensory experience: 43 cars powered by 500 or more horsepower make

DAYTONA ROARS
ALL YEAR LONG

As the headquarter city for the National Association for Stock Car Auto Racing, better known as NASCAR, Daytona celebrates auto racing year-round. So while the Daytona 500 happens just one day out of 365, there's plenty for you to see and do every day at the speedway's 480-acre complex. You can go to other races, go on a tour, or, as part of the Richard Petty Driving Experience, maybe even jump into a stock car yourself. Major races are held during nine weekends, and an assortment of other races take place throughout the year. On non-race days the Speedway is host to R&D of racing vehicles, car shows, and other events. For motorcycles, there's the Daytona 200 and the Daytona Supercross by Honda.

for a constant roar; there's the smell of hot rubber, fuel, and exhaust; and, if you happen to be down low by the track itself, you might be pelted by flecks of tire as the pack blasts by at speeds approaching 190 mph. Every so often, let your binoculars wander—you might just see a past champion or other celebrity.

The 2016 Daytona 500 will mark the unveiling of a $400 million "reimagining" of the iconic speedway, which opened in 1959. The 101,000 seats are wider and more comfortable, with improved viewing sight lines on the nearly mile-long stretch. Three concourses house "neighborhoods," where fans can socialize and dine without missing the action.

THE LAPS ALONG THE WAY

For more than 50 years, the world's top NASCAR drivers have competed in the Daytona 500, considered by many to be the sport's premier race.

The first official Daytona 500 was held on February 22, 1959, with 59 cars in front of 41,000 fans. It has been held each year in late February ever since. In the half century that followed, cash awards have grown from $68,000 to almost $20 million, with fewer drivers—43—but double the fans—150,000. Every year the 500-mile (200-lap) race marks the beginning of NASCAR's premier Sprint Cup series and generally offers the greatest monetary reward. Winning the Daytona 500 has been equated with a Super Bowl victory, and much as in that sport, the final moments can be the most memorable and most important.

GETTING TICKETS

For tickets to the Daytona 500 or any other races held at the speedway, contact the Daytona Speedway ticket office (✉ 1801 W. International Speedway Blvd., Daytona Beach ☎ 800/PIT-SHOP [748–7467] ⊕ www.daytonainternationalspeedway.com). Single adult tickets to the Daytona 500 range from $95 to $230, primo seats go quickly, so the sooner you order the better. Grandstand seats typically sell out days or weeks in advance.

NASCAR'S FINEST

David Pearson
"The Silver Fox"
105 NASCAR wins
retired in 1986.

Dale Earnhardt
"The Intimidator"
"Ironhead"
Killed during the
2001 Daytona 500.

Richard Petty
"King Richard,"
Most NASCAR wins
(200) and Daytona
victories (7).

Jimmie Johnson
Won his sixth
consecutive Sprint
Cup championship
in 2013.

EXPLORE THE WORLD CENTER OF RACING

Getting out and inspecting the track first hand is just one part of a Daytona Speedway tour.

You don't have to wait until race days to explore the World Center of Racing. Some of the best exploring can be done when the engines are silent. Narrated tours give you a look at the hallowed grounds where Fireball Roberts, Bobby Allison, Richard Petty, and Dale Earnhardt turned a regional sport into an international phenomenon.

The 90-minute All Access Tour ($23; hourly 10–3) brings you into the ritzy Daytona 500 Club and the Houston Lawing Press Box in the Sprint Tower, which features views not only of the 2.5-mile tri-oval, but also of the Atlantic Ocean nearby. You'll also visit the drivers' meeting room, the NASCAR Sprint Cup garages, Gatorade Victory Lane, and the Sprint FANZONE. There are three dramatic photo opportunities on the tour: Victory Lane, the start/finish line, and the daunting 31-degree banking in Turns 3 and 4.

Other options include the 30-minute Speedway Tour ($16; 11:30, 1:30, 3:30, and 4) and the three-hour VIP Tour ($50; by reservation on select days). ✉ 1801 W. International Speedway Blvd. ☎ 800/748–7467 ⊕ www.daytonainternationalspeedway.com.

If you're satisfied with merely viewing the historic speedway, driving opportunities are also available through the Richard Petty Driving Experience. You can ride shotgun—or, for more dough, drive yourself—in a stock car on Daytona International Speedway. You suit up, helmet and all, and slide into the car through the window, just like you're Jimmie Johnson. Be sure to get a photo afterward so your friends believe you when you tell them how you zoomed around at speeds in excess of 150 mph! Ride-alongs cost $144; call for driving prices and to reserve a ride. ☎ 800-BE PETTY (800/237–3389).

LADIES WELCOME

Stock-car racing has long been a male-dominated sport, but icons such as Dale Earnhardt Jr. and Jeff Gordon have been, on occasion, overshadowed by women. Danica Patrick, the pint-sized, telegenic driver of Indy Car fame made her NAS-CAR debut at Daytona in a 2010 Nation-wide Series race. Patrick, who made her Sprint Cup debut in 2012, is among a growing number of women entering motorsports but one of only a few to break into NASCAR.

rivers. It's on the site of a Timucuan Indian settlement discovered in 1605 by Spanish explorer Alvaro Mexia. ✉ *2099 N. Beach St., 3 miles north of, Ormond Beach* ☎ *386/676–4050* ⊕ *www.floridastateparks. org/tomoka* ▤ *$5 per vehicle, up to 8 people; $2 pedestrians* ⊙ *Daily 8–sunset.*

BOATING

Cracker Creek. At this eco-adventure park you can rent kayaks, canoes, hydrobikes, and pontoon boats or take ecotours or a Pirate Cruise on scenic Spruce Creek. There are also on-site picnic facilities. ✉ *1795 Taylor Rd., Port Orange* ☎ *386/304–0778* ⊕ *www.crackercreek.com* ⊙ *Wed.–Sun. 8–5; canoeing and kayaking by reservation only.*

FISHING

Sea Spirit Fishing. Four- to 12-hour private and group charters are options with this operator. ✉ *Inlet Harbor Marina, 133 Inlet Harbor Rd., Ponce Inlet* ☎ *386/763–4388* ⊕ *www.seaspiritfishing.com.*

GOLF

Club at Pelican Bay South Course. Golfers rave about the great value of Pelican Bay South, but one word of caution: what you save in greens fees you might give back in lost balls. No, this isn't the most difficult track. But the abundance of water—and challenging ocean breezes—can result in a lot of splashes for novices or overaggressive advanced players. Designed by Lloyd Clifton in 1984, the course is open to the public and features an island green on the par-4 15th. It's worth sticking around for lunch or dinner at the 19th Hole Bar & Grill. ✉ *350 Pelican Bay Dr.* ☎ *386/756–0034* ⊕ *www.pelicanbaycc.com* ▤ *$35* ⚑ *18 holes, 6385 yards, par 72.*

LPGA International. This is where aspiring women professionals compete to earn a place on the LPGA Tour. The qualifying tournament—Q-school—is held every January, but the meticulously maintained courses are open to the public year-round. The Jones Course, designed by Rees Jones, is a links-style course with large, fast, undulating greens. Fairways are tighter on the Hills Course, designed by Arthur Hills, with long, difficult par-5s due to long carries and well-guarded greens. Wildlife is abundant, with bald eagles, owls, and deer as well as rattlesnakes and gators (some quite large). The course has driving, putting, and short-game practice areas, and an excellent restaurant, Malcolm's. ✉ *1000 Champions Dr.* ☎ *386/523–2001* ⊕ *www.lpgainternational. com* ▤ *$69* ⚑ *Jones Course: 18 holes, 7088 yards, par 72; Hills Course: 18 holes, 6984 yards, par 72.*

Spruce Creek Golf & Country Club. Golfers distracted by loud noise might want to avoid this course, which is part of a fly-in community whose residents have included John Travolta and NASCAR star Mark Martin. Most, however, find the air traffic a unique amenity to this semiprivate course, considered one of the best golf values in the Daytona Beach area. The front 9 is challenging off the tees, with some tight, tree-lined fairways. Wind is more of a challenge on the more open back 9, where water lines 8 of the holes. A virtual tour on the club website gives golfers shot-by-shot advice in managing the course, which boasts a driving range as well as putting and short-game practice areas. ✉ *1900 Country*

Club Dr., Port Orange ☎ *386/756–6114* ⊕ *www.sprucecreekgolf.com* ☞ *$25 for 9 holes, $44 for 18 holes* ⚑ *18 holes, 6894 yards, par 72.*

MANATEE SPOTTING

Blue Spring State Park. January and February are the top months for sighting sea cows at this designated manatee refuge, but they begin to head here in November, as soon as the water gets cold enough (below 68°F). Your best bet for spotting a manatee is to walk along the boardwalk. The park, which is 30 miles southwest of Daytona Beach on Interstate 4, was once a river port where paddle wheelers stopped to take on cargoes of oranges. Home to the largest spring on the St. Johns River, the park offers hiking, camping, picnicking facilities, and two-bedroom cabins ($95 a night, 2-night minimum weekends and holidays). It also contains a historic homestead that's open to the public. ⊠ *2100 W. French Ave., Orange City* ☎ *386/775–3663* ⊕ *www.floridastateparks. org/bluespring* ☞ *$6 per vehicle, up to 8 people; $2 pedestrians, bicyclists* ⊗ *Daily 8–sunset.*

FAMILY **Manatee Scenic Boat Tours.** This Ponce Inlet operator takes you on narrated cruises of the Intracoastal Waterway. Kids will love looking for the creatures also known as "sea cows," and your guide might tell you how (sun-delirious?) sailors may have mistaken them for mermaids. ⊠ *133 Inlet Harbor Rd., Ponce Inlet* ☎ *386/761–2027, 800/881–2628* ⊕ *www.manateecruise.com* ☞ *$25.*

WATER SPORTS

Daytona Beach Parasail. Catch air with this Ponce Inlet outfitter. ⊠ *4936 S. Peninsula Dr., Ponce Inlet* ☎ *386/547–6067* ⊕ *www. daytonaparasailing.com.*

Maui Nix. This is one of several outfitters that rent surf and boogie boards. ⊠ *635 N. Atlantic Ave.* ☎ *386/253–1234* ⊕ *www.mauinix.com/ store.*

Salty Dog Surf Shop. You can rent surfboards or paddleboards here. ⊠ *201 E. Granada Blvd., Ormond Beach* ☎ *386/673-5277* ⊕ *www. saltydogsurfshop.com.*

NEW SMYRNA BEACH

19 miles south of Daytona Beach, 56 miles northeast of Orlando.

The long, dune-lined beach of this small town abuts the Canaveral National Seashore. Behind the dunes sit beach houses, small motels, and an occasional high-rise (except at the extreme northern tip, where none is higher than seven stories). Canal Street, on the mainland, and Flagler Avenue, with many beachside shops and restaurants, have both been "streetscaped" with wide brick sidewalks and stately palm trees. The town is also known for its internationally recognized artists' workshop and some of the best surfing on the East Coast.

EXPLORING

Arts on Douglas. In a warehouse that has been converted into a stunning 5,000-square-foot, high-ceiling art gallery, Arts on Douglas has a new exhibit of works by a Florida artist every month. Representing more than 50 Florida artists, the gallery has hosted exhibits on the handmade jewelry of Mary Schimpff Webb and landscape and still-life oils by Barbara Tiffany. The gallery also holds an opening reception every first Saturday of the month from 4 to 7 pm. ⊠ *123 Douglas St.* ☎ *386/428–1133* ⊕ *www.artsondouglas.net* ▨ *Free* ⊘ *Tues.–Fri. 10–5, Sat. 11–3, and by appointment.*

Atlantic Center for the Arts. With exhibits that change every two months, the Atlantic Center for the Arts has works of internationally known artists. Mediums include sculpture, mixed materials, video, drawings, prints, and paintings. Intensive three-week residencies are periodically run by visual-, literary-, and performing-master artists such as Edward Albee, James Dickey, and Beverly Pepper. ⊠ *1414 Art Center Ave.* ☎ *386/427–6975* ⊕ *www.atlanticcenterforthearts.org* ▨ *Free* ⊘ *Tues.– Fri. 10–4, Sat. 10–2.*

Canaveral National Seashore. Miles of grassy windswept dunes and a virtually empty beach await you at this remarkable 57,000-acre park on a barrier island with 24 miles of undeveloped coastline spanning from New Smyrna to Titusville. The unspoiled area of hilly sand dunes, grassy marshes, and seashell-sprinkled beaches is a large part of NASA's buffer zone and is home to more than 1,000 species of plants and 300 species of birds and other animals. Surf and lagoon fishing are available, and a hiking trail leads to the top of an American Indian shell midden at Turtle Mound. For an additional charge, visitors can take a pontoon-boat tour ($20) or participate in the turtle-watch interpretive program ($14). Reservations are required. A visitor center is on Route A1A at Apollo Beach. Weekends are busy, and parts of the park are closed when mandated by NASA launch operations at the Kennedy Space Center, so call ahead. ⊠ *Visitor information center, 7611 S. Atlantic Ave.* ☎ *386/428–3384* ⊕ *www.nps.gov/cana* ▨ *$5 cars; $1 pedestrians, bicycles* ⊘ *Nov.–Mar., daily 6–6; Apr.–Oct., daily 6 am–8 pm.*

Smyrna Dunes Park. In this park, on a barrier island at the northernmost tip of New Smyrna Beach peninsula, 1½ miles of boardwalks criss-cross sand dunes and delicate dune vegetation to lead to beaches and a fishing jetty. Botanical signs identify the flora, and there are picnic tables and an information center. It's also one of the few county parks where pets are allowed (on leashes, that is). ⊠ *2995 N. Peninsula Ave.* ☎ *386/424–2935* ⊕ *www.volusia.org/parks/smyrnadunes.htm* ▨ *$5 per vehicle, up to 8 people* ⊘ *Daily sunrise–sunset.*

BEACHES

Apollo Beach. In addition to typical beach activities, visitors to this beach on the northern end of Canaveral National Seashore can also ride horses here (with a permit), hike self-guided trails, and tour the historic Eldora Statehouse. From I-95, take Exit 220 and head east. **Amenities:** lifeguards (seasonal); parking (fee); toilets. **Best for:** solitude; swimming; walking. ⊠ *Rte. A1A, at southern end of New Smyrna Beach* ☎ *386/428–3384* ▨ *$5 per vehicle for national seashore.*

New Smyrna Beach. This public beach extends 7 miles from the northernmost part of New Smyrna's barrier island south to the Canaveral National Seashore. It's mostly hard-packed white sand, and at low tide can be stunningly wide in some areas. The beach is lined with heaps of sandy dunes, but because they're endangered, it's against the law to walk on or play in them or to pick the sea grass, which helps to stabilize the dunes. From sunrise to sunset cars are allowed on certain sections of the beach (speed limit: 10 mph). In season there's a $10 beach-access fee for cars. **Amenities:** food and drink; lifeguards; parking (some with fee); showers; toilets; water sports. **Best for:** sunrise; surfing; swimming; walking. ✉ *Rte. A1A.*

WHERE TO EAT

$$ SEAFOOD
🍴 **J.B.'s Fish Camp and Restaurant.** Better known simply as J.B.'s, this local landmark is on the eastern shore of the Indian River (i.e., the middle of nowhere). Crowds gather around the picnic-style tables inside and out, or belly up to the bar to dine on mounds of spicy seafood, Cajun alligator, J.B.'s famous crab cakes, and rock shrimp by the dozen. It's a great place to catch the sunset, and there's live music weekend afternoons. Five bucks says at least one person at your table says their hush puppies are the best he's ever eaten. [$] *Average main: $17* ✉ *859 Pompano Ave.* ☎ *386/427–5747* 🌐 *www.jbsfishcamp.com* ✍ *Reservations not accepted.*

$$$ SEAFOOD
🍴 **Norwood's Seafood Restaurant.** Fresh local fish and shrimp are the specialties at this bustling New Smyrna Beach landmark, open since 1946. Built as a gas station, the building later served as a general store and piggy-bank factory, but the remodeled interior belies this backstory; the place is replete with wood, from the chairs and booths to the walls and rafters. Order steak, pasta, or innovative seafood dishes such as seared grouper topped with wasabi cream and served over a Yukon gold potato cake (yeah, it's as good as it sounds). Prices are reasonable, and more than 3,000 bottles of wine are on hand. Don't be fooled by the fancy wine list and linen tablecloths; you can still wear shorts (business casual, however, is the norm). [$] *Average main: $21* ✉ *400 2nd Ave.* ☎ *386/428–4621* 🌐 *www.norwoods.com.com* ✍ *Reservations not accepted.*

$$ CUBAN
🍴 **Spanish River Grill.** Michele and Henry Salgado own this modern Cuban and Spanish eatery, which many locals think is the best restaurant in New Smyrna Beach. Though many consider the cuisine to represent fine dining, overall the restaurant is casual and unpretentious. Henry combines his Cuban grandmother's recipes with local ingredients for knockout results. Start with the fried green plantains with avocado salsa or local clams with Serrano ham, fresh mango, and tarragon cream. For your main course, try the yuca-crusted fresh fish or char-grilled chimichurri-marinated fillet. Be sure to save room for one of Michele's desserts. Sunday sees a brunch from 11 to 3. [$] *Average main: $20* ✉ *737 E. 3rd Ave.* ☎ *386/424–6991* 🌐 *www.thespanishrivergrill.com* ✍ *Reservations not accepted* 🕒 *Closed Mon.*

WHERE TO STAY

$ B&B/INN Fodor's Choice ★
🏨 **Black Dolphin Inn.** On a quaint residential street, this Spanish-style, three-story inn combines the charm and hospitality of a B&B with modern sensibilities and a chic, coastal-casual vibe. **Pros:** hospitable staff; river views; comfy beds. **Cons:** no pool; must drive to the beach. [$] *Rooms from: $169* ✉ *916 S. Riverside Dr.* ☎ *386/410–4868, 855/410–4868* 🌐 *www.blackdolphininn.com* 🛏 *14 rooms* 🍽 *Breakfast.*

The Florida Trail goes through Ocala National Forest, taking hikers past hardwoods, pines, and prairies.

$
B&B/INN
🖼 **Riverview Hotel and Spa.** A landmark since 1885, this former bridge tender's home is set back from the Intracoastal Waterway at the edge of the north causeway, which still has an operating drawbridge. **Pros:** on-site spa and dining; hospitable staff; homey feel. **Cons:** small rooms in main house; strict cancellation policy; blocks from the beach. Ⓢ *Rooms from: $149* ✉ *103 Flagler Ave.* ☎ *386/428–5858, 800/945–7416* ⊕ *www.riverviewhotel.com* ⤳ *17 rooms, 1 suite* ⵌ *Breakfast.*

OCALA NATIONAL FOREST

Eastern entrance 40 miles west of Daytona Beach, northern entrance 52 miles south of Jacksonville.

This breathtaking 383,000-acre national forest off Route 40 has lakes, springs, rivers, hiking trails, campgrounds, and historic sites. It also has the largest off-highway vehicle trail system in the Southeast and three major recreational areas: Alexander Springs, Salt Springs, and Juniper Springs. To get here, take Interstate 4 east to Exit 92, and head west on Route 436 to U.S. 441, which you take north to Route 19 north.

Alexander Springs Recreation Area. In this recreation area you'll find a stream for swimming, canoeing, and kayaking and a campground. ✉ *49525 Rte. 445 S, off Rte. 40, Altoona* ⊕ *www.fs.usda.gov/recarea/ocala* ⵌ *$5.50.*

Juniper Springs Recreation Area. Here you'll find a stone waterwheel house, a campground, a natural-spring swimming pool, and hiking trails. The 7-mile Juniper Springs run is a narrow, twisting, and winding canoe ride, which, although exhilarating, isn't for the novice. ⊠ *14100 Rte. 40 N, Silver Springs* ⊕ *www.fs.usda.gov/recarea/ocala* ⊠ *$5.*

Salt Springs Recreation Area. The draw here is a natural saltwater spring where Atlantic blue crabs come to spawn each summer. ⊠ *Visitor Center, 14100 Rte. 19, Fort McCoy* ☎ *352/685–3070* ⊠ *$6.*

SPORTS AND THE OUTDOORS

CANOEING

Juniper Springs Canoe Rentals. This operator inside the national forest offers canoe rentals. ⊠ *Juniper Springs Recreation Area, 26701 Florida 40, Silver Springs* ☎ *877/444–6777.*

FISHING

Captain Tom's Custom Charters. Charter fishing trips offered by this company range from two hours to a full day. You can arrange sightseeing cruises as well. Trips are by reservation only and are operated in a variety of areas within the national forest. ☎ *352/236–0872* ⊕ *www. captaintomscustomcharters.net/.*

HORSEBACK RIDING

Adopt a Horse Club. Located within the Ocala National Forest, this outfitter offers trail riding and lessons (walk, gait, and canter) for all ages. ⊠ *22651 S.E. Rte. 42, Umatilla* ☎ *352/821–4756, 800/731–4756* ⊕ *www.adoptahorseclub.com.*

GAINESVILLE

98 miles northwest of Daytona Beach.

The University of Florida (UF) anchors this sprawling town. Visitors are mostly Gator football fans and parents of students, so the styles and costs of accommodations are aimed at budget-minded travelers rather than luxury-seeking vacationers. The surrounding area encompasses several state parks and interesting gardens and geological sites.

GETTING HERE AND AROUND

Gainesville Regional Airport is served by American, Delta, United, and US Airways. From the airport, taxi fare to the center of Gainesville is about $20; some hotels provide free airport pickup.

Contact Gainesville Regional Airport (*GNV*). ⊠ *3880 N.E. 39th Ave.* ☎ *352/373–0249* ⊕ *www.gra-gnv.com.*

VISITOR INFORMATION

Contact Gainesville/Alachua County Visitors and Convention Bureau ☎ *352/374–5260, 866/778–5002* ⊕ *www.visitgainesville.com.*

EXPLORING

Devil's Millhopper Geological State Park. Scientists surmise that thousands of years ago an underground cavern collapsed and created this geological wonder that is designated as a National Natural Landmark. You pass a dozen small waterfalls as you head down 236 steps to the bottom of this botanical wonderland: exotic subtropical ferns and trees growing in a 500-foot-wide, 120-foot-deep sinkhole. You can pack a lunch to enjoy in one of the park's picnic areas. And bring Spot, too; just keep him on a leash. Guided walks with a park ranger are offered Saturday mornings at 10. ⊠ *4732 Millhopper Rd., off U.S. 441* ☎ *352/955–2008* ⊕ *www.floridastateparks.org/devilsmillhopper* 🖃 *$4 per vehicle, up to 8 people; $2 pedestrians and bicyclists* ⊘ *Wed.–Sun. 9–5.*

FAMILY **Florida Museum of Natural History.** On the campus of the University of Florida, the state's official museum of natural history and the largest natural-history museum in the Southeast has holdings of more than 40 million objects and specimens. In addition to active collections in anthropology, archaeology, botany, mammalogy, and ornithology, the museum features several interesting replicas, including nearly complete

fossil skeletons of a mastodon and mammoth from the last ice age as well as a full-size model of a Florida cave and mangrove forest. The Butterfly Rainforest houses 60 to 80 species in a 6,400-square-foot, screened, free-flight vivarium. Butterfly releases take place weekdays at 2, and weekends at 2, 3, and 4, weather permitting. The museum has changing temporary exhibits; kids eight and under will love Discovery Room, featuring interactive exhibits, a reading corner, and a building area. ⊠ *University of Florida Cultural Plaza, S.W. 34th St. and Hull Rd.* ☎ *352/846–2000* ⊕ *www.flmnh.ufl.edu* 🖃 *Free; Butterfly Rainforest $10.50; parking $4* ⊘ *Mon.–Sat. 10–5, Sun. 1–5.*

FAMILY **Marjorie Kinnan Rawlings Historic State Park.** One of America's most cherished authors found inspiration in this out-of-the-way hamlet about 20 miles outside of Gainesville. The 90-acre park, set amid aromatic citrus groves, has a playground for kids and short hiking trails, where you might see owls, deer, or Rawlings' beloved "red birds." But the main attraction is the restored Florida Cracker–style home, where Rawlings wrote classics such as *The Yearling* and *Cross Creek* and entertained the likes of poet Robert Frost, author Thornton Wilder, and actor Gregory Peck. Although the house is guarded closely by spirited roosters, guided tours ($3) are offered seasonally. ⊠ *18700 South County Rd. 325, Hawthorne* ☎ *352/466–3672* ⊕ *www.floridastateparks.org/marjoriekinnanrawlings* 🖃 *$3 per car; house tour is an additional $3* ⊘ *Daily 9–5; house tours Oct.–July, Thurs.–Sun. at 10, 11, 1, 2, 3, and 4.*

Samuel P. Harn Museum of Art. This 112,800-square-foot museum has five main collections: Asian, with works dating back to the Neolithic era; African, encompassing costumes, domestic wares, and personal adornments; Modern, featuring the works of Georgia O'Keeffe, William Morris Hunt, Claude Monet, and George Bellows; Contemporary, with original pieces by Yayoi Kusama and El Anatsui; and Photography, including the work of Jerry N. Uelsmann, a retired University of Florida professor. ⊠ *3259 Hull Rd.* ☎ *352/392–9826* ⊕ *www.harn.ufl.*

edu ✉ *Free* 🕒 *Tues.–Fri. 11–5, Sat. 10–5, Sun. 1–5, 2nd Thurs. evening of each month 6–9.*

WHERE TO EAT

$ ECLECTIC 🍴 **Bistro 1245.** You can get high-quality meals at bargain-basement prices at this trendy yet surprisingly down-to-earth restaurant, which shares a roof with Leonardo's by the Slice. Some call the small dining room cramped, while others find the close quarters romantic. However you look at it, the menu is full of comfort foods with a twist, such as maple-roasted chicken breast, spicy shrimp pasta, a seared-tuna club sandwich, and bison sirloin. In keeping with the bistro's lack of pretention, you're invited to pick your own wine from the restaurant's wine rack. For a lighter meal and a lighter price, order from the lunch menu in the evening. [$] *Average main: $13* ✉ *1245 W. University Ave.* ☎ *352/376–0000* 🌐 *www.leonardosgainesville.com.*

$$ LATIN AMERICAN 🍴 **Emiliano's Café.** Linen tablecloths and art deco–style artwork create a casual, elegant feel at this Gainesville institution serving Pan-Latin cuisine for more than 20 years. Dine indoors or beneath the stars at the sidewalk café. Start with the Spanish stew (a family recipe) and then move on to one of the chef's signature dishes such as Mofongo or Spanish saffron rice with shrimp, clams, mussels, fresh fish, chicken, artichoke hearts, peas, asparagus, and pimientos. Emiliano's also offers an extensive tapas menu with nearly 20 items to mix and match, and tempting desserts like the original chipotle brownie cake. Live jazz fills the air Monday and Wednesday nights. Weekends feature a brunch with $5 Bloody Marys and mojitos, and entrées such as the breakfast Cuban with eggs, pulled pork, and Swiss on pressed Cuban bread. [$] *Average main: $15* ✉ *7 S.E. 1st Ave.* ☎ *352/375–7381* 🌐 *www.emilianoscafe.com.*

$ ITALIAN 🍴 **Leonardo's by the Slice.** It's ironic that the kitschy pizza joint with 1950s flair is surrounded by a white-picket fence, since most of its patrons and employees are far from conventional. College students, especially the pierced and tatted kind, flock to the Gainesville landmark not only because it's cheap but because it has the best pizza in town. Available in thick or thin varieties, by the pie and, of course, by the slice, Leonardo's pizza comes in a handful of varieties (like veggie, pepperoni, Greek, and spinach tomato). It also offers calzones, salads, and pasta such as spaghetti and meatballs and fettuccine Alfredo, with no non-pizza entrée over $8.95. [$] *Average main: $12* ✉ *1245 W. University Ave.* ☎ *352/378–2001* 🌐 *www.leonardosgainesville.com* ✍ *Reservations not accepted.*

$$$ EUROPEAN Fodor's Choice ★ 🍴 **Paramount Grill.** This tiny, fine-dining restaurant may have single-handedly changed the perception of Gainesville from a college town fueled by pizza, chicken wings, and pitchers of beer to an up-and-coming culinary destination with imaginative menus driven by fresh Florida produce. What Paramount lacks in size and glitz it makes up for with its ever-changing menu. Try the organic beet salad and such entrées as grilled mahimahi over black beans, sweet potato and Cotija cheese enchiladas, or West Indian BBQ pork loin over white cheddar and corn pancakes. If you miss lunch here, try the Sunday brunch.

$ *Average main: $25* ✉ *12 S.W. 1st Ave.* ☎ *352/378–3398* ⊕ *www. paramountgrill.com* ⊘ *No lunch Sat.*

WHERE TO STAY

$
HOTEL
🏨 **Hilton University of Florida Conference Center Gainesville.** With 25,000 square feet of meeting space, the University of Florida's flagship hotel caters most obviously to business travelers, but its location on the southwest corner of campus also makes it a good choice for UF visitors. **Pros:** proximity to college; spacious rooms; free use of business center. **Cons:** spotty service; overrated restaurant; charge for Wi-Fi. $ *Rooms from: $143* ✉ *1714 S.W. 34th St.* ☎ *352/371–3600* ⊕ *www.hilton.com* ➨ *245 rooms, 3 suites* ⦿ *No meals.*

$
B&B/INN
🏨 **Laurel Oak Inn.** Guests at this 1885 Queen Anne–style dwelling say they're so comfortable and at ease they feel like they're in a home, not an inn. **Pros:** three-course breakfast; location; hospitable staff. **Cons:** processing fee for cancellations; no pool. $ *Rooms from: $140* ✉ *221 S.E. 7th St.* ☎ *352/373–4535* ⊕ *www.laureloakinn.com* ➨ *5 rooms* ⦿ *Breakfast.*

$
B&B/INN
Fodor's Choice
★
🏨 **Magnolia Plantation Inn.** Among only a handful of French Second Empire buildings in the southeastern United States, this inn consists of a main house, built in 1885, and six adorable cottages. **Pros:** friendly service; breakfast; nightly social hour. **Cons:** some small rooms; seven-day cancellation policy. $ *Rooms from: $145* ✉ *309 S.E. 7th St.* ☎ *352/375–6653, 800/201–2379* ⊕ *www.magnoliabnb.com* ➨ *5 rooms, 9 cottages* ⦿ *Breakfast.*

$
B&B/INN
🏨 **Sweetwater Branch Inn Bed & Breakfast.** Modern conveniences such as hair dryers, complimentary Wi-Fi, a new pool, and business services mix with Southern charm and hospitality, all wrapped up in two grand Victorian homes surrounded by lush tropical gardens. **Pros:** Southern-style breakfast; Jacuzzi suites. **Cons:** occasional noise issues; frequent on-site weddings. $ *Rooms from: $139* ✉ *625 E. University Ave.* ☎ *352/373–6760, 800/595–7760* ⊕ *www.sweetwaterinn.com* ➨ *12 rooms, 8 cottages* ⦿ *Breakfast.*

NIGHTLIFE

Lillian's Music Store. Gainesville's oldest bar has rock and Top 40 music, bands, and Jam Night every Monday. ✉ *112 S.E. 1st St.* ☎ *352/372–1010.*

1982 Bar. There's music, comedy, theater, and a wide variety of video games at this full-service café/bar. ✉ *919 W. University Ave.* ☎ *352/371–9836* ⊕ *www.1982bar.com.*

The Swamp Restaurant. This place attracts college students by the pitcher, especially on game day. ✉ *1642 W. University Ave.* ☎ *352/377–9267* ⊕ *www.swamprestaurant.com.*

SPORTS AND THE OUTDOORS

AUTO RACING

Auto Plus Raceway. The site of professional and amateur auto and motorcycle races, including Gatornationals in March, is also home to Frank Hawley's Drag Racing School (☎ *866/480–7223* ⊕ *www.*

frankhawley.com). ✉ *11211 N. County Rd. 225* ☎ *352/377–0046* ⊕ *www.autoplusraceway.com.*

FOOTBALL

Ben Hill Griffin Stadium. The University of Florida Gators play their home games in the largest stadium in the state, also referred to as "The Swamp." ✉ *Lemerand Dr. and Stadium Rd.* ☎ *352/375–4683.*

THE SPACE COAST

13

Updated by Jennifer Greenhill-Taylor

South of the Daytona Beach area and Canaveral National Seashore are Merritt Island National Wildlife Refuge, the John F. Kennedy Space Center, and Cape Canaveral—hence the name "Space Coast." This area is also home to the laid-back town of Cocoa Beach, which attracts visitors on weekends year-round because it's the closest beach to Orlando, 50 miles to the east.

VISITOR INFORMATION

Contact Space Coast Office of Tourism ☎ 877/572–3224, 321/433–4470 ⊕ *www.visitspacecoast.com.*

TITUSVILLE

34 miles south of New Smyrna Beach, 67 miles east of Orlando.

It's unusual that such a small, easily overlooked community could accommodate what it does, namely the magnificent Merritt Island National Wildlife Refuge and the entrance to the Kennedy Space Center, the nerve center of the U.S. space program.

EXPLORING

American Police Hall of Fame & Museum. Police officers deserve our respect, and you'll be reminded why at this intriguing attraction. In addition to memorabilia like the *Robocop* costume and *Blade Runner* car from the films, informative displays offer insight into the dangers officers face every day: drugs, homicides, and criminals who can create knives from dental putty and guns from a bicycle spoke. Other exhibits spotlight the gory history of capital punishment (from hangings to the guillotine to the electric chair) and crime scene investigation, terrorism, and a rotunda where more than 9,000 names are etched in marble to honor police officers who have died in the line of duty. A 24-stall shooting range provides rental guns. ✉ *6350 Horizon Dr.* ☎ *321/264–0911* ⊕ *www.aphf.org* 🎟 *$13* 🕐 *Museum: Tues.–Sun. noon–7. Shooting Range: Tues.–Fri. noon–8, weekends noon–6.*

FAMILY

Fodor's Choice
★

Kennedy Space Center Visitor Complex. America's space program—past, present, and future—is the star at this must-see attraction, just 45 minutes east of Orlando, where visitors are treated to interactive experiences, two spectacular IMAX movies, bus tours, and more. Located on a 140,000-acre barrier island, Kennedy Space Center was NASA's launch headquarters from the beginning of the space program in the 1960s until the final shuttle launch in 2012. Thanks to an invigorated NASA program and to high-tech entrepreneurs who have turned their interests to space, visitors to the complex can once again view live rocket

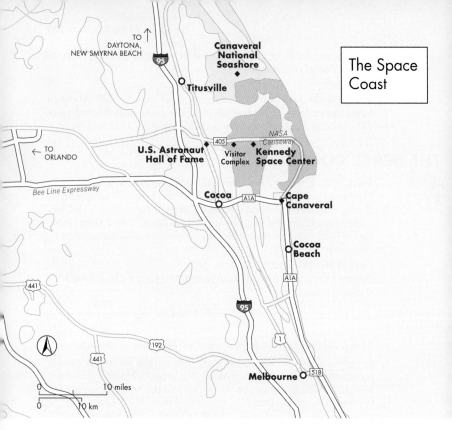

launches from the Cape. In fact, there were 24 launches scheduled in 2015—even more in 2016 (check the website for launch schedule).

The newest IMAX film, *Journey To Space*, narrated by *Star Trek* legend Sir Patrick Stewart, fills a five-story movie screen with dramatic footage shot by NASA astronauts during missions, accentuating the bravery of all space travelers while capturing the spirit of the human desire to explore and expand. The film honors the milestones of the Space Shuttle Program—deploying and repairing the Hubble Space Telescope, assembling the International Space Station—and then looks forward to the deep-space exploration missions to come, offering a glimpse of the Space Launch System rocket that will send the Orion crew capsule toward Mars.

The drama of the IMAX films gives you great background for the many interactive programs available at the complex. The bus tour included with admission (buses depart every 15 minutes) takes you past iconic spots, including the 525-foot-tall Vehicle Assembly Building and launch pads which are getting ready for future missions. Stops include the Apollo/Saturn V Center, where you can look up in awe at one of three remaining Saturn V moon rockets, the largest rocket ever built. Other exhibits include the Early Space Exploration display, which highlights the rudimentary yet influential Mercury and Gemini space programs;

and the Lunar Theater, which shows the first moon landing. Visitors can dine next to a genuine moon rock at the cleverly named Moon Rock Café.

Several Up-Close tours offer more intimate views of the VAB, the Shuttle Landing Facility, the runway where the shuttles landed (now slated for use by the Sierra Nevada *Dream Chaser,* one of the commercial spacecraft under development), and the Cape Canaveral launch pads, where NASA, SpaceX, and the United Launch Alliance rockets await takeoff. Other iconic images include the countdown clock at NASA's Press Site, a giant crawler transporter that carried Apollo moon rockets and space shuttles to the launch pad, and the Launch Control Center. The Then and Now Guided Tour (extra charge), visits America's first launch sites from the 1960s and the 21st century's active unmanned-rocket program.

The space shuttle *Atlantis* attraction offers views of this historic space-craft as only astronauts have seen it—rotated 43.21 degrees with pay-load bay doors open and its robotic arm extended, as if it has just undocked from the International Space Station. The attraction includes a variety of interactive highlights, including opportunities to perform an Extravehicular Activity (EVA), train like an astronaut, and create sonic booms while piloting *Atlantis* to a safe landing.

Don't miss the outdoor Rocket Garden, with walkways winding beside a group of historic vintage rockets, from early Atlas spacecraft to a *Saturn IB*. The Children's Playdome enables kids to play among the next generation of spacecraft, climb a moon-rock wall, and crawl through rocket tunnels. Astronaut Encounter Theater has two daily programs where retired NASA astronauts share their adventures in space travel and show a short film.

More befitting a theme park (complete with the health warnings), the Shuttle Launch Experience is the center's most spectacular attraction. Designed by a team of astronauts, NASA experts, and renowned attraction engineers, the 44,000-square-foot structure uses a sophisticated motion-based platform, special-effects seats, and high-fidelity visual and audio components to simulate the sensations experienced in an actual space-shuttle launch, including MaxQ, Solid Rocker Booster separation, main engine cutoff, and External Tank separation. The journey culminates with a breathtaking view of Earth from space.

A fitting way to end the day is a stop at the black-granite Astronaut Memorial, which honors those who lost their lives in the name of space exploration.

Other add-ons include Lunch with an Astronaut, where astronauts talk about their experiences and engage in a good-natured Q&A; the typical line of questioning from kids: "How do you eat/sleep/relieve yourself in space?" ✉ *Kennedy Space Center, Rte. 405* ☎ *877/313–2610* ⊕ *www. kennedyspacecenter.com* 🛥 *$50 (includes bus tour, IMAX movies, visi-tor complex shows and exhibits, and Astronaut Hall of Fame); specialty tours $21–$25; lunch with an astronaut $29.99* ☉ *Daily 9–5; last regu-lar tour 2½ hrs before closing. Call ahead if visiting on a launch day.*

United States Astronaut Hall of Fame. The original *Mercury 7* team and the later *Gemini, Apollo, Skylab,* and shuttle astronauts contributed artifacts and memorabilia to make the hall of fame the world's premium archive of astronauts' personal stories. Authentic equipment from their collections help tell the tale of human space exploration. You can watch videotapes of historic moments in the space program and see one-of-a-kind items such as Wally Schirra's *Sigma 7* Mercury space capsule, Gus Grissom's space suit (colored silver only because NASA thought silver looked more "spacey"), and a flag that made it to the moon. The exhibit First on the Moon focuses on crew selection for *Apollo 11* and the Soviet Union's role in the space race. Don't miss Simulation Station, a hands-on discovery center with interactive exhibits that help you learn about space travel. One of the more challenging activities is a space-shuttle simulator that lets you try your hand at landing the craft—and afterward replays a side view of your rolling and pitching descent.

If you want to live the life of an astronaut, consider enrolling in Astronaut Training Experience (ATX, $175). Held at the Hall of Fame, it immerses you in an exciting combination of hands-on training and preparation for the rigors of space flight. Veteran NASA astronauts helped design the program, and you hear first-hand from them as you progress through an exciting day of mission simulation and exploration at the busiest launch facility on Earth. The cost includes spaceflight simulators, full-scale space shuttle mission simulation, meet and greet with a NASA astronaut, and ATX gear. Age restrictions apply. Space is limited (no pun intended), so call well in advance. ⊠ *6225 Vectorspace Blvd.* ☎ *877/737–5235* ⊕ *www.kennedyspacecenter.com* ⊠ *$27 Hall of Fame only; included in KSC Visitor Complex admission ($50)* ⊙ *Opens daily at noon, closing times vary by season (call for details).*

Valiant Air Command Warbird Museum & Tico Airshow. Don't judge a book by its cover: what's inside this very ordinary looking building that is extraordinary. Operated mostly through the efforts of an enthusiastic team of volunteers, the museum is a treasure trove of aviation history, with memorabilia from World Wars I and II, Korea, and Vietnam, as well as extensive displays of vintage military flying gear and uniforms. There are posters that were used to help identify Japanese planes, plus a Huey helicopter and the cockpit of an F-106 that you can sit in. In the north hangar a group of dedicated aviation volunteers busily restores old planes. It's an inspiring sight, and a good place to hear some war stories. In the spring the museum puts on the Tico Warbird Airshow, featuring fighter and bomber aircraft that formerly flew in combat around the world. The lobby gift shop sells real flight suits, old flight magazines, bomber jackets, books, models, and T-shirts. ⊠ *6600 Tico Rd.* ☎ *321/268–1941* ⊕ *www.vacwarbirds.org* ⊠ *$20* ⊙ *Daily 9–5.*

BEACHES

Playalinda Beach. The southern access for the Canaveral National Seashore, remote Playalinda Beach has pristine sands and is the longest stretch of undeveloped coast on Florida's Atlantic seaboard. You can, however, see the shuttle launch pad at Cape Kennedy from the beach. Hundreds of giant sea turtles come ashore here from May through August to lay their eggs. Fourteen parking lots anchor the beach at

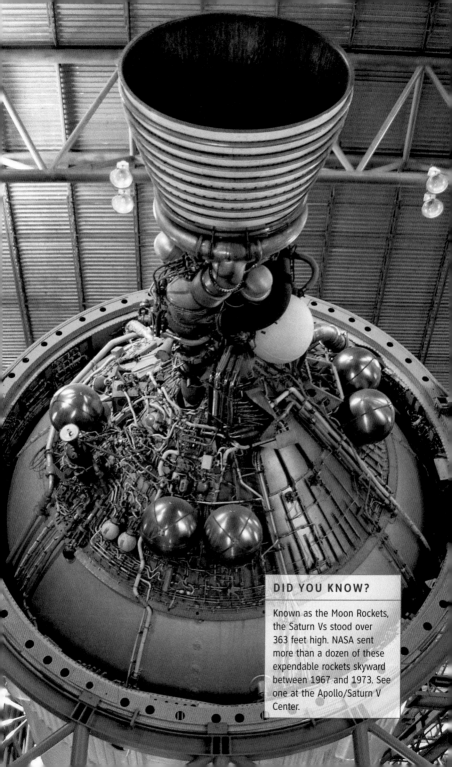

1-mile intervals. From Interstate 95, take Exit 249 and head east. Bring bug repellent in case of horseflies, and note that you may see some unauthorized clothing-optional activity. **Amenities:** lifeguards (seasonal); parking (fee); toilets. **Best for:** solitude; swimming; walking. ✉ *Rte. 402, at northern end of Beach Rd.* ☎ *321/267–1110* 🌐 *www.nps.gov/cana* 🎫 *$5 per vehicle for national seashore.*

WHERE TO EAT

$$ SEAFOOD 🍴 **Dixie Crossroads.** This sprawling restaurant is always crowded and festive, but it's not just the rustic setting that draws the throngs—it's the seafood. The specialty is rock shrimp, which are served fried, broiled, or steamed. Diners with a hearty appetite can opt for the all-you-can-eat shrimp or snow crab, or, if seafood isn't your choice, the menu offers steaks, chicken, pork and ribs. You might have to wait (up to 90 minutes) for a table, but if you don't have time to wait, you can order takeout or use the call-ahead seating option. A word to the wise: when that basket of corn fritters dusted with powdered sugar appears like magic on your table, try not to fill up on them. [$] *Average main: $23* ✉ *1475 Garden St., 2 miles east of I–95 Exit 220* ☎ *321/268–5000* 🌐 *www.dixiecrossroads.com* ✍ *Reservations not accepted.*

WHERE TO STAY

$ HOTEL 🏨 **Hampton Inn Titusville.** Proximity to the Kennedy Space Center and reasonable rates make this four-story hotel a top pick for an overnight near the center. **Pros:** free Wi-Fi; extra-comfy beds; convenient to I–95. **Cons:** thin walls; no restaurant on-site; no room service. [$] *Rooms from: $139* ✉ *4760 Helen Hauser Blvd.* ☎ *321/383–9191* 🌐 *www.hamptoninn.com* 🛏 *86 rooms, 4 suites* 🍽 *Breakfast.*

SPORTS AND THE OUTDOORS

Fodor's Choice ★ **Merritt Island National Wildlife Refuge.** Owned by the National Aeronautics and Space Administration (NASA), this 140,000-acre refuge, which adjoins the Canaveral National Seashore, acts as a buffer around Kennedy Space Center while protecting 1,000 species of plants and 500 species of wildlife, including 15 considered federally threatened or endangered. It's an immense area dotted by brackish estuaries and marshes, coastal dunes, hardwood hammocks, and pine forests. You can borrow field guides and binoculars at the visitor center (5 miles east of U.S. 1 in Titusville on State Road 402) to track down falcons, ospreys, eagles, turkeys, doves, cuckoos, owls, and woodpeckers, as well as loggerhead turtles, alligators, wild boar and otters. A 20-minute video about refuge wildlife and accessibility—only 10,000 acres are developed—can help orient you.

You might take a self-guided driving tour along the 7-mile Black Point Wildlife Drive. On the Oak Hammock Foot Trail you can see wintering migratory waterfowl and learn about the plants of a hammock community. If you exit the north end of the refuge, look for the Manatee Observation Area just north of the Haulover Canal (maps are at the visitor center). They usually show up in spring and fall. There are also fishing camps, fishing boat ramps, and six hiking trails scattered throughout the area. If you do want to fish, a free, downloadable permit is required. Most of the refuge is closed 24 hours prior to a launch.

✉ *Visitor center, Rte. 402, 5 miles east of U.S. 1 across Titusville Causeway* ☎ *321/861–0667, 321/861–0669 visitor center* ⊕ *www.fws.gov/ merrittisland* ✎ *Free; $5 per vehicle on Black Point Wildlife Dr. only* ⊗ *Daily sunrise–sunset; visitor center daily 9–4.*

COCOA

17 miles south of Titusville.

Not to be confused with the seaside community of Cocoa Beach, the small town of Cocoa sits smack-dab on mainland Florida and faces the Intracoastal Waterway, known locally as Indian River. There's a planetarium and a museum, as well as a rustic fish camp along the St. Johns River, a few miles inland.

Folks in a rush to get to the beach tend to overlook Cocoa's Victorian-style village, but it's worth a stop and is perhaps Cocoa's most interesting feature. Within the cluster of restored turn-of-the-20th-century buildings and cobblestone walkways you can enjoy several restaurants, indoor and outdoor cafés, snack and ice-cream shops, and more than 50 specialty shops and art galleries. The area hosts music performances in the gazebo, arts-and-crafts shows, and other family-friendly events throughout the year. To get to Cocoa Village, head east on Route 520—named King Street in Cocoa—and when the streets get narrow and the road curves, make a right onto Brevard Avenue; follow the signs for the free municipal parking lot.

EXPLORING

FAMILY **Brevard Museum of History & Natural Science.** This is the place to come to see what the lay of the local land looked like in other eras. Hands-on activities draw children, who especially migrate toward the Imagination Center, where they can act out history or reenact a space shuttle flight. Not to be missed are Ice Age era creatures such as a fully articulated mastadon, giant ground sloth, and saber-tooth cat. The Windover Archaeological Exhibit features 7,000-year-old artifacts indigenous to the region. In 1984, a shallow pond revealed the burial ground of more than 200 American Indians who lived in the area about 7,000 years ago. Preserved in the muck were bones and, to the archeologists' surprise, the brains of these ancient people. Nature lovers appreciate the museum's butterfly garden and the nature center with 22 acres of trails encompassing three distinct ecosystems—sand pine hills, lake lands, and marshlands. ✉ *2201 Michigan Ave.* ☎ *321/632–1830* ⊕ *www. brevardmuseum.org* ✎ *$9* ⊗ *Wed.–Sat. 10–5.*

WHERE TO EAT

$$$ ✕ **Café Margaux.** Eclectic, creative, and international is the best way
ECLECTIC to describe the cuisine and decor at this charming Cocoa Village spot,
Fodor's Choice featured in 2015 on the Food Network. The menu blends French, Italian, and Asian influences with dishes such as lollipop pork chop over
★ English pea–and–orzo risotto, sweet onion–crusted fresh red snapper, and braised veal scaloppine. Themed dining rooms are elaborately decorated with dramatic window treatments, wallpaper, and artwork. An outdoor courtyard with umbrella tables adds to the Continental flair.

$ *Average main: $26* ✉ *220 Brevard Ave.* ☎ *321/639–8343* ⊕ *www. margaux.com* ✆ *Closed Sun.*

$ ✕ **Lone Cabbage Fish Camp.** The word "rustic" doesn't even begin to
ECLECTIC describe this down-home, no-nonsense fish camp restaurant (translation: you eat off paper plates with plastic forks) housed in a weathered,
old, clapboard shack along with a bait shop and airboat-tour company.
Set your calorie counter on stun, as you peruse the plates of fried fish,
frogs' legs, turtle, and alligator (as well as burgers and hot dogs). Dine
inside or on the outdoor deck overlooking the St. Johns River with
live music every Sunday. Who knows, you might even see your dinner
swimming by. $ *Average main: $10* ✉ *8199 Rte. 520, at St. Johns River*
☎ *321/632–4199* ⚔ *Reservations not accepted.*

SHOPPING

Cocoa Village. You could spend hours browsing in the more than 50
boutiques here, along Brevard Avenue and Harrison Street (the latter
has the densest concentration of shops). Although most stores are of the
gift and clothing variety, the village is also home to antiques shops, art
galleries, restaurants, a tattoo parlor, and a spa. ✉ *Rte. 520 and Brevard
Ave.* ☎ *321/631–9075* ⊕ *www.visitcocoavillage.com.*

Renninger's Super Flea & Farmers' Market. You're sure to find a bargain at
one of the 800-plus booths at this market, which is held every Friday,
Saturday, and Sunday from 9 to 4. ✉ *4835 W. Eau Gallie Blvd., Melbourne* ☎ *321/242–9124* ⊕ *www.superfleamarket.com.*

SPORTS AND THE OUTDOORS
BOATING

Twister Airboat Rides. If you haven't seen the swampy, alligator-ridden
waters of Florida, then you haven't really seen Florida. This thrilling
wildlife tour goes where eagles and wading birds coexist with water
moccasins and gators. The Coast Guard–certified deluxe airboats hit
speeds of up to 45 mph and offer unparalleled opportunities to photograph native species. The basic tour lasts 30 minutes, but 60- and
90-minute ecotours are also available at an additional cost by reservation only. Twister Airboat Rides is inside the Lone Cabbage Fish
Camp, about 9 miles west of Cocoa's city limits, 4 miles west of Interstate 95. ✉ *8199 Rte. 520, at St. Johns River* ☎ *321/632–4199* ⊕ *www.
twisterairboatrides.com* ✆ *$22* ✆ *Daily 10–4:30.*

CAPE CANAVERAL

5 miles east of Cocoa via Rte. A1A.

The once-bustling commercial fishing area of Cape Canaveral is still
home to a small shrimping fleet, charter boats, and party fishing boats,
but its main business these days is as a cruise-ship port. The north end
of the port, where the Carnival, Disney, and Royal Caribbean cruise
lines set sail, has some good waterfront restaurants, with big viewing
decks. Port Canaveral is now Florida's second-busiest cruise port for
multiday cruises, which makes this a great place to catch a glimpse of
these giant ships. It's also a great place to catch sight of an unmanned
rocket being launched from Cape Canaveral Air Force Base.

13

EXPLORING

FAMILY **Exploration Tower.** The best view at Port Canaveral is no longer from the top of your cruise ship. In fact, the view from atop this towering seven-story structure, which opened in late 2013, makes the cruise ships look—well, not so massive after all. The tower, a short walk from the cruise port, is equal parts museum and scenic overlook. The seventh-floor observation deck offers impressive views of the cruise port, the Atlantic Ocean, the Banana River, and even the Vehicle Assembly Building at Kennedy Space Center. Other floors house exhibits highlighting cultural history of the area, from space flight to surfing, bird and sea life to the rich maritime history. Kids will enjoy interactive exhibits, including a virtual ship's bridge that allows you to pilot a boat through the Canaveral Channel and into the Atlantic. A theater shows a 20-minute film dedicated to the history of Brevard County, and a small café sells refreshments and baked goods. The ground floor houses a visitor information center. ✉ *670 Dave Nisbet Dr.* ☎ *321/394–3408* 🌐 *www.explorationtower.com* 🎟 *$6.50* 🕒 *Daily 10–7.*

BEACHES

Jetty Park. A wonderful taste of the real Florida, this 4½-acre beach and oceanfront campground has picnic pavilions, bike paths, and a 1,200-foot-long fishing pier that doubles as a perfect vantage point from which to watch a liftoff from Cape Canaveral or to glimpse the gigantic cruise ships as they depart the port for the Bahamas. Lifeguards are on duty year-round, and all manner of equipment from beach chairs and umbrellas to boogie boards to beach wheelchairs is available for rent. A jetty constructed of giant boulders adds to the landscape, and a walkway that crosses it provides access to a less populated stretch of beach. Real and rustic, this is Florida without the theme-park varnish. **Amenities:** food and drink; lifeguards; parking (fee); showers; toilets; water sports. **Best for:** sunrise; surfing; swimming; walking. ✉ *400 Jetty Rd.* ☎ *321/783–7111* 🌐 *www.jettyparkbeachandcampground.com* 🎟 *$5–$10 cars, $7–$15 RVs.*

WHERE TO EAT

$ SEAFOOD 🍴 **Seafood Atlantic.** Locals think of this casual waterfront seafood market/eatery as a well-kept secret, but more and more cruise patrons are making their way here for a pre- or postcruise treat. The market is connected to the restaurant, guaranteeing not only freshness but an array of choices. You don't just order a fish sandwich or plate of steamed shrimp; you choose from at least four varieties of fish (try the Golden Tile in season) and several varieties of shrimp (the Royal Reds may be the best you've ever tasted). Seating is alfresco, with views of the Port Canaveral waterway and passing cruise ships. Best for lunch or an early dinner, the restaurant closes at 8 on Friday and Saturday, earlier other nights. [$] *Average main: $15* ✉ *520 Glen Cheek Dr.* ☎ *321/784–1963* 🌐 *www.seafoodatlantic.net* ✍ *Reservations not accepted* 🕒 *Closed Tues.*

$$ THAI 🍴 **Thai Thai III.** The mouthwatering photos on the menu aren't just a marketing ploy. The pictures don't do the real stuff justice. Locals and cruise-ship vacationers frequent this casual Thai/Japanese eatery within walking distance of cruise-port hotels. Seafood is an emphasis here, with specialties like lobster pad thai and snapper with ginger and scallion.

The Thai curries, noodles, and soups can be prepared "Thai hot," but "medium" packs a subtle punch, too. On the sushi side, try the Beauty and the Beast roll: half tuna, half eel, with avocado, asparagus, scallions, and roe. Decor is eclectic and relaxing, with brightly painted walls and low-hanging sconces. Don't fret if you see a crowd out front. The place does a brisk take-out business. $ *Average main: $20* ⊠ *8660 Astronaut Blvd.* ☎ *321/784–1561* ⊕ *www.thaithai3.com.*

WHERE TO STAY

$ ▥ **Radisson Resort at the Port.** For cruise-ship passengers who can't wait
HOTEL   to get under way, this splashy resort, done up in pink and turquoise, already feels like the Caribbean. **Pros:** cruise-ship convenience; pool area; free shuttle; free Wi-Fi. **Cons:** rooms around the pool can be noisy; loud air-conditioning in some rooms; no complimentary breakfast. $ *Rooms from: $123* ⊠ *8701 Astronaut Blvd.* ☎ *321/784–0000, 888/201–1718* ⊕ *www.radisson.com/capecanaveralfl* ↦ *284 rooms, 72 suites* ¶◎¶ *No meals.*

$ ▥ **Residence Inn Cape Canaveral/Cocoa Beach.** Billing itself as the closest
HOTEL   all-suites hotel to the Kennedy Space Center, this four-story Residence Inn, painted cheery yellow, is also convenient to other area attractions such as Port Canaveral, the Cocoa Beach Pier, the Brevard Zoo, and Cocoa Village, and is only an hour from the Magic Kingdom. **Pros:** helpful staff; free breakfast buffet; free Wi-Fi; pet-friendly. **Cons:** less than picturesque views; street noise in some rooms. $ *Rooms from: $189* ⊠ *8959 Astronaut Blvd.* ☎ *321/323–1100, 800/331–3131* ⊕ *www.marriott.com* ↦ *150 suites* ¶◎¶ *Breakfast.*

SHOPPING

Cove Marketplace. Whether you're at Port Canaveral for a cruise or are just passing through, this retail marketplace on the south side of the harbor has enough shops, restaurants, and entertainment venues to keep you occupied. Since most of the bars and eateries are located on the public waterfront area, you'll have a view of the cruise ships—and their colorful passengers. ⊠ *Glen Cheek Dr., at Scallop Dr., Port Canaveral* ⊕ *www.portcanaveral.com/covemarketplace* ⊡ *Free* ⊙ *Hrs vary by business.*

COCOA BEACH

5 miles south of Cape Canaveral, 58 miles southeast of Orlando.

After crossing a long and high bridge just east of Cocoa Village, you drop down upon a barrier island. A few miles farther and you'll reach the Atlantic Ocean and picture-perfect Cocoa Beach at Route A1A.

In the early 1960s Cocoa Beach was a sleepy, little-known town. But in 1965 the sitcom *I Dream of Jeannie* premiered. The endearing show centered on an astronaut, played by Larry Hagman, and his "Jeannie" in a bottle, Barbara Eden, and was set in Cocoa Beach. Though the series was never shot in Florida, creator Sidney Sheldon paid homage to the town with local references to Cape Kennedy (now known as the Kennedy Space Center) and Bernard's Surf restaurant. Today the town and its lovely beach are mecca to Florida's surfing community.

VISITOR INFORMATION

Contacts Cocoa Beach Convention and Visitors Bureau ☎ *321/454–2022, 877/321–8474* ⊕ *www.visitcocoabeach.com.*

EXPLORING

Cocoa Beach Pier. By day, it's a good place to stroll—if you don't mind weather-worn wood and sandy, watery paths. Although most of the pier is free to walk on, there's a small charge to enter the fishing area at the end of the 800-foot-long boardwalk (even to look around), and a separate fishing fee. You can rent rods and reels here for an additional $15. Surf competitions can be viewed from the pier, as it's a popular surf spot. By night, visitors and locals—beach bums and surfers among them—head here to party. Weekends see live music. ■TIP→ **The pier is a great place to watch launches from Kennedy Space Center or Cape Canaveral.** ⊠ *401 Meade Ave.* ☎ *321/783–7549* ⊕ *www.cocoabeachpier.com* ⌂ *$2, $7 to fish.*

13

BEACHES

Cocoa Beach. This is one of the Space Coast's nicest beaches—and the place where the great professional surfer Kelly Slater got his start. The beach boasts one of the steadiest surf breaks on the East Coast and has wide stretches that are excellent for biking, jogging, power walking, and strolling. In some places there are dressing rooms, showers, playgrounds, picnic areas with grills, snack shops, and surfside parking lots. Beach vendors offer necessities, and lifeguards are on duty in the summer.

A popular entry road, Route 520 crosses the Banana River into Cocoa Beach. At its east end, 5-acre **Alan Shepard Park,** named for the famous astronaut, aptly provides excellent views of launches from Kennedy Space Center and Cape Canaveral. Facilities here include 10 picnic pavilions, shower and restroom facilities, and more than 300 parking spaces. Beach vendors carry necessities for sunning and swimming. Parking is $7, $10 on weekends and holidays March through Labor Day. Shops and restaurants are within walking distance. Another enticing Cocoa Beach entry point is 10-acre **Sidney Fischer Park,** in the 2100 block of Route A1A in the central beach area. It has showers, playgrounds, changing areas, picnic areas with grills, snack shops, and plenty of well-maintained, inexpensive parking lots ($5 for cars). **Amenities:** food and drink; lifeguards (summer); parking (fee); showers; toilets; water sports. **Best for:** sunrise; surfing; swimming; walking. ⊠ *Rte. A1A from Cape Canaveral to Patrick Air Force Base, 401 Meade Ave.*

WHERE TO EAT

$$$

GERMAN

✕ **Heidelberg.** As the name suggests, the cuisine here is definitely German, from the sauerbraten served with potato dumplings and red cabbage to the beef Stroganoff and spaetzle to the classically prepared Wiener schnitzel. All the soups and desserts are homemade; try the Viennese-style apple strudel and the rum-zapped almond-cream tortes. But if German specialties are not your favorites, there are other European-influenced dishes aplenty. Elegant interior touches include crisp linens and fresh flowers. There's live music Wednesday through Saturday evenings. You can also dine inside the jazz club, Heidi's, next

The Cocoa Beach Pier is a magnet for nightlife in Cocoa Beach.

door. $ *Average main: $29 ⊠ 7 N. Orlando Ave., opposite City Hall ☎ 321/783–6806 ⊕ www.heidelbergcocoabeach.com ♥ Closed Mon. and Tues. No lunch Sun.*

$ **✕ Keith's Oyster Bar.** At the only open-air seafood bar on the beach, at the
SEAFOOD entrance of the Cocoa Beach Pier, the main item is oysters, served on the half shell. You can also grab a fish sandwich or burger here, crab legs by the pound, or one of the popular buckets of steamed shrimp or coconut shrimp. Drinks range from beer (the best accompaniment to oysters) to cocktails sporting paper umbrellas. The atmosphere is ultracasual (e.g., plastic chairs) and laid back, just what you'd expect on a fishing pier. During high season, there's live entertainment on Wednesday, Friday, Saturday, and Sunday. $ *Average main: $14 ⊠ 401 Meade Ave., Cocoa Beach Pier ☎ 321/783–7549 ⊕ www.cocoabeachpier.com.*

WHERE TO STAY

$ **⚑ Best Western Oceanfront Hotel & Suites.** Families love this Best West-
HOTEL ern for its affordable suites; everyone loves it for its oceanfront location (just a half block from the Cocoa Beach Pier), the great views of launches from Kennedy Space Center and Cape Canaveral, and the fact that it's just five minutes from the cruise ships at Port Canaveral. **Pros:** free Wi-Fi and HBO; free parking; complimentary hot breakfast; cruise terminal shuttle. **Cons:** not all rooms have an ocean view; small bathrooms; noise from the pier. $ *Rooms from: $169 ⊠ 5600 N. Atlantic Ave. ☎ 321/783–7621, 800/962–0028 ⊕ www.bestwesterncocoabeach. com ⤴ 230 rooms, 62 suites ⑩ Breakfast.*

$$ **DoubleTree by Hilton Cocoa Beach Oceanfront.** Proximity to the beach
HOTEL and comforts like in-room microwaves and refrigerators—and Double-
Tree's famous chocolate-chip walnut cookies—make this six-story hotel
a favorite of vacationing families, particularly Orlandoans on weekend
getaways. **Pros:** private beach access; comfy beds; complimentary park-
ing. **Cons:** extra charge for beach-chair rental; thin walls; slow eleva-
tors. $ *Rooms from: $224* ✉ *2080 N. Atlantic Ave.* ☎ *321/783–9222*
⊕ *www.cocoabeachdoubletree.com* ⤳ *148 rooms, 12 suites* ¶◎¶*No
meals.*

$ **Hilton Cocoa Beach Oceanfront.** You can't get any closer to the beach
HOTEL than this seven-story oceanfront hotel. **Pros:** beachfront; friendly staff.
Cons: fees for Wi-Fi and parking; small pool and bathrooms; no bal-
conies; room windows don't open. $ *Rooms from: $179* ✉ *1550 N.
Atlantic Ave.* ☎ *321/799–0003* ⊕ *www.hiltoncocoabeach.com* ⤳ *285
rooms, 11 suites* ¶◎¶ *No meals.*

$ **Inn at Cocoa Beach.** This charming oceanfront inn has spacious, indi-
B&B/INN vidually decorated rooms with four-poster beds, upholstered chairs,
and balconies or patios; most have ocean views. **Pros:** quiet; romantic;
honor bar. **Cons:** no on-site restaurant; "forced" socializing. $ *Rooms
from: $165* ✉ *4300 Ocean Beach Blvd.* ☎ *321/799–3460, 800/343–
5307 outside Florida* ⊕ *www.theinnatcocoabeach.com* ⤳ *50 rooms*
¶◎¶ *Breakfast.*

$$ **The Resort on Cocoa Beach.** Even if the beach weren't in its backyard,
RESORT this family-friendly, oceanfront property offers enough activities and
FAMILY amenities—from tennis and basketball courts to a game room, pool, and
Fodor'sChoice 50-seat movie theater—to keep everyone entertained. **Pros:** kids activi-
★ ties; full kitchens; in-room washers and dryers; large balconies; free
Wi-Fi. **Cons:** check-in not until 4 and checkout at 10; not all rooms
are oceanfront; slow elevators. $ *Rooms from: $245* ✉ *1600 N. Atlantic
Ave.* ☎ *321/783–4000, 866/469–8222* ⊕ *www.theresortoncocoabeach.
com* ⤳ *124 suites* ¶◎¶ *No meals.*

NIGHTLIFE

The Cocoa Beach Pier has several nightspots as well as live-music sessions a couple of nights a week.

Heidi's Jazz Club. Local and nationally known jazz musicians (Boots
Randolph and Mose Allison have taken the stage) play Tuesday through
Sunday, with showcase acts appearing on weekends. ✉ *7 Orlando Ave.
N* ☎ *321/783–4559.*

SHOPPING

Merritt Square Mall. The area's only major shopping mall is about a
20-minute ride from the beach. Stores include Macy's, Dillard's, JCPenney, Sears, Foot Locker, Island Surf and Skate, and roughly 100 others. It's an indoor mall, a rapidly diminishing fixture in the Florida
landscape, making for comfortable shopping in the heat of summer.
There's a 16-screen multiplex, along with a food court and several
restaurant chains. ✉ *777 E. Merritt Island Causeway, Merritt Island*
☎ *321/452–3270* ⊕ *www.merritsquaremall.com.*

13

SPORTS AND THE OUTDOORS
KAYAKING
Adventure Kayak of Cocoa Beach. Specializing in manatee encounters, this outfitter organizes one- and two-person kayak tours of mangroves, channels, and islands. Tours launch from various locations in the Cocoa Beach area. Rates run about $30 per person. ⊠ *599 Ramp Rd.* ☎ *321/480–8632* ⊕ *www.kayakcocoabeach.com.*

SURFING
Cocoa Beach Surf Company. The world's largest surf complex sits inside the Four Points by Sheraton resort, and has three floors of boards, apparel, sunglasses, and anything else a surfer, wannabe-surfer, or souvenir-seeker could need. Also on-site are a 5,600-gallon fish and shark tank and the Shark Pit Bar & Grill. You can rent surfboards, bodyboards, and wet suits, as well as umbrellas, chairs, and bikes. And staffers teach wannabes—from kids to seniors—how to surf. There are group, semi-private, and private lessons available in one-, two-, and three-hour sessions. Prices range from $40 (for a one-hour group lesson) to $120 (three-hour private). All gear is provided. ⊠ *Four Points by Sheraton, 4001 N. Atlantic Ave.* ☎ *321/799–9930* ⊕ *www.cocoabeachsurf.com.*

Fodor's Choice **Ron Jon Surf Shop.** It's impossible to miss Ron Jon: it takes up nearly
★ two blocks along Route A1A and has a giant surfboard and an art deco facade painted orange, blue, yellow, and turquoise. What started in 1963 as a small T-shirt and bathing-suit shop has evolved into a 52,000-square-foot superstore that's open every day 'round the clock. The shop rents water-sports gear as well as chairs and umbrellas, and it sells every kind of beachwear, surf wax, plus the requisite T-shirts and flip-flops. ⊠ *4151 N. Atlantic Ave., Rte. A1A* ☎ *321/799–8820* ⊕ *www.ronjonsurfshop.com.*

MELBOURNE

20 miles south of Cocoa Beach.

Despite its dependence on the high-tech space industry, this town is decidedly laid-back. Most of the city is on the mainland, but a small portion trickles onto a barrier island, separated by the Indian River Lagoon and accessible by several inlets, including the Sebastian.

EXPLORING
FAMILY **Brevard Zoo.** At the only Association of Zoo and Aquariums–accred-
Fodor's Choice ited zoo built by a community, you can stroll along the shaded board-
★ walks and get a close-up look at rhinos, giraffes, cheetahs, alligators, crocodiles, giant anteaters, marmosets, jaguars, eagles, river otters, kangaroos, exotic birds, and kookaburras. Alligator, crocodile, and river-otter feedings are held on alternate afternoons—and no, the alligators don't dine on the otters. Stop by Paws-On, an interactive learning playground with a petting zone, wildlife detective training academy, and the Indian River Play Lagoon. Hand-feed a giraffe in Expedition Africa or a lorikeet in the Australian Free Flight Aviary, and step up to the Wetlands Outpost, an elevated pavilion that's a gateway to 22 acres of wetlands through which you can paddle kayaks and keep an eye open for the 4,000 species of wildlife that live in these waters and woods.

Adventurers seeking a chimp's-eye view can zipline through the zoo on Treetop Trek. ☒ *8225 N. Wickham Rd.* ☎ *321/254–9453* ⊕ *www. brevardzoo.org* ⌂ *$16.95; $20.50 with train and giraffe and lorikeet food; Treetop Trek $22–$57* ⊙ *Daily 9:30–5, last admission 4:15.*

BEACHES

Paradise Beach. Small and scenic, this 1,600-foot stretch of sand is part of a 10-acre park north of Indialantic, about 20 miles south of Cocoa Beach on Route A1A. It has a refreshment stand, volleyball courts, outdoor showers, a beachfront park with pavilions, grills, picnic tables, and lifeguards in summer. **Amenities:** food and drink; lifeguards (seasonal); parking; showers; toilets. **Best for:** sunrise; surfing; swimming; walking. ☒ *2301 N. Rte. A1A* ⊕ *www.brevardcounty.us/parksrecreation/ south/HowardFutch.*

Satellite Beach. This sleepy little community just south of Patrick Air Force Base, about 15 miles south of Cocoa Beach on Route A1A, sits on a narrow barrier island with the Atlantic Ocean on one side and the Indian River lagoon on the other. Its beach is protected by dunes, and sea turtles flock there to lay their eggs. A popular spot for family vacations because of its slow pace and lack of crowds, Satellite Beach has several beachfront parks with playgrounds, pavilions, and picnic facilities. One park, which teaches visitors about the importance of the dune system, has boardwalks that meander over the dunes to the beach. **Amenities:** food and drink; lifeguards; parking; showers; toilets; water sports. **Best for:** sunrise; surfing; swimming; walking. ☒ *Rte. A1A, Satellite Beach* ⊕ *www.satellitebeachfl.org.*

SPORTS AND THE OUTDOORS

BASEBALL

Space Coast Stadium. Even though they play in our nation's capital during the regular season, the Washington Nationals use this 8,000-seat stadium for their spring training site. For the rest of the season, the facility is home to the Brevard County Manatees, one of the Milwaukee Brewers' minor-league teams. ☒ *5800 Stadium Pkwy., Viera* ☎ *321/633–4487 stadium, 321/633–9200 Brevard County Manatees* ⊕ *www.viera.com.*

GOLF

Baytree National Golf Links. "Challenging but fair" is how golfers describe this award-winning, links-style course, designed by PGA legend Gary Player (aka "The Black Knight."). This semiprivate course, built in 1992, is known for its unique red shale coquina waste areas. A round can be something of a roller coaster ride, with an easy hole or two followed by a perplexingly challenging one. The 454-yard, par-4 18th, for instance, is rated among the toughest in Brevard County. It plays into the wind and requires an imposing carry over wetlands, followed by an approach into a green guarded by water on all sides. The club has a restaurant and full practice facility. ☒ *8207 National Dr.* ☎ *321/259–9060* ⊕ *www.baytreenational.com* ⌂ *$30 for 9 holes, $59–$70 for 18 holes* ⚑ *18 holes, 7043 yards, par 72.*

Viera East Golf Club. Rated among the best public courses—and values—on the Space Coast, Viera East reflects course architect Joe Lee's credo that "golf should be enjoyable, not a chore." Novices appreciate the forgiving, open layout with generous landing areas; more advanced players embrace the challenge of Lee's strategically placed bunkers (there are 66), water hazards, and expansive, undulating greens. The coastal breezes can make club selection tricky at times. Opened in 1994, the course is framed by marshlands, lakes, ponds, and pine and cypress trees. The par-5 14th is among the more picturesque and challenging holes, with a green surrounded by water. ⊠ *2300 Clubhouse Dr., Viera* ☎ *321/639–6500* ⊕ *www.vieragolf.com* ⊠ *$60* ⚑ *18 holes, 6720 yards, par 72.*

THE PANHANDLE

WELCOME TO THE PANHANDLE

TOP REASONS TO GO

★ **Snowy white beaches:** Most of the Panhandle's Gulf Coast shoreline is relatively unobstructed by high-rise condos and hotels, and the white-powder sand is alluring.

★ **Lots of history:** Spanish, Native American, and, later, French and English influences shaped the direction of this region and are well represented in its architecture, historic sites, and museums.

★ **Slower pace:** The Panhandle is sometimes referred to as "L.A.," or Lower Alabama. Southern through and through, the pace here is as slow as molasses—a fact Tallahassee plays up by claiming to be "Florida with a Southern accent."

★ **Capital sites:** As the state capital (chosen because it was midway between the two earlier Spanish head-quarters of St. Augustine and Pensacola), Tallahassee remains intriguing thanks to its history, historical museums, universities, and quiet country charm.

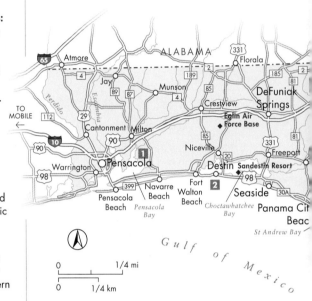

1 Around Pensacola Bay. By preserving architecture from early Spanish settle-ments, Pensacola earns points for retaining the influ-ence of these early explor-ers. The downtown district is compact, plus there's the city's Naval Air Museum and beaches nearby. Inland are some small towns with Old Florida appeal.

14

GETTING ORIENTED

The Panhandle is a large area, and there are a number of airports to access the largest cities. Two major east–west routes offer alternatives to Interstate 10. Roughly parallel to its modern cousin, U.S. 90 is an early byway that goes from Tallahassee through small Old Florida towns like Marianna and DeFuniak Springs on its way to Pensacola. From Pensacola, U.S. 98 generally skirts along the Gulf of Mexico through seaside towns and communities like Fort Walton Beach, Destin, Panama City Beach, and Apalachicola, providing some breathtaking waterfront drives.

2 The Emerald Coast. A nature reserve spans thousands of square miles of Gulf Coast land, and miles of shoreline between Pensacola and Destin is nearly void of development. The area is known for its blue-green waters and sugarlike sand beaches made of Appalachian quartz crystals. Panama City offers unique attractions.

3 Tallahassee. In the state capital you can see the old and new capitols, visit the state's historical museum, attend an FSU football game, and go for a country ride down canopied roads.

Updated by
Ashley Wright

The sugar-white sands of the Panhandle's beaches stretch 227 miles from Pensacola east to Apalachicola. Sprinkle in clear emerald waters, towering dunes, and laid-back small towns where the fish are always biting and the folks are friendly, and you have a region with local color that's beloved by Floridians and visitors alike.

There are sights in the Panhandle, but sightseeing isn't the principal activity. The region is better known for its rich history, ample fishing and diving, and its opportunities for relaxation. Here it's about Southern drawls, a gentle pace, fresh seafood, and more grits and old-fashioned hospitality than anywhere else in the state. Sleepy (and not so sleepy) beach towns offer world-class golf, deep-sea fishing, relaxing spa treatments, and unbeatable shopping.

There's glamour here, too. Look for it in winning resorts throughout the region and in the abundance of nightlife, arts, and culture—from local symphonies to boutique art galleries—particularly in the more metropolitan areas. And then there's the food: from fresh catches of the day to some of the nation's finest oysters to mom-and-pop favorites offering fried seafood goodness.

Jump in a car, rent a bike, or buy a spot on a charter boat—you're never too far from outdoor adventure, with more miles of preserved coastline than anywhere else in the state. Destin is, after all, dubbed "The World's Luckiest Fishing Village," and the sport of YOLO Boarding (this region's term for the popular paddleboarding craze) has invaded the area in full force, offering a unique waterborne view of the entire region's unspoiled, natural beauty.

Don't forget to veer off the beach roads and venture into some of the area's picturesque historic districts. Pensacola is known as America's first settlement, and the rest of the region follows suit with rich history dating from the first settlers. The state's capital, Tallahassee, has its own unique history woven of politics, varying cultures, and innovation. Between the local charm, natural splendor, outdoor adventures, and miles of coastline, it's no wonder that the Panhandle is so beloved.

PLANNING

WHEN TO GO

Peak season is Memorial Day to Labor Day, with another spike during spring break. Inland, especially in Tallahassee, high season is during the fall (football) and March to April. Vendors, attractions, and other activities are in full swing in the summer. There's a "secret season" that falls around October and November: things quiet down as students go back to school, but restaurants and attractions keep normal hours and the weather is moderate.

GETTING HERE AND AROUND

AIR TRAVEL

The region is home to two primary airports—Northwest Florida Beaches International Airport (ECP) and Pensacola International Airport—which offer flights from a number of major airlines. In addition, there are airports with regularly scheduled passenger service in Tallahassee, as well as a public airport—Northwest Florida Regional Airport—in Fort Walton Beach on the Eglin Air Force Base.

Contacts Northwest Florida Beaches International Airport (*ECP*). ✉ 6300 W. Bay Pkwy., Panama City ☎ 850/763–6751 ⊕ www.iflybeaches.com. **Northwest Florida Regional Airport** (*VPS*). ✉ Fort Walton Beach ☎ 850/651–7160 ⊕ www.flyvps.com. **Pensacola International Airport** (*PNS*). ✉ 2430 Airport Blvd., Pensacola ☎ 850/436–5000 ⊕ www.flypensacola.com. **Tallahassee Regional Airport** ✉ 3300 Capital Circle SW, Tallahassee ☎ 850/891–7800 ⊕ www.talgov.com/airport.

CAR TRAVEL

The main east–west arteries across the top of the state are Interstate 10 and U.S. 90. Interstate 10 can be faster but monotonous, while U.S. 90 routes you along the main streets of several county seats. U.S. 98 snakes eastward along the coast, splitting into 98 and 98A at Inlet Beach before rejoining at Panama City and continuing on to Port St. Joe and Apalachicola. The view of the gulf from U.S. 98 can be breathtaking, especially at sunset.

If you need to get from one end of the Panhandle to the other in a timely manner, drive inland to I–10, where the speed limit runs as high as 70 mph in places. Major north–south highways that weave through the Panhandle are (from east to west) U.S. 231, U.S. 331, Route 85, and U.S. 29. From U.S. 331, which runs over a causeway at the east end of Choctawhatchee Bay between Route 20 and U.S. 98, the panorama of barge traffic and cabin cruisers on the twinkling waters of the Intracoastal Waterway will get your attention.

HOTELS

Many of the lodging selections here revolve around extended-stay options: resorts, condos, and time-shares that allow for a week or more in simple efficiencies, as well as fully furnished homes. There are also cabins, such as the ones that rest between the dunes at Grayton Beach. In any case, these are great for families and get-togethers, allowing you to do your own housekeeping and cooking, and explore the area without tour guides.

14

Local visitors' bureaus often act as clearinghouses for these types of properties, and you can also search online for vacation rentals. On the coast, but especially inland, the choices seem geared more toward mom-and-pop motels in addition to the usual line of chain hotels. ■ TIP➜ During the summer and over holiday weekends, always reserve ahead for top properties.

Hotel reviews have been shortened. For full information, visit Fodors. com.

RESTAURANTS

An abundance of seafood is served at coastal restaurants: oysters, crab, shrimp, scallops, and a variety of fish. Of course, that's not all there is on the menu. This part of Florida still impresses diners with old-fashioned comfort foods such as meat loaf, fried chicken, beans and corn bread, okra, and fried green tomatoes. You'll also find small-town seafood shacks where you can dine on local favorites such as deep-fried mullet, cheese grits, coleslaw, and hush puppies. Restaurants, like resorts, vary their operating tactics off-season, so call first if visiting during winter months.

WHAT IT COSTS				
	$	$$	$$$	$$$$
RESTAURANTS	under $16	$16–$20	$21–$30	over $30
HOTELS	under $201	$201–$300	$301–$400	over $400

Restaurant prices are the average cost of a main course at dinner or, if dinner is not served, at lunch. Hotel prices are the lowest cost of a standard double room in high season.

PENSACOLA BAY

Nestled on the Gulf of Mexico at Florida's northwest tip, this region takes visitors back in time thanks to its rich cultural heritage. In 1559, Don Tristan de Luna first "discovered" the area, which today is divided into four distinct parts: North Pensacola, the walkable downtown historic district, Pensacola Beach, and Perdido Key. The historic district is the heart of the area. Just across the bay, Pensacola Beach is on Santa Rosa Island, while Perdido Key is farther west, hugging the Alabama state line.

PENSACOLA

59 miles east of Mobile, Alabama, via I–10.

Pensacola consists of four distinct districts—Seville, Palafox, East Hill, and North Hill—though they're easy to explore as a unit. Stroll down streets mapped out by the British and renamed by the Spanish, such as Cervantes, Palafox, Intendencia, and Tarragona.

An influx of restaurants and bars has brought new nightlife to the historic districts, especially Palafox Street, which is now home to a thriving entertainment scene. Taste buds water over fresh coastal cuisine from a number of award-winning, locally owned and operated restaurants, and the downtown entertainment district offers fun for any age throughout the year—festivals, events at bars and concert venues, and a growing Mardi Gras celebration.

At the southern terminus of Palafox Street is Plaza DeLuna, a 2-acre park with open grounds, interactive water fountains, and concessions. It's a quiet place to sit and watch the bay, fish, or enjoy an evening sunset.

GETTING HERE AND AROUND

Pensacola International Airport has dozens of daily flights and is served by American Airlines (American Eagle), Delta, Southwest, Silver Airways, United, and US Airways. From Pensacola International Airport via Yellow Cab, it costs about $14 to get downtown or about $32 to reach Pensacola Beach.

In Pensacola and Pensacola Beach, Escambia County Area Transit provides regular citywide bus service ($1.75), downtown trolley routes, tours through the historic districts, and free trolley service to the beach from mid-May to Labor Day on Friday, Saturday, and Sunday evenings as well as Saturday afternoon.

Contacts Escambia County Area Transit *(ECAT). ☎ 850/595–3228 ⊕ www.goecat.com.* **Yellow Cab** *☎ 850/433–3333.*

VISITOR INFORMATION

Contacts Pensacola Visitor Information Center *✉ 1401 E. Gregory St. ☎ 850/434–1234, 800/874–1234 ⊕ www.visitpensacola.com.*

EXPLORING

TOP ATTRACTIONS

Historic Pensacola Village. Within the Seville Square Historic District is this complex of several museums and historic homes whose indoor and outdoor exhibits trace the area's history back 450 years. The Museum of Industry (✉ *200 E. Zaragoza St.*), in a late-19th-century warehouse, is home to permanent exhibits dedicated to the lumber, maritime, and shipping industries—once mainstays of Pensacola's economy. A reproduction of a 19th-century streetscape is displayed in the Museum of Commerce (✉ *201 E. Zaragoza St.*). Also in the village are the Julee Cottage (✉ *210 E. Zaragoza St.*), the "first home owned by a free woman of color"; the 1871 Dorr House (✉ *311 S. Adams St.*); and the 1805 French-Creole Lavalle House (✉ *205 E. Church St.*).

Strolling through the area gives you a good (and free) look at many architectural styles, but to enter some of the buildings you must purchase an all-inclusive ticket at the Village gift shop in the Tivoli High House—which was once in the city's red-light district but now is merely a calm reflection of a restored home. A guided tour (at 11, 1, and 2:30 and lasting 60–90 minutes) lets you experience the history of Pensacola as you visit the Lavalle House, Dorr House, Old Christ Church, and 1890s Lear-Rocheblave House. ✉ *Tivoli High House, 205 E. Zaragoza St.* ⊕ *www.historicpensacola.org* 🎫 *$6* ⏲ *Tues.–Sat. 10–4.*

National Museum of Naval Aviation. Within the Pensacola Naval Air Station, this 300,000-square-foot museum has more than 140 historic aircraft. Among them are the NC-4, which in 1919 became the first plane to cross the Atlantic; the famous World War II fighter the F-6 *Hellcat*; and the Skylab Command Module.

Other attractions include an atomic bomb (it's defused, we promise), and the restored Cubi Bar Café— a very cool former airmen's club transplanted here from the Philippines. Relive the morning's maneuvers in the 14-seat motion-based simulator as well as an IMAX theater playing *Fighter Pilot, The Magic of Flight,* and other educational films. Pensacola, also known as the "Cradle of Naval Aviation," celebrated the 100th Anniversary of Naval Aviation in 2011. ✉ *Pensacola Naval Air Station, 1750 Radford Blvd.* ☎ *850/452–3604* ⊕ *www.navalaviationmuseum.org* 🖅 *Museum free, IMAX film $8.75* ⊙ *Daily 9–5.*

> **TOP GUN**
>
> The National Museum of Naval Aviation is one of only two locations nationwide that feature "Top Gun," four real F-14 military flight-training simulators with all the actual controls. Experience mock air-to-air combat, practice carrier landings, or simply cruise over Las Vegas; Iraq; Miramar, California; and other simulated sites during a 20-minute joyride. The $25 experience includes "cockpit orientation training."

Pensacola Children's Museum. The Pensacola Children's Museum is the newest museum in the West Florida Historic Preservation, Inc. complex. The museum offers a variety of programs for children of all ages, including story time, art projects, as well as a plethora of interactive historical exhibits from maritime to multicultural themes. ✉ *115 E. Zaragoza St.* ☎ *850/595–1559* ⊕ *www.historicpensacola.org* 🖅 *$6* ⊙ *Tues.–Sat. 10–4.*

Fodor's Choice ★   **Pensacola Naval Air Station.** Locals almost unanimously suggest this as *the* must-see attraction of Pensacola. As you drive near it, don't be alarmed if you're suddenly struck with the shakes—they're probably caused by the U.S. Navy's Blue Angels' aerobatic squadron buzzing overhead. This is their home base, and they practice maneuvers here on Tuesday and Wednesday mornings at 11:30 from March to November.

Then stay late—the pilots stick around after the show to shake hands and sign autographs. During the show, cover your ears as the six F/A 18s blast off in unison for 45 minutes of thrills and skill. Watching the Blue Angels practice their aerobatics is one of the best "free" shows in all of Florida (your tax dollars are already paying for these jets). It's also home to the National Flight Academy, which teaches the principles of Science, Technology, Engineering, and Math (STEM) during an immersive experience for students aged 11–17. ✉ *1750 Radford Blvd.* ☎ *850/452–3604, 850/452–3606.*

Seville Square Historic District. Established in 1559, this is the site of Pensacola's first permanent Spanish settlement (it beat St. Augustine's by six years). Its center is Seville Square, a live oak–shaded park bounded by Alcaniz, Adams, Zaragoza, and Government streets. Roam these brick streets past honeymoon cottages and homes set in a parklike setting. Many buildings have been converted into restaurants, bars, offices, and shops that overlook broad Pensacola Bay and coastal road U.S. 98, which provides access to the Gulf Coast and beaches. ☎ 850/595–5985.

FAMILY **T.T. Wentworth, Jr. Florida State Museum.** Even if you don't like museums, this one is worth a look. Housed in the elaborate, Renaissance revival–style former city hall, it has an interesting mix of exhibits illustrating life in the Florida Panhandle over the centuries. One of these, the City of Five Flags, provides a good introduction to Pensacola's history. Mr. Wentworth was quite a collector (as well as a politician and salesman), and his eccentric collection includes a mummified cat (creepy) and the size 37 left shoe of Robert Wadlow, the world's tallest man (not creepy, but a really big shoe). A wide range of both permanent and traveling exhibits include a rare collection of dollhouses, Black Ink (a look at African-Americans' role in printing), Hoops to Hips (a review of fashion history), Civil War exhibits, and a kid-size interactive area with a ship and fort where kids can play and pretend to be colonial Pensacolans. ✉ 330 S. Jefferson St. ☎ 850/595–5990 ⊕ www.historicpensacola.org 🎟 Free ⊙ Tues.–Sat. 10–4.

Vince J. Whibbs Sr. Community Maritime Park. The latest gem of the city sits on Pensacola's waterfront and offers a multi-use, public-private park development that is home to a 5,038-seat multipurpose stadium and Randall K. and Martha A. Hunter Amphitheater that overlooks beautiful Pensacola Bay. The stadium is also home to the Double-A Pensacola Blue Wahoos, part of Minor League Baseball's Southern League, and is considered one of the premier facilities in Minor League Baseball. Keep an eye out for tickets—they sell out fast—as well as a variety of other events that fill the stadium and surrounding park year-round. ✉ 301 W. Main St. ☎ 850/436–5670 ⊕ pensacolacommunitymaritimepark.com.

WORTH NOTING

Palafox Historic District. Palafox Street is the main stem of historic downtown Pensacola and the center of the Palafox Historic District. The commercial and government hub of Old Pensacola is now an active cultural and entertainment district, where locally owned and operated bars and restaurants attract flocks of locals and visitors. The opulent, renovated Spanish Renaissance–style Saenger Theater, Pensacola's 1925 movie palace, hosts performances by the local symphony and opera, as well as national acts.

On Palafox between Government and Zaragoza streets is a statue of Andrew Jackson, which commemorates the formal transfer of Florida from Spain to the United States in 1821. While in the area, stop by Veterans Memorial Park, just off Bayfront Parkway near 9th Avenue. The ¾-scale replica of the Vietnam Memorial in Washington, D.C., honors the more than 58,000 Americans who lost their lives in the Vietnam War.

Pensacola Museum of Art. Pensacola's city jail once occupied the 1906 Spanish revival–style building that is now the secure home for the museum's permanent collection of paintings, sculptures, and works on paper by 20th- and 21st-century artists—and we do mean secure: you can still

14

see the actual cells with their huge iron doors. Traveling exhibits have focused on photography (Wegman, Leibovitz, Ansel Adams), Dutch masters, regional artists, and the occasional art-world icon, such as Andy Warhol or Salvador Dalí. ✉ *407 S. Jefferson St.* ☎ *850/432–6247* 🌐 *www.pensacolamuseum.org* 🎟 *$7* 🕒 *Tues.–Sat. 10–5.*

BEACHES

Perdido Key State Park. Part of Gulf Islands National Seashore, this state park is on Perdido Key, a 247-acre barrier island. Its beach, now referred to as Johnson Beach, was one of the few beaches open to African-Americans during segregation. Today the park offers primitive camping year-round. It is within walking distance of dining and nightlife on the key and is a short drive from Alabama. **Amenities:** showers; toilets. **Best for:** sunsets; swimming; walking. ✉ *5 miles southwest of Pensacola off Rte. 292, Perdido Key* 🌐 *www.floridastateparks.org/perdidokey* 🎟 *$3 per vehicle.*

WHERE TO EAT

$ ECLECTIC 🍴 **Al Fresco.** Five different dining spots (including four airstream trailers serving as food trucks), complete with umbrella-shaded tables, sit within a sea of palm trees in downtown Pensacola. You will find a wide variety of flavors to suit any palate, with Shux Oyster Bar as the anchor and four airstream trailers including Z Taco Fresh Mex, Gouda Stuff Gourmet Melts, Gunshot BBQ, and Fusion World. Have a taco before a baseball game, or enjoy a chilled bottle of beer before walking through the shops downtown. Be warned: this is a fully alfresco dining experience. Hours vary by truck, but all are open for lunch and dinner daily. [$] *Average main: $8* ✉ *501 S. Palafox St.* ☎ *850/438–1999* 🌐 *www.eatalfresco.com.*

$$$ SEAFOOD 🍴 **Fish House.** Come one, come all, come hungry, and come at 11 am to witness the calm before the lunch storm. By noon the Fish House is packed with professionals, power players, and poseurs. The wide-ranging menu of fish dishes is the bait, and each can be served in a variety of ways: ginger-crusted, grilled, blackened, pecan-crusted, or Pacific-grilled, which puts any dish over the top. The attentive service, bay-front setting, and signature "Grits a Ya-Ya" (fresh gulf shrimp on a bed of smoked Gouda-cheese grits smothered with a portobello mushroom sauce) keeps diners in the net. Steaks, delicious homemade desserts, a sushi bar, more than 300 varieties of wine, and a full-service bar don't hurt the popularity of this restaurant either. [$] *Average main: $28* ✉ *600 S. Barracks St.* ☎ *850/470–0003* 🌐 *fishhousepensacola.com.*

$$$ ECLECTIC 🍴 **Global Grill.** Come hungry to this trendy downtown Pensacola restaurant, and fill your eyes, plate, and belly from the selection of more than 40 different tapas, 11 entrées, and eight salads. Among the tapas are the high-demand lamb lollipops, Israeli couscous, sundried tomato au jus, spicy seared tuna with five-pepper jelly, and the andouille-Manchego empanadas with cucumber cream. To jazz things up, entrées like filet mignon, gulf shrimp, duck breast, fresh fish, and New York strip compete with the light appetizers. [$] *Average main: $26* ✉ *27 S. Palafox St.* ☎ *850/469–9966* 🌐 *globalgrillpensacola.com* ✍ *Reservations essential* 🕒 *Closed Sun. and Mon. No lunch.*

Like an Old West town with a Victorian twist, historic Pensacola is eye candy for architecture buffs.

$$ IRISH Fodor's Choice ★ 🍴 **McGuire's Irish Pub.** Since 1977 this authentic Irish pub has promised its patrons "feasting, imbibery, and debauchery" seven nights a week. A sense of humor pervades the place, evidenced by the range of prices on hamburgers—$10–$100 depending on whether you want it topped with cheddar or served with caviar and champagne. Beer is brewed on the premises, and the wine cellar has more than 8,500 bottles. Menu items include corned beef and cabbage, great steaks, and a hickory-smoked prime rib. In an old firehouse, the pub is replete with antiques, moose heads, Tiffany-style lamps, and Erin-go-bragh memorabilia. As for the "richness" of the decor—on the walls and ceiling are nearly $1 million in bills signed and dated by "Irishmen of all nationalities." [$] *Average main: $20* ✉ *600 E. Gregory St.* ☎ *850/433–6789* 🌐 *www.mcguiresirishpub.com.*

WHERE TO STAY

$$$ HOTEL 🏨 **Crowne Plaza–Pensacola Grand Hotel.** On the site of the restored historic Louisville & Nashville (L&N) railroad passenger depot, the Crowne Plaza has a 15-story glass tower, attached to the train depot by a glass atrium, and incredible views of historic Pensacola. **Pros:** great location near downtown; amenities perfect for business travelers. **Cons:** it's a box; there are more intimate choices closer to downtown. [$] *Rooms from: $188* ✉ *200 E. Gregory St.* ☎ *850/433–3336, 800/348–3336* 🌐 *www.pensacolagrandhotel.com* 🛏 *200 rooms, 10 suites* 🍽 *No meals.*

$$ B&B/INN 🏨 **New World Inn.** If you like your inns small, warm, and cozy, with the bay on one side and a short two-block walk to the downtown historic area on the other, then this is the inn for you. **Pros:** perfect location downtown; unique boutique hotel. **Cons:** not well suited for kids or

large families. [$] *Rooms from: $109* ✉ *600 S. Palafox St.* ☎ *850/432–4111* 🌐 *www.newworldlanding.com* 🛏 *14 rooms, 1 suite* 🍴 *Breakfast.*

$$ HOTEL 🏨 **Solé Inn and Suites.** If you want to stay in the middle of downtown action but within reasonable distance of Pensacola's beaches, Solé Inn and Suites offers a bit of trendy style in a central location for a great price. **Pros:** unique decor; complimentary happy hour; free Wi-Fi. **Cons:** small bathrooms; during peak season downtown location can be loud. [$] *Rooms from: $109* ✉ *200 North Palafox St.* ☎ *850/470–9298, 888/470–9298* 🌐 *www.soleinnandsuites.com* 🛏 *45 rooms* 🍴 *Breakfast.*

NIGHTLIFE

Pensacola offers a wide variety of lively places to enjoy once the sun goes down, from Irish pubs to local watering holes that were once the haunts of old naval heroes. You can sample homegrown concoctions at upscale martini bars and the tunes of local and national music acts at numerous live-music venues.

Hopjacks Pizza Kitchen and Taproom. This restaurant and bar has one of the Panhandle's most extensive selections of specialty beers—more than 150, including 36 on tap. A second location has opened at 204 9 Mile Rd. in North Pensacola. ✉ *10 S. Palafox St.* ☎ *850/497–6073* 🌐 *www.hopjacks.com.*

McGuire's Irish Pub. Those of Irish descent and anyone else who enjoys cold home-brewed ales, beers, or lagers will feel at home in this restaurant and microbrewery. Its 8,500-bottle wine cellar includes vintages ranging from $14 to $20,000. If you want a quiet drink, steer clear on Friday and Saturday nights—when crowds abound and live entertainment enlivens the masses. ✉ *600 E. Gregory St.* ☎ *850/433–6789* 🌐 *www.mcguiresirishpub.com.*

Seville Quarter. In the heart of the Historic District is Pensacola's equivalent of New Orleans's French Quarter. In fact, you may think you've traveled to Louisiana when you enter any of its seven bars and two courtyards offering an eclectic mix of live music. College students pack the place on Thursday, tourists come on the weekend, and military men and women from six nearby bases are stationed here nearly all the time. This is a classic Pensacola nightspot. ✉ *130 E. Government St.* ☎ *850/434–6211* 🌐 *www.sevillequarter.com.*

Vinyl Music Hall. Music now fills the space of this 112-year-old former Masonic lodge. An impressive variety of bands and acts have floated through the intimate music venue, which offers mostly standing room. It's also home to 5½ bar, where mixologists create unique, handcrafted drinks from the classic to the contemporary in a swanky, downtown loft atmosphere. The box office is open weekdays between noon and 5 as well as before all events (one hour before start time). ✉ *2 S. Palafox Pl.* ☎ *850/607–6758* 🌐 *www.vinylmusichall.com.*

SHOPPING

The Pensacola area is home to a variety of shopping options. The Palafox and Seville historic districts are enjoyable areas for browsing or buying; here boutiques sell trendy clothing and imported and eclectic home furnishings. Meanwhile, the area's main shopping staple, Cordova Mall, contains national chain stores.

Cordova Mall. Ten miles north of the historic districts, this mall is anchored by large stores such as Dillard's, Dick's Sporting Goods, Best Buy, and World Market. There are also more than 125 specialty shops and a food court. ⊠ *5100 N. 9th Ave.* ☎ *850/477–5355.*

University Town Plaza. This renovated outdoor shopping center is anchored by Sports Academy + Outdoors, Toys R Us, Burlington Coat Factory, and Famous Footwear. Many dining options are nearby and in the complex. ⊠ *7171 N. Davis Hwy.* ☎ *850/477–7562* ⊕ *www.simon. com/mall/university-town-plaza.*

SPORTS AND THE OUTDOORS
CANOEING AND KAYAKING
The Pensacola Bay area is known as the "Canoe Capital of Florida," and the pure sand-bottom Blackwater River is a particularly nice place to paddle. You can rent canoes and kayaks from a number of local companies as well as from outfits on nearby Perdido Key, home to the picturesque Perdido Watershed.

Adventures Unlimited. This outfitter on Coldwater Creek rents light watercraft as well as campsites and cabins along the Coldwater and Blackwater rivers in the Blackwater State Forest. Though prime canoe season lasts roughly from March through mid-November, Adventures Unlimited rents year-round. ⊠ *8974 Tomahawk Landing Rd., Milton* ☎ *850/623–6197, 800/239–6864* ⊕ *www.adventuresunlimited.com.*

Blackwater Canoe Rental. Canoe and kayak rentals for exploring the Blackwater River are available from this outfitter northeast of Pensacola off Interstate 10 Exit 31. ⊠ *6974 Deaton Bridge Rd., Milton* ☎ *850/623–0235, 800/967–6789* ⊕ *www.blackwatercanoe.com.*

FISHING
With 52 miles of coastline and a number of inland waterways, the Pensacola area is a great place to drop a line. Bottom fishing is best for amberjack and grouper; offshore trolling trips search for tuna, wahoo, and sailfish; and inshore charters are out to hook redfish, cobia, and pompano. For a complete list of local fishing charters, visit ⊕ *www. pensacolafishing.com.*

Beach Marina. For a full- or half-day deep-sea charter, try the Beach Marina, which represents several charter outfits. ⊠ *655 Pensacola Beach Blvd.* ☎ *877/650–3474.*

GOLF
The bay area has a number of award-winning and picturesque golf courses. Some offer beach views, and others are local haunts.

Club at Hidden Creek. Hidden Creek is known for its lush landscape, rolling terrain, and scenic layout. The public course, designed by Ron Garl, offers challenging play for all levels of golfers with water throughout and well-guarded greens. It's rated one of the "Top 201 Courses to Play in North America" by *Golf Digest.* A natural grass practice facility with driving, putting, and chipping areas offers another unique feature.

14

✉ *3070 PGA Blvd., Navarre* ☎ *850/939–4604* ⊕ *theclubathiddencreek. com* 🖃 *$25–$47* ⛳ *18 holes, 6805 yards, par 72.*

Lost Key Golf Club. Framed by the natural beauty of Perdido Key, Lost Key is located a short drive from downtown Pensacola and features the new Sea Dwarf Paspalum grass from the tee through the green. The public Arnold Palmer Signature Design Course was the first golf course in the world to be certified as an Audubon International Silver Signature Sanctuary. The clubhouse has a full-service golf shop, men's and ladies' locker-room facilities with lounge areas, and a restaurant and bar with indoor and outdoor seating and panoramic views of the golf course. ✉ *625 Lost Key Dr.* ☎ *850/549–2160, 888/256–7853* ⊕ *www. lostkey.com* 🖃 *$35 for 9 holes, $69 for 18 holes* ⛳ *18 holes, 6801 yards, par 71.*

SCUBA DIVING

Also called the "Mighty O," the USS *Oriskany*, a retired aircraft carrier, was sunk 24 miles off the Pensacola Pass in 2006 to serve as the superstructure of the world's largest artificial reef. The "island" is accessible just 67 feet down, and the flight deck can be reached at 137 feet. A number of dive shops offer charter trips to take divers to the site.

PENSACOLA BEACH

5 miles south of Pensacola via U.S. 98 to Rte. 399 (Bob Sikes) Bridge.

One of the longest barrier islands in the world, Pensacola Beach offers a low-key, family-friendly feel with many local hangouts, fishing galore, and historic Fort Pickens. Connected to Pensacola by two long bridges, the island offers both a gulf-front and "sound" side for those seeking a calmer seaside experience. Public beaches abound in the area, including Casino Beach at the tip of Pensacola Beach Road, which offers live entertainment at its pavilion in the summer, as well as showers and bathrooms. Quietwater Beach Boardwalk, across the street from Casino Beach, also offers boutique shopping, eateries, and nightlife.

Long home to chain hotels as well as locally owned motels, the beach has opened a number of condominiums and resorts in recent years. Don't miss renting a bike or taking a drive to explore both Fort Pickens Road and J. Earle Bowden Way (connecting Pensacola Beach to the Navarre Beach area), which have reopened after many years of being closed to vehicular traffic. They offer breathtaking, unobstructed views of the gulf.

GETTING HERE

Pensacola Beach is a short drive (just 5 miles) from Pensacola across the Bob Sikes Bridge (Route 399).

EXPLORING

Fort Pickens. Constructed of more than 21 million locally made bricks, this fort, dating back to 1834, once served as a prison for Apache chief Geronimo. A National Park Service plaque describes the complex as a "confusing jumble of fortifications," but the real attractions here are the beach, nature exhibits, a large campground, an excellent gift shop, and breathtaking views of Pensacola Bay and the lighthouse across the inlet. It's the perfect place for a picnic lunch and a bit of history, too. ✉ *Fort Pickens Rd., at western tip of island* ☎ *850/934–2635* 💲 *$8 per car* ⊙ *Daily 7 am–10 pm.*

BEACHES

Casino Beach. Named for the Casino Resort, the island's first tourist spot when it opened in 1931 (the same day as the first Pensacola Beach Bridge), this beach offers everything from seasonal live entertainment to public restrooms and showers. You can also lounge in the shade of the Pensacola Beach Gulf Pier. Casino Beach has the most parking for beach access on the island and is just a short stroll from dining, entertainment, and major hotels such as the Margaritaville Beach Hotel and Holiday Inn Resort Beachfront Hotel. **Amenities:** food and drink; lifeguards (seasonal); parking (free); showers; toilets. **Best for:** swimming; walking. ✉ *735 Pensacola Beach Blvd.*

Langdon Beach. The Panhandle is home to the Florida District of the Gulf Islands National Seashore, the longest tract of protected seashore in the United States. At the Ft. Pickens area of the park on the gulf-side tip of Santa Rosa Island, this beach is one of the top spots to experience the unspoiled beauty and snow-white beaches this area is known for. Keep an eye out for wildlife of the flying variety; the Fort Pickens area is known for its nesting shorebirds. A large covered pavilion is great for picnicking and a few minutes of shade. **Amenities:** lifeguards; parking (no fee); showers; toilets; water sports. **Best for:** solitude; snorkeling; sunrise; sunset; walking. ✉ *Fort Pickens Rd.* ✛ *3 miles west of Pensacola Beach on west end of Santa Rosa Island* ⊕ *www.nps.gov/guis/index.htm.*

WHERE TO EAT

$$
SEAFOOD
✕ **Flounder's Chowder and Ale House.** The wide and peaceful gulf spreads out before you at this casual restaurant where, armed with a fruity libation, you're all set for a night of "floundering" at its best. Funkiness comes courtesy of an eclectic collection of objets d'art; tastiness is served in specialties such as seafood nachos and the shrimp-boat platter. Most signature dishes are charbroiled over a hardwood fire, and to cater to those who love the sea but not seafood, the extensive menu reveals more choices. Live entertainment is presented every night in season, with performances limited to weekends off-season. 💲 *Average main: $16* ✉ *800 Quietwater Beach Blvd.* ☎ *850/932–2003* ⊕ *www.flounderschowderhouse.com.*

$$$
SEAFOOD
✕ **Grand Marlin Restaurant and Oyster Bar.** This restaurant offers unforgettable views of Santa Rosa Sound and Pensacola Bay along with mouthwatering fresh local cuisine. Top-notch seafood shares the menu—printed daily—with specials. A creative oyster bar carries the finest oysters from Apalachicola, East Bay, and beyond, shucked to order. 💲 *Average main: $21* ✉ *400 Pensacola Beach Blvd.* ☎ *850/677–9153* ⊕ *www.thegrandmarlin.com.*

WHERE TO STAY

$
HOTEL
🛏 **Hilton Pensacola Beach Gulf Front.** The name is fitting; right on the gulf, this hotel offers incredible views at one of the beach's most affordable prices. **Pros:** impeccably well kept; great dining; affordable. **Cons:**

14

chain hotel. Ⓢ *Rooms from: $179* ✉ *12 Via De Luna* ☎ *850/916–2999, 866/916–2999* ⊕ *www.pensacolabeachgulffront.hilton.com* ⤢ *272 units* ⦿ *No meals.*

$$ ⌂ **Holiday Inn Resort Pensacola Beach.** Known for its 250-foot lazy
RESORT   river and cascading waterfall, this gulf-front hotel is one of the most family-friendly on the beach. **Pros:** indoor pool; beach-view fitness center. **Cons:** non-gulf-front rooms have views of the parking lot. Ⓢ *Rooms from: $200* ✉ *14 Via de Luna* ☎ *850/932–5331* ⊕ *www. myholidayinnbeachresort.com* ⤢ *206 rooms* ⦿ *No meals.*

$$ ⌂ **Margaritaville Beach Hotel.** This tropical getaway, inspired by the lyr-
HOTEL   ics of Jimmy Buffett, gives you the relaxed, fun Margaritaville experience with the amenities of a top-notch hotel that oozes barefoot elegance. **Pros:** clean, inviting atmosphere; lots of dining options; local spa services available. **Cons:** somewhat off the beaten path to other local dining and nightlife. Ⓢ *Rooms from: $299* ✉ *165 Fort Pickens Rd.* ☎ *850/916–9755* ⊕ *www.margaritavillehotel.com* ⤢ *162 rooms* ⦿ *Multiple meal plans.*

SPORTS AND THE OUTDOORS

DOLPHIN-SPOTTING CRUISES

Chase-N-Fins. Climb aboard this 50-foot navy utility launch, which cruises Pensacola Bay along Ft. Pickens, Pensacola Pass, and the Lighthouse at Pensacola Naval Air Station in search of friendly dolphins. ✉ *655 Pensacola Beach Blvd.* ☎ *850/492–6337, 800/967–6789* ⊕ *www. chase-n-fins.com* ⤢ *From $25.*

FISHING

Pensacola Beach Gulf Pier. The 1,471-foot-long pier touts itself as the "the most friendly pier around." It hosts serious anglers who find everything they'll need here—from pole rentals to bait—to land that big one, but those looking to catch only a beautiful sunset are welcome, too. Check the pier's website for the latest reports on what's biting. ✉ *41 Fort Pickens Rd.* ☎ *850/934–7200* ⊕ *www.fishpensacolabeachpier.com* ⤢ *$7.50 fishers, $1.25 observers.*

DAY TRIPS FROM PENSACOLA

Inland, where the northern reaches of the Panhandle butt up against the back porches of Alabama and Georgia, you'll find a part of Florida that goes a long way toward explaining why the state song is "Swanee River" (and why its parenthetical title is "Old Folks at Home"). Stephen Foster's musical genius notwithstanding, the inland Panhandle area is definitely more Dixie than Sunshine State, with few lodging options other than the chain motels that flank the Interstate 10 exits and a decidedly slower pace of life than you'll find on the tourist-heavy Gulf Coast.

But the area's natural attractions—hills and farmland, untouched small towns, pristine state parks—make for great day trips from the coast should the sky turn gray or the skin red. Explore underground caverns where aeons-old rock formations create bizarre scenes, visit one of Florida's up-and-coming wineries, or poke around small-town America in DeFuniak Springs. Altogether, the inland area of the Panhandle is one of the state's most satisfyingly soothing regions.

DEFUNIAK SPRINGS
77 miles northeast of Pensacola on U.S. 90 off I–10.

This scenic spot has a rather unusual claim to fame: at its center lies a nearly perfectly symmetrical spring-fed lake, one of only two such naturally circular bodies of water in the world (the other is in Switzerland). A sidewalk encircles Lake DeFuniak (also called Circle Lake), which is dotted by pine and shade trees, creating a very pleasing atmosphere for a long-distance mosey. In 1848 the Knox Hill Academy was founded here, and for more than half a century it was the only institution of higher learning in northwestern Florida.

In 1885 the town was chosen as the location for the New York Chautauqua educational society's winter assembly. The Chautauqua programs were discontinued in 1922, but DeFuniak Springs attempts to revive them, in spirit at least, by sponsoring a countywide Chautauqua Festival in April. Christmas is a particularly festive time, when the sprawling Victorian houses surrounding the lake are decorated to the nines.

14

There's not a tremendous amount to see here, but if you have the good sense to travel U.S. 90 to discover Old Florida, at least take the time to travel Circle Drive to see its beautiful Victorian homes. Also take a little time to walk around the small downtown area and drop in its bookstores, cafés, and small shops.

EXPLORING
Chautauqua Winery. Open since 1989, this winery and its vintages have slowly won respect from oenophiles wary of what was once considered to be an oxymoron at best: "Florida wine." The winery has won honors in national and international competitions, with wines that vary from dry, barrel-fermented wines to Southern favorites like sweet muscadine and blueberry wines. Fourteen vats ranging in size from 1,500 to 6,000 gallons generate a total of 70,000 gallons of wine. Take a free tour to see how ancient art blends with modern technology; then retreat to the tastefully decorated tasting room and gift shop. ⊠ *364 Hugh Adams Rd* ☎ *850/892–5887* ⊕ *www.chautauquawinery.com* ✉ *Free* ☉ *Daily 9–5.*

TAKE A TOUR

Circle Drive. Some of the finest examples of Victorian architecture in the state can be seen while you are walking or motoring around Circle Drive, the road that wraps around Circle Lake. The circumference is marked with beautiful Victorian specimens like the Walton-DeFuniak Public Library, the Dream Cottage, and the Pansy Cottage. Most of the other notable structures are private residences, but you can still admire them from the street.

FALLING WATERS STATE PARK
35 miles east of DeFuniak Springs via U.S. 90 and Rte. 77.

Falling Waters State Park. This site of a Civil War–era whiskey distillery and, later, an exotic plant nursery (some species still thrive in the wild) is best known for also being the site of the Falling Waters Sink. The 100-foot-deep cylindrical pit provides the background for a waterfall, and there's an observation deck for viewing this natural phenomenon. The water freefalls 67 feet to the bottom of the sink, but where it goes after that is a mystery. ⊠ *1130 State Park Rd., Chipley* ☎ *850/638–6130*

⊕ *www.floridastateparks.org/fallingwaters* ▧ *$5 per vehicle, up to 8 people* ⊙ *Daily 8–sunset.*

FLORIDA CAVERNS STATE PARK

13 miles northeast of Falling Waters off U.S. 90 on Rte. 166.

Florida Caverns State Park. A short drive from the center of Marianna, a cute and pristine community, you can see what's behind or—more accurately—what's beneath it all. Ranger-led cave tours reveal stalactites, stalagmites, soda straws, columns, rim stones, flowstones, and "waterfalls" of solid rock at these underground caverns, where the temperature hovers at an oh-so-pleasant 68°F year-round. Some of the caverns are off-limits to the public or open for scientific study by permit only, but you can still see enough to fill a half-day or more—and be amazed that caverns of this magnitude exist in the Sunshine State. Don't forsake the quiet, preserved, and peaceful woodlands, which encompass 10 distinct communities including upland glade, hardwood forests, floodplains, forests, and swamps. There are also hiking trails, campsites, and areas for swimming, horseback riding, and canoeing on the Chipola River. ✉ *3345 Caverns Rd., off U.S. 90 on Rte. 166, Marianna* ☎ *850/482–9598, 800/326–3521 for camping reservations* ⊕ *www.floridastateparks.org/floridacaverns* ▧ *Park $5 per vehicle, up to 8 people; caverns $8* ⊙ *Daily 8–sunset; cavern tours Thurs.–Mon. 9–4.*

THE EMERALD COAST

On U.S. 98, several towns, each with its own personality, are strung along the shoreline from Pensacola southeast to St. George Island. The side-by-side cities of Destin and Fort Walton Beach seemingly merge into one sprawling destination and continue to spread as more condominiums, resort developments, shopping centers, and restaurants crowd the skyline each year. The view changes drastically—and for the better—farther along the coast as you veer off 98 and enter Route 30A, the main coastal road that leads to a quiet stretch known as South Walton. Here building restrictions prohibit high-rise developments, and the majority of dwellings are privately owned homes, most of which are available to vacationers.

Continuing southeast on U.S. 98, you come to Panama City Beach, whose Miracle Strip, once crammed with carnival-like amusement parks, junk-food vendors, T-shirt shops, and go-kart tracks, has been nearly replaced by up-to-date shopping and entertainment complexes and new condos that have given the area a much-needed face-lift. Farther east, past the up-and-coming sleeper cities of Port St. Joe and Mexico Beach, is the quiet blue-collar town of Apalachicola, Florida's main oyster fishery. Watch oystermen ply their trade, using long-handled tongs to bring in their catch. Cross the Apalachicola Bay via the Bryant Patton Bridge to St. George Island. This unspoiled 28-mile-long barrier island offers some of America's most scenic beaches, including St. George Island State Park, which has the longest beachfront of any state park in Florida.

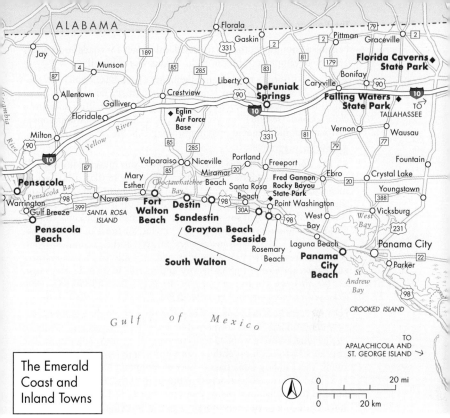

The Emerald Coast and Inland Towns

GETTING HERE AND AROUND

Northwest Florida Regional Airport, on Highway 85 in North Eglin, is served by American Airlines (American Eagle), Delta (Delta Connection), United Airlines (Express Jet), and US Airways. From here you can take a number of car and cab services, including Checker Cab, to destinations such as Fort Walton Beach ($18) or Destin ($24).

Contacts Checker Cab ☎ 850/650–8294.

VISITOR INFORMATION

Contacts Emerald Coast Convention and Visitors Bureau ☎ 850/651–7131, 800/322–3319 ⊕ www.emeraldcoastfl.com.

FORT WALTON BEACH

46 miles east of Pensacola via U.S. 98.

This coastal town dates from the Civil War but had to wait more than 75 years to come into its own. Patriots loyal to the Confederate cause organized Walton's Guard (named in honor of Colonel George Walton, onetime acting territorial governor of West Florida) and camped at a site on Santa Rosa Sound, later known as Camp Walton. In 1940 fewer than 90 people lived in Fort Walton Beach, but within a decade the city became a boomtown, thanks to New Deal money for roads and bridges and the development of Eglin Field during World War II.

Although off-limits to civilians, Eglin Air Force Base, which encompasses 724 square miles of land with 10 auxiliary fields and 21 runways, is Fort Walton Beach's main source of income. Tourism runs a close second. Despite inland sprawl, the town has a cute little shopping district with independent merchants along U.S. 98.

EXPLORING

Air Force Armament Museum. The collection at this museum just outside the Eglin Air Force Base's main gate contains more than 5,000 armaments (aka missiles, bombs, and aircraft) from World Wars I and II and the Korean and Vietnam wars. Included are uniforms, engines, weapons, aircraft, and flight simulators. You can't miss the museum—there's a squadron of aircraft including a B-17 Flying Fortress, an SR-71 Blackbird, a B-52, a B-25, and helicopters parked on the grounds in front. A continuously playing 32-minute movie, *Arming the Future*, features current weapons and Eglin's history and its role in their development. ⊠ *100 Museum Dr.(Rte. 85), Eglin Air Force Base* ☎ *850/651–1808* ⊕ *www.afarmamentmuseum.com* ⊠ *Free* ☾ *Mon.–Sat. 9:30–4:30.*

Eglin Air Force Base Reservation. The 250,000 acres of the Eglin reservation conditionally open to the public include 21 ponds and plenty of challenging, twisting wooded trails that are all open to exploration. The area appeals to outdoors enthusiasts who want to hunt, fish, canoe, and swim. You can buy a day pass to hike or mountain bike on the Timberlake Trail. In order to gain access to the areas of the reservation that are open to the public (and many areas are closed all the time, others just some of the time), you must obtain a permit from the Natural Resource Division (also known locally as the Jackson Guard). ⊠ *Jackson Guard, 107 Rte. 85 N, Niceville* ☎ *850/882–4164* ⊕ *jacksonguard.com* ☾ *Trail Mon.–Thurs. 7–4:30, Fri. 7–6, and Sat. 7:30–12:30.*

FAMILY **Gulfarium.** This marine adventure park has been a beloved attraction for locals and visitors alike for almost 60 years. In fact, it is the oldest continuously operating marine park in Florida. Species exhibited here include otters, penguins, alligators, harbor seals, and sharks. Meander through a range of exhibits and get up close and personal with marine life thanks to several new interactive experiences, from swimming with our watery friends to feedings. For the not so faint of heart, the Stingray Bay Snorkel offers a chance to swim with the creatures as well as sharks, but for an even more intensive experience, there's a five-hour one-on-one with a marine-mammal trainer. ⊠ *1010 Miracle Strip* ☎ *850/243–9046, 800/247–8575* ⊕ *www.gulfarium.com* ⊠ *$19.95, animal encounters extra* ☾ *Daily 9–4:30.*

BEACHES

John Beasley Park. This tranquil seaside park rests among the rolling dunes on Okaloosa Island. Two dune walkovers lead to the beach, where there are a dozen covered picnic tables, pavilions, changing rooms, and freshwater showers—plus lifeguards in summer. The city's hottest nightlife is just down the road, but families can enjoy the scenic beauty. There is also an emphasis on wheelchair beach access.

Amenities: lifeguards; parking; showers; toilets. **Best for:** sunset; walking. ⊠ *Okaloosa Island.*

WHERE TO EAT

$$

AMERICAN

✕ **Angler's Beachside Grill and Sports Bar.** Unless you sit in the water, you can't dine any closer to the gulf than at this casual beachside bar and grill next to the Gulfarium. Located at the entrance to Okaloosa Island Pier (and within a complex of other nightclubs and restaurants), Angler's houses the requisite sports bar with televisions broadcasting sports events, including in the elevators and bathrooms. Outside, a volleyball net tempts diners onto the sands. Snack on nachos and quesadillas, sample fresh-catch dishes such as king crab and prawns, or try the smoked tuna dip, a lightly smoked yellowfin tuna dip served with warm, crisp tortilla strips. The waterfront setting is the image of a picturesque Gulf Coast eatery. Ⓢ *Average main: $19* ⊠ *1030 Miracle Strip Pkwy.* ☎ *850/796–0260* ⊕ *www.anglersgrill.com.*

$$$

STEAKHOUSE

✕ **Pandora's Steakhouse and Lounge.** On the Emerald Coast, the name Pandora's is synonymous with prime rib. Steaks are cooked over a wood-burning grill, and you can order your prime rib regular or extra-thick cut; fish aficionados should try the char-grilled yellowfin tuna or one of the daily specials. Cozy up in an alcove to enjoy your meal in peace or head to the lounge, where the mood turns a bit more gregarious, with live entertainment Wednesday through Saturday. Ⓢ *Average main: $26* ⊠ *1226 Santa Rosa Blvd.* ☎ *850/244–8669* ⊕ *www.pandorassteakhouse.com* ⊗ *Closed Mon. No lunch.*

WHERE TO STAY

$$

HOTEL

🏨 **Holiday Inn Resort Fort Walton Beach Hotel.** Located directly on the beach facing the Gulf of Mexico, this family-friendly resort has enough activities to keep all ages entertained—from one of the best pools in the area to an interactive mermaid to a secret tie to the rich mlitary history of the Emerald Coast. **Pros:** steps from the beach; supervised kids programs; number of rooms with Gulf views. **Cons:** Pay extra for beach services; louder music in lobby and pool areas. Ⓢ *Rooms from: $276* ⊠ *1299 Miracle Strip Pkwy. SE* ☎ *850/301–9000* ⊕ *holidayinnresortfortwaltonbeach.com* ⇱ *152 rooms* ⏹ *No meals.*

$

RESORT

🏨 **Ramada Plaza Beach Resort.** If your family loves the water, splash down at this beachside extravaganza, where activity revolves around a 194,000-gallon pool (allegedly the area's largest) with a spectacular swim-through waterfall that tumbles down from an island oasis; there's also a separate kiddie Splash Garden, a beachwear and beach-toy shop, and an 800-foot private beach. **Pros:** extravagant offerings for a family-friendly vacation; the pool may please the kids more than the gulf. **Cons:** may be too busy for romance travelers or seniors seeking peace and quiet. Ⓢ *Rooms from: $199* ⊠ *1500 Miracle Strip Pkwy. SE* ☎ *850/243–9161, 800/874–8962* ⊕ *www.ramadafwb.com* ⇱ *335 rooms, 18 suites* ⏹ *No meals.*

NIGHTLIFE

The Boardwalk. This massive dining-and-entertainment complex at the entrance to the Okaloosa Island Pier includes several restaurants (Crab Trap, Oyster House, Floyd's Shrimp House, and Angler's) as well as

14

an assortment of nightclubs. ✉ *1450 Miracle Strip Pkwy.* ⊕ *www. theboardwalkoi.com.*

SPORTS AND THE OUTDOORS

FISHING

Okaloosa Island Pier. Don't miss a chance to go out to the end of this quarter-mile-long pier. There's an admission fee (and a fee to fish), and you can buy bait and tackle, and rent poles as well. ✉ *1030 Miracle Strip Pkwy. E* ☎ *850/244–1023* ⊕ *www.okaloosaislandpier.com.* 🖃 *$2; $7.50 to fish.*

SCUBA DIVING

Discovery Dive World. Run by military veterans, this full-service snorkeling and dive shop offers a variety of gear and lessons, though they specialize in spear fishing. ✉ *92 S. John Sims Pkwy., Valapariso* ☎ *850/678–5001* ⊕ *www.discoverydiveworld.com.*

DESTIN

8 miles east of Fort Walton Beach via U.S. 98.

Fort Walton Beach's "neighbor" lies on the other side of the strait that connects Choctawhatchee Bay with the Gulf of Mexico. Destin takes its name from its founder, Leonard A. Destin, a Connecticut sea captain who settled his family here sometime in the 1830s. For the next 100 years, Destin remained a sleepy little fishing village until the strait, or East Pass, was bridged in 1935. Then recreational anglers discovered its white sands, blue-green waters, and abundance of some of the most sought-after sport fish in the world. More billfish are hauled in around Destin each year than from all other gulf ports combined, giving credence to its nickname, the World's Luckiest Fishing Village.

But you don't have to be the rod-and-reel type to love Destin. There's plenty to entertain the sand-pail set as well as senior citizens, and there are many nice restaurants, which you'll have an easier time finding if you remember that the main drag through town is referred to as both U.S. 98 and Emerald Coast Parkway. The name makes sense, but part of what makes the gulf look so emerald in these parts is the contrasting whiteness of the sand on the beach. Actually, it's not sand—it's pure, powder-soft Appalachian quartz that was dropped off by a glacier a few thousand years back. Since quartz doesn't compress (and crews clean and rake the beach each evening), your tootsies get the sole-satisfying benefit of soft, sugary "sand." Sand so pure it squeaks.

ESSENTIALS

Visitor Information Destin Chamber of Commerce ☎ *850/837–6241* ⊕ *www.destinchamber.com.*

EXPLORING

FAMILY **Big Kahuna's Lost Paradise.** The water park is the big draw here, with the Honolulu Half Pipe (a perpetual surfing wave), flume rides, steep and slippery slides, and assorted other methods of expending hydro-energy appealing to travelers who prefer freshwater thrills over the gulf, which is just across the street. This complex also has dry family-friendly attractions: 54 holes of miniature golf, two go-kart tracks, an arcade, thrill

Live oaks draped with Spanish moss are most common in the Panhandle.

rides, and an amphitheater. ✉ *1007 U.S. 98 E* ☎ *850/837–8319* ⊕ *www. bigkahunas.com* ✆ *Grounds free, water park $37.99, miniature golf $6.99, go-karts $6.99, Sky Coaster or Cyclone $16.99* ☺ *Water Park: early May–Labor Day, varying days 10–5 or 6. Adventure Park: early May–Labor Day, varying days 2–9 or 10; late Mar. and early Apr., varying days 2–9.*

BEACHES

Crab Island. All of the sugary, white-sand beaches of Destin and the surrounding Emerald Coast garner worldwide attention, but this is the locals' favorite. Actually a sandbar in East Pass rather than an island, Crab Island draws water-lovers and boaters, who wade the sandbar or drop anchor in droves on fair-weather days, especially weekends. People are friendly, so it's a great place to make new friends, and the shallow waters are good for families. A food barge comes around the "island" seasonally. **Amenities:** food and drink; water sports. **Best for:** partiers; snorkeling; swimming. ✉ *North side of East Pass and Marler Bridge.*

WHERE TO EAT

$$$ ✕ **Marina Café.** A harbor view, impeccable service, and sophisticated
SEAFOOD   fare create one of the finest dining experiences on the Emerald Coast. An ocean motif is expressed in shades of aqua, green, and sand accented with marine tapestries and sea sculptures. The chef calls his creations contemporary Continental, offering diners a choice of thick USDA steaks, classic creole, Mediterranean, or Pan Asian dishes. One regional specialty is the popular pan-seared yellow-edge grouper with a blue-crab-meat crust. A special sushi menu is available, the wine list is extensive, and happy hour runs from 5 to 7. Ⓢ *Average*

main: $24 ✉ *404 U.S. 98 E* ☎ *850/837–7960* 🌐 *www.marinacafe.com* 🕒 *No lunch.*

WHERE TO STAY

$$$$ RESORT 🏨 **Emerald Grande at HarborWalk Village.** Even locals seek out the views at this harborfront destination within a destination, with luxurious hotel accommodations and a full menu of amenities, including a full-service spa, marina, health club, and indoor/outdoor pools. **Pros:** great for larger families and groups; many top-rated amenities are part of the complex. **Cons:** very family-oriented, so it's not ideal for a romantic couple's getaway; must water-taxi to the beach. [$] *Rooms from: $487* ✉ *10 Harbor Blvd.* ☎ *800/676–0091* 🌐 *www.emeraldgrande.com* 🛏 *269 rooms* 🍴 *No meals.*

NIGHTLIFE

AJ's Seafood & Oyster Bar. Folks come by boat and car to this supercasual bar and restaurant overlooking the marina. Nightly live music means young lively crowds pack the dance floor. ✉ *116 U.S. 98 E* ☎ *850/837–1913* 🌐 *www.ajs-destin.com.*

Harbor Docks. Affiliated with Pensacola's Dharma Blue, this favorite with the local seafaring set has been around since 1979. The incredibly casual feel is marked by picnic tables and hibachi grills. There's live music Thursday through Saturday. There's also a sushi bar. ✉ *538 U.S. 98 E* ☎ *850/837–2506* 🌐 *www.harbordocks.com.*

Hog's Breath Saloon. The festive atmosphere is enhanced by good live music from a solo performer during the week and more musicians on the weekend. The food—steaks, burgers, salads—isn't bad, either. ✉ *541 U.S. 98 E* ☎ *850/837–5991* 🌐 *www.hogsbreath.com.*

Nightown. This nightclub has an expansive dance floor, VIP access with bottle service, seven bars, live music, pool tables, and plenty of drink specials and themed evenings. It's open Wednesday through Saturday until 4 am. ✉ *140 Palmetto St.* ☎ *850/837–7625* 🌐 *www.nightown.com.*

SHOPPING

Destin Commons. Don't call it a mall. Call it an "open-air lifestyle center." More than 70 high-end specialty shops are here, as well as a 14-screen theater, Hard Rock Cafe, miniature train, and nautical theme park for kids. ✉ *4300 Legendary Dr.* ☎ *850/337–8700* 🌐 *www.destincommons.com.*

Silver Sands Factory Stores. One of the Southeast's largest retail designer outlets has more than 100 shops selling top-name merchandise. ✉ *10562 Emerald Coast Pkwy. W* ☎ *850/654–9771* 🌐 *www.silversandsoutlet.com.*

SPORTS AND THE OUTDOORS

FISHING

Destin has the largest charter-boat fishing fleet in the state. You can also pier-fish from the 3,000-foot-long Destin Catwalk and along East Pass Bridge.

Adventure Charters. This company represents more than 90 charter services that offer deep-sea, bay-bottom, and light-tackle fishing excursions. ⊠ *East Pass Marina, 288 U.S. 98 E* ☎ *850/837–1995* ⊕ *www.destinfishingservice.com* ✉ *From $120 per hr.*

Destin Dockside. It's a great place to pick up bait, tackle, and most anything else you'd need for a day of fishing. ⊠ *390 Harbor Blvd.* ☎ *850/428–3313* ⊕ *www.boatrentalsindestin.com.*

HarborWalk Marina. At this rustic-looking waterfront complex you can get bait, gas, tackle, and food. Regularly scheduled party-fishing-boat excursions are offered and are a much cheaper alternative to chartering or renting your own boat. ⊠ *66 Harbor Blvd. (U.S. 98 E)* ☎ *850/337–8250* ⊕ *www.harborwalk-destin.com* ✉ *From $55.*

GOLF

Indian Bayou Golf Club. Indian Bayou offers three 9-hole courses with wide, forgiving fairways accented by well-manicured, lush greens, tall pines, and numerous lakes and water features. With challenging options for all skill levels, it is one of the more affordable options in the area. ⊠ *1 Country Club Dr. E, off Airport Rd., off U.S. 98* ☎ *850/837–6191* ⊕ *www.indianbayougolf.com* ✉ *$35–$75 for nonmembers* 🚶 *Choctaw Course: 9 holes, 3464 yards, par 36; Creek Course: 9 holes, 3433 yards, par 36; Seminole Course: 9 holes, 3614 yards, par 36.*

Kelly Plantation Golf Club. Designed by Fred Couples and Gene Bates, this semiprivate course meanders along the Choctawhatchee Bay. The overall layout is encouraging for novice golfers from the forward tees, with hardly any forced carries; however, from the back tees, it's an entirely different game. Stretching 7,099 yards, the course offers a serious driving test for long hitters. Greens are unique on almost every hole. Keep an eye out for hole 4's spectacular, panoramic view of Choctawhatchee Bay, and take in the scents and sights of the surrounding magnolias and palmettos, native to the northwest Florida region. ⊠ *307 Kelly Plantation Dr.* ☎ *850/650–7600* ⊕ *www.kellyplantationgolf.com* ✉ *$59–$139* 🚶 *18 holes, 7099 yards, par 72.*

Regatta Bay Golf and Country Club. Here you'll find a semiprivate course nestled among nature preserves along Choctawhatchee Bay. You'll also enjoy the golf club's amenities, including a state-of-the-art Parview GPS system on golf carts, and small touches that make the course and club unique, like chilled apples on the 1st and 10th tees and mango-scented iced towels. It's a favorite course for players in northwest Florida. ⊠ *465 Regatta Bay Blvd.* ☎ *850/337–8080* ⊕ *www.regattabay.com* ✉ *Varies by times and season* 🚶 *18 holes, 6894 yards, par 72.*

SCUBA DIVING

Although visibility here (about 50 feet) isn't on par with the reefs of the Atlantic Coast, divers can explore artificial reefs, wrecks, and a limestone shelf at depths of up to 90 feet.

Emerald Coast Scuba. You can take diving lessons, arrange excursions, and rent all the necessary equipment through this operation. ⊠ *503 Harbor Blvd.* ☎ *850/837–0955* ⊕ *www.divedestin.com* ✉ *Dive trips from $65, snorkel cruises from $30.*

14

STAND-UP PADDLEBOARDING

GUSU Paddleboards. The biggest craze in the region is YOLO ("You Only Live Once") boarding, or stand-up paddling (SUP), on what looks like a surfboard. It can be found at many resorts in the region and also through businesses such as GUSU Paddleboards. The company's website offers a map of paddle trails throughout the region and state, as well as rates for lessons and tours. Try one out for $25 for a one-hour rental or a SUP-lates class. They're located inside "TheXperience," a store that sells paddleboards and other wares in Destin. ✉ *TheXperience, 111 Harbor Blvd.* ☎ *850/460–7300* 🌐 *www.thexperiencedestin.com.*

SOUTH WALTON

The 16 communities spread out along 26-mile stretch of coastline between Destin and Panama City Beach are referred to collectively as South Walton. Along this stretch of the Panhandle are monolithic condos of Destin and Panama City Beach in either direction, like massive bookends in the distance, flanking the area's low-slung, less imposing structures. A decidedly laid-back, refined mood prevails in these parts, where vacation homes go for millions and selecting a dinner spot is usually the day's most challenging decision. The South Walton neighborhood of Seaside is the birthplace of new urbanism and has been mimicked by several surrounding communities.

Accommodations consist primarily of private-home rentals, the majority of which are managed by local real-estate firms. Also scattered along Route 30A are a growing number of boutiques selling everything from fine art and unique hand-painted furniture to jewelry, gifts, and clothes.

ESSENTIALS

Visitor Information Visit South Walton Information Center ☎ *850/267-1216, 800/822-6877* 🌐 *www.visitsouthwalton.com.*

SANDESTIN

The resort community of Sandestin offers a one-stop shop for a family or quiet getaway offering everything from stunning golf courses to exceptional spa services. The Village of Baytowne Wharf offers a plethora of restaurants and nightlife options for those seeking entertainment. This is one of the areas in South Walton where you can also enjoy views of both the Gulf of Mexico and Choctawhatchee Bay a mere minutes from each other. Year-round events also make the area a draw for guests all four seasons.

WHERE TO STAY

$$$$ RESORT Fodor's Choice ★ 🏨 **Sandestin Golf and Beach Resort.** This place is its own little world—with shopping, charter fishing, spas, salons, tennis, water sports, golf, and special events—so it's no wonder newlyweds, conventioneers, and families all find something for them at this 2,400-acre resort. **Pros:** everything you'd ever need in a resort—and more. **Cons:** lacks the personal touches of a modest retreat. [$] *Rooms from: $211* ✉ *9300 Emerald Coast Pkwy. W* ☎ *850/267–8000, 800/277–0800* 🌐 *www.sandestin.com* 🛏 *1,400 rooms, condos, villas, and town homes* 🍴 *No meals.*

Continued on page 757

GONE FISHIN'

by Gary McKechnie

My favorite uncle has a passion for fishing.

It was one I didn't really understand—I'm more of a motorcycle guy, not a fishing pole–toting one. But one day he piqued my curiosity by telling me that fishing has many of the same enticements as motorcycling. Come again? He beautifully described the peaceful process of it all—how the serenity and solitude of the sport wash away concerns about work and tune him into the wonder of nature, just like being on a bike (minus the helmet and curvy highways).

I took the bait, and early one morning a few weeks later, my Uncle Bud and I headed out in a boat to a secluded cove on the St. Johns River near DeLand. We'd brought our rods, line, bait, and tackle—plus hot chocolate and a few things to eat. We didn't need much else. We dropped in our lines and sat silently, watching the fog hover over the water.

There was a peaceful stillness as we waited (and waited) for the fish to bite. There were turtles sunning themselves on logs and herons perched in the trees. We waited for hours for just a little nibble. I can't even recall now if we caught anything, but it didn't matter. My uncle was right: it was a relaxing way to spend a Florida morning.

REEL TIME

Florida is recognized as the "Fishing Capital of the World" as well as the "Bass Capital of the World." It's also home to some of the nation's most popular crappie tournaments.

Florida and fishing have a bond that goes back to thousands of years before Christ, when Paleo-Indians living along Florida's rivers and coasts were harvesting the waters just as readily as they were harvesting the land. Jump ahead to the 20th century and along came amateur anglers like Babe Ruth, Clark Gable, and Gary Cooper vacationing at central Florida fishing camps in pursuit of bream, bluegill, and largemouth bass, while Ernest Hemingway was scouring the waters off Key West in hopes of snagging marlin, tarpon, and snapper. Florida was, and is, an angler's paradise.

A variety of fish and plentiful waterways—7,800 lakes and 1,700 rivers and creeks, not to mention the gulf and the ocean—are just two reasons why Florida is the nation's favorite fishing spot. And let's not forget the frost-free attributes: unlike their northern counterparts, Florida anglers have yet to

When he wasn't writing, Ernest Hemingway loved to fish in the Florida Keys. He's shown here in Key West in 1928.

drill through several feet of ice just to go fishing in the wintertime. Plus, a well-established infrastructure for fishing—numerous bait and tackle shops, boat rentals, sporting goods stores, public piers, and charters—makes it easy for experts and first-time fishermen to get started. For Floridians and the visitors hooked on the sport here, fishing in the Sunshine State is a sport of sheer ease and simplicity.

An afternoon on the waters of Charlotte County in southwest Florida.

CASTING WIDE

The same way Florida is home to rocket scientists and beach bums, it's home to a diverse variety of fishing methods. What kind will work for you depends on where you want to go and what you want to catch.

From the Panhandle south to the Everglades, fishing is as easy as finding a quiet spot on the bank or heading out on freshwater lakes, tranquil ponds, spring-fed rivers, and placid inlets and lagoons.

Perhaps the biggest catches are found offshore—in the Atlantic Ocean, Florida Straits, or the Gulf of Mexico. For saltwater fishing, you can join a charter, be it a private one for small groups or a large party one; head out along the long jetties or public piers that jut into the ocean; or toss your line from the shore into the surf (known as surf casting). Some attempt a tricky yet effective form of fishing called net casting: tossing a circular net weighted around its perimeter; the flattened net hits the surface and drives fish into the center of the circle.

Surf casting on Juno Beach, about 20 mi north of Palm Beach.

FRESHWATER FISHING VS. SALTWATER FISHING

FRESH WATER

With nearly 8,000 lakes to choose from, it's hard to pick the leading contenders, but a handful rise to the top: Lake George, Lake Tarpon, Lake Weohyakapka, Lake Istokpoga, Lake Okeechobee, Crescent Lake, Lake Kissimmee, Lake George, and Lake Talquin. Florida's most popular freshwater game fish is the largemouth bass. Freshwater fishermen are also checking rivers and streams for other popular catches, such as spotted bass, white bass, Suwannee bass, striped bass, black crappie, bluegill, redear sunfish, and channel catfish.

SALT WATER

The seas are filled with some of the most challenging (and tasty) gamefish in America. From piers, jetties, private boats, and charter excursions, fishermen search for bonefish, tarpon, snook, redfish, grouper, permit, spotted sea trout, sailfish, cobia, bluefish, snapper, sea bass, dolphinfish (the short, squat fish, not Flipper), and sheepshead.

Tarpon

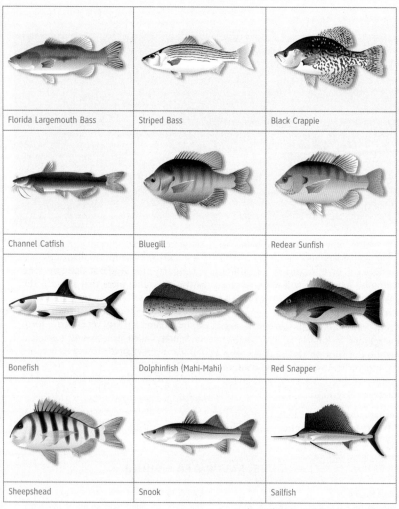

Florida Largemouth Bass | Striped Bass | Black Crappie

Channel Catfish | Bluegill | Redear Sunfish

Bonefish | Dolphinfish (Mahi-Mahi) | Red Snapper

Sheepshead | Snook | Sailfish

(top six) freshwater, (bottom six) saltwater

HERE'S THE CATCH

The type of fish you're after will depend on whether you fish in Florida's lake, streams, and rivers, or head out to sea. The Panhandle has an abundance of red snapper, while Lake Okeechobee is the place for bass fishing—although the largemouth bass is found throughout the state (they're easiest to catch in early spring, when they're in shallower waters). If you're looking for a good charter, Destin has a very large charter-boat fishing fleet. In the Florida Keys, you can fish by walking out in the very shallow water for hundreds of yards with the water only up to your knees; the fish you might reel in this way include bonefish, tarpon, and permit.

CHARTING THE WATERS

TYPE OF TRIP	COST	PROS	CONS
LARGE PARTY BOAT	Approx. $40/person for 4 hrs.	The captain's fishing license covers all passengers; you keep whatever you catch.	Not much privacy, assistance, or solitude: boats can hold as many as 35 passengers.
PRIVATE CHARTER	Roughly $1,200 for up to six people for 9 hrs.	More personal attention and more time on the water.	Higher cost ($200 per person instead of $40); tradition says you split the catch with the captain.
GUIDED TRIP FOR INLAND WATERS	Around $300–$400 for one or two people for 6 hrs.	Helpful if your time is limited and you want to make sure you go where the fish are biting.	Can be expensive and may not be as exciting as deep-sea fishing.
GOING SOLO	Cost for gear (rod, line, bait, and tackle) and license ($30–$100 depending on where you fish and if you need gear).	Privacy, flexibility, your time and destination are up to you; you can get fishing tips from your fellow anglers.	If you require a boat, you need to pay for and operate it yourself, plus pay for gear and a fishing license and find a fishing spot!

With a little hunting (by calling marinas, visiting bait and tackle stores, asking at town visitor centers), you can find a fishing guide who will lead you to some of the best spots on Florida's lakes and rivers. The guide provides the boat and gear, and his or her license should cover all passengers. A guide is not generally necessary for freshwater fishing, but if you're new to the sport, it might be a worthwhile investment.

On the other hand, if you're looking for fishing guides who can get you into the deep water for tarpon, redfish, snook, snapper, and dolphinfish, your best bet is to hang out at the marinas along the Florida coast and decide whether price or privacy is more important. If it's price, choose one of the larger party boats. If you'd prefer some privacy and the privilege of creating an exclusive passenger list, then sign up for a private charter. The average charter runs about nine hours, but some companies offer overnight and extended trips, too. Gear is provided in both charter-boat methods, and charters also offer the service of cleaning your catch. All guided trips encourage tipping the crew.

Most people new to the sport choose to do saltwater fishing via a charter party boat. The main reasons are expert guidance, convenience, and cost. Plus, fishing with others can be fun. Charter trips depart from marinas throughout Florida.

CREATING A FLOAT PLAN

If you're fishing in a boat on your own, let someone know where you're headed by providing a float plan, which should include where you're leaving from, a description of the boat you're on, how many are in the boat with you, what survival gear and radio equipment you have onboard, your cell phone number, and when you expect to return. If you don't return as expected, your friend can call the Coast Guard to search for you. Also be sure to have enough life jackets for everyone on board.

RULES AND REGULATIONS

To fish anywhere in (or off the coast of) Florida, you need a license, and there are separate licenses for freshwater fishing and saltwater fishing.

For non-residents, either type of fishing license cost $47 for the annual license, $30 for the 7-day one, or $17 for a 3-day license. Permits/tags are needed for catching snook ($10), spiny lobster ($5), and tarpon ($51.50). License and permit costs help generate funds for the Florida Fish and Wildlife Conservation Commission, which reinvests the fees into ensuring healthy habitats to sustain fish and wildlife populations, to improve access to fishing spots, and to help ensure public safety.

You can purchase your license and permits at county tax collectors' offices as well as wherever you buy your bait and tackle, such as Florida marinas, specialty stores, and sporting goods shops. You can also buy it online at ⊕ license.myfwc.com and have it mailed to you; a surcharge is added to online orders.

If you're on a charter, you don't need to get a license. The captain's fishing license covers all passengers. Also, some piers have their own saltwater fishing licenses that cover you when you're fishing off them for recreational purposes—if you're pier fishing, ask the personnel at the tackle shop if the pier is covered.

RESOURCES

For the latest regulations on gear, daily limits, minimum sizes and seasons for certain fish, and other fishing requirements, consult the extraordinary **Florida Fish and Wildlife Conservation Commission** (☎ 850/488–4676 ⊕ www.myfwc.com).

WEB RESOURCES
Download the excellent, and free, Florida Fishing PDF at www.visitflorida.com/guides. Other good sites:
www.floridafishinglakes.net
www.visitflorida.com/fishing
www.floridasportsman.com

NIGHTLIFE

Sandestin Village of Baytowne Wharf. You can find funky blues, great sushi, and a set of dueling pianos here any night of the week. Music guests have included Graffiti & the Funky Blues Shack and John Wehner's Village Door Nightclub. ⊠ *Sandestin Resort, 9300 Emerald Coast Pkwy. W* ☎ *800/622–1038.*

SHOPPING

Market at Sandestin. The two dozen or so upscale shops in this elegant Sandestin complex peddle everything from expensive chocolates to designer clothes. ⊠ *Sandestin Resort, 9300 Emerald Coast Pkwy. W* ☎ *850/267–8092.*

Shops at Grand Boulevard at Sandestin Town Center. This town center–style shopping and dining complex is on the area's main thoroughfare, just a hop, skip, and jump from the Sandestin Resort. For the high-end shopper, the center offers everything from Fusion Art Glass Gallery to Brooks Brothers Country Club. A number of boutiques, such as Hello, Sunshine and Magnolia House, carry fare you can't find anywhere else. Dining options include Mitchell's Fish Market, P. F. Chang's China Bistro, and Cantina Laredo Gourmet Mexican Food. ⊠ *600 Grand Blvd., Miramar Beach* ☎ *850/654–5929* ⊕ *www.grandboulevard.com.*

SPORTS AND THE OUTDOORS

For sheer number of holes, Sandestin tops the list with 72 (four courses): Baytowne Golf Club at Sandestin, the Burnt Pines Course, the Links Course, and the Raven Golf Club. For more information, see ⊕ *www.sandestin.com/golfers.*

Raven Golf Club. This picturesque course is a two-time home to the Boeing Championship—a stop on the PGA Champions Tour—and is carved through the marshes and pine trees of Sandestin Resort. Robert Trent Jones Jr. crafted the course as what he calls "a true modern traditional." The Raven Golf Club requires strategy on every tee as golfers are presented with a variety of shot options accompanied by changes in color and texture throughout the course. It will require almost every club and trick in your bag. ⊠ *9300 Emerald Coast Pkwy. W* ☎ *850/267–8155* ⊕ *www.sandestin.com/Golfers* ⌷ *$69* ⚑ *18 holes, 6931 yards, par 71.*

GRAYTON BEACH

18 miles east of Destin via U.S. 98 on Rte. 30A (Exit 85).

Inland, pine forests and hardwoods surround the area's 14 dune lakes, giving anglers ample spots to drop a line and kayakers a peaceful refuge. Grayton Beach, the oldest community in this area, was founded in 1890. You can still see some of the old weathered-cypress homes scattered along narrow, crushed-gravel streets. The secluded off-the-beaten-path town has been noticed with the addition of adjacent WaterColor, a high-end development of vacation homes with a stylish boutique hotel as its centerpiece. The architecture is tasteful, development is carefully regulated—no buildings taller than four stories are allowed—and bicycles and kayaks are the preferred methods of transportation. Stringent building restrictions, designed to protect the pristine beaches and dunes, ensure that Grayton maintains its small-town feel and look.

EXPLORING

Eden Gardens State Park. Scarlett O'Hara could be at home here on the lawn of an antebellum mansion amid an arcade of moss-draped live oaks in nearby Point Washington. Tours of the mansion are given every hour on the hour, and furnishings inside the spacious rooms date as far back as the 17th century. The surrounding grounds—the perfect setting for a picnic lunch—are beautiful year-round, but they're nothing short of spectacular in mid-March, when the azaleas and dogwoods are in full bloom. ✉ *Rte. 395, Point Washington* ☎ *850/267–8320* 🎟 *Gardens $4, mansion tours $4* 🕒 *Daily 8–sunset; mansion tours Thurs.–Mon. 10–3.*

BEACHES

Fodor's Choice ★ **Grayton Beach State Park.** This is the place to see what Florida looked like when only American Indians lived here. One of the most scenic spots along the Gulf Coast, this 2,220-acre park is composed primarily of untouched Florida woodlands within the Coastal Lowlands region. It also has salt marshes, rolling dunes covered with sea oats, crystal-white sand, and contrasting blue-green waters. The park has facilities for swimming, fishing, and snorkeling, and there's an elevated boardwalk that winds over the dunes to the beach, as well as walking trails around the marsh and into the piney woods. Notice that the "bushes" you see are actually the tops of full-size slash pines and Southern magnolias, an effect created by the frequent shifting of the dunes. Even if you're just passing by, the beach here is worth a stop. Thirty fully equipped cabins and a campground provide overnight options. **Amenities:** fishing; parking (fee); showers; toilets; water sports. **Best for:** snorkeling; sunrise; swimming; walking. ✉ *357 Main Park Rd., off Rte. 30A* ☎ *850/267–8300* 🌐 *www.floridastateparks.org/graytonbeach* 🎟 *$5 per vehicle, up to 8 people; $2 pedestrians/cyclists* 🕒 *Daily 8–sunset.*

WHERE TO EAT

$$$ ECLECTIC Fodor's Choice ★ 🍴 **Fish Out of Water.** Time your appetite to arrive at sunset and you'll witness the best of both worlds: sea oats lumbering on gold-dusted dunes outside and a stylish interior that sets new standards of sophistication for the entire Panhandle. Colorful, handblown-glass accent lighting that "grows" out of the hardwood floors, plush taupe banquettes, oversize handmade lamp shades, and a sleek bar area create an atmosphere worthy of the inventive cuisine. Menus are seasonal, but often range in influences from Southern (Low Country shrimp and scallops with creamy grits) to classic Continental, but all are convincingly wrought and carefully presented. The extensive wine list keeps pace with the menu offerings. [$] *Average main: $26* ✉ *WaterColor Inn, 34 Goldenrod Circle, 2nd fl., Santa Rosa Beach* ☎ *850/534–5050* 🌐 *www.watercolorresort.com* 🕒 *No lunch.*

$$ SEAFOOD 🍴 **The Red Bar.** You could spend weeks here just taking in all the funky-junky, eclectic toy-chest memorabilia—from Marilyn Monroe posters to flags to dolls—dangling from the ceiling and tacked to every available square inch of wall. The contemporary menu is small, although it includes what you'd expect to find in the Panhandle: crab cakes, shrimp, and crawfish, to name a few. It also serves breakfast. In season, it can feed hundreds of people a day, so expect a wait. Blues and jazz musicians play nightly in the Red Bar. You can't make up a place like this.

$ *Average main: $20* ⊠ *70 Hotz Ave., Santa Rosa Beach* ☎ *850/231–1008* ⊕ *www.theredbar.com* ⊟ *No credit cards.*

WHERE TO STAY

$

RENTAL

🏠 **Cabins at Grayton Beach State Park.** Back-to-nature enthusiasts and families love to visit these stylish accommodations set among the sand pines and scrub oaks of this pristine state park. **Pros:** rare and welcome preservation of Old Florida; pure peace and quiet; what a gulf vacation is meant to be. **Cons:** if you're accustomed to abundant amenities, you won't find them here. $ *Rooms from: $130* ⊠ *357 Main Park Rd., Santa Rosa Beach* ☎ *800/267–8300* ⤳ *30 cabins* ⭘⌐ *No meals.*

$$$

HOTEL

Fodor's Choice

★

🏠 **WaterColor Inn and Resort.** Nature meets seaside chic at this boutique property, the crown jewel of the area's latest—and largest—planned communities. **Pros:** perhaps the ultimate vacation experience on the gulf; upscale and fancy. **Cons:** you may feel like it caters exclusively to Ivy Leaguers and CEOs, which might make it hard to relax. $ *Rooms from: $333* ⊠ *34 Goldenrod Circle, Santa Rosa Beach* ☎ *850/534–5000* ⊕ *www.watercolorresort.com* ⤳ *60 rooms* ⭘⌐ *Breakfast.*

14

NIGHTLIFE

The Red Bar. The local watering hole presents red-hot blues or jazz acts every night. On Friday and Saturday nights it's elbow-to-elbow at the truly funky and colorful bar, which would be right at home on Miami's South Beach or in New York City's Greenwich Village. But credit cards aren't accepted. ⊠ *70 Hotz Ave., Santa Rosa Beach* ☎ *850/231–1008* ⊕ *www.theredbar.com.*

SHOPPING

Shops of Grayton. This quaint shopping area offers eight cottages in a colorful complex where you can buy gifts, artwork, and antiques. ⊠ *Rte. 283, 2 miles south of U.S. 98.*

SEASIDE

2 miles east of Grayton Beach on Rte. 30A.

This thriving planned community with old-fashioned Victorian architecture, brick streets, restaurants, retail stores, and a surfeit of art galleries was the brainchild of Robert Davis. Dubbed "new urbanism," the development style was designed to promote a neighborly, old-fashioned lifestyle. There's much to be said for an attractive, billboard-free village where you can park your car and walk everywhere you need to go. Pastel-color homes with white-picket fences, front-porch rockers, and captain's walks are set along redbrick streets, and all are within walking distance of the town center and its unusual cafés and shops. The community is so reminiscent of a storybook town that producers chose it for the set of the 1998 film *The Truman Show,* starring Jim Carrey.

The community has come into its own in the last few years, achieving a comfortable, lived-in look and feel that had escaped it since its founding in the late 1970s. Some of the once-shiny tin roofs are starting to rust around the edges and the foliage has matured, creating pockets of privacy and shade. There are also more signs of a real neighborhood with bars and bookstores added to the mix. Still, although Seaside's popularity continues to soar, it retains a suspicious sense of *Twilight Zone* perfection that can weird out some visitors.

If you saw *The Truman Show,* you may recognize several places in Seaside, where the movie was filmed.

Other planned neighborhoods, variations on the theme pioneered by Seaside's founders, have carved out niches along the dozen miles of Route 30A east to Rosemary Beach. The focus in the 107-acre planned community is on preserving the local environment (the landscape is completely made up of indigenous plants) and maintaining its small-town appeal. A nascent sense of community is sprouting at the Town Green, a perfect patch of manicured lawn fronting the beach, where locals gather with their wineglasses to toast the sunset. In total, South Walton touts 16 of these new urbanism–style beach communities and resorts.

WHERE TO EAT

$$$
EUROPEAN

✕ **Bud & Alley's.** This down-to-earth beachside bistro (named for a pet cat and dog) has been a local favorite since 1986. Tucked in the dunes by the gulf, the rooftop Tarpon Club bar makes a great perch for a sunset toast (guess the exact moment the sun will disappear and win a drink). Daily salad specials are tangy introductions to such entrées as grilled black grouper, seared diver scallops with creamy grits, a marinated pork chop with sweet-potato hash browns, and a taco and pizza bar. $ *Average main: $30* ⊠ *2236 E. Rte. 30A* ☎ *850/231–5900* ⊕ *www. budandalleys.com.*

$$$$
EUROPEAN

✕ **Café Thirty-A.** About a mile and half east of Seaside in a beautiful Florida-style home with high ceilings and a wide veranda, this restaurant has an elegant look—bolstered by white linen tablecloths—and impeccable service. The menu changes nightly and includes such entrées as wood-oven-roasted wild king salmon, sesame-crusted rare yellowfin tuna, and grilled Hawaiian butterfish. Even if you're not a Southerner, you should try the appetizer of grilled Georgia quail with creamy grits and sage fritters. With nearly 20 creative varieties, the martini menu alone is worth the trip. [$] *Average main: $32* ✉ *3899 E. Rte. 30A, Seagrove Beach* ☎ *850/231–2166* 🌐 *www.cafethirtya.com* ✍ *Reservations essential* ⏲ *No lunch.*

$$$ SEAFOOD ✕ **Great Southern Cafe.** Jim Shirley, founder of Pensacola's very popular Fish House, brought Grits a Ya Ya to this restaurant on Seaside's town square. Breakfast is served from 8 to 11, when the menu segues to regional fare, including gulf shrimp, Apalachicola oysters, and fresh sides such as collards, okra, black-eyed peas, fried green tomatoes, and sweet potatoes. Oysters and po'boys stuffed with shrimp bring a little of N'awlins to the beach. Beer and wine and a full liquor bar are here to boot. [$] *Average main: $24* ✉ *83 Central Sq.* ☎ *850/231–7327* 🌐 *www.thegreatsoutherncafe.com.*

14

WHERE TO STAY

Seaside Cottage Rental Agency. When residents aren't using their pricey one- to six-bedroom, porticoed, faux-Victorian cottages, they rent them out. Homes have fully equipped kitchens, TV/VCR/DVDs, and vacuum cleaners and are a perfect option for a family vacation or a large group. And the rental agency helps by throwing in a bottle of wine, golf discounts, bicycles, and other perks. With gulf breezes blowing off the water and proximity to unspoiled, sugar-white beaches, Seaside is an attractive vacation destination. And there are more than 200 different properties to choose from, sleeping from 2 to 14 people. What you won't find are the comforts of a full-service hotel. ✉ *2311 E. Rte. 30A, Santa Rosa Beach* ☎ *850/231–2222, 866/966–2565 reservations* 🌐 *www.cottagerentalagency.com* 🛏 *275 units* 🍴 *No meals.*

SHOPPING

Seaside's central square and open-air market, along Route 30A, offer a number of unusual and whimsical boutiques carrying clothing, jewelry, and arts and crafts. In the heart of Seaside in an area called Ruskin Place, there's a collection of small shops and artists' galleries that has everything from toys and pottery to fine works of art.

Perspicacity. This shop sells simply designed women's clothing and accessories perfect for easy, carefree, beach-town casualness. ✉ *178 Market St.* ☎ *850/231–5829.*

SPORTS AND THE OUTDOORS

Butterfly Bike & Kayak. A few miles from Seaside in Seagrove Beach, this outfitter rents bikes, kayaks, scooters, and golf carts and has free delivery and pickup. ✉ *3657 E. Rte. 30A, Seagrove Beach* ☎ *850/231–2826* 🌐 *www.butterflybikerentals.com* 🎫 *From $20 per day from $45 per wk.*

SeaOats Beach Service. Whether it's a beach fire or surf lessons, this local couple's love for the beach shows through in a wide variety of luxury beach services. They don't have a brick-and-mortar store, but will meet you on the beach in Rosemary Beach instead. ☎ *850/951–3632* 🌐 *www.seaoatsbeachservice.com.*

PANAMA CITY BEACH

21 miles southeast of Seaside off U.S. 98.

Although Front Beach Road, the so-called Miracle Strip, is lined by high-rises (about two dozen in total) built mostly during the early 2000s, Panama City Beach's ample 27-mile coastline still gives you opportunities to avoid the crowds and congestion. Spring-break season in March and early April can bring extra congestion and noise, but the sprawling beach is long enough to accommodate everyone. The one constant in ever-changing cityscape is the area's natural beauty, which, in many areas, helps you forget the commercialization in others.

The busiest section of Front Beach Road is book-ended by two undeveloped and fully protected state parks and their equally beautiful beaches. Stand on the pier and look in front of and behind you to see the abrupt end of the high-rises and the return of nature as far as the eye can see. The shoreline is so long that even when a mile is packed with partying students, there are 26 more where you can toss a beach blanket and find the old motels that have managed to survive. Or you travel inland, toward West Bay and find even quieter quarters, including expanses of undeveloped pinelands and a city park with ample biking trails. What's more, the beaches along the Miracle Strip, with their powder-soft sand and translucent emerald waters, are some of the finest in the state, so it's easy to understand why developers wanted to build here.

The busiest season stretches from spring (when college students descend en masse from neighboring states for spring break and a lot of raucous partying) to summer (when families and others come for the warm gulf waters and beautiful beaches). Come before mid-March, when the temperatures can still be chilly and definitely not conducive to water activities, or after Labor Day until mid-October, when the water is still warm and inviting, and you will find a much quieter vacation destination.

Cabanas, umbrellas, sailboats, WaveRunners, and floats are available from any of dozens of vendors along the beach. To get an aerial view, for about $30 you can strap yourself beneath a parachute and go parasailing as you're towed aloft behind a speedboat a few hundred yards offshore. St. Andrews State Park, on the southeast end of the beaches, is treasured by locals and visitors alike. Camp Helen State Park, on the northwest end of the beaches, is a popular wedding venue with an incredible beach. The beautiful white sands, navigable waterways, and plentiful marine life that once attracted Spanish conquistadors today draw invaders of the vacationing kind—namely families, the vast majority of whom hail from nearby Georgia and Alabama. ■TIP➔ **When coming here, be sure to set your sights for Panama City Beach. Panama City is its beachless inland cousin.**

GETTING HERE AND AROUND

The Northwest Florida Beaches International Airport on the east shore of Panama City's West Bay has only been open since 2010, with routes operated by Delta and Southwest, but it's the best of the region's airports. From the airport to the beach area, depending on the location of your hotel, it's about $15–$27 by taxi. Try Yellow Cab or Checker Cab.

If you're lucky, you may see a great blue heron foraging on Shell Island in St. Andrews State Park.

When navigating Panama City Beach by car, don't limit yourself to Front Beach Road—the stop-and-go traffic will drive you nuts. You can avoid the congestion by following parallel roads like Back Beach Road and U.S. 98. Also, anywhere along this long stretch of beachfront, look for "sunrise" signs, which indicate an access point to the beach. They're a treasure to find, especially when you happen across one in the midst of a quiet residential neighborhood and know that a private, quiet beach experience is just a few feet away. The Baytown Trolley serves Bay County, including downtown Panama City and the beaches ($1.50, $4 for an all-day pass); Panama City Beach is served by Route 7

Contacts Baytown Trolley ☎ *850/769-0557* ⊕ *www.baytowntrolley.org.* **Checker Cab** ☎ *850/236-6666.* **Yellow Cab** ☎ *850/763-4691.*

VISITOR INFORMATION
Contacts Panama City Beach Convention and Visitors Bureau ☎ *850/233-5070, 800/722-3224* ⊕ *www.visitpanamacitybeach.com.*

EXPLORING
FAMILY **Gulf World Marine Park.** It's certainly no SeaWorld, but with a tropical garden, tropical-bird theater, plus alligator and otter exhibits, the park is still a winner with kids. The stingray-petting pool and the shark-feeding and scuba demonstrations are big crowd pleasers, and the old favorites—performing sea lions, otters, and bottlenose dolphins—still hold their own. If you're particularly interested, consider a specialty program, such as Trainer for a Day, which takes you behind the scenes to assist in food preparation and training sessions and lets you make an on-stage appearance in the Dolphin Show. The $250, six-hour program

includes a souvenir photo, lunch, and trainer T-shirt. ✉ *15412 Front Beach Rd.* ☎ *850/234–5271* ⊕ *www.gulfworldmarinepark.com* ✉ *$28* ⊙ *Fall, winter, spring, daily 9:30–7; extended summer hrs vary.*

FAMILY **Miracle Strip Amusement Park.** You'll see the roller coaster and the Ferris wheel of this reborn 1960s-era amusement park as you drive around on the Miracle Strip. Although the original park closed in 2004, several of the rides have been refurbished here. The 14 acres of old-fashioned carnival rides and games are a throwback to a simpler time. In 2015 the park switched from individual ride tickets to a one-price admission policy. ✉ *284 Powell Adams Rd.* ☎ *850/230–5200* ⊕ *www.ms-pp.com* ✉ *$22.99.*

FAMILY
Fodor's Choice
★
St. Andrews State Park. At the southeastern tip of Panama City Beach, the hotels and condos and traffic stop, and there suddenly appears a pristine 1,260-acre park that offers a peek at what the entire beach area looked like before developers sank their claws into it. Here are beaches, pinewoods, and marshes with places to swim, pier-fish, and hike on clearly marked nature trails. A rock jetty creates a calm, shallow play area that is perfect for young children. There are also camping facilities and a snack bar. Board a ferry to Shell Island—a 700-acre barrier island in the Gulf of Mexico with some of the best shelling between here and southwest Florida's Sanibel Island. ✉ *4607 State Park La.* ☎ *850/233–5140* ⊕ *www.floridastateparks.org* ✉ *$8 per vehicle, up to 8 people* ⊙ *Daily 8–sunset.*

FAMILY **Shipwreck Island Waterpark.** Once part of the Miracle Strip Amusement Park operation, this six-acre water park has everything from speedy slides and tubes to the slow-moving Lazy River. Oddly enough, admission is based on height, with under 35 inches free. Wear flats. ✉ *12201 Middle Beach Dr.* ☎ *850/234–3333* ⊕ *www.shipwreckisland.com* ✉ *$33.99, 50 inches and above; $28.99, below 50 inches* ⊙ *Mid-Apr.– May, weekends and some weekdays 10:30–4:30; June–early Aug., daily 10:30–5; mid-Aug.–early Sept., Sat. and some other days, 10:30–4:30.*

BEACHES

Carillon Beach. You're likely to find absolute solitude at the powdery beach of this planned community west of Panama City Beach proper. Public parking is available at the entrance to the development, and then it's a several-block stroll to one of the seven over-dune walkways. You'll expend some effort, but it's worth it if you want to find a groomed beach without crowds. The development has several restaurants, but the only on-beach services are for members only. **Amenities:** restrooms. **Best for:** solitude; swimming; walking. ✉ *100 Market St., Carillon Beach* ⊕ *carillon-beach.com.*

Panama City Beach. With 27 miles of shoreline, the beaches of Panama City offer the same pure white sand and emerald-green waters as its neighbors. Here, however, the coastline is dotted with high-rises rather than unspoiled nature. On the plus side, there are plenty of places to play, swim, splash, and feast, and there's no excuse for getting bored or hungry. Although it was once known as party central, Panama City Beach is becoming more family-friendly. **Amenities:** lifeguards; parking; showers; toilets; water sports. **Best for:** partiers; swimming;

walking. ✉ *Front Beach Rd., between U.S. 98 and St. Andrews State Park* ☎ *800/722–3224.*

WHERE TO EAT

While you'll find an almost endless array of chain restaurants in Panama City Beach, the city does have some extremely good locally owned restaurants as well if you are willing to look beyond Pier Park and the Miracle Strip.

$$ SEAFOOD 🍴 **Billy's Steamed Seafood Restaurant, Oyster Bar, and Crab House.** Join the throng of locals who really know their seafood. Then roll up your sleeves and dig into some of the gulf's finest blue crabs and shrimp seasoned to perfection with Billy's special recipe. Homemade gumbo, crawfish, shrimp, crab claws, fish tacos, whole lobsters, and the day's catch as well as sandwiches and burgers round out the menu. It's no-frills dining, but you may get a kick out of hanging out with some real Florida folks who consider table manners optional. [$] *Average main: $16* ✉ *3000 Thomas Dr.* ☎ *850/235–2349* 🌐 *www.billysoysterbar.com.*

$$$ SEAFOOD 🍴 **Capt. Anderson's.** Come early to watch the boats unload the catch of the day on the docks and to beat the long line that forms each afternoon at this noted restaurant with a real family feel. Here since 1953, it doesn't seem to have changed much and that's a good thing. A nautical theme is reinforced by tables made of hatch covers in the attached bar, which attracts longtime locals. The Greek specialties aren't limited to feta cheese and shriveled olives. Charcoal-broiled grouper, amberjack, and yellowfin tuna; crab-stuffed jumbo shrimp; stuffed fillet of grouper; whole oven-broiled stuffed Florida lobster; and steaks are prominent on the menu as well. If you're visiting in the off-season, call to make sure it's adhering to the posted hours before venturing out. [$] *Average main: $30* ✉ *5551 N. Lagoon Dr.* ☎ *850/234–2225* 🌐 *www.captainandersons.com* ✍ *Reservations not accepted* ⏲ *Closed Sun. and Nov.–Jan. No lunch.*

$ AMERICAN 🍴 **Liza's Kitchen.** This local lunch favorite is popular with both locals and visitors for salads and delicious sandwiches on homemade focaccia bread; even many condiments, salad dressings, and all soups are made in-house. It's a casual spot, with seating both inside and out. During the high season, there's sometimes live music outside. On weekends, come in for brunch or breakfast and enjoy the popular French toast, egg sandwiches, or eggs Benedict. It's only open until 4 pm weekdays, 3 pm on weekends; breakfast is only offered on weekends. Ask about occasional cooking classes at night. [$] *Average main: $8* ✉ *7328 Thomas Dr., Suite L* ☎ *580/233–9000* 🌐 *www.lovelizas.com* ⏲ *No dinner.*

$$$ STEAKHOUSE 🍴 **Saltwater Grill.** One of the better upscale dining alternatives in Panama City Beach is this popular restaurant that specializes in steaks, lobster, and other seafood, including gulf grouper or whatever is available fresh from the seafood markets. There's also an extensive martini menu. Two dining rooms surround an enormous, 25,000-gallon saltwater aquarium, which provides a dramatic backdrop for the restaurant. A piano player entertains Tuesday through Saturday during high season in the city's only full-fledged piano bar. A daily happy hour brings in customers for half-price martinis. The restaurant is busy year-round but especially so in the high season, when reservations are a good idea.

[$] *Average main: $27* ✉ *11040 Hutchison Blvd.* ☎ *850/230–2739* 🌐 *www.saltwatergrillpcb.com* ⏲ *No lunch.*

$$ SEAFOOD 🍴 **Schooners.** This beachfront spot—which is really tucked away down a small avenue—bills itself as the "last local beach club," and more boldly, "the best place on Earth." Drawing a mix of locals and tourists, it's actually a perfect spot for a casual family lunch or early dinner: kids can have burgers and play on the beach while Mom and Dad enjoy grown-up drinks and simple fare such as homemade gumbo, steak, a burger, or seafood like crab-stuffed shrimp, fresh grouper, and grilled tuna steaks. At sunset, the ceremonial firing of the cannon is a favorite activity that draws big crowds for an all-around good vibe. Arrive early if you want to park your car in the lot or yourself at a table. Late-night folks pile in for live music and dancing. [$] *Average main: $17* ✉ *5121 Gulf Dr.* ☎ *850/235–3555* 🌐 *www.schooners.com.*

WHERE TO STAY

If you want a quieter experience, look for lodging on the bay side of Panama City Beach. You'll have a bit more traveling to get to the Miracle Strip and the beaches, but the quieter surroundings can be very pleasant, especially during the high season.

$$ RESORT 🏨 **Edgewater Beach Resort.** You can sleep at least four and as many as eight in the luxurious one-, two-, and three-bedroom apartments in beachside towers and golf course villas. **Pros:** variety of lodging options; 110 acres of beautiful beachfront property. **Cons:** overwhelming for those looking for a quiet getaway. [$] *Rooms from: $219* ✉ *11212 Front Beach Rd.* ☎ *855/874–8686 information, 877/278–0544 reservations* 🌐 *www.edgewaterbeachresort.com* 🛏 *520 apartments* 🍽 *No meals.*

$ HOTEL FAMILY 🏨 **Legacy by the Sea.** Nearly every room at this family-friendly, 14-story, pastel-peach hotel has a private balcony with commanding gulf views. **Pros:** shopping, dining, and attractions are within walking distance; all the amenities a family (or college kids) need. **Cons:** in the heart of a crowded and congested district; can be difficult to access in peak seasons. [$] *Rooms from: $179* ✉ *15325 Front Beach Rd.* ☎ *850/249–8601, 888/886–8917* 🌐 *www.legacybythesea.com* 🛏 *139 rooms and suites* 🍽 *Breakfast.*

$$ RENTAL 🏨 **Reflections at Bay Point.** If you're looking for a comfortable condo resort, this polished bay-side option offers expansive, well-equipped apartment units as well as a beautiful, large pool area and upscale spa. **Pros:** free Wi-Fi; beautiful pool area; nice spa. **Cons:** only one restaurant, which isn't open year-round; extra fee to use the gym; dining nearby but not within the hotel. [$] *Rooms from: $205* ✉ *4100 Marriott Dr.* ☎ *877/865–3890 reservations, 850/236–6190* 🌐 *www.sterlingresorts.com* 🛏 *87 units* 🍽 *No meals.*

NIGHTLIFE

Club La Vela. Among the offerings that guarantee a full-tilt party here are a slate of concerts (acts have included Aerosmith, Creed, and Ludacris); international DJs; 48 bar stations; swimming pools; a tropical waterfall; and dance halls with names like Thunderdome, Underground, Night Gallery, Rock Arena, and the Pussykat Lounge. At spring-break time this club is transformed into a whirlpool of libido. ✉ *8813 Thomas Dr.* ☎ *850/234–1061, 850/234–3866* ⊕ *www.clublavela.com.*

Pineapple Willy's. This eatery and bar is geared to families and tourists—as well as sports fans. The signature rum drink, the Pineapple Willy, was the inspiration for its full slate of tropical drinks and the hangout's tiki attitude. ✉ *9875 S. Thomas Dr.* ☎ *850/235–0928* ⊕ *www.pwillys.com.*

SHOPPING

Pier Park. Occupying a huge swath of land that was once an amusement park, this diverse 900,000-square-foot entertainment/shopping/dining complex creates the downtown feel that Panama City Beach otherwise lacks. Anchor stores including Dillard's, JCPenney, and Target keep things active during the day, and clubs like Jimmy Buffett's Margaritaville and the 16-screen Grand Theatre keep things hopping after dark. Other stores, such as Ron Jon Surf Shop and Fresh Market, offer even more reason to see this vibrant and enjoyable complex. ✉ *600 Pier Park Dr.* ☎ *850/236–9974* ⊕ *www.simon.com.*

SPORTS AND THE OUTDOORS

CANOEING

Econfina Creek Canoe Livery. Rentals for a trip down Econfina Creek—known as Florida's most beautiful canoe trail—are supplied by this outfitter, and they will pick you up from the end of the trail and bring you back to your vehicle (even if you bring your own canoe, albeit for a price). Single kayaks are $40; double kayaks and canoes rent for $50. No checks or credit cards. It's open by appointment only in the off-season (October–April). ✉ *5641 Porter Pond Rd., north of Rte. 20, Youngstown* ☎ *850/722–9032* ⊕ *www.canoeeconfinacreek. net* ✎ *From $40.*

GOLF

Bay Point Resort Golf Club. Two golf courses—the Nicklaus Course and the Meadows Course—are nestled on a 1,100-acre wildlife sanctuary and are open to the public. The Nicklaus Course is the only Nicklaus Design golf course in northwest Florida and features generous plateaus and uncharacteristic elevation changes unique to the Florida Panhandle region. A few holes offer panoramic views of the Grand Lagoon and St. Andrews Bay.

The Meadows Course is also picturesque, and its occasionally tight fairways, numerous lakes, and bunkers provide an ever-changing set of challenges. ✉ *4701 Bay Point Rd.* ☎ *850/235–6950, 877/235–6950* ⊕ *www.baypointgolf.com* ✎ *Nicklaus Course, $34–$109; Meadows Course, $26–69* ⚑ *Nicklaus Course: 18 holes, 7000 yards, par 72; Meadows Course: 18 holes, 6913 yards, par 72.*

Hombre Golf Club. The Hombre opened in 1989 with 18 holes and hosted its first PGA Tour event (The Panama City Beach Classic) in 1990. It now has a total of 27 holes; the 9-hole groupings are known as "Good," "Bad," and "Ugly," and they can be played in varying combinations that give golfers three different 18-hole options as well as four sets of tees for different levels of difficulty to best fit their game and handicap. The original 18 holes plays from 5,400 yards (senior tees) to 6,836 yards (championship tees) for the men, while the ladies' layout is 4,901 yards.

14

Each fall, Hombre hosts the PGA Tour Qualifying School, with the likes of Gary Nicklaus, Mike Weir, and Michael Campbell having come in the past. ✉ *120 Coyote Pass* ☎ *850/234–3673* ⊕ *www.hombregolfclub.com* ⌨ *"Good" course, $25; "Bad" and "Ugly" courses, $54* ⚑ *"Good" course: 9 holes, 3170 yards, par 35; "Bad" course: 9 holes, 3393 yards, par 36; "Ugly" course: 9 holes, 3427 yards, par 36.*

PADDLEBOARDING

Fodor's Choice
★

Walkin' on Water Paddleboards. One of the most popular activities in the Gulf area is stand-up paddleboarding, and the folks at WOW Paddleboards have a full-service operation, including guided paddling tours, equipment, instruction, and even equipment if you are in the business of buying. You can sign up for everything from cheaper group paddling trips to individual lessons. The instructors are competent and caring and can get almost anyone up onto a board, but you may find that you use muscles you never knew you had. ✉ *108 Carillon Market St.* ☎ *850/588–6230* ⊕ *www.wowpaddleboards.com* ⌨ *From $45.*

SCUBA DIVING

Snorkeling and scuba diving are extremely popular in the clear waters here. If you have the proper certification, you can dive among dozens of ships sunk by the city to create artificial reefs.

Panama City Dive Center. Here you can arrange for instruction, gear rental, and charters. Two-day "Wreck Daze," for those interested in wreck diving, include boat accommodations and guides. ✉ *4823 Thomas Dr.* ☎ *850/235–3390* ⊕ *www.pcdivecenter.com* ⌨ *From $34.*

WILDLIFE-WATCHING CRUISES

Fodor's Choice
★

Dolphin and Snorkel Tours. Captain Lorraine will take you on a cruise around the bay to see dolphins with stops for snorkeling and (on longer tours) lunch. Tours can be as short as two hours or as long as a full day. She knows all the best spots to find the most interesting sealife in the bay and, especially, around Andrews State Park and Shell Beach. She tries to make the trips educational and eco-friendly without causing undue disturbances for the wildlife. While she specializes in small private groups, Lorraine will work to put smaller groups together to avoid making trips unaffordable. ✉ *Bay Point Marina, 3824 Hatteras La.* ☎ *850/866–8815* ⊕ *www.dolphinandsnorkeltours.com* ⌨ *From $65.*

Paradise Adventures. Known for an array of dolphin tours, sunset sails, and half-day sightseeing cruises, Paradise Adventures has showcased the natural beauty of the area for visitors and locals alike. They also offer a Shell Island Adventure Tour. ✉ *3901 Thomas Dr.* ☎ *850/769–8663* ⊕ *paradiseadventurespcb.com* ⌨ *From $45.*

APALACHICOLA

65 miles southeast of Panama City Beach off U.S. 98.

It feels like a long haul between Panama City Beach and here. Add an odd name and a town's below-the-radar reputation to that long drive and you may be tempted to skip Apalachicola. But you shouldn't. It's a weirdly fascinating town that, for some reason, has a growing cosmopolitan veneer. And that makes it worth a visit.

Meaning "land of the friendly people" in the language of its original Native American inhabitants, Apalachicola—known in these parts as simply Apalach—lies on the Panhandle's southernmost bulge. European settlers began arriving in 1821, and by 1847 the southern terminus of the Apalachicola River steamboat route was a bustling port town. Although the town is now known as the Oyster Capital of the World, oystering became king only after the local cotton industry flagged—the city's extra-wide streets, built to accommodate bales of cotton awaiting transport, are a remnant of that trade—and the sponge industry moved down the coast after depleting local sponge colonies.

But the newest industry here is tourism, and visitors have begun discovering the Forgotten Coast, as the area is known, flocking to its intimate hotels and bed-and-breakfasts, dining at excellent restaurants, and browsing in unique shops selling anything from handmade furniture to brass fixtures recovered from nearby shipwrecks. If you like oysters or want to go back in time to the Old South of Gothic churches and spooky graveyards, Apalachicola is a good place to start.

VISITOR INFORMATION

Contacts Apalachicola Bay Chamber of Commerce ☎ *850/653–9419* 🌐 *www.apalachicolabay.org.*

WHERE TO EAT

$$ SEAFOOD 🍴 **Apalachicola Seafood Grill.** Where will you find the world's largest fish sandwich? Right here in downtown Apalachicola. Here since 1908, this is where the locals go for lunch and dinner, noshing on blue-crab cakes, seafood gumbo, fresh grouper, shrimp, and hamburgers. The decor is iconic diner, with a giant flamingo on the ceiling for that added Florida charm. [$] *Average main: $15* ✉ *100 Market St.* ☎ *850/653–9510* ⏲ *No dinner Sun.*

$$ SEAFOOD 🍴 **Boss Oyster.** "Shut up and shuck." That's the advice from this rustic Old Florida restaurant—and it should know, since many consider this the top oyster restaurant in Florida's oyster capital. Located at the Apalachicola River Inn, this is where you can eat your oysters fried, Rockefeller-style, on the half shell, or Greek, Mexican, English, with garlic, with shrimp, with crab, with hot peppers, with—oh, just eat 'em with gusto at this laid-back eatery overlooking the Apalachicola River. In addition to oysters, it lays down jumbo gulf shrimp, blue crabs, bay scallops, and fresh gulf grouper. Eat alfresco at picnic tables or inside in the busy, rustic dining room, but don't let the modest surroundings fool you—oysters aren't cheap here or anywhere in Apalach. The menu also includes such staples as steak and pizza. [$] *Average main: $20* ✉ *125 Water St.* ☎ *850/653–9364* 🌐 *www.bossoyster.com.*

$$$ AMERICAN 🍴 **Owl Café.** Located in a behemoth clapboard building on a prime corner in downtown Apalachicola, this old-fashioned, charming lunch-and-dinner spot pleases modern palates, both in the white-linen elegance of the dining room and in the colorful garden terrace. The food is an artful blend of old and new as well: the chicken wrap seems as much at home on the lunch menu as the crab quesadillas. Dinner seafood specials are carefully prepared and include lump-crab cakes, Atlantic salmon, and authentic jambalaya. Fine wines for adults and special

menu selections for children along with a cluttered gift shop make this a family-friendly place. Later, the mood shifts to a casual lounge setting with a full bar—and if the liquor bar lacks enough choices there's a 3,000-bottle wine cellar featuring 250 selections from around the world. [$] *Average main: $21* ✉ *15 Ave. D* ☎ *850/653–9888* 🌐 *www.owlcafeflorida.com.*

$$$ LATIN AMERICAN 🍴 **Tamara's Café.** Mixing Florida flavors with South American flair, Tamara, a native Venezuelan, opened this colorful bistro more than a decade ago. Now owned by her daughter and son-in-law, the restaurant resides in a 1920s-era building, complete with stamped-tin ceiling and original brick walls. For starters, try the creamy black-bean soup or the pleasantly spicy oyster stew; for dinner choose from seafood paella, prosciutto-wrapped salmon with mango-cilantro sauce, or margarita chicken and scallops with a tequila-lime glaze. All entrées come with black beans and rice, fresh vegetables, and focaccia bread, but if you still have room for dessert, try the fried-banana split or the *tres leches* (cake soaked in three types of milk), a South American favorite. The chef, who keeps watch over the dining room from an open kitchen, is happy to accommodate most any whim. [$] *Average main: $23* ✉ *71 Market St.* ☎ *850/653–4111* 🌐 *www.tamarascafe.com.*

WHERE TO STAY

$ RENTAL 🏨 **The Consulate.** These four elegant suites, on the second story of the former offices of the French consul, range in size from 650 to 1,650 square feet and combine a 19th-century feel with 21st-century luxury. **Pros:** large rooms; more character than you'd find in a chain hotel. **Cons:** a bit pricey, especially for Apalachicola. [$] *Rooms from: $155* ✉ *76 Water St.* ☎ *850/408–0556* 🌐 *www.consulatesuites.com* 🛏 *4 suites* 🍽 *No meals.*

$ B&B/INN 🏨 **Coombs Inn.** A combination of neighboring homes and a carriage house, this entire complex was created with Victorian flair. **Pros:** clean and comfortable; on-site, friendly owner who's happy to assist with travel tips and suggestions. **Cons:** be prepared to meet and greet other guests at the inn; if you favor complete privacy, a hotel may suit you better. [$] *Rooms from: $119* ✉ *80 6th St.* ☎ *850/653–9199* 🌐 *www.coombshouseinn.com* 🛏 *23 rooms* 🍽 *Breakfast.*

$ B&B/INN 🏨 **Gibson Inn.** One of a few inns on the National Register of Historic Places still operating as a full-service facility, this turn-of-the-20th-century hostelry in the heart of downtown is easily identified by its wraparound porches, intricate fretwork, and widow's walk. **Pros:** smack dab in the center of town; peaceful veranda. **Cons:** may get a little busy when weddings are taking place in the main lobby. [$] *Rooms from: $120* ✉ *51 Ave. C* ☎ *850/653–2191* 🌐 *www.gibsoninn.com* 🛏 *28 rooms, 2 suites* 🍽 *No meals.*

SHOPPING

The best way to shop in Apalachicola is just to stroll around the tiny downtown area. There are always new stores joining old favorites, and somewhere along the way you'll find something that'll pique your interest.

Grady Market. On the first floor of The Consulate inn is a collection of more than a dozen boutiques, including several antiques dealers and the gallery of Richard Bickel, known for his stunning black-and-white photographs of local residents. ✉ *The Consulate, 76 Water St.* ☎ *850/653–4099* 🌐 *www.gradymarket.com.*

ST. GEORGE ISLAND

8 miles southeast of Apalachicola via Bryant Patton Bridge off U.S. 98.

Cross the long, long bridge leading east out of Apalachicola and then look to your right for another lengthy span that takes you south to pristine St. George Island. Sitting 5 miles out in the Gulf of Mexico, the island is bordered by both Apalachicola Bay and the gulf, offering the best of both to create a nostalgic seaside retreat.

14

The rich bay is an angler's dream, whereas the snowy-white beaches and clear gulf waters satisfy even the most finicky beachgoer. Indulge in bicycling, hiking, canoeing, and snorkeling, or find a secluded spot for reading, gathering shells, or bird-watching. Accommodations mostly take the form of privately owned, fully furnished condos and single-family homes.

EXPLORING

Fodor's Choice ★ **St. George Island State Park.** This is Old Florida at its undisturbed best. On the east end of the island are 9 miles of undeveloped beaches and dunes—the longest beachfront of any state park in Florida. Sandy coves, salt marshes, oak forests, and pines provide shelter for many birds, including bald eagles and ospreys. Spotless restrooms and plentiful parking make a day at this park a joy. Campers and boaters also welcome. **Amenities:** parking; showers; toilets. **Best for:** walking; swimming. ✉ *1900 E. Gulf Beach Dr.* ☎ *850/927–2111* 🌐 *www.floridastateparks.org/stgeorgeisland* 🎟 *$6 per vehicle, up to 8 people* 🕒 *Daily 8–sunset.*

WHERE TO EAT

$ PIZZA 🍴 **BJs.** In any other locale you might think twice before dining at a restaurant that advertises "kegs-to-go" on the menu, but this is an island, so establishments tend to wear several hats (some even sell live bait). Fear not. This simple beach shack serves solid, if predictable, sandwiches (grilled chicken, turkey club, BLT), salads (Caesar, tuna, fried chicken), and appetizers (buffalo wings, cheese sticks, onion rings), but the pizza is definitely worth stopping for. Pies range from white pizza with chicken and bacon to shrimp-and-mozzarella to build-your-own personal pie (choose from 15 toppings). Beer and wine are available, and there are pool tables to pass the time while you wait for your order. [$] *Average main: $7* ✉ *105 W. Gulf Beach Dr.* ☎ *850/927–2805* 🌐 *www.sgipizza.com* ✍ *Reservations not accepted.*

$$ SEAFOOD 🍴 **Blue Parrot.** You'll feel like you're sneaking in the back door as you climb the side stairs leading to an outdoor deck overlooking the gulf (this is Apalach's only restaurant on the beach). Or if you can, grab a table indoors. During special-event weekends, the place is packed, and service may be a little slow. The food is hard to beat if you're not looking for anything fancy. Baskets of shrimp, oysters, and crab cakes—fried or char-grilled and served with fries—are more than one person can

handle. Daily specials are listed on the blackboard. $ *Average main: $20* ✉ *68 W. Gorrie Dr.* ☎ *850/927–2987* ⊕ *www.blueparrotsgi.com.*

TALLAHASSEE

103 miles east of Panama City, 78 miles northeast of Apalachicola.

Tallahassee is Florida with a Southern accent. It maintains a tranquillity quite different from the sun-and-surf coastal towns. The only Southern capital spared in the Civil War, Tallahassee has preserved its history. Vestiges of the city's colorful past are found throughout. For example, in the capitol complex, the turn-of-the-20th-century Old Capitol building is strikingly paired with the New Capitol skyscraper.

The canopies of ancient oaks and spring bowers of azaleas line many streets; among the best "canopy roads" are St. Augustine, Miccosukee, Meridian, Old Bainbridge, and Centerville, all dotted with country stores and antebellum plantation houses. Between March and April, flowers bloom, the legislature is in session, and the Springtime Tallahassee festival is in full swing.

GETTING HERE AND AROUND

Just 14 miles south of the Georgia border and nearer to Atlanta than Miami, Tallahassee is midway between Jacksonville and Pensacola. Tallahassee Regional Airport is served by American, Delta, United Express, and US Airways. From the airport to downtown is around $20 via City Taxi or Yellow Cab.

Contacts City Taxi ☎ *850/562–4222.* **Yellow Cab** ☎ *850/575–1022.*

VISITOR INFORMATION

Contacts Tallahassee Area Convention and Visitors Bureau ☎ *850/606–2305, 800/628–2866* ⊕ *www.visittallahassee.com.*

EXPLORING

DOWNTOWN

TOP ATTRACTIONS

FAMILY   **Challenger Learning Center.** Visitors of all ages can't help but get excited about math and science exploration at this museum that features a space mission simulator, an IMAX 3D theater, and the Downtown Digital Dome Theatre and Planetarium. Every kid, and kid at heart, can reenact a space mission with The Challenger Learning Center Space Mission Simulator. The next best thing to actual space flight, the simulator features a Mission Control room designed after NASA Johnson Space Center and an orbiting space station modeled after the laboratory on the International Space Station. Hands-on or demonstrational science techniques and equipment can be found throughout the museum. ✉ *200 S. Duval St.* ☎ *850/645–7796, 850/644–4629 IMAX* ⊕ *www.challengertlh.com* 🎫 *Planetarium $5, IMAX $6–$8* ⊗ *Show times vary.*

Museum of Florida History. If you thought Florida was founded by Walt Disney, stop in here. The displays explain the state's past by highlighting the unique geological and historical events that have shaped the

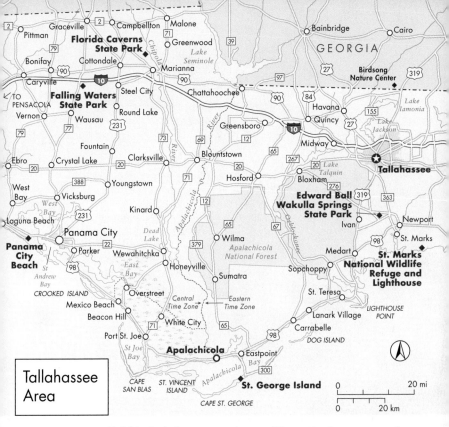

Tallahassee
Area

state. Exhibits include a mammoth armadillo grazing in a savanna, the remains of a giant mastodon found in nearby Wakulla Springs, and a dugout canoe that once carried American Indians into Florida's back-waters. Florida's history also includes settlements by the Spanish, British, French, and Confederates who fought for possession of the state.

Gold bars, weapons, flags, maps, furniture, steamboats, and other arti-facts underscore the fact that although most Americans date the nation to 1776, Florida's residents were building settlements hundreds of years earlier. If this intrigues you, one floor up is the Florida State Archives and Library, where there's a treasure trove of government records, manuscripts, photographs, genealogical records, and other materials. ■TIP→ It was in these archives that researchers found footage of a young Jim Morrison appearing in a promotional film for Florida's univer-sities. ⊠ 500 S. Bronough St. ☎ 850/245–6400, 850/245–6600 library, 850/245–6700 archives ⊕ www.museumoffloridahistory.com ⊠ Free ⊗ Weekdays 9–4:30, Sat. 10–4:30, Sun. noon–4:30.

New Capitol. In the 1960s, when there was talk of relocating the capi-tal to a more central location like Orlando, Panhandle legislators got to work and approved the construction of a 22-story skyscraper that would anchor the capital right where it was. It's perfectly placed at the crest of a hill, sitting prominently behind the low-rise Old Capitol. The

governor's office is on the first floor, along with the Florida Artists Hall of Fame, a series of plaques that pay tribute to Floridians such as Ray Charles, Burt Reynolds, Tennessee Williams, Ernest Hemingway, and Marjorie Kinnan Rawlings.

The House and Senate chambers on the fifth floor provide viewer galleries for when the legislative sessions take place (March to May). Catch a panoramic view of Tallahassee and the surrounding countryside all the way into Georgia from the fabulous 22nd-floor observation deck. Although budget cuts have stopped scheduled guided tours, a free brochure can get you around; if you're traveling in a group you can call ahead to have a guide usher you. To pick up information about the area, stop at the Florida Visitors Center on the plaza level, and check out the plaque on the north wall facing the elevators. It's dedicated to Senator Lee Wissenborn "whose valiant effort to move the Capitol to Orlando was the prime motivation for the construction of this building." ⊠ *400 S. Monroe St.* ☎ *850/488–6167* ⊕ *www.myfloridacapitol.com* ☒ *Free* ⊙ *Visitor center weekdays 8–5.*

> ## TALLAHASSEE HISTORIC TRAIL
>
> A route mapped and documented by an eager Eagle Scout is now a Tallahassee sightseeing staple. Start at the New Capitol, where you can pick up maps and descriptive brochures at the visitor center. You'll walk through the Park Avenue and Calhoun Street historic districts, which will take you back to territorial days and the era of postwar reconstruction. Along the way are landmark churches and cemeteries and outstanding examples of Greek Revival, Italianate, and prairie-style architecture. Some houses are open to the public.

Old Capitol. The centerpiece of the capitol complex, this 1842 structure has been added to and subtracted from several times. Having been restored, the jaunty red-and-white-striped awnings and combination gas-electric lights make it look much as it did in 1902. Inside, it houses a must-see museum of Florida's political history as well as the old Supreme Court chambers and Senate Gallery—a very interesting peek into the past. ⊠ *S. Monroe St. at Apalachee Pkwy.* ☎ *850/487–1902* ☒ *Free* ⊙ *Self-guided tours weekdays 9–4:30, Sat. 10–4:30, Sun. noon– 4:30; call for guided tours.*

AWAY FROM DOWNTOWN
TOP ATTRACTIONS
Alfred B. Maclay Gardens State Park. Starting in December, the grounds at this 1,200-acre estate are afire with azaleas, dogwood, Oriental magnolias, spring bulbs of tulips and irises, banana shrubs, honeysuckle, silverbell trees, pansies, and camellias. Allow half a day to wander past the reflecting pool into the tiny walled garden and around the lakes and woodlands. The Maclay residence (open January through April) is furnished as it was in the 1920s; picnic areas, gardens, and swimming and boating facilities are open to the public. ⊠ *3540 Thomasville Rd.* ☎ *850/487–4556* ⊕ *www.floridastateparks.org/maclaygardens* ☒ *$6 per vehicle, up to 8 people; garden extra $6 per person Jan.–Apr. (blooming season), free rest of yr* ⊙ *Daily 8–sunset.*

Guided tours are given daily at Florida's Old Capitol in Tallahassee. It sits in front of the 22-story New Capitol.

Fodor's Choice
★

Edward Ball Wakulla Springs State Park. Known for having one of the deepest springs in the world, this very picturesque and highly recommended park remains relatively untouched, retaining the wild and exotic look it had in the 1930s, when the films *Tarzan* and *Creature from the Black Lagoon* were shot here. Even if they weren't, you'd want to come here and see what Florida really looks like. Beyond the lodge is the spring where glass-bottom boats set off deep into the lush, jungle-lined waterways to catch glimpses of alligators, snakes, nesting limpkins, and other waterfowl. It costs $50 to rent a pontoon boat and go it alone—it may be worth it since an underground river flows into a pool so clear you can see the bottom more than 100 feet below. The park is 15 miles south of Tallahassee on Route 61. If you can't pull yourself away from this idyllic spot, spend the night in the 1930s Spanish Mediterranean–style lodge. ⊠ *550 Wakulla Park Dr., Wakulla Springs* ☎ *850/926–0700* ⊕ *www. floridastateparks.org/wakullasprings* ⊠ *$6 per vehicle, up to 8 people; boat tour $8* ⊙ *Daily 8–sunset; boat tours daily 9:30–4:30.*

Mission San Luis Archaeological and Historic Site. Long before New England's residents began gaining a foothold in North America, the native Apalachee Indians as well as Spanish missionaries settled here. On the site of a 17th-century Spanish mission and Apalachee Indian town, this museum focuses on the archaeology of the late 1600s, when the Apalachee village here had a population of at least 1,400. By 1704, however, threatened by Creek Indians and British forces, the locals burned the village and fled. About once a year, researchers conduct digs, and then they spend the rest of the year analyzing their findings. If you're here when they are, you can watch them dig. Otherwise, you'll have to be content with roaming around the re-creation of a 17th-century Spanish village and speaking with the living-history guides, who offer tours by advance arrangement. Even without seeing researchers digging for clues, this is still a cool experience and a great way to learn about Florida's impressive history. A 24,000-square-foot, state-of-the-art visitor center offers an expanded exhibit hall and gift shop. ⊠ *2100 W. Tennessee St.* ☎ *850/245–6406* ⊕ *www.missionsanluis.org* ✉ *$5* ⊗ *Tues.–Sun. 10–4.*

St. Marks National Wildlife Refuge and Lighthouse. As its name suggests, this attraction is of both natural and historical interest. Natural salt marshes, tidal flats, and freshwater pools used by early natives set the stage for the once-powerful Fort San Marcos de Apalache, which was built nearby in 1639. Stones salvaged from the fort were used in the lighthouse, which is still in operation. In winter the 100,000-acre-plus refuge on the shores of Apalachee Bay is the resting place for thousands of migratory birds of more than 300 species, but the alligators seem to like it year-round (keep your camera ready). The visitor center has information on more than 75 miles of marked trails. Hardwood swamps and pine woodlands also provide habitat for wood ducks, black bears, otters, raccoons, deer, armadillos, coyotes, feral hogs, fox squirrels, gopher tortoises, and woodpeckers. Twenty-five miles south of Tallahassee, the refuge can be reached via Route 363. ⊠ *1255 Lighthouse Rd., St. Marks* ☎ *850/925–6121* ⊕ *saintmarks.fws.gov* ✉ *$5 per vehicle* ⊗ *Refuge daily sunrise–sunset; visitor center weekdays 8–4, weekends 10–5.*

WORTH NOTING

FAMILY **Tallahassee Museum.** Not exactly a museum, this is really an expansive, bucolic park that showcases a peaceful and intriguing look at Old Florida, located about 20 minutes from downtown. The theme and presentation here is of a working 1880s pioneer farm that offers daily hands-on activities for children, such as soap-making and blacksmithing. A boardwalk meanders through the 52 acres of natural habitat that make up the zoo, which has such varied animals as panthers, bobcats, white-tailed deer, bald eagles, red wolves, hawks, owls, otters, and black bears—many of which were brought here injured or orphaned. Also on-site are nature trails, a one-room schoolhouse dating from 1897, and an 1840s Southern plantation manor, where you can usually find someone cooking on weekends. It's peaceful, pleasing, and educational. ⊠ *3945 Museum Dr.* ☎ *850/575–8684* ⊕ *www.tallahasseemuseum.org* ✉ *$7.50* ⊗ *Mon.–Sat. 9–5, Sun. 11–5.*

WHERE TO EAT

$$$ ✕ **Andrew's 228.** Part of a smart complex in the heart of the political
ITALIAN district, this two-story "urban Tuscan villa" (contradiction noted) is the latest of owner Andy Reiss's restaurant incarnations to occupy the same space (the last was Andrew's Second Act). Leaning toward upscale, the menu includes a range of chicken, steak, pasta, and fish dishes such as grouper picatta, pesto salmon, wild-mushroom risotto, chicken marsala, and double-cut pork chops. If you're so inclined, try the specialty

$6 martini. **$** *Average main: $26* ✉ *228 S. Adams St.* ☎ *850/222–3444* ⊕ *www.andrewsdowntown.com* ⊗ *Closed Sun. No lunch.*

$$$
SOUTHERN
✕ **Avenue Eat and Drink.** Elegant yet unpretentious, this cozy restaurant offers an eclectic mix of Southern fusion food that delights taste buds in small bites and larger plates. You can't go wrong with tuna two ways or the melt-in-your-mouth boneless short ribs served with mashed parsnip and potatoes with a rosemary-Cabernet reduction. There is an extensive wine selection and a specialty martini menu. **$** *Average main: $28* ✉ *115 E. Park Ave.* ☎ *850/224–0115* ⊕ *www.avenueeatanddrink.com.*

$
AMERICAN
✕ **Hopkins' Eatery.** Locals in the know flock here for superb salads, homemade soups, and sandwiches—expect a short wait at lunchtime—via simple counter service. Kids like the traditional peanut butter–and-jelly sandwich (with bananas and sprouts, if they dare); adults might opt for a chunky chicken melt, smothered beef, or garden vegetarian sub. The spearmint iced tea is a must-have, as is a slice of freshly baked chocolate cake. A second location on North Monroe Street offers the same menu; a third location has also opened at 1208 Capital Circle SE. **$** *Average main: $6* ✉ *1415 Market St.* ☎ *850/668–0311* ⊕ *www.hopkinseatery. com* ⊗ *Closed Sun. No dinner Sat.*

$$
CARIBBEAN
✕ **Kool Beanz Café.** The cuisine is as eclectic and cozy as the atmosphere at this Tallahassee staple, loved by locals and visitors alike. The decor is part of the charm, with a vibrant setting of dark pastels and modern art. The menu changes daily but typically includes seafood and vegetables served island-style. For a real treat, try brunch. **$** *Average main: $20* ✉ *921 Thomasville Rd.* ☎ *850/224–2466* ⊕ *www.kool-beanz.com.*

WHERE TO STAY

$$
HOTEL
▦ **Aloft Tallahassee Downtown.** This urban-chic hotel provides the tree-lined downtown district with a bit of trendy fun courtesy of loft-style rooms with bright, minimalist decor. **Pros:** convenient to downtown, universities, and nightlife/restaurants. **Cons:** small, utilitarian rooms; lobby can get packed from the bar on weekend nights. **$** *Rooms from: $139* ✉ *200 N. Monroe St.* ☎ *850/513–0313, 866/513–0313* ➷ *162 rooms* ⦿ *No meals.*

$$$
B&B/INN
▦ **Governors Inn.** Only a block from the capitol, this plushly restored historic warehouse is abuzz during the week with politicians, press, and lobbyists. **Pros:** well run and well placed, a few steps from museums, restaurants, and the capitol; the rooms and lobby are warm and inviting. **Cons:** during session and football season, the district can get crowded and busy, and accessing the area may be a challenge. **$** *Rooms from: $169* ✉ *209 S. Adams St.* ☎ *850/681–6855* ⊕ *www.thegovinn. com* ➷ *41 rooms, 8 suites* ⦿ *Breakfast.*

$$
HOTEL
Fodor's Choice
★
▦ **Hotel Duval.** This boutique hotel, a renovated version of the landmark build in 1951, sets a high standard for small luxury hotels in the capital. **Pros:** top-level amenities; good restaurants. **Cons:** not suited to families; small rooms. **$** *Rooms from: $109* ✉ *415 N. Monroe St.* ☎ *850/224–6000* ⊕ *www.hotelduval.com* ➷ *108 rooms, 9 suites* ⦿ *No meals.*

14

SHOPPING

Market District. Hop off I–10 at Exit 203 to head to this shopping and dining district filled with locally owned specialty shops, salons, cafés, and restaurants. My Favorite Things and Cotton Colors are popular, as are many other stores scattered around the area in smaller enclaves. Not to worry, though—most are within walking distance of one another. The Market District is the place for a taste of true local culture. It's slightly west of Thomasville Road at the intersection of Timberline Road and Market Street. ⊠ *Timberline Rd. at Market St.* ⊕ *www.themarketdistricttallahassee.com.*

Midtown District. This area mixes a little bit of Southern charm with city chic, offering everything from the stylish and cutting-edge fashions of Cole Couture and Divas and Devils to luxury beauty and spa services at Kanvas. Shops adorn the sides of North Monroe Street heading toward downtown, as well as some of the side streets. If you get hungry picking up purchases, try the delicious treats at Lucy & Leo's Cupcakery, featured on *Cupcake Wars.* ⊠ *Between North Moore St. and Thomasville Rd., between W. 7th Ave. and W. 4th Ave.*

TRAVEL SMART
FLORIDA

GETTING HERE AND AROUND

■ AIR TRAVEL

Average flying times to Florida's international airports are 3 hours from New York, 4 hours from Chicago, 2¾ hours from Dallas, 4½–5½ hours from Los Angeles, and 8–8½ hours from London.

AIRPORTS

Florida has 21 commercial airports, the busiest being Orlando International Airport (MCO), Miami International Airport (MIA), Tampa (TPA), and Fort Lauderdale–Hollywood International Airport (FLL). Flying to alternative airports can save you both time and money. Fort Lauderdale is close to Miami, Palm Beach International (PBI) is close to Fort Lauderdale, and Sarasota Bradenton International (SRQ) is close to Tampa. FLL is a 30-minute drive from MIA. And what you might lose in driving time between Sarasota and downtown Tampa, you'll make up for in spades with shorter security lines and fewer in-terminal navigation woes at SRQ.

■TIP➔ Flying to secondary airports can save you money, so price things out before booking. Sometimes one-way car rentals in Florida can be more cost-effective than shared van shuttles.

Airport Information Daytona Beach International Airport (DAB). ✉ 700 Catalina Dr., Daytona Beach, Florida ☎ 386/248–8069 ⊕ www.flydaytonafirst.com. Fort Lauderdale–Hollywood International Airport (FLL). ✉ 100 Terminal Dr., Fort Lauderdale, Florida ☎ 866/435–9355 ⊕ www.broward.org/airport. Jacksonville International Airport (JAX). ✉ 2400 Yankee Clipper Dr., Jacksonville, Florida ☎ 904/741–4902 ⊕ www.flyjax.com. Key West International Airport (EYW). ✉ 3491 S. Roosevelt Blvd., Key West, Florida ☎ 305/809–5200, 305/296–5439 ⊕ www.eywairport.com. Miami International Airport (MIA). ✉ N.E. 20th St. and LeJeune Rd., Miami, Florida ☎ 305/876–7000 ⊕ www.miami-airport.com. Northwest Florida Beaches

International Airport (ECP). ☎ 6300 W. Bay Pkwy., Panama City, Florida ☎ 850/763–6751 ⊕ www.iflybeaches.com. Orlando International Airport (MCO). ✉ 1 Jeff Fuqua Blvd., Orlando, Florida ☎ 407/825–2001 ⊕ www.orlandoairports.net. Palm Beach International Airport (PBI). ✉ 1000 Palm Beach International Airport, West Palm Beach, Florida ☎ 561/471–7420 ⊕ www.pbia.org. Sarasota Bradenton International Airport (SRQ). ✉ 6000 Airport Circle, Bradenton, Florida ☎ 941/359–5200 ⊕ www.srq-airport.com. Southwest Florida International Airport (RSW). ✉ 11000 Terminal Access Rd., Fort Myers, Florida ☎ 239/590–4800 ⊕ www.flylcpa.com. St. Petersburg–Clearwater International Airport (PIE). ✉ 14700 Terminal Blvd., Clearwater, Florida ☎ 727/453–7800 ⊕ www.fly2pie.com. Tampa International Airport (TPA). ✉ 4100 George J. Bean Pkwy., Tampa, Florida ☎ 813/870–8700 ⊕ www.tampaairport.com.

GROUND TRANSPORTATION

SuperShuttle service operates from several Florida airports: Miami, Orlando, Sarasota-Bradenton, St. Petersburg/Clearwater, Tampa, the Palm Beaches, and Fort Lauderdale. That said, most airports offer some type of shuttle or bus service.

If you book a shuttle from your hotel to the airport, allow at least 24 hours, and expect to be picked up at least 2½ hours before your scheduled departure.

Cab fares from Florida's larger airports into town can be high, and there can be a departure fee from an airport. (In Fort Lauderdale, that airport departure fee is $3.) Note that in some cities airport cab fares are a single flat rate; in others, flat-rate fares vary by zone; and in others still, the fare is determined by the meter. Private car service fares are usually higher than taxi fares.

Shuttle Service SuperShuttle ☎ 800/258–3826 ⊕ www.supershuttle.com.

FLIGHTS

American Airlines. Flies to Daytona Beach, Fort Lauderdale, Fort Myers, Fort Walton Beach, Gainesville, Jacksonville, Key West, Melbourne, Miami, Orlando, Pensacola, Sarasota, Tallahassee, Tampa, and West Palm Beach. ☎ *800/433–7300* ⊕ *www.aa.com.*

Delta. Flies to Daytona Beach, Fort Lauderdale, Fort Myers, Fort Walton Beach, Gainesville, Jacksonville, Key West, Melbourne, Miami, Orlando, Panama City, Pensacola, Sarasota, Tallahassee, Tampa, and West Palm Beach. ☎ *800/221–1212 for U.S. reservations, 800/241–4141 for international reservations* ⊕ *www.delta. com.*

Frontier. Flies to Fort Lauderdale, Fort Myers, Jacksonville/St. Augustine, Orlando, and Tampa. ☎ *800/432–1359* ⊕ *www.frontierairlines.com.*

JetBlue. Flies to Fort Myers, Jacksonville, Sarasota, Tampa, Key West, and West Palm Beach. ☎ *800/538–2583* ⊕ *www. jetblue.com.*

Southwest. Flies to Fort Lauderdale, Fort Myers, Jacksonville, Key West, Orlando, Panama City, Pensacola, Tampa, and West Palm Beach. ☎ *800/435–9792* ⊕ *www. southwest.com.*

Spirit Airlines. Flies from Fort Lauderdale to Fort Myers, Orlando, Tampa, and West Palm Beach, as well as assorted cities elsewhere across the United States. ☎ *801/401–2200* ⊕ *www.spirit.com.*

United. Flies to Daytona, Fort Lauderdale, Fort Myers, Fort Walton Beach, Gainesville, Jacksonville, Key West, Miami, Orlando, Pensacola, Sarasota/Bradenton, Tallahassee, Tampa, and West Palm Beach. ☎ *800/864–8331 for U.S. reservations, 800/538–2929 for international reservations* ⊕ *www.united.com.*

▌ CAR TRAVEL

Three major interstates lead to Florida. Interstate 95 begins in Maine, runs south through the Mid-Atlantic states, and enters Florida just north of Jacksonville. It continues south past Daytona Beach, the Space Coast, Vero Beach, Palm Beach, and Fort Lauderdale, ending just south of Miami.

Interstate 75 begins in Michigan at the Canadian border and runs south through Ohio, Kentucky, Tennessee, and Georgia, then moves south through the center of the state before veering west into Tampa. It follows the west coast south to Naples, then crosses the state through the northern section of the Everglades, and ends in Miami. Despite its interstate status, the Interstate 75 stretch between Naples and just west of Fort Lauderdale levies a toll each way per car, with higher tolls for motor homes, boat carriers, and such.

California and most Southern and Southwestern states are connected to Florida by Interstate 10, which moves east from Los Angeles through Arizona, New Mexico, Texas, Louisiana, Mississippi, and Alabama. It enters Florida at Pensacola and runs straight across the northern part of the state, ending in Jacksonville.

SUNPASS

To save time and money while on the road, you may want to purchase a SunPass for your personal or rental vehicle. It provides a discount on most tolls, and you'll be able to sail past collection booths without stopping. You also can use SunPass to pay for parking at Orlando, Tampa, Palm Beach, Miami, and Fort Lauderdale airports. (SunPass now interfaces with North Carolina's Quick Pass and Georgia's Peach Pass.) With SunPass—transponders can be purchased for $4.99 to $25, at drugstores, supermarkets, or tourism welcome centers—you can charge up with a credit card and reload as needed. For more info, check out ⊕ *www.sunpass.com.*

RENTAL CARS

Unless you're going to plant yourself at a beach or theme-park resort, you really need a vehicle to get around in Florida. Rental rates, which are loaded with taxes, fees, and other costs, sometimes can start around $35 a day/$160 a week, plus the aforementioned add-ons. In Florida you must be 21 to rent a car, must have a credit card, and need to know rates are higher if you're under 25.

CAR RENTAL RESOURCES

Local Agencies

Continental (Fort Lauderdale and Orlando)	800/221–4085 or 954/332–1125	www.continentalcar.com
Sunshine Rent A Car (Fort Lauderdale)	888/786–7446 or 954/467–8100	www.sunshinerentacar.com

Major Agencies

Alamo	877/222–9075	www.alamo.com
Avis	800/331–1212	www.avis.com
Budget	800/218–7992	www.budget.com
Hertz	800/654–3131	www.hertz.com
National Car Rental	800/227–7368	www.nationalcar.com

ROAD CONDITIONS

Downtown areas of major cities can be extremely congested during rush hours, usually 7–9 am and 3:30–6:30 pm or later on weekdays. ■ TIP➔ Florida has a website (⊕ www.fl511.com) with real-time traffic information for six regional zones.

RULES OF THE ROAD

Speed limits are generally 60 mph on state highways, 30 mph within city limits and residential areas, and 70 mph on interstates, some Orlando area toll roads, and Florida's Turnpike. Supervising adults must ensure that children under age seven are positioned in federally approved child car seats. Infants up to 20 pounds must be secured in rear-facing carriers in the backseat. Children younger than four years old must be strapped into a separate carrier or child seat; children four through five can be secured in a separate carrier, an integrated child seat, or by a seat belt. The driver will be held responsible for passengers under the age of 18 who aren't wearing seat belts, and all front-seat passengers are required to wear seat belts.

Florida's Alcohol/Controlled Substance DUI Law is one of the toughest in the United States. A blood-alcohol level of 0.08 or higher can have serious repercussions even for a first-time offender.

FROM-TO	MILES	HOURS +/-
Pensacola–Panama City	100	2
Tallahassee–Panama City	100	2
Tallahassee–Jacksonville	165	3
Jacksonville–St. Augustine	40	0:45
Cape/Port Canaveral–Orlando	60	1
Orlando–Tampa	85	1:30
Fort Lauderdale–Miami	30	0:45
Miami–Naples	125	2:15
Miami–Key Largo	65	1
Miami–Palm Beach	70	1:45
Key Largo–Key West	100	2

■ FERRY TRAVEL

If you would like to avoid road traffic to the Keys and make the trip a watery adventure, Key West Express ferries people from Fort Myers Beach on a daily basis (and Marco Island in season) to Key West's historic seaport. The trip, just under four hours, is cheaper than airfare, and doesn't require months-in-advance booking.

Contact Key West Express ⊠ *1200 Main St., Fort Myers* ☎ *888/539–2628* ⊕ *www.keywestexpress.us.*

ESSENTIALS

▪ ACCOMMODATIONS

In general, peak seasons are during Christmas/New Year's holidays and late January through Easter in the state's southern half, during the summer along the Panhandle and around Jacksonville and St. Augustine, and both time frames in Orlando and Central Florida. Holiday weekends at any point during the year are packed; if you're considering home or condo rentals, minimum-stay requirements are longer during these periods, too. Fall is the slowest season, with only a few exceptions (Key West is jam-packed for the 10-day Fantasy Fest at Halloween). Rates are low and availability is high, but this is also prime time for hurricanes.

Children are generally welcome throughout Florida, except for some Key West B&Bs and Inns; however, the buck stops at spring breakers. While many hotels allow them—and some even cater to them—most rental agencies won't lease units to anyone under 25 without a guardian present.

Pets, although allowed at many hotels (one upscale chain, Kimpton, with properties in Miami, Palm Beach, and Vero Beach, celebrates its pet-friendliness with treats in the lobby and doggie beds for rooms), often carry an extra flat-rate fee for cleaning and de-allergen treatments, and are not a sure thing. Inquire ahead if Fido is coming with you.

APARTMENT AND HOUSE RENTALS

The state's allure for visiting snowbirds (Northerners "flocking" to Florida in winter) has caused private home and condo rentals to boom in popularity, at times affording better options for vacationers, particularly families who want to have some extra space and cooking facilities. In some destinations, home and condo rentals are more readily available than hotels. Fort Myers, for example,

doesn't have many luxury hotel properties downtown. Everything aside from beach towels is provided during a stay, but some things to consider are that sizable down payments must be made at booking (15% to 50%), and the full balance is often due before arrival. Check for any cleaning fees (usually not more than $150). If being on the beach is of utmost importance, carefully screen properties that tout "water views," because they might actually be of bays, canals, or lakes rather than of the Gulf of Mexico or the Atlantic.

Finding a great rental agency can help you weed out the junk. Target offices that specialize in the area you want to visit, and have a personal conversation with a representative as soon as possible. Be honest about your budget and expectations. For example, let the rental agent know if having the living room couch pull double-duty as a bed is not OK. Although websites listing rentals directly from homeowners are growing in popularity, there's a higher chance of coming across Pinocchios advertising "gourmet" kitchens that have one or two nice gadgets but fixtures or appliances from 1982. To protect yourself, talk extensively with owners in advance, see if there's a system in place for accountability should something go wrong, and make sure there's a 24-hour phone number for emergencies.

Contacts American Realty of Captiva ✉ *11526 Andy Rose La., Captiva, Florida* ☎ *800/547–0121* ⊕ *www.captiva-island.com.* **Endless Vacation Rentals** ☎ *877/782–9387* ⊕ *www.evrentals.com.* **Florida Keys Rental Store** ✉ *MM 82, 81800 Overseas Hwy., Upper Keys, Islamorada, Florida* ☎ *800/585–0584, 305/451–3879* ⊕ *www.floridakeysrentalstore. com.* **Freewheeler Vacations** ✉ *MM 98.5, 98500 Overseas Hwy., Key Largo, Florida* ☎ *866/664–2075, 305/664–2075* ⊕ *www. freewheeler-realty.com.* **Interhome** ☎ *954/791–8282, 800/882–6864* ⊕ *www. interhomeusa.com.* **ResortQuest** ✉ *14 Sylvan*

Way, Parsippany, New Jersey ☎ *800/336–4853* ⊕ *www.resortquest.com.* **Sand Key Realty** ✉ *790 S. Gulfview Blvd., Clearwater Beach, Florida* ☎ *800/257–7332, 727/443–0032* ⊕ *www.sandkey.com.* **Suncoast Vacation Rentals** ✉ *224 Franklin Blvd., St. George Island, Florida* ☎ *800/341–2021* ⊕ *www.uncommonflorida.com.* **Villas International** ☎ *415/499–9490, 800/221–2260* ⊕ *www.villasintl.com.*

BED-AND-BREAKFASTS

Small inns and guesthouses in Florida range from modest, cozy places with home-style breakfasts and owners who treat you like family, to elegantly furnished Victorian houses with four-course breakfasts and rates to match. Since most B&Bs are small, they rely on various agencies and organizations to get the word out and coordinate reservations.

Reservation Services BedandBreakfast.com ☎ *512/322–2710, 800/462–2632* ⊕ *www.bedandbreakfast.com.* **Bed & Breakfast Inns Online** ☎ *800/215–7365* ⊕ *www.bbonline.com.* **Florida Bed & Breakfast Inns** ☎ *561/223–9550* ⊕ *www.florida-inns.com.*

HOTELS AND RESORTS

Wherever you look in Florida, you'll find lots of plain, inexpensive motels and luxurious resorts, independents alongside national chains, and an ever-growing number of modern properties as well as quite a few classics. All hotels listed have a private bath unless otherwise noted.

Hotel reviews have been shortened. For full reviews, visit Fodors.com.

▮ EATING OUT

Smoking is banned statewide in most enclosed indoor workplaces, including restaurants. Exemptions are permitted for stand-alone bars where food takes a backseat to libations.

One caution: Raw oysters pose a potential danger for people with chronic illness of the liver, stomach, or blood, or who have immune disorders. All Florida restaurants that serve raw oysters must post a notice

---

FLORIDA'S SCENIC TRAILS

Florida has some 8,000 miles of land-based routes (plus another 4,000 miles for paddling!). About 1,400 miles of these connect to create the Florida Trail, one of only 11 National Scenic Trails in the United States. Info on top segments is available at ⊕ *www.floridatrail.org,* and you can find a searchable list of all trails at ⊕ *www.visitflorida.com/trails.*

---

in plain view warning of the risks associated with their consumption.

MEALS AND MEALTIMES

Unless otherwise noted, you can assume that the restaurants we recommend are open daily for lunch and dinner.

RESERVATIONS AND DRESS

We discuss reservations only when they're essential (there's no other way you'll ever get a table) or when they're not accepted. It's always smart to make reservations when you can, particularly if your party is large or if it's high season. It's critical to do so at popular restaurants (book as far ahead as possible, often 30 days, and reconfirm on arrival).

We mention dress only when men are required to wear a jacket or a jacket and tie. Expect places with dress codes to truly adhere to them.

Contacts OpenTable ⊕ *www.opentable.com.*

▮ HEALTH

Sunburn and heat prostration are concerns, even in winter. So hit the beach or play tennis, golf, or another outdoor sport before 10 am or after 3 pm. If you must be out at midday, limit exercise, drink plenty of nonalcoholic liquids, and wear both sunscreen and a hat. If you feel faint, get out of the sun and sip water slowly.

Even on overcast days, ultraviolet rays shine through the haze, so use a sunscreen with an SPF of at least 15, and have children wear a waterproof SPF 30 or higher.

While you're frolicking on the beach, steer clear of what look like blue bubbles on the sand. These are Portuguese men-of-war, and their tentacles can cause an allergic reaction. Also be careful of other large jellyfish, some of which can sting.

If you walk across a grassy area on the way to the beach, you'll probably encounter the tiny, light-brown, incredibly prickly sand spurs. If you get stuck with one, just pull it out.

▮ HOURS OF OPERATION

Many museums are closed Monday but have late hours on another weekday and are usually open on weekends. Some museums have days when admission is free. Popular attractions are usually open every day but Thanksgiving and Christmas Day. Watch out for seasonal closures at smaller venues; we list opening hours for all sights we recommend, but these can change on short notice. If you're visiting during a transitional month (for example, May in the southern part of the state), it's always best to call before showing up.

▮ MONEY

Prices here are given for adults. Substantially reduced fees are almost always available for children, students, and senior citizens.

CREDIT CARDS

We cite information about credit cards only if they aren't accepted at a restaurant or a hotel. Otherwise, assume that most major credit cards are acceptable.

Reporting Lost Cards American Express
☎ 800/528–4800 ⊕ www.americanexpress. com. **Diners Club** ☎ 800/234–6377 ⊕ www. dinersclub.com. **Discover** ☎ 800/347–2683 ⊕ www.discovercard.com. **MasterCard** ☎ 800/622–7747 ⊕ www.mastercard.com. **Visa** ☎ 800/847–2911 ⊕ www.visa.com.

WORD OF MOUTH

Did the food give you shivers of delight or leave you cold? Did the resort look as good in real life as it did in the photos? Did you sleep like a baby, or were the walls paper-thin? Was the service stellar or not up to snuff? Rate and review hotels and restaurants or start a discussion about your favorite (or not so favorite) places on ⊕ www.fodors.com. Your comments might even appear in our books. Yes, you, too, can be a correspondent!

▮ PACKING

Northern Florida is much cooler in winter than southern Florida, so pack a heavy sweater or more. Even in summer, ocean breezes can be cool, so it's good to have a lightweight sweater or jacket.

Aside from an occasional winter cold spell (when the mercury drops to, say, 50), Miami and the Naples–Fort Myers areas are usually warm year-round and extremely humid in summer. Be prepared for sudden storms all over in summer, and note that plastic raincoats are uncomfortable in the high humidity. Often, storms are quick, often in the afternoons, and the sun comes back in no time. (This also means that it's best to get in your beach time earlier in the day; if it's nice in the morning in August, go to the beach. Don't wait.)

Dress is casual throughout the state—sundresses, sandals, or walking shorts are appropriate. Palm Beach is more polos and pearls, Miami is designer jeans, and elsewhere the Tommy Bahama–esque look dominates. Even beach gear is OK at a lot of places, but just make sure you've got a proper outfit on (shirt, shorts, and shoes). A very small number of restaurants request that men wear jackets and ties, but most don't. Where there are dress codes, they tend to be fully adhered to. Take note that the strictest places are golf and tennis clubs. Many ask that you wear whites or at least special sport shoes and attire. Be prepared for air-conditioning working in overdrive anywhere you go.

You can generally swim year-round in peninsular Florida from about New Smyrna Beach south on the Atlantic coast and from Tarpon Springs south on the Gulf Coast. Bring a sun hat and sunscreen.

▌SAFETY

Stepped-up policing against thieves preying on tourists in rental cars has helped address what was a serious issue in the mid-1990s. Still, visitors should be wary when driving in unfamiliar neighborhoods and leaving the airport, especially near Miami. Don't leave valuables unattended—and that can include food and drink—while you walk the beach or go for a dip. And never leave handbags, cameras, etc., in your vehicle. Visitors have reported theft of belongings while stopped for meals as they travel to or from the airport. Don't blatantly stow valuables in your car trunk just before walking away, either, since thieves can be adept at popping lids. And don't assume that valuables are safe in your hotel room; use in-room safes or the hotel's safety-deposit boxes. Try to use ATMs only during the day or in brightly lighted, well-traveled locales.

If you're visiting Florida during the June through November hurricane season and a hurricane is imminent, be sure to follow safety orders and evacuation instructions from local authorities.

▌TAXES

Florida has no state personal income tax, instead heavily relying on tourism revenues. The state sales tax rate in Florida is 6% (with exceptions of most groceries and medicine that go untaxed), combined with local taxes so that the total sales tax rate is between 6% and 7.5%. Hotel taxes, often called "bed taxes," "resort taxes," or "transient rental taxes," vary. In Central Florida including Orlando, for example, taxes on purchases range from 6.5% to 7%. A 6% resort tax is imposed on all hotel rooms in addition to the sales tax.

Palm Beach County has raised its bed tax to 6%, for a combined total of 12% with state sales tax. In Greater Fort Lauderdale, the bed tax is 5%, for a combined total of 11%.

▌TIME

The western portion of the Panhandle is in the Central time zone, and the rest of Florida is in the Eastern time zone.

▌TIPPING

Tip airport valets or hotel bellhops $1 to $3 per bag (there typically is also a charge to check bags outside the terminal, but this isn't a tip). Maids often get $1 to $2 per night per guest, more at high-end resorts or if you require special services, ideally left each morning since the person servicing your room or suite could change from day to day during your stay. Room service waiters still hope to receive a 15% tip despite hefty room-service charges and service fees, which often don't go to the waiters. A door attendant or parking valet hopes to get $1 to $3. Waiters generally count on 15% to 20% (on the before-tax amount) or more, depending on your demands for special service. Bartenders get $1 or $2 per round of drinks. Golf caddies get 15% of the greens fee.

▌VISITOR INFORMATION

Florida welcome centers, with maps and citrus juice, are on Interstate 10 (near Pensacola), Interstate 75 (near Jennings), Interstate 95 (near Yulee, north of Jacksonville), and U.S. 231 (near Campbellton), and in the lobby of the New Capitol in Tallahassee.

Contact Visit Florida ☎ *850/488-5607, 866/972-5280* ⊕ *www.visitflorida.com.*

INDEX

PHOTO CREDITS

Front cover: Anne Rippy / Alamy [Description: Buildings on 5th Avenue South, in Naples, Florida. Back cover, from left to right: Cheryl Casey/Shutterstock; Brian Dunne/Shutterstock; Andreas Prott/iStockphoto. Spine: BCritchley I Dreamstime.com. 1, Visit Florida. 2-3, Jiawangkun I Dreamstime.com. 5, PBorowka/Shutterstock. Chapter 1: Experience Florida: 8-9, S.Borisov/Shutterstock. 10, ACE STOCK LIMITED / Alamy. 11 (left), jeff gynane/Shutterstock. 11 (right), Jeff Greenberg/age fotostock. 12 (left), Cogoli Franco/SIME. 12 (right), Visit Florida. 13 (top left), Visit Florida. 13 (bottom left), Orlando CVB. 13 (top right), Universal Orlando Resort. 13 (bottom right), John Henshall / Alamy. 14 (top left), Jeremy Edwards/iStockphoto. 14 (bottom left), SeanPavonePhoto/Shutterstock. 14 (right), Visit Florida. 15 (left), Penumatsa Family/Flickr, [CC BY 2.0]. 15 (top right), RIEGER Bertrand/age fotostock. 15 (bottom right), Danita Delimont /Alamy. 16 (left), Jeff Greenberg / Alamy. 16 (top right), Ken Canning/ Shutterstock. 16 (bottom right), Cogoli Franco/SIME/eStock Photo. 17 (left), Robert Harding Picture Library Ltd / Alamy. 17 (right), Dominika Sebjan/iStockphoto. 18, The Breakers Palm Beach. 19 (left), Jeff Greenberg/age fotostock. 19 (right), Orlando CVB. 20, Cheryl Casey/Shutterstock. 21, St. Petersburg/Clearwater Area CVB. 28, GlyndaK, Fodors.com member. Chapter 2: Miami and Miami Beach: 29, iStockphoto. 30, Stuart Westmorland/age fotostock. 31, Jeff Greenberg/age fotostock. 32, Roxana Gonzalez/Shutterstock. 33 (top), JupiterImages/ Brand X / Alamy. 33 (bottom), Alena Haurylik / Shutterstock. 34, Ivan Cholakov/Shutterstock. 54, Robert Harding Picture Library Ltd / Alamy. 90, John Tunney I Dreamstime.com. 101 (left), dk/Alamy. 101 (right), Nicholas Pitt /Alamy. 103 (top), Nicholas Pitt/Alamy. 103 (2nd from top), Park Central Hotel. 103 (3rd from top), Ian Patrick Alamy. 103 (4th from top), Laura Paresky. 103 (bottom), ICIMAGE/Alamy. 104 (top), INTERFOTO Pressebildagentur/ Alamy. 104 (bottom left), Ian Patrick/Alamy. 104 (bottom right), culliganphoto/Alamy. 113, Pesky-Monkey/iStockphoto. Chapter 3: The Everglades: 117, David Lyons / Alamy. 118 (top), Visit Florida. 118 (bottom), Jeff Greenberg/age fotostock. 119 (top), FloridaStock/Shutterstock. 119 (bottom), Pamela McCreight/Flickr. 120-21, tbkmedia.de/Alamy. 124 (left), inga spence/Alamy. 124 (top center), FloridaStock/Shutterstock. 124 (bottom center), Andrewtappert/wikipedia. org. 124 (top right), wikipedia. org. 124 (bottom right), David R. Frazier Photolibrary, Inc./Alamy. 125 (top left), Larsek/Shutterstock. 125 (bottom left), Caleb Foster/Shutterstock. 125 (bottom center), mlorenz/Shutterstock. 125 (top right), umar faruq/Shutterstock. 125 (bottom right), Peter Arnold, Inc./Alamy. 126 (left), John A. Anderson/Shutterstock. 126 (top right), FloridaStock/Shutterstock. 126 (bottom center), Norman Bateman/Shutterstock. 126 (bottom right), FloridaStock/Shutterstock. 127 (top left), David Drake & Deborah Jaffe. 127 (bottom left), Krzysztof Slusarczyk/Shutterstock. 127 (bottom center), Norman Bateman/ Shutterstock. 127 (right), Jerry Zitterman/Shutterstock. 128, Patricia Schmidt/iStockphoto. 129, (top left), Brett Charlton/iStockphoto. 129, (bottom left, bottom center, and right), David Drake & Deborah Jaffe. 130 (left), Walter Bibikow/age fotostock. 130 (right), Stephen Frink Collection/Alamy. 131, Leatha J. Robinson/Shutterstock. 133, Larsek/Shutterstock. 141, Steven Widoff / Alamy. 147, Marc Muench / Alamy. 151, Sarah and Jason/Flickr, [CC BY-SA 2.0]. 158, Visit Florida. Chapter 4: The Florida Keys: 163, f11photo / Shutterstock. 164 (top), Pawel Lipiec/iStockphoto. 164 (bottom), David L. Amsler/iStockphoto. 165 (top), Sheri Armstrong/Shutterstock. 165 (bottom), Visit Florida. 166, Gregory Wrona / Alamy. 167 (top), Claudio Lovo/Shutterstock. 167 (bottom), Michael Ventura/Alamy. 168, iStockphoto. 175, Stephen Frink/ Florida Keys News Bureau. 182, flasporty/flickr. 190, Korzeniewski I Dreamstime.com. 192, PBorowka/Shutterstock. 193 and 194 (top), Douglas Rudolph. 194 (bottom), ANDY NEWMAN/Visit Florida. 195, M. Timothy O'Keefe/Alamy. 196 (top), Bob Care/ Florida Keys News Bureau. 196 (bottom), Julie de Leseleuc/iStockphoto. 197 (left), Visit Florida. 197 (right), Charles Stirling (Diving)/Alamy. 198 (top), Visit Florida. 198 (bottom), Gert Vrey/iStockphoto. 199, Scott Wilson, FKCC Student. 201, Melissa Schalke/iStockphoto. 210, Henryk Sadura / Alamy. 222, CedarBendDrive/Flickr. 224, Visit Florida. 226, John P Franzis. 237, Starwood Hotels & Resorts. 240, Laure Neish/iStockphoto. 242, Laure Neish/iStockphoto. Chapter 5: Fort Lauderdale: 249, James Schwabel / age fotostock. 250, Rick Gomez. 251 (top), Dean Bergmann/iStockphoto. 251 (bottom), Jeff Greenberg /Alamy. 252, Jorg Hackemann/Shutterstock. 262, Nicholas Pitt / Alamy. 272, Eric Gevaert/ Shutterstock. 281, Lago Mar Resort & Club. 291, Terrance Klassen / age fotostock. Chapter 6: Palm Beach and the Treasure Coast: 297, Rieger Bertrand/age fotostock. 299 (top), Perry Correll/Shutterstock. 299 (bottom), Bill Bachmann / Alamy. 300, FloridaStock/Shutterstock. 305, The Breakers Palm Beach. 309, mrk_photo/flickr. 311, FloridaStock/Shutterstock. 324, Andre Jenny / Alamy. 326, Morikami Museum and Japanese Gardens. 341 and 357, Visit Florida. Chapter 7: The Tampa Bay Area: 361, Sayran I Dreamstime.com. 362 (top), gppilot, Fodors.com member. 362 (bottom), Visit Florida. 363 (top), Marje Cannon/iStockphoto. 363 (bottom), gracious_tiger/Shutterstock. 364, iStockphoto. 370, Martin Bennett / Alamy. 389, Seymour Levy, Fodors.com member. 399, Ed Wolfstein/Icon SMI.

400 (top), Mtrommer | Dreamstime.com. 400 (bottom), Asklar | Dreamstime.com. 401 (top), Evan Meyer/Shutterstock. 401 (bottom) and 402 (bottom background photo), Mtrommer | Dreamstime. com. 402 (top), Gary I. Rothstein/Icon SMI. 403 (background photo), Bokdavid | Dreamstime.com. 406, watland, Fodors.com member. 409, Richard T. Nowitz / age fotostock. 419, Titon Donald / age fotostock. 421, cogito ergo imago/Flickr (CC BY-SA 2.0). Chapter 8: The Lower Gulf Coast: 431, Dan Leffel/age fotostock. 433 (top), FloridaStock/Shutterstock. 433 (bottom), Visit Florida. 434, Philip Lange/Shutterstock. 440, Visit Florida. 447, World Pictures/age Fotostock. 449, Walter Bibikow / age fotostock. 453, blewisphotography/Shutterstock. 454, Mitch Aunger/Shutterstock. 478, Dennis Guyitt/ iStockphoto. Chapter 9: Orlando and Environs: 489, Visit Florida. 491 (top), Nick Hotel. 491 (bottom), Universal Orlando Resort. 492, Universal Orlando Resort. 496, Orlando CVB. 500, Kissimmee - The Heart of Florida/Flickr. 502, spakattacks/Flickr. 535, Visit Florida. Chapter 10: Walt Disney World: 539, Disney. 540, d4rr3ll/Flickr. 541, vanguardist/Flickr. 542, Orlando CVB. 548, ckramer/ Flickr. 554, JoshMcConnell/Flickr. 565, Disney. 566, yeowatzup/Flickr. 583, tom.arthur/Flickr. 585, PrincessAshley/Flickr. Chapter 11: Universal Orlando: 589-90, Universal Orlando Resort. 591, bea&txm/Flickr. 592, divemasterking2000/Flickr. 602, Universal Orlando. 605, Jessica Walsh. 612, Universal Orlando Resort. 614, PCL / Alamy. 616, Wet 'n Wild. Chapter 12: SeaWorld Orlando: 619, SeaWorld Orlando. 620, Cybjorg/Wikimedia Commons. 621, Wendy Piersall (@eMom)/Flickr. 622, SeaWorld Orlando. 625, SeaWorld Orlando. 633, SeaWorld Parks & Entertainment. 634, Orlando CVB. Chapter 13: Northeast Florida: 637, Frilet Patrick/age fotostock. 638, The Freewheeling Daredevil/Flickr. 639, Diane Uhley/Shutterstock. 640 and 641 (both), Kennedy Space Center. 642, Visit Florida. 647, Karel Gallas/Shutterstock. 653, Jeff Greenberg/ age fotostock. 656, Therese McKeon/ iStockphoto. 666, funinthetub, Fodors.com member. 674, Arkorn | Dreamstime.com. 678, c) Paul65516 | Dreamstime.com. 696-97, Visit Florida. 698 (top) Visit Florida. 698 (bottom left), David Allio/Icon SMI. 698 (bottom 2nd from left), Jack Braden/wikipedia.org. 698 (bottom 3rd from left), Arni Katz/ Alamy. 698 (bottom right), Motorsports Images and Archives/Datona International Speedway. 699, Nancy Nally/Flickr, [CC BY-ND 2.0]. 704, greg pelt/iStockphoto. 713, yeowatzup/Flickr. 720, Louishenault | Dreamstime.com. Chapter 14: The Panhandle: 725, Cheryl Casey/Shutterstock. 726 (top), Cheryl Casey/Shutterstock. 726 (bottom), Visit Florida. 727, Todd Taulman/Shutterstock. 728, divemasterking2000/flickr. 735, Kathy Hicks/iStockphoto. 747, Judykennamer | Dreamstime.com. 751, Visit Florida. 752 (top), Ernest Hemingway Photograph Collection, John F. Kennedy Presidential Library and Museum, Boston. 752 (bottom), Visit Florida. 753 (top), Linda Brinck, Fodors.com member. 753 (bottom), George Peters/iStockphoto. 756, Andrew Woodley/Alamy. 760, Thor/Flickr, [CC BY 2.0]. 763, JNB Photography / Shutterstock. 774-75, imagebroker / Alamy. 777, Dennis MacDonald/age fotostock.

About Our Writers: All photos are courtesy of the writers except for the following: Kate Bradshaw, courtesy of Tess Chibirka; Jennifer Greenhill-Taylor, courtesy of Joseph Hayes; and Lynne Helm, courtesy of John Rude.

ABOUT OUR WRITERS

Tampa Bay updater and beach lover Kate Bradshaw lives in St. Petersburg, where she edits the news and politics section of *Creative Loafing,* the alternative weekly in the Tampa Bay area. Born in the Chicago area, Kate is proud to be a Florida resident and is in love with her adopted home.

Jacksonville and Space Coast updater Jennifer Greenhill-Taylor has been a journalist for more than two decades—working at both the *Florida Times Union* in Jacksonville and the *Orlando Sentinel.* Now an independent travel writer and editor, she has lived in four countries and a dozen states. She lives in Orlando.

After being hired sight unseen by a South Florida newspaper, Fort Lauderdale–based freelance travel writer and editor Lynne Helm arrived from the Midwest anticipating a few years of palm-fringed fun. More than a quarter century later, she's still enamored of Florida's sun-drenched charms. Lynne updated the Everglades chapter and Travel Smart.

Updating the Florida Keys and the Lower Gulf Coast is Miami native, Jill Martin. As a freelance writer, she has written for the state's tourism website, Visit Florida, and also for various travel sites and print magazines. She is the creator of Sunshine Brain Games, a trivia card game all about Florida. She resides full time in the Redland and part time on Sanibel.

Northeast Florida updater Steve Master lives in Daytona Beach, 10 miles west of famed Daytona International Speedway. Steve spent 20 years as a sports writer for the *Daytona Beach News Journal,* where he won many awards, including a 2007 national

honor from the Associated Press Sports Editors. He's an associate professor of communication at Embry-Riddle Aeronautical University in Daytona Beach.

Jan Norris, contributing editor of *Florida Food & Farm,* is a career food journalist and publishes the website ⊕ *JanNorris. com.* She writes about the South Florida food and dining scene as well as travel in the Sunshine State after a 26-year career as food editor at *The Palm Beach Post.* Jan's a fifth-generation Floridian and enthusiastically promotes her state, quirky bits and all.

Paul Rubio's travels have taken him to 107 countries and counting. He graduated from Harvard in 2002 with master's degrees in both Public Administration and Economics, but in 2008 he gave into his passion and became a full-time travel writer. An award-winning writer, he is the travel editor of *Palm Beach Illustrated, Naples Illustrated,* and *Weddings Illustrated* and regularly contributes to several other publications.

Panhandle updater Ashley Wright is a northwest Florida native and a master-of-all-trades in the publishing world. She contributes to a number of local and regional publications, and loves sharing the hidden treasures of her native coast with travelers both near and far.

The Orlando and Walt Disney World chapters were updated by a talented team of writers, including Rona Gindin (Where to Eat), Jennifer Greenhill-Taylor (Where to Stay), Jennie Hess (all of Disney World), Gary McKechnie (Universal, SeaWorld, and Sports & the Outdoors), and Joseph Hayes (Orlando and Environs exploring as well as Shopping and Nightlife).